The History of Higher Education
Third Edition

Lenoar Foster, Series Editor

Association for the Study of Higher Education

Edited by

Harold S. Wechsler
New York University

Lester F. Goodchild
University of Santa Clara

Linda Eisenmann
John Carroll University

PEARSON
Custom Publishing

Cover Illustration: *Tappan Hall*, by Margaret Drake Penfield, c. 1838-1841. Courtesy of the Oberlin College Archives.

Printed in the United States of America

10 9 8 7 6 5 4 3

ISBN 0-536-44341-6

2007220026

SB/MJ

PEARSON CUSTOM PUBLISHING
501 Boylston Street, Suite 900, Boston, MA 02116
A Pearson Education Company

COPYRIGHT ACKNOWLEDGMENTS

CONTENTS

ACKNOWLEDGMENTS

We owe a singular debt to the authors of the essays in this *Reader*. Reading the fruits of their scholarship made our editorial work exceptionally rewarding. Many authors deepened our understanding of significant events, institutions, and individuals, while others have synthesized the rich monographic literature published after the previous edition of this *Reader*.

We are grateful to the many colleagues who helped us find our way to this scholarship. We consulted the syllabi of many instructors:

William Barba, State University of New York-Buffalo
James R. Biddle, University of Dayton
V. R. Cardozier, University of Texas
Greg Dubrow, Florida International University
Thomas Dyer, University of Georgia
Lori Hunter-Union, Wesleyan University
Dennis E. Gregory, Old Dominion University
Jerlando F. L. Jackson, University of Wisconsin
Sharon McDade, George Washington University
Claire Major, University of Alabama
Paul H. Mattingly, New York University
W.R. "Bill" Ogden, Texas A & M University-Commerce
Jack Schuster, Claremont Graduate University
Ed Taylor, University of Washington
J. Douglas Toma, University of Georgia
Lucy Townsend, Northern Illinois University
Thomas S. Westbrook, Drake University
John B. Williams, University of Maryland

The members of our editorial board provided excellent counsel:

James Anderson, University of Illinois
Melissa Anderson, University of Minnesota
Joyce Antler, Brandeis University
M. Christopher Brown, Pennsylvania State University
Joan Burstyn, Syracuse University
John D. Burton, DePaul University
Katherine Reynolds Chaddock, University of South Carolina
Steven Diner, Rutgers University, Newark
John Douglass, University of California, Berkeley
Marybeth Gasman, University of Pennsylvania
Roger L. Geiger, Pennsylvania State University
Lynn D. Gordon, University of Rochester
Karen Graves, Denison University
Philo A. Hutcheson, Georgia State University
W. Bruce Leslie, State University of New York, Brockport
James McLachlan, Princeton, New Jersey

Kathryn Moore, North Carolina State University
Christine Ogren, University of Iowa
Patricia Palmieri, Teachers College, Columbia University
Robert Pedersen, Towson State University
Linda M. Perkins, Claremont Graduate University
Joseph Stetar, Seton Hall University
John R. Thelin, University of Kentucky
Barbara Townsend, University of Missouri
W. Paul Vogt, Illinois State University
Jennings L. Wagoner, Jr., University of Virginia
Cally Waite, Teachers College, Columbia University
Amy S. Wells, Teachers College, Columbia University

We profited from detailed exchanges with Sharon McDade, George Washington University, and Vicki Rosser, University of Missouri, Kansas City. Michael Bieze, of the Marist School, Atlanta, Georgia, supplied the website with documents relating to Booker T. Washington. Special thanks go to Philo Hutcheson, Jana Nidiffer, Christine Ogren, Linda Perkins, and other members of HASHE (Historians at ASHE), who provided advice, documents, and encouragement.

Karen Whitehouse and her staff at Pearson Custom Publishing found ways to include the extensive content before you, and to create the first website for an ASHE Reader.

The ASHE publications committee, chaired by Judith Glazer-Raymo, and Lenoar Foster, the editor for the *ASHE Reader Series*, established the standards for the series, and then counseled and encouraged us from the initial conceptualization of this *Reader* through its production.

We are most gratified by the feedback we've received from students and colleagues who have used prior editions of the *Reader*. This book is the product of a true collaborative effort.

Overview

The History of American Higher Education: An Overview and a Commentary

The 1838 painting of Oberlin College on our cover symbolizes a radical juncture in the history of the 4,200 institutions of higher learning in the United States. The founding of Oberlin in northern Ohio in 1833 launched a crusade for the advancement of education, religion, and abolition for both sexes from all races, as described in Robert S. Fletcher's renowned narrative, *History of Oberlin College.*[1] Two hundred years had passed since Harvard College was founded in 1636, which marked the beginning of higher learning in the colonies. Harvard's curriculum and clientele constituted an English pattern of liberal education and professional study for white males of intellectual and financial ability. Harvard and other colonial institutions laid the foundation for an American mandate for higher learning. However, a new Presbyterian sentiment in the Midwest—rather different from that of Eastern churches and colleges—inflamed the Oberlin educational reformers. Oberlin's 3,000-seat campus meeting house, central dormitory, and classroom building for theological students, and three other residence halls established a uniquely American institution of higher learning. Their college for all persons was an innovation in western English-speaking higher education. The Oberlin faculty proclaimed its values in an 1839 statement. Oberlin would assume unparalleled religious, intellectual, and social obligations in its mandate for higher learning, including

> . . . the hearty recognition of equal human rights as belonging to all whom God has made in his own image; a deep sympathy with the oppressed of every color, in every clime; and a consecration of life to the well-being of suffering humanity—finally this paramount principle, that the cultivation of moral feelings is the first object of education, Gospel love to God & man, the first of all acquisitions more precious than all other disciplines.[2]

The Oberlin faculty proclaimed the founding moment to democratize our colleges and universities. This mandate has continued for over a century and a half through rational persuasion, institutional diversity, lobbying, and litigation. The democratization of higher education thus began some 57 years after the signing of the Declaration of Independence and comprised one of the distinguishing features of the nascent American system.

In their classic work, *Higher Education in Transition: A History of American Colleges and Universities, 1636–1976,*[3] John S. Brubacher and Willis Rudy draw our attention to the development of this democratizing characteristic of our colleges and universities. They also identify other distinctive features: The extensive opportunities for all persons, young and old, to enroll in diverse institutions of higher learning; the broad scope of courses offered at colleges and universities; the institutional commitment to serve local communities and American society; the voluntary cooperation among colleges and universities in setting standards through accrediting associations; the corporate structure of postsecondary governance; and the extracurriculum. Each of these attributes arose out of a unique interplay between higher education and American life, as will be noted shortly.

The Organization of the Reader

As part of the Association for the Study of Higher Education (ASHE) Reader Series, the History of Higher Education, now in its third edition, offers the faculty and graduate students of higher education many learning aids. First, a preface on the nature of the historical inquiry and method in

American higher education (2004) from past President of the History of Education Society, Linda Eisenmann, invites the reader into American higher education's complex past. Second, a six-part extended introductory essay by Les Goodchild on the themes and readings of the book are presented in each part of this text. They provide an overview for each chronological period of American higher education. Third, the Reader's major contribution is the compilation of important journal articles, book chapters, and essays from the best higher education historians for each period. Fourth, Harold Wechsler identified approximately 300 primary readings to capture the flavor and meaning of important issues for each chronological period in this new edition, which may be used by faculty and students by going to our Reader's new companion website http://www.pearsoncustom.com/mi/msu_ashe These extensive readings are categorized in a parallel manner to the book: (1) General—Classic Statements and Overviews; (2) the European and Colonial Eras; (3) the Antebellum Era; (4) the 19th Century Proliferation Era; (5) the 1900 to 1950 Era; (6) the Post-World War II Era; and (7) Appendices—Bibliographies and Specialized Studies. The companion website also contains articles which were dropped from this edition of the Reader. We believe that this edition is a significant improvement over its predecessors because of recent historical studies on higher education and our extensive trove of primary documents.

The third edition of this Reader complements several comprehensive histories of higher education in the United States.[4] Faculty and students in the approximately 200 higher education programs across this country have found the Reader useful in filling out the major treatments offered by other historians of higher education. Again, the companion website provides numerous primary readings that can be supplemented further by Richard Hofstadter and Wilson Smith's classic *American Higher Education: A Documentary History.*[5]

Four principles of selection guided our editorial choices. First, the text is organized chronologically. After presenting a general history of global higher education and an overview of American higher education, the Reader covers five periods within North American higher education. Second, for each period, the Reader initially offers an overview article or chapter that canvasses major developments, and then offers specific readings put forth on the history of higher education. The readings attempt to cover four major research topics within this field of study: (1) the organizational development of institutions, (2) faculty life, (3) curricular considerations, and (4) student life. The Reader thus introduces students to the themes of other ASHE Readers on organizational theory, curriculum, faculty, student life, community colleges, and finance (see on the back cover of this book). Our third organizational principle consisted of making available the most recent trends in historiography and related research. Thus, we de-emphasized an elitist history of higher education, which has centered primarily on the rise of American research universities. We also included regional developments within higher education, especially southern and midwestern perspectives, and concise histories of western higher education, especially Californian higher education. Furthermore, we accentuated public colleges and universities that now enroll 75 percent of postsecondary students. The Reader also includes recent research on the education of female students, women's colleges, and coeducation, as well as some analyses of colleges and universities that serve different clienteles, such as Catholics, African-Americans, Native Americans, and Latinos. Finally, our fourth principle involved listening to historians of higher education in making our selections. The resulting collaborative process provides a rich compendium of source materials for the history of higher education courses in our higher education and student development programs across the country, as well as for other courses in American studies or intellectual history.

From the founding of Harvard College in 1636 to contemporary multi-campus, statewide systems of California, New York, Texas, Pennsylvania, Wisconsin, Illinois, and others, the development of American higher education is thus a fitting tribute—despite its problems and inequities—to a people's quest for the advancement of religion, morality, knowledge, and research during the past 371 years.

Lester F. Goodchild
San Jose, California

ENDNOTES

[1]Robert S. Fletcher, *History of Oberlin College: From Its Foundation Through the Civil War,* 2 Volumes (Oberlin, 1943) p. 11231.

[2]*Ibid.*

[3]John S. Brubacker and Willis Rudy, *Higher Education in Transition: A History of American Colleges and Universities* 1636–1976 (New York: Harper and Row Publishers, 1976).

[4]The following are some of the major works by educational historians: Frederick Rudolph, *The American College and University: A History* (New York: Vintage Books, 1962); Christopher J. Lucas, *American Higher Education: A History* (New York: St. Martin's Griffin, 1994); Arthur M. Cohen, *The Shaping of American Higher Education: Emergence and Growth of the Contemporary System* (San Francisco: Jossey-Bass, 1998); and John R. Thelin, *A History of American Higher Education* (Baltimore: Johns Hopkins University Press, 2004).

[5]Richard Hofstadter and Wilson Smith, *American Higher Education: A Documentary History,* 2 Volumes (Chicago: University of Chicago Press, 1961).

PREFACE

This Reader, like its two predecessors, introduces students to the history of American higher education. More than one-third of the content is new to this edition—a sign of continued scholarly vitality.

Institutions have traditional values and practices—some distinctive, and some derived from general historical trends—that affect their students, faculty and staff members, and trustees. In turn, institutions respond to the histories of the resident actors, disciplines, professions, and the larger academic world. Historical analyses help us to understand the encounters among the actors, the strength of academic norms, and institutional opportunities and constraints, and they permit administrators and faculty members to consider the long-term effects of a contemplated action.

This Reader does not adopt a specific historiographical approach. This eclecticism allows for complexity and uncertainty, and for multiple interpretation of the same phenomenon. History informs students—as well as policy makers and administrators—but does not dictate. The "latest" explanation is neither the only, nor the "correct," understanding.

Previous editions of this Reader includes "primary sources" or original records, including correspondence, memoranda, faculty and trustee minutes, speeches, official reports, accreditation materials, college catalogs—an oft-maligned resource—newspapers and magazines, and statistical materials. Historians analyze documents, generated by yesterday's and today's administrators, students, and faculty members to understand actors and their motives and events and their consequences. These documents allow students to explore the raw materials used in decision-making: Learning how a committee "constructed" or used a report shows students ways to use documents in their professional lives.

The 300 documents accompanying this edition of the Reader are located on a companion website http://www.pearsoncustom.com/mi/msu_ashe. Moving the documents to the web gives students and faculty members the flexibility to investigate topics in depth. A website format also permits updating of materials. The website includes specialized bibliographies on the history of higher education, including Jurgen Herbst's exhaustive compilation. Also featured are key U.S. government documents, including *120 Years of American Education* by Thomas Snyder. The website also includes links to many online public domain books and reports.

The address of this Reader's companion website ishttp://www.pearsoncustom.com/mi/msu_ashe. We hope you visit the site often.

Harold S. Wechsler
New York University

Lester F. Goodchild
Santa Clara University

Linda Eisenmann
John Carroll University

February, 2007

INTEGRATING DISCIPLINARY PERSPECTIVES INTO HIGHER EDUCATION RESEARCH

LINDA EISENMANN

The Example of History

Few would deny that higher education has matured as a field of study: dozens of higher education graduate programs now thrive, scholarly organizations and journals abound with enthusiastic contributors, and new scholars consider themselves higher education specialists. The *Journal of Higher Education* has entered an eighth decade of publishing, and the Association for the Study of Higher Education (ASHE) just celebrated a twenty-fifth anniversary as the most prominent research group devoted to postsecondary educational concerns.

Yet, higher education represents a fairly recent area for research, a field that has been built through the contributions of previously established disciplines. In recognition of this history, editor John C. Smart solicited a series of articles for the annual *Higher Education: Handbook of Theory and Research* which offer autobiographies of several "pioneers" of higher education research. In highlighting the work of Robert Pace (1998), W. J. McKeachie (1999), Burton Clark (2000), and Robert Berdahl (2001), Smart cites these "distinguished scholars from other disciplines whose cumulative contributions are seminal to the development of higher education research literature" (1998, p. 1). His contention—supported by the scholars' accounts—is that higher education coalesced into a research field when such psychologists, sociologists, and political scientists, joined by economists, historians, philosophers, and others, applied modes of inquiry from their home disciplines to postsecondary education.

This mix of methodological and epistemological contributions raises two questions for higher education research. First, as the field matures, does it continue to value, welcome, and integrate the perspectives offered by the disciplines? Some are doubtful. A recent survey of ASHE members (Aleman, 2002) reveals some disenchantment with higher education scholars' seeming penchant for studying increasingly smaller parts of collegiate issues without wider contextual analysis. This concern leads to the second methodological question: how can discipline-based scholars continue to use higher education to explore vital questions, questions that both advance their disciplines and extend our understanding of higher education?

This article uses the discipline of history to explore these questions. While not a teeming group, historians of higher education have employed their disciplinary lens to advance several lines of significant postsecondary inquiry (for example, issues of access, social mobility, professionalism, gender, and regionalism). This article first traces historians' early contributions to higher education, noting that most considered themselves scholars of history who happened to find higher education a fruitful spot for their investigations. Over time, a cadre of educational historians developed, scholars who focus intentionally on higher education; the next section explores their growing contributions. But this latter group faces its own methodological challenge: how to balance between generating research that is guided by the insights and problems of history versus allowing contemporary educational puzzles about students, leadership, organization, or markets to determine their research agenda. Recognizing this as a difficult choice for any disciplinary scholar, this article encourages historians to consider the value of the second approach, suggesting that it offers strong potential for strengthening higher education research.

Early Historical Contributions to Higher Education Research

Historian John Thelin, whose recent presidency of ASHE marks him as a scholar sensitive to the postsecondary present, explored the origins of historical scholarship on higher education in a 1985 review. He observed that most early contributors were historians first and higher education specialists only incidentally. Yet, as the field developed, Thelin worried that later scholars too frequently ignored the contemporary implications of their analyses.

Thelin tracked the field's serious origins to the 1960s, when historians began to examine the collegiate past within a "wider sphere of social context and change" (p. 350). They abandoned an earlier tendency to tell stories of individual campuses simply as parts of an unquestioned march of progress and instead pursued a deeper inquiry into the importance of collegiate organization, politics, growth, and conflict. Historians increasingly viewed colleges and universities as a structural element in the social history of the United States, one that traditionally served a professional, or at least privileged, class of students. Several of these 1960s historians produced classic interpretations that are still used by higher education scholars, including Frederick Rudolph's *The American College and University: A History* (1962) and Laurence Veysey's *The Emergence of the American University* (1965).

Thelin noted the strong "cross-fertilization" between history and sociology as a hallmark of higher education scholarship by the 1970s. Sociologists such as David Riesman, Christopher Jencks (1968), and Burton Clark found in higher education history examples of concepts like stratification, class, and functional analysis that expanded our understanding of how higher education affected social mobility. Historians Harold Wechsler (1977) and Marcia Synnott (1979) followed this lead in a specific direction, producing impressive analyses of how colleges had dealt over time with minority populations and selective admissions. This era, and the disciplinary collaborations it fostered, established the themes of access and mobility as one of higher education's strongest strands of inquiry.

Yet, assessing the field in the mid-1980s, Thelin was wary. He gauged the 1970s as the peak of history's influence, given the prominent scholars using the approach and the relative ease with which they attracted financial support. By 1985 Thelin judged that "the logic and methods of historical analysis remain accidental or marginal in higher education as a field of study" (p. 374). He worried that historians were ignoring potent current applications, perhaps from a fear of having their work labeled "presentist" by other historians who decry using current problems to drive historical questions.

Hoping to allay worry and encourage stronger collaboration, Thelin outlined a series of potential connections between historians and other scholars who wish to explore the role of collegiate institutions in American life. A study of the relationship of access and admissions, he suggested, could clarify the accumulated impact of each era's decisions about who constitutes a desirable student. Historians' explication of social context could provide information to help institutions in their long-range strategic planning. Likewise, clarity about the shifting historical role of financing and economics could inform policy analysis.

Thelin never suggested that historians let their scholarship be guided by purely utilitarian ends, choosing topics only for their contemporary relevance. Such an approach would deny the true nature of scholarly inquiry. However, he called on historians, higher education scholars, and practitioners to end their strategy of "mutual avoidance," encouraging historians to show how they could contribute to contemporary discussions of mission, student retention, remediation, marketing, and organizational context.

A New Assessment

How has the collaboration between history and higher education fared nearly two decades after Thelin's analysis? Have historians responded to Thelin's encouragement? This section traces an array of contributions, showing first how non-historians in higher education have used historical perspectives to clarify their own work. It then outlines how historians have provided "building blocks" for the field, sometimes examining specific issues, other times redefining a scholarly understanding. I suggest that, although only some historians have intentionally heeded Thelin's call for a more contemporary-focused inquiry, all their work demonstrates strong implications for understanding the present, thereby expanding the base of higher education scholarship.

As higher education research has matured, practitioners with an appreciation of history have applied a historical lens to their own work. The pioneers' autobiographies (Pace, 1998; McKeachie, 1999; Clark, 2000; Berdahl, 2001) offer one example, as does a twenty-year retrospective by members of the postsecondary research division, presented at the 2001 annual meeting of the American Educational Research Association (Morey, et al., 2001). Similarly, the *Journal of Higher Education* published an anniversary issue in 1999 that reprinted a collection of articles from the 1930s, its first decade. Editor Leonard Baird observed the ahistorical nature of this work, finding the early articles generally void of references to literature beyond higher education. Especially striking was that, for a group of pieces written in the Depression-era 1930s, so much of the surrounding tumult was "perplexingly absent." At best, Baird noted, 1930s authors presaged issues around administrative change, selective admissions, assessment techniques, and curricular innovation, but without much analytical prescience (*Journal of Higher Education*, 1999).

Such efforts are useful examples of higher education scholars applying a historical lens to the overall direction of the field. An additional contribution occurs when scholars who are not historians recognize the importance of exploring the historical bases of their own research. Robert Birnbaum (2000), for example, realizes the impact of historical cycles in analyzing how management "fads" have seduced higher education administrators over the last several decades, letting them conveniently forget the promises and pitfalls of previous solutions. Arthur Cohen (1998) recognizes how strongly the history of the community college movement has affected its current place—and challenges—within the higher education taxonomy. Susan Twombly and Marilyn Amey (1991) use a historical lens alongside a contemporary one in exploring how decisions by national community college leaders have affected local decision makers. James Hearn (2000) emphasizes contextual historical analysis when examining inconsistencies in the growth of four decades of federal student aid programs, showing the absence of expected demographic, managerial, fiscal, or political requisites. Patricia McDonough, Marc Ventresca, and Charles Outcalt (1995) begin a study of how institutions approach student access by first outlining how historians, including Veysey, have explained organizational change in higher education.

Such use of historical analyses by non-historians is a sign of the field's maturity. Clearly, historians of higher education have been creating building blocks and crafting new perspectives that others can tap as they explore contemporary concerns. How have historians developed these perspectives, and to what extent do they acknowledge, and even foster, implications to current issues?

Often, historians' inquiry is prompted by particular historical puzzles, situations, or developments, many of which are connected to the present. Connolly (2000), for example, examines the appearance over time of Native American nicknames and logos at various American colleges and universities and sorts periods of acceptance, offense, challenge, and change that resulted from attention to their symbolic meaning. Hutcheson (1997) acknowledges the ongoing significance of 1950s McCarthyism to understanding past and present faculty life but also highlights the historiographic problems that have kept scholars from fully understanding the impact of that movement. Historians like Wallenstein (1999) and Kean (1999) are beginning to refine the history of the 1950s and 1960s campus-based civil rights movement by adding the stories of individual black Southerners, including women, who challenged segregation before and after the 1954 *Brown* decision. These fuller stories affect the way that campuses view their own recent histories.

At times, the consideration of a group's experience attracts historians' attention. For example, the history of African Americans in higher education has been expanded by James Anderson's *The Education of Blacks in the South* (1988), a work that emphasizes the agency of black participants in dealing with white philanthropists and power brokers. Vanessa Siddle Walker's *Their Highest Potential: An African American School Community in the Segregated South* (1996) extends Anderson's analysis by stressing the significance of community to the development of African American institutions. Amy McCandless (1999) has done much the same for consideration of women's role in higher education. Her award-winning study of Southern women's education clarifies the roles played by both white and African American students and educators, even as it reclaims the history of the South in the development of postsecondary education.

Sometimes the analysis of an individual campus deepens or corrects contemporary understandings. Katherine Reynolds (1998), writing on Black Mountain College, David Potts (1992) on Wesleyan University, and John Rury (1997) on DePaul have all provided such deeply analytical campus histories, at times surfacing situations and memories that challenge a thoroughly positive picture. When historians take on the ultimate contemporary challenge by writing the history of their own campus, real political concerns and scholarly conflicts can emerge. A group of historians who have attempted institutional histories have written about the difficulties they face: sponsors can resist the uncovering of unsavory episodes, still living participants can be hurt by revelations or analyses, scholars can be pressured to conform to a specific preferred interpretation (Leslie, 2000). To combat these concerns, these historians recommend taking a strong scholarly stance, rather than being seen as public relations advocates. Like all good scholars, they attempt to challenge prevailing interpretations through analysis of strong data.

Other historians have done the same when redefining a larger issue in the field. The historical development of college and university administration offers a good example of how historians' rediscovery of forgotten elements has reoriented our understanding. Collegiate administration has a surprisingly underanalyzed history, given its growth throughout the twentieth century. Early contributor Veysey (1965) briefly examined increases in administrative roles while explicating the larger growth of the research university. More recently, Carolyn Bashaw (1999), Jana Nidiffer (2000), and Robert Schwartz (1997) have approached this history by examining the little-studied student affairs deanship. All three have found that women helped professionalize a field that had been staffed only haphazardly by men. Perhaps because men traditionally had more professional options, they overlooked the potential power of the dean's role; women, on the other hand, used it as an entering wedge into higher education administration. The new interpretation crafted by these historians changes our understanding of the place of student affairs within the wider postsecondary enterprise.

Nidiffer and Bashaw (2001) pursued the implications of knowing more about women's role in the development of administrative positions. They co-edited a book with the unusual goal of combining historical and contemporary analyses of women as educational leaders, presenting contributions by historians and practitioners in the same volume. Through a historical analysis of women's experiences, the authors not only highlighted a continuing issue of discrimination, but also identified places in collegiate administration where women—as presidents, deans, physical education teachers, and health professionals—claimed space, power, and influence for themselves and for female students.

Historians have similarly prompted a reinterpretation of the role of college athletics on contemporary campuses. Current observers worry about the disproportionate influence of athletics on curriculum, finances, and image, yet their critiques often miss the element of how sports acquired such a key role in college life. Historical analyses from scholars like Thelin (1994) and Toma and Cross (2000) assert that changes in current athletic policies must start by recognizing the contribution of sports, athletes, and coaches to the collegiate enterprise. Historical analysis reminds us, for example, that for many taxpayers, the fortunes of the state university team epitomize education's real "success," as well as the status of public commitment to education. Athletics have provided an unusual connection between higher education and the democratic polity that cannot be ignored, either historically or in the present.

A third area (in addition to administration and athletics) where historians have helped redefine contemporary understanding is the growth of systemic elements in higher education. Sometimes these elements are particular types of institutions; other times, they are state or national influences. For instance, Roger Geiger (1986, 1993) has investigated the growth of research universities over the course of the twentieth century. Nancy Diamond and Hugh Davis Graham (1997) are intrigued by the selective growth of such institutions after World War II, wondering how some schools benefitted so demonstrably from the era's rise of "big science," as well as how this growth affected collegiate missions. Their *The Rise of American Research Universities: Elites and Challengers in the Postwar Era* could be a primer for contemporary institutional planners by exploring how some schools seized new opportunities, redefining both their mission and curriculum, while others fumbled in responding to the new environment. John Aubrey Douglass (2000) interrogates the development and impact of a state-level system, analyzing the 1960s California Master Plan that served as a model for so many other states. When Douglass explores some of the costs from this planned reorganization of higher education, he helps explain current developments in California that result from decades of state-level planning. George Marsden (1994) and Philip Gleason (1995) have led a concerted effort to reexamine the development of Catholic institutions, considering them not only as a separate strand, but also investigating the effect of such a unique option within higher education. Each of these analyses is conducted by historians who see implications of the past for the present.

Occasionally, historians attempt a wide revision of the history of higher education, although few have done so since Rudolph and Veysey in the 1960s. This development may be slow because new historical methods like social history and quantitative analyses are providing complex basic analyses that make syntheses difficult. However, the history of women in higher education offers one example of a recently reconceptualized history. Historian Barbara Solomon's *In the Company of Educated Women* (1985) synthesized the increasingly sophisticated contributions being made by new developments in women's history. Using newly available research, Solomon offered a reconceived exploration of women's demand, use, participation, and effect on American higher education, emphasizing their varied successes amid long periods without welcome. Although Solomon's work is now old enough to merit revision of its own (Eisenmann, 1997, 2001), it nonetheless stands as a strong reanalysis of a large sweep of higher education, one that helps analysts better understand women's ongoing struggles for professional acceptance (e.g., "the glass ceiling").

Roger Geiger (1992) offers another wide-ranging new analysis in his exploration of collegiate growth and change throughout the nineteenth and twentieth centuries. His "matrix" approach to higher education examines consecutive periods of collegiate development according to changes in knowledge, institutions, and constituents. Such a conception invites other historians to provide additional building blocks and data points that can help affirm, disconfirm, or revise Geiger's analysis.

Recent historical work in higher education—whether closely focused on a single topic or widely conceived—has clearly enriched the field. At times historical scholars have intentionally applied their findings to contemporary situations; but often, the implications remain to be drawn. How might a historian more actively respond to issues of contemporary application that arise during research?

Using the Historical Lens

In this article, I have agreed with Thelin's (1985) suggestion that historians re-examine their solipsistic research inclinations, and I have highlighted examples that demonstrate how solid historical scholarship can—intentionally or not—inform current research. The challenge is not an easy one, however, for historians who must employ the methods, curiosity, themes, and inquiry of their discipline, whether or not the findings apply to the present. In this final section, I use my own current explorations of post-World War II higher education to examine how a historian can recognize a dialogue between historical findings and contemporary implications.

I am pursuing two lines of historical research on higher education from 1945 to the present. My main focus examines women's participation as faculty and students from 1945 to 1965, before the new women's movement took firm hold on American campuses (Eisenmann, 2002, 2003). I explore connections between women's more recent activism and a quieter period in their history. A second, more preliminary project investigates the history of comprehensive, urban universities (like the "Urban 13") that prospered and expanded during the high-growth 1960s.

We already know a great deal about some aspects of this "golden age" of American higher education. Richard Freeland (1992) and Roger Geiger (1993), among others, have traced the development of research universities through the postwar influx of federal research dollars, emphasizing the power of this new sector and its mission. The appearance of G.I. Bill veterans has provided another line of historical inquiry, with attention to how this new group altered the student profile (Olson, 1974; Clark, 1998). General education was also reinvigorated during the postwar landscape, partially prompted by Harvard's explorations (Harvard University, 1945; Rudolph, 1977). Work on all of these areas has helped redefine our understanding of contemporary institutions.

But other elements of postwar collegiate development—ones with equally strong contemporary applications—have attracted less attention from historians. For instance, looking at institutions, community colleges burst with growth as new populations, new needs, and new money coincided in the 1960s. Yet these schools lack a thorough exploration of their history (Hutcheson, 1999). Likewise, other significant institutions, like comprehensive universities and urban institutions, found added constituents, growing support, and invigorated missions in a burgeoning postwar period, but historians have yet to seriously analyze the effects of their development.

The shifting populations in higher education—which are intriguing to current scholars of access and financial aid—also lack a full examination through the lens of social history. Women, people of color, and middle-class students (beyond the veterans) changed the look of campuses; but what else did they change? How might deeper investigations of postwar organizations, students, and influences reveal antecedents or clarifications of current concerns?

The study of women's postwar educational participation promises clarity on a few of these questions. Women's postwar role has, perhaps surprisingly, been rather neglected, even with the last two decades of strong research. Perhaps the "Father Knows Best" stereotypes of the 1950s have encouraged us to accept Betty Friedan's (1963) picture of women carelessly abandoning college in favor of home and family. In fact, although women's percentage of the student body dropped immediately following World War II, their actual numbers in higher education grew steadily from 1945 to the present (with slight dips only in 1951 and 1952) (NCES, 1993). Simultaneously, women's participation in all segments of the labor market—including single women, married women, and older women—grew steadily (Goldin, 1990; Kessler-Harris, 1982). These two facts suggest how postwar women came to understand the economic power of collegiate training; they also inform the recent concern that women now "overpopulate" sectors of higher education at the expense of men (Eisenmann, 2003).

When current scholars and student affairs professionals lament the continuing lack of understanding about students of color, women, and gay and lesbian students, they might be informed by the studied indifference accorded these groups in the postwar era. African Americans and women generally attracted attention only from people holding direct responsibility for them, including administrators at historically black institutions and women's colleges. Most postwar observers and scholars regarded these groups as far too marginal to hold any explanatory power in larger models or policy recommendations.

For example, Caplow and McGee's influential analysis of *The Academic Marketplace* (1958), dismissed women entirely: "Women tend to be discriminated against in the academic profession, not because they have low prestige but because they are outside the prestige system entirely and for this reason are of no use to a department in future recruitment" (p. 111). Minority scholars met much the same fate. The authors did acknowledge the "inequitable treatment" that these scholars experienced, but they offered few suggestions for analyzing or amending the damage (see also Caplow & McGee, 2001).

Postwar organizations and commissions offer potentially fruitful avenues for exploring the actual situation for such scholars and students. Ad hoc groups like the President's Commission on Higher Education (also known as the Truman Commission) (President's Commission, 1947) and the Commission on the Education of Women of the American Council on Education (1953–1962) focused attention not only on these students but also on institutions and research that supported them, emphasizing the ongoing effects of discriminatory practice. Similarly, organizations like the National Association of Women Deans and Counselors, the American Association of University Women (Bashaw, 2001), and its African American counterpart, the National Association of College Women (Perkins, 1990), reveal historical antecedents of exclusion that help explain subsequent (and sometimes difficult) efforts to claim a place for women professionals. Examining these organizations allows us to trace, from past to present, the personal, professional, and research concerns surrounding these populations, as well as to reclaim the contributions of individual postwar scholars and activists.

We can also inform our understanding of how different groups of students have experienced college by investigating their treatment in the past. For example, postwar cultural norms preached heterosexuality and the preeminence of the family. Consequently, most gay and lesbian collegians and faculty were either closeted or persecuted for much of this period. The Kinsey reports of 1948 and 1953 signaled a slow acceptance of new approaches to sexuality on campuses (Bailey, 1999; D'Emilio, 1992). Similarly, countercultural groups like the Beats allowed women limited new options for self-expression (Breines, 1994).

The postwar growth of institutional "tiers" and the power of the research model help explain the "mission creep" that has been identified among many current institutions trying to redefine their place in the hierarchy. The history of Massachusetts offers an interesting example. Unlike many states, Massachusetts has a weak history of state-sponsored higher education. The five campuses of the University of Massachusetts were organized into a system only in 1991, and the state colleges have developed more autonomously than in many regions of the country. Currently, at least one of these state colleges aspires to university status; its president has proclaimed this institution as ready to "advance" to a new tier. Resistance and doubt have met the president's announcement. Certainly, Massachusetts' long history of strong private institutions that denigrate the former teachers colleges, along with the slow growth of state influence, help explain the reaction—and, perhaps, the college's chance of success.

Connecting History and Practice

Work like my own that attempts to clarify the "ecology" of a wider array of higher education populations and institutions holds considerable promise for the way we understand contemporary higher education. Examining how various sorts of institutions interacted, as well as how higher education met challenges posed by growing student populations, can better inform our appreciation of current concerns.

Yet not all historians would perceive such an easy conversation between examining the present via the past. Like all disciplinary scholars, historians generate their questions and organize their inquiry according to the tenets of their field. Thus, many would reject as presentist any suggestion that their analyses be dictated by the interests of practitioners and policymakers.

However, the material highlighted here demonstrates that there can be a symbiosis between rigorous historical analysis and careful contemporary application. Historians like Rudolph, Veysey, and Solomon used sound historical methods and produced work that is both ground-breaking to history and helpful to scholars of higher education. Likewise, more recent historians, working on challenges and puzzles found in the historical record, have prompted insights into the postsecondary present.

Perhaps the results are strongest when the responsibility for applying historical analysis is shared by those who *produce* it and those who *use* it. Historians must become more comfortable in highlighting, even pursuing, connections between past and present; but, at the same time, they must welcome and converse with other scholars—even those not trained in history—who apply elements of historical analysis to contemporary concerns. This approach never diminishes disciplinary inquiry but gains the added strength of extending the increasingly vital field of higher education research. Through such discussion, historians join disciplinary colleagues in economics, philosophy, law, psychology, and anthropology who intentionally apply their interpretive skills and methodological approaches to higher education.

Conclusion

It has taken some time for historians to recognize the fertile ground that higher education offers as a site for their analyses. Likewise, the field of higher education needed to mature before it fully appreciated the value of applying historical assessments to contemporary concerns. However, some traditional historians became intrigued with using higher education as a setting to examine their concerns, for example, with class mobility. Other times, higher education analysts turned to the tools and data of history to clarify their understanding, for example, of the power of athletics on collegiate campuses. Once the two approaches conjoined after the 1960s, a deeper understanding began to inform higher education's view of access, mobility, student populations, curriculum, institutional diversity, policymaking, and financing, to name only a few significant contributions.

The value of turning a historical lens on these concerns—whether it comes from asking a question specific to history or is generated by contemporary practice—is that practitioners and policymakers gain a fuller, more wide-angled view of the higher education enterprise. Worries about women's growing predominance as undergraduate students, for instance, can be clarified by learning the history of how and why they pushed for access to an identifiably equal collegiate curriculum. Or the complicated negotiations faced by many contemporary gay and lesbian students can be illuminated by understanding the treatment they experienced in the post-World War II era. Higher education—still a relatively young field—needs disciplinary contributions to stretch its analyses, both conceptually and methodologically. And, for the foreseeable future, higher education promises to offer a potent site for disciplinary inquiry, as the example of history promisingly demonstrates.

References

Aleman, A. M. (2002). *Report of the task force on the membership.* Association for the Study of Higher Education.

Anderson, J. D. (1988). *The education of Blacks in the South, 1860–1935.* Chapel Hill, NC: University of North Carolina Press.

Bailey, B. (1999). *Sex in the heartland.* Cambridge, MA: Harvard University Press.

Baird, L. L. (1999). A note from the editor on JHE's anniversary issue. *Journal of Higher Education, 70* (5), v–x.

Bashaw, C. T. (1999). *"Stalwart women": A historical analysis of deans of women in the South.* New York: Teachers College Press.

Bashaw, C. T. (2001). "To serve the needs of women": The AAUW, NAWDC, and the persistence of academic women's support networks. In J. Nidiffer & C. T. Bashaw (Eds.), *Women administrators in higher education* (pp. 249 –269). Albany, NY: SUNY Press.

Berdahl, R. (2001). Apologia pro vita mia. In J. C. Smart (Ed.), *Higher education: Handbook of theory and research* (Vol. 16, pp. 1–24). New York: Agathon Press.

Birnbaum, R. (2000). *Management fads in higher education: Where they come from, what they do, why they fail.* San Francisco, CA: Jossey-Bass.

Breines, W. (1994). The "other fifties": Beats and bad girls. In J. Meyerowitz (Ed.), *Not June Cleaver: Women and gender in postwar America, 1945–1960* (pp. 382–408). Philadelphia: Temple University Press.

Caplow, T., & McGee, R. J. (1958). *The academic marketplace.* New York: Basic Books.

Caplow, T., & McGee, R. J. (2001). *The academic marketplace* (with new introduction by the authors). New Brunswick, NJ: Transaction.

Clark, B. R. (2000). Developing a career in the study of higher education. In J. C. Smart (Ed.), *Higher education: Handbook of theory and research* (Vol. 15, pp. 1–38). New York: Agathon.

Clark, D. A. (1998). "The two Joes meet—Joe College, Joe Veteran": The G. I. bill, college education, and postwar American culture. *History of Education Quaterly, 38* (2), 165–189.

Cohen, A. M. (1998). *The shaping of American higher education: Emergence and growth of the contemporary system.* San Francisco: Jossey-Bass.

Connolly, M. R. (2000). What's in a name?: A historical look at Native American-related nicknames and symbols at three U.S. universities. *Journal of Higher Education, 71* (5), 515–547.

D'Emilio, J. (1992). *Making trouble: Essays on gay history, politics, and the university.* New York: Routledge.

Diamond, N., & Graham, H. D. (1997). *The rise of American research universities: Elites and challengers in the postwar era.* Baltimore: The Johns Hopkins University Press.

Douglass, J. A. (2000). *The California idea and American higher education: 1850 to the 1960 Master Plan.* Stanford, CA: Stanford University Press.

Eisenmann, L. (2003, April). *Reclaiming the "Incidental Students": Higher education and women in the 1950s.* Vice presidential address presented at the meeting of the American Educational Research Association, Chicago, IL.

Eisenmann, L. (2002). Educating the female citizen in a postwar world: Competing ideologies for American women, 1945–1965. *Educational Review, 54* (2), 133–141.

Eisenmann, L. (2001). Creating a framework for interpreting U.S. women's educational history: Lessons from historical lexicography. *History of Education, 30* (5), 453–470.

Eisenmann, L. (1997). Reconsidering a classic: Assessing the history of women's higher education a dozen years after Barbara Solomon. *Harvard Educational Review, 67,* 689–717.

Freeland, R. (1992). *Academia's golden age: Universities in Massachusetts: 1945 to 1970.* New York: Oxford University Press.

Friedan, B. (1963/1983). *The feminine mystique.* New York: Dell.

Geiger, R. L. (1986). *To advance knowledge: The growth of American research universities, 1900–1940.* New York: Oxford University Press.

Geiger, R. L. (1992). The historical matrix of American higher education. *History of Higher Education Annual, 12,* 7–28.

Geiger, R. L. (1993). *Research and relevant knowledge: American research universities since World War II.* New York: Oxford University Press.

Gleason, P. (1995). *Contending with modernity: Catholic higher education in the twentieth century.* New York: Oxford University Press.

Goldin, C. (1990). *Understanding the gender gap: An economic history of American women.* New York: Oxford University Press.

Harvard University. Committee on the Objectives of a General Education in a Free Society. (1945). *General education in a free society: Report of the Harvard committee.* Cambridge, MA: Harvard University.

Hearn, J. (1993). The paradox of growth in federal aid for college students, 1965–1990. In J. C. Smart (Ed.), *Higher education: Handbook of theory and research* (Vol. 10, pp. 94–153). New York: Agathon.

Hutcheson, P. A. (1997). McCarthyism and the professoriate: A Historiographic nightmare? In J. C. Smart (Ed.), *Higher education: Handbook of theory and research* (Vol. 12, pp. 435–460). New York: Agathon.

Hutcheson, P. A. (1999). Reconsidering the community college. *History of Education Quarterly, 39,* (3), 307–320.

Jencks, C., & Riesman, D. (1968). *The academic revolution.* Garden City, NY: Doubleday.

Journal of Higher Education. (1999). Special Anniversary Issue: A Look Back, *70* (5).

Kean, M. F. (1999). Guiding desegregation: The role of "the intelligent white man of the South," 1945–1954. *History of Higher Education Annual, 19,* 57–84.

Kessler-Harris, A. (1982). *Out to work: A history of wage-earning women in the United States.* New York: Oxford University Press.

Kinsey, A. C., Pomeroy, W. B., & Martin, C. E. (1948). *Sexual behavior in the human male.* Philadelphia: Saunders.

Kinsey, A. C., & Staff of the Institute for Sex Research (1953). *Sexual behavior in the human female.* Philadelphia: Saunders.

Leslie, W. B. (2000). Writing postwar institutional histories. *History of Higher Education Annual, 20,* 83–91.

Marsden, G. M. (1994). *The soul of the American university: From Protestant establishment to established nonbelief.* New York: Oxford University Press.

McCandless, A. T. (1999). *The past in the present: Women's higher education in the twentieth-century South.* Tuscaloosa: University of Alabama Press.

McDonough, P., Ventresca, M. J., & Outcalt, C. (2000). Field of dreams: Organizational field approaches to understanding the transformation of college access, 1965–1995. In J. C. Smart (Ed.), *Higher education: Handbook of theory and research* (Vol. 15, pp. 371–405). New York: Agathon.

McKeachie, W. J. (1999). Teaching, learning, and thinking about teaching and learning. In J. C. Smart (Ed.), *Higher education: Handbook of theory and research* (Vol. 14, pp. 1–38). New York: Agathon Press.

Morey, A., Leslie, D., Slaughter, S., Peterson M. W., & Clark, B. R. (2001). *A critical look at twenty years of postsecondary education research and thoughts for the future.* Unpublished panel at the annual meeting of American Educational Research Association, Seattle.

National Center for Education Statistics. (1993). *120 years of American education: A statistical portrait.* Washington, DC: Office of Educational Research and Improvement.

Nidiffer, J. (2000). *Pioneering deans of women: More than wise and pious matrons.* New York: Teachers College Press.

Nidiffer, J., & Bashaw, C. T. (2001). *Women administrators in higher education: Historical and contemporary perspectives.* Albany, NY: SUNY Press.

Olson, K. W. (1974). *The G.I. bill, the veterans, and the colleges.* Lexington: University Press of Kentucky.

Pace, C. R. (1998). Recollections and reflections. In J. C. Smart (Ed.), *Higher education: Handbook of theory and research* (Vol. 13, pp. 1–34). New York: Agathon.

Perkins, L. M. (1990). The National Association of College Women: Vanguard of Black women's leadership and education, 1923–1954. *Journal of Education, 172* (3), 65–75.

Potts, D. B. (1992). *Wesleyan University, 1931–1910: Collegiate enterprise in New England.* New Haven: Yale University Press.

President's Commission on Higher Education. (1947). *Higher education for American democracy: A report of the President's Commission on Higher Education.* New York: Harper & Brothers.

Reynolds, K. C. (1998). *Visions and vanities: John Andrew Rice of Black Mountain College.* Baton Rouge: Louisiana State University Press.

Rudolph, F. (1962). *The American college and university: A history.* New York: Random House.

Rudolph, F. (1977). *Curriculum: A history of the American undergraduate course of study since 1636.* San Francisco: Jossey-Bass.

Rury, J. L. (1997). The urban Catholic university in the early twentieth century: A social profile of DePaul, 1898–1940. *History of Higher Education Annual, 17,* 5–32.

Schwartz, R. A. (1997). Reconceptualizing the leadership roles of women in higher education: A brief note on the importance of the dean of women. *Journal of Higher Education, 68* (5), 502–522.

Smart, J. C. (Ed.). (1998). *Higher education: Handbook of theory and research* (Vol. 13, p. 1). New York: Agathon.

Solomon, B. M. (1985). *In the company of educated women.* New Haven: Yale University Press.

Synnott, M. G. (1979). *The half-opened door: Discrimination and admissions at Harvard, Yale, and Princeton, 1900–1970.* Westport, CT: Greenwood Press.

Thelin, J. R. (1985). Beyond background music: Historical research on admissions and access in higher education. In J. C. Smart (Ed.), *Higher education: Handbook of theory and research* (Vol. 1, pp. 349–380). New York: Agathon.

Thelin, J. R. (1994). *Games colleges play: Scandal and reform in intercollegiate athletics.* Baltimore: The Johns Hopkins University Press.

Toma, J. D., & Cross, M. E. (2000). Contesting values in American higher education: The playing field of intercollegiate athletics. In J. C. Smart (Ed.), *Higher education: Handbook of theory and research* (Vol. 15, pp. 406–455). New York: Agathon.

Twombly, S. B., & Amey, M. J. (1991). Leadership in community colleges: Looking toward the second century. In J. C. Smart (Ed.), *Higher education: Handbook of theory and research* (Vol. 12, pp. 376–419). New York: Agathon.

Veysey, L. R. (1965). *The emergence of the American university.* Chicago: University of Chicago Press.

Walker, V. S. (1996). *Their highest potential: An African American school community in the segregated South.* Chapel Hill, NC: University of North Carolina Press.

Wallenstein, P. (1999). Black Southerners and non-Black universities: Desegregating higher education, 1935–1967. *History of Higher Education Annual, 19,* 121–148.

Wechsler, H. S. (1977). *The qualified student: A history of selective college admission in America 1870–1970.* New York: Wiley.

PART I

HISTORIES OF GLOBAL AND AMERICAN HIGHER EDUCATION

Part I: Histories of Global and American Higher Education

A commentary on the Reader's selections offers an opportunity to identify the historical themes for each period of American higher education and the conceptual framework underlying its organization. The study of higher education as a graduate degree program began with Clark University President G. Stanley Hall's pioneering effort in 1893[1]—yet, the quest to achieve higher learning originated in the early fabric of human culture. While higher learning may be seen in the development of theological study and praxis in the ancient worlds of Mesopotamia and Egypt, the first institutions similar to our own are found in India. In 400 A.D., Buddhist monks created proto-universities with extensive course offerings and libraries. Even though there were rigorous admission policies, some 10,000 students attended Nalanda in India at one point.[2] Between the years 700–1300, Islamic centers of learning expanded to become universities, where faculty arrayed themselves into three ranks: assistant, associate, and full teachers. The force of this theological orientation in higher education continued.

In our first reading, Harold Perkin's expansive survey of the history of higher education begins with western universities in the medieval world and ends with contemporary post-secondary systems.[3] With the rise of universities at Bologna, Salerno, Paris, and Oxford in the twelfth and thirteenth centuries, Western civilization created institutions of higher learning to preserve, transmit, and discover knowledge. This evolutionary and comparative perspective enables us to place the development and growth of American colleges and universities within a world context. Next, Lester Goodchild's short history of American higher education from the recent two-volume encyclopedia, *Higher Education in the United States*,[4] offers the reader a comprehensive window into the complex history of American post-secondary education.

ENDNOTES

[1] Lester F. Goodchild, "Higher Education as a Field of Study: Its Origins, Programs, and Purposes, 1893–1960," in *Administration as a Profession*, edited by Jonathan D. Fife and Lester F. Goodchild, *New Directions for Higher Education*, No. 76 (San Francisco: Jossey-Bass Publishers, 1991), 15–32; idem, "G. Stanley Hall and the Study of Higher Education," *The Review of Higher Education* 20, No. 1 (1996), 69–99.

[2] Lester F. Goodchild, "Religious Vocations (Theological Schools and Seminaries)," in *The Encyclopedia of Higher Education*. Volume 2, *Analytic Perspectives: The Institutional Fabric of the Higher Education System*, 4 Volumes (Oxford: Pergamon Press, 1992), 1200–1217; 2nd ed., 1997.

[3] Harold Perkin, "History of Universities," *International Higher Education: An Encyclopedia*, Volume 1 (New York: Garland Publishing, 1991).

[4] Lester F. Goodchild, "History of Higher Education," *Higher Education in the United States*, 2 Volumes (Denver: ABC-CLIO Publishing, 2002), 1: 319–333.

CHAPTER 1

HISTORICAL PERSPECTIVES

HISTORY OF UNIVERSITIES

HAROLD PERKIN

All advanced civilizations have needed higher education to train their ruling, priestly, military, and other service elites, but only in medieval Europe did an institution recognizable as a university arise: a school of higher learning combining teaching and scholarship and characterized by its corporate autonomy and academic freedom. The Confucian schools for the Mandarin bureaucracy of imperial China, the Hindu *gurukulas* and Buddhist *vihares* for the priests and monks of medieval India, the *madrasahs* for the mullahs and Koranic judges of Islam, the Aztec and Inca temple schools for the priestly astronomers of pre-Columbian America, the Tokugawa *han* schools for Japanese samurai— all taught the high culture, received doctrine, literary *and/or* mathematical skills of their political or religious masters, with little room for questioning or analysis. The same might be said for the monastic schools of early medieval Europe that kept alive biblical studies and classical learning in the dark ages between the fall of Rome and the twelfth-century Renaissance. The athenaeums and lyceums of ancient Greece had some of the characteristics of the medieval European university, free speculative thought and the challenge to authority, and for much the same reason, the fragmentation of authority and possibility of escape for the dissident philosopher to another city, but they never achieved the corporate form that gave the university its permanence.

Only in Europe from the twelfth century onwards did an autonomous, permanent, corporate institution of higher learning emerge and survive, in varying forms, down to the present day. The university was the accidental product of a uniquely fragmented and decentralized civilization. The Europe that emerged out of the violence and chaos of the Germanic and Viking invasions was fractured and divided on every dimension: between church and state, and within them between multiple layers of authority from emperor and pope through baron and bishop down to knight's fee and borough. The Gelasian doctrine of the "two swords," temporal and spiritual (Pope Gelasius II, A.D. 494), split the allegiance of society and imposed two systems of law, canon and civil, with equal jurisdiction over the faithful. In the mutually destructive strife between empire and papacy, power was "up for grabs" and fractionated out in a hierarchy of competing authorities: king and archbishop, duke and abbot, free county and free city, manorial lord and parish priest. In the interstices of power, the university could find a modestly secure niche and play off one authority against another. Unintentionally, it evolved into an immensely flexible institution, able to adapt to almost any political situation and form of society. In this way it was able to survive for eight centuries and migrate eventually to every country and continent in the world.

Designed originally for a cosmopolitan world in which scholars from every part of the Christian West could gather at key centers and communicate in Latin, it outlived that world and adjusted itself to a succession of divergent social and political systems. After helping to destroy the medieval world order at the Reformation, the universities were "nationalized" by the emerging nation states in the religious wars between Catholic and Protestant, which they served as instruments of propaganda warfare. During the eighteenth-century Enlightenment, they declined to such an extent that they were bypassed by the Scientific Revolution and the rise of new philosophies and social sciences, and were in danger of disappearing altogether. Indeed, the French Revolution abolished them in France and the conquered territories, but resurrected them again in the form of the *grandes écoles* and the Napoleonic University of France. At the same time the old universities were revitalized in Scotland and above all in Germany, where a new model of professorial organization combining teaching and research emerged and came to be emulated all over Europe and eventually in countries overseas, including the United States and Japan. That form of university was especially suited to the needs of the new society produced by the Industrial Revolution, to which it belatedly but brilliantly adjusted. Meanwhile, the expansion of Europe by conquest and colonization spread the university to other continents, from the sixteenth century to the Spanish empire, from the seventeenth to the English and French colonies in North America, and later to other continents, including India, Australia and New Zealand, Africa, and even to China, the Middle East, and Japan. It became an instrument not only of modernization on the Western model but also in the shape of nationalist ideology and student unrest, of the anticolonial reaction against Western domination of Asia and Africa.

Finally, in the worldwide expansion of higher education that followed World War II, it transformed itself once again, into the pivotal institution of a new kind of society. In this new postindustrial or professional society, agriculture and manufacturing became so efficient, with the help of the scientific research produced by the university and its offshoots, the technical colleges and research institutes, that most people came to work in service industries, increasing numbers of whom would require specialized high-level training. This entailed the transition from elite to mass higher education, from a system catering to fewer than 3 percent of the student age group to one catering to more than 15 percent, and even for as much as 30 to 50 percent in the most advanced countries. Not all of these were in universities but in increasing numbers of technical colleges, community colleges, short-cycle institutions, and the like, which had first arisen to serve the needs of industrial society, and now came to train the second quartile below the university level. In most countries, however, the university and its children became so large and expensive, so dependent on the state, for resources, and, like the state itself, so bureaucratized that it was once more dominated by superior authority. The cost of becoming the axial institution of modern postindustrial society is that the university has become, or is in danger in many countries of becoming, an integral organ of the state and so of losing its autonomy and academic freedom.

The history of higher education, therefore, is largely the history of the European university and its evolution into an institution, or congeries of institutions, flexible enough to serve the needs of enormously different societies in every part of the world, culminating in its universal acceptance as the key institution of modern and developing societies everywhere. Its history can be told in five stages:

1. The rise of the cosmopolitan European university and its role in the destruction of the medieval world order at the Reformation (twelfth century–1530s)

2. The "nationalization" of the university by the emerging nation states of the Religious Wars, and its decline during the eighteenth-century Enlightenment (1530s–1789)

3. The revival of the university after the French Revolution and its belated but increasing role in Industrial Society (1789–1939)

4. The migration of the university to the non-European world and its adaptation to the needs of developing societies and the anticolonial reaction (1538–1960s)

5. The transition from elite to mass higher education and the role of the university and its offshoots in post-industrial society (1945–present)

The University and the Medieval World Order

The first universities grew out of the cathedral and municipal schools of the reviving cities of twelfth-century Europe. As life surged back to urban centers after the Germanic and Viking invasions, a demand arose for trained elites to serve the bureaucracies of church and state and the emerging professions of the clergy, law, and medicine. These urban schools supplemented or replaced the monastic schools that had kept Biblical studies and ancient classical learning alive during the Dark Ages. Education had always been a lesser concern of the monasteries, whose main function was, and remained, the salvation of souls by prayer and mediation through the saints, but they needed to train their own novices and, sometimes, also trained neighboring magnates' children. Where they were established in or near towns, they were only too willing to take advantage of the more specialized teaching of these new schools. The Franciscan and Dominican friars, after they came into existence in 1209 and 1215, often gravitated to cities with schools and provided students and teachers for them, especially in theology.

The new urban schools, called *studia,* came to serve the needs of a more secular, if still profoundly religious society, more settled if still warlike, for parish and diocesan clergy, lawyers and administrators, and medical practitioners. Most of them never became universities but taught the basic skills needed for the literate professions: grammar (the Latin used in all the business of church and state), rhetoric (persuasive reasoning used in sermons, lectures, and political speeches), and dialectic (logic, and by extension, philosophy, for analyzing texts and making policy). These three arts made up the *trivium.* The seven liberal arts were completed by the *quadrivium*—music, arithmetic, geometry, and astronomy—making up all that an educated man needed for the business of life. Such a man became a *magister,* a master qualified to teach others and to proceed to the higher faculties of theology, law, or medicine. An arts *studium* that added one or more of the higher faculties and attracted students from far and wide could claim to be a *studium generale* and, in the course of time, petition the emperor or the pope to confirm its status by imperial charter or papal bull and grant it the *jus ubique docendi,* the right of its masters to teach anywhere.

Salerno

The first school to enjoy this status, at least in medicine, was at Salerno. In southern Italy at the crossroads of Christian, Arab, Greek, and Jewish influences, it had a well-known medical school from the ninth or tenth century, teaching the works of Galen and Hippocrates through translations from the Arabic, some made by Constantine, the African who settled there about 1177. Although given a monopoly of medical teaching by Frederick II, king of Naples, in 1231 and recognized as a *studium generale* by his successor Charles II of Anjou in 1280, it faded in the thirteenth century and its claim to be the first university is still disputed.

Paris and Medieval Scholasticism

The first full universities in Europe were Paris and Bologna. In the twelfth-century renaissance of Greek philosophy, recovered through translations from the Arabic, the fame of the church schools of Paris— the schools of Notre Dame cathedral, St. Genevieve, and of the regular canons of St. Victor—attracted students from all over northern Europe. They came to sit at the feet of great masters like William of Champeaux, Hugh of St. Victor, John of Salisbury, and, above all, Peter Abelard.

Abelard, a charismatic Breton Augustinian canon, transformed the traditional arts course, and especially dialectic, into a pathbreaking instrument of philosophical analysis. The dialectic method of his book, *Sic et Non* (pro and con, thesis and antithesis) became the chief tool for deconstructing the meaning of sacred and classical texts and reconciling their contradictions. He and his followers set out to reconcile Holy Writ and the Christian Fathers with the recently recovered writings of Aristotle and, to a lesser extent, Plato. Scholasticism became the key to understanding the visible world of men and things and the invisible worlds of Christian revelation and Platonic ideas. Its promise of esoteric knowledge and wisdom and its training in intellectual analysis and subtle argument excited generations of young scholars who flocked to Paris and other universities to learn the meaning of life and eternity. It reached its apogee in the works of two Dominican doctors, Albertus Magnus (1193–1280) and his pupil Thomas Aquinas (1225–1274), who patiently reconciled the Arabic commentaries of Avicenna and Averroes on Aristotle with the Bible and the Fathers in two great syncretisms, the former's *De Unitate Intellectus* (On the unity of the intellect) and the latter's *Summa Theologiae* (Encyclopedia of theology), still the foundation of Catholic exegesis today.

The method had its dangers, physical as well as spiritual. Abelard was tried twice for his heretical questioning of church doctrine, as were many other academics down to Jan Hus and Giordano Bruno, some of whom were burned as heretics. For even the most abstruse philosophical argument could endanger the unity of the church. The most perilous question of all, strange to modern ears was the ancient Greek dispute between realism—not common-sense realism but the reality of the (Platonic) universals that underlay particular objects in the material world—and nominalism—the (more Aristotelian) belief that such ideas were mere names or abstractions. When applied to the theology of the Mass, the dispute over the reality or mere symbolism of Christ's body and blood in the bread and wine became the *cause célèbre* of theological disputes and heresy trials. Both realists like the protoprotestants, John Wyclif of Oxford and Jan Hus of Prague, and nominalists like Marsiglio of Padua, Rector of Paris University, and William of Ockham, the skeptical doctor of both Oxford and Paris, could become irreconcilable critics of papal orthodoxy. At the Reformation, belief in transubstantiation (the profoundly realist interpretation of the Mass) would become the litmus test between Catholic and Protestant. The intellectual daring and occasional martyrdom of the schoolmen established the tradition of academic freedom that was to shake the medieval church to its foundations.

By the thirteenth century, the schools of Paris had grown into a single *studium generale* with its privileges confirmed by the pope (1194) and the French King (1200). Royal and papal patronage were necessary to protect the scholars from the overbearing cathedral chancellor and the hostile citizenry of Paris. In 1200, for example, a tavern student riot that provoked the townsfolk to murder ended with the king imprisoning the provost (mayor) of Paris, hanging or banishing the murderers, and enforcing an oath on the citizens to respect the privileges of the university. In 1229, a carnival riot inciting the killing of students, in which the murderers were supported by the queen-regent Blanche of Castille, provoked the "great dispersion," a university strike and migration of students and masters to Orleans, Reims, and Angers (incidentally starting up universities in those cities) and causing an economic depression in Paris. Only after the pope ordered the young king in 1231 to punish the murderers, recalled the hostile papal legate, and granted the university a Great Charter of privileges did the scholars return.

With good reason, therefore, the university began to take on corporate form or, rather, forms. Both masters and students organized themselves against the cathedral clergy, the citizens, and against each other. The word *universitas* meant no more than a society or guild, like the contemporary guilds of craftsmen or merchants in most medieval towns. The university originally signified not the studium but, in Paris and northern Europe, the guild of masters and, in Bologna and the Italian universities, the guild of students. North of the Alps it followed the normal guild form, with the lowliest students, the undergraduates, equivalent to the apprentices of the crafts; those who passed the trivium became bachelors, equivalent to the craft bachelors or journeymen; and those fully qualified in all seven arts became masters, licensed to practice, that is, to teach the bachelors and apprentices. Later, elsewhere in France and in Italy, the arts would be taught outside the university and the *baccalaureate* would become a prerequisite for admission. The term university, meaning the organization of masters *and/or* students, eventually became attached to the *studium* itself.

In Paris a guild of masters was in existence by 1170, with formal statutes from 1210, whose main concern was to limit the control of the cathedral chancellor, who had the right to license masters. His claim to withhold the license and control the masters was denied by the pope in 1219 and 1222, who also abolished the bishop's right to imprison scholars or excommunicate the university.

At the same time the arts students began to organize in four "nations": the "French" (of the Ile de France), the Normans, the Picards, and the English (who included the Germans and other northerners). Each nation elected its own rector and two proctors, who took charge of discipline and finance, including funding the important appeals to Rome and setting lodging rents with the Parisians. By 1245 they had agreed to elect a single rector, usually a young master, who became, by the weight of supporting numbers, the effective head of the university. In time the nations, dominated by the young regent masters obliged to teach for the first two years while studying in a higher faculty, were able to impose their own rector upon the masters and doctors as the representative of the university to the outside world. Despite this anomaly, Paris became a "university of masters," unlike the Italian "university of students" discussed below.

The college system also evolved in Paris. Originally students lived in a lodging, hostel, or hall rented by one of them or a resident master. To maintain discipline and prevent quarrels with the locals, such a residence might be rented or purchased by a benefactor, for his kin or neighbors or clients, as Jean de Sorbon, chaplain to King Louis IX, endowed the "House of Sorbonne" about 1257. A model for such colleges already existed in the houses that the friars often maintained for their own scholars. The college tended to become a permanent society of masters and students, in which the older members tutored the younger, at first to supplement the university lectures and later to replace them. The college system, in varying forms, came to be imitated at Oxford and Cambridge and at many other universities in Italy, Germany, Scotland, and elsewhere, though it often took different forms in different places. In this and other ways, Paris became the model for most universities north of the Alps.

Bologna and the Student University

Bologna was the rival model. In the more advanced and sophisticated civilization of Italy, there was a greater demand for lawyers and administrators, and the university emerged from the municipal schools that taught the civil law of ancient Rome and the canon law of the papacy. Bologna, halfway between Ravenna, the last foothold of the Byzantine emperors in the West, and papal Rome, taught the *Corpus Juris Civilis* of the Emperor Justinian and the law of the supreme ecclesiastical courts in contemporary Rome. In the twelfth century it had two doctors of genius: Irnerius, who between 1116 and 1140 revived the study of the civil law, and Gratian, who codified the canon law in his great *Decretum* of about 1140. The two systems of law battled for supremacy down to and beyond the Reformation, when in Protestant countries canon law was abolished. Meanwhile, pope and emperor vied for the universities' support in their struggle for supremacy. The Emperor Frederick Barbarossa's *Autentica Habita* (1158) came to be regarded as the founding charter of Bologna university, and the pope granted the *jus ubique docendi* in 1291.

Like Paris and the northern universities, Bologna had its problems with the local townsfolk. Quarrels and riots led to migrations of scholars to Modena and Montpellier in the 1170s, to Vicenza in 1204, Arezzo in 1215, and Padua in 1222, thus establishing universities in those cities. In their quarrels with the city, the "foreign" (non-Bolognese) students were the first to organize effectively, since under Italian law they were legally aliens unprotected by rights of citizenship. As law students, rather older and wealthier than the arts students of the north, they were better placed to seize the initiative. They organized themselves into student guilds, somewhat like the Paris nations, for mutual protection but also to oppose their professors, who as Bolognese citizens shortsightedly took the side of the city. There arose four student "universities," representing the Lombards, the Tuscans, the Romans and Campanians, and the Ultramontane for those from beyond the Alps. Later they were reduced to two, the Cismontane for the Italians and the Ultramontane for the rest. Only in 1245, after many town and gown quarrels and migrations, were the students conceded equal civil rights by the city authorities and had their statutes and privileges recognized by the commune and the papacy (1252–1253).

The power acquired by the students, although falling short of control over the curriculum, was used to impose the most draconian discipline upon their teachers. The student rector and proctors determined the doctors' fees, levied fines on them for starting or finishing their lectures late, not keeping up with the syllabus, leaving the city without permission or without giving sureties for their return, and forced them to deposit large caution moneys from which to deduct the fines. This extraordinary system lasted, despite professorial protest, until the late fourteenth century, when income from student fees came to be supplemented by salaries paid by the commune (to discourage professorial emigration). Henceforward, Bologna and the other Italian universities gradually converged with the Parisian model, with power shared between professors and the student rector, but with an ongoing tradition of student protest that has lasted down to the present day.

Oxford and Cambridge

The brilliant success of Paris and Bologna led to emulation, often by the classic process of migration. Oxford arose spontaneously about 1167 from one of the many arts studia in English towns, perhaps helped by the return of English students from France around 1167 as a result of Henry II's quarrel with the pope and the French king over his recalcitrant archbishop, Thomas Beckett. Cambridge originated with a migration from Oxford after town and gown riots in 1209. Later migrations, to Northampton, Salisbury, Stamford, and other towns, failed to take root against the opposition of Oxford and Cambridge, backed by king and pope, and the two remained the only universities in England, as distinct from Scotland where four had appeared by Queen Elizabeth I's day, down to the nineteenth century. Distant from their diocesan bishops in Lincoln and Ely, they elected their own chancellors and became more independent than most continental universities. They never developed formal student nations, but acquired well-endowed colleges, like Merton (1264) and Peterhouse (1284), which gave the fellows and especially the heads of colleges great power and, eventually, wealth.

Oxford and Cambridge came to play a considerable role in the intellectual controversies of the later Middle Ages, especially in the disputes between realism and nominalism, with the renowned European figures of John Wyclif and William of Ockham, and between scholasticism and humanism, the revival of the Greek and Latin literary classics in the original languages, popularized by William Grocyn and Richard Foxe of Oxford and John Gunthorpe and the great Dutch humanist Desiderius Erasmus of Cambridge.

Other French Universities

In France, where Paris jealously guarded her supremacy in theology, her daughter universities, Orleans, Angers, and Toulouse, all benefiting from the great dispersal of 1229, tended to concentrate on law. Toulouse was founded that same year by Pope Gregory IX to support his crusade against the Catharist heretics of Aquitaine. Other French schools were recognized by the pope as *studia generales* at Montpellier (1289), Cahors (1332), Grenoble (1339), Orange (1365, but suppressed by the pope in 1475 at the instance of Montpellier), Dole (1422), Poitiers (1431), Caen and Bordeaux (at the instance of the occupying English in 1437 and 1459), Valence (1459), Nantes (1460), and Bourges (1464). They were in fact mostly royal foundations, confirmed by the pope, and somewhat less independent than Paris, Oxford, or Bologna. The bishop counted for more, but as in Paris, internal government was shared by the masters and doctors and a student-elected rector. As in Italy, arts students tended to be downgraded or taught outside, so that the baccalaureate was taken before entry.

Other Italian Universities

Many Italian cities competed for the honor and economic benefits of a university, and wooed scholars to set up schools. In 1188 Reggio contracted with a master, probably Bolognese, to import scholars, and acquired a *studium generale* in 1276, but it had disappeared by 1313. Migrations from Bologna founded Vicenza (1204), Arezzo (1215, defunct by 1373), Padua (1222), Pisa (1343), and Florence (1349, merged with Pisa, 1472). Scholars from Padua founded Vercelli (1228) and Siena (1246). Naples was founded in 1224 by the Emperor Frederick Barbarossa, who tried to suppress Bologna and transfer its scholars there, but his authoritarian university failed to attract many students until it was reformed by its Spanish rulers in 1507. A similar "pocket university" founded by the pope at the Roman Court about 1244 also languished, except as a home for professors of oriental languages, with the forlorn object of converting the Jews and the Turks.

Other Italian universities were recognized, usually by the city authorities who petitioned the pope for a bull, at Piacenza (1248), the City of Rome (1303), Perugia (1308), Treviso (1318), Pavia (1361), Ferrara (1391), Turin (1405), and Catania (1444). Nearly all the Italian universities followed the Bologna model of student government, but also reverted to professorial control in the later Middle Ages when municipal salaries and magnificent buildings liberated the professors from student control.

Spain and Portugal

The universities of the Iberian peninsula were nearly all royal foundations, endowed by the various monarchs with church revenues and taxes from their own estates. Although recognized by the pope, they were, with one famous exception, *studia generales respectu regni*, drawing students only from the king's territory. The first, Palencia, founded and refounded by the kings of Castille in 1178 and 1208, proved abortive and had disappeared by 1250. Vallodolid was a more spontaneous civic growth, endorsed by the king of Castille in 1293. The most famous, Salamanca, was founded by the king of Leòn in 1218 and granted by the pope in 1255 the privileges (a common seal, the right to award degrees, the *jus ubique docendi,* and so on) which, with the help of the university clauses of the general law code of Alfonso the Wise of Castille in 1263, were to make it a convenient model for university charters throughout the later Spanish empire. In 1298 it was recognized by the pope, along with Paris, Oxford, and Bologna, as one of the great universities of Christendom. The single university in Portugal was founded by the king in 1290 at Lisbon, but was continually shuttled between there and Coimbra before finally settling in the latter city in 1537. Aragon was especially prolific in foundations, and the kings established universities at Lerida (1300), Perpignan (1350), Huesca (1354), Barcelona (1450), and Palma, Majorca (1483). Alcalà was projected by the king of Castille in 1293 but not raised to a *studium generale* by the pope until 1499. Valencia, a municipal foundation, was projected in 1246 and recognized by the pope and James I of Aragon but came to nothing; in 1374, when the city hired a teacher he was promptly excommunicated by the bishop on the grounds that he was infringing the monopoly of neighboring Lerida. It led a checkered life, opposed by Lerida and the bishop, until Alexander VI, the famous Borgia pope and a Valencian citizen, granted it a bull in 1500. Spain was to become the parent of many institutions of higher education worldwide, as the Spanish conquerors exported the European university to other continents.

Germany and Beyond

Until the fourteenth century, students from beyond the Rhine and the Alps went to France or Italy for higher education, a result of the slower development of city life in northern and central Europe. Arts *studia* came into existence to prepare them, but the first *studium generale* in the empire was established only in 1347, by Charles IV, king of Bohemia and emperor-elect, in Prague. German as well as Czech students, poorer perhaps than those who went to France and Italy, flooded there, and by 1400 it was said to have two thousand or more "foreign" students alone, and four "nations" drawn from Bohemia, Poland, Bavaria, and Saxony. Unfortunately, the Czechs and the Germans began to quarrel, exacerbated in the fifteenth century by the religious and philosophical disputes between the followers of the Bohemian reformer and realist Jan Hus and the more Orthodox and nominalist Germans. When the Bohemian king Wenceslas IV tried to impose Czech hegemony on the university in 1409 the Germans seceded to Heidelberg, Cologne, and, above all, to Leipzig, adding to the new universities in the first two and causing a university to spring up in the last. From 1419 Prague became in effect the first Protestant university in Europe, protected by the kings of Bohemia. For two centuries it was disputed between the reformers and the orthodox, until it was finally handed over to the Jesuits in 1622.

Vienna, the first wholly German university, was founded by the Habsburg duke of Austria, Rudolf IV, in 1365 and soon took over the academic lead from Prague. Other German rulers joined in the competition with universities at Erfurt in the prince-archbishopric of Mainz (with papal bulls in 1379 and 1389 from the rival schismatic popes in Avignon and Rome), Heidelberg in the Rhine Palatinate (1385), in the free city of Cologne (1388), in the prince-bishopric of Würzburg (1402, closed after town and gown riots and the murder of the rector in 1413), in the Hanseatic city of Rostock (1419 by the Duke of Mecklenburg; it migrated to Greifswald in 1443–1473 and again in 1487–1490 because of urban uprisings, leading to a university there recognized by the pope in 1456), at Leuven (Louvain) in Brabant (in modern Belgium) which became one of the most famous universities of Europe (1425), at the free city of Basel (1432: confirmed by Pope Pius II, a Basel citizen, in 1459), in Freiburg-im-Breisgau by the Archduchess Machtildis of Austria (1455), at Ingolstadt near Munich by the Duke of Bavaria (1459), at Mainz by the prince-archbishop (1476), at Tübingen by the Count of Württemburg, son of the Archduchess Machtildis of Austria (1477), and finally at Wittenberg in Prussia by the Elector of Brandenberg (1502), just in time to give Martin Luther a platform for the Reformation.

With the increasing dynastic nationalism of the later Middle Ages, other nations vied with each other to found their own universities. The kings of Poland, Casimir the Great and Ladislaus, founded and refounded Cracow in 1364 and 1397, later to be made famous by the revolutionary astronomer Copernicus. Kings of Hungary founded Pecs (Funfkirchan) in 1367 but teaching had ceased there by

1400, "Old Buda" at Budapest in 1369, and Poszony (Pressburg) in 1467. In Scandinavia the Swedish bishops petitioned Pope Sixtus IV for a university on Bolognese lines at the archdiocese of Uppsala in 1477, and King Christian I obtained a bull for one in Copenhagen in 1478.

Scottish students commonly went to France and England for their education, but whenever the English were at war with Scotland or France (which was often) and travel became difficult, their thoughts turned to founding their own universities. The three medieval Scottish universities were founded at St. Andrews, Glasgow, and Aberdeen by their bishops with royal backing in such periods in 1409, 1450, and 1494. They were much influenced by French and German examples and were, like them, to play a considerable part in the theological and philosophical disputes that led to the Reformation.

The Destruction of the Medieval World Order

The original four informal universities that emerged in the twelfth century, Salerno, Paris, Bologna, and Oxford, grew to sixteen by 1300, thirty-eight by 1400, and seventy-two by 1500. By that time they were highly organized institutions with a rector or chancellor, a common seal and corporate personality that enabled them to own property and make contracts, formal faculties, usually of arts, theology, law, and medicine, often with student nations, increasingly with endowed colleges, and with privileges guaranteed by pope and secular ruler that protected them from arbitrary interference by bishop and civic authorities and from sporadic violence by their urban neighbors. Though some of them were very small, like St. Andrews or Naples, with a few score students, others, like Paris, Bologna, or Vienna, were very large, with several thousand. As the main service industry of many cities and as the alma mater of most popes, bishops, judges, and high administrators in church and state, they were influential at all levels of medieval life. They were also powerful enough to challenge the very bases of the medieval world order and shake it to its foundations.

This was because both lay and ecclesiastical authorities looked to the universities as their chief instruments of propaganda in their unending struggles for supremacy. They were the ideological heavy artillery in the intellectual wars between church and state. At times when the protagonists were more than usually divided, the universities and their academic stars might go beyond mere influence and become arbiters in their own right. During the Great Schism of 1378–1417 when the whole of Christendom was divided in allegiance between rival popes at Avignon, supported by the powerful French and English kings and many northern rulers, and at Rome itself, elected by the corrupt Italian cardinals, the theologians of Paris were appealed to for a solution. Their proposal that both popes should resign and make way for a fresh election led to the Conciliar movement, a series of ecumenical church councils of bishops and university theologians that nearly overturned the autocracy of the papacy and established a more democratic, or at least oligarchic, church. The Parisian theologians' solution was accepted at the Council of Pisa in 1409 and implemented, with the help of the balancing vote of the English delegates, at the Council of Constance in 1414. The papacy, reunited under the compromise Pope Martin V in 1417, reestablished autocratic rule but its defenses were fatally weakened. For a century the doctrine and organization of the church were disputed by reformers at Paris, Oxford, Louvain, Prague and many other universities, who condemned the power, greed, luxury, and corruption of the pope and the higher clergy and demanded a return to the poverty and simplicity of the early apostolic church.

The universities thus became almost a separate "intellectual estate," a third force between church and state. They were themselves divided several ways, between reformers and conservatives, realists and nominalists, Aristotelian schoolmen and the new humanists who challenged scholastic logic-chopping and introduced the "new learning," the rebirth of the ancient Greek and Latin literary classics, of the fourteenth-century Renaissance. These intellectual currents often flowed in contrary directions. Corrupt popes like Alexander VI of the Borgia family could be patrons of humanism and reforming humanists like Erasmus of Rotterdam and Sir Thomas More could become defenders of the unity of the church, while antipapists like Philip Melanchthon, Ulrich Zwingli, and Jean Calvin were also dedicated humanists. Ultimately, however, it was the schoolmen, both realists and nominalists, whose logic chopping arguments exposed the church not only to reform but to the perpetual schism of the

Reformation. Both the realists like Wyclif and Hus and the nominalists like Marsiglio of Padua and William of Ockham challenged the pretentions of the pope to control the keys of heaven, to sell forgiveness of sins through indulgences, to shorten purgatory through prayer and the intercession of saints, to excommunicate individuals and interdict communities for disagreeing with the pope, in short, to use all the supernatural sanctions that had given the spiritual sword its power. The academic schoolmen thus prepared the way for the revolutionary reformers of the sixteenth century—Luther, Zwingli, Calvin, John Knox, and the rest.

When Martin Luther, a student of William of Ockham, nailed his ninety-five theses to the church door at the University of Wittenberg in 1517, he was in a sense hammering home the triumph of the university over the unity of the church and with it the demise of the medieval world order. What the university had given, the ideological defense of church against the state, the university had taken away. At the same time it took away one of the foundations of its own independence, the divided authority that had enabled it to survive by appealing to two swords instead of one, its triumph paved the way for the monopoly of the temporal sword, the secular nation state, which was to become a greater threat to academic freedom than the heresy-hunting church. Only by doing the bidding of the state while skillfully exploiting its by now traditional claim to freedom of thought and scholarship could the university survive for the next three centuries.

Reformation and Decline

The university's experience in the Reformation of the church was ambivalent. On the one side it helped to defeat the papacy and rend the church apart. On the other it helped to bring about the resurgence of the Roman church in the Counter-Reformation. On both sides it became an instrument of the embattled states in the religious wars of the sixteenth and seventeenth centuries, and many new colleges and universities were founded for that purpose, before they declined into a complacent somnolence in the ensuing reaction against the "enthusiasm" of the eighteenth-century Enlightenment.

A Pyrrhic Victory

The power of intellectual thought has no better material example than the dissolution of the monasteries in Protestant countries. The Reformation was about many theological disputes: the means of grace, salvation by faith, works, or the inscrutable will of God, the two or seven sacraments, communion for the laity in one or both kinds, the implications of the omniscience and omnipotence of God for the predestination of the soul, and so on, all fought with weapons forged by the universities. None had such implications for a thousand year-old way of life and the ownership of great concentrations of property as the destruction by the Reformers of the doctrine of purgatory. Monasteries existed for the salvation of souls by prayer and the mediation of saints. If there was no purgatory, there was no point in praying for the souls of the dead, since their time there could not be shortened. Ergo, no purgatory, no monastery. Out of its collapse came, in England for example, the biggest land grab since the Norman Conquest, when Henry VIII and his young son Edward VI confiscated the possessions of the monasteries and chantries, one sixth of the land of England, and sold or gave away most of it to their secular artistocratic supporters.

Yet the Reformation was a Pyrrhic victory for the universities. They forged the weapons but the secular nation state took the spoils, not only in Protestant countries but in Catholic ones as well, like France, Spain, and Austria where the monarchs were able to impose tighter control over the church and its property and taxes, and squandered them on war, royal favorites, and a luxurious way of life. The only thing that saved the universities from complete subjection was the persisting pluralism of Europe, now divided more ferociously between rival dynastic states that strove to attract academics to their side.

The universities in England, for example, came within an ace of the fate of the monasteries. The Oxford and Cambridge colleges were quasi-monastic institutions and were often obliged by their foundations to say prayers for the souls of the founder and his kin and successors. They were saved from the covetousness of their neighbors by King Henry himself, who declared: "I judge no land in England better bestowed than that which is given to our universities, for by their maintenance our land will be well-governed when we be dead and rotten." And he founded great new colleges, Christchurch, Oxford, and Trinity College, Cambridge, partly on the spoils of the nearby monasteries. But the price of survival was a loss or change of function. In 1535 the teaching of canon law was banned, thus abolishing the largest graduate faculty. With civil law already concentrated in the Inns of Court in London, the two universities, apart from a handful of unpractical physicians, were relegated to teaching arts and theology to the Anglican clergy. Their solution was to annex the training of the lay and often amateur administrators of the state and the localities, drawn increasingly from the landed gentry. From the Reformation of the 1530s to the Civil War of the 1640s, sons of the gentry and the wealthier middle classes began to go in large numbers to Oxford and Cambridge, more for the general training in manners and political awareness than for intellectual improvement, for they often did not stay long enough to take the degree. Thus in England, as elsewhere, the universities adapted themselves to a new social function, the general education of the ruling elite.

Under the principle of *cuius regio, eius religio* (the ruler determines the religion), confirmed by the Peace of Augsburg, 1555, lay rulers everywhere turned the universities into instruments of propaganda for their particular faith and training schools for statesmen and civil servants. Those in Scandinavia and north Germany became Lutheran, and those in Switzerland, Scotland, and the northern Netherlands (after they achieved independence from Spain from 1580 onwards) became Calvinist. The Prince of Translyvania even converted an old college at Cluj-Napoca (now in Romania) in 1556 to Unitarianism.

The Catholic Counterattack

Both Catholic and Protestant rulers rushed to found new educational institutions to reinforce their hold on their subjects' minds. The Emperor Charles V, chief lay protagonist on the papal side, and his successors in his Spanish dominions founded nine new Catholic universities in Spain itself, from Granada (1526) to El Escorial (1587), five in Italy, from Genoa (1513) to Cagliari in Sardinia (1606), two in the Spanish Netherlands including Douai (1560), the chief training school of Catholic missionaries to England, and Maastricht (1617), Besançon in Franche-Comte (1564, later annexed by Louis XIV of France), and the first universities in the New World, in Santo Domingo (1538), Lima, Peru, and Mexico City (1551), and Bogotá, Colombia (1580). Charles V and his successors at the Austrian end of his divided dominions founded six new universities, including Dillingen (1553), Innsbruck (1562), Graz (1585), and Lubljana (1595). Other German Catholic princes founded their own, such as Duke Julius of Braunschweig-Wolfenbuttal at Helmstedt (1575) and the prince-archbishop at Salzburg (1617).

The spearhead of the Catholic counterattack was the Society of Jesus, which infiltrated or took over many of the older universities and founded many new ones. The Jesuits, founded by Ignatius Loyola, a Spanish ex-soldier dedicated to following Christ's path, in 1504, were "the shock troops of the Counter-Reformation." They fought on three fronts: as confessors to royal families and courts to stiffen their resistance to reforming subjects; as overseas missionaries across the globe from the Americas to the Philippines and Japan; and above all as educators of the young, in gymnasia, seminaries, colleges, and universities. With their numbers rising from about a thousand at Loyola's death in 1556 to 15,544 in 1626, and to 22,589 in 1749, they became by far the largest organized bodies within the Roman church, and dominated education at all levels until the order was suppressed by the pope in 1773. From their three great centers, Cologne, where they began to lecture in 1542, the Gregorian University, founded at Rome by Loyola himself in 1553, and Ingolstadt, near Munich, taken over by them in 1556, they spread throughout Europe. They established or took over institutions as far afield as Evora, Portugal, about 1559, Olomouc, Bohemia, in 1566, Vilnius in Polish Lithuania in 1579, the great University of Vienna in 1622, Breslau, Silesia, in 1659, and Lvov, Poland, in 1661. Even Paris was not immune: they founded two colleges there in 1540 and 1561 which were incorporated into the university in 1564, but they were unwelcome guests and were expelled in 1594.

Overseas they founded colleges in Argentina in 1613, Ecuador and Bolivia in 1622, Colombia in 1623, and Québec in 1635. Their infiltration tactics, aggressiveness, and sophistry made them unpopular not only with Protestants but also with their own co-religionists. In the skeptical eighteenth century, they were to be expelled from Portugal and Spain and their colonies, the Habsburg empire, France, and the two Sicilies, and were suppressed by Pope Clement VII in 1773. (The Order, however, was revived again in 1814, after the atheistic excesses of the French Revolution and Napoleon's Concordat with Rome.)

The Protestant Response

On the Protestant side, the north German principalities, the Swiss cantons, the Dutch provincial estates, and the monarchs of Scotland and England also founded new educational institutions to spread the gospels of Luther, Zwingli, Calvin, and the Arminian Anglicans. German Protestant universities were founded by the duke of Prussia at Konigsberg (1541), by the elector of Saxony, who had already turned Leipzig Lutheran, at Jena (1539), by the margrave of Baden at Durlach (1586), by the margrave of Hesse-Darmstadt at Giessen (1605), by the free city of Hamburg (1613), by the great elector Frederick William of Brandenberg-Prussia (where Luther's own university of Wittenberg had been taken over by his rival Melanchthon at Duisberg (1664), and by his successor, Frederick III, soon to be king of Prussia, at Halle (1685).

Swiss Protestant academies were established at Zurich by Zwingli (1525), at Bern by the city authorities (1528), and at Lausanne and Geneva by Calvin (1537 and 1559). Although the Protestant Netherlands did not have a university by name until 1876, every Dutch province founded an *illustre school*, from Leiden (1575) to Zutphen (1686), England's Queen Elizabeth I founded Trinity College, Dublin, in newly conquered Ireland (1592), her successor-to-be James VI of Scotland chartered the Tounis College, later Edinburgh University (1583), and Protector Oliver Cromwell tried unsuccessfully to found a university in Durham (which was to have England's third university in 1832). The kings of Sweden, then heading a considerable empire, founded colleges at Dorpat (Tartu) in Esthonia (1632), Åbo (Turku) in Finland (1640), and at Lund in southern Sweden (1668), but later lost the first two to the Russians.

The Frontier Zone

Meanwhile, as the religious wars swayed back and forth, many universities found themselves in the frontier zone between the armies and changed their political and religious allegiance, some more than once. The Hussite University of Prague, where the Jesuits founded a college in 1556, was finally handed over to them in 1622 after the suppression of the Protestant Bohemian rising by the Habsburg Emperor Ferdinand III. Heidelberg, turned Calvinist by the elector palatine in the 1550s, was Romanized by the Catholic League in 1631, converted to Lutheranism by the Swedes in 1631, and after a twenty-year suspension was finally returned to Calvinism by the returning elector in 1652. Protestant colleges established at Klagenfurt and Linz by local estates in Austria in 1552 and 1574 were handed over to the Jesuits by the Habsburgs in 1604 and 1629, as was the Protestant university at Eperjes (1665) in Upper Hungary in 1685.

In France the large number of Huguenot colleges tolerated by the early Bourbon kings, like Nimes (1539) and Die (1601), were suppressed by Louis XIV in 1685, as were the Protestant institutions, like Montauban (1598), Montbéliard (1598), and Sedan (1599), annexed by the French. The only exception was the University of Strasbourg (1621), which, after the French conquest of Alsace, was confirmed by Louis XIV as the only Protestant University in France.

The Dark Age of the Enlightenment

As long as the religious wars lasted and required the ideological support of the universities, they thrived, and student numbers surged to new heights down to the mid-seventeenth century. From then onwards a period of decline set in, as students and their elders wearied of the religious disputes of the last century and began to repudiate "enthusiasm." By the 1680s, Oxford, for example, was "very dead for want of students," fewer than at any time before the Civil War. By the eighteenth century, universities everywhere were in the doldrums, confined to the training of priests or pastors, a few civil servants, and those gentry too poor to educate their sons by private tutors and the increasingly popular "grand tour" of the Continent. In Germany student numbers in the 1780s, at about seven thousand, were smaller than a century and a half earlier. One reason was the sheer exhaustion with religious controversy, but the principal cause was the rise of a new skeptical outlook associated with the "Enlightenment," a critical, rationalistic view of the world that eschewed the emotional fanaticism, as they saw it, of the old doctrinal wars. It was associated with the new "cooler" view of the universe attributed (perhaps mistakenly) to Newton and the Scientific Revolution, in which God had made the world like a perfect clock that needed little or no intervention by the great Clock-maker, and man's role was not to quarrel over it but to understand it by tracing out his work through the application of scientific reasoning. This rational cosmology undermined the universities as the homes of outmoded theoretical knowledge, still based largely on Aristotle and the medieval school-men and increasingly out of touch with observed reality. Why go to a University, it was argued, to learn old doctrine of little use outside a career in the church?

The Enlightenment affected life at all levels, from the new monarchs like Frederick II of Prussia, Catherine II of Russia, and Joseph II of Austria who took their political methods from Machiavelli ("whatever works is right") to the *philosophes* and *savants* who scoffed at the Aristotelians of the universities and pursued scientific truth outside them. The Scientific Revolution, except for a few aberrant geniuses like Galileo and Newton, took place outside the universities, in new and mainly amateur institutions like Gresham College, London (1575), where Francis Bacon, the great empiricist, and Humphrey Gilbert of magnetism fame operated, the Academia dei Lincei in Rome (1603), where Galileo and his disciples disputed, the Royal Society of London (1661), where Sir Robert Boyle demonstrated his vacuum experiments, the French Académie des Sciences (1666), and other scientific societies in Berlin (1700), Uppsala (1710), Peter the Great's new capital at St. Petersburg (1724), Stockholm (1739), Göttingen (1742), Copenhagen (1743), and Munich (1759). In France the *philosophes* and *encyclopédistes* led by Voltaire, Rousseau, and Diderot set out to challenge all traditional interpretations and collect from scratch all practical and useful knowledge. Their scorn for the *ancien régime* and its supporting academics culminated in the French Revolution and its abolition of the universities. In England pioneers of modern knowledge like Richard Price, Joseph Priestley, and John Dalton developed unorthodox ideas like Unitarianism, the chemistry of gases, and the atomic theory of matter at new dissenting academics at Warrington, Daventry, and Northampton. The Society of Arts (1754) gave prizes for "the encouragement of arts, manufactures and commerce," and in 1799 the American adventurer Count Rumford founded the London Institution, where Humphrey Davy and Michael Faraday demonstrated their experiments in gases and electricity.

The universities could not escape the new developments altogether and a few pioneers of modern science operated there, though often under difficulty. Fabrizius and Vesalius pioneered observational anatomy at Padua, La Ramée mathematics at the Collège de France but was expelled for his Protestantism, Galileo and his pupil Toricelli at Pisa and Florence under constant persecution from the Aristotelians, and Newton in optics and astronomy as well as alchemy and the prophesies of the Book of Daniel at Cambridge. At Glasgow and Edinburgh, the "Scottish historical school of philosophy," including Adam Ferguson, David Hume, Dugald Stewart, Adam Smith, and John Millar, virtually founded modern skeptical philosophy and the modern social sciences. In the Netherlands, Leyden and other universities pioneered new, more practical systems of teaching medicine and the natural sciences and sent scientific missionaries out to Edinburgh, Vienna, and Göttingen. In Germany, Halle (refounded in 1694), Göttingen (1734), and Erlangen (1743) tried to update the curriculum and let the Enlightenment into the ivory tower. For the most part the Scientific Revolution passed the universities by, and managed to conquer them only after their reform in the nineteenth century.

Apart from the few exceptions in Scotland, the Netherlands, and Germany, most universities in eighteenth-century Europe were moribund, with idle professors feebly teaching a medieval curriculum without much relevance to modern life, and despised by the intellectuals of the Enlightenment.

In England, the historian of the Roman empire, Edward Gibbon, described his student days at Oxford as "the fourteen months the most idle and unprofitable of my whole life," and his teachers, "the monks of Magdalen," as "decent, easy men who supinely enjoyed the gifts of the founder." In Germany, civil servants and politicians seriously discussed whether universities did more harm than good and ought to be abolished. Even the students lacked the energy to protest: perhaps because there was so little to protest against, there were fewer student riots in that century than before or after. In France, the revolutionaries did abolish the universities, and all those in the territories they conquered. Paradoxically, however, the French Revolution paved the way for their revival, not only in France but also in the rest of Europe.

The University and Industrial Society

The Industrial Revolution, which started in eighteenth-century Britain and spread from there to Europe, America, and the rest of the world, began outside the universities and for a long time was ignored by them. In the first half of the nineteenth century, most universities were still seminaries for the clergy and a few lawyers and administrators of the nation state. The medieval curricula in the arts, theology, law, and medicine were still largely intact, if somewhat updated, and Aristotle and Plato were still more important than Newton or Kant. So much was this the case that the applied science and technology needed for the new manufacturing, mining, and transport industries had to be taught in new institutions: mechanics' institutes in Britain, *technische hochschulen* in Germany, and *grandes écoles* in France, where Napoleon's new University of France (1806) embraced the whole education system down to the *lycées* (secondary schools) but still did not modernize the syllabus. Only gradually did the old universities catch up with the new natural and social sciences, and only then when they had been shamed into it by new institutions, including a new wave of universities.

Industrial society, nevertheless, eventually recreated the university in its own image. It invented, or took over the accidental invention of the modern research university, the technical college, and the research institute. New natural sciences like chemistry, biology, and geology, new applied sciences like engineering, mineralogy, electricity, and practical medicine, and new versions of the humanities like archive-based history, modern languages, and vernacular literature, came into the curricula of new universities and spread to the older ones. In the later nineteenth century, student numbers expanded all over Europe from Britain and France to Germany and Russia, and dramatically in the United States, and for the first time women students began to appear in more than token numbers. Higher education at its widest was still very elitist, but in the twentieth century the change was large enough to bring in some students from the lower layers of society. Taking every kind of tertiary institution, numbers in Europe expanded from less than 1 in 200 (0.46 percent) of the student age group in 1860 to nearly 1 in 100 (0.88 percent) in 1900, and to 1 in 50 (2.07 percent) in 1940. In the United States, from this time onwards ahead of Europe in education, they increased from 1 in 90 (1.1 percent) in 1860 to 1 in 44 (2.3 percent) in 1900, and to 1 in 11 (9.1 percent) in 1940. Of these, women formed an increasing proportion, in Europe from negligible percentages before 1900 to 14 percent in 1920 and 22 percent in 1940, and to about 30 percent in the United States. These figures reflected the changing social function of higher education in industrial society, from educating the ruling elite and its religious supporters to training a much wider range of leaders in industry, commerce, finance, expanding state bureaucracies, and the growing professions, including many kinds of engineering, accountancy, social administration, and education itself.

The Emergence of the Research University

The modern university combining teaching and research (rather than the conservation of traditional knowledge) began almost by accident in two poor and at that time marginal countries, Scotland and Germany. Each independently invented the same device for saving money, the specialized, single-subject professor, replacing the traditional regent master who taught the whole syllabus. In time the demands of industrial society would have necessitated this anyway, but the new approach began before industrialism took hold. The unintended by-product was that the specialist professors, like Adam Smith's specialist craftsmen in the industrial division of labor, became not only more skilled but active innovators in their specialized fields.

In eighteenth-century Scotland the new professors revolutionized old disciplines and pioneered new ones, like Colin Maclaurin, Newton's pupil, in mathematics, David Hume and Dugald Stewart in philosophy, William Robertson in history, Adam Smith in political economy, John Millar in sociology, Joseph Black in chemistry, the Hunter brothers in surgery, and so on. The Scottish historical school became renowned throughout Europe and America for its pioneering social science, including Smith's political economy and Millar's economic interpretation of history and social structure, both of which influenced Ricardo and Marx.

The Scottish model had a profound influence on the new English universities of the nineteenth century. University College was founded in London in 1826 by Henry Brougham, Thomas Campbell, and other Edinburgh graduates, with a slate of single-discipline professors in medicine, jurisprudence, political economy, chemistry, physics, modern languages, logic and philosophy, with others planned in engineering, mineralogy, design, and education. Its example was followed by its rival, King's College (1833), united with it in the federal University of London (1836), by Durham University (1832) and the colleges at Manchester (1851), Leeds (1874), Bristol (1876), Sheffield (1879), Liverpool and Nottingham (1881), and Birmingham (1891), which eventually became the great civic universities of England.

The University of London acted as midwife and nurse to many of these provincial universities, as it was also to do to many colonial universities, especially in Africa, India, the West Indies, and Malaya. From 1858 it offered external degrees to individual and college students anywhere in Britain or the Empire, and enabled colleges to earn their university status by taking its degrees for a generation or more before becoming independent. Its admission of women to the external degree in 1878 was a landmark in women's education, not only enabling women's colleges to follow the same path, but also setting the precedent for other universities to admit them. Other new universities, in Ireland, Wales, India, South Africa, New Zealand, and elsewhere were founded on the same federal principle with affiliated colleges. London thus became the mentor or the pattern for a very large number of universities throughout the Empire and Commonwealth. The Queen's University of Ireland was founded on the London model by the Westminster government in 1850, with affiliated colleges at Belfast, Cork, and Galway. The rival Catholic University of Dublin was founded in 1854, with John Henry Newman as its rector. The three colleges at Aberystwyth, Bangor, and Cardiff united in the federal university of Wales in 1893. All these new universities adopted the cheap and effective Scottish and London device of the single-subject professor, and many of them pioneered new departments of civil, mechanical, chemical, mining, and electrical engineering, textile sciences, dyestuffs chemistry, brewing, agriculture, architecture, and other technologies, and acted as innovators and consultants for their local industries.

The older universities at Oxford and Cambridge dragged their feet but were eventually shamed by external critics, internal reformers, and royal commissions in the 1850s and 1870s into modernizing themselves. With the building of the Clarendon and Cavendish Laboratories in 1870 and 1872, Oxford and Cambridge began to play a leading role in science and technology. But the professorial system never became as dominant there as in Scotland, Wales, Ireland, and the English provinces. The English tradition of liberal education by college tutors, as much concerned for the moral character as for the intellectual development of a governing elite, was intensified by famous tutors like Benjamin Jowett at Oxford and Oscar Browning at Cambridge, and continued to influence University education throughout Britain and the Empire, as it had already done in the United States.

The German and French Models

Most German universities in the eighteenth century were as moribund as elsewhere, and were lucky to escape abolition like the French. A few, led by the elector of Brandenburg-Prussia's foundation at Halle in 1693, George II of England's at Göttingen in 1733, and the elector of Bavaria's at Erlangen in 1743, were revitalized by the device of the specialist professor and soon drew students from all over Germany.

When Halle was suppressed after Napoleon's victory at Jena in 1806, King Frederick William III of Prussia declared: "The state must replace by intellectual powers what it has lost in material ones." He appointed Wilhelm von Humboldt, brother of the famous scientist-explorer Alexander von Humboldt, to reform the Prussian education system and found the University of Berlin (1810). Humboldt saw the university as the moral soul of society at the source of the nation's culture and survival. To ensure the highest form of knowledge *(Wissenschaft)*, absolute freedom of teaching and learning *(Lehrfreiheit* and *Lernfreiheit)* was imperative. Thus began one of the paradoxes of the modern university, that it increasingly came to depend on the state both for material support and for defense of its freedom from its most dangerous threat, the state. The paradox was intensified by the fact that academic freedom was most self-consciously proclaimed in Germany, the most authoritarian state east of Russia. Dependence was to cost it dear, not only in Hitler's Germany and Stalin's Russia but elsewhere, even in democratic countries, where democracy could be turned against the elitism of a privileged profession.

Wissenschaft meant something broader than science. It was an approach to learning, a method of scholarship aimed at active intellect, sound judgment, and moral feeling. So "pure" was it that German medical professors were not allowed to treat patients, and applied science and technology were hived off into *technische hochschulen* and *gewerbe instituten* (technical college and trade schools). In practice, however, the individual professors with their separate research institutes and unpaid assistants *(privat docenten)* produced a surge of research with far-reaching consequences. Professors like Liebig in chemistry, Thaer in agricultural economics, Wundt in experimental psychology, even Ranke in history, had an effect on German development that was the envy of other countries. The new model attracted students in large numbers, far more than in any other country in Europe, though less than in the United States. German university students increased from 12,188 in 1860 to 33,739 in 1900 and 97,692 in 1930 (a 23-fold rise), compared with from 3,385 to 17,839 and 37,255 at the same dates in Britain (a 16-fold rise), and from 5,000 to 16,357 and 43,600 in Russia (a 9-fold rise at less than half the level in a population over four times the size of Germany). To these should be added nonuniversity students in technical and teachers colleges, who multiplied in Germany 17 times, from 5,797 in 1860 to 37,199 in 1930, compared with 13 times in Britain, from 2,129 to 28,954, and in tsarist Russia 8 times, from about 3,750 in 1860 to 30,990 in 1910 (and 66 times, to 247,300 in 1930 under the soviet regime).[1] With good reason, the German research university became the model for advanced higher education in northern Europe, Russia, the United States, and Japan.

It was not the only continental model. The French also had one to offer, which was much admired in southern Europe, especially Italy and Spain, and also in Latin America, and some of its elements, like the *grande école* and the research institute, had influence as far afield as Russia and Japan. The French model after the Revolution was a two-tier system, with an upper tier of *grande école*, like the *École des mines*, the *École Polytechnique*, the *École des langues orientates vivantes*, and other specialized schools of elite studies, to which high-status research institutes were later added, over a lower tier of the Parisian and regional faculties of the Napoleonic University of France. Although originally not so intended, it was a logical solution to the problems of industrial society, and led to the intensely competitive and meriocratic French system of education, tempered as elsewhere by privileged middle-class access to the secondary *lycées,* by the "cultural capital" of the bourgeois family, and by the special tutoring required to get into the *grandes écoles.* It deserved better results than the slowing up of French economic growth during the nineteenth century, though it began to pay off in the twentieth.

The German model was more widely followed in other countries, especially later in the century when German industrialization began to overtake that of Britain and France, and the military strength of the newly united German empire (1871) began to be feared and emulated. All over northern and eastern Europe, from Scandinavia to Greece (Athens University, 1837) and Turkey (the Istanbul House of Science, 1863), and into tsarist Russia, the German specialized professor and the single-discipline department were imitated, and universities became geared, to varying extents, to the combination of teaching and research. During the migration, the model often suffered a sea change, and was modified to meet the differential political, social, and cultural ethos of the importing society. In the United States, Russia, and Japan, for example, the results were very different from the intentions, and their universities took over the professorial principle and the research function without the German professors' independence or domination of the university, which in the first case belonged to the university president and trustees or regents, in the second to the state, and in the third was divided between the state and the private university board.

The Tsarist Russian Solution

In Russia, the tsarist autocracy always had an ambivalent attitude toward higher education, as it did toward modernization, which for them meant Westernization, in general. Education and research were necessary for Russia to catch up with the wealth and military power of western rivals, but students and intellectuals were a disruptive force that might become dangerous to the regime. They were well aware that students had taken a leading role in the French Revolutions of 1789, 1830, and 1848 and in the German and Austro-Hungarian rising of 1848, and were apprehensive—rightly, as it turned out in 1905 and 1917—that they would do the same in Russia.

Academies existed at Kiev from 1627 and in Moscow from 1681, and Peter the Great's widow Catherine I proposed a university attached to her imperial Academy of Sciences in 1726, but at the opening of the nineteenth century Russia had only one university, Moscow, founded by the Empress Elizabeth in 1755. Alexander I refounded Dorpat in conquered Finland in 1802 and Vilnius in captured Polish Lithuania in 1803, and established new ones at Kharkov and Kazan in 1804 and St. Petersburg in 1819. But the next century added only five more, at Kiev (1835), Odessa (1865), Warsaw (1869), Tomsk (1880), and Saratov (1909), though no less than 105 technical institutes. University education became mandatory for promotion to the higher levels of Peter the Great's famous table of ranks in 1809, and in 1834 all ranks were close-coupled to levels of education. Tsar Nicholas I imposed severe restrictions on enrollments in the state universities in 1850 but exempted a dozen specialized technical institutes. Even the educational-reforming Tsar Alexander II closed down the universities in 1861, but gave them new charters granting a measure of self-rule in 1864, which began a new period of expansion. Later expansion in Vyshnegradsky and Witte's industrializing period (1885–1903) was concentrated in the technical institutes and polytechnics, which came to hold nearly as many students as the universities. By 1914 there were about 58,000 students, mostly men, in technical institutes, compared with about 35,000 men in universities and about 34,000 women in "higher courses."[2] If the universities followed the German model, and produced many eminent scholars and scientists, the technical institutes followed the French model, at a less prestigious level. But tsarist higher education was a tiny elite system, with about 127,000 students perched on top of a huge population of 174 million, two-thirds of whom were illiterate. This combination led not to modernization but to revolution: as Count Witte, architect of Russian industrialization, said, "Education foments social revolution, but popular ignorance loses wars." The tsarist regime was impaled on both horns of that dilemma.

The German model was most admired and emulated in the United States and Japan, but this was part of the spread of the European university to the wider world, discussed below. Meanwhile the modern university, the technical college, and the research institute had, belatedly but successfully, been created by and helped to create that industrial society which, until Europe nearly destroyed itself in two world wars, gave the West almost complete mastery over the rest of the world.

Higher Education for the Excluded

One of the most important features of industrial society was its opening up of higher education to groups of the population previously excluded. This was partly because, even at the level of elite education achieved by the end of the period, talent needed to be sought wherever it could be found. More directly, the Industrial and French Revolutions combined to accelerate the trends toward democracy and equality, as working-class and feminist movements claimed rights denied them in earlier societies. In Europe down to and including most of the nineteenth century, students from the classes below the landed gentry and the professions were rare indeed, usually less than 1 percent of enrollments, and women were excluded altogether. By 1910 working-class students were still only 1 percent of the student body in England, 3 percent in Denmark, 5 percent in Italy, and 11 percent in Sweden.

By 1930 the proportion had changed little, except in Sweden with 16 percent, and England where it had suddenly surged to 29 percent due to new state and local government scholarships.[3] The widening of access was only a small beginning, but it laid the foundations for the post-World War II expansion of higher education. There was better hope for the disadvantaged student in nonuniversity and part-time education, particularly in vocational education, which expanded in most countries in the early twentieth century, though very erratically, and foreshadowed the massive expansion of nonuniversity education after World War II.

Before the mid-nineteenth century, it was almost unheard of for women to go to university. The best they could hope for was attendance at finishing schools or seminaries, where academic work was discouraged. In the second half of the century, beginning in Britain and the United States, normal schools, teachers colleges, and academic women's colleges were founded and the universities for the first time began to admit women, though often under restrictive conditions as to studying alongside men and taking full degrees. In England, Bedford College for Women was established in 1849 by feminists and later incorporated in London University. Girton College moved to Cambridge in 1869, but although sharing teaching and, from 1922, "titular degrees," women were not accepted as full members of the university until 1948. Four women's colleges were founded at Oxford between 1878 and 1893, but women were not formally admitted to the university until 1920. London was the first university to admit women, via its external degrees in 1878, and was soon followed by most provincial, Welsh, and Scottish universities, often against the wishes of many professors and most male undergraduates. In the United States, women were confined to seminaries, mostly founded between 1820 and 1850, until the last quarter of the century, when the leading women's colleges like Vassar and Mount Holyoke evolved from them. In 1880 there were sixty-two women's seminaries and twenty-nine colleges; by 1920 there were twenty-two seminaries and 191 colleges, plus 291 coeducational colleges awarding degrees to both sexes. In Western Europe as a whole, including Britain, women in 1910 averaged about 12 percent of university students—12 times more than working-class men—ranging from 4 percent in Germany and 9 percent in France to 17 percent in Italy and 22 percent in Switzerland. By the eve of World War II, they averaged 20 percent, ranging from 12 percent in Spain to 27 percent in Britain and 34 percent in France.

The extension of higher education to sectors of the population other than the male governing and professional elites was an expanding feature of industrial society, driven by the need for talent and the demands of the excluded. It was still, however, very limited until after World War II when, in a different, postindustrial society, the demand for much larger numbers of highly educated personnel would raise it to a higher level.

The University in the Wider World

The university first spread to the non-European world on the backs of conquerors and colonists, and only later by the force of its own double-edged attraction. Its initial function there was to educate the priests and ministers of the colonists and their governing and merchant elites. When it was later adapted to the education of the subject peoples, it imposed on them European intellectual and cultural values that they welcomed for the wealth and employment opportunities they promised but resented for the threat to native culture and values they imported. They had an unintended effect, however, which was to train and empower the local people to demand their own independence and reject European domination. This operated differently at different times in different places, according to the mix of settlers and indigenous peoples and the prior strength and literacy of the native culture. But everywhere the university and its preparatory schools and satellites became the instruments of nationalism and anticolonialism, and heralded the demise of four hundred years of Western hegemony.

Latin America

Spain, the first European power to achieve world supremacy, began to export education to its colonies from the beginning. Unlike the English, French, and Dutch in North America, the conquistadors sought not to drive out the native peoples but to convert them to Christianity and European culture.

Soon after the conquest of the Americas the Spaniards founded universities in Santo Domingo on the island of Hispaniola in 1538, Lima, Peru, and Mexico City in 1551, and Bogotà, Colombia, in 1580, along with Jesuit and Dominican schools in virtually all their colonies. The Jesuits also founded a Philippine university in Manila in 1629. There were soon said to be more institutions of higher education in Spanish America than in Spain itself. At least another sixteen universities were founded there, from Cordoba, Argentina (1613), to Panama (1749), as well as numerous other colleges and seminaries, before Latin America achieved independence in the early nineteenth century. The universities were modeled on the charter and statutes of Salamanca, which supplied many of them with professors and administrators, and were open equally to Indians, Creoles, and Spaniards. The last century of Spanish rule, with cities larger and more splendid than any in contemporary North America, was the golden age of Latin American higher education, with chairs of Indian languages as well as arts, philosophy, theology, and medicine. The native Americans, though exploited by the Spanish landlords and missionaries, were better protected by the Spanish crown than they were to be under the successor republics and, officially at least, were eligible for the same honors, dignities, and appointments as the natives of Castille.

Portugal was less active in colonial education than Spain, and the first Brazilian university, at Rio de Janeiro, was not founded until 1920, nearly a century after independence. The Latin American universities after independence mainly served the European elites, landlords, and the priesthood; the emerging professional schools in agriculture, forestry, veterinary medicine, engineering, and so on were mainly for a second level of technicians and administrators who rarely aspired to high rank. The Latin American republics became to all intents and purposes economic colonies of Britain, whose entrepreneurs developed their towns, railways, mines, and oil fields, until after World War I. From 1918 their universities became famous for student unrest, with demands for participation that anticipated the 1960s student movement elsewhere, but in 1950 they were described as "untended gardens of obsolete learning,"[4] and only later blossomed into their current liveliness.

The French and Dutch Empires

Apart from the Jesuit college at Laval (1635) in Québec the French founded no universities in their colonies until one for French *pied-noirs* in Algiers in 1879, which was considered an integral part of France and therefore merited a regional campus of the Napoleonic University. A new policy was adopted from 1945, when the other colonies became part of Metropolitan France and institutes of higher education were founded in Tunisia, Morocco and Sènègal, those in Dakar and Tunis becoming universities in 1957 and 1960, just before and just after independence.

The Dutch were also slow to export higher education. In the Dutch East Indies (Indonesia), no university was founded until independence in 1947, when the University of Indonesia in Batavia (Jakarta), projected in 1942 but delayed by the Japanese invasion, was formed by the amalgamation of various colleges, including the Engineering College at Bandoeng (1920), the Law, Medical, and Literary Colleges at Batavia (1924, 1927, and 1940), and the Agricultural College at Buitenzorg (1940).

British North America

The British were quick to export higher education to their North American colonies, not because of the home government's policy but because the English colonists, often dissenters in religion, needed to train their own pastors, as dissident and intolerant as themselves. All nine colonial colleges founded before the American Revolution began as religious seminaries, instruments of the community and its faith: Harvard College at Cambridge, Massachusetts (1636), William and Mary College at Williamsburg, Virginia (1639), Yale College at New Haven, Connecticut (1701), Princeton College, New Jersey (1748), King's College (later Columbia), New York (1754), the University of Pennsylvania at Philadelphia (1754), Brown University at Providence, Rhode Island (1764), and Dartmouth College at Hanover, New Hampshire (1769). They naturally followed the models they knew, Oxford and Cambridge and the Scottish universities, emphasizing general education and the training of moral character. In time they evolved from seminaries into liberal arts colleges, educating young gentlemen of the planter and business classes as well as of the cloth, and set the pattern for that general education that has been the mark of the American undergraduate experience down to the present.

In English-speaking Canada, the first universities seem to have been stimulated by the need of Canadians, reinforced by Loyalist refugees from the infant United States, to safeguard their offspring from the republicanism of their neighbors. The University of New Brunswick was founded as the Provincial Academy of Arts and Sciences at Fredericton in 1785, the first state institution in Canada, and received a royal charter as King's College in 1828. Another King's College was founded by United Empire Loyalists at Windsor in 1789 and given a royal charter, in 1802 (it moved to Halifax, Nova Scotia, in 1920), and another at York, Ontario, in 1827, which became the University of Toronto in 1849. St. Mary's College, the first Catholic institution apart from French-speaking Laval (1635), was founded at Halifax in 1802 (becoming a university in 1841), where the two most famous, Dalhousie College (University since 1863) was founded by the governor of Canada, the ninth earl of Dalhousie in 1818, and McGill University in Montreal was founded by the will of James McGill, fur trader, in 1821. When Canada achieved Dominion status and virtual internal independence in 1867, there were eighteen degree-awarding institutions (including the French ones), most of them religious foundations; only Dalhousie and McGill were lay foundations. By 1939 there were thirty-eight universities with 35,903 students, about a quarter of them women. By 1987 there were eighty-three universities, sixty-one English-speaking, seventeen French-speaking, and five bilingual, with about three-quarters of a million students, more than half of them women, representing over 50 percent of the age group.

The United States

After the American Revolution three overlapping developments built on the foundations laid by the colonists. First was the rise of the state university, beginning with the universities of North Carolina and Georgia, opened in 1795 and 1801, secular institutions with all the strength of public funding behind them but also under the monitoring eye of the state legislature. Second was the creation, under the Morrill Act of 1862, of the land-grant colleges, among the earliest being Ezra Cornell's college at Ithaca in upper New York State (1869), where "any person can find instruction in any study," particularly in those applied sciences so useful to a newly industrializing society as agriculture and engineering. American education had an eye for the practical as well as the intellectual and moral, but the great leap forward resulted from the third development, the import of the German research university, beginning with Johns Hopkins in 1876 and soon to be imitated by Harvard, Yale, Columbia, Northwestern, Michigan, and other universities, state and private, all the way across to Stanford and Berkeley on the West Coast. Yet the American research university bore little resemblance to the German model. Its highly funded research professors with their large teams and departments were able to bring to bear much larger resources than elsewhere on scientific and technological problems, with spectacular results. The United States in the twentieth century became the mecca for scholars from the whole world over, especially for European refugees from Hitler and Stalin.

The overwhelming features of American higher education have been its diversity and its restless expansion. Not only could any person find any study but, particularly after the U.S. Supreme Court ruled against New Hampshire's attempt to impose state control on Dartmouth College in 1819, any individual, group, church, city, state, or private firm could found a college and open its doors to anyone willing to pay the tuition fees. The American cornucopia, born after the Civil War of free or cheap land, mass production, and endless opportunity, poured out part of its riches into hundreds and later thousands of colleges and universities across the continent. Every state and large city had its state-funded university, often with several campuses, and private universities sprang up to suit every kind of student. The nine colleges at the American Revolution grew to 560 in 1870 and to 1,220 in 1928, and students in higher education as a whole increased from 1,237 in 1800 (about 1 percent of the white males between 18 and 21) to 32,364 (3.1 percent) in 1860, 256,000 (5 percent) in 1900, and 1,174,400 (15 percent of both sexes aged eighteen to twenty-one) in 1928—over five times the average percentage in Europe. Of these, women constituted an increasing proportion, from 28 percent in 1870 to no less than 49 percent in 1928, although many more were in teachers colleges and the like than in universities.[5] Today there are over 3,100 institutions of higher education, with more than twelve million students, over 50 percent of the age group.

Nor were African-Americans left out altogether, though they were far behind the rest. There were no black colleges, as distinct from vocational and secondary schools, before the Civil War. Emancipation from slavery precipitated the founding of black colleges in Atlanta, Nashville, and Washington, D.C., between 1865 and 1867. Others followed, and the Morrill-McComas Land-Grant Act of 1890 added seventeen more. In 1900 there were only 750 black students, rising to 3,500 in 1910 and 22,000 in 1930. Despite the long campaign of the National Association for the Advancement of Colored People from 1909; in 1938, 97 percent of the black students were in segregated colleges. It would take a Supreme Court decision in 1954 and the Civil Rights Movement of the 1960s to open up white universities, particularly in the South, to Afro-Americans, and even then to less than their share in the population. In the 1980s Afro-Americans constituted about 8 percent of American students, compared with their 11 percent share in the population.

The White Dominions

In the white settler colonies of Britain that became virtually independent Dominions between 1867 and 1910, the Europeans wanted their own higher education, as they did in North America. In Australia the government of each colony, later federated state, set up its own university. New South Wales founded Sydney University in 1850, Victoria, Melbourne University in 1853, South Australia, Adelaide University in 1874; Tasmania its University at Hobart in 1890; Queensland, Brisbane University in 1909; and Western Australia its own at Perth in 1911. Apart from the Australian National University founded as Canberra University College in 1930, and a handful of offshoots of state universities like Armidale, New South Wales (1938), progress was slow until after World War II when, in 1947, students numbered 28,558, over a quarter of them women. By 1987 there were 181,000 students, nearly half of them women, over a quarter of the age group.

New Zealand was quick off the mark with the University of Otago at Dunedin in 1869, twenty-one years after the first European settlement, which soon merged with Canterbury College to form the federal University of New Zealand, on the London University pattern, in 1874. Affiliated colleges followed, at Auckland (1882), Wellington (Victoria College, 1898), and Canterbury and Massey Agricultural colleges (1870 and 1926). By 1947 there were about 12,000 students in the seven colleges, only about 15 percent of them women. In 1987 there were 62,000 students, just over half of them women, over a quarter of the age group.

In white South Africa, higher education began with the South African College in 1829, fifteen years after the Dutch ceded the Cape of Good Hope to the British, which in 1918, after the Union of South Africa achieved Dominion status (1910), became the University of Cape Town. Grey College at Bloemfontein followed in 1855, later (1935) the University College of Orange Free State. In 1873 the Federal University of the Cape of Good Hope, patterned on the University of London, was set up, to which most of the South African colleges became affiliated: Cape Town (1873), Grey College (1916), Potchefstroom (1869, affiliated 1921), Rhodes College (1904, affiliated 1916), Pretoria (1908), Natal (1909), and Pius XII Catholic University in Basutoland (1945), the first university institution for black Africans. Only the University of Stellenbosch (1874) remained outside the federal University, until the latter was broken up in 1951. The only black college within the Union was the African Native College at Fort Hare, founded by the Free Church of Scotland in 1916. In 1947 there were about 16,000 white students, of whom about a quarter were women. After the election of the Nationalist government in 1948, apartheid was imposed on higher education in 1951. In 1960 black Africans were no longer allowed at Cape Town and Witwatersrand universities, the only mixed-race institutions, and were confined to the three Bantu colleges of Fort Hare, the College of the North at Turfloop, and Zululand College, and to a non-European Medical School at Durban, while colleges were provided for "Coloreds" at Cape Town and Indians at Durban. South Africa educates about 5 percent of the age group, one of the smallest percentages in the developed world, but this represents perhaps four times that proportion of the white population.

Though neither tropical nor technically a Dominion, Southern Rhodesia was an internally independent white settler territory from 1924 until 1980 when it became the African Republic of Zimbabwe. It did not have a university college (of Rhodesia and Nyasaland) until 1955, and the white settlers generally sent their children to South Africa or Britain for their higher education. After the breakup of the Central African Federation in 1964 and the declaration of unilateral independence in 1966, the college threw off its link with London University and became the University of Rhodesia in 1970. It always accepted both black and white students, as its successor the University of Zimbabwe (1980) does under the African republic. It now has about eight thousand students, about one-fifth women. Zambia (Northern Rhodesia) and Malawi (Nyasaland) set up their own universities after independence in 1964, with about 2 percent of the student age group in 1981.

The Non-White British Empire

Outside the white Dominions and white-dominated South Africa and the Rhodesias, there were two kinds of colonies in the British Empire. In all of them there were few white settlers, as distinct from officials, soldiers, and missionaries, to lobby for higher education or provide their own. In Africa, the west Indies, and other tropical areas, where most of the indigenous peoples were preliterate, the main concern of the colonial officials and missionaries was to teach literacy for the purpose of preaching Christianity and the virtues of work rather than higher forms of learning, and the natives too could only progress to higher education through basic preliminary schooling. The ancient civilizations of India and south Asia, on the other hand, had a long history of advanced education going back to Buddhist monasteries of the seventh-century B.C., to the third-century A.D. Hindu *Nalanda,* and to the eleventh-century Islamic *madrasahs,* although by the time of the British Raj such colleges were in low water. Both kinds of colony developed a love-hate relation to their imperialist rulers, however. Both wanted the advantages of education, at different levels, the more literate to compete for positions, however lowly, in the conquerors' system of administration and business, the unliterate to grasp at whatever means of gaining a living they could find in a poverty-stricken environment. At the same time they both sought ways of conquering the conquerors, of learning from them ways to turn the tables and throw them out. Schools and colleges provided the most promising way to arm themselves ideologically and acquire the necessary intellectual and moral means to gain independence.

India and Southeast Asia

India under the British possessed at least three traditions of advanced scholarship, in the Hindu *gurukulas,* the Buddhist *vihares,* and the Koranic *madrasahs* of her three great religions. In the eighteenth century the British encouraged native culture, and Warren Hastings founded a new Islamic *madrasah* at Calcutta in 1781 and John Duncan a Hindu college at Benares in 1792. In the early nineteenth century, however, the influential James Mill and the English Utilitarians dismissed Indian culture as moribund and doubted the utility of "teaching mere Hindoo, or mere Mohammedan literature," and, after a generation-long dispute between the "Westerners" and the "Orientalists," persuaded the Indian government to found colleges of Western learning. The British Raj developed a policy, based on Lord Macaulay's famous minute of 1835, of educating the Indians in English language, literature, and science with a view to state employment and perhaps a distant prospect, expressed as early as 1865, of self-government. After much debate between the home and Indian governments, the Raj set up in 1857 three federal examining universities on the London pattern in Calcutta, Bombay, and Madras, surrounded by affiliated colleges. Others, including the Muslim universities at Aligarh (1875) and Lahore (1882), followed; nineteen in all by independence in 1947, plus scores of affiliated colleges.

The Indian universities became immensely popular, with about 60,000 students by 1921, and twice that number by 1936. They served two major purposes, that of educating Indians, especially Brahmins and Muslims, for the professions and for minor posts in the Indian Civil Service, and that of preparing the way for independence. That preparation came most forcefully in ways not anticipated by the British rulers. As an Indian academic put it in 1917, "The University of Calcutta is a foreign plant imported into this country, belonging to a type that flourished in foreign soil. . . . the new system was introduced in entire ignorance and almost in complete defiance of the existing social order regulating the everyday life of an ancient people." The unintended effect was to provide recruits for the Indian Congress Party and the Muslim League and to fuel the nationalist movements that agitated for independence from before World War I until after World War II. By independence in 1947, there were nearly 200,000 students in India. In 1987 there were 3.6 million students, nearly a third of them women, about 8 percent of the age group. At independence, Pakistan had three federal universities: Panjab (1882), Dacca (1921), and Sind (1947), with 106 affiliated colleges and perhaps 100,000 students, mostly men.

Outside British India itself, Rangoon College (1920, affiliated to the University of Calcutta) became the University of Rangoon after the separation of Burma from India in 1937, with over 4,000 students, a quarter of them women, at independence in 1948. Ceylon University College (1921), affiliated to the University of Calcutta, amalgamated with the Ceylon Medical College (1870) to form the University of Ceylon in 1942, six years before the independence of Sri Lanka in 1948, when there were 1,577 students, including 251 women. In the University of Sri Lanka and its associate institutions, there were in 1987 almost 20,000 students, nearly half of them women, about 3 percent of the age group. In Malaya the King Edward VII College of Medicine (1905), Raffles College (1928), named for the founder of Singapore, and the College of Agriculture at Selangore were amalgamated as the University of Malaya only in 1949, when there were 696 students, ninety-four of them women. The affiliated college at Singapore became a separate university shortly before Malaysia and Singapore became independent in 1963 and 1965. In 1981 they had about 5 percent and 8 percent of the age group, respectively, in higher education. The University of Hong Kong was founded by the colonial government in 1911, and refounded in 1946 after its destruction by the Japanese. In 1947 it had 507 students, 125 of them women, and there were another 784 in other colleges of agriculture, teacher training, engineering, and commerce. A separate Chinese University was founded in 1963. In the two universities in 1987, there were 15,795 students, two-fifths of them women, about 10 percent of the age group.

Thailand, the only independent country in Southeast Asia, did not escape Western influence, and its universities were based on the English model: Chulalongkorn (1917), the University of Moral and Political Sciences (1933), Kaesetsart (1943), and the University of Medical Sciences (1943), all four in Bangkok, with about 16,000 students in 1947. By 1981 no less than 20 percent of the age group were in higher education.

British Tropical Africa and the West Indies

Long before the Europeans arrived, Africa had famous Muslim colleges in the mosques of Sankoré in Timbuctu, Qarawiyin in Fez, and Ál-Azhar in Cairo, but they were naturally conservers of tradition rather than instruments of modernization. Until after World War I, British governments took little interest in higher education in the tropics, believing that what largely nonliterate societies needed first was elementary and vocational education. Most schooling of any kind was provided by missionaries, the (Anglican) Church Missionary Society, the Wesleyan Methodists, and the Scottish churches. The first and, until after World War I, only college in British West Africa was Fourah Bay College near Freetown in Sierra Leone, the British colony for slaves recaptured from the banned slave trade. It was founded in 1818 as a seminary for prospective clergy by the Church Missionary Society to serve students from all over West Africa. Many attempts were made during the nineteenth century to raise it to university status, including a vigorous campaign in the 1870s by the Reverend Edward Blyden, a West Indian of African descent, who later (1881) became president of Liberia College in the American-sponsored republic for ex-slaves. It finally succeeded in 1876 with its affiliation for examination purposes to the University of Durham, but it averaged only between four and fourteen degree students a year from then until 1926. Technical schools or departments were founded at Freetown in Sierra Leone, Accra on the Gold Coast, and Lagos in Nigeria in the 1890s, but nothing more was done before World War I. In East Africa, where school education was even more backward, the only higher education institution was Gordon Memorial College in Khartoum, founded by General Kitchener after defeating the late Mahdi's forces in 1898. It was only after World War I that Britain began to take seriously the question of higher education for Africans.

Between the wars, colonialism came under increasing attack from both liberal Westerners and the subject peoples themselves, and the principles of national self-determination and trusteeship proclaimed by President Wilson's Fourteen Points and the League of Nations made the imperial powers think more carefully about their responsibilities, After a critical report by the American missionaries' African Education Commission in 1922, the British Colonial Office decided to appoint a permanent advisory committee on native education in tropical Africa, and later extended its scope to all the British colonies. This led to a white paper on *Education Policy in British Tropical Africa* (1925) and to a series of official inquiries, including the Currie Report (1933), which recommended that the existing colleges in Uganda, Sudan, Sierra Leone, the Gold Coast, and Nigeria be raised to university status. Against the reluctance of the local governors, however, nothing was done until the Asquith and Elliot Commissions (1943–45) recommended a full scheme of higher education for East and West Africa, with university colleges at Makerere, Khartoum, Fourah Bay, Achimota, and Ibadan in Nigeria. These "Asquith colleges" were duly established after the war, with British government finance and the help of London University, which tailored its examination offerings to African needs.

With the independence of Ghana in 1957 and the other African colonies in the 1960s, their university colleges threw off the tutelage of London and Durham universities and became full universities. Unfortunately, their British constitutions only worked when operated by British conventions, and some of the newly independent politicians, like Kwame Nkrumah in Ghana and Nnamdi Azikiwe in Nigeria, did not appreciate the need for academic freedom and university autonomy, and interfered rather too readily in appointments and day-to-day operations. (The French, who maintained an interest in their ex-colonial universities, argued that state-employed professors had better safeguards for their freedom.) This was partly due to the African politicians' frustration with the British and, increasingly, American traditions of academic studies which still dominated their institutions, an inevitable by-product of their foreign origin, and to their anxiety for rapid economic development. In 1981 Ghana and Sierra Leone had 1 percent of the student age group in higher education and Nigeria 3 percent.

In the West Indies the only institution of higher education before World War II was the Imperial College of Tropical Agriculture in Trinidad (1921), which had only fifty-one students in 1948. As a result of a British educational commission in 1938, it became a constituent of the University College of the West Indies, founded in 1949 to offer London external degrees to students from the fourteen islands, eventually with three campuses in Jamaica, Trinidad, and the Bahamas. Despite the immediate dissolution of the West Indies Federation after independence (by the withdrawal of Jamaica and Trinidad) in 1962, it became a separate university still serving the whole archipelago. It grew to 7,621 students, about half of them women, by 1987, about 5 to 6 percent of the age group.

China

By the early twentieth century, very few areas of the globe outside Europe and its offshoots in the Americas and Australasia were still independent, and those few were heavily penetrated by European economic, cultural, and intellectual influences. Even China, pioneer of professional education for two millennia, saw the collapse of the imperial examination system in 1905 and the creation before the 1911 Revolution of three Western-style universities and thirty-eight other institutions of higher education. By 1928 there were seventy-four university institutions, and by 1937, when the Japanese invaded, 108. Despite the destruction of the war, at the Communist Revolution in 1948, there were fifty-five universities, seventy-nine independent colleges, and eighty-one technical institutes, a total of 215 institutions with about 130,000 students—in a population of 450 million. As in Soviet Russia, the Communist government harnessed education to modernization and propaganda, but decoupled it by closing the universities during the Cultural Revolution, whose effects have become a negative proof of the connection between education and development. In 1981 there were still only 1 percent of the student age group in higher education.

The Middle East

In the Middle East, where most countries in the early twentieth century were only nominally free, Iran, divided into British and Russian "spheres of influence," established Western-style universities in Tehran in 1934 and Tabriz in 1947, with about 5,000 students in 1948 and 50,000 in 1970. Iraq, a British protectorate, did not have a unified university but founded modern faculties of law, commerce and economics, agriculture, music, and fine arts in the 1930s, with about 3,000 students in 1948 and 35,000 in eleven institutions by 1967. Even remote Afghanistan established a Western-style university at Kabul in 1932, another in Jalalabad in 1963, and the Kabul Polytechnic in 1968. In 1981 Afghanistan had 2 percent, Iran 5 percent, and Iraq 9 percent of the student age group in higher education.

Turkey, which had a Koranic university in Istanbul since its conquest of the Byzantine Empire in 1453 and a naval engineering school since 1773 which developed other engineering faculties during the nineteenth century, built the "House of Science" in Istanbul in 1863 and acquired the same year Robert College, an American institution with Western staff, and an American College for Girls in 1890. Only after the overthrow of the sultan and the establishment of Ataturk's republic in 1923 did modern higher education take off in earnest, with use of the Roman alphabet in 1928 and instituted equality for women. By 1950 there were three universities and nine technical and professional schools, with about 20,000 students, about a fifth of them women, and by 1969 nine universities and eighty other colleges, with about 120,000 students. Between 1960 and 1980 the percentage of the student age group in higher education rose from 2 percent to 5 percent.

Egypt broke away from the Turkish empire under Mehemet Ali Pasha in 1830 and began to Westernize education but, apart from the Ál-Azhar *madrasah* in the great mosque of Cairo, no modern university was founded before the American University in 1919. That was followed, after official independence from the British in 1922, by Fouad I University in 1925, Farouk I and Alexandria Universities in 1942, and Asyut University in 1957. By 1969 there were about 125,000 students, plus 18,748 at Ál-Azhar, where they covered the whole span from primary to higher education. The proportion of the student age group in higher education rose from 5 percent in 1960 to 15 percent in 1981.

In Syria and Palestine, there was little higher education under the Turks, and the first universities came after World War I under the British and French Mandates, the Syrian University at Damascus in 1923 and the Hebrew University in Jerusalem, first projected by the Zionist movement in the 1880s, in 1925. The Technion, the Hebrew Institute of Technology at Haifa founded in 1912, was also raised to university status in 1925. By 1970 the two Syrian universities, at Damascus and Aleppo, had about 39,000 students, and the proportion of the age group in higher education rose from 4 percent in 1960 to 18 percent in 1980. In the new state of Israel, the two universities at independence in 1948 grew to four plus two university colleges and a research institute by 1973, with over 50,000 students, rising from 10 percent of the age group in 1960 to 26 percent, a very Western level, in 1980.

Japan

The most spectacular example of Westernization in higher education, as in much else, was of course Japan. The revolutionary samurai who restored the Emperor Meiji in 1868 eagerly imported Western science, technology, and education, in Prime Minister Ito's words "to maintain the nation's strength and to guarantee the welfare of the people." "A rich country and a strong army" was the watchword, and the *han* schools for samurai bureaucrats were replaced by imperial universities, at Tokyo (1886), Kyoto (1897), Fukuoka on Kyushu (1903), Sapporo on Hokkaido (1903), and Nagoya (1939). They were followed by many other colleges and institutes, more of them private than public. Initially on French lines with attached but separate research institutes, they soon ostensibly followed the German model of the combined teaching and research university. But the German model, like everything Western, was quickly modified to fit Japanese culture and society. *Wissenschaft* became purely practical and harnessed to Japanese development, *Lehrfreiheit* and *Lernfreiheit* were unknown, and the professorial chair, in the spirit of Japanese teamwork and group psychology, was transformed into a sofa. Student numbers surged, and on the eve of American reorganization in 1947 there were nearly half a million in 648 institutions; only 15 percent were women, most of them in nonuniversity institutions. Since World War II they have soared still higher, with 1,645,000 students, 28 percent of them women, in 1970, in 1,345 institutions. With 30 percent of the age group going to college in 1985, Japan is one of the first countries to reach mass higher education, as befits the most successfully developed nation outside the West.

In higher education as in technology, management, and industrial relations, Japan set the pattern for postindustrial society. By the end of World War II, most advanced and developing nations had adopted or were in the process of adopting, if in a highly modified form, the Western type of higher education that had done so much to reinforce, and in later cases to midwife, industrial society, with its promise of wealth and power but its heavy costs in drudgery and maldistribution of rewards. The world, unknowingly perhaps, was poised for another great leap forward, into a postindustrial phase in which the university and its satellites would become the key to further the development of human society.

The University and Postindustrial Society

The period since World War II has seen the greatest expansion of higher education in the history of the universities since the twelfth century. Everywhere old universities have doubled and trebled in size, new institutions have come into existence in practically every country in the world, and student numbers have increased to embrace ever larger proportions of the adolescent age group. According to one estimate, in Europe both east and west (excluding Russia) students as a percentage of the twenty- to twenty-four-year-old age group increased tenfold between the 1930s and the 1970s, from 2.1 percent in 1940 to 21.5 percent in 1978; in the United States, already with nearly four times the European figure, more than fourfold, from 9.1 to 40.0 percent.[6] More recent figures from the World Bank show dramatic increases worldwide between 1960 and 1985. Even the poorest thirty-four countries, with average per capita incomes in 1982 of $280, including India and China (which suffered from the setback to higher education during the Cultural Revolution), more than doubled their percentage of the twenty- to twenty-four-year-old age group in higher education, from 2 to 5 percent. The lower-middle income group of thirty-eight countries, with per capita incomes of $840, including Egypt, Peru, Turkey, and Zambia, quadrupled theirs, from 3 to 13 percent. The twenty-two upper-middle income countries, including Brazil, Greece, Korea, and Yugoslavia, with average incomes of $2,490, also quadrupled theirs, from 4 to 16 percent. The high-income oil producers of the Middle East with average incomes of $14,820, which after the oil price rise of the 1970s could buy anything they liked, including professors, multiplied theirs eleven-fold, from 1 to 11 percent. The nineteen "industrial market economics," the rich OECD countries of North America, Western Europe, Australasia, and Japan, with average incomes of $11,070, already at much higher levels, more than doubled their percentage, from 16 to 39 percent. The Eastern bloc, too, which no longer reported their per capita income (except for Hungary and Romania $2,270 and $2,560), nearly doubled their percentage, from 11 to 21 percent.[7]

From Elite to Mass Higher Education

In the advanced countries, at least, these figures represent what Martin Trow has called the transition from elite to mass higher education, from under 5 percent to over 15 percent of the student age group. Unlike previous increases, it embraces much larger sections of the population, including women for the first time in something approaching equal numbers, and working-class students in significant numbers, though still much less than their share in the population. Between 1950 and 1975, women as a proportion of the student body have risen in Western Europe from 21 percent to 37 percent, in Eastern Europe from 34 percent to 48 percent, in Japan from 11 percent to 32 percent, and in the United States from 30 percent to 45 percent.[8]

Working-class students of either sex are much less recognizable than women, and few countries make returns of their percentage in the student body. In Western Europe, according to sociological surveys of different nations at different dates, they increased considerably from about 1950 to about 1970 but with enormous variations between countries. In France and West Germany they increased from 4 percent to 13 percent, by the Netherlands from 1 percent to 14 percent, in Denmark from 7 percent to 16 percent, in Italy from 11 percent to 20 percent, in Sweden from 14 percent to 23 percent; in England, where working-class students had reached 29 percent of an admittedly small student body in 1930, the percentage actually shrank by the postwar period and remained stationary at around 23 percent.

When the working-class share is shown as a percentage of the age group rather than of the student body, it is much less impressive, since the working-class, despite its shrinkage as a proportion of the work force in postindustrial societies, is still the largest class in most countries. Before World War II, working-class students as a percentage of the twenty- to twenty-four-year-old age group in most European countries were a negligible figure (from 0.06 percent in Germany to 0.9 percent in England), and it was still less than 1 percent around 1950. By about 1970, it had risen sharply everywhere, but was still an unequal proportion, usually from a quarter to a third of the overall average for a class that was at least half the population (e.g., Germany 2.1 percent out of 13.5 percent; England 3.1 percent out of 14.1 percent; France 4.5 percent out of 15.8 percent; Sweden 7.3 percent out of 21.3 percent). This was not perhaps surprising, given the unequal distribution of income and opportunities, the biased effect of "cultural capital," and the fact that the middle classes are in a better position to exploit the increased access. It is a salutary reminder that expansion does not necessarily bring greater relative equality, but against this absolute opportunities have increased all round.

The Postindustrial Revolution

The reasons for the unprecedented expansion of higher education are twofold: the demand of a more complex and highly geared economy for applied science and technology and for the social and administrative sciences for managing large institutions and corporate structures; and the demand in a postindustrial society providing more sophisticated services for highly educated personnel to operate and service them. Both are the product of a new kind of society, a further stage in human development, based more on services than on agriculture and manufacturing. It is in fact a third industrial revolution in the line of the prehistoric Neolithic Revolution that introduced settled agriculture and the Industrial Revolution of the last two centuries that inaugurated the mass production of goods. It is not that the service industries have replaced manufacture, any more than manufacturing in the Industrial Revolution replaced agriculture. On the contrary, what is happening to manufacturing in the Postindustrial Revolution is what happened to agriculture in the last Industrial Revolution, when food production became so efficient that it could feed the majority of the population with a minority of the work force, and release most of the people for work in other industries. Now manufacturing, with the aid of automation and electronic technologies, is becoming so efficient that it takes a minority of the work force to produce the material goods for the majority, so that most people can be released for work in other areas, notably in service industries. Professional experts are needed not only for the service industries but also for the more sophisticated operation of high technology agriculture and manufacturing industry.

This of course presents the same dilemma as the first two industrial revolutions: will there be enough jobs for all the displaced workers, and will those jobs be intellectually and emotionally satisfying, and financially rewarding? It is true that many of the new service industries offer mainly low-grade, low-paid jobs in fast food catering, retail distribution, hotel work, transportation, and the like. But the evidence suggests that on balance there are far more high-grade, well-paid jobs in management, administration, finance, and all the burgeoning professions than ever before, including the high technology professions previously unknown to the economy. In what Ulrich Teichler has called the highly educated society, the percentage of college-educated people in the work force of leading countries has risen steeply since World War II without any loss of job opportunities. In Germany the percentage of college-trained persons in the occupied population has risen from 4 percent in 1960 to 10 percent in 1987, and in the entering labor force from 13 percent to over 20 percent. In Japan the first percentage has risen from 5.4 percent in 1960 to 13.1 percent in 1980, and the second from 8.7 percent to 39.4 percent. In the United States the first figure has risen from 13 percent in 1970 to 22 percent in

1984, and during the 1990s about half the American work force will have completed at least one year of college and a quarter four years or more.

At the same time there is no evidence that the highly educated are not finding suitable jobs. Gloomy forecasts of graduate unemployment have not been fulfilled, and although many have had to accept positions not traditionally occupied by graduates, surveys have shown that they have not found them undemanding or unrewarding, and many have enriched their jobs by upgrading their performance in them. Average differential salaries between graduates and nongraduates have narrowed, but this is in large part a statistical artifact from comparing an expanding upper tier with a shrinking lower one. As the World Bank figures of per capita national income show, the highly educated countries have much higher average incomes than the less educated ones, so that both tiers have materially benefited. It may be that graduates have displaced nongraduates and forced them into lesser occupations, but overall unemployment has not increased to anything like prewar levels, particularly in the most highly educated societies like the United States, West Germany, and Japan, and the rate of changeover from a nongraduate to a graduate work force does not seem to have got out of balance with job opportunities.

Moreover, the highly educated society, in which the college-educated occupy the top quartile of positions, does not altogether neglect the second quartile, of technicians, office workers, and other highly skilled workers. This second quartile is increasingly educated in high schools and technical institutions, often part-time or by "distance learning" in such institutions as the Open Universities in Britain and the Netherlands, the new British Open College (1987) for vocational courses, or Deakin University in Australia. In West Germany more than half the young workers receive some two to three years' training via apprenticeship and part-time vocational schooling, which, compared with France enables German industry to employ fewer supervisors. In Britain there is a long tradition of part-time vocational education for higher national diplomas and certificates below the degree level, and the same is true of many other countries. Training on-the-job is also increasingly supplemented by what has been called the "corporate classroom," formal teaching provided by business firms for manual workers and for office staff and junior management, and in their own staff colleges or short courses at business schools for higher management, too. In this more highly educated society, there is a trickle-down effect, extending education and training to larger and lower layers of the work force. It also affects the growing area of nonvocational, not-for-credit education, an expansion of the traditional adult or continuing education for self-improvement and pleasure, which has been a feature of university extension work, philanthropic bodies like the Workers Educational Association, and local government provision in Britain, Scandinavia, and other countries.

All this means that in postindustrial society the production of knowledge and of what Daniel Bell has called "knowledge workers" is itself one of the biggest service industries, producing an increasing share of the national income and taking an increasing share of government spending. Although government expenditure accounts for only part of the cost, the percentage of national budgets spent on education as a whole has significantly increased since World War II. This is because no government in the postindustrial world can afford to neglect human capital wherever it can be found, which is why higher and further education has not only expanded but widened its access to include women and working-class students as well. Those countries that fall behind in the educational competition find themselves declining on every other dimension: cultural, economic, political, and military. The rise and fall of great powers are not unconnected with the exploitation of their human capital as well as their material resources.

The Axial Institution of Professional Society

The competitive production of new knowledge and of knowledge workers has made the university and its offshoots the key institutions of the new society. In Daniel Bell's phrase, the university has become the axial institution of postindustrial society. That society is best described as professional society, a society dominated by professionals, including professional bureaucrats and managers, as preindustrial society was dominated by landed aristocrats and industrial society by industrial capitalists. At the head of each industry, service, and career hierarchy—government, defense, health, welfare services, education, manufacturing, transportation, commerce, finance, art, music, sport, entertainment, even religion—stand the professionals who have effectively replaced the owner-managing capitalist as the initiator and organizer of productive activity. Even if the educational system, as some cynics believe, merely acts as a screening device directing the talented toward the career ladders, it is still at the lowest estimate, the gatekeeper of the new economy. On a more realistic view, higher education, which trains and socializes as well as selects most of the professionals and provides them with the research-based knowledge for further development, is the key profession of this new professional society.

The Drawbacks of Professional Society

It is not all gain. There are three overlapping drawbacks to professional society as far as the universities are concerned. First, higher education has become much more expensive and dependent on the state, and therefore has become more vulnerable to government pressure. Second, the universities themselves have become much larger institutions and subject to the same bureaucratic tendencies as other large organizations. Third, as pivotal institutions of the new society, they have become targets for politicization by student radicalism of a kind that can have widespread national and international effects and be counter-productive for higher education.

First, mass higher education and "big science" have become so expensive that, in the predominantly state systems, and even in countries like the United States, India, and Japan with large private sectors, the universities have become increasingly dependent on the state for financial aid, research grants, and student support. In 1981 the nineteen industrial market economies were spending 5.1 percent of their central government budgets (plus unknown amounts of local government expenditure) on education, the low-income economies 5.9 percent, and the middle-income economies no less than 14.3 percent, an increasing part of it on higher education.[9] Understandably, governments have demanded a greater share of control over the uses to which this massive expenditure is put. This in turn leads to government intervention into university and college activity, "guidance" of research, "suggestions" for curriculum change, control over student admissions and professorial numbers, with the danger, already evident in the Eastern bloc and many third-world countries, of direct government interference in academic decisions. Society has always, of course, demanded some say in what the universities have given in exchange for its support, but now that higher education has become a significant item in the national budget, the temptation to control it in the name of accountability, with its implications for university autonomy and academic freedom, is often too great to be resisted, even in countries with so long a tradition of academic freedom as Britain, Australia, and Canada. Democracy itself is no defense: the democratic electorate may think academic freedom another name for privilege and feel itself entitled to control the universities in the name of the nonacademic majority. The only hope for the universities is to engage in a constructive dialogue with the politicians and the public and convince them that academic freedom is not only a right but a necessity if the best and most fearless work is to be performed for the benefit of the nation and the world as a whole.

Burgeoning expenditure and accountability exacerbate the second drawback, the bureaucratization of the university itself. The increasing size and complexity of the university, and its greater need to raise resources from the state and from private or corporate donors, make professional management inevitable, and the traditional informal organization is replaced by bureaucratic systems of control. Paradoxically, this has been the case longer in such democratic systems as the American, where the power of the university president and trustees has made academics more like employees than in Europe, where the professors have traditionally held sway over academic decisions, but even in the latter the officials are becoming much more powerful, especially as state financial controls have put pressure on university budgets. Since the essence of academic production is the freedom to work on one's own problems at one's own pace, the institution itself is in danger of becoming a threat to the academic enterprise. University autonomy, defined as the independence of the university administration, may be in conflict with the freedom of the individual academic. Again, the remedy is closer contact and better understanding between academics and administrators as the main hope of fending off the interventionist state or corporation.

Greater size and expense, dependence on the state and the public, and bureaucratic management—all contribute to the third drawback, the political implications of student unrest. Students, being young and literally irresponsible, have always been restless, and since the twelfth century have clashed with their elders, both within the university and without. The town and gown riots in medieval Paris, Oxford, and Bologna that led to murder and the migration of scholars elsewhere brought intervention by kings and popes. The students of the Renaissance universities played their part in the murderous religious quarrels of the Reformation. Thomas Hobbes blamed the students and dons of Oxford and Cambridge for the English Civil War. Students played a leading role in all the European revolutions from the great French Revolution of 1789, through the German, Austrian, and French ones of 1848, to the Russian revolutions of 1905 and 1917. They also helped to bring down the two-thousand-year-old Chinese Empire in 1911. In Latin America the Cordoba Manifesto of 1918 demanding university reform swept through the whole continent between the wars. Right-wing German students took part in the rallies that swept Hitler and the Nazis into power. And the famous Oxford Union resolution of 1934 "that this house would in no circumstance fight for its King and Country" gave Hitler the idea that Britain was finished as a great power.

By comparison with these past irruptions the student unrest of the 1960s, though it contributed to the fall of de Gaulle and to Mao's Cultural Revolution in China, seems almost trivial and, outside the United States at least, more concerned with student participation in institutional government than with national political matters like the Vietnam War and the Civil Rights movement. The achievement of tripartite university government in West Germany, Scandinavia, and Latin America (with equal representation for students, professors, and nonprofessorial staff) and a smaller measure of student participation elsewhere was a high price to pay for the backlash that followed.

The student movement in Europe and America had a dramatic and, in the end, counterproductive effect on the universities. Given the greater size and expense of what was still a small privileged minority of mostly well-to-do young people, the mass demonstrations, strikes, and sit-ins alienated the public and contributed in many countries to a disillusion with the promised benefits of higher education that set the stage for cuts in government funding. Student activists are few, student generations short, and student unrest still shorter and, since the deceleration in university expansion and the rise in unemployment associated with the oil crises and world recession of the 1970s and early 1980s, most students have once again settled down to preparing themselves for professional careers. But public memory is long and in many countries a mood of caution toward university expansion has persisted, allied to a skepticism about the economic promises of higher education and research. Again, the universities have a major public relations exercise to perform, to convince the wider society that supports them that they give value for money and deserve the autonomy and academic freedom they claim.

Despite the drawbacks, the university and its offshoots are essential to a professional society. If the university did not exist, it would have to be invented under another name. Many alternatives have been tried—British polytechnics, French *instituts universitaires de technologie* (IUTs), German *Fachhochschulen*, Russian research institutes, American corporation schools for business executives, and so on—but most of them drift back to the original university model. No institution so flexible and productive of new knowledge and adaptable graduates has yet been discovered. Yet this flexibility and productivity still depend, as in the days of Abelard, Aquinas, Luther, Galileo, Newton, Descartes, Adam Smith, Kant, Humboldt, or Einstein, on the academic freedom to pursue knowledge wherever it can be found. If the overbearing state or the over mighty corporation crushes that freedom, it may well kill the goose that lays the golden eggs.

Notes

1. K. H. Jarausch, ed., *The Transformation of Higher Learning, 1860–1930* (Chicago: University of Chicago Press, 1982), 13, 15.
2. Ibid., 98.
3. Hartmut Kaelble, *Social Mobility in the 19th and 20th Centuries* (Leamington Spa, England: Berg, 1985), 54, 67–68, 71–72.

4. Eric Ashby, *Universities: British, Indian, African* (Cambridge, Mass.: Harvard University Press, 1966), 10.
5. Jarausch, 111, 115.
6. Kaelble, 42–3.
7. World Bank, *World Development Report, 1984* (Washington, D.C.: World Bank, 1985), Table 25.
8. Kaelble, *Social Mobility*, 86–87.
9. World Bank, *World Development Report*, Table 26.

History of Higher Education in the United States

Lester F. Goodchild

To advance learning, knowledge, and professional practice may appropriately characterize the mission of North American higher education since 1636. Beginning with the nine colleges of the English Colonies to the approximately 4,000 postsecondary institutions of the present, men and women have struggled to provide opportunities for others to become highly educated. Such historic efforts have enabled students to achieve baccalaureate, master of arts or science, professional master's, specialist, and doctoral degrees to further their lives and careers as well as society and culture in the United States and elsewhere. These higher education opportunities occurred initially through a remarkable development of adapting European institutions of higher learning to the demands and needs of the expanding American landscape and population. Once established, colleges and universities changed, as waves of major influences from church bodies, accreditation agencies, state and federal governments, and student demands reshaped their institutional public or private missions. Institutional transformations also occurred, reflecting particular U.S. needs. Academies and schools became colleges. Colleges expanded to embrace university stature through advanced degrees and research. Most dramatically, specialized institutions arose to satisfy special educational needs and later broadened the scope of their missions: junior colleges became community colleges, normal schools expanded to become state universities, trade schools transformed into proprietary and nonprofit postsecondary education institutions, and correspondence programs led to virtual universities through distance education. The former president of Harvard University, Derek Bok, in his book *Higher Learning* (1986), rightly pointed to institutional responsiveness as one of the enduring characteristics of U.S. higher education. This drive to serve various local, regional, national, and later international constituencies has led to greater higher educational opportunity through the creation of a complex array of colleges and universities. In this system, some 15 million U.S. citizens and others are currently furthering their learning, advancing knowledge through research, and beginning their careers for the betterment of a global society.

The history of U.S. higher education may be understood by reviewing the establishment of the Colonial colleges, the development of pioneering colleges during the new Republic, and the rise of modern U.S. universities during the Civil War. Later in the nineteenth century, various groups demanded their own more "democratic" postsecondary institutions to further their academic and professional aspirations. The resulting confused array of academies, junior colleges, colleges, and universities entered the twentieth century ready for reform and reorganization. Various movements would reshape these institutions to configure the contemporary system. In the Progressive Era of the early twentieth century, accreditation associations and institutional consortia brought about an orderly sequence to these institutions. The system transformed again in the last half of the twentieth century as federal and state policies recast the largely autonomous enterprise to be more responsive first to societal needs and later to national priorities. During the 1960s and thereafter, in response to federal laws, institutions allowed students to adopt a consumerist approach to their educational aspirations. Campus leaders and faculty struggled to accommodate these major forces for change during these eras, while maintaining their academic professional callings to teach, do research, and perform public service. Nonetheless, their creation and adherence to academic traditions—as well as their willingness to make appropriate accommodations—have created the North American system of higher education.

The Colonial Colleges, 1636–1775

At the tricentenary of Harvard University in 1936, campus leaders struck a medallion to proclaim and remember this extraordinary achievement. The oldest institution of higher learning in the United States pressed its motto on the one side of this medal: an open book emblazoned with the Latin inscription *Veritas*, indicating that all pursuit of liberal knowledge involved and encountered divine truth. On the other side, a Puritan saying epitomized the religious ethos that was pervasive at the time of its first buildings: "Out of smalle beginnings greater things have been prodused by his hand that made all things of nothing and give being to all things that are." This enduring spirit of U.S. higher education, combining the search for truth with strong religious roots, originated from a small group of Puritan settlers who included 140 university graduates, the largest number being from Emmanuel College at Cambridge University. As Frederick Rudolph showed in his classic *The American College and University* (1962), these enlightened Protestants had fled Anglican England to establish their own Christian society. The mission of their college in creating this grand utopia involved preparing men for ministering to their own community and educating the colonists to become a "lettered" people.

As other religious groups came to the colonies, they followed this initial pattern, eager to expand learning opportunities in their own communities. In 1693, the Anglicans established the College of William and Mary in Virginia, offering higher education in the southern colonies. Others followed: the Collegiate School at New Haven in 1701 (now Yale University in Connecticut), the College of Philadelphia in 1740 (University of Pennsylvania), the College of New Jersey in 1746 (Princeton University), King's College in 1754 (Columbia University in New York), the College of Rhode Island in 1764 (Brown University), Queen's College in 1766 (Rutgers University in New Jersey), and last, Dartmouth College in 1769 in the wilderness of New Hampshire. Presbyterian, Baptist, Dutch Reformed, and Congregationalist communities thus founded their own schools of higher learning, being strongly influenced to do so by the Great Awakening, a call for religious renewal and revival emanating from Jonathan Edwards's fervid preaching of Calvinism in New Jersey.

By the late eighteenth century, however, as this wave of fervor subsided, the nine colleges loosened their ties to their founding churches and reduced their pietistic demands on students. Their presidents and tutor faculty shifted their interests more to curricular and pedagogical issues: Obtaining a sufficient student body and offering a classical liberal arts curriculum in Greek and Latin became their main concerns. Science through the study of mathematics and natural philosophy also entered this humanistic course of study, especially at the College of Philadelphia. This development came largely from European scholars and professors from Scotland.

The common teaching approach in all subjects remained recitation. Students chafed under the burdens of memorization and its recall during the day and confinement to the school and dormitories at night. Discipline problems, such as leaving the grounds at night, and rebellions, usually against bad food, erupted often among these restive older students. College life, though, served many social functions; for example, it offered the best opportunity to meet other enlightened men—and their sisters, who were perceived as having great potential as future brides. During this first century and a half of U. S. higher education, some 3,000 male graduates provided important local intellectual leadership to these increasingly rebellious colonies as the Revolutionary War approached.

The Pioneering Colleges of the New Republic, 1776–1861

Although the Revolutionary War disrupted the operation of the nine colleges, a new nation looked even more to these small schools to produce the next generations of democratic leaders for the new Republic. As the country expanded westward, the first settlers created new villages and towns with their churches and schools; those with higher aspirations began colleges. Such boosterism occurred as waves of migration crossed the Allegheny Mountains into the Mississippi Valley and Mississippi Basin, only to go further west with President Thomas Jefferson's huge addition of the Louisiana Territory in 1803. These pioneering colleges, begun on the edge of the frontier, reflected their local communities' religion and educational needs. Presbyterians, Congregationalists, Methodists, and Baptists initially and Catholics and Lutherans later were most active in spreading the educational aspects of their missionary work to Native Americans and to more recent settlers. In the 1830s, they began making their new schools available to women and African Americans.

Both Colin Burke in *American Collegiate Populations* (1982) and Roger Geiger in *The American College in the Nineteenth Century* (2000) described these new institutions as "multipurpose" colleges, displacing the former terms—"old-time" or "antebellum" college—that scholars once employed. This new label designated the variety of studies found at these schools—classical studies at the baccalaureate level, secondary education, training for the trades—depending on the desires of the church and community. Tests of who controlled these new colleges came quickly, as state legislatures and governors sought to clarify their rights over these schools and their fiscal obligations. Generally, towns and their churches wanted local control rather than significant influence from far-away state capitals. In 1819, U.S. Supreme Court Chief Justice John Marshall, in the famous *Dartmouth College v. Woodward* case, decided after an impassioned defense of the small college by Daniel Webster, that local sovereignty remained with the trustees of the corporation. They held the right to govern the institution and protect its autonomy, thereby rebuffing state intrusions into its very workings. As Jurgen Herbst argued in *From Crisis to Crisis: American College Government, 1636–1819* (1982), this decision finally put to rest an almost two-centuries-long conflict by defining the legal nature of the U.S. corporation and its invulnerability to external claims, with particular relevance to governance of local colleges.

Such educational desires and legal freedoms allowed founders and trustees to create institutions where all citizens could gain higher learning. Catholics began very early to establish their own schools with the founding of Georgetown College in 1789, St. Louis University in 1818, and the University of Notre Dame in 1842; some twelve other Catholic colleges had opened by 1860. Women also found doors open to them at their own institutions, beginning with Troy Female Seminary in 1822, Georgia Female College in 1836, and Mount Holyoke College in 1837, as well as at coeducational schools at Oberlin College in 1834 and Antioch College in 1853. The enlightened Congregationalists at Oberlin also held strong abolitionist beliefs. They allowed African Americans to enroll. In so doing, they created the quintessential U.S. college. In 1849 in Pennsylvania, African Americans created the first of their own institutions, Avery College, which began secondary studies. In 1854, Presbyterians began collegiate studies for African Americans at Lincoln University, and two years later the Methodists opened Wilberforce University. Others would follow.

Yet the question as to what constituted baccalaureate studies perplexed all during the first fifty years of the new Republic. Generally, presidents and faculty considered Greek and Latin works from the European Enlightenment humanities tradition to be what was needed to educate students to be cultured citizens or to train them for the ministerial, medical, or legal professions. Increasing threats, from several reformers, to this liberal arts course of study by adding science, geometry, and more practical subjects finally led Yale's President Jeremiah Day, Professor James L. Kingsley, and their faculty to defend the traditional college curriculum. In their Yale Report of 1828, they claimed that "intellectual culture" occurred through the "discipline and furniture of the mind" by which they meant that lectures about and recitations of the great classical works expanded the mind's powers and stored it with knowledge. The object of the college was to provide students with a "superior foundation" for these professional studies, and the Yale Report claimed that studying the liberal arts would do just that. The report's success among U.S. colleges in maintaining the dominance of the classical course for the rest of the nineteenth century resulted from the fact that at this time, Yale had graduated most of the college presidents in the country. This course also allowed the new nation's small institutions of higher learning to offer intellectual breadth at a very reasonable cost.

Students, however, chafed under this rigid curriculum, eager for more literary and scientific studies. Unable to study about these subjects in greater detail during the school day, they created their own literary and dramatic societies, which met after class to explore these areas, and they developed their own related libraries. Further need for diversions led them to create their own residence system through Greek houses for men or women and to establish club, intramural, and eventually intercollegiate sports. The first contest between Harvard and Yale in 1852 involved a crewing competition in New Hampshire; baseball, football, and other intercollegiate sports greatly enlivened college life. However, not until Harvard's successful challenges to the fixed curriculum in the 1860s and in the 1910s did this traditional liberal arts course fade across college campuses. Its last vestiges disappeared in the 1970s, when several private universities dropped their requirement that all undergraduates take Latin. Its passing would allow a new intellectual vitality to accompany the frenzied activity occurring outside of the classrooms on college campuses.

In retrospect, the nineteenth century was the age of the small, residential, liberal arts colleges, with their rural students, where many different types of studies could be found. The demand for college education had become so great by the end of the century that institutional leaders chose to construct classroom buildings rather than residences. Thus, at most institutions, only about 25 percent of the students remained on campus rather than living in town. Moreover, by this time, an increasing number of academies and high schools were entering the educational institutional thicket to accommodate students in the growing urban areas, and it became harder to distinguish the differences among these schools, except in the oldest colleges. Nevertheless, institutions of higher learning had grown exponentially as the western migrations continued throughout the century. By 1900, approximately 110,000 students attended some 1,030 colleges and other schools of higher learning; 43 percent were coeducational, 20 percent were for women, and 37 percent were for men. Other types of higher education would offer new alternatives.

The Modern U.S. University, 1862–1945

In the first half of the nineteenth century, various reformers—Thomas Jefferson, Alexander Hamilton, Francis Wayland, Eliphalet Nott, George Ticknor, and Henry Phillip Tappen—sought to change the rigid college curriculum. Their efforts helped to create new institutions of higher learning— particularly public colleges and universities—and to alter the collegiate course by introducing more scientific, mathematical, and applied studies. Several states had begun their own schools of higher learning or had begun granting credentials to institutions shortly after the Revolutionary War. The University of Georgia in 1789 and University of Vermont in 1791 were founded on state charters, while the University of the State of New York allowed institutions in the state to grant degrees as early as 1787, four years after an initial university plan had been put forward. The curricula at these state-sponsored institutions did not reflect these new curricular innovations; they remained similar to the typical collegiate programs elsewhere. Rather, new institutional missions and curricular innovations would come initially from Rensselaer Polytechnic Institute in 1824, the University of Virginia in 1825, the University of Michigan in 1837, Yale University in 1860, and Harvard University in 1869. Their combined efforts led directly and indirectly to the modern U.S. university.

After Thomas Jefferson's efforts to change the curriculum at the College of William and Mary failed, he created a new institution of higher learning in Charlottesville, Virginia. In 1825, when the university opened, it proclaimed a true university mission of advanced studies and allowed students to choose from among eight different courses of study in separate schools (from the older professions of law and medicine to the classical studies of ancient languages, natural philosophy, and moral philosophy to the newer studies of modern languages, mathematics, and natural history), and it remained secular in all aspects. These developments reflected Jefferson's understanding and experience of the best innovations from the Scottish and French Enlightenments. As John Brubacher and Willis Rudy note in their comprehensive *Higher Education in Transition* (1997), this university influenced not only southern institutions but also major innovators at northern institutions, such as Ticknor at Harvard, Wayland at Brown, Woodward at Michigan, and Eliot at Harvard. More colleges, especially after the 1850s, began to adopt the so-called parallel course plan, in which students could elect to study either the classical curriculum or a scientific one. The creation of the scientific schools at both Harvard and Yale made these developments increasingly part of the college landscape.

Similarly, Henry Tappen, after he became president of Michigan in 1852, introduced Prussian and German ideas of what university education meant. His interest in promoting research led to replacing the common teaching form (i.e., recitation) with lectures, encouraging faculty research, and establishing a graduate course of study. After 1871, further advancements at Michigan under President James B. Angell led to a clear distinction between graduate and undergraduate studies, the creation of the seminar, and demands that the faculty carry out original research. State universities thus offered significant innovations not found at the typical private college.

Private universities would further provide curricular developments that helped configure the modern U.S. university. Yale College challenged all other institutions of higher learning in 1860 by inaugurating the doctor of philosophy degree and moving toward becoming a university. After returning from two years of study in Germany, Daniel Coit Gilman proposed in 1856 that the Sheffield Scientific School at Yale offer a Ph.D. with the expectation that students would take two years of graduate course work, achieve a competency in foreign languages, pass a comprehensive examination, and write a dissertation. In July 1860, Dean John Porter of the school persuaded the Yale trustees to approve the plan. The first U.S. Ph.D.'s graduated the following year. It was a higher education milestone, for German university ideas and curricula were assimilated and then tailored to academic traditions in the United States. This doctoral course thus followed the parallel curricular pattern, namely, creating a graduate program after the college course. Still, curricular flexibility had not been achieved.

Finally, Charles Eliot's demand in his 1869 inaugural address for electivism at Harvard University provided the most flexible curriculum mechanism to introduce new courses into college and graduate studies. By allowing students to create their own courses of studies and by no longer requiring a fixed curriculum, faculty were free to teach any subject area, including the sciences. He called for a "New Education" consisting of the sciences, modern languages, and mathematics. Over the next two decades, electivism was implemented completely in Harvard's collegiate studies: By 1893, only the freshman writing course remained compulsory. The next president, Abbott Lawrence Lowell, constrained this electivism and revised the undergraduate curriculum to provide two years of general education and a major in a particular subject area. By the second decade of the twentieth century, Harvard had thus created the national pattern for undergraduate studies for the rest of the century.

These four nineteenth-century developments created sufficient innovations for higher education leaders to embark on the creation of two modern U.S. institutional types, each with a new mission: (1) land-grant colleges and universities, with the passage of the Morrill Land-Grant Acts of 1862 and 1890, and (2) graduate research-oriented universities, with the founding of Johns Hopkins University in 1876. The missions of these modern universities centered on the discovery, transmission, and application of higher practical, humanistic, scientific, and professional knowledge. Each institutional type increasingly adhered to a new intellectual ideology associated with its mission. Pragmatism supported agricultural, mining, mechanical, and military studies of the new land-grants. Research (or the more familiar German ideal of *Wissenschaft*) described the value-free inquiry and advancement of pure knowledge, namely, learning for its own sake, associated with research universities, as Laurence Veysey explored so well in his definitive *The Emergence of the American University* (1965).

When the northern Congress during the Civil War passed the first land-grant act, it ceded approximately 17.5 million acres of federal lands to all participating states. These lands were then sold to support the creation of what would eventually be fifty-one new institutions, one for each state and Puerto Rico. Iowa State University, founded in 1858, in 1862 became the first university to take advantage of this law. Its founding commitment to women's education as well as to men's also meant that it was the first land-grant institution to be coeducational and to create studies in domestic science. This openness to applied and vocational studies spoke to the mission of these institutions. With his half-million-dollar gift, Cornell's new president, Andrew White, implemented this ideal, even though it took decades for these institutions to determine what exactly applied and vocational studies were and how they related to liberal education.

The public enthusiasm for higher practical studies that assisted the state and its citizens was best epitomized in the espousal of the Wisconsin Idea. In 1874, President James Bascom of the University of Wisconsin provided religious zeal to this movement. He saw that the power of a state in collaboration with its land-grant university and faculty could educate and train its citizens to create a moral and productive agricultural Christian society. A later, more secularized, Wisconsin Idea under President Charles R. Van Hise empowered the presidents of many land-grant institutions. The movement's fiscal stability finally came from George W. Atherton, president of Pennsylvania State University, who ensured the passage of the Hatch Act in 1887, which allocated federal funds for the operation of these institutions. He also created the National Association of State Universities and Land-Grant Colleges in the same year to discuss the act's implementation, as Hugh Hawkins's helpful *Banding Together: The Rise of National Associations in American Higher Education, 1887–1950* (1992) describes. As the oldest higher education association, it not only became the driving force to further the land-grant movement, but it also became the model for other consortia. Atherton and the presidents of other land-grant institutions encouraged the passage of the Second Morrill Land-Grant Act in 1890, which created or affiliated seventeen additional land-grant colleges and universities for African Americans in the South (for example, Prairie View A&M University in Texas, Florida A&M University, and Tuskegee University in Alabama) to blunt the failures of Reconstruction. All offered secondary education initially; the establishment of collegiate studies at the 1890 land-grant colleges took more than twenty-five years.

Another distinctive institution of higher learning arose on the international academic landscape, an institution that would influence U.S. scientific research. Beginning in 1810 with the founding of the University of Berlin, Germany's universities became famous for their single-minded focus on research and the advancement of scientific and humanistic knowledge. Some 9,000 U.S. students went to German universities during the nineteenth century to attend lectures and seminars from leading scholars, gain research training, and earn Ph.D. degrees. As Americans returned to the United States, they clamored for greater academic freedom by demanding that their own institutions take up such studies. Gilman's success at Yale led to the presidency of the University of California and made him, by the 1870s, the ideal candidate to create a new institution along German lines. The $3.5 million railroad fortune that Johns Hopkins bequeathed to an enlightened group of trustees led to the founding in 1876 of the first U.S. institution focused primarily on research and graduate studies. As Johns Hopkins University's first president, Gilman acquired an international faculty dedicated to research. It offered doctoral degrees in nineteen humanistic and scientific areas, launched the first U.S. research journals, and created national disciplinary associations.

Leading U.S. industrialists saw that the United States needed to train its own researchers and scientists if it was to compete successfully in a developing global market and defend its national interests. As Roger Geiger's *To Advance Knowledge: The Growth of American Research Universities, 1900–1940* (1986) describes in detail, their philanthropy fueled this new drive toward the development of the research universities and the creation of advanced graduate studies. G. Stanley Hall launched Clark University, which offered exclusively graduate programs, including eight doctoral programs, in 1889 with a $1 million gift from Jonas Clark. Bishop John Joseph Keane began the Catholic University of America, which also offered only graduate programs, including nine doctoral programs, in the same year with a half-million-dollar gift from Mary Gwendoline Caldwell. Eventually, these institutions also started undergraduate programs when financial difficulties beset them. Other new research universities were founded with even larger gifts, which allowed all levels of study to be offered. Stanford University, launched under the leadership of President David Starr Jordan in 1891, benefited from Leland Stanford's $20 million gift in memory of his son. Sponsored by the liberal Northern Baptist church, the University of Chicago began under the presidency of William Rainey Harper in 1892 with the massive funding of $35 million from John D. Rockefeller. The institution soon offered twenty-nine doctoral programs. Older institutions also greatly enhanced their graduate and professional studies, as may be seen from the $40 million gift by John William Sterling to Yale University in the 1920s.

Following the strategy of graduate students who had banded together nationally to facilitate their studies through the Federation of Graduate Clubs, the research university presidents formed the Association of American Universities in 1900 to ensure the quality of doctoral degrees, to allow only member institutions to offer the Ph.D. degree, and to set standards for doctoral education. Similarly, university faculty sought to protect their rights to advance knowledge through research, academic freedom, participation in institutional governance, and fairness in employment contracts and disputes by creating the American Association of University Professors in 1915. Their efforts established the academic profession, as Richard Hofstadter and Walter Metzger described in their definitive work, *The Development of Academic Freedom in the United States* (1955).

Finally, in the first decades of the twentieth century, the largest philanthropic foundations in the nation began to take an interest in higher education and its faculty. The Carnegie Foundation's $135 million and the Rockefeller Foundation and its General Education Board's $200 million recast U.S. higher education. These foundations used their money to expand college and university endowments, update administrative practices, inspect professional schools, and establish faculty pension funds. In 1910, for example, the Carnegie Foundation, under Abraham Flexner, inspected all 155 medical schools in the country and subsequently recommended that only 31 remain open and that as many as possible affiliate with universities. Later demands for this "new professionalism" forced greater academic preparation for all professional education by requiring that a student have a four-year baccalaureate degree before entering medical, legal, engineering, divinity, or social work schools, by facilitating the organization of professional educational associations, and by instigating the dramatic move of professional schools to university campuses.

The rise of the modern U.S. university thus involved the development of state, land-grant, and research universities. As the twentieth century began, many academic leaders considered it to be the age of the university. The next forty-five years saw these institutions weather world wars, economic recessions, and the Great Depression, yet they did not falter in their missions. Rather, campus life was enriched as students augmented their academic lives through the expansion of Greek life and intercollegiate sports, particularly football, during the Roaring Twenties. Nevertheless, these universities became increasingly integral to the advancing educational and national agendas in U.S. society and government.

The Democratic Colleges and Universities, 1865–1945

Spanning the developments of the pioneering colleges and modern U.S. universities was another type of institution of higher learning that arose after the Civil War. It was particularly created for persons who were increasingly unable to enter older, more established institutions. Women, African Americans, Native Americans, Jews, Catholics, and poor or rising-middle-class students found admission to traditional white Anglo-Saxon Protestant private higher education gradually unobtainable in the last half of the nineteenth and the early twentieth centuries. As Harold S. Wechsler in his *The Qualified Student: A History of Selective College Admission in America, 1870–1970* (1977) and David O. Levine in his *The American College and the Culture of Aspiration, 1915–1940* (1986) showed, "undesirable" groups were selectively being denied admission to elite institutions. In response, these groups funneled their energy and resources into creating their own private colleges and universities for their students, often patterned after one of their pioneering colleges. Interestingly, William Rainey Harper at the University of Chicago saw the problem, especially for poorer urban students, and suggested the development of junior colleges as part of the answer. This founding responsive spirit often came from Christian churches that created boards of education to oversee and extend higher learning throughout the country to meet these new educational needs.

The continuing legacy of these more democratic colleges thus made higher learning aspirations possible for disenfranchised and excluded groups. As women initially entered state, land-grant, and research universities, they found increasing discrimination from other students, faculty, and administrators. In response, women went to four-year colleges and normal schools as they could. In the 1869/1870 academic year, 11,000 women attended institutions of higher learning. Lynn Gordon pointed out in her valuable *Gender and Higher Education in the Progressive Era* (1990) that some 6,500 attended women's colleges and normal schools, and the other 4,600 enrolled in coeducational institutions. Women campus leaders, such as Martha Carey Thomas, Alice Freeman Palmer, and

Elizabeth Cady Stanton, created these new institutions and spoke eloquently to blunt the growing Victorian bias against women going on to higher education. Following the lead of Mount Holyoke College, Swarthmore College, Vassar College, Wellesley College, Smith College, Bryn Mawr College, and Radcliffe College formed the Seven Sisters colleges as models for women's higher education elsewhere. Similarly, normal schools offered women opportunities to obtain higher education by becoming teachers. Some fifty schools existed by 1875, and the number had grown to close to two hundred by 1920, as these institutions developed into state teaching universities. Twenty years later, in 1940, the tide had turned so much that women made up 40 percent of postsecondary students, and for a couple of years during World War II they even were in the majority.

Racial minority groups also found higher education difficult to enter. As African Americans began increasingly to avail themselves of postsecondary education, as noted by James Anderson in his insightful *The Education of Blacks in the South, 1860–1935* (1988), historically black colleges and universities arose with the support of various Christian missionary associations. Fisk University in Nashville in 1866, Talladega College in Alabama and Morehouse College in Atlanta in 1867, Howard University in Washington, D.C., in 1868, and Tougaloo College in Mississippi in 1869 began the movement all over the South to educate the newly liberated citizens of color at hundreds of institutions, later greatly supported by the ideas of W. E. B. Du Bois, who encouraged higher education rather than vocational training. Although educating Native Americans had ostensibly been the reason for founding many of the Colonial and pioneering colleges, Native Americans actually received little postsecondary education there. Later church efforts on reservations or tribal lands created institutions particularly for them, such as Sheldon Jackson College in 1878 in Alaska and Bacone College in 1880 in Oklahoma. Greater success would come later in founding two-year tribal colleges, as Paul Boyer showed in his groundbreaking *Native American Colleges* (1997).

As new waves of European immigrants entered the United States after the 1860s, religious groups struggled to obtain higher learning. Catholics founded more of their own colleges and universities to accommodate their expanding populations, such as Christian Brothers University in Memphis in 1871, Gonzaga University in Spokane in 1887, DePaul University in Chicago in 1898, and Loyola University in New Orleans in 1912. In 1900, almost one hundred colleges and universities—many of them women's colleges (e.g., the College of St. Catherine in St. Paul, founded in 1905) or men's colleges (e.g., Belmont Abbey College in North Carolina, founded in 1876)—with their sixteen thousand students, had been established to educate Catholics for the priesthood, religious life, and secular careers through the efforts of French and German orders and societies (such as the Jesuits, Marianists, Vincentians, Benedictines, and Christian Brothers) or local Catholic dioceses. As Philip Gleason showed in his comprehensive *Contending with Modernity: Catholic Higher Education in the Twentieth Century* (1995), undergraduate and graduate expansion continued, reaching almost two hundred institutions, with some 160,000 students, in 1940. As the Jewish community grew, it too sought to establish rabbinical seminaries to provide rabbis for their major traditions, such as Hebrew Union College in New York City in 1875. Some of the seminaries later became colleges and then universities, such as Yeshiva University in New York City in 1886, and some Hebrew-language postsecondary schools were founded, such as Gratz College in Philadelphia in 1887, Dropsie College of Hebrew and Cognate Learning in Philadelphia in 1906, and the Spertus College of Judaica in Chicago in 1924. Most attention, however, as Paul Ritterband and Harold Weschsler pointed out in their groundbreaking *Jewish Learning in American Universities* (1994), went to establishing advanced studies in Judaic Semitics, Jewish history, and medieval Jewish philosophy, as it turned out, at six research universities: Brandeis, Columbia, University of Chicago, Harvard, Johns Hopkins, and University of Pennsylvania.

Finally, as first-generation college students found it too expensive to enter four-year colleges at the turn of the century, they learned that Joliet Junior College in 1901 was open to them. President William Rainey Harper had worked with the public schools in Joliet, a city just south of Chicago, to expand one of their high schools to offer the first two years of college. As Steven Brint and Jerome Karabel explored in their valuable *The Diverted Dream: Community Colleges and the Promise of Educational Opportunity in America, 1900–1985* (1989), the movement to establish public junior colleges reached some eighty-five institutions by 1918, and they enrolled some 4,500 students by 1925.

For example, Sacramento Junior College in 1916, North Iowa Area Community College in 1917, Trinidad State Junior College in Colorado in 1925, and Temple Junior College in Texas in 1926 offered lower-middle-class students opportunities to live at home for the first two years of college, while saving their money before transferring to a four-year college to finish their degree. The rise of junior colleges and the need for administrators to operate them created considerable growth in the new higher education administration programs that were developing in the 1920s at Ohio State University, the University of Chicago, Teachers College at Columbia, the University of California, Berkeley, and the University of Michigan. These democratic colleges responded to the higher educational needs of these various groups and thus moved higher education beyond its earlier elite student social and economic patterns. Yet now this educational array of high schools, academies, normal schools, junior colleges, colleges, professional schools, land-grant colleges, and research universities proved bewilderingly overlapping and complex.

The Progressive Era of Standardization, 1885–1948

As U.S. higher education approached the three hundredth anniversary of its beginning in 1936, the more democratized institutional system had been determined in these overlapping movements. However, order, funding, and greater student responsiveness among these schools, colleges, and universities were still needed in the twentieth century. The growth of the U.S. population and its needs required greater order in all of its economic, social, and governmental institutions. Educational leaders for their part pointed to progressive reform of schooling and higher education as a way to meet the nation's challenges. Gradually, standardization through accreditation of colleges and universities became the means to bring order to the evolving system. Private regional associations organized to standardize college admissions, to differentiate secondary schools from colleges, to certify whether colleges' course work was of sufficiently high quality to be transferred to different institutions, and to certify that institutions had programs sufficient to offer bachelor's and master's degrees. The New England Association of Colleges and Preparatory Schools, founded in 1885; the North Central Association of Colleges and Secondary Schools, founded in 1895; and eventually four other associations representing the southern, middle Atlantic, western, and northwestern regions brought order to the system through site visitations by a group of inspectors who were either school and district administrators, for high schools, or college officers and professors, for postsecondary institutions. The North Central Association published the first list of accredited colleges in 1913, certifying that these institutions had met the standards of adequacy in their curricula for degrees, numbers of degreed faculty and departments, library holdings, endowment sufficiency, and suitable buildings. Other regional associations followed suit. In 1938, the American Association of Universities also turned over accreditation of specific Ph.D. programs to the regional associations, finding it too difficult to ensure that standards for quality were in place for the forty universities offering the highest degree. During this time, specialized accreditation also began. The American Medical Association, the American Bar Association, and others developed affiliated bodies for assessing and accrediting their own professional schools. For example, the Association of American Law Schools (AALS), founded in 1900, gradually established norms for its schools. After the release of the Carnegie report by Alfred Reed on law schools in 1921, which was similar to the Flexner Report of 1910 on medical schools, the fifty AALS-accredited schools forced the other hundred nonmember schools to join or lose their accreditation. By 1940, only ninety-one schools retained AALS accreditation. Both regional and specialized accreditation thus transformed U.S. higher education—and would continue to do so—for the betterment of society. The system was now ready for national service.

The Public Policy Era of Federalism, 1935–1980

Although the federal involvement in higher education had resulted in the funding of military academies as well as land-grant colleges and universities during the nation's first two centuries, public support for higher education remained primarily the responsibility of the states. However, national crises of the twentieth century required significant federal action in all aspects of society. To blunt the continuing Depression, Congress passed the National Youth Administration fund, which enabled 620,000 students to attend colleges and universities, at the cost of almost $100 million between 1935 and 1945. Federalism, in the form of major public policies, had begun. A grateful federal government further sought to reward U.S. soldiers for their military service in winning World War II. In 1944, Congress passed the Servicemen's Readjustment Act, popularly known as the GI Bill. It provided funding for a college education, unemployment benefits, and medical care for 2 million veterans during the next six years. In 1947, 2.3 million students were thus enrolled in some 1,800 colleges and universities. These developments led President Harry Truman to authorize the American Council on Education, under the leadership of George Zook, to report on the future role of higher education. The 1947 six-volume Truman Commission Report (formally, *The Report of the President's Commission on Higher Education for American Democracy*) transformed the mission of public higher education in U.S. society. It called for increased federal funding in the sciences, doubling of student enrollments to 4.6 million, and the expansion of junior colleges to become community colleges. The new era of public policy had begun in earnest.

This development also came at a price. As Ellen Schrecker described so well in her *No Ivory Tower: McCarthyism and the Universities* (1986), the House of Representatives' Un-American Activities Committee sought to identify and jail communist sympathizers and suspected agents in all walks of life. College and university professors came under considerable fire, as hundreds were hauled before the committee. Some were jailed for refusing to testify. Many lost their positions or were blacklisted from promotion. States joined in the fray by creating loyalty oaths for state employees. Such campus and faculty scrutiny caused a chilling effect on the exchange of ideas everywhere. Academic freedom came under extraordinary attack. The American Association of University Professors failed to blunt this extensive intrusion into academe or defend its suspected faculty, as many academics initially acquiesced to these government actions. The years of investigation, however, yielded no subversives. Public criticism finally put an end to these federal witchhunts. Perhaps in response to this legislative zealousness, the U.S. Supreme Court's 1957 *Sweezy v. New Hampshire* decision finally upheld the university as a marketplace of all ideas, especially in faculty lectures and classroom activities. Justice Felix Frankfurter's concurring opinion in the case established the faculty's "four essential freedoms": Faculty had the right "to determine for itself on academic grounds who may teach, what may be taught, how it shall be taught, and who may be admitted to study" (*Sweezy v. New Hampshire*, 354 U.S. 234; 77 S. Ct. 1203; 1L. Ed. 2d 1311). This precedent-setting case and its citation in later court rulings provided the legal foundation for an academic culture of faculty professionalism. Rightly so, Christopher Jencks and David Riesman declared in their book, *The Academic Revolution* (1968). The faculty had succeeded in becoming central to the mission of the U.S. university and college.

Indeed, faculty research became the key to advancing university development and responding to national imperatives. Governmental funding of research in the sciences that had been necessary during World War II expanded, reaching some $150 million for universities in 1950. The same year, Congress established the National Science Foundation to coordinate much of this activity. Eight years later, Congress's passage of the National Defense Education Act to counter the Soviet space and intercontinental missile threat gave $1 billion to colleges and universities to improve math and science education and to expand their facilities. By 1960, the federal government wished to advance higher education not only to serve its national defense needs in the Cold War but also to accommodate a huge increase in college-bound students resulting from the postwar baby boom. The Kennedy and Johnson administrations funneled billions of dollars into higher education through the Higher Education Facilities Act of 1963 and the Higher Education Act of 1965 to accommodate the ballooning postsecondary enrollments, which rose from 3.7 million in 1960 to 8.5 million in 1970 to 12 million in 1980, and to hire faculty to teach them. Fueled by these larger undergraduate populations, institutions enhanced their research capacities and graduate programs, thereby becoming research universities. In his significant 1963 book, *The Uses of the University*, Clark Kerr, the president of the University of California, best characterized what was happening nationally to U.S. higher education by describing the expansions of state, land-grant, and research universities during this time as the creation of multiversities. Ohio State University and the University of Minnesota epitomized this development as they reached some 50,000 students on their campuses; huge academic divisions and large professional schools became their own minicampuses with thousands of faculty. Finally, the 1972 Amendments to the Higher Education Act required states to establish governing, coordinating, or planning boards for expanding public higher education to facilitate the increasingly complex institutional relations with state governments. Decreases in federal funding of higher education began in 1981 with the Reagan administration, as military spending gained exponentially in order to overcome the Soviet Union. The era of massive federal support for higher education thus had ended, as Roger Geiger noted in his valuable *Research and Relevant Knowledge: American Research Universities since World War II* (1993). Yet its legacy continued.

The Consumerist Student Era of Mass Higher Education, 1965–2000

The Higher Education Act of 1965 brought about a significant relational change between campuses and the U.S. government. Previously, funding had gone directly to institutions for research, graduate programs, and facilities. Federal research funding continued in this way after the passage of the Higher Education Act, with approximately one hundred universities receiving 80 percent of these dollars, some $9 billion by 1996. However, after the act most federal moneys given to institutions came from student financial aid through grants and loans. Millions of students now determined which colleges and universities gained these dollars. Although universal higher education had not become a federal policy, a new era of mass higher education had begun, as, after 1965, 50 percent of the high school graduating cohort attended college annually. In 1964, all financial aid had come to only $550 million; however, by 1990, federal student financial aid alone brought $34.6 billion to campuses, as Arthur Cohen noted in his helpful commentary on higher education, *The Shaping of American Higher Education* (1998). The consumerist student era had commenced; student choice played a key role in institutional development. Campuses swiftly changed their residential rules, faculty accommodated to student curricular interests, and administrations sought to satisfy student demands in order to attract and retain students.

The quintuple expansion of student populations by 1980 to 12 million students forced huge growth spurts on public college campuses, which now educated 80 percent of the student population. Traditional, adult, women, and minority students all found higher education accessible. The U.S. Supreme Court's desegregation of education through the 1954 *Brown v. Board of Education of Topeka, Kansas*, decision and the use of affirmative action in postsecondary admissions after the 1978 *Regents of the University of California v. Bakke* case opened campuses to new student populations. Title IX of the 1972 Educational Amendments to the Higher Education Act further demanded sex equity in college admission and sports. By 1979, women permanently made up more than 50 percent of the student body. Demands for student power and black power arose on campuses during the 1960s, as they became battlegrounds in protest against the Vietnam War and racial discrimination. Student activism, as described by Philip Altbach's comprehensive treatment in *Student Politics in America* (1974), started with Berkeley's free speech movement in 1964, shifted to campus takeovers and building burnings at Columbia and Cornell with protests against the war, and resulted in the killing of four students by the National Guard at Kent State University in 1970. With the end of the war, student radicalism declined and refocused on environmental issues, such as Earth Day. Traditional campus social activities had generally continued during this difficult decade. In fact, the expansion of collegiate football, basketball, and other sports made campuses lively, as John Thelin pointed out in his *Games Colleges play* (1994). Later student generations turned more to academic and career preoccupations, making campuses much quieter places.

Higher education had secured its place in U.S. life as an essential passport to the intellectual and academic life, professional careers, and most specialized business opportunities. Growing demand for these studies advanced institutional expansion. Defined by the newly developed 1970 Carnegie Classification of Institutions of Higher Education, the universe of institutions consisted of research and doctorate-granting universities, comprehensive universities, liberal arts colleges, community colleges, and advanced professional schools. Seven hundred and sixty-two institutions together made up the first three groups. There had been many more liberal arts colleges in the past. They had declined in number to 719 by 1970, but they had not declined in spirit; despite regular accusations that they were irrelevant to a system dominated by universities, they continued as a vital component of the array of U.S. institutions. Conversely, the number of junior and community colleges soared to 1,091 in 1970, later rising to 1,236 with the inclusion of 29 Native American tribal colleges that became land-grant community colleges in 1994. By the end of the twentieth century, 15 million students attended some 4,000 institutions of higher learning that required some $200 billion annually to operate. Students earned annually more than 1 million baccalaureate degrees, 500,000 master's and professional degrees, and 50,000 doctorates. Colleges and universities were remade not only by these student expansions but also by growing numbers of different faculty and staff. The 1964 Civil Rights Act and President Lyndon Johnson's 1965 executive order on affirmative action had made legal inroads on campuses to promote equal opportunity in higher education employment. Soon diversity became paramount for students, faculty, and administrators, as the nation sought to prepare the new leadership through its colleges and universities for the future multicultural society. U.S. colleges and universities had thus been transformed through these three eras by the turn of the millennium. This massive social institution of higher learning still advanced and transmitted knowledge; furthered the academic, professional, and career goals of its students; and enabled the next generations to develop socially. Furthermore, it assisted federal and state governments in achieving their educational and research goals for the betterment of the nation. The growing influx of international students during this time finally pointed to the increasing global attraction of and praise for the U.S. higher education system, which had become the envy of the world.

—Lester F. Goodchild

Sources and further reading:

Altbach, Philip. 1974. *Student Politics in American: A Historical Analysis.* New York: McGraw-Hill.

Anderson, James D. 1988. *The Education of Blacks in the South, 1860–1935.* Chapel Hill: University of North Carolina Press.

Bok, Derek, 1986. *Higher Learning.* Cambridge, MA: Harvard University Press.

Boyer, Paul. 1997. *Native American Colleges: Progress and Prospects.* Princeton: Carnegie Foundation for the Advancement of Teaching.

Brint, Steven G., and Jerome B. Karabel. 1989. *The Diverted Dream: Community Colleges and the Promise of Educational Opportunity in America, 1900–1985.* New York: Oxford University Press.

Brubacher, John S., and Willis Rudy. 1997. *Higher Education in Transition: A History of American Colleges and Universities.* 4th ed. New Brunswick, NJ: Transaction Publishers.

Burke, Colin. 1982. *American Collegiate Populations.* New York: New York University Press.

Christy, Ralph D., and Lionel Williamson, eds. 1992. *A Century of Service: Land-Grant Colleges and Universities, 1890–1990.* New Brunswick, NJ: Transaction Publishers.

Cohen, Arthur M. 1998. *The Shaping of American Higher Education: Emergence and Growth of the Contemporary System.* San Francisco: Jossey-Bass.

Geiger, Roger L. 1986. *To Advance Knowledge: The Growth of American Research Universities, 1900–1940.* New York: Oxford University Press.

_____. 1993. *Research and Relevant Knowledge: American Research Universities since World War II.* New York: Oxford University Press.

_____, ed. 2000. *The American College in the Nineteenth Century.* Nashville, TN: Vanderbilt University Press.

Gleason, Philip. 1995. *Contending with Modernity: Catholic Higher Education in the Twentieth Century.* New York: Oxford University Press.

Goodchild, Lester F., and Harold S. Wechsler, eds. 1997. *ASHE Reader: The History of Higher Education.* 2nd ed. Needham Heights, MA: Simon and Schuster Custom Publishing.

Gordon, Lynn. 1990. *Gender and Higher Education in the Progressive Era.* New Haven: Yale University Press.

Hawkins, Hugh. 1992. *Banding Together: The Rise of National Associations in American Higher Education, 1887–1950.* Baltimore: Johns Hopkins University Press.

Herbst, Jurgen. 1982. *From Crisis to Crisis: American College Government, 1636–1819.* Cambridge, MA: Harvard University Press.

Hofstadter, Richard, and Walter P. Metzger. 1955. *The Development of Academic Freedom in the United States.* New York: Columbia University Press.

_____. 1961. *American Higher Education: A Documentary History.* 2 vols. Chicago: University of Chicago Press.

Jencks, Christopher, and David Riesman. 1968. *The Academic Revolution.* New York: Doubleday.

Kerr, Clark. [1963] 2001. *The Uses of the University,* 5th ed. Cambridge, MA: Harvard University Press.

Levine, David O. 1986. *The American College and the Culture of Aspiration, 1915–1940.* Ithaca, NY: Cornell University Press.

Lucas, Christopher J. 1994. *American Higher Education: A History.* New York: St. Martin's Griffin.

President's Commission on Higher Education. 1947. *Higher Education for American Democracy: A Report of the President's Commission on Higher Education.* New York: Harper and Brothers.

Ritterband, Paul, and Harold Weschsler. 1994. *Jewish Learning in American Universities: The First Century.* Bloomington: Indiana University Press.

Rudolph, Frederick. 1981. *Curriculum: A History of the American Undergraduate Course of Study since 1636.* Carnegie Council Series. San Francisco: Jossey-Bass.

_____. [1962] 1990. *The American College and University: A History.* 2nd ed. Athens, GA: University of Georgia Press.

Schrecker, Ellen W. 1986. *No Ivry Tower: McCarthyism and the Universities.* New York: Oxford University Press.

Solomon, Barbara M. 1985. *In the Company of Educated Women: A History of Women and Higher Education in America.* New Haven: Yale University Press.

Sweezy v. New Hampshire, 354 U.S. 234; 77 S. Ct. 1203; 1L. Ed. 2d 1311.

Thelin, John R. 1994. *Games Colleges Play: Scandal and Reform in Intercollegiate Athletics.* Baltimore: Johns Hopkins University Press.

Veysey, Laurence R. 1965. *The Emergence of the American University.* Chicago: University of Chicago Press.

Wechsler, Harold S. 1977. *The Qualified Student: A History of Selective College Admission in America, 1870–1970.* New York: John Wiley and Sons.

Yale University. 1828. *Reports on the Courses of Instruction in Yale College by a Committee of the Corporation and the Academical Faculty.* New Haven: Yale University.

PART II

COLONIAL HIGHER EDUCATION IN THE AMERICAS, 1538–1789

Part II. Colonial Higher Education in the Americas, 1538–1789

After the discovery of the New World in the 15th century, European settlers soon established institutions of higher learning. Colonial higher education in the Americas began with the papal chartering of Santo Domingo's University of St. Thomas Aquinas in 1538, following the Spanish Catholic pattern described by Perkin (in Part I of this Reader). Almost one hundred years later, English colonists founded Harvard College to advance Puritan Christianity. Harvard followed European university patterns, especially Cambridge University in England and Scottish governance and curricular ideas. John R. Thelin's chapter from his *The History of American Higher Education*[1] gives us a complete picture of the first colonial colleges, their faculty, students, curricula, and finances, reflecting the basic structure of the Reader's organization. The first colonial college soon was followed by the founding and chartering of eight other colleges before the American Revolution: the College of William and Mary, 1693; the Collegiate School at New Haven, 1701 (renamed Yale College); the College of Philadelphia, 1740 (renamed the University of Pennsylvania), the College of New Jersey, 1746 (renamed Princeton College), King's College, 1754 (renamed Columbia College); the College of Rhode Island, 1764 (renamed Brown University); Queen's College, 1766 (renamed Rutgers College); and Dartmouth College, 1769. Meanwhile to the north of these colonies, New France established a theological seminary in Quebec in the 1660s that later became Laval University. Colonial higher education, which embodied characteristics of both secondary and higher learning (as also may be seen at the Jesuit school established in Newton, Maryland in 1677), brought European liberal and professional knowledge to this hemisphere.

The English colonists established their nine colleges to satisfy local educational needs that arose from pastoral and missionary demands within various Christian denominations. Unlike the state church of European countries, several religious communities lived within the same province. As their numbers grew, pleas for tolerance became more pressing. Yale President Clap was forced to accept student requests for freedom of worship. When Queen's College was founded as the second collegiate institution in New Jersey, its Anglican president admitted men of all religious persuasions.

Such changes in policy and governance began the process of Americanization, as old world structures were tailored to meet new demands within the colonies. Jurgen Herbst's article, "From Religion to Politics," chronicles and comments on these changes as the colleges slipped from their religious moorings to be left tied mainly to colonial governments. In this shift, the original mission of these institutions waned. Bobby Wright in "For the Children of the Infidels," scrutinizes how these transformations in the first colonial colleges eclipsed the then Indian missionary purposes to Christianize these indigenous peoples. Wright contends that the proselytizing and educating of these populations was used mainly to gain financial support from English churches and benefactors rather than being truly apostolic.[2]

The rise of colonial collegiate faculty and their varied duties may be understood in the development of Harvard tutors and professors in the 17th and 18th centuries. John Burton offers us an in-depth look at the early professional development of these groups and their implications for other colonial institutions. This focused article may be placed within a larger national picture by reviewing Martin Finkelstein's *The American Academic Profession*,[3] which distinguishes the colonial and antebellum faculty transformation from the models of English tutor to the teaching scholar. Generally unacknowledged, Scottish ideas and curricular patterns played a significant role in developing eighteenth and early nineteenth century colleges, especially in the sciences. Douglas Sloan is one of the few scholars who have described this important contribution. The chapter from his book, *The Scottish Enlightenment and the American College Ideal*,[4] offers a glimpse of an intellectual and institutional bridge that would link the colonial colleges to the inchoate departmental structure created at the University of Virginia by Thomas Jefferson. During this early period, students not only studied but also interacted with the town where some even resided. Nevertheless, overseers and presidents maintained collegiate legal autonomy in most disciplinary matters. Burton's article provides an interesting study of these "town-gown" relationships, which became more strained at commencement times when drinking and dancing caused considerable friction, requiring assistance from local constables. As the social function of these colleges grew, they provided the means to acquire stature within the colonies. Phyllis Vine thus shows how these institutions enabled students to assume leadership roles, marry into the best families, and make social contacts that assisted their future career success. This social function became even more important during the nineteenth century. The primary readings for this section, for example, explore Harvard's early student rules and charter. Such mandates established the mission of these colonial institutions and the means to control their "inmates," as students were called in the eighteenth century.

These colleges embraced a different *raison d'etre* after the American Revolution. Now their mandate centered on creating religious and lay leadership for a new nation. The effects of this profound transition may be learned from David Robson's *Educating Republicans: The College in the Era of the American Revolution, 1750–1800,* and John Roche's *Colonial Colleges in the War for American Independence.*[v] This epic event resulted in a new westward focus for American higher education, as the next 70 years saw a tremendous growth in collegiate institutions on the frontier.

ENDNOTES

[1] John R. Thelin, *A History of American Higher Education* (Bultimore, MD), Johns Hopkins University, Press, 2004. See also

[2] As the first of our revisionist articlers, Wright's article follows the lead of James Axtell in his *The European and the Indian* (New York: Oxford University Press, 1981) and the *Invasion Within* (New York: Oxford University Press, 1985).

[3] Martin Finklestein, *The American Academic Profession* (Columbus, OH: Ohio State University Press, 1984).

[4] Douglas Sloan, *The Scottish Enlightenment and the American College Ideal* (New York: Teachers College Press, 1971).

[5] David Robson, *Educating Republicans: The College in the Era of the American Revolution, 1750–1800* (Westport, Conn.: Greewood Press, 1985) and John Roche, *Colonial Colleges in the War for American Independence* (Millwood, NY: Association Faculty Press, 1985).

CHAPTER 2
ESTABLISHING COLONIAL COLLEGES

COLLEGES IN THE COLONIAL ERA

JOHN R. THELIN

Colleges and the Colonial Revival

The historic colleges founded in the colonial era enjoy a special place in our national memory. Our oldest corporation, for example, is Harvard College, not a commercial business. Not only are these colleges old, they also are influential and vivid in the American imagination. When President Dwight D. Eisenhower visited the Dartmouth campus in 1953 he exclaimed, "Why, this is how I always thought a college should look!" Most Americans understood his response and shared his sentiment. Red brick Georgian buildings with slate roofs, white trim, and mullioned windows, clustered around a green, provided an academic archetype indelibly linked with a real and imagined colonial past.

This presence meant that the surviving colleges founded before 1781—familiar today as Harvard, William and Mary, Yale, Princeton, Columbia, Brown, Dartmouth, Rutgers, and Pennsylvania—stand out as institutions that have acquired prestige along with longevity. Their oldest buildings, including Princeton's Nassau Hall, Brown's University Hall, Harvard's Massachusetts Hall, Yale's Connecticut Hall, and the Wren Building at William and Mary, have become monuments that convey dignity and command respect. These buildings ascend to the status of national shrines because early on, their academic operations were heroically fused with the larger events of social and political history. Their space was transformed dramatically to play a central role in the American campaign for independence. Classrooms became sites of legendary patriotic oratory, and dormitories were pressed into service as hospitals and barracks for troops during the Revolutionary War. As one alumni society's bumper sticker proclaimed in 1981, they were the "Alma Mater of a nation."

The obvious prestige that the colonial heritage gives to these colleges today, however, has been neither inevitable nor unbroken. The historic colleges themselves had from time to time been indifferent to connections between their past and present. In other words, it has only been since around 1890 or 1900 that the colleges founded in the colonial era rediscovered and then asserted this legacy as part of their contemporary educational mission and appeal. Once again, the architectural record provides a good clue to this change. Most of their original buildings from the seventeenth and eighteenth centuries had been either torn down or destroyed by fire. Those that survived into the nineteenth century were in disrepair. Many of their original design elements became hidden over the years as college officials, for example, added a porch in the 1850s or plastered over windows in the 1870s. Photographs of the academic building at the College of William and Mary from as late as 1925 show the original college edifice, constructed in 1695, with plaster crumbling, electrical cords dangling from the ceiling, and window frames rudely covered by either brick or plywood.

The important element of the colonial success story is that between 1890 and 1960, Americans, including officials at the old colleges, rediscovered and then revitalized their colonial heritage. The momentum was provided in part by the centennial celebration of 1876, and by 1890 it had gained formal status with the creation of such organizations as the Daughters of the American Revolution. In numerous cities and states along the Atlantic coast, voluntary associations formed groups dedicated to "preserving antiquities," and the old colleges benefited from this movement, which energetically combined historical preservation, ancestor worship, and patriotism. Renovating the handful of surviving seventeenth- and eighteenth-century college structures was the first step, with attention to sprucing up the neglected sites, and the preservation ethos dictated that this was to be done so as to convey some approximation of allegedly *authentic* historic forms and colors. The growing fascination with and respect for the colonial connection surfaced in other visual forms, too. When Brown University, for example, celebrated its sesquicentennial in 1914, its official poster depicted a thoughtful colonial gentleman in a tricorn hat kneeling next to a modern scholar wearing a mortarboard and academic gown.

Resurrection of colonial motifs as part of academic strategy gained appeal elsewhere. In Williamsburg, Virginia, the college campus benefited from the colonial restoration sponsored by the Rockefeller family starting in the late 1920s. Not only was the academic building restored; there was also a commensurate restoration of ceremonies and rituals as students and administrators increasingly emphasized colonial roots in college publications and public events. Festive colonial costume balls were initiated, as well as such solemn events as "Charter Day," with readings from original college documents. Before the 1930s, catalogues, diplomas, and library stamps had shown little connection with historic names and often referred to the institution as William and Mary College. But now names and titles were codified and standardized to reflect a distinguished past. Henceforth the institution would be known as the College of William and Mary in Virginia. The official language on diplomas took the historicism an additional step: deference to the real and imagined classical curriculum of the eighteenth century meant that the twentieth-century parchment would carry the name Collegium Guillamus et Marius, even though the study of Latin had long ceased to be a requirement for the bachelor's degree.

At the College of William and Mary, revitalized historic pride also displayed itself in the name and tone of the student yearbook, *The Colonial Echo*. Editors of the 1936 edition showed their admiration for the founding fathers by using seventeenth-century typefaces and spelling in a volume "in which Ye editors attempt to intensify the reverberations of the Glorious Past of the College." The college president reinforced the spirit of the student project as he noted in his preface to the yearbook, "Like a great Artery throbbing and pulsing from the Heart of Life, the Aims, the Obligations, the Courage and the Will of 1693 animate the William and Mary of 1936."

Indeed, 1936 was a very good year for colonial celebration. At the same time that William and Mary was echoing its seventeenth-century heritage, to the north in Massachusetts, Harvard was celebrating its three hundredth anniversary with a yearlong slate of academic ceremonies, special events, and guest speakers. At all the historic colleges, officials began to update their admissions brochures and "view books" so as to draw increasing attention to an account of founding, of struggle and perseverance, a mix of heroic events and legendary figures.

Why is it important to delineate this colonial revivalism as part of the colleges' self-characterization in the twentieth century? First, one must bear in mind that invoking an inspired colonial heritage had become potent but had not always been so. For example, in 1888, representatives of William and Mary urged Virginia's legislators to fund this historic institution that had fallen on hard times. Surely the legislature would recognize its duty to help the college reclaim its original colonial commitment to the liberal education of future leaders. This historical imperative might have been self-evident to the college representatives, but they were surprised to find that their campaign held little appeal to the Virginia General Assembly. Legislators ignored the case for colonial resurrection and instead opted to provide annual subsidies so that the historic college could tend to the immediate and modern problem of educating a cohort of white male schoolteachers to staff the state's emerging public school system. Fifty years later, though, invoking a colonial legacy would become effective in both academic fund-raising and admissions.

A second reason to consider closely the historic colleges as part of a larger movement of colonial revivalism is that the movement fostered standards of academic honor and imitation. Brown University reminded prospective students of its heritage with the following reminder in its 1956 admissions brochure: "Brown is an old institution—older, actually, than the nation itself—and it derives great strength from its rich tradition and heritage. There is a distinctive flavor about very old colleges, something that comes from vast experience, from the durability of ancient ideas and ideals, from a spirit that has persisted long before the memory of living man and even from the ivy which climbs the walls." Colleges and universities of all ages and types across the United States acknowledged this heritage and often attempted to incorporate it into their own ethos.

The American public, as well as academics, has subscribed to this characterization of colonial tradition as a source of educational excellence. When the historic colleges banded together to form an "Ivy League" athletics conference in 1956, the group was nicknamed the "Ancient Eight" by sportswriters. Jumping from the popular activities of spectator sports to movies, one finds a comparable awareness of collegiate heritage among Hollywood studio executives. In 1934 a movie director insisted on sending an entire film crew from Los Angeles to New England to shoot scenes of "college life." When asked to justify the inordinate time and expense involved, he said bluntly, "I want the richness, the fine old atmosphere of the Ivy League."

A good example of this revivalism and emulation took place at Miami University of Ohio. The university's splendid Marcum Conference Center combines a twentieth-century interior and amenities with an exterior that reproduces the Wren Building of the College of William and Mary. Even the historic colleges themselves followed the formula of colonial revivalism. For example, Thomas Mott Shaw, one of the primary architects of the colonial Williamsburg town restoration, also designed new residential quadrangles at Brown University. In 1934, William and Mary replaced a non-descript field with a colonial-style "sunken garden" to complement its newly renovated Wren Building. By the time Harvard was ready to celebrate its tercentennial in 1936, it had completed an extensive neo-Georgian environment, relying on the architectural firm of Coolidge, Shepley, Bulfinch, and Abbott to create its new residential "house" system, which would accommodate over thirty-five hundred undergraduates. Here, as at other historic colleges, it was not sufficient merely to renovate existing buildings. When new construction was required, even it had to look old.

Exhuming and Examining the Glorious Past

Although campus visitors and yearbook editors may have been satisfied with the atmosphere and imagery of the glorious past projected by the colonial colleges, the revivalism movement merely starts our historical inquiry. Monuments and motifs are important, but they are only one layer of historical analysis. The challenge here is to use the colonial celebration as the lens through which to look critically and closely at the substance of these institutions founded prior to the Revolutionary War.

The first research question the colonial-revival colleges raise is: What were the distinctive features and contributions of these colleges that make them central to the *American* heritage? Reconstructing the collegiate past gets increasingly complicated when this question coincides with another finding: the attraction of the early American colleges is in part due to their historic association with England. For example, a recent guide to Harvard's architecture described Holden Chapel (built in 1744) as a "Georgian Gem" that stands out as a "solitary English daisy in a field of Yankee dandelions." When academic leaders at William and Mary completed their historic college building, they called it the Sir Christopher Wren Building, even though there was no record that the great English architect had anything to do with its construction or that his name was ever used to describe it in the seventeenth and eighteenth centuries. So we are left with the reminder that American heritage included a formidable strand of Anglophilia. It was, after all, a colonial region that included a self-proclaimed "New England."

Anglophilia is a recurring theme in the history of American higher education. One important interpretation is that the distinction and success of the colonial colleges was associated with their having transplanted the Oxford-Cambridge ideal to America. This was the intriguing argument made by historian Frederick Rudolph in his classic account of the "collegiate way." It is also a theme often presented by the colleges themselves today. In 1963, Harvard College described the legacy as follows: "Students lived together in the college building in constant contact with their teachers. They worked and played together, creating the very special kind of community which has been characteristic of the American residential college ever since. American colleges, following Harvard's early example, have adopted the Cambridge-Oxford pattern rather than that of the continental universities." The late George W. Pierson, long-time historian of Yale, summed up the legacy with this account of the "college system":

> Another essential in Yale's code from the start was the collegiate ideal. That is, young men should eat, sleep, study, play, and worship together, make friends, compete against each other and learn to stand on their own two feet, in loyalty always to the larger community. As at Oxford and Cambridge, books were to be but a part of the education. Or, as Yale's younger Timothy Dwight (1886–99) would insist, the truth can be "but dimly seen by the intellect alone."
>
> Whatever the present differences of opinion on this matter, the historic fact is that from the earliest times the College had tried to keep all of its students together—and the youthful society thus formed had promptly and enthusiastically set to work to create its own system of self-improvement, a second or social curriculum.

This intriguing interpretation, persistently presented by a formidable group of college historians, however, is not the whole story. In order to understand precisely what was being praised and invoked as the model for the American colonial colleges, it is useful to reconstruct the character and condition of Oxford and Cambridge in the seventeenth and eighteenth centuries.

Oxford and Cambridge in Perspective

It is true that the "collegiate system" of mixing living and learning was at the heart of the Oxford and Cambridge pedagogy, and this vision was seminal in the plan for higher education that college founders pursued in the American colonies. Equally true, however, was that Oxford and Cambridge were distinctive in their governance and formal legal structures. This unique arrangement was that the "colleges" were privately endowed, relatively autonomous units that were linked in a federation. In short, the twelve or so residential "colleges" of eighteenth-century Oxford and Cambridge were the famous sites of student learning and living. College names, including Balliol, Trinity, Clare, Caius, Pembroke, Emanuel, Magdalene, Oriel, and Christchurch, were the primary sources of affiliation for students and faculty alike. The overarching structure—the "university"— was the degree-granting entity, defined and protected by a royal charter. At Oxford and Cambridge, students may have had their academic instruction and extracurricular activities centered in their respective "colleges," but it was the "university" that conducted examinations and awarded degrees.

Why is this important? First, the American colonial colleges fused instruction with certification— a practice wholly alien to Oxford and Cambridge. Second, Oxford and Cambridge were remarkable in that within each university there was a honeycomb network of "colleges," each with its own heritage, tradition, funding, and emphases. According to Cambridge University's historical brochures, by 1596 it included sixteen endowed colleges, and "the founders of colleges were various—but all were extremely wealthy." In contrast, no American institution ever went beyond providing a single "college," and founding donations were modest when measured against the standards of benefactions for England's universities. America's colleges took a long time—more than two centuries—to match the appearance of Oxford and Cambridge. Construction of the Harvard "houses" and the Yale "colleges" in the 1930s was a belated architectural fulfillment of this collegiate ideal.

Architecture also is a useful approach to reconstructing the colonial colleges because the surviving buildings graphically display both the strengths and the limits of the Oxford-Cambridge model in America. The defining form for the Oxford and Cambridge educational and "collegiate" system was the quadrangle: an enclosed, total institution with a courtyard or grassy interior. The historic colonial academic buildings, for all their grandeur, also demonstrated the limits of transplanting England's academic architecture to the New World. Each building was at the time of construction probably the largest, most expensive structure in its host colony. At the same time, neither the architecture nor the pedagogy could completely replicate the Oxford-Cambridge ideal. In most cases, the colleges ran out of money before they could complete the construction of a planned quadrangle that would extend behind and around the main building to create the "total environment" for living and learning associated with the "collegiate way." King's College (now Columbia University) in New York City first used Trinity

Church Schoolhouse for its instruction. There is no compelling evidence of plans for elaborate construction of quadrangles. In Philadelphia, local fund-raising was intended to pay for what was called "New Building," a large preaching hall and charity school. Work on this monumental structure, hailed as the city's largest building, was suspended first for lack of money and later for hospital and military operations during the Revolutionary War. Even from its origin, it carried out the distinctive educational ideas and plans of Benjamin Franklin, who hardly sought to emulate the English residential college curricular scheme.

Reservations about the extent to which the colonial academics sought to create truly residential collegiate environments are found in Virginia. The early statutes for William and Mary explicitly stated that students who were paying their bills were *not* required to live at the college: "We leave their parents and guardians at liberty whether they shall lodge and eat within the college or elsewhere in the town, or any country village near the town. For it being our intention that the youth, with as little charge as they can, should learn the learned languages and the other liberal arts and sciences; If any have their houses so near the college, that from thence the college bells can be heard and the public hours of study be duly observed, we would not by these statutes hinder them from boarding their own children, or their friends, or from lodging them at their own houses."

Adaptation to scarcity was part of the story. Running out of money was a pervasive problem, but not the only factor. Even if the New World college founders had acquired additional resources, they would not necessarily have considered Oxford's architecture of the eighteenth century to be a very pleasing model. Accounts from England indicate a great deal of self-indulgent, ostentatious building at the universities. Magnificent stables for gentleman scholars who brought more horses than books to university was one Oxford contribution. Laboratories and provisions for scientific research were marginal at Oxford, if provided at all. Libraries were built more for the sake of monumental decor than utility. Diaries of university scholars indicate time and time again that for well over a half-century, commitment to serious scholarship had ceased to be "fashionable" among Oxford undergraduates and masters alike. In conclusion, although Oxford and Cambridge influenced and inspired the college founders in America, the British universities also provided some examples of educational practices that the colonists deliberately rejected. The colonial colleges were both more and less than "little Oxfords and Cambridges."

This general claim about the "collegiate way" must be tempered by a close look at varieties of historical evidence. First, institutional transplants seldom have been perfect, so for all the invocation of a "New England," well-intentioned college builders fell short in their efforts to recreate Cambridge or Oxford in America. Furthermore, the various colonial colleges also embodied indigenous efforts at innovation and reform. In fact, the American colleges of the colonial era were remarkable and complex, a hybrid of legacies, transplants, deliberate plans, and unintended adaptations. As historian James Axtell has argued, the New England colonists aspired to create a "school upon the hill" as part of their social ideal of a "city upon the hill." The preceding brief profile of seventeenth- and eighteenth-century Oxford and Cambridge has already hinted at some defining characteristics of the colonial colleges. It is a good preface to a detailed consideration of religion, philanthropy, governance, curriculum, and student life up to the Revolutionary War.

Governance and Structure

Understanding the philosophy and structure of the colonial colleges requires consideration of legacies beyond Oxford and Cambridge. For example, although the residential "collegiate way" appealed to the New World college founders, they detested the sloth and autonomy of the Oxford scholars. They therefore looked to the Scottish universities' reliance on an external board—rather than faculty control—to give legal definition to the college as an incorporated institution. In matters of charters and academic codes, the medieval universities of the Continent also had an influence that has often been underappreciated by historians. And given the range of Protestant denominations accommodated within the colonies, one would do well to look at the influence of England's "dissenting academies": institutions of advanced learning founded by Methodists and other groups that were ineligible for royal charters and hence excluded the power to confer degrees.

This provision for ultimate control by an external board built in a mechanism for continual accountability. Equally important was the board's vesting the office of the college president with administrative authority. This was a radical departure from academic governance at the historic British universities. In England the custom had been that the colleges were self-perpetuating associations of faculty, with perhaps some rotational authority given to a master who would be "first among equals." The English universities had no strong central administrative officer. Even to this day, it remains an Oxford pastime to try to decipher what precisely, if anything, the chancellor is expected to do. The American colleges could not have been more different.

Whereas Oxford and Cambridge masters had endured and ignored kings, queens, and bishops for centuries, the colonial college faculty faced daily scrutiny by, and little indulgence from, a stern governing board and its appointed administrators. A president reported to the board of trustees or the board of visitors, not to the faculty. Reading through the early college statutes and bylaws, one finds other evidence of a systematic effort to confine faculty authority. For example, at one institution there was official provision for a "College Senate," but the bylaws defined its membership as being drawn exclusively from the board of visitors and college governors, not the faculty. Little wonder, then, that academic freedom and instructors' rights in matters of hiring and firing received minimal consideration. This element in the structure and accountability of the colleges was an innovation that had enduring consequences. One could argue that the creation and refinement of this structure—the external board combined with a strong college president—is a legacy of the colonial colleges that has defined and shaped higher education in the United States to this day.

College Finances

During an extended period in which colonies were saturated with taxes from the British crown, it seems remarkable that colonial revenues were used to support the colleges at all. Relative to other civic or public services, each college tended to be blessed with government funding. The General Court of the Massachusetts Bay Colony dedicated one-fourth of the colony's annual tax levy—about £400—to help Harvard College get started. The College of William and Mary, which enjoyed the privilege of a royal charter, was the most abundantly assisted institution, King William having provided almost £2,000 and other subsidies for founding the college in 1693. Either crown or colony provided the colleges with land. In several cases, when founders of a new college grew unhappy with its original site, they considered moving elsewhere. Such cases gave rise to battles between towns, with the host town literally fighting to keep the college in its original place. If persuasion or incentives did not work, townspeople relied on other means. Citizens of Saybrook, Connecticut, "unhitched the Oxen, [and] broke down some bridges" in an effort to block that colony's college from carting its books to New Haven. Meanwhile, rival New Haven offered incentives of land and subsidies to persuade a college to relocate. In New Jersey, the town of New Brunswick lost out to Princeton in the competition to be the home of the Presbyterians' College of New Jersey. This did not deter the New Brunswick contingent, which eventually persuaded the Dutch Reform church leaders to build their new Queen's College (now Rutgers) in their town.

Bridge tolls, surcharges on licenses, tobacco poundage, lottery proceeds, and gifts of land were among the varied and sundry subsidies colonial governments relied upon for collegiate funding. But if the system and intentions were strong, the actual record of regular support was erratic and (at least from the colleges' perspective) marginal if not insufficient. From the start, then, American colleges perpetually depended on tuition payments and donations as well as subsidies to operate. The colleges also learned through experience the need for accountability and good record keeping, particularly as they came to acquire substantial resources. During the Revolutionary War, for example, Harvard's treasurer absconded with college funds, an action that one economic historian has described as "disturbing."

Religion and the College

Religion occupied a central but confined place in the colonial colleges. Although the New World provided some opportunities for religious freedom not found in England or Europe, it does not follow that the colonies were hospitable to religious tolerance. Rhode Island was an anomaly on two counts. First, its founding by a Baptist put it outside the orbit of not only the Church of England but even the "accepted" learned Protestant denominations. Second, its allowance for religious practice by a number of groups was exceptional. This tolerance worked its way into Rhode Island's collegiate charter, with the explicit provision that "there shall never be admitted any Religious Tests but on the Contrary all members hereof shall forever enjoy full free absolute and uninterrupted Liberty of Conscience," and that "the Sectarian differences of opinions shall not make any Part of the Public and Classical Instruction."

Even this accommodation had strict limits. The colonies were a Christian world, and more accurately a Protestant world. Well into the eighteenth century, few colonial governments accommodated Quakers. We find no establishment of a Roman Catholic–affiliated college in the colonies. Judaism did not enter into the discussions, even though college scholars sometimes studied Hebrew. Appointments to the governing board of the tolerant College of Rhode Island were set by statute to follow a strict formula that limited membership to Baptists, Presbyterians, Congregationalists, and Anglicans. New Jersey—along with Rhode Island, probably the most diverse and tolerant of the colonies—was home to two colleges: color the College of New Jersey, founded by and for Presbyterians, and Queen's College, tied closely to the Dutch Reform denomination. At the College of William and Mary, all masters and scholars were required to take an oath of allegiance to the crown and to the Church of England. What we find, then, especially in the seventeenth and early eighteenth centuries, is a precarious balance in which each colony and its college were staked out by followers of a particular Protestant denomination.

Was this a "theocracy?" Contrary to conventional wisdom, it was not. The Massachusetts Bay Colony had restrictions on clergy and government. Harvard College's statutes for appointments to the college's board made a clear distinction between "ministers" and "magistrates." Although divines were influential and powerful figures in the life of the colonies, including the colleges, ordained clergy could not hold government office. Hence, there were some structural checks and balances with respect to clerical power. This provision, however, did not prohibit one religious group from dominating institutions. The College in Connecticut, later renamed Yale, was founded by Congregationalists who had become displeased with what they thought was theological laxity of the Harvard divines. In their new venture as "wilderness prophets," they soon faced some bad news: college board members were surprised to discover that their newly selected rector and their one tutor, upon whom they had relied to uphold a strict Congregational orthodoxy, had publicly declared for Episcopacy. Anglicans were not welcome in Connecticut or at its college. Illustrating the power of the external board, both the rector and tutor were dismissed immediately, and henceforth all those who were appointed to the faculty were required to subscribe to a "confession of Congregational orthodoxy."

There was an important change in the politics of religion and colleges by the mid-eighteenth century. The aim at some of the newer colleges was to allow some diversity and balance of representation among sects in an effort to keep any single group from gaining hegemony. The original proposal for the creation of King's College in New York had called for it to be an Anglican institution, but by 1753 a group of Presbyterians, many from the nearby College of New Jersey, had effectively blocked this measure. The compromise was that the charter required the King's College president to be Anglican, but its board members were to be drawn from other Protestant denominations, and its admissions requirements showed no favoritism toward any one sect.

These episodes and resolutions indicate that within the ranks of the colonial colleges there was no love lost and little tolerance extended between competing denominations. According to historian Jurgen Herbst, the religious disputes in matters of college governance were a result of the proliferation of Protestant denominations, which led to increased diversity within the colonial population, especially in the Middle Atlantic region. Colonial governments tried to avoid social disruption by encouraging denominational tolerance, even in college admission policies. In the mid-eighteenth century, however, this practice broke down when the dominant denomination at a particular college clashed with the varied mix of Methodists, Baptists, and Quakers among students and their parents. Herbst claims that the breakdown of interdenominational tolerance in college governance laid the groundwork for the nineteenth-century trend in which each religious group would seek to found its own colleges.

Philanthropy

Philanthropy was closely tied to religion—a partnership of which colleges were major beneficiaries. This partnership worked in several interlocking ways. First, devout donors in England who may not have been specifically interested in endowing a college were nevertheless intrigued by the prospects for missionary work among the American Indians. Such donors were generous in their support of programs designed to provide a Christian education to those they considered to be savages. Colonial colleges were an available, appropriate vehicle to administer such funds and to carry out these charitable programs.

Resourceful college officials were adept at gaining permission to implement flexible interpretations of wills and bequests. Perhaps the best illustration of this sort of philanthropic windfall is the estate of the wealthy English chemist Sir Robert Boyle. Boyle's will designated that rents from his estate, the Brafferton, were to be used to support "pious and charitable works." The executor of the estate had license to define this directive as including scholarships for Indian students in the wilderness of America. And representatives of two colonial colleges—Harvard and the College of William and Mary—were eager to let the executor know that their colleges were available to help carry out Boyle's charitable wishes. In addition to the scholarship funds, each college also claimed a sum for operating expenses (probably a forerunner to "overhead" accounts). Later, ingenious college officials argued successfully that the scholarships could also be used to educate colonial students who aspired to become missionary teachers among the Indians.

Assessing the motives and measure of early donations is not easy. John Harvard and his fellow Cambridge University alumni, whose early gifts of books and money were crucial to the founding of the college in the Massachusetts Bay Colony, are depicted as devout and serious of purpose. The college's fund-raising prospectus indicated that good works—namely, support for a college—might help one to a place in heaven. This was not always the only incentive for generosity, as some donors sought and received their rewards immediately on earth. In London, for example, three convicted pirates agreed to give the College of William and Mary a gift worth £300, and in return they were spared the gallows.

At best a college donor could simultaneously gain both perpetual fame and eternal salvation. One fascinating glimpse at the biographical profile of a philanthropist who combined the two goals comes from the epitaph that Elihu Yale wrote to describe himself before his death in 1721:

Born in *America*,
in *Europe* bred,
In *Africa* Travell'd,
and in *Asia* wed,
Where long he liv'd,
and thriv'd;
at *London* dead.
Much good, some ill, he did;
so hope all's even,
and that his soul,
through mercy's gone to heaven.
You that survive,
and read, take care
For this most certain exit to prepare:
For only the actions of the just
Smell sweet
and blossom in the dust

Elihu Yale, described by George Pierson as a "London Yankee who had been a nabob in India," gave the financially struggling collegiate school in Connecticut a gift of "nine bales of goods" worth about £562, along with 417 books and a portrait and arms of King George I. Although this donation represented only a small part of his mercantile wealth, the college trustees changed the institution's name to Yale College as a sign of both gratitude and hope for additional gifts from this new namesake patron. But much to the college officials' disappointment, Yale's will did not mention the college. Unknown to college representatives at the time, Elihu Yale had never really considered the college to be a primary interest among his numerous projects and philanthropies. Religion also probably played a role. As an Anglican, he had reservations about being a benefactor for a college that represented a dissenting denomination.

Donations to support faculty were rare during the colonial period, but there were some landmark episodes. At Harvard in 1721, Thomas Hollis donated money to endow a chair of divinity. This was an important, controversial area of scholarship, and the gift ushered in a classic battle between college and donor over who had the right to define the curriculum and to pick the scholar to occupy the chair. The legacy of this episode of philanthropy was charges on both sides of abuse and self-dealing. The acrimony that the episode generated was fortunately dissipated when Harvard readily accepted, and adhered to the conditions of, Hollis's later gift to endow a faculty chair in the sciences and mathematics.

One can piece together from ledgers and journals the skeletons of college budgets. However, the records are incomplete and misleading. First, currencies varied greatly in their worth. Silver and gold coins from England were worth more than domestic currency of comparable face value. Second, economic historians rely on rough estimates based on "comparable worth" from one era to another. This strategy runs into problems when an item that might have been essential in the eighteenth century is in little demand in the twentieth. Third, a great deal of a college's income was in the form of "country pay"—namely, gifts in kind of crops, firewood, or livestock. Before one dismisses such practices as obsolete, it is worthwhile to note that even in the twenty-first century the practice of prosperous farmers and ranchers donating livestock for university football team dining halls persists as a generous and welcome custom.

The colonial colleges were lean operations. Salaries for most instructors (called "tutors") were marginal, often less than the wages for artisans. Professorial positions were scarce. The one academic appointment that commanded good compensation was that of college president. The salary was relatively high and was often paid directly from the colonial general courts. The job's perquisites included a house and grazing rights in the college yard for one's cows.

Colleges subsisted from year to year and were dependent in part on paying students. However, according to most estimates, charges for tuition plus room and board were relatively modest, and no college could have paid all operating expenses from student fees. When Samuel Johnson wrote an advertisement for the opening of King's College in 1754, he went on eloquently about lofty aims "to teach and engage the children to know God in Jesus Christ, and to love and serve him in all sobriety, godliness, and righteousness of life." Then he closed with the less lofty but very emphatic note, "The charge of the tuition is established by the trustees to be only 25s [hillings] for each quarter." Another source of income was endowed scholarships for "poor but able youth." The colleges seem to have worked hard at keeping tuition low and to have used financial aid to recruit applicants. What is remarkable about the colonial colleges is that they managed to survive despite their lean budgets. This was due in part to their fiscal conservatism and also to the legal protections and occasional subsidies provided by governments of the era. But most of all they owed their survival to their tireless fund-raising efforts.

The Curriculum

We have few written records to help us reconstruct the colonial curriculum. Each college published admission requirements and usually spelled out the specific classical languages, ancient authors, and levels of mathematics the student was expected to have mastered. Published requirements are one matter, but strict adherence is quite another. Entrance examinations were usually administered verbally by the college president. Since there was no reliable system of primary or secondary education in place, precisely how prospective college students were to gain a preparatory education remained uncertain. Sometimes the colleges simply allowed boys to matriculate, often as young as fourteen or fifteen years old. Most of the colonial colleges both bent admissions requirements and provided preparatory and elementary instruction as a way of gaining revenues and cultivating future student cohorts.

As for pedagogy, students faced a mix of classroom recitations and oral disputations in which they were subject to immediate critical evaluation by both masters and fellow undergraduates. Often the motivation for a young man to put aside games and indolence in order to study biblical texts, solve mathematical problems, or conjugate Latin verbs was to avoid the jeers that greeted poor public speaking, flawed logic, or faulty translations. The capstone event of the academic year was the series of speeches and disputations presented during commencement week. Varied accounts indicate an impressive level of intellectual discourse and critical analysis. One newspaper account of the commencement exercises at King's College in 1758 praised the presentations dealing with such topics as metaphysics. Contemporary science was given a central place, with the audience hearing a treatise on the revolution of the earth around the sun that was based on both astronomical observations and the theory of gravity. Although the college had made concessions to the vernacular by allowing disputations to be conducted in English, guardians of standards were reassured to learn that the valedictory oration was in Latin. The program ended with prayers and blessings, reconciling secular learning with Christian faith. The newspaper writer concluded that all was well with the young college and urged citizens to "promote so useful, so well regulated an institution." What the newspaper account did not mention was that in addition to the academic events, commencement exercises were often an occasion for extended celebrations and drinking by both town and gown in the colonial era.

The kinds of lectures and presentations that were central to the King's College commencement ceremonies illustrated exciting international developments. At the highest levels of their scholarship and pedagogy, the colonial colleges were influenced by the academics at Edinburgh and Glasgow more than by the practices of Oxford or Cambridge. Political oratory based on classical allusions and sound logic helped to develop the critical analytic skills that defined political economy as a discipline, a discipline that would be central to the college education of future statesmen in the New World.

There also was a fluidity in the collegiate environment that indicates a breadth of learning and inquiry beyond the formal course of study. Undergraduates, including a young Thomas Jefferson, noted in diaries their lessons and discussions with mentors in such fields as law or even medicine, even though such subjects were not always a central part of the official curriculum. (King's College in New York claims to have established a medical school in 1767, but this was an exceptional innovation.) The College of Rhode Island was adventurous in its relatively broad intentions for the curriculum. Its charter explicitly stated that "the Public teaching shall in general respect the Sciences." At all the colleges the young scholars who served as tutors evidently had interests and learning far beyond the requirements of their formal teaching. From time to time there is evidence that they pursued on their own studies in "natural philosophy," forerunner to our contemporary notion of the physical sciences.

One peculiar characteristic of the colonial colleges in their first decades is that there was little emphasis on completing degrees. Many students matriculated and then left college after a year or two, apparently with none of the stigma we now associate with "dropouts." College students probably constituted less than 1 percent of the population. Enrollments were modest even in terms of the eighteenth-century population. When the College of Rhode Island opened in 1765, only one student enrolled. Two years later, the total enrollment was ten. By 1707 Yale College had conferred bachelor's degrees upon a total of eighteen students. At the College of William and Mary so few undergraduates petitioned for graduation that in 1768 a new governor of Virginia, Lord Botetourt, resolved to provide both a push and a pull to the conferring of the bachelor of arts degree. His strategy was to put up substantial prize money and medallion awards for commencement week oratory contests. The governor, who surprised both himself and the colonists by his unexpected fondness for the college, insisted on the interesting requirement that only degree candidates were eligible to participate. Botetourt's plan was appealing. Several students completed degrees, and the fortunate few who won prizes left the college wiser and wealthier than their less academically ambitious fellows. Historian Phyllis Vine has argued that the ascent of commencement ceremonies as a solemn, prestigious event coincided with the increased recognition by colonial leaders that a college education signaled a young man's entry into a position of power and responsibility in adult life.

Reconstructing the academic life of colonial instructors and students is surprisingly difficult because although many of the elements seem familiar, colonial practices were in fact markedly different from their modern counterparts. For example, one pervasive mode of instruction was classroom recitations. In more advanced courses, lectures on such topics as political economy found favor among both instructors and students. This was probably the clearest link to the remarkable teaching legacy of the universities of the Continent and Scotland. At the same time, the colonial colleges did draw from the pedagogy associated with Oxford and Cambridge: reliance on tutors and tutorial sessions. Across all these instructional variations, books and paper remained dear commodities, so most work was oral. Instead of the written examinations familiar to us today, declamation and oratory dominated the educational life of the colonial colleges. Colleges took great pride in their book collections, but these collections remained small and were hardly intended to be a library in the modern sense, with volumes circulating to undergraduates.

Even the most prosperous and successful colleges—namely, Harvard, Yale, the College of New Jersey, and the College of William and Mary—remained small as to enrollments and limited as to constituency and mission. There is little evidence that any of the colonial colleges ever enrolled more than a hundred students in a single year. Many of the colleges expanded their courses of study to include a grammar school as well as the bachelor of arts course. The bachelor of arts curriculum did not include fine arts. Some of the colleges' charters and documents talk about intentions to add advanced studies in, for example, theology, but such plans seldom if ever materialized. A fictionalized example of the curricular limits of undergraduate studies may be found in Kenneth Roberts's best-selling historical novel of 1937, *Northwest Passage*. The narrator is a young man who has been expelled from Harvard and ends up serving as a cartographer with the famous Rogers Rangers in the British wars against the French and Indians. He was forced to leave Harvard for violating two college regulations: he had first ridiculed college masters and then, to compound this crime of disrespect, had drawn caricatures of the president and instructors. Neither art nor insubordination had a place in the college.

The incident, although fictional, is telling because it illustrates the extent to which colonial college life was characterized by perpetual tensions between students and faculty. Despite the glorification of the "collegiate way" as a haven for youth and a harmonious arrangement for learning, it also was a recipe for conflict characterized by student riots and revolts. These outbursts frequently were triggered by what we would call "consumer complaints" about matters ranging from bad food in the dining commons to restrictions on student activities and autonomy. Presidents, assisted by tutors, were constant disciplinarians. Student offenders were subject to a range of punishments. "Rustication," for example, meant that a student literally had to "go to the country"—that is, move his person and possessions off the college property for some stated period of time. A more enduring, formal punishment was "degradation," the lowering of a student's ranking in his class. The dispensing of academic penalties in the colonial colleges appears to have lacked the humor and goodwill that often characterized student life in the medieval universities. In fourteenth-century Paris, for example, a young scholar found guilty of some offense such as speaking in the vernacular or missing vespers might be "punished" by having to provide wine for masters and fellow students alike.

Food and discipline did not exhaust the list of student complaints about college life. In addition to these perennial sources of student malaise, by the mid-eighteenth century an increasing number of intense, thoughtful students had become restless and critical of the collegiate order and curriculum. This shift was promoted in part by a change in the nature of student misconduct. Whereas in 1720, for example, college students often were boys guilty of childish mischief, by 1770 or thereabouts an older and more politically savvy generation of students were young men who challenged the principles and premises of their elders. There was a growing student interest in Republicanism and ideas outside the academic orthodoxy. Furthermore, a tendency for college officials to be loyal to the unpopular crown escalated the conflicts between students and administration.

The elaborate extracurriculum of athletics teams and musical groups later associated with the "collegiate way" were not part of the colonial colleges. There was one important organized activity, however, that did flourish in the latter part of the colonial era: student debating and literary societies. The first such group, Phi Beta Kappa, was founded at William and Mary in 1776. Accounts indicate that this student society met and drafted its charter and bylaws in the Apollo Room of the Raleigh Tavern, not on the college grounds or in a college building. Its spirit of fraternity and political discussion was evident in its provision for welcoming fellow students at other colleges to join in starting their own chapters. Hence by 1781, undergraduates at Yale and then Harvard had accepted the invitation to establish their own Phi Beta Kappa chapters. In a similar spirit, undergraduates at the College of Rhode Island formed their own "Society of the Federal Adelphi" to promote literary discourse and scholarly fellowship.

Whatever the boundaries of the formal academic course of study, American college students had from the start exhibited an interest in political discussion and oratory. When a college happened to be located near its colonial capital, it provided a convenient outlet for the young gentleman to observe and emulate the leading lawyers and statesmen of the day. The interest in politics and law, both within and beyond the formal course of studies, also signaled another important change in the colonies and the colleges: the gradual but persistent decline of clergy as public leaders, with a drift toward the ascendancy of the lawyer as statesman.

Although the social composition of the collegiate student body was relatively homogeneous, there were clear reminders of social class. College rolls listed students not alphabetically but by family rank. And, following the Oxford tradition, academic robes identified socioeconomic position. "Commoners"—literally, those students who dined in commons—wore long robes, as distinguished from the short academic robes of "servitors," scholarship students who waited on tables. Little wonder, then, that the College of Rhode Island was considered a bit radical in 1769 when the broadside for its commencement exercises bore the headline, "Nomine alphabetice disposita sunt." Although the college had retained the curricular elitism of Latin, it had made a concession to democracy by publishing the names of its graduating students in alphabetical order. Elsewhere, Harvard and the other colleges continued to list graduates by social rank.

College Students: From Christian Gentleman to Gentleman Scholar

The preceding account of the collegiate curriculum has, naturally, included some observations about student life and the composition of the student body. The characteristics of these students reveal a great deal about the purposes of the colleges, and about the reasons for colonies being established in the first place. If one looks at the colonies associated with the founding of Harvard, Yale, and Princeton, it is evident that college-building was serious business. Congregationalists and Presbyterians—what might be collectively described as Puritans—had definite ideas about collegiate education as part of a large, important social, religious, and political vision. As a group, Puritans had tended to be dissenters in matters of religion. This put them at odds with the crown and often meant that their sons were not eligible to matriculate at the royal universities. From time to time all Oxford students were required to swear an oath of allegiance to the monarchy and to the Church of England. The former was acceptable to Puritans; the latter was not.

The family background of the students at colonial Harvard, Yale, and Princeton tended to be one of mercantile wealth. Prosperous and successful, the Puritan merchants were also devout. They hardly wanted to lose their sons to the depravity of Oxford, where "Cavaliers" and "rakes" represented the worst of two worlds: indecent behavior combined with Anglican affiliation. From time to time during the lengthy wars of religion and civil wars of the Tudor and Stuart reigns in England, the Puritans might gain a foothold in the universities. As a general rule, though, the two historic universities, especially Oxford, were not hospitable to the Puritan sense of propriety, religion, or education.

The Puritans as college founders were committed to a rigorous, demanding education of young men who would become Christian gentlemen. They were in line to inherit family commercial enterprises in shipping and selling. The tradeoff was that fathers wanted assurance that Congregationalism or Presbyterianism was integral to their sons' daily and eternal life. So the early collegians were sons of privilege who at the same time were expected to inherit grave responsibilities as leaders and men of influence in a new world where their religion was central and not subject to government or ecclesiastical constraints. Learning was serious, and there was great emphasis placed on the ability to analyze and to be articulate. The crucial ingredient, though, was that all learning ulti-mately was to coalesce into the values and actions of a Christian gentleman.

Who went to the colonial colleges? As the preceding profile suggests, it was a relatively privi-leged group of young men who were expected to be serious about their studies and their religion. In the early decades, college tuition charges were not prohibitive, and there was some scholarship money available for poor, able youth. However, in the seventeenth and early eighteenth centuries, economic conditions in the Massachusetts Bay Colony and Connecticut were austere. Few families could afford the loss of an able-bodied young man from the family farm or business.

There were significant differences among the colonies that shaped their respective colleges. South of New England and the Middle Atlantic area, patterns of settlement in Virginia and what was known as the Chesapeake were markedly different from what one would have found in Cambridge or New Haven. By the late seventeenth century, Virginia had attracted and nurtured a conspicuous planter class—a group whose religious heritage was Anglican and whose ancestors had been large landholders in England, gentry who loved horses and hunting. Not surprisingly, these legacies shaped their notion of colony and college. Plantations and waterways, not townships and roads, defined the colonial world in Tidewater Virginia and into the coastal Carolina region.

By the mid-eighteenth century, colonial economies in all the regions, ranging from New England to Virginia, enjoyed substantial growth and prosperity. Local communities had each devel-oped their own networks and hierarchies of regional elites and favored families. By about 1750 or so, a college affiliation connoted prestige and high social status. The combination of forgone income and the cost of two or three years of college tuition and expenses made a college education unaf-fordable, or at least unappealing, to the vast majority of colonists. Class distinctions within the colony were sharp, and the colleges became increasingly distant from the world and experience of most American families. Clearly, a main purpose of the colleges was to identify and ratify a colo-nial elite. The college was a conservative institution that was essential to transmitting a relatively fixed social order.

The colleges' acquisition of this enhanced role in creating a colonial elite was not altogether direct or immediate. According to Phyllis Vine, there was widespread concern among colonial lead-ers and elders that parents were not always providing the appropriate upbringing for boys who were likely to hold responsible positions when they became adults. One solution was to shift the social-ization function away from the family to formal institutions, including grammar schools and, ultimately, the colleges. The colleges, with their concentration of strong male adults—ministers, alumni, government officials, and tutors—were charged with transforming little boys into little men. The historical importance of this enhanced responsibility for the colleges is that it marked a significant transition in colonial society. In 1960, Bernard Bailyn's seminal work *Education in the Forming of American Society* prompted a generation of scholars to regard families as the primary agents to educate children both in literacy and in social values. Vine does not reject that perspective, but she concludes that by the early eighteenth century the college had supplemented, and perhaps replaced, the family as the transmitter of social lessons.

Given this socializing role, one challenge in accurately analyzing the colonial colleges is to try to look beneath the pejorative modern connotations of *elitism*. In other words, the remarkable fea-ture of the colonial colleges was not their elite character. Rather, it was the fact that established wealthy families and frugal colonial governments and representatives of the crown put so much discretionary time and resources into trying to impart to their privileged sons a sense of responsibility and pub-lic service. It is true that the colonial colleges ratified and perpetuated an elite that would inherit positions of influence in communities. One could also argue that the son of a wealthy Virginia planter or Boston merchant was going to be wealthy and powerful whether he went to college or not. The colonial college was an insurance policy guaranteeing that these favored young men would acquire not only literacy but also a sense of leadership and service by about their twentieth birthday. Democ-racy in the modern sense of the word had little support among colonial leaders—a disparity that remains difficult for us today to accept. The forthright statement of one Virginian sums up the world-view of the young men who typically went to the colonial colleges: "I am an aristocrat. I love lib-erty; I hate equality."

The colleges stepped in to nurture and harness this attitude. King's College described its mission as being to provide to future colonial leaders an education that would "enlarge the Mind, improve the Understanding, polish the whole Man, and qualify them to support the brightest Characters in all the elevated stations in life." A comparable commitment and justification were conveyed by John Witherspoon in 1772 when he wrote about the founding and mission of the College of New Jersey (later renamed Princeton) to prospective donors in the West Indies:

> The children of persons in the higher ranks of life, and especially of those who by their own activity and diligence, rise to opulence, have of all others the greatest need of an early, prudent and well-conducted education. The wealth to which they are born becomes often a dangerous temptation, and the station in which they enter upon life, requires such duties, as those of the finest talents can scarcely be supposed capable of, unless they have been improved and cultivated with the utmost care. Experience shows the use of a liberal Education . . . to those who do not wish to live for themselves alone, but would apply their talents to the service of the public and the good of mankind.

Did the colonial colleges in fact provide their communities with an effective, responsible elite? If one looks at the disproportionate contribution of colonial college alumni to the discussions, debates, and political activity associated with the Revolutionary War and the creation of the United States, it is not unreasonable to give the colleges high marks. College alumni certainly did not monopolize the intellectual and political leadership of the Revolution, but they were a formidable presence. Secular leadership characterized by the ability to debate in the public forum and to write effectively on matters of political philosophy and law was no small achievement.

The religious emphasis of the college founders raises some questions about collegiate purpose. It is important to dispel the stereotype that the colonial colleges were largely concerned with the education of clergymen. The seventeenth-century document "New Englande's First Fruits," in which Harvard officials stated their "dread fear" of leaving future generations an unlettered ministry, is frequently cited as proof of Harvard's central commitment to the education of the clergy. In fact, this interpretation is inaccurate because it fails to acknowledge the tone and context of the document. "First Fruits" was essentially a fund-raising broadside, distributed in England as an emotional appeal to potential donors who had little if any firsthand knowledge of the New World, let alone its colleges. It emphasized the religious element because college founders knew this commitment would be especially appealing to potential donors.

The argument that colonial colleges were devoting a substantial part of their curricula to education of the clergy runs into trouble when one considers that these colleges did not confer divinity degrees. Nor did they ordain ministers or priests. In Virginia, for example, although the royally chartered College of William and Mary was loyal to the crown and the Church of England, it would have been impossible for the college to serve as a seminary. Ordination of an Anglican priest had to be carried out by a bishop. Any aspirant would have had to sail back to England for examination and other ecclesiastical requirements. One must also consider the important distinction between collegiate plans and collegiate achievements. The charter for the College of William and Mary referred to a course of study in divinity, an advanced curriculum following the bachelor of arts degree, but there is no record that the program was ever implemented.

This debate about the relation between the colleges and the ministry was connected to issues of conservative elitism, as discussed earlier. Colonial leaders had an unabashed distrust of an unlearned clergy. Since colleges were the necessary prelude to advanced divinity study and clerical ordination, they were the thin line that protected the colonies from the excesses of populist religion. Harvard College did not ordain ministers, but about half of its graduates eventually entered the clergy. The hope among the governors of the Massachusetts Bay Colony and their counterparts in Connecticut, New Jersey, and other colonies was that college alumni who became clergy would provide an antidote to the threat of uneducated or "unlettered" revivalist preachers. The cautious, critical, scholarly clerics of Presbyterianism and Congregationalism were concerned that "enthusiasm," not reasoned belief, would come to dominate colonial religion and society. What the established clergy did not see was that by the mid-eighteenth century their influence even among the traditional college constituencies had started to erode, with power and prestige becoming increasingly concentrated among an educated secular leadership.

There was, in short, a discernible separation of the state from colleges and churches by the end of the colonial era.

Religious Revivalism and the Colonial Colleges

A number of prominent historians, including George M. Marsden, have argued that the colleges and universities of today have unwisely ignored the importance of religious belief or abolished its place in the core of higher education. One variation of this lament is that faculty and curricula have been allowed to stray from the original religious, and specifically Christian, values of the "founding fathers." The implication is that reform is in order—that it would be good to restore the religious spirit and emphasis of the original colleges.

What is problematic about such revivalism as a reform mandate is that its historical references and antecedents are unclear, and perhaps dubious. First, the "founding fathers" of the colleges must not be confused with the "founding fathers" of the nation. As noted earlier, by the time of the Revolutionary War the collegiate mission had already undergone a discernible shift away from religious orthodoxy toward secular learning and leadership. The leading educational thinkers of the mid-eighteenth-century colonial colleges were hardly of a single mind on the primacy of some set of religious beliefs. Benjamin Franklin and Thomas Jefferson, for example, were worlds apart from John Winthrop or Increase Mather. Above all, it is not evident that the values espoused by the Puritan college builders were especially humane or tolerant. The college founders were impatient with or at best indifferent to disagreements within Congregationalism and Presbyterianism, and they were downright hostile toward Anglicanism and Roman Catholicism.

A recurring pattern in the progression of college founding is that disputes over religious beliefs were a driving force for groups either to be expelled from an established college or to leave it because they felt that it had fallen from religious grace. Cotton Mather, dissatisfied with both the religion and the politics of Harvard College, saw the young Collegiate School in Connecticut as a welcome opportunity to restore to Congregationalism the purity that he and others felt Harvard had lost. The subsequent efforts of Connecticut's Congregationalists to purge the colony and its college of Anglican stirrings demonstrated that the fusion of religion and higher education in the eighteenth century placed more importance on orthodoxy than on interdenominational goodwill. The later founding of the College of New Jersey by New Light Presbyterians was in large measure an effort to create an institution that acknowledged some elements of the Great Awakening, as established Harvard and Yale did not. Indeed, the College of Rhode Island stands as the major exception to this relative lack of tolerance and accommodation within collegiate communities of the seventeenth and eighteenth centuries. To reiterate a point made earlier in discussing Jurgen Herbst's scholarship on college governance of the mid-eighteenth century, the concerted efforts of colonial governors to promote denominational tolerance in college admissions in the Middle Atlantic region ultimately failed.

On balance, then, the religious policy of most colonial colleges was one of favoritism toward established denominations, with a drift toward exclusion of dissenters and evangelicals. This policy would leave a legacy of conflict and fragmentation. Dissatisfaction and departure were precedents established early in the histories of these colleges. Just within the confined world of Protestantism, they were characterized by distrust, wrangling, and crystallization into warring factions. As such, they provide a dubious model for the restoration of religion to a central place on the American campus of the twenty-first century, especially in a society characterized by religious diversity.

Expansion and Experimentation: The Limits of Student Diversity

Instead of being preoccupied with conjecture about the colonial colleges as clerical seminaries, a fresh historical account ought to include attention to activities that extended the scope of the colleges. Experiments such as grammar schools and Indian schools indicate the pragmatism and creativity that the early college presidents and boards brought to the task of devising plans to increase the enrollments and resources of their institutions. Once again, philanthropy was center stage, as the education of Native Americans, including their conversion to Christianity, had great appeal to donors in England. The problem was that such experiments were usually disastrous, and most enterprising college officials who got involved in these ventures quickly looked for ways to get out. Most of the Indian students who showed up at the colleges succumbed either to measles, consumption, or alcoholism. Pedagogically and philosophically, they became trapped between worlds. After a few years of high attrition among Native American students, the colleges had to construct a strategy for holding on to the missionary endowments while shifting attention away from educating heathens and back toward instilling knowledge and responsibility into young gentlemen. Tellingly, the council of Indian chiefs who had initially agreed to send their sons to the colleges felt that the colonial education had rendered their future chiefs "good for nothing." They refused the colleges' offers to renew the scholarship program and politely suggested that colonial officials might want to send young Englishmen to the tribes for a truly beneficial education in leadership.

If a missionary zeal for the Christian education of Native Americans characterized the colonists and their working connections in England, there is little evidence that this commitment extended to a comparable concern for African Americans. Nothing in their attitudes or actions with respect to race relations or slaveholding sets college officials and alumni apart from other colonists. There is no record of colonial commitment to the collegiate education of black students, whether in the regular course of study or at special affiliated schools.

Women were excluded from the colleges by statute. There are occasional accounts of young women who were considered for entrance examinations—strange, because there would never have been any intention to allow the woman to matriculate, even if she had excelled in the admissions examination. For example, George W. Pierson wrote about one "Miss Lucinda Foote whose knowledge of classical authors and New Testament scripture in 1784 was declared to be worthy of admission by the Yale President. She was given a parchment to document that achievement"—and nothing else. One is left, then, with several intriguing historical riddles: What was the reason for this partial acknowledgment of talent without conceding educational opportunity? What would Lucinda Foote gain or do with the consolation prize that gave testimony to her academic skill? Equally mysterious are the alternative modes of education that enabled at least a significant minority of women to acquire a high level of literacy and professional skills, no thanks to the formal schools or colleges.

The Limits of Institutional Purpose and Educational Mission

From time to time historians have uncovered fragmentary records that prompt a reinterpretation of the colleges' scope and mission. For example, is there evidence that such "applied" fields as engineering and science had a place at the college? My curiosity about this possibility was aroused when I learned that the College of William and Mary issued a surveyor's license to George Washington. Was this evidence that the eighteenth-century college had perhaps provided instruction and certification in civil engineering? In fact, the evidence did not support the hypothesis. The issuing of a surveyor's license by the college proved to have no connection with the curriculum. It was merely a convenience that benefited the college: the crown and the colonial government allowed the college both to issue the license and, more important, to keep the licensing fee as well as some percentage of the proceeds from a surveyor's land sales.

Furthermore, there is not much evidence that the colonial colleges provided advanced instruction in the learned professions. A college might have had a professor who delivered lectures on law, but the subject was combined with such topics as "police," a field that was most likely a forerunner to what is known today as political science and public administration. There were no law degrees or coherent courses of legal study. Going to college was not a prerequisite to the practice of the learned professions. Learning often took place outside the academy in various forms of apprenticeship.

In short, the established colleges were not the only places where advanced learning took place in this era. The fact that a college degree was seldom if ever a prerequisite for the practice of any learned profession, including law and medicine, underscores the limited mission and scope of the colonial colleges. The colleges did, especially in the mid-and late eighteenth century, undertake admirable ventures to assure that undergraduates studied mathematics, history, natural sciences, political economy, and moral philosophy. They were not averse to innovation, as indicated by accounts from the 1750s about disputations sometimes being held in English as well as in Latin. But advanced scientific inquiry and what we would call "research" were beyond the resources (if not the intentions) of the colleges. Probably the best opportunities for such endeavors were in private societies, museum groups, or investigations by independent naturalists and investigators. The separation of advanced professional study and certification from the American college was not inherently a problem. Why *not* have other institutions—Inns of Court, teaching hospitals, apprenticeships, or a College of Surgeons or Royal Society—handle such pursuits?

Attempts to reform and expand the academic curriculum usually met with failure. One conspicuous case was Thomas Jefferson's failure to persuade his alma mater to embrace new fields of study, let alone a comprehensive plan of educational reform. The so-called Jeffersonian Reorganization of the College of William and Mary in 1779 was an earnest attempt to transform the historic college into a "university." But here as elsewhere, conservatism among the board of visitors and the unfortunate timing of the war meant that many such innovative reforms had to be tabled or scrapped. Jefferson would have to wait several decades to put into place his plan for an "academical village."

External Relations and the Paper Chase

Constructing a clear picture of the colonial colleges can be problematic for historians in the twenty-first century because these institutions did not adhere to the categories of "public" and "private" that shape our thinking about organizational taxonomies today. Even though Harvard, Yale, Brown, and Princeton all claim to be "independent" institutions today, in the seventeenth and eighteenth centuries each was indelibly linked to its colonial government. This linkage was reflected in the original names. Princeton was the College of New Jersey, Brown was the College of Rhode Island and Providence Plantations. No Harvard commencement ceremony could begin without the procession led by the sheriff of Middles County, and no degree could be awarded without approval of a board whose membership by statute included the governor of Massachusetts Bay Colony. The academic procession outlined for King's College specifically mentioned the lieutenant governor's place in the marching order. The charter of the College of William and Mary explicitly recognized the crown and royal emissaries. In most colonies only a single institution received a charter, and overproliferation of new colleges was strongly resisted. Herein lie the roots of an interesting and significant cluster of government-campus relations, ranging from oversight to financial support.

The accounts of the founding and early decades of the nine colonial institutions attest that college leaders were constantly required to plunge into external politics. Many college presidents were skilled at this endeavor and seemed to relish the intrigue and negotiations with constituencies outside the college. The earlier discussion of institutional governance and philanthropy hints at a distinctively American tradition of college relations. It was in the external relations of college-founding and then college-building and political involvement that the leaders of the colonial colleges most conspicuously displayed their genius and expended their energies. On balance, the American college was an indigenous and exciting institution that historian Jurgen Herbst has perceptively called the "Provincial College."

One finds in the numerous early accounts of colonial college life a stark split within the ranks of presidents. There seem to have been many who were temperamentally unsuited to the job or who misread its emphases. In this category one places the hapless presidents who were mired in the policing of student life or, to an even more depressing extreme, intent on gouging students through petty abuses such as skimping on the dining commons or levying fines. Numerous diaries and other accounts indicate that those students often literally voted with their feet and gave such presidents the boot.

In contrast, such presidents as James Manning of Rhode Island College, James Blair at William and Mary, Thomas Clap at Yale, and Eleazar Wheelock at Dartmouth understood and relished the essentially political character of the institution. They grasped the opportunities and understood the problems that accompanied this new American institutional form: its strong legal protections, the alliance of an external board with a strong administrative president. And they understood its peculiar challenge: funding was not so much meager as uncertain and subject to vacillations. This indigenous form of American leadership was personified in Benjamin Franklin, founder of the Publick Academy of Philadelphia (later known as the College of Philadelphia and later still as the University of Pennsylvania). In short, the American college president from the start had to be an entrepreneur in the broadest and best sense of the word.

The successful presidents were indefatigable. James Blair, who persuaded his board of visitors to have him named president-for-life, coexisted with colonial governors over the course of decades and usually gained an advantage for his beloved College of William and Mary. James Manning, who served as president of the College of Rhode Island from its founding in 1765 until his death twenty-six years later, established a reputation as a civic leader, as the pastor of an influential urban congregation, and, in 1786, as a member of Congress. He was an expert stonemason and scythe-wielder, as well as a superb conversationalist and orator, and students held him in high esteem as an instructor. Manning cultivated the enduring financial and political support of the Brown family, Providence's leading commercial family for whom the college was eventually renamed.

Perhaps the most intriguing member of this group of lively, long-term college presidents was Eleazar Wheelock. His grasp of the political life of the colonies was matched only by his opportunism. He parlayed Moor's Indian School, chartered in Connecticut, into Dartmouth College in New Hampshire. Later, when farmers and merchants in the western part of Massachusetts expressed resentment at their exclusion from the politics and privileges of the Boston-Cambridge area, Wheelock advanced a bold proposition: he urged the dissidents to secede from Massachusetts and create a new colony. His contribution would be to bring with him the collegiate charter for Dartmouth—on the condition that he would then be installed as governor of the new colony.

The paper chase and the thrill of the hunt, whether for charters, donors, or political allies, were the lifeblood of the colonial college presidents who endured and whose institutions thrived. Architects are fond of debating the relation between form and function. The same concept can help us understand how and why an institutional model allegedly transplanted from Oxford and Cambridge ended up so markedly different in its dynamics. At Oxford and Cambridge, where the endowed "college" was the crucial unit, the structure was comparable to that of a lobster: a strong external shell (including a hefty endowment) that provided the sustenance and armor to allow the growth and vitality of the institution to take place inward. In contrast, the radical structural innovation of the American colonial college left it with a strong skeleton, yet its growth and activities took place externally. American college presidents, who had no counterpart at Oxford or Cambridge, did not have the luxury of retreating inward. Their charters and statutes may have protected them from their faculty and students, yet these instruments also gave them both the freedom and the obligation to tend to matters with legislatures, governors, sheriffs, bishops, merchants, and monarchs.

Timing, of course, was important in charting college presidential fortunes. By the eve of the Revolutionary War, many college presidents were in an untenable position. On the one hand, if their charters or funding were at all dependent on loyalty to the British crown, their flexibility to negotiate in provincial and local matters was obviously constrained. The advantage associated with being president of an institution called King's College or Queen's College in 1766, for example, had most likely become a local liability by 1776. Americans (including Tories) of the 1770s have been described as "vexed and troubled Englishmen"—a mood that did not bode well for any of the colleges whose charters included an oath of loyalty to the crown.

Indeed, the advent of revolution and war put the colonial colleges in a paradoxical position. On the one hand, it was a heroic time for the colleges. They provided students and alumni to serve as soldiers and political leaders, as well as academic buildings to serve as barracks and hospitals. On the other hand, the War of Independence suspended academic operations and, predictably, drained off funding for the war effort. And, of course, support in the form of the royal taxes that had once come from the crown was forfeited. By the end of the war almost all the colleges either had closed down or were greatly reduced in resources and energy. Queen's College probably fared the worst of the historic colleges. A proposal to save the struggling college by merging it with the College of New Jersey was voted down in 1793. Two years later the trustees considered moving to New York, but lacking both funds and tutors, they closed the institution. The timing of the war explains in part the college's failure or inability to respond to the exciting ideas about curricular expansion and institutional innovation put forward by Thomas Jefferson and others who wanted to create a distinctive modern university for a new nation.

The Essence of the Colonial Colleges

On balance, then, what was distinctively "American" about the colonial colleges? Here we encounter a series of paradoxes if not contradictions. In the aggregate, the colonies and their colleges showed some religious diversity, but not necessarily religious tolerance. The colleges were concerned with educating their students for "public service," but these students were neither egalitarian nor democratic.

Oscar and Mary Handlin captured the subtleties of the collegiate role in their profile of the young John Adams:

> For young men like Adams, the value of a higher education lay not in professional training but elsewhere. It derived from the belief that a course of learning endowed those who completed it with cultural attributes that were signs of superior status. This was by no means a crude, calculating attitude, but rather one composed of multiple, scarcely conscious, sets of values. The ability to quote a Greek maxim in a legal brief was not essential but helpful. More important was the prevailing conviction that those who had sharpened their minds on the complexities of Greek thought would be better able as a result to deal with the day-to-day problems of trespass and contract. Most important was the awareness that colonial society still put a premium on and assigned practical rewards to people who could display such signs of gentlemanly rank as command of the classics.

Along with refining the politically ambitious and financially privileged young men of the colonies, colonial college-building made a significant, positive contribution to the ideas and actions of the generation that shaped the American Revolution. As Gordon S. Wood has argued, impact of the colleges stands out when one contrasts the aspirations of fathers and sons in the mid-eighteenth century. Thomas Jefferson, for example, inherited from and shared with his father the benefits of life as a Virginia planter. Yet many of the founding fathers attended college and were the first in their families to do so. A college education with its emphasis on informed argumentation, classical languages, and political economy supplemented the landed gentry's ethos with a political and intellectual awareness largely absent from the previous generation. Wood elaborated:

> Both the Scottish and North American leaders felt compelled to think freshly about the meaning of being civilized, and in the process they put a heightened emphasis on learned and acquired values at the expense of the traditional values of blood and kinship. Wanting to become the kind of gentlemen that their contemporaries Jane Austen and Edmund Burke idealized, they enthusiastically adopted the new enlightened eighteenth century ideals of gentility—grace without foppishness, refinement without ostentation, virtue without affection, independence without arrogance. They struggled to internalize the new liberal man-made standards that had come to define what it meant to be truly civilized—politeness, taste, sociability, learning, compassion, and benevolence—and what it meant to be good political leaders—virtue, disinterestedness, and an aversion to corruption and courtier-like behavior.

The colonial college, then, was the right institution in place at the right time to nurture this predisposition. Its impact was neither complete nor infallible, nor even indispensable. It was, however, significant. The preamble to the charter for the College of Rhode Island and Providence Plantations (later renamed Brown University) captured the convictions of the college-builders: "Institutions for liberal Education are highly beneficial to Society, by forming the rising Generation to Virtue, Knowledge and useful literature and thus preserving in the Community a Succession of Men duly qualified for discharging the Offices of Life with usefulness and reputation." There is a touching sense of high purpose in the mottoes adopted by these small, struggling institutions: "Veritas," "Lux et veritas," "In deo speramus," "Vox clamantis in deserto." These were admirable voices crying out in the New World wilderness, looking for light and truth—and not without strong Christian faith combined with secular resolve. No right-minded builder of a new, better world could disagree with the University of Pennsylvania's motto: "Leges sine moribus vanae" (Laws without morals are useless). Despite numerous obstacles and poor odds, these colleges educated several generations of bright, articulate young men, and probably did so far more effectively and efficiently than their academic counterparts in England during the same era.

Historical memory is, of course, dominated by the perspectives of those who survived and triumphed. Harvard College's founding in 1636 shines brightly today because the college endured. This contrasts to the false start or stillbirth of college-building in Virginia in 1619. The Virginia Company had endowed ten thousand acres of land and arranged with King James I to receive donations of £1,500 for founding a university and an Indian School near Henrico. However, the educational plans were abandoned after Indians massacred 347 settlers, including the deputy in charge of the college lands.

It is difficult to find a wholly satisfactory explanation as to why colleges were established in some places but not in others. For all the commerce, trade, agriculture, and population that existed south of Tidewater Virginia, for example, why did wealthy planters not found a college in Savannah or Charleston for their sons? Was Maryland's strong Catholic composition a factor that prompted either an Anglican monarchy or adjacent Protestant governors to block a college there? The absence of colleges in such underserved colonies as Georgia was not due to lack of effort. Thomas G. Dyer has reconstructed the prolonged campaign by the evangelist George Whitefield from about 1755 to 1770 to have Bethesda School in Savannah enhanced in its mission so that he could petition the English crown to have it chartered as Bethesda College. For a while Whitefield's attempts to gain the college charter seemed well timed because the idea was attractive to constituencies both in England and in Georgia. Georgia's colonial government was intrigued by the prospect of having a bona fide college close to home so that the colony's future leaders would not have to head north to Princeton or King's College to be educated. According to Dyer, the crown's distrust of a college with evangelical roots was evidently the primary obstacle to the granting of a charter. Even though this attempt at college-founding came to nothing, the commitment that the Bethesda College plan commanded reinforces the general observation that creating a college was an important proposition in the southern colonies as well as in the north.

Contrasts in Colonization and Colleges: New England and New Spain

Thus far our historical discussion has been limited to the British colonies. To put the experience of these colonies in perspective, it is useful to look at other parts of the North American colonial world. In 1538, almost a century before the founding of Harvard College in the Massachusetts Bay Colony, Spanish settlers in the Caribbean had established the University of Santo Domingo. As early as the mid-sixteenth century one finds that Spanish settlers had utilized the support of both the king of Spain and the pope to open universities in their colonies, including the Universidad Nacional Autonoma de Mexico and the Universidad Nacional Mayor de San Marco in Peru, both established in 1551. Some records indicate that the oldest continuously operating American university is in Mexico: the Colegio de San Nicolas Hidalgo. By the early seventeenth century, the Spanish had established universities in Chile, Argentina, and Bolivia.

Imperial Spain probably surpassed Britain in its commitment to institution-building, educational programs, and missionary work among indigenous peoples in the New World. And although the collegiate architecture of the British colonies was impressive, it paled in comparison with the network of missions—elaborate "total institutions"—that Franciscan monks from Spain established along the Pacific Coast at about the same time that the British colonists were founding colleges. The Spanish colonies had the advantage of a concentrated official policy of both crown and church to fund and supervise distinct programs and goals. But although the Spanish settlers may have built magnificent coordinated systems of churches, missions, and forts, it was as part of an imperial blueprint that was not strongly committed to bringing settlers from the Old World to establish civilian towns and to pursue agriculture and local trade. And the Spanish imperial model evidently had little if any provision for founding and nurturing universities as part of the colonial vision in the vast area of America north of Mexico.

The missions in what we know today as California warrant some comparison with the Indian Schools that were a feature of many colonies on the Atlantic coast. The California missions administered by the Franciscans were well organized and dedicated (although not always effective) in their efforts to "educate" Native Americans, in the sense of converting them to Roman Catholicism and socializing them into a work ethic tied to raising and processing local agricultural crops. In contrast, the Indian Schools at Dartmouth, Harvard, and William and Mary relied on uncertain private donations and were characterized by reluctant commitment. But when one looks beyond missionary efforts and into the realm of higher learning, the Spanish educational initiatives in California are dwarfed by those of the British colonists. The colleges stretching from the Massachusetts Bay Colony to Tidewater Virginia were distinctive in the imperial scheme. The contrast between the British and Spanish colonies in North America reinforces the point that college building was not inevitable, and the efforts and achievements of college founders in the British colonies gain in historical significance as exceptional endeavors.

After the Revolution: Colonies and Colleges in a World Turned Upside Down

When the British troops of Cornwallis surrendered to George Washington at Yorktown, the fifers for the defeated army were ordered to play "A World Turned Upside Down." True, the victory of the colonists over the imperial troops upset the conventional political order. Long before that, however, the colonial colleges had turned the educational world upside down. And they had taken the Oxford-Cambridge corporate structure and turned it inside out by shifting control from faculty to an external board of trustees and a president. They had founded and maintained eight colleges in a country where higher education might not necessarily have been a high priority. The most incredible finding of all is an obvious and basic one: each colony built its beloved "school upon a hill" as a *college*, without a strong, coherent base of elementary and secondary education even among its elite families, let alone its general population.

By the close of the colonial period the American colleges were characterized by two features: their charters and legally incorporated structures were strong; and their structures and protections ensured flexibility and endurance. This was fortunate because the college's future survival and health would depend on their capacity for resilience.

An interesting postscript to this discussion of the legacies of the colonial colleges is that the "colonial revival" impetus that started around 1890 ultimately proved to be limited in its ability to invigorate a university. In 1960 a Harvard faculty report on admissions suggested that college brochures and publicity items needed a change of tone. The report warned that "chilly Puritan prose" might be sending the message that Harvard was seeking only "eggheads." In other words, the prestige of historic Harvard was in danger of losing its appeal to talented, lively prospective students. Evidently, the report made an impact on the graphics and images projected by the historic institution. In 1970 one commentator observed the shift away from somber prose and colonial motifs: "Until very recently Harvard's official publications looked to have been designed by a Pliocene typographer whose idea of the beautiful was different from our own. Most of them still are in appearance strongly reminiscent of another epoch. Though brave new things are announced within them, they proclaim by the grayness of their pages, that the University is stoutly resisting change. But a few official publications have turned over a new leaf and put a bold face on it."

So, in both 1780 and 1980, academic leaders at the historic colleges realized that reliance on heritage without attention to the changing social and political environment was a blueprint for institutional erosion. How American colleges fared under the auspices of a new nation and a new set of legal ground rules after the Revolutionary War is the next theme for consideration.

From Religion to Politics: Debates and Confrontations over American College Governance in Mid-Eighteenth Century America

Jurgen Herbst

Growing religious diversity during the middle decades of the eighteenth century challenged traditional forms of governance at the colleges in the English colonies of North America. At the beginning of that century, the secular government and the established church jointly exercised authority over each college. In subsequent decades, the arrival of Baptists, Anglicans, and Quakers in New England, and the influx of Presbyterians and Quakers in Virginia threatened the entrenched dominance of Congregationalists at Harvard, Presbyterians at Yale, and Anglicans at the College of William and Mary and placed great strains on the working agreements between the authorities of church and state.[1]

The middle colonies' religiously and ethnically mixed populations precluded college governance on the Reformation model of *cuius regio, eius religio*, by which a sovereign's denomination determined both the ecclesiastical allegiance of his or her subjects and the religious policies of colleges. Instead, the aggressive evangelism of the supporters of the Great Awakening—that pan-Protestant arousal of enthusiastic religiosity in the late 1730s and early 1740s which swept the colonies from Massachusetts to Virginia—and the heterogeneity of the people combined to produce a colonial variant of the English policy of toleration. As understood in the colonies, toleration meant the tacit recognition that the dominant church in each province was the established ecclesiastical authority. Yet, in contrast to traditional Reformation policy, members of minority denominations were guaranteed religious liberty while attending the college of the dominant religion. Thus, a colony's college was entrusted with stewardship for all Protestants. The adoption of a policy of toleration in college governance constituted a recognition that, under conditions of pluralism, accommodation and conciliation were mandatory in order to end and avoid conflicts.

In addition to problems caused by the growth of diversity, toleration had inherent defects and weaknesses; as a policy, it did not survive into the nineteenth century. In the colonies it quickly proved to be an elusive and unattainable ideal. Its pursuit led to tension and polarization between ecclesiastical authorities and secular leaders and frequently provided convenient cover for political power struggles. Questions of college governance became indistinguishable from political debates and battles, and the alliance of secular and ecclesiastical interests ultimately broke asunder.

As the Revolution approached, new distinctions were drawn between private and denominational colleges on the one hand and public colleges on the other. The beginnings of this new alignment could be seen as early as the 1760s, when Queen's College was chartered in New Jersey as a rival to the provincial college at Princeton. The trend, however, reached its full development only in the 1780s and 1790s with the chartering of the first state universities in New York, Pennsylvania, Georgia, and Vermont and with the founding of the first private colleges in Virginia, Kentucky, and Pennsylvania.[2] Yet in the mid-eighteenth century, the major issues surrounding college development stemmed from tension between the defenders of ecclesiastical authority and proponents of secular control. Under the pressure of demographic forces, toleration became an outmoded policy by the end of the eighteenth century, and the religious disputes became transformed into political battles involving the colleges in the larger social and political issues of the colonies.

The Great Awakening and College Governance

The Great Awakening was the catalyst for breaking the mold of joint ecclesiastic-secular college governance. Its very nature as an evangelical movement welcoming students and teachers from all Protestant denominations placed it in opposition to the idea of an established church order in colony and college. Its leaders, expecting the benefit from population growth and geographic expansion, pressed the colleges to be inclusive with regard to the religious persuasions of their students and encouraged them to accept denominational differences.[3]

Even though authorities in England were committed to the concept of joint establishment of state and church, their endorsement of a policy of toleration and their political consideration for the welfare of the colonial populations posed few serious obstacles to interdenominational cooperation. Thus, in 1763, when the Crown recommended an Anglican fund-raising effort for King's College and for the College of Philadelphia, it spoke of "the various denominations of other Protestants" who, in addition to the Anglicans, were jointly committed to "the support and extension of the reformed religion."[4]

To be sure, this statement of royal support came decades after the flood tide of the Awakening had passed. Crown authorities had been somewhat less accommodating in the 1740s when the Awakening first affected the colleges of New England. But even then the main opposition arose less from the crown than from the colonial clergy—Congregational at Harvard and Presbyterian at Yale. At the Massachusetts college, the effects were comparatively mild. There was no change in the governance of the college, other than an increasing influence of the magistrates on the Board of Overseers and a strengthening of the liberal ministers at the expense of their orthodox brethren.[5] At Yale, however, the Awakening ushered in a grave crisis. Throughout Connecticut it pitted against each other partisans and opponents of the demand for ecclesiastic-secular college governance.

At the beginning of the 1740s, the Collegiate School (as Yale was then officially known) differed in its form of governance from other colleges in the Western world. Its administration, unlike that of Harvard or William and Mary, included no representatives of the provincial government. Yale's exclusively clerical board of trustees exercised the functions of directors of a corporate body; without having been legally established as such, it constituted a quasi-corporation. While acknowledging the Connecticut Assembly as their source of funds, the trustees were prepared to accept its direction only as a court of equity in controversial matters.

In 1745, however, under the leadership of their recently elected rector, Thomas Clap, the trustees exchanged their relative freedom from legislative supervision for the security and privilege of full incorporation as The President and Fellows of Yale College. Even then they did not count civil representatives of the colonial government among their number. But under the new charter the assembly had the right to inquire into or repeal the trustees' legislative and administrative rules "when they shall think proper." Perhaps Clap thought that the legislature's pledge of annual cash grants to the college "to continue during the pleasure of this Assembly"[6] amply compensated for this unavoidable concession to the assembly. Whatever his motives, the fact remained that in 1745, only five years after his election, Clap had succeeded in formally incorporating the Collegiate School and bringing it under the authority of both Connecticut's established Presbyterian churches and its legislature. The governance of the provincial college now conformed in principle, if not in every detail, to that of other colleges founded after the Reformation.[7] However inconsequential or weighty the concession to assembly oversight really was, its effects could only become apparent in the future.

Clap cherished the participation of the legislature in college affairs because he had found assembly support invaluable during the late 1730s, the tumultuous years of the Awakening. Initially, he had welcomed the arrival of such well-known revivalists as George Whitefield and Gilbert Tennent, but he changed his mind when he witnessed their effects on the Yale students. Encouraged by these visiting "New Lights," as they were called, the students began to question the piety of their "Old Side" teachers and ministers. This led the Yale trustees to decree in September 1741 "that if any student of this college shall directly or indirectly say that the rector, either of the trustees or tutors are hypocrites, carnal or unconverted men, he shall for the first offense make a public confession in the hall, and for the second offense be expelled."[8]

Clap soon found occasion to apply the ordinance and expel David Brainerd for having said of his tutor that he possessed no more grace than a chair. But the turmoil persisted, split the New Haven church, and led Clap to send the student body home. In April 1742, a committee of the legislature, alarmed that students had "fallen into several errors in principle and disorders in practice," recommended that the General Court grant funds to hire a college minister.[9] A month later the assembly intervened with its "Act for Regulating Abuses and Correcting Disorders in Ecclesiastical Affairs" and attempted to ban itinerant ministers from Connecticut churches.[10] Clap and the college trustees were wholly in sympathy with these drastic and repressive measures against the New Lights. In their desire to uphold the Old Side establishment of state, church, and college, they perceived the legislature as their strongest and most reliable ally.

Highlighting once more the existing college-church-state nexus, the most acute crisis involving the college directly in the turmoil of the Awakening came late in 1744. Two students, the brothers John and Ebenezer Cleaveland, while on college vacation at home in Canterbury, Connecticut, had attended New Light worship services with their parents. When Clap and the tutors heard of this, they charged the brothers with having violated the rules of the Gospel as well as the laws of the colony and college. John Cleaveland apologized for his ignorance of the laws as Clap had defined them but refused to admit that the meetings he had attended were anything other than gatherings of a legally constituted church. He objected strenuously to what he considered the unwarranted application of college laws outside the confines of Yale: "For we always thought," he told Clap, "that when we were out of New Haven we had full liberty to go to what meeting we pleased without a thought of transgressing any college law." But Clap would have none of this. "All college laws," he retorted, "excepting a few little ones extend farther than New Haven bounds."[11] Speaking for the tutors and himself, he added:

> We conceive that it would be a contradiction in the civil government to support a college to educate students to trample upon their own laws and break up the churches which they establish and protect, especially since the General Assembly in May 1742 thought proper to give the governors of the college some special advice and direction upon that account; which was to this effect, that all proper care should be taken to prevent the scholars from imbibing those or such like errors; and that those who would not be orderly and submissive, should not be allowed the privilege of the college.[12]

Pressed to justify punishing students for violating a law which could be said to exist only by implication, Clap accused the Cleaveland brothers of knowing that their actions were contrary to his judgment, "and if you do not go according to my judgment you can't expect to enjoy college privileges."[13] With this statement Clap presumed to personify both the law of the college and the law of the colony. Only the students and a few sympathizers protested. The New York *Post-Boy* published a letter by an author who was "a little warm upon this late stretch of college power,"[14] and the Yale students printed and distributed John Locke's *Essay on Toleration*. But this had little impact on the common front of college administration, Old Side establishment, and General Court.[15]

During 1745, the Cleaveland affair and the possibilities of renewed rebellion among students and young tutors pushed Clap to seek incorporation for the college. Once incorporation was accomplished, he could rest both his own authority and that of the board of trustees on the charter rights of a corporation backed by the General Court.

The terms of the Yale charter broke new ground. This was not because of the appointment of a group of nonresident ministers to the corporation, as had been stated,[16] but because of the exclusion of any and all tutors and professors from membership. At the two colonial colleges founded prior to Yale, nonresident governors served among the overseers at Harvard and among the visitors at William and Mary. However, at Harvard one professor and some of the tutors were members of the corporation, while at the Virginia college the entire faculty and the president constituted the corporation.[17] Clap barred all teachers at Yale because he recognized that threats to the Old Side establishment were more likely to arise among young, inquisitive college tutors than among established ministers. Perhaps Clap was also reminded of the rebellion of the Harvard tutors in the 1720s or of ex-President Cutler's and tutor Samuel Johnson's defections to Anglicanism, a shock that had nearly led to the closing of the college two decades earlier.[18] Regardless of his motivation, Clap rested his faith on responsible external governors, whom he placed directly under legislative oversight, and openly demonstrated his distrust of college teachers.

The same concern for keeping the college a law unto itself, for minimizing the possibilities of internal rebellion and thereby of outside interference, is manifest in the 1745 laws of the college drawn up by Clap.[19] Under these laws students were made subjects of the college and the church of New Haven, and the president, tutors, fellows, and the General Court held disciplinary authority over them. Students were specifically prohibited from attending any religious services not approved by the president or public authority. In addition, they were denied the right to enter complaints or bring suit in civil court against other members of the college unless they first obtained permission from the president or fellows. Clap sought to ensure the autonomy of the college as a provincial institution against intervention by municipal authorities or inferior courts. Narrowly circumscribing the spheres of action assigned to teachers and students, he anchored the college firmly in the bedrock of its associated institutions of church and state.

It is supremely ironic that Clap's stormy presidency eventually terminated in strife, riots, and the near collapse of the college as a result of his decision in 1753 to desert his own guidelines. Losing sympathy with his brethren in the Connecticut churches and with the assembly, Clap himself began to loosen the connections that held the college to church and state. In 1747, he wrote proudly that his charter and laws had "reduced the college to a much more perfect state" and that the former trustees, "not so proper or usual a title for the governors of a college in a more mature and perfect state,"[20] had become corporation fellows. But pride over internal changes could do little to prevent the outside world from challenging Clap's claim of autonomy for the college and autocracy for himself.

The challenge to Clap's authority began in 1753 with the opening of an Anglican church in New Haven. Clap abruptly terminated the relationship between Yale and New Haven's First Presbyterian Church by ordering all students to worship and receive religious instruction within the college. He obviously meant to respond to the Anglican threat by drawing the college community ever closer upon itself, even if that meant reversing his previous policy of integrating the college into the existing establishment of Presbyterian church and state. His ban offended Connecticut Presbyterians as much as Anglicans, and both groups protested strongly. Clap's only response was to note that no community could exist without enforcing uniform rules for all of its members. He now began a "go-it-alone" policy, despite its potential for splitting the college from the church and the state.[21]

Anglican reaction to Clap's new ordinance came quickly and effectively from Samuel Johnson, newly elected president of King's College in New York. Johnson, a Yale alumnus, ex-tutor, and—after his Episcopal ordination—an influential spokesman for Connecticut's Anglicans, warned Clap:

> Tell it not in Gath, much less in the ears of our dear mother-country, that any of her daughters should deny any of her children leave to attend on her worship whenever they have opportunity for it. . . . For God's sake do not be so severe to think in this manner, or to carry things to this pass! If so, let Dissenters never more complain of their heretofore persecutions or hardships in England, unless they have us tempted to think it their principle, that they ought to be tolerated, in order at length to be established, that they may have the sole privilege of persecuting others.[22]

Johnson was blunt. He reminded Clap that New England's Anglicans might have to complain to "our superiors at home." The English officials could conclude, in turn, that Yale College, which was incorporated by the colonial assembly rather than the crown, was "a nullity in itself."[23] Moreover, the colony's act of incorporation might have been illegal, endangering its own status in law. And as if that were not enough, Johnson added, Yale College had been funded with the aid of such

Anglican donors as Elihu Yale, Bishop Berkeley, and, through the annual contributions of the Connecticut Assembly, the colony's Anglican taxpayers. As much as Clap must have resented being reminded of Connecticut's changing demography, of English law, and of his own earlier views of college-church-state relationships, he had to concede the points. Johnson's threat of appeal to the crown was too formidable a risk.[24]

Clap's concession, however, came neither gracefully nor enthusiastically. Without announcing any change in policy, he began to grant permission for Anglican students to attend services of their faith if they so requested. Clap combined his reversal with a spirited defense of his original position and a novel reading of college history. He declared that the laws of the college and the rules of peace and charity demanded preservation of the original purpose and order of the college. There was no violation of liberty of conscience involved in this, Clap told Johnson: Anglicans who entered the college did so by their own free will and, by entering, accepted the college rules.[25] In a twenty-page pamphlet especially prepared for the occasion, Clap argued that "the original end and design of colleges was to instruct, educate, and train up persons for the work of the ministry." Though colleges since the Reformation had been chartered by civil government, they were run by ecclesiastical persons for spiritual purposes and were therefore religious societies. Because their purpose was to train ministers, he argued, colleges were superior to ordinary churches, which trained the common people.[26]

Clap went on to announce that, since 1746, the trustees had been accumulating an endowment fund for a professor of divinity; in the meantime, they had asked the president to perform that role. As for Messrs. Yale and Berkeley, they surely knew, wrote Clap, that their contributions to the college were supporting the intent of the original donors and could not alter the college's foundation. He added that Connecticut's taxpaying Anglicans were amply repaid by the education of Episcopal ministers.[27] In this interpretation of college history, Clap virtually ignored the effects of the Reformation, which had left the purpose more secular and had weakened governance by ministers. He angered the Anglicans by substituting insult for injury, and he offended Presbyterian ministers and magistrates as well with his arrogant claim for the superiority of colleges to churches. All he accomplished was to isolate himself.

Clap's sparring with the Anglicans was but a prelude to a far more serious battle in the 1760s. Building on his announcement that colleges were superior to religious societies, Clap argued that colleges could carry on religious instruction, worship and ordinances "within their own jurisdiction, by their own officers, and under their own regulation."[28] This was his jurisdiction for withdrawing students from the New Haven church and subsequently for organizing a separate college church under his direct supervision. In March 1756, the trustees installed Naphtali Daggett as professor of divinity, and on July 3, 1757, Daggett preached his first sermon as the pastor of the newly established Church of Christ in Yale College.[29] Thus, between 1753 and 1757, Clap succeeded in redefining the society over which he had presided for sixteen years. If he could have his way, Yale College for the training of civil servants for state and church was going to become a church seminary, and its first senior professor would become its chaplain. In attempting to carry out this transformation, Clap not only affronted members of the assembly and others in Connecticut who believed in the original purpose of the college, but he also violated the Saybrook Platform, which gave the consociation of churches a voice in all matters of church separation.[30] To make matters worse, in 1757 Clap sought to oust Joseph Noyes, minister of New Haven's First Church, from the college corporation by accusing him of heresy and requesting a trial.[31] In this instance, Clap was forced to back down by a gathering storm of protest and resistance to his high-handed, arbitrary administration. As Louis Tucker, Clap's biographer, reports, the Yale controversy began as a religious issue, spilled over into politics, and "in the course of the dispute, weighty questions were raised relative to the nature and purpose of Yale, the relationship of the school to the General Assembly, and the extent of authority of the Corporation and President Clap."[32] When these questions were finally taken up in the assembly, the college entered the political arena, where Clap was to experience his greatest triumph and his ultimate defeat. I will return to these events after discussing some parallels and differences among issues of college governance in other colonies.

Toleration and the Role of the State

Clap's regime at Yale contrasted markedly in two ways with the initiatives sought in New Jersey, New York, and Pennsylvania: in its repudiation of the college's integration into the network of established institutions of state and church, and in its singular determination to reject compromise with either Anglicans or Presbyterians. In each of the three Middle Atlantic provinces, a college came into existence after the high tide of the Awakening had receded during the late 1740s. But the College of New Jersey, King's College, and the College of Philadelphia all emerged in colonies where religious diversity was the norm rather than a new development.[33] These colleges, therefore, found accommodation to various denominational groups to be in their own interest. The denomination in nominal control on each board of trustees—the Presbyterians in New Jersey, the Anglicans in New York, and both of them together in Philadelphia—emphasized its stewardship rather than its possession of the institution. The New Jersey charter proclaimed hospitality to students "of every religious denomination" with "free and equal liberty and advantage of education . . . notwithstanding any different sentiments in religion."[34] In New York, President Samuel Johnson assured parents that he had "no intention to impose on the scholars the peculiar tenets of any particular sects of Christians, but to inculcate upon their tender minds the great principles of Christianity and morality in which true Christians of each denomination are generally agreed."[35] In Philadelphia, too, the trustees agreed in 1764 to the official adoption of a policy of nondiscrimination which was to be "perpetually declaratory of the present wide and excellent plan of this institution."[36] Thus, in the middle colonies the new colleges founded at mid-eighteenth century endorsed the English policy of toleration as best suited to their particular circumstances.

The origins of the College of New Jersey present a case study in toleration of and accommodation to the secular and religious desires of diverse groups. The struggle over the college's founding took the form of a contest among Presbyterian factions in the colonies of New York, New Jersey, and Pennsylvania. Members of the New York presbytery wanted to establish a provincial institution on the model of the New England colleges or European universities. In the New Brunswick presbytery—joined with the New York and New Castle presbyteries in the synod of New York—revitalist New Light ministers hoped to strengthen the so-called Log College, an evangelically oriented academy founded by William Tennent, Sr., sometime between 1728 and 1730. A third group, Old Side in inclination and centered around Philadelphia, was organized into a synod named after that city. They were suspicious of their brethren in New York and in New Brunswick. In fact, their insistence on a synodical examination of ministerial candidates led in 1745 to a formal split of the synod.[37] During this time members of the New York presbytery proceeded with their plans for the New Jersey College and hoped for an eventual reconciliation among the warring factions. Consulting with Presbyterian laypersons in New York City, they were confirmed in their belief that they must not found a seminary. What was needed was a degree-granting college incorporated by the government. They declared:

> Though our great intention was to erect a seminary for educating ministers of the gospel, yet we hope it will be a means of raising up men that will be useful in other learned professions—ornaments of the State as well as the Church. Therefore we propose to make the plan of education as extensive as our circumstances will admit.[38]

Like the colleges in Massachusetts, Connecticut, and Virginia, the projected institution was to produce graduates who could "sustain with honor the offices they may be invested with for the public service."[39] In order to attract young men of Presbyterian, Quaker, Dutch Reformed, German Reformed, and Anglican backgrounds, the curriculum had to compare favorably with those of Harvard and Yale. Finally, the planners felt that their chances for success depended heavily on ready financial support. Consequently, they began a subscription drive in New York and New Jersey, which by March 1745 netted pledges of £185 in New Jersey currency.[40] The New Lights of the New York presbytery had come to feel that they could succeed only if they avoided sectarian and exclusively religious objectives; therefore, they proposed a college that would serve all interests in the middle colonies. Events proved them right. Not only did they found their college, but by 1758 they also could participate in the reconciliation of the once-hostile Presbyterian factions.

With a parallel desire to avoid identification with particular secular interests, the founders also stressed their intercolonial character. When John Hamilton, the acting governor, signed the charter of the College of New Jersey on October 22, 1746, the fourth colonial college came into existence. It was incorporated under a trusteeship form of government familiar to Presbyterians from the dissenting academies in England, the academies of Scotland, and the 1701 charter of Connecticut's Collegiate School. All seven of the trustees named were Presbyterians; three of them held pastorates in New Jersey and one in New York, and three were New York laymen. These men constituted the first intercolonial governing board of an eighteenth-century college. Their number was permitted to grow to twelve, the remaining five to be chosen by the original seven. When the choice was made in the summer of 1747, all five of the new trustees were graduates of the Log College, representing the frontier areas of Pennsylvania and New Jersey.

Even though New Light clergymen dominated the board, the institution was a college and not a religious seminary. Its charter did not refer to church, presbytery, or synod, nor did it mention the training of ministers. The college also shunned ties of the colony's government. None of the trustees served in an *ex officio* capacity, and the charter neither contained nor hinted at any promise of financial aid from the legislature. The charter, in fact, had been authorized by the governor without legislative action.

It did not take long, however, for the colony of New Jersey to assert its authority as guardian of the rights of all its inhabitants and to insist on a voice in college governance. The guiding force for reform of the college's charter was Governor Belcher, who had recently arrived from Massachusetts and was intimately acquainted with the governance of Harvard College. Anxious to strengthen the position of the College of New Jersey, his "adopted daughter," he advocated tightening the relationship between school and colony. During the early part of 1748, he negotiated with the trustees, insisting both on *ex officio* membership on their board for the governor and members of his council and on the role of board president for himself. Such an organization would have resembled that of the Harvard overseers, with four ministers and four councillors balancing the interests of church and state. The New Jersey ministers on the Board, however, objected strongly to the *ex officio* membership of the magistrates. They did not object to Belcher personally, but they could not be sure of his successors. Eventually, they reached a compromise which named the four councillors as individuals but placed the governor on the board *ex officio* as its presiding officer.

The new charter enlarged the board of trustees from nine ministers and three laymen to twelve ministers, ten laymen, and the governor. Compared to the first charter, the 1748 document gave greater emphasis to secular and intercolonial representation by adding the New Jersey governor, his council, and three prominent Pennsylvanians—thus more than doubling the lay membership. These men served in addition to the three New Yorkers appointed under the first charter. The inclusion of the college president on the board elevated his position from that of academy headmaster to one comparable to the presidency of other colonial colleges. In this and other ways, Belcher helped bring the new college more in line with its sister institutions.

Though there were magistrates of three colonies on the board, the designation of the New Jersey governor as presiding officer and the required presence of at least twelve New Jersey board members underlined acceptance of the institution as New Jersey's provincial college.[41] To the dismay of many of the college's backers, however, this official status brought neither legislative funding nor an authorization for a colonial lottery. The college had to rely on financial gifts from friends, on lotteries conducted outside New Jersey, and on fund-raising efforts among English dissenters and Presbyterians in Scotland and Ulster.[42] The New Jersey governor and councillors confined themselves to protecting the college's interests; they also sought to ensure that the college would serve young men of diverse Protestant denominations from New Jersey and its neighboring colonies.

In New York, arguments over the prospect of founding a college revolved around different interpretations of the principle of toleration. Could this English policy continue to grant preferential treatment to the Anglicans? Or, given the religious diversity of New York's population, should it be applied evenhandedly to Protestants of all denominations? But earlier in the late 1740s, few of these kinds of questions were raised. Neither the city's Anglicans nor their secular-minded opponents had any use for the enthusiastic proponents of the Great Awakening. And yet the dour Presbyterian orthodoxy of President

Clap at Yale was equally unappealing. When in 1746 and 1748 the legislature authorized lotteries for a college, most interested citizens merely hoped that such an institution would bring prestige, wealth, and political stability to the province by training future civil and ecclesiastical officers. In 1749, William Livingston, reader in the Dutch Reformed church of Albany and a 1741 graduate of Yale, wrote that a college would "demolish enthusiasm and superstition" along with vice, drunkenness, and vandalism, and would "cause a surprising alteration in the behavior of our young gentry."[43] Samuel Johnson, then an Anglican missionary in Connecticut, expected the college to revitalize the colony's political, social, and economic life.[44] To govern the college, an anonymous contributor to the *New York Evening Post* proposed a board of trustees composed, like Harvard's overseers, of magistrates and ministers but with private persons added.[45] There was agreement in the city that the new institution was to be neither an academy under denominational control nor a college with an incorporated faculty.

When in November 1751 the legislature authorized a board of trustees for the lottery funds, they appointed to its membership the colony's senior councillor, the speaker of the assembly, the judges of the supreme court, the mayor of New York City, the colony's treasurer, and Messrs. James Livingston, Benjamin Nicoll, and William Livingston.[46] All three of the named members were lawyers; all of the office holders and Benjamin Nicoll, the stepson of Samuel Johnson, were active members of the Anglican church. The board reflected accurately the realities of political life in New York, where Anglicans exerted an influence quite out of proportion of their numbers. For these board members to claim a strong voice in the affairs of the projected college was but to follow traditional models already in force in Massachusetts, Virginia, and Connecticut. The New York college was to be a provincial institution under the guidance of the established church and state.

Nevertheless, the Anglican preponderance among the lottery trustees created uneasiness among non-Anglicans. Their sentiments found expression in a series of letters in the spring of 1753 in William Livingston's *Independent Reflector*.[47] Livingston and three collaborators, all Yale graduates, vowed to fight any Anglican influence over the college. The four men asserted that the connection of Anglican church and crown spelled potential tyranny, and they championed the assembly as the defender of the people's liberties. Early in 1753, in a letter to another Yale friend, Livingston outlined their program and essays yet to come in the *Reflector*. If the New York college were to fall under the management of churchmen, wrote Livingston, the consequence would be "universal priestcraft and bigotry in less than half a century." He complained that all the men proposed as trustees were Anglicans "and many of them the most implicit bigots" at that. He continued:

> The Church can assign no color of reason to have the direction of the affair in preference of any other sect, but I would not have it managed by any sect. For that reason I would have no charter from the Crown but an act of Assembly for the purpose. Nor, for the same reason should divinity be taught at college because whoever is in the chair will obtrude his own notions for theology. Let the students follow their own inclinations in the study of divinity and read what books they please in their chambers or apply themselves to it after they leave the college. Their religious exercises should consist of reading the scriptures, and hearing a prayer in which all Protestants may join.[48]

Livingston's essays constituted the first sustained argument against the English policy of toleration. Toleration, he reasoned, was unworkable and unfeasible. The process of moving away from the Reformation triad of established church, state, and college should not stop halfway by assigning ownership or governance of a college to one particular church or denomination and requiring that group to "tolerate" the presence and religious rights of other Protestants. Foreshadowing arguments that would be voiced in New York in the 1840s, Livingston asserted that there could be no such thing as nondenominational or nonsectarian religious instruction. In short, neither government by a religious group nor religious instruction was a possible alternative in a college intended to serve the interests of a religiously and ethnically heterogeneous society. Only a secular college with no official religious ties would do.

The counterpart to the *Reflector*—at least in the eyes of New York Anglicans—was *A General Idea of the College of Mirania*, a small volume by William Smith, a recent immigrant from Scotland who later became provost of the College of Philadelphia. Smith agreed with Livingston that the diversity of

New York's population called for public institutions to counteract splintering tendencies. He wrote: "Nothing could so much contribute to make such a mixture of people coalesce and unite in one common interest as the common education of all the youth at the same public schools under the eye of the civil authority." The government should suppress private schools and see to it "that youth, who are the property of the state . . ., be educated according to the intention of the state." But unlike Livingston, Smith assigned part of this educational task to the established church. The Anglicans, as well as the president, he thought, might well furnish the ritual and order of religious services in the college, although the president should not also serve as parish minister.[49] Smith and other Anglicans like Samuel Seabury and Samuel Johnson thought that Livingston's notion of equal toleration of all churches was preposterous. As Seabury put it, it was impossible to agree on "a scheme of public worship for our college which shall not be liable to all the confusions in the building of Babel." Only the Church of England, he declared, was disinterested enough to furnish an acceptable kind of worship.[50] Smith protested against "unbridled liberty of conscience" and proclaimed the impossibility of governing a college once the incentive of preferment or the threat of disestablishment was removed.[51]

Thus, at the heart of the issue between Livingston and Smith were their differing interpretations of the policy of toleration. Their dispute centered on whether it was possible to have nondenominational worship and religious instruction in an institution intended to serve all members of the population. For Smith there could be no such thing as equal toleration; toleration had to be wedded to preferment. For Livingston, to whom preferment was anathema, equal toleration could be achieved and guaranteed only under secular, public auspices. In 1754, Smith's Anglican point of view prevailed. King's College obtained a royal charter which provided for an Anglican president and for worship services according to the prayer book of the Church of England.[52]

In Philadelphia, still another interpretation of the toleration policy spawned a third variant of a provincial college. The College of Philadelphia almost entirely a product of secular initiatives and interests, was the middle-colony college that was least dependent on ecclesiastical support. While it performed the functions of a provincial college, it remained a municipal institution devoted to the prosperity of Philadelphia. In 1749, a group of prominent Philadelphians had sponsored a subscription campaign for a "public academy in the City of Philadelphia."[53] The twenty-four largest subscribers functioned as trustees. Eight were wealthy merchants, four were well-known physicians, and many of the others—among them Benjamin Franklin—were active in the political life of the city and the colony. Like the trustees of such English grammar schools as St. Paul's and Merchant Taylors, they were laypersons who served as stewards of a public trust. They insisted that, with regard to the admission of students, considerations of "sect or party" be excluded. George Whitfield, the famed English revitalist of the Great Awakening, sensed correctly that the trustees had not contemplated placing the doctrines of Christianity at the school's center. He complained to Franklin that "there wants *aliquid Christi* in it, to make it so useful as I would desire it might be."[54] To be sure, the majority of the trustees were Anglicans and parishioners of Philadelphia's Christ Church, and Franklin preferred Anglicans to Presbyterians precisely because he did not cherish the latter's "narrow" and strife-ridden denomination. As trustees, however, these men acted as laypersons and prominent citizens, not as representatives of a religious denomination or church. Their concern was public and secular, not private or ecclesiastical.[55]

Despite these secular credentials, the College of Philadelphia could not quite avoid being drawn into denominational controversies. The school was incorporated as a college in 1755 with a charter drawn up by William Smith and Francis Alison. The former was made the college provost and the latter vice provost and rector of the academy. The alliance of Anglican priest and Old Side Presbyterian minister was meant to underscore the nondenominational character of the college and, at the same time, to distinguish the school from the New Light College of New Jersey. But Smith was rarely reluctant to engage in denominational infighting, and in 1756 he happily confided to an Anglican correspondent in England that "the Church, by soft and easy means, daily gains ground in [the college]."[56] So much did denominational jealousies enter the picture that in 1764 the Archbishop of Canterbury, the proprietors of the colony, and a representative of English dissenters presented recommendations to the trustees for "some fundamental rule or declaration to prevent inconveniences."[57] The trustees promptly adopted the recommendation from England as their own official policy declaration. It is hard to determine whether they did so out of genuine commitment to interdenominational cooperation, or in obedience to English policy, or simply in hopes of avoiding the kind of deadlock that had bedeviled the college founders in New York. It is clear, in any case, that the Philadelphia trustees sought to give little cause for religious resentment. They were happy that they had initially avoided a clear-cut identification of the college with a particular church, and they were not eager to invite difficulties over religious questions.

The difficulties that beset the Philadelphia trustees were mainly political. They derived chiefly from the constant threat of Indian warfare at the province's frontiers, from the resulting feud between the Quaker-dominated assembly and the proprietors' allies, and from the corresponding clashes in their own organization over the provost's activities. In 1756, Smith was accused of having violated the trust of his office by partisan indoctrination of his students, but both trustees and students absolved him of the charge. The students testified that he had never introduced "any thing relating to the parties now subsisting in this province, or tending to persuade us to adopt the principles of one side more than another."[58] When, two years later, the assembly found the provost in contempt and had him jailed, the trustees again came to his support and authorized him to teach his classes in jail. At the end of the year, they gave him permission to go to England, where he successfully presented his case before the crown.[59]

Late in 1758, attacks came from a different direction. Pennsylvanicus, an anonymous writer in the *Pennsylvania Journal*, attacked Smith for writing political pamphlets and also censured the trustees, ministers, and magistrates of Philadelphia for having permitted a lottery for the college. Faculty members wanted to reply in the press, but the trustees vetoed that proposal. It was undignified, they argued, to respond to "low creatures who wrote from passion and resentment."[60] Pennsylvanicus, however, returned to the attack, condemned the college charter as "narrow" and "confined," criticized the trustees for being mesmerized by unlimited power, and, in a manner reminiscent of the New York *Reflector* five years earlier, called for a new charter "more safe and generous" than the old.[61] Just as the emotions unleashed by the Awakening had rocked the colleges of other colonies in preceding decades, the passions of political warfare came to engulf the College of Philadelphia. As the 1760s approached, religious disputes gave way to political ones.

Polarization and Secularization

The culmination of the religious and political controversies over colonial college governance occurred in the 1760s. In New York, Connecticut, and Virginia these confrontations reached crisis proportions. They led to resolutions which, with local variations, emphasized the secular nature of the colleges and the role played by provincial governments. But these confrontations also led to the founding of a new type of college: one entirely under private or ecclesiastic sponsorship, without any involvement of civil authorities other than through the act of incorporation.

In New York, the Anglican victory at King's College had sown the seeds for the first denominational college. This development had begun in October 1754, when the Dutch Reformed Church of New York petitioned the assembly for a professorship of divinity at King's College. The Dutch argued that they constituted "the greatest number of any single denomination of Christians in this province."[62] In May of the next year, Domine John Ritzema, prominent leader of the conservative wing of the Dutch church and a member of the board of governors of King's College, single-handedly moved the college board to apply to New York's governor for an additional charter containing the professorship. This charter was granted. But Ritzema's consistory repudiated it, charging that it had been "prepared incontestably without our knowledge, advice, or counsel" and did not answer "to our conception of what would be advantageous for the upbuilding of our church."[63]

Ritzema correctly felt that his opposition came from members of his church who sought a college of their own in the middle colonies. The main power behind this move was Theodore Frelinghuysen who, in attacking Ritzema, had expressed his amazement at "the astonishing imposition of the encroaching party [the Anglicans] that would monopolize our intended college" and at "our own infatuation, stupidity, and lethargy" in allowing Ritzema's project to proceed unhindered. Frelinghuysen did not believe in uniting with other denominations or churches in college efforts. He concluded: "We have no business with their colleges; they may erect as many as they please, and must expect to maintain them too, themselves. Let every one provide for his own house."[64]

Frelinghuysen's appeal in 1756 expressed a growing number of Americans' disenchantment with the task of coping with diversity. The game, Frelinghuysen seemed to say, was not worth the candle. Perhaps the Dutch in New York could afford such sentiments since they had the numbers to build their own house; perhaps, also, Frelinghuysen was simply tired of the bickering and impatient with the slow process of seeking cooperation. No matter how approached or understood, the English policy of toleration was difficult to implement in the pluralistic society of the colonies.

Frelinghuysen's suggestion bore fruit ten years later when Queen's College, later to be known as Rutgers, was founded in New Jersey to serve the Dutch Reformed churches of the middle colonies. Breaking the tradition of a provincial college monopoly, this new collegiate model marked the transition from the provincial colleges of the seventeenth and eighteenth centuries to the private institutions of the nineteenth.

The establishment of the chair of divinity for the Dutch Reformed at King's College and the subsequent founding of Queen's College constituted one kind of collegiate model arising out of the New York struggle over toleration. Livingston's project for a public college in New York foreshadowed the emergence of a second model. Livingston's proposal, officially introduced in a bill in the New York Assembly, called for a college run entirely by the government.[65] The college's trustees would need the consent of the governor, council, and assembly for any grant or sale of college property and for the appointment of college officers. They would be required to submit to the three branches of the provincial government their annual financial reports, bylaws, plan of instruction, and their plans for providing nondenominational worship services. The assembly also reserved the right to fix the location of the college and declared that new appointments to the twenty-four-member trustee board should be made by the legislature. During recess of the assembly, a majority of the trustees might temporarily appoint a president or treasurer of the college, but such a decision would have to be confirmed by the legislature at its next session. As one might expect, the bill expressly prohibited any religious tests or discrimination against Protestants. There was to be no public instruction in divinity, but both the Anglican and the Dutch Reformed churches of New York could elect professors of divinity who might privately instruct those students who so desired. Students and officers could sue the trustees, the president, and other officers of the college "in any court of law within this colony."[66]

With this bill, Livingston mounted the most radical challenge to established forms of college governance yet devised in the colonies. He brushed aside both English notions of collegiate autonomy and the Reformation concept of joint church-state-college establishment as well as the modifications of the latter in New Jersey and at King's College. By allowing appeals to civil courts he would emancipate both students and officers from their total submission to college authority, contrary to Clap's policy at Yale. Had his college seen the light of day, it would have been the first genuine state college in the American colonies. But the time was not yet ripe. However, when New York's state university was created after the Revolution in 1784, its roots led back to Livingston's bill of 1754. Together with the Queen's College charter of 1766, the 1754 bill marked the outer limits of the now polarized field into which the provincial colleges of the eighteenth century had moved.

It was in Connecticut during the 1760s that the most dramatic confrontations over the issue of college governance took place. When Clap terminated Yale's relationship to the First Church of New Haven, ordered the sons of Anglicans not to attend nearby services, and established the college church, he fueled the suspicions and ill will of the Connecticut Assembly. In 1755, the assembly refused to make the annual £100 grant to the college. One of its members, Dr. Benjamin Gale, physician and deputy from Killingworth, vigorously rejected Clap's statement that Yale had been founded "principally by the ministers." He accused the president of falsely claiming that the assembly had been "neither the founder nor visitor of that house," and he disputed the legal status of the college as a corporation. He also rejected Clap's contention, derived from canon law, that Yale College was an ecclesiastical corporation. Gale and the legislators insisted on the college's accountability to the public. In striking similarity to Livingston's arguments in New York and to the views of the antiproprietary party in Philadelphia, he also asserted the legislature's rights of oversight and visitation.[67]

By 1761, disciplinary action against some students brought forth a written protest in which Connecticut citizens urged the legislature "to turn your eyes upon the society you have founded, fed, and nourished, and for the honor of what is good, great, and noble, subject it to such like visitation as other collegiate schools in this land or devise some method of redress."[68] Again the college escaped such action; the General Court "resolved in the negative." But matters went from bad to worse. By November 1762, student rebellion engulfed the college; the corporation fought back by expelling some students and placing others on probation. In the following spring, more protest memorials reached the assembly. They spoke of the college's "deplorable state" of "notorious" facts, of the uneasiness of students and parents, and of "the resentments and prejudices the youth generally bring from thence." They charged that the college law forbidding students and faculty to sue the college in civil court violated "the natural rights of Englishmen." The college, they wrote, was "an *imperium in imperio,* as shall be rather dangerous than serviceable to the community." Their numerous and specific complaints all led to one chief demand: the legislature must appoint a commission of visitation.[69] Such action would force an answer to one key question: To what extent was a college a law unto itself, and to what degree must the college be governed by the wider body politic which had authorized and supported it?

The confrontation over the issue of college autonomy took place on Sunday, May 15, 1763. Before the General Court, Clap answered the charges against this rule and concentrated on two chief items among his accusers' demands: visitation by the General Court, and students' right to appeal the corporation's disciplinary rulings to the governor and council. In a brilliant disquisition, filled with learned references to English law, Clap maintained that though the assembly held a general supervisory authority over all institutions of the province, it did not have the right of visitation over the college. He based his conclusion on a contention—doubtful, to be sure, but not contradicted in 1763—that the ministers had founded the college before it had been chartered by the General Court.[70] On the question of appeal, Clap remained equally adamant. An appeal to authorities outside the college "would occasion a great dely in government and mispence of time." The same disadvantages of "a great expense of time and money and . . . many mischiefs and confusions" would result, Clap held, if students were allowed to sue each other or the college officers.[71] On no point, in fact, did Clap budge.

Clap's intransigence was not simply a show of strength or the result of confidence in his considerable legal knowledge. He saw correctly that visitation and appeal were issues inextricably linked to each other and that the question of appeal could be used to put the General Court on the defensive. If the court decided on visitation or permitted students to appeal Clap's disciplinary judgments, Clap warned the legislators, the college might file a complaint with authorities in London. Do not encourage the students to appeal from my jurisdiction to the governor and council, Clap seemed to be saying, lest you suggest that I appeal the colony's court decision to king and parliament. Order a visitation of the college by the assembly and you open the door to visitors from England appearing in Connecticut "with full power in themselves to redress everything in our laws or courts which they might esteem to be abuses."[72] The risk of royal interference in Connecticut affairs might have been minor in 1763, but it was nonetheless a risk, and Clap craftily and successfully made the most of it. On May 15, 1763, the General court conceded defeat. In his 1766 *Annals or History of Yale College,* Clap allowed himself the luxury of reporting his own triumph:

> When the arguments were considered by the Honorable the Great Assembly but very few appeared to be of the opinion that the Assembly were the founders of the College, and so they acted nothing upon the memorial, [sic] And it is generally supposed that the question never will be publicly moved again.[73]

Clap was wrong in his guess for the future, but in 1763 he was the man of the hour and the victory was his.

In the light of Yale's subsequent history, however, the confrontation of 1763 was at best a winning battle at the turning point in a war that was about to be lost. As other historians have pointed out, the students accomplished what the legislature had failed to do; a few years later they brought down Clap's administration in utter ruin.[74] But more was involved in their battle than student high jinks or adolescent rebellion against an obstinate old man. Behind the students stood their parents and the other people of Connecticut. Gale and the memorialists had expressed sentiments that enjoyed wide currency beyond the immediate vicinity of the college or even the colony. When they had criticized Clap's rule against student access to the courts and objected to paying for new college buildings, they had referred to the natural rights of Englishmen and spoken of taxation without representation. Demanding visitation by the assembly, they had echoed Livingston's call in New York for a public college under the direction of the legislature and Pennsylvanicus's quest for a broader and more generous charter for the College of Philadelphia. They had clearly indicated their belief that the Fellows' assumed rights to self-visitation were anachronistic. Clap's manner and policies did nothing to help dispel the aura of autocracy surrounding him, and it is therefore difficult to agree with those who have argued that his defiance of the memoralists constituted a victory for academic freedom.[75] On the contrary, Clap's defiance was a victory for the concepts of a college as a sectarian seminary and of college governance as paternal absolutism.

Neither of Clap's concepts blended well with the prevailing temper of 1763, and it was but a matter of a few years until his world came to grief.[76] In February 1766, students accused Clap of being in his dotage and showing arbitrariness and partiality. They demanded his ouster. When the corporation failed to act on their petition, they tore up college buildings, burned furniture, threatened the tutors with bodily harm and drove them out of the college. In July, Clap offered his resignation. This the corporation accepted, effective at commencement in September. With the college nearly in ruins, the Clap regime had come to its end.

Now matters changed quickly. The members of the assembly asserted their oversight. In October they ordered the corporation to submit its accounts annually before the General Court if it expected to receive any funds from them.[77] Benjamin Gale and his friends had won after all. In a letter to Ezra Stiles, then a minister in Newport, Gale wrote proudly of "our gentle visitation of Yale College, in which we touch'd them so gently that till some time after the assembly, they never saw they were taken in, that we had made ourselves visitors, and subjected them to an annual visitation."[78] Gale could feel satisfied. Everything Clap had resisted, with the sole exception of the students' right of appeal to the General Court, had now been accepted. Most of the vestiges of Clap's autocratic reign had been overcome, Clap's myth of Yale as a religious seminary had been laid to rest, and the school was acknowledged again as Connecticut's provinical college.

In Virginia, too, the secular-versus-ecclesiastical controversy over college governance ended with the triumph of a secular model. The College of William and Mary, like the colleges of Oxford and Cambridge, was legally a corporation composed of the president and masters who were faculty members. Unlike its sister institutions in Massachusetts, Connecticut, New Jersey, New York, and Pennsylvania, it had a board of external governors—called the visitors—that was unincorporated. The board of visitors, however, not the corporation, dominated college governance. This arrangement made a struggle between corporation and visitors unavoidable.[79] The struggle, which began in the 1750s, pitted the Oxford-educated clergymen of the corporation against the representatives of the Virginia gentry who constituted the visitors. It demonstrated once more that a body of clergymen standing on prerogative and corporate rights could not prevail against lay representatives demanding that the college serve the interests of a secular society.

On September 14, 1763, the visitors issued a statute granting themselves the right, by majority vote, to discharge the president and masters and exercise direct and final authority over the internal management of the college. The statute also prohibited faculty members from taking parish assignments while holding office in the college, required their residence at college, and ordered the president and masters to take an oath pledging support of the statute.[80] There can be little doubt that these requirements constituted a severe infringement on the charter rights of the masters. The new statute placed tenure rights of the members of the corporate body at the mercy of an outside board, and it abrogated the members' basic right to administer their own affairs. If the visitors claimed that they asked for no rights other than those enjoyed by the governing boards of other colonial colleges, they ignored the fact that these other boards were themselves the college corporations; in Virginia, the faculty was the legally incorporated body. The Virginia dispute had all the earmarks of a constitutional confrontation.

The first round came in 1764, when the visitors cited their new statute and asked Professor Camm, a faculty member at William and Mary, to choose between his professorship and his parish. Refusing to respond to the question, Camm argued that he was confronted with a charge and demanded the right to submit a written defense. After considerable hesitation, the visitors agreed, and Camm severely condemned their statute, chided President Horrocks for having taken an oath on it, and announced that he would appeal the whole affair to the crown. As in Connecticut, this threat was effective; the visitors dropped their demands.[81] Later, on May 1, 1766, they agreed to amend the statute. The day-to-day administration of the college was left to the faculty under the supervision of visitors. Nothing was said about the visitors' power of dismissal, and the prohibition of parish employment was determined not retroactively applicable. Camm could keep both his parish and his professorship. Some observers agreed with Governor Fauquier, who complained that the visitors had allowed "Mr. Camm [to] lead them by the nose."[82] The requirement of an oath on the statute, however, and the prohibition of future outside employment remained. The visitors held fast to their claim to supervision over internal college affairs and, by continuing to demand the oath, upheld the principle of their action.

The 1766 amendment accommodated Professor Camm and tried to protect the visitors' claim to their rights of governance, but it did not resolve any of the key issues raised by the statute of 1763. So the struggle continued fruitlessly, its very lack of resolution underscoring the importance of the masters and the *de facto* power of the visitors. In 1768, the faculty petitioned for a change in the college's charter in order to clarify the roles of professors and visitors.[83] The petition met with silence on the key issue of power to govern and discipline. Concerning their request to administer charitable scholarships, the petitioners were insulted by the response that such an administrative arrangement would be "impiety to the dead and injustice to the living.[84] Instead they were offered a crumb they had not asked for—free hot suppers in the college. President Horrocks reported to the masters that the visitors had asserted their full control over the appointment of officers and servants and on the issue of parish appointments by faculty members. The masters were understandably upset. They appealed to Bishop Terrick of London, the College Chancellor:

> It seems impossible for us . . . to make any other conclusion but that the visitors mean to keep the grand points of power, on which the practical utility of a college must turn, unsettled and in confusion, and to leave us without the authority which is necessary for obtaining the discipline and regularity which the visitors are desirous should be enforced. . . .[85]

They concluded that they saw no solution other than to petition the crown for a new charter or to appeal to the king as the supreme visitor of the college.[86]

Here, as in Connecticut, an appeal to London was the last ace the college party could play, but after the Stamp Act crisis even that card began to lose its value. Issues of home rule versus the prerogatives of the crown and established church were becoming less threatening. Excited by the tremors of the approaching Revolution, Virginians were ill-disposed to listen to the faculty's complaints. The visitors saw no reason to desist from their attempts to place tighter reins on the faculty. They rebuked masters for having married and moved off campus, and they interfered with student discipline and curriculum. They proposed abolishing the requirement for classical studies and wanted to permit students to take mathematics without prior work in the classics.[87] Such a plan, the masters protested, would depart from the program "hitherto approved of in the most famous universities" and would do "abundantly more injury than benefit to the public."[88] But there was little the masters could do to retain the powers due them under their college charter; the Virginia visitors were in control. These members of the colony's gentry had little patience with Oxford-educated Anglican clergymen. They wanted William and Mary to function as their provincial college, intended for the education of their young men who were to become useful citizens and professionals of a society ready to break its ties to the mother country.[89]

There can be little doubt that the political agitation of the American Revolution in the late 1760s and 1770s helped to clarify and sharpen the issues of college governance. There should also be no question that the colonies' changing social structure and increasing ethnic and religious heterogeneity were fundamental factors which had already begun to transform the Reformation pattern of college governance. College governors modified the assumptions they had inherited from the Reformation in order to accommodate young men of diverse Protestant denominations without discrimination or infringement upon religious liberties. Under the new policies of equal toleration and preferment, legislators and the public held on to the Reformation view of the college as a civil institution for the training of a province's leadership. In the colonies, where clergymen of all Protestant denominations were included among the professional elite, this view implied that no one church or denomination should claim exclusive privileges.

In Massachusetts, Connecticut, New Jersey, New York, Pennsylvania, and Virginia, each college reacted differently to its particular situation in meeting the demands of a heterogenous population. In Virginia and Connecticut, those who protested against policies of toleration in the name of academic autonomy were locked in losing battles with their legislatures. In New York and New Jersey, those who rebelled against domination by their orthodox brethren broke with the established tradition of one province, one college. Their actions laid the foundation for a nineteenth-century model of the private or church-related college.

Thus, the middle decades of the eighteenth century proved to be critical years in the shaping of colleges. The second half of the eighteenth century saw the gradual emasculation of governing schemes based on the idea of toleration. A polarization of denominational and secular concerns in the 1780s gave rise to public colleges and universities which, in turn, provoked the proliferation of private or church-related colleges in the nineteenth century. That, however, takes us far beyond the confines of the eighteenth century and is, as the phrase has it, another story altogether.

Notes

1. Jurgen Herbst, "The First Three American Colleges: Schools of the Reformation," *Perspectives in American History*, 8 (1974), 7–52.
2. Jurgen Herbst, "The Eighteenth-Century Origins of the Split between Private and Public Higher Education in the United States," *History of Education Quarterly*, 15 (1975), 273–280.
3. On the Great Awakening and its impact on education, see Lawrence A. Cremin, *American Education: The Colonial Experience, 1607–1783* (New York: Harper & Row, 1970), ch. 10; Douglas Sloan," ed., *The Great Awakening and American Education: A Documentary History* (New York: Teachers College Press, 1973); William W. Sweet, *Revivalism in America: Its Origin, Growth, and Decline* (New York: Charles Scribner's Sons, 1944); and Alan Heimert and Perry Miller, eds., *The Great Awakening: Documents Illustrating the Crisis and Its Consequences* (Indianapolis, Ind.: Bobbs-Merrill, 1967).
4. "Order in Council," rpt. in *Circular of Information*, No. 2 (Washington, D.C.: U.S. Bureau of Education, 1893), pp. 77–78.
5. On Harvard College during this period, see Samuel Eliot Morison, *Three Centuries of Harvard, 1636–1936* (Cambridge, Mass.: Harvard Univ. Press, 1936), pp. 53–100; and John Maynard Hoffmann, "Commonwealth College: The Governance of Harvard in the Puritan Period," Diss. Harvard Univ. 1972.
6. Quotations from 1745 charter of Yale in Edward C. Elliott and M. M. Chambers, eds., *Charters and Basic Laws of Selected American Universities and Colleges* (New York: Carnegie Foundation, 1934), p. 592.
7. For the 1701 and 1745 charters of Yale, see Franklin B. Dexter, ed., *Documentary History of Yale University* (New Haven, Conn.: Yale Univ. Press, 1916), pp. 20–23; and Elliott and Chambers, pp. 588–93. For Yale's early history, see Richard Warch, *School of the Prophets: Yale College, 1701–1740* (New Haven, Conn.: Yale Univ. Press, 1973), p. 310.
8. Franklin B. Dexter, ed., *Biographical Sketches of the Graduates of Yale College with Annals of the College History* (New York: H. Holt and Company, 1885), I, 663.
9. The committee report of 1742 may be found in Dexter, *Documentary History*, p. 356. For narratives of the events in Connecticut, New Haven, and the college, see Benjamin Trumbull, *A Complete History of Connecticut* (New Haven, Conn.: Mastby, Goldsmith and Co., 1818), II, 160–175; Brooks M. Kelley, *Yale: A History* (New Haven, Conn.: Yale Univ. Press, 1974), pp. 49–72; and Louis L. Tucker, *Puritan Protagonist: President Thomas Clap of Yale College* (Chapel Hill, N.C.: Univ. of North Carolina Press, 1962), pp. 123–141.
10. Rpt. in Stephen Nissenbaum, ed., *The Great Awakening at Yale College* (Belmont, Calif.: Wadsworth, 1972), pp. 136–139.
11. Nissenbaum, p. 239.

12. Nissenbaum, p. 231.

13. Nissenbaum, p. 240.

14. Nissenbaum, p. 222.

15. The Cleaveland affair is described and documented in Nissenbaum, pp. 219–250; Trumbull, II, 182–83; Richard Hofstadter and Wilson Smith, eds., *American Higher Education* (Chicago: Univ. of Chicago Press, 1961), I, 74–82; and Dexter, *Documentary History,* pp. 370–372.

16. See Richard Hofstadter, *Academic Freedom in the Age of the College* (New York: Columbia Univ. Press, 1961), pp. 134–144.

17. Clap's account of the drafting of the charter and laws is contained in his "Annals of Yale College in New Haven," 1747 ms. in the Yale Archives; the Harvard charter of 1650 is reprinted in Samuel Eliot Morison, *Harvard College in the Seventeenth Century* (Cambridge, Mass.: Harvard Univ. Press, 1936), part 1, pp. 5–8; and the charter of the College of William and Mary is represented in Edgar W. Knight, ed., *Documentary History of Education in the South before 1860* (Chapel Hill, N.C.: Univ. of North Carolina Press, 1949), I, 400–439.

18. On the defection of Cutler and Johnson, see Warch, pp. 96–117; on the tutor rebellion at Harvard, see Morison, *Three Centuries,* pp. 69–74.

19. The laws are printed in Dexter, *Biographical Sketches,* II, 2–18.

20. Clap, p. 48.

21. Tucker, pp. 166–83.

22. Herbert Schneider and Carol Schneider, eds., *Samuel Johnson, President of King's College: His Career and Writings* (New York: Columbia Univ. Press, 1929), I, 178.

23. Schneider and Schneider, I, 178.

24. Schneider and Schneider, I, 178–82.

25. Schneider and Schneider, I, 175.

26. Thomas Clap, *The Religious Constitution of Colleges* (New London, Conn.: T. Green, 1754), pp. 1–4.

27. Schneider and Schneider, I, 190–91.

28. Clap, *Religious Constitutions,* p. 4.

29. Ralph Henry Gabriel, *Religion and Learning at Yale* (New Haven, Conn.: Yale Univ. Press, 1958), pp. 3–6.

30. See Kelley, p. 66; Tucker, p. 192.

31. Tucker, p. 190.

32. Tucker, p. 199.

33. For the College of New Jersey, consult Thomas J. Wertenbaker, *Princeton, 1746–1896* (Princeton, N.J.: Princeton Univ. Press, 1946), pp. 3–46; and G. Howard Miller, "A Contracting Community," Diss. Univ. of Michigan 1970, I, 2–195. The history of King's College is best presented in David C. Humphrey, "King's College in the City of New York, 1754–1776," Diss. Northwestern Univ. 1968, pp. 2–244; a brief summary may be found in John H. Van Amringe, "King's College and Columbia College," in *A History of Columbia University, 1754–1904* (New York: Columbia Univ. Press, 1904), pp. 1–41. The most recent history of the College of Philadelphia is Ann Gordon, "The College of Philadelphia, 1749–1779: The Impact of an Institution," Diss. Univ. of Wisconsin 1975; see also Edward P. Cheyney, *History of the University of Pennsylvania 1740–1940* (Philadelphia: Univ. of Pennsylvania Press, 1940).

34. Both the 1746 and the 1748 charters of the College of New Jersey are reprinted in Wertenbaker, pp. 396–404.

35. Samuel Johnson, "Advertisement," in *Charters, Acts of the Legislature, Official Documents and Records,* ed. John B. Pine, rev. and enl. ed. (New York: 1920), pp. 32–35.

36. Neda M. Westlake, ed., *Minutes of the Trustees of the College, Academy and Charitable Schools, University of Pennsylvania, Vol. 1, 1749 to 1768* (Wilmington, Del.: Scholarly Resources, 1974), p. 262.

37. The situation among middle-colony Presbyterians is described in Archibald Alexander, *Biographical Sketches of the Founder and Principal Alumni of the Log College* (Princeton, N.J.: J. T. Robinson, 1845); Leonard J. Trinterud, *The Forming of an American Tradition* (Philadelphia: Westminster Press, 1949), pp. 53–108; Elijah R. Craven, "The Log College of Neshaminy and Princeton University," *Journal of the Presbyterian Historical Society,* 1 (1902), 308–14; and Douglas Sloan, *The Scottish Enlightenment and the American College Ideal* (New York: Teachers College Press, 1971), pp. 36–102.

38. Quoted in Wertenbaker, pp. 19–20.

39. Wertenbaker, p. 20.

40. Wertenbaker, p. 21.

41. Wertenbaker, pp. 23–27; John Maclean, *History of the College of New Jersey, 1746–1854* (1877; rpt. New York: Arno Press, 1969), I, 70–113; see also Jonathan Edward's account of the charter negotiations in *The Works of President Edwards* (New York: G. & G. & H. Carvill, 1830), I, 266–68, 275.

42. Wertenbaker, pp. 30–35; Maclean, I, 147–54; see also Alison B. Olson, "The Founding of Princeton University: Religion and Politics in Eighteenth-Century New Jersey," *New Jersey History*, 87 (1969), 133–150.
43. Hippocrates Mithridates, Apoth. (pseud. for William Livingston), *Some Serious Thoughts on the Design of Erecting a College in the Province of New York* (New York: J. Zenger, 1749), pp. 1–7.
44. Schneider and Schneider, I, 135.
45. *New York Evening Post*, 18 May 1747, n. pag.
46. Commissioners of Statutory Revision, eds., *Colonial Laws of New York from the Year 1664 to the Revolution* (Albany, N.Y.: James B. Lyon, State Printer, 1894), HI, 607–616, 679–688, 731–732, and 842–844.
47. See Milton M. Klein, ed., *The Independent Reflector* (Cambridge, Mass.: Harvard Univ. Press, 1963).
48. Klein, pp. 36–37.
49. William Smith, *A General Idea of the College of Mirania*, ed. Edward M. Griffin (1753; rpt. New York: Johnson Reprint Corp., 1969), pp. 10, 66–67, 71, 75.
50. *New York Mercury*, 30 April 1753, n. pag.
51. Leonard W. Labaree, ed., *The Papers of Benjamin Franklin* (New Haven, Conn.: Yale Univ. Press, 1962). IV, 467–70, 475; Klein, pp. 201–203.
52. Hugh Hastings, ed., *Ecclesiastical Records: State of New York* (Albany: J. B. Lyon, 1905), V, 3508–3514; Schneider and Schneider, IV, 24–25.
53. See Cheyney, p. 30.
54. Labaree, III, 467.
55. See Cheyney, pp. 17–40; Labaree, III, 385–88, 397–429, 462, 467; and Westlake, I, 2–5.
56. Horace W. Smith, ed., *Life and Correspondence of the Rev. William Smith* (Philadelphia: Ferguson Brothers, 1879), I, 143.
57. Westlake, I, 260.
58. Horace W. Smith, ed., *Life and Correspondence of the Rev. William Smith* (1870; rpt. New York: Arno Press, 1972), I, 126.
59. Bruce R. Lively, "William Smith, the College and Academy of Philadelphia, and Pennsylvania Politics, 1753–1758," *Historical Magazine of the Protestant Episcopal Church*, 38 (1969), 237–58; Westlake, I, 68, 70–72, 91, 97, 99; and Labaree, VII, 12, and VIII, 416.
60. Westlake, I, 99.
61. *Pennsylvania Journal and Weekly Adviser*, 28 Sept. and 30 Nov., 1758; 25 Jan., 8 Feb., 1 March, and 15 March, 1779.
62. Hastings, V, 3505.
63. Hastings, V. 3576.
64. Frelinghuysen's statement was published under the pseudonym David Marin Ben Jesse, *A Remark on the Disputes and Contentions in this Province* (New York: Hugh Gaine, 1755), pp. 6, 11–12. Consult also Hastings, V, 3501, 3542–45, 3554–56, 3574–77, 3605, 3611–13; Nelson R. Burr, *Education in New Jersey 1630–1871* (Princeton, N.J.: Princeton Univ. Press), pp. 19–21; William H. S. Demarest, *A History of Rutgers College, 1766–1924* (New Brunswick, N. J.: Rutgers, 1924), pp. 25–50; Richard P. McCormick, *Rutgers: A Bicentennial History* (New Brunswick, N.J.: Rutgers Univ. Press, 1966), pp. 1–8; and Pine, pp. 26–27.
65. *Journal of the Votes and Proceedings of the General Assembly of the Colony of New York*, published by order of the General Assembly (New York: Hugh Gaine, printer, 1766), II, 412–419.
66. *Journal of the Votes; Colonial Laws*, III, 1927; and Hastings, V, 3525–3526.
67. See Dexter, *Biographical Sketches*, II, 357; Thomas Clap, *A Brief History* (New Haven, Conn.: James Parker, 1755), p. 9; and Benjamin Gale, *The President State of the Colony of Connecticut Considered* (New London, Conn.: T. Green, 1755), pp. 7, 9–11.
68. Thomas Fuller, Moses Bartlett, and Thomas Skinner, "Letter to the Assembly, 6 Oct., 1761," ms. in Yale Univ. Archives.
69. Ebenezer Devotion, Stephen White, James Cogswell, Josiah Whitney, and Benjamin Throop, "Memorial of April, 1763," ms. in Yale Univ. Archives and in *Connecticut Archives*, pp. 67a–b; and Edward Dorr, Jedediah Elderkin, Eleazer Fitch, Hezakiah Bissell, Jonathan Marsh, Josiah Talcott, Ebenezer Grant, Daniel Sheldon, and Titus Horsmer, "Memorial of March 10, 1763," ms. in Yale Univ. Archives and in *Connecticut Archives, Colleges and Schools*, 1st ser., II, 66a–h.
70. The story of the May 15 meeting is told by Clap himself in his "Annals of Yale College in New Haven," 1766 ms. in Yale Univ. Archives, also printed as *The Annals or History of Yale College* (New Haven, Conn.: John Hotchkiss and B. Mecom, 1766). See also Trumbull, II, 327–33; Dexter, ii, 780–781; *Connecticut Archives*, p. 67b; and, for greatest detail, Tucker, pp. 224–231.
71. "Answer of President and Fellows," Connecticut Archives, pp. 71g, 71h, 71s.

72. "Answer of President and Fellows," *Connecticut Archives,* pp. 71t, 71u.

73. Clap, *Annals* (1766), pp. 76–77.

74. Tucker, pp. 232–70.

75. See Dexter, *Biographical Sketches,* II, 790–791; and compare with Hofstadter, pp. 175–176; and Gabriel, p. 29.

76. See Trumbull, II, 333.

77. Tucker, p. 257; see also Charles J. Hoadley, ed., *The Public Records of the Colony of Connecticut from May 1762 to October 1767* (Hartford, Conn.: Case, Lockwood and Brainard, 1881), pp. 513–514.

78. Franklin B. Dexter, ed., *Itineraries of Ezra Stiles* (New Haven, Conn.: Yale Univ. Press, 1916), p. 492.

79. Knight, I, 400–439.

80. William S. Perry, ed., *Virginia,* Vol. I of *Historical Collections Relating to the American Colonial Church* (New York: AMS Press, 1869), p. 518; William W. Manross, ed., *The Fulham Pavers in the Lambeth Library: American Colonial Section—Calendar and Indexes* (Oxford: Clarendon Press, 1965). The paper described by Manross are in the Lambeth Palace Library, American Colonial Section.

81. Perry, p. 523; Manross, XIV, 95–102.

82. Manross, XIV, 91–92.

83. "Journal," *William and Mary Quarterly,* 1st ser., 5 (1896–1897), 83–89.

84. "Journal," p. 226.

85. "Journal," p. 229.

86. See also Fulham Papers, XIV, 147–152, 155–160.

87. Manross, XIV, 161–196, 199–202; "Minutes of the Visitors," *William and Mary Quarterly,* 1st ser., 17 (1919), 239–240.

88. "Journal," *William and Mary Quarterly,* 1st ser., 13 (1904), 150–154.

89. For an excellent analysis of the situation at the College of William and Mary, see Robert P. Thomson, "The Reform of the College of William and Mary, 1763–1780," *Proceedings,* American Philosophical Society, 115 (1971).

The author gratefully acknowledges support received in preparation of this paper from the National Institute of Education. The opinions expressed do not necessarily reflect the position of the Institute, and no official endorsement by the Institute should be inferred.

THE HARVARD TUTORS: THE BEGINNING OF AN ACADEMIC PROFESSION, 1690–1825

JOHN D. BURTON

Richard Hofstadter identified Harvard's transition from the seventeenth to the eighteenth century as a paradox. According to Hofstadter, "the seeds of Harvard liberalism were actually planted within Puritanism itself, and they sprouted not long after the first generation of American Puritans had passed on to their rewards." Unfortunately, the study of the intellectual changes at Harvard has overshadowed the beginning of an important social transformation in the American professorate occurring at the same time. At Harvard, the tutors formed the primary teaching staff during the seventeenth and eighteenth centuries. Most historians, however, have dismissed the colonial tutors as a group of transient instructors with little commitment to teaching and date the rise of professional faculty to the 1750s. In fact, a pattern of increasing stability among the tutors began to appear at Harvard in the 1690s. The changes in the composition of the Harvard tutors was part of a larger series of trends in Anglo-American education that saw the separation of the teaching profession from that of the ministry.[1]

English universities had a tradition of faculty control. Tutors (or "fellows" as they were sometimes called) were usually permanent faculty responsible for both instruction and college governance. Professorships, which also existed within the English universities, were endowed positions, and were no more permanent than many tutorships or fellowships. At the beginning of the eighteenth century, New England society in general was undergoing a period of Anglicization, a process wherein colonial institutions were reformed to more closely replicate English norms. The changes in Harvard's governance structure and the position of its tutors were part of this larger process. The tutorship at Harvard was the only one to begin to replicate English models because only Harvard was old enough to have the financial resources, stability, and student body to support permanent faculty in the early eighteenth century. Yale, in comparison, had a stormy history during the early 1700s. Both its site and its faculty were transitory and resources to support even a full-time rector-president were often lacking. The Yale tutors were further discredited by the frequent student riots that occurred during vacancies in the rectorship when they were ostensibly in control. The Yale tutorship, therefore, never had the opportunity to begin to professionalize before other faculty models became the accepted norm in the American colonies.[2]

Colonial Harvard had two types of teachers. Professors, first appearing in the 1720s, taught in specific disciplines and lived off-campus. Tutors, active in the college since the 1640s, were responsible for teaching the entire basic curriculum, lived in the college, and supervised the students' curricular and extracurricular activities. The difference in instructional responsibilities was important; the distinction in living arrangements should not be overstressed, however. The 1734 college laws specified that "the professors shall constantly reside in Cambridge near the college." Before the American Revolution, Harvard professors lived in homes adjacent to the college grounds at the east end of the current Harvard Yard. Many of the professors took as boarders the overflow of Harvard students. Life in the professors' homes replicated life in the colleges in many respects. Both the professors and the tutors were expected to dine in commons. The chief distinction in the professors' living arrangements was their ability to marry (tutors were expected to remain single). Moreover, the Harvard tutors should not all be lumped into a single category. The seventeenth-century tutorship was very different from the eighteenth and reflects the increased professionalization of college teaching.[3]

Wilson Smith first noted the important transition the Harvard tutorship underwent from the seventeenth to the eighteenth century. Where most seventeenth-century tutors only remained at the college for less than three years, in the eighteenth century many of the tutors remained at Harvard for fifteen or more years. He cited the careers of a number of Harvard tutors, highlighting their activities at the college, their long-term dedication to teaching, and their long tenure at the college. He noted that most eighteenth-century tutors were not necessarily waiting for calls to the pulpit. Unlike the seventeenth-century tutors who virtually all went into the ministry, the eighteenth-century tutors sought a wider-range of careers. By the middle of the eighteenth century, more than a third of the tutors remained in education. Moreover, by the eighteenth century, the pay for tutors (all single men) was relatively good. Tutors were paid between £90 and £100 pounds in the mid-eighteenth century, less than many ministers, but unlike rural clergymen, the tutors knew they would receive their pay without resort to lengthy court action. In spite of these trends, however, Wilson concludes that "college teaching was clearly not a profession" in the mid-eighteenth century.[4]

Other historians of the eighteenth century have dismissed the tutorship altogether. William Carrell, in his study of eighteenth-century professors, places the rise of the professional academic in the later half of the eighteenth century. Carrell's study focuses exclusively on professors and college presidents. He dismisses the tutorship as a transient office, in spite of the increased longevity of the eighteenth-century Harvard tutors. Similarly, in comparing the tutors and professors, Martin Finkelstein points at "permanence" as the chief distinction between the two groups of academics. Professors remained in office longer, usually until death, and Finkelstein also placed the rise of the professionalization of the faculty with the beginning of the professoriate.[5]

Historians of higher education studying the rise of the academic profession have used a more narrow view of the professional idea. Using a more traditional view of professionalization as the rise of a middle-class or high-class occupation, Samuel Haber, for example, looked to the late nineteenth century as the formative period for the American professoriate. In looking for the colonial roots of professionalization, historians have focused on the establishment of faculty chairs in the mid-eighteenth century and ignored the existence of other types of faculty, specifically the tutors who carried out much of the teaching burden in colonial colleges. Much of the discussion of the academic profession in colonial America has been colored by the rise of research universities and discipline-based education in the late nineteenth century. This anachronistic view of colonial America has missed the multiplicity of models for the academic professional in the eighteenth century.[6]

Other models for understanding professionalization shed new light on the status of the eighteen-century tutors. Bruce Kimball, in *The 'True Profession Ideal' in America*, has provided one interpretation of the development of American professions. Kimball overcomes the narrow interpretations of earlier historians who defined professionalization in late nineteenth- and early twentieth-century terms, thereby making the rise of professions a "modern" occurrence. Instead Kimball used a fluid definition of "profession" and "professionalization." One important insight of Kimball's is that the "rhetoric or cultural ideal" of the profession has undergone important changes from the fifteenth to the twentieth century. For example, in the eighteenth century, professions took on a more pronounced vocational character, replacing the older religious concepts. Although professions continued to be identified by communities of like-minded individuals, the concept of professions as occupations requiring a functional expertise, or having a strong connection with the development of the American middle-class were more modern interpretations of the ideal of the professions, inappropriate to interpreting their development in the eighteenth century. Professional expertise as specialized knowledge was a nineteenth-century concept; the eighteenth century stressed universal, general knowledge as the basis of all the professions. Thus, professions should not be equated with middle-class consciousness in the eighteenth century. Moreover, the development of professions needs to be understood as a continuing, developmental process, rather than a single event in time. Unfortunately, Kimball included little discussion of the eighteenth century tutors in this discussion of the professionalization of the faculty in the eighteenth century. This paper hopes to fill in his analysis.[7]

Ignored as a post for transient instructors who taught for several years and then left teaching for other careers, usually as ministers, the tutorship at Harvard in fact was undergoing a transformation in the late seventeenth and early eighteenth century from a temporary job to a semi-permanent or permanent career. The tutorship often served as the first stage of a teaching career followed by service as a professor or a schoolmaster. Instead of placing the rise of professionalism in academia to the 1750s, many of these trends can be dated to the 1690s, when tutors first displayed an increased interest in and commitment to the teaching profession. The eighteenth century actually saw the development of two models of the academic profession, one more individualistic with discipline-based instruction carried out by professors living independently outside the college and the other more communitarian, with tutors living in the college and proving a broad-range of instruction. Both models increasingly allowed for lifetime careers, a strong sense of identity and vocation, had specific training, and the potential for a significant role in collegial governance. Only one survived to the nineteenth century, however.[8]

The changes in the composition of the Harvard tutors were part of a larger trend in Anglo-American education that saw the separation of the teaching profession from that of the ministry. Important to this professionalization was the pattern of increasing stability and involvement in college life, which started to appear among the Harvard tutors. The college records chronicle the role of the tutors in Harvard's educational life and greater control over the governance of the college. This study suggests that the professionalization of the teaching staff at Harvard coincided with and often preceded the creation of the other professions including law and medicine in colonial New England. In particular, the professionalization of the tutors needs to be viewed as part of the creation of a teaching profession that included school teachers and grammar school masters.[9]

***

Until 1722, Harvard did not have any endowed chairs or professorships; tutors were entrusted with the bulk of the teaching load. For most of the seventeenth century, Harvard appointed two tutors. In 1699, the number was increased to three and in 1720 to four. Until 1716, the tutors were given permanent appointments subject to good behavior. Each tutor saw one or two classes of students and saw the class through the entire undergraduate curriculum. This integrated instruction should not be viewed as a limitation in the professional development of the tutors. In fact, these expectations show the broad competence that college-educated men were expected to have in a variety of subjects. At the same time, the emphasis of institutional historians on the role and power of the college's various governing authorities has obscured the almost absolute power the tutors had over the everyday life of Harvard's students. *The Lawes Libertyes and Orders of Harvard College* for the years 1642–1646 made the tutors responsible for the religious supervision of students, the students' conduct in commons, and in their chambers. Permission of the tutors or the president was required for students to "live or board in the family or private house of any Inhabitant in Cambridge" or to "be present at or in any of the publick civill meetings or concourse of People as Courts of Justice, Elections, ffayers, [or] military Exercise in the time or hours of the colledge exercise." Furthermore, the tutors had authority over the scholars as long as the students were within the town of Cambridge. If a student lived off-campus illegally, the college authorized the tutors to take action against him "by Admonition & private correction." Tutors were also authorized to use mild forms of corporal punishment. These responsibilities extend beyond those of the professors and other instructors. For example, the Hebrew instructor was required to refer students to the tutors for corrections in "matters of greater importance." Similarly the professors were eventually granted the powers of correction described as the same as the tutors. Thus, the tutors supervised the totality of the students' activities at Harvard. For their efforts, tutors received a free room and a small salary set by the college Corporation. In the seventeenth century, the college did not pay the tutors directly; each was responsible for collecting fees from his students. When these fees did not cover the agreed-upon salary, the college made up the difference.[10]

During the second half of the seventeenth century, the two Harvard tutors also occupied two of the seven positions on the Corporation, the college's chief governing body. Neighboring ministers usually held three positions, and the treasurer and president of the college the other two. In spite of the responsibilities assigned to the tutors on paper for the college's governance and operation, the tutorship was neither professional nor a powerful position in the seventeenth century. Samuel Eliot Morison described the typical seventeenth-century tutor as "a very young man, appointed to the fellowship after taking his Bachelor's degree. He was a candidate for the ministry, and he resigned his tutorship as soon as a ministerial opening appeared." There was little separation between the preaching and teaching professions. Some 73 percent of the tutors serving before 1680 became ministers after leaving the college.[11]

Furthermore, the seventeenth-century tutors were a transient group. Where most Harvard presidents held office for lengthy tenures (Henry Dunster for fourteen years and Charles Chauncy for more than seventeen), few tutors remained in their post for more than three years (see Table 1). Age provided another contrast: unlike the presidents, who were mature, established ministers, most tutors were fairly young at the time of their appointment, usually under the age of twenty-five (see Table 2). At the end of the seventeenth century, however, the role and position of the Harvard tutors began to change.

With the appointment of John Leverett and William Brattle as Harvard tutors in the 1680s, the tutorship began to fill a more professional position within the college. Although both men were only twenty-three when appointed to the tutorship in 1685, each remained at Harvard for about twelve years. After leaving their positions at Harvard, Brattle's career followed the traditional path for seventeenth-century tutors; he entered the ministry and served the Cambridge church. Leverett, on the other hand, chose to study law, settled in Cambridge, and eventually returned to Harvard as president in 1708. With the tenure of Brattle and Leverett, the rapid turnover in incumbents came to an end, and the tutors increased their role in the operation of the college.[12]

The political instability of the colony in the late seventeenth century led to the tutors assuming a larger role in the governance of the college. Leverett and Brattle's influence can be seen in the changing intellectual environment at Harvard. Beginning in the 1690s, Harvard moved away from strict Puritan theology and became increasingly liberal in its orientation. This was accomplished through the increased power and authority of the tutors during a period of political instability in

TABLE 1
Length of Service of the Harvard Tutors by Year of Appointment

Years of Service	1650–1659	1660–1679	1680–1699	1700–1719	1720–1739	1740–1759	1760–1779	1780–1795
1–3	16	16	2	3		2	8	16
4–6	4	3	2	3	1		8	4
7–9				1	2		1	1
10–12				2	1	1	1	
13–15								
16–19					2			
20–25								
over 25			1					
Total Number of Tutors	20	19	7	8	6	5	17	21
Average Years of Service	2.7	2.6	13.3	5.6	11.2	11.7	3.5	2.5
Without Flynt		6.3						

Sources: *Publications of the Colonial Society of Massachusetts* (Boston, 1925), 15:clvii-clix.
Corporation Records, Harvard University Archives.
John Sibley and Clifford Shipton, *Biographical Sketches of Graduates of Harvard University in Cambridge, Massachusetts*, 17 vols. (Boston: Massachusetts Historical Society, 1873-).

TABLE 2
Age of Harvard Tutors at Year of Appointment

Age	1640–1659	1660–1679	1680–1699	1700–1717	1720–1739	1749–1759	1760–1779
Less than 20	7	1					
20–24	9	13	5	3	1	2	3
25–29	1	4	2	3	5	1	8
30–34				1		2	4
35–40				1			
Unknown	3	1					2
Total Number of Tutors	20	19	7	8	6	5	17
Average age at appointment	20	22	24	27	26	28	27

Sources: *Publications of the Colonial Society of Massachusetts* (Boston, 1925), 15:clvii–clix.
Corporation Records Harvard University Archives.
John Sibley and Clifford Shipton, *Biographical Sketches of Graduates of Harvard University in Cambridge, Massachusetts*, 17 vols. (Boston: Massachusetts Historical Society, 1873-).

the colony. In 1685, the Crown annulled the Massachusetts charter and created the Dominion of New England. Because the colony had issued Harvard's 1650 charter, the crown's action also canceled its charter. What followed was perhaps the most complex chartering episode ever experienced by any college in America. The General Court proposed five charters between 1692 and 1700; the Crown or the royal governor rejected four, and the fifth was lost in the bureaucracy in London. Meanwhile, Harvard operated under temporary legislative acts and several temporary governing boards. Increase Mather, Harvard's president, was out of the country during much of the dispute, serving as the colony's deputy in England beginning in 1688. When Mather returned to Massachusetts in 1692, he did not take up residence in Cambridge, but instead remained in Boston. In 1701, he resigned the presidency; his successor, Samuel Williard, also remained in Boston. Consequently, the tutors were left with much of the oversight for the college for almost twenty years. What stability Harvard enjoyed at the turn of the century was achieved by the continuity in office of its two tutors, Leverett and Brattle.[13]

The tutors used their increased authority to change Harvard's theological orientation. After the Crown annulled the college's charter, the President and Council of New England met on July 23, 1686 and confirmed Increase Mather as rector of the college and instructed him to "make his usual visitations." They also declared "that Mr Jon Leverett & Mr Wm Brattle be the Tutors, & enter upon the Governmt of the Colledge, & manage the public reading in the hall." The council also confirmed the salaries of the tutors.[14] Leverett and Brattle, in Richard Hofstadter's words, "were members of mercantile and magisterial families that were in short order aligned against Mather. They were relatively liberal in their attitudes, and for twelve years the future intellectual elite of the Bay Colony passed under their tutelage and theirs alone."[15]

Although Increase Mather might have supported some reform at the college, Perry Miller noted that Leverett and Brattle "entertained notions still more 'enlarged'" than the college president would have supported.[16] The eighteenth century ushered in an American Enlightenment. Norman Fiering writes that Puritan scholastic thought was replaced by a

"new moral philosophy," a discipline that was neither an exposition of Aristotle, as the old academic moral philosophy had been for four hundred years, nor an overt presentation of practical theology, such as many Protestants in the seventeenth century had hoped would succeed the old Aristotelian ethics. The new moral philosophy was a Christian ethics of sorts . . . but it was not Christ centered or dogmatic. One might call it a post-theological, but not a post-Christian, morals.[17]

TABLE 3
Occupation After Service at Harvard by Year of Departure

Occupation	1640–1679	1680–1719	1720–1759	1760–1779
Minister	22	10	4	7
Law/Government	4	2	1	1
Physician	3		1	
Merchant	1	2	1	
Education*			3	3
Total Number of Tutors	30	14	9	13

*Education includes tutors who remained in office until retirement, became professors, or schoolmasters.
Eight tutors died during their appointments.
Sources: *Publications of the Colonial Society of Massachusetts* (Boston, 1925), 15:clvii-clix.
Corporation Records, Harvard University Archives.
John Sibley and Clifford Shipton, *Biographical Sketches of Graduates of Harvard University in Cambridge, Massachusetts*, 17 vols. (Boston: Massachusetts Historical Society, 1873-).

The Harvard tutors were the leaders of the intellectual revolution at Harvard that moved the curriculum away from an exclusively classical education designed for theological education to a more humanistically-oriented one that could encompass training for a wide-variety of professions. These curricular changes in turn helped to separate college attendance and college teaching from the ministerial profession. By the mid-eighteenth century, tenure as a college tutor would be valued as preparation for careers in law, business, and school teaching (see Table 3).

The clearest articulation of this sense of new professionalism among the Harvard tutors occurred between 1716 and 1722 in the tutors' dispute with the Harvard Corporation. They had two complaints. Until 1712, the tutors had kept separate accounts for each of their students, collecting tuition and then settling with the college on a regular basis for any shortfall from their stated salaries. In effect, the tutors were responsible for an important part of the financial operations of the college. In 1712, however, the college took over the collection of tuition and the tutors were instead paid a set salary. Similarly, until 1716, the tutors had a permanent appointment subject only to good behavior. In April 1716, the Corporation voted: "no tut[o]r or Fellow of the House [a title to distinguish tutors from fellows of the Corporation] now or henceforth to be chosen shall hold a fellowship with Salary for more than Three years, Except continued by a New Election." The Corporation was attempting to assert greater control over the college faculty. These actions were the first steps in the attempt to reduce the authority and status of the tutors. The tutors' response displayed their professional resentment to the downgrading of their status within the college. In March 1718, the tutors attempted to take direct control of the revenues of the college.[18]

The controversy expanded to the tutor's right to sit on the Corporation. In 1707, when the Corporation was reestablished under the 1650 charter, Governor Dudley had chosen from among the members of the temporary Corporation, seven to sit on the reconstituted board. He chose only two of the three tutors. The third tutor, John Whiting, was elected to the Corporation at the next vacancy. Because tutors did not always give up their fellowship immediately after leaving the tutorship, there could be some lag between appointment to the tutorship and election to the fellowship. Nevertheless, usually at least two and sometimes all three tutors sat on the Corporation after 1707. In 1716 and 1717, three vacancies occurred within the Corporation and two of the tutors not yet sitting on the Corporation expected that these positions would fall to them. After the experiences of Leverett and Brattle, the tutors increasingly expected to play a central role in the governance and operation of the college. But Harvard had become a pawn in a provincial struggle over which religious faction would control the college. Traditional Puritans from Mather's camp sat on the college's Overseers while liberal Congregationalists dominated the Corporation. The Corporation chose to elect three prominent liberal Congregational ministers to solidify liberal control of the college, rather than the two tutors.[19]

Nicholas Sever, one of the two tutors not yet on the Corporation, felt especially slighted by the Corporation's actions. Sever was already an ordained minister when he became a tutor at the age of thirty-six (he had to leave the pulpit because of strained vocal cords). When the college passed him over for a seat on the Corporation, Sever examined past practices of the college and found that in the seventeenth century, tutors had automatically served as fellows of the Corporation. He therefore argued that all tutors should automatically be considered fellows. His argument implied that the tutors should be viewed not only as the primary instructors of the college, but also as its governors.[20]

In March 1718, Sever wrote a lengthy protest to the Corporation on his treatment as a Harvard tutor. His sentiments display an increasingly professional attitude. Sever argued that "Mr. President [Leverett] had encroached upon the rights of the Fellows." Sever explained that Leverett was usurping the authority of the tutors; Leverett had fined freshmen for not attending readings in the hall, even though Sever had excused the students in accordance with the regulations of the college. Furthermore, Sever contended that the triennial act requiring the reelection of the tutors every three years rather than making permanent appointments, "appears to me to be an additional weakening" of the tutors' position. Because the workload of the tutors had increased with the size of the student body, it would make more sense "to set the follows [tutors] higher . . . and make them stronger, and the contrary to weaken, and lessen them must in my humble opinion have a bad tendency." Sever's protest of 1718 is the first outburst from Harvard's faculty to protect their rights in the governance process.[21]

Sever specifically complained about the lack of collegial behavior from the president (the former tutor, John Leverett). He noted that Leverett was taking the decision-making power of the college "intirely into his own hands." Sever also complained that he had been improperly treated when his tutorship was not proclaimed in the college hall. He also felt slighted by the size of his salary which was less than Leverett had received as tutor twenty years earlier (Brattle and Leverett had received a supplement to their salary while the president was absent from the college). Ultimately, Sever feared that the tutors were being left with only the responsibility for governing the houses (or dormitories) at Harvard: "if we are left with little more than a Name to govern the house, we must needs become despicable in the eyes of those we ought to govern." Sever concluded by calling for the tutors to be appointed to the vacant positions on the Corporation. Sever's fear of the loss of status is similar to that later experienced by late nineteenth-century professionals who saw the gradual decline of their power and authority within the community. The tutors had been able to achieve an increased sense of professionalism in the first decades of the eighteenth century. That new-found professionalism was put in jeopardy by the college president and external forces (the liberal Congregational ministers) who wanted to control Harvard's governance.[22]

The tutors did not let the matter drop; in 1720 all three tutors (Henry Flynt, Nicholas Sever, and Thomas Robie) presented a memorial to Leverett and the Corporation. The tutors argued that although the Charter of 1650 did not explicitly state that the tutors were to be considered fellows of the Corporation, such was the tradition of European universities. Although he already sat on the Corporation, Henry Flynt joined the other two tutors in their challenge to the Harvard authorities. The three tutors showed remarkable solidarity against the president and Corporation. Not getting satisfaction from the president, the tutors turned next to the Overseers.[23]

The tutors' dispute rapidly developed larger ramifications. The Overseers were composed of magistrates and ministers and met infrequently, the Corporation being the main governing body by the early eighteenth century. The Overseers were authorized, however, to intervene in college affairs on extraordinary occasions. In 1721, Sever asked the Overseers to review the tutors' protest. Although traditional Puritans dominated the Overseers and evidence suggests that Sever and his fellow tutors were theological liberals, the Overseers nevertheless took up the tutors' cause as a way of displacing at least two of the liberal Congregationalists on the Harvard Corporation. The controversy quickly turned into a battle for religious control of Harvard by factions outside the college, and the professional concerns of the tutors were lost in the rhetoric of the religious struggle. The event's importance in the religious history of the period has obscured the basis of the tutors' original protest.[24]

The inability of the tutors to regain their seats on the Corporation did not signal their defeat. One or two tutors continued to sit on the Corporation, and they played an important role in Harvard's decision-making. They were frequently entrusted with college business that directly affected the town community. For example, in 1722, the Corporation appointed tutors Flynt and Robie (now both fellows of the Corporation) to represent the college in the laying out of a road through the college farm. Similarly, in early 1723, the Corporation asked Henry Flynt "to take with him Mr Sever and Mr Welsteed to View the College Lott in Cambridge neck and observe what trespass has bin committed thereupon." Three tutors were to inquire who was responsible and report back to the Corporation. Unlike most of the ministers on the board, the tutors were resident in Cambridge so were better situated to transact and oversee college business.[25]

The average length of service for the various tutors in the eighteenth century obscures the fact that a number of them served the college for substantial parts of their career. Although some tutors only served three or four years, others remained in the college for more than a decade. Henry Flynt was the longest-serving tutor (fifty-five years). Flynt is normally viewed as the exception (Finkelstein refers to him as a "permanent tutor" as if his status and appointment was different from the others at Harvard; it was not), but others served lengthy careers as well. Nathan Prince served for nineteen years (from 1723 to 1742) and would have served longer if not removed by the Harvard authorities. Thomas Marsh served twenty-five years and only resigned when the Corporation demanded it after his marriage. Marsh was so attached to the tutorship that he tried to keep his marriage a secret for a time. He turned to schoolteaching after his resignation. Belcher Hancock also served twenty-five years, and retired in his post. A core of the mid-eighteenth-century tutors are better characterized by their longevity and dedication to teaching than by brief and transient service.

Eighteenth-century tutors were also older at the time of their appointment (see Table 2). Where the seventeenth-century tutors had been recent college graduates in their early twenties, by the mid-eighteenth century, the tutors were in their late twenties and early thirties when appointed to office. Almost all had already received their masters degrees; many had served as librarians or butlers at the college before their service as tutors and were, therefore, more experienced in the operations of the college. Given the greater age differences, the students' relationship with the tutors changed in the eighteenth century. According to Morison, students "chummed" less with the tutors and started to view them as enemies, rather than allies. In addition, teaching was less likely to precede an entry into the ministry. Where before 1680, 73 percent of the tutors became ministers, by the mid-eighteenth century, only 33 percent did and as many as 40 percent remained in educational careers, serving as tutors, schoolteachers, or college professors until their death or retirement (see Table 3). The eighteenth-century tutorship was becoming a permanent career for some and the first stage of an emerging educational career track for others.[26]

The establishment of faculty chairs at Harvard in the 1720s continued the trends the tutors had begun. Like the tutors, the average age of appointment for the professors was in their late twenties. Initially, the professors were also given term appointments of five years, but by the late 1720s, the term was changed to life tenure. The careers of the professors closely replicated those of the longest-serving tutors. All of the professors appointed prior to 1770 except one served until illness or death forced their retirement. Unlike the senior tutors, however, the professors were for the most part excluded from the Corporation. In fact, during the 1730s, two of the tutors sat on the Corporation while Isaac Greenwood, the Hollis professor of mathematics and natural history, did not. In many cases between 1720 and 1760, the tutors on the Corporation were actually responsible for selecting and electing the professors to their chairs. But no more than one professor served on the Corporation at any given time in the eighteenth century.[27]

Ultimately, the increased professionalization of the tutors led to conflict with the newer professors. Like school masters, the tutors remained generalists, teaching all parts of the curriculum to a single set of students. Nevertheless, some of the tutors continued to hold positions as members of the Corporation and could, theoretically, control the governance of the college. Therefore, the tutors serving on the Corporation in the 1730s and 1740s actually directed the activities of the professors who did not. The tutors also held administrative responsibility for supervising the students both in college and in the town of Cambridge. The professors, on the other hand, were bound more tightly to their specific disciplines and did not provide general instruction, differentiating them from schoolteachers and grammar schoolmasters. After the creation of faculty chairs and the establishment of an externally-controlled Corporation in the mid-eighteenth century, the Harvard authorities began a concerted effort to reduce the tutorship to secondary importance in institutional governance and decrease its professional status. Tutors became the adjuncts to the endowed professorships.

As the size of the faculty increased in the eighteenth century, and most were excluded from the Corporation, separate faculty governance appeared at Harvard. The tutors and professors jointly formed the faculty. No distinction was made between the two types of positions. They began to meet regularly as a group distinct from the Corporation in 1725. Both had an equal voice in the meetings of the faculty. The new organization usurped some responsibilities formerly assigned to the tutors, however, including student discipline and oversight of the college's physical plant. The 1750s saw further, purposeful reduction in the authority of the tutors. In the hierarchy of the college records, the professors were listed after the tutors until 1758, but were moved above the tutors in that year. In 1755, the Corporation ordered "that (excepting those who are already Tutrs in Harvard College) no person whatsoever, that shall be hence forward chosen into sd office, shall abide therein more than eight years from his sd choice." Although the professors were appointed for life, the tutors were now appointed to fixed-term, terminal positions. In 1766, the tutorship was reconstructed. The tutors no longer followed a single class and instead each taught a single subject, mirroring the disciplinary organization of the professors. Although the tutors now had the same disciplinary allegiance as the faculty, they were restricted in their length of service. After mid-century the tutorship became a temporary career, distinct from the professors. Tutors had to find another post at the conclusion of eight years at Harvard. With Hancock and Marsh's retirement in the 1760s, the length of service started to decline to less than four years on average, a return to the seventeenth-century pattern.[28]

The professors finally subjugated the tutorship in the early nineteenth century. In a final bid for faculty control of the Corporation, in 1824, the professors, calling themselves the "resident instructors" used the tutors' earlier service on the Corporation to justify their attempt to secure faculty appointments to the Corporation. The Overseers rejected the professors' claims but did respond by reorganizing the faculty into departments, each headed by a professor with tutors or instructors assisting. Moreover, student discipline was reassigned from the tutors to a faculty board headed by a professor. Disciplines and professors now ruled academic governance.[29]

Although influenced by the religious divisions of the period, the tutors' dispute with the college was primarily an outgrowth of the increased professional self-image of the tutors. In the 1690s, the Harvard tutors had assumed primary control for Harvard, and had successfully changed the intellectual climate, opening the door for more liberal theology and more progressive thought. The tutors who began teaching in the following years remained longer, a number for the bulk of their professional careers. The theological disputes opened in the 1690s came back to haunt the tutors. In spite of their professional expansions, the tutors were excluded from governance and their authority lessened, in order to secure liberal control of the college.[30]

The development of a professional professoriate at Harvard extended over the entire eighteenth century. It began with the increased professionalism of the tutors in the first half of the eighteenth century and can be seen in their struggle with college authorities. In the second half of the century, the professors extended and continued these professionalizing trends. Ironically, the tutorship was reduced in authority after mid-century and returned to being a short-term, temporary teaching assignment. Without examining both the tutorship and the professorship, however, the process of professionalization becomes truncated.

✳✳✳

It is true that Harvard may be exceptional. Because of its early founding, it had an institutional maturity by the first half of the eighteenth century that its sister institutions lacked. Nevertheless, the trends at Harvard often have been a precursor for other institutions. It was by no means preordained that the tutors would become second-class faculty. In fact, during the first half of the eighteenth century, their career paths suggested that two different, but not necessarily unequal, types of professional faculty might develop at Harvard as in England. But the case of eighteenth-century Harvard demonstrates the difficulty higher education has with sustaining multiple forms of the professoriate.

Given the changes in the professoriate during the last twenty-five years, the increased professionalization of the tutors during the colonial period can provide important insights for colleges today. In spite of the tutors' position of strength in the early eighteenth century, including seats on the Corporation, life-appointments, and operating responsibility for the college, dual faculty models led to the creation of faculty hierarchies. The professors were able to obtain first-class status, either through their more favorable teaching conditions, the prestige of the named chairs, or the greater freedom to marry, raise families, and settle outside the college. The tutorship was purposefully made a second tier teaching assignment, its tenure restricted and its authority reduced. The Harvard faculty in the eighteenth century was faced with multiple models and with competing interests. The Harvard faculty included both specialists and generalists. Just as the interests of teaching and research-oriented faculty can clash today, the professional standards and models of the tutors and professors clashed in the eighteenth century. The professors won.

Notes

1. Richard Hofstadter and Walter Metzger, *The Development of Academic Freedom in the United States* (New York: Columbia Univ. Press, 1955), 81.
2. Kathryn Moore, "The War with the Tutors: Student-Faculty Conflict at Harvard and Yale, 1745–1771," *History of Education Quarterly* 18 (1978): 115–125; Richard Warch, *School of the Prophets: Yale College, 1701–1740* (New Haven, Conn.: Yale Univ. Press. 1973), 59–60, 69, 75, 245–46; John M. Murrin, "Anglicizing an American Colony: The Transformation of Provincial Massachusetts" (Ph. D. diss., Yale Univ., 1966). Harvard's founders may have initially embraced a short-term tutorship because of their prior experience at Emmanuel College, Cambridge. The desire to train ministers at Emmanuel (a Puritan foundation) was so strong that the fellows were to resign their posts within one year of finishing their last degree and seek positions as ministers. Emmanuel's model was the exception, however. See "Extracts from the Statutes of Emmanuel College, Cambridge," in *Puritanism in Tudor England*, ed. H. D. Porter (Columbia, S.C.: Univ. of South Carolina Press, 1971), 132–94.
3. *Publications of the Colonial Society of Massachusetts* (Boston, 1925), 15:152–153; Corporation Records, Harvard University Archives, 2:227–229.
4. William Smith, "The Teacher in Puritan Culture," *Harvard Educational Review* 36 (1966): 399–405.
5. William Carrell, "Social, Political, and Religious Involvement of American College Professors, 1750–1800" (Ph.D. diss., George Peabody College for Teachers, 1967); William Carrell, "American College Professors, 1750–1800," *History of Education Quarterly* 8 (1968): 289–305; Martin Finkelstein, "From Tutor to Specialized Scholar: Academic Professionalization in Eighteenth and Nineteenth Century America." *History of Higher Education Annual* 3 (1983): 99–122.
6. Samuel Haber, *The Quest for Authority and Honor in American Professions* (Notre Dame, Ind.: Univ. of Notre Dame Press, 1988).
7. Bruce Kimball, *The 'True Professional Ideal' in America: A History* (Cambridge, Mass.: Blackwell, 1992), 1–17, 304.
8. The dichotomy I am describing is not one of teaching and research. All eighteenth-century faculty focused on instruction. The difference between tutors and professors was one of pedagogy, teaching style, and relationship to students.
9. For a larger discussion of the separation of school teaching from the ministry in the early modern period, see Rosemary O'Day, *Education and Society, 1500–1800* (London: Longman, 1982), 79.
10. *Pub. Of the Col. Soc. Of Mass.*, 15: 190, 192, 203, 16:456, 490, 603, 16:528.
11. Samuel Eliot Morison, *Harvard in the Seventeenth Century*, 2 vols. (Cambridge, Mass.: Harvard Univ. Press, 1936), 1:51–53.
12. John Sibley and Clifford Shipton, *Biographical Sketches of Graduates of Harvard University in Cambridge Massachusetts* 17 vols. (Boston: Massachusetts Historical Society, 1873 to 1975), 3:183, 200. Leverett's career also extended to governance in the town of Cambridge. Before leaving his position as tutor at the college, Leverett was chosen one of the agents for the town's common land. He also served as Cambridge's

representative to the General Court. Leverett's political activities set the foundation for the professor's political involvement during the American Revolution. See, *Cambridge Proprietor's Records* (Cambridge, Mass.: John Wiley and Son, 1901) 208.

13. Jurgen Herbst, *From Crisis to Crisis* (Cambridge, Mass.: Harvard Univ. Press, 1982), 15–16; Morison, *Harvard in the Seventeenth Century*, 479–536.

14. *Pub. Of the Col. Soc. of Mass.*, 16:827.

15. Hofstadter and Metzger, *Academic Freedom*, 101.

16. Perry Miller, *The New England Mind: From Colony to Province* (Cambridge, Mass.: Harvard Univ. Press, 1953), 238.

17. Norman Fiering, *Moral Philosophy at Seventeenth Century Harvard* (Chapel Hill, N.C.: Univ. of North Carolina Press, for the Institute of Early American History and Culture, 1981), 295. This view disagrees with Morison who argued that the 1723 Harvard curriculum was substantially the same as that of President Dunster's tenure in the seventeenth century. See Morison, *Harvard in the Seventeenth Century*, 1:147.

18. *Pub. Of the Col. Soc. of Mass.*, 16:434; Samuel Eliot Morison, *Three Centuries of Harvard*, (Cambridge, Mass.: Harvard Univ. Press, 1936), 64–73; Margery Somers Foster, *"Out of Smalle Beginings. . .": An Economic History of Harvard College in the Puritan Period* (Cambridge, Mass.: Harvard Univ, Press, 1962), 136.

19. Morison, *Three Centuries of Harvard*, 64–73; Shipton, *Sibley's Harvard Graduates*, 5:92–93.

20. Shipton, *Sibley's Harvard Graduates*, 5:91–93.

21. *Pub. of the Col. Soc. of Mass.*, 49:266–267.

22. *Pub. of the Col. Soc. of Mass.*, 49:267–270; Richard Hofstadter, *The Age of Reform: From Bryan to F.D.R.* (New York: Alfred A. Knopf, 1955), 148–162.

23. *Pub. of the Col. Soc. of Mass.*, 49:317–320. The tutors also argued that "in the first dayes of the College the Corporation consisted of persons in the College and in the Town Wholly." In the seventeenth century, only two of the Fellows, the two tutors, had actually been residents in the college. It had been Harvard's practice to fill the other three seats in the Corporation with clergymen from the Cambridge area. The president and treasurer filled the other two seats. The treasurer was also from Cambridge until the late seventeenth century.

24. Morison, *Three Centuries of Harvard* 64–73.

25. *Pub. of the Col. Soc. of Mass.*, 16:470, 480.

26. Shipton, *Sibley's Harvard Graduates*, 8:137–140, 9:67–70; Morison, *Three Centuries of Harvard*, 179. Living in the colleges led to the requirement that the tutors maintain a single state. The Corporation once made an exception to this rule in 1701, allowing Samuel Angier to live "from the Colleg" and appointing a "scholar of the House" to take Angier's place in the college. This is the model that would reappear in the late eighteenth century with the creation of the permanent tutorship. See *Pub. of the Col. Soc. of Mass.*, 15:368.

27. *Pub. of the Col. Soc. of Mass.*, 16:682.

28. *Corporation Records*, Harvard University Archives, 2:70, 113.

29. *Report of a Committee of the Overseers of Harvard College on the Memorial of the Resident Instructors, May 4, 1824* (Cambridge, Mass., 1824), 7–10; Hofstadter and Metzger, *Academic Freedom*, 234.

30. *Pub. of the Col. Soc. of Mass.*, 15:clvii-clix.

"FOR THE CHILDREN OF THE INFIDELS"?: AMERICAN INDIAN EDUCATION IN THE COLONIAL COLLEGES

BOBBY WRIGHT

Wild and savage people, ... they have no Arts nor Science, yet they live under superior command such as it is, they are generally very loving and gentle, and doe entertaine and relieve our people with great kindnesse: they are easy to be brought to good, and would fayne embrace a better condition.
—*Robert Johnson,* Nova Britannia, *1609*

We must let you know . . . the Indians are not inclined to give their Children Learning. We allow it to be good, and we thank you for your Invitation; but our customs differing from yours, you will be so good as to excuse us.
—*Canassatego (Iroquois), 1744*

Schemes to deliver higher education to American Indians arose sporadically throughout the colonial period. Within a decade of the first permanent European settlement at Jamestown, plans were already underway for an Indian college, and similar designs continued periodically throughout the seventeenth and eighteenth centuries. Indians, in fact, offered the impetus for establishing and maintaining the nation's most enduring and prestigious halls of higher learning—such elite institutions as Harvard College, the College of William and Mary, and Dartmouth College.

The lofty aspirations to provide higher education arose amidst conflicting interests among the stay-at-home English, the colonists, and the native people for whom the colleges were intended. The English, mindful of the Crown's desire to spread the gospel among the "heathens" of America, generously endowed the educational missions in a true spirit of piety. The colonists, eager to maintain British sanction of their struggling settlements and institutions, capitalized on the religious fervor of the English, but for the most part neglected to fulfill their professed pious mission. Meanwhile, the Indians, tenacious in their cultural persistence, were rigidly resistant to the white man's interest in their spiritual welfare. Only when war and disease had disintegrated tribal integrity and left Indian communities vulnerable to English domination did Indians embrace Christianity and European culture.

Despite the prevailing literature glorifying these efforts to convert and "civilize" American natives, close examination of the several schemes to establish colonial Indian colleges reveals a drama of deception and fraud, in which the major players betrayed motives that were less than honorable. Most historians of the colonial era would have us believe that piety was the moving force behind the early colleges. After all, in Virginia as in New England, the officially proclaimed purpose of English colonization of America was the conversion of native "heathens" to Christianity. King James I, in the 1609 charter of the Virginia Company of London, reaffirmed his mandate that "the principal Effect, which we can desire or expect of this Action, is the Conversion and Reduction of the People in those Parts unto the true Worship of God and Christian Religion."[1] Similarly, the 1629 Charter of the Massachusetts Bay Company proclaimed its purpose to "wynn and incite the natives . . . to the knowledge and obedience of the onlie true God and Saviour of mankinde."[2]

In assuming their missionary charge, colonists viewed education as a primary means not only to Christianize Indians, but also to civilize and remake them in the image of the European. As early as 1609, Robert Gray advocated this means since "it is not the nature of men, but the education of men, which makes them barbarous and uncivill, and therefore chaunge the education of men, and you shall see that their nature will be greatly rectified and corrected."[3] Yet, despite this avowed pious calling, the colonists either ignored their mandate or failed miserably in their meager attempts to fulfill it. The most enterprising among them, however—those who promoted the Indian colleges—were able to capitalize handsomely on this mission.

In settling Jamestown in 1607, the Virginia Company had more than devotion to religious duty in mind. It was, after all, a profit-making venture, financed by the most daring entrepreneurs. Yet in *A True and Sincere Declaration of the Purpose and Ends of the Plantation* (1609), the Company declared that its principal aim was "to preach and baptize into the Christian Religion, and by propagation of the Gospell, to recover out of the armes of the Divell, a number of poore and miserable soules, wrapt up unto death, in almost invincible ignorance."[4] However, a dissenting faction within the Virginia Company later declared that, despite assurances to the contrary, "conversion of those Infidels did not happen in those first 12 years during which time the English were allmost allso in continuall Hostilitie wth ye Infidells."[5] Indeed, the Jamestown colonists spent much more energy in seizing Indian lands than in spreading the gospel.

Indian conversion nevertheless proved fertile ground for reaping other benefits. Duly impressed with a carefully contrived visit from Pocahantas, the first and only Jamestown Indian convert, King James ordered in 1617 a special collection in churches throughout the realm. The proceeds were to be delivered to the Virginia Company for "the erecting of some Churches and Schooles, for the education of the children of those Barbarians."[6] Accordingly, the Virginia Company in 1618 ordered "that a convenient place be chosen and set out for the planting of a University . . . in time to come and that in the mean time preparation be there made for the building of the said College for the Children of the Infidels." The company then endowed the college with 1,000 acres of land seized from the natives at Henrico, some 50 miles upriver from Jamestown.[7]

Against this backdrop entered one of this drama's most crafty and enterprising players, Sir Edwin Sandys, treasurer of the Virginia Company. Sandys reported in 1619 that the bishops' collections had already netted 1,500 pounds. However, only about half of that sum was available in cash, since the Company had borrowed the remainder for its own financial needs. By May, 1620, augmented by considerable private donations to the college, the collections grew to 2,043 pounds.[8] Despite this substantial and growing benefaction, Sandys advised a postponement in building the college. He justified the delay by proposing to invest the funds to create an endowment for the college. Evidence suggests, however, that he planned to employ the capital to further the Virginia Company's ambitious economic plan.

To save the Company, which continually wavered on the brink of bankruptcy, Sandy's new economic policy aimed to rapidly increase the population settled on the public lands and to stimulate the production of new commodities. Accordingly, he announced his intention to use the Indian college funds to ship indentured tenants for the college lands. Sandys incidentally noted that this use of the charity "may save the joint stock the sending out a [supply] Shipp this yeare."[9] Instead of reaping income for the college at Henrico, half of the tenants who arrived in 1619 were assigned to private plantations. When the scattered tenants were finally resettled on the college lands, they served another aim of the Company—the production of new staples, silk and wine. With the remaining college funds, Sandys invested not in education but in yet another economic scheme, an ironworks on a plantation owned by himself and another investor. Two years later, one significant benefactor complained about the use of his donation by private investors, "contrary to my minde."[10]

By 1620, although nearly three-fourths of the money raised in England to educate Indians had been disbursed, Treasurer Sandys had diverted the charity and thwarted all intentions to construct the college. Not a penny went toward the conversion and education of would-be native scholars. Meanwhile, a native uprising in 1622 put an end to the grandiose plan for the Indian college at Henrico. Considering this scheme, an eighteenth-century historian concluded that "we do not find that the money was employed as those Religious Persons would have had it"—an understatement indeed and a better than warranted reflection on the dubious character of Sir Edwin Sandys.[11]

The New England colonists, settling their new world with the same godly mission, learned from the Virginia experience. They learned, foremost, to manipulate and capitalize on the charitable impulses of the pious English. Their enterprising machinations resulted in the construction of the Harvard Indian College, which advantaged English scholars more than it did the natives for whom it was ostensibly intended. Also like their Virginia predecessors, the New England colonists—neglectful of their chartered mission—spent more effort in seeking funds for Indian conversion than in actually spreading the gospel. Publishing several pieces of promotional literature, which greatly exaggerated their success in converting Indians and even more their desire to do so, New England leaders embarked on a plan to link the needs of the fledgling Harvard College with the proven solicitations for Indian conversion. In fact, the first promotional tract, published in 1643, recommended that contributions for the Indian work be sent to the College president.

Under pressure from New England lobbyists, in 1648 the House of Commons began to debate a bill to charter a new philanthropic corporation for Indian missions in the Puritan colonies. One debate focused on an opportunistic amendment to alter fundamentally the character of the bill, placing Indian conversion in a position of importance secondary to that of Harvard College. In this amendment, the New England colonists advocated allocating the charity "for the maintaining of the universities of Cambridge in New-England, and other schools and nurseries of learning there, and for the preaching and propagating of the Gospel among the natives." However, this attempt to include assistance for the College was thwarted, as Parliament approved the final bill designating funds solely for "the preaching and propagating of the Gospel of Jesus Christ amongst the natives, and also for maintaining of schools and nurseries of learning, for the better educating of the children of the natives."[12] Thus, in 1649 Parliament created the Society for the Propagation of the Gospel in New England, commonly called the New England Company, charging the London-based Society to raise and administer funds for Indian conversion.

Against this backdrop, a behind-the-scenes player, Harvard President Henry Dunster, entered center stage. Although he had provided much of the information for the 1643 tract designed to create a climate of favorable support in England, Dunster made an even more strategic move by engineering Harvard's charter in 1650. The charter provided for the "education of the English and Indian Youth of this country in knowledge: and Godlines."[13] (It is instructive that, although Harvard College was established in 1636, it had not yet professed a commitment to Indian education.) In 1651, this maneuver accomplished, he inquired of the Commissioners of the United Colonies, overseer of the New England Company's disbursements in the colonies, whether the charitable funds might in some measure benefit the College. The Commissioners responded with a letter to their London agent suggesting that "an eye may bee had in the destrebutions to the enlargement of the Colledge at Cambridge wherof there is great need and furtherance of learning not soe Imediately Respecting the Indian Designe." The interests and intentions of Dunster as well as those of the colonial commissioners were clear; foremost among them was the struggling and financially strapped Harvard College.

Whatever their motives, the solicitations were fruitful. In 1653 the trustees of the missionary fund ordered "the building of one Intyre Rome att the College for the Conveniencye of six hopfull Indians youths . . . which Rome may bee two storyes high and built plaine but strong and durable." The Indian college was accordingly completed in 1656.[14]

In this use of charitable funds, several factors arouse suspicion regarding the Commissioners' intentions for the Indian college. First, the building did not cost one hundred pounds as initially proposed. Twice enlarged beyond the original design—this, to accommodate English, not additional Indian students—the total cost was some four hundred pounds. Such a sum would have supported ten missionaries for four years at the prevailing twenty-pound annual rate paid through 1656.[15] Second, there were no Indian students identified to occupy the Indian college, a situation surely known to Harvard's president and to the Commissioners. Three years after construction of the Indian college building, the New England Company wanted to know

> what number of Indians there are att the university and what progresse and profisiency they make in their learning; and to what degree and measure therin they have attained; and we hope wilbee such as will give good satisfaction unto divers well affected heerunto.

Although the Commissioners encouragingly reported that "there are five Indian youthes att Cambridge in the lattin [preparatory] Schoole," they made no mention of any at the Indian college.[16] Not until 1660 did an Indian student enter Harvard for the bachelor's degree, and never did more than two occupy the Indian College at any given time. Indeed, during the nearly four decades of its existence, the college housed only four Indian scholars.

Nevertheless, the building did not stand vacant. As soon as it was completed, Harvard's next President, Charles Chauncy, proposed that its rooms be used to accommodate English students. Later, a contemporary observer described the Indian College as "large enough to receive and accommodate about twenty scholars with convenient lodgings and studies; but not hitherto hath been much improved for the ends intended. . . . It hath hitherto been principally improved for to accommodate English scholars."[17]

Despite receiving encouraging reports and testimony from the colonial Commissioners, the New England Company questioned the progress relative to expenditures, reporting that "it is wondered by some heer that in all this time there are noe more in regard it appeers by the account sent; . . . we desire therfore that . . . you would please to bee more particular in youer next accounts." They also warned that "we shalbee slow to take many more English or Indian youthes upon our charge for education till wee have some experience of those on whom soe much hath bine bestowed."[18]

If the Society was suspicious of the Puritan effort by 1660, certainly the negligible progress through the remainder of the college's life to 1693 afforded no evidence to allay their misgivings. Indeed, by 1675 there was but one Indian student at the College, and the last Indian attended in 1685. The professed interest in educating Indians at Harvard merely concealed the intention to use the Indian cause to exact English funds for the survival of the colonists' college. This was a lesson learned from the earlier Virginia enterprise at Henrico, and it was once again destined to be employed in that same colony. Ironically, when the Indian College at Harvard was demolished in 1693, the College of William and Mary in Virginia received its royal charter—once again, purportedly for the education of Indian youth.

As was the case in other missionary enterprises, the promise of funds incited greater concern for the education of Indians—again under the initiative of a cunning, enterprising individual; in this case, the Commissary of Virginia, James Blair. While soliciting contributions from the merchants of London for the founding of a college in Virginia, Blair proposed in 1690 the possibility of "perhaps" creating "a foundation for ye Conversion of our neighbouring Heathen to ye Christian Faith."[19] Since there is no evidence that the proposed college was intended for Indians, it is likely that the mention of conversion was a bid to enlist the merchants' pious impulses.

A twist of fate then forced Blair to play his hand openly. In January 1691, while Blair was in London seeking a royal charter for the College of William and Mary, the Governor of the New England Company, Robert Boyle, died, leaving 5,400 pounds for unspecified "Charitable and other pious and good uses." Boyle's will recommended "the Laying out of the greatest part of the same for the Advance or propagation of the Christian religion amonst Infidells."[20] Prevailing upon the executor of Boyle's estate to direct the fund toward the support of an Indian school at the prospective college in Virginia, Blair reported from London that "Mr. Boyle died about the beginning of last month, & left a considerable Legacy for pious uses, which, when I understood, I made my interest with his executors by means of the Bishop of Salisbury, and I am promised 200.1. [pounds] of it for our college."[21]

Ultimately, Blair's solicitations proved even more successful. From the proceeds of an investment of the Boyle bequest, the executors specified an annuity to

> keep art the said Colledge soe many Indian Children in Sicknesse and health in Meat drink Washing Lodgeing Cloathes Medicines bookes and Educacon from the first beginning of Letters till they are ready to receive Orders and be thought Sufficient to be sent abroad to preach and Convert the Indians.[22]

Thus, when Blair obtained in 1693 a royal charter for the establishment of the College of William and Mary, he duly contrived that, among other ends, the College would exist so that "the Christian faith may be propagated amongst the Western Indians."[23] Despite the semblance of a pious mission, no evidence survives of Indian enrollment at William and Mary prior to 1705. Clearly, during his fifty years as the college president, Blair made no serious attempt to fulfill the intent of the Boyle legacy. Instead, he devised other than the intended uses for the charity.

By 1716 Indian students were so few that their college master requested "the liberty of teaching such English Children as shall be put to him" and that a partition be erected to separate English students from Indians.[24] By 1721, William and Mary College had no native students, and the "Indian Master" rendered his services exclusively to English scholars.[25] There is no evidence that Indians attended the college in the later 1720s.

In the face of an untapped and rapidly accumulating Boyle fund, President Blair began to contrive further uses for the account which might revitalize the struggling and financially strapped William and Mary College. In 1723, reviving the appearance of commitment to Indian education, Blair constructed a building for an Indian school which did not in fact exist. Built at a cost of 500 pounds, the structure, called the Brafferton, was a handsome two-and-a-half story brick house. This accomplished, Blair devised yet another tactic to capitalize on the Boyle bequest to aid the College. Using the fund to build its severely deficient library, in 1732 he authorized a London agent to spend up to 300 pounds on books for the general use of William and Mary scholars. Blair rationalized this diversion by sarcastically noting that "as we do not live in an age of miracles, it is not to be doubted that Indian scholars will want the help of many books to qualifie them to become good Pastours and Teachers."[26] Little did it matter that there would be no Indian scholars at William and Mary for over a decade.

Efforts to engage Indian students were negligible throughout the remainder of President Blair's administration. On Blair's death in 1743, William Dawson became the new president. That same year, the College enrolled perhaps half a dozen Indian students.[27] From the 1750s until the Revolution, when funds from England halted and the Brafferton "Indian College" simultaneously ceased to exist, William and Mary maintained a small but steady enrollment of between three and five Indian students. But, throughout the course of James Blair's presidency, the Indian School at the College of William and Mary was, in the words of College historian J. E. Morpurgo, "an entry in the ledgers through which charitable funds could be funneled to extraneous activities."[28]

The final and most lucrative scheme for the advanced training of Indians during the colonial period resulted from the machinations of Eleazar Wheelock, called—perhaps mistakenly— the founder of Dartmouth College. A Congregational minister in Lebanon, Connecticut, Wheelock in 1754 established Moor's Charity School for Indian students, unquestionably a successful venture which operated for nearly a century. In 1763, seeking a land grant of thirty to thirty-five square miles, Wheelock sent to England "A Proposal for Introducing Religion, Learning, Agriculture, and Manufacture among the Pagans in America," suggesting "a large farm of several thousand acres of and within said grant be given to this Indian school [and] that the school be an academy for all parts of useful learning: part of it a College for the Education of Missionaries, Schoolmasters, Interpreters, etc., and part of it a School for reading and writing, etc."[29] This proposal reflected Wheelock's growing passion for establishing a college as well as his then waning interest in educating Indians.

The efforts of Wheelock's most successful Indian protégé provided the money needed to finance his scheme. Samson Occum, Wheelock's "black son," embarked on a fund-raising mission to England and Scotland from 1765 to 1768. He thus raised over 12,000 pounds in the mistaken belief that the funds were to be employed "towards building and endowing an Indian academy for cloathing, boarding, maintaining, and educating such Indians as are designed for missionaries and schoolmasters, and for maintaining those who are, or hereafter shall be employed on this glorious errand."[30] These funds represented the largest amount that any college up to that time had been able to raise by direct solicitation abroad.

Yet Wheelock had become disillusioned with his Indian students because of what he called their "Sloth," "want of Fortitude [and] Stability," and "doleful Apostasy."[31] He set into motion his plans to relocate to New Hampshire, where he had secured a substantial land grant for his college. With an ample treasury at his disposal, his next task was to obtain a royal charter for the so-called "Indian achademy." On December 13, 1769, Wheelock secured the charter for Dartmouth College. In writing the charter, Wheelock had to deal with several potentially volatile matters. One centered on defining the purpose of the school. On the one hand, he had to assure the Society in Scotland for Propagating Christian Knowledge, trustees of Samson Occum's collections, that their funds would be employed solely for the education of Indians. On the other hand, he had to deal with the expectation among the people of New Hampshire that the school would supply local ministers. Wheelock had already decided that Dartmouth would emphasize the education of English scholars, but in writing the charter, he disguised his intentions well. The first charter draft defined the school's purpose as providing "for the education & instruction of Youths of the English and also of the Indian Tribes." After carefully considering that numerous English benefactors had contributed thousands of pounds to a school for Indians—*not* white colonists—he revised the reference to English youth as if to indicate their subordinate position in his scheme. Accordingly, the final draft of the charter read that the college would exist

> for the education & instruction of Youth of the Indian Tribes in this Land in reading wrighting and all parts of Learning which shall appear necessary and expedient for civilizing and christianizing Children of Pagans as well as in all liberal Arts and Sciences; and also of English Youth & any others.[32]

The business of the charter settled, Wheelock completed his move to New Hampshire in 1770. During that year the number of Indian students in Wheelock's Connecticut school had conveniently diminished to three, while the number of English scholars had grown to sixteen.[33] The school continued to admit Indians after the move to New Hampshire, although with an increasing influx of white students. During the entire decade of the 1770s, the reverend was responsible for educating some forty Indians, while during the same period he had more than 120 white students at Dartmouth College and many more at the charity school. By 1774, Wheelock had exhausted all of Occum's collections for Indian education.

While Wheelock's sophistry led to the fulfillment of his dream to establish a college, it shattered the vision of his Indian protégé. Samson Occum maintained that the English funds were raised solely for his brethren, as "we told them that we were Beging for poor Miserable Indians." Occum further complained that he had been duped, having previously been warned in England that "You have been a fine Tool to get Money for them, and when you get home, they won't Regard you the'll set you a Drift,—I am ready to believe it Now," he wrote.[34] A nineteenth-century critic was even more harsh in his condemnation. The charitable collection for Indian education, he wrote,

> is all expended; and excepting in new lands, Dartmouth College is without funds. It was intended that only the interest should be annually spent, but the fund itself is consumed. Though this was primarily designed for Indians, yet the only Indian that has graduated there was obliged to beg elsewhere towards supporting him the last year of his college residence. . . . Such a mixture of apparent piety and eminent holiness, together with the love of riches, dominion, and family aggrandizement, is seldom seen.[35]

When the sincerity of the professed commitment to Indian education in the colonial colleges is measured by comparing announced intentions against actual effort and money expended, there is reason to seriously doubt the genuineness of pious motivation. While the presence of some measure of concern for the Indians' spiritual welfare is unquestionable, other factors clearly motivated the major figures responsible for the advancement of Indian education and conversion. Certainly the colonists played cunningly on the religious impulses of stay-at-home Englishmen, capitalizing successfully on the image of "lost heathen" souls. In doing so, they were able to further their own political, economic, and educational agendas, which included Indian education as an ancillary aim at best, while all the time professing their own piety as if this were their singular motivation. The Virginia Company leaders were thus able to invest charitable funds in their new economic program, intended more to revitalize the colonial enterprises than to establish the Henrico Indian college. College presidents Henry Dunster of Harvard and William and Mary's James Blair capitalized on Christian philanthropy to enhance the growth of their floundering and financially strapped colleges. So, too, was Reverend Wheelock able to profiteer and thus fulfill his desire to found Dartmouth College. Consequently, the colonial experiments in Indian higher education were not simple expressions of unblemished piety. Rather, they characterize a drama of self-righteousness, deception, and neglect enacted on a stage of failure in Indian education.

Notes

1. Willaim MacDonald, ed., *Select Charters and Other Documents Illustrative of American History, 1660–1775* (New York: MacMillan Co., 1906), 16.
2. Nathaniel B. Shertleff, ed., *Records of the Governor and Company of the Massachusetts Bay in New England,* 5 vols. (Boston: William White Press, 1853–84), 1:17, 384.
3. [Robert Gray], *A Good Speed to Virginia* (London: Felix Kyngston, 1609); reprinted in J. Payne Collier, ed., *Illustrations of Early English Popular Literature,* 2 vols. (London: Privately Printed, 1864), 2:18.
4. Robert Hunt Land, "Henrico and Its College," *William and Mary Quarterly,* 2nd ser. 8 (1938): 470–171.
5. Susan Myra Kingsbury, ed., *The Records of the Virginia Company of London,* 4 vols. (Washington, D.C.: Government Printing Office, 1906–1935), 2:395.
6. Peter Walne, "The Collections for Henrico College, 1616–18," *Virginia Magazine of History and Biography* 80 (1972): 260.
7. Kingsbury, *Records of Virginia Company,* 3:102.
8. *Ibid.,* 1:220, 263, 335; 3:117, 576.
9. *Ibid.,* 1:220–221.
10. *Ibid.,* 1:586.
11. John Oldmixon, *The British Empire in America, Containing the History of the Discovery, Settlement, Progress and State of the British Colonies on the Continent and Island of America,* 2 vols. (London: John Nicholson, Benjamin Tooke, Richard Parker, and Ralph Smith, 1708), 1:300; cited by Arlyn Mark Conard, "The Christianization of Indians in Colonial Virginia" (Th. D. diss., Union Theological Seminary, 1979), 224.
12. Leo Francis Stock, ed., *Proceedings and Debates of the British Parliament Respecting North America,* 5 vols. (Washington, D.C.: Carnegie Institution, 1924), 1:209.
13. *Harvard College Records* (Boston: Colonial Society of Massachusetts, 1925; 1935).
14. David Pulsifer, ed., *Records of the Colony of New Plymouth in New England: Acts of the Commissioners of the United Colonies of New England,* 2 vols. (Boston: n.p., 1859), 2:107, 120, 128, 168.
15. George Parker Winship, *The New England Company of 1649 and John Eliot* (Boston: The Prince Society, 1920), 17.
16. William Kellaway, *The New England Company, 1649–1776: Missionary Society to the American Indians* (1961; reprint ed., Westport: Greenwood Press, 1975), 110; Pulsifer, *Acts of the Commissioners,* 2: 216–217.
17. Daniel Gookin, "Historical Collections of the Indians in New England," *Collections of the Massachusetts Historical Society,* 1 (1792): 176.
18. Pulsifer, *Acts of the Commissioners,* 2:242.
19. "Papers Relating to the Founding of the College," *William and Mary Quarterly,* 1st ser. 7 (1898–1899): 161.
20. A Contemporary Copy of the Will of Robert Boyle, 18 July 1691, William and Mary College Papers (Williamsburg: College of William and Mary), folder 7.
21. Herbert Lawrence Ganter, "Some Notes on 'The Charity of the Honourable Robert Boyle, Esq., of the City of London, Deceased'" *William and Mary Quarterly,* 2nd ser. 10 (1930): 68.
22. "Supplementary Documents Giving Additional Information Concerning the Four Forms of the Oldest Building of William and Mary College," *William and Mary Quarterly,* 2nd ser. 10 (1935): 14.
23. Robert Fitzgibbon Young, *Comenius in England: The Visit of Jan Amos Komensky (Comenius) The Czech Philosopher and Educationist to London in 1641–1642; It's bearing on the Origins of the Royal Society, on the Development of the Encyclopedia, and on Plans for the Higher Education of the Indians of New England and Virginia* (London: Oxford University Press, 1932), 267.
24. *Virginia Magazine of History and Biography* 4 (1897): 172.
25. J. E. Morpurgo, *Their Majesties' Royall Colledge: William and Mary in the Seventeenth and Eighteenth Centuries* (Washington, D.C.: Hennage Creative Printers, 1976), 69.
26. "Instructions from the President and Masters of William and Mary College in Virginia, to John Randolph Esq.," William and Mary College Papers, f. 12.
27. James Axtell, *The Invasion Within: The Contest of Cultures in Colonial North America* (New York: Oxford University Press, 1985), 194.
28. Morpurgo, *Their Majesties' Royall Colledge,* 67.
29. Wheelock Papers ([microfilm edition], Hanover: Dartmouth College Archives), 763427.2
30. Frederick Chase, *A History of Dartmouth College and the Town of Hanover,* 2 vols., ed. John K. Lord (Cambridge: John Wilson and Sons, 1891), 1:59; James Dow McCallum, ed., *The Letters of Eleazar Wheelock's Indians,* Dartmouth College Manuscript Series, no. 1 (Hanover; Dartmouth College Publications, 1932), 305; James Dow McCallum, ed., *Eleazar Wheelock, Founder of Dartmouth College,* Dartmouth College Manuscript Series, no. 4 (Hanover: Dartmouth College Publications, 1939), 164–65.

31. Wheelock Papers 769274.2, 769255; Eleazar Wheelock, *A Continuation of the Narrative of the Indian Charity-School in Lebanon, in Connecticut; From the Year 1768, to the Incorporation of it with Dartmouth-College, and Removal and Settlement of it in Hanover, in the Province of New-Hampshire, 1771* (n.p.: n.p., 1771), 19–20.

32. Wheelock Papers 769663.2; Jere R. Daniell, "Eleazar Wheelock and the Dartmouth College Charter," *Historical New Hampshire* 24 (Winter 1969): 3.

33. Harold Blodgett, *Samson Occom,* Dartmouth College Manuscript Series, no. 3 (Hanover: Dartmouth College Publications, 1935), 121–122; Chase, *History of Dartmouth College,* 88.

34. Wheelock Papers 771424.

35. Cited by Chase, *History of Dartmouth,* 559.

SCIENCE, SOCIETY, AND THE CURRICULUM

DOUGLAS SLOAN

This study has been concerned with those Scottish educational influences in eighteenth-century America associated primarily with the Presbyterian academies and the College of New Jersey. A larger pattern of Scottish influences on American higher education, however, has also been glimpsed from time to time. Although it would fall outside the scope of this study to appraise the full impact of Scotland upon the American college, the major configurations of this larger pattern can be drawn. The task that remains, therefore, is to relate the early Princeton traditions to some of the wider issues and developments in eighteenth-century American higher education.

Four areas are especially worthy of attention. First, the late eighteenth century saw the emergence in American higher education of a genuine academic scientific community. Second, the American college became one of the central arenas in which the conflicting claims of the Enlightenment and of traditional religious points of view were mediated. Third, major efforts were made toward enunciating a social theory of education appropriate to the specific situation and needs of the new American nation. Finally, American educators applied themselves self-consciously, and often with considerable success, to the task of constructing a modern college curriculum. In all four areas Americans concerned with education found themselves frequently guided and informed by Scottish ideas and examples.

I

One strand in the wider network of Scottish influences on American higher education, which this study has touched upon in the career of Benjamin Rush, deserves a few pages of special attention. This was the appearance in late eighteenth-century America of an embryonic community of professional, academic scientists. Two major sources of Scottish scientific thought in the American college must be considered: the Scottish scientists and physicians who immigrated to America, especially during the first half of the century; and the American students who returned from their medical studies in Scotland during the latter half of the century.

Scottish intellectuals and university-educated persons came to America for a variety of reasons in the eighteenth century. Many able Scotsmen found opportunities in the colonies for political service and advancement that they would not have found open to them in Scotland; hence, they were often readier to live abroad than their fellow Englishmen, who enjoyed ample opportunities for themselves at home. In their comparison of the similar provincial status of Scotland and America, Bernard Bailyn and John Clive have stressed the crucial role in America of the royal officials and agents of the British government. They point out that the colonial agents of British imperialism were frequently the social leaders in the major town, "cultural go-betweens" with immense influence on the fashions, styles, and thought in the provinces.[1] America and Scotland were much alike in this regard. There was, however, one essential difference between the two. Clive and Bailyn neglect to point out that many of the royal officials and government agents in the American colonies were themselves Scotsmen. During the eighteenth century, there was a total of about thirty Scottish-born governors and lieutenant governors in charge of American colonial affairs. In many instances, these officials were surrounded and supported by strong Scots factions which enjoyed considerable political and financial influence.[2] Even English army units serving in America often found themselves placed under Scots officers, much to the discontent of the troops; and many of the military doctors were Edinburgh-trained Scotsmen.[3]

As might be expected, the activities of Scots creditors and royal agents in the colonies did not always inspire good feelings toward Scotsmen, particularly during the last years before the Revolution. Nevertheless, the intellectual and educational contributions of Scottish colonial officials, frequently men of learning, should be noted. Probably the most famous of these men was Cadwallader Colden, a leading figure in colonial intellectual circles, and author of important scientific and philosophic treatises. A graduate of the University of Edinburgh and a trained physician, Colden was Lieutenant Governor of New York from 1760 to 1775. In North Carolina, Governor Gabriel Johnstone, a zealous protector of royal interests, displayed a concern with colonial education. Born in Dundee, Johnstone was a graduate of the University of St. Andrews, where he had studied medicine and oriental languages. As Governor, he repeatedly enjoined the North Carolina Assembly to set up a comprehensive system of schools. Even in Virginia, the Presbyterians received some early crucial assistance from Scottish-born officials. The Synod of Philadelphia in 1738 was encouraged by Governor William Gooch, also a Scot, to begin its educational and missionary activities in the Great Vallye of Virginia. And, when Samuel Davies arrived in Scotland in 1753 to raise funds for the College of New Jersey, he was pleasantly surprised to discover that the way had been smoothed for him by letters of recommendation to the Provost and other leaders of Glasgow from the Scottish-born Governor of Virginia, Robert Dinwiddie.[4]

Most striking, however, in the first two thirds of the century, were the scientific and intellectual contributions made by Scottish physicians in the colonies. Several names stand out. In Boston, there was William Douglass; in Annapolis, Alexander Hamilton; in Charleston, John Lining, Alexander Garden, and Lionel Chalmers; in Urbana, Virginia, John Mitchell; in Philadelphia, and later New York, Adam Thomson; and also in New York, Peter Middleton and, of course, Cadwallader Colden. All of these men, trained physicians, settled in the colonies before 1750, most had been born in Scotland, and all had received the whole or a major part of their higher education at Scottish universities.[5]

Three things about these men were especially significant. First, they were instrumental in helping to form the beginnings of an inter-colonial community of intellectuals. Together with such other leading American scientists as Franklin, James Logan, and John Bartram, they corresponded regularly among themselves, exchanging ideas, proposing new schemes, and offering their comments and criticisms of one another's work. The Scots were early identified in the colonies as a group. The editors of the *American Medical and Philosophical Register* later in the century, for example, expressed recognition that the contributions of these men were related. Referring to John Mitchell, the editors wrote that "with Chalmers and Lining of South Carolina and Alexander and Colden of New York he has done much for the advancement of medical and physical science on this side of the Atlantic."[6] Early impetus to organize colonial science and scientists also came from the Scots. According to Brook Hindle, it was Colden who, writing to William Douglass in 1728, first made the suggestion for a colonial scientific academy; and eight years later Douglass communicated to Colden news of the formation of a medical society in Boston.[7]

The naturalists, furthermore, were especially active in establishing close and early links with major European thinkers. It was with the encouragement of Peter Collinson, one of Franklin's favorite London correspondents, that Colden completed and published his treatise on the Indians. Both John Mitchell and Alexander Garden, as well as Colden, maintained a long-standing and intimate correspondence with Gronovius in Holland and Linnaeus in Upsala, sending them new specimens from America for investigation and classification.[8]

Second, the academic background of these Scottish physicians set them apart from most of their fellow American scientists. Whereas the majority of American scientists—like John Bartram and Benjamin Franklin—were exceptionally gifted, but basically amateurs, the Scots were university-trained, and, what is more, aware of the difference. For example, as Hindle points out, Colden and Garden were in agreement that John Bartram was doing pioneer work in natural history, but they also felt that Bartram was seriously hindered by a weak command of the systematic principles of botany.[9]

Finally, these physician-scientists consciously maintained their identity as Scotsmen. All were active members of the St. Andrew's Societies or other Scottish Charitable organizations which existed in most of the larger cities. Adam Thomson was, in fact, a founding member of the St. Andrew's Societies in both New York and Philadelphia; William Douglass and Alexander Hamilton both wrote descriptions of the Societies in their cities, Boston and Annapolis respectively.[10] More important, however, than the patriotic and charitable sentiments involved in their promotion of the Scottish Societies was the strong sense displayed, especially by Garden, Colden, Lining, and Mitchell, of the intellectual debt they owed to their Scottish professors. All appear to have kept in close touch with their former professors at Edinburgh.[11]

The presence in the colonies of these outstanding Scottish physicians probably encouraged Americans to seek professional medical training in Scotland, as growing numbers did. The most immediate effect of American study at Edinburgh was, of course, the founding of the first American medical schools by Edinburgh graduates: at Philadelphia in 1765, at New York in 1767, and at Boston in 1782. The short-lived attempt of James McClurg (Edinburgh M.D., 1770), to establish a medical department at William and Mary, where he taught as Professor of Anatomy and Medicine from 1779 to 1783, should also be included in this list.[12]

The story of the founding of the first medical schools in America has been told often, and need not be repeated. It is sufficient here merely to underscore the importance of the Edinburgh institutional ideal as the pattern for the American schools. The plan for an American medical school began to take concrete shape in the circle of colonial students at Edinburgh.[13] John Morgan, who had been a member of this Edinburgh group, presented the idea of putting science and medicine on a firm institutional footing at the 1765 commencement services of the College of Philadelphia. The scheme for a medical faculty, which Morgan, with William Smith's help, succeeded in persuading the College of Philadelphia to adopt, was based upon the Scottish tradition of a school connected with an arts college, rather than the London form of a hospital-school.[14] The medical school at King's College, New York, also was modeled closely after the Edinburgh school, with even a stone hospital," after the plan of the Royal Infirmary of Edinburgh," to provide clinical lectures.[15]

The impact of medical study in Edinburgh on American higher education extended far beyond the inspiration to found medical schools, however. For one thing, the study of medicine fostered the development of many of the specialized sciences such as chemistry, botany, paleontology, and geology. For another, medicine led the way in the early academic institutionalization of science.

These developments were interrelated, and were directly encouraged by the experience of American medical students at Edinburgh. In the first place, Americans there had every incentive to view medicine as a subject to be studied within the context of the total university curriculum. This incentive derived only in part from the traditional connection between the Edinburgh medical school and the university. It came also from the exposure of American students to a range of intellectual stimulation beyond that of their medical studies through their contacts with other intellectuals in the university and city. Besides his work in medicine, John Morgan, for example, made a point of sitting in on the lectures on rhetoric and *belles lettres* delivered by Hugh Blair in the university. "Thou won't be satisfied," Morgan's friend Professor William Hewson chided him from London, "without being a Physiologist, Chemist, Physician, & Rhetorician. Mercy upon us, where will you end."[16] Future American academicians were making acquaintance with Scottish intellectual life at the very moment of its full bloom, and seeing it as an integrally related whole. In the second place, the Edinburgh requirement that students pass through the entire medical program also meant that future American professors of medicine would return home ready to offer instruction in a wide spectrum of scientific subjects. Finally, the achievements of their university professors impressed the Americans with the importance of the sciences' having strong institutional support.

In his 1765 *Discourse Upon the Institution of Medical Schools in America*, John Morgan wrote: "Private schemes for propagating knowledge are unstable in their nature, and the cultivation of useful learning can only be effectively promoted under those who are patrons of science, and under the authority and direction of men incorporated for the improvement of literature." Morgan also presented as one of the compelling reasons for the establishment of a medical school the advances it would bring in other fields of science, especially those connected with natural history.[17] Morgan himself insisted that medical students should be accepted only after they had received a thorough grounding in the general arts and sciences. Although the College of Philadelphia dropped Morgan's premedical requirements in 1787, and though many of his ideas about the professional standards of physicians were either never realized or severely compromised, Morgan had given expression to two trends that would continue. After the Revolution, specialized scientific studies previously connected with medicine continued to develop on their own, and became increasingly implanted in academic institutions.

The outstanding work in natural history, theretofore mainly the province of American amateurs, was more and more carried out by professors of materia medica. Benjamin Waterhouse in Boston, Samuel Latham Mitchill in New York, Benjamin Smith Barton in Philadelphia, and Henry Muhlenberg at Franklin College dominated the field. Chemistry was also entering a new phase. Benjamin Rush, his pupil James Woodhouse, Samuel Latham Mitchill again, and John Maclean at Princeton were leading the way in America. All of these men were, incidentally, known to Rush, and all, with the exception of Muhlenberg and Woodhouse, had studied at Edinburgh.

The developments taking place in natural history are well illustrated by the career of Benjamin Smith Barton. Brook Hindle has contrasted the world of difference that separated the academic work of Barton from his predecessors, the gentlemen naturalists, John and William Bartram.[18] Barton graduated from the College of Philadelphia, going from there to two years of study at Edinburgh in 1786, followed by a year at Goettingen. The letter of introduction which Barton carried with him from Rush to William Cullen flatteringly informed Cullen of Barton's desire to graduate from Edinburgh "where (unfortunately for all the other universities in the world) degrees have a kind of exclusive preeminence."[19] Barton found Edinburgh congenial, and in his letters to his brother, Barton frequently spoke with admiration of Joseph Black. He distinguished himself by winning the coveted Harveian prize for his dissertation in materia medica. As a student, he also published in Edinburgh Part One of his *Observations on Some Parts of Natural History*, and edited the Edinburgh version of Samuel Stanhope Smith's *Essay*.[20]

Returning from Europe in 1789, Barton was asked to teach botany and the first American course in natural history.[21] For twenty years (1795–1815), Barton held the chair of materia medica, referring to himself as "Professor of Materia Medica, Natural History, and Botany," Barton was as instrumental as anyone in putting the study of natural history upon a systematic basis. He authored numerous works and in 1803 brought out the first American textbook in botany, his *Elements of Botany or Outlines of the Natural History of Vegetables*. In 1813, two years before his own death, he added to his teaching duties the professorship of the "practice of Physic," left vacant by the death of Benjamin Rush.[22]

In the field of chemistry, the beginnings of a real community of scientists in the late eighteenth century were even more strikingly apparent than in natural history. The study of combustion and the use of the balance were bringing about a genuine revolution in the subject of chemistry. For Americans, the 1794 arrival in Philadelphia of Joseph Priestley, famed for his attainments as divine, educator, and scientist, was a great event. An outstanding and imaginative chemist, Priestley was the leading spokesman in the defense of phlogiston against "Old Oxygen." That American chemistry was already acquiring the characteristics of a mature science is shown by the fact that there were a number of chemists who, despite their respect for Priestley, were ready to challenge his theories.

Most of those who led in arguing the theories of Lavoisier against Priestley had been trained, like Rush, under Joseph Black in Scotland, and several were protégés of Rush himself. One of the first, according to Edgar Fahs Smith, to actually use the terminology of Lavoisier was Samuel Latham Mitchill. Mitchill was not a student of Rush, but he had studied under Black at Edinburgh. Appointed to the chair of chemistry at Columbia in 1792, Mitchill came to dominate scientific circles in New York. A fascinating man, Mitchill is worth mentioning here, if for no other reason than to indicate another of the important academic and scientific ties with Scotland in the early years of the Republic.[23]

Benjamin Rush, of course, enjoyed a special place among American chemists as the first professor of the subject. Both Rush and Black were slow in coming round to a full acceptance of the French theories, but Rush must have been cognizant of them and sympathetic, since his own students quickly took up the new ideas of combustion, respiration, and oxidation.

James Woodhouse, Rush's student and his candidate for the chair of chemistry at Philadelphia, performed several important tasks for the future of the science. Woodhouse led in the founding of the Chemical Society of Philadelphia in 1792, and through his careful experiments and published papers helped to bring about the final defeat of the doctrine of phlogiston in America, all the while remaining on friendly terms with Priestley. Like Rush, Woodhouse was immensely interested in applied chemistry and laboratory methods of instruction. His laboratory achievements were such as to gain the admiration of many, including Thomas Cooper, then the professor of chemistry at Dickinson College. Woodhouse was also the teacher of both Robert Hare, one of the most imaginative American scientists in the early nineteenth century, and Benjamin Silliman of Yale.[24] As Morgan, Rush, and others had envisaged, medical education was, indeed, encouraging advances in other subjects.

Rush, it will be remembered, was also the first to alert Samuel Stanhope Smith to the qualifications of John Maclean and to advise Maclean to settle at Princeton. Maclean, shortly thereafter, joined the faculty at the College of New Jersey and immediately entered the lists against the doctrine of phlogiston.[25] The far-reaching implications of the spreading network of Scottish scientific influences during this period is vividly illustrated in the relationship between John Maclean and Benjamin Silliman. As Professor of Chemistry at Yale, editor of *The American Journal of Science and Arts,* and a founder of the Sheffield Scientific Institute, Benjamin Silliman was to exert immense influence on American science before the Civil War.

As a young man, Silliman received his first real introduction to chemistry in correspondence and talks with John Maclean at Princeton. "Dr. Maclean," Silliman later wrote,

> was a man of brilliant mind, with all the acumen of his native Scotland; and a sprinkling of wit gave variety to his conversation. I regard him as my earliest master of chemistry, and Princeton as my first starting-point in that pursuit; although I had not an opportunity to attend any lectures there.[26]

Silliman then studied under James Woodhouse at Philadelphia, and finally went to Edinburgh for two years. Later Silliman and Maclean collaborated in bringing out the first American edition of William Henry's *An Epitome of Chemistry.*[27]

Although natural philosophy and the scientific subjects associated with it were firmly established in the American college curriculum by 1740, the pursuit of science in America throughout the eighteenth century, and into the nineteenth, was also much dependent upon the work of amateurs. By 1802, however, all of the twenty-one full-time jobs in science in America were in academic institutions, including medical schools. There were only about sixteen colleges of any real importance in America at the time; yet the number of professional scientists was still relatively small.[28] It reflected the growing trend, nevertheless, away from the amateur pursuit of science toward its academic and professional development.

It would take nearly another half century for a true scientific community to appear, but a skeletal framework was being raised in the late eighteenth century. In this early phase of development, the Scottish university made direct and decisive contributions: First, the Scottish university provided important intellectual substance. Sometimes, as in the case of Cullen's theories, the results left much to be desired; in other instances, as with Black's chemistry and Hope's materia medica, the contributions were invaluable. Furthermore, the Scottish university furnished strong support and inspiration for the institutional ideal of the systematic pursuit of science in close connection with the liberal arts and with the colleges of the nation. And finally, it should be stressed again, the Scottish university offered confirmation and example to the Enlightenment and Republican faith in the college as an active agent of social progress and as more than a guardian of tradition.

II

Before the arrival of John Witherspoon, both the Old Side and New Side Presbyterians had established important links with Scotland. Each, however, drew upon those Scottish traditions which, across the distance of the Atlantic, appeared most congenial to their own outlooks and interests. Edwards, Davies, and the Tennents corresponded with Evangelical, revival-minded Scottish ministers; Alison and his Old Side colleagues sought help from Hutcheson and other Moderate leaders in the Church of Scotland. From the beginning, these transatlantic contacts helped to bring the new American colleges into an international intellectual community and to prevent them from being locked too tightly into the provincialism of their own religious and social antagonisms. William Smith and Francis Alison, for example, fought intensely over the religious control of the colonies and the College of Philadelphia, but they shared similar intellectual interests and backgrounds, and remained together on the faculty of a college that continued to grow under their leadership. The leaders of the College of New Jersey differed in outlook from both Smith and Alison on many points, but they too were members of a larger international community that opened to them still wider horizons in the person of John Witherspoon.

Witherspoon's blending of the Scottish Enlightenment with the viewpoints of both the Old Side and the New Side ushered in an entirely new situation. After Witherspoon, the full intellectual resources of the Scottish Enlightenment became increasingly available to Presbyterians of every stripe. The old theological distinctions no longer seemed to govern what was to be selected from Scottish thought. Witherspoon had helped to show that the very achievements of the Moderate literati could be put to the service of true religion. Americans soon seemed to forget that the culture-loving Scottish ministers had at one time been suspect to the devout.

At least three characteristics of Scottish thought, as it was introduced by Witherspoon, made this change possible. In the first place, the eclecticism of his own outlook was broad and flexible enough that it could be made to include a wide spectrum of viewpoints. Moreover, Scottish thought itself was broad and inclusive, and could be put to various uses. Both Old Side and New Side, for example, were able to tap aspects of Scottish thought that appeared to support or to follow logically from their own concerns and convictions. Finally, the Scottish Enlightenment never severed its roots in its religious past. The close alliance between the Church of Scotland and the representatives of culture also eventually gave to Scottish thought an added element of religious respectability. As religious issues in America shifted increasingly from conflicts among the faithful to a growing need to reconcile belief itself with modern science and philosophy, Scottish thought appeared all the more attractive.

Purportedly rational and scientific, yet rejecting skepticism and affirming the reality of the world and the evidences of a divine creator, Scottish common sense realism, for example, could commend itself to a wide range of theological views. By the beginning of the nineteenth century, as Sydney Ahlstrom has shown, the apologetic resources proffered by common sense philosophy had been recognized and taken up by American theologians and churchmen as varied as William Ellery Channing, Bishop William White of the Episcopal Church, and Timothy Dwight and Nathaniel Taylor of Yale, as well as by the Old School Calvinists of Princeton Theological Seminary and others.[29] Years before, however, John Witherspoon had demonstrated the potential in Scottish thought for effecting the needed reconciliation between religion and the modern spirit. The different forms this reconciliation could take were illustrated by Samuel Stanhope Smith, who sought to reveal the transcendent dimensions of science, and by Benjamin Rush, who appealed to the testimony of the moral faculty and the sense of deity as scientific justification for his religious progressivism.

There was also no reason why Scottish natural science, and Scottish scientists, should not find favor among Americans of varying persuasions. Scottish science and psychology, for example, carried neither the stigma of atheism, frequently associated with the French materialists, nor even the stain of religious heterodoxy of such Englishmen as Joseph Priestley and David Hartley. This was especially important in the American colleges where churches were strongly represented, if not in complete control. At the same time the genuine abilities and accomplishments of Scottish scientists could satisfy any demands for scientific competence.

By way of illustration, both sides of Scottish science were exemplified in Walter Minto, Professor of Mathematics and Natural Philosophy at the College of New Jersey from 1787 to 1796. As a youth,

Minto attended the University of Edinburgh under Ferguson, Robertson, and Blair, and, after a period of theological studies, took up his lifelong career in mathematics. When he came to Princeton, he had already achieved an outstanding reputation in Scotland as a mathematician, was a recipient of an honorary degree of Doctor of Law from Aberdeen University, and was the co-author with the Earl of Buchan of a biography of John Napier, the inventor of logarithms. A friend of Franklin and Rush, Minto was elected to the American Philosophical Society in 1789. At the college commencement in September 1788, Minto delivered the inaugural oration, "On the Progress and Importance of the Mathematical Sciences." Minto's oration closed with a prayer for America addressed to the "Father of truth and reason and of everything that lives." Minto's successor at the college, John Maclean, was no less accomplished in his own field of chemistry, and was perhaps even more devout.[30]

American scientists in the nineteenth century almost unanimously took the position that science was a true handmaiden to theology. In doing so, they too relied upon Scottish realism. According to George H. Daniels, one explanation for the concern of nineteenth-century American scientists to affirm that their work complemented theology rather than competed with it was the need of a growing scientific community to avoid conflict with its chief rival profession, the Protestant clergy.[31] Whatever the merits of this sociological explanation, the scientists were using basic arguments already sketched in the eighteenth century by the theologians—the sublimity of science celebrated by Samuel Stanhope Smith being a case in point. The ultimate results, however, appear to have been beneficial neither to science nor to theology, and to have robbed both of a needed inner dynamic and self-direction.[32]

The socially and intellectually conservative uses to which Scottish common sense realism seems to have been put in the nineteenth century have encouraged similar interpretations of the introduction of the philosophy in the eighteenth century.[33] In this light, the initial welcome accorded to common sense is then also seen as a reactionary attempt on the part of the orthodox to neutralize the corroding acids of science and critical philosophy. There is enough truth in this interpretation to make it especially tempting.

It is only part of the truth, however, and its anachronistic simplification produces unfortunate results, particularly for the historian of education. In the first place, the role played by Scottish realism in the early Princeton tradition seems to defy the neat application of the conservative-liberal categories. Witherspoon, Smith, and, for that matter, Rush were all in their ways certainly conservative enough, and their reliance upon Scottish thought had its full quota of reaction. At the same time, Witherspoon mediated many of the values dear to his Moderate opponents; Smith incurred charges of heresy and infidelity; and Rush produced a rather unorthodox combination out of the medical theories of Cullen, the Scottish faculty psychology, his political republicanism, and his New Side Calvinist background. By no stretch of the imagination did any of the three speak disparagingly or grudgingly of science and the scientific temper.

Even when the conservative characteristics of each are duly acknowledged, the use of Scottish thought by Smith and Rush, especially, can be viewed as a somewhat adventuresome attempt—"bold" would perhaps be too strong a word—not merely to buttress religious faith, but also to move it into the mainstream of what were taken to be the most progressive currents of the age. Scottish philosophy in the eighteenth century had both liberal and conservative components. If the conservative did, indeed, later come to predominate, the earlier picture at any rate seems to have been much more complex.

Another, still more important problem is involved in appraising Scottish influences upon education in the eighteenth century, as distinct from the nineteenth century. In the latter period, it was apparently Scottish realism itself—the so-called Scottish school of Reid, Stewart, Hamilton, and Brown—that was of prime importance to Americans. Philosophical realism in the earlier period, however, was only one among several Scottish offerings that Americans found attractive.

Scottish social thought was at least as important to eighteenth-century Americans as Scottish epistemology. American educators who turned their attention after the Revolution to the problems of the new nation confronted the task of reconciling the need for social change and the need for stability. The new science, the new politics, even a new and changing population, held the promise of great progress; yet, at the same time, each posed a potential threat to social order. Just as Scottish philosophy had offered a means of reconciling religious concerns and secular learning, so, too, Scottish social thought presented a concept of progress that appeared to strike a balance between change and order, and between the needs of the individual and the needs of society.

In the first place, Scotsmen, such as Ferguson, tended to see progress in terms of the interaction between the individual and the larger community. The appeal of the alternative French emphasis, as represented by Condorcet, for example, upon the individual and his discoveries as the primary forces of progress was weakened and discredited in the eyes of many Americans by the events of the French Revolution.[34] In the second place, the Scottish view of the pliability of human nature within the limits of the social and natural environment made a special place for education, but accorded it both a progressive and a conserving function. Finally, in addition to this broad—even vague—notion of education, which in itself could serve as a source of motivation and needed rhetoric, Scotland offered concrete examples and models: a system of feeder schools, progressive universities, learned professors, and modern pedagogy.

It is particularly interesting that Scottish social and educational theory was broad enough that Americans could make of it what they needed for their own situation. Furthermore, in the variety of Scottish educational practices, Americans of differing persuasions could find examples to meet their own liking and demands. So it was that the Federalist, liberal-conservative Samuel Stanhope Smith, and the Jeffersonian, conservative-liberal Benjamin Rush, could both draw upon Scottish thought and practice. Even concerning the point on which they differed most, the priorities in republican education, both could appeal to Scotland for support: Smith emphasizing the stabilizing classical tradition fundamental to Scottish philosophy; Rush promoting the utility of the modern languages made respectable by Scottish teachers.

The range of Scottish influences has been most apparent in this study in American attempts to build a modern college curriculum. Scottish educators in the eighteenth century were already seeking solutions to three of the most perplexing problems in modern higher education. The first problem was the rapid expansion of knowledge that was beginning to press upon institutions of higher education. In response to the mounting specialization in nearly every field of inquiry and the proliferation of new subject areas, the Scottish universities were among the first to abolish regenting and to introduce the specialized professorship. The Scottish emphasis upon system and method, no less present in moral philosophy than in medicine, also reflected the concern of Scotsmen to find some integrating and unifying framework or principles that would relate the different disciplines to each other.

The second problem had to do with the relevancy of knowledge and its application to the realities of life and society. Here, especially, Scotsmen appeared to have provided some clear answers. Their scientists had excelled in relating theory to Scottish social and economic needs, and their philosophers were engaged in analyzing human nature and society. The development of the common sense philosophy itself rested upon the pragmatic orientation of Scottish thought and the fear that Hume's philosophy would dissolve the grounds for practical action. Hume himself, of course, pursued his inquiry into the human mind out of a similar concern "to free learning" from "abstruse philosophy and metaphysical jargon"—and "such airy sciences."[35]

Scotsmen, finally, devoted much attention to the moral uses of knowledge. Learning should be promoted because of its morally beneficial effect alone, if for no other reason. "It is certain," Hume said, voicing a common conviction, "that a serious attention to the sciences and liberal arts, softens and humanizes the temper, and cherishes those fine emotions, in which true virtue and honour consists."[36] The significance of moral philosophy was precisely that it promised to uncover natural ethical laws that would enable men in all circumstances to decide how they ought to act and to what purposes they should apply their knowledge.

Indeed, one explanation, perhaps, for the importance attached to moral philosophy, both in Scotland and America, was that it touched squarely upon all three educational problems. Not only was moral philosophy by its nature concerned with the relevance and moral uses of knowledge, but, as developed by the Scotsmen, it seemed to solve the problem of integrating knowledge. Included within the compass of moral philosophy were the nascent social sciences of economics, political science, and psychology, which Scotsmen took an early lead in developing.[37] In applying to each of these subject areas the inductive, scientific method, Scottish moral philosophy suggested that an integrating principle of knowledge was at hand.

The inductive method of attempting to move from particular to general laws was extended from science and moral philosophy to the entire curriculum. Both in the teaching of individual subjects and in the structure of the overall course of study the desire to follow the inductive method provided an underlying unity in the development of the eighteenth-century Scottish university. The Aberdeen reforms, it will be recalled, deliberately tried to arrange the curriculum so that students would be introduced to concrete, factual studies in their early years, and ascend gradually to the more abstract and general philosophical courses in their last years. The same principle was applied in the organizing and teaching of individual subjects, such as logic and literature and rhetoric, as well as science and moral philosophy.

The attempt to apply a general scientific method to all courses has already been observed in the moral philosophy lectures of Alison, Witherspoon, and Smith, and in the use of the logic of William Duncan at the Colleges of New Jersey and Philadelphia, and elsewhere. Witherspoon's lectures on eloquence also seem to have been based upon the procedure of deriving systematic literary categories from the examination of specific authors, then using those categories as basic critical tools for further literary analysis. This method was highly developed, though in somewhat different ways, by Lord Kames in his *Elements of Criticism* (1762) and by Hugh Blair in his *Lectures on Rhetoric and Belles Lettres* (1783). Both Kames and Blair insisted that their critical method was one of ascending from observation and experience to general principles. After Witherspoon, the works of Kames and Blair were both used fairly extensively in the American colleges.[38] It is the judgment of Carl Albert Hangartner that the influence of the method of Kames and Blair, with all of its shortcomings, "appears to have been one of the factors which raised the study of English literature to the status of a separate area of study and teaching and prepared the way for the establishment of departments in the colleges in the nineteenth century."[39]

The introduction of modern courses into the curriculum, which has been observed at Princeton, Philadelphia, and Dickinson, was general in most American colleges by the end of the century.[40] Curriculum expansion, however, was only a part of the story, for this expansion does not appear to have taken place haphazardly or by mere accretion. Eighteenth-century Scottish educators thought they possessed in the inductive scientific method a guiding principle both for teaching individual courses and for relating courses to one another in the curriculum as a whole. It is possible to see the eighteenth-century fascination with system in the Aberdeen-type of curriculum that was repeated with variations at Philadelphia and Princeton. The macrocosmic structure of the large curriculum was replicated in the microcosm of the teaching and organization of individual subjects. Although the ideal was seldom realized in full in the American colleges, partly because of limited resources and partly because the ideal itself was not without its own problems, a definite model, nevertheless, did exist.

Snow sees Harvard, Yale, Brown, and Columbia all following a curriculum pattern by 1825 similar to the one introduced at Philadelphia in 1756.[41] Although Snow's claims for the direct influence of the ideas of William Smith seem extravagant, the organizing principles were, nevertheless, essentially the ones first instituted at Aberdeen University. If by 1825, as is sometimes maintained, this curricular scheme had lost its innovative character and had hardened into a kind of inflexible educational orthodoxy,[42] the causes are probably to be sought as much in changing expectations for the colleges as in the inherent limitations of the system itself.[43]

It remains for someone to undertake a careful examination of the relationships among the early American colleges, and of their mutual influence upon one another.[44] One especially intriguing question, for example, concerns the possible influence of the Aberdeen model on Thomas Jefferson's 1779 curricular reform proposals for the College of William and Mary.[45] Although there appears to be no evidence linking the influence of William Smith to William and Mary, another close personal connection between Jefferson and Aberdeen has attracted the notice of historians.

In 1758, William Small, a graduate of Marischal College (1755), subscribed his oath as Professor of Natural Philosophy at William and Mary. For six years Small taught mathematics and natural philosophy at the college. At the end of this time, perhaps because he was disappointed about not being made president of the college, he returned to Great Britain, where he was associated with the Lunar Society of Birmingham, a prominent group of leading British educational and scientific figures. Upon his return to Great Britain Small carried out a commission to purchase scientific equipment for the college.[46]

Among the little extant information regarding Small's influence at William and Mary, the most important comes from Thomas Jefferson himself. Jefferson, Small's student from 1760 until 1762, included a well-known tribute to his Scottish teacher in his account of his college years:

> It was my great good fortune, and what probably fixed the destinies of my life, that Dr. William Small of Scotland, was then Professor of Mathematics, a man profound in most of the useful branches of science, with a happy talent of communication, correct and gentlemanly manners, and an enlarged and liberal mind. He, most happily for me, became soon attached to me, and made me his daily companion when not engaged in the school; and from his conversation I got my first views of the expansion of science, and of the system of things in which we are placed. Fortunately, the philosophical chair became vacant soon after my arrival at college, and he was appointed to fill it per interim: and he was the first who ever gave, in that college, regular lectures in Ethics, Rhetoric, and Belles Lettres.[47]

The extent to which Jefferson may have obtained specific ideas for his 1779 curriculum from William Small remains a tantalizing question. Jefferson's proposals, however, were not unlike other American college programs that had similar links to the Scottish universities.

By the end of the eighteenth century, Americans were asserting their own cultural, as well as political, integrity. The many plans put forth in the years of the early Republic for national systems of education and for a federal university reflected American desires to keep abreast, and wherever possible, ahead of European cultural achievements. These educational schemes told much, to be sure, about American hopes, fears, and fantasies at the beginning of the nineteenth century. In higher education, however, the stillborn proposals for a federal university were much less significant than the changes that had actually been taking place at more fundamental levels: in the curriculum, in teaching, in the founding of new colleges, in American intellectual concerns and outlooks. Whatever indigenous qualities had come to characterize the eighteenth-century American, they had not developed in isolation from a genuine transatlantic community that extended from beyond the Susquehanna to the Thames—and, in education, to the Firth of Forth and above the River Tay.

Notes

1. John Clive and Bernard Bailyn, "England's Cultural Provinces: Scotland and America," *The William and Mary Quarterly*, 3rd ser., XI (April 1954), 208.
2. Opportunities for trade also attracted many Scots businessmen and merchants to the colonies. By mid-century nearly every American port of any importance had its Scots business community of merchants, clerks, and shopkeepers. Scottish business influence, while not negligible in the northern coastal cities, was, of course, strongest in the South, where representatives of Glasgow shipping firms dominated the Chesapeake tobacco trade. The factors, or agents, of the great Glasgow firms set up stores and trading posts in the back country where they became not only the chief engrossers of American tobacco, but also extended credit to the planters, and, by 1775, controlled the distribution of imports in Maryland and Virginia. Ian Cargill Graham, *Colonists from Scotland: Emigration to North America, 1707–1783* (Ithaca: Cornell University Press, 1956), pp. 117, 142.
3. See James Hayes, "Scottish Officers in the British Army, 1714–1763," *Scottish Historical Review*, XXXVII (1958), 23–33. Army doctors provided some of the most important early links between the colonies and the Scottish universities. Many Scottish physicians came into the colonies as military men in the French and Indian Wars, and then decided to stay. For example, Dr. Hugh Mercer (M.D. Aberdeen), a practicing physician in Pennsylvania and Virginia, who later died fighting the British, and Dr. James Craik (M.D. Edinburgh), raised to physician-general of the army under Washington, both initially came to the colonies as members of Braddock's expedition. See Theodore Diller, "Pioneer Medicine in Western Pennsylvania," *Annals of Medical History*, VIII (1926), 141–155.
4. Peter Ross, *The Scot in America* (New York: The Raeburn Book Co., 1896), p. 82; Carl Bridenbaugh, *Mitre and Sceptre* (New York: Oxford University Press, 1962), p. 131; W. H. Foote, *Sketches of Virginia* (2 vols.; Philadelphia: William S. Martien, 1850–1855), I, 263.
5. These individuals were included in the innermost circles of American intellectual life. Most of them were outstanding in at least one field; several were prolific writers in a wide range of subjects. William Douglass, educated at Edinburgh and Leyden, settled in Boston in 1718, and discovered that he was the only

physician in that city with an M.D. degree. Notorious for his controversy with Cotton Mather over small-pox inoculation, Douglass is more favorably remembered for his work, *A Summary, Historical and Political . . . of the British Settlements in North America* (1760), as well as for his careful descriptions of scarlet fever. See Brook Hindle, *The Pursuit of Science in Revolutionary America, 1735–1789* (Chapel Hill: The University of North Carolina Press, 1956), pp. 38, 48–50, 58–61.

In 1750, in what Carl Bridenbaugh says may have been the first public medical lecture in this country, Adam Thomson presented his method of preparing the body for inoculation. Thomson's system, which was defended in print by Dr. Alexander Hamilton, was widely adopted in Europe, where it was known as "the American method." Carl Bridenbaugh, *Cities in Revolt* (New York: Alfred A. Knopf, 1965), pp. 200–201.

Dr. Peter Middleton, another Edinburgh-trained Scotsman, settled in New York in 1730. Together with John Bard, also Edinburgh-trained, Middleton performed the first dissection before students in America, and, with Samuel Bard, helped in 1767 to set up the medical school at King's College in New York. James Thacher, *American Medical Biography* (2 vols.; Boston: Richardson and Lord and Cotton and Barnard, 1828), I, 384.

In South Carolina, Lionel Chalmers practiced medicine, sent papers on various subjects to the old American Society at Philadelphia, and in 1776 published his *Essays on the Weather and Diseases of South Carolina*, one of the finest general medical works in the colonies. Bridenbaugh, *Cities in Revolt*, p. 410. John Lining of Charleston wrote on botanical and meteorological subjects, but his influential *History of the Yellow Fever* was his most important work. F. C. Bing, "John Lining, An Early American Scientist," *Scientific Monthly*, XXVI (1928), 249–252. Also see Hindle, *The Pursuit of Science in Revolutionary America*, pp. 50–51.

Cadwallader Colden, John Mitchell, and Alexander Garden did especially important work in natural history, and were among the first in the colonies to grasp and apply the Linnaean system of classification. Colden and Mitchell were known for their publications on a variety of other subjects as well. Mitchell's "Map of North America" and Colden's *History of the Five Indian Nations,* for example, were considered authorative works on both sides of the Atlantic for many years. Lewis Leonard Gitin, "Cadwallader Colden," *New York History*, XVI (1935), 169–177. Hindle, *The Pursuit of Science in Revolutionary America,* pp. 50–58; Wyndham B. Blanton, *Medicine in Virginia in the Eighteenth Century* (Richmond: Garrett & Massie, 1931, *passim:* also see John C. Greene, "American Science Comes of Age, 1780–1820," *The Journal of American History,* LV (June 1968), 22–28.

6. Quoted in Blanton, *Medicine in Virginia in the Eighteenth Century,* p. 139.
7. Hindle, *The Pursuit of Science in Revolutionary America,* pp. 60–61.
8. *Ibid.,* pp. 38–43; Blanton, *Medicine in Virginia in the Eighteenth Century,* pp. 137–141.
9. Hindle, *The Pursuit of Science in Revolutionary America,* p. 26.
10. See Graham, *Colonists from Scotland,* pp. 131–133.
11. John Lining, for example, published on botanical subjects in the *Edinburgh Essays* and the *Edinburgh Medical Journal* and exchanged letters with his former teachers at the university, Robert Whytt and Charles Alston. Bridenbaugh, *Cities in Revolt,* p. 200. On the close relationship which Colden, Lining, Mitchell, and Garden maintained with Alston and Whytt, also see Hindle, *The Pursuit of Science in Revolutionary America,* pp. 26, 46–47, 51–52; Blanton, *Medicine in Virginia in the Eighteenth Century,* p. 127; J. Gordon Wilson, "The Influence of Edinburgh on American Medicine in the Eighteenth Century," *Institute of Medicine of Chicago,* VII (January 15, 1929), 135.
12. Blanton, *Medicine in Virginia in the Eighteenth Century,* p. 330.
13. As already noted, Morgan and Shippen, and the Virginians, Arthur Lee and Theodorick Bland Jr., along with other colonial students at Edinburgh, often discussed the need for an American medical school. Whitfield J. Bell, Jr., *John Morgan, Continental Doctor* (Philadelphia: University of Pennsylvania Press, 1965), pp. 72–73. Samuel Bard could hardly contain his disappointment at being too young to be included in the plans for the first school. "I own I feel a little jealous of the Philadelphians," Bard wrote to his father, "and should be glad to see the College of New York at least upon an equality with theirs." Carl Bridenbaugh, *Cities in Revolt,* p. 230. Bard lost no time and his medical school at King's College, New York, opened in 1767 with a six-member faculty, five of whom were also Edinburgh graduates.
14. John Morgan, *A Discourse Upon the Institution of Medical Schools in America* (Philadelphia: University of Pennsylvania Facsimile Reprint, 1965; first published 1765), pp. 29, 36. Also see Richard Shryock, *Medicine and Society in America, 1660–1860* (New York: New York University Press, 1960), p. 24. Edinburgh also

appears to have supplied the model for the founding of the Pennsylvania Hospital a few years earlier. In 1760 Benjamin Franklin wrote to his friend, Sir Alexander Dick in Edinburgh: "I inclose you one of our Philadelphia Newspapers, supposing that it may give you and my good Lord Provost some Pleasure, to see that we have imitated the Edinburgh Institution in that remote Part of the world." *Writings of Benjamin Franklin,* edited by Albert Henry Smyth (10 vols.; New York: The Macmillan Company, 1902), IV, 1–2. The plan of examination for degree candidates at Philadelphia was also the same as that used at Edinburgh. The Edinburgh procedure is described in full by Samuel Bard in a letter to his father, May 15, 1765, reprinted in B. C. Corner, *William Shippen, Jr., Pioneer in American Medical Education* (Philadelphia: American Philosophical Society, 1951), p. 152.

15. Bridenbaugh, *Cities in Revolt,* p. 280.
16. Quoted in Bell, *John Morgan,* p. 67.
17. Morgan, *Discourse,* pp. 29, 36, 52–54, 58–59.
18. Hindle, *The Pursuit of Science in Revolutionary America,* pp. 308–311.
19. Benjamin Rush, *Letters of Benjamin Rush,* edited by L. H. Butterfield (2 vols.; Princeton: Princeton University Press, 1951), I, 392.
20. An important article on Barton is Francis Pennell's "Benjamin Smith Barton as Naturalist," *Proceedings of the American Philosophical Society,* LXXXVI (1942), 108–122. Also see Edgar Fahs Smith, "Benjamin Smith Barton, 1766–1815," Lancaster County (Pa.) Historical Society, *Papers,* XXVIII (1924), 59–66.
21. The development of natural history itself into systematic and specialized fields of study is well illustrated by the work of Casper Wistar in anatomy. Wistar, a graduate of the College of Philadelphia, received an M.D. from the University of Edinburgh in 1786. While a student at Edinburgh, Wistar was a favorite of Professors Charles Stewart and William Cullen. He served as President of the Royal Medical Society in Edinburgh for two successive years, and dedicated his Edinburgh M.D. thesis to Benjamin Franklin and William Cullen. Thacher, *American Medical Biography,* II, 207–208. Three years after his graduation from Edinburgh he succeeded Rush to the chair of chemistry in the newly reopened College of Philadelphia— Rush having been appointed Professor of the Theory and Practice of Medicine. In 1792 Wistar took over the chair of anatomy, surgery, and midwifery in the medical faculty of the University of Pennsylvania. As with Barton and so many of Rush's colleagues, Rush's initial friendship with Wistar dissolved in a quarrel in the 1793 yellow fever epidemic when Wistar failed to give public support to Rush's cures. Wistar is perhaps best known as the author of the first American *System of Anatomy* (1811), but his pioneer work in the field later to be known as vertebrate paleontology was also significant. One of the earliest in America to become interested in the study of fossils was George Croghan, Scotch-Irish immigrant and one of the foremost Indian agents in America. Croghan collected specimens from the Big Bone Lick on the Ohio River in 1766, and sent them to Lord Shelburne, Franklin, and others in London. Croghan's specimens created a stir of excitement in scientific circles, and during the rest of the century the Big Bone Lick continued to attract the attention of others, including Caspar Wistar. The difference between the gifted amateur and the academic specialist is vivid in the contrast between Croghan and Wistar. According to George Gaylord Simpson, the papers written by Wistar, though only two in number, were the first technical studies of paleontology of professional quality to be done in America. Much of the credit for fossil study that has been given to Jefferson, Simpson says, should rightfully go to Wistar, as Jefferson himself urged. See G. G. Simpson, "The Beginnings of Vertebrate Paleontology in North America," *Proceedings of the American Philosophical Society,* LXXXVI (1942), pp. 13–188.
22. Despite Rush's original sponsorship of Barton, the two were seldom on friendly terms, mainly because Rush took offense at Barton's membership in the circle of professors surrounding William Shippen. See Rush, *Letters,* II, 225.
23. Edgar Fahs Smith, *Samuel Lathom Mitchill—A Father in American Chemistry* (New York: Columbia University Press, 1922), p. ii. Also see Courtney Robert Hall, *A Scientist in the Early Republic: Samuel Latham Mitchill, 1764–1831* (New York: Columbia University Press, 1934), especially pp. 19, 47–48.
24. On Benjamin Rush, James Woodhouse, and their connections, see Edgar Fahs Smith, *Chemistry in Old Philadelphia* (Philadelphia: J. B. Lippincott Company, 1919). Also see Edgar Fahs Smith, *Chemistry in America* (New York: Appleton & Company, 1914).
25. See John Maclean, *A Memoir of John Maclean, M.D.* (Princeton: at the "Press" office, 1876), p. 18.
26. From a letter quoted in John F. Fulton and Elizabeth H. Thompson, *Benjamin Silliman, 1779–1864* (New York: Henry Schuman, 1947), pp. 30–31.
27. Maclean, *A Memoir of John Maclean, M.D.,* p. 53.
28. See Theodore Hornberger, *Scientific Thought in the American Colleges, 1638–1800* (Austin: University of Texas Press, 1945), pp. 6–15; also George H. Daniels, *American Science in the Age of Jackson* (New York:

Columbia University Press, 1968), pp. 34–35. The amateur status of much science in colonial America is admirably treated by Hindle, *The Pursuit of Science in Revolutionary America.*

29. See Sydney E. Ahlstrom, "The Scottish Philosophy and American Theology," *Church History,* XXIV (1955), 257–272. Even Thomas Jefferson, an admirer of the writings of Lord Kames, combined the Scottish realism of Dugald Stewart with the ideology of Destutt de Tracy in his own thought. See Adrienne Koch, *The Philosophy of Thomas Jefferson* (Gloucester, Mass.: Peter Smith, 1957), pp. 17, 49–53.

30. Maclean, *Memoirs of John Maclean,* pp. 56–57. Luther P. Eisenhart, "Walter Minto and the Earl of Buchan," *Proceedings of the American Philosophical Society,* XCIV (June 1950), 282–294.

31. See Daniels, *American Science in the Age of Jackson,* p. 51. Daniels points repeatedly to the important part played by Scottish realism in the outlook and method of many nineteenth-century American scientists.

32. See the judgments of Ahlstrom and Daniels regarding the final effect of the Scottish philosophy upon theology and science respectively. Ahlstrom, "The Scottish Philosophy and American Theology," pp. 268–269; Daniels, *American Science in the Age of Jackson,* pp. 100–101.

33. The classic statement is that of J. Woodbridge Riley, who described the movement of Scottish realism into the Middle and Southern states as "a kind of intellectual glacier" and its triumph as "the glacial age in American thought." J. Woodbridge Riley, *American Philosophy; The Early Schools* (New York: Dodd, Mead, & Company, 1907), p. 478.

34. I have relied upon the discussion of Condorcet in Kingsley Martin, *The Rise of French Liberal Thought* (New York: New York University Press, 1954), pp. 289–292.

35. David Hume, *Enquiries Concerning the Human Understanding and Concerning the Principles of Morals,* edited by L. A. Selby-Biggs (Oxford: The Clarendon Press, 1902), p. 12.

36. Quoted in John Stewart, *The Moral and Political Philosophy of David Hume* (New York: Columbia University Press, 1963), p. 357, n. 31.

37. Gladys Bryson calls moral philosophy in relation to the subjects which emerged from its subdivisions, "the matrix discipline." See Gladys Bryson, *Man and Society: The Scottish Inquiry of the Eighteenth Century* (Princeton: Princeton University Press, 1945), pp. 239–245. Also see three articles by Gladys Bryson: "The Emergence of the Social Sciences from Moral Philosophy," *International Journal of Ethics,* XLII (April 1932), 304–323; "The Comparable Interests of the Old Moral Philosophy and the Modern Social Sciences," *Social Forces,* XI (October 1932), 19–27; and "Sociology considered as Moral Philosophy," *Sociological Review,* XXIV (January 1932), 26–36.

38. At Yale, Kames was in use as early as 1777 and Blair as early as 1785. See Carl Albert Hangartner, "Movements to Change American College Teaching, 1700–1830," (Ph.D. dissertation, Yale University, 1955), p. 193. Blair was in use at Harvard in 1788, at Columbia in 1792, at Princeton in 1800, and at Brown in 1803. See Louis F. Snow, *The College Curriculum in the United States* (New York: Printed for the author, 1907), pp. 83, 97, 116, 113.

39. Hangartner, "Movements to Change American College Teaching, 1700–1830," p. 192. For an assessment of the importance of Scottish literary criticism in the early nineteenth century in America, see William Charvat, *The Origins of American Critical Thought 1810–1835* (Philadelphia: University of Pennsylvania Press, 1936).

40. See Snow, *The College Curriculum in the United States,* pp. 82–140.

41. *The College Curriculum in the United States,* pp. 96, 123. Also compare the Dartmouth curriculum; see Herbert D. Foster, "Webster and Choate in College: Dartmouth under the Curriculum of 1796–1819," in *The Collected Papers of Herbert D. Foster* (Privately printed, 1929), pp. 213–249.

42. This is the position assumed by Snow, for example. Snow, *The College Curriculum,* pp. 141 ff.

43. If these speculations are at all accurate, the similarity between the development of the college curriculum and the interpretation of the changing function of Scottish realism suggested above is obvious.

44. To cite one example of the kind of data needing analysis: Rhode Island College (founded 1764) reproduced Samuel Finley's Princeton curriculum under its first president, James Manning, who graduated from the College of New Jersey under Finley. Texts in use at Rhode Island in 1783 included Kames' *Elements of Criticism,* Hutcheson's *Moral Philosophy,* Duncan's *Logic,* and several Scottish mathematical works. Snow, *The College Curriculum,* pp. 108–109.

45. A chair of medicine was established at Marischal in 1700; wide-ranging reforms in natural philosophy were attempted in 1726, but were not successfully instituted until 1753; a chair of Oriental languages was established in 1741; and history, natural and civil, belles lettres, ethics, jurisprudence, and politics were also included in the 1753 curriculum. Jefferson's plan of 1779 contained all of these emphases in one form or another. For Jefferson, see Roy J. Honeywell, *The Educational Work of Thomas Jefferson* (Cambridge: Harvard University Press, 1931), pp. 110–111.

46. See Herbert L. Ganter, "William Small, Jefferson's Beloved Teacher," *William and Mary Quarterly,* 3rd ser. (1947), 505–507; also "Portion of Physical Apparatus, Purchased by Dr. William Small in 1767," *William and Mary Quarterly,* XVI (1907–8), 166–168.

47. Andrew A. Lipscomb, ed., *The Writings of Thomas Jefferson* (Washington, D.C.: The Thomas Jefferson Memorial Associates, 1903), I, 3. A few years earlier Jefferson had written that Dr. Small was "to me as a father. To his enlightened and affectionate guidance of my studies while at college, I am indebted for everything. . . . He first introduced into both schools [of philosophy and mathematics] rational and elevated courses of study, and, from an extraordinary conjunction of eloquence and logic, was enabled to communicate them to the students with great effect" (*ibid.,* XIV, 231).

COLLEGIATE LIVING AND CAMBRIDGE JUSTICE: REGULATING THE COLONIAL HARVARD STUDENT COMMUNITY IN THE EIGHTEENTH CENTURY

JOHN D. BURTON

This article discusses the ways Harvard College and Cambridge, Massachusetts cooperated in the eigh-teenth century in order to regulate the student community. The leadership of the two communities was successful in maintaining order through much of the eighteenth-century, but with the outbreak of the American Revolution and the changing social structure of the two communities in its aftermath, the ability to enforce student regulation broke down by the end of the century.

Students and townspeople have often come into conflict in America. During the 1960s, student protests spilled over into local communities, increasing tensions between town and gown. Student unrest is not a product of the sixties, however, and has a long history. Students have traditionally engaged in activities that disturbed the peace of their surrounding communities. Kathryn Moore has provided a thorough overview of student regulation for seventeenth-century Harvard. The question remains how did student regulation change as both the college and Cambridge grew in the eighteenth century. This article attempts to understand the role of local authorities in regulating student life at eighteenth-century Harvard. In Cambridge, academic and town leaders cooperated, much like their twentieth-century counterparts, to ensure peace and order, with the result that, prior to the 1760s, student activities did not often lead to student unrest. This harmony was not the result of a separation of town and gown, but grew out of Harvard's integration with the local judicial structures.[1]

New England Puritans believed in consensual order, rule rising naturally from within the community, not imposed from outside it. Town constables, justices of the peace, and county courts were designed to maintain harmony in local communities. Harvard's students had to be similarly regulated, and the college and the town cooperated to ensure peace. The tutors combined with local magistrates and constables to discipline students, investigate offenses, and monitor individual behavior. Harvard's reliance on local authorities mirrored the actions of its English counterpart. Rather than create a separate police force as Oxford did, the University of Cambridge used the local constabulary to monitor its student population. But the English university's powers were more wide-ranging than Harvard's. The Oxford and Cambridge vice-chancellors were authorized not only to call out the local police but to arrest local inhabitants and, under some circumstances, to try them in university courts. Harvard's charter did not grant the college separate legal jurisdiction, nor did the president or fellows have specific rights to judge or punish students. Instead, the Harvard authorities were free to discipline their charges only as long as the students cooperated and remained at the college to be punished.[2]

The need to regulate student life outside the classroom developed from Harvard's decision to embrace a collegiate lifestyle, albeit imperfectly implemented. The college operated in some ways

History of Higher Education Annual 23 (2004): 83–105.
©2004. ISBN: 0-7658-0839-0

as a separate community, with Cambridge and Middlesex County surrounding but not controlling it. Seventeenth-century Harvard authorities chose collegiate living less from a need to govern and control unruly students than from a desire to create a collegial community. Particularly in the seventeenth century, Cambridge authorities, like any Puritan leaders, were prepared to enforce order and to discipline any of their citizens. The more important benefit the leadership may have sought from collegiate living was the development of personal connections between the students as part of a self-defined intellectual community.[3]

Disciplining students had been a common occurrence at Harvard since its founding. Written regulations described an ideal society; in fact, students regularly broke the rules and had to be corrected. Although Harvard drew upon a much narrower set of punishments than did the local judiciary, college authorities emulated the magistrates by stressing verbal persuasion, not physical force, to maintain peace and only flirted briefly with corporal punishment in the seventeenth-century. For more serious infractions or for intransigent students, the college had either to rely on local authorities or expel the scholars. Moreover, the town magistrates and local minister were usually also members of Harvard's governing bodies, creating an interlocking group of community leaders to ensure the peace. Most problems in the seventeenth century involved young male townsmen disturbing the peace of the college, not rowdy students disrupting the town. When complaints did occur from the town, Harvard responded quickly to punish the offenders. The college also confirmed that the town watch had "at all times . . . full powr of inspeccon into the manners and orders of all persons related to the Coll, whether wth in or wth out the precints of said Coll . . . any usage, or custome to the contrary not withstanding," but the Corporation did restrain the watch from laying "violent hands on any of the students" in the Yard. Thus Harvard defined the town watch's authority over scholars broadly when they were in the town but more narrowly within the college precincts. Although the watch was allowed to enter the Yard, if students were seized within college bounds, town authorities could secure them only until the president and fellows were notified.[4]

By the early eighteenth century, Cambridge youth were no longer posing a significant nuisance to collegiate life. Instead, Harvard authorities focused primarily on the regulation of their own young men. After abandoning whipping and flogging in the seventeenth century, the college officials could still handle a wide variety of infractions without recourse to the local officers or courts. By 1734, the regulations had further expanded to enumerate punishments for lying, stealing, and breaking open "any Chamber, Study, Cellers, Ches[t,] Desk or any place under lock & key." Students were not to keep distilled liquor on campus or entertain strangers (non-college members) in their rooms. They could be fined for being absent from prayers in the college hall, public worship in the Cambridge meetinghouse, or the divinity professor's lectures. Missing the Sunday church service was the most serious of these offenses; the fine was three shillings.[5]

At the same time, the students were beginning to resist the authority of the faculty. Their resistance brought into question the relative jurisdictions of both the college and the county counts. Not only were professors added to the faculty in the eighteenth century, but the tutors, who lived with the students and were responsible for much of their instruction, were older, remained at the college longer, and were more comfortable with exercising their powers. In 1718, one of the tutors, Nicholas Sever, charged one of the masters students, Ebenezer Pierpont, with "contemning, reproaching and Insulting the Governmt of the College." Pierpont had been the Roxbury schoolmaster for several years while waiting to apply for his second degree, during which time complaints had come to the attention of the fellows of the Harvard that the students from the Roxbury school were ill prepared for college. When Harvard rejected two of Pierpont's students in 1717, one of the students' fathers accused Sever of rejecting his son for personal reasons. Pierpont complained that the Harvard fellows were a set of "Rogues, Dougs & tygars." The Corporation, in turn, denied Pierpont his masters degree. To forestall Pierpont's appeal to the Overseers, Harvard President John Leverett reported the case to them himself, and the Overseers concurred with the college's actions stating, "Well, there is an End of it, and no more to be sd." Pierpont, unsatisfied, took his case to court.[6]

The college authorities were reluctant to accept judicial oversight. When Leverett received a summons from Pierpont for the Corporation to appear before the governor, he petitioned the executive to refer the case back to the Overseers, arguing that if the matter were carried into the courts, it "wilbe hurtfull to the rights and Privileges of the College, and tends to weaken the Governmt therof." But Pierpont had some powerful allies, including Cotton Mather, who still resented the choice of Leverett over himself as Harvard president. At the Overseers' meetings, Mather made a strong appeal to Governor Samuel Shute on behalf of Pierpont. The Overseers held two meetings, the governor presiding, to persuade the two to settle their differences. Because Pierpont's defense was so weak and poorly presented, the Overseers urged him to sign an apology. Above all, the Harvard authorities wanted to get the case out of the local courts and included in the agreement a clause that Pierpont would promise to stop "any further prsecutions in the Law against Mr. Sever." Sever agreed to sign, but Pierpont refused. The case went forward in the Middlesex County court, which denied Pierpont satisfaction, noting that the matter had "already had an hearing according to the Charter of Harvard College and Laws & Customs there of before the Corporation and Overseers of the sd college." The county court preferred to respect the rights and privileges of the college and was unwilling to press its advantage in the situation.[7]

The Pierpont-Sever case did not close the door to civil suits involving the college and its personnel. In 1733, Leonard Vassall sued tutor Daniel Rogers for striking Vassall's son, a student at Harvard. Young William Vassall had passed his tutor while walking on the streets in Cambridge; Rogers had doffed his hat but Vassall had kept his hat on his head. Rogers, in accord with college custom, retaliated by boxing Vassall's ear. Vassall sued Rogers, arguing the tutor's authority did not extend beyond the college. Ultimately, the Supreme Court found for Rogers, leaving intact Harvard's right to regulate students within both the college and the town.[8]

In 1734, the year after the Vassall-Rogers case, the Corporation voted that "no Scholar (or his Parent, or Guardian in his behalf) Shall exhibit to any Other Authority, than that of the College, a complaint Against any of the Governours or resident members thereof, for any injury cognizable by the Authority of the College, before he has sought for redress to the President and Tutors." If the student and his family could not get relief from the Corporation, they were to appeal to the Overseers. Any scholar who went directly to the courts "shall forthwith be expelled." Although Harvard had used the county court in the past for its own interest, it was now doing all it could to maintain its judicial independence when the court might be used against it. These requirements did not allow students to flout local authority, however. Harvard's regulations of 1734 required scholars to show "due respect & honou[r] in speech and behaviour" not only to the president and fellows but also to the "Magistrates . . . and Elders" of the town.[9]

Court cases in the seventeenth century had closed the door to collegiate oversight of townsmen. To prevent undesirable contact between scholars and Cambridge residents in the eighteenth century, Harvard had to focus on the scholars. For example, in 1735, William Woodhouse, a barber, kept showing up at the college and promoting improper behavior among the students. The college labeled Woodhouse as "a person of a dissolute life" but could not take direct action against him. Although Woodhouse was the chief problem, the cautions and potential punishments were directed at the scholars. Woodhouse was "strictly forbidden coming to the College," but the scholars were also "publickly charged upon their peril not to keep his company, nor receive him into their chambers upon any pretence wtsever." Woodhouse must not have heeded the college's warning, because five years later, the students were once again reminded not to "Entertain or associate, with, Either Wm Woodhouse of this town, or Titus, a Molattoe slave of the late Revd. Presdt Wadsworth's." The two potential trespassers' names were posted in the buttery as a daily reminder to the students to shun them.[10]

Just as Harvard expected students to respect the Cambridge authorities, officials would not tolerate unruly behavior either on campus or in the town. In 1749, for example, the college punished two students for "a Disturbance to certain Persons met for a Private Worship At the house of Mr. Wm. Morse." Harvard was willing to discipline students for infractions within Cambridge and responded to complaints from townsmen about the behavior of scholars.[11]

To better control its students, Harvard tried to co-opt some of the power of local authorities by having the tutors or other college officers appointed justices of the peace. Harvard personnel could then hear cases and punish offenders not only as officers of the college but also as officers of the local court. Leverett had been a justice of the peace but had resigned his office on becoming president. Henry

Flynt was commissioned a justice of the peace for Cambridge while a Harvard tutor and had the "full power of any Justice in Cambridge for the advantage and better government of the Colledg." But Flynt hesitated to use these powers. When Josiah Parker, a tavern keeper in Cambridge, was accused in 1722 of "abusing [one of the students] by blows etc," Leverett asked Flynt to hear the case. In spite of the tutor's clear right to do so, he refused to conduct a trial alone, explaining, "I was a Stranger to such things and might take wrong stepps." Flynt also felt his duties at the college prevented his giving proper attention to the law because he "was not Engaged in a particular Study and could not attend to aquaint myself as I should." Leverett, who was probably prepared to give all the guidance that was needed, retorted, "You know how to Judge of a matter that is before you." He suggested further that if Flynt "did not now begin," he would "never do anything," and that "these things were as plain as could be desired." But the president had no luck persuading Flynt to exercise his judicial authority, and the college had to continue to rely on the Cambridge magistrates to discipline the townsmen and keep peace in the larger community. In spite of his unwillingness to exercise the powers of his office, Flynt continued to be appointed a justice of the peace as late as 1737.[12]

Thus, in cases extending beyond the college, Harvard called on the magistrates for assistance. One such case occurred in 1751. One evening, tutor Jonathan Mayhew was "disturbed by the rowlling of a Logg twice down the Stairs leading to his Chamb. from above." Mayhew got out of bed to investigate and, in the dark, was "pushed down from the Top of the Stairs by a Stranger, whm he found standing on them." Mayhew asked for the help of another tutor, Belcher Hancock. The tutors then called on Samuel Danforth, the Cambridge magistrate, to investigate because "of a Stranger's being found to be concerned with this Insult." Danforth came to the college and accompanied the tutors to the room of Joseph Gerrish, one of the suspected students. There they found Stephen Miller of Milton and Ebenezer Miller of Braintree, brothers of another student, John Miller. Danforth led the examination of the students and two "strangers." The malefactors blamed "One Browne of Providence" for rolling the log down the stairs and pushing tutor Mayhew after it. After questioning by the two tutors, however, John Miller confessed that Mr. Brown was fictional. In fact, it was Benjamin Gerrish, Joseph's brother, "who did what they had charg'd upon this Browne," and the others finally agreed with Miller in front of Danforth and the two tutors. Although Danforth had been called to investigate, the case was then turned over to the college authorities; Miller was degraded eighteen places in his class and Gerrish was expelled. Gerrish's more severe punishment was due to his "giving false Testimony upon Oath, before one of his Majesties Justices of the Peace." Although the college did not want the local authorities appearing on campus unrequested, when the Harvard officers called upon them, the tutors expected the students to pay appropriate respect. Gerrish missed his commencement in 1752, but he made a public confession the following year, was restored to his rank, and received his degree. The "strangers" apparently went unpunished. In spite of Danforth's presence during the investigation, the case was not recorded in the Middlesex County court.[13]

Although the aims of the magistrates and the college authorities were the same, Harvard made a clear distinction between punishments imposed by the town and punishments imposed by the college. For the most part, students did not come before the local authorities, but from time to time exceptions did occur. In 1758, James Lovell, a resident graduate studying for his master's degree, was living in the college but taking his meals with Jonathan Hastings, a Cambridge tanner, who lived at the north end of the commons. Hastings's daughter Susanna died giving birth to an illegitimate child, and she may have named Lovell as the father. Although Lovell at first denied paternity, the next year he confessed in the Cambridge church to fornication. The college was not satisfied with this confession, and the faculty ordered Lovell to make another one "publicly in the [college] Chapel." The Puritan reliance on public confession satisfied both groups. Not only was Lovell restored to his privileges at the college but he was also admitted to full communion at the Cambridge church the next year. By the 1760s, Harvard had gained a *de facto* autonomy, even if the local courts had *de jure* authority. Although the college resisted local judicial oversight, its officials urged local authorities to restore order in the town when the peace of the college was threatened, punished students for local complaints, and required scholars to have proper respect for local magistrates. This balance between autonomy and peaceful cooperation became difficult to preserve in the decade preceding the Revolution.[14]

By the late 1750s, Harvard was once again in the midst of a housing shortage. The Corporation noted in 1759, "There are now so large a number of students belonging to the College, that a very considerable part of them, are oblig'd to live out of the College in the town." About seventy students were taking lodgings in Cambridge in 1759; sixty-four would do so in 1760. The Corporation again petitioned the General Court for "some inlargement of the College buildings." By the 1760s, most of each freshmen class had to stat their college careers in town lodgings, moving into college housing their second or third year. Harvard at the same time was relaxing its requirement that all students dine in the college. Students living in the college were required to eat in commons, but students living in town were now allowed to dine with householders "upon the invitation of any housekeeper in the town to dine or sup gratis."[15] Corporation Records, Harvard University Archives, 2:123, 130, 139; Overseers Records, Harvard University Archives, 2:70; Faculty Records Harvard University Archives, 2:116, 5:139.

Not only was the college housing more of its students in town, but the regulations also began allowing scholars to leave Cambridge on occasion. In 1763, the Corporation decided that students could leave town for one day without permission of the tutors and that seniors could leave for two days so long as they did not miss any of their lectures. Not everyone approved of this new leniency. The visiting committee of the Overseers complained in 1765 that students living in town should be "prevented [from] breakfasting in the town's people's houses" and asked that the Corporation provide those students with breakfast in the college hall. Likewise, when the Overseers approved the college's new calendar in 1766, they asked that students not be allowed to leave Cambridge except during official college breaks. It was supposed to be the professors' responsibility (since they lived in Cambridge) to oversee the students living in the town, but the Overseers reported that professors Wigglesworth and Sewall were not visiting the chambers of the town dwellers. Wigglesworth was partially excused for his oversight, as his "bodily infirmities" prevented him from doing so, but close oversight of students living in private homes was probably unreasonable. The Corporation did not respond to the Overseer's criticisms.[16]

Although Harvard began to relax some of its regulations, the changes did not occur fast enough to suit the students. In 1761, the college eased restrictions on students' entertainments, allowing the scholars to "entertain one another & strangers with punch." The Corporation explained that punch "as it is now usually made is no intoxicating liquor." Whether punch as the students made it was not intoxicating was another matter. Overall, students were socializing more, and the number of infractions for drinking and card playing rose. The infractions in 1761 were not unusual. For example, several students stole "boards and tools" from the Cambridge church construction site, but after a complaint from the housewright building the church, the youths confessed and made full restitution. By the end of the decade, however, student unrest and disorders had reached unprecedented proportions.[17]

This relaxation in student regulation came at an unfortunate time. Although the tutorship at Harvard College had been a strong and stable position at Harvard through much of the eighteenth century, the average tenure for tutors dropped from more than eleven years in the 1740s and 1750s to less than four years in the 1760s. The shorter length of service left both less experienced tutors in charge of the students and increased the turnover of faculty. Moreover the tutorship underwent a curricular transformation. Up until the 1760s, each tutor taught the entire curriculum to a given class, making the connections between a tutor and his students quite strong and lasting over four years of college. In 1767, the tutors began to teach specific subjects, reducing the connection between tutors and a specific class and so probably weakening faculty oversight. Coincidentally, the length of service for Cambridge selectmen also dropped after the 1760s from an average of more than seven years in mid-century to less than five years in the 1760s and 1770s. Both the college and the town went through several decades of weakened leadership around the years of the American Revolution.[18]

In response to this student unrest and weakened faculty oversight, Harvard tried to strengthen collegiate living. During the second half of the eighteenth century, the college built several new buildings to accommodate its students. The General Court appropriated €2500 in 1762 for one new dormitory, Hollis Hall. Most students were living on campus, but some still lived in town. The construction of new housing failed to accomplish Harvard's goals. Ultimately, after a century of struggling with strict enforcement of a collegiate lifestyle that was more an ideal than a reality, the college shifted its focus. By the end of the century, Harvard was paying more attention to the types of homes in which students were living than to getting all scholars on campus. The college now turned to local family homes as a positive alternative to other types of housing, particularly private boarding houses and taverns. The faculty ordered that "no student be permitted to occupy a room in any house in the town of Cambridge where a family does not reside, nor in any building where Spirituous liquors are retailed or a tavern is kept." Students were also barred from dining in these establishments. Although Harvard remained primarily residential, the administration became reconciled to some students living in the town.[19]

Pre-Revolutionary Student Disorders

Harvard students in the 1760s were older than their predecessors had been a generation before, entering college at about age seventeen rather than around age fourteen or fifteen. They chafed under administrative paternalism and felt their lives too closely regulated because they could not leave Cambridge without permission and had to eat in commons. Moreover, after decades of strong presidential rule, leadership weakened when President Holyoke's health deteriorated before his death. The tutors, now less experienced, were unprepared for the vacuum in executive leadership, and discipline suffered. One student reported that there "was much deviltry carried on in College" during this period. In 1766, students complained to the senior tutor about the quality of the butter served in commons. The tutor rejected the complaints. When the same rancid butter appeared at table the next morning, the students walked out of commons and breakfasted in town. The faculty was able to restrict this first protest to a single incident. As was Harvard's preference, the Cambridge authorities were not called for assistance. Instead, Holyoke and the faculty drew up a written confession of guilt to be signed by each of the participants if they wanted to remain at college.[20]

The faculty could not handle the next set of protests so easily. In spite of a liberalizing of the regulations in 1767, a rebellion broke out again in 1768. This time the spark was recitations. Until 1768, unprepared students had been able to avoid recitations by answering "nollo," or "I don't want to." Beginning in March 1768, the Corporation decreed that only seniors could refuse to recite. The scholars stonewalled the new regulation by refusing *en masse* to participate. Some then vandalized their tutors' rooms. When it was reported that tutor Joseph Williard had shut up a freshman, Thurston Whiting, in the tutor's room all day without food in a vain effort to tell who was behind the disorders, the college went up in a storm. Sixty or seventy students attacked Williard's room, breaking his windows.[21]

The faculty panicked when it appeared that the demonstration could not be contained within the college bounds, and someone called for the Middlesex County sheriff. When the students heard rumors that the county militia was approaching the Yard, they armed themselves and set off to meet the soldiers at the commons. Confrontation was averted when one of the students, Stephen Peabody, learned that the guard had been sent to protect college property, not to arrest the students. The protest fell apart after Whiting recanted his accusations against Williard, explaining that he had not been held against his will. Harvard did not have to seek further assistance from Middlesex or Cambridge authorities. Instead, it handled the matter itself as it had for the past century: the scholars publicly confessed and were reintegrated into the Harvard community.[22]

Two years later, student disorders spread out of the Yard, across the commons and into Cambridge. In March 1770, five Harvard students were charged in Middlesex County court with breaking into the home of John Nutting and assaulting and threatening to kill the occupant, Samuel Butterfield. The reasons for the attack are unknown. The event's chief historian, Theodore Chase, believes that Nutting was not the intended victim. Moreover, although the events occurred two weeks after the Boston Massacre, no specific political cause can be identified. Chase suggests that the event was an outgrowth of personal animosities between scholars and townsmen. Butterfield was about the same age as the college students, and some personal antagonism may have existed between him and them. All of the students involved in the incident had histories of disciplinary problems. John Frye, a master's candidate and probably one of the leaders, had already been admonished by the faculty for disturbances within the college that had also affected "many Inhabitants of the Town." On March 21, Frye had been especially busy violating the college regulations. In addition to breaking into Nutting's house, he had entertained "women of ill Fame" in his room at Harvard.[23]

As if they were not in enough trouble already, on May 9, Frye and two other students assaulted Captain William Angier, a tanner, in order to persuade him not to give evidence in the forthcoming trial. Angier subsequently testified to the college authorities that he had seen Frye, Winthrop Sergeant, and Thomas Saunders entertaining prostitutes in March. He stated that the three students did "assult, illtreat, and threaten the said Capt Angier, in such a manner, that he apprehend himself in danger from them." They also "threatened his wife." Such treatment of town residents by students was unparalleled. The college officials were particularly concerned that the scholars' actions would make it more difficult for the faculty to procure the testimony of town residents in the future. In the upshot, the Corporation "rusticated" all three students, sending them to study with rural pastors.[24]

Had the case ended there, it would have been only an example of extreme student violence, highlighting town-gown tensions but not suggesting any changes in the balance of power between the college and the local judiciary. But the same day, violence broke out when students tried to stop local authorities from arresting the three culprits. Although the town's actions may seem justified today, they were unprecedented in 1770. No Harvard student had ever been arrested by local authorities in the eighteenth century, nor had any been punished except by college officials since Goodman Healey had been hired to whip students under President Hoar in the 1670s. The students rescued their fellows, but the accused were later apprehended and required to give bond to appear the second Tuesday in May at the Middlesex County courthouse. Though the case was subsequently dropped, the offenders protested the college's punishment later in May by walking out of the college chapel.[25]

The county then brought in a second indictment of disrupting the peace against four of the students who had tried to stop the earlier arrest. The court described the defendants as "infants above the age of fourteen years and all students now residing at Harvard College in Cambridge." They were accused of participating, along with "fifty other evil minded & disorderly Persons," as "Rioters, Routers, and Disturbers of the Peace." The jury found all four guilty. The students then appealed to the Superior Court, but the outbreak of the Revolution intervened. Although the case was dismissed in 1776, it was unique in the colonial era as the only occasion when students were called into the Middlesex County court. A possible precedent had been set: students were not immune from prosecution in the local courts. Moreover, punishment by the college authorities did not necessarily preempt action by local officials.[26]

Student disorders persisted in the post-Revolutionary period, but civil authorities did not prosecute any scholars, Harvard handling most complaints directly. When Harvard officials received a complaint from Edward Richardson of Watertown that Daniel Murry, a student, was "abusing, in language" Richardson's wife and son, Murry was quickly degraded in order to "deter . . . all the Members of this society . . . from maletreating any person in the vicinity of Harvard College." Further student infractions took place, but punishment was left to college authorities. Wine was stolen from a Cambridge resident; the college privies were set on fire, endangering homes in the town; and a student was found to be keeping "at his own expense" a "lewd Woman" in a local house. In the 1780s, the faculty began keeping a set of "student disorder papers," outlining each offense. Most of the violations affected only the college, but the loud noise and disturbances often drifted into the town as well. At first, Harvard tried to expand its own authority into the town in order to rein in the students. The college saw the taverns as the main culprit and believed that if their regulation was transferred to Harvard, peace would return to the community.[27]

Harvard Students and Cambridge Taverns

Puritans were not teetotalers and taverns were an accepted part of life, but students were barred from frequenting them throughout the colonial period. As early as President Dunster's time, Harvard had protested tavern keepers "harbouring students unseasonably," and Dunster made an agreement with local tavern owners to keep student purchases to a minimum. Scholars were only to purchase bread and beer from local ordinaries when supplies at the college were inadequate. Although students occasionally were chastised for frequenting ale houses in the early eighteenth century, it was not until mid-century that Harvard began to express concern. Taverns had become a focus of debate in New England life. In 1738, the *Boston Evening Post* defended taverns as "very Necessary and Beneficial" for the "Entertainment of Strangers and Travellers" but criticized them as haunts of town residents. In Cambridge, the total number of establishments had increased significantly. In 1650, the town had one authorized tavern, by the 1670s, three, in 1700, seven, and by 1750, eleven. This figure amounted to one tavern for every 135 inhabitants, approaching Boston's ratio of one for every 100.[28]

At first, Harvard turned to the town authorities for assistance with the problem of student patronage of taverns. In 1751, the Corporation asked the "Justices and Selectmen of the town of Cambridge, that they would use their interest that neither the retailers nor inn-holders of said town, do sell to any of the students of Harvard College being undergraduates any rum or spirits whatsoever." In 1763, the Overseers expressed different fears about the students frequenting taverns. In their annual visitation of the college, the Overseers instructed the Corporation "to project some method for preventing Innholders & Retailers from Supplying the Undergraduates with Wine & Spirituous Liquors upon Trust or Credit." They recommended that the General Court pass a law requiring the Middlesex County Court of General Sessions (which approved licenses for the Cambridge taverns) to cancel the licenses of establishments that fell under the disapproval of the college authorities. The Overseers were as much worried about the students' pocketbooks as about their sobriety.[29]

Harvard reacted to these concerns by reissuing regulations that required students to refrain from frequenting local taverns, and the Corporation "earnestly requested of his Majesty's Justices of the Peace of the County of Middlesex, on whom the keepers of the public houses and Retailers . . . have dependence for their licenses, that they would be pleased to enforce the observation of this law . . . within three miles of the college." Because students were adept at leaving Cambridge to find entertainment, Harvard also asked the Charlestown selectmen to "exert themselves effectively to suppress all Practices within their Township so immoral in their Nature & of such dangerous Tendency." More directly, they asked the Charlestown authorities to take action against the Ship Tavern, "a House of bad fame" that employed one or more "lewd" women. By 1767, Harvard no longer had only liquor and prostitutes to worry about. The concerns of River City, Iowa, had reached eighteenth-century Cambridge: a pool table had been installed in one of the taverns! The Harvard faculty protested to the selectmen that "we are inform'd that a Billiard Table hath lately been set up in Cambridge not far from the College viz. at the house of Capt. Samuel Gookin, by a Person who is not an Inhabitant of this Town." The Corporation asked that the selectmen "take such steps as they in their Wisdom may judge necessary to prevent, the dangerous Effects wch may Naturally be expected from gaming Houses." There is no record of the town taking any action against Gookin. Harvard continued to complain to the town authorities about taverns throughout the 1760s, and the town tried to rein in abuses. For example, the selectmen voted in 1773 "that they earnestly Entreat all such who shall have approbation or Recommendation to sell strong drink, that they would not allow young men. . . to have Strong Drink or intertain them." Although townsmen occasionally complained to the college of the drunken activities of the students, they were more interested in the profit the taverns brought to the community.[30]

The Corporation also asked the selectmen to help enforce its regulations against dancing. In 1766, the Corporation protested that "a dancing school hath lately been open'd in Cambridge & diverse scholars of this house have attended it, without leave from the Governmt of the College." The Corporation asked the selectmen to close the school, as "the continuance of sd school will be of bad consequences to this society." The selectmen were not convinced of the dangers and took no action. Dancing continued. Elizabeth Cranch reported on visiting Harvard in 1771 that "all such as Learn to dance are so taken up with it, that they can't be students."[31]

After the Revolution, Harvard authorities threatened direct action against both taverns and dancing. In 1783, the Corporation directed the president to "write the Select Men of the town of Cambridge, requesting them not to permit any of the students of the College to have use of the Town Hall for a Ball." These dances may have been part of larger community problem. The selectmen were concerned about outsiders coming to Cambridge for "entertainment," and they appointed a committee, including James Winthrop, the Harvard librarian, to devise ways of restricting the events. Neither the selectmen nor the Harvard authorities were able to stop dancing and other student entertainments. John Quincy Adams reported attending horse races, dances, militia meetings, and teas in Cambridge during his student years in the late 1780s.[32]

Harvard authorities took more direct action against taverns. The Corporation distributed copies of the college laws respecting student drinking to the Cambridge establishments and asked the innkeepers to help enforce the college regulations, or else Harvard would oppose the renewal of their licenses. February and March 1789 were particularly trying months. Drunken students regularly returned to the college in a "noisy and tumultuous manner." To the tavern keepers' credit, in at least one instance the scholars found the Cambridge taverns closed to them and had to ride "two or three miles to a public house from whence they did not return 'till about four o'clock the next morning." Harvard decided more forceful action was necessary and asked the legislature to transfer the right to license taverns from the county to the college. In their petition, the Overseers inquired

> whether it be not needful to the welfare of the university that the Governors of it, or some of them, should have some control over the appointment of Innholders within a given distance from the College and that application should be made for the appointment of a Magistrate or Magistrates from among the immediate Governors of the college to prevent or suppress the disorderly conduct of those who do not belong to it.

At this possible expansion of college authority, the Cambridge selectmen sat up, took notice, and petitioned that Harvard's request "might not be granted, & that they [the selectmen] might be allowed an hearing." The legislature received both sets of petitions and chose a course of inaction. Harvard did not receive expanded licensing or judicial powers, and the life of the college continued to be plagued by liquor and loose women. Maintaining order in the community, even during Harvard-sponsored events, required the cooperation of both the town and college authorities.[33]

Commencement and Cambridge Disorders

Commencement was one of the most important of these occasions. Graduating seniors celebrated with their families and friends, and many alumni returned to the college. The crowds attracted merchants and peddlers, so that the whole event had the trappings of a county fair. Morison estimates that by the late seventeenth century, several hundred visitors came to Cambridge at commencement, and "hucksters and cheap-jacks came too, in order to cater to the crowd in its lighter moments." Beginning in 1687, the commencement ceremony moved from the college hall, which had become too small to house the crowd, to the Cambridge meetinghouse. Dinner was served in the hall to the graduates, and parties continued in their lodgings into the evening.[34] As early as 1681, Harvard recognized that it needed assistance in patrolling the college and policing visitors because the student revelries were getting out of hand. There was too much drinking, and too many strangers were coming in and out of the college. In response, the Overseers appointed Samuel Andrew, a resident master, "to execute the office of Proctor for the commencement week." His new assignment was to keep intermixing between the scholars and uninvited visitors at a minimum by ensuring that no one lingered in the college during the commencement service and that all "strangers" left by nine o'clock on commencement evening. The proctor then closed the college to all except the students, reminding visitors that "the usual recourse of any to the college . . . excepting scholars is displeasing to the hon. & Revd Overseers."[35]

The college was successful at self-regulation into the eighteenth century, but by the 1720s, Harvard authorities were finding the crowds, festivities, and noise of commencement more than they could handle. They therefore instituted "private" ceremonies restricted to graduates and their families, in which public events were kept to a minimum, hoping to discourage visitors from coming to Cambridge. To keep the crowds down, the college no longer held commencement on a fixed date (traditionally the first Wednesday in July). Instead, it announced the date of the ceremony in the Boston newspapers only a couple of weeks in advance of the event, hoping the peddlers and non-academic visitors would be unable to attend at short notice. At the same time, the Corporation tried to restrict the student's private parties by limiting the list of beverages and provisions the students could offer their guests, with strong punch specifically forbidden.[36]

These efforts failed to reduce the problems at commencement. In 1732, the Overseers instructed the Corporation "to consult with the Justices of the peace that Live in Cambridge about the Time of Commencement particularly on the Commencement day & the Night following." President Wadsworth described a meeting between the Corporation and two of the local officials "about proper means to prevent disorders at Commencement." The justices suggested that the college ask the undersheriff, a constable, and four or five assistants to attend commencement, estimating that "furnish'd with a Warrant from the Justices, [they] would be a sufficient number to watch and walk as there should be occasion toward evening on Commencement day, and the night following." The college would pay the men's salaries of ten shillings apiece and twenty shillings for the "captain" of the guard. In 1736, with new provisions for security, Harvard returned to holding commencement on the first Wednesday of July.[37]

Throughout the rest of the century, Harvard paid the local constabulary to secure the streets of Cambridge during commencement. At first, the guards' responsibilities were to patrol the town while Harvard's faculty maintained order within the college. Because disorders continued on commencement night, in 1737 the guards were charged with preventing "the disorders both in the town & college." The guards were usually Cambridge townsmen headed by the local constable. Over time, their number increased from the constable and four assistants in the 1730s to ten assistants in the 1780s. To end the festivities, the guard was charged in 1766 "not only to strike the Booths on Commencement evening" but to direct visitors to remove their belongings and be out of town by the next morning.[38]

Harvard further restricted students' activities on the evening of commencement. Punch was allowed in 1759, but larger "entertainments" were not permitted. In spite of these precautions, a riot broke out after commencement in 1761, and four students had to be rusticated. Drinking, entertainments, and dancing were all feared by the college authorities, who restricted graduates' receptions to students and family members. Some students and their parents circumvented the college regulations by holding parties in town, but these affairs were subsequently banned, except when hosted by students whose parents lived in Cambridge. Given that the scholars had already graduated, the only penalty the Corporation could inflict was withholding the graduates' master's degrees, a severe punishment that was usually overturned a year or two later.[39]

After the Revolution, Harvard began to ask that the local magistrates remain in town through the day following commencement "to preserve peace and good orders." The town also began to show increased concern about the students' parties. In 1786, the selectmen formed a committee "to devise by-laws to prevent these entertainments." The guard was increased to twelve in the 1790s, with at least two magistrates in attendance. Over the course of the eighteenth century, commencement had been transformed from a Harvard-regulated activity to a community-wide event. It fell to local authorities to preserve the town's peace. Balls also became an accepted part of student life, by the 1790s, Harvard allowed students to use rooms at the college for these events.[40]

✳✳✳

In the aftermath of the American Revolution, cooperation between Harvard and Cambridge to maintain order in the community began to break down. Visiting the United States in 1788, J. B. Brissot de Warville reported that "Boston has the glory of having given the first college or university to the new world." As an afterthought, he mentioned that the college was actually located "four miles from Boston in a place called Cambridge." Brissot de Warville's view of Harvard as Boston's college was a sign of a larger transformation in town-gown relations. In the new republic, Harvard was increasingly tied to the metropolis of Boston and less its own town. Faculty members were connected to a Beacon Hill elite and students were mostly sons of Boston merchants and traveled regularly to the city for parties and shopping. At the same time, Cambridge was becoming a working-class suburb with interests increasingly divergent from that of the college. People visiting Harvard during this period should be excused for not realizing they had left Boston.[41]

By the late eighteenth and early nineteenth century, a sense of gentility and refinement extended to Harvardians—both faculty and students. In the 1770s, John Winthrop, professor of natural history, chronicled his adoption of the custom of taking tea in the afternoon and entertaining dining companions in the evening. Most of his guests were either faculty members or provincial politicians; he had little interaction with other Cambridge elites, and the Harvard faculty withdrew from town life. The social life of students also changed. Drinking and card playing became popular entertainments. The increase in tavern attendance in the eighteenth century did not solidify town-gown relations, but put Harvard at odds with Cambridge. The economic benefits of the taverns outweighed the town's desire for orderliness and control. Harvard's attempt to usurp the power of local courts to license taverns was defeated, but not without forcing overt confrontation between town and college authorities.[42]

Because Harvard was unable to regulate the community, it worked instead to reduce student interaction with townsmen. This battle became all the more important as Cambridge went through a social transformation of its own. In the final decades of the eighteenth century, the town began to grow quickly. The new neighborhoods to the east and north were mostly working-class communities with few ties to the college or to the central settlement. Many of the new inhabitants were Baptist or Roman Catholic, rather than Congregationalist, Unitarian, or Episcopalian like the students. Harvard responded to the newcomers by sequestering the students. Although they were allowed to worship in the churches in Old Cambridge, they were barred from those in east Cambridge. Students were urged to mix with faculty members and a few socially prominent townsmen rather than with the new town dwellers. The best symbol of this new attitude toward the community was the orientation of Holsworthy Hall, a dormitory built in 1811. For the first time, Harvard built a building that did not face or give direct access to the Cambridge common. Holsworthy turned its back on the town and opened into the Yard. Later in the century, Harvard raised the height of the wall surrounding the campus and added iron gates to keep out townsmen.[43]

By 1800, Harvard College could not effectively isolate its students from the temptations of the surrounding community. Although the college resisted town oversight in the eighteenth century, it had to rely on local police to maintain order in unusual circumstances, particularly at commencement. Moreover, students came to Harvard expecting to participate in local entertainments—dances, balls, and other social events. Although scholars continued to be punished for infractions, they regularly went to taverns, played cards, and brought liquor into their rooms. College attendance was no longer merely a scholarly endeavor; it was also a social experience. The separation of oversight between the college and the town and these new social temptations increased frictions. But the case of Harvard's regulation of student life demonstrates the importance of studying college life, not in isolation, but within a larger community context. Students were not only subject to collegiate oversight but also that of local authorities. Similarly, infractions could occur both within the college and outside it. If the academic and town leadership could cooperate, student life could be successfully regulated, and town-gown tensions minimized. Colleges were community institutions, and the regulation of student life involved the entire community.

Notes

1. Kathryn McDaniel Moore, "The Dilemma of Corporal Punishment at Harvard College," *History of Education Quarterly* 14 (fall 1974): 335–39.
2. David Hackett Fischer, *Albion's Seed: Four British Folkways in America* (New York: Oxford University Press, 1989), 189; Jurgen Herbst, *From Crisis to Crisis: American College Government, 1636–1819* (Cambridge, Mass.: Harvard University Press, 1981), 5–8; Harvard Charter of 1650, in *American Higher Education: A Documentary History*, eds. Richard Hofstadter and Wilson Smith, vol. 1 (Chicago: University of Chicago Press, 1961), 10–12.
3. Corporation Records, Harvard University Archives, vol. 2, p. 139; Clifford Shipton, *Sibley's Harvard Graduates: Biographical Sketches of those Who Attended Harvard College* (Boston: Massachusetts Historical Society, 1873–1975), vol. 4, p. 381, vol. 7, p. 517. The Massachusetts leadership's own experience at the University of Cambridge highlighted the importance of interpersonal contact during collegiate education to the creation of a Puritan intellectual elite. See Francis Bremer, *Congregational Communion: Clerical Friendship in the Anglo-American Puritan Community, 1610–1692* (Boston: Northeastern University Press, 1994), 17.
4. Moore, "Corporal Punishment," 335–39; *Harvard Records*, Colonial Society of Massachusetts, *Collections* 15 (1925): 44–45, 205; Samuel Eliot Morison, *Harvard in the Seventeenth Century*, vol. 1 (Cambridge, Mass.: Harvard University Press, 1936), 24.
5. *Harvard Records*, Colonial Society of Massachusetts, *Collections* 15 (1925): 142–44; 16 (1925): 593.

6. *Harvard Records*, Colonial Society of Massachusetts; *Collections* 16 (1925): 441; 49 (1975): 285–87; Shipton, *Harvard Graduates*, vol. 6 (1942), 99.

7. *Harvard Records*, Colonial Society of Massachusetts, *Collections* 16 (1925): 441–42; Overseers Records, Harvard University Archives, 1:13–14; John Leverett, Diary, Harvard University Archives, 172, 178; Shipton, *Harvard Graduates*, vol. 6 (1942), 100.

8. *Harvard Records*, Colonial Society of Massachusetts, *Collections* 16 (1925): 610–15; Overseer Records, Harvard University Archives, 1:133–34; Shipton, *Harvard Graduates*, 350.

9. *Harvard Records*, Colonial Society of Massachusetts, *Collections* 15: 137, 145.

10. Faculty Records, Harvard University Archives, 1:82.

11. Ibid., 1:228.

12. Henry Flynt, Diary, Typescript, Harvard University Archives, 403–4. In 1737, President Holyoke was also appointed justice of the peace for Middlesex County. Neither Flynt nor Holyoke appears to have actually heard cases; see *Boston Evening Post*, 14 November 1737.

13. Faculty Records, Harvard College Archives, 1:347–55. Shipton provides a brief account of the incident in Shipton, *Harvard Graduates*, vol. 13, 231–32, 271–72.

14. Faculty Records, Harvard University Archives, 2:100; Shipton, *Harvard Graduates*, vol. 14, 31.

15. Corporation Records, Harvard University Archives, 2:123, 130, 139; Overseers Records, Harvard University Archives, 2:70; Faculty Records, Harvard University Archives, 2:116, 5:139.

16. Corporation Records, Harvard University Archives, 2:167–8, 253; Overseers Record, Harvard University Archives, 2:173, 3:9.

17. Corporation Records, Harvard University Archives, 2:143; Faculty Records, Harvard University Archives, 2:142. This section of the chapter benefits from two previous studies of Harvard disorders by Shelden Cohen and Theodore Chase. I have focused on the town and county involvement in the student disturbances. For greater detail on the student disturbances, see Cohen, "The Turkish Tyranny," *New England Quarterly* 47 (December 1974): 564–83, and Chase, "Harvard Student Disorders in 1770," *New England Quarterly* 61 (March 1988): 25–54.

18. John Burton, "Harvard Tutors: The Beginning of an Academic Profession," *History of Higher Education Annual* 16 (1996): 5–20; John Burton, "Puritan Town and Gown: Harvard College and Cambridge, Massachusetts, 1636–1800" (Ph.D. diss., College of William and Mary, 1996), 18. 42.

19. Faculty Records, Harvard University Archives, 2:355; Bainbridge Bunting and Robert Nylander, *Survey of Architectural History in Cambridge, Report Four: Old Cambridge* (Cambridge, Mass.: Cambridge Historical Commission, 1973), 150–54. By the mid-eighteenth century, rooming off campus was more than just a residential option. Edmund Trowbridge, a Cambridge lawyer, offered not only rooms but also optional legal study for those students choosing to live with him. Trowbridge usually had only one or two students in residence, but from the 1730s to 1770s, at least a dozen scholars combined their studies at the college with Trowbridge's legal tutelage. See Shipton, *Harvard Graduates*, vol. 8, 510.

20. Cohen, "Turkish Tyranny," 564–66.

21. Ibid., 567–70.

22. Ibid., 571–74.

23. Faculty Records, Harvard University Archives, 3:153–54; Court of General Sessions of the Peace, Middlesex County, Record Book, 1748–1777, Microfilm, Massachusetts Archives, 495–98; Theodore Chase, "Harvard Student Disorders," 30–34. Winthrop Sergeant, another of the students, was not content with his infractions of March. In May, he "fired pistols charged with ball in the town of Cambridge in such a manner as to endanger the lives and Property of the Inhabitants." Surprisingly, the town did not bring formal actions.

24. Faculty Records, Harvard University Archives, 3:153–54; Chase, "Harvard Student Disorders," 37–38. Chase does not include much discussion of the Corporation meeting of May 1770.

25. Chase, "Harvard Student Disorders," 39–41.

26. Court of General Sessions of the Peace, Middlesex County, Record Book, 1748–1777, Microfilm, Massachusetts Archives, 495–98; Chase, "Harvard Student Disorders," 43–45. For an evaluation of the effect of the American Revolution on student life at Harvard, see Sheldon S. Cohen, "Harvard College on the Eve of the American Revolution," Colonial Society of Massachusetts. *Publications* 59 (1982): 187–90.

27. Faculty Records, Harvard University Archives, 3:185, 193–95, 4: 185–88; Student Disorder Papers, Harvard University Archives. In 1790, a Harvard student called in the Cambridge constable when an altercation broke out among some of the scholars. The malefactors were brought before James Winthrop, Cambridge justice of the peace, but Winthrop dismissed the case "as too trivial to require the cognizance of a court of law." See Dennie-Vose Correspondence, Massachusetts Historical Society, 7–27 May 1790.

28. Morison, *Seventeenth Century*, vol. 1, 93; *Boston Evening Post*, 16 June 1738; Pulsifer Transcript, Massachusetts Archives. 3:216, 4:150; Middlesex Court of Sessions, Record Book, 1686–1746, Massachusetts Archives, 86, 212; Record Book, 1748–1777, 112; David W. Conroy, *In Public Houses: Drink and the Revolution of Authority in Colonial Massachusetts* (Chapel Hill: University of North Carolina Press for the Institute of Early American History and Culture, 1995), 9.

29. Corporation Records, Harvard University Archives, 2:12–13; Overseers Records, Harvard University Archives, 2: 140, 187.

30. Overseers Records, Harvard University Archives, 2:200; Corporation Records, Harvard University Archives, 2:208; Faculty Records, Harvard University Archives, 3:51, 229; Selectmen Records, 1769–83, Microfilm, Early Massachusetts Records Series.

31. Corporation Records, Harvard University Archives, 2:260; John Adams, *The Works of John Adams, Second President of the United States*, ed. Charles Francis Adams (Boston: Little, Brown and Company, 1850), vol. 2, p. 289.

32. Faculty Records, Harvard University Archives, 5:131; Town Records B, 26 June 1786, Microfilm, Early Massachusetts Records Series; John Quincy Adams, *Diary*, ed. D. Gray Allin et al. (Cambridge, Mass.: Belknap Press of Harvard University Press, 1981), vol. 2, pp. 10, 109, 120, 139, 142, 161.

33. Corporation Records, Harvard University Archives, 3:274; Faculty Records, Harvard University Records, 6:16–17, 22–24: Cambridge Selectmen's Records, 1788–1804, Microfilm, Early Massachusetts Records Series, 10 June 1789; Overseers Records, Harvard University Archives, 4:22–24. Copies of the petitions can be found in the Belknap Papers 161.B. 13c, 161.B.14c, Massachusetts Historical Society.

34. Morison, *Seventeenth Century*, vol. 2, pp. 465–67.

35. *Harvard Records*, Colonial Society of Massachusetts, *Collections* 15 (1925): 242.

36. Ibid., 16 (1925): 549–50, 583; Shipton, *Harvard Graduates*, vol. 8, p. 110.

37. Overseers Records, Harvard University Archives, 1:116; *Harvard Records*, Colonial Society of Massachusetts, *Collections* 16 (1925): 648, 33:487.

38. Faculty Records, Harvard University Archives, 1:94, 2:250, 4:240–42.

39. Corporation Records, Harvard University Archives, 2:120, 127–28, 329; Faculty Records, Harvard University Archives, 2:141–42; Overseers Records, Harvard University Archives, 3:19.

40. Corporation Records, Harvard University Archives, 3:233, 265, 285, 307; Faculty Records, Harvard University Archives, 6:81, 312; Letters of Curtis Chamberland to Francis Cabot Lowell, 5 February 1793, 2 April 1793, Francis Cabot Lowell Papers, Massachusetts Historical Society.

41. J. P. Brissot de Warville, "The Air of Cambridge is Pure," *The Harvard Book: Selections from Three Centuries*, rev. ed., William Bentick Smith, ed. (Cambridge, Mass.: Harvard University Press, 1982), 441. For the changes at Harvard, see Ronald Story, *Harvard and the Boston Upper Class: The Forging of an Aristocracy, 1800–1870* (Middletown, Conn.: Wesleyan University Press, 1980), chapters 3, 4, and 6.

42. Shipton, *Harvard Graduates*, vol. 9, p. 247; John Winthrop, Diaries, Harvard University Archives.

43. Henry Binford, *The First Suburbs: Residential Communities on the Boston Periphery* (Chicago: University of Chicago Press, 1985), 18–44. Until the 1810s, views of Harvard inevitably were from the vantage point of the commons, showing the college open to the community. By the 1820s, views of the interior of the Yard were as common; see Hamilton Vaughan Bail, *Views of Harvard: A Pictorial Record to 1860* (Cambridge, Mass.: Harvard University Press, 1949), pl. 36–41. Similar changes occurred at Yale, which also built walls around the campus and reoriented the buildings inward. See Juliette Guilbert, "Something That Loves a Wall: The Yale University Campus, 1850–1920," *New England Quarterly* 68 (June 1995): 247–77.

THE SOCIAL FUNCTION OF EIGHTEENTH CENTURY HIGHER EDUCATION

PHYLLIS VINE

Since the appearance of Bernard Bailyn's provocative essay, *Education in the Forming of American Society*, scholars have been acknowledging their debt to him with the most enduring form of flattery: they have heeded his call for a re-examination of the meaning of education in American society. In the years since his work appeared, students have rewritten the history of different schools, of eminent educators, and of the host of goals and purposes for education.[1] Yet, in an important way some of the questions raised by Bailyn's work still have not been addressed. What new socializing roles did educational institutions perform as the family shed itself of old functions after 1700? This essay will attempt to deal with that question as it inquires into the social function of eighteenth-century college education.

The rhetoric of educators, the hopes of parents, and the behavior of students indicate that a changed social function for education emerged after the 1740s. Educators perceived a moral crisis sweeping all of society and laid the blame to improper training within the family. They pinned their hopes for social stability on a pacific, orderly generation of youth. Parents recognized the increased difficulty in transmitting to their sons the advantages of class and wealth which could then be applied to leading a heterogeneous society. The concerns of each group intersected to project the college into a new role in which it would be endowed with greater responsibilities for training youth. Gradually, the college was seen and came to serve as an institution which was best suited to inculcate virtue and promote social sponsorship among the privileged.

Three colleges which were founded in the 1740s and 1750s provide the basic evidence for this discussion: The College of New Jersey, 1746; The College of Philadelphia, 1754; and King's College, 1755.[2] Taken together they represent the most viable choices for higher education for the sons of the urban wealthy and landed gentry in the middle Atlantic region. Although founded by enclaves of denominational strength, each school promoted itself as having a colony wide appeal and clientele which would transcend sectarian differences in the process of promoting public well-being.

The combined impact of geographical mobility, cultural and political squabbles, religious declension and family reorientation led to fears that social disorder was growing and virtue and morality in decline in the middle of the eighteenth century.[3] Those who spoke to these issues directly, such as Princeton's President Aaron Burr, noted what must have been obvious to those who lived during the discord between Governor Lewis Morris and the elected New Jersey Assemblies in the 1740s. Burr lamented "contention between Governors and Assemblies," and instructed his listeners to put aside "all private and selfish Designs."[4] William Livingston, the New York based social reformer and critic of the proposed Anglican domination of King's College, sounded the same theme. He proclaimed himself a "reformer of public abuses," and founded the *Independent Reflector* in 1752 to reveal the villainy of those who "owe their Prosperity to the Violation of their Trust."[5] Each man devoted his life to serving the public and each helped to create institutions which would foster public order. They represent a generation of leaders who were convinced that one way to stop the expansion of stability, or perhaps to permit social change to proceed according to their own visions, was through

139

a collegiate education. They would take it upon themselves to teach individual male youth how to "serve the Public with honor to themselves and to their Country"[6] by educating them in institutions of higher learning.

With few exceptions, those who headed the eighteenth-century colleges started their careers as ministers. Moving from the church to the school, these men began shepherding young males through a course of learning and in the process they became ministers-of-education. Also, they questioned the ability of the family to produce the training needed during such times of stress. Heaping scorn upon the family, Aaron Burr of Princeton noted in 1755 that "almost all prevailing corruptions of the times" come from a "want of proper government and instruction in families." He proposed that "parents and governors of families . . . use their authority and influence, for the reforming [of] a corrupt and wicked generation." Burr represented one set of opinion about reforming youth by purifying the family; one of his successors at Princeton, John Witherspoon, represented another. In contrast to Burr, Witherspoon asked that youth be removed from the family. During a fund-raising trip to the West Indies in the 1770s, the eminent Scottish educator argued that the greatest distance from home promoted the best education. In his experience, "those who come from the greatest distance, have in general behaved with most regularity." The reason was simple. Unable to rely on the support or comfort of familial ties, students were forced to behave within the guidelines established by the college. Also, educators at a distant college received less pressure from parents who wanted special considerations granted their sons. As Witherspoon told his listeners, it was necessary for students "to support a character, as they find themselves treated by their companions, teachers, and indeed all other persons, according to their behavior."[7]

Other educators fell somewhere between Burr's attitude of trying to reform the family and Witherspoon's of extricating the student from it. Wherever they stood, educators agreed that a low quality of public leadership could be attributed to a deficiency in the way youth were prepared for adult responsibilities. The bluntness with which a College of Philadelphia trustee, Richard Peters, identified the problem suggests how deeply this attitude ran. For Peters, the problem could be firmly affixed to the mother. Mothers were too indulgent to discipline spirited youth. When a child misbehaved, rather than being corrected "he is taken into the arms of his mother, tenderly caressed, and commended for a boy of spirit." Peters lamented that the unhappy woman had no idea "what numerous evils will flow from this ill judged [sic] indulgence."[8] Akin to Puritans who feared that too much love could interfere with preparation for sainthood, educators in the eighteenth century thought too much indulgence created a generation of weak leaders. In contrast to their Puritan forebears who shifted youth from one family to another, or other critics who found fault with the family, these men created a new institution to further their aims.

Since they doubted the mother's ability to teach the child to behave with decisiveness and authority, it became important for boys to learn how to command authority from those who claimed to know: their teachers. Part of the explanation for educators' desire to remove youth from the influence of mothers and the family may be inferred from the importance of emulation in eighteenth-century pedagogical theory. As one educational theorist noted, "Without numbers there can be no emulation. It is founded on the love of distinction. In a private family this distinction cannot be acquired." Teachers had to be of "irreproachable characters; men whose lives should be a daily comment on their precepts," noted Philadelphia's Provost William Smith in the Utopian tract about education in the mythical state of Mirania.[9] In short, emulation presumed that one learned how to behave by watching the example of others, and boys could receive the wrong impressions at home.

John Witherspoon's advice on correcting misbehaving children nicely illustrates these assumptions. In *Letters on Education* (1775) Witherspoon stressed the need for fathers, or other males, to enforce discipline in the home. "The mother or any female attendant," he said, "will necessarily be obliged to do things displeasing to the child." He warned his readers that the "mother or nurse should never presume to condole with the child, or show any signs of displeasure at his being crossed." On the contrary, both ought to give "every mark of approbation of their own submission to the same person."[10] Witherspoon spoke to the possibility that women would contradict the process by which boys learned how to work within a patriarchal society and a society in which those in power might have to make hard decisions.

In the college and away from the influence of mothers, Mirania's boys would learn what William Smith called "a manly turn of thought." These educators were apprehensive about future leaders acquiring unmanly traits. Ebenezer Pemberton, a trustee of the College of New Jersey wrote a promotional tract in 1760 in which he announced that methods of instruction attempted to prevent "idleness, effeminacy, vanity . . ." Aaron Burr noted that of the numerous vices sweeping the land, idleness and effeminacy along with discontent and contempt of authority "sap the very foundation of society." It was not only educators, however, who noted the potential problem with effeminacy. Edward Antill, the wealthy New Jersey patron of King's College, made clear that the ideal parent had no "false love or effeminate fondness for children. "[11] Antill's remarks further emphasized the need for schools since few parents were ideal.

When speaking of manly characteristics, educators placed their concerns within the eighteenth-century context of the debate between passion and reason. Reason was that agency or faculty which allowed for calculation and prudence in solving difficult problems; it directed man to his duty to God and to society. Its antithesis, passion, encompassed ambition, envy, covetousness, pride, selfishness, vanity, and indulgence—to name but a few. Both passion and reason resided in each person, and it was the goal of education to teach youth how to use reason to harness passion, how to behave properly.[12] One of the impulses which emanated from passions, and which was frequently attributed to parents, was that of indulgence. If parents had a tendency to indulge their children, women had a greater predisposition toward indulgence since they had not been taught how to control this passion. Reverend Richard Peters, the only minister who was a trustee at the College of Philadelphia, opened the Academy in 1751 with a sermon charging that parents' partiality made them "unfit to be trusted with the sole care of their children's education."[13] The mother's passion might predominate and through emulation boys might learn to act in an unmanly fashion.

It was not enough simply to remove boys from the family and the presence of indulgent mothers. Efforts to provide male role models became an important issue and this may be seen in the living arrangements colleges established. Although in 1761 King's College allowed the families of stewards and faculty to reside in the college, in 1763 the Board of Governors abolished this practice, noting that "no woman under any pretense whatever (except a cook) be allowed to reside within the college for the future, and that those who are now there be removed as conveniently as may be." At the College of New Jersey when Walter Minto, professor of Mathematics and Natural Philosophy, married in 1789, he moved out of the college. In fact when looking for a new teacher of classics and mathematics, Samuel Johnson of King's College specified that the candidate should be "a good and eloquent preacher, with a strong voice . . . a truly exemplary person . . . well acquainted not only with all parts of polite literature, but also with Hebrew Scripture, and . . . unmarried."[14] The presence of women posed a problem for training adolescent boys, whether they remained at home or at school. In the eyes of the college officials, the only way to assure that young men received the proper education away from the corrosive influence of indulgent mothers was to remove them from the family and place them in a predominantly male institution.

Why would parents consent to relinquish control over their sons as they came under this criticism? What were educators offering, in addition to their scorn, that would impel parents to bestow their confidence in the college? Some explanations seem compelling. Parents appear to have sensed their growing inability to manage adolescent sons through the traditional, weakened, dependency based on the distribution of land.[15] For them, the college which promised to pay strict attention to manners and morals may have seemed like a reasonable alternative to land-discipline.

Even for those who could control their sons, evidence indicates that fathers questioned their own abilities to teach sons the skills that the heterogeneous, mobile, and secular society required. The care with which Ralph Izard solicited help in 1787 from William Samuel Johnson, President of Columbia College, illustrates parental insistence that higher education must assist elite children. Izard, who was one of South Carolina's wealthiest men and whose career included station and power, told Johnson that he was sending his sons to Columbia in the hopes that an education there would afford him the prospect of "their being useful, valuable citizens of their country."[16] Izard confirmed what educators had been saying when they asserted that wealth alone would not guarantee success. It was no secret that "those of superior talents from nature, by mere slothfulness and idle habits, or self-indulgence, have lived useless and died contemptible."[17] A parent of one student and supporter of King's College, Edward Antill noted in 1761 that "riches without wisdom to use them, without skill to direct them to their proper end . . . only become sneers to us, and prove our destruction."[18] In fact, it was even more important that those born to privilege have higher education. As John Witherspoon informed his audience in Jamaica, "the station in which they enter life requires such duties, as those of the finest talents can scarcely be supposed capable of, unless they have been improved and cultivated with the utmost care."[19]

In addition to offering vague and imprecise statements about teaching students how to use riches and talents, colleges characterized themselves as offering another advantage which might seem more compelling. "Persons of Leisure and Public spirit," wrote Benjamin Franklin about the people who founded the Academy of Philadelphia, would "zealously unite, and make all the Interest that can be made to establish [students], whether in Business, Offices, Marriages, or any other thing for their advantage."[20] Franklin stated what others keenly knew: proper connections were essential for success. He offered the hope that the right schools could provide the means through which connections could be made. Thus, the emergence of the college and its attraction for parents can be related to the emergence of a need for intra-colonial structures, which would institutionalize alliances which the family was hard-put to secure. Even those as well-placed as the New York DeLancey family had difficulty in 1755 finding a good merchant with whom young Stephen could learn the trade, according to Mrs. Peter DeLancey. Although Stephen was apprenticed to Beverly Robinson, within a year the family had to go through the identical process, with similar difficulty, when trying to place John.[21]

How did the process work through which the college facilitated such associations? The life of Benjamin Rush provides one illustration. Rush was graduated from the College of New Jersey in 1760, and his one year of matriculation coincided with Richard Stockton's tenure as trustee (1757–1781). At the end of an apprenticeship, the aspiring physician continued his education by attending medical lectures at the University of Edinburgh (1766–1768) during the time that the College of New Jersey was actively soliciting John Witherspoon for its president. If Rush had not met Trustee Stockton before, it is certain that they met during their simultaneous efforts to attract Witherspoon. Rush's subsequent marriage to seventeen-year old Julia Stockton occurred shortly after he visited Stockton at his New Jersey estate, Morven, on the edge of Princeton.[22] James Francis Armstrong illustrates the process again. He was prepared for college by John Blair, at Fagg's Manor, one of the academies which often sent students to the College of New Jersey. After Armstrong graduated from college in 1773, he continued to study with President John Witherspoon until he was licensed for the ministry in 1777. He married Susannah Livingston, the sister of William Smith Livingston (A.B., 1772), whose two years at Princeton coincided with his.[23]

The examples of Benjamin Rush and James Francis Armstrong illustrate how the eighteenth-century college was providing the means through which student associations were cemented. Preliminary findings based on an investigation of a sample of 368 students from Princeton, Philadelphia, and King's indicate that about one-quarter of the students married sisters of classmates or daughters of trustees or presidents. Other examples from the College of New Jersey include the marriage of Aaron Burr (A.B., 1772), son of the president, to Esther Edwards, daughter of another president, Jonathan Edwards. Their daughter, Sarah, married Tapping Reeve (A.B., 1763), who was a student and later became the family tutor. In other instances, David English (A.B., 1789) married Lydia Scudder, daughter of trustee Nathaniel Scudder; Samuel Blair, Jr., (A.B., 1760) married Susan Shippen, sister of William Shippen, Jr., (A.B., 1754); David Rice, Jr, (A.B., 1761) married Blair's sister, Mary, making the schoolmates brothers-in-law. At the College of Philadelphia a similar pattern may be seen in the marriage of Jacob Duché (A.B., 1757) to Elizabeth Hopkinson, sister of Duché's classmate Francis Hopkinson (A.B., 1757). Hopkinson's son, Joseph (A.B., 1786), married Emily Mifflin, whose father Thomas Mifflin (A.B., 1760) entered school while Francis Hopkinson was still matriculating. The Mifflin-Hopkinson ties to the college were cemented later when their tenure as trustees overlapped during the 1770s. Finally, examples from King's College include Peter Van Schaak (A.B., 1768) who eloped with Elizabeth Cruger, daughter of King's Governor Henry Cruger. Beverly Robinson, Jr., (A.B., 1773) married the sister of his classmate, Thomas Barclay (A.B., 1772), who married into the DeLancey family. Richard Hofstadter's observation that intermarriage among the Board of Trustees of the College of Philadelphia "provides us with a microcosm of the economic and social world of the colonial elite" can be applied to the patterns among the students as well.[24]

The personal connections formed in college which led to future marriages also led to apprenticeships. Again, Benjamin Rush can serve as an illustration. President Davies, Rush's mentor at Princeton, recommended him for an apprenticeship with Dr. John Redman, one of Philadelphia's leading physicians. Rush studied with Redman for the five and a half years between graduation and going to Edinburgh in 1766. Another Princeton student, Tapping Reeve, studied law with classmate William Paterson (both A.B., 1763), who was trained by Trustee Richard Stockton.[25]

The manner in which Philip Vickers Fithian (A.B., 1772) secured a job as a tutor after leaving the College of New Jersey illustrates another aspect of the ways in which colleges were becoming important institutions where one acquired social amenities and appropriate certification in addition to contacts. When John Witherspoon received a request for a tutor from Robert Carter of Westmoreland, Virginia, the inquiry was passed on to Fithian. He took the job and served the family for two years before he became licensed by the Presbyterian church. Before he left, however, he turned the job over to another classmate. About to leave Carter Hall, the experienced tutor wrote to his successor, John Peck, about the immense social value of having attended the College of New Jersey "With a well confirmed testimonial of your having finished with credit a course of studies at Nassau-Hall, you would be rated without any more questions asked, either about your family, your estate, your business or your intention, at £10,000."[26]

Viewing eighteenth-century colleges as institutions that served a social purpose in addition to teaching sheds light on the pervasive disdain of a foreign education after the American Revolution. Prior to Independence, students were educated and graduated from European universities. Afterward, various spokesmen insisted that an education abroad would undermine character by allowing students to emulate and perhaps acquire foreign habits. This concern speaks to "education" as the process by which one inculcates the values of society. The desire to educate students at home also speaks to another concern, one arising from the knowledge that institutional education enhanced social contacts. John Jay, for example, who wrote to Robert Morris to argue that the Morris sons ought to attend college in America, will help explain. Jay noted that "connections founded at School and College have much influence, and are to be watched at that period—If judiciously formed, they will endure and be advantageous through life." Jay emphasized that schools facilitated students getting to know "those with whom they are often engaged in the business of active life."[27]

Jay's remarks reflect an attitude which was based on his own experience of how the system operated. Some of the associations he made during his years as a student at King's College proved advantageous to him as well as others. Recommending a friend for a military post in 1776, he recalled "an opinion of his abilities" drawn from an "early acquaintance with him at College." Throughout his life, Jay maintained cordial relationships with many of his schoolmates, entered into a partnership with classmate Robert R. Livingston, often saw other classmates through the Debating Society, the Social Club, and even helped those whose loyalty to Britain conflicted with his own patriotic activities.[28]

The above examples illustrate that the purpose of going to school extended beyond the classical authors and included a strong social component. By the middle of the eighteenth century, teachers and parents began to view the college as an institution which would abet weaknesses in the family's socialization of youth. As educators removed students from the immediate influence of parents, and provided opportunities for a broader range of personal and professional contacts, they established an institution that functioned to solidify an elite while training students to serve the public arena.

A final dimension of the new social function for the college may be seen in the increasing importance attached to commencement ceremonies as a public means of displaying the new baccalaureates to the larger community. Educators gradually invested commencement ceremonies with a symbolic significance that told students and the community that they were "now about to step into life." In addition to marking an important *rite-de-passage* for a select group of young men, the commencement ceremonies denoted, as Samuel Johnson told King's College students, that they would hence be "called to act a more important part of life."[29] In both respects, graduation became a way of informing the world beyond the college of the new importance attached to higher education.

By the middle of the century, the ritual of commencement ceremonies was systematically established as a part of the requirements for receiving a degree. This is not to suggest that previously there was no such thing as college commencement. Rather, its significance grew and its form assumed a new meaning. The commencement ceremony itself is a medieval rite.[30] An important difference between the medieval ceremony and its eighteenth-century modification involves the audience for whom the graduates performed. In the medieval university, the bestowal of a degree was an event within the college. Toward the end of the eighteenth century, graduation became an event for the community. In 1701, Increase Mather tried to discourage the president of Yale College from holding commencement services. As a Puritan, Mather thought they "proved very expensive & are occasion of much sin." He suggested that commencements "may be done privately as well as publickly," [sic] as they often were in England.[31] While Harvard College sporadically entertained commencement exercises, it was not until the 1767 revision of College Laws that it became important to the institution, and then it became a criterion for receiving the degree.[32]

By the time several new schools were founded in the second half of the century, the ceremony of graduation was a necessary part of the established rules for governing the college. The ritual bears striking resemblance to the owning of the covenant in the early New England churches, something which had become almost defunct by the time colleges adopted its form.[33] By the middle of the eighteenth century, those ministers who became educators turned to the college to evoke a chorus confirming the secular community. Instead of beginning one's religious rebirth and committing oneself to God's dictates, the visible saint in the eighteenth century began his secular life in public view from the college stage.

If it were not for the communal importance of the service, the actual commencement ceremony would be perfunctory.[34] The ceremony was preceded by two different examinations. The first was a private rehearsal for the second public examination, before men of learning. Just as with the confession of faith in the New England church, here the communicant was questioned by elders. After completion of these two examinations, the student was permitted to prepare for his graduation oration. He deposited a copy with various officials before he delivered it. Generally, the ceremony took place in September. The procession included candidates, masters, tutors, professors, the president, trustees, and invited officials—in that order. Students wore a special robe, their heads remained uncovered until after the service. Nothing was left to chance, and at the College of New Jersey Samuel Finley codified it by writing *The Process of Public Commencement* in 1764.

By the middle of the century, graduation was becoming a ceremony for the elite community. The 1759 Valedictorian at the College of New Jersey noted:

> The transactions of this day have been public testimonies of its beauty, influence and popularity. . . . Of its influence and popularity, from the respect paid to this seat of the muses, by every rank and degree of men; to that I may venture to say, the sentiments of every one present, are in favour of learning; and should every one speak, each voice would be a testimony of its attractive excellence. Else whence this unusual concourse? Why have so many gentlemen of employment in church and state, from various parts, condescended to grace this occasion with their presence?[35]

The observation about gentlemen from high station was made frequently. John Witherspoon mentioned that commencement had become a "fixed annual" event which was "attended by a vast concourse of the politest company."[36] In 1775, the College of Philadelphia moved the date for commencement "as Delegates from the different colonies are now assembled in *Congress* in this city, it might be proper to invite them." The following year they cancelled public commencement "on account of the present unsettled state of public affairs." At Yale College, public commencement ceased throughout the entire Revolution, even though commencement was the favorite ceremony of President Ezra Stiles. Finally, in order to attend the first ceremony at Columbia College after the American Revolution, the Continental Congress and both houses of the New York legislature suspended business for the day.[37]

The service had to be performed on the public stage for the benefit of the college and the community. Commencement was a place to see and to be seen. The diary of the peripatetic Reverend Ebenezer Parkman (Harvard, A.B., 1721) contains accounts of the various individuals who were present, of the festivities, and of any unusual circumstances at the Harvard commencements he dutifully attended. It was also a place where employment could be secured, as in the case of John Adams. In his autobiography Adams notes: "Mr. Maccarty of Worcester . . . [who] was empowered by the Select Men of that Town to procure them a Latin Master for their Grammar School engaged me to undertake it."[38] The attention of the community, local politicians and dignitaries, and future employers, served to underscore the newfound significance of the college. Had the college performed its investiture in private, it would have denied itself the opportunity to assert its role in uniting culture and its important task of presenting newly-accomplished students in their ascribed role.

The importance attached to graduation ceremonies symbolized the significance of the college as a public institution designed by ministers-of-education who sought to reform youth and correct deficient family training. Educators wanted to teach adolescents to behave in a manly fashion—something they thought only they could do. They also offered the institution as a conduit for the mixing of upper echelons, and those with aspirations to the elite, by the available connections for business and marriage opportunities. Throughout a torrent of criticism, parents acquiesced as they too began to recognize that intra-colonial institutions of higher education would benefit their sons. Toward the end of the century it appeared that a new function, defined in social terms, was beginning to characterize the need for higher education.

Notes

An earlier version of this paper was presented at the meetings of the American Educational Research Association, April, 1976, San Francisco, California, where it benefited from David Allmendinger's criticism. Also, I would like to thank friends and former colleagues at Union College, Manfred Jonas, David Potts, and Robert Wells, who offered encouragement and suggestions.

1. The literature which acknowledges a debt to Bailyn since the appearance of *Education in the Formation of American Society* (New York, 1960) is legion. The most comprehensive work which expands upon a number of Bailyn's insights, is Lawrence Cremin, *American Education: The Colonial Experience, 1607–1783* (New York, 1970). This work also contains an excellent and extensive bibliography. Between Cremin's bibliography, and a recent essay by David B. Potts, "Students and the Social History of American Higher Education," *History of Education Quarterly*, XV (Fall, 1975): 317–327, most of the literature is discussed. Relevant works published after Cremin, and not contained within the subject of Potts' essay include: Carl F. Kaestle, *The Evolution of an Urban School System, New York City, 1750–1850* (Mass., 1973); Joseph J. Ellis, *The New England Mind in Transition: Samuel Johnson of Connecticut, 1696–1702* (New Haven, 1973); Richard Warch, *School of the Prophets, Yale College, 1701–1740* (New Haven, 1973); James Axtell, *The School Upon a Hill: Education and Society in Colonial New England* (New Haven, 1974).

2. The standard histories of these schools may be found in the following: For the College of New Jersey, see Varnum Lansing Collins, *Princeton* (New York, 1914); John Maclean, *A History of the College of New Jersey*, 2 Vols. (Philadelphia, 1877); Thomas J. Wertenbaker, *Princeton, 1746–1896* (Princeton, 1946). More recently the College of New Jersey has received attention by Howard Miller's book, *The Revolutionary College: American Presbyterian Higher Education, 1707–1837* (New York, 1976); Douglas Sloan, *The Scottish Enlightenment and the Early College Ideal* (New York, 1971). For King's College consult: Howard Van Amringe, et. al., *A History of Columbia University, 1754–1904* (New York, 1904); Clement Clarke Moore, *The Early History of Columbia College* (New York, 1940 ed); and most recently, David C. Humphrey, *From Kings College to Columbia, 1746–1800* (Columbia University Press, 1976). The history of the College of Philadelphia may be found in Edward Potts Cheney, *The University of Pennsylvania, 1740–1940* (Philadelphia, 1940); Thomas Montgomery, *A History of the University of Pennsylvania from its Founding to 1770* (Philadelphia, 1900); Thomas L. Turner, "The College, Academy and Charitable School of Philadelphia: The Development of a Colonial Institution of Learning, 1740–1770," University of Pennsylvania, Ph.D. Thesis, 1952; Ann D. Gordon, "The College of Philadelphia, 1740–1779: The Impact of an Institution," University of Wisconsin, Ph.D. Thesis, 1975.

3. For examples consult: Jack Greene, "Search for Identity: An Interpretation of the Meaning of Selected Patterns of Social Response in Eighteenth-Century America," *Journal of Social History* 3 (1970): 189–220; N. Ray Hiner, "Adolescence in 18th Century America," *History of Childhood Quarterly*, 3 (1975): 252–280; Richard Bushman, *From Puritan to Yankee: Character and the Social Order in Connecticut, 1690–1765* (Cambridge, 1967).

Works which discuss these concerns after the American Revolution are: Gordon Wood, *The Creation of the American Republic* (Chapel Hill, 1969); Miller, *The Revolutionary College*; John Howe, "Republican Thought and the Political Violence of the 1790s," *American Quarterly* XIX (1967): 147–165.

4. Aaron Burr, *A Discourse Delivered at New-Ark* (New York, 1755), pp.28–29. For background consult: Donald L. Kemmerer, *Path to Freedom: The Struggle for Self-Government in New Jersey, 1703–1776* (Princeton, 1940), chapter X; John E. Pomfret, *The New Jersey Proprietors and Their Lands, 1664–1776* (Princeton, 1964), chapter X; and, Pomfret's more recent work *Colonial New Jersey: A History* (New York, 1973), chapter 7; Alison B. Olson, "The Founding of Princeton University: Religion and Politics in Eighteenth-Century New Jersey," *New Jersey History,* LXXXVII (1969): 135–150,

5. William Livingston, et al., *The Independent Reflector,* ed., Milton M. Klein, (Cambridge, 1963), pp. 55–59. Background on New York may be found in Dorothy R. Dillon, *The New York Triumvirate; A Study of the Legal and Political Careers of William Livingston, John Morin Scott and William Smith, Jr.* (New York, 1949); Stanley Nider Katz, *Newcastle's New York: Anglo American Politics, 1732–1753* (Mass., 1968); Patricia Bonomi, *A Factious People: Politics and Society in Colonial New York* (New York, 1971); Ruth L. Higgins, *Expansion in New York, with Especial Reference to the Eighteenth Century* (Ohio, 1931); Bernard Bailyn, *The Origin of American Politics* (New York, 1967), pp. 107–114.

6. Benjamin Franklin, "A Proposal for Promoting Useful Knowledge. Among the British Plantations in America," in L. Jesse Lemisch, ed., *Benjamin Franklin: The Autobiography and Other Writings* (New York, 1961), 210.

7. Burr, *Discourse,* 33; John Witherspoon, "An Address to the Inhabitants of Jamaica," in *Works* (Edinburgh, 1815), VIII: 311; Other examples of this attitude may be found in John Witherspoon to Nicholas Van Dyke, May 12,1786, Mss., Firestone Library, Princeton University; Charles Nisbet to the Trustees of Dickinson College, July 9,1799, Founders Collection, Dickinson College. At Union College, President John Blair Smith went so far as to argue that there were more immoral influences at home than at school. See "Inaugural Address, 1795," Shaffer Library, Union College.

8. Richard Peters, *A Sermon on Education, Wherein Some Account is Given of the Academy* (Philadelphia, 1751), 5, 6, 11–13, 14.

9. Samuel Harrison Smith, *Remarks on Education . . .* (1797) in Frederick Rudolph, ed., *Essays on Education in the Early Republic* (Cambridge, 1965), 207. William Smith, *A General Idea about the College of Mirania* (1752), in *Discourses on Public Occasions* (London, 1822), 80. For a discussion of the role of emulation in pedagogical practice, see Phyllis Vine Erenberg, "Change and Continuity: Values in American Higher Education, 1750–1800," University of Michigan, Ph.D. Thesis, 1974, 123–141.

10. Witherspoon, "Letters on Education," in *Lectures on Moral Philosophy* (Philadelphia, 1822), 225.

11. [Ebenezer Pemberton], "A Short Account of the rise and State of the College in the Province of NEW JERSEY, in America," *The New American Magazine* XXVII (March, 1760), 103; Burr, *Discourse,* 28; Smith, *Mirania,* 42; Edward Antill to Samuel Johnson, December 13, 1758, College Papers, Columbia University Library.

12. Eighteenth-century Enlightenment philosophy debated whether reason was an innate or an acquired faculty. Even though the basic orientation of these theories differed significantly, colonial educators betrayed an eclecticism borrowing from each school to make the point that from reason came judgment. Several works discuss the history of psychology in the eighteenth century. For an emphasis on colonial America, see I. Woodbridge Riley; *American Philosophy: The Early Schools* (New York, 1907); A. A. Roback, *History of American Psychology* (New York, 1952), 3–55. To place the colonial context in a larger perspective see George Sidney Brett, *A History of Psychology,* Vols. I and II (London, 1921).

13. Peters, *A Sermon,* 5–6.

14. Minutes of the Governors, March 1, 1763, Columbia University Library; Princeton University Trustee Minutes, September 30, 1789, Princeton University Library; Milton Halsey Thomas, "The King's College Building," *New York Historical Society Quarterly* XXXIX (1955), 429; Herbert and Carol Schneider. eds., *Samuel Johnson, President of King's College* (New York, 1929), IV: 59–60.

15. For illustration of changing patterns of land distribution and declining patriarchalism, see Philip Greven, *Four Generations: Population, Land and Family in Colonial Andover, Mass.* (Ithaca, 1970), 222–258, 272–273. For other indications of perceptions of increasing inability to control adolescents, see Daniel Scott Smith and Michael S. Hindus, "Premarital Pregnancy in America, 1640–1970; An Overview and Interpretation," *Journal of Interdisciplinary History* V (1975), 537–570; Hiner, "Adolescence in 18th Century America." I am indebted to Robert Wells for allowing me to read his forthcoming article, "Illegitimacy and Bridal Pregnancy in Colonial America," which will appear in a collection of essays edited by Peter Laslett. Also see F. Musgrave, "The Decline of the Educative Family," *Universities Quarterly* XIV (1960), 337–405.

16. Ralph Izard to William Samuel Johnson, December 20, 1787, in Schneider and Schneider, *Johnson,* IV: 196.

17. Witherspoon, "An Address to the Senior Class Preceding Commencement, September 23, 1775," in *Lectures*, 182.

18. Antill to Leonard Lispenard, February 19, 1761. Antill to Johnson, December 13, 1758. Both are located in College Papers, Columbia University Library.

19. Witherspoon, "Address to the Inhabitants of Jamaica," in *Works*, Vol. VIII (Edinburgh, 1815), 311.

20. Franklin, "Proposals," 210–211, On this point see an article by sociologist Ralph Turner, "Modes of Social Ascent through Education; Sponsored and Contest Mobility'," in A. H. Halsey, J. Floud, C. A. Anderson, eds., *Education, Economy and Society* (London, 1967), 121–139. Also see Lawrence Stone, "Social Mobility in England, 1500–1700," *Past and Present* 33 (1966), 16–55.

21. This is discussed in Kaestle, *The Evolution*, 11.

22. Rush mentioned Stockton's efforts in a letter to Jonathan Bayard Smith who was Rush's classmate. *Letters of Benjamin Rush*, ed., Butterfield, I: 38–43. The efforts to attract Witherspoon may also be found in Maclean, *History*, I: 285–300; L. H. Butterfield, ed., *John Witherspoon Comes to America* (Princeton, 1953). For Rush's life, see David Freeman Hawke, *Benjamin Rush, Revolutionary Gadfly* (Indianapolis, 1971), especially 139–140 for details of the courtship.

23. Information on Armstrong and the other students from the College of New Jersey comes from student files in the Princeton University Archives. I would like to thank James McLachlan for graciously allowing me to use the material which he and his staff collected in preparation of the forthcoming biographical dictionary of Princeton's early students.

24. Richard Hofstadter, *Academic Freedom in the Age of the College* (New York, 1955), 150. For students from the College of New Jersey, see *ibid.* Information on students from the College of Philadelphia comes from *Dictionary of American Biography*; University of Pennsylvania, *Biographical Catalogue of the Matriculates of the College, 1749–1893* (Philadelphia, 1894); W. J. Maxwell, ed., *General Alumni Catalogue of the University of Pennsylvania, 1917* (Philadelphia, 1917); Thomas Montgomery, *The University of Pennsylvania* (Philadelphia, 1900); Gordon, "The College of Philadelphia." The network of marriage patterns among students parallels the pattern which exists among the trustees as well. Gordon's recent study indicates that when the Academy opened in 1749 only two of the trustees were related through marriage. Between 1751 and 1779, however, of the thirty-one who were appointed, twenty-three were related somehow (p. 14).

    Data on students from King's College comes from Leonard F. Fuld, "King's College Alumni-II," *Columbia University Quarterly* 9 (1907), 54–60; Milton Halsey Thomas, comp., *Columbia University Officers and Alumni, 1754–1857* (Columbia University Press, 1936); Walter Barrett, *The Old Merchants of New York City* (New York, 1885), I: 67; Richard B. Morris, ed., *John Jay, The Making of a Revolutionary* (New York, 1975) 81, 331–332. Through David Humphrey's discussion of King's College another aspect of the marriage alliances emerges. Humphrey notes the high incidence of students who were related to the Governors. During the 1750s, about sixty percent were related as sons or nephews; by the 1770s, the figure fell to less than twenty percent. See *From King's College*, 117, 137, *passim*.

    A final note on this point comes from work on Yale. In a recent study, Richard B. Warch notes that of the 386 students who attended between 1701 and 1740, the daughters of Yale alumni married 87 other Yale graduates. See *School of the Prophets, Yale College, 1710–1740* (New Haven, 1973), 276.

25. Whitefield Bell, Jr., "A Portrait of the Colonial Physician," in Bell, Jr., ed., *The Colonial Physician & Other Essays* (New York, 1975), 31; William Paterson, *Glimpses of Colonial Society and the Life at Princeton College, 1766–1773*, W. J. Mills, ed., (Philadelphia, 1903); also see relevant Princeton sources in *ibid.*

26. Philip Vickers Fithian, *Journal and Letters*, 1757–1774, ed., John Rodgers Williams (Princeton, 1900), 287; Gordon, "The College of Philadelphia," 133–134 also discusses this point.

27. John Jay to Robert Morris, October 13, 1782, quoted in Max M. Mintz, "Morris and Jay on Education," *Pennsylvania Magazine of History and Biography*, 74 (1950), 343.

28. Quoted in David Humphrey, *From King's College*, 209. The reference is probably to Edward Nicoll (A.B., 1766). See Alexander McDougall to John Jay, 20 March, 1776, in Morris, ed., *John Jay*, 240 fn. 1, 331–332, 87, 113–114.

29. William Smith, "A Charge to the Graduates," in *Discourses*, 130–131; Samuel Johnson, "To the Graduates," in Schneider and Schneider, *Johnson*, Vol. IV: 278.

30. Samuel Eliot Morison notes that the "incorporation of a newcomer into the society of masters, and his formal entrance upon his functions by the actual performance of its duties" was a part of Roman law which was essential for all forms of investiture. By the time Harvard College was founded the original significance of the "Act' had been forgotten." See *Harvard College* (1935), 12–13, fn. 2, 34, 72–73.

31. Increase Mather to [Rev. James Pierpont], Sept. 15, 1701, in Franklin Bowditch Dexter, ed., *Documentary History of Yale College* (New Haven, 1916), 7. Also see the early proposals for Yale College which stipulated; "Let there be no such expensive *Commencements,* as those in other *Universities,*" in *ibid.,* 3.

32. Samuel Eliot Morison, et al., "Harvard College Records," in *Publications Of the Colonial Society of Massachusetts,* XXXI (1935); 332–334, 380–383; XVI (1925): 551, 562, 722, 746, 751, 761, 772, 819.

33. Edmund Morgan, *Visible Saints* (New York, 1965 ed.), 88–89, 61, 62. Perry Miller noted that by the end of the seventeenth century the new world ritual had become a communal chant, and the minister's role depended "not upon a scholastic definition of their place in the hierarchy of being, but upon a revived community, upon the ability to evoke from year to year an answering chorus." See *The New England Mind: From Colony to Province* (Boston, 1961 ed.), 116, 118.

34. On the significance of public behavior and communal experience, see Rhys Isaac, "Dramatizing the Ideology of Revolution: Popular Mobilization in Virginia, 1774 to 1776," *William and Mary Quarterly,* 3rd. Ser., XXXIII (1976), 357–385.

35. _____, *Valedictory Oration Pronounced at the Commencement in Nassau Hall in New Jersey, September 26, 1759* (New York, n.d.), 4–5.

36. Witherspoon, "Address to the Inhabitants," 320.

37. College of Philadelphia Trustee Minutes, January 24, 1775, May 23, 1776; Edmund Morgan, *The Gentle Puritan, A Life of Ezra Stiles, 1727–1795* (New Haven, 1962), 361; New York Journal and Weekly Register, April 13, 1786.

38. Francis G. Walett, ed., *The Diary of Ebenezer Parkman* (Worcester, 1974), 6, 49, 38, *66,* 80, 120, 179, 219, 278; L. H. Butterfield, ed., *The Adams Papers: Diary and Autobiography of John Adams* (New York, 1964). Vol. III: 263.

PART III

HIGHER EDUCATION DURING THE ANTEBELLUM PERIOD, 1790–1860

Part III: Higher Education During the Antebellum Period, 1790–1860

The historiography of antebellum colleges and universities is controversial. Scholars disagree on the number of institutions founded, the reason for their establishment, the meaning and the pattern of their curricula, the type of student enrolled, and the effect of these institutions and their graduates on society. Robert Church and Michael Sedlak's overview, "The Antebellum College and Academy,"[1] from *Education in the United States* adopts the Tewksbury thesis of collegiate proliferation, describes the differences between colleges and academies, stresses the importance of the *Dartmouth College Case* (decided by the U.S. Supreme Court in 1819) for understanding collegiate privatization, offers a positive interpretation of the *Yale Report of 1828*, and notes the revival of denominationalism among the colleges after the Civil War. Church and Sedlak derived many of their conclusions from the revisionist historical scholarship done in the 1970s. However, James Axtell's "The Death of the Liberal Arts College" (1971) had successfully challenged the classic interpretations of Tewksbury, Hofstadter, and Rudolph as being Whiggish. Further support for this new interpretation—that local "boosterism" explains the rash of collegiate foundations in the first half of the 19th century—comes from David Potts's argument in our readings. This development can be seen in the creation of the University of Virginia in 1819, as state demands for higher learning increased—lead by no less an important national figure than Thomas Jefferson.[2] One of the crucial developments in this period is the *Dartmouth College Case*. Francis Stites's legal interpretation of this case points to the significant role that Chief Justice John Marshall played in resolving a dispute between the trustees and the president of the institution. Its resolution in American jurisprudence created the definition of a corporation, clarified the use of state power, and confirmed the protection of private charters.

Understanding the curricular development of antebellum institutions beyond Church and Sedlak's and Potts's analyses may be gained by reading longer treatments, such as Douglas Sloan's article, "Harmony, Chaos, and Consensus: The American College Curriculum"[3] or selections from Rudolph's *Curriculum*.[4] For our purposes, a more focused study of the *Yale Report of 1828* is needed because of its pervasive effect on undergraduate curricula for the remainder of the nineteenth century. The rationale and significance of the *Report* has been debated extensively; for instance, Jack Lane's neo-republican thesis points to the Yale authors' plea to educate the future leaders of this new nation by requiring classical humanistic ideas of the past in an emerging country wedded to entrepreneurial spirit.[5] This interpretation points to the *Report* as a responsive rather than reactionary document. Readers are encouraged to make their own assessments by exploring the full *Report* in the primary documents for this era by using this edition's companion website.

In his work, Axtell (1971) points to the culture of academic life as a means to understand antebellum colleges. Adhering to his insight, we chose to include other institutional perspectives, such as the beginning of women's higher learning and student life to fill out this period. During the first two centuries of American higher education, higher learning was for men. However, the establishments of Troy Female Seminary in 1822 and Mount Holyoke College in 1837 and the actual enrollment of women at Oberlin College opened the door to baccalaureate education for women. Patricia Palmieri's analysis provides a perspective on the development of women's higher education from 1820 to 1920. Linda Perkins discusses the origins of black women's education with a particular emphasis on Oberlin's role and developments in the South after the Civil War. These efforts pointed to how women's education became essential in creating a middle class, as Margaret Nash maintains in her chapter from *Women's Education in the United States, 1780–1840*;[6] such a sociological endeavor was "to improve the morality" of the developing republic.

By the Civil War, some of the distinguishing features of American higher education had thus begun to appear: a classical curriculum, collegiate governance structures which were separate from the state, service to local communities, and the access of persons from both sexes and all races to higher learning. These developments, as evidenced at the University of Virginia and Oberlin College, constituted the first major steps in the Americanization of higher education, as Continental or European patterns gave way to state or local practices. Paul Mattingly offers a concluding coda (1997) to this spate of recent revisionist interpretations of the American college by the mid-nineteenth century. His balanced assessment breathes new freshness and enthusiasm into the importance of these educational institutions and their roles in creating a new republican nation.

ENDNOTES

[1] Robert Church and Michael Sedlak, "The Antebellum College and Academy," in *Education in the United States* (New York: Free Press, 1976).

[2] Jennings L. Wagoner, Jr., "Honor and Dishonor at Mr. Jefferson's University: The Antebellum Years," *History of Education Quarterly* 16 (1986), 155–179.

[3] "Harmony, Chaos, and Consensus: The American College Curriculum," in *Teachers College Record,* 73 (December 1971), 221–298.

[4] Frederick Rudolph, *Curriculum* (San Francisco: Jossey-Bass, 1977).

[5] Jack C. Lane, "The Yale Report of 1828 and Liberal Education: A Neorepublican Manifesto," *History of Education Quarterly* 17 (Fall 1987), 325–338.

[6] Margaret Nash, "Possibilities and Limitations: Education and White Middle-Class Womanhood," in *Women's in Education in the United States,* 1789–1840 (New York: Palgrave, 2004).

CHAPTER 3
THE ANTEBELLUM PERIOD

THE ANTEBELLUM COLLEGE AND ACADEMY

ROBERT L. CHURCH AND MICHAEL W. SEDLAK

I

At the same time that t[...] s of equality in a relatively complacent community, [...] ere being rapidly founded in growing communitie[...] to superiority in a society increasingly committed, [...] emies and colleges shared with the district school [...] e academies and colleges recruited from larger are[...] an a district—in that they were very much creatur[...] oung people for roles in that community. But, qu[...] ges offered an education whose prime function w[...] as superior to the mass. Although the conferring [...] ry announced purpose— as we shall see, they had [...] most significant accomplishment.

In this chapter, we w[...] making little distinction between them, for in esse[...] vere fundamentally similar. Both offered post-ele[...] he approximate ages of 10 and 40. Most students, [...] d terminal education in that they claimed to provi[...] young person needed for life. Tuition at these private institutions was generally minimal, but the student and his family had to bear the burden of the student's refraining from wage-earning employment while he pursued additional years of schooling. These foregone earnings, rather than the cost of tuition and maintenance, generally restricted institutions of higher learning to the middle and upper classes. Additional expense, and additional restrictions, grew from the fact that most students had to live away from home in order to attend these institutions.

The colleges and academies founded after the Revolution were, unlike their predecessors in the colonial period, located in most cases in small towns far from major population centers. The colleges and academies recruited from fairly wide areas surrounding these small towns—colleges, for example, recruited students from areas within a fifty-mile radius. Students came to live in the town housing the institution but, for the most part, they did not live in the institutions themselves. The boarding school became widespread only after the Civil War. Despite the fact that the students did not live "on campus," their lives were closely disciplined by the colleges and academies. Schools often licensed the boarding houses in which the students lived and constantly regulated what students could eat, how they should dress, and what they could do with the very little free time that the school program—which usually began with a chapel program at dawn and went straight through a full day to a chapel service at nightfall—left them. In all cases, the institutions were expected to stand *in loco parentis*; discipline, academic and extracurricular, was very tight. Set off in a small town with little entertainment available, faced with seemingly endless and meaningless memorizing of texts, subject to constant faculty interference with their social and religious lives, without

154

the release of organized athletics, students no doubt sometimes found higher education a pretty grim business.

It is little wonder that the pre-Civil War college and academy experienced a series of outbreaks of student violence—outbreaks which ranged from the killing of a professor at Princeton (unpremeditated) and the firing of a cannon into a college building to the more normal harassment of authority and the throwing of food in commons. This violence gradually subsided, especially after 1830; it is not clear why. The advent of organized athletics and the broadening of the curriculum possibly had something to do with it. The rising age of the student body also contributed. Relief was also found in the relaxation of the college's commitment to a rigorous interpretation of *in loco parentis*—a relaxation that grew from a general softening of nineteenth-century society's view of the sinfulness of children and society's gradual renunciation of force as a means of enforcing personal morals. In the first half of the nineteenth century, colleges and academies came more and more to rely, not on physical force, but on the power of religion to control their students. As Frederick Rudolph has so dramatically pointed out, the ideal college experience for every student would include the experience of one revival on the campus in which that student experienced the saving light of the Lord. Masters and students sought to encourage such revivals—and, of course, the conscious effort to do away with sinful behavior was thought one of the most effective means of encouragement. Thus, schoolmasters were able to develop a desire for religious experience among their students and to depend on that desire to make the students themselves enforce a great deal of the institution's disciplinary code. This change made the colleges and academies appear less openly oppressive than earlier when they depended on physical constraints over their students, but whether revivalistic constraints were any less restrictive from the students' point of view is unclear.

The status of women in higher education was a point of much controversy in this period. Academies were most often coeducational while the colleges—with the exception of Oberlin, which, from its establishment in 1833, admitted all comers regardless of race or sex, and a few others— resisted the admission of women well into the second half of the nineteenth century. A large number of academies were opened exclusively for women, several of which offered courses of study equivalent to that offered by most men's colleges. The most famous, perhaps, were Emma Willard's Troy Female Seminary, opened in 1821, and Mary Lyon's Mount Holyoke Seminary, opened in 1837 (it gained collegiate status only in 1893). There women studied the same advanced subjects as men. In teaching women at an equal level with men, Lyon and Willard undermined the assumption that women were intellectually inferior to men that prevailed even among educators of women. The first women's college (Vassar) was not founded until 1865, the next (Smith and Wellesley) in 1875. In most schools, women were taught subjects thought likely to improve their performance as housewives, mothers, and elementary school teachers. Their work emphasized English grammar rather than the classics and higher mathematics. The practice in oratory and elocution that was part of the rhetoric course for men was dropped, as women were not supposed to speak in public (Lucy Stone refused to write a commencement part at Oberlin in 1842 because a male student would have to read it to the audience). Simple arithmetic, geography, the other elementary school subjects, and work in household arts such as sewing or embroidery rounded out the English course for women. Within the co-educational schools, women were often segregated both socially and in the classroom. Contact between the sexes, inside or outside of class, was minimal—or at least was supposed to be minimal.

Whatever its shortcomings, "higher education" for women in the first half of the nineteenth century marked a great improvement on the colonial finishing school for young ladies. And the broadening of women's education greatly influenced education in general in the United States. First, it hastened the day when women would be considered intellectually equal to men. Second, it gave thousands of young women destined to teach the elementary grades some post-elementary-school training. Much of higher education for women in this era grew out of a generally recognized need to recruit better educated members to the steadily feminizing teaching force.

Like the district schools, academies and colleges in this era were community oriented and controlled, but as the colleges and academies recruited from and served far wider communities, the nature of community control was somewhat different. The average man did not have the same sense of control over the academy in his area as he had over the district school (although he might take a good deal more pride in having an institution of higher learning in his community than he did from the existence of a district school). Leadership and control of these institutions generally resided with the social elite of the area—the upper and upper middle classes. Academies and colleges were privately owned by boards of self-perpetuating trustees who appointed the president or master and his subordinate teachers and who had the power to establish educational policy. This form of educational polity was at that time uniquely American, one that had developed in the early colonial era when it was found that traditional ways of governing institutions of learning did not fit the conditions of the country. European precedents suggested either educational institutions governed closely by the church and state or educational institutions largely autonomous from any outside control and governed by the institution's faculty.

The Massachusetts colonists attempted to bring the latter arrangement over from England and established Harvard College on that basis. But the Bay Colony's leaders found that they disliked entrusting their sons and the fate of the college to the young transient "faculty" at Harvard, which consisted almost exclusively of young graduates of the college awaiting a "call" from a congregation to take up their proper role as ministers. Furthermore, early American colleges had no steady sources of support like those upon which Oxford and Cambridge could depend. American colleges were from the very start dependent on the gifts of their immediate communities. Community financial involvement, especially when accompanied by the absence of permanent and mature college faculties, inevitably undermined the autonomy of the colleges and led to a system of lay governance whereby community leaders assumed financial and educational responsibility for their operations. At times these lay boards of trustees were composed of community officials and area clergymen—the idea being that those men responsible for maintaining community interests in other areas would be most capable of doing so in the case of educational institutions. At other times, boards of trustees of colleges were composed simply of influentials in the community, appointed because they were instrumental in founding the college or in rendering it financial support. This system of governance, which began to emerge from the very first years of Harvard's existence, was pretty well confirmed there by the 1680s when the last Harvard faculty member to serve as trustee (with a brief exception in the 1880s) was forced off the board. The second and third American colleges—William and Mary chartered in 1693 and Yale in 1701—were established with boards of trustees totally distinct—except for the college president—from the teaching body. This pattern has persisted in virtually every American college until the late 1960s when various campus crises brought tentative efforts to give faculty (and students) more "power over their lives" by including them on college boards of trustees. This pattern of governance was, from the first, the one that controlled the development of academies in the United States.

The colleges and academies of the early national period were also similar in that, although they were "private" institutions, they had a public aspect and received a certain amount of public support. Ideally, a college or academy was to apply for a charter from the state before it opened its doors (although hundreds, perhaps thousands, of academies existed for years without a state charter). The chartering process was a hold-over from a period in which the state tightly controlled economic and social life to the extent that no man was allowed to do business until the state had determined that his efforts would help the state. In that mercantilist age, the state was supposed to determine or plan its own economic development and virtually assign individuals to the roles necessary for accomplishing that plan. Any group that drew together to manufacture glass or build a bridge or found a school or fight fires (even voluntarily) had to petition either the local or national government for a charter which would grant them the privilege of carrying out their plans. Such a grant of privilege came only when the government had determined that the activity was in the public interest. Charters also often granted monopolies. If the government granted a group the privilege of building a toll bridge in a certain place, it was likely to promise not to allow any other group to build a competing bridge nearby. Monopolies of this kind were granted in order to insure the success of the first venturers on the assumption that, if building a bridge was in the public interest, it was also in the public interest to insure that the bridge builders found the venture profitable enough to continue. In the last half of the eighteenth and the first half of the nineteenth century—the very time when thousands of colleges and academies were receiving state charters—the chartering system and the system of economic and social control that supported it were being challenged and were breaking down in England and the United States.

This period in England saw the increasing elaboration of the laissez-faire theories of Adam Smith and David Ricardo, which held that the public and state interest is best served by allowing the maximum feasible individual freedom in economic activity. A state's economy would be strongest when every individual pursued his own economic self-interest unimpeded by the state. Thus, Smith could argue that the pursuit of self-interest was also the pursuit of public interest, and that the public interest suffered whenever the state interfered with the individual pursuit of self-interest. Smith's ideas came to dominate nineteenth-century academic thought but became only partially implemented in the economies of Western Europe in that or any other century. In the United States, the story was somewhat different as the weakness of centralized government in a sparsely settled country with poor internal communications made laissez-faire a governmental practice long before the classical economists developed the theory. Colonial governments and early state governments had neither the enforcement machinery to regulate effectively the economic activities of widely scattered citizens nor the foresight and financial resources to understand and serve the public interest in a new and rapidly developing country. So although governments, both colonial and state, continued to issue charters and grants of privilege, they did so largely symbolically. Few entrepreneurial ventures were stopped because the state refused to grant a charter or because it effectively regulated the venture, once established: likewise with educational institutions. Colonial and state governments in almost all cases issued charters to all who requested them and, once having granted the privilege of establishing an educational institution, the governments interfered in no way with the running of the institution. Indeed, by a strange piece of irony, freedom from interference became a privilege, made famous in the Dartmouth College case in 1819, that accompanied a state charter. This complex legal case was one of several which arose when state governments, following the Revolution, had sought either to take control of or to impose new conditions, more in line with revolutionary democratic doctrine about public control, on "private" colleges originally chartered by colonial governments. In the Dartmouth College case, the Supreme Court ruled that since the Constitution had explicitly guaranteed that the new government would honor all contracts made under the colonial governments and that, since a charter was a contract, it was illegal for a state or local government to interfere in any way with a chartered institution except insofar as the original charter provided for such interference. In other words, a charter was a contract in perpetuity and, except under provisions written into the original contract, the state could not abridge that contract in any way. Although the charter was originally granted in recognition of the public service nature of the institution, it was now interpreted as an assurance of the essential privateness of the institution. Thus, the charter was vital because it insured the trustees and potential donors that, despite the election of new governments every few years, the college would continue as planned. In an era when democracy was new and when shifts in European governments had often meant upheavals in all institutions, this kind of assurance was significant; some historians have argued that the assurance given by the Dartmouth College case was the spark which accounts for the ever increasing rate of educational institution founding after 1820. It is doubtful that the Dartmouth College decision "sparked" this movement, but it surely gave the private sector the confidence necessary to sustain the movement.

The charter had another value for an educational institution. It symbolized the fact that the institution carried out a public function—the education of the young, which was in the interest of the society as a whole. The charter symbolized this relation of the private institution to the public interest. As often as not, the charter also brought with it a certain amount of public support for the educational institution. When it chartered a public service institution, the state government would often grant the institution some public land that the school could sell to raise revenue, or a portion of the income from a state or local tax, or sometimes, when the state was feeling especially poor, a guarantee (seldom fulfilled) that the school would have a monopoly on higher education in its region. Thus, Harvard College received part of the income from tolls, first on the ferry and then on the bridge across the Charles River, many academies received land in Maine from the Massachusetts legislature upon chartering, and academies in many states received money from the liquor tax or from the fines paid by those guilty of certain misdemeanors in their area. Williams College thought the state promised it a monopoly on higher education in western Massachusetts when it was chartered in 1793, and in 1821 angrily and unsuccessfully fought the establishment of Amherst forty-four miles away as a violation of its charter. Thus, the charter served both to protect the private nature of the educational institution and to establish its public service character. It is this very ambiguity that is most crucial to understanding the institutional shape of the academy and college in the early nineteenth century; this ambiguity about the publicness of private educational institutions is far from being resolved even in the present day, as we can see in the battles over state support for parochial education and over the issue of the relation of government to the "private" universities.

✳✳✳

Another area in which the college and academy resembled each other was curricular. That they should be so similar in this respect is ironic, for the academy was first suggested in America as an alternative form of higher education that was to offer modern and practical subjects—like English, modern foreign languages, navigation, surveying—instead of the classical training of the grammar school and college. The model for the American academy, defined as a secondary institution which combined instruction in the classics with more practical, "modern" subjects, came from the ideas of the poet John Milton as institutionalized in the Puritan dissenting academies in England during the Restoration. Benjamin Franklin had those dissenting academies in mind when he published, in 1749, his *Proposals Relating to the Education of Youth in Pennsylvania,* in which he suggested that Philadelphia needed an institution with a broader curriculum than that of the classical grammar school. He proposed a school where the students would "learn those Things that are likely to be *most useful* and *most ornamental,* Regard being had to the several Professions for which they are intended." Franklin's suggestions for practicality were more radical than most: "While they are reading Natural History, might not a little *Gardening, Planting, Grafting, Inoculating,* &c. be taught and practised; and now and then Excursions made to the neighbouring Plantations of the best Farmers, their Methods observ'd and reason'd upon for the Information of Youth. The Improvement of Agriculture being useful to all, and Skill in it no Disparagement to any."[1] English, mathematics, history and civil government, and natural history were the most important parts of the curriculum; learning foreign languages was also necessary, but Latin and Greek were accorded only equal status with French and German. Franklin's suggestions and arguments were ignored and his planned "English academy" became nothing but a preliminary adjunct to the classically oriented University of Pennsylvania and its attached grammar school.

Franklin's experience was to be repeated time and again in the next hundred years. Proposals for more practical curricula in both colleges and academies and plans for more modern schools were ignored or scrapped in order to meet the demand from faculties and apparently from students (or their parents) for the traditional Latin and Greek. Theoretically, the academy was supposed to be more modern and more practical; in fact, it seems in general to have been about as traditional as the grammar schools and the colleges. Several things may account for this. First, as Franklin found, teachers and parents wanted Latin and Greek taught. These were the subjects of elite education and few parents wanted any less for their own children. Furthermore, it is not clear that Latin and Greek were such impractical subjects from the point of view of the personal success and mobility of the students in the academies.

The practicality of the practical curricula of those academies that did claim to offer these subjects must be questioned. In most cases the practical and modern subjects in a school's catalogue or advertisements were listed only for advanced students and often it turned out that no students were advanced enough to take them. In other academies, the practical subjects received cursory treatment—not through observation and induction, as Franklin suggested, but through memorization and rote recitation from a book. In the early nineteenth century, we also find little pedagogical knowledge or concern about the effective teaching of modern subjects such as natural history or trigonometry. Texts in these subjects started to appear only in the thirties, and they stressed the memorizable rather than the practical. Botany became the study of the names of the classifications rather than a study of how plants grow. These problems with the "practical" subjects were compounded by the fact that few teachers were even minimally trained to teach these modern subjects. All in all, what practical instruction there was was not likely to be very practical.

So far as historians know, however, most academies made hardly any effort to teach the modern or the practical. It was too expensive. The more subjects a school taught, the more books, equipment, and teachers it needed. And modernity and practicality seemed to call especially for expensive equipment, such as surveying instruments and laboratories. Latin and Greek, on the other hand, were fairly cheap to offer. Any man with some college education could teach them since he had learned them in college—and, as "teaching" was largely the hearing of recitations and the grading of papers and tests, special pedagogical training was not very relevant. Furthermore, a school with a traditional classical curriculum could get by with a single teacher, as any educated man was expected to know all the classical subjects. But the modern and practical subjects, if they were to be taught at all well, needed specialists at added expense. Had there been a real demand from students and parents for modern and practical subjects, academies would undoubtedly have passed the extra expense on to the students; that so few did so suggests how little effective demand there was. The marginal economic position of most academies prevented them from taking the time and the risk to cultivate a demand for a different curriculum among the communities they served.

These same arguments explain the colleges' experience in this era—the expense and difficulties of teaching modern and practical subjects and the lack of effective demand for that kind of training prevented almost all colleges from departing from the traditional curriculum. Indeed, the colleges argued quite effectively that the traditional curriculum was the most practical teaching that a young person could receive. In 1828, the faculty of Yale College prepared a report to justify that faculty's rejection of an alumnus' suggestion that Yale add several "practical subjects" to its curriculum. The Yale Report argued that the mental discipline that the student received while studying the classics best prepared him to think for himself about other problems that he would encounter. "First exercise the mind and then furnish it," the professors wrote. "Furnishing" would most often come later, on the job or in a special training school like a seminary. The college's function was to exercise the mind and Latin and mathematics were the supreme tools for that purpose. They were pure, abstract, and complete. If a student could master a systematic, ordered, rounded body of knowledge like Latin or mathematics, he then had mastered a system of thought applicable to other, less complete subjects. Study of these traditional and well-ordered subjects gave the student a standard of knowledge, system, and completeness which he could use in seeking knowledge in other subjects. In a sense it was advantageous that Latin was a dead language since it was no longer subject to changes brought about by usage, regional corruptions, and slang. It could safely be treated and studied as a completed, logical, internally consistent, and perfect system—a closed system. Mathematics, of course, possessed the same advantages. Furthermore, the classical languages and mathematics were difficult, and it was thought best to train people on difficult subjects, as it was easier to go from the difficult to the more simple (as the modern subjects were designated). Difficult subjects also had a greater disciplinary value; the harder the subject, the greater disciplining of will power necessary to master it. The Yale Report rested on the faculty psychology and on the assumption of transfer of training—that is, the idea that exercising the mind in the study of one subject would make the mind more adept at studying other subjects, that memorizing Latin would improve the mind's ability to memorize French should the student want to do so at some future date. Thus, according to the Yale Report, disciplines which gave the mind the most rigorous and the most general exercise were the most practical school subjects. And those subjects— happily for the professors—were the traditional Greek, Latin, and mathematics.

The Yale Report came at a critical time for the fate of the classical languages in higher education. From the founding of the universities in Western Europe in the Middle Ages, the classical languages had been recognized as the languages of communication among educated men. Treatises in medicine, law, education, theology, and even science were written in Latin; the "wisdom of the ancients" was constantly called upon and applied in everyday situations. Thus, the most practical education a would-be professional or a well-rounded gentleman could hope for would be one that taught him the language and literature of primary communication. In the eighteenth century, the vernacular gradually replaced Latin as the language of communication among even the most educated men. Although scholars and professional specialists still wrote and read Latin in their work, the well-rounded educated man took his ideas and his knowledge of the world from works written in the vernacular. Men still believed in the importance of the wisdom of the ancients—note the constant parallels Americans drew between their own democratic experiment and classical forms of government—but that wisdom was generally thought to be available in translation. Thus, the obvious rationale for the emphasis on the classics in education was undermined. The classics were no longer practical, some argued, and should be replaced with more useful subjects. Had the classics continued to justify their position in the curriculum on the basis of their usefulness as languages of communication and as sources of great classical ideas and ideals, they would surely have been replaced. But the Yale Report subtly but clearly changed the rationale for keeping the curriculum classical; argued, indeed, for a higher form of practicality than did the advocates of the modern subjects.

The ideas of the Yale Report were not original with the professors at Yale, but their report, widely publicized as a statement of positive educational progress (not the reactionary defense of the old that most modern historians term it), set the tone and rationale of higher education for the greater part of the remainder of the century. Although written by college professors as a manifesto about college education, the report had as great an impact on academies as it did on colleges. Here was a report that accomplished everything; it reconciled the financial interests of the schools and the cultural pretensions of the teachers with the practical tendencies of a developing nation and reconciled, perhaps more importantly, the conflict within parents and students between the desire to share the cultural training of the elite and the desire for practical training for the business of life.

There are some exceptions to the generalizations about curriculum made in the preceding pages, just as there are to all the generalizations made in this volume. The most important exceptions were the few technical schools founded for the training of engineers in early America—the United States Military Academy (1802) and Rensselaer Polytechnic Institute (1824) being the most famous. Both, because they were established to deemphasize the classics, took the name of academy or institute in order to distinguish themselves from the colleges. Also exceptional were the normal schools or teacher training academies founded in this period. These schools offered occupationally oriented secondary education (their training was hardly of professional grade, however) and as such carried out the utilitarian mandate of the original academy model. In most cases, however, the normal school was not as advanced as the academy; its curriculum concentrated largely on reviewing the elementary subjects in order to train students to teach in elementary schools.

The colleges and academies in the period 1780–1860, then, largely shaped their curricula according to the traditional classical model. The student occupied the greatest part of his time learning Latin, Greek, and mathematics. Rhetoric and forensics—training in the writing and speaking of English—took up a smaller portion of his day. The lower the level of the school, the more time it devoted to English rather than classical languages. As the period progressed, science—natural philosophy (physics and chemistry) and natural history (geology and biology)—received more attention, especially in the wealthier institutions. Benjamin Silliman gave lectures and laboratory demonstrations in chemistry at Yale in the first decade of the nineteenth century, at least twenty years before the publication of the Yale Report. The colleges and most of the academies conducted some work in mental and moral philosophy—generally in the capstone course in the curriculum where the college president or academy principal guided the graduating class through a book like Francis Wayland's *The Elements of Moral Science* (1835), a treatise that sought to cover the ethical aspects of all phases of an educated man's life. It included discussions of how the mind was formed and how it functioned, of the sources of moral ideas and ideals, of political economy and civil government, and finally of marriage and the family. Here, more than in any other class in the school, the instructor did more than simply listen to and mark recitations. Instead, he discussed and advised his charges on the moral issues of their time.

With this exception, however, pedagogy in institutions of higher learning was not markedly better than it was in the district schools. Rote recitation—in which the student memorized a passage from the text or his translation of a passage from the text and repeated it to the teacher—was a standard practice. Only in rhetoric and forensics was there much student creativity; even the few science laboratories established in the first half of the nineteenth century were used mostly to demonstrate experiments to students, not to let them *do* them. Students' creativity and imagination were stimulated much less by the curriculum and teaching of the schools than by what Frederick Rudolph has called the "extracurriculum"—the network of literary clubs, secret societies, fraternities, debating clubs, and voluntary agencies which students established and ran with a high level of intellectual rigor. Literary and debating clubs, for example, often had larger and better libraries than the college or academies—with especially strong collections of modern works, including novels, a class of frivolous books excluded from most college libraries. Whereas college libraries opened perhaps only an hour or two a day and discouraged the circulation of books, the club libraries were much more accessible and consequently much more intellectually influential. As the Yale Report had insisted, the institutions of higher learning were more concerned with disciplining and training the mind than with furnishing it; students turned to the clubs and societies for information about the world around them.

el of curriculum and instruction, it is difficult to distinguish
erally, of course, colleges tended to admit a slightly older
vanced and rigorous curriculum. But only slightly and not
udents is a very complicated one. We do know that academies
he and that colleges matriculated many students under fif-
stered substantial numbers of students over thirty. But about
ical student—we know next to nothing. Some colleges kept
m which historians have been able to discover that the aver-
1800 to the Civil War. The increasing age of college students
tist colleges and of the recruitment patterns of the American
young men to college in return for their promise to become
has been done with respect to academy matriculants. It is
at since the academy was not seen principally as a prepa-
, academy students would not necessarily be younger than

s normal practice of establishing its own secondary school
s for college work. Colleges often sprang up in areas in
; and had to accept students directly out of district school
and offer them a secondary course. Throughout the period some colleges had far more students in their precollege sections than in the colleges themselves; some had no students registered in college courses. Furthermore, less than half—probably fewer—of the students who attended the secondary portion ever went on the register in the college. These colleges were academies in everything but name, as they offered terminal secondary schooling to the majority of their students. While some schools labeled academies gave courses at a level commensurate with those at all but the best colleges, others functioned only as private elementary schools. Academies, especially those located in sparsely settled rural or frontier areas, were desperate for tuition money, and if paying students needed elementary work, the academy, however reluctantly, taught it.

Thus, although we can speak in the abstract of varying levels of higher education, we cannot associate those levels firmly with institutional titles. Greek, Latin, mathematics, forensics, rhetoric, natural history, and moral philosophy could be taught at the advanced or the basic level, a distinction corresponding to the tertiary and the secondary levels of schooling. But many institutions labeled colleges taught only at the basic level and many labeled academies taught both the basic and the advanced. Thus, the name "college" or "academy" did not necessarily indicate what kind of school existed under that title or what kind of instruction it provided. Specific institutions chose to title themselves as they did, apparently, more in accordance with local prejudices toward the rhetorical "practicality" of the academy or the intellectual elitism of the college than in accordance with the kind of instruction they offered. Many institutions found they had made a mistake and changed their designation—the usual change, as would be expected, from the lower to the higher, from academy to college. Firm demarcation of secondary from tertiary education, however, would not come until the beginning of the twentieth century.

II

Many more colleges and academies were established in the period between the Revolution and the Civil War than were needed to fulfill the demands for higher education among the population of the period. Only by understanding why there was more popular demand for the building of these institutions than there was demand for their educational facilities will we understand the place of higher education in the early American republic.

How many academies were there? We do not really know, for the only way to count is to find copies of academy charters among neglected state legislative records. No one has made this examination as of yet. Moreover, a charter will tell us only that an academy was contemplated; it does not tell us that it was actually founded. Further complicating the statistical picture, there were many more unincorporated (unchartered) academies than incorporated ones. Perhaps the best estimates that we have are those compiled by Henry Barnard in the 1850s.[3] Barnard found that there were over 6,000 academies enrolling more than 250,000 students. He found, on the other hand, that there were 239 colleges enrolling a little over a tenth of that number. Albert Fishlow estimates that in 1850 approximately 4 million children were enrolled in public common schools.[4] This attendance figure, according to Fishlow, is equal to approximately 56 percent of the common-school-age population. On the other hand, if we take Barnard's figure of a quarter of a million children attending academies as relatively accurate, which it probably is, and compare it to the estimated total white population in the 15–24 age group—4.1 million—we find that the academies served at any one time approximately 6 percent of the available population. The chances were that about 12 percent of the population coming of age at the time had attended academies for four years during some part of their careers. Perhaps more went to academies, for it is very probable that a majority did not complete a four-year course. These figures help us to understand that the magnitude of the academy movement, in terms of institutions and students, was not insignificant. Moreover, they point out that the academies serviced a far larger proportion of the population than did their predecessors, the Latin Grammar Schools, which were limited in number and located almost exclusively in densely populated areas and which in the colonial era required substantial intellectual achievement and social status for admission. The academy movement saw the founding of literally thousands of institutions devoted primarily to secondary schooling and the spreading of secondary education from cities to the small towns.

The pattern in the growth in numbers of colleges and in numbers of students attending college presents a somewhat different picture. Nine colleges were founded in the American colonies. Between the Revolution and the Civil War, the United States saw the founding of 173 colleges that were to survive until the 1920s—when Donald Tewksbury studied and counted antebellum colleges.[5] Actually, many more than 173 were founded, for a majority of these did not survive into the twentieth century—Tewksbury estimates that, for every college that survived, three or four others died.

The figures on the founding of the more hardy institutions reveal a rapidly increasing rate of growth. Only 28 of these colleges were founded before 1820; 12 in the 1820s; but 35 in the thirties, 32 in the forties (there was a steep depression in the late thirties and early forties which slowed down the rate of investment in and the survival capabilities of colleges), and 66 in the 1850s. Another historian has estimated that in 1800, 18 of every 10,000 Americans were college trained (i.e., they had spent some time at an American college but had not necessarily graduated) and that in 1830, 17 of every 10,000 were college trained.[6] Although these estimates do not account for European training that some Americans had received, it is probable that no more than two tenths of a percent of the American population was college trained in the first quarter of the century. By mid-century, as Barnard's figures for 1850 suggest, considerable expansion had occurred, yet even then the colleges enrolled less than 2 percent (1.25%) of the population in the 20–24 age group. In terms of enrollments, then, the colleges were small; but their symbolic importance, their wide dispersion over the country, and the prominence of their graduates make them significant for the historian measuring American attitudes toward education and the effects of education on American society.

All the available statistics demonstrate that institutions of higher education greatly expanded in number and enrollment in the first eighty years of nationhood.[7] The most dramatic increase, however, was in the number of institutions, an increase far greater than that necessitated by increasing enrollments. The academies and colleges were seriously overbuilt. This overbuilding—the fact that not enough tuition-paying students existed to fill the numerous institutions to the "breakeven" point—accounts for the extremely high mortality rate among colleges and what seems, so far as we can tell, a similar mortality rate among academies. The cries of educators lamenting the pinch caused by lack of students and their tuition money are universal during the period. At the college and at the academy level, trustees and presidents contemplated desperate schemes to assemble capital to get a school established or over a financial hurdle. One such scheme provided that initial donors to the college received in return a "perpetual scholarship" for their children and *their* children. Some colleges that had financed their beginnings in this manner found in the next generation that all the original contributions had been eaten up by initial building expenditures and that most of their students were descendants of original contributors who attended without charge. Northwestern University was forced to honor such a pledge and admit a student free of charge as late as the early 1970s. Most commonly, however, faculty members were forced to bear the financial burden of overbuilding. There are scores of harrowing tales of faculty members going for years without pay or with greatly reduced pay in order to help their institution stay alive. And of course students bore a considerable burden in consequence of this overbuilding. Although tuition remained surprisingly low—competition for students dictated that—educational quality and educational facilities like libraries suffered greatly because of this underfinancing.

One evidence of the overbuilding is that colleges were often founded right on the frontier line—not a generation after the founding of a town or of a state, but at the same moment as the founding of the town or state. Thus in states like Kentucky, Kansas, and Minnesota, colleges were founded before the population of the states rose above the 100,000 mark—if the 18 in 10,000 figure for college-trained people can be said to apply uniformly across the country, each of these states established colleges before there were 200 college-trained residents in the state. At the 1850 rate of enrollment for colleges in the 20–to–24 age group—less than 2 percent—there were less than 300 students available to go to college in these states. Nor is there any reason to believe that the rate of enrollment in these frontier communities reached nearly as high a figure as 2 percent. The same pattern holds true for academy foundings—Iowa's first appeared in 1836, ten years before statehood and when that territory (which included part of what is now Minnesota) boasted less than 40,000 inhabitants. In 1850 Texas, with a population of only 213,000, was reported to have 97 academies. Assuming that 6 percent of the young people 15–24 attended an academy and, adjusting for the likelihood that frontier regions would contain a larger cohort of that age group than older locales (young people tended to migrate much more frequently than older, more settled people), each Texas academy could expect about 40 students at a time and Iowa's lone academy had to recruit from a potential 720 students dispersed through the vast territory.[8] And again, as in the case of the frontier colleges, there is every reason to expect that in the frontier areas where young men were especially important in helping families begin new farms and new enterprises, fewer youngsters sought higher education than in more settled regions.

The rapidity with which colleges and academies sprang up did not reflect a realistic appraisal of the educational needs of the communities they were designed to serve. Rather, this overbuilding must be seen as a product of the entrepreneurial, cultural, moral, and status aspirations of their founders and patrons. When we come to understand these reasons for overbuilding this kind of institution—there was, we must note, no similar overbuilding at the common or district school level—we will come to understand the underlying functions of higher education in the United States in the first half of the nineteenth century.

✳✳✳

Founding of institutions of higher education was one product of the overoptimistic boosterism that characterized the American development of space in the antebellum period. Daniel Boorstin in the second volume of his trilogy, *The Americans* (1965), describes this booster spirit with great verve and insight.[9] Every settlement, every "wide spot in the road," "claimed the name of 'city,'" he points out. No one seems to have paid any particular attention to the real meaning of the word. "Every place that claimed the honors of a city set about justifying itself by seeking to conjure up suitably metropolitan institutions." Among these metropolitan institutions were a hotel, a newspaper, and, almost as important, an institution of higher learning—whether an academy or a college. Boston, New York, Philadelphia had colleges; why should not Georgetown, Kentucky (1829), and Galesburg, Illinois (Knox, 1837)? And each got a college—when its population had barely reached 1,000.

The efforts to build Athenian cities in the West were somewhat paradoxical. As the founders of these colleges and academies sought to upgrade the towns in which they lived into cities, they brought about a diffusion of culture which would challenge the very definition of a city as a center of culture. The scattering of colleges and similar cultural institutions among hundreds of western towns represented a significant departure from the idea of centralized urban culture which had pervaded Western civilization from its beginning. The founders of colleges and academies were not even content to choose a single town to be the cultural capital of each state. Every town, they seemed to say, should be a cultural center.

The cultural leaders of the West viewed the city ambiguously. On the one hand, they wanted institutions like those located in New York or Boston; on the other, they felt urban environments to be evil. Many westerners thought of Boston and New York in much the same way that Jefferson thought of Paris and London. Noah Webster was but one of many who believed that "large cities [even those in America] are always scenes of dissipation and amusement, which have a tendency to corrupt the hearts of youth and divert their minds from their literary pursuits."[10] Urban educational entrepreneurs agreed with Webster about older large cities, but felt that their own cities—absolutely imaginary as they were—would be free of such corrupting influences and thus safe places in which boys and girls could learn and where a pure culture could be maintained (although they often acknowledged the pervasive distrust of urban influence by placing their institutions on the edge of the city, in a protected place such as on a hill that overlooked the city but was somewhat isolated from it). Henry Nash Smith has described the American vision of the West as a virgin land, a new Eden, where men could begin all over again in a state of innocence, where men could be reborn. He describes this image as a kind of pastoral vision which saw the West as an agricultural heaven.[11] But the urban boosters of the antebellum period felt that the western cities-to-be could foster this same sense of innocence and rebirth. Establishing educational institutions became one way of insuring that the new urban units would live up to the cultural, moral, and Edenlike aspirations of these boosters.

The building of institutions of higher education in these areas also served to fulfill more mundane aspirations. Among these aspirations, the quest for financial profit dominated. The unflagging preoccupation with land speculation determined educational investment. A school raised the price of nearby land. One frontiersman explained that land developers "are shrewd enough to know that one of the most successful methods to give notoriety to an embryo town, and induce New England settlers, is forthwith to put in operation some institution of learning with a high sounding name." One public elementary school administrator in Madison, Wisconsin, complained that establishment of a female academy "would do more to raise the price of village lots and secure a better class of people for the future city of Madison than any amount of money expended in building school houses and providing teachers for the public schools."[12] This complaint that academies and colleges rather than public elementary schools attracted settlers and investment explains, in part, why higher education was so overbuilt relative to elementary education. It also suggests that settlers were attracted less by the quality of the education offered than by the titles of institutions and their superficial claims to "culture."

The contributions educational institutions made to an area's economic health were well recognized in the antebellum period. Localities actually bid for such institutions—and the institutions chose to locate where they received the best financial guarantees. The University of Missouri was established only when Boone County—where Columbia is located—outbid five other Missouri River counties. The citizens of Boone County raised pledges of $82,000 in cash and $35,000 in land—the contributions coming "from over 900 individuals, of whom nearly a hundred gave five dollars or less."[13] Such patterns of contribution, as Boorstin points out, served to tie the college to the community very closely—the University of Missouri was Columbia's own college because the people of the town and its environs had "bought" it.

What financial advantages did an institution of higher learning offer a community? It would raise land values by attracting settlers who were interested in sending their children to school. Probably more important to the people who bid for the presence of a college or academy was the fact that these establishments, by attracting students and faculty from the outlying regions and from neighboring towns, would assemble more customers for the local merchants—would pump, in modern parlance, more buying power into the town's economy. Academies and colleges of the period were small, no doubt, but the towns were also small. Thus the influx of forty or fifty students could make a great difference in the town's economy. Before the colleges and academies learned that they could make a profit from renting dormitory rooms to students, the students from the outlying regions were forced to purchase room and board from townspeople. Some colleges deliberately refrained from building dormitories to house their students so that the student board revenue would be distributed throughout the town, convincing the townsmen of the college's importance to the town's economy.

If the overbuilding of higher educational institutions rested on an exaggerated optimism about the development of new areas of the United States, it also rested in large part on an overblown fear that the movement away from the old areas of settlement and their established ways would bring about a barbarism, a lack of community, and a breakdown of culture among those who made the move. Men beginning new communities in new areas felt the need for reassurance that they could maintain, in a new environment, the values and culture they had left behind. Like the erection of a church just like the one they had left behind, the building of a school on the older model served to reaffirm the community's commitment to older values and its capability of achieving traditional standards of morality and culture. This eagerness to affirm that they were still part of civilization, still capable of living up to the old morality and culture, accounts for the rapidity with which communities established institutions of learning. Like the habit of building schools in order to enhance land values, the habit of building schools as symbols of the aspiration to morality and culture and civilization was applicable at all levels. In the earliest years of community settlement, thousands of district schools were founded as just such a symbol. But just as institutions of higher education had greater economic value than the district school, so did they have greater symbolic value as commitments to culture.

While participants in the new community ventures worried about what was happening to them, benevolent groups in the older communities worried about them also. The college president of the early nineteenth century was no less a slave to money-raising responsibility than is his modern counterpart, and part of his obligations included frequent trips to the east coast (and sometimes to England) to raise funds for the college. The educational institution's fund-raiser was most successful at home by appealing to the economic interests and community pride of the local community; he was most successful in the East in appealing to the philanthropists' and the churches' concern with the morals and manners of the westerner and frontiersman. When citizens left one community to venture to a new frontier or a new community in a less settled region, they and more particularly those who remained behind felt that the movers were breaking, or at least severely straining, the social code which emphasized loyalty and subordination of self to the interests of the group. Some of the less trusting easterners felt that the pioneers had left "civilized and religious society for the simple purpose of getting out of its restraints." By moving to the West, these people had excluded themselves from the community, from "society," and from its control. They had become different and, as such, came to seem more or less dangerous to the settled ways of those living in the traditional communities.

In response to this crisis of "outsiders," several religiously oriented organizations sprang up to supply ministers, schools and Sunday schools, Bibles, and tracts to the outsiders in the hopes of influencing their morals. As the executive committee of the Home Missionary Society, in appealing for funds in 1839, put it: "The Gospel is the most economical police on earth." The most important of these benevolent societies were the American Home Missionary Society (founded in 1826), the American Tract Society (1825), the American Bible Society (1816), the American Education Society (1816), and the American Sunday School Union (1824). These, plus a host of small institutions, individual churches, and individual philanthropists, similarly concerned that the movement away from a set-tled community effected a deleterious character change in people, provided much of the capital for the overexuberant expansion of higher education in the first half of the nineteenth century. They did so in hopes that such educational institutions would reassert the authority of religion and civi-lization on a population that seemed to those unfamiliar with it—as the easterners largely were—a dangerous source of disorder and political and social disruption.[14]

Religion and religious instruction were very much a part of the work carried on by most of the academies and colleges founded before the Civil War—as they were of those founded after. This religious orientation manifested the concern many of the supporters of higher education in this period felt for the morals and character of those for whom the institutions were being built. The character of this religious orientation was largely nondenorninational, although distinctly Protestant and militantly anti-Catholic. But it is not particularly helpful to describe this period in the history of higher education as one of denominational rivalry in the founding of schools and to attribute the overbuilding of the era to that competition. Each denomination, the argument goes, in adjusting to the voluntarism necessitated by the separation of church and state formalized by the Bill of Rights, sought to gain and keep converts. One important device for furthering this evangelistic enterprise was the denominational school and college. Thus, the argument continues, each denomination rushed to found schools in as many areas as possible so that each school could inculcate the religious dogma of the denomination which controlled it and win for the denomination a much firmer hold on the students who passed through the school. These students, thanks to their training, would be less likely to break the voluntary bonds of denominational membership. Furthermore, it is argued, the vari-ous sects sought schools in which to train ministers.

Although this argument from denominational competition has a certain superficial logic, it does not adequately fit the facts of the first half of the nineteenth century. Denominational competition was not an important characteristic or cause of the development of institutions of higher education in that era. The historian of higher education in the antebellum period finds the typical school under a nom-inal denominational identification, but open to all without tests of religious faith. The school served a geographic rather than a religious community and was attended by students from the surrounding ter-ritory, no matter what their religious affiliation—if any. The school engaged in no doctrinal inculca-tion beyond commonly accepted tenets of Christian morality. Most of the colleges founded before the 1840s took on the denominational coloring of their backers because these backers stipulated that a majority of the institution's trustees must belong to a certain denomination. Often, however, another denomination was given perpetual minority status on the board of trustees in order to secure support for the new venture among town leaders who did not share the denominational affiliation of most of the backers. At the same time, in order to make the college as attractive as possible to all comers, the backers prohibited religious tests for either faculty or students. As Frederick Rudolph has pointed out, the "nineteenth-century American college could not support itself on a regimen of petty sectari-anism; there simply were not enough petty sectarians or, if there were, there was no way of getting them to the petty sectarian colleges in sufficient numbers."[15]

On the other hand, there was little likelihood that Americans would maintain nondenomina-tional colleges in this era. Virtually every educational institution established in the nineteenth century set out to instill piety and virtue in students and to explain to them the power and the beauty of God. All the colleges were Christian. But such a designation was hardly enough in that era—a person was, after all, a Christian in a particular way—a Methodist or a Congregationalist or what-have-you. There was no recognized general Christian way of serving God or of worshipping Him. One served and worshipped as a member of a denomination. After all, chapel services had to take some form—a form of communion and a form of the Lord's Prayer had to be agreed upon. "Nondenominational" forms of worship had yet to be invented. Even the ostensi-bly nonsectarian state colleges, perhaps with the exception of the University of Virginia, were thought to have been "captured" by denominations. But the nature of this "capture" reveals how unimportant denomination affiliation was from the evangelistic point of view. A college was con-sidered captured whenever a majority of the trustees belonged to a single denomination, but the denominational affiliation of the conquerors need not have effected any change in the operation or the personnel of the college.

Denominational identification in the years before 1830 or 1840 seems largely to have been accidental in that the new institution took whatever denominational form that most of its trustees favored. Some denominational identification was virtually necessary to the functioning of the institution, and the natural and simple thing to do was to adopt the religion of the social leaders, the boosters, of the community in which the institution was housed. These were the men who became the trustees. Between 1830 and the Civil War, events become somewhat more complicated. Some academies and colleges, desperate for money, sought to emphasize their denominational leanings in order to convince churches that they merited financial support. These solicitations met with varying success— one college changed its identification three times in as many years in hopes of appealing successfully to some denomination. Also, very gradually after 1830, regional and national administrators of the various denominations grew interested in seeking or building schools in each area with which to affiliate. They took the first steps toward building a network of schools to which members of the denomination could send their children and be sure they were receiving proper religious instruction. But only after the Civil War did the denominations begin to play a central role in organizing, locating, and supporting higher education. By then the spirit of community involvement had weakened considerably. In explaining the overbuilding of colleges and academies in the antebellum period, however, general concern for morality and social control are much more important than denominational competition.

The fourth reason that academies and colleges were so overbuilt in the decades before the Civil War was that local social leaders and their children derived considerable social status from these institutions. Institutions of higher education had economic value for these social leaders in that they increased the wealth of the community. Just as important was the fact that those institutions confirmed (or established) the social leaders' status in that community. The social leaders were, of course, the influentials in the community. They might be like the people responsible for the founding of Phillips Andover and Phillips Exeter, in 1778 and 1783 respectively, or like the founders of Lafayette College in Pennsylvania. Samuel Phillips, Jr. was descended from a long line of Harvard-trained Puritan clergymen; his father was a prominent Massachusetts businessman and politician. Samuel was a member of the General Court of the Massachusetts Bay Colony; he was a member of the convention that framed the constitution of Massachusetts; he became a judge, a state senator, and, at the time of his death, lieutenant governor. Two other members of the family assisted Samuel in establishing the two academies which still bear the family name—one a doctor, the other a leading judge in New Hampshire. The fact that the Phillips family could afford to give the two academies an endowment estimated somewhere between $100,000 and $150,000—a lot of money at the time— attests to the family's prominence.

In underdeveloped regions, the patterns of influence and leadership were somewhat different. Whereas the Phillipses had both the influence and the money to start their ventures virtually alone, leaders in new towns depended on their ability to mobilize support from others. These leaders, typically, did not have deep social and economic roots in the community. They were men who hoped to establish their wealth and their prestige by developing the communities to which they had recently moved. James Madison Porter, lawyer, canal promoter, and leading citizen-booster of Easton, Pennsylvania, is a case in point. Recently settled in that small underdeveloped community seventy miles north of Philadelphia, Porter took note of the economic stimulus that colleges provided such a small town. In 1824 he published an advertisement calling on all interested citizens to meet to discuss the founding of such a college. The meeting was a success and a board of thirty-nine men was appointed. "This number included several promoters, a number of businessmen, lawyers, a physician, two newspapermen, and two hotelkeepers. Not one of the number had been born in Easton; only one had attended college."[16] The four ministers in the town were excluded so as to prevent any appearance of clerical control. Porter and the other trustees felt that their personal success depended on Easton's growth. In 1824 the town's prospects seemed good. The town, largest in eastern Pennsylvania north of Philadelphia, lay across wagon routes to the West at the confluence of the Lehigh and Delaware rivers upon which coal and shipbuilding materials were sent to Philadelphia. They expected Lafayette College, as it was called, to draw needed attention to their community. Easton was in an eastern locale but was a town similar in its newness, pretension, and leaders to hundreds of similar towns newly founded in undeveloped regions from Maine to Minnesota.

Status was an important motive in the founding of the academies and colleges. The Phillipses looked on higher education as a way of maintaining the traditional social order and the traditional separation of classes in a society awash with revolutionary theory and paeans to the dignity and equality of all men. Samuel Phillips wholeheartedly supported the revolutionary impulse to secure liberty and purity for Americans, but he did not think that his sons were better than any other men living in America. He felt that the greatest weakness of the Dummer School, which he had attended between 1765 and 1767, was that it sought to educate charity students along with paying ones.[17] Academy training would give his sons a refinement, an esprit, and a sense of moral character and social responsibility that would make manifest the separation in which he believed. For a man like James Madison Porter, ambitiously trying to carve an upper-middle-class status for himself, sending his offspring to an academy or college would lend them a refinement and a status to help set them (and him) above most of the people living in northeastern Pennsylvania.

Noah Webster noted how differences in language abilities separated people. In one sense, this is what the academies and colleges were all about. The most characteristic feature of their instruction was its emphasis on the classical languages. American educational reformers and theorists from Benjamin Franklin on stressed the need for instruction in more practical subjects in the academies—they argued that the study of English and of the arithmetical skills necessary to the merchant and the engineer should form the core of the academy curriculum. Francis Wayland repeated these injunctions and applied them to the colleges in 1842. But Wayland's efforts at reforming the curriculum in the 1840s came to naught just as Franklin's had one hundred years earlier, and the study of Latin and Greek continued as the most important aspect of instruction in these schools.

Why? Because a knowledge of Latin and Greek, however superficial, gave its possessor something—a skill, but more important a sense of refinement—that his fellow citizens did not have. Speeches and conversations of the period were filled with gratuitous snippets of Latin or Greek that served to manifest the culture and the refinement of the speaker. Ability to include such quotations served as a kind of badge of status, just as proper pronunciation of English served to separate the classes from the masses. Thus, while the elementary schools, at least in theory, sought to break down class barriers by stressing common training in English, institutions of higher education continued to erect other linguistic separations.

A knowledge of the classics, superficial or not, became a key means of access to the professions and to positions of leadership that society felt should be restricted to educated men. Although the academies and colleges served primarily the children of social leaders, they did not restrict their admissions to these people—they could not afford to. Thus, they afforded a means of mobility to young men bent on bettering themselves. Attendance at these institutions furnished the upwardly mobile youngster with all the patina of culture and refinement that a classical education could give plus the opportunity to mix with and adopt the values of the offspring of social leaders.

A great deal of the mixing, the sharing of values, and the building of cohesion among these upper-middle-class students and those who aspired to that status occurred in the student-organized clubs that appeared in the academies and colleges soon after the turn of the century. At the colleges, Greek letter fraternities appeared in the late twenties and thirties, but literary and debating societies had appeared long before. These societies functioned much as did fraternities in later years. All these clubs, societies, and fraternities carried out some of the most important goals of higher education in this period. The constitution of Phillips Exeter proposed to prepare students for "the Great End And Real Business Of Living" and stressed that "the *first* and *principal* object of this Institution is the promotion of true Piety and Virtue; the *second,* instruction in the English, Latin, and Greek Languages, etc."[18] In the literary and debating clubs, the students gathered to exercise their language skills and to discuss contemporary issues of morality and government—issues affecting the "real business of living." In a curriculum that was dominated by rote memorization, these clubs served an important function by transmitting common social values to students.

Thus, where the elementary schools may have been preparing students to enter comfortably the local power structure in the middling and lower ranks, the colleges and academies were preparing students to enter the local leadership group—to become influentials themselves. They provided badges of status and a sense of cohesiveness among the leaders-to-be. These higher institutions in effect socialized the students to the leadership function and to the values of the local leadership group. They also socialized students to the spirit of local boosterism—there the students were at the very center of the issue, their schooling and their future careers often dependent on whether local promoters could assemble enough money to pay the professors and keep the school in business. They lived in the midst of fund-raising campaigns and all the inevitable huckstering connected with selling the future of the town and its institutions. The schools also socialized the future leaders to the sense of separateness between themselves and others—that they stood somewhat above the common man with special privileges and special responsibilities, with opportunities and duties different from those of the common man. In the early 1840s, Isaiah Boott came home from college for summer vacation to visit friends and relatives. "Here for the first time did I begin to feel how perceptibly education separated those of equal age. Tho I had been but two years at college, it seemed that my schoolmates had gone backward half a century. I saw there was a wide difference between us. I supposed that society was becoming rough and going back to heathenism as fast as possible. But the fact was that my comrades were where I left them and I had gone forward."[19] And this, of course, was for many of the students, parents, and founders of institutions of higher learning the whole point of the experience—that these institutions would foster a spirit of separateness, of leadership, and of social responsibility among those lucky enough to attend them.

The academies and colleges were not intent on forming an aristocracy in America; rather, they were contributing to the formation of a broad American middle, or upper middle, class. Their students would become the promoters, the land developers, the lawyers, doctors, ministers, and teachers, the merchants and manufacturers, and the statesmen and politicians of the future. The very diffuseness of the academy and college movement prevented those institutions from assuming aristocratic pretensions. There were too many schools and too many pupils.

Evaluation of the effects of this overbuilding on higher education is very difficult. A number of historians have lamented the fact that the overbuilding of institutions of higher education in the antebellum period caused a serious decline in the quality of education at the secondary and tertiary level. Some historians have seen the antebellum period as the nadir of higher education in which anti-intellectual evangelicals displaced qualified educators and the value of higher education became debased. Much of what these historians say is true—higher education during this period was lamentably bad, for serious overbuilding did cause educational considerations to suffer because of financial and other reasons. And it is possible to argue that, had the money spent on higher education been concentrated on a few institutions, the United States would have had colleges and secondary schools ranking with the best in the world.

On the other hand, one must note that the diffusion of cultural and educational institutions and the intertwining of local economic and cultural interests vastly increased the population's interest in cultural activity. For all the superficiality of this interest in culture, for all the interest in form and disregard of content, such diffusion and such stress on the economic and local advantages of education contributed a great deal in teaching Americans to value education. Further, it is quite possible that the diffusion of higher education—however debased—may have played a major role in encouraging the economic growth of the United States in the nineteenth century and in strengthening its institutions. What higher education may have lost in intellectual quality through diffusion of effort, it may have gained in popular support and interest.

Notes

1. Benjamin Franklin, *Proposals Relating to the Education of Youth in Pennsylvania* (Philadelphia, 1749), quoted in Theodore Sizer, ed., *The Age of the Academies* (New York, 1964), 71, 75.
2. David F. Allmendinger, *Paupers and Scholars: The Transformation of Student Life in Nineteenth-Century New England* (New York, 1975), and David Potts, "Baptist Colleges in the Development of American Society, 1812–1861" (Unpublished Dissertation, Harvard University, 1967).
3. Henry Barnard, "The Educational Interest of the United States," *American Journal of Education*, I (March, 1856), 368, Table III.
4. Albert Fishlow, "The American Common School Revival: Fact or Fancy?" in Henry Rosovsky, ed., *Industrialization in Two Systems: Essays in Honor of Alexander Gerschenkron* (New York, 1966), 40–67.

5. Donald G. Tewksbury, *The Founding of American Colleges and Universities Before the Civil War: With Particular Reference to the Religious Influence Bearing upon the College Movement* (New York, 1932).

6. Sydney Aronson, *Status and Kinship in the Higher Civil Service: Standards of Selection in the Administrations of John Adams, Thomas Jefferson, and Andrew Jackson* (Cambridge, Mass., 1964), 122–123.

7. On the relative decline in college enrollment in the nineteenth-century, see Frederick Rudolph, *The American College and University: A History* (New York, 1962), 99, 118–140, and John S. Whitehead, *The Separation of College and State: Columbia, Dartmouth, Harvard, and Yale, 1776–1876* (New Haven, Conn, 1973).

8. Twenty-one percent of the national population was aged 15–24 in 1850; we have figured the frontier percentage at 30 percent (which is probably too high). We have made no adjustment for the presence of blacks in the Texas population.

9. Daniel Boorstin, *The Americans: The National Experience* (New York, 1965), especially chapters 16, 17, 20, 21. The sentence quoted below is from p. 152.

10. Noah Webster in Frederick Rudolph, *Essays on Education in the Early Republic* (Cambridge, Mass., 1965), 52.

11. Henry Nash Smith, *Virgin Land* (Cambridge, Mass., 1950), *passim.*

12. Lloyd Jorgenson, *The Founding of Public Education in Wisconsin* (Madison, Wis., 1956), 34.

13. Boorstin, *National Experience*, 159.

14. The best discussion of these societies is Clifford Griffin, *Their Brothers' Keepers: Moral Stewardship in the United States, 1800–1865* (New Brunswick, N. J., 1960); quotations are from pp. 59–60, 111. Griffin quotes on p. 111 *The Home Missionary*, XII (May, 1839), 9–10.

15. Rudolph, *American College and University*, 69.

16. Boorstin, *National Experience*, 156. A more detailed discussion can be found in David B. Skillman, *Biography of a College* (Easton, Pa., 1932), which confirms Boorstin's account.

17. Andover's first president preceptor, Eliphalet Pearson, modified Phillips' stand on this issue to the extent that the academy did provide some scholarship funds for indigent students. On Samuel Phillips and his academies, see especially James McLachlan, *American Boarding Schools: A Historical Study* (New York, 1970).

18. Quoted in Elmer E. Brown, *The Making of Our Middle Schools: An Account of the Development of Secondary Education in the United States* (New York, 1903), 195.

19. Quoted in David Potts, "Baptist Colleges" (dissertation draft, chapter 4, p. 29).

References

Guide to Further Reading

Frederick Rudolph, *The American College and University: A History* (New York, 1962), remains the most thorough analysis of the antebellum college in the United States. His bibliography of institutional histories is the best and most conveniently available. The early chapters of Oscar and Mary Handlin, *The American College and American Culture: Socialization as a Function of Higher Education* (New York, 1970), and more generally their essay on *Facing Life: Youth and Family in American History* (Boston, 1971) examine, with a good deal of perception, the experience of leaving home. Richard Hofstadter and Walter P. Metzger, *The Development of Academic Freedom in the United States* (New York, 1955), Part I (published separately by Hofstadter in 1961), is the best account of that topic and a useful introduction to the antebellum academic experience in general. Richard Hofstadter and Wilson Smith, eds., *American Higher Education: A Documentary History*, 2 vols. (Chicago, 1961), is a model collection of primary sources. An investigation of the sources of support for antebellum institutions, and an excellent introduction to the concepts of "public" and "private," are included in John S. Whitehead, *The Separation of College and State: Columbia, Dartmouth, Harvard, and Yale, 1776–1876* (New Haven, Conn., 1973). In *Professors and Public Ethics: Studies of Northern Moral Philosophers before the Civil War* (Ithaca, N.Y., 1956), Wilson Smith examines ethical theorists and public policy in several antebellum institutions. Collegiate innovations based upon student requirements are explored in David F. Allmendinger, *Paupers and Scholars: The Transformation of Student Life in Nineteenth-Century New England* (New York, 1975). David Madsen, *The National University: Enduring Dream of the U.S.A.* (Detroit, 1966), remains the standard survey.

Donald G. Tewksbury, *The Founding of American Colleges and Universities Before the Civil War: With Particular Reference to the Religious Influence Bearing Upon the College Movement* (New York, 1932), remains the standard introduction to antebellum college founding, but should be supplemented by Natalie A. Naylor's critique, "The Ante-Bellum College Movement: A Reappraisal of Tewksbury's Founding of American Colleges and Universities," *History of Education Quarterly*, XIII (Fall, 1973), 261–274. David Potts examines the impact that localism had upon the secular nature of denominational institutions before the Civil War in "Baptist Colleges in the Development of American Society, 1812–1861" (Unpublished Dissertation, Harvard University, 1967) and "American Colleges in the Nineteenth Century: From Localism to Denominationalism," *History of Education Quarterly,* XI (Winter, 1971), 363–380. Daniel Boorstin, *The Americans: The National Experience* (New York, 1965), suggests the influence of local "boosterism" upon the antebellum movement to establish institutions of higher learning. George P. Schmidt's volumes on *The Old Time College President* (New York, 1930) and *The Liberal Arts College: A Chapter in American Cultural History* (New Brunswick, N. J., 1957) remain useful.

The American academy and other nonpublic school educational institutions are surveyed in Robert Middlekauff, *Ancients and Axioms: Secondary Education in Eighteenth-Century New England* (New Haven, Conn., 1963), Theodore R. Sizer, ed., *The Age of the Academies* (New York, 1964), Robert F. Seybolt, *The Evening School in Colonial America* (Urbana, Ill., 1925), Seybolt, *The Public Schools of Colonial Boston, 1635–1775* (Cambridge, Mass., 1935), and Elmer E. Brown, *The Making of Our Middle Schools: An Account of the Development of Secondary Education in the United States* (New York, 1903).

"COLLEGE ENTHUSIASM!" AS PUBLIC RESPONSE: 1800–1860

DAVID B. POTTS

Standard histories of higher education typically picture the early nineteenth-century college as an institution becoming increasingly unpopular with parents, students, public officials, politicians, and businessmen. Religious leaders and their most avid followers may have been happy with a curriculum dominated by Greek and Latin, the argument goes, but few others in this early era of technological takeoff could find relevance in classical studies. As a result of ignoring public needs and desires, these hundreds of antebellum colleges enrolled a dwindling portion of the population. The multitude of institutions founded is seen as proof of zealous insensitivity to the lack of individual and public interest. Many colleges never opened or were soon forced to close their doors. Only with the rise of the late nineteenth-century universities offering curricula of practical appeal, the textbook interpretation concludes, was a significant portion of the public persuaded to patronize higher education. The almost century-long love affair between middle-class America and its various alma maters presumably began with such phenomena as the steady growth of engineering enrollments in land-grant colleges during the 1870s, the strengthening of links between state universities and public high schools in that same decade and the next, and the surge in enrollments in almost all institutions beginning around 1890.[1]

More than fifteen years after Bernard Bailyn provided the first major stimulus to conceptual awareness in the history of American education,[2] we are close to the point where a very different interpretation based on substantial research can be substituted for this century-old picture of early nineteenth-century higher education. As research on antebellum colleges moves from a prolonged period of historiographical criticism into an exciting phase of monographic contributions, a clearer view of the complex relationships between colleges and their constituencies has emerged. Continued reliance on the standard account of our heritage in higher education can be shown to yield only meager and distorted understandings. The chief distortion, as this essay will emphasize, concerns the capacity of educational institutions, even in difficult times, to generate public enthusiasm for their services.

Criticism and an Alternative Overview

A major portion of the historiographical case against the predominant interpretation of antebellum colleges is contributed by scholars subjecting the standard primary and secondary sources to a close and skeptical reading. This scrutiny exposes a reformer bias in the major primary documents cited and a closely related university bias in the historians basing their conclusions on a sympathetic reading of these sources.[3] The uses of writings by Francis Wayland provide a good example. Given the large extent to which Wayland's perceptions were shaped by rigid economic doctrines, a millennial vision, and peculiar problems as president of Brown University (1827–1855), one can question the use of his commentaries by Richard Hofstadter and his readers as an unquestioned source of information and insights concerning early nineteenth-century colleges.[4] Younger historians familiar with the handful of fine monographs on late nineteenth-century colleges also detect a general Whiggism in the Wayland-based picture of an earlier age of inadequacy followed by the dramatic rise of the university. They find the functionalist model employed to be simplistic, and the general interpretation at some points quite contrary to "common sense."[5] Even the data foundation for the traditional interpretation supplied by Donald G. Tewksbury in *The Founding of American Colleges and Universities Before the Civil War,* long regarded as the most useful and trustworthy monograph in the field, proves to be defective. A reappraisal of this work reveals distortions, inaccuracies, and omissions which flaw its extensive use by historians over a period of more than four decades.[6]

A second source of explicit historiographical criticism is located in the work of scholars beginning to report during the last decade that their research findings fail to support many of the most basic conclusions of the accepted interpretation. Studies of sixteen Baptist colleges, fifteen northeastern colleges, early Catholic colleges, nonreformer observations of higher education, and major education societies find little or no evidence of narrow sectarian zeal or denominational proselytizing.[7] Work on the social origins of students and on college costs produces no signs of aristocratic dominance or tendencies.[8] Investigations of curricula yield no indications of hostility to change, resistance to science, or antagonism between religion and science.[9] Comprehensive tabulations of enrollments fail to expose colleges as institutions declining in importance and public favor.[10]

More important than these negative findings are the data and generalizations in many of the same recent studies which enable us to construct the major outlines of a new alternative interpretation. Antebellum colleges can now be seen as broadly based local enterprises, deeply rooted in the economic and cultural life of hundreds of towns, counties, and surrounding areas in states extending from the east coast westward through the Mississippi Valley.[11] Access to a college education, it appears, was relatively easy compared to the years before 1800, and an increasing number of students from humble family backgrounds were enrolling and making their presence felt.[12] The curricula of these institutions, it can be argued persuasively, was intellectually vital and responsive within the cultural context of this period.[13] Especially interesting is the discovery that a constantly increasing proportion of potential college students in the national population is found to be enrolling at these institutions during the four decades preceding the Civil War.[14] When measured along all these dimensions, colleges emerge as demonstrably popular educational enterprises.

College-Community Alliances

The key to understanding this popularity resides in the many ways in which college-community relationships developed. A study of Baptist colleges[15] illustrates the intricate alliances forged between college promoters and a particular town or county. Although many of the examples cited below are found in the histories of particular Baptist-affiliated colleges, the representativeness of these examples and the validity of generalizations they support were checked against data on more than a dozen other colleges of this type, as well as available evidence in the few older studies of colleges affiliated with the Methodist, Presbyterian, and Episcopal denominations.[16] The comparison verifies that Baptist colleges were sufficiently typical to warrant their extensive use as illustrations in a brief synthesis of current scholarship on antebellum colleges.[17]

Unusually extensive information concerning close college-community cooperation in the founding years can be found in the history of Colby College, the first Baptist-affiliated institution of nineteenth-century origin to offer college-level instruction.[18] At least three non-Baptist residents of Waterville, Maine, played important roles in securing the college for their town and in providing for continued broad-based support of the institution. One, a Unitarian minister and state legislator, argued successfully for state aid to the college on the same grounds that aid was granted to common schools. Colleges, he argued in 1828, are "designed for the good of all," with "all classes of the community, rich and poor . . . equally interested in them."[19] Another non-Baptist active in the early years of Colby was a wealthy merchant and landowner who helped secure the college for his town by personally guaranteeing a major portion of the town's bid. Joining him in this effort to persuade the predominantly Baptist board of trustees to locate their college in Waterville was a prototype of the nineteenth-century local booster, Timothy Boutelle.

Boutelle, a lawyer who became a Waterville resident in the first decade of the nineteenth century, had by 1820 acquired title to much of the future business section and adjacent water rights in this promising young town. During his fifty years in Waterville, Boutelle was a major figure in establishing the town's first bank, building the first bridge across the Kennebec River to the neighboring town of Winslow, providing land for a Baptist meetinghouse and the town academy, and extending the Androscoggin and Kennebec Railroad to his town. In raising local money to supplement his own generous subscriptions to Colby College, Boutelle argued that this institution would make important contributions to the commonwealth. The college, he noted, would help improve the area's common schools by supplying competent teachers and by promoting a general respect for learning. In a growing nineteenth-century town such as Waterville, the private and public interests of a man like Timothy Boutelle were tightly interwoven. By bringing a college, a bridge, and a railroad to Waterville, Boutelle improved not only his own cultural and economic status, but also that of the town and region to which he had committed his talents and energies.[20]

With substantial assistance from non-Baptist citizens like Boutelle, college promoters in many towns established institutions that were primarily the products of local forces and circumstances. Even when a Baptist state convention founded the college, as in the cases of Wake Forest, Mercer, and Furman, local ties were sought and proved helpful in establishing a viable educational enterprise. With Bucknell, Rochester, and Mississippi Colleges, the community took the initiative and then solicited denominational support for its planned or existing school. Except for George Washington and Richmond, both urban colleges, the basic element in college founding was a bargain struck between the trustees of each institution and a town or county. Usually, this agreement determined the location of the college and ranged in formality from the "solemn compact" between Hamilton, New York, and the New York Baptist Education Society to the verbal understanding between Bucknell and the citizens of Lewisburg, Pennsylvania, and vicinity who contributed to it. The financial terms of these written and implied contracts ranged from the less than $2,000 bid by Franklin, Indiana, in the mid-1830s, to the $100,000 offered by Rochester, New York, little more than a decade later.[21]

These initial alliances were continuously reinforced by the subsequent policies of college trustees and presidents. In recommending that construction of additional dormitory rooms and a commons be postponed, the building committee of Bucknell's board of trustees calculated that "boarding and lodging the Students with the Citizens of the Town, will interest them in the College, by the strongest plea, self-interest."[22] College presidents frequently reminded townspeople that students and teachers injected money into the local economy and that a college improved local land values. These educational leaders were well aware of the advantages derived from being in a community small enough, as President Ransom Dunn of Hillsdale College observed, for "the people [to] appreciate such an institution" yet large enough for them to "do something handsome for it."[23] Although the financial status of individual contributors has yet to be carefully assessed, evidence on the numbers of contributors found in small towns, the many local people benefiting from a college's presence, and even the large and socially diverse attendance at commencements suggests a broad base of active support. In 1835, British visitors noted that Colby College enlisted "the sympathies of every class of the community,"[24] an observation that could probably be applied to the large majority of antebellum colleges. College agents did much of their fundraising within a forty- to sixty-mile radius of each institution, the region from which a majority of students were drawn.[25]

Removal Controversies

When denominational leaders proposed that colleges be moved to new locations outside these carefully cultivated zones of support, community responses clearly demonstrated the strength and importance of local connections with colleges.[26] Each of the six major removal controversies at Baptist-affiliated colleges in the late 1840s and 1850s produced a direct confrontation between recently developed statewide denominational plans and well-established community interests. Removalists usually argued that colleges could attain increased prominence and support within the denomination if transferred to a more convenient location and reorganized to insure a larger degree of denominational control. Communities fighting to retain colleges developed an argument stressing the local role in institutional origins. This position was fully expressed in the confrontation at Colgate in the late 1840s. Replying to the removalist argument that Colgate was "the creature and handiwork of the churches throughout the state," an editorial in the Hamilton, New York, newspaper asserted that the school was "in fact the *creature and handiwork* of a few individual Baptists *and others* in Hamilton and the surrounding country."[27] Commenting more generally on the topic, this newspaper observed in 1849:

> It is local feeling, religious and secular, that has given birth to all the institutions in our land. . . . It is seldom that even a denominational institution receives aid first from the denomination as such; by it the beginnings of such institutions are frequently regarded with indifference. A few farsighted men lay the foundation. . . . They first look well to the "local interest"—create a nucleus, deeply imbedded in the "local feeling"—in congenial soil, where the plant can take deep root.[28]

Since Hamilton residents had not only nurtured but also successfully bid for the college in competition with other towns, it would be both immoral and illegal, the anti-removal argument concluded, for the denomination to break this "solemn contract."[29]

Important financial and cultural interests were at stake for college towns threatened by removals. Granville, Ohio, stood to lose the tens of thousands of dollars annually injected into the local economy by the students and faculty of Denison. Local leaders "clearly understood that the college was the chief factor of the prosperity in Granville,"[30] and local Baptists knew that without the college they would no longer have ministerial talents comparable to those supplied to their pulpit by Denison's president. Realizing that the removal of Colgate would "deeply and permanently" injure the "intellectual, moral, social, and pecuniary interests" of their "flourishing village,"[31] Hamilton residents estimated that "from *thirty* to *forty thousand dollars* are annually expended in our vicinity by the officers and students of the University"[32] and that its removal would cause local property to "depreciate a fourth in value."[33] In addition, "our elegant Bookstore will hardly remain a month."[34] Local investments in the colleges would also be lost; Hamilton's citizens had contributed more than $30,000 to their college, and Granville's had contributed more than $15,000 to Denison.

With these interests threatened, community resistance took many forms. The initial reaction was sometimes a mass meeting at which the citizens organized to "fight. . . nobly, Baptist and non-Baptist alike, as a community."[35] The committee appointed at such a meeting in Hamilton to defend community interests consisted of three lawyers, two businessmen, a physician, and the editor of the local newspaper; none of them belonged to the Baptist church. Lewisburg, Pennsylvania's interests were well represented because close to a majority of Bucknell's trustees were drawn from within a twenty-mile radius of the college. Unable to control a majority of the Hillsdale College board, some residents of Spring Arbor, Michigan, attempted to seize the college records and install a new slate of trustees. When this maneuver failed, citizens even confiscated books and apparatus and threatened to tar and feather one of the professors.

The most effective tactic employed by threatened college communities was to question the legality of removal.[36] They constructed a legal argument that rested largely on the way Baptist colleges originated. It was generally contended that contributions to a college, especially those made by local residents during its early years, were given with the understanding that the school would always remain at its original site. Removal of the institution would constitute a breach of trust to contributors no longer living and a breach of contract unless it was consented to by those still alive. In the case of Colgate, an actual written contract bound six citizens representing the town of Hamilton to pay $6,000 to the Baptist Education Society of the State of New York in return for the permanent location of the school in their community. Implied contracts between denominational groups and local residents who successfully bid for a school can be identified at four of the other five colleges. These local contractual arrangements were strengthened by subsequent community contributions, and in the case of Mercer were initiated by sale of land near the campus to create a college community.

In varying forms and with divergent emphases, the basic legal argument played a major role in at least four out of six removal controversies.[37] Hamilton took its case to the courts in early 1849 and on April 23, 1850, a New York State Supreme Court judge issued the permanent injunction which prevented removal of Colgate. The decision in this case was based on technicalities, but also contained the judge's observation that anti-removalists who were parties to the original contract between the town and the founders of the institution had "the right to restrain the removal of the university."[38]

Removalists abandoned the possibility of further legal action at this point and proceeded to found and charter a new institution, the University of Rochester. Participants in the Denison controversy were well acquainted with the Colgate case, and the legal question pervaded this debate from start to finish. The failure of the removalists to agree on a new location and the pledge of the anti-removalists to conduct an ambitious fund drive that would begin in the immediate vicinity of the college helped to prevent removal. But the clinching argument offered by anti-removalists just prior to the denomination's final decision not to remove the college featured the legal opinion that "Granville College could not be removed."[39] Similar legal opinion also occupied a prominent place in the debate at the Georgia Baptist Convention of 1857 and the decision not to attempt a removal of Mercer. In most of these cases, it was the prospect of prolonged and institutionally damaging legal controversies that ultimately discouraged the removalists.

The one removal effected during this period occurred after a Michigan circuit court judge in late 1854 dissolved an injunction preventing removal of the college at Spring Arbor to Hillsdale. Claiming that they were stockholders in the college corporation, probably by virtue of their contributions, Spring Arbor citizens had obtained a preliminary injunction in mid-1853. The judge who subsequently dissolved this injunction did so on the grounds that "there were no stockholders of the corporation to be protected by a court of equity."[40] To avoid further legal difficulties the college trustees obtained a new charter in 1855. The few thousand dollars' worth of college property and equipment in Spring Arbor was abandoned. Little more was removed than the faculty, students, records, and reputation of the college. The removal to establish Hillsdale College is therefore an exception to the general pattern of success enjoyed by antebellum college communities in retaining the Baptist-affiliated institutions so deeply rooted on the local level.

The victories of anti-removalists, however, did not mean that Baptist colleges would continue as primarily local institutions.[41] Although legal opinion in the 1850s confirmed the essentially nondenominational origins and functions of Baptist colleges up to that time, it soon recognized the changing nature of these institutions. In 1871, the United States Supreme Court ruled that state legislatures usually had the right to "amend, alter, or modify"[42] corporate charters. This was a valid procedure for effecting college removals. Anyone making a contract with a private corporation such as a college, through donations, purchase of scholarships, or other means, generally did so with tacit assent to this legislative authority being part of the contract. Citing the Colgate decision, the court held that there might be some exceptional cases involving contributions to colleges that would require "judicial discretion,"[43] but subsequent court decisions tended to acknowledge legislative powers regarding charters and were characterized by increasing leniency toward college removals. A favorable county court decision and certain compensations to Penfield, Georgia, enabled Mercer to move to Macon in 1871. Howard College encountered no local legal resistance in the mid-1880s when it relocated on the outskirts of Birmingham, Alabama.

Most removal controversies, however, concluded with Baptists deciding to transform loosely affiliated local colleges into strong state denominational schools without further efforts at changes in location. The accumulation of buildings and other facilities quickly strengthened commitment to an original site. Once a removal issue was settled and denominational interest was directed toward institutional improvement, the ironic result was a decline in the importance of local contributions when compared to the increased financial support from distant sources.[44]

Egalitarian Trends

The widely dispersed and initially local nature of early nineteenth-century colleges, illustrated by the circumstances of their founding and mid-century removal controversies, rendered antebellum higher education much more accessible than colleges had been in previous centuries. In recent studies of colonial colleges, there is substantial agreement on the elitist objectives and control of these earlier institutions and on the higher proportion of students from prominent families. These students, privileged by means of family social status achieved through politics, profession, or wealth, were joined by only very limited numbers from the lower ranges of the middle class. Some signs of increasing proportions of college students from outside the ranks of wealth, power, and prestige are detected from the mid-eighteenth century through 1800, but the picture, especially for the post-Revolutionary decades, is not yet very clear.[45] Most of the evidence for a contrast between eighteenth- and nineteenth-century college students resides in a study which uses student ages as an indicator of family background. This work suggests that the percentage of graduates from late eighteenth-century Harvard and Yale who were older and poorer than the average college graduate of that time is significantly exceeded by the percentage of such students for the early nineteenth century at a group of less prominent New England colleges.[46]

Contemporary observations and quantitative data collected during the last decade support the related argument that this increased proportion of students from the middle and lower ranges of the middle class was large enough to be a distinguishing characteristic of antebellum higher education. "Little colleges," a Southern writer noted in the mid-1840s, "are the means of affording liberal education to numerous youth . . . within forty miles of [their] walls, who would never go to Cambridge."[47] Geographical proximity and modest fees were especially advantageous for families of modest means. "Men with their thousands," commented a midwestern newspaper, "can send their sons where they please; but men with only their hundreds must have a place near home, and where expenses will be at least reasonable."[48] A pamphlet published in Boston just before mid-century contained the estimate that a "full three-fourths of the members of the country colleges are from families with small means,"[49] families described by a midwestern college president as those with "small but well cultivated farms" and "economical shops."[50]

Although direct college costs were not low enough to permit easy access for children of the poor unless they were among the considerable number aided by education societies, expenses were kept at levels which made colleges increasingly more available to an expanding middle class. During most years of the early nineteenth century, significant overall gains were made in collegiate accessibility. By the 1850s, according to a recent quantitative analysis, liberal arts colleges were subsidizing students "at a percentage level higher than the most egalitarian of college systems in the United States in the 1960s."[51]

Studies for Secular Success

Despite their major commitment of resources to maintaining low direct student costs, antebellum colleges also managed to develop curricula characterized by steady growth in breadth and diversity. The academic programs of these colleges—including preparatory departments, partial and parallel courses, and a basic bachelor-of-arts curriculum that contained a wide range of courses in addition to those usually labeled classical—were designed to attract widespread attendance and support. Even the short-lived manual-labor experiments at many colleges in the 1830s and 1840s can be viewed in this light. And courses within the basic curriculum proliferated at such a pace that educational reformers soon began to perceive need for an elective system.[52]

Of primary importance for increasing breadth in the basic curriculum was development in the area of science. A study of scientific curricula at fifteen northeastern colleges finds a dramatic "awakening" from 1820 to 1860 in contrast to the relatively limited efforts and achievements of the colonial and post-colonial eras. From the "somewhat undirected revolution" of the 1820s came a proliferation of science courses in the prescribed curriculum to the point where college students devoted "more time to science than they ever had before or would again." By 1838, four of seven professorships at Williams were in science and mathematics, with most other colleges approximating this proportion. Assuming a mutually beneficial interaction between science and religious belief, colleges established a "dynamic relationship" with science which provided a firm foundation for scholarly as well as curricular developments in the late nineteenth century.[53]

A recent study reports that "trends toward a modernized higher educational system were well established by the 1830s," except in technical-vocational subjects.[54] Another analysis finds that almost one-third of students in Baptist-affiliated colleges during the 1850s were enrolled in nonclassical degree programs.[55] Yet the most interesting and vital relationship between curriculum and a modernizing society may have as its key element the basic program for a bachelor of arts degree.

Central to understanding this program's contribution to the popularity of early nineteenth-century higher education is a new analysis of the curricular philosophy expressed by the very document historians have frequently used to demonstrate the lack of rapport between colleges and the public.[56] The Yale Report of 1828 was the most prominent and influential statement of educational philosophy in America prior to 1860. In this document, the faculty defined a college's prime function as the training of mental faculties, such as reason, imagination, and communication, through emphasis on classical studies. Anachronistic readings of the Report are now yielding to interpretations that find it a thoughtful, realistic, and effective approach to pre-Civil War collegiate education.[57] Recent discussions of the Report have taken into account widespread acceptance of the psychological theory upon which the authors' argument was based, the appropriateness of basic-skills training in an era when individuals frequently changed occupations or even professions,[58] and the wide variety of educational programs already provided by other contemporary institutions. These considerations lead to conclusions that the Report, despite its emphasis on classical studies, was "comprehensive, open-minded, and liberal,"[59] or at least "a reasonably modern document by the lights of its time."[60] The link between mental discipline and secular success, a pervasive theme in the Report, is particularly important in assessing this document's impact.[61] Throughout the antebellum years, college promoters stressed this success theme.[62] With "intellectual faculties properly strengthened,"[63] they argued, a graduate would find that traditional college studies "do 'pay' professional men . . . a large dividend, and that immediately."[64]

Increasing Enrollments

The final and most important evidence for this reinterpretation of antebellum colleges is provided by enrollment data. Scholars critical of Whiggish interpretations of the antebellum institutions have been frustrated in their search for reliable statistics. Almost all footnote trails lead to incomplete enrollment figures[65] compiled by college president-reformers plagued with peculiar problems at their own institutions.[66] And the data available are heavily concentrated in New England, the region with least growth in student population.[67] Until very recently, the paucity of compiled data might have given further reason for skepticism but could not carry a historian very far toward claiming demographic evidence that either weakened or strengthened the traditional interpretation.

Current studies are beginning to generate data that suggest antebellum college enrollments comprised a steadily increasing proportion of the college-age group in the general population. Largely through the multiplication of institutions outside of New England, the annual growth rate for enrollments in higher education from 1800 to 1860 is estimated to exceed that for either the second half of the nineteenth century or the first half of the twentieth. The growth rate for liberal-arts enrollments alone is found to be 1.7 times that of the general population.[68] A new study limited to New England colleges found that even in this region the numbers of early nineteenth-century college graduates expanded at a faster rate than that found in the growth of the region's total population.[69] The accelerating pace of college enrollment expansion is suggested by a calculation for Baptist colleges, where the number of students in the traditional curriculum increased fourfold between 1845 and 1860.[70]

Starting from a small base in 1800, this rate of expansion did not produce totals by 1860 which are impressive by twentieth-century standards. Estimates of national college enrollments for 1860 vary from about 25,000 to a little more than 30,000.[71] While much demographic work remains to be done, it is clear that, when compared with the unchanging nature of enrollment-population ratios for the last half of the eighteenth century,[72] developments in the antebellum years can now be viewed as initiating significant growth in public esteem for higher education.

College Enthusiasm

One essential task remains if we are to formulate a comprehensive reinterpretation of early nineteenth-century higher education. We need an interpretive model to replace the mechanistic one that has dominated scholarship in the field since it was spawned by the classical economics of Francis Wayland.[73] The simple, national needs-and-demands formulation, according to which institutions merely accommodate or ignore popular opinions and the perceptions of reformers, has contributed more distortion than understanding to the analytical record. A knowledge of the "social forces" often cited in functionalist models of this type can, when extensively investigated, help to define the broad constraints influencing institutional and individual behavior.[74] But an approach limited to this level of generalization obscures some of the institutional initiatives and intricate college-community interactions crucial to the viability and vitality of antebellum colleges.

One alternative to the old approach would be for historians to explore the possibilities of viewing colleges in the manner Bernard Bailyn has indicated would be appropriate for academies—as a folk movement.[75] The sources of increasing collegiate popularity seem to reside in a variety of local and regional circumstances that suggest certain affinities between colleges and academies. A foreign observer, noting in the early 1850s the local impulses that led to the founding of both colleges and academies, found "most worthy of attention . . . the great sums which have often been accumulated by means of very small contributions."[76] Particularly important to an analysis of college founding as a folk movement would be a careful delineation of the economic and cultural benefits perceived by many college supporters who never set foot in a classroom. Research designs that once assumed the hilltop college was an early version of the ivory tower should now yield to investigation of the ways in which colleges served as symbols and sources of local pride and prosperity.

Student studies would also provide information and insights of great importance for the development and testing of a more satisfying model and persuasive interpretation of antebellum colleges. In tracing the impulses to found and nurture colleges and in assessing the consequences of efforts by college agents to create increased demand for higher education in various local and regional contexts, historians will need many more investigations of geographical distribution, family background, curricular choices, and patterns of enrollment growth within the student population.[77]

The most important element in formulating a new and more complex model may be increased attention to the ways in which local sentiments were stimulated and shaped by college promoters attempting to create sufficient demand for their nascent institutions. Even contemporaries of Wayland within his own denomination disputed the assumption that demand in education was stationary while the supply of colleges multiplied. Education is different from "mercantile affairs," they argued, because "its very diffusion creates for it an increased demand."[78] The process was described with illuminating detail in the mid-1850s:

> Denominational colleges . . . derive their existence in the first instance from efforts made among the people; and their endowments are raised, and their patronage secured and continued, by employment of just such means as must necessarily increase the number of educated men. Agents, . . . sent out from time to time to secure students, . . . talk at the public gatherings and around the firesides of the masses of people. They enlist by their explanations and persuasions men who not appreciating education themselves would never have sent [sons] to any College, but for these efforts. They raise their endowments by free will offerings, which when made, secures their interests, and to obtain which requires a discussion on the subject of education in all its bearings. Many additional minds are thus enlisted by appeals to their patriotism, their benevolence, and their interests—those perhaps who never dreamed of educating their sons before such efforts went made.[79]

Given the fluidity and dispersion reflected in the population patterns, political structure, and religious institutions of early nineteenth-century America, the local role of college agents in creating a widespread faith in general education deserves intensive investigation.

"College Enthusiasm!," the words used by Ezra Stiles when reacting in 1770 to colonial college-founding,[80] may be more aptly applied to higher education in the early nineteenth century. The scholarship currently probing antebellum college enthusiasm exposes some of the major reasons why the American public began to value collegiate institutions. Further exploration of this question within a model of multiple college-community interactions should provide us with a clearer understanding of the degree to which early nineteenth-century colleges were locally prominent, economically accessible, academically attractive, and generally popular in the eyes of a significant and increasing portion of the American public.

Notes

1. For the standard account, see Frederick Rudolph, *The American College and University: A History* (New York: Knopf, 1962) and the works cited therein, especially those of Richard Hofstadter. Portions of the standard account persist in John S. Whitehead, *The Separation of College and State: Columbia, Dartmouth, Harvard, and Yale, 1776–1876* (New Haven, Conn.: Yale Univ. Press, 1973), ch. 3; Stanley M. Guralnick, *Science and the Ante-Bellum American College* (Philadelphia: American Philosophical Society, 1975), p. 141; Robert L. Church, *Education in the United States: An Interpretive History* (New York: Free Press, 1976)., p. 38; and John S. Brubacher and Willis Rudy, *Higher Education in Transition*, 3rd ed., rev. and enl. (New York: Harper & Row, 1976), pp. 35, 69–74.

2. *Education in the Forming of American Society: Needs and Opportunities for Study* (Chapel Hill: Univ. of North Carolina Press, 1960).

3. George E. Peterson, *The New England College in the Age of the University* (Amherst, Mass.: Amherst College Press, 1964), pp. 2–3; David B. Potts, "Baptist Colleges in the Development of American Society, 1812–1861," Diss. Harvard Univ. 1967, pp. 1–10; James Axtell, "The Death of the Liberal Arts College," *History of Education Quarterly*, 11, (1971), 341–342; David B. Potts, "American Colleges in the Nineteenth Centry: From Localism to Denominationalism," *History of Education Quarterly*, 11 (1971), 364–366; and Colin B. Burke, "The Quiet Influence: The American Colleges and Their Students, 1800–1860," Diss. Washington Univ. 1973, pp. 1–13.

4. For data on these characteristics of Wayland and his problems at Brown, see Joseph L. Blau's introduction to Francis Wayland, *The Elements of Moral Science* (Cambridge, Mass.: Harvard Univ. Press, 1963); Theodore R. Crane's introduction to Francis Wayland, *The Education Demanded by the People of the United States* (Schenectday, N. Y: Union College, 1973); Walter C. Bronson, *The History of Brown University, 1764–1914* (Providence, R. I.: Brown Univ., 1914), ch. 7; and Donald Fleming, *Science and Technology in Providence, 1760–1914: An Essay in the History of Brown University in the Metropolitan Community* (Providence, R. I.: Brown Univ., 1952), pp. 34–43. For an example of Wayland being used more extensively than any other single source, see Richard Hofstadter and Wilson Smith, eds., *American Higher Education: A Documentary History* (Chicago: Univ. of Chicago Press, 1961), I, II. In the introduction provided for one of the documents, Wayland is identified as "one of the great figures in nineteenth-century American education" and credited with a "searching appraisal of the aims and services of American colleges" (p. 334).

5. Axtell, pp. 242–245; Douglas Sloan, "Harmony, Chaos, and Consensus: The American College Curriculum," *Teachers College Record*, 72, (1971), 225–227; and Miles Bradbury, "Colonial Colleges: The Lively Communities," paper presented at the Annual Meeting of the Organization of American Historians, Boston, 17 April 1975.

6. Donald G. Tewksbury, *The Founding of American Colleges and Universities Before the Civil War* (1932; rpt. New York: Archon, 1965). The critique is presented by Natalie A. Naylor, "The Ante-Bellum College Movement: A reappraisal of Tewksbury's Founding of American Colleges and Universities," *History of Education Quarterly*, 13, (1973), 261–274.

7. Potts, "Baptist Colleges," chs. 2–3; Potts, "American Colleges"; Guralnick, pp. 152–153; Philip Gleason, "From an Indefinite Homogeneity: The Beginnings of Catholic Higher Education in the United States," paper presented at the Catholic History Seminar, Univ. of Notre Dame, 15 March 1975, pp. 13–20; David F. Allmendinger, Jr., "The Strangeness of the American Society: Indigent Students and the New Charity: 1815–1840," *History of Education Quarterly*, 11 (1971), 3–32; Naylor, pp. 268–70; Harvey R. Bostrom, "Contributions to Higher Education by the Society for the Promotion of Collegiate and Theological Education at the West," Diss. New York Univ. 1960; Charles E. Peterson, Jr., "Theron Baldwin and Higher Education in the Old Northwest," Diss. Johns Hopkins Univ. 1970; Travis K. Hedrick, Jr., "Julian Monson Sturtevant and the Moral Machinery of Society: The New England Struggle Against Pluralism in the Old Northwest, 1829–1877," Diss. Brown Univ. 1974; and Daniel T. Johnson, "Financing the Western Colleges, 1844–1862," *Journal of the Illinois State Historical Society*, 65 (1972), 43–53.

8. Potts, "Baptist Colleges," pp. 236–237, 240–241; Burke, pp. 50–95; David F. Allmendinger, Jr., *Paupers and Scholars: The Transformation of Student Life in Nineteenth-Century New England* (New York: St. Martins, 1975), pp. 1–27, 129–138.

9. Potts, "Baptist Colleges," pp. 162–167, 323; Sloan, pp. 240–241; Burke, pp. 56–67, 96, 167; Guralnick, chs. 7–8.

10. Potts, "Baptist Colleges," pp. 322–23; David B. Potts, "Liberal Arts Colleges, Private," *The Encyclopedia of Education* (New York: Macmillan, 1971), pp. 500–501; Burke, pp. 15–24.

11. Potts, "American Colleges," pp. 367–368.

12. Allmendinger, *Paupers*, chs. 1, 6–7; Burke, pp. 50–78.

13. Potts, "Liberal Arts Colleges," pp. 499–500; Sloan, pp. 323–347; Guralnick.

14. Potts, "Liberal Arts Colleges," pp. 500–501; Burke, pp. 18–20.

15. Colleges in this study include all but a few of the institutions of higher education affiliated with the Baptists, founded after 1800, and in operation for at least a decade prior to the Civil War. For a discussion of how accurately these colleges represent widely shared characteristics of antebellum higher education, see Potts, "American Colleges," pp. 371–373.

16. Sylvanus M. Duvall, *The Methodist Episcopal Church and Education up to 1869* (New York: Teachers College, Columbia Univ., 1928); C. Harve Geiger, *The Program of Higher Education of the Presbyterian Church in the United States of America* (Cedar Rapids, Iowa: Laurance Press, 1940); Hikaru Yanagihara, "Some Attitudes of the Protestant Episcopal Church in America: A Historical Study of the Attitudes of the Church and Churchmen Toward the Founding and Maintaining of Colleges and Schools Under Their Influence Before 1800," Diss. Columbia Univ., 1958; Paul M. Lambert, *Denominational Policies in the Support and Supervision of Higher Education* (New York: Teachers College, Columbia Univ., 1929).

17. New perspectives found in the most recent studies cited throughout this essay have generally been derived from investigating a group of institutions at a common point in time. These research designs created opportunities to raise and explore interesting questions at a level of generalization usually unavailable to the historian of an individual institution and yet with a degree of precision and documentation unattainable by the author of a survey history.

18. Institutions are designated here by their current names, even though in many cases different names were in use during the early nineteenth century. Related to the interpretation presented here is the fact that original names were almost always those of the towns or counties in which the colleges were located. Thus, Colgate was first known as Hamilton [New York] Literary and Theological Institution; then as Madison [County] University, and finally as Colgate University after 1890. Similarly, Colby was originally known as Waterville, Bucknell as Lewisburg, and Denison as Granville.

19. "Waterville College," *Waterville Intelligencer,* 21 Feb. 1828.

20. Potts, "Baptist Colleges," pp. 12–30.

21. Potts, "Baptist Colleges," pp. 76–77.

22. Quoted in Louis Edwin Theiss, *Centennial History of Bucknell University, 1846–1946* (Lewisburg, Pa.: Bucknell Univ., 1946), pp. 63–64.

23. Ransom Dunn, "The Story of the Planting: A Reminiscence of the Founding and Early History of Hillsdale College," *Reunion,* 6 May 1885.

24. Francis A. Cox and James Hoby, *The Baptists in America: A Narrative of the Deputation From the Baptist Union in England to the United States and Canada* (New York: Leavitt, Lord, 1836), p. 342.

25. Potts, "Baptist Colleges," ch. 3.

26. Potts, "Baptist Colleges," pp. 286–306.

27. "Baptist Educational Society," *Democratic Reflector,* 28 June 1848.

28. "Provided There Are No Legal Obstacles," *Democratic Reflector,* 24 May 1849.

29. "A Fraternal Address," *New York Baptist Register,* 9 Aug. 1849.

30. Nathan S. Burton, Granville's Indebtedness to Jeremiah Hall," *Old Northwest Genealogical Quarterly,* 8 (1905), 381.

31. State of New York, *Memorial in Relation to Madison University,* State Senate Document No. 37, 16 Feb. 1849.

32. "Madison University," *Democratic Reflector,* 2 Dec. 1847.

33. "Removal of Madison University, No. II," *Democratic Reflector,* 27 July 1848.

34. "Removal of Madison University. A Last Appeal," *Democratic Reflector,* 3 Aug.1848.

35. George W. Eaton, "Historical Discourse Delivered at the Semi-Centenary of Madison University, Wednesday, August 25, 1869," in *The First Half Century of Madison University (1819–1869) or the Jubilee Volume* (New York: Sheldon, 1872), p. 67.

36. Potts, "Baptist Colleges," pp. 306–10.

37. The legal question appeared several times in the course of the Bucknell controversy but probably did not exert a decisive influence. No mention of legal considerations can be found in the very small amount of information available concerning the dispute at Franklin College.

38. Hascall v. Madison University, 8 Barbour (N.Y.), 174 (1850).

39. "Meetings at Cleveland," *Journal and Messenger,* 29 Oct. 1852.

40. John C. Patterson, "History of Hillsdale College," *Collections and Researches Made by the Michigan Pioneer and Historical Society,* 6 (1883), 154.

41. Potts, "Baptist Colleges," pp. 310–311.

42. Pennsylvania College Cases, 13 Wallace (U.S.), 218 (1871).

43. Id. at 219.

44. Of the more than $130,000 subscribed to Colgate's semi-centennial fund in the late 1860s, only about $6,000 came from Hamilton residents. Lewisburg citizens provided slightly more than ten percent of the $100,000 subscribed to Bucknell's endowment fund a few years earlier. A contemporary campaign at Denison raised over $100,000, with $5,000 of this coming from Granville. Potts, "Baptist Colleges," pp. 311–312.

45. Donald O. Schneider, "Education in Colonial American Colleges, 1750–1770, and the Occupations and Political Offices of Their Alumni," Diss. George Peabody Univ., 1965; Richard Warch, *School of the Prophets: Yale College, 1701–1740* (New Haven, Conn.: Yale Univ. Press, 1973); David C. Humphrey, *From Kings College to Columbia, 1746–1800* (New York: Columbia Univ. Press, 1976); Guy Howard Miller, *The Revolutionary College: American Presbyterian Higher Education, 1707–1837* (New York: New York Univ. Press, 1976); Robert Polk Thomson, "Colleges in the Revolutionary South," *History of Education Quarterly,* 10 (1970), 339–412; Robert Polk Thomson, "The Reform of the College of William and Mary, 1763–1780," *Proceedings of the American Philosophical Society,* 115 (1971), 187–213; Margaret W. Masson, "The Premises and Purposes of Higher Education in American Society, 1745–1770,' " Diss. Univ. of Washington, 1971; James Axtell, *The School Upon a Hill: Education and Society in Colonial New England* (New Haven, Conn.: Yale Univ. Press, 1974); Phyllis Vine [Erenberg], "Change and Continuity: Values in American Higher Education, 1750–1800," Diss. Univ. of Michigan 1974; David W. Robson, "Higher Education in the Emerging American Republic, 1750–1800," Diss. Yale Univ. 1974; and Howard Miller, "Evangelical Religion and Colonial Princeton," in *Schooling and Society,* ed. Lawrence Stone (Baltimore, Md.: Johns Hopkins Univ. Press, 1976).

46. Allmendinger, *Paupers.*

47. "The Columbian College, D. C," *Christian Index,* 16 Jan. 1846.

48. "Franklin College," *Christian Messenger,* 13 Nov. 1845.

49. Charles Haddock, *Collegiate Education* (Boston: Press of T. R. Marvin, 1848), pp. 7–8, quoted in Guralnick, p. 139.

50. "Franklin College."

51. Burke, pp. 47, 78, 124, 127.

52. Potts, "Baptist Colleges," pp. 162–167, 216–224; Burke, pp. 56–57; Guralnick, pp. 126–129; and Sloan, pp. 246–248.

53. Guralnick, pp. vii–viii, 25, 138, 37, 116, 152–247, xii–xiii.

54. Burke, p. 96.

55. Potts, "Baptist Colleges," p. 323.

56. For comments on the Yale Report as the "villain in the rape of American scholarship," see Peterson, *New England College,* pp. 213–214.

57. Potts, "American Colleges," p. 368, and "Liberal Arts Colleges," pp. 499–500; Sloan, pp. 226, 242–46; and Guralnick, pp. 28–33. For an earlier sympathetic reading, see Ralph Henry Gabriel, *Religion and Learning at Yale: The Church of Christ in the College and University, 1757–1957* (New Haven, Conn.: Yale Univ. Press, 1958), ch. 6.

58. Burke, pp. 145–50.

59. Guralnick, *Science,* p. 30.

60. Sloan, "Harmony," p. 246.

61. *Reports on the Course of Instruction in Yale College* (New Haven, Conn.: Hezekiah Howe, 1828), pp. 15, 17, 28, 29, 36–37, 54.

62. Potts, "Baptist Colleges," pp. 228–32.

63. "Schools and Colleges," *Journal and Messenger,* 16 July 1858.

64. "Shurtleff College," *Christian Times,* 23 Feb. 1859.

65. [Francis Wayland], *Report to the Corporation of Brown University, on Changes in the System of Collegiate Education, Read March 28, 1850* (Providence, R.I.: George H. Whitney, 1850), pp. 29–30; and [F. A. P. Barnard], *Analysis of Some Statistics of Collegiate Education* (New York: printed for the use of the Trustees, 1870), pp. 6–15.

66. Bronson, pp. 258–59; and Marvin Lazerson, "F. A. P. Barnard and Columbia College: Prologue to a University," *History of Education Quarterly,* 6 (1966), 49–64.

67. Burke, p. 171.

68. Burke, pp. 15–16, 88, 97.

69. Allmendinger, *Paupers,* p. 3.

70. Potts, "Baptist Colleges," pp. 322–323.

71. Potts, "Liberal Arts Colleges," p. 401; and Burke, pp. 21–22.

72. Vine [Erenberg], pp. 1–2.

73. Some links between Wayland's economic and educational ideas are suggested by Joseph L. Blau in his introduction to Wayland, *Elements*, p. xix, and by Sloan, p. 248.

74. Burke, ch. 1.

75. Bernard Bailyn, "Education as a Discipline: Some Historical Notes," in *The Discipline of Education*, ed. John Walton and James L. Kuethe (Madison: Univ. of Wisconsin Press, 1963), p. 135. For an excellent beginning in the direction suggested by Bailyn, see Church, *Education*, ch. 2.

76. P. A. Silijestrom, *Educational Institutions of the United States: Their Character and Organization*, trans. Fredrica Rowan (London: John Chapman, 1853), p. 312.

77. For a survey of reported research and a listing of studies currently in progress, see David B. Potts, "Students and the Social History of American Higher Education," *History of Education Quarterly*, 15 (1975), 317–327.

78. "Richmond College—No. 5," *Religious Herald*, 28 Dec. 1843.

79. "The Comparative Advantages of Denominational and State Colleges Reviewed," *Biblical Recorder*, 12 July 1855.

80. Franklin B. Dexter, ed., *The Literary Diary of Ezra Stiles* (New York: Scribner's, 1901), I, 45–46.

THE YALE REPORT OF 1828 AND LIBERAL EDUCATION: A NEOREPUBLICAN MANIFESTO

JACK C. LANE

In recent years, historians of higher education have mercifully taken us beyond the pinched and narrow conventional view of the nineteenth-century college curriculum to a more meaningful contextual interpretation of that much maligned institution. In the process they have reinterpreted the "Old College's" principal manifesto: the Yale Report of 1828. Earlier studies had depicted the Yale Report as either a document cementing a collegiate education to the past or as one aimed at maintaining "a numerically tiny social elite against the hostile pressure of a rising Jacksonian equalitarianism." Recent studies have revised this interpretation, on the one hand by arguing that the report simply reaffirmed the liberal arts as taught through the classical curriculum, and on the other by contending that it was "actually a thoughtful, responsible attempt to consider the place of the undergraduate college in the totality of the American educational scheme." Instead of representing the last "bulwark of educational reactionism, elitism, and authoritarianism," the revisionists argue, the report did not significantly differ "in its essentials from the vision held by most of America's foremost champions of university reform."[1]

The revisionists thus have allowed us to see the Yale Report as a response rather than a reaction to early nineteenth-century educational developments. Still an issue remains unresolved. No one has considered the report within the specific context for which the writers intended it—that is, within the framework of the historical development of liberal education. After all, as it originally appeared in print in the *American Journal of Science and Arts*, it was entitled "A Report on the Course of Liberal Education," and in the second part the writers began with a definition of liberal education.[2] If then the report was in part a disquisition on the meaning and nature of liberal education as these educators saw it in 1828, it behooves us to understand it as the writers intended: to explicate the philosophical rationale of the prevailing course of study, but more importantly to find a role for this program in the larger republican culture and particularly in the new developments in the republican era.

At the center of these developments were transformations, especially economic ones, that seemed life-threatening to a society shaped by republican ideology. Americans initially responded by attempting to adapt these changes to republican structures, desperately trying to salvage republican ideals while enjoying the fruits of the new developments. The result was a fusion that one historian has termed neorepublicanism, an "off-spring of the uneasy alliance between the new unrestrained private enterprise" and the republican ideals of civic virtue.[3] The Yale Report, I contend, was a significant, though heretofore unrecognized, neorepublican attempt to accommodate a republican institution—classical liberal education—to the changing, dynamic economic and social conditions of the early nineteenth century. Like most similar attempts, it speaks two languages, hoping to reconcile conflicting views of life. The document contains several arguments that express a classical republican position on liberal education. But as I hope to show, it faces not a republican past but an entrepreneurial future. This essay will explore this perspective, first by discussing in what form liberal education came to America in the seventeenth century and how early colonials and revolutionaries transformed it, second by explaining how the Yale Report interpreted this heritage, and third by evaluating the nature and meaning of this effort and its potential impact on the future of American liberal education.

The writers of the Yale Report were the recipients of an extensive American experience with liberal education. As the Puritans began construction of a new provincial college—Harvard College—they had two liberal education traditions to draw upon: 1) an institutional one growing out of the medieval university that used liberal education for the purposes of acquiring knowledge and of training the intellect, relying on Christian piety for moral training; and 2) the Renaissance humanist tradition that saw liberal education not merely as a way of instilling knowledge, but essentially as a moral process that would develop such personal traits as civility and sociability, and such public virtues as integrity and wisdom.[4]

Early American colonists approached liberal education from the scholastic-institutional perspective. The charter establishing Harvard College in 1650 frankly proclaimed the training of ministers as the institution's primary purpose, as did the charter of William and Mary some fifty years later.[5] But we ought not to interpret this in too narrow terms. In their community-building efforts, the Puritans clearly intended that the college would serve the broader leadership needs of the new society. On the basis of their Oxbridge experience, they were convinced that the courses of study of Cambridge and Oxford, which emphasized the institutional approach and purposes of liberal education, would serve both their religious and secular needs, particularly since the Puritans made little distinction between the two. In the early colonial years, ministers served both as magistrates and preachers and, more importantly, as guardians of public order and stability. Although the thrust of their approach was Christian education, the Puritans saw little contradiction between institutional and humanist liberal education tradition. The charter of Yale College, originally secured in 1701, a generation after Harvard's founding, perhaps best expressed this Puritan fusion of institutional-humanist traditions: its course of study would emphasize "the Arts and Sciences," which would train students "for Public employment both in Church and Civil State."[6]

Although colonial liberal education never lost its religious orientation, during the eighteenth century emerging republican thought suggested a significant shift in the concept. Influenced by European Enlightenment and English Whig thought and spurred by the conflict with England, the American revolutionary generation began to formulate a secular system of thought historians now characterize as classical republicanism, an ideology, states Gordon Wood in oft-quoted phrases, that "meant more for Americans than simply the elimination of a king and the institution of an elective system. It added a moral dimension, a utopian depth, to the political separation from England—a depth that involved the very character of their society."[7] Revolutionary Americans came to believe that the survival of a republic depended not on force of arms but on the character and spirit of the people and their leaders, both of which must be prepared to "sacrifice individual interests to the greater good of the whole." Prior to and after the Revolution, the republicans used the concept of classical republicanism not only to justify the break with England, but also as the ideological foundation for the creation of the American republican society. The concept was a central unifying force, for both revolutionaries and founders: "The [colonial] beliefs in virtue as the most worthy goal of mankind and as the essential ingredient of the good society united [those] who in other areas could hold divergent views."[8]

Having placed public good at the center of their ideological beliefs, not surprisingly the republicans found in the classical liberal education system an established means for training virtuous leadership necessary for a stable republic.[9] Educated in ancient literature and immersed in a "neo-classical revival," they turned invariably to the classics as the means for achieving republican purpose. For the republicans, the classical literature served both didactic and mimetic functions: it was a source of moral instruction and a model for virtuous conduct.[10] Significantly, new colleges founded during this period consciously emphasized virtue training in their purpose statements. Rhode Island College proclaimed "liberal education" to be "highly beneficial to society by forming the rising generation to virtue, knowledge, and useful literature." The University of Georgia was founded in 1785 in order to "place the youth under the forming hand of society that by instruction they may be molded to the love of virtue and good order."[11]

But even as the revolutionaries and postrevolutionaries expounded republicanism, historical forces were reshaping American culture and drastically altering the concept. In a revolutionary war dedicated in part, at least, to the preservation of republican values, the conflict ironically opened the door to grasping personal ambition and private profiteering, behavior that classical republicans always considered as corrupting vices. After the founding of the new nation, expanded economic development in commerce and industry not only further opened the door to similar behavior but actually seemed to depend on personal drive and ambition for its survival. As society came to see these developments as evidence of progress, and progress as a public good, Americans were forced to reconcile earlier republican values with these new realities. Historians are only now realizing how complicated this process was, but clearly by 1830 that intellectual challenge had been met. Manufacturing and commerce, viewed by classical republicans as corrupting economic endeavors, were by 1830 acknowledged as essential to the republic's economic well-being.[12] Republican forms must of necessity don new clothing. Thus, writes Isaac Kramnick, "Citizenship and the public quest for the common good were replaced by economic productivity and hard work as the criterion of virtue." Kramnick notes that this transformation was not simply a withdrawal from "public activity to a private self-centered realm," though in time this would be the logical outcome. Instead, he argues, the transformation involved a change in the emphasis on the nature of human behavior. "The moral and virtuous man was no longer defined by his civic activity, but by his economic activity. One's duty was still to contribute to the public good, but this was best done through economic activity which actually aimed at private gain. Self-centered economic productivity, not public citizenship, became the badge of the virtuous man."[13]

Concomitantly, the concept of republican virtue also changed. Hard work and frugal living, which republicans had seen as means to virtuous independence, were now viewed as ends in themselves; such behavior demonstrated "the right republican character," or to employ a more commonly used phrase, a "business-like character." Here was a modern view of republicanism, "a bastard-republicanism," in Rowland Berthoff's critical phrase, based on the conception that virtuous individuals were those who, through hard work and self-discipline, had achieved material success.[14]

These winds of cultural change that were transforming American society by the 1820s brought challenges to the traditional concept of liberal education. Based as it was on the classical republican idea that knowledge was the "handmaid of virtue," that a "study of human nature and of social institutions" should be "combined with that of morals," such an education hardly seemed appropriate for the emerging economic and social developments that called for expertise and enterprise and a conceptual transformation that turned these qualities into virtues.[15] In the 1820s many began to sense this apparent dichotomy between the moral/public thrust of traditional liberal education as taught through the classical curriculum and the requirements and needs of an entrepreneurial society. Educationists such as Philip Lindsley of the University of Nashville, George Ticknor of Harvard, and James Marsh of the University of Vermont sought reforms that would speak to this cultural dissimilarity; changes that would open the colleges to a larger segment of the society, that would create distinct departments of knowledge, that would allow for a less severe system of discipline, for more meaningful and effective examinations, and for the replacement of the recitation-textbook pedagogy with that of lecture, discussion, and inquiry. Even more significantly, the reformers wanted traditional liberal education to share the curriculum with English, modern foreign languages, and the new sciences.[16] Such courses were viewed as more appropriate to America's prevailing needs.

The implication of these demands for reform was explicitly articulated by Amherst College faculty reports in 1827. The colleges, it charged, were not preparing young men to live and work in the emerging entrepreneurial corporate world. "While everything else is on the advance, our Colleges are stationary; or, if not quite stationary . . . they are in danger of being left far behind, in the rapid march for improvement." This last phrase struck the proper chord. In this "age of improvement," as George Ticknor called it, where material success seemed open to all who could take advantage of it, it was a serious matter to be charged with clinging to the past, to holding on "tenaciously to prescriptive forms of other centuries," and to be tied to a curriculum from which students derived "no material advantage." The faculty of Amherst wanted to introduce a shockingly practical course of study that would include science courses with emphasis on their "application to the more useful arts and trades . . . and to the domestic economy." It also wanted lectures on labor-saving machines, on bridges, on locks and aqueducts and architecture, and it proposed a "department of theoretical and practical mechanics."[17]

Whatever others might have thought of these proposals (few of them succeeded), at least the Yale Corporation took them seriously. In September 1827 it asked a corporation committee (which in turn gave the issue over to a faculty group) "to inquire into the expediency" of restructuring the liberal education curriculum with the possibility of dropping the classical course of study based on "dead languages" and substituting another program.[18] The charge was narrow, but sensing that the issue was not just another quarrel between ancients and moderns over appropriate courses of study, that in fact it raised a more fundamental question of liberal education's role in the new republic, the faculty committee proposed to explore the broader issue of the purposes of liberal education. In the process it would show how those objectives were not only not incompatible with the prevailing cultural transformations, but could actually be made to serve the entrepreneurial needs of those developments.

The faculty committee divided its chores into three parts. President Jeremiah Day defined the purposes of a liberal education, classics professor James Kingsley defended the classical curriculum as appropriate to those purposes, and a trustee, in a third part, reaffirmed the committee's recommendations as being the position of the corporation. Day began, as one writer has noted, by "conceding a certain legitimacy to the enemy."[19] In this age of improvement, of course, the college would change and in fact had changed. It was certainly not the same college that had been established over one hundred years earlier; in fact, it was not even the college that some living alumni would recognize and, given the more rigid requirements, would now be able to attend. But change, Day suggested, should take the form of a response not a reaction. For that reason, he argued, the discussion should begin not with the curriculum itself, but with the larger purposes of a liberal education. In this sense, Day clearly understood that the enemy was not innovative educational theories or carping educational utilitarians, but changing society itself. What was called for was a rationale for classical liberal education that would convince the society that such an education was not merely useful but essential to its needs.[20]

Day gave direction and set the tone of the report in the initial discussion on purposes: "We shall in vain attempt to decide on the expediency of retaining or altering our present course of instruction, unless we have a distinct apprehension of the object of collegiate [read liberal] education." In an oft-quoted unequivocal declaration, he declared that the appropriate objective of such an education was

> the discipline and the furniture of the mind; expanding its powers, and storing it with knowledge. The former of these is, perhaps, the more important of the two. A commanding object, therefore, in a collegiate course, should be to call into daily and vigorous exercise the faculties of the student. Those branches of study should be prescribed, and those modes of instruction adopted which are best calculated to teach the art of fixing the attention, directing the train of thought, analyzing a subject proposed for investigation; following, with accurate discrimination, the course of argument; balancing nicely the evidence presented; awakening, elevating, and controlling the imagination; arranging with skill the treasures which memory gathers; rousing the powers of genius.[21]

Later, in part 2 ("an inquiry into the expediency of insisting on the study of the ancient languages"), the writers specifically defined liberal education in almost precisely the same terms: "Liberal education . . . has generally [been] understood, [as] such a course of discipline in the arts and sciences, as is best calculated . . . both to strengthen and enlarge the faculties of the mind, and to familiarize it with the leading principles of the great objects of human investigation and knowledge."[22] In the first part of the report, the writers enlarged upon the meaning of mental discipline as an objective, and in the second, they discussed the classical curriculum as the most effective method of disciplining the mental faculties.

In these discussions the report drew upon the widely accepted ideas of faculty psychology, a theory which claimed that certain mental faculties—memory, accuracy, observation, attention, etc.— could be trained if the mind was properly exercised. It also contended that such mental skills were transferable from one subject to another and even from subjects to other activities. Nineteenth-century society regarded classical languages as the most effective way of stimulating the mental faculties because these subjects were seen as ideal in compelling students to develop orderly, systematic, and accurate habits of thought.

Such ideas were fully in accord with the classical republican concept of liberal education. Few republicans would have disagreed with the objective of mental discipline or with the report's insistence that the classical curriculum best served that objective. It was the writers' emphasis of (perhaps even obsession with) mental discipline that distinguished the report as a neorepublican statement. For classical republicans, liberal education was not just a matter of acquiring knowledge and strengthening the intellect, though they thought that essential; it was also one of ensuring that virtuous conduct ensued from mental training. Left to itself, without standards or guidance, one Federalist republican warned, society was "apt to sink into effeminacy and apathy."[23] No republican would think of turning loose in the world a trained intellect without first providing it with virtuous principles and purposes. Along with knowledge, a young man must be provided with virtues that would direct that knowledge toward moral public goals.

On this point the Yale Report was at best ambivalent. It does admit that "the models of literature put in the hands of the young student can hardly fail to imbue his mind with liberty; to inspire the liveliest patriotism, and excite noble and generous action."[24] The writers did not trust narrow professional education to inculcate "those liberal and comprehensive views, and those fine proportions of character which are found in him whose ideas are always confined to a particular channel." They also could rise to the noble heights of classical republican rhetoric when defining man's higher responsibilities: "Is man to have no other object than to obtain a living by professional pursuits? Has he not duties to perform to his family, to his fellow citizens, to his country?" Yet even in appealing to republican ideals, they used the language of neorepublican reality. The requirements for meeting these noble duties, they argued, were "various and extensive intellectual furniture."[25] Thus, their bows to republican ideals occupy a secondary place in the report. Its thrust, its first language if you will, is that of neorepublicanism. Its concern is not so much with the ends of liberal education (much less moral purposes) but with the means. Mental discipline, which teaches how to analyze, synthesize, evaluate, is a skill and therefore a *means* to some unspecified end. Such an objective may have social use, but it leaves unanswered the question: disciplined for what identifiable moral purpose? Significantly, the word "virtue" does not appear in the entire report.

Nothing shows this stress on intellectual means as does the report's discussion of the specific objectives of the courses in the classical curriculum. The student learned from mathematics the art of reasoning, from physical sciences the methods of induction and the varieties of probable evidence, from logic the art of thinking, and from rhetoric the art of speaking.[26] One need only compare this list of objectives with that of a leading colonial figure, Samuel Johnson, first president of King's College, to see how thoroughly the Yale Report had intellectualized liberal education. For Johnson, all subjects had to serve the ultimate goal of virtue training. He justified physical sciences on the basis that they gave the students a "sense of beauty, harmony, and order appearing in the whole of the system of nature." Logic, he argued, taught students to "distinguish truth from falsehood" and thus to "determine virtuous courses of action in their personal and public lives," and classical literature taught the students the "great maxims" which guide them toward right conduct.[27] In Johnson's classical republican perspective courses in a liberal education program provided students with a set of common moral precepts essential to a society's well-being.

The writers of the report, thus, had taken the basic structure of republican liberal education—the classical curriculum—and made it the instrument not of virtue nurturance but of mental discipline. In doing so they gave liberal education a rationale palatable to the new entrepreneurial society. If mental training had no identifiable social/moral purposes, it certainly had a social usefulness. As one historian has suggested, it happily reconciled seriously conflicting interests: the "cultural pretensions of teachers with practical tendencies of a developing nation," and the elitist desires of middle-class parents with students' desires for career training.[28]

In a recent study on early nineteenth-century private institutions, Peter Hall has pointed to an additional neorepublican social usefulness for mental discipline: it could be used to socialize "dependable and predictable, disciplined and internally controlled" potential managers into the emerging world of large-scale corporate enterprises. Moreover, Hall contends, in an entrepreneurial world that valued highly independent, self-reliant, self-initiated individuals, the Yale Report's emphasis on mental discipline was a "remarkable peroration on the subject of how to educate people for autonomy," that is, to think and act independently.[29] These are important insights for our purposes because they help us understand how thoroughly the Yale Report turned liberal education from public moral ends (in classical republican terms, public virtue) into a process that was intended to prepare the individual for personal success. The student facing a world of indefinite opportunities, where he would be thrown upon the "resources of his own mind" (to use a phrase in the report) could expect success only if that mind were properly trained. As Daniel Boorstin has suggested, in a world where roles were still relatively undefined, where the criteria for "professional eminence" were still so vague, mental training seemed to provide the only possible career preparation.[30] In the words of the report, "the active, enterprising character of our population, renders it highly important that this bustle and energy should be directed by sound intelligence."[31]

The Yale Report, then may be seen as one of those attempts among many others to accommodate essential republican institutions to the new economic and social conditions. If longevity is a criterion for success, then the effort must be deemed successful. The prescribed classical curriculum remained the dominant course of study in colleges until the turn of the century, and most everyone, even its detractors, gives the Yale Report credit (or blame) for this development. If the new concept of liberal education lacked clear public/moral purposes, it did, nevertheless, give liberal education social utility. It could prepare young men to enter a profession, in this case an unspecified career in an undifferentiated, competitive society. The curriculum at Yale, the report argued, had no courses in business, technology, agriculture, or the professions as such; on the other hand, a classical education laid a foundation preparatory to the study of these "practical arts." By establishing principles to guide the student in his chosen calling, a Yale education would aid the graduate in "arranging plans of business, of new combinations, of mechanical processes," all of which must come from "the mind's more highly and systematic" cultivation. Not surprisingly, much of the language and tone of the report was that of entrepreneurialism. It saw education as a commodity when it argued that by concentrating the college's efforts on the prescribed classical curriculum, the institution aimed "at doing its work with greater precision, and economy of time, just as the merchant who produces but one kind of fabric executes his business more perfectly than he whose attention and skills are divided among a multitude of objects." In this sense then—that is, that a classical education would serve the public good by fitting young men to pursue successfully their chosen careers—the Yale Report was expounding the ideology that saw public virtue in professional, economic terms, that is, in neorepublican terms.[32]

The concept of liberal education as formulated by the Yale Report, then, was patently not a reactionary plea for a return to an idealized past. It was a conservative effort aimed at preserving the structure of a tradition—the classical curriculum—while it reshaped that structure to fit the present and future needs of an expanding entrepreneurial society. In a pluralistic, restless, enterprising society, bereft of a common core of values, where material success was the measure of an individual's worth, intellect alone seemed capable of securing such success. True to its republican tradition, the report could propose noble purposes. As one writer has noted, it was in part a "plea for quality," growing out of a fear that democratic pressures would leave the nation "at the mercy of superficially educated demagogues and uncouth millionaires."[33] But its tendency was to drift toward more personal purposes. Ministers, lawyers, and physicians had a better "chance for success" with a liberal education than they would without one.[34] In their willingness to make education serve personal purposes, in the belief that such purposes served the public good, the writers of the Yale Report were at one with the emerging liberal capitalist ideology that would capture the imagination of American society in the Age of Jackson and reach maturity in the late nineteenth century.

The report's effect on historical liberal education is more problematic. True enough, by making adjustments to changes, it saved the concept as a meaningful and functional educational experience. A truly reactionary stance might have destroyed liberal education altogether. But this gain was not without its costs. The report's inflexibility toward a prescribed course of study had serious repercussions. It revived the ancient/modern quarrel over courses appropriate to a liberal education, a fruitless debate over means rather than ends that still plagues American education. Day's twenty-page discussion of the object of liberal education made it appear that the centrality of the classical curriculum followed from the objective, when actually it was the other way around.

The writers wanted to save the classical curriculum, and mental discipline justified that course of study. This was a grave mistake because it played into the hands of the enemy, those clamoring for an instrumental collegiate education. They now had only to sever the umbilical connection that the report had established between the classics and mental discipline, or they could discredit mental training and thus collapse the arch of classical liberal education. Actually, they did both. Although forced to the fringes of American higher education by the Yale Report, new fields and disciplines slowly but surely made their way into the college curriculum during the nineteenth century. Late in the century when psychologists discredited faculty psychology and the natural and social sciences won academic respectability, most of them entered the curriculum as discrete professional disciplines bereft of larger moral/public ends.

Perhaps more importantly, the report's doctrine of mental discipline left liberal education without a focused moral direction. The report had stated that to catch the breeze the republican ship of state would have to be directed with intelligence. Surely, but according to whose moral compass? The report did not tell us because it had concerned itself not with the ends of education but with its processes. To rephrase its metaphor, the ship of liberal education, since early colonial times propelled by the prevailing winds of virtue and piety, was set adrift in the nineteenth century on the swirling waters of pluralism, individualism, the cult of improvement, and the gospel of success. Buffeted by storms of material values and dashed by the tidal waves of university education, professionalism, careerism, and technocracy, the fragile vessel has drifted deeper and deeper into the seas of ambiguity, perhaps lost to us forever.

Notes

Jack C. Lane is Weddell Professor of American History at Rollins College.

1. The first quotation ("tiny social elite") is from Laurence Veysey, "Stability and Experiment in American Undergraduate Curriculum," in *Content and Context: Essays on College Education*, ed. Carl Kaysen (New York, 1973), 2. The other quotations are from Douglas Sloan, "Harmony, Chaos, and Consensus: The American College Curriculum," *Teachers College Record* 73 (Dec. 1971): 221–51. See pages 242–47 for a discussion of the Yale Report.

   Other writers who have interpreted the Yale Report as a conservative, even reactionary, statement are Richard Hofstadter and E. Dewitt Hardy, *The Development and Scope of Higher Education in the United States* (New York, 1952), 15–16; Melvin I. Urofsky, "Reforms and Response: The Yale Report of 1828," *History of Education Quarterly* 5 (Mar. 1965): 53–67; George P. Schmidt, *The Liberal Arts College: A Chapter in American Cultural History* (New Brunswick, N.J., 1957), 55–57, and especially "Intellectual Crosscurrents in American Colleges, 1825–1855," *American Historical Review* 42 (Oct. 1936): 46–47; Frederick Rudolph, *The American College and University: A History* (New York, 1962), 134–35; Rudolph was more generous with the report in his later work, *Curriculum: A History of the American Undergraduate Course of Study since 1636* (San Francisco, 1977), 67–76, but still depicted it as a retreat to the past; John Brubacher and Willis Rudy, *Higher Education in Transition: A History of American Colleges and Universities, 1636–1976* (New York, 1958), 101–2; R. Freeman Butts, *The College Charts Its Course: Historical Conceptions and Current Proposals* (New York, 1939), 118–25; Louis Franklin Snow, *The College Curriculum in the United States* (New York, 1907), 149–54.

   Less harsh in their judgments of the report are, in addition to Sloan, Brooks M. Kelley, *Yale: A History* (New Haven, Conn., 1974), 160–65; Ralph Gabriel, *Religion and Learning at Yale: The Church of Christ in the College and University* (New Haven, Conn., 1958), 98–108, who correctly see the report as reaffirming the liberal arts as taught through the classical curriculum; Robert L. Church, *Education in the United States: An Interpretive History* (New York, 1976), 32–33; Lawrence A. Cremin, *American Education: The National Experience, 1783–1876* (New York, 1980), 272–73; and Peter Dobkin Hall, *The Organization of American Culture, 1700–1900: Private Institutions, Elites, and the Origins of American Nationality* (New York, 1982), 151–67.

2. "Original Papers in Relation to a Course of Liberal Education," *American Journal of Science and Arts* 25 (Jan. 1829): 197–351. Hereafter cited as the Yale Report.

3. Rowland Berthoff, "Peasants and Artisans, Puritans and Republicans: Personal Liberty and Communal Equality in American History," *Journal of American History* 69 (Dec. 1982): 579–98.

4 For a seminal study of the meaning of liberal education in eighteenth-and nineteenth-century England and Europe, see Sheldon Rothblatt, *Tradition and Change in English Liberal Education: An Essay in History*

and Culture (London, 1976). For a history of the idea of liberal education from the ancient world to the present, see Bruce A. Kimball's recent book, *Orators and Philosophers: A History of the Idea of Liberal Education* (New York, 1986).

5   Richard Hofstadter and Wilson Smith, *American Higher Education: A Documentary History* (Chicago, 1961), I: 10-12, 33.

6   Quoted in Richard Warch, *School of the Prophets: Yale College, 1701–1740* (New Haven, Conn., 1973), 186. For a discussion of the role of ministers in colonial society, see Darrett B. Rutman, *American Puritanism: Faith and Practice* (Philadelphia, 1970), 91–97.

7   Gordon A. Wood, *The Creation of the American Republic, 1776–1787* (Chapel Hill, N.C., 1969), 47–53. The literature on republicanism is extensive and growing. For an evaluation of the most recent, see Robert E. Shalhope, "Toward a Republican Synthesis: The Emergence of an Understanding of Republicanism in American Historiography," *William and Mary Quarterly* 29 (Jan. 1972): 49–80, and "Republicans and Early American Historiography," *William and Mary Quarterly* 39 (Apr. 1982): 334–56. See also the *American Quarterly* 37 (1985), which devotes the entire fall issue to "Republicanism in the History and Historiography of the United States."

8   Wood, *Creation of the Republic, 69.*

9   David W. Robson, "College Founding in the New Republic, 1776–1800," *History of Education Quarterly* 23 (Fall 1983): 323–42, and his recent book, *Educating Republicans: The College in the Era of the American Revolution, 1750–1800* (Westport, Conn., 1985). Robson points out that the major topic of college commencement addresses during this period was the role of virtue in the new republic.

10 Robson, "College Founding," 323, 325. For a discussion of the neo-classical revival, see Wood, *Creation of the Republic, 47.*

11 Robson, "College Founding," 326.

12 Cathy Matson and Peter Onuf, "Toward a Republican Empire: Interest and Ideology in Revolutionary America," *American Quarterly* 37 (Fall 1985): 496–531; Jean Baker, "From Belief into Culture: Republicanism in the Antebellum North," ibid., 532–50. For an extended discussion of this issue, see Drew R. McCoy, *The Elusive Republic: Political Economy in Jeffersonian America* (Chapel Hill, N.C., 1980).

13 Isaac Kramnick, "Republican Revision Revisited," *American Historical Review* 87 (June 1982): 629–64.

14 Berthoff, "Peasants and Artisans," 579–98.

15 See chapter 4, "Salvaging the Classical Tradition," in Linda K. Kerber, *Federalists in Dissent: Imagery and Ideology in Jeffersonian America* (Ithaca, N.Y., 1970), for a good discussion of the debate over classical learning after the Revolution.

16 For a general discussion, see Rudolph, *American Colleges,* 116–24; and Brubacher and Rudy, *Higher Education,* 97–110. Criticism of the prescribed classical curriculum was by no means new. Meyer Reinhold found discontent with it as early as the first decade of the eighteenth century, and evidence of scattered charges that the "dead languages" were of little benefit in the American environment could be found throughout the century. The "classical revival" during the revolutionary period stilled criticism momentarily until it broke out anew immediately after the Revolution and reached greater intensity during the 1820s. Meyer Reinhold, "Opponents of Classical Learning in America during the Revolutionary Period," *Proceedings of the American Philosophical Society* 112 (1968): 221–34. See also Robert Middlekauff, "A Persistent Tradition: The Classical Curriculum in Eighteenth-Century New England," *William and Mary Quarterly* 18 (Jan. 1961): 54–67. For the debate after the revolutionary period, see Kerber, *Federalists in Dissent.*

17 William Tyler, *A History of Amherst College . . . 1821 to 1891* (New York, 1895), 65. See also George Ticknor, *Remarks on Changes Lately Proposed or Adopted in Harvard University* (Boston, 1825).

18 Yale Report, 298.

19 Rudolph, *Curriculum, 67.* For an evaluation of Day's presidency at Yale and background to the report, see Kelley, *Yale,* 156–66.

20 Yale Report, 300–301.

21 Ibid.

22 Ibid., 324.

23 Quoted in Kerber, *Federalists in Dissent,* 118–19.

24 Yale Report, 345.

25 Ibid., 309.

26 Ibid., 301–2.

27 David D. Humphrey, *From King's College to Columbia, 1746–1800* (New York, 1976), 158; Joseph J. Ellis, *The New England Mind in Transition: Samuel Johnson of Connecticut, 1696–1772* (New Haven, Conn., 1973), 239–40.

28 Church, *Education in the U.S.*, 35. For a full discussion of this topic, see Walter B. Kolesnik, *Mental Discipline in Modern Education* (Madison, Wis., 1958). My thinking on mental discipline as a means not an end was shaped by Rothblatt, *Tradition and Change*.

29 Hall, *Organization of American Culture*, 160.

30 Daniel J. Boorstin, *The Americans: The National Experience* (New York, 1967), 34.

31 Yale Report, 324.

32 Ibid., 303, 307, 323.

33 Rudolph, *Curriculum*, 71.

34 Yale Report, 309.

PRIVATE INTEREST & PUBLIC GAIN: THE DARTMOUTH COLLEGE CASE, 1819

FRANCIS N. STITES

"The doctrines of *Trustees of Dartmouth College* v. *Woodward,* announced by this court more than sixty years ago have become so imbedded in the jurisprudence of the United States as to make it to all intents and purposes a part of the constitution itself."

—Chief Justice Morrison R. Wait, 1880

Despite modification through reservation clauses in corporate charters, strict construction of such charters, and the state powers of eminent domain, police, and taxation, *Dartmouth College* v. *Woodward* stands as one of the most important precedents in the history of the Supreme Court. It infused the doctrine of vested rights into the contract clause of the national Constitution. It restricted state power, and rendered the corporation serviceable to the needs of a developing national economy. Reverence for property rights and concern that state legislatures might infringe those rights caused the Marshall Court to expand the contract clause into a constitutional shield for vested rights.

1

The *Dartmouth College* rule that corporate charters were contracts protected by the Constitution was a statement on property that gave legal form to the social and economic axioms of America. Attachment to property represented not a reactionary devotion to the status quo at public expense, but a conviction that restriction on government power was necessary to protect the most valuable right of the individual, the right "to acquire property, to dispose of that property according to his own judgment, and to pledge himself for a future act."[1] The liberal individualism of John Locke and its concern with natural law and social contract formed a climate of opinion that society existed to preserve the rights an individual possessed before he entered society and the corollary that society benefited or prospered in direct proportion to the protection afforded individual rights. Protection of the basic right, property, either of private individuals or groups of private individuals would encourage the productive labor necessary to open the continent and develop the economy. Nineteenth-century American law absorbed this belief in the tie between individual rights and public welfare. From a conviction that the legal order should protect and promote this productive energy and that it should help create an environment that would increase opportunity and limit circumstance, legislatures passed laws concerning canals, turnpikes, banks, and railroads, and courts built a body of doctrine—the doctrine of vested rights—founded on judicial support of the sanctity of private property.[2] The Marshall Court was no exception.

Marshall's proclamation in *Dartmouth College* that the contract clause of the national Constitution protected vested rights climaxed the expansion of that clause initiated in *Fletcher* v. *Peck* (1810), and it is this that constitutes the importance of the *College* case in 1819. The Chief Justice, imbued with a belief in eighteenth-century natural law and a conservative distrust of state legislatures, continually sought to protect private property by using the contract clause to limit state interference.[3] *Fletcher* v. *Peck* represented the first step toward employing the contract clause to protect vested rights.

In that case, Marshall enlarged the idea of contract by declaring that public contracts, those to which a state is a party, were as much within the limitations of the contract clause as private contracts. He failed to base the decision on a specific constitutional provision, ruling that state interference with a grant was voided "either by general principles [natural law] . . . or by the particular provisions of the Constitution."[4] There was no such subtle or ambiguous blend of natural law and constitutional provisions in *Dartmouth College*. Charters of incorporation, Marshall declared in unequivocal terms in 1819, were contracts, "the obligation of which cannot be impaired, without violating the constitution of the United States."[5]

Corporations were important to the decision not as the principal beneficiaries but as the species of private property that epitomized the wedding of individual rights and public welfare. *Fletcher* v. *Peck*, as even the New Hampshire court admitted in 1817, left little room to doubt that charters of incorporation were contracts. There was no need to establish that and there was no pressing need to single out business corporations from other types. Marshall's definition of a corporation as "an artificial being, invisible, intangible, and existing only in contemplation of law" applied to all.[6] Moreover, it highlighted the close relation between state and corporation—the fact that this association of individuals owed its existence to the state and had to organize and conduct itself as the state required. Marshall realized that every corporation of the period, whether bank, turnpike, or college, was tinged with a public interest. Preambles to corporate charters suggested that a claim to public usefulness was important, and there was a contemporary belief that the corporate form should not be resorted to unless the public interest were involved.[7] So, when he said that the objects of incorporation were "universally such as the government wishes to promote," he was expressing his belief that the goals of the community were essentially the same as those of the individual and his concern that the New Hampshire court's use of the objects of incorporation as a standard for determining justifiable legislative meddling could affect all corporations and impede progress. In overturning that standard and ruling that the charter of Dartmouth College, in which the state had a considerable interest, was private property, Marshall was saying that a public interest in the objects, the uses, of private property was insufficient ground for state interference.[8] Protection of private vested rights would better serve the public interest.

The consequences of the decision in 1819 were for the moment confined to the College. Dartmouth University, never more than embryonic, collapsed. President Allen became president of Bowdoin College, where he got involved in a strikingly similar controversy and successfully invoked the *Dartmouth College* decision for redress.[9] President Brown, whose feeble health had been weakened by his exertions during the controversy, died in July 1820.[10] The College, saved from the reorganization embodied in the legislation of 1816, continued to suffer from financial difficulties incurred during the litigation.[11]

There was little notice of the decision in the public press outside New England, but this scant notoriety indicated contemporary appreciation of Marshall's purpose.[12] Although newspapers reflected indignation at the blow to state power, they never mentioned the decision's effect on business corporations. Even as a restriction on state power, the other two landmark cases of 1819, *McCulloch* v. *Maryland* and *Sturges* v. *Crowinshield*, overshadowed *Dartmouth College* v. *Woodward*.[13] The obscurity was doubtless due to the insignificance of colleges and business corporations in 1819, at least in comparison with the Bank of the United States and bankruptcy legislation.[14]

Some of the principals in the case did realize its importance. Early in the controversy, the College had decided to publish a report of the conflict to attract public moral and financial support. Work on the project did not proceed in earnest until after the decision in 1819, and Farrar and Webster assumed major responsibility.[15] Story also assisted in the preparation; and when the book appeared in August 1819, he asked Kent to review the work in hope that the Chancellor might impress upon the public "the vital importance to the well being of society, and the security of private rights, of the principles on which that decision rested." Story was confident those principles would "apply with an extensive reach to all the great concerns of the people, and will check any undue encroachments upon civil rights, which the passions or the popular doctrines of the day may stimulate our State Legislatures to adopt."[16] Kent declined, but in his *Commentaries* concluded that the decision was the most important step in securing all rights and franchises derived from a government grant and in making solid and inviolable the "literary, charitable, religious and commercial institutions of our country."[17]

The emphasis on the importance of *Dartmouth College* to business corporations has obscured its impact on higher education.[18] Before 1819, the most practical way to introduce a measure of public responsibility into colleges had been for states to bring existing colleges under some sort of government control, either by exercising visitatorial rights or by amending college charters. The increasing probability of state interference was of considerable concern to the denominational colleges, and the *College* decision provided some assurance of immunity. After 1819, if a state wanted to control institutions such as colleges, it would have to found them. There was no middle ground. The *College* case, then, suggested the alternative of state colleges. It is impossible to determine the extent to which the decision contributed to the growth of state colleges. It might, though, have actually retarded educational development in the United States by providing a legal base for the proliferation of small private and denominational colleges, which characterized mid-nineteenth-century America.[19] After state colleges developed, the decision raised the question whether these institutions were even corporations, and if so, of what species. In some cases, they were held to be private corporations; in a few instances, they were regarded as non-corporate departments of state government. Most of the time, they were regarded as strictly public corporations.[20] Finally, in defending the Trustees, faculty, and students against legislative encroachment, the Supreme Court was unwittingly erecting a symbol of academic freedom.[21]

The *Dartmouth College* decision did not, as critics have charged, rob the states of all regulatory power over corporations.[22] It established some restriction on state power with its rulings that certain powers must be granted a corporation to enable it to function and that a donor has the right to prescribe the uses of his charity. Beyond these, the state was free to set whatever limits it deemed appropriate. Neither state nor federal courts had the power to grant corporate charters. The granting of rights and privileges which constituted a corporate franchise was entirely a legislative prerogative. Dicta in the *College* case stressed this, declaring that if the legislature meant to amend corporate charters so as to control or restrict corporate power, it would have to reserve the authority in the charter grant.[23]

The Court in *Dartmouth College* was simply reminding the legislature that the wisdom of grants was not a matter for judicial determination. This was no innovation. State courts had ruled similarly as early as 1806, and legislative practice in reserving powers dated back to 1784.[24] Beginning with a New York statute in 1827, it became common practice to insert reservation clauses in general statutes or in state constitutions and so make them applicable to corporations generally.[25] Improvident legislative grants, not the *Dartmouth College* rule, robbed states of regulatory power.

The first important modification of the *Dartmouth College* doctrine came also in 1827 when the Court in *Ogden* v. *Saunders* decided that state laws in existence at the time a contract was entered into became part of the obligation of contract.[26] This decision is generally understood as the turning point in Marshall's contract clause decisions because it undermined the logic of his position that the obligation flowed from natural instead of positive law. It was also pivotal for the *Dartmouth College* doctrine since the Court, by extension, was also saying that reservation clauses in state constitutions and general statutes became part of the contract and that subsequent exercise of that power would not impair the contract obligation.[27] Reserved powers became part of constitutional law.

After 1827 the Marshall Court took additional steps toward modifying the implications of the *Dartmouth College* rule. The most significant was *Providence Bank* v. *Billings* (1830).[28] The Bank was chartered in 1791, and in 1822 the Rhode Island legislature enacted a general tax on banks. Arguing that the Bank's charter implied an exemption from taxation, counsel for the Bank pleaded an impairment of contract. Marshall had said in *McCulloch* that the power to tax involved the power to destroy, and the Bank's counsel argued from this that if the federal supremacy clause had deprived Maryland of the power to destroy the Bank of the United States, the contract clause, as interpreted in *Dartmouth College* v. *Woodward*, should deprive Rhode Island of the power to destroy the Providence Bank.[29]

Marshall considered the taxing power vital to government and said the relinquishment of such a power could never be assumed. He could not say, without overruling *New Jersey* v. *Wilson*, that the power could not be relinquished. But "as the whole community is interested in retaining it undiminished; that community has a right to insist that its abandonment ought not to be presumed, in a case in which the deliberate purpose of the state to abandon it does not appear."[30] The state, Marshall said, granted charters of incorporation to confer the characteristics of individuals on collective bodies. Except for the stripulations in their charters, corporations were the same as individuals. They were members of the body politic, and legislative power, including taxation, operated on all members of that body. The individual's right was never so absolute that it exempted him from sharing the public burdens—a share for the legislature to determine. The corporate individual possessed only those privileges conferred by its charter. Marshall found no "express contract" for tax exemption in the Bank's charter and ruled that the state's tax law did not impair the contract's obligations.[31]

This was an important decision because, without discussion, Marshall was applying the *Dartmouth College* doctrine to business corporations, although not until *Planters' Bank* v. *Sharp* (1848) did the Court strike down a statute as an unconstitutional impairment of the contract in a commercial charter.[32] Moreover, the Chief Justice was announcing that, at least in some regards, corporate charters must be strictly construed in favor of the state. He admitted a state's right to contract away part of its sovereign power by "express grant," but he left the states free to determine what portion, if any, they would dispose of. Corporate rights were not to be extended beyond the obvious meaning of their charters. With the legislatures thus free from any implied expansion of corporate power, it is difficult to blame the *Dartmouth College* rule for the failures of public policy that led to widespread abuse of corporate immunity in the late nineteenth century. Not even Marshall was willing to see corporate power larger than state power.

2

Corporate vested rights presented more difficult problems to the Taney Court than to Marshall, not only because of the more complex character of corporate enterprise but because the Court's personnel reflected the individualism and economic and political egalitarianism of the Jacksonian era. Like his colleagues, Taney was not an implacable foe of corporations, only of monopoly and special privilege. His concern for the security of private property and his disdain for state legislative interference with what he viewed as legitimate property rights led him to accept the philosophy underlying Marshall's interpretation of the contract clause, although an equally strong concern for state's rights caused him to restrict that interpretation on occasion. From 1837 to 1863 the number of contract cases increased rapidly and the proportion of cases in which state legislation was invalidated remained the same as in the Marshall period.[33] This extended use of the contract clause manifested increasing state concern about corporations and the Jacksonian imperative to enlarge individual rights, in this case property rights. The Taney modifications of the *Dartmouth College* rule also indicated these concerns.

The Taney Court had to allow the state authority to cope with changing economic conditions, such as the building of railroads parallel to old canals. At the same time, it had to preserve precedents with which it was in essential agreement. This could only be accomplished in contract cases by denying the validity of the contract—declaring that the state was not free to contract away certain sovereign powers. In some cases, like those involving eminent domain, this strategy succeeded because there were no Marshall precedents. In others, notably the taxing-power cases, there were irksome precedents. Where it was impossible to deny the contract, the Taney Court relied upon strict interpretation of corporate charters in favor of the state.

The classic statement of this dilemma facing the Taney Court was strikingly similar to Marshall's *Providence Bank* decision. In *Charles River Bridge* v. *Warren Bridge* (1837),[34] Taney relied on strict construction in ruling that a charter to build and operate a toll bridge did not imply an exclusive grant which would prevent the erection of another bridge nearby. The words of the charter did not convey an exclusive right, and the Court would not infer such a right. The growing economy of the United States, he maintained, daily demanded "new channels of communication." If the country were not to be shackled to improvements of the last century for the benefit of old canals and turnpikes, public grants must be strictly construed. Nothing should pass by implication and any ambiguities should be interpreted in favor of the state. "While the rights of private property are sacredly guarded," the Chief Justice said, "we must not forget that the community also have rights, and that the happiness and well being of every citizen depends on their faithful preservation."[35] Despite heavy criticism from old vested-rights stalwarts, the decision was not a blow to the doctrine of vested rights. Quite the contrary, it manifested concern for the rights of the new group of private investors which an implied monopoly would have restricted. There were few cases during the Taney period applying the *Charles River Bridge* rule.[36] One of these, decided in his last term, carried the rule further by holding that even express grants of monopolies would not be interpreted as granting anything by implication.[37]

For its effect on the *Dartmouth College* doctrine, counsel's discussion of eminent domain—a subject Marshall's contract cases did not mention—in the *Charles River Bridge* case was more important.[38] Marshall had been unwilling to admit the inalienability of some state powers. He did say the contract clause was never intended to restrain the states in regulation of their internal affairs or to embrace contracts other than those respecting property rights.[39] But, for Marshall, regulation of internal affairs meant civil institutions adopted for internal government, and a grant to such an institution was a grant of political power such as that found in charters to municipal corporations. He saw no reason to infer that, because a contract involved an exemption from some state power, it was concerned with political power, not property rights.[40] The most he would say was that the grant of state powers should not be assumed.

Counsel for Warren Bridge argued that eminent domain could not be bargained away. Webster, for the Charles River Bridge, maintained that when the national contract clause and the state's power of eminent domain conflicted, the contract clause would be superior. Taney did not see fit to rule on the question, and postponed any judicial pronouncement on the subject to 1848. In *West River Bridge* v. *Dix* (1848), a near unanimous Court held that all contracts were subject to the power of eminent domain.[41] Even so, the Court upheld the *Dartmouth College* precedent. It did not deny the contract, but asserted that into all contracts "there enter conditions which arise out of the literal terms of the contract itself; they are superinduced by the preexisting and higher authority of the laws of nature, of nations, or of the community." Every contract is made subordinate to them. The exercise of those conditions "does not impair the contract . . . but recognizes its obligation to the fullest extent, claiming only the fulfilment of an essential and inseparable condition."[42] The Court was still using Marshall's equation of individual and corporate rights within society. This precedent has stood unchallenged ever since.[43]

Probably the most perplexing problem for the Taney Court's application of the *Dartmouth College* decision was the taxing power. Logically, if eminent domain were inalienable, the taxing power should have been also. But there were troubling Marshall precedents. In *New Jersey* v. *Wilson* (1812), the Court had sustained an express tax exemption under the contract clause. The *Dartmouth College* case made this precedent applicable to corporations, which proved to be the principal beneficiaries. Finally, *Providence Bank*, though emphasizing the necessity of the taxing power, upheld the state's right to bargain it away.[44] The Taney Court refused to abandon these precedents. The question of the inalienability of the taxing power first came up in *Piqua Bank* v. *Knoop* (1853).[45] In striking down a state tax as an impairment of the charter obligation, Justice McLean ruled that the question of taxes and tax exemptions was one of state policy and not state power. If the state chose to grant a tax exemption, it was exercising and not surrendering its sovereignty. The same rule applied through the century, though not without vigorous dissents.[46] Justice Miller's dissent in *Washington University* v. *Rouse* (1869)[47] argued that no legislature had the right to alienate its taxing power any more than eminent domain and reprimanded the Court for being "slow to perceive that what were claimed to be contracts were not so, by reason of the want of authority in those who profess to bind others."[48] But Miller was too harsh, for the Court still adhered to strict construction and held that tax exemptions had to be clear.[49]

3

The post-Civil War years witnessed the gradual decline of the contract clause and the *Dartmouth College* doctrine. Prior to 1865, the Court completed the doctrinal expansion of the contract clause and modified the *Dartmouth College* doctrine.[50] State legislatures began to regret their liberal grants to corporations and to seek methods of avoiding the implications of that doctrine. From 1888 to 1910, under Chief Justice Melville W. Fuller, the contract clause declined and was replaced by the more comprehensive protection for vested rights found in the due process clause of the Fourteenth Amendment. The most interesting and important modification of the *Dartmouth College* doctrine came in these years with the doctrine of the inalienability of the police power—the state's power to provide for the protection of the lives, health, and property of citizens, and the preservation of good order and morals.[51]

In this era, the Vermont supreme court provided a precedent on the police power which the Court at Washington often cited with approval.[52] In *Thorpe* v. *Rutland & Burlington R.R. Co.* (1854),[53] Judge Isaac Redfield admitted that there would be no question of such power were it reserved in a charter or the general laws of the state. What if the legislature exercised this power without reservation and after the date of the charter? Citing *Dartmouth College* with approval, Redfield noted that Marshall's statement that the charter privileges which could not be abrogated were those expressly conferred by the charter or incidental to the charter's existence did not settle the question. He referred to the *Providence Bank* decision and the rule that the corporation, like the individual, must share the public burden, and Taney's *Charles River Bridge* declaration of the need to protect the rights of the community. These precedents, he felt, justified his decision that the state police power was sufficient for regulation of corporations, so far as necessary to prevent injury to persons or property, without regard to charter provisions.[54]

The Supreme Court took an important step toward using the police power to regulate corporations in *Munn* v. *Illinois* (1877).[55] Like Taney, Chief Justice Waite faced the problem of reconciling the community's need to cope with changing economic conditions and precedents upholding vested rights. His solution was the rule that when private property is "affected with a public interest," it is subject to public regulation. This "public interest" doctrine repudiated the *Dartmouth College* decision. Although Waite had expressed adherence to that precedent and insisted that the two doctrines were compatible, the "public interest" doctrine abandoned Marshall's rule that the origin of the corporation determined its character and adopted Richardson's rule concerning the objects of incorporation.[56] Waite was occupying the middle ground that Marshall in 1819 would not admit. He created a new class of corporations, the quasi-public corporation whose franchise and property were private but whose business was "affected with a public interest" and subject to regulation. Most corporations receiving public franchises were of this character. With legislative regulation possible in the public interest, the implication of *Munn* was application of the police power to the many important beneficiaries of the *Dartmouth College* decision. Within three years, the Court had applied the police power to uphold state regulation of corporations.

The leading case here is *Stone* v. *Mississippi* (1880).[57] There were other cases between 1877 and 1880, but *Stone* was the first where the police power was the only ground for sustaining the state statute.[58] In 1867, Mississippi had chartered a lottery company. In a revised constitution, the state then prohibited the lottery business and passed an act subjecting that business to prosecution. The lottery protested that the statute impaired the obligation of contract. Waite began his opinion with a statement on *Dartmouth College*. It was too late, he said, to contend that a charter was not a contract. That doctrine announced by the court more than sixty years ago had "become so imbedded in the jurisprudence of the United States as to make it to all intents and purposes a part of the constitution itself."[59] He maintained that instead of protecting the corporate charter, the Constitution protected only contracts contained within the charter. No one, he said, could doubt that a charter existed. The existence of a contract, however, depended upon the authority of the legislature to bargain away the subject of the grant. Property rights were valid and proper subjects of contract; government rights were not. Pointing to Marshall's *Dartmouth College* declaration that the contract clause was not intended to restrain the states in the regulation of their internal affairs, Waite contended that no legislature was free to bargain away public health and morals. He admitted the police power lacked definition, but asserted that it extended to matters affecting public health and morals. Consequently, when a corporate charter was granted subject to this power, there was no contract, only a suspension of government rights, which was subject to withdrawal at will.[60]

These decisions on eminent domain, police power, and taxation affirmed the Court's adherence to the *Dartmouth College* doctrine, while they reserved to the Court the power to determine in every case the nature of the corporation and the validity of the legislation. There was little apparent difference between the property rights inherent in a college and those in a brewery and as much alienation of state power in a tax exemption as in a license to conduct a lottery. Yet these inconsistencies only demonstrated the magnitude of the problem facing the Supreme Court in reconciling private rights and public welfare, not to mention the judicial dilemmas produced by adherence to precedents in the face of a drastically changed environment.

Many viewed these modifications, especially the Granger cases and the police power, as taking the life out of the doctrine of vested rights as embodied in the *Dartmouth College* decision. It seemed that the protection given corporations had been removed and that it would be a rare case in which a decision could be obtained voiding any conceivable legislative interference. As one critic phrased it: "this historic cause has been embalmed in spices, and laid carefully away upon a shelf, like the corpse of an Egyptian king."[61]

While there was some truth in these assertions, the Court had by no means abandoned either corporations or vested rights. Accompanying this mummification of the *Dartmouth College* doctrine was gradual application of the due process clause of the Fourteenth Amendment to corporate vested rights. An important move in this direction was the 1886 decision that corporations were persons within the meaning of that clause—a decision facilitated by the long-standing equation of individual and corporate property rights initiated in *Dartmouth College*.[62] Not long after, the Court invalidated state regulatory measures on due process grounds.[63] Often in these due process cases the *Dartmouth College* decision continued to exert influence through a corollary that the charter of a private or quasi-public corporation implied a contract by the state to allow the corporation to enjoy the reasonable exercise of its franchise. In *Smyth* v. *Ames* (1898), this corollary was one of the grounds on which the Court struck down a state statute regulating freight rates. When a railroad had been incorporated and had built its road in a proper manner and at reasonable cost, the Court said, the state violated the implied contract if it regulated rates to the point of denying the corporation a reasonable return on its investment.[64] More important for the decision was the Court's declaration that such regulation deprived the corporation of property without due process.

While *Smyth* v. *Ames* left no doubt that a corporation could not be deprived of its property without due process of law—the position of both Mason and Webster before the Superior Court in 1817—the police power continued to whittle away at the *College* doctrine as protection for public grants. In *Home Building and Loan Association* v. *Blaisdell* (1934), the Court used the police power to sustain the 1933 Minnesota Mortgage Moratorium Law, a temporary and conditional interference with contracts to offset the effects of the Great Depression, and sounded the knell for the application of the contract clause and due process as protection for corporations.[65] Chief Justice Charles Evans Hughes justified the statute as an exercise of the reserved police power of the state. All contracts, he said, are subject to the future exercise of the state's regulatory power. "The policy of protecting contracts against impairment presupposes the maintenance of a government by virtue of which contractual obligations are worth while,—a government which retains adequate authority to secure the peace and good order of society."[66] The state was not free to destroy the obligations of contract, but in times of severe economic distress it could employ the police power to prevent the immediate and literal enforcement of that obligation. In short, the remedy could certainly be modified as the national wisdom directed without impairing the obligation.[67]

Ironically, this decision upheld a statute of the sort the framers of the contract clause had intended to prohibit, and did so in a case involving not a contract to which a state was a party but one between private individuals. The idea of the police power, which it had used, had developed after 1787 in large measure as a response to Marshall's expansion of the contract clause to embrace public contracts. Yet the reasons for the *Blaisdell* decision were substantially the same as those guiding the framers in 1787, Marshall from 1810 to 1819, and later Courts. The history of the Court's contract decisions, Hughes said, demonstrated a "growing appreciation of public needs and of the necessity of finding ground for a rational compromise between individual rights and public welfare." The question was "no longer merely that of one party to a contract as against another, but of the use of reasonable means to safeguard the economic structure upon which the good of all depends."[68] John Marshall could have made that statement.

Few Supreme Court decisions have had more influence through American history than *Dartmouth College* v. *Woodward*, and it deserves serious consideration on at least that ground. Originating in a small college president's forlorn venture into local politics in 1815, the case enhanced the reputation of the Marshall Court, restricted the power of the states, confirmed the rights of private colleges and the academic freedom of their faculties, and provided the leading precedent regulating the scope of legislative power over corporations through the nineteenth century. Its principal importance lay more in its relation to private property than to corporations. Other decisions have equal claim to stimulating the growth of corporate enterprise.[69] Marshall's equation of individual and corporate rights not only shifted the doctrine of vested rights from the vague ground of natural law, but it enabled later Courts to modify the *College* doctrine and to provide the more comprehensive protection of the due process clause of the Fourteenth Amendment.

The constitutional safeguards for vested rights provided by the *Dartmouth College* doctrine and the Fourteenth Amendment grew less important as widespread abuse of corporate privilege at the turn of the twentieth century caused belief in the sanctity of private property to give way to increased demands for government regulation. So the *Dartmouth College* case, though never overruled, has been tucked away. Yet the concern for the protection of individual rights, which the Marshall Court expressed in the *Dartmouth College* case, continues. The concern has shifted from individual rights of property to individual rights of free speech and other personal freedoms, but the emphasis is the same. That much of the *College* case still operates in the American constitutional system.

Notes

1. Marshall's dissent in *Ogden* v. *Saunders*, 12 Wheaton 346 (1827).
2. A vested right is a legal claim to ownership which comes to exit or "vest" in one party through a legitimate contract with another. See Robert Kenneth Faulkner, *The Jurisprudence of John Marshall* (Princeton, 1968), 3–44; James Willard Hurst, *Law and Conditions of Freedom in Nineteenth-Century United States* (Madison, 1956), 11–18, 22–29, 39–45.
3. Faulkner, *Jurisprudence of John Marshall*, 3–44; Charles Grove Haines, *The Revival of Natural Law Concepts* (Cambridge, Mass., 1930), 79–88; Edward S. Corwin, "The Basic Doctrine of American Constitutional Law," *Michigan Law Review*, 12 (1914), 246–76; Nathan Isaacs, "John Marshall on Contracts: A Study in Early American Juristic Theory," *Virginia Law Review*, 7 (1921), 413–28. During Marshall's tenure, nine states adopted contract clauses, of the federal model. When added to the three states already possessing such contract clauses, this indicates popular suspicion of legislative tyranny over legitimate property rights. See Wright, *Contract Clause*, 60–61.
4. 6 Cranch 139. In addition to natural law and the contract clause, Marshall also referred to the prohibitions in Article I, section 10 against bills of attainder and *ex post facto laws*—the latter despite Justice Chase's ruling in *Calder* v. *Bull*, 3 Dallas 386 (1798), that *ex post facto* applied only to accusations of crime and not to civil suits. On *Fletcher* v. *Peck* see C. Peter Magrath, *Yazoo; Law and Politics in the New Republic; The Case of Fletcher v. Peck* (Providence, 1966).
5. 4 Wheaton 650.
6. *Ibid.*, 636.
7. George H. Evans, Jr., *Business Incorporations in the United States, 1800–1943* (New York, 1948), 21; Oscar and Mary Handlin, "Origins of the American Business Corporation," *Journal of Economic History*, 5 (1945), 22; see also Davis, *American Corporations*, 1; and Samuel Williston, "History of the Law of Business Corporations Before 1800, "*Harvard Law Review*, 2 (1888), 105–66. The existence of such an attitude was evident in Hopkinson's statement in his argument in *Dartmouth College* that "there may be supposed to be an ultimate reference to the public good in granting all charters of incorporation; but this does not change the property from private to public." 4 Wheaton 616–17. Even Richardson shared this attitude for he included turnpikes and canals under the heading "private." In the late nineteenth century, these would have been labelled public or at least "affected with a public interest." The term "public" for Richardson meant an agency of government. Williard W. Smith, "The Relations of College and State in Colonial America," (Ph.D. diss., Columbia University, 1950) shows a large amount of state aid to colleges.
8. For criticism of Marshall's statement about the objects of incorporation, see Norman J. Small and Lester S. Jayson, eds., "The Constitution of the United States of America, Analysis and Interpretation, Annotations of Cases decided by the Supreme Court of the United States to June 22, 1964," 88 Cong., 1st sess., *Senate Document No. 39* (Washington, 1964), 391. This is a revision of the 1952 edition by

Edward S. Corwin. Henry J. Friendly, "The Dartmouth College Case and the Public-Private Penumbra," *Texas Quarterly*, 12 (1969), 7–41, criticizes Marshall's dichotomy between public and private. Story's specific reference to banks in his concurring opinion in *Dartmouth College* was intended only to bolster his distinction between the popular and strictly legal meanings of the term "public."

9. *Allen* v. *McKean*, 1 Fed. Cas. 489 (1833).

10. Wood, "Life of President Brown," 143.

11. It must be noted that the 1816 reforms, much to Plumer's chagrin, did not remake Dartmouth College into a state college. The Governor grew continually more disappointed with the University and, in 1818, had despaired of its ever approaching his liberal goals. Plumer to Hale, Dec. 28, 1818, Letter Book, 9 (LC).

12. Charles Warren, *The Supreme Court in United States History*, 2 vols. (Boston, 1926), 1:488–91; Warren, "An Historical Note," 671–75. Hill's protest that the Supreme Court had subordinated the public welfare to the benefit of a privileged few forecast the criticisms of the decision during the Granger Movement.

13. *McCulloch* v. *Maryland*, 4 Wheaton 316, and *Sturges* v. *Crowninshield, ibid.*, 122.

14. An unsuccessful attempt was made in *Benjamin Foster and Another, Executors, &c.* v. *The President, Directors and Company of the Essex Bank*, 16 Massachusetts Reports 244 (1819) to apply the *Dartmouth College* rule to a bank charter. The Essex Bank was incorporated on July 1, 1799 for a term of twenty years. Before expiration of the charter, the legislature passed a law on June 19, 1819 extending the lives of corporations three years beyond charter expiration for purposes of suing and being sued and settling and closing their affairs; but not for continuing the business for which they were established. Using the *Dartmouth College* doctrine that a law which altered any part of a contract contained in a corporate charter was of no effect, the Bank protested the act's constitutionality on the ground that it continued the existence of the corporation without the consent of the members. Interestingly, Webster argued for the state and against the attempt to use the *College* precedent. He argued that the purpose of the law was to protect creditors' rights, not to violate rights—an interesting switch from the *Dartmouth College* case where the purpose of the law was not germane. Webster distinguished the cases by pointing out that in the *College* Case the legislature, by a special act, had undertaken to abolish a private corporation and give its property to others. This 1819 statute was general, and its provisions beneficial to all parties, and hence within the proper exercise of legislative power. The Court, through Chief Justic Parker, concurred.

15. Timothy Farrar, *Report of the Case of the Trustees of Dartmouth College Against William H. Woodward* (Portsmouth, 1819); on the preparation of the *Report* see Baxter, *Daniel Webster*, 104–06; Shirley, *Dartmouth College Causes*, 290–98; Farrar's *Report* was used by Henry Wheaton in preparing his report of the Supreme Court decision and by the New Hampshire reporters in preparing their later report of the case.

16. Story to Kent, Aug. 21, 1819, Story, *Life and Letters*, 1:330.

17. Kent, *Commentaries*, 1:419; on Kent's refusal to review the book see Kent to Story, Aug. 3, 1819, *Proceedings of the Massachusetts Historical Society*, Second Series, 14 (190), 413.

18. Eleemosynary corporations have been involved in six contract cases before the Supreme Court, excluding *Dartmouth College*, and only three of these concerned colleges: *Vincennes University* v. *Indiana*, 14 Howard 268 (1852); *Pennsylvania College Causes*, 13 Wallace 190 (1872); and *Bryan* v. *Board of Education*, 151 U.S. 639 (1894). The other cases involved a church, a hospital, and a benevolent association. See Wright, *Contract Clause*, 129.

19. Hofstadter, *Academic Freedom*, 219–20; Donald G. Tewksbury, *The Founding of American Colleges and Universities Before the Civil War* (New York, 1932), 64–5, *passim*; Lester Bartlett, *State Control of Private Incorporated Institutions of Higher Education* (New York, 1926); Gordon L. Clapp, "The College Charter," *Journal of Higher Education*, 5 (1934), 79–87.

20. *The State, ex rel. Robinson* v. *Carr, Auditor of State*, 111 Ind. 335 (1887); *Trustees of the University of Alabama* v. *Winston*, 5 Stew. and P. (Ala.) 17 (1833). For a thorough discussion of these and related cases, see Edward Charles Elliott and M. M. Chambers, *The Colleges and the Courts: Judicial Decisions Regarding Institutions of Higher Education in the United States* (New York, 1936), 115–18, *passim*.

21. Hofstadter, *Academic Freedom*, 219–20.

22. Thomas M. Cooley, *Constitutional Limitations*, 338, says that under the protection of the *College* doctrine, "the most enormous and threatening powers in our country have been created. . . . Every privilege granted or right conferred—no matter by what means or on what pretence—being made inviolable by the Constitution, the government is found frequently stripped of its authority in very important particulars, by unwise, careless, or corrupt legislation; and a clause of the federal Constitution, whose purpose was to preclude the repudiation of debts and just contracts, protects and perpetuates the evil." Hugh E. Willis, "The Dartmouth College Case—Then and Now," *St. Louis Law Review*, 19 (1934), 185, is critical of Marshall for not ruling that even though a charter was a contract, it was subject to the state's

sovereign powers of eminent domain, police, and taxation. Between Cooley and Willis, the number of such commentators and of grounds upon which they criticize the decision is legion.

23. 4 Wheaton 636, 675, 708, 712.

24. *Wales* v. *Stetson*, 2 Mass. 143 (1806); Dodd, *American Business Corporations*, 141, refers to a Pennsylvania charter of 1784 containing such a reservation.

25. Dodd, *American Business Corporations*, 141; Wright, *Contract Clause*, 169–70.

26. 12 Wheaton 213.

27. In *Greenwood* v. *Freight Co.*, 105 U.S. 13 (1881) the Supreme Court ruled this way. In *Allen* v. *McKean*, 1 Fed. Cas. 489 (1833), Story invalidated a Maine statute altering the charter of Bowdoin College, despite a reserved power to amend, on the ground that the statute went beyond mere alteration. Nearly all cases involving reserved power arose after the Civil War, and in all of them, except those involving public utilities, the Court ruled for the state. See *Pennsylvania College Cases*, 13 Wallace 109 (1871). The Court has stated, but never ruled, that reserved powers must be exercised reasonably and that alteration must be consistent with the object of the grant. See *Phillips Petroleum Co.* v. *Jenkins*, 297 U.S. 629 (1936).

28. 4 Peters 514.

29. *Ibid.*, 535.

30. *Ibid.*, 561.

31. In *Beaty* v. *Lessee of Knowler*, 4 Peters 168 (1830), Marshall concurred in McLean's opinion that "a corporation is strictly limited to the exercise of those powers which are specifically conferred on it. . . . The exercise of the corporate franchise, being restrictive of individual rights, cannot be extended beyond the letter and spirit of the Act of Incorporation." Marshall made a similar statement in *Dartmouth College*, 4 Wheaton 636 (1819).

32. 6 Howard 301 (1848). This was not the first contract case to involve a commercial corporation. It was the first involving state regulation of a commercial corporation in which the decision was for voiding the state legislation. An earlier decision of unconstitutionality involving a bank tax exemption was *Gordon* v. *Appeal Tax Court*, 3 Howard 133 (1845).

33. Wright, *Contract Clause*, 63, 245, notes that there were eight such cases in Marshall's thirty-four years and eighteen in Taney's twenty-eight years.

34. 11 Peters 420 (1837).

35. *Ibid.*, 547–48.

36. Wright, *Contract Clause*, 65–66.

37. *Bridge Proprietors* v. *Hoboken Co.*, 1 Wallace 116 (1864).

38. 11 Peters 455, 466, 505, 515, 535.

39. *Dartmouth College* v. *Woodward*, 4 Wheaton 629 (1819).

40. *Providence Bank* and *New Jersey* v. *Wilson* are conclusive on this point.

41. 6 Howard 507.

42. *Ibid.*, 532–33.

43. The Court continually stressed this point in dicta throughout the century. In 1917 it went so far as to apply the rule to a case involving an express contract not to exercise the right of eminent domain. See *Pennsylvania Hospital* v. *Philadelphia*, 245 U.S. 20 (1917). An interesting development from the inalienability of eminent domain was the decision in *Illinois Central Railway Co.* v. *Illinois*, 146 U.S. 387 (1892) that a state may revoke an improvident grant of public property without recourse to eminent domain— especially interesting in view of *Fletcher* v. *Peck*.

44. In view of subsequent taxation cases, *Providence Bank* looms as an important precedent upholding the state tax.

45. 16 Howard 369 (1853).

46. See the other Ohio Bank Cases; *Home of the Friendless* v. *Rouse*, 8 Wallace 430 (1869); in *Given* v. *Wright*, 117 U.S. 648 (1886) the exemption at issue in *New Jersey* v. *Wilson* was ruled invalid, but this did not affect the precedent which still binds. See *Georgia R. Co.* v. *Redwine*, 342 U.S. 299 (1952).

47. 8 Wallace 439; for a discussion of the dissenting opinions in the tax cases during the Taney period see Robert L. Hale, "The Supreme Court and the Contract Clause," *Harvard Law Review*, 57 (1944), 642–52.

48. 8 Wallace 442.

49. Small and Jayson, "Constitution Annotated," 395–96.

50. Wright, *Contract Clause*, 127; Wright also discusses the different kinds of corporations affected in this litigation, 128–30. For a statistical breakdown of cases under the contract clause after 1865, see Small and Jayson, "Constitution Annotated," 409–10.

51. Small and Jayson, "Constitution Annotated," 410, believe that the subordination of public grants to the police power and the expansion of due process contributed to the decline of the contract clause. In his

chapter on the later history of the contract clause, Wright, *Contract Clause*, 91–100, believes the reserved power was more important.

52. Marshall suggested the idea that was later designated as "police power" with his statement in *Dartmouth College* that the contract clause was not intended to restrain the states in the regulation of their internal affairs, 4 Wheaton 629. The idea became more explicit in *Gibbons* v. *Ogden*, 9 Wheaton 1 (1824); *Brown* v. *Maryland*, 12 Wheaton 419 (1827); and in *Wilson* v. *The Blackbird Creek Marsh Co.*, 2 Peters 245 (1829). See also Webster's argument in *Wilkinson* v. *Leland, ibid.*, 627. Taney implied such a power with his statement about the state promoting the public happiness in *Charles River Bridge* v. *Warren Bridge*, 11 Peters 420 (1837); he was more succinct in *The License Cases*, 5 Howard 504 (1847).

53. 27 Vt. 140 (1854).

54. *Ibid.*, 155; Redfield also doubted the state's right to alienate its taxing power.

55. 94 U.S. 113 (1877).

56. In view of late nineteenth-century criticisms of Marshall for his lack of understanding of common law and his selective choice of precedent, it is instructive to note the manner in which Waite arrived at the "public interest" doctrine. He borrowed from a treatise by the seventeenth-century English jurist Lord Chief Justic Hale. The treatise, *De Portibus Maris*, was not published until 1787, and it is not representative of Hale's jurisprudence. The synthesis of Hale's position was his *Analysis of the Civil Part of Our Law*, which was the foundation for Blackstone's *Commentaries*. It was not coincidental that Waite did not use Blackstone and that Blackstone never mentioned anything being "affected with a public interest." Waite chose the antiquated *De Portibus Maris* and quoted a phrase pertaining to the regulation of fees charged by enterprises in public ports: "For now the wharf and crane and other conveniences are affected with a public interest, and they cease to be *juris privati* only." By translating the particulars— "the wharf and crane"—into the generic term "private property," Waite completely transformed the quotation's meaning. Moreover, there were five cases involved, and all but *Munn* concerned railroad corporations. *Munn* concerned a grain elevator partnership and so did not raise the question of a corporate charter. Yet Waite decided the other cases on the basis of *Munn*. See Breck P. McAllister, "Lord Hale and Business Affected with a Public Interest," *Harvard Law Review*, 43 (March, 1930), 759–91; Walton H. Hamilton, "Affectation with Public Interest," *Yale Law Journal*, 34 (June, 1930), 1089–1112.

57. 101 U.S. 814 (1880).

58. The other cases involved reserved power or grants which, if strictly construed, warranted abolition of the grant. See *Boyd* v. *Alabama*, 94 U.S. 645 (1877); Bradley's definition of the police power in *Beer Co.* v. *Massachusetts*, 97 U.S. 25 (1878); and *Fertilizing Co.* v. *Hyde Park, ibid.*, 659.

59. 101 U.S. 814.

60. In *Butchers Union Co.* v. *Crescent City*, 111 U.S. 476 (1884), the Court applied both the *Fertilizing Company* and *Stone* rulings in striking down the New Orleans slaughterhouse monopoly which it had sustained in the *Slaughterhouse Cases*, 16 Wallace 36 (1873).

61. Aldace F. Walker, "A Legal Mummy, or the Present Status of the Dartmouth College Case," *Proceedings of the Vermont Bar Association* (1885), 32; William P. Wells, "The Dartmouth College Case," *American Bar Association Report*, 9 (1886), 229–56. See also Justice Stephen Field's dissent in *Munn* v. *Illinois*, 94 U.S. 148 (1877).

62. *Santa Clara County* v. *Southern Pacific Railroad*, 118 U.S. 394 (1886).

63. *Chicago &c. Railway Co.* v. *Minnesota*, 134 U.S. 418 (1890). See also Charles Wallace Collins, *The Fourteenth Amendment and the States* (Boston, 1912), 126–38, 188–207.

64. 169 U.S. 526 (1898).

65. 290 U.S. 398 (1934). The *Blaisdell* decision insofar as it affected due process must be considered together with *Nebbia* v. *New York*, 291 U.S. 502 (1934). The death blow for economic due process came in *West Coast Hotel* v. *Parrish*, 300 U.S. 379 (1937).

66. 290 U.S. 435.

67. In *Sturges* v. *Crowninshield*, 4 Wheaton 200 (1819), Marshall said: "Without impairing the obligation of the contract, the remedy certainly be modified as the wisdom of the nation shall direct."

68. 290 U.S. 442.

69. This was particularly true of the decisions facilitating corporate transactions on an interstate scale and those giving corporations standing in federal courts. See *Bank of Augusta* v. *Earle*, 13 Peters 519 (1839) and *Louisville Railroad Co.* v. *Letson*, 2 Howard 497 (1844).

From Republican Motherhood to Race Suicide: Arguments on the Higher Education of Women in the United States, 1820–1920

Patricia A. Palmieri

> Why is it, that, whenever anything is done for women in the way of education it is called "an experiment,"—something that is to be long considered, stoutly opposed, grudgingly yielded, and dubiously watched,—while, if the same thing is done for men, its desireableness is assumed as a matter of course, and the thing is done? Thus, when Harvard College was founded, it was not regarded as an experiment, but as an institution. . . . Every subsequent step in the expanding of educational opportunities for young men has gone in the same way. But, when there seems a chance of extending . . . the same collegiate advances to women, I observe that . . . the measure [is spoken of] as an "experiment."
>
> Thomas Wentworth Higginson

Scholars studying American social and intellectual history are just beginning to address the question of why women's higher education has perennially been conceptualized as a revolutionary experiment, as the social critic and reformer Thomas Wentworth Higginson observed in 1881.[1] Before the last decade, American educational history was peripheral to the study of American history. Moreover, educational history was dominated by booster portraits of elite male institutions, usually seen through the eyes of their presidents. The exceptions to the male bias of educational history, Thomas Woody's two-volume *A History of Women's Education in the United States*, written in the late 1920s, and Mabel Newcomer's *A Century of Higher Education for American Women*, issued in the 1950s, stood alone for many years, although they too demonstrated the conceptual difficulty of studying American women's higher education.[2]

A progressive historian, Woody was interested in "out-groups," in this case women, and chronicled their struggle to gain access to institutions of education created mainly for men. For Woody, access meant success and progress; women, by virtue of being admitted to a formerly male educational bastion, would ultimately achieve intellectual, social, and even political liberation.

Newcomer, a professor of economics at Vassar College, sustained this liberal outlook. Focusing on the women's colleges, she cited their propensity for innovation and noted the high proportion of notable women achievers they produced. For Newcomer, as for Woody, women's entry into higher education was a significant positive marker.

The social and political events of the 1960s, the concomitant rise of a new social history, and the emergence of many more educated, articulate women interested in the status of women gave birth to a revisionist school of women's higher educational history. Aggrieved by the documented discrimination against educated women and angered by the meager victories of even the most educated women in the professions, these social and intellectual historians saw the history of women's education darkly. They began to question the equation of access with progress, arguing that coeducation and even the separate women's colleges reinforced patterns of women's subordination in academe.[3]

At the same time, a vocal chorus of disaffected graduates of the Seven Sisters also lambasted women's education. They wrote popular books like *Peculiar Institutions* and *I'm Radcliffe! Fly Me!*

The Seven Sisters and the Failure of Women's Education, books whose titles testify to their authors' disgruntlement.[4]

Beginning in the 1970s, post-revisionist scholars have struggled to shed both booster arguments and dark diatribes. Their concern with women's experiences as students and faculty and their analysis of the development of women's culture within coeducational and single-sex colleges display a new appreciation for the complexity of their subject.[5] To these approaches historians must add another: a focus on arguments for and against women's higher education. Only then can we better understand the interaction between the historical context and real changes in the lives of educated women. Such an examination of the ongoing discussion and its social and intellectual setting will make clear the need to reevaluate the periodization of the history of American women's education in the nineteenth and early twentieth centuries. Moreover, exploration of this realm reveals that in the complex history of women's education there is a central paradox: that success, overwhelming success, triggered as many problems (within the movement and without) as would have total failure.

In what follows I will briefly discuss the arguments covering women's higher education in three significant periods:

1. The Romantic period (1820–1860) or, to use Linda Kerber's term, the era of "Republican Motherhood."

2. The Reform era (1860–1890), which saw the opening of the women's colleges and a vigorous debate about women's higher education. In this period I find the rise of Respectable Spinsterhood.

3. The Progressive era (1890–1920), in which the first generation of college women began entering the professions, triggering a conservative reaction that I term the "Race Suicide Syndrome."

The Romantic Period: 1820–1860

Historians have documented that Puritan culture was suspicious of women; it classified women as evil. Woman's intellect was also considered inferior to man's, and extensive learning for women was deemed inexpedient and dangerous. In a religiously oriented society, higher education meant the production of ministers; thus males could immediately attend Harvard and Yale with a view toward assuming ministerial roles. Women, locked in a private sphere, were barred from all formal education.[6]

By the 1820s, a major shift had occurred in women's roles in American culture. Post-revolutionary American society was permeated with an optimism about individuals derived from two sources: liberal enlightenment thinking and romanticism. Rather than stressing women's evil nature, the new ideology elevated and idealized women's capacity to be pure, moral, and sentimental. What impact did this new cultural definition of women have on women's education? In "The Cult of True Womanhood" and other essays, the historian Barbara Welter argues that the romantic image of woman was anti-intellectual. A woman was supposed to be passive, to indulge in domesticity, and to lead a circumscribed intellectual life. Innocence and emotionalism reigned to the detriment of intellect. The virtuous female was thought to be threatened by too much education.[7]

However, it is clear that this same romantic image could work on women's behalf. Romanticism put an emphasis on perfectionism. Educational reformers began to pit romantic images of women against the frivolous "ornamental" woman who lacked education and was nothing other than a dilettante.

In *Women of the Republic,* Linda Kerber notes that the new republic, anxiously seeking to produce a virtuous citizenry, assigned women roles as influential caretakers. Although women were not expected to participate in the public domain, they were given access to education and drawn, if only indirectly, into the new republican experiment by their responsibility to educate their sons. In this period, seminaries like Emma Willard's Troy and Mary Lyon's Mount Holyoke opened; the historian Anne Firor Scott finds that Willard's Troy was a seedbed of feminism rather than a citadel of domesticity.[8]

The new romanticism operated on women's behalf in other ways. Romantic ideology, a phenomenon discussed by Susan Conrad in *Perish the Thought,* equated genius with such qualities as intuition, emotional empathy, and insight, qualities preeminently associated with women. By laying claim to special emotional and moral traits, women could cultivate intellectual roles as teachers, translators, and social reformers.[9] Concomitant with these cultural changes, economic factors were also operating to provide a rationale for women's education. By the 1820s, America was becoming increasingly industrialized, and factory work was beginning to replace family production. In New England, at least, young women were not needed as much as before to tend farms; neither were they expected to busy themselves in home crafts or to devote themselves to domestic chores. As men moved into the urban economy or ventured West, they delayed marriage. Sensing these changes, families in the 1840s seem to have engaged in what David Alimendinger calls a "life-planning" strategy which promoted the education of daughters. A seminary education would allow women to teach, add to the family income, and support themselves until they entered marriage.[10] The common-school movement, with its demand for a cheap labor pool, dovetailed nicely with other social and economic changes that encouraged, indeed forced, women to become educated for teaching roles in the public sphere.[11]

The Era of Reform: 1860–1890

Thus far historians studying women's history in general and educational history in particular have concentrated their attention on the pre-Civil War era. Our understanding of the links between the Civil War and the growing demand for women's higher education are thus minimal. In general, we know that war causes disruption in social values and also allows some crossover in sex roles. Moreover, in wartime women often are allowed access to careers because their skills are in demand. During the Civil War, for example, women figured more prominently in public activities such as nursing. We also know that contemporaries believed that a superfluity of single women existed in New England as a result of the war. Addressing Mount Holyoke graduates in 1873, William Tyler claimed that there were 30,000 more young women than men in the region; he thus welcomed the opening of colleges for women. Vassar's president, John Raymond, spoke in 1870 on the "Demand of the Age for the Liberal Education of Women and How It Should Be Met." He declared that "statistics in our time place it beyond a peradventure that multitudes of women must remain unmarried." Moreover, Raymond sounded a new cultural note. He coupled the statistical reality with the conclusion that it would be an "insult to woman" if she had to sit and wait for a man. As he noted, "Under certain circumstances it is good *not* to marry." According to Raymond, it was one of woman's unquestionable rights to serve her country. Hence women, no less than men, should be provided with the kind of education that promoted independent activity and prepared them for work. The Vassar curriculum with its innovations in science training reflected his concern that women be capable of taking their place in an increasingly professionalized society. While Raymond often envisioned women as helpmates in science, rather than as leaders, he still broke with a tradition in stressing that single women had a right to their autonomy and to education.[12] By the 1870s, then, "respectable spinsterhood," not "republican motherhood," was seen as the raison d'être of women's higher education.[13]

Beyond a demographic shift, what had caused such a tremendous transition in arguments for women's higher education? Historians have not pursued this question sufficiently. In 1870, John Raymond astutely connected the movement for women's higher education with the pre-Civil War women's rights movement. He admitted that a vanguard had awakened the public's attention to women's quest for autonomy. While he personally found some of the women's rights leaders to be "vixens and viragos," he noted that "extremists always precede and herald a true reform." Those who followed in the wake of the original agitation might "gather whatever fruit it may have shaken from the tree of truth."[14] To what extent was the opening of women's colleges an attempt to forestall more radical social change? To what extent was this movement part of a larger social reform history? These questions have yet to be sufficiently explored.

In 1868, John M. Greene, in encouraging Sophia Smith to endow a women's college in Massachusetts, stated: "The subject of women's education, woman's rights and privileges, is to be the great step in the progress of our state."[15] In the late nineteenth century, the desire for women's higher education took on the quality of a millennial-like reform movement, not unlike other communitarian reforms that dotted the American landscape in the pre-Civil War era.[16] Conventionally, most social historians conclude that the post-Civil War era was a kind of dark ages, bereft of social reform or behavior. Ronald Walters, for example, concludes that the reform impulse had entirely spent itself by the 1870s. Moreover, to many the Gilded Age has been, in the words of Geoffrey Blodgett, "a vast gray zone of American history, monotonous and inconclusive, an era of evasion, avoidance and postponement, . . . one sterile of purposes."[17]

This standard interpretation is based on a tainted vision of politics in the post-Civil War era and on a paucity of studies in cultural and social history. Women's history and social history are just beginning to challenge this stereotype. The movement for women's higher education must be seen as an extension of the romantic and evangelical reform tradition. It was also an effort to achieve women's equality. Hence, those historians who have focused narrowly upon the history of the organized suffrage movement and view the 1870s and 1880s as the doldrums also miss the import of the social movement for women's higher education.[18]

Indeed, by the 1870s, the debate about women's educability had become, at least in middle-class American society, what the abolitionist debate was before it and the suffrage debate after it—a large-scale movement, amorphous, with different intellectual strands, involving the energies of many middle-class women and men. Vassar president John Raymond alluded to this movement when asserting that "the whole world is astir with a sense of the coming change."[19]

Like those other organized movements, the movement for women's higher education had its "antis," in particular a set of doctors and educators who continuously unleashed fears about the deleterious effects on women's biological and social roles. The ideology of the anti-movement, like the ideology of the movement for women's higher education, deserves serious attention, which it has not received from scholars as yet. Most historians cite as the chief malefactor Dr. Edward Clarke of Harvard University, who in 1873 published *Sex in Education: A Fair Chance for the Girls*, in which he argued that higher education would damage women's health and ultimately inhibit their reproductive capacity. Clarke's book caused quite a stir; within a year it went through twelve printings.[20]

Clarke's book and the ensuing controversy are commonly cited by historians of higher education as illustrative of the negative climate surrounding the founding of the women's colleges in the 1870s and 1880s. Historians suggest that as a result, many of these women's institutions became defensive; they compromised their lofty educational ideals and succumbed to genteel domesticity, health regimes, and upholding rather than revolutionizing the cultural norms of "true womanhood."[21] This is, I think, misleading. Clarke's book stimulated a debate which if anything only heightened the revolutionary quality of the struggle for women's higher education. M. Carey Thomas recalled that as a young girl she was "haunted by the clanging chains of that gloomy little specter, Dr. Edward Clarke's *Sex in Education*." Alarmed by his rhetoric, the adolescent Thomas encouraged her mother to read his book and was relieved to learn from her that broken-down invalids like those described by Clarke did not really exist. That her mother scorned Clarke's dire predictions and encouraged Thomas in her quest for collegiate training demonstrates important information about women's ambitions in the late nineteenth century and the intergenerational context of women's higher education, and introduces the historical questions of family strategies—the relationship between family culture and women's higher education.[22]

It also made the first generation of women students extraordinarily conscious of their pivotal role in proving to the world that women were men's intellectual equals. As one alumna of Wellesley's class of 1879 recalled: "We were pioneers in the adventure—voyagers in the crusade for the higher education of women—that perilous experiment of the 1870s which all the world was breathlessly watching and which the prophets were declaring to be so inevitably fatal to the American girls."[23] Here we return to Higginson's theme of "experiment," for the first generation of college women confronted the experimental, revolutionary and adventuresome quality of women's higher education. While Higginson noted its negative implications—that women always had to prove themselves to a suspicious male world—there is of course another aspect to experiment: that daring, bravado, and adventure, that sense of being a pioneer and of course that desire to uphold extraordinarily high norms. Subsequent generations of women lost that excitement, and the nature of women's higher education changed. Clarke's dire predictions did not dampen the women's college movement. Wellesley and Smith opened in 1875, and others followed soon after.

The Progressive Era and the Backlash—The "Race Suicide Syndrome": 1890–1920

Most historians view the Progressive era as a period of advance when college women entered the professions of medicine, law, social work, and academe. But it was also a period of reaction. This reaction took different forms and emanated from a variety of groups. In 1908, boasting of the remarkable success of women's higher education, Bryn Mawr's president, M. Carey Thomas, took note of the changing public perception of college women: "Our highest hopes are all coming gloriously true. It is like reading a page of Grimm's fairy tales. The fearsome toads of those early prophecies are turning into pearls of radiance before our very eyes. Now women who have been to college are as plentiful as blackberries on summer hedges."[24] Whereas her generation had been ignominiously labeled fearsome toads, the new college woman was rapidly becoming a prized pearl. The pioneer band of college women had been so successful in weathering the dangerous experiment that in the twentieth century college attendance for women was not a sacerdotal or strange experience, but a socially sanctioned endeavor. Vassar professor Elizabeth Hazelton Haight commented on this success in 1917, stressing that unlike the "stern pioneer" many women now "wear their learning lightly like a flower."[25]

But herein lay a paradox and a dilemma. Soon the staunch pioneers, especially the first generation of academic women at the women's colleges, would be as troubled by their amazing success as they might have been over their failure. As early as 1900 many of them viewed the rising tide of more socially acceptable college girls as a grim fairy tale indeed—one that spelled death to the dedication they deemed requisite for the intellectual life and the spread of a disease they termed dilettantism.

If women faculty winced at the price of success within the internal college climate, they would soon find themselves confronted by an even thornier set of problems stemming from the growing popularity of college life. In the words of Mary Cheyney, secretary of the Western Association of Collegiate Alumnae, the "very success of the movement, which amounts to a great revolution affecting one-half the human race, has roused men to resist its progress."[26] Not so surprisingly, the 1900s saw a backlash against the women's colleges. Many male educators and doctors viewed the lengthening lines of candidates in the secondary schools with alarm. They believed the women's colleges were "institutions for the promotion of celibacy," producing a disappearing class of intellectual women who were not marrying and hence were committing race suicide.[27]

In 1908, coincident with Thomas's speech about formerly fearsome toads turning into pearls, G. Stanley Hall, a professor of psychology at Clark University, published an article entitled "The Kind of Women Colleges Produce." In it he lambasted Thomas and other "spinster" presidents and faculty who called upon women to be self-supporting and to uphold in high regard the ideal of scholarship and to train for a definite career. Hall railed: "The ideal of our colleges for young women, especially those whose regimentation is chiefly feminine, is not primarily wifehood and motherhood, but glorified spinsterhood." Women's colleges were, according to Hall, in the hands of misguided feminists."[28]

By 1905, a diffuse but increasingly outspoken group of educators, psychologists, doctors, and journalists had registered their alarm at the low marriage rates of women's college alumnae. Even President Theodore Roosevelt was concerned about celibacy. In a 1905 speech before Congress in which he condemned low marriage rates and the equally scandalous practice of birth control, he popularized the term "race suicide." The incapacity or unwillingness of the Anglo-Saxon race and particularly its highly educated members to marry and reproduce unleashed fears that within a generation or two they would die out. Presumably the leadership of the nation would then be left in the hands of immigrants from Central and Eastern Europe whose fertility was quite high, but whose intellect was deemed inferior.[29]

Viewed from this angle, M. Carey Thomas's statement about toads turning into jewels takes on another meaning: no doubt she hoped to assuage the fears of opponents who continued to relish and rely on the image of the college woman as a peculiar creature. In effect, then, from the very beginning the women faculty at the women's colleges had been battling a psychological war on two fronts: they hoped to challenge the larger culture and to change women's role in society, and in so doing they were engaging in a subversive, radical act. At the same time they wished to maintain the image of women's colleges as reputable and respectable institutions, a difficult task given that they were functioning within an inhospitable social climate for women's higher education, and professionalization.

In this tangled conversation about women's education, it is extremely significant that often the first generation of college-educated women who became academics wound up fueling their enemies' arguments. They had built their identities on the ideology of the select few: so long as there were only a token handful of women seeking intellectual careers, a system of special patronage and fatherly advising favorable to their careers had operated. Moreover, the tolerance for the select few meant that only someone like Madame Curie might succeed; faculty women could never settle for being average. They set appallingly high standards for themselves and for their students.

Shocked and dismayed by how few women wanted to follow the scholarly path, some faculty balked at what they called the universalization of collegiate norms. Average women were getting the B.A. and coming to symbolize the "College Type." But as Margaret Deland astutely noted in 1910: "[The] occasional women who did so-called unwomanly things, that is, unusual things generally left to men . . . who have distinguished themselves . . . were conspicuous, because they were strays. Achieving women are not very conspicuous now, simply because there are more of them."[30]

Ironically, then, on one level, proponents and detractors of women's higher education had a mutual investment in the ideology of the select few. For the faculty at the women's colleges, any dilution of the norms or shift from the high standards threatened their status. So long as a raison d'être for college attendance was scholarship and was wrapped up in vows of renunciation, successful academic women appeared irrefutably to be geniuses and would be tolerated. Wary opponents of women's higher education were also satisfied with this equation; they could always explain away or dismiss (even while they praised) the remarkable rare exceptions. But the popularization of collegiate life caused them alarm. They were distraught because more women than they had expected were earning Phi Beta Kappa keys and seeking entry into the professions. However, only rarely did these antifeminists focus directly on their fears of feminization of colleges and professions. In 1901, Hugo Munsterberg, a professor of philosophy at Harvard, voiced his alarm: "In the colleges and universities men still dominate, but soon will not if things are not changed; the great numbers of young women who pass their doctoral examinations and become specialists in science will have more and more to seek university professorships, or else they will have studied in vain. And here, as in the school, the economic conditions strongly favour the woman; since she has no family to support, she can accept a position so much smaller that the man is more and more crowded from the field. And it may be clearly foreseen that, if other social factors do not change, women will enter as competitors in every field where the labour does not require specifically masculine strength. So it has been in the factories, so in the schools and so, in a few decades, it may be in the universities. . . ."

While in 1904 Munsterberg could acknowledge with relief that "professional chairs for the most part belong to men," he still worried over the ultimate feminization of American culture. Any success he attained would be devalued because women had demonstrated equal achievement. "The triumph in . . . competition is no honour if it consists in bidding under the market price. In fact, it is not merely a question of the division of labour, but a fundamental change in the character of the labour."[31] Such fears confirm the argument made by Margaret Rossiter in *Women Scientists in America:* that the growing numbers of women in the professions threatened many academic men who were caught up in defining their career paths as professional rather than amateur.[32] Like other professional men, Munsterberg was anxious to divorce himself from the cheapening effect that feminization has on the status of any profession.

Ultimately, the pioneers would discover that there was a price to be paid for an explanation of college generations that revolved around the fact that a first generation of staunch scholars were, happily or unhappily, passing from the scene. Defenders of the women's colleges were giving their opponents some potent psychological weapons. By 1920, critics and advocates agreed that the experience of the first cohort of college-educated women who went into the professions and who remained single was not representative of normal womanhood. This kind of defense was at one level useful in soothing fears and dismissing doubts about the future status of women's higher education, but it also helped to mythologize the select few, and worse, it labeled them as deviant. Of course the ideology of the select few had always had this vulnerable underbelly—one was intellectually select and prized, but one stood apart and was different from ordinary women.

The negative implications of this "extraordinary woman" approach can be clearly seen in a defense of women's higher education entitled "Education and Fecundity," written by Nellie Seeds Nearing and published in 1914 by the American Statistical Association. She argued that the "average woman . . . who went to college in the early days . . . was not the type who would have been apt to marry in any case." Just who were the pioneers? They "consisted largely of the woman who had some special talent which she wished to develop and practice, the woman of strong intellectual proclivities, who preferred not to engage in the domestic occupations usually relegated to women, and the woman who, because of personal unattractiveness, knew or feared her lack of popularity among men." The contemporary college woman, somehow, was irrefutably different. "Today it is the normal, not the unusual girl who goes to college. . . . It has become a common comfort. . . ." Nearing also believed that a college education had become desirable because it polished off a woman's cultural education.[33]

Mollifying the opponents of women's colleges by emphasizing the conventionality of the collegiate experience for women drew attention away from the fact that marriage rates for college-educated women remained lower than those for the rest of the eligible population. In 1923, Vassar economics professor Mabel Newcomer found that as of the summer of 1922, of 4,424 alumnae surveyed, only 55.6 percent had married. Although Vassar women, she noted, were marrying more, and marrying at younger ages, the total picture was one of deviation from the national averages of marriage rates, which usually hovered around 90 percent.[34] Nellie Nearing had understood this, but she took pains to explain the tremendous disparity by factors other than education. She was led back to economic arguments that noted that educated people expected a high standard of family living and that it was difficult for women to find husbands who could meet this elevated standard.

The constant need to explain away such potent statistics highlights as well the culturally charged climate of the first quarter of the twentieth century, in which marriage and family were deemed by Freudian dicta to be universally desirable experiences craved by all normal women. World War I temporarily masked the shifting social scene that produced hostility toward professional women. Writing in 1938, Marjorie Nicholson, a professor at Columbia University who had received her B.A. in 1914, commented: "We of the pre-war generation used to pride ourselves sentimentally on being the 'lost generation,' used to think that because war cut across the stable path on which our feet were set we were an unfortunate generation. But as I look back upon the records, I find myself wondering whether our generation was not the only generation of women which ever really found itself. We came late enough to escape the self-consciousness and belligerence of the pioneers, to take education and training for granted. We came early enough to take equally for granted professional positions in which we could make full use of our training. This was our double glory. Positions were everywhere open to us; it never occurred to us at that time that we were taken only because men were not available. . . . The millennium had come; it did not occur to us that life could be different. *Within a decade shades of the prison house began to close, not upon the growing boy, but upon the emancipated girls* [emphasis added]".[35]

By the end of the 1920s, renunciation of marriage in favor of professional life was equated with a race of "warped, dry creatures."[36] Reconciliation of marriage and career became the watchword of the 1920s. Educated women "wearing their learning lightly like a flower" attempted to combine career and marriage. But lacking the support of institutions and bereft of a feminist movement, such attempts were often thwarted.

In the 1920s and continuing into the 1930s and 1940s, critics still questioned the value of women's higher education. Detractors insisted that college attendance posed innumerable dilemmas for modern American women. Thus, at some level, higher education for women was still being discussed as an experiment, the view that Higginson had castigated some forty years before. Unwilling to accept the permanency of women's entrance into academia as students or as scholars and unable to accept professional advancement of women in a wide range of careers, critics still dubbed such advances by women as "revolutionary," their worth still to be proved. But despite doubts, American women's entry into and success within higher education permanently altered their life courses and changed as well the social and intellectual course of the nation.

Notes

1. Thomas Wentworth Higginson, "Experiments," *Common Sense about Women* (Boston: Lee and Shepard, 1882), p. 199.
2. Thomas Woody, *A History of Women's Education in the United States* (New York: Farrar, Straus and Giroux, 1980; originally published by Science Press, 1929); Mabel Newcomer, *A Century of Higher Education for American Women* (New York: Harper and Brothers, 1959).
3. See, for example, Jill Conway, "Perspectives on the History of Women's Education in the United States," *History of Education Quarterly* 14 (Spring 1974): 1–12; P. A. Graham, "So Much to Do: Guides for Historical Research on Women in Higher Education," *Teachers College Record* 75 (February 1975): 421–29; P. A. Graham, "Expansion and Exclusion: A History of Women in American Higher Education," *Signs* 3 (Summer 1978): 759–773.
4. Elizabeth Kendall, *Peculiar Institutions* (New York: G. P. Putnam's Sons, 1975); Liva Baker, *I'm Radcliffe! Fly Me! The Seven Sisters and The Failure of Women's Education* (New York: Macmillan, 1976).
5. For example, see Lynn Gordon, "Coeducation on Two Campuses: Berkeley and Chicago, 1890–1912," in *Women's Being, Woman's Place: Female Identity and Vocation in American History,* ed. Mary Kelly (Boston: G. K. Hall, 1979), 171–94; Patricia Foster Haines, "For Honor and Alma Mater: Perspectives on Coeducation at Cornell University, 1868–1885," *Journal of Education* 159 (August 1977): 25–37; Patricia Ann Palmieri, "Here Was a Fellowship: A Social Portrait of the Academic Community at Wellesley College, 1890–1920," *History of Education Quarterly* 23 (Summer 1983): 195–214.
6. Laurel Thatcher Ulrich, "Vertuous Woman Found: New England Ministerial Literature, 1668–1735," *American Quarterly* 28 (Spring 1976): 19–40.
7. Barbara Welter, "The Cult of True Womanhood" in *Dimity Convictions: The American Woman in the Nineteenth Century* (Athens: Ohio University Press, 1976), pp. 21–41.
8. Linda Kerber, *Women of the Republic: Intellect and Ideology in Revolutionary America* (Chapel Hill: University of North Carolina Press, 1980).
9. Susan Conrad, *Perish the Thought: Intellectual Women in Romantic America, 1830–1860* (Secaucus, N.J.: Citadel Press, 1978).
10. David Allmendiger, "Mount Holyoke Students Encounter the Need for Life Planning, 1837–1850," *History of Education Quarterly* 19 (1979): 27–47.
11. On the common school movement, see Carl F. Kaestle, *Pillars of the Republic: Common Schools and American Society, 1780–1860* (New York: Hill and Wang, 1983). Also see Nancy Hoffman, *Women's True Profession* (New York: Feminist Press, 1981).
12. John Raymond, "The Demand of the Age for the Liberal Education of Women and How It Should Be Met," in *The Liberal Education of Women,* ed. James Orton (New York: A. S. Barnes, 1873), pp. 27–58.
13. For a discussion of the culture of spinsterhood before the Civil War, see Lee Chambers-Schiller, *Liberty, A Better Husband: Single Women in America. The Generations of 1780–1840* (New Haven, Conn.: Yale University Press, 1984); Patricia Ann Palmieri, "'This Single Life': Respectable Spinster-hood" *American Quarterly* forthcoming (review of Chambers-Schiller, 1984).
14. Raymond, "Demand for Liberal Education," p. 50.
15. John M. Greene to Sophia Smith, January 7, 1868, Smith College Archives.
16. On the reform spirit, see John L. Thomas, "Romantic Reform in America 1815–1865," *American Quarterly* 17 (Winter 1965): 656–681.
17. Ronald G. Walters, *American Reforms, 1815–1860* (New York: Hill and Wang, 1978). Geoffrey Blodgett, "A New Look at the Gilded Age: Politics in a Cultural Context," in *Victorian America,* ed. Daniel Walker Howe (Philadelphia: University of Pennsylvania Press, 1976).
18. The traditional interpretation that views the 1870s and 1880s as a quiet era can be found in Aileen Kraditor, *The Ideas of the Woman Suffrage Movement, 1880–1920* (Garden City, N.Y.: Doubleday, 1971), p. 4. Recently, some scholars studying women's higher educational history have challenged this conclusion. See Sally Gregory Kohlstedt, "Maria Mitchell: The Advancement of Women in Sciences," *New England Quarterly* 51 (March 1978): 39–63.
19. Raymond, "Demand for Liberal Education," pp. 50–51.
20. Edward Clarke, *Sex in Education or A Fair Chance for the Girls* (Boston: J. R. Osgood, 1874).
21. Sheila Rothman, *Woman's Proper Place* (New York: Basic Books, 1978).

22. M Carey Thomas, "Present Tendencies in Women's College and University Education," *Educational Review* 25 (1908): 64–85, reprinted in *The Educated Woman in America*, ed. Barbara Cross (New York: Teachers College Press, 1965), p. 162.

23. Louis McCoy North, "Speech for '79 and the Trustees at Semi-Centennial" (Wellesley, Mass.: North Unprocessed Papers, Wellesley College Archives, 1979).

24. Thomas, "Present Tendencies," p. 162; See also Julia Ward Howe, ed. *Sex and Education: A Reply to Dr. E. H. Clarke's "Sex in Education"* (Boston: Roberts Brothers, 1874).

25. Elizabeth Hazelton Haight, "Pleasant Possibles in Lady Professors," *Journal of the Association of Collegiate Alumnae*, 11 (September 1917): 10–17.

26. Mary Cheyney, "Will Nature Eliminate the College Woman?" *Association of Collegiate Alumnae*, 3rd ser., 10 (January 1905): 1–9.

27. William L. Felter, "The Education of Women," *Educational Review* 31 (1906): 360.

28. G. Stanley Hall, "The Kind of Women Colleges Produce," *Appleton's Magazine*, September 1908, p. 314.

29. On race suicide and its relationship to immigration and other cultural issues, see Linda Gordon, *Woman's Body, Woman's Right: A Social History of Birth Control in America* (New York: Grossman, 1976).

30. Margaret Deland, "The Change in the Feminine Ideal," *Atlantic Monthly* 105 (March 1910): 289.

31. Hugo Munsterberg, *The Americans* (New York: McClure, Phillips, 1904), p. 5.

32. Margaret Rossiter, *Women Scientists in America* (Baltimore: Johns Hopkins University Press, 1982) pp. 73–100.

33. Nellie Seeds Nearing, "Education and Fecundity," *American Statistical Association* 14 (June 1914): 156.

34. Mabel Newcomer, "Vital Statistics from Vassar College," *American Journal of Sociology* 29 (July 1923–May 1924): 430–442.

35. Marjorie Hope Nicholson, "The Rights and Privileges Pertaining Thereto," *Journal of the American Association of University Women* 31 (April 1938): 136.

36. Ethel Puffer Howes, "Accepting the Universe," *Atlantic Monthly*, 129 (April 1922): 453.

The Impact of the "Cult of True Womanhood" on the Education of Black Women

Linda M. Perkins

This paper compares the primary purposes and functions of educating black and white women in the nineteenth century. For white women, education served as a vehicle for developing homemaker skills, for reinforcing the role of wife and mother, and a milieu for finding a potential husband. For black women, education served as an avenue for the improvement of their race or "race uplift." The economic, political, and social conditions which contributed to these purposes are discussed within a historical context.

To better understand the education of black women vis-a-vis the education of women of the larger society, it is important to place black women within a social and historical context. This essay examines the impact of the "true womanhood" philosophy on the education of white women, and the black philosophy of "race uplift" on the education and development of black women in the nineteenth century. Although blacks considered the women of their race "women" in the early and mid-nineteenth century, by the end of the century they began to place more emphasis on them being "ladies." This shift in attitudes toward women by many educated male blacks will also be discussed.

The Nineteenth Century Context: The Antebellum Period

Observers of the early nineteenth century frequently cite the emergence of the "cult of true womanhood" as significantly shaping women's education during this period. This concept of the "true woman" emphasized innocence, modesty, piety, purity, submissiveness, and domesticity. Female education was necessary for the molding of the "ideal woman." Such education reinforced the idea of women's natural position of subordination and focused upon women being loving wives and good mothers. Literacy was deemed important for the reading of the Bible and other religious materials. And needlepoint, painting, music, art, and French dominated the curriculum of "female" education (see Cott, 1977, Rosenberg, 1982, Rothman, 1978; Welter, 1966).

This "true womanhood" model was designed for the upper and middle-class white woman, although poorer white women could aspire to this status. However, since most blacks had been enslaved prior to the Civil War and the debate as to whether they were human beings was a popular topic, black women were not perceived as women in the same sense as women of the larger (i.e., white) society. The emphasis upon women's purity, submissiveness, and natural fragility was the antithesis of the reality of most black women's lives during slavery and for many years thereafter.

Not surprisingly, whites of the early nineteenth century developed an educational philosophy to correspond with their attitudes towards women. At the same time, blacks espoused a philosophy of education for "race uplift." This education was for the entire race and its purpose was to assist in the economical, educational, and social improvement of their enslaved and later emancipated race (For a detailed discussion see, Perkins, 1981). Unlike their white counterparts, blacks established coeducational schools and similar curricula for both males and females.

The early decades of the nineteenth century witnessed a dramatic shift in the social and economic fabric of the nation. The growth of factories and increased industry provided employment outside homes and altered the colonial self-sustaining family. With the coming of urbanization and industrialization, a new role for women emerged. Unlike the colonial period, when single and married white women worked without stigma, the early nineteenth century emphasized women's "proper sphere" as being within the home (see Rothman, 1978). Throughout the antebellum years, white women were deluged with sermons and speeches, which stressed the "duty" of a "true woman." These speeches and sermons were reinforced by a proliferation of magazines, journals and other printed materials that focused upon instructing women of their proper sphere (Cott, 1977).

During the period of the development of the norm of "true womanhood," antebellum blacks struggled to abolish slavery and obtain equality in the nation. The theme of "race uplift" became the motto within the black communities of the nation. It was expected that blacks who were able to assist, i.e., "uplift," other members of their race, would do so (Perkins, 1981).

Although white society did not acknowledge the black women as female, the black race did. During the first half of the nineteenth century, black women's educational, civic, and religious organizations in the north bore the word "ladies" in their titles, clearly indicating their perceptions of self. One of the earliest black female educational societies, the Female Literary Association of Philadelphia, combined educational and civic objectives for the group's purposes. The Preamble of the organization's constitution reflected the women's commitment to the philosophy of race "uplift." They wrote, it was their "duty . . . as daughters of a despised race, to use our utmost endeavors to enlighten the understanding, to cultivate the talents entrusted to our keeping, that by so doing, we may in a great measure, break down the strong barrier of prejudice, and raise ourselves to an equality with those of our fellow beings, who differ from us in complexion." (reported in the *Liberator*, December 3, 1931). Clearly, the women spoke of their oppression as a result of their race and not sex.

Unlike women of the white society, black women were encouraged to become educated to aid in the improvement of their race. An 1837 article entitled "To the Females of Colour" in the New York black newspaper, *The Weekly Advocate*, (Jan. 7, 1837), urged black women to obtain an education. The article stated, "in any enterprise for the improvement of our people, either moral or mental, our hands would be palsied without woman's influence." Thus, the article continued, "let our beloved female friends, then, rouse up, and exert all their power, in encouraging, and sustaining this effort (educational) which we have made to disabuse the public mind of the misrepresentations made of our character; and to show the world, that there is virtue among us, though concealed; talent, though buried; intelligence, though overlooked," (To the Females of Colour, 1837). In other words, black females and males would demonstrate the race's intelligence, morality, and ingenuity.

It should be understood that during the antebellum period, free blacks lived primarily in an occupational caste. The men were relegated to menial positions while women were primarily domestic workers. Although blacks perceived education as "uplifting," most whites viewed education of blacks as threatening to their position of dominance.

By the time of emancipation in 1863, every southern state had laws that prohibited the education of slaves, and in many instances free blacks as well (Woodson, 1919/1968). There were scattered opportunities for both free blacks and slaves to become literate prior to the 1830s in the nation. However, education for blacks was viewed as dangerous after the fiery *Appeal* of David Walker in 1829 and the 1830 slave revolt of Nat Turner—both literate men. After the 1830s, all southern states instituted laws prohibiting the education of blacks, and such activities were thereby forced underground (Woodson, 1919/1968).

The decades of the 1830s and 1840s in which free blacks sought access to educational institutions in the North paralleled the founding of seminaries for white women. Historian Ann Firor Scott (1979) points out in her study of Troy Female Seminary, the first such institution to open, that the school combined the "true womanhood" ideal with feminist values from its opening in 1822. Under the direction of Emma Willard, the institution sought to preserve the traditional social and political status of women while challenging the notion of women's inferior intellectual status. Despite this challenge to society's view of the intellectual inferiority of women, Troy instilled within its students that "feminine delicacy . . . was a primary and indispensable virtue."

Other such seminaries proliferated in the nation prior to the Civil War. These institutions began the professional training of female teachers. However, few opened their doors to black women on a continuous basis. The lone exception was Oberlin College, which received notoriety in 1833 when it decided to admit both women and blacks on an equal basis with white men. As a result, most of the earliest black college graduates, male and female, were Oberlin graduates (DuBois, 1900). It was not atypical for black families to relocate to Oberlin for the education of their daughters. For example, when Blanche V. Harris was denied admission to a white female seminary in Michigan in the 1850's, her entire family moved to Oberlin (Henle & Merrill, 1979). Similarly, Mary Jane Patterson, who in 1862 became the first black woman to earn a college degree in the United States, moved from North Carolina in the 1850s to Oberlin with her family because of the educational opportunities at the College. Three Patterson females and one male graduated from Oberlin. Fanny Jackson Coppin, the second black woman to earn a college degree in the nation, was sent from Washington, D.C. to Newport, Rhode Island, where her educational opportunities were greater. After completing the Rhode Island State Normal School, she also went to Oberlin and graduated in 1865. Bishop Daniel Payne of the African Methodist Episcopal Church was so impressed with the ambition of Fanny Jackson Coppin that he aided her with a scholarship to Oberlin (see Coppin, 1913). This financial assistance is not insignificant when one remembers that when Fanny Jackson Coppin entered Oberlin in 1860, no black women in the nation had a college degree and very few black men attempted higher education. Bishop Payne's enthusiasm and support for Coppin's education contrasts with the debates on the danger of higher education that surrounded the question of education for white women. These arguments stated that higher education not only reduced a woman's chance of marriage but also resulted in physical and psychological damage (Woody, 1929).

As early as 1787, Benjamin Rush in his publication, *Thoughts on Female Education,* stated that women should be educated to become "stewards, and guardians" of the family assets. And Noah Webster warned that "education is always wrong which raises a woman above her station." Even as high schools for women became available after the Civil War, historian Thomas Woody, in his seminal history of women's education (1929) notes that the primary purposes of such institutions were to (1) extend the scope of "female education," (2) increase the social usefulness of women, and (3) train teachers for the lower grades as opposed to the preparation for college which was the primary aim of the male high school.

Studies of the students and graduates of white female high schools and seminaries confirm that marriage usually terminated employment of the women. Teaching, the predominant profession of these women, was merely a way-station until matrimony. Scott's work on Troy women students and graduates during the period 1822–1872 indicates that only 6 percent worked during marriage and only 26 percent worked at any time during their life. David Allmendinger's (1979) research on Mt. Holyoke students from 1837–1850 is consistent with Scott's data. Although the majority of the student population taught at some point in their lives, most did so for less than five years. Only 6 percent made teaching a lifetime profession. Although data on black women for these periods are inconclusive, the literature on black attitudes towards education strongly takes the view that educated black women and marriage were not incompatible. W. E. B. Du Bois' study of 1900 of the black college graduates indicates that 50 percent of the black women college graduates from 1860–1899 were married. Similarly, census statistics in 1900 report that ten times as many married black women than married white women were employed. (Du Bois, 1900) This disproportionate ratio is no doubt a reflection of the economic necessity of black women to their families.

After the Civil War

For several thousand New England white women who journeyed South to teach after the Civil War, it appears that the "cult of true womanhood" was a significant impetus. The women were overwhelmingly single, upper and middle-class, unemployed, and educated in New England seminaries and Oberlin College (McPherson, 1975). Their letters of application to the missionary societies sponsoring teachers to the South often reflected a deep need to escape idleness and boredom. A letter stating, "my circumstances are such that it is necessary for me to be doing something" was the common theme (Jones, 1980). In contrast, black women who applied were overwhelmingly employed and financially supported families. Their letters of application consistently reflected a theme of "duty" and "race uplift." While the tenure of the white female educator in the South was normally two to three years, the black female expressed a desire to devote their entire lives to their work and most did (Perkins, in press).

Although conscious of their gender, the earliest black female college graduates repeatedly stated their desire for an education was directly linked to aiding their race. Fanny Jackson Coppin expressed in her autobiography of 1913 that, from girlhood, her greatest ambition was "to get an education and to help [her] people." Anna J. Cooper (1882), an Oberlin graduate of 1884 whose papers are housed at Howard University, stated she decided to attend college while in kindergarten and devote her entire life to the education of her race. Affluent Mary Church Terrell, also an Oberlin graduate of '84, jeopardized her inheritance when her father, who wished her to model her life on the upper-class white "true womanhood" ideal, threatened to disinherit her if she worked after graduating from Oberlin. Terrell wrote years later (1968) of this dilemma: "I have conscientiously availed myself of opportunities for preparing myself for a life of usefulness as only four other colored (women) had been able to do . . . All during my college course I had dreamed of the day when I could promote the welfare of my race." Although she was forced by law to forfeit her public school teaching post after marriage, she taught voluntarily in an evening school and became a widely known lecturer and women's club leader.

"Race uplift" was the expected objective of *all* educated blacks; however, after the Civil War, the implementation of this philosophy was placed primarily on the shoulders of black women. Women were prominent among the many educated blacks who migrated or returned south after emancipation to aid in the transition of emancipated blacks from slavery to freedom. For example, Louise DeMontie, a noted lecturer who migrated from Virginia to Boston in the 1850s, moved to New Orleans in 1865 to open the city's first orphanage for black youth. Mary Shadd Cary, who migrated to Canada in the 1850s, returned to the United States after the outbreak of the War to serve as a scout for the Union army. Scores of other black women went South to engage in the massive effort to educate the newly emancipated blacks (Blassingame, 1973; Williams, 1883).

Throughout the War and afterwards, northern black women raised money and collected clothes to send South. On one occasion the Colored Ladies Sanitary Commission of Boston sent $500 to blacks in Savannah. Similarly, in Washington, D.C., Elizabeth Keckley, the mulatto seamstress of First Lady Mary Lincoln organized the Contraband Relief Association of Washington in 1862. With forty other black women, in its first two years of existence, the group sent nearly one hundred boxes and barrels of clothing to southern blacks and spent in excess of $1600 (McPherson, 1965).

Perhaps more impressive were the efforts of black women in the South to aid themselves. Viewing charity primarily as an activity for the fortunate to aid the unfortunate, white missionaries frequently recorded with astonishment the establishment of black self-help groups. One such report in *The National Freedmen* in 1865 (May 1, 1865, Number 4) cited a group of poor black women in Charleston who formed an organization to aid the sick. After working all day, members of the group devoted several hours to duty in the hospitals. In fact, *The National Freedmen*, the organ of the National Freedmen Relief Society, often reported the general charity among blacks in general and black women in particular. One such missionary report stated:

> I have been greatly struck with the charity of these colored people. There are few of them even comfortably situated for this world's goods. Yet, their charity is the most extensive, hearty, genuine thing imaginable. They have innumerable organizations for the relief of the aged, the helpless or needy from whatever. (*The National Freedmen*, December 15, 1865, Number 11).

The observer was greatly impressed by the work of black women. He wrote that he witnessed black women "past the prime of life and with no visible means of support" who took in whole families of orphaned children. These stories were found repeatedly in missionary letters.

Despite the significant contributions of black women to the economic, civic, religious, and educational improvement of the race, after emancipation there was a noticeable shift in the attitudes towards the role of women by many members of the race.

Schools for blacks in the South proliferated after the close of the Civil War and, by the 1870s, those founded by northern missionaries and the federal Freedmen's Bureau became the backbone of the public schools for blacks (Bullock, 1970). Du Bois, in his 1900 study of the *Negro Common School,* reports that in 1890 there were over 25,000 black teachers. Half of this number were women. With education being placed at the top of the race's agenda for progress, a huge number of black teachers was necessary. By 1899, more than 28,500 black teachers were employed in the nation.

While public schools for blacks were overwhelmingly coeducational, and girls received primarily the same instruction as boys, the black men greatly outnumbered black women in higher education. By 1890, only 30 black women held baccalaureate degrees, compared to over 300 black men and 2,500 white women. In this same year, white women constituted 33 percent of the undergraduate collegiate student bodies (Cooper, 1892; Graham, 1975). Whereas prior to the Civil War education was viewed as important for all members of the race, during and after Reconstruction, those black women who were educated were trained almost exclusively to become elementary and secondary school teachers. In contrast, the small number of educated black men had more encouragement and access to institutions of higher education. Further, employment options of black men were greater than those of black women (Johnson, 1938).

The issues of sexism and racism were confronted head on in 1892 by Anna Julia Cooper in her book, *A Voice from the South.* Citing all of the well known arguments against higher education of women promulgated by whites in the past, Cooper stated that most black men had accepted these arguments and also believed women to be inferior to men. Cooper wrote, on the women question: "[Black] men drop back into sixteenth century logic." These men, according to Cooper ascribed to the view that "women may stand on pedestals or live in doll houses . . . but not seek intellectual growth." Cooper continued, "I fear the majority of colored men do not yet think it worth while that women aspire to higher education." (Cooper, 1892, p. 75).

Cooper's observations were correct concerning the view of many educated black men. The passage of the fourteenth amendment in 1870 which granted black men the right to vote, signaled the first major gender distinction acknowledged by society towards them. As a result, black men during the latter decades of the nineteenth century moved temporarily into high political offices. Twenty-two black men served in the nation's Congress by 1900 and scores of others held local and state political positions (Franklin, 1969). As black men sought to obtain education and positions similar to that of white men in society, many adopted the prevailing notion of white society, of the natural subordination of women.

Sexism and the Education of Black Women

Given the unique history of black women in their race, to view them as less than men was not only retrogressive but absurd. Even though the prevailing economic deprivation of blacks at the end of the nineteenth and early twentieth centuries demanded that black women work, many elite blacks nevertheless embraced the Victorian "true womanhood" ideal of the 1820s and 1830s (see Williamson, 1971). As were New England white women of the antebellum period, black women were expected to be self-sacrificing and dutiful. (Prior to emancipation, *all* blacks were expected to do so). Speeches and articles abound citing black women as the nurturers and the guardians of—not the thinkers or leaders of the race. Most black women educators accepted that charge. (See Laney, 1899.)

By the end of the nineteenth century, sexism had increased significantly among educated blacks. When the first major black American Learned Society was founded in 1897, by a group of well known black men, the constitution of the organization limited membership to "men of African descent." The issue of female membership was debated by the group, and they resolved that the male stipulation would be rescinded; however, this was never done (Moss, 1981). It was clear by the end of the nineteenth century that many black men viewed women as their intellectual subordinates and not capable of leadership positions. When Fanny Jackson Coppin eulogized Frederick Douglass in 1896 (included in *In Memoriam: Frederick Douglass*), she praised him for "his good opinion of the rights of women . . . that women were not only capable of governing the household but also of elective franchise." The fact that she made this the point of her praise for Douglass indicates that his view of women was the exception rather than the rule.

Fanny Coppin headed the prestigious Institute for Colored Youth in Philadelphia, the oldest black private high school in the nation from 1869–1901. After she was forced to retire in 1901, the school was henceforth headed by black men. (For details on Coppin's years at the Institute for Colored Youth, see Perkins, Note 1.) Likewise, the prestigious, oldest black public high school in the nation, M Street School in Washington, D.C. was initially headed by a black woman, Mary Jane Patterson. Patterson served as Assistant Principal to Coppin at the Institute for Colored Youth from 1865–1869 and was appointed principal of M Street in 1869 (Perkins, Note 1). She was removed several years later so that a male could head the institution. Anna Julia Cooper also served briefly at Principal of M Street from 1901–1906 but was dismissed for her refusal to adhere to the inferior curriculum prescribed for black students. Like the Institute for Colored Youth, by the turn of the century and thereafter, M Street was headed by black men (Anna J. Cooper Papers, Howard University).

As the century came to a close, "race uplift" was synonymous with black women. With the formation of the National Association of Colored Women 1896, educated black women focused their activities on community development. Reflecting the century old race philosophy, the group chose as their motto "lifting as we climb." Throughout the South, the organization founded orphanages, homes for the elderly and educational institutions, and supported religious programs. The crusade against lynching of this period was also spearheaded by a black woman, the fearless Ida B. Wells-Barnett.

In 1894, the black Senator John Mercer Langston from Virginia recalled his visits in the South after Emancipation and noted:

> They (black women) were foremost in designs and efforts for school, church and general industrial work for the race, always self-sacrificing and laborious . . . Through all phases of his advancement from his Emancipation to his present position of social, political, educational, moral, religious and material status, the colored American is greatly indebted to the women of his race. (Langston, 1894, p. 236)

Later, black scholar W. E. B. Du Bois (1969) would also write, "after the war the sacrifice of Negro women for freedom and black uplift is one of the finest chapters in their history." Yet, today this chapter is rarely found in black, women's or educational histories.

Even into the twentieth century, the focus on educating black women to "uplift" and primarily to educate the race continued. In 1933, dean of women at Howard University, Lucy D. Slowe wrote a piece entitled "Higher Education of Negro Women" which addressed many of the same issues raised by Anna J. Cooper in 1892. Slowe voiced concern for the lack of opportunity for college educated black women to get leadership training within black colleges. Noting that while black men college graduates were found in the fields of ministry, law, medicine and other professions, teaching constituted the largest occupation of black women college graduates. After surveying the responses of forty-four black coeducational institutions, Slowe found that black women received little in courses, activities, or role-models to aid them in leadership development. Slowe conceded that many black families were conservative when it came to the issue of independent and assertive women; however, black colleges aided in fostering this paternalistic and conservative view of women. She wrote: "The absence of women or the presence of very few on the policy-making bodies of colleges is also indicative of the attitude of college administrators toward women as responsible individuals, and toward the special needs of women (Slowe, 1933, p. 357).

Despite the feminist writings of Anna J. Cooper and Lucy Slowe, the education of black women into the twentieth century continued to be focused towards teaching and "uplifting" the race. In a 1956 study of the collegiate education of black women, Jeanne L. Noble observed that the education of black women continued to be basically utilitarian—to provide teachers for the race. One of the 412 women in her study commented on this professional isolation.

> There are entirely too many fine Negro women in the teaching profession. There should be vocational guidance to encourage them into new fields. Around this part of the country middle-class women go into teaching because this is the highest type of position for them (Noble, 1956, p. 87).

Unlike black women of the mid and late nineteenth century who consciously prepared themselves for leadership positions, as Lucy Laney stated in 1899, to many black women in the twentieth century such a role had become a burden. Rhetaugh Graves Dumas indicates in her (1980) essay "Dilemmas of Black Females in Leadership," that their leadership has been restricted to primarily female and youth organizations most often surrounding the black community. Recent work by sociologist Cheryl Townsend Gilkes also confirms that the education of black women leaders has been focused to meet the black community needs (Gilkes, 1980).

The shift in attitude towards women in the black community and the role they were expected to assume vis-a-vis men paralleled the acceptance by black men of the dominance of man after Emancipation. Although black women have worked far out of proportion to their white counterpart, out of economic necessity, sexism and paternalism among the men of their race have resulted in relegation of black women to the roles of nurturer and "helpmate." The recognition of sexism within the black community has been slow. Recently (Summer, 1982, Volume 51), the *Journal of Negro Education* (1982) devoted a special issue to the Impact of Black women in Education—the first such issue in the journal's fifty-one year history.

Although the shift from egalitarian to sexist views of black women can be explained historically, sociologically, and psychologically, the continued depressed economic and educational status of blacks demands that race "uplift" return to its original meaning to include both men and women.

Note

1. Perkins, L. M. *Fanny Jackson Copping and the Institute for Colored Youth: A model of nineteenth century black female educational and community leadership, 1837–1902.* Unpublished dissertation, University of Illinois, Champaign-Urbana, 1978.

References

Blassingame, J. W. *Black New Orleans, 1860–80.* Chicago, IL: University of Chicago, 1978.

Bullock, H. A. *A history of negro education in the South: From 1619 to the present.* Cambridge, MA: Harvard University Press, 1970.

Cooper, A. J. *A voice from the South.* Xenia, OH: Aldine, 1892.

Coppin, F. J. *Reminiscences of school life and hints on teaching.* Philadelphia, PA: African Methodist Episcopal Church, 1913.

Cott, N. *The bonds of womanhood: "Woman's sphere" in New England, 1780–1835.* New Haven, CT: Yale University Press, 1977.

Du Bois, W. E. B. The college bred Negro. In *Proceedings of the fifth conference for the study of the negro problems.* Atlanta, GA: Atlanta University Press, 1900.

Du Bois, W. E. B. *Darkwater: Voices from within the veil (1920).* New York: Schocken, 1969.

Dumas, R. G. Dilemmas of black females in leadership. In L. F. Rodgers-Rose (Ed.), *The black woman.* Beverly Hills, CA: Sage, 1980, 203–215.

Franklin, J. H. *From slavery to freedom.* New York: Vintage, 1969.

Gilkes, C. T. Holding back the ocean with a broom: Black women and community work. In L. F. Rodgers-Rose (Ed.) *The black woman.* Beverly Hills, CA: Sage, 1980, 217–231.

Graham, P. A. Expansion and exclusion: A history of women in American higher education. *Signs,* 1978, 3, 766.

Henle, E., & Merrill, M. Antebellum black coeds at Oberlin College. *Women's Studies Newsletter,* 1979, 7, 10.

In memoriam: Frederick Douglass. Philadelphia, PA: John C. Yorston, 1895.

Johnson, C. S. *The negro college graduate.* College Park, MD: McGrath, 1938.

Jones, J. *Soldiers of light and love: Northern teachers and Georgia blacks, 1865–1873.* Chapel Hill, NC: University of North Carolina Press, 1980.

Journal of Negro Education. Special Issue on the impact of black women in education, Vol. 51, Summer, 1982.

Laney, L. The burden of the educated colored woman. In *Hampton Negro Conference,* No. 3, Hampton, VA: Hampton Institute Press, 1899.

Langston, J. M. *From the Virginia plantation to the national capital.* Hartford, MA: Hartford, 1894.

McPherson, J. M. *The negro's Civil War: How American negroes felt and acted during the war for the Union.* New York, NY: Vintage, 1965.

Moss, A. A. *The American negro academy: Voice of the talented tenth.* Baton Rouge, LA: Louisiana State University Press, 1981.

Noble, J. L. *The negro woman's college education.* New York: Teachers College, Columbia University, Bureau of Publications, 1956.

Perkins, L. M. Black women and racial "uplift" prior to emancipation. In F. C. Steady (Ed.), *The black woman cross-culturally.* Cambridge, MA: Schenkman, 1981, 317–334.

Perkins, L. M. The black female American missionary association teacher in the South, 1860–70. In *The history of blacks in the South.* Chapel Hill, NC: The University of North Carolina Press, in press.

Rosenberg, R. *Beyond separate spheres: Intellectual roots in modern feminism.* New Haven, CT: Yale University Press, 1982.

Rothman, S. M. *Woman's proper place: A history of changing ideals and practices, 1870 to the present.* New York: Basic Books, 1978.

Rush, B. *Thoughts upon female education, accommodated to the present state of society, manners and government in the United States of America.* Philadelphia, PA: Prichard & Hall, 1787.

Scott, A. F. The ever widening circle: The diffusion of feminist values from the Troy female seminary, 1822–1872. *History of Education Quarterly,* Spring, 1979, 3–25.

Slowe, L. Higher education of negro women. *Journal of Negro Education,* 1933, 2, 352–358.

Terrell, M. C. *A colored woman in a white world.* Washington, DC: National Association of Colored Women's Clubs, 1968.

Welter, B. The cult of true womanhood: 1820–1860. *American Quarterly,* 1966, *18*, 151–174.

Williams, G. W. *A history of the negro race in America.* New York: Bergman, 1883.

Williamson, J. Black self-assertion before and after emancipation. In N. I. Huggins, M. Kilson, & D. M. Fox (Eds.), *Key issues in the Afro-American experience.* New York: Harcourt Brace & Jovanovich, 1971.

Woodson, C. G. *The education of the negro prior to 1861 (1919).* New York: Arnon, 1968.

Woody, T. *A history of women's education in the United States.* New York: Science Press, 1929.

Possibilities and Limitations:

Education and White Middle-Class Womanhood

Margaret A. Nash

Advanced education for women and men was more similar than it was different in both curricula and pedagogy between 1780 and 1840. Although there were those who believed that brains were sexed and that women's brains were less capable of study, the predominant rhetoric was one of equal ability. Educators believed that the type of learning that would best prepare women for their future roles was basically the same education that prepared men for theirs. There was a general consensus that women had the same intellectual capabilities as men, could enjoy intellectual pursuits as much as men, and that their lives would be similarly enriched. Teachers and students alike were motivated by a strong belief in the value of learning for its own sake, and the joys inherent in learning.

The most salient difference in educational opportunities was that of class and race, not gender. Only a small group of mostly white and middle-class people attended academies, seminaries, and colleges. By the 1820s and 1830s, that experience became part of the formation of a middle-class identity and the consolidation of middle-class cultural imperatives. Expanded higher education was an essential component of the new middle-class's self-creation. By common practice, the cost of schooling, and sometimes by law, institutions of higher learning excluded the poorest parts of the population and virtually all African Americans.

As white middle-class women gained cultural capital through their education, some grew dissatisfied with their political and social subordination within their class group. Intended or not, advanced education equipped women with the confidence and skills they needed to forge a women's rights movement in the late antebellum period.

Education and the Respectability of the Middle Class

In spite of the proliferation of institutions for higher learning, relatively few women were able to avail themselves of the opportunities that did exist. The women who attended academies, seminaries, high schools, and collegiate institutes were an elite group. Virtually all of them were white and middle or upper class. Even if these schools had been free, which none of them were, most poorer families could not survive without the earnings of teenagers or young adults who might have attended seminaries. Some students paid tuition by alternately working in factories or teaching for a few months, and then attending school for a term, but the poorest families could not manage even this.[1]

Some schools provided opportunities for girls and women from lower income families. Mount Holyoke kept costs low by instituting a system in which students and faculty performed all the domestic labor. Its founder, Mary Lyon, intended to provide high-quality education for those in the "common walks of life."[2] Oberlin College also kept costs low by having students perform manual labor.[3] In addition, some schools provided scholarships for a number of students, and literary societies worked to fund education for members of the "deserving poor."[4] Troy Female Seminary provided scholarships for poorer students who intended to become teachers, but scholarship students only comprised about ten percent of the student body.[5] While these scholarships no doubt had a huge impact on the lives of those women who received them, the majority of Troy's students were from wealthy enough families that they did not need scholarships. In fact, when Emma Willard approached the New York state legislature asking for funds for female education, she did not argue that the state should help provide education for those who otherwise could not afford it. She argued that state funding would improve the quality of education for women, and that the state had as much of a responsibility to provide funds for female as for male education.[6]

Opportunities for advanced education were particularly slim for African American women, although exact data are difficult to compile. Fifteen African American women graduated from Oberlin College before the Civil War, and others attended without graduating.[7] The Lexington (Massachusetts) Normal School accepted African American students, both male and female, when it opened in 1839.[8] But support among whites for the education of African American females was so low that when the white Quaker teacher Prudence Crandall admitted one black student into her school in Connecticut in 1832, white parents withdrew their daughters. When Crandall then reopened the school as a school for "Young Ladies and Little Misses of Color," white townspeople harassed students and jailed Crandall.[9]

African American women's desire for education was as great as that of white women's. Certainly these women pursued learning with the same assiduity, even when their options were more limited. African American women organized literary societies in Lynn and Boston, Massachusetts, in Providence, Rhode Island, and in Rochester, Buffalo, and New York; in the 1830s there were at least three such societies in Philadelphia alone.[10] Perhaps Maria Stewart made the most poignant statement of this longing in an 1831 essay for *The Liberator* in which she asked, "How long shall the fair daughters of Africa be compelled to bury their minds and talents beneath a load of iron pots and kettles?"[11] The situation improved slightly in the North in the 1850s, when several more normal schools admitted African American women, but clearly most whites considered higher education as appropriate primarily for themselves.[12]

Seldom explicitly discussed, one of the most important functions of antebellum academies and seminaries was their role in class formation and consolidation. Schools may have offered scholarships to the genteel poor, but seldom if ever to the abjectly destitute, women of color, or immigrants. Most seminaries made clear that they were educating women to be *ladies*, and the word "ladies" was in the name of many schools.[13] That word included an implicit understanding that ladies were white and that they shared certain middle-class values.[14] The process of class formation included "an impulse toward self-definition, a need to avow publicly one's own class aspirations."[15]

Middle-class status was not solely linked to economic position. Indeed, as discussed earlier, "vicissitudes of fortune," in the form of a volatile market meant that one's economic situation could change drastically. Class status, therefore, had to be linked to something other than finances. Instead of material wealth alone, the middle class created an identity as a group that subscribed to certain sets of principles. One set of values revolved around a work ethic and a sense of personal responsibility. Industriousness, hard work, punctuality, and sobriety all figured prominently. Another set of values revolved around self-improvement, appropriate use of leisure time, and ideas about what it meant to be cultured. Education, therefore, was a major key to class status. The newly forming middle class defined itself against the urban poor, which it typed as "ignorant, careless," rife with "inebriation, squalid wretchedness, Sabbath profanation, and vices."[16] One way that the middle classes separated themselves from the "lower" classes and inculcated its own values was by education.[17]

Demonstrating that middle-class status was about more than economic condition, New England female factory workers established themselves as members of the middle class in the 1820s and 1830s. Tough economic times meant that the "factory girls" could not, at that moment, anyway, be domestic "ladies." But they could exhibit the morals and habits of their class. Visitors to factory cities commented on the workers dressing like ladies, wearing "scarves, and shawls, and green silk hoods," and carrying parasols. Visitors defined the workers against perceptions of what lower class women should look like; the "superior" factory workers were "not sallow, nor dirty, nor ragged, nor rough. They have about them no signs of . . . low culture . . . ."[18] Proponents of industrialization encouraged women to come work in the mills by representing factory workers as embodying middle-class values. When their factory shift ended, the workers played the pianos in their boarding house parlors, studied together, formed reading and self-improvement circles, and even published their original essays and poems in journals of their own making. In short, industrialists projected the image of workers living a middle-class life that included cultural activities and the pursuit of knowledge.

If factory owners capitalized on these middle-class values, proprietors of academies and seminaries certainly also vied for students on these grounds. Few schools were as blunt in their appeal to class biases as New Haven Young Ladies' Institute. Its catalogs from 1829 and 1830 stated that a benefit of a boarding school education, as opposed to private tutoring at home, was "well regulated intercourse with virtuous and intelligent associates." Boarding school life would prepare students for social life as adults. However, the proprietor asserted, "it is not to every kind of society that we would attach so great a value. . . . A school must be select," he went on, choosing only the "children of families, who are themselves refined, and who value refinement."[19]

Even without strong class assertions, many academies and seminaries trumpeted their adherence to and promotion of middle-class values of respectability, morality, industry, thrift, and order. Respectability was key to middle-class status, and referred to a person's good character and conduct; someone could be respectable in this sense even while being in material straits due to economic cycles.[20] Because respectability was so central to middle-class identity, some schools advertised that they would produce ladies who were "respected."[21] Even the students' visitors had to pass muster, as, for instance, South Carolina Female Institute would admit only "respectable female relatives" during visiting hours.[22] Alabama Female Institute promised to operate the government of the school based on appealing to students' "principles of obvious propriety and obligation, and to the better feelings of the soul" and to "discipline the social and moral feelings."[23] A speaker at a New Jersey seminary praised the "propriety" of education for women.[24] Students at Rhode Island's Arcade Ladies' Institute received an "appropriate" education that encouraged "the highest moral culture."[25] Promotional literature for Ballston Spa Female Seminary promised that an education there would "improve and refine both [a student's] social and moral nature."[26] Students at seminaries would learn to "improve their own style of manners and general deportment," and to value "personal neatness and cleanliness."[27]

Attention to manners coexisted with academic study. Lexington Female Academy, which taught such academic subjects as mathematics, Latin, and Greek, also promised that "Manners and Morals will form a prominent object of attention, throughout the whole course of studies."[28] Similarly, Roxbury Female School, which promoted "the very laborious and unfashionable task of *intense thinking*," also gave rewards for "lady-like deportment."[29] Brooklyn Collegiate Institute for Young Ladies taught "*elegance* and *propriety* of conversation and manners" along with Livy, Horace, logic, and intellectual philosophy.[30] A writer for Young Ladies' Association of the New-Hampton Female Seminary cautioned students not to slip into "inattention to personal appearance, uncouthness of manners, and a neglect of the elegant and graceful."[31] The proprietor of one seminary assured parents that "rudeness and dissipation of manners" were "controlled."[32] Another writer for the same organization despaired over the "intemperate and profane" teachers she encountered in Kentucky and Indiana.[33]

Female education, wrote the head of a ladies' seminary in New Hampshire, should promote "industry and economy."[34] Abigail Mott, author of an 1825 treatise on female education, also believed that women must be "virtuous, industrious, and economical."[35] Boston's Mount Vernon Female Seminary sought to instill "a conscientious sense of duty" in its students.[36] "Perfect punctuality, promptness, and order, is the standard presented to every pupil on entering the Seminary," wrote the principal of Le Roy Female Seminary, while Townsend Female Seminary promised to form "habits of industry, punctuality, good order, and strict economy in the use of time."[37] An advertisement for Greenfield High School for Young Ladies noted that its students came from homes where they had "been trained to habits of industry and propriety."[38]

Rhetoric emphasized values that set the middle class apart from the wealthy as well as from the poor. As discussed in an earlier chapter, some discourse ridiculed boarding schools that turned out "fops" and "dandies." Adherents of middle-class values disparaged the frivolity and wastefulness they associated with the wealthy. "All who have consumed much time in the frivolous pursuits of what is called fashionable life, must ultimately feel," said one writer in 1831, "that these things are both debasing to the character and unsufficing [*sic*] to the heart."[39] The middle class valued moderation, a mode of behavior that they thought separated them both from the licentiousness of the poor and the wasteful consumption of the wealthy. "Regulating the passions" was a value that educators claimed students would learn through higher education.[40]

Nor was this a phenomenon that pertained only to female education. Men's schools, too, created and reflected an assumption that educated men were gentlemen, but not in the aristocratic sense.[41] Promotional literature for a boys' high school in New York promised that the school would teach everything an "educated man ought" to know, because "[s]o much . . . of our respectability . . . depends upon a knowledge of the material world, and its inhabitants, and of the arts of civilized life." The moral and republican values that the principal promised to inculcate while preparing "lads" for either college or the "counting house" were "industry, prompt obedience, and exact discipline."[42] A commencement speaker at Philadelphia Academy admonished students to remember that "your future enjoyment of life, your usefulness and respectability in society, and the formation of your respective characters" depended on how they spent their time in their youth.[43]

Higher education in the 1820s and 1830s, then, was largely a class project. Far more marked than differences between men and women were differences of class and race. The white middle classes believed in education for a wide array of reasons. As concerned citizens, they saw education as a way to improve the morality of the republic. Religious devotees saw education as a way to spread their Christian beliefs, while people concerned with status saw it as a means of ensuring upward mobility. For many people, the love of learning was an end in itself. Largely unspoken as a goal, higher education also functioned as a delineator of social classes. For all these reasons, curricula and pedagogy did not need to be starkly differentiated for women and men. Indeed, for class consolidation, similarities between men and women of the same social class were as important as differences between the middle class and those outside their class.

The Power and Limitations of Intellectual Equality

Before the late 1840s, few women or men agitated for full political or legal rights for women, yet many asserted women's intellectual equality, their right to have a good education, and the freedom to put their education to good use. Historians often date the beginning of the women's rights movement to the Seneca Falls convention in 1848, and indeed that probably marked the first time that women and men gathered publicly to discuss the rights of women. But discourses on women's rights began long before then. As Catharine Sedgwick wrote in *Means and Ends*, an advice book for young women published in 1839, "There has been a subject much agitated of late years. . . . As you come into life and mingle in society, you will hear much talk of the '*rights of women*.' "[44] Discussion of women's intellectual abilities, and the opportunities they should have to exercise those abilities, played a prominent role in the emerging discourse on women's rights.

Thomas Gisborne and Charles Butler both opposed women's political equality. In *An Enquiry into the Duties of the Female Sex*, Thomas Gisborne took note of "some bold assertors [*sic*] of the rights of the weaker sex stigmatizing, in terms of indignant complaint, the monopolozing [*sic*] injustice of the other; . . . upholding the perfect equality of injured woman and usurping man in language so little guarded, as scarcely to permit the latter to consider the labours of the camp and of the senate as exclusively pertaining to himself." Gisborne wrote this attack on advocates of women's rights in 1796, demonstrating the existence of this debate by at least that date. Forty years later, Gisborne's language continued to resonate. Charles Butler lifted this passage verbatim (as he did much else of Gisborne's work) and included it in his book *An American Lady*, published in 1836.[45] Clearly neither Gisborne nor Butler had any patience for women who thought they could step in to men's roles.

Yet both of these opponents of women's social or political equality were strong champions of women's intellectual excellence. Gisborne urged women with "strong mental powers" to exert them.[46] Butler, for his part, roundly took to task women who "foolishly affect to be thought even more silly than they are," and who "exhibit no small satisfaction in ridiculing women of high intellectual endowments, while they exclaim, with much affected humility, . . . that 'they are thankful *they* are not geniuses.' " Butler wryly commented that, "though we are glad to hear gratitude expressed on any occasion, yet the want of sense is really no such great mercy to be thankful for."[47] To Gisborne and Butler, female intellectual abilities and attainments were laudable, yet were not a basis for political or social equality.

The realm of intellect was not the only arena in which some people urged forms of equality while stopping short of proclaiming full political and social equality. The evangelical fervor that swept much of the nation in the 1820s and 1830s included many advocates of female preaching, as well as advocates of female church members' right to vote on matters of church business. Historian Catherine Brekus documented sects that allowed women to vote in church, but also noted that "these sects never claimed that women should be allowed to vote in state [elections] as well." Further, ministers who allowed women to preach and teach still maintained a belief in female subordination to men. Some men and women agreed with the minister Ephraim Stinchfield who believed that "if a woman has a gift, she has as good a right to improve that gift as a man," but exercising that gift, even in the pulpit, did not change the essential structure of men as "the head in the affairs both of church and state, as well as in his family."[48]

The three most famous school founders, Emma Willard, Catharine Beecher, and Mary Lyon, held views that emphasized sex-based differences. For none of them, however, did their beliefs that there should be political and social distinctions between men and women lead to a belief in intellectual difference. Regardless of their religious views or their views on shaping the social or political role for women, Willard, Beecher, and Lyon clearly believed in women's high intellectual capacities and their right to have those capacities fully developed.

Emma Willard used ideologies regarding men's and women's different responsibilities in life to argue for improved education for women. Willard began teaching in a village school in Connecticut in 1804. Three years later she moved to Middlebury, Vermont, where she was struck by the differences between educational opportunities available to men in Middlebury College and what had been available to her. Here she first began formulating her desire to open "a grade of schools for women higher than any heretofore known."[49] As early as 1809 she wrote a plan for state support of women's education, which she proposed to the New York state legislature in 1818. In this plan, she argued that female education suffered from the vagaries of a market system that forced proprietors to teach only courses for which parents and students were willing to pay. State support of male education, on the other hand, allowed instructors to focus on academic excellence.[50] Willard, then, argued that men and women had equal rights to a good education and had an equal claim to state financing of that education. She based this argument on women's roles as mothers who "have the charge of the whole mass of individuals, who are to compose the succeeding generation," and who therefore needed a solid education to prepare for this work.[51]

Willard's professional life supported her belief in intellectual equality without overtly challenging middle-class women's social roles. The school that Willard established, Troy Female Seminary, "bore a remarkable resemblance to the contemporary men's colleges." The curriculum included geometry, algebra, botany, chemistry, modern languages, Latin, history, philosophy, geography, and literature.[52] She deliberately chose, however, not to call her institution a college so that it would "not create a jealousy that we mean to intrude upon the provence [sic] of man."[53] To reassure parents and the public generally that she did not intend for women to renounce their own station, students at Troy also learned embroidery and other forms of needlework.[54] Willard did not plan to disrupt the social order. She referred to men as "the only natural sovereign" of a family, and told students to "above all preserve feminine delicacy." She sat down during the public speeches she gave because she considered it unfeminine for women to address a crowd; seated, she was merely engaging in conversation.[55] One scholar of Willard stated that " 'subordination' was one of her favorite words."[56]

Yet Willard also engaged in a wide array of activities beyond motherhood and rarely subordinated herself to anyone. She not only founded and ran a high-caliber institution for women, and took it upon herself to propose legislation to the State of New York, but she also wrote a dozen highly successful texts. Her geography textbook was published in 14 printings between 1822 and 1847; her U.S. history text enjoyed 53 reprintings between 1828 and 1873, and was translated into German and Spanish; and her world history text had 24 printings between 1835 and 1882.[57] She ran for, and was elected to, the office of supervisor of schools in Kensington, Connecticut—an election in which women could not vote. In the 1840s, she traveled extensively (reportedly 8,000 miles just in 1846) promoting the common school reform movement.[58] Closer to home, Willard insisted that her fiancé sign a marriage settlement that denied him access to any of the substantial property she brought to the marriage, in addition to any money or property she might acquire during the marriage. In 1839, after less than a year of marriage, she claimed fraud and cruelty, and filed for divorce in a highly publicized case.[59] Thus, Willard embodied complicated notions of womanhood. She built a seminary largely on the argument that women needed education to prepare for their all-important work as mothers, and she promoted ideals of gentility and demure femininity. Yet she also argued that women and men were equally capable intellectually and needed the same type of education, even if they put it to different uses. She wrote and published numerous books and amassed a small fortune, from which she consciously and adroitly prevented her husband from benefiting.

Catharine Beecher, daughter of the renowned minister Lyman Beecher, widely publicized her views that women were morally superior to men, and that because of this moral superiority, their work as wives, mothers, and teachers was crucial for forming and sustaining the virtue of the nation. Beecher believed that women preserved their moral superiority in part by their removal from the temptations of the world. Confined to the domestic sphere, they could not be sullied by the iniquity of the outside world. In order to retain their moral superiority, therefore, Beecher opposed women working publicly for most reform movements, including women's rights and abolition. However, she actively promoted the expansion of women's roles and opportunities in the profession of teaching. As teachers, she urged women not only to leave their hearths for the schoolroom, but she also urged them to leave New England altogether and move to the West to help Christianize the nation. Her vision then was of women as people with a special moral calling, which they should put to use within the home and the schoolroom.[60]

At the same time, Beecher attempted to elevate women's domestic roles. She openly discussed the hard labor of housework and the essential contributions of women as the backbones of society. She also pushed for higher wages for female teachers, promoted teaching as a profession for women, and argued that women should be able to be financially self-sufficient through their labor. Furthermore, her statements regarding women's sphere being that of the domestic circle did not imply a base subservience of women to men. Instead, Beecher argued, the "true attitude to be assumed by woman, not only in the domestic but in all our social relations, is that of an intelligent, immortal being, whose interests and rights are *every way* equal in value to that of the other sex. . . . And every woman is to *claim* this, as the right which God has conferred upon her."[61] Beecher, then, believed that "woman's sphere" was in the home and the classroom, and that women should leave the realm of politics to men. At the same time that she emphasized women's morality, though, she also emphasized women's intelligence. A "True Woman," for Beecher, was not merely pious, and certainly was not abjectly servile. She was an intelligent person with a right to both education and a means to support herself.

Mary Lyon, founder of Mount Holyoke Female Seminary, refused to be hemmed in by notions of appropriate behavior for middle-class women. When she was criticized for riding from town to town in her fundraising efforts, she responded, "What do I that is wrong? I ride in the stage coach or cars without an escort. Other ladies do the same. . . . If there is no harm in doing these things once, what harm is there doing them twice, thrice, or a dozen times? My heart is sick, my soul is pained with this empty gentility, this genteel nothingness."[62] Unlike Beecher, Lyon had little interest in fitting in to higher status society.

Lyon believed that a God-ordained difference between the sexes required distinctions in some respects but not in others. She set out her position clearly in a private letter to Catharine Beecher in 1836. Beecher had begun advocating higher salaries for female teachers, urging teaching as a respectable way for women to gain social status and financial independence. Lyon disagreed. She was not interested in issues of women's equal right with men to attain financial self-sufficiency. "Let us cheerfully make all due concessions," she wrote to Beecher, "where God has designed a difference in the situation of the sexes, such as woman's retiring from public stations, being generally dependent on the other sex for pecuniary support, &c."[63] This was not particularly a comment on women's right to earn money. Lyon was not arguing about whether women had a right, relative to men's right, to earn an income. That question simply did not interest her. Lyon was deeply religious and believed that leading a Christian life and leading others to that life were the only matters of real import. Her disinterest in the salaries of teachers was not a result of her belief about female subordination, or her opposition to a movement to raise women's status. Instead, it reflected her lifelong renunciation of material comfort for *all* Christians, male or female. A supporter of the revival of the theology of Jonathan Edwards, Lyon believed in self-denial and in the "doctrine of disinterested benevolence."[64] Women's motivation to become teachers, she felt, should not be monetary but rather should be to fulfill the biblical injunction to love thy neighbor as thyself.

Lyon apparently had a narrow definition of the "public stations" from which women ought to retire, given that there were many public arenas in which she thought women belonged. She trained women to be both teachers and missionaries, both of which took women away from their firesides. Lyon herself traveled alone in her fund-raising ventures for Mount Holyoke Female Seminary, wrote articles promoting the seminary, and organized a coalition of men to support her venture. She was also more than willing to work behind the scenes when this seemed most politically expedient. In a private letter to Zilpah Grant about building public support for a new seminary, Lyon wrote, "It is desirable that the plans relating to the subject should not seem to originate with *us*, but with benevolent *gentlemen*."[65] She did not say that, as women, they had a moral duty to stay behind the scenes. Like many female activists, her position was strategic, not ideological.

Although Lyon was not interested in pressing for a culture in which women could take credit publicly for their ideas, or in which women took on explicitly political roles, she also did not believe that every aspect of men's and women's lives should be different. If women were to agitate for equal treatment in any regard, Lyon hoped it would be within the contexts of education and religion. She wrote, "O that we may plead constantly for her religious privileges for equal facilities for the improvement of her talents, and for the privilege of using all her talents in doing good!"[66] She spent her life trying to provide those "equal facilities" in the institutions in which she taught.

Willard, Beecher, and Lyon, then, held some similar and some different views of what realms of activity were appropriate for women and what were not. All seemed to fit an acceptable model of middle-class womanhood, especially by virtue of their piety. All three also modeled assertiveness and independence. Historiographical debate has centered on whether these three seminary founders promoted or challenged the ideology of domesticity and whether domesticity had feminist potential.[67] Instead of furthering that debate, the ubiquity and power of an ideology of domesticity must be interrogated. Various school founders, teachers, students, and parents had different purposes, intents, and views of womanhood. There may indeed have been a "cult of true womanhood" emphasizing piety, purity, obedience, and domesticity, but simultaneously there were people who believed that a "true" woman was strong, courageous, self-sufficient, rational, assertive, and, above all, intelligent.[68]

Many historians have provided evidence of these alternative visions of womanhood in the early nineteenth century. Frances Cogan documented a definition of womanhood that she called the ideology of "real womanhood." According to Cogan, those who believed in this ideology valued self-sufficiency, intelligence, and physical fitness and health, and their beliefs were reflected in popular magazines and novels.[69] Mary Kelley concluded that most of the female characters who appeared in over two hundred novels, stories, and essays in the antebellum era had the attributes of strength, activity, and independence.[70] Laura McCall, analyzing the premier women's magazine *Godey's Lady's Book*, found that of 234 characters in stories and essays, "*not one* possessed all four features [of piety, purity, submissiveness, and domesticity] that purportedly made up the 'true woman.'" McCall's analysis further showed that only 14 characters had 3 of the 4 determinants of "true women," and 85 had none at all.[71] When McCall analyzed 104 bestselling antebellum novels, she found that over 70 percent of the authors of these bestsellers, both male and female, created female characters who were celebrated for their independence and ingenuity.[72]

Examination of the discourse surrounding advanced education for women suggests that many seminaries promoted visions of womanhood that included attributes of independence, intelligence, and strength. As described in previous chapters, writers of prescriptive literature promoted self-sufficiency for women in both the late eighteenth and early nineteenth centuries. Further, rather than emphasizing "femininity," some people in evangelical circles praised women, especially those who worked as teachers, for being "manly." For instance, in a eulogy for educator Martha Whiting, her minister said she was "distinguished for manly and Christian independence. As a Christian, she endeavored to think and act for herself."[73] Catherine Brekus found that many evangelical groups "lauded women for their 'masculine' acts of courage as well as their 'feminine' nurture of their families."[74]

Promoters of advanced education for women often cited as a benefit of education that women would be confident enough to assert themselves and take action. For instance, in a treatise called *Observations on the Importance of Female Education*, Abigail Mott told the story of a quick-thinking woman who assertively corralled the labor of neighbors to save a house from fire. "That [women] should be taught timidity," Mott moralized, "or to consider it as an accomplishment to shrink from the appearance of danger, is a great error." The qualities she listed as important for women to have were prudence, fortitude, and presence of mind, along with virtue, industriousness, and the ability to economize.[75] Seminaries advertised that they would train students to "form a general character of self-reliance," to "depend on themselves," or to "cultivate a proper reliance on her own powers."[76] Private letters as well as published essays reinforce that many people shared these views. Marcus Stephens, a Southern plantation owner, wrote to his granddaughter who was in school in North Carolina that "women have not been treated with Justice by the male sex. . . . [H]er mind is equally vigorous as his . . . and I have known several instances in private life where women have exhibited full as much courage, prudence and strong sense as any man in like circumstances."[77] A vigorous mind, courage, prudence, and strong sense may not have been the defining characteristics of "true women," but they were attributes that many held in high esteem for women.

Whatever the intentions of educators or parents, the experiences some women had in the academies, seminaries, high schools, and colleges may have created a desire for social or political equality while simultaneously providing the foundation from which to articulate those sentiments. Advocates of higher education clearly promoted a view of men and women as intellectual equals. Furthermore, many educators inspired in students a sense of certitude in their abilities. Students remembered learning self-respect and a "stubborn faith in the capacity" of women at these institutions.[78] Men, too, encouraged women to have self-respect and confidence. A male speaker at a female seminary in 1840 told students that their minds were like steam ships: an educated woman, he said, "has within herself the power . . . of progressing and keeping her course despite . . . opposing winds and waves."[79] Another male speaker concluded an address to a women's literary society by exclaiming, "To sum up the whole in one concise rule, which, I hope, you will treasure up in your memory, and practise [sic] in your lives, I would say—*in your intellectual and moral being, 'call no man master'*."[80] In these ways, women were encouraged to take themselves and their ideas seriously.

The government structure in many institutions taught responsibility, and encouraged students to think for themselves rather than simply to obey rules. The structure consistently was one of "*self-government*" based on "the dictates of enlightened reason . . . [and not] mere submission to authority."[81] The "great object of all intellectual and moral culture," according to the trustees of Uxbridge Female Seminary, was "*entire self-government*."[82] School government must be "rational," not simply blind obedience, said a flyer for a female collegiate institute in western Pennsylvania.[83] The Roxbury Female School had its own constitution for students to adhere to, drawn up by a committee of students. The constitution included a system of appeals for students who felt they had been given a demerit unjustly. Clearly, Roxbury's students were actively involved in the school government.[84] Many institutions of higher education encouraged women to rationally assess the wisdom and fairness of rules, and some created a system in which women participated fully in the establishment of the regulations by which they would live. For some women, this situation no doubt contrasted bitterly with their relationship to state and federal government, and possibly their relationships with male members of their own families, as well.

Higher education also fostered a belief in the superior morality, not only of women, but also of the white, native-born, middle class. Not surprisingly, by the late 1840s, some educated women objected to men of "inferior" classes gaining political rights that were denied to white women. The 1848 "Declaration of Sentiments" criticized men for withholding from women "rights which are given to the most ignorant and degraded men—both native and foreigners."[85] In 1854, Elizabeth Cady

Stanton said in a speech, "We [white women] are moral, virtuous, and intelligent, and in all respects quite equal to the proud white man himself, and yet by your laws we are classed with idiots, lunatics, and negroes. . . . Can it be that you [in the New York state legislature] . . . would willingly build up an aristocracy that places the ignorant and vulgar above the educated and refined . . .?"[86] Although these attitudes existed by the late 1840s, because the antebellum woman's rights movement was so linked with abolition, this theme did not predominate until after the War.[87]

In addition to, unwittingly or not, nursing in women a dissatisfaction with their political and social status, higher education also gave students the tools to build a women's movement. At a minimum, higher education gave women confidence in their intellectual abilities. Many seminaries required students to write compositions, thereby honing their writing skills and their abilities to formulate coherent arguments. Many seminaries asked students to display their intellectual skills before large crowds at public examinations, and some students also read compositions at these proceedings. Hundreds of seminary students went on to organize institutions of their own.[88] In the process, they learned organizational skills, fund-raising, management, budgeting, and networking. Historians have suggested that leaders of the women's movement learned their speaking and organizational skills from their prior work in the abolition movement, temperance, and missionary work, and indeed many women's leaders had labored in these fields.[89] But many women's leaders, including Elizabeth Cady Stanton, Antoinette Brown Blackwell (the first female ordained minister in the United States), Lucy Stone, and Abby Kelley applied the skills and knowledge gained from their advanced educations in the creation of their roles as public activist women.[90] Their experiences in seminaries were as important in launching their activism for women's rights as their experience in abolitionism.

Feminized Men and Masculinized Women: Opposition to Women's Education

This study ends in 1840, the year by which the three most famous female seminaries were established. In the following decades, women's education continued to expand. The greatest growth in seminaries occurred in the 1850s, when hundreds of such schools sprang up across the country. This decade also saw an increase in the number of women's schools willing to take on the name "college" rather than "seminary," as well as an increase in the number of coeducational colleges. In the 1850s, there were more than 45 degree-granting colleges open to women.[91]

Advanced education for women did not face much overt opposition until the late nineteenth century. One of the opening volleys was lobbed by Dr. Edward Clarke. Clarke, a Harvard Medical School professor, published *Sex in Education* in 1873, in which he argued that by studying too much, females misdirected blood from their "female apparatus" to their brains, resulting in "neuralgia, uterine disease, hysteria, and other derangements of the nervous system," along with eventual sterility.[92] Tied in with the newly emerging eugenics movement and a racist fear of the decline of the "white race," Clarke and his allies attacked women's education.

In the 1870s, too, women's rights activists more vocally turned to the issue of suffrage than they had in the antebellum era. Activists who had referred to their movement as the "woman's rights movement" in the antebellum era began referring to it as the "woman suffrage movement" after the Civil War.[93] Activists more often and more vociferously linked suffrage and education in this later period. In the 1820s and 1830s, before any organized women's rights movements, women and men argued for women's right to education, and educators specifically argued for increased opportunities for education, without calling for political equality. In the late 1840s and 1850s, activists began to appeal to class and racial biases. After the war, women's rights advocates more often used the education already attained by middle- and upper-class white women as an argument in support of women's right to vote. Education demonstrated women's intellectual capacity for making clear and rational decisions, and also connoted the moral center that was deemed peculiarly female and middle class. The moral sensibilities and cultural refinement, along with mental discipline, that white middle-class women acquired through education qualified them for the franchise. One faction of the woman's suffrage movement resorted to racism, classism, and nativism, warning "American women of wealth, education, virtue and refinement" about "the lower orders of Chinese, Africans, Germans and Irish" who would make laws for them.[94] Education became a symbol of white middle-class women's claim to political and social rights. This push for women's rights came at a time when white middle-class men were experiencing challenges from many fronts.

By the late nineteenth century, some historians argue, masculinity was "in crisis." While other historians criticize the hyperbole, most do agree that there was intense interest in this period in redefining manhood.[95] Economic downturns and cycles of severe depressions in the 1870s, 1880s, and 1890s meant that a man's financial status was not as secure as in an earlier generation. A growth in low-level clerical work meant that men might be less likely to move up the ladder in business.[96] Self-employment, which had been a hallmark of middle-class manhood, dropped precipitously; the percentage of middle-class men who had been self-employed declined from 67 percent in 1870 to 37 percent by 1910.[97] Meanwhile, working-class men—against whom middle-class men defined themselves—were in open revolt. In the last two decades of the nineteenth century, there were nearly 37,000 strikes involving seven million workers, and many of the strikes were violent.[98] Furthermore, the political clout of immigrant groups grew in this period, as immigrants "wrested political control from middle-class men in one city after another."[99] According to historian Gail Bederman, the "power of manhood, as the middle class understood it, encompassed the power to wield civic authority, to control strife and unrest, and to shape the future of the nation"; each of these meanings of manhood was now being threatened.[100]

White middle-class men responded to these threats by redrawing the boundaries of manhood. Millions of men joined male-only organizations, either secret or civic societies, such as the Freemasons and Oddfellows, and they signed their sons up for groups dedicated to turning boys into men, such as the Boy Scouts.[101] Athletics flourished as men devoted themselves to bodybuilding, fighting, and football; also flourishing were vigorous outdoor adventure groups comprised of men seeking the "strenuous life" advocated by Theodore Roosevelt. Even as Christians, men needed to be "muscular" in their faith.[102] In short, the lines "separating masculinity and femininity had become more sharply drawn; less permeable and elastic" than they had been in the early republic and antebellum eras.[103] It was precisely at this moment that women were making some of their greatest strides toward formal education.

From the 1870s on, the number of women attending institutions for higher education increased dramatically. In 1870, approximately 11,000 women were enrolled in seminaries or colleges. By 1880, the number had jumped to 40,000, and in the next 20 years, it more than doubled, reaching 85,000 in 1900.[104] Not only that, but the majority of these female students enrolled in coeducational institutions, where some professors and male students viewed them as "the feminine equivalent to the yellow peril in education."[105] In this context, there was a backlash against higher education for women.

The hostility toward women in coeducational colleges took several forms. Some universities, such as the University of Chicago and the University of Wisconsin, established sex-segregated classes for men and women. Stanford banned women from some liberal arts courses, and instituted a ratio restriction of at least three males to every female student enrolled in the university. The University of California established a junior college system for women. Other institutions set up "coordinate colleges" for women on separate campuses. Examples of this system of keeping women out of "men's" schools include Barnard for women who otherwise might have attended Columbia, Radcliffe at Harvard, Pembroke at Brown, Sophie Newcomb at Tulane, Jackson at Tufts, and the Women's College at the University of Rochester.[106] Admission restrictions and quotas did not disappear entirely until after passage of Title IX of the Education Amendments of 1972, which outlawed gender discrimination in educational institutions that accepted federal money.

Outright hostility to women's education reached its peak around the turn of the twentieth century. Even then, few argued that women should not be educated. Rather, the most strident objections were to men and women being educated together, in coeducational settings. In the creation of coordinate colleges, for instance, the implication was that it was acceptable for women to get a college education, as long as they did not get it in the same classrooms as men. Opponents of coeducation feared either the feminization of men or the masculinization of women, or both. They feared either that women's lesser abilities would slow men's academic progress by holding entire classes back, or else that women's superior abilities would demoralize men who could not achieve the same level of academic success. They simultaneously feared that women would come to coeducational colleges simply to seek husbands, and that coeducation would take the "mystery" out of heterosexuality and result in fewer marriages altogether.[107]

People who became hostile to advanced education during this period did so for many reasons. Suffrage activists were more vocal, and perhaps presented more of a threat of social disruption than agitators for women's rights had in the 1820s and 1830s. Suffrage activists also made an explicit link between women's education and their right to vote. Because birth rates for educated women were lower than for those who had not pursued advanced study, some people worried that white women would refuse—or be unable—to propagate the "white race." Finally, the proportion of women attending schools of higher learning before the Civil War was very small, but increased dramatically at the end of the nineteenth century. Not only might such women not reproduce, but they also might take over the formerly male institutions.

None of this pertained to earlier periods, however. The late nineteenth century hostility was a backlash specific to that period, and not indicative of what had come before. There was less opposition to women's education in the early republic and antebellum era than there was at the end of the nineteenth century. In the absence of immediate threats to the gender order and drawing on popular ideas derived from the Enlightenment, the Revolution and evangelicalism, antebellum higher education for women matured in a relatively friendly atmosphere. This is not to say that these were golden years for women's education. Women certainly did not have broad access to higher education, and that sad fact may partially explain why women's education was not dramatically opposed. Women did not face stiff antagonism until they achieved a critical mass, comprising roughly one-third of the student body of coeducational institutions in the late nineteenth and early twentieth centuries.

The academies and seminaries of the early republic and antebellum era paved the way for the women's college movement, not by proving women's intellectual capabilities, but by institutionalizing women's *right* to education and setting in motion a commitment to access to equal education for women. Before the twentieth century, only a tiny proportion of either men or women earned college degrees (even today, only 25 percent of the population has a college degree). Advanced education in the early republic and antebellum era included only a very small number of women, most of whom were white and either middle or upper class. Within that small group, however, most educators held an assumption of intellectual equality. Educators and students alike held an ideal of learning as one of life's great pleasures, a pleasure that was of equal value to women and men alike.

Notes

1. Carl F. Kaestle, *Pillars of the Republic: Common Schools and American Society, 1780–1860,* (New York: Hill and Wang, 1983), 118; Thomas Dublin, ed., *Farm to Factory: Women's Letters, 1830–1860* (New York: Columbia University Press, 1981), 21–22.
2. Mary Lyon to Hannah White, February 26, 1834, in Marion Lansing, ed., *Mary Lyon Through Her Letters* (Boston: Books, Inc., 1937), 129.
3. *First Circular of the Oberlin Collegiate Institute, March 8, 1834* (Oberlin: n.p., 1834), 1.
4. For examples, see *Catalogue of the Officers and Students of Bradford Academy, Bradford, Massachusetts, October, 1839* (Haverhill, MA: E. H. Safford, 1839), 12; reports of the Young Ladies' Association of the New-Hampton Female Seminary; and the Ipswich Society for the Education of Females.
5. Nina Baym, "Women and the Republic: Emma Willard's Rhetoric of History," *American Quarterly* 43 (March 1991), 6–7.
6. Emma Willard, *An Address to the Public: Particularly to the Members of the Legislature of New York, Proposing a Plan for Improving Female Education* [1819] (Middlebury, VT: Middlebury College, 1918); Baym, "Women and the Republic," 7–8.
7. Ellen N. Lawson and Marlene Merrill, "The Antebellum 'Talented Thousandth': Black College Students at Oberlin Before the Civil War," *Journal of Negro Education* 52 (Spring 1983), 154.

8. Madelyn Holmes and Beverly J. Weiss, *Lives of Women Public Schoolteachers: Scenes from American Educational History* (New York and London: Garland Publishing Inc., 1995), 63, 192.

9. For one account of the incident, see Shirley J. Yee, *Black Women Abolitionists: A Study in Activism, 1828–1860* (Knoxville: University of Tennessee Press, 1992), 50–51. Also see Bonnie Handler, "Prudence Crandall and Her School for Young Ladies and Little Misses of Color," *Vitae Scholastica* 5 (Winter 1986), 199–210; Philip S. Foner and Josephine F. Pacheco, *Three Who Dared: Prudence Crandall, Margaret Douglass, Myrtilla Miner: Champions of Antebellum Black Education* (Westport, CT: Greenwood Press, 1984).

10. See *Freedom's Journal* (August 24, 1827); Sarah Mapps Douglass, "Address," *The Liberator* (July 21, 1832); "Constitution, Female Literary Association," *The Liberator* (December 3, 1831); Dorothy B. Porter, "The Organized Educational Activities of Negro Literary Societies, 1828–1846," *Journal of Negro Education* 5 (October 1936), 555–576; Julie Winch, " 'You Have Talents—Only Cultivate Them': Philadelphia's Black Female Literary Societies and the Abolitionist Crusade," in *The Abolitionist Sisterhood: Women's Political Culture in Antebellum America*, Jean Fagan Yellin and John C. Van Home, eds. (Ithaca, NY: Cornell University Press, 1994), 101–118; Yee, *Black Women Abolitionists*; James Oliver Horton and Lois E. Horton, *In Hope of Liberty: Culture, Community, and Protest among Northern Free Blacks, 1700–1860* (New York: Oxford University Press, 1997). Also see Mary Kelley, " 'A More Glorious Revolution': Women's Antebellum Reading Circles and the Pursuit of Public Influence," *New England Quarterly 76* (June 2003), 163–196.

11. Maria W. Stewart, "Religion and the Pure Principles of Morality, The Sure Foundation on Which We Must Build," reprinted in *Maria W. Stewart, America's First Black Woman Political Writer: Essays and Speeches*, Marilyn Richardson, ed. (Bloomington: Indiana University Press, 1987), 38.

12. Fanny Jackson Coppin, principal of the Institute for Colored Youth, went to the Rhode Island State Normal School in 1859, prior to attending Oberlin. Charlotte Forten Grimke, who became well known for the journals she kept while she taught recently freed people as part of the Port Royal Project in South Carolina, attended the Normal School at Salem (Massachusetts) in 1854. Sarah Smith, who married Henry Highland Garnet, attended several normal schools in the New York City area in the 1850s, although we do not know which ones. Myrtilla Miner's School for Colored Girls in Washington, DC opened in 1851, training women to be teachers. See Linda M. Perkins, "Heed Life's Demands: The Educational Philosophy of Fanny Jackson Coppin," *Journal of Negro Education* 51 (Summer 1982), 181; Janice Sumler-Edmond, "Charlotte L. Forten Grimke," in *Black Women in America: An Historical Encyclopedia*, Darlene Clark Hine et al., eds. (Bloomington: Indiana University Press, 1993), 505; "Sarah S. T. Garnet," in *Black Women in America*, 479; Dorothy Sterling, *We Are Your Sisters: Black Women in the Nineteenth Century* (New York and London: W. W. Norton & Co., 1984), 190.

13. For example, Arcade Ladies' Institute (Rhode Island), Brooklyn Collegiate Institute for Young Ladies, Greenfield High School for Young Ladies (Massachusetts), Newark Institute for Young Ladies, New Haven Young Ladies' Institute, Van Doren's Collegiate Institute for Young Ladies, Western Collegiate Institute for Young Ladies (Pennsylvania), the Young Ladies' High School (Boston), the Young Ladies' Seminary (Keene, New Hampshire). Most seminaries, however, used the terms "female" or "women."

14. Political scientist Pauline Schloesser describes the process of the construction of white women as a "racialized sex group that lost consciousness of itself as bounded by race and class." Pauline Schloesser, *The Fair Sex: White Women and Racial Patriarchy in the Early American Republic* (New York and London: New York University Press, 2002), 53.

15. Christine Stansell, *City of Women: Sex and Class in New York, 1789–1860* (Urbana and Chicago: University of Illinois Press, 1987), 68. For other work on class formation in this era, see Stuart M. Blumin. Robert Fogel, and Stephan Thernstrom, eds., *The Emergence of the Middle Class: Social Experience in the American City, 1760–1900* (New York: Cambridge University Press, 1989); Linda Young, *Middle Class Culture in the Nineteenth Century: America, Australia and Britain* (New York: Palgrave Macmillan, 2003); Jonathan Daniel Wells, *The Origins of the Southern Middle Class, 1800–1861* (Chapel Hill: The University of North Carolina Press, 2004); Heidi L. Nichols, *The Fashioning of Middle-Class America: Sartains Union Magazine of Literature and Art and Antebellum Culture* (New York: Peter Lang, 2004); T. Walter Herbert, *Dearest Beloved: The Hawthornes and the Making of the Middle-Class Family* (Berkeley: University of California Press, 1993); Burton S. Bledstein and Robert D. Johnston, eds., *The Middling Sorts: Explorations in the History of the American Middle Class* (New York and London: Routledge Press, 2000).

16. New York City Tract Society reports of 1837, 1838, and 1839, quoted in Stansell, *City of Women*, 63.

17. See Kaestle, *Pillars of the Republic*, especially ch. 6; William J. Reese, *The Origins of the American High School* (New Haven, CT and London: Yale University Press, 1995), especially ch. 3.

18. Michael Chevalier, *Society, Manners and Politics in the United States: Being a Series of Letters on North America* (Boston: Weeks, Jordan & Company, 1839), 137; Anthony Trollope, *North America* [1861]

(New York: St. Martin's, 1986), 249; Amal Amireh, *The Factory Girl and the Seamstress: Imagining Gender and Class in Nineteenth Century American Fiction* (New York and London: Garland, 2000), 7. Also see Gerda Lerner, "The Lady and the Mill Girl: Changes in the Status of Women in the Age of Jackson," *Midcontinent American Studies Journal* 10 (Winter 1969), 5–15.

19. *Catalogue of the Instructors and Pupils, in the New Haven Young Ladies' Institute, During Its First Year* (New Haven, CT: n.p., 1830), 7–8.

20. For discussions of respectability, see Richard L. Bushman, *The Refinement of America: Persons, Houses, Cities* (New York: Random House, 1992); Blumin et al., *The Emergence of the Middle Class*; Daniel A. Cohen, "The Respectability of Rebecca Reed: Genteel Womanhood and Sectarian Conflict in Antebellum America," *Journal of the Early Republic* 16 (Fall 1996), 419–461.

21. For examples, see *Newark Institute for Young Ladies* (Newark, NJ: n.p., 1826), 7.

22. Elias Marks, *Hints on Female Education, with an Outline of an Institution for the Education of Females, Termed the So. Ca. Female Institute; under the direction of Dr. Elias Marks* (Columbia, SC: David W. Sims, 1828), 42.

23. *Catalogue of the Alabama Female Institute, Tuscaloosa, Ala. For the Year Ending 14th July, 1836* (Tuscaloosa, AL: Marmaduke J. Slade, 1836), 11.

24. Baynard R. Hall, *An Address Delivered to the Young Ladies of the Spring-Villa Seminary, at Bordentown, N.J. At the Distribution of the Annual Medal and Premiums: on the Evening of the 29th of August, 1839* (Burlington NJ: Powell & George, 1839), 8.

25. *Arcade Ladies' Institute, Providence, R.I.* (Providence, RI: n.p., 1834?), 7.

26. *Ballston Spa Female Seminary* (Albany, NY: Packard & Van Benthuysen, 1824), 5.

27. *Catalogue of the Greenfield High School for Young Ladies, for the Year 1836–37* (Greenfield, MA: Phelps & Intersoll, 1837), 9; John W. Scott, *An Address on Female Education, Delivered at the Close of the Summer Session for 1840, of the Steubenville Female Seminary, in Presence of its Pupils and Patrons* (Steubenville, OH: n.p., 1840), 6.

28. *Prospectus of the Lexington Female Academy* (Lexington, KY: n.p., 1821), 2.

29. *Roxbury Female School* (Boston? n.p., 1830?), 11, 13; emphasis in original.

30. *Brooklyn Collegiate Institute for Young Ladies; Brooklyn Heights, Opposite the City of New York* (New York: n.p., 1830), 8; emphasis in original.

31. *Second Annual Report of the Young Ladies' Association of the New-Hampton Female Seminary, for the Promotion of Literature and Missions; with the Constitution, etc. 1839–40* (Boston: Freeman and Bolles, 1836), 29.

32. *Arcade Ladies' Institute*, 8.

33. *Third Annual Report of the Young Ladies' Association of the New-Hampton Female Seminary, for the Promotion of Literature and Missions; with the Constitution, etc. 1835–36* (Boston: John Putnam, 1837), 22.

34. *Catalogue of the Young Ladies' Seminary, in Keene, N.H. for the Year Ending October, 1832* (Keene, NH: J. & J. W. Prentiss, 1832), 13.

35. Abigail Mott, *Observations on the Importance of Female Education, and Maternal Instruction, with their Beneficial Influence on Society. By a Mother* (New York: Mahlon Day, 1825), 14.

36. *Mount Vernon Female Seminary* (Boston: n.p., 1836), 11.

37. *Catalogue and Circular of the LeRoy Female Seminary* (Rochester, NY: David Hoyt, 1840), 11; *Catalogue of the Officers and Students of the Townsend Female Seminary, for the Year Ending March, 1839* (Boston: John Putnam, 1839), 3.

38. *Catalogue of the Greenfield High School for Young Ladies, for the Year 1836–37*, 8.

39. Mrs. Townshend Stith, *Thoughts on Female Education* (Philadelphia: Clark & Raser, 1831), 13.

40. Almira Hart Lincoln Phelps, *The Female Student; Or, Lectures to Young Ladies on Female Education* (New York: Leavitt, Lord & Co., 1836), 29. See also James M. Garnett, *Lectures on Female Education, Comprising the First and Second Series of a Course Delivered to Mrs. Garnett's Pupils, At Elm-Wood, Essex County, Virginia. By James M. Garnett. To Which is Annexed, The Gossip's Manual* (Richmond, VA: Thomas W. White, 1825), 58–62.

41. Some coeducational academies specified that they were for "young gentlemen" and "young ladies." See, for instance, *Catalogue of the Officers, Teachers and Members of Day's Academy for Young Gentlemen, and Seminary for Young Ladies from March 6, 1834, to January 14, 1835* (Boston: Beals & Greene, 1835).

42. William J. Adams, *Circular* (New York: n.p., 1829), 2, 4, 5.

43. James Abercrombie, *A Charge Delivered, after a Public Examination, On Friday, July 27, 1804, to the Senior Class of the Philadelphia Academy, upon Their having Completed the Course of Study Prescribed by that Institution* (Philadelphia: H. Maxwell, 1804), 8.

44. Catharine M. Sedgwick, *Means and Ends, or Self-Training* (Boston: March, Capen, Lyon & Webb, 1839), 267; emphasis in original.

45. Thomas Gisborne, *An Enquiry into the Duties of the Female Sex* (London: T. Cadell and W. Davies, 1798), 19; Charles Butler, *The American Lady* (Philadelphia: Hogan & Thompson, 1836), 19. Butler plagiarized

so completely that even the pagination remained the same for much of the two books. However, in the passage quoted here, Butler added the hostile phrase "the supposed lords of creation" to his description of women's views of men.

46. Gisborne, *An Enquiry into the Duties of the Female Sex*, 107.

47. Butler, *The American Lady*, 185; emphasis in original.

48. Catherine A. Brekus, *Strangers & Pilgrims: Female Preaching in America, 1740–1845* (Chapel Hill: University of North Carolina Press, 1998), 136.

49. Henry Barnard, ed., *Memoirs of Teachers, Educators, and Promoters and Benefactors of Education, Literature, and Science. Reprinted from the American Journal of Education* (New York: F. C. Brownell, 1861), 133.

50. Nancy Beadie, "Emma Willard's Idea Put to the Test: The Consequences of State Support of Female Education in New York, 1819–67," *History of Education Quarterly 33* (Winter 1993), 543–545.

51. Quoted in Thomas Woody, *A History of Women's Education in the United States*, I (New York: The Science Press, 1929), 308.

52. For quotation, see Anne Firor Scott, "The Ever-Widening Circle: The Diffusion of Feminist Values from the Troy Female Seminary, 1822–1872," *History of Education Quarterly 19* (Spring 1979), 7. For curriculum, see ibid., 7; Lucy Forsyth Townsend, "Emma Willard: Eclipse or Reemergence?" *Journal of the Midwest History of Education Society 18* (1990), 289–290.

53. Quoted in Scott, "The Ever-Widening Circle," 22, fn. 8.

54. Townsend, "Emma Willard," 290.

55. Scott, "The Ever-Widening Circle," 11–12.

56. Baym, "Women and the Republic," 6.

57. Ibid., 5–6.

58. Scott, "The Ever-Widening Circle," 11–12.

59. Lucy F. Townsend and Barbara Wiley, "Divorce and Domestic Education: The Case of Emma Willard," Unpublished paper, 10, 19–20; Townsend, "Emma Willard," 285.

60. The best works on Beecher are Kathryn Kish Sklar, *Catharine Beecher: A Study in American Domesticity* (New Haven, CT: Yale University Press, 1973), and Jeanne Boydston, Mary Kelley, and Anne Margolis, *The Limits of Sisterhood: The Beecher Sisters on Women's Rights and Woman's Sphere* (Chapel Hill and London: University of North Carolina Press, 1988).

61. Catharine Beecher, *The True Remedy for the Wrongs of Women* (Boston: Phillips, Sampson, 1851), quoted in Boydston, Kelley, and Margolis, *The Limits of Sisterhood* 139; emphasis in original.

62. Quoted in Elizabeth Alden Green, *Mary Lyon and Mount Holyoke: Opening the Gates* (Hanover, NH: University Press of New England, 1979), 160.

63. Mary Lyon to Catharine Beecher, July 1, 1836, in *Mary Lyon Through Her Letters*, Marion Lansing, ed. (Boston: Books, Inc., 1937), 199.

64. Joseph A. Conforti, *Jonathan Edwards, Religious Tradition, and American Culture* (Chapel Hill and London: University of North Carolina Press, 1995).

65. Mary Lyon to Zilpah Grant, February 4, 1833, in *Mary Lyon Through Her Letters*, Lansing, ed., 110; emphasis in original.

66. Mary Lyon to Catharine Beecher, July 1, 1836, 199.

67. See chapter 1 in this book for a discussion of this.

68. The "cult of true womanhood" was first defined by Barbara Welter in her "The Cult of True Womanhood," *American Quarterly 18* (Summer 1966), 151–174.

69. Frances B. Cogan, *All-American Girl: The Ideal of Real Womanhood in Mid-Nineteenth-Century America* (Athens: University of Georgia Press, 1989).

70. Mary Kelley, "The Sentimentalists: Promise and Betrayal in the Home," *Signs 4* (Spring 1979); Mary Kelley, *Private Woman Public Stage: Literary Domesticity in Nineteenth-Century America* (New York: Oxford University Press, 1984).

71. Laura McCall, " 'The Reign of Brute Force Is Now Over': A Content Analysis of *Godey's Lady's Book, 1830–1860*," *Journal of the Early Republic 9* (Summer 1989), 235; emphasis in original.

72. Laura McCall, " 'Shall I Fetter Her Will?': Literary Americans Confront Feminine Submission, 1820–1860," *Journal of the Early Republic 21* (Spring 2001), 97–99.

73. Rev. H. Hutchins, quoted in Catharine Naomi Badger, *The Teacher's Last Lesson: A Memoir of Martha Whiting, Late of the Charlestown Female Seminary. Consisting Chiefly of Extracts from Her Journal, Interspersed with Reminiscences and Suggestive Reflections* (Boston: Gould and Lincoln, 1855), 263.

74. Brekus, *Strangers & Pilgrims*, 153.

75. Mott, *Observations on the Importance of Female Education*, 49, 13.

76. *General View of the Plan of Education Pursued at the Adams Female Academy* (Exeter, NH: Nathaniel S. Adams, printer, 1831), 5; *Catalogue of the Greenfield High School for Young Ladies, for the Year 1836–37*, 9; *Catalogue of the Officers and Members of the Utica Female Academy* (Utica, NY: Bennett, Backus, & Hawley, 1840), 17.

77. Marcus Cicero Stephens to Mary Ann Primrose, November 7, 1841, Stephens Papers, Southern Historical Collection.

78. See, e.g., Scott, "The Ever-Widening Circle," 8, 23, fn. 12.

79. Scott, *An Address on Female Education*, 10.

80. S. S. Stocking, *An Address, Delivered Before the Young Ladies' Literary Society of the Wesleyan Academy, June 8, 1836* (Boston: David H. Ela, 1836), 22; emphasis in original.

81. *A Catalogue of the Abbot Female Seminary, Andover, Mass* (Andover, MA: Gould, Newman and Saxton, 1840), 11; emphasis in original; *Catalogue of the Alabama Female Institute, Tuscaloosa Ala. For the Year Ending 14th July, 1836*, 11. For more examples of self-government in female seminaries, see *Greenfield High School for Young Ladies* (Greenfield, MA: n.p., 1840), I. "Our authority is sustained by reason": *Outline and Catalogue of the Steubenville Female Seminary for the Year Ending in October, 1840* (Steubenville, OH: n.p., 1840), 6.

82. *Catalogue of the Trustees, Instructors and Pupils in the Uxbridge Female Seminary, at Uxbridge, Mass* (Providence, RI: H. H. Brown, 1838), 9.

83. *Western Collegiate Institute* (Pittsburgh: n.p., 1837), 1.

84. *Roxbury Female School*, 13.

85. "Declaration of Sentiments," reprinted in *Women's America: Refocusing the Past*, 2nd ed., Linda K. Kerber and Jane DeHart-Mathews, eds. (New York and Oxford: Oxford University Press, 1987), 472.

86. Elizabeth Cady Stanton, "Address to the Legislature of New York on Women's Rights," February 14, 1854, in *The Elizabeth Cady Stanton-Susan B. Anthony Reader: Correspondence, Writings, Speeches*, Ellen Carol DuBois, ed. (Boston: Northeastern University Press, 1992), 45.

87. Some activists had already pitted "women's" issues (i.e., white middle-class women) against the issue of abolition as early as 1840. Abby Kelley and Frederick Douglass, for instance, were on opposing sides of this issue that effectively caused the "first grand division" in the antislavery movement. See Dorothy Sterling, *Ahead of Her Time: Abby Kelley and the Politics of Antislavery* (New York and London: W. W. Norton & Co., 1991), ch. 14. However, the issue became much more heated and divisive after the Civil War. There are many accounts of the racism within the women's rights campaigns of the post-Civil War era. See Ellen Carol DuBois, *Feminism and Suffrage: The Emergence of an Independent Women's Movement in America, 1848–1869* (Ithaca, NY and London: Cornell University Press, 1978); Andrea Moore Kerr, *Lucy Stone: Speaking Out for Equality* (New Brunswick, NJ: Rutgers University Press, 1992), ch. 8.

88. See Reports from Young Ladies' Association of the New-Hampton Female Seminary, the Ipswich Society for the Education of Females, and Scott, "The Ever-Widening Circle," 10–12, for examples.

89. For instance, Sara Evans writes, "Most important, however, the antislavery movement provided women with both an ideological and a practical training ground in political activism for democratic and egalitarian change." Sara M. Evans, *Born for Liberty: A History of Women in America* (New York: The Free Press, 1989), 80–81.

90. Stanton attended Troy Female Seminary, Lucy Stone and Antoinette Brown Blackwell attended Oberlin College, Abby Kelley attended the New England Friends Boarding School, and Susan B. Anthony attended a seminary in New York.

91. Woody, *A History of Women's Education*, 1,395; Barbara Miller Solomon, *In the Company of Educated Women: A History of Women and Higher Education in America* (New Haven, CT and London: Yale University Press, 1985), 23–24; Roger Geiger, "The Superior Education of Women," Unpublished section from "The Transformation of the Colleges," Presented at the 1995 meeting of the History of Education Society, 61.

92. Edward H. Clarke, *Sex in Education; Or, a Fair Chance for the Girls* (Boston: J. R. Osgood, 1873), quoted in Solomon, *In the Company of Educated Women*, 56.

93. Evans, *Born for Liberty*, 122.

94. Elizabeth Cady Stanton, "The Sixteenth Amendment," *Revolution* (April 29, 1869), 264–265. For discussion of this, see DuBois, *Feminism and Suffrage*.

95. Joe L. Dubbert, "Progressivism and the Masculinity Crisis," in *The American Man*, Elizabeth H. Pleck and Joseph H. Pleck, eds. (Englewood Cliffs, NJ: Prentice-Hall, 1980), 303–320; John Higham, ed., "The Reorientation of American Culture in the 1890s," *Writing American History: Essays on Modern Scholarship* (Bloomington: Indiana University Press, 1978), 73–102; Michael S. Kimmel, "The Contemporary 'Crisis' of Masculinity in Historical Perspective," in *The Making of Masculinities*, Harry Brod, ed. (Boston: Allen &

Unwin, 1987), 121–154; James R. McGovern, "David Graham Phillips and the Virility Impulse of the Progressives," *New England Quarterly* 39 (September 1966): 334–355.

96. Blumin et al., *The Emergence of the Middle Class*, 290–295.

97. Peter G. Filene, *Him/Her/Self: Sex Roles in Modern America* (Baltimore: Johns Hopkins University Press, 1986), 73.

98. Alan Trachtenberg, *The Incorporation of America: Culture and Politics in the Gilded Age* (New York: Hill and Wang, 1982), 80.

99. Gail Bederman, *Manliness & Civilization: A Cultural History of Gender and Race in the United States, 1880–1917* (Chicago and London: The University of Chicago Press, 1995), 13.

100. Bederman, *Manliness & Civilization*, 14.

101. Mark C. Carnes, *Secret Ritual and Manhood in Victorian America* (New Haven, CT: Yale University Press, 1989); Jeffrey P. Hantover, "The Boy Scouts and the Validation of Masculinity," in *The American Man*, Elizabeth H. Pleck and Joseph H. Pleck, eds. (Englewood Cliffs, NJ: Prentice-Hall, 1980), 285–302.

102. Harvey Green, *Fit for America: Health, Fitness, Sport, and American Society* (Baltimore: Johns Hopkins University Press, 1986), 182–215; E. Anthony Rotundo, *American Manhood: Transformations in Masculinity from the Revolution to the Modern Era* (New York: Basic Books, 1993), 231–239, 251.

103. McCall, "Shall I Fetter Her Will?," 112.

104. U.S. Bureau of the Census statistics, quoted in Solomon, *In the Company of Educated Women*, 63.

105. Solomon, *In the Company of Educated Women*, 60.

106. Solomon, *In the Company of Educated Women*, ch. 4; Lynn D. Gordon, *Gender and Higher Education in the Progressive Era* (New Haven, CT and London: Yale University Press, 1990), ch. 1.

107. Solomon, *In the Company of Educated Women*, 60–61.

THE POLITICAL CULTURE OF AMERICAN'S ANTEBELLUM COLLEGES

PAUL H. MATTINGLY

In spite of local and denominational variations, the American college experienced historical commonalties and a conceptual cohesion before the Civil War. The antebellum college achieved its institutional character by drawing from both evangelical and political cultures of the period but also by resisting and recreating features of both traditions into a newly idealized, civic education. This essay assesses the distinctive and problematic context within which both new-founded and older colleges operated; it also put familiar episodes like the Dartmouth College case and the Yale Report in a newly critical light.

I

Schooling in early nineteenth-century America, especially beyond the district or common school, assumed an increasingly important role in both the moral and the commercial life of the nation.[1] Much historical scholarship has approached the American college, in particular, with twentieth-century assumptions of its importance, its place in a calibrated educational ladder, and its necessity in the training of social leaders and professionals. However, the centrality of the college in the American republic was the product of vigorous nineteenth-century competitions, which often shared little of the meaning and conceptions that later generations would attribute to college instruction. During the antebellum period, the service of the largely denominational college to the republic was not obvious. Had not the majority of Americans achieved literacy with minimal or no formal schooling?[2] What service could any advanced instruction provide when work and experience offered basic learning skills to every citizen? For the American college to become a pivotal institution in the American republic, its spokesmen had to avoid both religious and political indoctrination, had to engage and retool local traditions without indulging parochialism, had to convince a skeptical public that unencumbered study was a necessity rather than a privilege. How did the American college shift from an uncertain commodity in the American marketplace to a constructive ingredient of republican civic virtue?

The nineteenth-century college became a pivotal device in a major cultural shift of this period by yoking together two disparate traditions. First, its spokesmen reformulated a highly competitive, evangelical tradition into a consciously "educational" ideology that transcended denominational boundaries. Second, commentators with Whiggish political values included the college into their ideological matrix. These values favored hierarchical organizations, legalistic compromise, and a gradual process of constitutional change. In spite of diverse regional variations, the antebellum college drew from both of these traditions to promote an idealized educated citizen, inspired by national republican values yet rooted in locally resonant priorities. The new tradition was thought to be distinctively voluntary, adaptive yet disciplined, factually informed yet inquiring, socially engaged yet undemogogic.[3] The new collegiate ideal both arose out of and promoted this American voluntary tradition, while resisting any sharp generic or dogmatic inscriptions about antebellum colleges or college life.

To explore this transition, this essay will examine several episodes involving "collegiate values" in the antebellum period. First, the essay establishes a broad economic context within which any college, denominational or otherwise, necessarily had to compete. Next, the peculiar pressures of the antebellum period, I am assuming, arose more clearly in the cases of newly founded institutions rather than those with explicit denominational inheritances. Hence the case of Girard College and its novel rationale of civic production. How the prevalent denominational colleges dealt with such an alternative can be explored by examining resonant episodes of the period but from a newly critical stance. In particular, the often-studied Dartmouth College case (1816-19) and the equally familiar Yale Report (1828) played an important role in demonstrating how the denominational college began its own reconstruction and accommodation of new secular arguments about advanced instruction. Out of an intensive economic and ideological competition a transformed sense of the American college and its republican commitments arose by mid-century.[4]

II

Alongside official addresses of the nation's leadership and recent speeches of the U.S. Congress, the *National Intelligencer*, which became Washington D.C.'s self-proclaimed newspaper of record, also filled its pages with random advertisements of equal importance to the antebellum national readership: steamship schedules and rates; rewards for runaway slaves; legal notices of land transfers and equity actions; obituaries; special cargoes (plows, fodder, etc); lottery announcements; and of course, especially in August and September before classes began, school promotions—seminaries, medical departments, academics, tutorials, and colleges. Georgetown College in the nation's capital, for example, boasted its "university" status, under boldface headings, like "Georgetown College" with no sense of incongruity. Roman Catholic Georgetown underscored its commercial pitch by trumpeting its 1815 charter from the U.S. Congress and its receptivity to non-Catholic students. By the 1830s, the American college had become an attractive, though imprecise, commercial value, aggressively competing for a special discretionary priority among American consumers.[5] The antebellum "college" in America had not yet achieved a distinctive generic meaning and consequently was regularly overextended by multiple, even contradictory, claims.

The founding rationale of Girard College illuminates one of the original strands of this emerging collegiate identity. The Girard case demonstrates not only the problematic meaning of "college" itself but also the conceptual pressures on such institutions to broaden their appeal beyond a traditional, sectarian service.[6] On July 4, 1833, the *National Intelligencer* published Nicholas Biddle's address at the dedication of Girard College in Philadelphia. Biddle assured his listeners that out of the beneficence of Stephen Girard, self-described Philadelphia "Merchant and Mariner," would rise, "the spirit which may more influence the destiny of ourselves and our children than all else the world now contains. . . . It is that knowledge, which trampling down in its progress the dominion of brutal force and giving to intellect its just ascendancy, has at length become the master power of the world." Biddle associated the multiplying example of Girard's philanthropy and moral discipline with the "safety" of the republic and "the public spirit of community at once enlightened and generous."[7] The inaugural speech was nationally propitious not only for its timing and association with the origins of the American Republic but also for other associations made explicit by Biddle's address. The force of Biddle's view articulated values which would embed themselves in the ubiquitous voluntary associations of the period and which would dramatically affect all institutions shaped by American Whig culture, most especially colleges.[8]

Several features of Girard's benevolence made it both extraordinary and problematic for a democratic republic. The sheer amount of money involved—two million dollars—provided in a stroke an endowment that exceeded the sum of all other American colleges.[9] The beneficence projected an image of cultural and architectural influence commensurate with values of Greek culture and polity. The school would be spatially as well as fiscally autonomous. All activities of schooling and residence were contained, according to Girard's will, within a single institution. If further guarantees of endurance were required, Nicholas Biddle, the chairman of the college's Board of Trustees, served as the President of the Bank of the United States. Biddle's stewardship of the new college would have also suggested to the Bank's Jacksonian critics an expansion of Whig elitism in the nation's commerce and republican values.[10] At issue quickly was the basic public benefit to the republic of a new institution—a "college"—that did not directly serve all of the people. Its endowment and implicit durability as well as its sponsoring elite made Girard's school unique among American institutions at that time.[11]

Least remarkable at the time—but surprising from a twentieth century viewpoint—was its appropriation of the term, "college," for the instruction of orphans of district school age. Indeed, Girard's will had specified poor white male orphans between the ages of six and ten. Girard had insisted that the school was neither to be an almshouse nor a charity school but a "college." It would provide the various branches of sound education in reading, writing, grammar, arithmetic, geography, navigation, surveying, practical mathematics, astronomy, natural, chemical, and experimental philosophy, and the French and Spanish languages. The founder's only caveats opposed uniform dress and excessive stress on Greek and Latin. In his will Girard also incorporated the stipulation that "no ecclesiastic, missionary or minister of any sect whatsoever" should have any capacity in his institution.[12] The result would embrace "everything necessary to form a well-educated man," producing in the process an institution which will be "the civil West Point of the country."[13]

Significantly, Biddle professed an admiration, not for Girard's administrative specifications, but for his enlarged spirit of benevolent, public stewardship, the centerpiece of antebellum Whig republicanism.[14] This notion of stewardship, in particular defined both the conceptual breadth of collegiate expectation and the elasticity of the word, "college," for the antebellum period. For Girard the term contained no implications for subject sorting or institutional rank; it connoted nothing of the historic, British meanings of college, namely, a collection of youthful students studying beyond basic levels or even a residence hall where such students lived: it implied no official or legal degree-granting authority. Its practical aims were to have fatherless youth trained for employment by ages fourteen to eighteen. However, its profound ("irradiating") social impact followed from the example-setting voluntarism of Girard and the dynamic consequences of a morally informed educational purpose.[15] This dynamic of voluntarism yoked to an expansive Whig republicanism, not some generic blueprint of a "college," formed the common ground that Girard College shared with virtually all other social and cultural institutions of the antebellum period. Whig republican institutions, like most antebellum colleges, stressed the benevolent esprit—they called it "character"—which ideally softened the sharp, self-interested edges of elitism and selectivity associated with new antebellum institutions.[16]

This voluntary standard, so rooted in denominational didactics and practice, nevertheless had shed much of its pointedly denominational aspects during the antebellum period. Still, it retained a secularized missionary fervor, a didactic "non-denominational" message, an espoused preference for the indirect persuasion of example, and a substitution of civic benevolence for sectarian piety. The residuary inheritance of antebellum voluntarism thus retained older features of religious evangelism in its basic structure and in its increasingly widespread educational and political ventures, while contending with other more practical and mundane concerns.[17] However adamant Girard's stipulation against direct denominational proselytizing, his effort to internalize the moral compass of civic behavior was but a variant on an older process of evangelical conversion. His Girard College demonstrated the degree to which a diluted evangelism had become a part of America's cultural fabric by the 1830s. The novelty of antebellum voluntarism like Girard's lay with the effort to disseminate a new republican civility through schools rather than by the narrow didacticism of the pulpit. The historic achievement of this new voluntarism was the substitution of a "non-denominational" moral code for an older dogmatic sectarianism and its adoption even by consciously denominational colleges.

Girard College represented a bold form of this new Whig republicanism by proposing a public service unallied with any denomination. Since most education and especially antebellum colleges had been driven by a denominational elan, how representative was Girard's school? It is essential to recognize the ongoing power of America's evangelical tradition here without becoming overly distracted by its denominational roots. Each denomination and each denominational college confronted the incontestable fact of vigorous and often wasteful competition with each other in the antebellum period. Several denominations made a post-Revolutionary effort to broaden the aegis of the Christian religion to the new Republic as a whole.[18] The peculiar antebellum organizations that followed—"the Voluntary System"—even when they resulted in a less broad denominational consciousness, paralleled non-sectarian outreaches like Girard's. Only in the most narrow sense was this transformation of all antebellum schooling a secularization of religious indoctrination. Rather, it represented a reworking of older evangelical practices into a distinctively republican institutional tradition, epitomized by the ubiquitous voluntary organizations of the antebellum period. Both denominational and non-denominational colleges evinced a new (overstated) voluntarism like Girard's that would appear to accommodate the competitive spirit of America's antebellum republic.

The antebellum "college" encompassed schools instructing youth from ages anywhere between six and thirty. Its curricular offerings varied substantively, from the sacred to the profane, depending on region and local priorities. Many were consciously and aggressively denominational, while others, like both Girard College and the University of Virginia, explicitly distanced themselves from religious association. Nearly all had fiscal problems that sometimes compelled them to close their doors, often reopening, sometimes under new names. These mercurial economics forced more than one, like Transylvania University in Kentucky, to be transferred successively to competing Protestant denominations or, in effect, to suffer the tenuousness of many American businesses.[19] Between 1800 and 1860 their student bodies fluctuated from several dozen to several hundred. Few schools could afford to be so selective that they achieved associations with definable elites; most adopted ringing statements of standards and purpose, then sought to fill their classrooms with students of widely different preparations.[20]

III

Historians have often overcompensated for this apparent disorder by latching on to a few dramatic figures and special episodes to impose a heroically thematic but decontextualized order to American collegiate history. The historical variety of collegiate "models" has promoted an entire literature to characterize the pre-Civil War patterns as "disordered."[21] Both legal and denominational history have given most scholars of the American college an overly precise, that is, oversimplified, categorical framework for the antebellum period. The most powerful legal definition of the early republican college in America has emanated from the Supreme Court decision known as the Dartmouth College Case (1819), which clarified the distinction between a "public" and a "private" corporation. However, like Girard's legacy, the court decision said more about the problematic transition of an eighteenth-century denominational college into its nineteenth-century mode of non-denominational voluntarism than it did a new "private" tradition of collegiate operation.

The Dartmouth College case arose in 1816 when William Plumer, the New Hampshire governor and political associate of Thomas Jefferson, supported a revision of Dartmouth's collegiate charter that had been awarded by the British king via his colonial assembly in 1769. The college president, John Wheelock, son of the school's founder, had clashed with his trustees in several staff appointments and curricular changes. The trustees' opposition implicitly raised questions about how responsive and adaptable a college should be to the public. Direct accountability to politically elected leaders struck both the Governor and Dartmouth's president as particularly desirable and civic in America's post-revolutionary period. But the royal charter, the college's trustees retorted, represented a special brand of public autonomy, attuned to but not whiplashed by the political whims of party and faction. From the trustees' viewpoint, a college was a privately-held charity, influential in its community but not directly answerable to its leadership.

In actual fact, the antebellum fears of any institution—educational, commercial, or otherwise—becoming distinctly "private," that is, a self-perpetuating monopoly, raised the specter of monarchical exploitation that the Revolution was thought to have redressed. Jefferson himself had taken great pains to specify how "public" universities in a democracy must remain subordinate and politically accountable to the elected representatives of the people.[22] Similarly concerned, the New Hampshire legislature passed a formal revision of the colonial charter giving the Governor special powers to appoint trustee and overseers for the college, which was thus construed as a state and civic rather than an eleemosynary institution. The new law also defined the school as a university and gave it legal authority over the management of Dartmouth's property holdings and resources. For a time, with the trustees resisting, Dartmouth College and Dartmouth University operated side by side.

The Dartmouth trustees, who were Congregationalist in religion and Federalist in politics, appealed to the New Hampshire Supreme Court, which upheld the new charter's revision. This new decision considered Dartmouth the only college in the state and hence a state institution. The trustees appealed the state decision to the U.S. Supreme Court to recover their property and hired the eminent Dartmouth alumnus and future Whig, Daniel Webster, to defend them. The Supreme Court's decision reversed the state legislative and judicial judgement; it upheld the trustees and the original colonial charter on the grounds that "no state shall pass any . . . law impairing the obligation of contracts." By this precedent, the chartered American college became a private, charitable corporation in a decidedly proto-Whig political tradition, and corporate contracts were held inviolate from direct state or public interference, a distancing from Jeffersonian institutional assumptions.[23] The ownership of the college was firmly set with the trustees. The Supreme Court's decision also presaged a new relationship between colleges and the state. However, the Court decision left the "public" responsibility of such "private" institutions an unsettled issue.

The ultimate importance of the Dartmouth College case rested with later interpretations of a legal charter for American business. When promulgated, the Dartmouth case only affected voluntarism in so far as it formalized organizational options implicit within this tradition. The case did not, as Frederick Rudolph has suggested, release a lengthy string of autonomous colleges, while subordinating state power to communal rights and putting the college beyond public passions.[24] A few subsequent colleges, most with eighteenth-century roots (e.g. Harvard, Union College, University of Maryland, and Bowdoin College), explicitly used the Dartmouth precedent in analogous struggles, but many newer nineteenth-century college founders evinced little knowledge or explicit encouragement from the Dartmouth legal precedent.[25] Colin Burke has persuasively argued that some states continued to restrict the role and place of private colleges and charitable institutions, and, on their part, private colleges like Bowdoin, University of Pennsylvania, Amherst, Williams, and Columbia, continued to petition states for funds though with declining success.[26] More important, the case had little import for the Southern states and some Northern ones, like New York, which sustained restrictive statutes against private endowments like colleges. New England's distinctive cultural and economic dynamics, by contrast, gave rise to private corporations and private colleges, creating a regional hub of Boston. That city thus integrated new fiscal and cultural powers, which advanced learning aggressively and would put Boston in a singularly advantageous position at the end of the nineteenth-century.[27]

In essence, the Dartmouth College case gave legal expression to a powerful intellectual tension concerning organizational voluntarism, most pronounced in New England and its Midwestern satellites with Congregational inheritances.[28] The competitions of early nineteenth-century life in America made individual initiatives increasingly problematic, particularly in so far as sharp practices of individuals or single-interested groups drove fissures into the neighborly well-being of a cohesive community. Embedded in both political oratory and evangelical revivalism, antebellum voluntarism channeled itself into the operations of the American college and necessitated tangible evidence that such institutions benefited the public. From the collegiate viewpoint, the crucial instrument of power had to be either internal, variously called moral or pietistic in the nineteenth century, or some external, paternalist monitor, like the state or its representatives.[29] The Dartmouth College case did not reduce the elasticity of the college as a voluntary organization but rather made social outreach a promotional feature of all the actual colleges founded after the Dartmouth College case, including Girard's model of civic stewardship.[30]

The immediate, historic significance of the Dartmouth College case was not its distinction between public versus private colleges, but rather the ongoing legitimation of contentious claims that affected all antebellum institutions. The court actually engineered a translation of the Dartmouth trustees' Congregational tradition into Daniel Webster's nascent Whig values. It also permitted Webster's version to triumph over elected state politicians. But even more, the Dartmouth College case sustained the problematic nature of the college by publicizing two legitimate but competing "public" traditions: the college as a charitable creation and the college as a politically-attuned service. The court decision did little to settle how colleges could guarantee a different brand of leadership while avoiding the divisive partisanship of denominations and political factions. The decision did not formalize Whig biases on behalf of property owners and a weakened governing executive, so much as it continued the conundrum about the kind of education that a republic needed. Exactly how did college training benefit a republic and its leaders?

Subsequently, state governments would assume a more detached role in the face of citizens' legitimate organizational ventures, but these new processes emerged slowly, largely out of economic considerations, not with the thunderclap of a courtroom decision. States willingly chartered new schools and colleges but regularly resisted any responsibility for financial support. As historian John Whitehead has noted, Dartmouth's trustees requested that the state legislature pay their legal costs, after supposedly winning a clear distinction between the public and private sectors. Indeed, Dartmouth like many other financially strapped "private" colleges continued to appeal for state support throughout the antebellum period, sometimes offering state representation on the trustee board in exchange.[31] Few legal scholars relied on the public/private distinction in subsequent pre-Civil War arguments, precisely because the intent of those arguments was to distinguish two brands of "public" organization: one charitable, dominated by citizens' voluntary associations and the other civil, dominated by state organization, like Jefferson's conception of a state university.[32] Neither connoted "private" in any twentieth-century sense.

IV

Not only did antebellum colleges resist easy categorization as "public" or "private," but most emphatically resisted identification as local or sectarian (while cultivating both and becoming denominationally affiliated). For instance, Wesleyan University's charter prohibited restrictions against any other denomination in spite of its explicitly Methodist identity. Initially, various denominations were represented on any number of trustee boards and in their student populations. Similarly, Georgetown University, the oldest Roman Catholic college in the United States (f. 1789), admitted into their earliest classes all denominations and advertised the point boastfully through the 1830s. For the first three decades of the nineteenth century, one-quarter to one-third of Georgetown's student body were non-Catholic. While Wesleyan and Georgetown relied substantively in their early years on local benefactors, both schools worked from the outset to reach interdenominational audiences at regional, national and even international levels.[33]

In spite of varied efforts to project a distinctive autonomy, antebellum colleges did not become isolated communities. This period publicized images of institutions with fences and walls separating town and gown, residential dorms, refectories and collegiate chapels on a definable "campus." Despite this physical autonomy, a college often connected itself organizationally with broader, translocal, denominational networks. Early on, it became clear that local resources were insufficient to sustain not only colleges but also many other educational levels beyond the common school: academies, female seminaries, normal schools, and literary institutes.[34] Financial stability necessitated continual outreach, and the success of such enterprises often resulted in spawning more intensive competition. Wesleyan, for example, cultivated Methodist donors in Boston until one of these benefactors decided to found Boston University in 1869. This Boston competitor siphoned off Wesleyan's New England donations and forced it to shift its constituency to New York City friends and alumni.[35] Similarly, Randolph-Macon College in Virginia originally anticipated wide support from several Methodist conferences, but the competition from Pennsylvania's Dickinson College (f. 1783) eroded its earlier support from the Baltimore Conference. Further, the creation of Emory (f. 1836) in Georgia, narrowed Randolph-Macon's geographical base to central and southern Virginia and parts of North Carolina.[36] Changes in the network stabilized for attracting funds and students often resulted in a geographical constriction of the meaning of "college community."

The tension between grand vision and local realities during the antebellum period became clearly expressed in an oil portrait of New York University, founded in 1831 in the heart of the nation's emergent commercial metropolis. One of the first members of the faculty, artist/inventor Samuel F. B. Morse, depicted his newborn University as an ancient Gothic oasis in an idyllic Tuscan landscape.

The overstated historic roots of his conception projected the image of autonomy, stability, and safety in a natural countryside that fit easily into many national or cultural canons. The connotations of composure and isolated self-sufficiency required standards of conception and technique that transcended not only local but also American boundaries. And in spite of ambitious national and international promotions, within a few short years New York University was scrambling for its financial life and sharing the mercurial history of its antebellum collegiate counterparts.[37]

The history of most antebellum colleges reflected regular fluctuations of money and student enrollment. The universal fact of collegiate life was competition for a modest pool of basically trained youth that required active solicitation and constant cultivation.[38] Virtually all colleges consciously imitated the recruitment and endowment campaigns pioneered in the early nineteenth century by itinerant college agents. The Congregational network, which eventually formed itself into the American Education Society, operated out of Andover Theological Seminary (f. 1808) and extended to college and universities in the South and Midwest.[39] Few ministers rode circuit, preaching the gospel of Christ alone. Most were empowered to solicit funds for various institutions, to sell perpetual scholarships to substantial donors, to discount or waive tuition to promising but impoverished youth, and to advertise the distinctive merits of "non-denominational" schools without abrogating their continuing denominational ties.[40] These networks differentiated eighteenth-from nineteenth-century colleges, the difference between "surprising," that is, unplanned versus engineered evangelical traditions.

However calculated these collegiate dynamics were, their voluntary mandates make them appear in retrospect as encompassing rather than as exclusive and differentiating. It was as if both institutions and individuals came into their respective identities by their network of associations rather than by their distinctive attributes or achievements. Princeton, for example, counted an expanding network of schools in its Southern outreach and made minor distinctions between academies and colleges. Not only did these institutions serve as feeder schools, however loosely affiliated with Princeton, but their networks also served to bolster Presbyterian congregations and at times the salaries and careers of ministers.[41] The career of Robert Baird (1798–1863) illuminates the trajectory of these loosely connected but highly efficient voluntary networks. Born in western Pennsylvania, Baird attended first a local Uniontown (Pa.) academy, then for several terms Washington and Jefferson Colleges. Though degreeless, he had sufficient preparation for entering and graduating from Princeton Theological Seminary (f. 1812)[42] in 1822. His subsequent ministerial work led him to the principalship of the Princeton Academy, civic work in the 1820s to create the first New Jersey public school system, service as general agent for the American Sunday School Union, and international agent in Paris and Rome for the American and Foreign Christian Union, which promoted temperance and educational reforms world-wide. Virtually none of his positions were distinctly specialized or thought to be progressive advancements but rather mixed charitable and civic work, a harmonizing standard of stewardship common to both local and national organizational leadership.[43]

One of the corollary features of antebellum voluntarism was its distinctive organizational structure, particularly its overlapping informal networks. Promoting temperance in a particular locale did not suggest it ranked ahead of collegiate solicitation. Like newspaper advertisements, local priorities shaped the precedence among reform enterprises. Increasingly, a particular college's interests shared the social saddle-bag of the American evangelist with other worthy causes. But emphatically regional concerns mixed kaleidoscopically with other worthy issues connected with constructing a Republican, Christian commonwealth.[44]

Within the 1801 Plan of Union forged by the Presbyterian and Congregational denominations, churchmen created voluntary organizations of a national scope. Their intention was to project their special brand of Protestantism and make it coincident with the malleable, local voluntary associations still developing in the East and, more important, about to develop in the West. In 1843, the Society for the Promotion of Collegiate and Theological Education at the West (SPCTEW) began its work, at the center of which was funneling small-donor support and didactic, revivalistic-oriented printed matter across the trans-Appalachian West. What resources this East Coast network generated would be channeled to select Western colleges. By 1874, when the organization dissolved, the SPCTEW had buttressed twenty-six colleges and provided a model for competing Baptist and

Methodist organizations.[45] The basic voluntary mode of organization extended to kindred associations, like the American Tract Society, the Sunday School Union, and the American Bible Society, which made their mark powerfully, though indirectly, on the collegiate enterprise.[46] Officials of these organizations were generally themselves college graduates and were sought out, not only by college presidents for collegiate donations but for advice and arbitration of knotty inter-denominational collegiate disputes. Thus, one of the crucial attractions of the voluntary tradition was the mixture of moral coercion and persuasion within a personalized, informal style, as if knotty issues could still be settled short of contentious, political confrontations.

Antebellum colleges, originating from select denominational roots, local resources and merchant capitalists, nevertheless participated in broader, voluntary networks that clarified a common reality of collegiate culture: collegiate survival could not depend for long on local resources alone.[47] Even among denominations, like the Baptists, the Methodists, and the Disciples of Christ, who came late to the value of advanced instruction, college leadership resulted in a permanent tension between a college's moral goals and the practical, worldly concerns of the college's business patrons. Randolph Macon College (f. 1830) was one of some 229 schools founded by the Methodists before 1860, all but ten after 1830, but it avoided creating a theology professorship and wholly Methodist trustee board in order to obtain a charter from the Virginia state legislature.[48] Still, the individuals with regional connections were often precisely those who boosted local values, since their status in local elites often depended directly on their ability to command influence and money from outside a given local community.[49] Similarly, Stephen Girard whose "local" college contributed to Philadelphia pride, not only drew upon his own international experience but projected with his philanthropy an unspecified, broader implication for a new American republic. In these features Girard provided a two-way, local-national trajectory for antebellum collegiate voluntarism, imitated even by his nemesis, the ubiquitous denominational college.

Unmistakably regional rather than local or national boundaries became the forceful parameters of the antebellum college in America.[50] Early on New England began to develop highly restrictive admissions standards, whereas in the South and Midwest before the Civil War, institutional survival necessitated fairly unrestrictive policies with respect to age or previous schooling. Oberlin College (f. 1831) in Ohio, for example, admitted literally hundreds of students and was noted for the earliest admission of both women and blacks to collegiate instruction. However, within Oberlin's aegis there were multiple departments, accommodating students in primary and "normal" (i.e., teacher-preparatory) instructional groupings as well as in the college and theological seminary. Most institutions outside the Northeast, as Colin Burke has compellingly demonstrated, were scaled-down versions of Oberlin.[51] High tuitions in the East compounded the expense of city residence, permitting some coastal colleges to charge three times the costs of instruction outside New England.[52] In the Midwest and South, fiscal anxiety, student access, and evangelical piety kept tuition low.[53]

In large part, colleges with expansive preparatory and collegiate departments appeared in the Midwest and South in sparsely or recently settled areas, particularly where the New England model of the state-supported common school had not yet penetrated. The varied levels of "collegiate instruction" responded to all comers, averaging about twenty students at their collegiate level, when their Eastern counterparts enrolled up to 400 students. With such a student pool, Eastern colleges early on could dispense with preparatory classes and project a distinctive collegiate identity.

Those communities that could not raise sufficient funds, even using a particular denominational network, responded with an adaptive, multipurpose academy. Such schools were often the taproot of later colleges.[54] Amherst Academy, for example, founded in 1814 as a coeducational school, led within a decade to the founding of an exclusively male classical college with a state charter. Still, Amherst's early curriculum resembled the collegiate affinities of many academies, and one of its early presidents, Edward Hitchcock, assumed the collegiate leadership with theological rather than regular collegiate training. Probably more important than any degree was Hitchcock's experience as principal of nearby Deerfield Academy and as a self-taught geologist.[55]

The distinction between academy and college became sharper as the nineteenth century wore on, a function first of age grouping, then curricular organization, and ultimately socio-cultural distinctions. In *The National Intelligencer* (2 November 1833) the flourishing Brookville (Md.) Academy publicized its refusal to admit students over seventeen, while a month earlier the same newspaper printed the University of Virginia's announcement of a cutoff age of no younger than sixteen. Though academies and colleges often offered complementary studies, subjects in science, mathematics, language, and philosophy had begun to receive greater specification at institutions striving for university status in these years.

Until the sharpening of North-South division after the 1830s, college leaders strove to reach out beyond their regional boundaries. Physical traffic moved constantly between the two regions, in many ways heightening rather than breaking down regional consciousness of distinctive cultures. By midcentury, however, the South had foregone an earlier aspiration to create expansive state-supported public school systems modeled on Massachusetts' example. The rising dichotomy between Cavalier and Yankee compelled the South to rely more heavily upon elitist support for both private academies and denominational colleges as well as their public universities, subordinating earlier Southern commitments to tax-supported public schools.[56]

For the first half of the nineteenth century and later, the American college lacked any single, formal standard of structure or operation; rather, it fluctuated competitively between local dynamics and regional pressures, often of a denominational sort. In the competition for students and donors, overstated goals and ambitions abounded, masking the strategic force of local elites and sectarian priorities. In the process of survival, schools depended on localities and denominations in spite of lofty republican, even national, aspirations. At any given point, a college could strum multiple chords to woo students, trustees, or financial resources. And at times, with minimal regard to educational theory, different institutions transformed themselves, from academy to college, from local to regional, from sectarian to functioning non-denominational institutions, all within Girard's original "college" conception of an agency converting youth to responsible citizenship, a voluntary venture in civic evangelism.

V

In this erratic and fluctuating context. Yale College emerged as distinct, not simply for amassing the largest student body before the Civil War,[57] but for aggrandizing the meaning of the antebellum college itself. In the justly touted Yale Report of 1828, three college faculty members—the president, Reverend Jeremiah Day, its distinguished scientist, Professor Benjamin Silliman, and its classicist, Professor James L. Kingsley—posed an argument that consciously refashioned a merger of the school's inherited evangelical values with the competitive demands of the day. Like virtually all other antebellum colleges, the coiners of the Yale argument had to explain to their several constituencies how the moral mantic handed down to them from their Congregational founders would survive in a world that was incompletely Congregational. In addition, they needed to explain why anyone should bother to commit himself to two to four years of costly study, when the jobs and careers of America's economy could be had and exploited with little more than the basic instruction of the district school.

The Yale Report addressed the dilemmas of their community's moral and secular culture with an argument that won the allegiances of many colleges in vastly different circumstances. Their *apologia* began with a disarming admission that colleges must not offer a "blind opposition to salutary reform" but rather must be adaptable "to the spirit and wants of the age." Their commitment needed to avoid rigid defensiveness and to adhere "to some of its original features . . . from a higher principle." Every institution, it suggested expansively, should re-examine its original purpose and should entertain the possibility of breaking up its older system. Most important, they implicitly asked, how much of an inherited brand of eighteenth century instruction could antebellum Yale condone in the nineteenth?

The Yale Report also confronted charges that antebellum Yale housed elitist pretensions, incompatible with republican values. Its argument took the high road and insisted no college could gear itself to those whose ambitions concentrated on political leadership or specific vocational skills. "In this country, where offices are accessible to all who are qualified for them, superior intellectual attainments ought not to be confined to any description of persons." In actual fact, like most New England colleges, Yale graduates throughout the first half of the nineteenth century were not all wealthy. One-third to nearly one-half of its students graduated at age twenty-three or older.[58] Many of these "mature" students, originating from New England's poorer hill country villages with ministerial aspirations, completed their college study only after delays and disruptions of their educations. Many left college to teach common school or academies and required charitable assistance to finish; others pursued a string of cul-de-sac jobs before returning to study with substantially younger classmates. The Yale Report thus made a civic virtue out of the widely shared age mix of college students rather than probing the implied pedagogical problems.[59]

Yale's defensive protestations against elitism only heightened the problematic character of collegiate service and worth. If it were so completely adaptable to the spirit of the age, how could anyone discern whether or not the college was actually meeting its obligations? Who or what locale would determine the adjudicating "spirit of the age?" Yale established two priorities for its collegiate purpose: first, everyone must receive "thorough education" through the cultivation of a discipline and "furniture of the mind." Second, education would be "inculcated" by "daily and vigorous exercise" and the subjects taught would best "fix attention, directing the train of thought, analyzing a subject proposed for investigation." These claims and their institutional applications resisted any sharp prediction of behavioral or vocational results; their conceptual authority, like that of evangelism itself, lay primarily within each individual's disposition.[60]

Throughout, the Yale Report stressed the outcomes of order and stability in training the faculties with words like "arranging," "balancing," "guiding," "controlling," "directing," "fixing the attention," "establishing the tone." The central terms revealed, perhaps unconsciously, a concern about the actual turmoil and riot that characterized so much of student life in the antebellum college, exacerbated by the melange of youth and young adults.[61] Ultimately, collegiate education would throw the individual, so the Report argued, on the resources of his own mind, resulting ideally in the "sublimest efforts of genius." The diffusion of knowledge, so central to Jefferson's eighteenth-century educational values, had been consciously replaced with "inculcation," which assumed an internalization of both method and information, in its way, the production of a civic conversion.

If "inculcation" represented a non-denominational modification of Yale's eighteenth-century support of revivalism, the Yale Report went on to claim a new nineteenth-century, evangelical space. Collegiate knowledge, it argued, was unlike professional learning; it was transferable and ultimately realized only later in specific local communities. Professional knowledge and occupational training, which so many colleges were pressured to adopt, belonged to training in situ, a special vocational apprenticeship adapted exclusively to a particular geographical locus; it was a finished education, whereas the conclusion of a college education resulted in a "commencement," a beginning of long-term work prospects. A college education concerned itself with foundations and discipline, was local without becoming parochial, and most important, should precede professional instruction, lest learning result in rigidity, self-serving myopia or "extravagance." The college continued its role as a quasimoral institution without adopting any distinct sectarianism (whatever its Congregational inheritances) and, in the process, laid claim to education more basic than training in law, medicine, ministry, public school teaching, or business.[62]

But, of course, such assertions were meaningless without some specification about how, compared with other schools, the college would achieve its goals. The heart of collegiate discipline, as many educators had already insisted, was the classics. "Should the time come," antebellum defenders of the classics intoned, "when Latin and Greek should be banished from our Universities, and the Study of Cicero and Demosthenes, of Homer and Virgil, should be considered unnecessary for the formation of a scholar, we should regard mankind as fast sinking into absolute barbarism, and the gloom of mental darkness as likely to increase until it should become universal."[63] Educational backsliding followed a perilously similar course to moral backsliding, The kinds of control that colleges produced were ideally not dogmatically imposed. The sanctions of a collegiate community were thought to be most instructive when natural, informal, and indirect; in a word, voluntary.

The Yale Report synthesized much of an inherited educational wisdom by reaffirming the classics not only as foundational but as a concrete means for inculcating moral character without resorting to any denominational or sectarian interpretation of piety. The deference to the classics was not an uncritical deference to tradition or conservative biases; rather it reflected a cultural anxiety about guaranteeing constructive changes which educators could not assess precisely or technically. The classics substituted for an older Biblical *lingua franca* and became the educational and linguistic code of a new republican, educated elite before the Civil War. The emerging importance of the classics did not connote a relaxation of denominational fervor but rather a reformulation of it into a wider republican sphere.[64]

Of course, the promulgation of the Yale Report did not substantively interfere with the rising importance of mathematics, science, literature, philosophy, or even consciously vocational training, which had already reduced the doctrinal orientation of Yale's eighteenth-century instruction.[65] Colleges continued to fluctuate between harsh times and flush times throughout the period, while the Yale Report offered a curricular and organizational priority that would not have been possible a generation earlier and was indeed aggressively new in 1828. At Yale itself the Report did not result in a dogged entrenchment of the classics. The college gradually modified its classical requirements to make way for advanced mathematics, experimental science, and history. These curricular emphases emerged more as a consequence of the well-trained individuals whom President Jeremiah Day and his nineteenth-century successors hired than any curricular or "market" policy.[66]

The intellectual influence of the Report spread through the work of Yale's graduates, whose missionary pattern continued in an evangelical vein, whether carried by ministerial alumni or not. At the time of the Report's publication, Yale had the largest enrollment in the country (c 250), when large colleges averaged 150 students. Yale also had the largest living and most geographically dispersed alumni, giving it the most legitimate claim to a national constituency. In addition, many of its faculty produced widely-used textbooks, codifying subjects and methodologies and associated Yale with their disseminated reputations. In 1840 Yale and Princeton graduates filled many of the presidencies of American colleges. The so-called Yale Band founded colleges across the Midwest, like Beloit College in Wisconsin, Illinois College in Illinois or Depauw in Indiana, Berea College in Kentucky, Miami in Ohio, and Hobart in New York. Some of these satellite schools explicitly cited the Yale Report in their college brochures.[67] But again, like their counterparts, their ability to deliver on the blueprint was a function of dynamics often beyond their control.[68] The Report's rhetorical and political value likely exceeded its service as a concrete administrative paradigm until late in the nineteenth century, particularly given the frequency of raucous and disorderly student behavior.[69] Still, the ingenuity of the Report's argument about a basic, principled discipline and (classical) furniture of the mind was widely disseminated and had much to do with the reconceptualization of the college's place in American society; it was hardly the conservative impediment to reform that has often been claimed.[70]

The Yale Report's key dilemma remained the connection between education and its civic promises; it never really clarified how its classical offerings could guarantee the foundational equipment for varied students' civic life and future work. Its central problem was the common dilemma of the antebellum period, determining the meaning of college and its fit in the educational panoply. Given the range of options, Yale's insistence that the college must be viewed as a family with the president and teachers as substitute parents took risks by using an established congregational metaphor. In most Calvinist denominations the congregation, the ultimate device for probing spiritual matters, was a special moral entity, and Calvinist ministers used familial metaphors to explain the organic relationship of members to church. However, given the character of the antebellum college, the usurpation of the familial mantle, not only as metaphor but as practice, had to be an exercise in risk-taking. Such familial authority must have come more easily to colleges like Girard with students not yet in their teens. For Yale, admitting students from ages fourteen through twenty-three, familial deference had to be not only jarring but inappropriate to Yale's espoused goals of training self-possessed and morally-informed citizens.

The very diversity, diffuseness, and fragmentation of the antebellum collegiate experience have distracted scholars from the cohering sense that an inculcated voluntarism provided to the shapers and practitioners of the nineteenth century collegiate tradition.[71] The thread that links most antebellum collegiate institutions, in spite of their variation, was the supra-denominational energy, which sought to influence, if not control, a new republican spirit in America, It was impossible to insist on dogmatic, denominational correctness in such a competition, especially among and between many Protestant sects. The coerced embrace of a modified doctrinal evangelism, which ministers themselves depicted as the "Voluntary Principle," served to extend many conceptual and traditional features of an older missionary fervor. However, once channeled toward an indeterminate public good, a major inheritance of the American Revolution, many denominations engineered a crucial sharing of power between churches and schools in an effort to "train up the character" of the next generation.

The competition for students and resources ironically led many colleges to a restrictive geographical scope at the very moment when their rhetoric and energies became centrifugal. Still, the powerful image of the autonomous, local college matched a new educational leadership that was, like Stephen Girard, more stewardly than ministerial. His civic example seemed to make the force of his money secondary; it illuminated the central instructional standard of the nineteenth century; the power of persuasion, rhetoric, and example, that accepted ubiquitous differences of opinion and behavior but idealized a society of self-disciplined citizens, harmonized by their distinctly (Whiggish) republican commitments. This new civic religion became coincident with a collegiate voluntarism that simultaneously (and often contradictorily) promised both individualized morality and its institutionalized dissemination. Before the model of tax-based public schooling, the antebellum college carried the burden of that aspiration. Its antebellum years can be best understood as a spirited episode in promoting education as a special republican power before Americans had the institutional apparatus for achieving it.

Notes

1 The author wishes to express his sincere thanks to Professors James E. Scanlon and Roger Geiger for especially close and face-saving critiques of this essay in earlier drafts. Two anonymous readers of the *History of Higher Education Annual* also contributed substantively to this final version.

2 Harvey Graff, *The Literacy Myth: Literacy and Social Structure in the Nineteenth Century City* (New York: Academic Press. 1979).

3 Cf. Gregory H. Singleton, "Protestant Voluntary Organizations and the Shaping of Victorian America." in *Victorian America*, ed. Daniel Walker Howe (Philadelphia: University of Pennsylvania Press, 1976). 47-58. The career of Horace Mann, which moved from Whig politics to public schooling, concluded with the presidency of Antioch College. One can see in his writings as well as in the proceedings of major voluntary associations of the period, like the American Institute of Instruction (to which Mann and most other nineteenth-century educational leaders belonged), the process of shaping a general allegiance to voluntarism into generically distinct institutions like the American college. Cf. Paul H. Mnttingly, *The Classless Profession: American Schoolmen in the Nineteenth Century* (New York: New York University Press, 1975).

4 Cf. Jack C. Lane, "The Yale Report of 1828 and Liberal Education: A Neorepublican Manifesto," *History of Education Quarterly* 27, no. 3 (Fall 1987): 325-33. This article contributes constructively to a rejection of early interpretations that made the Report a conservative atavism but overstates the historical agency of the Report on both American college and American culture.

5 *The National Intelligencer* (9 September 1835). For a collegiate history that should serve as a model of the historical genre, see Robert Emmett Curran, SJ, *The Bicentennial History of Georgetown University: Vol I, From Academy to University, 1789-1889* (Washington D.C.: Georgetown University Press, 1993). The college had been founded in 1789 as the first Roman Catholic college in America and operated until 1815 without a charter. For the first several decades of the nineteenth century non-Catholic students variously comprised one-quarter to one-third of the student body.

6 Thomas Bender, Peter D. Hall, Thomas Haskell and Paul H. Mattingly, "Institutionalization and Education in the Nineteenth and Twentieth Centuries," *History of Education Quarterly* 20, no. 4 (Winter 1980): 449–72.

7 *The National Intelligencer* (Wednesday, 10 July 1833). Due to stipulations in Girard's will as well as trustee interpretation of it, Girard College did not begin its actual operation until January, 1848, when it admitted 100 orphans. Within little more than a year its students numbered about 300. Most of these were assigned to a "preparatory" department (ages 6–10) while plans were afoot for intermediate (ages 10–14) and collegiate departments (14–18). Cf. Henry W. Arey, *The Girard College and Its Founder* (Philadelphia: C. Sherman, 1854).

8 See Daniel Walker Howe, *The Political Culture of American Whigs* (Chicago: University of Chicago Press, 1979), esp. 182–84. Of course, de Tocqueville remarked extensively on the ubiquitous voluntary associations in *Democracy in America*, considering them major devices for countering divisive party organization in a democracy.

9   Colin B. Burke, *American Collegiate Populations* (New York: New York University Press, 1982), 43–50, discusses antebellum endowments, stressing that most colleges thought themselves fortunate to have endowments whose interest covered the president's salary (usually averaging between $1500 and $2000). See also Merle Curti and Roderick Nash, *Philanthropy and the Shaping of American Higher Education* (New Brunswick: Rutgers University Press, 1965). Girard fully expected his legacy would pay building costs as well as operational expenses. The will has been, in part, anthologized in Edgar Knight and Clifton Hall, eds., *Readings in American Educational History* (New York: Appleton Century Crofts, 1951), 247–55.

10 Bray Hammond, *Banking and Politics in the Jacksonian Era* (Princeton: Princeton University Press, 1957). The connotations of endurance and power were short-lived for the Bank, which was vetoed by President Jackson in 1830 and which only survived until 1836. In spite of its failure, the Bank served antebellum orators as a metaphor of centralized institutional power for well over a generation afterward. Even in Girard College, designed for orphans, crucial choices emerged by the late 1850s and early 1860s, which privileged some by permitting a small elite for the Collegiate Department, and sent the majority off into apprenticeship and the world of work. Cf. Louis Romano, "Manual and Industrial Education at Girard College, 1831–1865: An Era of American Educational Experimentation" (Ph.D. diss., New York University, 1975), chap. 3.

11 Until Colin Burke's path-breaking book (n. 9), the conventional wisdom of Frederick Rudolph's *The American College and University* followed Donald Tewkesbury's argument that early nineteenth century colleges experienced an extraordinary pattern of "failure." Tewkesbury made his calculations based on the number of college charters awarded by state legislatures, without ever reflecting on how promotional and political such exercises were. In terms of colleges actually founded and operative— Burke's methodology—antebellum colleges experienced surprisingly little failure, however erratic their funding and administration. But these contextual features of varied resources meant that the "college" was not a functional, generic school even in the antebellum era.
    Cf. Rudolph's *The American College and University: A History* (New York: Vintage Books, 1962), esp. chap. 1; Tewkesbury's *The Founding of Colleges and Universities before the Civil War* (New York: Columbia University, 1932). See also Natalie Naylor's insightful "The Ante-Bellum College Movement: A Reappraisal of Tewksbury's Founding of American Colleges and Universities," *History of Education Quarterly* 13, no. 3 (Fall 1973): 261–74.

12 Paul Monroe, ed., "Girard College," *Cyclopedia of Education*, vol. 3 (New York: Macmillan, 1912), 113. Girard College gradually assumed features more common to other colleges after the Civil War. The process by which its organization grew beyond service to youth between the ages of 6 and 10 and reworded Stephen Girard's original will is detailed in Romano, "Girard College." See also Cheeseman Herrick, *History of Girard College* (Philadelphia: Girard College, 1927).

13 *The National Intelligencer* (10 July 1833). In Girard's will he explicitly proclaimed the civic sweep of his educational goals: "I would have them . . . by every proper means a pure attachment to our republican institutions, and to the sacred rights of conscience, as guaranteed by our happy constitution, shall be formed and fostered in the minds of the scholars." "Girard College and Its Founder," *American Journal of Education* 27 (1897): 593–616.

14 Ibid. Peter Hall makes the definitive argument about the place of trusts in college development, a major tenet of antebellum Whig politics as well as the nemesis of their Jacksonian opponents. Sec Peter D. Hall, *The Organization of American Culture* (New York: New York University Press, 1982), chap. 6.

15 Girard explicitly charged the College "to instill into the minds of the scholars the *purest principles of morality*, so that, on their entrance into active life, they may, *from inclination and habit*, evince *benevolence towards their fellow creatures*, and *a love of truth, sobriety and industry*, adopting at the same time such religious tenets as their *matured reason* may enable them to prefer." Cf. Knight and Hall, eds., *Readings*, 254.

16 Howe, *The Political Culture of the American Whigs*, 181–84; sec also Hall, *The Organization of American Culture*, chap. 8. Put very simply, Jacksonian republicanism in the antebellum period favored publicly supported and locally rooted institutions, hence Jackson's antipathy to the Bank of the United Slates. The Whig republican tradition regularly stressed a translocal, if not national perspective, which accommodated a range of institutional genres, from the Bank of the United Stales to nascent bureaucracies like Horace Mann's Massachusetts public school system.

17 Perry Miller, "The Voluntary Principle," in *The Life of the Mind in America* (New York: Harcourt Brace & World, 1965), 40–43. For the broader educational co-option of the evangelical tradition, see Mattingly, *The Classless Profession* and David Tyack and Elizabeth Hansot *Managers of Virtue: Public School Leadership in America. 1820–1980* (New York: Basic Books, 1982).

18 Mark A. Noll, *Princeton and the Republic, 1768–1822* (Princeton: Princeton University Press, 1989).

19 Daniel Boorslin, "Culture with Many Capitals: The Booster College," chap. 20 in *The Americans: The National Experience* (New York; Vintage Books, 1965).

20 David Allmendinger, *Paupers and Scholars: The Transformation of Student Life in New England, 1760–1860* (New York: St. Martin's Press. 1975).

21 Rudolph, *The American College and University*, chaps. 5–10.

22 Roy J. Honeywell, *The Educational Writings of Thomas Jefferson* (Cambridge, Mass.: Harvard University Press, 1931), esp. chap. 2.

23 John Whitehead, *The Separation of College and State* (New Haven: Yale University Press. 1973), chap. 2: Jean Edward Smith, *John Marshall: Definer of a Nation* (New York: Henry Holt, 1996), 433–38; Paul Monroe, ed., "Dartmouth College Case," *Cyclopedia of Education*, vol. 2 (New York: Macmillan, 1912), 252.

24 Frederick Rudolph, *The American College and University*, 211.

25 Cf. Ronald Story. *The Forging of an Aristocracy* (Middletown, Conn.: Wesleyan University Press, 1980), 148–49; Codman Hislop, *Eliphalet Nott* (Middletown, Conn.: Wesleyan University Press, 1971), 201–202. I am obliged to Roger Geiger for noticing these Dartmouth College case connections.

26 Burke, *American Collegiate Populations*, 41.

27 Hall, *The Organization of American Culture*, esp. chap. 6. See also the same author's essay, "The Spirit of the Ordinance of 1787: Organizational Values, Voluntary Associations and Higher Education in Ohio, 1803–1830," in *"Schools and the Means of Education Shall Forever Be Encouraged:" A History of Education in the Old Northwest, 1787–1880*, eds., Paul H. Mattingly and Edward W. Stevens (Athens, Ohio: Ohio University Libraries, 1987), 97–114.

28 Perry Miller, *The Life of the Mind in America*, Book 1.

29 Steven Novak, "The College in the Dartmouth College Case: A Reinterpretation," *The New England Quarterly* 47 (1975). Novak's defense of "pietistic" I would extend beyond his denominational meaning to include both individuals like Girard and Jefferson. Both of these individuals claimed a "moral discipline" in their versions of essential education, however different their meanings of "piety."

30 Girard's will took more than a decade to be realized, due to financial and interpretive problems. In virtually all of the major issues, the College's priorities gravitated ever more deeply into an explicitly Whig tradition. The first president, Alexander Dallas Bache, was sent to Europe to study educational precedents and returned to publish a powerful Whig-leaning report, *Education in Europe* (1839). Similarly, when Girard trustees sought additional educational advice, they turned to Francis Lieber, whose *A Manual of Political Ethics* (1838) had a shaping influence on Whig institutional assumptions. Bache and Lieber went on to distinguished scholarly careers and were instrumental members of the Lazzaroni who successfully promoted the creation of the Smithsonian Institution and the American Social Science Association. Cf. Romano, "Girard College," chap 2; also Howe, *The Political Culture of American Whigs*, 86–87; Thomas Haskell, *The Emergence of Professional Social Science* (Urbana: University of Illinois Press, 1977), esp. 70–74.

31 John Whitehead and Jurgen Herbst, "How to Think About the Dartmouth College Case," *History of Education Quarterly* 26, no. 3 (Fall 1986): 334.

32 Howe, *The Political Culture of the American Whigs*.

33 David Potts, *Wesleyan University, 1831–1910* (New Haven: Yale University Press, 1992); Curran, *Georgetown University*. For the efficacy of Catholic collegiate training of Protestants, see Alexis de Tocqueville's reported 1831 conversation with Benjamin LaTrobe in *Alexis de Tocqueville: Journey to America*, ed. J. P. Meyer (New Haven: Yale University Press, 1962), 78.

34 Many of such institutions reflected the history of the Troy Female Seminary, so well presented in Anne Firor Scott, "The Ever Widening Circle: The Diffusion of Feminist Values from the Troy Female Seminary, 1822–1872, *History of Education Quarterly* 19, no. 1 (Spring 1979): 3–46. Many of these comparable dynamics endured beyond the antebellum period. See W. Bruce Leslie, "Localism, Denominationalism and Institutional Strategies in Urbanizing America: Three Pennsylvania Colleges, 1870–1915," *History of Education Quarterly* 17, no. 3 (Fall 1977): 235–56.

35 Potts, *Wesleyan*, 127.

36 Scanlon, *Randolph-Macon College: A Southern History* (Charlottesville: University Press of Virginia, 1983), chap. 2. Later Trinity College, now Duke University, commandeered Randolph-Macon's North Carolina constituency, further reducing its geographical aegis.

37 Theodore Jones, *New York University* (New York: New York University Press, 1933). For most of the nineteenth century, N.Y.U.'s student population remained the size of comparable colleges. In spite of initial plans to orient itself to the city, the school quickly reverted to the orbit of the Calvinist, Dutch Reformed denomination.

38 Letter of George Ticknor to Thomas Jefferson, 28 March 1825, cited in *American Higher Education: A Documentary History*, vol. 1, eds. Richard Hofstadter and Wilson Smith (Chicago: University of Chicago Press, 1961), 268. "These [New England] colleges," Ticknor confided to Jefferson, "are now very numerous and under one pretext or another, are constantly becoming more so. Competition, therefore, is growing more and more active among them, and all are endeavoring to find new and better modes of instruction with which to contend against their rivals."

39 Natalie Naylor, "The Theological Seminary in the Configuration of American Higher Education: The Ante-Bellum Years," *History of Education Quarterly* 17 (Spring 1977): 17–30.

40 David F. Allmendinger, *Paupers and Scholars*; Mattingly, *The Classless Profession*, esp. chap. 2; Howard Miller, *The Revolutionary College* (New York: New York University Press, 1975), 218–33.

41 Miller, *The Revolutionary College* includes in Princeton's loose voluntary network, largely fostered by its graduates or members of the Presbyterian denomination, Liberty Hall [now Washington and Lee University] (1774) and Hampden-Sydney (1776) in Virginia, Dickinson College (1784) in Pennsylvania, Transylvania Seminary (1794), Centre College (1819) and Kentucky Academy in Kentucky, and Cumberland College (1823) in Tennessee. Miller persuasively argues that denominational proselytizing forced a break from an older late eighteenth century conception of religious harmony toward a tolerance of religious competition, which characterized the antebellum period.

Colin Burke, *American Collegiate Populations*, 35, has noted that schools in the loose "academy" genre increased from 3200 in 1840 to over 6700 by 1860, increases commensurate with primary school expansion.

42 Miller, *The Revolutionary College*, 249; Sidney E. Ahlstrom. *A Religious History of the American People* (New Haven: Yale University Press, 1972), 462.

43 *Who Was Who in America: Historical Volume* (Chicago: A. N. Marquis Co., 1967), 104. The western schools of the Presbyterian network tended to be more consciously and aggressively denominational but the generic character of its work takes on a peculiarly historical character. Although chartered as Jefferson College in 1802, Baird's alma mater was long known as Canonsburg Academy but retained a theological department recognized by the Virginia synod of the Presbyterian Church. Miller, *The Revolutionary College*, 250. See Miller. *The Life of the Mind in America* for Baird's contribution to the nineteenth century meaning of "voluntarism," 40–43; Ahlstrom, *A Religious History of the American People*, 859, uses Baird's writing to demonstrate how ingeniously American evangelicals adapted their religious style—"the activity, the bustle and the lay support of the churches"—to a larger American ethos. My thanks to Peter Wosh of N.Y.U. for drawing attention to Baird.

44 In the antebellum period, primary education and collegiate instruction were equally pressing issues, often promoted by the same individuals. See Mattingly, *The Classless Profession*; Timothy Smith, "Protestant Schooling and American Nationality," *Journal of American History* 53 (March 1967): 679–95; Tyack and Hansot, *Managers of Virtue*; Clifford Griffin, *Their Brothers' Keepers: Moral Stewardship in the United States* (New Brunswick: Rutgers University Press, 1960).

45 James Findlay, "The SPCTEW and Western Colleges: Religion and Higher Education in Mid-Nineteenth Century America," *History of Education Quarterly* 17 (Spring 1977): 39. Among the colleges which received SPCTEW aid were Lane Theological Seminary as well as Marietta and Western Reserve Colleges in Ohio, Wabash College in Indiana, and Illinois College in Illinois. After the Civil War, the organization also supported black Wilberforce College in Ohio.

46 Peter Wosh, *Spreading the Word* (New York: Cornell University Press, 1994); Anne Boylan, *Sunday School* (New Haven: Yale University Press, 1988).

47 Roger L. Geiger, "The Era of Multipurpose Colleges in American Higher Education, 1850–1890," *History of Higher Education Annual* 15 (1995), 51–92 [64 f]. In this extremely important essay, Geiger provides extensive documentation on the number and variety of college-founding in this and the later nineteenth century. His "multipurpose" formula, however, obscures what, if anything, these multi-purposed institutions had in common, culturally or historically. This essay prodded me to ask, whether the prevalence of the classical curriculum or of evangelical influences didn't document deeper, structural continuities amidst the colleges' multipurposes. And also, exactly how did such shared patterns connect to the "market revolution" or political influences of the antebellum period?

48 Scanlon, *Randolph Macon College*, 33. Scanlon has claimed that 34 of these schools were Methodist colleges, rapidly gaining on the Presbyterians with 49 and ahead of the Baptists with 25, the Congregationalists with 21, the Episcopalians with 11, and the Roman Catholics with 14. See also Jennings W. Wagoner. "Constraint and Variety in Virginia Higher Education," *History of Education Quarterly* 25 (Spring-Summer 1985): 181–193.

49 Peter Wosh, *Spreading the Word*, esp. chap. 3.

50 Burke, *American Collegiate Populations*, 194–200.

51 Ibid., 38.

52 One needs to qualify the putative democratic interpretations of popular accessibility by noting that college tuition nationwide had shifted from one-third of a skilled laborer's annual wage in 1800 to two-thirds by 1860. Ibid., 50.

53 Cf. John Barnard, *From Evangelicalism to Progressivism at Oberlin College, 1866–1917* (Columbus: Ohio State University Press, 1969), 17–18. Cf. Robert Fletcher, *A History of Oberlin College* (Oberlin; Oberlin College, 1943), 2 vols. Until the end of the century, these patterns only widened, and the costs of college attendance greatly exceeded tuition fees. Still, in the 1870s Oberlin charged $30 for a year's collegiate instruction, when Yale reportedly mandated $90. Brown and Amherst $75, and Dartmouth $60. Cf. W. C. Bronson, *A History of Brown University, 1764–1914* (Providence, R.I.: Brown University Press, 1914), 368.

54 Burke, *American Collegiate Populations*, 37–38. Burke estimated that the cutoff point in dollars was about $2600 for communities planning a "college." If communities could not command amounts above that, it was less likely that a "college" would ensue. See also James McLachlan, *American Boarding Schools* (New York: Charles Scribners & Sons, 1969). For enrollment figures cited here, see Burke, ibid., 49. This study is the definitive, quantitative synthesis of the antebellum collegiate experience.

55 Claude Fuess, *Amherst: The Story of a New England College* (New York: Little Brown & Co., 1935), chaps. 3 and 12, esp. 127. Hitchcock did hold a (1820) degree from Yale but in the theological department (Yale Theological Seminary was not founded until 1822). He built his reputation via instruction in natural history at Amherst for ten years before assuming its presidency. But his reputation ranged beyond Amherst village because of his scientific textbooks, used equally by academies and colleges, and his spirited defense of the ante-bellum academy. Cf. *Who Was Who in American History*, 323. See also Theodore Sizer, ed., *The Age of the Academies* (New York: Teachers College Press, 1964), which includes Hitchcock's forceful 1845 address, "The American Academic System Defended," itself a dedication of a new academy at Williston, Massachusetts. See also "Edward Hitchcock," in *Dictionary of American Biography*, vol. 5, ed. Dumas Malone (New York: Charles Scribner's, 1932), 70.

56 William R. Taylor, "Toward a Definition of Orthodoxy: The Patrician South and the Common Schools," *Harvard Educational Review* 36 (Fall 1966): 412–26; see also Michael Sugrue, "We Desired Our Future Rulers to be Educated Men: South Carolina College, the Defense of Slavery, and the Development of Secessionist Politics." *History of Higher Education Annual* 14 (1994): 39–72; E. Merton Coulter, *College Life in the Old South* (Athens: University of Georgia Press, 1979 [1st ed. 1928]). Of course, in some states, like Virginia, slave-owner dominance prevented taxation for public schooling earlier than states like Georgia.

57 Yale College had 325 enrolled college students in the year the Report was published. In addition, there were another 149 students—"resident graduates"—studying medicine, law, and theology. The size and differentiated units gave "Yale College" a "university" complexion during this period. Again my thanks to Roger Geiger for this insight.

58 Allmendinger, *Paupers and Scholars*. It may well have been this feature that compelled the authors of the Yale Report to acknowledge the merits of "partial education" for those unable to complete a "thorough" course of collegiate study. See "Original Papers in Relation to a Course of Liberal Education," *The American Journal of Science and Arts* 15 (January 1829): 312. "The Yale Report" has become a convenient scholars' reference to this essay, written in 1828 and published in 1829.

59 The Yale Report noted that its charter permitted admission to youth no younger than fourteen but occasionally dispensed with the rule. "Original Papers. . . ," 317.

60 Notable efforts to explain how an older evangelical rhetoric translated into specific actions are Wilson Smith, *Professors and Public Ethics* (Ithaca, N.Y.: Cornell University Press 1956); Richard J. Carwardine, *Evangelicals and Politics in Antebellum America* (New Haven: Yale University Press, 1993); and more recently, Paul Conkin, *The Uneasy Center: Reformed Christianity in Antebellum America* (Chapel Hill, N. C.: University of North Carolina Press, 1995).

    For an insightful commentary on important theoretical aspects of institutionalization, see W. W. Powell and Paul DiMaggio, *The New Institutionalism in Organizational Analysis* (Chicago: University of Chicago Press, 1991).

61 Steven Novak, *The Rights of Youth: American Colleges and Student Revolt, 1798–1815* (Cambridge: Harvard University Press, 1977).

62 "Original Papers in Relation to a Course of Liberal Education," 308–9.

63 Quoted in Melvin L. Urofsky, "Reforms and Response: The Yale Report of 1828," *History of Education Quarterly* 5, no. 1 (1965): 57.

64 Yale graduate, Rev. Lyman Beecher, illustrates the point with his *A Plea for Colleges* (Cincinnati, Ohio: 1836). Beecher's career as a widely-admitted missionary model for this antebellum generation receives

an insightful treatment in Donald M. Scott, *From Office to Profession: The New England Ministry, 1750–1850* (Philadelphia: University of Pennsylvania Press, 1978), 69–75.

65 Brooks Mather Kelley, *Yale: A History* (New Haven: Yale University Press, 1974).

66 Kelley, ibid., Chaps. 10 and 11.

67 Urofsky, "The Yale Report of 1828," *History of Education Quarterly* 5 (March 1965): 53–69. p. 62. Urofsky, misquoting George P. Schmidt, claimed that either Yale (36) or Princeton (22) graduates led four-fifths of the colleges in operation in 1840. These schools did impress Schmidt with the number of their graduates in college presidencies, but his study offered no four-fifths specification. Schmidt used an undiscussed sample of 75 colleges, leading Urofsky to his erroneous calculation of four-fifths or 58 graduates of Princeton and Yale. However, the 75 did not represent the total of antebellum colleges. See George P. Schmidt, *The Old Time College President* (New York: Columbia University Press, 1930), 96. 146. My thanks to Roger Geiger for initiating this correction.

   Even where the Yale Report was not explicitly endorsed nor operated as a part of the loose voluntary network out of Yale, the classics were defended for their special pedagogical role. Wilbur Fisk, a graduate of Baptist Brown and first president of Methodist Wesleyan University, as well as his Southern counterpart, Stephen Olin, a graduate of Congregational Middlebury and first president of Methodist Randolph-Macon, both echoed sentiments of the Yale Report and endorsed the classics in the inaugural speeches at their respective colleges. Cf. Scanlon, *Randolph-Macon College*, 55–57.

68 Lawrence Cremin, *American Education: The National Experience* (New York: Harper & Row, 1980), 405–09.

69 Joseph Kett, *Rises of Passage* (New York: Basic Books, 1977). chap. 2.

70 Rudolph, *The American College and University*, 131–35. More persuasive are the insightful arguments of Peter Hall in "Institutionalization and Education in the Nineteenth and Twentieth Centuries." *History of Education Quarterly* 20, no. 4 (Winter 1980): 461–63; or of Louise Stevenson. *Scholarly Means to Evangelical Ends: The New Haven Scholars and the Transformation of Higher Learning in America, 1830–1890* (Baltimore: Johns Hopkins University Press, 1986), which argues the creative force of nineteenth century evangelical culture.

71 Geiger, "The Era of Multipurpose Colleges in American Higher Education."

PART IV

THE PROLIFERATION OF POSTSECONDARY INSTITUTIONS: LATE NINETEENTH AND EARLY TWENTIETH CENTURIES

Part IV: The Proliferation of Postsecondary Institutions: Late Nineteenth and Early Twentieth Centuries

After the Civil War, the societal demands on higher education in the East and Midwest created new missions for institutions of higher learning. The rise of American universities, described by Carol Gruber in her introductory chapter of *Mars and Minerva*,[1] captures the institutional differentiation that occurred during the nineteenth century as state, land-grant, and research universities were founded. Providing an overview chapter for this period, she accepts the standard "consensus" argument of Laurence Veysey in his *The Emergence of the American University*,[2] which presented the view that these universities arose out of a reform movement against the antebellum college. This view has been challenged by Axtell (1971) and other revisionists. Later research on the scientific schools at Harvard and Yale disclosed a more gradual development of these new institutional ideals.[3] Yet, the desire for practical scientific knowledge as opposed to classical education led to the founding of the University of Virginia and later land-grant universities after 1862, such as Iowa State, Kansas State, and Michigan State. Daniel Lang's article (1978) chronicles this developing land-grant movement by describing the founding of People's College in 1858, the movement's relation to the Morrill Land-Grant Act of 1862, and the establishment of Cornell University. Other institutional developments further expanded this new science orientation. The desire for scientific inquiry, particularly espoused by American graduates of German universities since 1810, encouraged early efforts to launch research-oriented institutions of higher learning. Not until the founding of Johns Hopkins University in 1876, the establishment of all-graduate Clark University and Catholic University of America in 1889, and the re-establishment of the University of Chicago in 1892 did a university mission totally dedicated to research commence. Both new types of American institutional missions encouraged the professionalization of knowledge through the rise of national disciplinary associations, institutional advancement through creating consortial groups such as the Association of American Universities (AAU) in 1900, and faculty professionalization through the formation of the American Association of University Professors (AAUP) in 1915. Nevertheless, the college continued to be the central institution of higher learning for most students during the nineteenth century even with the rise of these universities—though it was not untouched by societal pressures and demands.

The differences between standard and revisionist arguments have been addressed by recent reassessments of these institutional types. To begin our presentation of state and land-grant universities in the Reader, Eldon Johnson's revisionist article further clarifies how these institutions fit within the developing context of American higher education. He argues that the land-grant idea and curricula developed gradually at these universities. Johnson contends that state universities still resembled antebellum colleges until the turn of the twentieth century. Joseph Stetar next discusses the higher education of southern whites during the Reconstruction period that resisted land-grant and research ideals. These works support a gradual differentiation of institutional types thesis during the latter part of the nineteenth century. Successful development of these new state institutions devoted to science and agriculture would not have occurred without George W. Atherton. In his congressional role, he assured the passages of the 1887 Hatch Act and the 1890 Second Morrill Land-Grant Act, which provided annual federal subsidies to these institutions and founded southern land-grant institutions for African-Americans, respectively. Roger L. Williams's short introductory chapter from his book, *The Origins of Federal Support for Higher Education*,[4] gives us a new understanding of Atherton's importance.

The major works on American research universities,[5] describe the beginnings of this unique American institution in our next chapter. Learning new methods of scholarship from German universities and institutes, American scholars advanced the ideals of "knowledge for its own sake," (i.e., pure research) when they began teaching at American institutions of higher learning. At the same time they placated demands for its practical application. In the Reader, Roger Geiger provides a review of the forces that created these new research universities. His interpretation centers on how philanthropy and funded research fueled their development through the 1980s. His chapter offers a framework for understanding how the discovery and expansion of knowledge occurred at these universities.

In an earlier article, Geiger (1984) discussed how much time faculty devoted to research rather than administration.[6] This new professoriate strove to professionalize knowledge through doctoral programs as well as their research. In their classic work, *Higher Education in Transition: A History of American Colleges and Universities*,[7] Brubacher and Rudy discuss the beginnings of academic administration as a new breed of presidential and decanal officers sought to lead research universities. This new internal constituency challenged the faculty in academic matters. By the end of the second decade of the twentieth century, this more professionalized faculty confronted the founders and presidents of these new institutions. The captains of industry and the presidents who created these research universities initially treated faculty as research labor—sometimes firing prominent professors. Bitter struggles between these two groups arose and led finally to the creation of the American Association of University Professors in 1915, which secured certain faculty rights and privileges—and eventually tenure. Christopher Newfield's chapter in his provocative *Ivy and Industry* points to how "divided governance" became the actual norm as only some faculty ascended to management, while most became labor as knowledge workers.[8] This critical theorist study offers an insightful portrayal of developing faculty life in the first half of the century, providing the necessary historical argument for understanding the dramatic faculty actions during the 1960s. Nevertheless, this faculty group not only reshaped how graduate education was delivered but also how external groups exerted pressures for reform. By the turn of the century, accrediting groups became the most powerful agents for institutional change for most institutions. On the other hand, Hugh Hawkins's chapter, "Toward System," discusses the AAU's role in maintaining the elite club of research universities and safeguarding the doctorate from overextension.

The unique character of the American research university can be readily seen through some of our primary readings. Harvard's president, Charles W. Eliot, argued for an elective undergraduate curriculum in his 1869 inaugural address, a key feature in the development of research universities. Further analysis of this important dynamic may be found in Hawkins's *Between Harvard and America: The Educational Leadership of Charles W. Eliot*.[9] Similarly, the protection of academic freedom through the AAUP encouraged the growth of the American professoriate—its principles are as important today as they were then. Daniel Coit Gilman's model for Johns Hopkins University brought forth a new institutional mission in American higher education. His vision of a university for advanced studies changed the direction of American higher education. Adding to the developing distinctive features of American higher education during this period were extensive curricular options and courses of study available to students as well as the earned graduate education, which began to require comprehensive written examinations and theses.

While this period has often been labeled the "Age of the University," other collegiate and precollegiate institutions still held center stage for most students. Roger Geiger's (1995/2000) significant reinterpretation of the college's place during the nineteenth century thus demarcates higher education historiography, as he relabeled the old college and antebellum college beginning in the 1850s as the "multipurpose college," which continued through the 1890s. These schools also offered many types of studies other than the classical curriculum, such as preparatory studies, science studies, or normal studies for teachers; and they often enrolled women alongside men. Bruce Leslie in his summary chapter from his important book, *Gentleman and Scholars*,[10] claims it was also another age—as he describes how these older traditional colleges expanded their administrative personnel, modernized their curricula, and broadened their student clienteles. On the other hand, Christine Ogren explores how 180 state normal schools, with their generally poorer students, provided instruction in the emerging field of teacher education across the country in mostly coeducational settings. Her research adds an important dimension in understanding how education became professionalized.

These three types of collegiate and pre-collegiate institutions comprised most of higher education in the nineteenth century, as the more specialized state and land-grant colleges evolved and research universities came into being. The Americanization of the higher education landscape thus had been furthered through this dramatic modern institutional differentiation over the century. The next period would see even more institutional change, as the more modern form of American higher education took hold.

ENDNOTES

[1] Carol Gruber, *Mars and Minerva* (Baton Rouge: Louisiana State University Press, 1975).

[2] Laurence Veysey, *The Emergence of the American University* (Chicago: University of Chicago Press, 1965).

[3] Robert Bruce, *The Launching of Modern American Science, 1846–1876* (New York: Knopf, 1987) and Francesco Cordasco, *The Shaping of American Graduate Education: Daniel Coit Gilman and the Protean Ph.D.* (Towanta, NJ: Rowman and Littlefield, 1973).

[4] Roger L. Williams, *The Origins of Federal Support for Higher Education* (University Park, PA: Penn State University Press, 1991).

[5] Laurence Veysey, *The Emergence of the American University* (1965); Jurgen Herbst, *The German Historical School in American Scholarship: A Study in the Transfer of Culture* (New York: Cornell University Press, 1965); and Roger Geiger, *To Advance Knowledge: The Growth of the American Research University, 1900–1940* (New York: Oxford University Press, 1986).

[6] Roger Geiger, "The Conditions of University Research, 1900–1920," in *History of Higher Education Annual* 5 (1987), 3–29.

[7] John S. Brubacher and Willis Rudy, *Higher Education in Transition: A History of American Colleges and Universities* (New York: Harper and Row Publishers, 1976).

[8] Christopher Newfield, "The Rise of University Management," in *Ivy and Industry: Business and the Making of the American University* (Durham, NC: Duke University Press, 2003).

[9] Hugh Hawkins, *Between Harvard and America: The Educational Leadership of Charles W. Eliot* (New York: Oxford University Press, 1972).

[10] W. Bruce Leslie, *Gentlemen and Scholars* (University Park, PA: Penn State University Press, 1992).

BACKDROP

CAROL S. GRUBER

It is commonplace to describe the emergence of the modern university in post-Civil War America as a phenomenon of revolutionary proportions, marked not only by the erection of great new institutions of higher learning but by the thorough transformation of the existing liberal arts college as well. The decades from the late 1860s to the turn of the century saw the rise of new universities, the construction of universities on the base of existing colleges, the founding of centers of professional, technical, and graduate training, and the invasion and profound alteration of the curriculum of the college itself.[1] "By contrast with England and the Continent, the problem [in America] was one of creation, not capture or redirection."[2] To be sure, the ideas and institutional devices were imported from abroad, but not before the social and material preconditions were established in the United States, and the product that resulted was stamped with the unmistakable imprint of the American environment.

The old liberal arts college that dated from colonial times was an adaptation of the English model. Its inspiration came from Oxbridge; but, because the American land was so vast and financial resources were so few and because of local and sectarian rivalries, the English pattern of great universities composed of clusters of independent, autonomous colleges never was duplicated. Instead, the American college assumed its own character, which it retained, not unchallenged but essentially unchanged, until the university revolution of the late nineteenth century.

The American liberal arts college was a sectarian institution designed to perpetuate a class of educated gentlemen. Staff members either already wore the cloth or were in training for the ministry. Its curriculum was prescribed and reflected the view that knowledge was a fixed body of truth to be acquired by rote through the discipline of the faculties of which the human mind was held to be composed: reason, memory, imagination, judgment, and attention. It was thought that these faculties could be developed best by drill in the classics, which consequently made up the heart of the curriculum. Because the course of study was fixed and because teaching chiefly was by recitation, there was no need for teachers to be specialists, and it was not uncommon for a tutor to take his students through the whole curriculum for the year (or longer, if he remained at the institution). Discipline, also under the tutor's charge, was enforced rigorously; attendance in class and chapel was compulsory and a tight rein was held on the students' behavior. The college, with its rigidly prescribed general education, its tone of moral piety, and its exclusive constituency, was isolated from the world around it. There was little, if any, articulation between college and career, school and society. Richard Shryock has observed that, in their educational level, their isolation from each other, and their pattern of lay government, pre-Civil War American colleges resembled the public schools (preparatory schools) of England more than its universities. "For more than two centuries," he concluded, "there was nothing 'higher' about American higher education."[3]

Beginning in the early nineteenth century, there were serious attempts to reform the American college in conformity with the expansion of knowledge and changing social conditions and needs, but the attempts met with enormous resistance and were brought to an end by the Civil War. The commitment to general education was too firm, the colleges were too poor to restructure even if they had had the will to do so, and the business community, which might have supplied some of the necessary funds, saw no relationship between higher education and its own interests. College still was viewed as a luxury for a minority, whose needs were met by traditional liberal education.

Following the Civil War, several material and social factors converged to produce a change in conditions and convictions sufficient to precipitate the restructuring of American higher education. The acceleration of urbanization and industrialization and the settlement of the continent created a demand for scientific and technical knowledge by both business and the federal and state governments. The accumulation of great fortunes made private capital available just at the time that the business community was beginning to identify education with material success. The increasing recognition by federal and state authorities of the social value of higher education made public funds available as well. The level of original and experimental work in science and engineering began to be sufficiently high to command respect in comparison with the classical curriculum, and the expansion of knowledge exposed the limitations of that curriculum to increasingly critical view. The challenge to the classical curriculum and the intellectual foundations on which it rested further was facilitated by an erosion of religious influence and an advancing secularism to which the impact of Darwinism contributed. All of these factors made American educational theorists receptive to the influence and example of university developments in Europe, particularly in Germany.

We have been cautioned against viewing the modern university of the 1870s, 1880s, and 1890s as a totally new type of institution established on foreign models. Laurence Veysey reminds us of the important legacies left by the old-time college, and Arthur Bestor insists that the university revolution essentially was a process of assimilation and integration of already present ingredients.[4] Granting the legitimacy of these caveats, it nevertheless is true that the modern university fundamentally was different in character and purpose from the college it superseded. The small, residential, closely regulated undergraduate colleges were supplanted by educational centers comprised of professional schools in law, medicine, theology, and higher arts and sciences, whose ideal intellectual climate was one of free inquiry. These centers were dedicated to the education of a mass society, to the expansion rather than mere perpetuation and transmission of knowledge, and to the teaching of technical and vocational skills. Their curricula were diversified and specialized, with scientific, technical, and vocational subjects assuming equal rank with liberal humanistic studies. The new objectives in higher education gave rise to new teaching techniques and special facilities, such as laboratories and research libraries. The universities recruited specialists in the new branches of knowledge, and the faculties were organized into departments along the lines of the various scholarly disciplines and technical and vocational subjects.

These developments were not confined to the university; they spilled over into the college itself, which was transformed in the process. Beginning with the reforms of Charles W. Eliot at Harvard in the 1870s, the new and higher studies were gradually introduced into the college curriculum. By the turn of the century, and after considerable controversy, the required classical curriculum had been invaded even in the most conservative colleges; it gave way to a program of varied studies from which the student could choose his courses. Adopting the elective system brought about the modernization of the undergraduate college along the lines laid down by the university revolution.

By 1900 the great changes had been accomplished. New university centers had been built across the country—Cornell in 1869, Johns Hopkins in 1876, Clark in 1889, Chicago in 1890, and Stanford in 1891; established institutions like California, Michigan, Minnesota, Wisconsin, Columbia, Harvard, Yale, and Princeton had been turned into modern universities; and the character of the undergraduate college had been transformed. Within these institutional changes and in reciprocal relationship to them, equally profound changes had taken place in the various branches of knowledge and in the profession of their practitioners. Two distinct but inseparable processes of professionalization had occurred: the professionalization of knowledge characterized by the emergence of discrete scholarly disciplines and the development of an academic profession characterized by the definition of standards of preparation, performance, protection, and rewards.

The professionalization of knowledge in part reflected the impact of science on American thought. The grip of theology and ethics on all branches of knowledge was weakened by the belief in rational causation, discoverable by induction from data accumulated by observation and experimentation. As knowledge expanded, it became defined and specialized into discrete subject areas. The process began with the professionalization of science itself in the second half of the nineteenth century; simultaneously, philosophy sloughed off its allegiances to theology; psychology was grounded on an experimental basis; the hodgepodge curriculum in moral philosophy broke up into the new disciplines of economics, political science, and sociology; and history, moving away from literature and philosophy, attempted to establish itself on a scientific basis.[5]

Specialists in the disciplines were trained in the new graduate schools of arts and sciences, where they were imbued with the ideal of research and instructed in its techniques. University presses and scholarly journals were founded to provide outlets for the results of their investigations. Finally, an institutional framework for the newly professionalized disciplines was provided by the establishment of associations to define standards and goals in the various fields of learning. Supplanting the pre-Civil War learned societies that were local in membership, generally open to anyone who wished to join, comprehensive in scope, and sometimes confused between scientific and humanitarian aims, the new professional associations functioned like guilds, setting standards for admission and performance on a national scale and giving the scholar a new persona as a practitioner of his discipline.[6] Organizations such as the Modern Language Association, American Historical Association, American Economic Association, American Psychological Association, and American Sociological Society, established between the last decades of the nineteenth century and the first years of the twentieth century, were indications of the professionalization of scholarship. The founding of the American Association of University Professors in 1915 signified a professional consciousness that transcended discipline boundaries to define the academic occupation.

As the academic setting changed with the emergence of the modern university, so did the character and vocation of the faculty. The academic career previously had been relatively unstructured and accessible; it was available to cultivated men of letters who did not need to give evidence of special training or competence in scholarly subjects. The professionalization of knowledge and diversification of the curriculum created the need for a specially trained and certified faculty, which led to the establishment of standards for entry into the profession, itself becoming increasingly structured and defined. Specialized training was provided by the graduate schools of arts and sciences and the Ph.D. degree became the certificate of entry into the profession, whose division into ranks provided a structure for measured advance. Finally, reflecting these changes, the general character of the calling also was changed. A vocation that previously had been confined to the teaching function was infused with the ideal of research and scholarship. The teacher no longer was an isolated instructor of immature minds; he was a member of a community of scholars dedicated to the expansion of learning as well as to its preservation and transmission.[7]

The uncertainties in the new profession, as well as its clearly emerging outlines, created a need to define its relationship with the constituent members of its own community and with the outside world. The AAUP was founded in 1915 to satisfy this need. When John Dewey defended the new association against charges of "trade unionism" and "sordid economic self-interest" by likening it to the American Medical Association and the American Bar Association,[8] he was voicing the emergent professional consciousness of the academic community. By the second decade of the twentieth century, professors had overcome their habitual individualism sufficiently to organize into a pressure group to protect their professional status. They were acknowledging that the revolution in higher learning had turned their vocation into a profession. The president of the AAUP announced at the second annual meeting:

> The truth is that we are a single profession—the most responsible branch of that profession which Fichte forever exalted with his inspired essay on 'The Nature of the Scholar.' And, to adapt a phrase of his from 'The Vocation of Man,' 'It is the vocation of our profession to unite itself into one single body, all the parts of which shall be thoroughly known to each other and all possessed of similar intellectual standards.' . . . Separated as we have been by the distinctions of our several sciences, and sundered as we still are and will be by distances of space and by independence of institutions, the professional bond of the University Scholar and Teacher must become and remain the strongest; for it is the one common and fundamental element in our careers. We need no charter to unite us; this bond is stronger and freer than a chartered law. Circumstances, and the ripeness of the times, have destined us to this union.[9]

Any description of the sources and contours of the university revolution that omits the German influence must be incomplete. To be sure, change could not occur before the ground was prepared at home; nevertheless, there was no single influence on the direction that change would take as great as that provided by the example from Germany. The influence was exerted directly on American students who, beginning in the early nineteenth century, went to the universities of Germany to acquire the professional and advanced education that was not yet available at home.

Between 1820 and 1920 almost nine thousand Americans studied in German universities—the majority during the last decades of the nineteenth century—either receiving advanced training as part of an American doctoral program or, more typically, taking a German Ph.D. degree. Among them were men who would become architects of the modern university in America, including Andrew Dickson White, Daniel Coit Gilman, and G. Stanley Hall. They returned to America inspired by the idea of the university as a community of students and scholars engaged in the free transmission and expansion of knowledge, and they proceeded to translate the idea into institutions modeled after the German example. The erection of the graduate school of arts and sciences reflected the Germanization of American higher education, as did the introduction of such teaching techniques and research devices as lectures, seminars, libraries, and laboratories. The establishment of knowledge on a scientific basis also reflected the influence of Germany, for it was there that the pioneering work was done in the various scholarly disciplines, and it was there that Americans learned to apply the methods of science to the accumulation and analysis of data. It was there, too, that they were introduced to the concept, which would become a foundation of their profession, that knowledge can be advanced only in a climate of absolute intellectual freedom. Finally, Americans who earned German Ph.D. degrees returned home as fully trained professionals in their disciplines. Their view of the vocation of scholarship contributed to the establishment of an academic profession, with precise standards and goals and with a high sense of social value.[10]

The German influence was particularly great on the American social sciences. It promoted not only a scientific methodology but also a conviction that knowledge has a social function, and it impressed upon scholars in the new disciplines a keen sense of responsibility to the public welfare.[11] Many of the pioneering American social scientists of the late nineteenth and early twentieth century—including the economists Richard T. Ely, Henry W. Farnam, and E. R. A. Seligman, the sociologists Albion W. Small and E. A. Ross, and the historians Herbert Baxter Adams, John W. Burgess, and James Harvey Robinson—did graduate work in Germany. German-trained social scientists were in the vanguard of those who developed graduate departments in their disciplines and founded professional associations and publications. They dominated the faculties of the social sciences departments of the new universities.

That Germany was the nation to vitally influence the emergence of the modern American university is not difficult to explain. From the early nineteenth century until the advent of Nazism, the excellence of the German universities and their high level of achievement made them "model academic institutions."[12] The prestige of a German doctorate was very high, and the degree was relatively easy to acquire. Americans were drawn by the intellectual vitality of nineteenth-century German university scholarship and by the reputation of individual scholars. Furthermore, the cost of living in Germany was attractively low. By comparison, the universities of France and Britain had little to offer.[13] Indeed, although British universities were emerging from a period of "torpor and ossification" and were beginning to improve in the early twentieth century and to attract American attention,[14] the advances they made were influenced by the German example.[15] Josiah Royce beautifully described the centrality of the German experience during the formative years of university building in America. Speaking of the late 1870s, he recalled a professor at Johns Hopkins telling him that "when he dealt with young American scholars he found them feeling as if not England, but Germany, were their mother-country. . . . One went to Germany," he continued, "still a doubter as to the possibility of the theoretic life; one returned an idealist, devoted for the time to pure learning for learnings' sake determined to contribute his *Scherflein* to the massive store of human knowledge, burning for a chance to help build the American University."[16]

Americans did not hesitate to acknowledge the influence of German higher education and scholarship. For example, in 1904 the University of Chicago for its fiftieth convocation chose the theme "Recognition of the Indebtedness of American Universities to the Ideals of German Scholarship." The principal address of the occasion, delivered by Professor John M. Coulter, held up the German university as "a model to other nations." The great principles on which the German university rests, Coulter said, must be the basic principles of universities everywhere.[17] In his letter of greeting to the assemblage, President Theodore Roosevelt hailed Germany as "the mother of modern science and learning."[18] The following year, an annual exchange professorship between German and American universities was established, expressing a mutual desire to preserve and promote the affinities between the higher educational world in the two countries.

In 1914, German representatives in the United States counted on these affinities to make American university scholars sympathetic to Germany's cause in the war. These representatives founded the German University League, with the purpose of uniting "those who have enjoyed the privilege of a German university education" in efforts "to strengthen the regard for the Germans and for their aims and ideals, and to secure for them . . . fair play and proper appreciation."[19] A letter from the philosophers Rudolf Eucken and Ernst Haeckel to the universities of America was distributed with the league's first announcement, expressing confidence in "the friendly feeling of the American universities," whose members, as a result of their training in Germany, the exchange of scholars, and the bonds created by scholarly research, "know what German culture means to the world." Eucken and Haeckel concluded with the expectation that American scholars would reject the Allied interpretation of the war and accept that of the Central Powers.[20]

This expectation, aside from overlooking the influence of the war's political and diplomatic issues on American scholars, was based on a mistakenly simple view of the influence of Germany on American higher education. What had been involved was a complicated process of interpretation, even misinterpretation, selection, and alteration to adapt the German example to the American environment. Americans transported the organizational structure of German scholarship—the graduate school and the instructional techniques and research devices associated with it, the professional association, and professional publications—and the new scientific methodology almost intact; but they eschewed the idealist context in which these operated in Germany. Walter P. Metzger observes, "Most Americans who went to study in Germany . . . took home the methods of her seminars and laboratories, but left the *Anschauung* of idealism behind."[21] According to Veysey, Americans who, under the influence of Germany, became dedicated to scientific research missed "the larger, almost contemplative implications of *Wissenschaft*" and transformed the German ideal of "pure learning," unaffected by utilitarian demands, into an American version, "pure science," assuming that "investigation meant something specifically scientific." The Germans' lofty evocation of underlying spiritual unity was ignored by research-minded Americans, who found the inspiration for their academic theorizing on the level of German practice and became deeply inspired by the rigorous and precise examination of phenomena. "An insufficiently differentiated Germany, partly real and partly imaginary," Veysey concludes, "became the symbol for all scientific claims upon American education."[22]

Furthermore, the process of cultural transfer was ambivalent, particularly in the social sciences. Jurgen Herbst demonstrates that it was largely the influence of German methods of empirical research and inductive generalization that professionalized history in late nineteenth-century America. But, he continues, the philosophic assumptions and political ideas that were central to German historical writing at the time were incompatible with American tradition and values. Consequently, the attempt to transfer to the United States a German science of history and politics failed in the long run.[23] The writings of the first generation of German-trained historians, chief among them Herbert Baxter Adams and John W. Burgess, applied German ideas and values—statism, rejection of natural rights and the social contract, Aryan superiority—to the history of the United States. In order for the next generation of American historians to understand the dynamics of a democratic society, they had to reject the approach of Adams and his followers. Herbst declares that Adams himself came to realize the incompatibility of German ideas with American history and ended his contacts with his German mentors, drawing closer to "democratic" colleagues in England. Herbst quotes W. Stull Holt's conclusion from this fact that "the orthodox account of the dominant influence of German scholarship in America during this period [1876–1901] may need revision."[24]

Herbst maintains that it was easier to accomplish cultural transfer in the fields of economics and sociology, where the object of inquiry was society and not the state and where, consequently, the problem of antagonism between the individual and the state did not necessarily have to be confronted.[25] But even in these disciplines Americans responded with discrimination to the influence of German scholarship. For example, Joseph Dorfman points out that, although the German historical school had a seminal influence on modern economics in America, the Germans' political philosophy of centralized authority was rejected by Americans, who substituted ideas more congenial to a pluralistic society.[26]

Finally, the manner in which Americans simultaneously adopted the German principle of academic freedom and adapted it to the American environment illustrates the selectivity of the process of cultural transfer. The German ideal of the free pursuit of knowledge, without religious, political, or administrative control, exacted both praise and envy from Americans from the time they first began to study in German universities.[27] By the time they organized the AAUP, professors in America had concluded that academic freedom was the prerequisite of the profession. But their application of the principle was vastly different from that of the Germans. For one thing, unlike the Germans, they were relatively unconcerned with the issue of student freedom (*Lernfreiheit*) and restricted their efforts to the definition and protection of the freedom of the faculty (*Lehrfreiheit*). Furthermore, the Americans restricted a professor's freedom within the classroom, insisting that he confine his subject matter to his field of competence and that he maintain a "neutral" posture in presenting it. At the same time, they extended the definition of academic freedom to protect freedom of expression outside university walls, insisting that a professor should no more be penalized for exercising his constitutional right of free speech than any other citizen. In this fashion, academic freedom in the United States became associated with civil liberty.[28]

One aspect of the experience of American students in Germany should at least be mentioned in connection with any evaluation of the German impact on American scholars. It was not uncommon for Americans who received their professional training in Germany and who were enormously impressed by German scholarship and culture to be at the same time disturbed, even repelled, by other traits of German society, particularly the high esteem accorded to the military establishment and the authoritarianism that characterized German political and social life. A high regard for German learning and culture, in other words, could go hand in hand with a rejection of other German values and institutions.[29]

Taken together, the increasing discrimination with which Americans came to view German education and scholarship and the simultaneous improvement in American graduate education led to a waning of German influence on American higher education after the 1890s. Veysey concludes that, "despite the inauguration of exchange professorships between the two countries, American and German academic circles increasingly lost contact with each other well before the advent of the First World War."[30] Nevertheless, by this time an acknowledged prior debt to Germany was part of the record of American higher education and, in the case of individual American professors, there were warm professional and personal relationships with German scholars and their families that had been established when the Americans had studied abroad and that endured during the early years of the twentieth century.

Professors Eucken and Haeckel and the founders of the German University League erred not only in viewing the influence of Germany on American higher education with an undiscriminating eye, but also in failing to consider other influences on American higher education and other deep and enduring influences on American culture that would help determine American sympathies in the war. Although the erection of the modern university in America was a process of Germanization, the base on which it was imposed derived from England, and the traces of the English college and the values it represented never disappeared from the American system. Historically, from the time of its inception in the seventeenth century, the American college had belonged to the English type. In its dedication to education rather than training and to the cultivation of moral and social as well as intellectual attributes, the American college exemplified the English ideal of liberal education.[31] It was this ideal that had to be combated by the proponents of the modern university. A French observer of the American educational scene in the late nineteenth century described it as a great battlefield on which English (liberal education) and German (laboratory science) influences fought.[32] Richard Hofstadter demonstrates that, although the German ideals of scholarship and academic freedom were at the heart of the university revolution, English influences persisted even after the revolution had been accomplished. He describes these influences as follows: concern with the development of character in undergraduates and with "atmosphere" in the institutions; a passion for imposing buildings, separated if possible from the urban community; an emphasis on teaching as opposed to research; a commitment to the centrality of the college among the various parts of the university; an aim of creating a broadly educated leadership as opposed to a body of specialists; and a zeal for undergraduate sports. These influences, he concludes, remained "especially strong in the better colleges and in some universities, like Yale and Princeton."[33] The regular attendance of American Rhodes Scholars at Oxford University beginning in 1902 suggests that British ideals of higher education continued to be relevant for Americans even after they had revamped their universities largely along German lines.

The cultural and intellectual affinities between America and Britain stretched far beyond the area of educational influences and interchange and present an even more complicated picture of cultural transfer than that already described between Germany and America. Only the broad outlines of that picture can be sketched here. In his study *The American Image of the Old World*, Cushing Strout demonstrates that Americans traditionally experienced acute ambivalence toward England. From the time of the Revolution, he argues, England provoked a kind of schizophrenic response from America; it was both America's oldest and most detested enemy, the prime target of America's antipathy toward the Old World, and the mother country, the source of America's language, culture, and many of its most cherished institutions.[34] Throughout the nineteenth century, Anglophobia lay at the heart of American patriotism, its persistence was demonstrated every Fourth of July and was revealed in virtually every school text in American history. This Anglophobia was reinforced by the fact that it was England with whom America was engaged in the most frequent and most dangerous diplomatic controversies. But there also was a strong strain of Anglophilia in nineteenth-century American culture, which was shared by those who recognized America's profound cultural debt to Britain and by trading and financial interests that had close economic ties with England.

Toward the end of the century, as a result of developments in both countries, relations between America and England began perceptibly to improve. Anglophilia in America was strengthened considerably as white Protestant Americans became increasingly fearful of the effects of the new immigration and as popularizers of Anglo-Saxonism played on the racial and cultural affinities of the English and American peoples. When the United States joined the ranks of imperialist powers, with its own overseas possessions and expanding interests in Latin America and the Far East, Americans grew increasingly aware of the necessity to cement the relationship with Great Britain, potentially the country's most dangerous foe. Britain was interested in improved relations because of its own imperial problems, particularly the threat of an expanding Germany. The possibilities of mutual benefit were demonstrated when Britain's benevolent neutrality in the Spanish-American War forestalled intervention by hostile European powers and Secretary of State John Hay reciprocated during the Boer War by making sure that America would take no action that would hurt the British cause.[35]

Bradford Perkins concludes that, in spite of the persistence of antipathy to England in the American popular imagination, during the years 1895–1914 a "great rapprochement" had taken place between America and Britain. With most of the concessions being made by Britain in response to challenges it faced elsewhere and with the American political elite in advance of American public opinion, the slate of more than a century of antagonism and conflict was wiped clean after the Spanish-American War, and a new spirit of understanding and accommodation between the two countries came to prevail.[36] A recent study of the intellectual roots of this Anglo-American "alliance" demonstrates that the turn-of-the-century accord reflected more than the political, economic, and strategic considerations from which it originated. Concentrating on the ideas of Theodore Roosevelt and some of his English correspondents, David H. Burton portrays a shared conviction that, despite superficial differences between England and the United States, there were deep, underlying political and cultural similarities between the two countries. The accord, these Anglo-Saxonists believed, was a "natural" response to the threats of the alien culture and polity of the dynamic, new German Empire, the uncertain future direction of the Russian state, and the chaotic conditions in China. St. Loe Strachey spoke for Anglo-Saxonists in both countries when he said: "We speak the same language, recognize the same common law principles in our law and administration, and are inspired by the same political and moral ideals."[37]

American Anglo-Saxonists were in a good position to combat continuing popular tendencies in their country to twist the lion's tail, for they were well represented in the sectors of society that influenced foreign policy opinions and decisions—in presidential administrations, in the army and navy, in the leadership of Congress, and among the intelligentsia.[38] Anglophilia flourished in America's pressrooms and publishing houses and on American campuses. Among professors the close intellectual tie with England exerted great sway, "stretching in memory," as Veysey observes, "all the way back to the first importation of 'liberal education' from Cambridge to Harvard in colonial times."[39] It was the persistence of the English gentlemanly social ideal among professors that ultimately intertwined with the newer impulse toward professionalization. Finally, the concept of "civilization," which was so important to American professors' interpretation of the war, meant to them the political, legal, economic, and cultural accomplishments of the English-speaking peoples and the prospective benefits to the rest of the world from the spread of their influence.

After the influences from Germany and England have been acknowledged, the fact remains that the character of American universities from the time of their origin has been unique and has stemmed from the special circumstances of the American environment. Compared to universities elsewhere in the Western world, American institutions of higher learning have been exceptionally responsive to conditions in the surrounding community. This is partly a result of the American departure from the pattern of national universities. The concomitant decentralization of decision making in American institutions of higher learning (that is, their freedom from central planning) and the extreme heterogeneity of their quality and character have made them responsive to social and economic forces in their local environments.[40] Furthermore, American universities, Allan Nevins points out, always have been peculiarly regional, in the sense of having "relevance to a special community." The idea that universities in America should have a regional function took root from the beginning, Nevins observes, as Harvard was planted for the special inspiration of Massachusetts Bay and William and Mary for the Old Dominion. The country was so large that as higher education spread westward, it had to find a state or regional pattern. This pattern was most characteristic of state universities, but not confined to them alone.[41] Finally, American universities have been particularly responsive to outside influence because of their pattern of lay government and their dependence for funds on donors in the case of private institutions and on legislative bodies in the case of public institutions.

Because the emergence of the modern university in America was associated so closely with the needs of a democratic, industrializing society, it is not surprising that its function should be defined largely in terms of serving those needs. The singularity of American institutions of higher learning stems more from the ideal of service with which they are permeated than from any other factor in their history. Although there never has been agreement about goals within the academic community, the ideal of service was pervasive in educational circles at the time of the university revolution and afterwards; it continues to be a distinguishing feature of American higher education. Indeed, Veysey makes it clear that the initial impetus toward the modern university came from those—like Charles W. Eliot of Harvard and Andrew Dickson White of Cornell—who viewed its function as serving the surrounding community. The concept of service sprang in part from the recognition by administrators of their need for support from public and private sources, from prevailing theories about the nature and function of knowledge, and from moral idealism in the faculty.[42]

The service-oriented educators made the primary assumption "that the patterns of behavior which flourished outside the campus were more 'real' than those which most often prevailed within it." "Reality" increasingly was defined as "democratic" and given a vocational tinge, and the university was to mirror that democratic reality in several ways: by establishing all fields of learning on an equal basis; by treating all students as equals; by providing easy admission; by portraying itself as an agency for individual success; by emphasizing its function to widely diffuse knowledge throughout society; and by embracing the idea that it should take its orders directly from the citizenry.[43] The commitment to service was reflected in student bodies drawn not from an intellectual elite seeking initiation into the mysteries of pure science, arts, and letters, but from those among the general population interested in acquiring an increasingly functional degree; in curricula that were highly differentiated and offered a wide range of practical training (extending downward in the education hierarchy from training for the professions of medicine, law, and engineering to training in the "science" of business administration and the "economics" of homemaking); and in faculties whose members freely donated their talents as expert advisers to municipal, state, and federal agencies.

The articulation of interest between the university and society was both appreciated and promoted by the federal government. Beginning in 1862 with the passage of the first Morrill Act and continuing with the Hatch Act of 1887 and the second Morrill Act of 1890, the federal government pledged its support to the promotion of education in the useful—agricultural and mechanical—arts, for the common man. The first Morrill Act was designed to provide improved techniques and trained operatives for the industry and agriculture upon which the northern national economy rested.[44] Grants of land under the act went both to existing institutions (in Wisconsin, for example, the state university was the beneficiary) and to newly established agricultural and technical colleges, and it was these land-grant colleges and other state institutions that came particularly to stand for the "all-purpose" curriculum and for service to the community.[45] Clark Kerr describes the Morrill Act as "one of the most seminal pieces of legislation ever enacted" and states, "Nowhere before had universities been so closely linked with the daily life of so much of their societies."[46]

The "Wisconsin Idea" was one of the earliest, most fully developed, and best publicized expressions of the service ideal and has come to stand as its archetype.[47] To be sure, the Wisconsin Idea neither significantly affected state politics nor ensured harmonious relations between the university and the legislature, educational authorities, and other officials in the state.[48] But the wide-ranging extension program and the substantial faculty advisory service to the many branches of the state government testified to the university's highly developed commitment to an organic relationship between itself and its surrounding community. However, the service ideal should not be associated exclusively with land-grant and state institutions or with universities, like Wisconsin, that established carefully planned and executed programs to put the ideal into practice. Even private institutions and those that had a more traditional focus on undergraduate liberal education or research-oriented graduate work in the pure sciences and in arts and letters appeared before the public in a garb of social service. It was not uncommon to use the idea of "service," loosely defined, to legitimize the American university.[49]

Since the revolution in higher learning was a process and not an event, it is not possible to say precisely when it was completed. But we can safely say that by 1910 the period of greatest change in the world of higher learning had taken place. By then the period of new university building had passed its peak, as had the influence of the elective principle on the undergraduate curriculum, and a professional outlook had come to characterize the scholarly disciplines and the academic vocation. That a great transformation had been accomplished, however, is not to say that a uniform product had emerged capable of clear definition or characterized by inner harmony and tranquillity. The opposite, in fact, was true. The modern university in America did not have clear goals or a common sense of purpose; aspects of the university revolution stood in contradictory relationship to each other and resulted in dysfunctional tension and antagonism; and, although the professional disciplines and a professional consciousness had been born, they were in their infancy and their future direction was unclear.

To speak at all of "the college" or "the university" in America at the time of the great transformation and down to the present can be misleading. In a country so vast where there came to be such a great emphasis on skill and where education became identified with success, there was room for an apparently unlimited number of higher educational institutions of very uneven character and quality. The world of higher education presented a varied face. In addition to the new and reformed private universities, the reformed liberal arts colleges, and the state institutions and their far-flung extension divisions, there were various vocational and technical schools, municipal colleges, separate schools for Negroes and for women, and the old-style denominational colleges, which, no longer in the mainstream, continued to exist. Higher educational institutions were, and remain, so heterogeneous in character and quality that a contemporary observer has concluded that "there is a college somewhere in America for everybody."[50] Too, the rate of development in the period of growth, particularly among the state institutions, was uneven, reflecting the uneven material and cultural progress of their states and the particular political and social circumstances in their environments.[51] Within this decentralized and continually expanding world of higher education, and particularly among the "successful" institutions, a state of keen competition came to prevail for financial support, students, faculty, and prestige.[52]

A salient fact emerges from the history of the university revolution: it failed to replace the unified pattern of the old-time college, which it shattered, with a clear pattern of its own. Veysey's work is a massive elaboration precisely of this point. It demonstrates the competing goals that characterized the early period of the university revolution, when the proponents of liberal culture, of research, and of utility struggled to stamp their vision on the face of the new institution. The debate over goals had quieted by about 1890, he concludes, but never was settled; rather than a clear sense of purpose, only "unacknowledged confusion," "hazy generalities," and an accommodation of conflicting purposes under the general rubric of social service had resulted. To this day the university remains in a state of "uneasy balance" from its embodiment of conflicting ideals: the German ideal of research and graduate and professional education; the English ideal of liberal culture and undergraduate education; and the American ideal of "lesser professional" (other than legal and medical) education and public service.[53] "The university is so many things to so many people," concludes Kerr, "that it must, of necessity, be partially at war with itself."[54]

Tensions that sprang from the internal development of the university as a social system were as significant as those that resulted from the lack of a unified sense of purpose within and between the institutions of higher learning. The chief tensions resulted from the bureaucratization of the university in the last decades of the nineteenth century. As the university grew in size and complexity, the old "familial" pattern of management was replaced by a bureaucratic structure embodied in an elaborate administrative hierarchy.[55] By the early 1900s, the universities had come to look like business corporations, with their directors (trustees), executives (administrators), and employees (faculty).[56] Within this process of bureaucratization, the changing role of the president had the most dramatic consequences. Although the president's legal rights had not expanded since 1870 (legally he still was the chief executive of the trustees), his stature had grown enormously with the expansion of the institutions and their administrative personnel. So, too, had the nature of the office changed, from the president being "first among equals," who shared with his faculty a religious purpose, a teaching function, a common intellectual background, and an intimacy of daily contact, to his becoming managerial overlord of a complex organization.[57]

The change in the presidential office destroyed the homogeneity of academic society by dividing it into two vocations—administration and teaching—with clearly demarcated spheres of influence. The faculty was given hegemony over the classroom, but vital policy decisions affecting the functioning and future development of the institution were the province of the administration, even though it might assign the faculty an advisory role in these areas. During the first decades of reform, the innovative presidents and the faculty often were allies against resistant conservative forces; but significant faculty resistance to presidential authority had developed by the early twentieth century, when a new generation of managerial consolidators occupied the presidential office.[58]

Tensions between the faculty and the president reflected more than competition for power over decision making; they reflected the deep-lying and often subtle tensions that grew out of the peculiar position of the faculty member as both professional and employee. The concept of professionalism resists easy definition, but sociologists seem to agree that autonomy—control by professionals themselves of the development and application of their field of special competence—is its essential condition. Because authority in an organization is enforced through "superordinate control," tension inevitably arises when professional roles confront organizational necessities.[59] These confrontations occurred frequently in academia; not only were subtle forms of rendering the faculty subservient involved, but head-on collisions as well.[60] The dual professional-employee position of the faculty has implications beyond the confines of the institution of higher learning. When he discusses the relative social status of university professors and other professional men like physicians and lawyers, Shryock observes that the general prestige of professors is lowered by their "quasi-employee" status.[61]

The simultaneous emergence of the modern university and professionalization of scholarship and the academic vocation offers a clue to internal tensions in the system. In many respects the two revolutions, in university structure and professionalism, were complementary, even interdependent.

The new disciplines and their practitioners needed the resources of the new universities to become established, gain recognition, and extend their influence. They were enormously strengthened by being recognized in the expanding curriculum, being given departmental status (with separate budgets and considerable control over standards and staffing), and having laboratory and library resources at their command. So, too, did the universities depend on the professionals for their advance. A faculty with a high professional reputation commanded students, financial support, and prestige for its institution. In another respect, however, the two revolutions were contradictory. For, as the university revolution climaxed in the triumph of administrative bureaucracy, with its descending lines of command, this bureaucracy conflicted with the increasing professional consciousness of the faculty. Indeed, the more accomplished and professionally distinguished the faculty, the more it would resist the enlarged powers of the president, insist on a voice in university management, and demand greater freedom. The tensions created by the dual professional-employee status of the faculty were an important factor in the academic freedom cases of the late nineteenth and early twentieth centuries.

It should not be concluded from the above observations that by the early twentieth century the academic vocation was characterized by a fully developed sense of group solidarity and professional élan or that there were no tensions and strains within the academic profession itself. The division of the vocation into ranks was one index of professionalism;[62] but the establishment of a rank hierarchy introduced considerable differences of status and outlook between individuals in the lower and higher positions. The individuals on the lower rung of the occupational ladder, instructors and assistant professors, were in a precarious occupational position characterized by uncertainty and insecurity.[63] Their number among the nation's professoriate had undergone a marked proportional increase between the late nineteenth and early twentieth centuries.[64] Their lot, according to a 1910 study of a selected group of assistant professors, was one of retarded advancement and exploitation, which benefited their seniors.[65] And it was the small core of senior professors who exercised whatever influence and power the faculty had.[66]

The history of the founding of their professional association itself reveals the problematic professional solidarity of university scholars, which persists to this day. Discussing the origins of the AAUP, Metzger points out that, although there was an enormous variety of proposals for the direction the new association should take, there was consensus about what the association should *not* do: deal with the question of salaries. "Collective bargaining was unthinkable," he says; "even a collective statement was presumed to suggest trade union tactics."[67] Although this response may, in part, suggest the presence of a professional self-image, the opposition to a united front on remuneration also suggests an absence of professional solidarity. Logan Wilson quotes a study that explains this opposition as a product of the preprofessional "tradition of dignity" inherited from the professor's previous ecclesiastical function, with its resulting notions that a gentleman does not bargain, that learning is its own reward, and that the life of a scholar necessarily is one of poverty and sacrifice. The study attributes the opposition further to a spirit of individualism among professors that indicates, it says, little conception of cooperative or unified welfare. This spirit was encouraged by rank cleavages, which produced a different occupational outlook between individuals in the lower and higher ranks, and by the departmental structure, which resulted in each department seeking to advance its own interests. That the AAUP operates under much heavier odds than the American Medical Association or the American Bar Association, Wilson observes, can be attributed to the absence of an overriding commitment to broad, professional interests among university scholars. Typically, a scholar's primary professional interest is his own discipline.[68] The limited resources and facilities of the AAUP, Shryock concludes, reflect "the fact that the first interest of professors is usually in their special fields, while their concern for the academic profession as a whole is secondary. The academic guild is, in a sense, a collection of a score or more of distinct professions." He contrasts this situation with "the solidarity of medical men who are physicians first and specialists thereafter."[69]

The scholarly disciplines themselves were in an inchoate condition in the early years of the twentieth century. Only recently established on a scientific basis and in a rudimentary state, they were characterized not only by a lack of clear definition of the substance and nature of the disciplines, but also by a lack of certainty about their limits and the lines of demarcation between them.

The problems of definition and demarcation were most apparent in the social sciences, the "new body of studies" as Dewey called them, that emerged out of the moral philosophy curriculum in the late nineteenth century. John Higham locates the origin of the ill-conceived, post-World War I "schism in American scholarship" between the humanities and the social sciences partly in the fluidity of categories in the subjects of the human studies and in the embryonic organization of scholarship during the early years of the century. The division between the modern humanists and social scientists, he argues, began in the effort of the new disciplines to define themselves as the classical curriculum broke down in the late nineteenth century. A student of the new science of sociology has described "the whole atmosphere of social science" between about 1885 and 1915 as "one of struggle for legitimacy against adversaries."[70]

In the attempts during the late nineteenth and early twentieth centuries to define and delimit the disciplines, historians found themselves in an ambiguous position: on the defensive against assaults on their legitimacy by the new social scientists and divided among themselves about the nature of their discipline and its proper relationship to the social sciences. Higham attributes considerable significance to the prewar quarrel among historians about the extent to which they should ally themselves with social scientists, seeing in the disagreement a premonition of the larger schism in American scholarship that would develop after the war.[71]

History in America became professionalized by differentiating itself from philosophy and literature and establishing itself on a scientific basis. The first generation of professional historians adopted not only the methods of science—empirical research, a critical approach to evidence, and inductive generalization—but its spirit as well: the repudiation of romantic idealism and its search for ultimate meaning. Misreading Leopold von Ranke, they drew a sharp distinction between the science and the philosophy of history, eschewed an interpretive approach and a search for laws to explain historical development, and confined themselves to a rigid factualism in an effort to recreate the past as it actually was.[72] Scientific history soon drew fire from the social sciences on the grounds that it was, in fact, highly unscientific, if not thoroughly meaningless. For example, at a session of the American Historical Association (AHA) annual meeting in 1903 devoted to the relation of history to the social sciences, Albion Small "contended that the historians . . . spend all their time in indexing dreary, profitless details about inconsequential folk, in developing their technical skill for the discovery of insignificant objects, in learning so much about how to investigate that they have forgotten what is worth investigating." Continuing the assault, Lester Ward charged that history was not a science because it was not concerned with causation, only with facts. Delivering the coup de grâce, "he declared [history] to be an agreeable occupation and a pleasant pastime."[73]

Considering the severity of the attack, it is not difficult to understand the heated tone in which George Burton Adams defended orthodox scientific history in his presidential address to the AHA in 1908. Using the language of conflict, he characterized the approach to history of political scientists, geographers, economic determinists, sociologists, and social psychologists as "a hostile movement," an "aggressive and vigorous school of thought" that threatened to drive the traditional historian from the field. This "disturbance in our province," he declared, represented a passing from the age of investigation to the perilous age of speculation (from which, he might have added, the first generation of professional historians had labored so assiduously to emerge). "What should the historian do," Adams asked, "in view of the threatened invasion of his domain by ideals and methods not quite his own?" He answered, in essence, that the historian must stick to his task of scientifically gathering the facts because, in the final analysis, if ever a philosophy of history was to emerge it could do so only on a firm foundation of fact. "At the beginning of all conquest of the unknown," he declared, "lies the fact. . . . The field of the historian is, and must long remain, the discovery and recording of what actually happened."[74]

The assault on scientific history came not only from hostile outsiders; by the early twentieth century there was defection within the ranks, as historians themselves divided along the lines suggested by the social scientists. A comparison of the address of Adams with those of his fellow historians at the International Congress of Arts and Science in St. Louis in 1904 offers evidence of this division. The remarks of Woodrow Wilson, James Harvey Robinson, and Frederick Jackson Turner at the congress were collectively a plea for interpretive history, for a rejection of narrative political history in favor of the study of history as a never-ending process of social development, which could be understood only by studying all aspects of human life and relying on all the allied sciences of human behavior. In contrast, Adams' paper amounted to an argument that history is fixed, there to be discovered by the historian, who mines the facts and from them constructs a narrative good for all time.[75]

The sources of the challenge by historians to scientific history, dubbed "the new history" by Robinson in 1912, were varied. Nurtured in the Progressive era and reflecting its spirit of democratic reform, infused with a "softened," nonideological version of Marxism, which was apparent not only in its emphasis of economic factors but in its view of causation and law in history, the new history was responding also to the prospect of the desertion of history by the social scientists. In its main outlines, the new history comprised a deliberate subordination of the past to the present by selecting and emphasizing those aspects of the past most relevant to present needs; a widening of the scope of history away from the institutional focus of scientific history to embrace all aspects of human affairs; and an enthusiastic alliance with the social sciences, with a view toward discovering laws of human development.[76] Particularly in their emphasis on the present, the new historians were expressing their conviction that the discipline derived its legitimacy from being a "useful" science. This conviction was expressed perfectly in a frequently quoted sentence from the introduction to James Harvey Robinson and Charles Beard's *The Development of Modern Europe*. Admitting that they "consistently subordinated the past to the present," the authors averred that it had been their "ever-conscious aim to enable the reader to catch up with his own times; to read intelligently the foreign news in the morning paper; to know what was the attitude of Leo XIII toward the Social Democrats even if he has forgotten that of Innocent III toward the Albigenses."[77] The new historians self-consciously emphasized the practical utility of their discipline; they "wanted history to prove itself."[78]

The orthodox and reform historians shared the field before World War I and frequently were tainted in "the common cause of superseding amateur scholarship." Furthermore, in many areas the reformers accepted the basic principles of orthodoxy.[79] Nevertheless, their attack on scientific history was sharp, even belligerent, and the discipline clearly was divided. In the emerging split between the humanities and the social sciences, history stood somewhere in the middle, unsure of its essential character. Paradoxically, those who opposed the "adulteration" of history with social science were speaking in the name of "scientific" history; those who argued in favor of an alliance with the social sciences were speaking of introducing meaning (i.e., value) into history; all the while, the social sciences themselves deliberately were moving away from the realm of value into that of empiricism.

The issue of the relationship between fact and value was a large one in early twentieth-century American thought; in almost all its branches there was a quest for a means to unite science and ethics in the interest of social reform. To be sure, the "new" social theorists in economics, sociology, philosophy, political science, history, and jurisprudence sought first to divorce science from morality, to make science "objective," because the two united traditionally had been an instrument of conservatism. But their objective was to establish morality on a scientific foundation by making science the arbiter of ethical problems. As non-revolutionary critics of "the glaring evils of capitalism," the "new" scholars sought to apply the scientific method to social problems and thus to formulate a science of reform.[80]

Similar concerns about the nature and function of knowledge were reflected in efforts to reestablish the unity of knowledge after the great fragmentation and specialization of the late nineteenth century. The urgency of the problem of unification was suggested by the attempts in nearly every field of thought to reconcile factual and normative knowledge and to consider the significance of rapidly accumulating "facts," their relationship to each other, and their place in the whole realm of knowledge and experience. The 1904 International Congress of Arts and Science, which brought together leading scholars in all fields of thought to consider the problem, approached it from an idealist perspective: reconciliation was to be accomplished by recognizing the "inner unity" of all branches of learning and acknowledging the human intellect and "psychical" causes as the chief social determinants.[81]

Theorists who rejected the idealist view were equally committed to the quest for unity, as Jean Quandt's study, *From the Small Town to the Great Community* makes clear. Quandt demonstrates the dedication of Progressive intellectuals to offset the individual isolation and fragmentation of life in urban, industrial America and to restore a sense of community, purpose, and shared value; she points out that they saw in the restoration of the unity of knowledge a means to this end. Their commitment to the new scholarship was not a random pursuit of truth for its own sake; they firmly believed that free inquiry would reveal the essential unity of knowledge and the oneness of man, nature, and society. Using Dewey as a prime example of this point of view, Quandt shows how he opposed the split between the cultural and the useful and the overspecialization of knowledge. Knowledge was power, according to Dewey; therefore its expansion certainly was not to be halted. But it was to be tied to action and available for use rather than compartmentalized and separated from the totality of experience.[82] The "new" theorists became the ideologists of Progressivism; they provided the intellectual foundation for attacks on laissez-faire capitalism and contributed to the prevailing faith in knowledge as an instrument of social change.[83] As individuals, they participated in reform movements of all sorts, exulting in action to such an extent that "active participation in politics, economics, and social reform became a professorial hallmark."[84]

According to Hofstadter, the Progressive era was a high-water mark of rapprochement between the intellectual and American society. The new complexity of government and administration that was a consequence of the need to control the economy, he argues, resulted in a widely acknowledged dependence on expertise. The interests of democracy itself led to an abatement of the suspicion of the expert that had originated in the democratic ethos of Jacksonian America. In the Progressive era, Hofstadter affirms, "partly as expert, partly as social critic, the intellectual now came back to a central position such as he had not held in American politics for a century." The ferment in ideas, although it did not bring a social revolution, created a widespread confidence among intellectuals that the gulf between the world of thought and the world of action finally had been bridged, affecting the morale even of those scholars whose work was far removed from the bustle of everyday life. Hofstadter concludes that "the most abstracted of scholars could derive a sense of importance from belonging to a learned community which the larger world was compelled to consult in its quest for adequate means of social control."[85] Higham, noting the relative decline in status of humanistic scholars during the early years of the twentieth century, considers Hofstadter's characterization "too simple [a] picture." Although the new type of professor, the practical man, the expert, was winning public approval, he argues, "the humanistic scholar more often felt elbowed aside" and by the time of World War I was being dramatized as a self-denigrator in the new academic novels and had become the prime butt of popular jokes about absentmindedness.[86]

The differences between Hofstadter and Higham suggest some of the difficulties in dealing with the subject of the academic intellectual's status in American society. In their social origins, the World War I generation of professors still represented a fairly homogeneous group. Existing evidence suggests that the chief breeding ground for the first and second generations of professional university scholars (those reaching maturity between the 1870s and the First World War), as for their preprofessional predecessors, still was the New England Protestant middle class.[87] But there was no single professorial "class" in America, no cultural elite with recognized social status and authority, no equivalent of the German "mandarinate."[88] Writing in 1906, William Graham Sumner pointed to the ambivalence of American attitudes toward intellect. On the one hand, he noted, Americans laud education and the multiplication of educational institutions; on the other hand, they reserve their admiration for the "common man," with his supposedly superior store of native wisdom.[89] Merle Curti has dubbed this simultaneous faith in the rational and suspicion of the life of reason, which he sees continuing to our own time, an "American paradox."[90] Without probing the question of the sources of the paradox, a clue to the status of professors during the time of this study—the period of America's involvement in the First World War—may be found in Shryock's observation that the prestige of professors has risen during periods of involvement by them in the affairs of the "real" world. If professorial prestige periodically has risen, he argues, it is "not because Americans have ceased to prize action above thought, but rather that more academicians have qualified for recognition by becoming men of action."[91] Academicians in large numbers became "men of action" during United States involvement in the First World War. There is every indication that they were well aware of the correlation between their "usefulness" and their legitimacy in the eyes of American society.

In this respect and in many others, the response of American professors to the challenge of World War I provides a valuable test case for the subjects covered in this chapter and can be understood only in reference to them. When the war came upon America, the modern university in this country only recently had been established and lacked a clear identity and sense of purpose. It drew heavily on English and particularly on German influences, but derived its special character and claim to legitimacy from a commitment to the ideal of service. Within the university, the position of the faculty was insecure; its dual professional-employee status created tensions that could and did lead to confrontations and conflict. The scholarly disciplines themselves were in a rudimentary state and were seeking to define their character and limits. Professional consciousness too was rudimentary; the AAUP had just been founded in 1915 and commanded neither widespread support in the profession nor influence in the infrastructure of university politics. The social status of the newly professionalized professoriate was uncertain, reflecting the ambivalence of American society to the life of the mind. The challenge of war both exposed and sharpened many of the tensions, contradictions, and uncertainties in the academic community. Furthermore, it confronted professors with a challenge to their loyalties. They found that loyalties that could be maintained simultaneously during normal times—to one's country, institution, professional standards and ideals, to the cause of peace, and to friends and colleagues—suddenly came into conflict in the crucible of war, and choices were forced on the basis of priorities that were not necessarily acknowledged or even recognized. The challenge of war brought into sharp focus questions concerning the uses of knowledge and the uses of the university in modern America.

Notes

1. The indispensable source for the subject is Laurence R. Veysey, *The Emergence of the American University* (Chicago, 1965). See also Richard Hofstadter, "The Revolution in Higher Education," in Arthur M. Schlesinger, Jr., and Morton White (eds.), *Paths of American Thought* (Boston, 1963), 269–90; Frederick Rudolph, *The American College and University: A History* (New York, 1962); John S. Brubacher and Willis Rudy, *Higher Education in Transition: A History of American Colleges and Universities, 1636–1968* (New York, 1958); George W. Pierson, "American Universities in the Nineteenth Century: The Formative Period," in Margaret Clapp (ed.), *The Modern University* (Ithaca, 1950), 59–94; and Richard J. Storr, *The Beginnings of Graduate Education in America* (Chicago, 1953). The following account is based largely on these sources; citations will be given only in the case of quotations or if otherwise indicated.
2. Pierson, "American Universities in the Nineteenth Century," 62–63.
3. Richard Shryock, "The Academic Profession in the United States," *American Association of University Professors Bulletin*, XXXVIII (Spring, 1952), 38.
4. See Veysey, *American University, 55*, and Arthur E. Bestor, Jr., "The Transformation of American Scholarship, 1875–1917," *Library Quarterly*, XXIII (1953), 164–179.
5. See Edward Lurie, "Science in American Thought," *Journal of World History*, VIII (1964–65), 638–665, and "An Interpretation of Science in the Nineteenth Century," *Journal of World History*, VIII (1964–1965), 681–706; Dorothy Ross, *G. Stanley Hall: The Psychologist as Prophet* (Chicago, 1972); Geraldine Joncich, *The Sane Positivist: A Biography of Edward L. Thorndike* (Middletown, Conn., 1968); Jurgen Herbst, *The German Historical School in American Scholarship: A Study in the Transfer of Culture* (Ithaca, 1965); John Higham *et al.*, *History* (Englewood Cliffs, 1965); and Merle Curti (ed.), *American Scholarship in the Twentieth Century* (Cambridge, Mass., 1953).
6. For the pre-Civil War learned societies see Merle Curti, *The Growth of American Thought* (New York, 1943), 570–571; for the guildlike character of the professional associations see Herbst, *German Historical School*, 40.
7. For the emergence of the academic profession see Walter P. Metzger, "Expansion and Profession" (Paper delivered before the Committee on the Role of Education in American History, Symposium on the Role of Education in Nineteenth-Century America, Chatham, Mass., June, 1964).
8. See Robert P. Ludlom, "Academic Freedom and Tenure: A History," *Antioch Review*, X (March, 1950), 18–19.
9. John H. Wigmore, "Presidential Address," *American Association of University Professors Bulletin*, II (March, 1916), 8–9.
10. See Herbst, *German Historical School*; Charles F. Thwig, *The American and the German University: One Hundred Years of History* (New York, 1928); and Walter P. Metzger, "The German Contribution to the

American Theory of Academic Freedom," *American Association of University Professors, Bulletin*, XLI (Summer, 1955), 214–230.

11. See Herbst, *German Historical School,* and Ernest Becker, *The Lost Science of Man* (New York, 1971).

12. Joseph Ben-David and Awraham Zloczower, "Universities and Academic Systems in Modern Societies," *European Journal of Sociology,* HI (1962), 47. The authors argue that the unique success of the German university sprang less from the "idea of the university" in Germany than from circumstances that historically had shaped it, particularly the decentralization of the higher educational system.

13. See Herbst, *German Historical School,* Chap. 1.

14. Veysey, *American University,* 196.

15. See George H. Haines IV, *Essays on German Influence Upon English Education and Science, 1850–1919* (Hamden, Conn., 1969).

16. Josiah Royce, "Present Ideals of American University Life," *Scribner's,* X (1891), 383.

17. John M. Coulter, "The Contribution of Germany to Higher Education," *Chicago University Record,* VIII (March, 1904), 348.

18. *Ibid., 354.*

19. Hugo Kirbach to "Dear Sir," January, 1915, in Richard T. Ely Papers, State Historical Society of Wisconsin.

20. Rudolf Eucken and Ernst Haeckel to the universities of America, August 31, 1914, sent with O. J. Merkel to A. Lawrence Lowell, December 26, 1914, both in A. Lawrence Lowell Papers, Harvard University Archives.

21. Metzger, "German Contribution to Academic Freedom," 227.

22. Veysey, *American University,* 128.

23. Herbst, *German Historical School,* Chap. 5. He concludes that the failure was a direct consequence of the American's misunderstanding of *Ideengeschichte.* Had they correctly read Wilhelm von Humboldt and Leopold von Ranke, he maintains, "they would have realized that not only the facts but the ideas of American history had to come from American sources." (p. 128).

24. *Ibid.,* 126.

25. *Ibid.,* Chap. 6.

26. Joseph Dorfman, "The Role of the German Historical School in American Economic Thought," *American Economic Review: Papers and Proceedings,* XLV (May, 1955), 17–28.

27. See Metzger, "German Contribution to Academic Freedom," 220. For an interesting development of the observation that academic freedom always was severely limited in Germany, see Ben-David and Zloczower, "Universities and Academic Systems," 56–61.

28. See "Report of the Committee on Academic Freedom and Academic Tenure," *American Association of University Professors Bulletin,* I (December, 1915), 20–43. Metzger's "German Contribution to Academic Freedom" provides a detailed exposition of the reasons for the modifications of the German model in America.

29. See Melvin Small, "The American Image of Germany, 1906–1914" (Ph.D. dissertation, University of Michigan, 1965), 118.

30. Veysey, *American University,* 131.

31. For a description of English higher education in the nineteenth and twentieth centuries see Charles C. Gillispie, "English Ideas of the University in the Nineteenth Century," in Clapp (ed.), *The Modern University,* 27–55, and Albert H. Halsey, "British Universities," *European Journal of Sociology,* III (1962), 85–101.

32. See Veysey, *American University,* 196–197n.

33. Hofstadter, "The Revolution in Higher Education," 565n.

34. Cushing Strout, *The American Image of the Old World* (New York, 1963), 134.

35. See *ibid.,* Chap. 8, and Harry C. Allen, *Conflict and Concord; the Anglo-American Relationship Since 1783* (New York, 1959), 221–224.

36. Bradford Perkins, *The Great Rapprochement: England and the United States, 1895–1914* (New York, 1968).

37. See David H. Burton, "Theodore Roosevelt and His English Correspondents: The Intellectual Roots of the Anglo-American Alliance," *Mid-America,* LIII (January, 1971), 12–34.

38. See Small, "American Image of Germany."

39. Veysey, *American University,* 196.

40. See Martin Trow, "The Democratization of Higher Education in America," *European Journal of Sociology,* III (1962), 232–234.

41. Allan Nevins, *The State Universities and Democracy* (Urbana, 1962), 18, 19.

42. See Veysey, *American University,* Chap. 2. Although Veysey prefers the term "utility" to "service," I choose to retain the latter because it was the term used by the professors with whom I deal. The very ambiguities

in the concept of "service" are a clue to understanding the role of the academic community during the war.

43. *Ibid.,* 61–64.
44. See Curti, "The American Scholar in Three Wars," 260.
45. See Brubacher and Rudy, *Higher Education in Transition,* 158.
46. Clark Kerr, *The Uses of the University* (Cambridge, Mass., 1963), 46–47.
47. For a detailed description of the Wisconsin Idea by one of the participants in its development, see Charles R. McCarthy, *The Wisconsin Idea* (New York, 1912).
48. See Merle Curti and Vernon L. Carstensen, *The University of Wisconsin* (Madison, 1949), II, 99–104. See also Veysey, *American University,* 108.
49. See, for example, Woodrow Wilson, "Princeton in the Nation's Service," *Forum,* XXII (December, 1896), 450–466, and "Public Service of University Officers," *Columbia University Quarterly,* XVI (March, 1914), 169–182.
50. Trow, "Democratization of Higher Education," 234.
51. See Nevins, *The State Universities and Democracy,* 78–79.
52. See Veysey, *American University,* 317–332.
53. See Kerr, *The Uses of the University,* 17–18, and Trow, "Democratization of Higher Education," 234.
54. Kerr, *The Uses of the University,* 8–9.
55. For a description of the rise of administration, see Veysey, *American University,* 305–17; Metzger, "Expansion and Profession," 27–31; and Shryock, "Academic Profession," 43–50.
56. Shryock, "Academic Profession," 45. Thorstein Veblen's *The Higher Learning in America* (New York, 1957) is the classic contemporary discussion of this development.
57. Metzger, "Expansion and Profession," 27.
58. *Ibid.,* 29–30.
59. Bernard Barber, "Some Problems in the Sociology of the Professions," *Daedalus,* XCII (Fall, 1963), 679. That the academic profession possesses the common attributes of the major professions is demonstrated in Logan Wilson, *The Academic Man: A Study in the Sociology of a Profession* (London, 1942), 114.
60. For an excellent treatment of the theme of subserviency and dependency see James McKeen Cattell, "Academic Slavery," *School and Society,* VI (October, 13, 1917), 421–426.
61. Shryock, "Academic Profession," 54.
62. Metzger, "Expansion and Profession," 52n.
63. For a description of the occupational implications and psychological consequences of rank divisions see Wilson, *The Academic Man,* 60–70.
64. Metzger, "Expansion and Profession," 17.
65. Guido Marx, "The Problem of the Assistant Professor," *Association of American Universities Journal of Proceedings and Addresses,* XI (1910), 18, 32.
66. Veysey, *American University,* 304.
67. Metzger, "Expansions and Profession," 19.
68. Wilson, *The Academic Man,* 140, 132–33.
69. Shryock, "Academic Profession," 68. It remains to be seen whether the present financial crisis in the colleges and universities and the tensions it spawns will be sufficiently threatening for professors to overcome their resistance to professional solidarity.
70. John Higham, "The Schism in American Scholarship," *American Historical Review,* LXXII (October, 1966), 1–21, and Becker, *The Lost Science of Man,* 9n.
71. Higham, "The Schism in American Scholarship," 13.
72. Higham *et al., History,* 92–103.
73. "What Is History?" *American Historical Review,* IX (1904), 449, 450.
74. George Burton Adams, "History and the Philosophy of History," *American Historical Review,* XIV (January, 1909), 224, 227, 229, 235, 236.
75. Cf. Woodrow Wilson, "The Variety and Unity of History," James Harvey Robinson, "The conception and Methods of History," Frederick Jackson Turner, "Problems in American History," and George Burton Adams, "The Present Problems of Medieval History," all in Howard J. Rogers (ed.), *Congress of Arts and Science, Universal Exposition, St. Louis, 1904* (Boston and New York, 1905, 1907), II, 3–20, 40–51, 183–194, 125–138.
76. Higham *et al., History,* 104–116, 171–182.
77. James Harvey Robinson and Charles Beard, *The Development of Modern Europe* (New York, 1907–1908), I, iii.
78. Higham *et al., History,* 112.

79. *Ibid.,* 183, 104, 114–115.
80. Morton G. White, *Social Thought in America: The Revolt Against Formalism* (New York, 1949), 28–29, 46. In *The Lost Science of Man,* Becker locates the central problem of the emergent discipline of sociology in efforts to make the "indignant ethical man" compatible with the "detached scientist" and thus to end the glaring disproportion between science and ethics. See pp. 20, 22.
81. George H. Haines IV and Frederick H. Jackson, "A Neglected Landmark in the History of Ideas," *Mississippi Valley Historical Review,* XXXIV (September, 1947), 201–20. The authors point out that, in fact, the contributors to the congress delved into their own fields of specialization, giving lip service only to the grand theme of unity.
82. Jean B. Quandt, *From the Small Town to the Great Community: The Social Thought of Progressive Intellectuals* (New Brunswick, 1970), especially Chap. 8. The book includes an intellectual who did not reject the idealist view; Josiah Royce plays a large part in the study.
83. Sidney Fine, *Laissez-Faire and the General Welfare State* (Ann Arbor, 1956), 169–288, and White, *Social Thought in America.*
84. Herbst, *German Historical School,* 162.
85. Richard Hofstadter, *Anti-Intellectualism in American Life* (New York, 1963), 198, 205.
86. Higham *et al., History,* 65n, 65. Higham attributes this status decline in large part to social and professional changes attendant on the breakup of the aristocracy of culture.
87. Metzger, "Expansion and Profession," 54n.
88. See Veysey, *American University,* 301, and Shryock, "Academic Profession," 33. A penetrating portrait of the "mandarinate" in Germany may be found in Fritz K. Ringer, *The Decline of the German Mandarins: The German Academic Community, 1890–1933* (Cambridge, Mass., 1969).
89. William Graham Sumner, *Folkways* (Boston, 1906), 205–206.
90. Curti, *American Paradox.* The theme is treated in greater depth in his essay "Intellectuals and Other People."
91. Shryock, "Academic Profession," 53.

CHAPTER 4
PUBLIC HIGHER EDUCATION

Misconceptions About the Early Land-Grant Colleges

Eldon L. Johnson

The universities called "land grant" have cut a wide swath in the history of American higher education. They deserve to be acclaimed, but they ought also to be better understood. Paradoxically, their long struggle for recognition and respectability has been so fully won that criticism has turned to unthinking acceptance. As a result, some misconceptions have arisen and flourished alongside the neglect of other matters of great significance, past and present.

What is both overestimated and underestimated really does matter if we have regard, not merely for the truth, but also for a balanced view of university development at home and of what is being imported by developing countries abroad. The misconceptions arise as we roll history back, proceeding from what we have fixed in our minds now; hence, we attribute to the early land-grant colleges the characteristics that exist today. What the colleges now *are* is merely what they *were* writ large. Far from it.

These colleges of humble origin, all derived from land grants to the states under the Morrill Act of 1862, are extremely important and do have a claim to uniqueness, but not always for the reasons assumed. They are no longer colleges. They are, in the main, full-fledged universities. They exist in every state and in most of the territories. They comprise a national system, derived from national policy. As a category, they supply eight of the ten largest undergraduate campuses in the United States and enroll more than one-seventh of all university students. They and the state universities together produce two out of every three doctoral degrees granted nationally. In other words, they are prime actors at both extremes: in mass education with its emphasis on "equal access," and in graduate training with its emphasis on research specialization. They are the bulwarks of scientific and technological education. By the terms of the enabling act, they encompass agriculture and mechanic arts; but whatever their beginnings, they now embrace a much broader curriculum—either science and technology generally, with the related professions, or the whole complement indistinguishable from the most comprehensive and traditional universities. In their original rebellion against classical instruction only, they put things scientific at the center, around which an unusually strong research orientation has developed, with an emphasis on application and problem solving. Thus was born the now famous academic trilogy: instruction, research, and service—a mission description that virtually every institution, public or private, now embraces, however different the interpretations.

These are the characteristics in which misconceptions have become embedded as history is neglected or time ignored. Concurrently, some decisive considerations have dropped almost entirely from our awareness. Four of the common misconceptions and two of the neglected considerations will be treated here. The sources used are the individual institutional histories of the early land-grant colleges, taking 1890 as the approximate terminal date. Such histories, taken together, give a composite picture that strikes the reader with insights that are not so conspicuous in the individual histories because they are understandably introspective.

Land Grant Uniqueness

It is quite erroneous, first, that use of land grants was or is the distinguishing characteristic of the so-called land-grant colleges, despite the inseparable name. Nor was the practice by any means novel.

Indeed it was so well established that Senator Justin Morrill, the legislative author, and his hundreds of intellectual allies were merely making a special application in 1862. That the impact was revolutionary in the end derived from a host of other considerations, not from a new social invention.

The precedents were ancient, numerous, and of high visibility. The colonies received the heritage from the English Crown. In fact, within twelve years of the founding of Jamestown, ten thousand acres of land were set aside in an abortive attempt to establish a university [10, pp. 2–4]. As states replaced colonies, they continued the practice of giving land grants for higher education, with Harvard, Yale, William and Mary, Dartmouth, and Michigan all the beneficiaries of either colonial or state gifts. Meanwhile, the vast western lands were ceded to the new national government, and because of abundant land riches, it became the chief donor. No reader need be reminded that grants in lieu of appropriations were given for great internal improvements and that the Northwest Ordinance of 1787 led to the practice of giving to each newly admitted state (unless carved out of the original thirteen) two entire townships for a "seminary of learning." What may not be remembered is that by the Civil War, and hence two years before the Morrill Act, no less than seventeen states had received two townships each, or a total of more than 4 million acres, and had spawned almost a score of state colleges and universities [39, p. 44; 1, p. 25]. Indeed many of these institutions of pre-Morrill land-grant origin were the trunk onto which the *new* land-grant shoot was grafted, always with revitalizing and sometimes life-preserving consequences.

Therefore, it is clear that the land-granting technique had become so pervasive before 1862 that turning to the federal government for educational help, instead of to the states, had become a dominant fashion. As an alert representative and senator, Justin Morrill had only to heed his eyes and ears to become the author of the famous act that bears his name, without awaiting a blinding vision that would make him "The First," as he sometimes implied in old age and as myth-makers came to believe. Insight on the times is also shown by President Lincoln's role and attitude. He did not turn a hand for the plans of Morrill, Jonathan Baldwin Turner, Horace Greeley, and all the others. He endorsed but did not promote; he signed the act but made no recorded comment. As a product of his time and place, with his free-soil ideas, he was said to have favored land grants "for all purposes and under any available condition" [43, p. 56].

If land grants were not new as a device for educational support, neither were they resorted to for purely educational reasons. Education was often the legitimizing factor, while the real objective was something else, perhaps pioneer settlement, speculation, or economic development. Citizens in Minnesota objected to having pine and farm lands chosen for universities because there were "higher" uses possible [18, p. 56]. Likewise, the unseemly emphasis on land as mere largess produced such interinstitutional scrambles among both public and private colleges that they were variously dubbed "Ohio's great land-grant sweepstakes" and Virginia's "War of the Colleges" [26, p. 51; 25, p. 21].

None of this is to deny Senator Morrill's great contribution, but rather to point it in another direction. Instead of siring the land-grant idea, even for colleges, he put together a timely political alliance that used the tried and true support mechanism for something new in higher education, certainly new in emphasis, and often new even in the kind of institution elicited. He helped establish a national policy, permissive though it was, which offered irresistible incentive to all the states at one time, old and new, to join a country-wide system of state-based institutions that had the potential we know only today. That *was* something new.

Student Demand

Another facile misconception is that the land-grant colleges were born of student demand. "People's colleges" must have had a popular base, and when established, they must have had a popular response. On the contrary, a case could be made that the new colleges were created by reformers, not practitioners, and for an ideal, not for an established need. Reaching out to sons, and later daughters, of farmers and artisans, to indigent students, and to whomever the existing system passed by was a noble egalitarian ideal that remained just that—an ideal—for decades, with laborious progress toward its realization. Dormancy or decline in enrollments had actually set in, with surprising results in the new colleges [46, p. 486; 13, pp. 66–68]. When Ohio's land-grant college opened, its public predecessor,

Miami University, was forced to close its collegiate department for want of enrollment, to resume only a dozen years later [26, pp. 54, 56].

One understandable obstacle was the inadequacy of the educational underpinnings: the land-driven reform outran the public school system. This extension of education from the top down, hastily induced by land grants, caused some sparsely settled western states to open the new colleges when few, if any, high schools existed. Arizona opened with none and Nevada with two [31, p. 38; 11, p. 52]. Other states were not too different. The University of Wisconsin was itself called "a High School for the village of Madison"; Pennsylvania State University, which began as "Farmers' High School," despite its collegiate intentions, met the student shortfall through preparatory work reaching down to the common-school level [38, p. 140; 12, pp. 21, 42]. In fact, preparatory departments became established collegiate features, and their enrollments were often merged into total student figures to assuage public hostility. When the president of the University of Arkansas boasted of the fourth largest enrollment in the nation during 1879–80, he counted 300 preparatory students in his total of 450 [42, p. 122]. Not until this nationwide problem was ameliorated did the new colleges have the student "demand" for which they were built.

The test is in their success in reaching the number and kinds of students intended. The best called for apology; the worst was appalling. In New Hampshire literally no new registrant showed up for the fall opening in 1877 [56, p. 58]. Missouri had the same experience during the first week of the opening term in 1866, although 40 did appear later [41, p. 25]. Pennsylvania's opening "capacity attendance" had dropped to 22 in 1869 and then took almost thirty years to reach 150 [12, pp. 25, 67, 135–136]. Massachusetts had drastic ups and downs, with twenty years required to get the enrollment back to the modest 1870 level [7, p. 63]. Neighboring Connecticut opened in 1881 with twelve "on the ground or on the way" [53, p. 144]. In its first twenty years, Nevada never exceeded 35 [11, p. 33]. A decade after the Civil War, no less than five institutions in Baltimore had "an enrollment at least double that of the little farmer's College" (University of Maryland), which in eight postwar years had five presidents under whom six students actually were graduated [4, p. 174]. Florida's college had a particularly difficult time: the 38 who began in 1884 were all in the preparatory department, and only 57 were in collegiate classes as late as 1898 [37, p. 278].

Some colleges did better, indeed well by national comparisons of the time, but the best had monumental troubles. Aided by an ideal combination of beginning assets and by advertising in three hundred newspapers, Cornell got off to the best beginning with the largest entering class ever admitted in the United States—412, or twice the lodging space. But after a quick ascent to a total of 600, all classes sank back to only 312 in 1882 [22, p. 184]. Minnesota and California likewise experienced huge declines after early enrollment gains, although the latter again took off to 500 by 1883 and four times that number by 1898 [18, pp. 47, 68; 52, pp. 93, 115; 16, p. 374]. Illinois did not attract the "hundreds" its head expected, but it began with about 50 (76 by the year's end) and moved rapidly in four years to 400 [51, pp. 99, 105]. Because of special fervor specially concentrated, the separated "agricultural and mechanical arts colleges," distinct from the state university in the same state, had some special drawing power—again, often without maintenance of the auspicious beginnings. Although Kansas State never reached 125 in any of its first ten years, it progressed with remarkable steadiness to 500 in the 1878–1890 period [58, pp. 22, 79]. Michigan Agricultural College enjoyed "overcrowding" for only two years, and although enrollment was parlayed into a respectable 340 in the 1880s, that was far short of the intended 500: the following decade the board was looking into "the seeming lack of popularity of our College" [27, pp. 23, 187, 188].

That there was no groundswell of student demand is shown by the many stratagems used to build enrollment. Necessity bred invention. The new college in North Carolina offered a month's free board to any student who would bring in another [29, p. 64]. Missouri relied on double-sized catalogs, five thousand circulars, and faculty forays into the country to "sell" the university [54, p. 300]. Scholarships with all degrees of financial support and equitability of selection were universally used, and, not uncommonly, available awards outran the total number of students. Only one-third of the Arkansas potential was taken up in 1873 [42, p. 74]; and before 1880, New Hampshire's enrollment never exceeded thirty-three, although thirty-four scholarships were available for instate students [56, p. 10; 48, pp. 8, 12]. In the impoverished economy of the Reconstruction, Louisiana State did attract students by the "charity" system of full-support "beneficiaries," but, reciprocally, enrollment dropped to thirty-one when politics terminated the arrangement [17, pp. 204, 221]. Some students were made automatic recipients of enrollment inducements, such as ministers, ministry students, and maimed Confederate soldiers in Georgia [23, p. 98]. Where land-grant funds were originally entrusted in New England to existing private universities, it was common to devote a share of the proceeds (half at Dartmouth) to dragooning the necessary students under state auspices [56, p. 10].

The student yield from all this frenetic effort shows that the ideal of an open sesame for neglected students was tardy in its realization. In their avowed and ready egalitarianism, the land-grant colleges differed from the traditional, but student demand was anemic everywhere, yielding the nation's topmost enrollment of 637 at Harvard in 1872, not much more than half that at Princeton, 124 at Columbia, and 88 at the University of Pennsylvania [32, p. 109]. Nothing did more *eventually* for mass or democratized education, but the land-grant colleges did little initially. It took them thirty years, or fifty, depending on one's standard for earning entitlement to what we now honor. They were committed, they opened their doors, and they pressed fate with action. Their early contribution was the ardent conviction and the provision of opportunity, the expectation, and the ideal, not the actual achievement. They were ahead of their times, not the slaves of popular demand. When the ideal did blossom, it did so magnificently, and these new institutions were often pacesetters. Within two decades of the general takeoff in both enrollment and state support, Edwin Slosson was to include Wisconsin, California, Illinois, Minnesota, and Cornell among the fourteen in his *Great American Universities* [50]. As one historian was to say, "Higher education for the masses . . . really dates from the early years of the Twentieth Century"—the tardy fruition of an early ideal [36, p. 1].

National Development Role

A third major misconception attributes to the new land-grant colleges the role of supreme force in national development after the Civil War—the prime mover in the American agricultural and industrial revolutions that became the envy of the world. If the colleges ever had that capacity, it was much later, certainly after the Hatch Act of 1887 with its emphasis on research, and probably not until well into the twentieth century. The colleges' *own* development had to precede their impact on national development. That is an oversight often found among admirers in the developing countries who are looking for importable, ready-made, time-defying instruments of progress.

Since agriculture was a "leading object," the greatest impact would presumably have been on the so-called "agricultural revolution." However, the status of agricultural education was indeed low, and the trained manpower produced was generally not distinguishable from that of other educational institutions. Agricultural colleges had birth pangs that have left us lurid descriptions: "a bundle of whimsies," an "undernourished abortion," "mere symbolic patches of hay or grass," and "an Agricultural College without Agriculture in it" [28, pp. 234, 253; 35, p. 62; 32, p. 124]. Agriculture played little part in the institutional evolution in West Virginia, Louisiana, and Nevada, and a difficult role even in some of the strongest farm states. Minnesota's trustees condoned growth within the cracks, in pieces, and against odds, with resulting "hostility between university and farm community that was to plague the administration for fifty years" [18, p. 33]. Students of that discipline never exceeded three a year and then relapsed to zero in 1880. In 1874 there were no agriculture students at Wisconsin, California, Minnesota, or Missouri—all established prior to the Morrill Act, all farm states, and all committed to doing something special for agriculture. In fact, Wisconsin graduated no agriculture student until 1878, with many years before the next. Thirty years after President Lathrop had begun urging agricultural education, one student was pursuing that field in contrast to sixty in law [9, pp. 463–464]. Where brand new institutions were founded under the Morrill Act, particularly if they were separated from the state university, agriculture generally fared better; and in some places it was clearly dominant. In Michigan, Pennsylvania, Mississippi, Massachusetts, and Kansas, agriculture was the driving force in the founding or in early emphasis, or both. In the northeastern states, where the land-grant funds (except in Maine and Massachusetts) were given to existing private universities, even if to a scientific college therein, agriculture was clearly a stepchild. But in all states, the unpromising state of agriculture as a profession or science was a serious obstacle. Professors of agriculture could not be found because the subject did not yet exist. It could be taught only in the guise of something else—botany, chemistry, or physiology. One president said it was "simply a mass of empiricism" [34, p. 57].

For potential application to national development, what kind of trained manpower did the land-grant colleges produce? The best agriculture showing by far was made at Michigan Agricultural College. By 1892, it had produced six hundred agricultural graduates, one-fifth of the national figure and exceeding the total for twenty-five other states, while other Midwestern colleges were averaging from ten to twenty-four each [27, p. 171]. Ohio State was very different; only two out of ninety-three graduates from 1870 to 1886 were in agriculture, whereas twenty-seven received engineering degrees, twenty-seven bachelors of science, and thirty-seven bachelors of arts and philosophy [26, p. 131]. Maine had only thirty-four in agriculture and allied industries out of 348 living alumni in 1892, or 10 percent as compared with 41 percent in engineering; also the professions, business, and editorial/literary work compared favorably with agriculture [15, p. 93]. Purdue University in Indiana averaged one graduate in agriculture a year until 1893, only one-sixth as many as in civil and mechanical engineering [21, p. 191]. The Wisconsin Board of Visitors in 1880 lamented "finding no students in and learning of no graduates from the agriculture department" [9, p. 465]. In the heart of the farm belt, Illinois had no enrollment in agriculture/horticulture in 1890, and its new college almost expired before being revitalized by the Hatch and Second Morrill Acts [51, pp. 239–241]. The Rutgers Science School turned out ninety-nine graduates in fifteen years, six of whom in farming [32, p. 92]. Of seventy graduates at Maryland between 1865 and 1892, two were farmers and six engineers [4, p. 198]. At the nadir, it took Arkansas thirty years to produce the first bachelor of science in agriculture, and Nevada did little better [19, p. 37; 8, p. 16].

It must be concluded, therefore, that the manpower training done by these new colleges turned out to be, both by student choice while in college and by employment choices after graduation, much more conventional than expected—it was chiefly for liberal education and for the common professions. Even in the exceptions found in institutions that deliberately restricted their curricula to a narrow interpretation of the Morrill Act, the "related" fields often did better than the explicit specialties.

No reputable history of American agriculture or of industry bears out the assumption that the new-type colleges virtually created modern America on the material side by their applications of knowledge to agriculture and industry. The ideal of development was always held by the land-grant colleges and their most evangelistic spokesmen, but the realization had to await both the generation of knowledge to apply and the development of staff to share. The volumes of *Agricultural History* contain several articles about the nineteenth century "agricultural revolution" but none assigns a significant role to the new land-grant colleges. These articles show that significant change was already evident by 1850, the century's greatest increase in agricultural productivity per worker occurred between 1860 and 1870, and a host of non-agricultural factors were at work [6, p. 121; 49, pp. 161–162; 40, pp. 193–195]. Likewise, American economic histories give more attention to natural conditions, inventions, canals, railroads, market developments, urbanization, and land policies than to land-grant education, which gets surprisingly little attention, and sometimes none at all [5, p. 101; 2, p. 452].

Before 1890, the developmental contributions of the land-grant colleges were fortuitous and indirect. They were a boon to frontier settlement and an important ingredient in the frenzy of "internal improvements" in many states. Many were ploys in the legislative maneuvering for scattering internal improvements around the state, with "equitable" distribution of college, capitol, penitentiary, insane asylum, and normal school. They gave powerful impetus to an improved and balanced school system, uplifting high schools particularly. Most potent of all was their relevance for and attachment to a particular geographical place: they served what their place names generally implied and designated. It was no accident that Kansas State scientifically demonstrated that winter wheat, among many other crops, was an answer to a harsh environment and that Florida Agricultural College experimented with semitropical fruits and vegetables [24, p. 289; 37, pp. 204, 346].

This points to the missing link. It was the absence of tested principles and verifiable knowledge that came from research. Before 1890 the colleges did not have that capacity, or more than a minuscule amount, and the concomitant capacity for systematic diffusion lagged still further. To contend otherwise is to perpetuate a myth that impedes our understanding of the developmental process and education's role in it. The direct developmental impact of the early colleges came after the agricultural experiment stations were established, after research knowledge was given an extension mechanism, after the engineering schools were equipped and well patronized for both training and applied research, and after enrollments in the practicing professions generated thousands, not merely scores, of leaders and specialists. It was a long road from the early unrealized ideal to the contemporary interlocking of development and education. The early colleges were within the system, not outside or above it. They were in some respects the product, not the cause. That may tell us more about national development and the university role in it, both past and present, both in the United States and overseas, than anything else.

State Support and Control

A fourth misunderstanding about early land-grant colleges assumes that between the federal role and state role, the latter was dominant and determining. Why else "state" universities? It is easy to infer now that the states eagerly stepped up to the federal challenge, embraced and discharged their constitutional responsibility for education, and perforce put their tax dollars behind an accepted public remedy for the deficiencies of the traditional private colleges. That is not what happened. Starting a college did not mean supporting it, and supporting a college did not mean controlling it. Support and control both had to evolve. As the giving of land grants by the federal government was a substitute for money, so the acceptance of land grants by the states was a substitute for taxes. In fact, full college adoption and reasoned tax support by the state was a phenomenon of the early twentieth century [44, p. 184].

The federal role has been neglected and underestimated. Federal land did more than entrap the states into sometimes unwanted responsibilities; its proceeds were the lifeblood in the early decades or even the sole support. The Morrill Act made a tremendous impact. Eventually, every state accepted its terms. By standards of that day, not of the present, it provided a "munificent grant," "a very handsome endowment," "a permanent fund," and "a bounty of the national government" [41, p. 23; 26, p. 21; 23, p. 12; 15, p. 361]. Indeed, 17.5 million acres was a handsome bounty nationwide, even if the income did fall below expectations. That bounty was "the salvation of the University of Georgia," it "helped the Maryland Agricultural College struggle to its feet," it aided Iowa Agricultural and Mechanical Arts College "in its desperate struggle for perpetuation," and in New Jersey "the foundations were laid for the new Rutgers" [23, p. 85; 4, p. 164; 45, p. 34; 32, p. 82].

For both politicians and educators in many states, the federal land grants had another strong appeal, but of a negative kind: they were an escape from state responsibility and taxation. Bad times caused some states to propose to "sell" the new college or repeal its charter as a tax-relief measure [45, p. 33; 27, p. 49]. More moderate politicians accepted the new-type college as frugal and easy on the public purse [30, p. 11; 45, p. 74]. Much legislative effort went into the search for some self-sustaining formula for the new colleges—tuition charges, sale of produce from the college farm, piggybacking on existing institutions, and aid from the highest bidder for the college location. Counties and cities were encouraged to compete with proffered cash, loans, buildings, or whatever other attractions human ingenuity could devise. The bids made and the deals struck were awe-inspiring— and tax saving. Arkansas endured paroxysms of salary-cutting, legislated faculty terminations with some rehiring at lower pay, library deprivations, and appropriations in warrants with value dropping as low as 30 percent [19, pp. 35–39, 55]. Wealthy creditors or benefactors also gave saving aid: for example, John Pillsbury in Minnesota and John Purdue in Indiana [18, pp. 25–31; 21, p. 32]. Citizens of Lincoln were persuaded to advance money to keep Nebraska's main building from falling down, with the expectation of legislative repayment, but the confidence proved to be misplaced [30, p. 64]. Most of the New England states hoped to avoid start-up costs, even for buildings, by assigning the land-grant funds to existing private institutions.

Thus regarding the land grants as a federal replacement of their responsibility, the states devoted many years to evasion, temporizing, reneging, and borrowing against what was neither matched nor supplemented. Even a quarter century after his famous legislation, Senator Morrill complained that his own state of Vermont was not doing its part by relying on federal proceeds solely, while Vermont's president lamented that the state had "not helped by one acre or one cent" [28, pp. 223, 236].

Having tried loans, other indebtedness, fees, and nominal salaries, Missouri reached its watershed of state support almost thirty years after its founding with legislative hands forced by the conditions set by the incoming president [57, p. 113]. Until settled as damages through the courts and a special commission, Yale received "not a dollar" from the state while it administered Connecticut's land grant [53, p. 72]. Some states, like Wisconsin, entrapped themselves into a precedent for annual appropriations by having to repay easy loans taken from the federal endowment [9, p. 127]. After having waited eleven years to open the doors of the college that the Morrill Act contemplated, Ohio took eighteen more to provide a direct state levy [36, p. 1]. Worse still, it took New Jersey thirty years [32, p. 93]. The "neglected stepchild" was the dominant countrywide image left by the states' relations with the early land-grant colleges [12, p. 111; 17, p. 304; 11, p. 22; 38, pp. 30, 35–36].

It must be concluded, therefore, that the original federal land grants were not effective in priming the state pump. The states, with few exceptions, did what they had to, minimally (i.e., erected buildings that were denied the use of federal income), thus avoiding annual outlays; but an increasingly self-conscious democratic spirit gradually came to the colleges' rescue, along with agitation and reminders from the colleges and their leaders. Some crisis or emergency or appeal to fair play usually led to an appropriation for some operational purpose, and what had thus begun could then be repeated. The spasmodic gradually became habitual. Two new extensions of federal assistance, the Hatch Act of 1887 and the Second Morrill Act of 1890 (the latter, with its money rather than land for a "more complete endowment"), pulled the colleges over the financial hump and gave the states their final reprieve while adjusting to the inescapable. A new era dawned. The takeoff point had been reached in state assumption of the major role in public higher education.

State control developed more or less in tandem with state support, replacing the early practice of state chartering with essentially private control through self-perpetuating boards of trustees. This evolution, beyond the space available here, gives still more evidence that state support and state control were public tastes that had to be acquired. Whether entrapped or not by accepting the Morrill Act's conditions, all states eventually conceded, however reluctantly and tardily, that state patronage should follow, that the new institution was a child of the state, and that the full faith and credit of the state were involved; but "eventually" was the key. Torn between emerging democracy and established tax resistance, the states needed time. They took it.

In addition to these major misconceptions, two significant historical developments have been omitted or grossly underestimated. One is the obverse of the state role discussed above; the neglected significance of the *national* system of state-based colleges and the national role in the formative years. The other is the great contribution of the incremental state-by-state educational upgrading that these humble colleges left in their wake enroute to becoming strong universities.

Neglected National Role

Nowadays, when the states and localities have come to be the educational bulwarks and the Congress has gone to such lengths to deny national responsibility, it is difficult to reconstruct from an earlier era the national role and its determining impact on educational reform. Born of the wartime nationalizing spirit, the Morrill Act was a masterpiece of nondirective federal aid. It was clear enough to guarantee a state-initiated college in every state but vague enough to let the college accommodate to local reality. It wanted agriculture and mechanic arts—the neglected concerns of neglected students—targeted for attention, but it did not exclude anything, however conventional. Yet the national intent showed through: a new emphasis, a new clientele, a permanent endowment, and an expected state commitment to fit into the loosely drawn national network against the alternative of refunding the income. Using their options freely, the states created all kinds of institutions, some maximizing the "leading object" of the Morrill Act and some minimizing it. It is significant that Senator Morrill himself emphasized the national purpose and role and later sought to enhance the endowment of what he called the "national colleges for the advancement of scientific and industrial education"—both "national" and, for greater breadth, "scientific" instead of "agricultural." He perceived a national educational obligation that was not to "be avoided by the cranky plea that Government has nothing to do with education" [33, pp. 3, 7, 13].

Ample evidence shows that the new colleges were regarded by their advocates and founders as a national system or network, and were so developed. The enabling act itself gave an unmistakable clue: a little-noted section provided that an annual informational report should be made by each college to every other college and to the Secretary of the Interior—that is, to others, thus serving the countrywide system, and to a national educational office, thus symbolizing the intended scope. The colleges, in parallel development with the U.S. Department of Agriculture, became the linchpin in the national "system" concept in agricultural education, research, and extension that has won world acclaim. That concept gained further cohesion by a groundswell of sentiment that culminated in the formation of the Association of American Agricultural Colleges and Experiment Stations in 1887, which brought the pieces together in both fellowship and professional advancement. With subsequent name changes, that organization promoted a host of interinstitutional objectives country-wide and lobbied vigorously for common national interests with a potency that has long been noted by academic and governmental onlookers. An informal system or network existed, too. Nationwide correspondence and meetings provided the original impetus for the colleges, for the association, and for closer relations with U.S. government officials. College officials visited other places for ideas, plans, curricula, and faculty and presidential recruitment. Arkansas built its Old Main directly from the Illinois plans [42, p. 103]. Colorado Agricultural College was slavishly patterned after the Michigan Agricultural College and Michigan law [20, p. 25]. Clearly, the national system was also a network of common philosophy and sentiment.

There were other evidences of a national system. A curricular core was imposed nationwide—agricultural and mechanic arts education and military training, whatever the fate of classical education might be. The wartime imposition of military training best symbolized the national aspects again. There was something common beyond the required core, too: the ready-to-develop ideals that would cater to the "industrial classes" and practical professions, assure the centrality of science (since it was the base for the "leading objects"), and use both experimentation and service as the cement for mutual relations with the states in which located. If one interpretation of American educational evolution after the Civil War held that there is no "great central idea" but at bottom something "formless, chaotic, and full of contradictions," as historian S. Willis Rudy has written [47, p. 156], it could accurately be said that the new colleges came closer to a "great central idea" than any others. They also had a keen and proud awareness of what they did hold in common across the nation.

Finally, it should be noted again that the national influence took tangible form, as previously noted, in the dominant financing of the early land-grant colleges. While the state fraction of the total support steadily mounted, after a tardy start, the national dominance was not overcome until the turn of the century. At that time, the catalogs for Rhode Island still boasted that all salaries were paid wholly from federal funds, and the University of Nevada still derived approximately three-fourths of its support from the "liberal aid" of the national government [14, p. 83, 8, p. 11]. A 1903 report showed that land-grant proceeds, then including federal appropriations under the 1890 Morrill Act, came to just under $2 million, whereas the states appropriated slightly less than $2.5 million for operating purposes [55, p. 11].

However, time shifted the balance against too much "nationalizing" as the Civil War receded. Senator Morrill, overtaken by political realities, eventually dropped "national" from his legislative proposals for further aid to his colleges and contented himself with the national effect from a network of state-based, federally aided institutions. While the balance thus shifted and the state role became much stronger, the national role left indelible marks. These and their history should not be forgotten nor minimized. Some such national impetus could alone have produced such a nationwide crop of colleges in so short a time. The country-wide impact on incipient institutions, on states relating thereto, and on national opportunities and rewards coming therefrom is the enduring heritage.

Incremental Improvement

The other neglected feature of the early land-grant colleges was their pragmatic, step-by-step progress, internally driven rather than externally inspired, toward better education in all the states. As a foreign observer, Lord Bryce was more prophetic than critical when, in *The American Commonwealth,* he cited the burgeoning state universities as often "true universities rather in aspiration than in fact" but still "better than nothing" [3, vol. 2, p. 681]. If they had awaited the evolution of high schools and despaired of standards below Harvard and Oxford, higher education in the United States would have been long delayed and immeasurably impoverished. Instead, the hope of incremental educational salvation sprang eternal in the new colleges. In state after state they were not much, but better than nothing—and often better in the newer states than any alternative.

While the new colleges, like most of the older ones, were running preparatory departments to undergird some pretense of university work, they were also locked into the upgrading processes whereby public school systems came into being. As soon as possible, they cut the Gordian knot of how to elicit acceptable high schools while providing a substitute. Many of the college presidents assiduously worked to make the college the leader, teacher-supplier, and upward-pulling magnet of the whole educational system of the state and found careers wending in and out of the upper layers of the emerging public school systems and their normal schools. Nebraska's chancellor said to a state teachers' convention: "I see the common school stuck in the mud and the university suspended in the air. If we are to have a system of education, the word is 'Close up'" [30, p. 90].

The modest incremental road to higher standards was clearly envisioned by President Chadbourne of Wisconsin, who said that instead of telling students what they ought to do, "We must take them as they are and do the best we can with them" [9, p. 230]. Others, like President Minor of Virginia Agricultural and Mechanical College, agreed that the problem was to encourage students "to seek the honour of a diploma not placed so high as to be beyond their reach" [25, p. 96]. The author of Nebraska's charter said his "prime objective was to get the institution at work as early as possible with as high a grade as the finances would permit, and then improve upon the general foundation as experience warranted or indicated modification" [30, p. 15]. No statement could better portray the prevailing pragmatic incrementalism—to get to work as soon as possible, to reach as high a grade as could be afforded, and to improve by experience. That ever-upward ideal was the constant and crucial factor.

As the new colleges ratcheted forward, step-by-step, opportunity by opportunity, not only was the public school system perfected, but the collegiate work was spread into a broader curriculum; professional schools and liberal arts education were given new balance; research and nonbook learning were embraced; the material instruments of learning (buildings, libraries, laboratories) burgeoned; only the "best" faculty became "good enough"; alumni successes proved that trained intelligence was a dormant resource in every state; intercollegiate rivalry and emulation nationwide added an upward impetus—until each state had a full-fledged comprehensive university (or the components shared in two, if a separate state university already existed). That was inherent in the statutory amplitude and in the linkage with public educational aspirations and the slow-but-eventually-sure public capacity for support.

This spreading around of the educational good, this doing what could be done toward an unswerving ideal, was a monumental achievement of the initial national policy and subsequent state support that flowed from the Morrill Act of 1862. Attempts to clear up misconceptions and to understand what has been neglected in our perception of the early land-grant colleges does not detract from the overall achievements, but, rather, confirms them from another perspective. When only a glimmer of the future had yet become apparent, the committee on education of the House of Representatives reported in 1890 that the land-grant colleges "have turned out a body of men who, as teachers, investigators, and leaders of industry, rank well up with the same class of men everywhere in the world," while at the same time bringing the older institutions "more closely into harmony with the spirit and purpose of the age" [58, p. 89]. This was only a modest forerunner of what was still ahead for the step-by-step incrementalism that was to change the face of American higher education. The historical adaptation of the "new education" has been remarkable. It has left something different and enduring—and something that is no longer confined to institutions called "land grant."

References

1. Becker, C. L. *Cornell University: Founders and the Founding.* Ithaca, NY: Cornell University Press, 1944.
2. Bidwell, P. W., and J. I. Falconer. *History of Agriculture in the Northern United States, 1620–1860.* Washington: Carnegie Institution, 1925.
3. Bryce, J, *The American Commonwealth.* Third edition. New York: Macmillian, 1904.
4. Callcott, G. H. *A History of the University of Maryland.* Baltimore: Maryland Historical Society, 1966.
5. Carman, H. J., and R. G. Tugwell. "The Significance of American Agricultural History." *Agricultural History,* 12 (April 1938), 99–106.
6. Carter, H. L. "Rural Indiana in Transition, 1850–1860." *Agricultural History,* 20 (April 1946), 107–121.
7. Cary, H. W. *The University of Massachusetts: A History of One Hundred Years.* Amherst: University of Massachusetts, 1962.
8. Church, J. E., Jr. (ed.). *Nevada State University Tri-Decennial Celebration, May 28 to June 2, 1904.* Reno: Barndollar and Durley, n.d.
9. Curti, M., and V. Carstensen. *The University of Wisconsin, 1848–1925.* Madison: University of Wisconsin Press, 1949.
10. Dexter, E. G. *A History of Education in the United States.* New York: Macmillan, 1904.
11. Doten, S. B. *An Illustrated History of the University of Nevada.* Reno: University of Nevada, 1924.
12. Dunaway, W. F. *History of the Pennsylvania State College.* Lancaster, PA: Lancaster Press, 1946.
13. Eddy, E. D., Jr. *Colleges for Our Land and Time: The Land-Grant Idea in American Education.* New York: Harper, 1956.
14. Eschenbacher, H. F. *The University of Rhode Island: A History of Land-Grant Education in Rhode Island.* New York: Appleton-Century-Crofts, 1967.
15. Fernald, M. C. *History of the Maine State College and the University of Maine.* Orono, Me.: University of Maine, 1916.
16. Ferrier, W. W. *Origin and Development of the University of California.* Berkeley: Sather Gate Book Shop, 1930.
17. Fleming, W. L. *Louisiana State University, 1860–1896.* Baton Rouge: Louisiana State University, 1936.
18. Gray, J. *The University of Minnesota, 1851–1951.* Minneapolis: University of Minnesota Press, 1951.
19. Hale, H. *University of Arkansas, 1871–1948.* Fayetteville: University of Arkansas Alumni Association, 1948.
20. Hansen, J. E., II. *Democracy's College in the Centennial State: A History of Colorado State University.* Fort Collins, Colo.: Colorado State University, 1977.
21. Hepburn, W. M., and L. M. Sears. *Purdue University: Fifty Years of Progress.* Indianapolis: Hollenbeck Press, 1925.
22. Hewett, W. T. *Cornell University.* New York: University Publishing Society, 1905.
23. Hull, A. L. *A Historical Sketch of the University of Georgia.* Atlanta: Foote and Davis Company, 1894.
24. Jones, C. C. "An Agricultural College's Response to a Changing World." *Agricultural History,* 42 (October 1968), 283, 295.
25. Kinnear, D. D. *The First 100 Years: A History of Virginia Polytechnic Institute and State University.* Blacksburg, Va.: Virginia Polytechnic Institute Educational Foundation, 1972.
26. Kinnison, W. A. *Building Sullivant's Pyramid.* Columbus: Ohio State University Press, 1970.
27. Kuhn, M. *Michigan State: The First Hundred Years, 1855–1955.* East Lansing, Mich.: Michigan State University Press, 1955.
28. Lindsay, J. I. *Tradition Looks Forward, The University of Vermont: A History 1791–1904.* Burlington, Vt: University of Vermont State Agricultural College, 1954.
29. Lockmiller, D. A. *A History of the North Carolina State College of Agriculture and Engineering of the University of North Carolina, 1889–1939.* Raleigh: Edwards and Broughton Company, 1939.
30. Manley, R. N. *Centennial History of the University of Nebraska,* Vol 1, *Frontier University (1869–1919).* Lincoln: University of Nebraska Press, 1969.
31. Martin, D. D. *The Lamp in the Desert, the Story of the University of Arizona.* Tucson: University of Arizona Press, 1960.
32. McCormick, R. P. *Rutgers: A Bicentennial History.* New Brunswick, N.J.: Rutgers University-Press, 1966.
33. Morrill, J. S. "Speech of Hon. Justin S. Morrill of Vermont in the Senate of the United States." Reprint headed "Educational Fund." Washington, April 26, 1876.
34. Nevins, A. *The State Universities and Democracy.* Urbana: University of Illinois Press, 1962.
35. Perry, G. S. *The Story of Texas A and M.* New York: McGraw-Hill, 1951.

36. Pollard, J. R. *History of the Ohio State University: The Story of its First Seventy-Five Years, 1873–1948.* Columbus: Ohio State University Press, 1952.

37. Proctor, S. *The University of Florida: Its Early Years, 1853–1906.* Microfilm. Gainesville: University of Florida, 1958.

38. Pyre, J. F. A. *Wisconsin.* New York: Oxford University Press, 1920.

39. Rainsford, G. N. *Congress and Higher Education in the Nineteenth Century.* Knoxville: University of Tennessee Press, 1972.

40. Rasmussen, W. D. "The Civil War: A Catalyst of Agricultural Revolution." *Agricultural History,* 39 (October 1965), 187–195.

41. Read, D. "Historical Sketches of the Universities and Colleges in the United States." In *Contributions to the History of Education,* edited by F. B. Hough, pp. 15–72. Washington: Bureau of Education, Department of Interior, 1883.

42. Reynolds, J. H., and D. Y. Thomas. *History of the University of Arkansas.* Fayetteville: University of Arkansas, 1910.

43. Ross, E. D. "Lincoln and Agriculture." *Agricultural History,* 3 (April 1929), 51–66.

44. ———. "The 'Father' of the Land-Grant College." *Agricultural History* 12 (April 1938), 151–186.

45. ———. *A History of the Iowa State College of Agriculture and Mechanic Arts.* Ames: Iowa State College Press, 1942.

46. Rudolph, F. *The American College and University.* New York: Alfred A. Knopf, 1962.

47. Rudy, S. W. "The 'Revolution' in American Higher Education, 1865–1900." *Harvard Educational Review,* 21 (Summer 1951), 155–173.

48. Sackett, E. B. *New Hampshire's University.* Somersworth, N.H.: New Hampshire Publishing Company, 1974.

49. Saloutos, T. "The Agricultural Problem and Nineteenth-Century Industrialism." *Agricultural History,* 22 (July 1948), 156–174.

50. Slosson, E. E. *Great American Universities.* New York: Macmillan, 1910.

51. Solberg, W. U. *The University of Illinois, 1867–1894.* Urbana: University of Illinois Press, 1968.

52. Stadtman, V. A. *The University of California, 1868–1968.* New York: McGraw-Hill, 1970.

53. Stemmons, W. *Connecticut Agricultural College—A History.* Storrs, Conn.: Connecticut Agricultural College, 1931.

54. Stephens, F. F. *A History of the University of Missouri.* Columbia: University of Missouri Press, 1962.

55. True, A. C, and D. J. Crosby. *The American System of Agricultural Education.* Washington: U. S. Government Printing Office, 1904.

56. University of New Hampshire. *History of the University of New Hampshire, 1866–1941.* Rochester, N.H.: University of New Hampshire, 1941.

57. Viles, J. *The University of Missouri: A Centennial History.* Columbia: University of Missouri, 1939.

58. Walters, J. D. *History of the Kansas State Agricultural College.* Manhattan, Kans.: Kansas State Agricultural College, 1909.

In Search of a Direction: Southern Higher Education after the Civil War

Joseph M. Stetar

The South did not share in the enormous expansion of American higher education in the years following the Civil War. Nationally, higher education enrollments grew over five-fold in the decades following the War. In 1870, there were 62,000 students in colleges, universities, professional, normal and teacher colleges in the United States. By 1890, the total higher education enrollment was 157,000 and by 1910 had risen to 355,000.[1] Multipurpose institutions with programs characteristic of the leading twentieth-century universities began to appear in the East, West, and Midwest. No such development was evident in the nineteenth-century South where colleges struggled to remain alive. Left virtually destitute by the War and lacking students, buildings, and assets, college leaders clung more to romantic dreams and were unable to share in the bold expansion experienced by other regions. The point is etched clearly when one realizes that about the time Charles W. Eliot began to chart the transition of Harvard College to Harvard University, Landon C. Garland, President of the University of Alabama, and later of Vanderbilt, wrote:

> The University buildings are all burned. Nothing was saved but the private residence of the officers. The most valuable part of my library . . . was consumed. This is a great loss to me just now.
> I do not know that the University of Alabama will be rebuilt—if at all, it will be several years hence. I cannot await the final results, but must look for some employment.[2]

Indeed an attempt to reopen the University of Alabama was made in 1865, but failed when only one student (son of the former Governor Thomas H. Watts) arrived for classes. Reconstruction compounded the political problems confronting the University of Alabama. In November of 1867, a new state constitution transferred control of the University of Alabama from its trustees to an elected board, The Board of Regents of the State University. These Regents were delegated broad powers of governance including the appointment of a president and faculty;[3] there were widespread reports of the dismissal of the ante-bellum faculty for political rather than scholarly reasons.[4]

In Oxford, Mississippi, the state University closed for a portion of the War and faced debilitating financial problems and political entanglements upon reopening. Control of the Board of Trustees had passed into the hands of Reconstructionists, and there was the widespread fear that the policies of the new board would undermine the University. Alexander J. Quinche, Secretary of the Faculty and Professor of Ancient Languages, spoke for many of the faculty in his assertion that the new trustees could destroy the University if they radicalized the faculty. Support for the institution, Professor Quinche insisted, came from old line Southerners and, should these patrons be alienated to the point of withdrawing their support, the University would atrophy.[5] The situation was also quite troubled in Spartanburg, South Carolina, where Wofford College watched its endowment, invested heavily in Confederate bonds and certificates, evaporate.[6] In North Carolina, the trustees of Trinity College (antecedent of Duke University) expressed some optimism, born of sheer-determination, about the future of the college while contending with the effects of a war which destroyed their financial resources and saw their 1861 student body of over 200 reduced to fifty.[7]

At the close of the War, 4,000 Union soldiers occupied the village and campus of the University of North Carolina at Chapel Hill, while the University possessed $200,000 in worthless securities and debts of over $100,000. To compound the problem, the Reconstruction government dismissed the ante-bellum faculty in 1868 and attempted to reestablish the University with a small group of carefully chosen professors. Nevertheless, it was unable to gain adequate financial support and the institution again officially closed its doors in 1871. In 1873, friends of the University led by Alexander McIver, then North Carolina Superintendent of Public Instruction, and an honors graduate of the University, sought legislative and public support to reopen the University. Their efforts met with limited success: in September of 1875 instruction was resumed with a faculty of seven and approximately seventy students,[8] considerably reduced from the ante-bellum University's 1857–1858 enrollment of over four hundred students in nine departments.[9]

In 1866, the trustees of Wake Forest College were faced with the task of reopening an institution which had been closed for four years. Preparatory work, phased out before the War, was reinstated, and only twenty-two of the sixty-seven enrolled in 1866 were classified as collegiate level students. The campus buildings were badly in need of repair, and all but approximately $11,000 of the $100,000 ante-bellum endowment had been lost.[10]

South Carolina College, antecedent of the University of South Carolina, found rebuilding the institution to be a herculean ordeal. Declining enrollment in the early months of 1862 had forced the college to close in the spring of that year.[11] The termination of fighting did not lessen the problems confronting the College. Reconstruction forces understandably pursuing a policy of racial integration and political intervention threatened, given the explosive social situation at that time, the very existence of the College,[12] which was forced to close or reorganize several times in the ensuing years. A report by President Frederick A. P. Barnard to the Trustees of the University of Mississippi in November of 1861 describes the changes effected by the War at the University of Mississippi, and throughout Southern higher education:

> The ambitions . . . entertained for its growth in reputation and usefulness, and for the enlargement of its scope, evaluation of its aims, and its ultimate recognition as one among the honored agencies whose function is to be, not merely by education to diffuse knowledge among men, but by original investigation to add to the priceless mass [of knowledge]. . . . But the fond dreams of so many anxiously hopeful years have been at length rudely dissipated, and the convulsions which have shaken . . . the country to its centre, have removed afar off the prospect of that distinguished preeminence in science which seemed but recently to be opening up before the University of Mississippi.[13]

The War and its social and economic consequences had a profound influence upon Southern higher education. The region's colleges were all but destroyed, and their clientele and financial support lost. Colleges that prospered in the ante-bellum era entered the latter years of the 1860s with great apprehension and little cause for optimism. Endowments had disappeared, students and faculty were in disarray, and facilities were often in ruins. The War resulted not only in the closing of colleges but in a complete reversal of the pattern of ante-bellum expansion and prosperity.

In their attempts to rebuild, Southern academics entered into a discussion regarding the values and philosophies which would shape their future. This debate will be examined in the context of the same general categories utilized by Laurence Veysey in his examination of the development of American universities: mental discipline and piety, utility, research, and liberal culture.[14] As in Veysey's study, there are numerous subgroups and considerable overlap among the categories. Within any of these categories and on most campuses many people were speaking and not all were saying the same thing. Motivations clearly differed, and on many campuses one could find proponents of each point-of-view. Nevertheless, categories do emerge which provide a highly useful perspective for examining the development of late nineteenth-century higher education. While this debate followed the general categories developed by Veysey, the results of these discussions were in many ways unique to the South.

The distinctiveness of Southern cultural life itself contributed to the uniqueness of Southern higher education. Due to the impoverishing effects to the Civil War and the South's relative cultural isolation from the rest of the nation, changes in higher education evolved at a slower pace than was true elsewhere.[15] The shared common cultural life of the South added to the region's insularity; in the years preceding the Civil War, when collectively the North, Midwest, and West were becoming more alike culturally, the South—rural, isolated, and dominated by slavery—was developing a uniquely regional way of life.[16] So great was this cultural difference that Wilbur J. Cash concluded:

> There exists among us . . . a profound connection that the South is another land, sharply differentiated from the rest of the American nation, and exhibiting within itself a remarkable homogeneity.
>
> As to what its singularity may consist in, there is, of course, much conflict of opinion. . . . But that it is different and that it is solid—on these things nearly everybody is agreed.[17]

Surrender at Appomatox and Reconstruction did little to bring the region into the mainstream of American life; in many ways the military defeat coupled with the tensions of Reconstruction widened the chasm between the South and the rest of the nation.[18] The post-war South, set apart by significant "differentials in per capita wealth, income and living standards that made it unique among the regions,"[19] possessed a degree of cultural solidarity and political cohesiveness perhaps never attained in the ante-bellum years.

In summary, both Southern culture and higher education were, in the latter third of the nineteenth century, distinct from those in other sections of the nation. The development of colleges and universities in this period did not replicate the process in the rest of the nation whereby research and utility dominated higher education and relegated mental discipline, piety, and liberal culture to marginal positions. The contest was much closer and markedly idiosyncratic to the South. Discipline and piety joined with liberal culture and Christian education to create a potent, viable educational philosophy which retained its strength well into the twentieth century. Although utility made significant inroads, research did not.

I

Mental Discipline and Piety

For mental disciplinarians, the mind was subdivided into faculties, each of which required systematic and balanced development. Exercising certain faculties to the neglect of others, they argued, deprived students of the qualities of wholeness and balance. In the view of James Henry Thornwell, antebellum president of South Carolina College, and other Southern educators, the most effective course of study was one which stimulated all the various faculties of the mind and developed habits of systemic thinking. He believed that through direct exposure to classics, the original writings of the ancient Greek and Latin authors, students developed sound habits. Few antebellum Southerners disagreed; the discipline of the mind, rather than the acquisition of knowledge, was the aim of education. He saw each student as the focus for this education, for in his words, it was "his perfection as a man simply, being the aim of his education." During his tenure (1852–55), undergraduate education at South Carolina consisted of a fixed course of study emphasizing the classics: the sole criterion for the inclusion of a particular subject in the curriculum was its contribution to mental discipline. Undaunted by charges that education emphasizing mental discipline failed to prepare one for a particular career, Thornwell insisted upon the efficacy of a well-disciplined intellect; colleges were not to have a vocational orientation but rather the inclusion of any subject in the curriculum was to be based on its ability to perfect the mind, nothing else.[20] The War would not alter this thinking.

Nothing more seriously violated the canons of mental discipline than the charge that higher education should respond directly to the social and economic needs of society. Significant among these challenges was utilitarian-inspired legislation passed in 1865 by the South Carolina Legislature which called for ten separate schools within the College (i.e., University of South Carolina) and supported the right of students to elect areas of study. While this forced the College to adopt a more practical curriculum, it engendered significant controversy. Fisk Brewer, Professor of Ancient Languages and Literature, chastised the Legislature for capriciously abandoning the classical curriculum and for introducing fragmented schools and electives which failed to ensure symmetrical development.[21]

Evidence suggests that Professor Brewer's discontent was not as widely shared by his colleagues as he might have preferred, for eight years later, in October of 1873, the faculty had arranged for a four-year classical course to be taught jointly by all professors. The new program included an alternative to the classical course which permitted the substitution of the modern languages for Greek and Latin. The alternative curriculum proved the more popular and its enrollment quickly eclipsed that of the classical program. Brewer's own notes indicate that of fifty-six freshmen and sophomores enrolled in the Spring of 1877, only seventeen were in the classical course on a full or conditional basis, while the remaining thirty-nine were in the modern language program.[22] However, to advocates of mental discipline, student enrollment—or lack of it—was of little importance; they attached "more value to quality of instruction than to the number of students; the latter will inevitably follow the former. Let the institution lift the students up, not the students drag the institution down."[23]

This concession to modern languages was significant, and it stirred considerable opposition among mental discipline's staunchest advocates. In their view, substituting modern languages for the classical permitted a student to replace the difficult and essential with the easy and unnecessary. For the truest classicist, all technical and professional instruction would be confined to special institutions so as not to violate the classical course. In opposing the substitution of modern languages for the classics, the rigid mental disciplinarians actually weakened their credibility. The modern languages had grown in popularity due to their literary importance, cognition with the native language, and proclaimed disciplinary value, and their advocates pressed for equal status with the ancient languages. Undaunted, mental disciplinarians remained adamant in their opposition, holding that "close mental labor . . . required in studying Latin and Greek is not found in studying the modern languages,"[24] and only mastery of the classics "develops the reasoning faculty and secures the power of careful, incisive and discriminating thought. . . ."[25] Thus, mental disciplinarians fought a constant and increasingly difficult battle against any encroachment on the exclusive position of the classics.

The press for limited or free electives and the inclusion of modern languages was not limited to South Carolina. John Waddel, Chancellor of the University of Mississippi from 1865–1874 and staunch mental disciplinarian, believed the classical course of study should be rigidly and universally imposed upon students. He insisted that the curriculum ". . . be compulsory, or the majority of students will neglect it."[26] The wisdom of a fixed program was considered to be self-evident and any alteration of the litany of moral and mental discipline, mathematics and the classics was unthinkable. Not surprisingly, attempts by reform-minded professors at the University of Mississippi to broaden the curriculum were soundly denounced by mental disciplinarians. In 1884, Professor Robert B. Fulton sponsored a resolution calling for an elective system in all classes of the University and permitting students to receive a B.A. degree without studying Latin and Greek. The University of Mississippi faculty were not ready for such an abrupt change, however, and the measure was defeated by nearly two to one.[27]

The massive social, political, and economic problems encountered by the post-war South did little to deter mental discipline's advocates from opposing almost any and all curricular change. Five years after President Barnard's 1861 statement that all hopes for significant educational advancement at the University of Mississippi had been destroyed by the War,[28] Chancellor Waddel reaffirmed mental discipline as the basis for higher education at Mississippi. However, in 1866 more than half of the 244 students attending the University of Mississippi were Confederate Army veterans, ill-prepared to undertake even rudimentary classical studies. These post-war students were a different breed, not the traveled sons of the country gentry but seasoned soldiers hard pressed to pay the fifty-dollar University fee and anxious to rebuild their lives and fortunes. Classical education to these students was surely rather curious and remote. However, Waddel was firm. The acquisition of knowledge was of secondary consideration to the disciplining and training of the mind.[29]

At Trinity College, mental discipline was an essential element of the institutional character during the late nineteenth century. Announcements for the 1885–1886 academic year reminded students that anyone deficient in the classics should not expect to receive his B.A., and William T. Gannaway, Professor of Latin and French at Trinity, averred, ". . . [since] it is believed that mental training and discipline can best be secured by a *patient* and thorough *study* of the Ancient Classics, the use of translations is strictly forbidden."[30] A concession to the realities of the times was made at

Wofford, where in the postwar years the number of students unwilling or unable to master Greek and Latin increased to the extent that an alternate degree program was initiated. Although the new degree, the Bachelor of Science, was considered inferior to the Bachelor of Arts degree, it proved quite popular. The B.S. students must have proved especially vexing to Wofford's President Shipp, who nonetheless continued his practice of delivering the annual commencement address in Latin; it was not until James H. Carlisle assumed the presidency of Wofford in 1873 that the graduation address was delivered in the vernacular.[31]

In Columbia, South Carolina, the Reconstruction government opened the University to blacks. While these students also lacked proper prerequisite education, they nonetheless sought the opportunity preparatory classes provided for remedial work, and substantial interest in the University developed among the black community. But even this change in student population had little impact upon mental disciplinarians such as South Carolina's Fisk Brewer, who insisted everyone had to experience the joy and discipline of reading the original Caesar's war and Xenophon's march in Latin.[32]

The 1871 graduating class of the College of Charleston was reminded that the classical curriculum should be placed at a high point of elevation, and be rigorously maintained. But there was little reason to fear the College of Charleston would abandon classical studies. Henry E. Shepherd, President of the Faculty from 1882 to 1897, vigorously supported the classical curriculum, asserting with some pride that the College of Charleston was one of the few institutions in the United States which had not caved in to the pressures for an elective or optional course of study.[33] Mental discipline also occupied a secure position at Emory College (later Emory University) in Georgia, where three of its post-war presidents conceived of education almost exclusively in terms of the classical curriculum. Luther M. Smith (1868–1871), Osborn L. Smith (1871–1875), and Atticus G. Haygood (1873–1884) made few concessions to new, emerging values and were generally committed to an education which, in the words of Luther Smith, sought the development of intellectual power through mental discipline and exercise.[34]

The classicists opposed the notion of producing merchants, lawyers, farmers or physicians as too narrow and too limited an aim for higher education. They sought instead to develop broadly cultured, symmetrical men, although the irony of attempting this by means of a rigidly fixed curriculum escaped them. In their view, vocationalism threatened the essence of higher education by turning colleges into workshops and learning into technical training. If preparation for a profession meant simple acquaintance with detail and mastery of technicalities, the colleges could be of little help; if, however, the professions required a fine, disciplined intellect capable of infinite adaptation, then a classical education was critical. Thus, despite the massive rebuilding task ahead, classicists dismissed utilitarian programs as frivolous. In this, their singular narrowness and detachment is remarkable. Unruffled by the demands of students and society, they sought to provide postwar students with the same gentlemanly education offered in the 1850: ". . . not culture alone . . . but mental discipline added to it."[35]

Concerned with educating the whole man, advocates of mental discipline also necessarily addressed themselves to the development of character and the inculcation of Christian values, often fearing a student's mental development might outpace his moral growth. Southern mental disciplinarians generally agreed that the most rigorous classical education was useless if moral and religious stamina were lacking. A classical education leavened with rigorous moral training was believed optimal for both the individual and the larger society, and a dire future was predicted for the student whose mind, "degenerated in its aims and crippled in its powers . . . flutters, like a bird of feeble wing, over the stagnant pools of sensualism."[36] Such reasoning was wholly consistent with the pervasive religious influence in the South.[37] And while such thinking seems to parallel that occurring in other sections of the nation, the South clung to these values longer and with greater intensity than did other regions.

In their efforts to ensure a moral, Christian atmosphere, advocates of mental discipline and piety sought to exercise control of the campus environment. This fusion of the academic and religious was the *raison d'etre* for Wofford College. William M. Whitman, a prominent figure in the establishment of Wofford, reminded his audience at a cornerstone-laying ceremony that a prime objective of the College was the development of moral character: "which grows out of a knowledge of Christian truth . . . [and a] cultivated understanding which is the product of thorough scholarship."[38]

The University of Mississippi prided itself on its positive "moral influences, freedom from temptation to vice, and the [exemplary] conduct of her students." Every faculty member was a professed Christian, tiny Oxford boasted five churches,[39] and an 1877 committee vigorously sought to prohibit the establishment and operation of billiard saloons or "tin pan alleys" within five miles of the University.[40] Regulating students' personal lives consumed a significant amount of the faculty's time. With students ranging in age from those fifteen or younger to those in their twenties, the rigorous enforcement of discipline was a major undertaking. The University of Mississippi's Trustees required faculty to visit student rooms at irregular hours, "with a view of seeing that students are . . . not engaged in anything improper," and faculty, of course, were expected to respond to all calls from the chancellor for assistance in the maintenance of order.[41] Intent upon protecting students from pernicious influences and anxious to insure a strong sense of morality and propriety in North Carolina, Trinity's President Craven (1872–1882) soundly denounced those institutions which tolerated misbehavior and thus arrested moral development.[42]

In retrospect it is clear that Southern mental discipline and piety did not atrophy after 1865. But the rigidity which precluded its easy adaptation to the exigencies of the post-war South, its antipathy to elective studies, and its total preoccupation with the classical curriculum increasingly isolated its proponents not only from the mainstream of society but from many of its students. Yet, it retained a substantial degree of support and proved capable, especially with its spawning of liberal culture/Christian education, of checking the development of newer, competing educational philosophies.

II

Liberal Culture and Christian Education

While the narrow and rigid mental discipline and piety of the Thornwell and Waddel genre faced rough sledding in the post Civil War era, their philosophical successors were able to draw sustenance from the literary, cultural, and religious traditions of the South to forge a new philosophy for higher education: liberal culture and Christian education. Rooted in Southern literary, cultural, and religious traditions,[43] liberal culture combined with Christian education in the South to foster a point of view toward the curriculum and toward teaching which is distinct from the conception of liberal culture found in the emerging universities of the North and West. In general, advocates of liberal culture and Christian education were critical of the major educational values of the era. They rejected mental discipline because of its adherence to faculty psychology and its reliance upon the classical curriculum as a means of disciplining the mind. They opposed a utilitarian brand of higher education because of its emphasis upon practical studies and an elective curriculum. Finally, they rejected research because of its advocacy of graduate study and specialization.

Throughout the South advocates of liberal culture and Christian education expressed their opposition to the other educational values. Karl P. Harrington and Henry F. Linscott of the University of North Carolina and Wofford College joined numerous other Southerners of the 1880s and 1890s in calling for a return to fixed curriculum. Rooted in a liberal education tradition, these scholars advocated the study of the great books and the classical languages for their intellectual breadth rather than mental discipline properties. They argued that students must not be permitted to choose their courses whimsically since colleges were obliged to guide students toward the accomplishments of the greatest human minds. They believed in building a foundation which enabled the undergraduate to discriminate between literary masterwork and mediocrity.[44]

Despite their mutual attention to literature and the classics, liberal culture sympathizers in the South strongly differed from such university-leaders of liberal culture as Irving Babbitt, Charles Eliot Norton and Barrett Wendell—all of whom rejected the religious and moral overtones of antebellum educational philosophies. Inspired by Matthew Arnold, these university leaders outside the South generally accepted culture as "a wide vision of the best things which man has done or aspired after," which capsulized their concern with "breadth, taste, heritage and idealism."[45] Yet the old established Southern college had been founded on piety and, while a few of the more liberated Southern proponents of liberal culture either avowedly rejected formal religion or permitted it to slip into the background, there was no significant move in the South to downgrade Christian theology.

Thus, it appears at least two versions of liberal culture existed: one, identified by Veysey, was rooted in the emerging universities of the North, West, and Midwest and rejected or minimized the religious and moral influences in education; a second, centered in the South, retained a central regard for the study of humanities and development of moral and religious principles, hence the term "liberal Christian education." However, common threads united all versions of liberal culture, its advocates were, in principle, sharply opposed to the emerging university and its alien values while they identified with the traditional commitment to a required course of study. They denounced the elective system which permitted a student to graduate without studying such areas as Latin, the modern languages, history, economics, and philosophy, and they advocated a return to a fixed curriculum.[46]

Despite the apparent detachment of some Southern colleges toward the technical and utilitarian needs of the region, there was genuine concern for its cultural life; numerous faculty viewed higher education as a vehicle for the preservation and advancement of Southern culture. As a new socioeconomic system gradually replaced the old, as the vast plantations were subdivided and the slaves set free, men of learning were challenged to preserve the best of Southern culture. Thus, the Southern colleges and universities of the late 1800s were called upon to serve as repositories for the region's history, mythology, and traditions.[47] As David Bertelson suggests in his study, *The Lazy South*,[48] while Southerners chafed under the stereotype of an idle and self-indulgent lifestyle, they successfully sought an accommodation with the economic order which emerged after the war. Clearly, the gentleman-scholar ideal (for both the planter and industrialist) remained an attractive one for the region and Southern higher education presented a means for preserving that image.[49] The notion of mental and spiritual integration and wholeness became a guiding principle in the education of cultivated, disciplined men; narrow specialists and professionals were not considered the proper product of higher education.

The immediate post-war period witnessed little popular demand for a "new South" and rather seemed to strengthen the determination of those who sought to resurrect at least part of an era that had passed away. Moreover, the post-war period witnessed an emphasis upon preserving Southern culture and included a substantial aversion for anything "Yankee."[50] In the absence of a comprehensive school system no better vehicle existed for preserving ante-bellum culture than the Southern college; rebuilding the old South required that the traditions of ante-bellum colleges be preserved and strengthened. Southern society, militarily defeated, called upon the colleges to blunt the invasion of Northern culture. At most Southern institutions, articulate and outspoken advocates of a concept of education based on religious principles held key positions throughout the post-war era, and their philosophy was deeply rooted in Southern culture.

The position of liberal Christian education with respect to research and scholarship was straightforward and clear. In the words of John Carlisle Kilgo, President of Trinity "all truth was dependent upon ultimate religious truth, and . . . literature, science, history [are] incomplete without religion." It may have been as Kilgo and others believed, that a Christian college was inherently free because it was beyond political power,[51] but liberal Christian education also had a decidedly doctrinaire flavor as exhibited by its emphasis upon the development of character and its desire to protect students from pernicious ideas. In Kilgo's view, presenting Christian views of human nature countered the false materialism of Locke, the unhealthy idealism of Kant, and the wretched agnosticism of Herbert Spencer.[52]

This tendency of liberal Christian education to declare certain fundamental intellectual questions off-limits demonstrates that the South lacked the basic orientation to the essentially non-theological frame of reference associated with the German-modeled graduate centers which were developing in other regions. While Southerners variously denounced education as too restrained or too free, as lacking practicality or as overly utilitarian, it was rarely permissible to question basic Christian assumptions. The search for truth in liberal Christian education was to a great extent confined to the theological framework of the particular sect involved. Truth was ultimately defined by the scriptures, and it was generally accepted by advocates of Christian education that religious truth was ultimate truth. Thus, while the literary and cultural aspects of liberal culture appealed to the South, its long tradition of religious fervor demanded that an acceptable educational philosophy accommodate itself to and include Christian philosophy as well. Thus, the concept of liberal Christian education which gained wide popularity and support throughout the region was an apparent synthesis of liberal culture and the old concept of discipline and piety which had infused Southern higher education.

Liberal Christian educational values were strong throughout the South, where it was insisted that: ". . . if both intellectual power and moral power are to be fully effective, the one must be thoroughly moralized and the other thoroughly intellectualized."[53] Neither the narrow classicist of the ante-bellum era nor the modern researcher was capable of providing the blend of scholarship and religious fervor these institutions sought: "The scholarship of the college instructor should be not only broad, but must also have refined itself into the grace and strength of that culture which is human and which humanizes. . . ."[54] Faculty were typically judged by their ability to share their knowledge and Christian principles with students rather than by external demonstrations of scholarship. Becoming an excellent teacher or role-model was generally believed to be the most important career objective in any young instructor's life.[55]

As an institution, Wofford College provides an illuminating case study for what emerged as the Southern philosophy of liberal Christian education. Traditionally, Wofford sought to combine both the intellectual and moral traditions of the South, for this was considered most efficacious in the development of learned Christian gentlemen. Piety and character building were the primary concern of James H. Carlisle, professor at the College from its founding and president from 1875 to 1902. Carlisle borrowed equally from discipline and piety, liberal culture, and Christian education, placing primary emphasis upon instructive personal relationships with his students, and he often wrote of the educated, disciplined mind capable of adjusting to all exigencies with an enthusiasm reminiscent of Thornwell or Waddel. Opposing premature specialization, Carlisle was more concerned with winning students to the "pure and right; and wise and good," than with erudition and scholarship.[56] Symbolic of the differences between Southern higher education and the emerging universities of other regions was the reaction of Carlisle's son to Charles W. Eliot's visit to Wofford in March of 1909:

> . . . there stood the most distinguished educator of New England, representing the very last word in the educational thought of the North . . . whose five foot book shelf had no room for the Bible, looking into the face of one of the greatest educators of the South, [James H. Carlisle] with a firm belief in the Bible as the word of God. . . ."[57]

Carlisle's contribution to the cause of liberal Christian education was recognized throughout the South. In a career spanning one of the most important periods in the history of American higher education, Carlisle was able to forge an eclectic position. He effectively opposed extreme utilitarianism on the one hand, while recognizing the need for practicality on the other. He maintained a balance in the educational program at Wofford, according some legitimacy to the broad concept of utility and accommodating the scholar, but his emphasis upon teaching and the development of character left little room for research. His philosophy of education drew significantly upon the precepts of mental discipline but was more flexible than Thornwell's or Waddel's. Carlisle's emphasis upon character and piety clearly illustrates the divergence between the university-centered liberal culture of the North and liberal Christian education in the South under his influence.

Wofford's curriculum was not based solely on traditional principles of mental discipline but rather on the liberal culture premise that the classics exposed students to the most profound works of the human intellect. Still the College proved capable of accommodating the new academicians, German educated scholars Charles F. Smith, who later taught at Vanderbilt and Wisconsin, and William Baskerville, who also later taught at Vanderbilt, and who both added intellectual force to Wofford. Capable of undertaking advanced research projects and conversant with the great intellectual and academic forces of the era, these scholars earned the respect of their peers and gained regional if not national status.[58] However, their presence caused some Wofford professors to protest that the research-oriented professor, "cabined, cubbed and confined in the narrow house of his own department,"[59] would force premature specialization on students and diminish the appeal of the traditional curriculum which had served the South so well in earlier years, and Carlisle agreed to a great extent. Thus, under his stewardship Wofford for the most part resisted the pressures of utility and research and remained serenely committed to literary-Christian values.

The impact of liberal Christian education was, as previously indicated, not confined to institutions with formal religious ties but was felt at state institutions as well. An excellent example is the University of Mississippi, which proclaimed its intention to educate "good scholars of industrious and frugal habits, well grounded in the principles of a high Christian morality. . . ."[60] Mississippi took pride in the moral climate of Oxford and in the fact that all members of the University faculty were active in church affairs.[61] The thrust of the University was guided by the goal of moral rather than intellectual development; a goal which permitted students to graduate who could neither spell nor write grammatically correct sentences. Edward L. Mayes, president of the University in 1889, spoke for many when he professed a desire to develop a "true manly dignity, to awaken a perception of the necessity for self-pause and self-restraint, to inculcate the nobility involved in a voluntary observance of the social and moral codes"[62] in his students.

In many ways, the University of Mississippi bore a striking resemblance to church-related institutions, for while Mississippi catered more to utility than did others, it was decidedly a culturally-oriented institution. Because the University of Mississippi retained the philosophy of liberal Christian education, the traditions of gentlemanly behavior, moral rectitude, and spiritual enlightenment became necessary correlatives of all intellectual endeavors there. Moreover, as at many other institutions, the faculty at University of Mississippi imposed strict codes of moral and personal conduct upon their students.

Thus, across the South liberal culture/Christian education drew sustenance from its antecedent mental discipline and piety to continue as a distinct and important educational value. Its appeal was clearly due to its cultural foundation, its central acceptance of the importance of Christian doctrine, and its complementarity to mental discipline. The final decade of the nineteenth century witnessed increased attacks upon liberal Christian education in the South. The emergence of science was inhospitable to liberal Christian education, and the rapid multiplication of disciplines began to force major adjustments in higher education throughout the region. No longer unchallenged as the supreme course of study, the future of the humanities provoked widespread discussion. Questions such as "Is Science an Incentive to Poetry?"[63] and "Does the Study of Science Tend to Suppress the Spirit . . . of Romance?"[64] were debated in colleges throughout the South.

After the turn of the century, the Southern tradition of the gentleman scholar, supported by liberal Christian education, was in some jeopardy. Increasingly, students sought higher education in an effort to secure financially adequate, if not lucrative, technical or professional positions. Moreover, as the new age of science emerged, its impact, measured by the growing influence of the research and utilitarian institutions, imposed increasing pressure on liberal Christian education. Indeed, liberal Christian education began to be viewed by its opponents as a frivolous and slightly droll remnant of the ante-bellum era.

III

Utility

Outside of the South the movement toward a more practical, useful, and service-oriented education increased in the decades after 1863; according to Veysey virtually every "change in the pattern of American higher education lay in the direction of concession to the utilitarian type of demand for reform."[65] The idea of a multipurpose educational institution serving the practical interests and needs of a diverse population ran counter to that of the classical college; predictably the concept of utility evoked a good deal of controversy.

In the South, insurgent utilitarians rejected the notions of mental disciplinarians and pressed for direct societal services through more practical studies. Following the War, they forced ante-bellum classical professors to share the campus with a growing number of social and applied scientists who sought to restructure education. Many saw the "new South" as needing individuals capable of accomplishing practical tasks. Viewing classical studies as anachronistic, they sought to reshape higher education in a more meaningful and responsive form. Professor Charles W. Hutson of the University of Mississippi perhaps best captured the movement's spirit:

> Against the spirit of the ancient world, which looked down upon commercial and manufacturing industries and all mechanical pursuits, must be erected the modern spirit of material progress, with all the modern appliances for furthering the advance of trade and the trades.[66]

The strong press for a more practical education is not surprising. The War had exacted a significant economic toll upon the region; widespread poverty and desolation were clearly evident.[67] Yet from this destruction arose the push for economic development, and by 1879 conditions seemed opportune in the South for a strong effort toward attaining a diversified industrial economy characteristic of the North.[68] This effort found strong support and sustenance among progressive Southerners, who generally accepted the idea that regional progress would require rapid economic growth and development of a diversified economy.[69] However, the expectations for economic development in the late nineteenth- and early twentieth-century South exceeded the reality of what actually occurred; the region continued to lag economically behind the rest of the nation.[70] Nevertheless, the push for economic development permitted the region to reconcile the competing ideologies of agrarianism and industrialism[71] and helped create an atmosphere throughout the region which would both permit and encourage Southern colleges and universities to pursue the service ideal that characterized much of American higher education.[72]

Thus, it is not surprising that in numerous instances after 1870, advocates of the classical curriculum were incrementally forced to accommodate the utilitarians. At Wofford, where mental discipline seemed especially entrenched, a course in English philology was felt to be a significant response to demands for practicality in education.[73] It was evident, however, that Wofford and other colleges would have to provide more than a course in philology to satisfy utilitarian demands. The growing influence of the utilitarian curriculum threatened to alter the course of Southern higher education.[74] In the post-war society, higher education was increasingly considered a proper instrument for social and economic development in the region. Southern wealth and power were shifting from plantation owners to the businessmen who organized and directed industrial enterprises; thus while the late nineteenth-century Southern economy remained basically agrarian, it was evident to those with foresight that this was changing and education would have to change with it.[75]

In 1875, dedication speeches at the new Vanderbilt University in Nashville focused on that institution's recognition "of every department of true thought, every branch of genuine knowledge, every mode of thorough scholarship"[76] and challenged other colleges to become involved in social, cultural, and economic development. Years later, Vanderbilt's Chancellor Kirkland, mindful perhaps of the University of Wisconsin and its relationship with the state, suggested that, among other things, higher education ought to assist state legislatures and other governmental bodies and commissions in conducting studies on public policy matters. Kirkland saw such involvement relating theory to practice, as enabling higher education to demonstrate its potential for public service. Moreover, he sought to increase Vanderbilt's effectiveness in dealing with external groups by cultivating ties with industry. The work of the physician, mechanic, farmer, navigator, engineer, and merchant was of concern to Vanderbilt which, although neither seeking nor achieving the degree of direct service attained by some state institutions, nonetheless was clearly aware of its responsibility to a society which lay beyond the campus.[77]

Trinity College also recognized its responsibility to offer a utilitarian education. Speaking in Orangeburg, South Carolina in 1899, President Kilgo expressed an interest in bringing to the College those who had grappled with the pressing, practical problems of the day.[78] He encouraged Trinity professors to involve themselves in state and national governmental affairs, thus making themselves available to agencies and organizations which addressed regional problems. In this, he realized that Trinity could not remain isolated from society if it was to be of service:

> Let colleges lay off their coats, defy all kinds of hardships and persecutions and toil with the banker to make his bank safer; work with the manufacturer to keep his machinery in motion; contend with the merchant to secure a fair market; burn his midnight lamp with the editor to save the government from the hurt of false doctrines and evil men; join the collier in his efforts to feed and educate his child; and stand by the laborer that his day may be full of sunshine.[79]

William H. Glasson, Professor of Economics and Social Sciences at Trinity, echoed Kilgo's views in his *South Atlantic Quarterly* article which asserted that only through direct societal involvement could the resources of higher education be fully utilized. Furthermore, he viewed public service as complimentary to the teaching function despite the problems inevitable in such an educational posture.[80]

By the late 1880s, Trinity's curriculum contained clear evidence of an accommodation to the more practical orientation of utility, with such courses as Civil Government (increasing knowledge of government, courts, justice, education and taxation) and "Roads and Road Building" (dealing with the location, construction, and theory of roads) and a ten-month business program appearing in the catalogue. In addition, professional schools of Civil Engineering and Mining Engineering were established, the former offering instruction in theoretical and practical areas and the latter preparing one for "work in practical engineering and the actual management of mines."[81] There was little danger, however, that Trinity would fall victim to the extreme manifestations of utilitarianism (such as Ezra Cornell's unfulfilled ambition to build campus factories operated by students), for the opposing forces were far too strong.

It was the Southern state-supported institutions, however, which faced the greatest pressures to provide a more practical education. As early as 1871, demands for utilitarian education led the University of Mississippi to issue a report outlining its resolve to meet the needs of the state's diverse population. It was recognized, however, that service to heterogeneous groups required the development of multiple educational foci, which threatened mental discipline's fixed curriculum.

Two models were weighed by the faculty of the University of Mississippi in its efforts to respond to pressures for agricultural education. The first was the Sheffield School at Yale with its theoretical and laboratory orientation. The second was the practical field work emphasized by Midwestern state universities. Neither was considered entirely acceptable. The Yale model was deemed too impractical for a farm constituency, while the state university model was dismissed because of an overemphasis on practice to the detriment of theory. The prospects of working in the fields to gain experience generated resentment among Southern students who sought the traditional classroom experiences they had come to expect of higher education. Ultimately Mississippi embarked upon a middle course. Professor Eugene W. Hilgard, whose own Ph.D. was earned from Heidelberg, stated this position when he encouraged the University:

> . . . to impart, besides a general education a thorough knowledge of the principles of agriculture, combined with such acquaintance with its practice as will enable . . . graduates . . . to know [not only] how things should be done, but to do [things] themselves in the field.[82]

In the final analysis, however, the liberal subjects were so entrenched at Mississippi that the agricultural and mechanical subjects called for by the Morrill Act could *not* readily be accommodated; it was necessary to establish the Mississippi Agricultural and Mechanical College in 1878 as an adjunct to the University.[83] In Columbia, however, South Carolina College president John McLaren McBryde, assured the state legislature in 1883 that it had a strong school of agriculture which was effectively meeting the state's needs for improved agricultural methods. The College served the farmer, analyzing his fertilizer and feed, testing new machinery, and assisting in the development of new breeds of farm animals and varieties of plants. McBryde indicated that of the 153 students then in attendance at the College, 53 were pursuing agricultural studies. He proclaimed a balance had been struck between theory and practice: South Carolina students were engaged in laboratory, classroom, and field activities.[84]

It was in this milieu that Kemp Battle, President of the University of North Carolina, affirmed that University's role as an active force for societal betterment. As early as 1866, Battle realized that industry, agriculture, and government required a work force capable of applying knowledge to practical problems, and he believed the modern farmer should be acquainted with the principles of chemistry and agricultural science. Therefore, schools of agriculture similar to the land-grant agricultural schools in the Midwest and West were needed in the South. Moreover, Battle urged that the services of the University not be limited to students at Chapel Hill but extended to constituents throughout the state.[85] By the turn of the century, Battle's successor, Edwin A. Alderman, affirmed that while the South could not contemplate extensive graduate education and research, public service was a most worthy mission for a state university.[86]

In the final analysis, the movement toward utility in the South was a powerful one by the turn of the century. By then Southern state universities under the spreading aegis of utility were, in the words of Alderman, seeking to reach the "public school, the factory child, the hand's hire, the village library, the home, the field . . . the shop . . . with a more practical education."[87] The utilitarian movement brought together advocates of an education centered on the agricultural and mechanical arts with those who defined reform as the development of an elective system that would provide students with greater opportunities to study history, modern languages, or literature. Despite the disparate composition of the reform movement, its members forged a single common objective: to remove the classical course of study from its position of preeminence. They were as we have seen moderately successful.

IV

Research

Although the emphasis of American higher education decidedly favored undergraduate studies, a trend toward research and graduate education had strong support outside the South. In the 1880s and 1890s, advocates of the German-based commitment to research and specialized knowledge loosely joined with those favoring utility to challenge effectively the position of mental discipline. By 1910, the values of research and utility exerted considerable leverage upon higher education outside of the South. Graduate studies became a major endeavor of such emerging universities as Harvard, Columbia, Stanford, Wisconsin, Chicago, and California. In the wake of the pioneering effort at Johns Hopkins, research became the *sine qua non* of academic respectability. American scholars, captivated by the scientific specialization and research indigenous to the German university, returned from Europe with a dedication to recast higher education in the German mold.

In contrast to the rest of the nation, however, the concept of research met with little enthusiasm in the South. Its milieu of detachment and aloofness appeared antithetical to Southern values and needs. Instead, Southern reformers addressed themselves to the problems inherent in introducing scientific knowledge, raising the levels of basic education and cultural awareness, and improving deplorable professional standards.[88]

By almost any measure, Southern colleges were poor and lacked the academic and financial capital to build the graduate research centers which were beginning to emerge in other parts of the nation. College proliferation was especially pronounced in the South, which in the 1880s could boast of more colleges than New England and the Middle Atlantic states combined.[89] Endowments were grossly inadequate or nonexistent at Southern colleges, which were forced to compete among themselves and with the high schools for the only available revenue—tuition. At the turn of the century:

> None of the eighteen American institutions that had endowments of $1,500,000 . . . were [*sic*] in the South; and of the thirty with as much as $1,000,000 the South had only two, Vanderbilt and Tulane.[90]

Moreover, the region was badly lacking in preparatory education. As Trinity's President Kilgo suggests, one cannot readily build a university in a region where preparatory education is woefully inadequate and the bachelor degree is offered by many colleges "whose entire scientific apparatus can be hauled away in a one-horse dray."[91]

While specialization and research may have gained support in other parts of the nation, Southern colleges retained a strong bias towards teaching. Southern colleges could not harbor academics who confined themselves to a library or laboratory:

> . . . the principal function of our colleges must be to teach . . . and each [professor] is required to cover a great deal of ground. He . . . does not . . . have the leisure that is necessary for carrying on work of his own, and even less often has the library or laboratory facilities for original work. So the conditions make it inevitable that the best Southern colleges should mainly tend to develop in their teachers and students not scholars and specialists, but men of ideas and power.[92]

The fate of research at Vanderbilt University is illustrative of the difficulties its proponents faced throughout the South. Founded at approximately the same time as Johns Hopkins and less than twenty years before Chicago, Vanderbilt was more a college than a university. Generally recognized as a leader of the Southern but not national university movement, Vanderbilt, plagued with inadequately prepared undergraduates, was unable and unwilling to deploy the resources necessary to build a first-rate university. Instead of developing an extensive graduate program, Vanderbilt made plans for a high school.[93]

Preparing students profoundly influenced Vanderbilt. Substantial tutorial work was thrust upon the faculty and the boyish character of the student body made research and graduate education all but impossible.[94] In 1893, when institutions in other sections of the country were prodigiously expanding their graduate offerings, Chancellor Kirkland, himself a graduate of Leipzig, strongly reaffirmed the undergraduate mission of Vanderbilt in his inaugural address. Nevertheless, research remained an unrealized aspiration for Vanderbilt. Despite Kirkland's interest in collegiate education he did not oppose graduate training and research *per se*; indeed, he recognized the contribution of advanced scholarship to higher education in hastening conversion of the theoretical into the practical.[95] But the fact that Kirkland was compelled to wrestle with the problems of establishing a basic system of secondary and elementary schools discouraged Vanderbilt and other Southern institutions from considering anything so ambitious as basic research. It was not until the 1920s that Kirkland found conditions suitable for an advanced graduate research center.[96]

John F. Crowell, Trinity's president from 1887 to 1894, was similarly committed to providing a superior undergraduate education. He recognized the need for a more qualified faculty and appreciated the fact that professors trained at graduate institutions both in America and abroad would make significant contributions to Trinity. Crowell actively recruited professors who brought a variety of skills and perspectives to bear on the various disciplines, and he deemed no instructor worthy to hold a position at Trinity who did not actually contribute to research and scholarship in his discipline.[97]

Evidence of Crowell's commitment emerges from an analysis of the academic preparation of Trinity faculty, which demonstrates a steady increase in the number of faculty members holding the Ph.D. In 1889, Trinity did not have a single Ph.D. on its faculty, while Mississippi, North Carolina, and South Carolina, for example, could collectively count slightly more than ten percent in this category. By 1896, the percentage of earned Ph.D.'s at Trinity (16.7 percent) compared favorably with others (Mississippi, 17.6 percent; North Carolina, 16.1 percent; South Carolina, 18.2 percent). By 1903, a greater percentage of the faculty (36.8 percent) held the terminal degree at Trinity than at any of the other three institutions (Mississippi, 22.7percent; North Carolina, 27.7 percent; South Carolina, 15.8 percent). While upgrading the educational level of its faculty, Trinity increasingly recruited from a broader geographic area. In contrast to prior years (1875 and 1882) when the entire faculty had received its undergraduate training in North Carolina, this number declined to less than forty percent by 1903.

Recognition of scholarly pursuits coupled with the desire to move the institution from rural Randolph County to the flourishing city of Durham are indicative of the university influence upon Trinity,[98] but these advances were merely flirtations with the university model. In plans for an envisioned (but never realized) Methodist University of North Carolina, Crowell saw Trinity, theoretically its major unit, focusing on advanced work while the schools and other colleges of the state concentrated on preparatory and collegiate work respectively.[99] In practice, Crowell sought to elevate Trinity to a first-rate college but he did not envision a university patterned after Johns Hopkins or Yale.

Any attempts to divert Trinity from its undergraduate and service mission to a graduate, research-oriented one would have been doomed to failure since the South lacked the social, intellectual, and economic base to sustain such an effort. An inadequate school system would frustrate plans for a graduate/research center for years to come. In 1892–1893, for example, only ten students were enrolled in Trinity's senior class while sixteen were sub-freshman.[100] Secondary schools developed so slowly after the War that little seems to have changed from the 1870s, when most students lacked suitable preparation, to the 1890s when the College was accused of an inability to enforce entrance standards. Conditions began to change after the turn of the century, however, as Trinity College, with the infusion of the Duke family fortune, eventually became a true university. Graduate departments developed, and the possibility of building a richly endowed university in the South[101] was realistically assessed. With the passing of years, both Trinity and Vanderbilt evolved into graduate universities with regional, if not national, missions, but throughout the nineteenth century the focus of their resources was almost solely on undergraduate studies.

Numerous problems also precluded substantial research and graduate study at other Southern institutions. As early as 1879, the faculty of the University of Mississippi, recognizing the value of research and the need for preparing specialists, charged a faculty committee with formulating "Requirements and courses of Study for the Post-graduate degree of Doctor of Philosophy (Ph.D.)."[102] Yet at the time the institution lacked the resources to support a substantive graduate program. Moreover, unlike their colleagues in the North, whose research led to a declining interest in undergraduate education and a greater demand for professional autonomy, Southern faculty retained a preeminent interest in undergraduate education and were seldom afforded comparable professional autonomy. At Mississippi the Trustees hired and fired professors capriciously, stipulating not only the courses to be taught but often the length of time for which they should meet (i.e., one semester, two years, etc.) In addition, they frequently declared all positions vacant at the end of the term in order to reorganize and recruit new staff.[103] This atmosphere, far from conducive to research, imposed many distractions; instructors at Mississippi spent a good deal of time policing the students[104] and could hardly find time to immerse themselves in a discipline. Yet, despite all obstacles, some graduate education existed at Mississippi. Prior to 1900, seventeen students enrolled in doctoral programs and three degrees were granted, one each in 1893, 1894, and 1895. Generally, however, Mississippi remained a small, localized institution, with a relatively homogeneous faculty concerned primarily with undergraduate education and harboring few pretentions of research excellence.[105]

While the experiences of Trinity and Mississippi were repeated throughout the South, there nevertheless remained a clear understanding of the importance of research as reflected in the popularity of Johns Hopkins as the primary source of Southern doctorates by 1903.[106] In 1901, 236 of the 465 advanced students at Johns Hopkins came from the South, and it seemed it would be the true Southern graduate university. The freedom of students and professors and the emphasis upon research at Johns Hopkins was stimulating to the graduates of Southern colleges. A graduate of Trinity attending the Baltimore institution described a great university scattered throughout the city which actually permitted students to abstain from chapel attendance. Unlike Trinity's emphasis on a structured undergraduate experience, Johns Hopkins encouraged independent research by both professor and student. And, unlike the infamous reputation some Southern colleges had earned by lowering their standards in an effort to increase enrollment, Johns Hopkins was known because of Gildersleeve, Newcome, Remsur, Adams, and their colleagues and the work they were doing, rather than for the size of an incoming freshman class.[107]

Professors educated at Johns Hopkins held many key positions in Southern colleges at the turn of the century, and a 1921 article in the *Sewanee Review* proclaimed that:

> . . . educational history of the [South] for the past quarter of a century has been largely that of the Johns Hopkins University. It is rare, indeed, to find in the South any college of note whose faculty has not been drawn largely from Baltimore, to say nothing of the impetus given everywhere to original research and to the publication of the results of such investigations.[108]

Certainly Johns Hopkins stimulated and influenced Southern higher education; however, lacking the necessary secondary school foundation, the region found it difficult to contemplate general implementation of graduate education. The secondary school problem would have to be resolved before graduate work could be introduced on a wide scale. The absence of quality secondary schools forced Southern higher education to direct substantial resources to the preparation of students for undergraduate studies and the remaining resources were often directed to the general improvement of the undergraduate program.

In conclusion, the destruction following the War and the attendant educational and financial problems set the South back many years. It was not until the 1920s that a revitalized South witnessed real attempts to build true universities in Nashville, Chapel Hill, and Durham. Research universities emerged so slowly in the South that the University of Virginia was the only Southern institution to hold membership in the prestigious Association of American Universities in the eighteen years from 1904 until 1922 when it was joined by the University of North Carolina.[109] Thus, Southern higher education in the latter third of the nineteenth century did not replicate the process in the rest of the nation whereby research and utility dominated higher education and relegated mental discipline and piety, and liberal culture to marginal positions. The contest was much closer. Discipline and piety joined with liberal culture and Christian education to create a potent, viable educational philosophy which retained its strength well into the twentieth century; and utility, not research, made significant inroads.

V

Conclusion

In retrospect, the last third of the nineteenth century was a transitional period in the development of Southern higher education. The traditional collegiate emphasis upon discipline and piety peaked in the years immediately preceding and following the War and thereafter declined. The mental discipline and piety of the Thornwell or Craven genre had little chance for survival in the post-war era; narrow and rigid, it could not withstand the pressures generated by a changing South. However, the importance of mental discipline and piety can be measured in part by its progeny, liberal Christian education, that peculiar brand of liberal culture which found its roots in the South. Mental discipline and piety were thus expanded and incorporated into a philosophy more in tenor with the time and region.

Utility found a gradual, if grudging, acceptance in a South confronting the debilitating effects of the war and an agrarian economy. Drawing sustenance from a more progressive South, utility's strength was expressed by the development of substantial agricultural programs at state-supported institutions such as South Carolina and Mississippi and eventually provided the rationale for the elective system at both state and private institutions. Institutions such as Trinity, Vanderbilt, North Carolina, Mississippi, and Wofford eventually accommodated utilitarian concerns in a positive if at times subdued manner.

Research, handicapped by the region's need to divert substantial resources to preparatory schools and sub-collegiate classes, failed to secure a foothold in the South during the nineteenth century. No major university was established in the region, and the history of Southern higher education in the nineteenth century is therefore one of a continued domination by the college as contrasted with the emergence of the university in other sections of the nation. In the twentieth century, a vastly improved financial picture, the development of the publicly-supported high school, and the increased demand for highly specialized personnel in all sectors of society finally enabled Vanderbilt, Duke, and North Carolina to create strong graduate components. In the nineteenth century, however, the emphasis in Southern higher education was decidedly undergraduate.

The university-centered, secular liberal culture described by Veysey found the South inhospitable. A distinctly college-centered liberal Christian education emerged instead, and its merits were extolled throughout the South. Its strong concern for the development of religious principles and gentlemanly character suited the region; with roots in both sectarian and public institutions, liberal Christian education constituted a significant force in Southern higher education.

By attempting to meet the needs of the greater society, however, Southern higher education engaged in a penetrating and potentially explosive evaluation of its goals, objectives, and methods. Furthermore, regardless of size or source of support, only a few institutions could be neatly placed in a single category; on most any campus one could find proponents of mental discipline and piety, liberal culture, Christian education, utility, and research. This recognition of and willingness to deal with a multifarious population and diverse societal needs naturally undermined the essence of the ante-bellum classical college while creating a new sense of dynamism in higher education. Had Southern higher education unanimously elected to retreat from contemporary concerns, it is likely that mental discipline would have reigned supreme for several decades after the War. This was not the case, however, for with each outward thrust, each attempt to meet the needs of the people, came new ideas and more intensive debate over the future direction of higher education in the region. But one thing is certain: Southern higher education did not follow the pattern of university development that emerged in other regions of the nation. It ultimately moved into the mainstream of American higher education, but its course was decidedly different.

Notes

1. C. B. Burke, "The Expansion of American Higher Education," in *The Transformation of Higher Learning 1860–1930*, ed. K. H. Jarausch (Chicago, 1983), p. 111.

2. Letter, L. C. Garland to his father, May 30, 1865. Joint University Library, Vanderbilt University, John James Tiger IV Collection.

3. J. B. Sellers, *History of University of Alabama, Vol. I: 1818–1902* (University of Alabama, 1953), pp. 292–313.

4. R. Somers, *The Southern State Since the War 1870–1871* (New York, 1871) pp. 159–160. Somers, a visiting Englishman, stated, "The professors at the close of the war were put under the ban of political proscription . . . and new men of inferior attainments were set down in their chairs. The consequence is that Alabama has still a University, with buildings and libraries, and professors, and expenditure, but no students. . . ."

5. Letter, A. J. Quinche to J. L. Johnson, February 1, 1873, Southern Historical Collection, University of North Carolina, John Lipscomb Johnson Papers. *Note:* John Lipscomb Johnson joined the University of Mississippi faculty in 1873.

6. D. D. Wallace, *History of Wofford College* (Nashville, 1951), p. 152.

7. N. C. Chaffin, *Trinity College, 1839–1892: The Beginnings of Duke University of North Carolina* (Durham, 1950), pp. 255–256.

8. K. P. Battle, *The Struggle and the Story of the Rebirth of the University* (Chapel Hill, 1901), pp. 3–11. Also see H. M. Wagstaff, *Impressions of Men and Movements at the University of North Carolina* (Chapel Hill, 1950).

9. "The curricula of the university 1857–1858 and 1897–1898," *University* [North Carolina] *Record*, January, 1898.

10. G. W. Paschal, *History of Wake Forest College, Vol. II: 1865–1898* (Wake Forest, 1943), pp. 2–22 and 419.

11. D. W. Hollis, *University of South Carolina, Vol. I: South Carolina College* (Columbia, 1951), pp. 214–222.

12. D. W. Hollis, *University of South Carolina, Vol. II: College to University* (Columbia, 1956), pp. 44–79.

13. F. A. Barnard, *Report on the organization of military schools, Made to the Trustees of the University of Mississippi* (Jackson, 1861), p. 31. University of Mississippi Library, Mississippi Collections.

14. L. R. Veysey, *The Emergence of the American University*, (Chicago, 1970). For a critique of Veysey, see P. Mattingly, "Structures Over Time: Institutional History," in *Historical Inquiry in Education*, ed. J. H. Best (Washington, D.C., 1983), pp. 34–55.

15. C. V. Woodward, *Origins of the New South, 1877–1913*, (Baton Rouge, 1951), pp. 436–438.

16. C. Degler, "The Two Cultures and the Civil War," in *The Development of an American Culture*, eds. S. Cohen and L. Ratner (Englewood Cliffs, 1970), pp. 92–119.

17. W. J. Cash, *The Mind of the South*, (New York, 1941), p. vii.

18. Degler, "Two Cultures and Civil War," p. 117.

19. Woodward, *Origins of the New South*, p. x.

20. B. M. Palmer, *The Life and Letters of James Henley Thornwell*, (Richmond, 1871), p. 357. *Also* J. N. Waddell, *Nature and Advantage of the Course of Study in Institutions of Higher Learning* (Natchez, 1866), p. 13.

21. F. Brewer, "South Carolina University," (manuscript, 1876), South Carolinian Library, University of South Carolina, Fisk Brewer Manuscript Collection.

22. F. Brewer, "Assorted class notes and notebook," *ca.* 1877, South Carolinian Library, University of South Carolina, Fisk Brewer Manuscript Collection.

23. W. D. Porter, *College and Collegians*, (Charleston, 1871), p. 19. Potter was a Trustee of South Carolina College from 1858 to 1868.

24. W. A. Pusey, "Should the classics still be studied," *Vanderbilt Observer*, 8, October, 1885, p. 2.

25. "The Study of Latin and Greek," *Trinity Archive*, VI, April 1893, p. 283.

26. Waddel, *Nature and Advantage*, p. 1.

27. Minutes of the Faculty Meeting, University of Mississippi, April 22, 1884. *Note:* Fulton joined the University of Mississippi in 1871 as a tutor and from the 1892 to 1906 served as Chancellor.

28. Barnard, *Report to the Trustees of University of Mississippi*, p. 31.

29. A. Cabaniss, *The University of Mississippi: Its First Hundred Years*, (Hattiesburg, 1971), p. 64.

30. *Catalogue of Trinity College*, 1885–1886, p. 9.

31. D. D. Wallace, *History of Wofford College*, (Nashville, 1951), pp. 77–78.

32. Brewer, "South Carolina University."

33. J. H. Easterby, *A History of the College of Charleston*, (Charleston, 1935), p. 164.

34. H. M. Bullock, *A History of Emory University*, (Nashville, 1936), pp. 154–174. *Also see:* M. Bauman, "Confronting the New South Creed: The Genteel Conservative as Higher Educator," in *Education and the Rise of the New South*, eds. R. K. Goodenow and A. O. White (Boston, 1981), pp. 91–113.

35. C. W. Hutson, "The South Carolina College of the late fifties," Compiler: Yates Snowden, *Sermon and Lectures South Carolina College and University, 1830–1910,* South Carolinian Library, University of South Carolina.

36. J. W. Taylor, *The Young Men of the New South: The Education, Duties and Rewards,* (Memphis, 1869), p. 8. Mississippi Collection, University of Mississippi Library.

37. W. Cash, *Mind of the South,* p. 80.

38. W. M. Whitman, "Address of the laying of the cornerstone of Wofford College," (manuscript, July 4, 1851). Sandor Teszler Library, Wofford College Archives.

39. *Catalogue of the officers and students of the University of Mississippi, 1879–1880,* pp. 74–75. *Also see:* Trustees of the State University, *Where shall I send my son?* (Oxford, 1876), pp. 3–4, Mississippi Collection, University of Mississippi Library.

40. Minutes of the Board of Trustees Meeting, University of Mississippi, June 24, 1886.

41. Minutes of the Board of Trustees Meeting, University of Mississippi, June 23, 1879.

42. B. Craven, "Mental discipline," (eight page manuscript, n.d.), Perkins Library, Duke University, Braxton Craven Papers.

43. C. V. Woodward, *Origins in the New South,* pp. 142–174 provides an excellent analysis of Southern literary and religious values in the decades following the Civil War. For a highly relevant look at higher education and Southern culture see J. L. Wagoner, "Higher Education and Transitions in Southern Culture: An Exploratory Apolgia," *Journal of Thought,* 18, Fall, 1983, pp. 104–118.

44. D. P. Harrington, Requirements of an A.B. Degree. Contained in *Proceedings of the first annual session of the College Association of North Carolina, North Carolina Teacher,* May 1892. H. F. Linscott, "Pure Scholarship—Its Place in Civilization," *South Atlantic Quarterly,* 1 (October, 1902): 341–350.

45. H. Hawkins, *Between Harvard and America,* (New York, 1972), p. 264.

46. B. J. Ramage, "The Limitations of Elective Work in School and College," *Sewanee Review,* 9 (July 1901): 319.

47. T. D. Witherspoon, *The appeal of the South to its educated men,* (Memphis, 1867), pp. 8–9. Mississippi Collection, University of Mississippi Library.

48. D. Bertelson, *The Lazy South,* (New York, 1967), pp. 75 and 182–183.

49. C. N. Degler, *Place Over Time* (Baton Rouge, 1977), pp. 99–132. Degler outlines the substantial economic and cultural continuity between the pre and post war South.

50. C. Degler, "Two Cultures and Civil War," p. 119.

51. E. W. Porter, *Trinity and Duke,* (Durham, 1964), pp. 70–144.

52. J. C. Kilgo, "Christian Education: Its Aims and Superiority," *ca.* 1896, Perkins Library, Duke University, John C. Kilgo Papers.

53. J. C. Kilgo, Untitled typescript, n.d., p. 5, Perkins Library, Duke University, John Carlisle Kilgo Papers.

54. H. N. Snyder, "The Denominational College in Southern Education," *South Atlantic Quarterly,* 5 (January 1906): 9.

55. H. N. Snyder, "The Case of the Denominational College," *Methodist Review,* 58 (January, 1909): 14.

56. J. H. Carlisle, An undated clipping from the Florence, South Carolina *Centenary* (January, 1892), Sandor Teszler Library, Wofford College, James H. Carlisle Papers. *Also see:* H. N. Snyder, "James H. Carlisle—Educator," *South Atlantic Quarterly,* 9 (January, 1910): 10–20.

57. J. H. Carlisle, Jr., "Memories of Wofford College," (manuscript, n.d.), Sandor Teszler Library, Wofford College, Wofford College Archives.

58. J. B. Henneman, "The Late Professor Baskerville," *Sewanee Review,* 8 (January, 1900): 26–44.

59. H. N. Snyder, "The college literary society," *Sewanee Review,* 12 (January, 1904): 83.

60. *Catalogue of the Officers and Students of the University of Mississippi, 1876–1877,* p. 46.

61. *Historical and current catalogue of the officers and students of the University of Mississippi, 1886–1887,* p. 152.

62. Minutes of the Board of Trustees, University of Mississippi, August 6, 1889.

63. G. T. Pugh, "Is Science an Incentive to Poetry?" *Wofford College Journal,* 7 (June, 1897): 284–291.

64. J. B. Wiggins, "Does the Study of Science tend to Suppress the Spirit of Poetry and Romance?" *Wofford College Journal,* 9 (June, 1898): 46–52.

65. Veysey, *Emergence of American University,* p. 60.

66. C. W. Hutson, *The Southern Renaissance,* (Columbia, 1885), p. 29.

67. For a contemporary's view of the South in the decade after the Civil War see C. H. Otken, *Ills of the South,* (New York, 1894). Reprint (New York, 1973). *Also see:* Woodward, *Origins of the New South,* pp. 107–112.

68. R. N. Current, *Northernizing the South,* (Athens, 1983), p. 84.

69. D. W. Grantham, *Souther Progressivism: The Reconciliation of Progress and Traditions,* (Knoxville, 1983), p. xviii.

70. Woodward, *Origins of the New South*, pp. 139–141.

71. M. O'Brien, *The Ideas of the American South, 1920–1941*, Baltimore, 1979), p. 6.

72. Grantham, *Southern Progressivism*, p. 84. Also see pp. 268–270 for an examination of the development of the utility in Southern higher education and pp. 5–8 for the impact of urbanization and industrialization upon the professions.

73. *Catalogue of Wofford College, 1876–1877*, p. 18. For a relevant analysis of President Eliot and the elective system at Harvard see: E. S. Joynes, "President Eliot's inaugural address," *Educational Journal of Virginia*, 1 (March, 1870): 136–140.

74. J. M. McBryde, *Agricultural education*. An address before the South Carolina State Legislature, December 12, 1882, (Columbia, 1883), pp. 12–15.

75. E. S. Joynes, "Relation to the state of higher education in colleges and professional schools," a paper read before the Southern Educational Association in Chattanooga on July 9, 1891, South Carolinian Library, University of South Carolina.

76. P. P. Lipscomb, *Dedication and inauguration of Vanderbilt University* (Nashville, 1875), p. 76.

77. J. H. Kirkland, *The service of citizenship*, 1911, Joint University Library, Vanderbilt University, James H. Kirkland Addresses.

78. J. C. Kilgo, "Up to date education," *State*, Columbia, South Carolina, April 14, 1899. Clipping contained in Perkins Library, Duke University, John C. Kilgo Papers.

79. J. C. Kilgo, "The mission of Trinity College," *The Trinity Archive*, 15 (November 1901): 127.

80. W. H. Glasson, "The college professor in the public service," *South Atlantic Quarterly*, 1 (July 1902): 254.

81. *Catalogue of Trinity College, 1887–88*, pp. 31–44.

82. E. W. Hilgard, Report on Organization of the Department of Agriculture and Mechanical Arts, 1871, Mississippi Collection, University of Mississippi Library.

83. R. A. McLemore, "The Roots of Higher Education in Mississippi," *Journal of Mississippi History*, 26 (August 1964). *Also* J. K. Betterworth, *People's College: A History of Mississippi State University* (Tuscaloosa, 1953), pp. 8–11.

84. J. M. McBryde, *Agricultural education*, (Columbia, 1883), pp. 22–23. South Carolinian Library, University of South Carolina. *Also see:* J. M. McBryde Papers, Southern Historical Collection, University of North Carolina Library.

85. K. P. Battle, *The head and the hand*, (June 23, 1886), pp. 5–6. Pamphlet located in the South Carolinian Library, University of South Carolina.

86. E. A. Alderman, "The university: Its work and its needs, University of North Carolina," *Record 1901–1902* (Chapel Hill, 1901), p. 51.

87. E. A. Alderman, Inaugural address, January 27, 1897. North Carolina Collection, University of North Carolina, p. 29.

88. A. E. Shepherd, "Higher education in the south," *Sewanee Review*, 1 (May 1893): 287.

89. J. D. Dreher, "Colleges North and Colleges South," National Educational Association, *Journal of Proceedings and Addresses 1886*, pp. 370–375.

90. Woodward, *Origins of the New South*, p. 437.

91. J. C. Kilgo, "Some Phases of Southern Higher Education," *South Atlantic Quarterly*, 2 (April 1903): 141.

92. W. P. Few, "Trinity College and Her Present Opportunity," *Trinity Archive*, 15 (November, 1901): 113. Few elsewhere states: "For the good of the country as a whole [educational] centers should be distributed over the country rather than concentrated in sections. Draw a line across the map of the United States from a point just below the latitude of Washington and Baltimore on the Atlantic coast, and all the leading centers of research will be north of the line. The Northeast has Harvard, Columbia, Yale, and other great centers. Johns Hopkins is near the border line. The Central West has the University of Chicago, University of Michigan, University of Wisconsin, and other centers of note. The Pacific coast has the University of California, Stanford University, and California Institute of Technology. The South is making progress in four or five places and in some of these centers the progress is apt to be notable. Even so, it will be a good while before the southern states can do their share in scientific study and research." W. P. Few, "The Beginnings of an American University," (typescript, n.d.), Perkins Library, Duke University, William Preston Few Papers.

93. Minutes of the Board of Trustees, Vanderbilt University, April 29, 1874.

94. Minutes of the Board of Trustees, Vanderbilt University, June 19, 1876.

95. J. H. Kirkland, *Proceedings and addresses at the installation and inauguration of James Hampton Kirkland, Ph.D.* (Nashville, 1893), p. 37.

96. J. H. Kirkland, "Sketch of Vanderbilt University," unpublished paper (1926). Joint University Library, Vanderbilt University, James H. Kirkland Papers.

97. W. K. Boyd, "Trinity College before its removal in Durham," (typescript copy, n.d.) Perkins Library, Duke University, William Kenneth Boyd Papers.

98. W. K. Boyd, "Trinity and Duke," (typescript copy, n.d.) Perkins Library, Duke University, William Kenneth Boyd Papers.

99. J. F. Crowell, "Plan of a Methodist University in North Carolina," (manuscript, *ca.* 1890), Perkins Library, Duke University, John F. Crowell Papers.

100. *Catalogue and Announcements of Trinity College, 1892–93.*

101. W. P. Few, "Trinity College and her Present Opportunity," p. 113.

102. Minutes of the Faculty Meeting, University of Mississippi, November 25, 1879.

103. Minutes of the Board of Trustees, University of Mississippi, June 22, 1886. *Also see:* Minutes of the Board of Trustees, University of Mississippi, June 27, 1889.

104. Minutes of the Board of Trustees, University of Mississippi, June 22, 1891.

105. M. R. Brown, *Graduate programs in Mississippi in 1900,* unpublished Master's thesis, History, University of Mississippi, 1968, pp. 15–16.

106. According to my research of the twenty-eight members with the Ph.D. at the University of South Carolina, University of Mississippi and University of North Carolina in 1903, seven received their doctorate from Johns Hopkins, six from German Universities, four from the University of North Carolina, four from Harvard University, three from other Eastern universities, two from other Southern universities, one from a Midwestern university and one was unknown.

107. D. C. Branson, "Letters from Johns Hopkins," *Trinity Archive,* IV, March, 1891.

108. B. S. Ramage, Notes, *Sewanee Review,* 9 (July, 1901): 379.

109. Wagoner, "Higher Education and Transitions," p. 114.

The Origins of Federal Support for Higher Education

Roger L. Williams

A New Interpretation

The American land-grant college movement, the context for this study, is not easily defined. In simple, concrete terms, the movement is the collective story of the emergence of seventy-one colleges and universities that were predicated on an exclusive relationship with the federal government and a shared set of obligations to their respective states. In more complex terms, the land-grant movement is the expression and diffusion of certain political, social, economic, and educational ideals. The motives typically attributed to the movement involve the democratization of higher education; the development of an educational system deliberately planned to meet utilitarian ends, through research and public service as well as instruction; and a desire to emphasize the emerging applied sciences, particularly agricultural science and engineering.

Of the original motives, the strongest was the urge to provide a "useful" form of higher education that would hold some appeal for the so-called "industrial classes." In 1862, when the enabling legislation was signed by Abraham Lincoln, that economic stratum included four of every five Americans—whether farmers, artisans, mechanics, or laborers. The vocation in which the majority of Americans were engaged—and with which the land-grant colleges were most strongly identified—was agriculture, which explains why the land-grant colleges were usually located in rural settings, far from the "corrupting" influences of cities. For some, including many land-grant college presidents, the agricultural orientation was overwrought. Even the father of the legislation, Senator Justin S. Morrill, was reputed to have disparaged the term "agricultural." He said the word "would never have been applied to the institution except that it happened to suit the casual convenience of an index clerk."[1]

The land-grant college movement must also be considered as a historical construct, an invention by scholars to give form and meaning to otherwise nebulous and uncertain developments. This becomes apparent when examining the literature on land-grant college history—when one can find it. The difficulty of defining the land-grant movement is compounded by the dearth of scholarship, especially recent scholarship, on the subject. While the history of American higher education has undergone substantial revision within the last fifteen years,[2] the history of the land-grant movement has remained largely untouched by the process. The corpus of land-grant history does contain a number of institutional histories, and an occasional biography of a land-grant college president or a prominent agricultural scientist, yet the quality of the works in both categories is uneven.[3]

There are only four major works on the history of the land-grant college movement proper: Joseph B. Edmond's *Magnificent Charter: The Origin and Role of the Morrill Land-Grant Colleges and Universities* (1978); Allan Nevins's *State Universities and Democracy* (1962); Edward D. Eddy's *Colleges for Our Land and Time: The Land-Grant Idea in American Education* (1957); and Earle D. Ross's seminal *Democracy's College: The Land-Grant College in the Formative Stage* (1942). Considered as a whole, the work of Ross, Eddy, Nevins, and Edmond tends toward a perspective of land-grant history that is evolutionary, impersonal, deterministic, and—especially—romantic. The overriding implication of their work is that the land-grant movement was inevitable, the colleges called into being by the educational

310

demands of a rapidly expanding and democratizing nation. This growing nation, they averred, had been badly served by the ante-bellum college, which they depicted as unresponsive, inflexible, retrogressive, and—worst of all—undemocratic.

Those assumptions about the ante-bellum college have been challenged by such revisionists as Stanley Guralnik, Colin Burke, and David Potts.[4] This revisionism is yet to be applied to land-grant historiography, however, so the deterministic bias there reigns unchecked. Certain histories of U.S. agricultural science add valuable insights regarding the land-grant movement, but on balance they are contextually deficient, focusing on agricultural issues to the exclusion of all else.[5] In short, the complete land-grant movement history worthy of the canons of scholarship now prevailing in the field of higher education history has not been written.

Limited as the land-grant histories are, they do agree that the first quarter-century after the 1862 Morrill Act was a dismal period for the land-grant movement. The colleges did not fail in the sense of having to close their doors—indeed, by 1870 all thirty-seven states had founded or had laid the groundwork for establishing a land-grant college. But the colleges did not flourish. Enrollments—a high percentage of them college preparatory courses—grew slowly, and student attrition remained high. Professors were asked to endure low salaries, heavy workloads, and primitive facilities. State support was slim, if forthcoming at all. The land-grant colleges also attracted powerful enemies. Congress launched an investigation of the institutions in 1874. The Grange followed with a similar inquest, condemning the colleges for their inability to attract agricultural students and vowing to oppose the schools in every way.

Between 1887 and 1891, the colleges finally began to stabilize. Through two acts of Congress, the Hatch Act in 1887 and the second Morrill Act in 1890, continuous federal appropriations began to flow, and the example of the national government encouraged state governments to begin or renew their support. The Hatch Act, providing for establishment of agricultural experiment stations, presented the colleges with the means to serve their agricultural constituencies in practical ways and inadvertently provided some general financial underpinnings. The 1890 Morrill Act provided what the Hatch Act did not: annual federal appropriations for general academic programs, from English to engineering. With the increased funds came growing numbers of students; by 1900, some 19,268 baccalaureate students were enrolled in sixty-five land-grant colleges.[6]

Land-grant historiography notwithstanding, these acts, and the political climate that gave rise to their passage, did not simply evolve. The study that follows tries to correct errant or incomplete interpretations of the lengthy transition from the era of strain and struggle to that of growth and relative prosperity.

It does so by examining the contributions to the land-grant movement of George Washington Atherton, seventh president (1882–1906) of the Pennsylvania State College, now The Pennsylvania State University, and its so-called "second founder." Atherton's work at the Pennsylvania State College is well documented. Three Penn State historians have credited him with effecting a "complete transformation" of a foundering school during his twenty-four-year tenure.[7]

Yet Atherton is virtually a forgotten figure in the history of higher education in the United States, despite his role as the leading land-grant college advocate of his day. His most important contributions to the land-grant movement lay not in his "local" work at Penn State, but in his activity on the national stage. He played the pivotal role in instigating and promoting the legislation that started the flow of continuous federal financial support to higher education. In addition, his leadership within the fledgling national association of land-grant colleges and agricultural experiment stations was critical to the progress of those institutions during the period 1885–1905.

Atherton was the motive force behind the Hatch Act, which encouraged establishment of agricultural experiment stations at land-grant colleges and provided an annual appropriation of $15,000 for the stations' work. And although the Department of Agriculture historian Alfred C. True stated that a legislative committee headed by Atherton was largely responsible for the success of the legislation,[8] Atherton's role was actually that of prime mover. His role in the campaign for the 1890 Morrill Act was equally significant. A group of land-grant college presidents, led by Henry E. Alvord, president of Maryland Agricultural College, and Atherton, worked unremittingly through the spring and summer of 1890 to bring the legislation to fruition. After passage of the second Morrill Act, which guaranteed annual appropriations that ultimately reached $25,000 for a range of educational programs, Atherton received a glowing letter from a colleague at Ohio State:

> We are much elated over passage of the Morrill Bill with our own amendment. Too much praise cannot be given to Major Alvord and yourself for your wise and prudent direction of the forces which have wrought so noble a result. Some day we will build a monument to you.[9]

The successful passage of both acts was inextricably tied to the tight network of land-grant college presidents and agricultural scientists that became the Association of American Agricultural Colleges and Experiment Stations, the first organization of peer higher education institutions in the nation. In this collectivity, Atherton also played the leading role, particularly in the 1885–1890 period. At the Association's preliminary meeting in 1885, for example, he was named chairman of the executive committee and appointed to chair a three-member committee charged with securing experiment station legislation. During the Association's founding convention in 1887, which was called to discuss implementation of the Hatch Act, Atherton was elected the Association's first president, and he served two terms through November 1889. Informally, Atherton was the Association's chief legislative architect and emissary to Congress and the federal administrative agencies, and he also involved himself in Association work on a variety of other fronts.

Aside from his work with Congress and the federal agencies, George Atherton played the critical role in keeping the Association intact. Early on, the organization gave rise to an internal power struggle between the college presidents and the experiment station directors. Atherton first articulated and later epitomized the presidents' position, which sought to keep the stations in their place as subordinate "departments" of the colleges—with the attendant responsibilities for teaching, research, and service that such a relationship implies. The station directors, most forcefully represented by Pennsylvania State College's Henry P. Armsby, argued that the stations should focus exclusively on research.

The Association itself is fertile ground for scholarly study, as it sheds new light not only on the nature and value of higher education associations, but on land-grant historiography as well. In the main, higher education historians have overlooked the institutional associations.[10] Yet it would have been impossible to conduct this study without a careful examination of this seminal organization, as it provided the matrix for Atherton's national advocacy on behalf of the land-grant movement.

The Association of American Agricultural Colleges and Experiment Stations (hereafter, the Association) preceded the founding of the National Association of State Universities by eight years and the Association of American Universities (AAU) by thirteen. Whether the Association, by its own example, had an effect on the formation of the AAU in 1900 is difficult to determine, but it is significant that the Association was the first in a sequence of similar organizations. The final chapter in this book presents some evidence that the Association did influence the formation of the National Association of State Universities in 1895. Although the two organizations eventually merged in 1963 as the National Association of State Universities and Land-Grant Colleges, their initial relationship was competitive rather than cooperative. Indeed, the old-line state universities—those without benefit of the land-grant in their respective states—flared with envy over the land-grant colleges' success in winning annual federal appropriations from Congress and sought to do likewise.

The Association not only helped to build the stature of the land-grant colleges, but also contributed to standardized entrance requirements, balanced curricula, and rationalized methods. Through a variety of initiatives involving graduate education, military instruction, mining engineering, and curriculum reform, and through the evolving relationships with the federal departments of Agriculture, Interior, and War, Atherton and his presidential colleagues used the Association to forge their vision of the land-grant college as a comprehensive institution attending to the liberal, scientific, and even civic education of well-rounded men and women, not merely the technician or vocationalist.

In fact, Atherton's view of land-grant colleges did not differ dramatically from the perception of the mainstream developing universities of his day, most of which had already adopted science in their curricula.

From the early 1870s, Atherton contended that the term "agricultural college" was a misnomer and that "national schools of science" was the more accurate term. Indeed, Atherton and his close colleagues were fully aware of the extent to which the popular conception of land-grant colleges as mainly "agricultural colleges" had impeded the institutions' broader development, and they sought to use the Association to effect their vision of the land-grant colleges as mainstream institutions in the forefront of liberal and scientific education. This is not to imply that Atherton disdained agricultural science, for he worked tirelessly in its cause. He did, however, resent its powerful capacity for characterizing the land-grant colleges as single-mission institutions.

While the efforts of the Association of American Agricultural Colleges and Experiment Stations offer a new lens for examining the land-grant college movement, and thus the beginnings of federal support for higher education, this study's main interest is a critical examination of George W. Atherton's nationally significant contributions on the colleges' behalf. Without the impetus provided by the Hatch Act and the 1890 Morrill Act, for which Atherton worked so hard, the development of land-grant colleges into consequential research universities would have been far more difficult. An investigation that focuses on the champion of the legislation not only provides insight into the motivations for such initiatives, but also makes the overtones of inevitability in the land-grant saga quickly fade away when the thoughts and actions of the movement's principals are brought to light.

The history of higher education has not been remiss in its valuation of outstanding leaders. The premier work on the nineteenth-century university movement, Laurence R. Veysey's *Emergence of the American University* (1965), examines the themes of the movement largely through the contributions of the leading institutional presidents: Charles Eliot of Harvard, Noah Porter of Yale, Nicholas Murray Butler of Columbia, James McCosh of Princeton, Daniel Coit Gilman of California and Johns Hopkins, Andrew White of Cornell, and others. Burdened by its deterministic historiography, land-grant history has been not nearly so concerned with identifying its "great men" (although this is not to argue for a "great man" theory of land-grant history). In fact, the most ambitious attempt to identify the "great men" of the land-grant movement was made by historian Earle D. Ross in a 1961 article. His "Great Triumvirate of Land-Grant Educators" included Daniel Coit Gilman, Andrew D. White, and Francis Walker.[11] Gilman is cited for his presidency of the land-grant institution that became the University of California at Berkeley; for his 1867 seminal article about land-grant colleges, in which he prescribed the means for their emergence as "national schools of science"; and for the first comprehensive survey of land-grant institutions, which he undertook in 1871 for the Bureau of Education. White's direct service to land-grant education was his role in the founding and shaping of Cornell, the "first visible spectacular fruit of the Morrill Act."[12] Walker's contributions to land-grant education lay in bringing the Massachusetts Institute of Technology (which received the engineering share of that state's divided land-grant endowment) to the apex of instruction and research in applied science and technology.

Drawing inspiration from Ross, this book searches for other leading lights. Indeed, it suggests a second and even more central "great triumvirate": George W. Atherton, of the Pennsylvania State College; Henry E. Alvord, president of Maryland Agricultural College; and Henry H. Goodell, president of Massachusetts Agricultural College. It also suggests a different criterion for determining "greatness," for none of this latter triumvirate built a leading university during his lifetime. Rather, this second triumvirate was responsible for securing important legislation and leading the Association of American Agricultural Colleges and Experiment Stations into the early twentieth century. Thus, their "greatness" stems from systemic contributions. They were key to transforming a stalled movement into a vigorous system of colleges with similar purposes, curricula, standards and constituencies—and a shared relationship with the federal government.

However justified Ross may have been in choosing his triumvirate, his selection is ultimately flawed. Gilman, White, and Walker reigned during the difficult first quarter-century of land-grant college struggle, but by 1885, Gilman and White, both of whom had a high regard for Atherton, had left the land-grant college scene. They played no role in the passage of the Hatch Act and the 1890 Morrill Act, which ushered in the new age. To ignore the principals, such as George Atherton, who brought this seminal "enabling" legislation to fruition is to leave a serious void in land-grant history.

The American land-grant saga was not so deterministic or romantic as it has been portrayed. It involved the rough-and-tumble of politics, including pressure tactics, aggressive lobbying, persuasion, agitation, and of course compromise. It resounded with the clash of competing ideas and interests—inside the movement as well as outside. And it is a story rife with paradox, inconsistency, and ambiguity. After twenty-five hard years of struggle and disappointment, the land-grant colleges turned the corner about 1890. This happened not because the institutions were destined to do so in response to some vague national demand, but because certain individuals were resolved to create the means—through federal legislation and through an organization of peer institutions—for the colleges' sustenance. And no one was more prominent in this work than George W. Atherton.

Notes

1. Quoted in George W. Atherton, *The Legislative Career of Justin S. Morrill,* An address delivered at New Haven, Connecticut, November 14, 1900 (Harrisburg, Pa.: J. Horace McFarland, 1900), 32.

2. See Bruce A. Kimball, "Writing the History of Universities: A New Approach," *Minerva* 24 (Summer-Autumn 1986), 375–389.

3. Some of the biographies in question are: Calvin Stebbins, *Henry Hill Goodell* (Cambridge, Mass.: Riverside Press, 1911); Mabel Hardy Pollitt, *A Biography of James Kennedy Patterson, President of the University of Kentucky, 1869 to 1910* (Louisville, Ky.: Westerfield-Bonte Co., 1925); Joseph C. Bailey, *Seaman A. Knapp: Schoolmaster of American Agriculture* (New York: Columbia University Press, 1945), Jean Wilson Sidar, *George Hammell Cook: A Life in Agriculture and Geology* (New Brunswick, N. J.: Rutgers University Press, 1976).

4. Stanley M. Guralnik, *Science and the Ante-bellum College* (Philadelphia: American Philosophical Society, 1975), Colin B. Burke, *American Collegiate Populations: A Test of the Traditional View* (New York: New York University Press, 1982); and David B. Potts, "Curriculum and Enrollments: Some Thoughts on Assessing the Popularity of Ante-bellum Colleges," *History of Higher Education Annual* 1 (1981), 88–109.

5. Land-grant history, such as it is, has been buttressed by some notable works on the history of agricultural science. Seminal among them are Alfred C. True's *History of Agricultural Education in the United States, 1785–1925,* U.S. Department of Agriculture, Misc. Pub. No. 36 (Washington, D.C.: Government Printing Office, 1929), and his *History of Agricultural Experimentation and Research in the United States, 1607–1925,* U.S. Department of Agriculture, Misc. Pub. No. 251 (Washington, D.C., Government Printing Office, 1937). To those have been added such modern studies as H. C. Knoblauch, E. M. Law, and W. P. Meyer, *State Agriculture Experiment Stations: A History of Research Policy and Procedure,* U.S. Department of Agriculture, Misc. Pub. 904 (Washington, D.C., Government Printing Office, 1962), as well as two recent books written in anticipation of the 1987 centennial of the Hatch Act: Alan I. Marcus, *Agricultural Science and the Quest for Legitimacy* (Ames: Iowa State University Press, 1985), and Norwood A. Kerr, *The Legacy: A Centennial History of the State Agricultural Experiment Stations, 1887–1987* (Columbia: University of Missouri at Columbia, 1987).

   Although these works are valuable in revealing the tensions between land-grant college presidents and their agricultural scientists, they treat the emerging colleges only within an agricultural context. Because the colleges are analyzed for their involvement with agricultural research and instruction in general and for their relationship with the agricultural experiment stations in particular, these books tend to reinforce prevailing but erroneous "cow college" assumptions about the nature of the early land-grant institutions. For example, in terms of student interest and enrollments, engineering far outweighed agriculture on most land-grant college campuses.

6. Alfred C. True, *Statistics of the Land-Grant Colleges and Agricultural Experiment Stations of the United States, 1900.* U.S. Department of Agriculture, Office of Experiment Stations, Bulletin No. 97 (Washington, D.C.: Government Printing Office, 1901), 8.

7. See esp. Wayland F. Dunaway, *History of the Pennsylvania State College* (Lancaster, Pa.: Lancaster Press, 1946), 165–166.

8. True, *Agricultural Education,* 208.

9. Alexis Cope to George W. Atherton, August 20, 1890, Box 7, Folder C, Atherton Papers (MSG 6).

10. See Hugh Hawkins, "Problems in Categorization and Generalization in the History of American Higher Education: An Approach Through the Institutional Associations," in *History of Higher Education Annual* 5 (1985), 45.

11. See Earle D. Ross, "The Great Triumvirate of Land-Grant Educators," *Journal of Higher Education* 32, (December 1961), 480–488.

12. Quoted in Roger L. Geiger, *To Advance Knowledge: The Growth of American Research Universities, 1900–1940* (New York: Oxford University Press, 1986), 6.

CHAPTER 5

RESEARCH UNIVERSITIES

RESEARCH, GRADUATE EDUCATION, AND THE ECOLOGY OF AMERICAN UNIVERSITIES: AN INTERPRETIVE HISTORY

ROGER L. GEIGER

The Formative Generation: The Civil War to 1890

A century ago American higher education was emerging from a generation of momentous changes. Much of what constitutes the American system of higher education today took shape and definition in the years between the outbreak of the Civil War and the last decade of the century. The land-grant colleges provided publicly maintained higher education across the entire country. Cornell University, among the earliest of the many major foundings of these years, showed that agriculture and the mechanic arts could be taught alongside the liberal arts and sciences. The elective system, effectively championed at Harvard by Charles Eliot (1869–1909), was clearly triumphant by the end of the 1880s. It unchained manifold possibilities concerning what could be learned in college and, just as importantly, what could be taught. Professional schools blossomed as expected components of forward-looking universities. Within the arts and sciences, the disciplines took their modern forms by organizing into professional disciplinary associations. The nature of college-going was transformed as well between the end of the Civil War and 1890. Higher education for women attained parity with that of men, whether in separate colleges or in co-educational settings. Students generally shed the compulsory piety and discipline of the ante-bellum colleges, and instead elaborated an extracurriculum of their own devising, not the least of their innovations being American football.[1]

Perhaps overshadowing all these changes was the long-awaited establishment of graduate education and research within American higher education. In the half-century before 1860, Richard Storr has written, 'the need, as distinct from the demand, for graduate education had been declared loudly and repeatedly'.[2] Increasingly, the inspiration for those who defined this need was the growing prowess of the German universities. The international hegemony of German academic learning and the concrete examples of German university practices presented compelling precedents, not just for American reformers, but for scientists and scholars everywhere. When Yale conferred the first American PhDs in 1861, it was consciously imitating the German degree, in part to spare would-be scholars from having to go abroad.[3] When the Johns Hopkins University was founded in 1876, it was perceived to be, and prided itself on being, a "German-style" university. This influence continued to grow into the next decade, making the 1880s the high tide of German influence on American universities. The number of Americans studying in Germany continued to swell into the 1890s; but as these ambitious and motivated scholars returned to their home campuses, they would spend the next generation adapting the ideals of German learning to the realities of higher education as they found them in this country.[4] Chiefly, this meant assimilating advanced study and research with the nature of the American college.

Graduate study in the United States is as venerable as higher education itself. At seventeenth-century Harvard, students for the master's degree prepared themselves by independently reading in the science of theology and then demonstrated their learning in public presentations. These undertakings were part of the responsibility of the college—in fact only Harvard bachelors were eligible—but they were administratively, pedagogically, and financially separate from what we would call the undergraduate college.[5] This pattern of separateness would endure for two centuries.

Insofar as an actual demand for higher learning existed in Ante-bellum America, it was pursued outside of the colleges. In the eighteenth century, the locus for advanced knowledge was in the learned societies, like the American Philosophical Society founded by Benjamin Franklin. This tradition of the pursuit of learning outside of higher education persisted through the first half of the next century and included the establishment of the American Association for the Advancement of Science (1848) and the National Academy of Sciences (1863).[6] Would-be reformers who tried to bring higher learning into the college curriculum met with little success. George Ticknor, for example, was unable to induce reforms at Harvard in the 1820s that would have made the teaching of advanced subjects possible, although he did succeed in raising the level of instruction in his own department.[7] Generally, however, scholarship or research was forced outside of the college. The first approximation of graduate professional training occurred in theological seminaries in the early nineteenth century. The best of these institutions recruited many of their students from among college graduates, became a home for Biblical scholarship, and trained a disproportionate number of future educational leaders.[8] Even more important were the scientific schools that later developed at Harvard and Yale in the 1840s. The Lawrence School at Harvard became the outlet for the scientific studies of a few Harvard faculty. The Sheffield School at Yale was broader, combining both instruction in practical subjects such as agricultural chemistry and advanced studies in science and arts. By being established separate from their respective colleges, these schools transcended the limitations of the fixed curriculum. The PhDs awarded in New Haven in 1861 were not the product of Yale College but of the Sheffield Scientific School—even though one of the degrees was in philosophy and another in classical languages.[9]

The very nature of the American college was the chief impediment to the incorporation of the higher learning. The problem—and it only constituted a "problem" for those who wished this institution to be something different—was the complete adaptation of the "old-time college" to its singular purpose of forming the minds of young men. According to the accepted contemporary doctrines of faculty psychology, the chief aim of the college training was to instill "mental discipline"—the capacity to learn. This capacity was best mastered, it was believed, by learning the classical languages, essentially by rote. Such learning was conducted and monitored through classroom recitations. Knowledge under this system was not the end of education, but a means. Only after this salutary preparation would a young man be expected to begin acquiring the rudiments of an actual profession. The curriculum also included a smattering of information about science and society—the "furniture of the mind" in the words of the Yale Report of 1828, the principal rationalization of these practices.[10] Over time, these materials were expanded and updated, particularly through a greater inclusion of scientific subjects. But even at those few fortunate institutions possessing sufficient wealth to augment their faculty and their offerings, the superficial character of these subjects was never overcome. Daniel Coit Gilman reported that he was introduced to twenty subjects during his senior year at Yale.[11]

The singular purpose of the old-time college, then, greatly limited its possibilities. Since the aims were identical for each student, so was the curriculum. A single, fixed set of courses in turn precluded advanced or specialized subjects. The requirements of imposing mental discipline upon recalcitrant youths molded the pedagogy of the colleges as well, making them ill-suited for anything else.[12] The colleges nevertheless, in spite of the charges of contemporary critics, largely had the sanction of society. In the population centers of the East, a college education was the accepted prerequisite for professional careers, and those careers were the path to a respectable social status. On the other side of the Allegheny Mountains, the colleges tended to fill an educational void for post-primary instruction. Although their purposes in these locales were more diverse, they still held the promise of social (and geographical) mobility, if not automatic high status. Thus, the upper levels of ante-bellum American society largely regarded the colleges as appropriate institutions for the perpetuation of social position, irrespective of what students actually learned there.[13] Reformers who directly attacked this social institution were largely frustrated: to pursue different purposes usually meant as in the case of Yale's Sheffield School, to operate on its periphery.

Much of the essential nature of the old-time college persisted after the Civil War. As late as the 1880s, when the classical curriculum was clearly losing its sway, university-builders inspired by the German model saw no place for advanced learning in the American college. They regarded collegiate studies as largely equivalent to what was taught in the Gymnasium in Germany. 'True university work', according to this view, could only commence on the graduate level. Prior to 1890, the chief experiments in American higher education reflected this view. Daniel Coit Gilman shaped Johns Hopkins as an institution in which the emphasis was on graduate education and research, although he realized that prevailing opinion would not allow him to dispense with an undergraduate college. G. Stanley Hall attempted to carry the experiment further by launching a purely graduate institution at Clark University. And William Rainey Harper envisioned the University of Chicago not only as a pinnacle of learning, but also as the capstone of a system of feeder colleges. Unprecedented acts of philanthropy made these bold departures from traditional colleges possible; but the circumstances of American higher education tended to pull them back toward the norm. Graduate students were few in number, and a faculty of specialized professors was expensive to maintain. Clark was not viable as a graduate institution; Hopkins reverted over time to a more traditional (although still small) undergraduate college; and Chicago, the best supported of the experiments, spent the next two generations debating how best to reconcile undergraduate education and the higher learning.[14]

The Generation of the American University: 1890 to World War

The 1890s brought what Laurence Veysey called a "boom" in university development and with it emerged the standard model of the American university.[15] At its center, still, was the college. Education for utilitarian or professional purposes, however, was largely hived off into separate compartments, at first called "departments" and eventually known as "schools." The proliferation of these professional compartments was an important contribution to the overall growth of universities; in fact, institutions that resisted this trend like Hopkins, Princeton, and for a time Stanford, remained comparatively small. As for research, each type of professional school developed at its own pace. Schools of agriculture, as a result of the experiment stations created by the Hatch Act (1887), developed an extensive research enterprise well before they had an appreciable number of students. Research in medical schools grew markedly after 1900, as the pattern set by Harvard and Johns Hopkins was increasingly imitated at other universities. Graduate study and research in education also had a narrow base, Teachers College at Columbia University (founded 1888) being the outstanding pioneer in this respect.[16] In other parts of the university, however, professional research and graduate education were slower to develop. Arts and sciences nevertheless remained at the core of the American university, and there research and liberal culture—representing, respectively, graduate and undergraduate education—were nevertheless linked. Separate graduate schools were created to minister to the needs and requirements of graduate students, but the "graduate faculty of arts and sciences"—the title chosen by Harvard in 1890—was coextensive with the senior faculty of the college. This essential pattern was adopted elsewhere: graduate education and research were inextricably joined with the undergraduate college through the faculty.

The separateness and the connectedness of graduate education and research *vis-à-vis* the college—this was the situation that bedevilled the first generation of university builders during the decades prior to the First World War. The thousands of Americans who earned degrees at German universities had directly experienced a situation in which the advancement of knowledge through research and graduate education was the highest value in university life. German professors had State-funded institutes attached to their university chairs. These institutes provided the resources needed for the conduct of research, made research the central commitment of their position, and permitted them to work directly with advanced students and assistants.[17] Back in the United States all these prerequisites of research—resources, faculty time, and advanced students—were problematic.

At the beginning of this century, the facilities for conducting research in this country were decidedly primitive in comparison to Germany. American professors who incurred extraordinary expenses in their research customarily met them out of their own pocketbooks or sometimes raised subscriptions in the local community. Such arrangements were an obvious constraint, and their inadequacy became increasingly apparent after 1900.[18] By that date, the Germans were already using the term *Grosswissenschaft* (or "Big Science"); research in the natural sciences required significant ongoing expenditures.

For American faculty, moreover, teaching and research were almost mutually exclusive activities.[19] The burden of teaching undergraduate introductory courses to poorly prepared, often weakly motivated students absorbed most of the time and energy of most of the faculty. American colleges and universities were essentially open to all who met the lenient qualifications. The clientele of the prestigious Eastern colleges was powerfully shaped by self-selection, but even there the actual admissions process was a low barrier. Potential students might qualify on either of two sets of admissions examinations, and then might be allowed to enter with conditions. Failing that, a determined young man might enroll in another institution and then easily transfer. By 1890, most of the state universities had adopted a less complicated scheme by automatically admitting graduates of "certified" high schools. Standardization proceeded further when the philanthropic Carnegie Foundation (founded 1906) defined "units" of secondary school study that any self-respecting college ought to require.[20] None of these procedures did much to discourage the burgeoning numbers of secondary school graduates. That group constituted 2.5 percent of the age cohort in 1880; 6.4 percent in 1900; and 16.8 percent in 1920.[21] Before the twentieth century, an ubiquitous concern of American colleges had been finding enough students (as well as retaining them!), and this fact of life had contributed to the basic openness of the system. Not until after the War would a few institutions wrestle with the problem of how to select from an overabundance of applicants. The indubitable fact of American higher education was that many students entered having rudimentary training and much to learn.

Would-be researchers in American universities needed funds for material and equipment, as well as a redefinition of their responsibilities so that they might have the time to utilize these things. Since the support of American institutions was largely tied to teaching, another source of funds was required.

From the time of the establishment of the Hollis Professorship of Divinity at Harvard (1721), it was gifts, and particularly gifts permanently preserved as endowments, that permitted American colleges to do things that were not strictly encompassed in the education of undergraduates. In the nineteenth century, the true research institutes of American colleges—the observatories and the museums—were established in this way.[22] As already noted, it was the burgeoning philanthropy for higher education that had launched the bold experiments at Johns Hopkins, Clark, and Chicago. To university presidents of this era, it was axiomatic that research needed its own, specifically earmarked funds if it were to flourish. Arthur Twining Hadley of Yale announced that "the research of a university should be as far as possible endowed research." Charles Eliot regularly invited Harvard's benefactors to provide for the needs of research. And Charles Van Hise of Wisconsin envisioned the day when his university's alumni would be numerous and wealthy enough to provide for the institution's research needs with a steady stream of gifts. Most ambitious of all was Jacob Gould Schurman of Cornell, who invited contemporary philanthropists to provide million-dollar endowments for each of Cornell's academic departments.[23]

Another possibility for facilitating research lay with the differentiation of the teaching role. Larger academic departments allowed at least some teachers to be emancipated from the travail of undergraduate instruction. As the universities grew, such differentiation was also accompanied through stratification. After the Civil War, two-thirds of the teachers in American colleges held the title of professor, but in the first decade of the twentieth century only one quarter would hold that rank at leading research universities.[24] New faculty positions were largely filled with instructors and assistant professors during these years, and these junior appointments were disproportionately responsible for introductory courses. This was the era of autocratic department heads who, like the German mentors with whom many had studied, assigned much of the drudgery to their subordinates. Some considered pushing differentiation even further. After the turn of the century the idea of "research professorships" became widely discussed. Such positions were actually created for a time at Cornell, Chicago, Wisconsin, California, Indiana, and Ohio State. This experiment was counterbalanced by attempts to create specialized teaching posts. The Princeton preceptors, at least as originally envisioned by President Woodrow Wilson (1902–1909), and the tutors created at Harvard by President A. Lawrence Lowell (1909–1933), were intended to fulfill such roles. Both these approaches fit awkwardly with the supposed egalitarianism of academic departments. In practice, university leaders generally followed a tacit policy of actively discriminating between assignments for "teaching men" and "research men."[25]

The unification of instruction and research at a high level nevertheless proved to be an elusive goal. Graduate study remained a distressingly minor component of even the foremost universities. As the American PhD replaced the German degree as the norm in this country, the number of doctorates awarded rose above 300 for the first time in 1897, although half of them were awarded by just six universities. But that total did not surpass 400 for another dozen years.[26] Graduate students at the turn of the century typically numbered less than 10 percent of undergraduates at those few institutions producing the majority of PhDs. Not very many American students possessed the resources or the dedication to devote themselves exclusively to advanced studies. And not everyone thought this desirable. In "The PhD Octopus," the Harvard philosopher William James penned the most celebrated condemnation of alleged Germanic tendencies toward pedantry and overspecialisation in American graduate studies. A substantial number of humanists defended an ideal of liberal culture against the growing trend toward specialized erudition.[27]

The fundamental difficulties that beset the infancy of the American university were increasingly overcome after 1900, but not in the ways foreseen by the advocates of the higher learning. American universities received comparatively few endowments for purposes of research, and those they did receive were largely confined to medicine. But they did become decidedly larger and wealthier over the course of this generation, and the undergraduate college was the key to both these developments.

Philanthropy has played a fundamental role in the development of higher education in the United States.[28] Prior to 1900, however, fundraising had been a sporadic and often difficult matter for even the most successful of institutions. After the turn of the century, this picture was altered by developments at Yale and Harvard. The Yale Alumni Fund, which had been started in 1891 in order to collect small contributions, began receiving gifts in such volume that a separate endowment fund was created in addition to the annual donation given to the university. At this same juncture, the Harvard class of 1880 gave $100,000 to the university on the occasion of its twenty-fifth anniversary. Every subsequent class would give at least as much.[29] Substantial magnitudes of gifts thus became for the first time a recurrent and dependable source of income. Both institutions were launched upon a course that would make them easily the country's wealthiest universities; and there was no doubt as to where the money was coming from—the graduates of the college.

The growing affluence of a few universities stood in contrast to the financial constraints facing many others, but it was those few that would lead the way in the expensive business of graduate education and research. The importance of their alumni in this process naturally tended to enhance the importance of the undergraduate college within the university. Although those universities assiduously cultivated the college and its culture, this emphasis was not necessarily inimical to research. As new laboratories and libraries were built, as the size of the faculty was expanded, the inherent capability of these fortunate institutions for supporting research was immeasurably strengthened.

The growth of undergraduate enrollments was a crucial factor for the advancement of the leaders among both public and private research universities. At private institutions, the tuition paid by the overwhelmingly undergraduate clientele roughly approximated the cost of faculty salaries during these years.[30] More students made it possible to employ more teachers in more subjects. An analogous process occurred in the leading state-supported universities. There, the expansion and extension of undergraduate instruction tended to be rewarded by state legislators with the provision of additional resources.[31] By about 1905 they had grown in size to equal their older and more prestigious private counterparts.

From 1905 to 1915 the major public and private research universities were all approximately the same size—3,000–5,000 regular students.[32] This was a period of consolidation for American higher education which contrasted sharply with the wide dispersion of resources that occurred throughout the Ante-bellum years. In 1894, the combined enrollment for the eleven largest research universities (Chicago, Columbia, Cornell, Harvard, Penn, Yale, California, Illinois, Michigan, Minnesota, and Wisconsin) was roughly 21,000; in 1904 it exceeded 35,500; and in 1914 they counted 53,000 students. In 1894 this total represented 15 percent of all students in American higher education, and from 1904 to 1914 their share constituted 17.5 per cent. This growth allowed the research universities to expand their faculties, to offer new subjects, and to accommodate greater specialization within established ones. This was a process that Walter Metzger has labeled as "substantive growth" of the academic profession.[33] At the same time, the increasing affluence of these schools permitted them to lower the teaching burden of faculty. Student-faculty ratios in the first decade of the century declined from 14:1 to 12:1 in state universities and from 10:1 to 8:1 in private universities.[34] In addition, larger and more specialized faculties facilitated a change in the nature of academic departments from the autocratic German model to a collegial, American model. Instead of a single "head" professor, reigning over subordinates, the American academic department came to have several full professors, together with junior faculty who might aspire to that rank, each individual intellectually sovereign in his specialty. In the American research university, all faculty members were expected to be experts on some facet of their field and to contribute to its advancement. This development was crucial for the promotion of graduate education and research, but it was principally made possible by the growth of undergraduate education.

Graduate education expanded too, but from quite a small base. It was aided considerably by one of the great unsung inventions of American higher education. In 1899, Harvard received a substantial bequest designated for the general purpose of encouraging research. The university chose to use these funds to create thirty fellowships for graduate students, which included the obligation of teaching half-time. Thus was born the graduate teaching fellow. This was a striking departure from the prevailing pattern, modeled upon German practices, which expected the graduate student to be dedicated exclusively to study. For a time this innovation was controversial—G. Stanley Hall accused Harvard of instituting a "sweating system."[35] But the graduate teaching fellow fitted the needs of American universities so perfectly that it soon swept the day. It provided needed support for graduate students, while further relieving scholarly faculty of the much-resented burden of teaching introductory courses. The state universities, with their growing instructional obligations, soon found the use of teaching fellows to be a means for equalizing conditions somewhat with their wealthier private counterparts.

By the time of the First World War, the American university had evolved a distinctive pattern that was quite different from what had been envisioned by the university purists of the preceding generation. Instead of eschewing the undergraduate college, it capitalized upon its popularity, upon the deep loyalties that it inspired, and upon the possibilities it presented for a fruitful division of labour. The pattern was anything but neat, and the university system still lacked funds for research *per se*; but because this model reflected powerful indigenous trends, it held great potential for the future.

The Inter-War Generation

The American university truly came of age during the inter-war years. Still in the thrall of European learning after World War I in most major fields, American scientists and scholars had established themselves at the frontiers of knowledge in virtually all fields by the eve of World War II. This accomplishment essentially took place within the universities, where research and graduate education were expanded in scope and made more rigorous in character. During the decade of the 1920s, for example, the production of American PhDs roughly tripled; and in the penurious environment of the 1930s, it increased by another 50 percent. Research is less readily measured, but there can be little doubt that it traced a similar path, accelerating greatly during the 1920s and then augmenting that level of activity further during the Great Depression. Overall, this change was made possible by the strengthening of the universities through their own efforts and through the assistance they received from external agencies.

The 1920s were the key to university development. Starting from the depths of the post-war depression, the decade ended with a flourish that brought American universities the greatest prosperity that they had ever known. Moreover, despite the onset of the Depression, these gains were permanent. Interestingly, they were achieved in two different ways.

In the decade prior to the First World War, the public and private universities had been more alike in terms of size and conditions than at any time before or since. After the war their respective developmental strategies diverged.[36] For the state universities, the dictum that "bigger is better" remained in force. By expanding their enrollments, and by utilizing increasing numbers of teaching fellows, they were able to have both larger, more specialized faculties, and more graduate students for advanced instruction. The private universities, however, partly in conformance with the preferences of their alumni, restricted their intake and concentrated their growing resources upon a selected group of students.[37] Both strategies were focused primarily upon the undergraduate college, and both succeeded during the 1920s. The image projected by the wealthiest private universities, particularly the group that became identified as the "Ivy League," was extraordinarily successful in attracting alumni gifts. This affluence permitted the cultivation of both distinguished faculties active in scientific research and a remarkable array of amenities for undergraduates.

The pivotal development of the 1920s, nevertheless, was the interest taken in university research by the great philanthropic foundations, particularly the Rockefeller group of trusts. The turning point for this development occurred in 1922, when Beardsley Ruml became director of the Laura Spelman Rockefeller Memorial, and when Wickliffe Rose was named director of the General Education Board (as well as a newly created International Education Board). For the remainder of the decade these two men would be the chief patrons, respectively, of the social and the natural sciences. Although completely independent of one another, their motives and their actions were closely parallel. Ruml reasoned that an adequate knowledge base was lacking for dealing intelligently with existing social problems. The only way to remedy this for the long term, he felt, was to build basic social scientific knowledge, and this could only be done by developing these subjects within the universities.[38] Rose too wished to stimulate basic research in the universities. His thinking undoubtedly reflected a prevailing post-war optimism about pure research leading to technological improvements (or, the "advancement of civilization," in the parlance of the day). He also had a long association with the highly successful Rockefeller programmes in public health. Ultimately Rose, more so than Ruml, seemed motivated by a belief in the advancement of science as an end in itself.[39]

Both Ruml and Rose spent the first several years of their directorships carefully assessing their fields and judiciously making grants. Then, in the years before the reorganization of the Rockefeller trusts, which occurred in 1929, they made grants on an increasingly massive scale. With small staffs and limited knowledge of the actual content of the many fields in which they operated, this was a sensible, although by no means the only, manner of distributing the millions of dollars at their disposal. The largest of their grants provided capital to support various aspects of research, primarily at the leading private universities. This was a strategy, in Rose's words, of "making the peaks higher;" and this deliberate elitism in fact proved highly effective in terms of allowing the favoured institutions to bring their programmes up to the highest international standards. Grant-making on such a scale, however, was unsustainable for long.

Both Ruml and Rose stepped down in 1929 when their trusts were folded into the reorganized Rockefeller Foundation, which then assumed responsibility for the advancement of knowledge in all fields. Their deeds nevertheless lived on as the Foundation had to meet the commitments they had made, even as its income was shrinking as a result of the Depression. A further reevaluation of the Foundation's activities was needed by 1934, and a scaling back of its grant-making resulted. In both the Social Science and Natural Science Division, a policy was established of supporting specific research projects in strategically chosen areas. The difference from the Rose-Ruml era was that now Foundation research grants were smaller in size and more closely specified; but they were also available to a much larger number of institutions. All of the prewar research universities were receiving foundation support by the end of the 1930s.[40]

Private industry also became a regular supporter of university research during the inter-war years. In contrast with the foundations' role, however, funds from industry tended to support research *per se* and did less to boost the research capacity of the universities. An exception to this generalization would be the support to graduate students in selected fields. During the 1920s, flourishing centers for conducting engineering research for industry emerged at Michigan and MIT, among others. Linkages with university research became commonplace in the chemical industry, electric power, pharmaceuticals, and, through the single firm of the America Telephone and Telegraph Company (AT&T), telecommunications.[41]

The role of foundations, and to a lesser extent industry, transformed the circumstances of university research. For the first time American universities could look to a regular, recurrent source of support for the direct expenses of conducting organized research. A separate "research company" had emerged, which not only resolved the chief impediment to conducting research on university campuses, but also made the research activities of faculty even more valued for university leaders. This last point deserves emphasis. In a decade in which higher education was dominated by the "collegiate syndrome"—the pronounced emphasis upon peer culture, athletics, and the extracurriculum in college life—foundation support for research gave tangible backing to the academic side of the university. The academic accomplishments of faculty became a facet of university prestige that universities—although not colleges—could scarcely afford to neglect. This consideration was reinforced in 1925, when Raymond Hughes published the first quality ranking of graduate departments.[42] From that day onward, the academic prestige hierarchy would be measured by attainments in graduate education and research.

The growth of university research naturally had a positive effect upon graduate studies. The handful of universities that regularly received research funding were able to enroll and support larger numbers of graduate students. One facet of foundation support, however, made a crucial contribution to the development of American science—the creation of post-doctoral fellowships. The first "postdocs" were established by the Rockefeller Foundation and the National Research Council (NRC) in 1919 in an almost accidental way when agreement could not be reached over the matter of founding research institutes. The fellowships were limited to just mathematics, physics, and chemistry. In the first dozen years of this program, one of every eleven PhDs in these fields was awarded an NRC post-doctoral fellowship, and 80 percent of these fellows subsequently taught in American universities. Post-doctoral fellowships were soon extended to medicine and biology as well. These awards bolstered American higher education at one of its weakest points—the transition from graduate study to faculty status. These new PhDs, instead of being relegated in the usual manner to extensive introductory instruction, were able to extend mastery of their fields at the most advanced centers of research. Such experience was far more effective in producing first-rate scientists; indeed, these fellows largely comprised the next generation of leadership for American science.[43]

While extraordinary opportunities were opening up for the best and the brightest products of American graduate schools, graduate education in general suffered from a lack of organization and definition. Throughout the 1920s, there were undoubtedly fewer graduate students than university departments would have liked. Thus, even while the colleges were establishing selective admissions, the graduate schools remained open to the brilliant and the plodding alike. Most schools attracted a major portion of their graduate students from among their own recent bachelors. Prominent among this group was always a number of June graduates who had failed to find employment. Many had not compiled very distinguished undergraduate records. Attrition, for this and other reasons, tended to be high. Even at Harvard, one half of the beginning graduate students failed to appear for the second year.[44]

The beginnings of a rationalization of graduate study did not occur until the 1930s. Harvard imposed restrictive standards upon its incoming students for the first time in 1930. Progress was uncertain, however, due to the lack of reliable criteria for judging applicants and the appetites of academic departments for students. An excess demand for places was clearly the prerequisite to meaningful selection. By the late 1930s, this condition was beginning to be met at some institutions. In 1937, Columbia, Harvard, Princeton, and Yale cooperated in the development of the Graduate Record Examination, an effort to improve the standard of graduate admissions.

When the rationalization of graduate education is considered together with the greater financial support for graduate students, the existence of post-doctoral fellowships, and the coeval rationalization of faculty career structures, a significant transformation becomes apparent. By the end of the 1930s, the potential university teacher was subject to evaluative hurdles at recurrent intervals. Selection upon entry to graduate school, discrimination in the award of financial support, post-doctoral opportunities for the most able—all added up to a competitive process that would govern the allocation of the most valuable opportunities for productive scholarship and research. By 1940, this process, which is now taken for granted, was firmly rooted within research universities.[45]

By that date, the conditions just described pertained in large measure to perhaps sixteen institutions—the research universities that to varying extents competed with one another for faculty, sometimes graduate students, and resources from the research economy.[46] To compete in this arena required a level of financial strength that was largely lacking outside of this circle. At least three other institutional types are sufficiently closely related to the research universities to deserve mention. Some relatively wealthy institutions, like Dartmouth and Brown, preferred to emphasize undergraduate education rather than graduate education and research. A second group of institutions had been captured by the late nineteenth century enthusiasm for graduate education and research but failed to develop the kind of financial strength needed to realize such ambitions. At Northwestern, for example, President Henry Wade Rogers (1890–1900) was constrained by financial limitations from seeking to emulate the established research universities of the East; and in the nation's capital, the efforts of Columbian University (George Washington University) to make the transition to full university status brought the institution instead to the brink of bankruptcy.[47] The state universities, as a third type, presented a full grant of financial and research capabilities. Below the top five—California, Michigan, Wisconsin, Minnesota, and Illinois—significant research efforts tended to be localized within a few departments even in the stronger institutions. Furthermore, when their productive scholars were recruited by other institutions, they were seldom able or inclined to attempt to match the offered salaries.[48] These last two groups of universities, in particular, expanded graduate education during the inter-war years; however, the sixteen principal research universities, which awarded 69 percent of doctorates before the First World War (1909), still awarded 54 percent of them in 1939.[49]

During the course of the inter-war generation, the basic pattern of the American university remained intact. That is, the bulk of university resources were derived from its instructional role, but to varying extents some portion of these were utilized to accommodate graduate education and research as well. Maintaining this research capacity became more costly in terms of resources devoted to faculty and facilities during these years; but because of foundation support for university research, it became more rewarding as well. A symbiotic relationship existed between the college and the graduate school that would take on new dimensions after World War II.

The Post-War Generation

During the three decades that stretched from the end of World War II to the mid-1970s, the American university built rapidly and monumentally upon the foundations that had been laid by the end of the 1930s.

The end of the war brought far-reaching change. A flood of discharged servicemen flocked into the country's colleges and universities assisted by federal aid (the 'G-I Bill'). Most sought bachelor's degrees, but enough persisted through graduate school to double the level of PhD output from 1940 to 1950. University research was increased by an even greater multiple, as the federal government's investment in war-time research became a permanent legacy. The character of that research nevertheless for long caused disquiet among the universities.

The critical technologies of World War II, particularly radar and atomic energy, were such that they could not be put aside with the cessation of hostilities, regardless of the state of international tension. Other lines of research were sustained through the promise of public usefulness. A wide spectrum of war-time research thus continued, which resulted in five broad channels of federal support for the university research economy.[50] The first of these, agricultural research, was the only prewar legacy, and it remained comparatively unchanged. The second was research sponsored by the military services that more or less fulfilled their immediate and particular needs. The responsibilities of the Atomic Energy Commission, which encompassed all radioactive materials, comprised a third and highly important channel. The continuation of war-time medical research by the Public Health Service (the National Institutes of Health) was a fourth channel, one that would in time allow university medical schools to join physics departments as the most research-intensive academic units. All this support, welcome as it was to its recipients, was focused upon specific, rather delimited areas of investigation. Whether this research was basic or applied in character, it chiefly reflected the programmatic needs of its sponsors. For a time after the war, there seemed to be no federal recognition of responsibility for a fifth channel—support for the lifeblood of academic science, research intended primarily for the advancement of basic knowledge.

This last channel was to have been filled, according to Vannevar Bush's blueprint for post-war research, *Science—The Endless Frontier,* by a national research foundation.[51] Political wrangling, however, prevented the establishment of this institution during the critical post-war legislative session that produced seminal enactments covering the other emerging channels of federal support—the Atomic Energy Commission, the Office of Naval Research, and the organization of research in the Public Health Service. The National Science Foundation did not come into being until 1950 and did not have significant funds to allocate until the latter years of that decade. In the interim, the Office of Naval Research became the generous and benign patron of basic academic research. This role, however, was anomalous and consequently temporary. For more than a decade after the war, basic academic research had no secure source of federal support.[52] As a result, complaints about the nature of the post-war research economy were widespread throughout the academic community in spite of the large federal investment in university research. Federal research funds were highly concentrated in a handful of universities, and they were narrowly targeted upon programmatic purposes. Funding was quite inadequate for both basic scientific research and support for sustaining the research capacity of universities.

In the decade of the 1950s, despite the gradual expansion of activities by the National Science Foundation and the large investments of the Ford Foundation, the output of PhDs rose by just 50 percent. The case was persistently argued for a greater national investment in basic academic research as the seedbed for technology, and in graduate education to augment the inadequate supply of scientists and university teachers.[53] In addition, after the Korean War, for the first time in almost a generation, a buoyant economy appeared to make such an investment feasible. Still, a catalyst seemed to be needed. It came in the form of a small sphere orbiting the earth emitting electronic "beeps."

The Soviet launch of Sputnik triggered a massive federal commitment to upgrade the nation's scientific capacity. In this process the federal government met and then exceeded the prescriptions of the post-war critics. In the decade after Sputnik (1958–68) federal support for *basic* research in universities increased by a factor of seven (from $179 to $1,251 million). In just eight years (1960–1968), university research doubled in relationship to GNP. The Higher Education Facilities Act of 1963 assisted the construction of $9 billion worth of college and university buildings. And, buoyed by federal fellowships, the nation's output of PhDs tripled during the 1960s, just as it had in the 1920s.[54]

In fact, the developments of the 1960s bear an intriguing similarity to those of the 1920s. In both decades substantial new money became available from external sources for the support of basic academic research; in both cases, one result was the enhancement of the value placed upon research within the university. Both decades also experienced substantial enrollment growth—expansive environments that were conducive to institutional advancement. In addition, the gains in both decades, although threatened by subsequent events, proved to be lasting. Given these similarities, the changes of the 1960s nevertheless had a more profound effect upon the ecology of the American university.

In those years for the first time, the values and outlook of the graduate school gained ascendancy over those of the undergraduate college for a significant portion of American higher education. This change was apparent to contemporaries. For Talcott Parsons and Gerald Platt the prototypical American university had become dominated by "cognitive rationality" expressed through research and graduate education by and of "specialists."[55] Christopher Jencks and David Riesman declared that an "Academic Revolution" was underway. Instead of the investigative potential of universities being constrained by the nature and extent of the undergraduate college, they perceived the graduate schools to be "by far the most important shapers of undergraduate education."[56]

To some degree this shifting relationship can be borne out through quantitative changes. Graduate-level education became a much larger component of the activities of most of the major research universities. At private institutions, the proportion of graduate students commonly approached 50 percent; at the much larger state research universities that figure might surpass 30 percent. If undergraduates were seldom an actual minority on these campuses, they often felt themselves to be a minority interest.

A second important trend was the broadening of the "Academic Revolution." Unlike the 1920s, when Wickliffe Rose set out to "to make the peaks higher," at the beginning of the 1960s the President's Science Advisory Committee recommended that the country needed more peaks.[57] At different times special programs to develop additional centers of university research were undertaken by the Ford Foundation and by the principal federal agencies that funded research.[58] More important than these explicit programs was the fact that the conditions tending to restrict the number of research universities no longer obtained in the 1960s. Whereas before Sputnik programmatic federal research funds had been highly concentrated, the sudden abundance of research support and the growing incentives linked with research lured additional universities into meaningful participation in the research economy. Whereas earlier the post-war shortage of scientists had led to their concentration in comparatively few universities, now increasing numbers of research-minded PhDs became available to other would-be research universities. In addition, whereas the availability of research facilities had been a limiting condition favoring the wealthier institutions, now federal support and the general context of growth resulted in up-to-date facilities being built throughout the country. The peaks of the established research universities did not get any lower—in fact, most of them continued to rise; but they were joined during the 1960s by other institutions increasingly committed to the advancement of knowledge.[59]

These achievements seemed to augur the fulfillment of the aspirations of America's original university builders: for the first time, American society made available ample resources chiefly for the advancement of knowledge. Universities responded with alacrity. Faculty threw themselves into the research puzzles of their disciplines as never before. They trained ever larger cohorts of graduate students to carry these investigations further. If ever German *Wissenschaft* found a home in America, it was during the 1960s. David Riesman and Christopher Jencks wrote at the time that the graduate academic department had become "autotelic;" and furthermore that "to suggest that the advancement of a particular academic discipline [was] not synonymous with the advancement of the human condition [was] to be regarded as myopic."[60] One can readily detect a note of incredulity in their language—a scepticism that this hypertrophy of pure research could prosper, let alone endure, in American universities. Their doubts in this case were not unfounded.

In a quantitative sense, the gains of the 1960s were permanent: overall federal support for university research, in real terms, eroded only slightly and temporarily; graduate education continued to expand into the early 1970s; and the number of universities significantly involved with research continued to increase. But the climate of expectations of that era somehow evaporated.

Undergraduates were the first to resist the hegemony of the autotelic graduate department. The student rebellion of the late 1960s was a complex phenomenon, but one of its central themes was the accuation of irrelevance leveled at disciplinary scholarship as reflected in the university curriculum. This was followed in the 1970s by a mass exodus from those disciplines. Students voted with their computer registration cards for vocational subjects of concentration, particularly majors related to business.[61] The reverberations from these developments are still being felt. Universities have had to wrestle with the dilemma of refashioning a curriculum for freshmen and sophomores that would instill more general kinds of skills and knowledge without actually abjuring the edifice that disciplinary scholarship has built.

TABLE 1
Percent of Total Academic R&D by Source, 1960–1989

	Federal government	State/local governments	Industry	Institution funds	Other sources
1960	62.7	13.2	6.2	9.9	8.0
1970	70.5	9.4	2.6	10.4	7.1
1980	67.5	8.2	3.9	13.8	6.6
1989	59.9	8.3	6.6	18.1	7.2

A second significant change occurred in graduate schools themselves. For the first time in their history, they actually ceased to grow. In 1973 almost 34,000 doctorates were awarded; that figure was not surpassed until the end of the 1980s. Even this level of output has only been possible due to a rising proportion of foreign students receiving degrees (from 15 to 26 percent with much higher proportions in fields like engineering). The principal cause for this stagnation can be readily identified—the weakness in the demand for college and university teachers. Dismal career prospects also had a disheartening effect upon graduate study itself—thinning the ranks of students and causing self-doubt and anxiety to replace the exuberance that reigned during the 1960s. Even though the market for new faculty has improved of late, and shortages have even emerged in some fields, 4,000 fewer doctorates were awarded to U.S. citizens in 1990 than in 1973.[62] Historically, the two decades of no-growth in doctorates is an unprecedented and somewhat ominous development.

A third significant change since the 1960s also becomes evident in historical perspective. Roughly speaking, throughout much of this century, decades of vigorous expansion of the university research enterprise have alternated with decades of relative consolidation. Thus, the relationship of the 1960s to the 1970s repeated the basic pattern of the 1920s and 1930s, or the 1940s and 1950s. According to this timetable, the 1980s were scheduled to be a decade of renewed growth. After a rather belated start, they fulfilled this destiny. Real expenditures of university research turned up sharply since about 1983. When measured against GNP, university research has attained the levels reached during the halcyon days of the late 1960s.[63] It is noteworthy, however, that the impetus for this upswing has not come from the federal government. The federal portion of total university research funding rose from 63 percent in 1960 to 73 percent in 1967. Through the 1970s, the federal contribution remained above two-thirds of the total, but by 1989 it had shrunk to just 60 percent. Industrial funding of university research, which was only 2.5 percent in 1967, has risen to 6.6 percent (1989); and the category "institutional funds" has advanced from 10 to 18 percent. Moreover, the expectations associated with the expansion of the 1980s nevertheless resemble the 1940s rather than the 1960s.

Instead of faith in the worth of basic research, the current expansion has been fueled by programmatic goals—by the expansion of military research and development during the first part of the 1980s and generally by hopes for pay-offs in technology transfer to industry that might augment international competitiveness in the relatively near term. Research sponsored by industry has been the fastest growing single component, although still a small portion of the total. The influence of private industry on the research universities is nevertheless larger than its 6+ percent share of R&D would indicate. Gifts to higher education from private corporations have also been the fastest growing component of voluntary support to higher education, having grown to 20 percent of the total.[64] When federal sources are considered, the Department of Defense has supplied the principal growth component, having tripled in constant dollars from the mid-1970s to the mid-1980s—a time when total federal obligations for academic research have risen by just 20 percent.[65] Viewed from the angle of the kinds of research that universities actually perform, the drift toward programmatic research and the relatively restrained growth of research in the basic sciences becomes evident. The interesting disclosure from Table 2 is that the programmatic shift in research funding is not just a federal policy: non-federal funds have been favoring engineering and computer sciences to an even greater extent than has the government. Philip Abelson, from his unexcelled viewpoint as long-time editor

TABLE 2
Percent Changes in Real University R&D Expenditures and Federal
Obligations for University Research, 1976–1986

	Total	Life sciences	Engineering math/comp. sciences	Other sciences
R&D	59	51	121	45
Federal Obligations	49	42	78	45

of *Science*, has aptly summarized this change: "the strong campus bias of the 1960s and 1970s against applications and industry has diminished and will not be reestablished soon." [66]

Concluding Observations

In the current era, research and graduate education within American universities seems to be influenced by three pervasive trends—the revolt of undergraduates against the autotelic department, the stagnation in graduate studies, and the increasingly utilitarian rationale for university research. Taken together they represent not just a movement away from the ascendancy of graduate-school values that occurred during the 1960s, but also a movement toward an amalgamation of forces and interests that is more typical historically of the American university. The recent spate of public interest in the matters affecting the college and its curriculum is testimony of sorts that the undergraduate college remains the true center of gravity in American higher education. Since about 1980, campus attitudes about relations with private industry have undergone a transformation, as indicated by Philip Abelson's comment. The protracted anemia of graduate schools of arts and sciences has been compensated in part by the robust health of the graduate-professional schools. These forces, however, are refracted through the American university in different ways.

Martin Trow captured one major facet of this when he wrote of the long-standing unwritten treaty between the State of California and its university: "we will support your ambitions to be a world-class research university if you will look after our bright children." [67] In many of our wealthiest private universities there exists a similar unwritten understanding with alumni that they will support the university's research ambitions if it will also cultivate the highest quality undergraduate college. In both these patterns, then, the research role of the university, particularly a specialized faculty of arts and sciences, has been maintained despite weaknesses in the graduate school by its symbiotic relationship with undergraduate education.

These two patterns, however, do not exhaust the possibilities. In most of the country's metropolitan areas can be found universities that have specialized increasingly in the offering of graduate-professional education. Their mission has been to provide programs offering a variable combination of intellectual elevation and professional advancement to a clientele that is or recently has been employed in middle-level positions, in government, industry, and the non-profit sector. These students frequently comprise the majority of an urban university's enrollments and commonly take some or all of their degree programs as part-time students. Most significant for this context, these students typically do not aim to devote themselves to *Wissenschaft*. Rather, they seek advanced education in order to be more effective leaders and practitioners in an increasingly knowledge-intensive world of affairs. In this type of research university, a somewhat different symbiosis occurs—in this case between graduate-level professional education and faculty involvement with research and scholarship.

Graduate education remains closely linked with research, at least in the PhD programs of the arts and sciences. But the example of the graduate-service universities underlines the fact that graduate study has also assumed a larger role. It now routinely assists individuals to catch up with the rapid proliferation of specialized knowledge in a variety of fields; and it is frequently utilized by persons seeking professional advancement and/or occupational mobility. These purposes are fully in keeping with the traditions of American higher education. The great success of graduate education and research in the American university over the past 100 years has not occurred because American society accepted very much or for very long the value of learning for its own sake. But rather, universities have of necessity found ways to make themselves both useful and learned at the same time. Entering its second century, this feature of the American university does not appear about to change.

Notes

1. Laurence R. Veysey, *The Emergence of the American University* (Chicago, 1965); Hugh Hawkins, *Between Harvard and America: The Educational Leadership of Charles W. Eliot* (New York, 1973); Barbara Miller Solomon, *In the Company of Educated Women: a History of Women and Higher Education in America* (New Haven, CT, 1985), 43–61; Ronald A. Smith, *Sports and Freedom: The Rise of Big-Time College Athletics* (New York, 1988).

2. Richard J. Storr, *The Beginnings of Graduate Education* (Chicago, 1953), 35.

3. Russell Chitenden, *A History of the Sheffield Scientific School* (New Haven, CT, 1928), I, 70–1, 86–88; coeval German influences in France, for example, are discussed in Roger L. Geiger, 'Prelude to Reform: The French Faculties of Letters in the 1860s', *The Making of Frenchmen: Current Directions in the History of Education in France,* ed. Donald Baker and Patrick Harrigan (Waterloo, Ontario, 1980), 337–361.

4. Hugh Hawkins, *Pioneer: A History of the Johns Hopkins University, 1874–1889* (Ithaca, NY, 1960), 127–128, 189; Veysey, *Emergence,* 125–133.

5. Samuel Eliot Morison, *Harvard College in the Seventeenth Century* (Cambridge, MA, 1936), 69–71, 148–150.

6. John C. Greene, 'Science, Learning, and Utility: Patterns of Organization in the Early American Republic', and Sally Gregory Kohlstedt, 'Savants and Professionals: The American Association for the Advancement of Science, 1848–1860', both in *The Pursuit of Knowledge in The Early American Republic: American Scientific and Learned Societies from Colonial Times to the Civil War,* ed. Alexandra Oleson and Sanford C. Brown (Baltimore, 1976), 1–20; 299–325. For the decay of this tradition, see A. Hunter Dupree, 'The National Academy of Sciences and the American Definition of Science', in *The Organization of Knowledge in Modern America, 1860–1920,* ed. Alexandra Oleson and John Voss (Baltimore, 1979), 342–363.

7. David B. Tyack, *George Ticknor and the Boston Brahmins* (Cambridge, MA, 1967), 107–128; Samuel Eliot Morison, *Three Centuries of Harvard* (Cambridge, MA, 1936), 232–238.

8. Natalie A. Naylor, 'The Theological Seminary in the Configuration of American Higher Education: The Ante-Bellum Years', *History of Education Quarterly,* 17 (1977), 17–30.

9. Stanley M. Guralnik, *Science and the Ante-bellum College* (Philadelphia, 1975).

10. 'The Yale Report of 1828', in *American Higher Education: A Documentary History,* ed: Richard Hofstadter and Wilson Smith (Chicago, 1961), 275–291; Douglas Sloan, 'Harmony, Chaos, and Consensus: The American College Curriculum', *Teachers College Record,* 73 (1961), 221–251; Jack C. Lane, 'The Yale Report of 1828 and Liberal Education: A Neorepublican Manifesto', *History of Education Quarterly,* 27 (1987), 325–338.

11. Daniel Coit Gilman, *The Launching of a University* (New York, 1906), 8–9.

12. The historical critique of the old-time college was best articulated by Richard Hofstadter, *Academic Freedom in the Age of the College* (New York, 1951), 209–61. This critique is now regarded as too sweeping, even though the revisionists focus on rather different issues from Hofstadter's concern with intellectual vitality See David B. Potts, '"College Enthusiasm!" As Public Response: 1800–1860', *Harvard Education Review,* 47 (1977), 28–42, and Colin B. Burke, *American Collegiate Populations: A Test of the Traditional View* (New York, 1982). For a balanced discussion, see Walter P. Metzger, 'The Academic Profession in the United States', in *The Academic Profession: National, Disciplinary, and Institutional Settings,* ed. Burton R. Clark (Los Angeles, 1987), 123–196.

13. Ronald Story, *The Forging of an Aristocracy: Harvard and the Boston Upper Class, 1800–1870* (Middletown, CT, 1980); Peter Dobkin Hall, *The Organization of American Culture, 1700–1900: Private Institutions, Elites, and the Origins of American Nationality* (New York, 1984); Burke, *American Collegiate Populations*; Potts, '"College Enthusiasm!"'; and for Virginia, Jennings L. Wagoner, Jr., 'Honor and Dishonor at Mr. Jefferson's University: The Ante-bellum Years', *History of Education Quarterly,* 26 (1986); 155–79.

14. W. Carson Ryan, *Studies in Early Graduate Education: The Johns Hopkins, Clark University, and the University of Chicago* (New York, 1939).

15. Veysey, *Emergence,* 263–268. The 'standard' features of the American university were noted by Edwin E. Slosson, *Great American Universities* (New York, 1910), 522. They included high school graduation required for admission; two years of general work in a college of arts and sciences, followed by two years of specialized work; five departments granting the Ph.D.; and at least one professional school. These criteria were taken from a statement by the National Association of State Universities: *Report of the U. S. Commissioner of Education* (1909), 89.

16. Roger L. Williams, *The Origins of Federal Support for Higher Education: George W. Atherton and the Land-Grant College Movement* (University Park, PA, 1991); Alan I. Marcus, *Agricultural Science and the Quest for Legitimacy: Farmers, Agricultural Colleges, and Experiment Stations, 1870–1890* (Ames, Iowa, 1985); Norwood A. Kerr, *The Legacy: A Centennial History of the State Agricultural Experiment Stations, 1887–1987* (Columbia, MO, 1987). Rosemary Stevens, *American Medicine and the Public Interest* (New Haven, CT,

1971), chapters 2–3; Donald Fleming, *William H. Welch and the Rise of Modern Medicine* (Boston, 1954). Lawrence A. Cremin, David A. Shannon, and Mary E. Townsend, *A History of Teachers College, Columbia University* (New York, 1954); Geraldine Joncich Clifford and James W. Guthrie, *Ed School: A Brief for Professional Education* (Chicago, 1988), 74–84.

17. Joseph Ben-David, *The Scientist's Role in Society* (Chicago, 1984); Charles E. McClelland, *State, Society, and University in Germany, 1700–1914* (Cambridge, 1980).

18. Roger Geiger, 'The Conditions of University Research 1900–1920', *History of Higher Education Annual*, 4 (1984), 3–29.

19. Hugh Hawkins, 'University Identity: The Teaching and Research Functions', in Oleson and Voss (eds), *Organization of Knowledge*, 285–312.

20. Harold Wechsler, *The Qualified Student: A History of Selective Admissions in America* (New York, 1977).

21. *Digest of Education Statistics, 1985–86* (Washington, DC, 1986), 69.

22. Howard Miller, *Dollars for Research: Science and Its Patrons in Nineteenth Century America* (Seattle, 1970); Roger Geiger, *To Advance Knowledge: The Growth of American Research Universities, 1900–1940* (New York, 1986), 80–82.

23. Geiger, *To Advance Knowledge*, 83–87.

24. Walter P. Metzger, 'The Academic Profession', 123–208, esp. 145; Alan Creutz, 'From College Teacher to University Scholar: The Evolution and Professionalization of Academics at the University of Michigan, 1841–1900', unpublished Ph.D. dissertation, University of Michigan, 1981,192–218.

25. Hawkins, 'University Identity', 292–293; Geiger, *To Advance Knowledge*, 72–74.

26. The six were Chicago, Columbia, Cornell, Harvard, Johns Hopkins, and Yale; however, Penn too was a large producer. These institutions dominated the granting of PhDs until after World War I. See Geiger, *To Advance Knowledge*, 276–277; National Research Council, *A Century of Doctorates* (Washington, D.C.: National Academy of Sciences, 1978), 7. Before 1900 the number of doctorates was somewhat inflated: Robert E. Kohler, 'The PhD Machine: Building on the Collegiate Base', *Isis*, 81 (1990), 638–662.

27. William James, 'The PhD Octopus', in *The Harvard Monthly* (1903), reprinted in *Educational Review*, 55 (1918), 149–157; Veysey, *Emergence*, 180–203; Hawkins, 'University Identity', 302–304.

28. See Jesse B. Sears, *Philanthropy in the History of American Higher Education* (New Brunswick, NJ, 1990, first published 1922); Merle Curti and Roderick Nash, *Philanthropy in the Shaping of American Higher Education* (New Brunswick, NJ, 1965).

29. Discussed in Geiger, *To Advance Knowledge*, 43–57.

30. Trevor Arnett, *College and University Finance* (New York, 1922). Institutional revenues from tuition are given in Geiger, *To Advance Knowledge*, 273–275.

31. *Ibid.*; Richard Rees Price, *The Financial Support of State Universities* (Cambridge, MA, 1923).

32. Full-time fall enrollments are given in Geiger, *To Advance Knowledge*, 270–271.

33. Metzger, 'Academic Profession', 147.

34. Geiger, *To Advance Knowledge, 272*. See also Metzger, 'Academic Profession', 146–147.

35. Association of American Universities, *Journal of Proceedings and Addresses*, 8 (1906); Geiger, *To Advance Knowledge*, 76–77.

36. Discussed in Geiger, 'After the Emergence: Voluntary Support and the Building of American Research Universities', *History of Education Quarterly*, 25 (1985), 369–381.

37. Marcia G. Synnott, *The Half-Opened Door: Discrimination in Admissions to Harvard, Yale, and Princeton, 1900–1970* (Westport, CT, 1979); Wechsler, *Qualified Student*; Geiger, *To Advance Knowledge*, 129–139, 215–219.

38. Joan Bulmer and Martin Bulmer, 'Philanthropy and Social Science in the 1920s: Beardsley Ruml and the Laura Spelman Rockefeller Memorial, 1922–29'. *Minerva*, 19 (1981), 347–407.

39. Robert E. Kohler, *Partners in Science: Foundations and Natural Scientists, 1900–1945* (Chicago, 1991).

40. *Ibid.*, 265–357.

41. John P. Swann, *Academic Scientists and the Pharmaceutical Industry: Cooperative Research in Twentieth Century America* (Baltimore, 1988); David C. Mowery and Nathan Rosenberg, *Technology and the Pursuit of Economic Growth* (Cambridge, 1989), 35–97; John W. Servos, 'The Industrial Relations of Science: Chemical Engineering at MIT, 1900–1939', *Isis*, 71 (1980), 531–549; David F. Noble, *America By Design* (New York, 1977). The differing patterns of MIT and CalTech are discussed in Geiger, *To Advance Knowledge*, 174–189.

42. Raymond M. Hughes, *A Study of Graduate Schools of America* (Oxford, OH, 1925); David S. Webster, 'America's Highest Ranked Graduate Schools, 1925–1982', *Change* (May/June 1983), 14–24.

43. Nathan Reingold, 'The Case of the Disappearing Laboratory', *American Quarterly*, 29 (1977), 79–101; Fosdick, *Rockefeller Foundation*, 145–146; National Research Council, *Consolidated Report upon the Activities*

of the National Research Council, 1919 to 1923 (Washington, DC: National Research Council, 1932); Geiger, *To Advance Knowledge,* 222, 235–238; Kohler, *Partners in Science,* 87–104.

44. Discussed in Geiger, *To Advance Knowledge,* 219–223.
45. Cf. Logan Wilson, *Academic Man: A Study in the Sociology of a Profession* (New York, 1942).
46. These sixteen universities are monitored in Geiger, *To Advance Knowledge:* CalTech, Chicago, Columbia, Cornell, Harvard, Johns Hopkins, MIT, Penn, Princeton, Stanford, Yale, California, Illinois, Michigan, Minnesota, and Wisconsin. They varied widely in the magnitudes of research and doctoral education. The patterns they evinced were naturally evident in other universities but to a lesser extent prior to 1940.
47. Elmer Louis Kayser, *Bricks Without Straw: The Evolution of George Washington University* (New York, 1970), 147–212; Harold F. Williamson and Payson S. Wild, *Northwestern University: A History, 1850–1975* (Evanston, 1976), 71–84, 93–99.
48. For example, A. B. Hollingshead, 'Ingroup Membership and Academic Selection', *American Sociological Review,* 3 (1938), 826–833.
49. *A Century of Doctorates,* 7; Geiger, *To Advance Knowledge,* 276–277.
50. Discussed in Roger Geiger, *Research and Relevant Knowledge: American Research Universities Since World War II* (New York, forthcoming, 1993).
51. Vannevar Bush. *Science—The Endless Frontier* (Washington, DC: National Science Foundation, 1960); see also Nathan Reingold, 'Vannevar Bush's New Deal for Research, or The Triumph of the Old Order', in *Science, American Style* (New Brunswick, NJ, 1991), 284–333.
52. J. Merton England, *A Patron For Pure Science: The National Science Foundation's Formative Years, 1945–1957* (Washington, DC, 1982), 45–106; Harvey M. Sapolsky, *Science and the Navy: The History of the Office of Naval Research* (Princeton, 1990).
53. *Basic Research—A National Resource: A Report of the National Science Foundation* (Washington, DC, 1957); Bernard Berelson, *Graduate Education in the United States* (New York, 1960).
54. *National Patterns of Science and Technology Resources: 1987* (Washington, DC, 1988).
55. Talcott Parsons and Gerald Platt, *The American University* (Cambridge, MA, 1973), 106.
56. Christopher Jencks and David Riesman, *The Academic Revolution* (Chicago, 1968), 247.
57. President's Science Advisory Committee, *Scientific Progress, the Universities, and the Federal Government* (Washington, DC, 1960). This document, known as the Seaborg Report, advocated doubling the number of research universities from the current level of 15–20 to 30–40.
58. National Science Foundation, *The NSF Science Development Programs* (Washington, DC, 1977); see also Geiger, *Research and Relevant Knowledge,* chapters 4 and 7.
59. Geiger, *Research and Relevant Knowledge,* chapter 7.
60. Jencks and Riesman, *Academic Revolution,* 250.
61. Roger Geiger, 'The College Curriculum and the Marketplace: What Place For Disciplines in the Trend for Vocationalism?,' *Change* (Nov/Dec. 1980), 17–23ff.
62. *Council of Graduate Schools Communicator,* 24 (May–June, 1991), 4–6; Bruce L. R. Smith, *The State of Graduate Education* (Washington, DC, 1985), esp. 1–83; John Brademas, *Signs of Trouble and Erosion: A Report on Graduate Education in America* (New York, 1984).
63. National Science Foundation, 'Selected Data on Academic Science/Engineering R&D Expenditures, Fiscal Year 1989' (October 1990), 90–321.
64. Council on Financial Aid to Education, *Voluntary Support for Education* (New York, 1989).
65. *Science and Engineering Indicators, 1987,* 253; National Science Foundation, *Federal Support to Universities, Colleges, and Selected Nonprofit Institutions,* Fiscal Year 1986, 24; Fiscal Year 1983, 44.
66. Philip H. Abelson, 'Evolving State-University-Industry Relations', *Science,* 231 (1986), 317.
67. Martin A. Trow, 'Reorganizing the Biological Sciences at Berkeley', *Change* (Nov/Dec. 1983), 52, 44–53.

TOWARD SYSTEM

HUGH HAWKINS

For academia, the years 1895 to 1920 can aptly be designated "The Age of Standards." During those years, regional associations strengthened their work in accrediting secondary schools and began accrediting colleges. Professional associations began to declare what was acceptable in schools that trained physicians, engineers, and lawyers. A new private foundation used its pension program to gain leverage in regularizing the nation's institutions of higher education. The U.S. Bureau of Education attempted to rate the nation's colleges and, although blocked, went on to publish elaborate data on institutions. In revealingly diverse ways, the institutional associations became part of this drive for standards or, as leaders often phrased it, for a system of American education.[1]

"The Age of Standards" stretched old terms and created new ones. *Standard,* for instance, characterized consensual common units of measurement ("a credit hour"), or terms (calling graduate programs by the name *school* and not *college*), or devices (the regular issuance of catalogues). But *standard* readily took on stronger valuational connotations and could mean an acceptable minimum, a requirement for respectability. To be a "standard college," one association determined, an institution must require (among other things) 120 credit hours for the bachelor's degree. The term *system* could be used to indicate whatever educational forms happened to exist. Increasingly after 1895, however, *system* meant that (through the operation of some authoritative body) institutions met common standards, could identify each other by type, and connected with each other in rationalized ways. *Accreditation* meant authentication of an educational unit by an external authority as meeting certain standards and (at least by implication) thereby fitting into a system.[2]

In their earliest gatherings, associations presented themselves as free institutions loosely grouped to seek limited purposes. But the rhetoric of these new organizations increasingly stressed higher education as a rational system, at least an emerging one, into which the association and its members fit. There was, however, no desire for a centralized national pattern like the one developed in France. Academic leaders were trying to create a system with multiple, nongovernmental centers of authority. This pluralistic, systemic approach allowed for differences among categories of institutions, each good in its place.

There was something talismanic in the frequent use at association meetings of the word *system,* with its denial of untidiness, its implied negation of mere persistence in traditional or locally determined practice. The NASU (National Association of State Universities) sometimes defined its members as capstones of state systems, but the AAACES (Association of American Agricultural Colleges and Experimental Stations), the only association with members in every state, had its own special claims as a national body. The AAU (Association of American Universities) sought to regularize distinctions between undergraduate and graduate study, while the late-emerging AAC (Association of American Colleges) began with an awareness that the maturing system threatened to omit or demean liberal arts colleges. All of the associations dwelt on gaining recognition for their members. The message, though often left implicit, was not hard to discern. We are this special, acknowledged sort of institution. We connect with the other sorts. Not only is our mission plain, but it has great value to society. The foundings of two other bodies, the Association of Urban

332

Universities (1914) and the American Association of Junior Colleges (1920), witnessed similar justifications. Although associations sometimes portrayed their membership as the linchpin of the whole, the implications of having multiple associations remained clear. With this increasing mutual acceptance and quest for coherence, it was reasonable to join in an umbrella organization like the ACE (Association Council on Education).[3]

The Land-Grant Institutions' Search for Common Identity

Although first to found a national association of institutions of higher education, the land-grant colleges had difficulties in establishing common ground. Their very spread into every state invited different practices, depending on such factors as a state's wealth and the maturity of its public high school system. But the land-grant institutions had one immense advantage in shaping an identity. In a nation that based its existence on revered founding documents, it was easier to justify an undertaking with a national charter. Again and again a retelling of the saga of the first Morrill Act marked the conventions of the land-grant college association. The fact that Lincoln had signed the act and done so in crisis times endowed the Morrill-grant institutions with a mythic quality. Besides Lincoln, the association could venerate Justin S. Morrill as a founding father. Remaining in Congress until his death in 1898, Morrill was long a spokesman for the new institutions and a fount of democratic aphorisms. After his death, recollections of his wisdom lent a special aura to institutions that benefited from the laws he had promoted.[4]

Given difficulties in attracting students and the primitive state of agricultural science, there was danger that some early Morrill-supported institutions would be mistaken for high schools. In 1888, South Dakota State College required for entrance only one year of preparation beyond the eighth grade. Only after 1913 did Connecticut Agricultural College require high school graduation. In 1896, the association accepted a committee's recommendations for more nearly uniform entrance and graduation requirements, with a strong general education component, but one-fourth of the members voted against the plan and nothing was made mandatory.[5]

Another problem of identity for the Morrill colleges was connection to state universities. Was it better to be part of a larger, more complex institution? As membership in both the AAACES and the NASU by the University of Kentucky, the University of Illinois, and others demonstrated, land-grant college and state university were not mutually exclusive categories. At times this overlap was awkward for the system-minded, but neither association wanted to sacrifice its special role. For over sixty years, the presidents tolerated increasing redundancy in the activities of the two groups. Members came to the defense of whichever arrangement they were associated with. For William Oxley Thompson of Ohio State, the unified institution prevented antagonisms and broadened student perspective, but Albert Boynton Storms of Iowa Agricultural College insisted that creating colleges of agriculture and mechanic arts independent of state universities was wiser pedagogically and truer to the spirit of the Morrill Act. The president of Mississippi Agricultural College could testify that, when the state university had received the Morrill funds (until 1878), agriculture had been scorned and neglected.[6]

The term *agricultural* in the association's title proved a handicap to the ambitions of its members. It was narrower than the curricular mandate of the Morrill Act, which also named "mechanic arts," as well as scientific, classical, and military studies. Because of its link with agriculture, the land-grant association was sometimes regarded as representing a vocationally separated branch of education, as would a grouping of normal schools. The link, although giving the association a base in Washington through the Department of Agriculture, also invited constraints. President Henry Suzzallo of the University of Washington, who wanted his state to have "one great university and one great vocational college for agriculture," condemned as disloyal to agriculture the efforts of "slyly ambitious" educators at State College to enter the state university's terrain.[7]

To be an association of "colleges" also implied limitation. In 1925, what was then called the Association of Land-Grant Colleges added the phrase "and Universities" to its title. If support for research was what made a university, the association could point to work in the experiment stations, which one president claimed had inspired the adoption of research in older private universities. Although there were comforts in being precisely placed within a category within a system, institutions tended to expand their functions beyond categorical boundaries. The example of complex research universities with their prestige and wealth was a magnet hard to resist.[8]

External acknowledgment was necessary if the group's identity was to be firmly established, and for some time the AAACES was worried about inadequate recognition. In 1900, after much correspondence, the association managed to get a place on the NEA program "in order to present the mission and scope of the land-grant colleges in the American system of education." By 1907, it was possible for a member of the executive committee to declare, "The land-grant colleges stand before the public as a well-defined group of institutions."[9]

But a year later, Henry S. Pritchett, the influential head of the Carnegie Foundation, criticized the group for relying thoughtlessly on the term *land-grant* and avoiding shared standards. The association thereupon resumed its interest in categorical clarification, including reconsideration of entrance and graduation requirements. The president of Iowa Agricultural College insisted in 1909 that "decent self-respect" required four years of secondary preparation, thus meeting the "standards established by long experience for classical and liberal arts schools." Another president recommended as a route to coherence the identification of members as "national" institutions, united by "national legislation, by the fact that they are to a certain extent under national control, that they are beneficiaries of the national fund, and that they represent a truly national spirit."[10]

Those pressing for uniform standards and a shared national identity encountered objections from others who emphasized the value of special adaptation to the needs of each state. During a reconsideration of entrance requirements following Pritchett's castigation of the association, Winthrop Ellsworth Stone of Purdue maintained that land-grant colleges properly had many students who were not degree candidates. Besides, he insisted, "the whole problem of college entrance requirements is . . . something which can not be standardized for the whole country. . . . There are state problems, local problems." Such a view had earlier helped bring the tabling of a plan to invite annual inspection of land-grant institutions by the Bureau of Education.[11]

The Ambitions of State Universities

Like the land-grant association, the National Association of State Universities, with a highly diverse membership, felt pressure to clarify member institutions' place within a system. The younger association urged recognition of the state university as a fixed part of American education, dismissing the lack of this institution in a few eastern states as a regional oddity that probably would not persist. Unlike the AAACES, the NASU did not have representation from every state. In 1918, it had no members from four New England states (Connecticut, Massachusetts, New Hampshire, and Rhode Island) or from four middle states (New Jersey, Pennsylvania, Maryland, and Delaware). Drawing on arguments developed to gain support for tax-supported, graded, free schools, the NASU emphasized the state university's place on an educational ladder of public education. The vital matter of learning for a democratic people should not be left to the efforts of competing religious denominations or to "the caprice and uncertainty of private generosity." Nor should public education lack comprehensibility and order. Such order was promoted when state universities set standards for other institutions, notably through undergraduate and graduate admission requirements that impinged on high schools and independent liberal arts colleges. At NASU meetings, Kentucky's James K. Patterson shared horror stories about a high school in Louisville authorized to give the B.A. and a one-year degree program at "National University" in Lebanon, Ohio.[12]

The Carnegie Foundation for the Advancement of Teaching (CFAT), aggressively concerned with the educational system, had done much to sharpen interest in standards among the major institutional associations. About the time of the CFAT's founding, both the NASU and the AAU set up committees on standards. When the NASU's Committee on Standards of American Universities, established in 1905, proved slow in reporting, it was urged not to dally. The state university presidents were clearly worried that some other body might preempt important functions within the emerging national system. George E. MacLean of Iowa warned that agencies lacking the NASU's breadth, such as national professional associations, were beginning to set standards. There was particular concern over the vigorous interest in defining a standard university displayed by "the so-called Association of American Universities," as the president of the University of Illinois, not yet a member of the AAU, phrased it.[13]

When the committee reported in 1908, it foresaw development of "a typical institution of learning which we may not improperly call the Standard American University" and called for quantifiable criteria: completion of sixty "year-hours" for the bachelor's degree, two undergraduate years of preparation before admission to professional courses, and Ph.D. programs in at least five departments. But the application of the definition should not be mechanical. In recommending an institution, an examining body should weigh "the character of the curriculum, the efficiency of instruction, the scientific spirit, the standard for regular degrees, conservatism in granting honorary degrees, and the spirit of the institution." The committee suggested that the NASU might issue certificates to nonmembers adhering to its standards. Partly because the recent admission of more state universities to the AAU had moderated interassociational antagonisms, the NASU drew back from the more ambitious plans of its committee and directed it to cooperate with a parallel AAU group. Between 1911 and 1913, Kendric C. Babcock of the USBE (United States Bureau of Education) conducted inspections at the NASU's request, but these were limited to state universities. Reporting the NASU's criteria, a journalist foreshadowed later resistance to standardization by derisively suggesting that American universities were already more alike than they ought to be.[14]

During this assertive period, the NASU had taken the lead in national efforts to coordinate standardization programs. It called the original meeting (1906) of the National Conference Committee on Standards of Colleges and Secondary Schools, familiarly known as the Williamstown Conference after the site of its early meetings. Here, in conjunction with regional accrediting associations and the College Entrance Examination Board (and shortly also the CFAT and the U.S. Commissioner of Education), the representatives of the NASU promoted a full system of regional accrediting bodies, common admission requirements, and common terminology (most influentially, the definition of a *unit* as "a year's study in any subject in a secondary school, constituting approximately a quarter of a full year's work").[15]

A pioneer in amassing educational statistics, the NASU began about 1905 compiling data on all state universities and land-grant colleges. Later it redesigned its questionnaire in consultation with Pritchett of the CFAT. The assembled information allowed creation of "practicable standards" and development of statistical comparisons that proved useful in influencing state legislators. Complaints about overdetail in questionnaires began jocularly; as their number multiplied, however, beleaguered administrators called for simplification and centralization. There was some relief when the USBE, advised by a committee that included institutional associations, began in 1915 to publish elaborate data from colleges and universities.[16]

The NASU never lived up to the expectations held by its more ardent members for influence as a system-maker and standardizer. Even colleagues who voted for their programs expressed doubts, one warning that future crystallization would turn the elevation of standards into tyranny and arguing that, to serve its constituency properly, each institution needed strong individuality with "a large freedom as to the method of its organization and work." In the Age of Standards, some educators made the case for diversity, even if it was branded provincialism.[17]

Against Confusion: The AAU

In 1908, the AAU declared its intention to undertake "the standardization of American universities" by insisting that those admitted to membership not only have a strong graduate department, but also require at least one year's undergraduate work for admission to professional programs. At the same time, the association expressed its interest in the standards of American colleges, reasoning that since it called for undergraduate work as prerequisite to graduate and professional study, it ought to identify genuine colleges. Moreover, since some foreign universities recognized bachelor's degrees only from members of the AAU, it behooved the association to inform the world that other institutions provided equivalent undergraduate education. The program of college recognition already under way by the Carnegie Foundation won AAU praise, and Pritchett was named a member of the association's committee on standardization.[18]

For a time the AAU hoped that the USBE would perform the desired college-accrediting function. In 1910, Kendric C. Babcock, newly added to the bureau as Specialist in Higher Education, attended the AAU meeting. Although what Samuel Capen called his "cold-blooded cocksureness" had turned some officials against him, the graduate deans praised his provisional classified list of colleges, findings its criteria well suited to help graduate-school admission decisions. But after this list of 344 institutions, hierarchized into four groups, reached the newspapers, representatives of institutions not placed in Group I raised vigorous objections. Chancellor James R. Day of Syracuse University charged unfair procedures and misleading results, hinting that Babcock, "an obscure man" (he had in fact taught at Minnesota and California and been president of the University of Arizona), was the tool of others. Day named Boston University, New York University, and the University of North Carolina as similarly dissatisfied. Like Syracuse, these had been barred from the honors of AAU membership. Early in 1913, President Taft ordered publication of the list halted, and the AAU's efforts to have President Wilson reverse the decision failed.[19]

Insulated from democratic politics, the AAU decided to perform the task itself. Through a committee chaired by Babcock, who had left the USBE for the University of Illinois, the AAU in 1913 issued its own list of approved colleges. More precisely, it adopted the Carnegie Foundation list (including colleges barred from the Carnegie pension program only because of religious connections). The AAU's approved list, justified as giving evidence of readiness for graduate study and not expanded until 1917, was recognized as more conservative than those of the regional associations, the first of which, from the North Central Association, had also appeared in 1913. Indeed, such lists were becoming something of a fad, and the AAU was not immune. In 1907, it had drawn up a list of Latin American universities "of approximately equal rank to each other."[20]

Babcock described AAU accreditation as "purely a voluntary act of a voluntary Association," but in fact the process coerced institutions not on the list to strive toward the AAU's standards. Without the prestige of certain of its members, the association could hardly have succeeded in asserting such quasi-governmental power. Soon catalogues of some colleges on the list were prominently mentioning their authentication by this national authority. Although other bodies also served accrediting functions, the AAU's list was particularly visible. Its undertaking became far more elaborate after 1924, when its Committee on Classification began visiting institutions. The dropping of Fordham University from the list after inspection in 1935 precipitated a contretemps between the institution's defensive president and the educational *commissarius* recently appointed by the Jesuit General. Acceding to recommended changes, Fordham regained the list a year later. Financial support came from the inspection fees and from the Carnegie Corporation, with the understanding that the AAU was continuing the classification program begun by the CFAT. Between 1923 and 1924, AAU expenditures had more than tripled, with two-thirds of the total resulting from the new inspection visits. In fact, the program required the AAU for the first time to have a salaried employee.[21]

The accrediting function caused the AAU many difficulties, nicely summarized by William K. Selden:

> It underwent the agony of establishing standards for educational institutions, of sending teams to visit colleges, of deciding what types of institutions should be included, of re-evaluating colleges, of warning and removing colleges from its list, of obtaining sufficient funds to conduct these operations, of responding to reams of correspondence, and of defending its decisions against innumerable criticisms.

In the late 1930s, the AAU was caught by a wave of resentment against accrediting bodies. Within its membership, some were complaining of the high-handedness of professional associations that sought to accredit universities, while others were defending the AAU against insinuations that its accrediting program was arbitrary and elitist. Despite evidence of weakening resolve among the membership, the AAU continued its program.[22]

Degrees, the academic currency in most general circulation, could hardly escape the attention of standardizers. The thought of confusion over American degrees in Europe, where education was so much more systematic, as well as the fear of charlatans and degrees mills, doubtless encouraged this part of the AAU's activities. To base institutional identification on degrees granted promised an orderly comparability and some semblance of system.

From its beginning, the AAU had concentrated on the Ph.D. degree, the standards for which had virtually determined the original choice of members. Concern about the proliferation of ill-defined professional degrees, especially those that represented no more than four years of undergraduate study, led the AAU in 1915 to set up a "Committee on Academic and Professional Higher Degrees," chaired by Dean Armin Leuschner of the University of California. Leuschner had shown interest at the time of the AAU's founding in extending the associational impulse to professional education by creating "separate sections in all the learned professions, including the technical sciences." He won acceptance for neither this suggestion nor his companion proposal that the association seek "federal or uniform state legislation for the upholding of the standard of the various professions." After meeting with representatives of professional associations and gathering data on current practices, the committee reported that, whereas "the academic Masters' and Doctors' degree have assumed a somewhat definite significance through the co-operation of this Association," there was an alarming proliferation of professional degrees. Among the members of the AAU alone, over 130 differently named degrees had been granted between 1914 and 1916. The committee, whose reports became a staple of the annual meeting, continued to confer with representatives of the professional associations, urging fewer degree designations and higher standards.[23]

In 1920, the committee was authorized to formulate clearer standards for the Ph.D. to set it off even more sharply "as a research degree, as distinguished from professional Doctors' degrees." In this matter, efforts were largely successful. The Masters' degree, however, seemed hopelessly diverse. The bedrock of institutional categorization remained the Bachelor of Arts as the degree expected of colleges, and its regional accrediting associations and the CFAT, with the AAU playing a role through its "Approved List." As to systematizing professional education, this the AAU sought through collaboration with other associations. It accepted the rationale of medical and other professional doctorates, but carefully reserved the Ph.D. as a symbol of achievement in research, a function increasingly identified as the sine qua non of a university.[24]

Standardization is too strong a word for some of the means by which members of the AAU came more closely to resemble each other. Often discussion raised a question of practice, and the administrators present freely exchanged information. Member universities could at least learn if they were unusual in their handling of such matters as department headship, salary differentials within ranks, or the teaching load of assistant professors. As usage spread through imitation, anomalies dwindled. Similar exchanges went on in other institutional associations, but the relative smallness and elitist ethos of the AAU bound its members with unusual closeness. Sometimes, of course, an institution took pride in being different. After describing the Harvard custom of mingling undergraduates and graduates in the same courses, Eliot declared this atypical arrangement to be delightful evidence of nonstandardization. The trend, however, was in the other direction.[25]

The drive for statistical conformity found an early champion in Frederick P. Keppel, then secretary to the president of Columbia. In his 1902 paper for the AAU, "Uniformity of University Statistics of Enrolment and Expenditure," Keppel advocated the department as the primary unit in both expenditure and enrollment statistics, providing the basis for calculations of cost per student. In pressing for fuller and more uniform tables of income and outgo, he admonished the gathered administrators: "We cannot expect an institution to announce that it is spending one hundred thousand dollars a year for, say, conchology, simply because it is conchology or nothing with some particular benefactor; but there is no reason why an opportunity should not be given to read the fact between the lines." Keppel's suggestions led some institutions to modify procedures, and Eliot praised his work as an aid in preventing padding of enrollment figures in catalogues.[26]

The hope for standardized nomenclature, with its expected benefits to interinstitutional communication and comparison, brought the creation of a special AAU committee in 1908. Citing wide divergences, the committee argued that "the institutions which are supposed to systematize and advance knowledge, which ought to illustrate the principles of education in their organizations as far as practicable, have permitted without protest a hopeless confusion of nomenclature which would not be tolerated in any of the sciences." With this rationale, the committee proposed standard meanings for the terms *department, course, college,* and *school.* In a spirit of interassociational comity, aided by overlapping membership, the NASU shortly agreed to accept these definitions. In making the case for all this regularization, the convenience of student transfers was rarely emphasized. Perhaps easing the departure of students was not a particularly good selling point to institutional leaders.[27]

In the wake of World War I, during which institutional variations had made national "manpower" programs harder to administer, representatives of the University of Wisconsin urged the AAU to consider the adoption of uniform opening and closing dates in higher education and a common decision as between semesters and trimesters. But wartime urgency had ebbed. The resulting committee never reported and was discharged after two years.[28]

The Ambivalence of the AAC

Early meetings of the AAC revealed members' anxiety over the processes of standardization already affecting them. Particularly worrisome was the labeling by the U.S. commissioner of education of some colleges as "sectarian." Colleges had, in fact, been barred from the Carnegie pension program because of this identification. The first AAC meeting urged the commissioner to change classification by control from "state-controlled, sectarian, and non-sectarian" to "tax-supported and non-tax-supported," with the latter divided into "church controlled, church affiliated, and independent."[29]

Although unsuccessful in this effort, the new association remained in close touch with the bureau, which had sent its specialist in higher education to the opening meeting. Capen gave words of comfort to presidents of institutions beleaguered by standardizers. It would be unwise to define a "standard college" just now, he declared. "After all most colleges are local institutions." Why should there be only one type? Williams and Reed need not be the same. A college had no obligation to commit suicide because some agency had set standards impossible for its local or regional constituency. Still, Capen justified certain classifications and urged that private colleges open their records as public institutions were obliged to do. In a cooperative spirit the AAC joined Capen's recently founded "Committee on Higher Educational Statistics" at the USBE, as did several other associations. The committee's work indicated limits to toleration of local variation. Although there was no classification, the first report followed its statistics on colleges with the declaration, "To the eye of the initiated the entries in this table tell their own story." The report included thirteen "Suggested Requirements for a Successful College of Arts and Sciences."[30]

Only by admitting an institution to membership did the AAC in any sense serve as an accrediting body. It lacked the authoritative self-confidence that allowed the AAU to publish rankings of nonmembers. Reluctant to sit in judgment, the AAC rejected an early proposal that it evaluate credits offered by transfer students. As the only national association of colleges, however, the AAC joined in the definitional movement already under way. One of its earliest committees drew up criteria for a "minimum college" and for an "efficient college," criteria designed, it was said, to be helpful in institutional self-analysis. At first, AAC membership was to be limited to those meeting the minimum, but waivers were soon allowed. Legislatures, noting the minimum criteria, were expected to "retard the birth rate of institutions with vastly inferior standards." As with trade associations, limiting competition was an AAC goal, a goal aided by the sometimes irritating standardization movement.[31]

Some AAC members were familiar with external appraisal through the work of church boards of education, whose programs of inspection had begun, in the case of the Methodists, as early as 1893. The council of these boards, the CCBE (Council of Church Boards of Education), it will be remembered, was the matrix in which the AAC originated. Like the AAC, the CCBE was interested in both uplift and efficiency. Its "Forward Movement" campaign of 1916 was designed not only to promote students' religious life but also "to assist in defining the function of the independent (non-tax-supported) college in America, and to assist in securing more definite recognition of it as a natural and permanent part of our developing system of education."[32]

Although they gave prominence to spiritual aspects of college education, the AAC leaders still urged the case for standard definitions and shared statistics. The AAC participated in an interassociational Committee on Standard Reports, which emerged in 1930 from work of the CCBE. Kelly begged the presidents to adopt similar methods in their annual reports "so that significant totals and averages may be arrived at and conclusions reached of actual scientific value." Among the ultimate results might well be "a science of college administration." A Quaker and a bureaucrat, Kelly wanted guidance from both the inner light and the lamp of classified knowledge. Like other administrative progressives, he linked hope for human betterment with a dedication to ordered institutions.[33]

The ACE and the Reshaping of Standardization, 1920–1940

California institutions did not belong to a regional association and the New England Association did no accrediting. The regionals were nevertheless considered by the 1920s to be the heart of accreditation in the American system. There was little complaint about their work from the institutional associations, whose own prerogatives in accreditation had been clarified. The AAU backed its prestigious "Accepted List" with elaborate criteria and inspections. Although the AAC denied that it accredited, its membership list gave institutional validation, and in 1925 the AAC turned the tables on the AAU when a committee presented ratings of graduate departments in universities as judged by college professors. The NASU and the land-grant association continued to urge standard entrance and graduation requirements, but without requiring these for membership. As for the ACE, it quickly rose to prominence in the accreditation movement, emphasizing its special capacities for national coordination.[34]

Even before he had formally assumed the directorship of the ACE in 1919, Capen forecast that it would standardize the standardizing agencies, of which a recent study had discovered no fewer than seventy-three. The council's initial venture into the field was considerably more modest, however. On the ground that it had an obligation to inform foreigners of the status of various colleges, the ACE entered what Capen called "perhaps the most dangerous of all sports" and published annually the lists of approved colleges issued by the AAU, the regionals, and the University of California. Although maintaining that it was not an accrediting agency, the ACE stood ready to answer inquiries. The response from a central national organization that a certain institution appeared on none of the approved lists was doubtless effective.[35]

But the ACE was not a passive compiler of lists. It quickly moved into a dominant position within the National Conference Committee on Standards (the Williamstown Conference), which in 1923 merged into the ACE's Committee on Standards. Beginning in 1922, the ACE issued guidelines for accrediting bodies, largely substantive criteria (such as a maximum teaching schedule of sixteen hours), which were soon adopted by various regionals, church boards of education, and state education departments. Four years later it led the exposure when some diploma mills sought to accredit each other through a fly-by-night "National Association of Colleges and Universities." Denouncing "Degrees for Dollars," the ACE's assistant director made sport of Helmut P. Holler and his "Oriental University," located in his home.[36]

In an uncharacteristic direct institutional appraisal, the ACE in 1934 published lists compiled by its Committee on Graduate Instruction which identified graduate departments with adequate or outstanding programs. The lists, based on the judgment of specialists in each field, gained extra notoriety when they were covered by the *New York Times*. The committee's work was not continued. The ACE gained little influence among professional associations that accredited programs in their fields, although some of them, such as the Council on Medical Education of the American Medical Association, became constituent members of the ACE.[37]

The idea of standards remained integrally tied to that of an educational system. The standards drawn up for junior colleges by the regionals and the ACE assumed that these institutions were part of a system through which students could move without encountering barriers peculiar to one institution. With the course credit as the medium of exchange, the United States had in fact developed an unusual if not unique system of educational "free trade."[38]

Besides promoting minimal standards, the ACE pressed for the adoption of common usage in terminology and statistics. Terms such as *semester* and *credit* were regularized to the point that noncomplying institutions had to adapt or issue defensive statements. The benefits of uniform statistics seemed plain to the system-minded, and studies sponsored by the Carnegie Foundation (1910) and the General Education Board (1922) sought to advance that cause. Without comparable figures, it was hard to test the accommodation to standards, to reward achievers and stimulate laggards, or to analyze "the system as a whole." Such views inspired the labors of the National Committee on Standard Reports, formed in 1930 by a merger of similar committees working under the auspices of the AAC-CCBE and the USOE and including representatives from associations of business officers, registrars, and teachers colleges. Its crowning work, *Financial Reports for Colleges and Universities* (1935), proposed uniformities that offered some relief to academic administrators beset by variously designed reporting requirements from external authorities.[39]

Although college and university presidents had helped launch the standardization movement, they came to have second thoughts as it exerted troublesome outside pressure on the institutions they headed. "University presidents," Harold Orlans has wryly observed, "have responded to accrediting agencies much as a dog responds to fleas—and with as little ultimate success." The institutional associations were apt forums for expressing the presidents' rising irritation. What had originally been praised as a way to elevate standards and give systemic coherence began to evoke warnings of "a stifling of initiative and experimentation and an unfortunate crystallization of the whole educational structure." Sometimes, presidential complaints seemed directed at the regionals, as when President Harry Pratt Judson of the University of Chicago protested that even the emphasis on four years of college represented inflexibility. But it was specialized, professional accrediting programs that roused militant opposition. Besieged presidents could imagine that virtually every occupation was determined to become a profession and that the chosen means was to be advanced education authenticated by accreditation.[40]

The lustrous model of the standardizer of professional schools, exemplified by Abraham Flexner with his 1910 study of medical schools, was beginning to tarnish. In the NASU, discussion of "the attempt of outside agencies to 'standardize' us" followed a 1923 address by Minnesota's Lotus D. Coffman and led the next year to passage of a resolution against the growing tendency "seriously to limit both local initiative and that freedom of experimentation which is necessary for educational advance." The president of the University of Washington returned home to fulminate against "groups of specialists having no acquaintance with general university administration who, by the threat of classification, are taking administration out of our hands and forcing us to new expenses." That the chief irritant was not the regionals became all the clearer when the NASU-authorized study of standardizing agencies appeared in 1926, focusing its attack on accreditation of professional schools. Besides undemocratically limiting the number who could enter a profession, the report alleged, the new procedures gave disproportionate leverage within a university to its professional schools.[41]

His embrace of this NASU report brought Samuel Capen to the fore as a critic of accreditation, a paradoxical role for the leading standardizer of ten years before. His apostasy owed much to his new perspective as a university president beset by accrediting agencies, but also something to his experience on committees with "persons of bureaucratic temper . . . who like to apply mechanical rules, to whom a rule becomes sacred as soon as it is adopted, persons who lack vicariousness and constructive imagination." The accreditors, he protested, used not educational standards but those of engineering, organization, or politics. Increased autonomy for institutions was the proper route to genuine advance of learning.[42]

The regionals with their accreditation of undergraduate programs did not escape the mood of counterreformation. As usual, it was the North Central Association that took the lead, beginning in 1928 with an admission that present standards failed to measure the real worth of colleges. A thorough reconsideration led to the adoption six years later of nonnumerical standards, designed to meet an institution's own sense of its mission. Shortly before it was published, the director of this study, George F. Zook, had become director of the ACE. In that office, he proselytized for the new cause: qualitative rather than quantitative standards and flexibility in accrediting procedures. Under Zook the ACE discontinued its statement of accrediting standards, many of which were quantitative. Although he encouraged various associations as they moved against mechanical or excessive standardization, he praised the voluntaristic origins of accrediting agencies and rejected suggestions for their abolition. Stimulation of institutional self-development was one of his ideals for accreditation reform; restricting practitioners' interference in professional education was another.[43]

Functioning a good deal like the regionals in accreditation of colleges, the AAU felt similar winds of change. Perhaps the AAU should itself give up accrediting to encourage similar restraint by professional associations, since those outsiders functioned "from the standpoint of aggrandizing a particular field of work and without understanding the problems of particular institutions." Such was the advice from one University of California dean to another, who was preparing a talk on accreditation for an AAU meeting. The resulting paper used medical education to exemplify problems of imposed curricular rigidity, although its author thought that newer professions with their social insecurities posed a greater threat to university freedom. The aggressiveness of pharmacists seemed particularly troublesome at the moment, and their stiff inspection fees added offense. In 1938, the AAU announced that it did not apply standards mechanically and that a course of study not measurable in quantitative units might be acceptable, but the association retained numerical criteria and continued to insist on inspection.[44]

Changed attitudes toward accreditation marked a report published in 1940 by the USOE at the suggestion of the Association of Chief State School Officers. Emphasizing state responsibilities, the report declared that voluntary associations should limit themselves to improving colleges, which could be done better if not accompanied by accrediting functions. The report skirted the issue of national comparability that had motivated much of the work of the institutional associations. Deans at the AAU received a preliminary version skeptically, but evidence was mounting that the AAU's glory days as an accrediting agency were over.[45]

As early as 1924 the NASU formally warned that the standardization movement suffered from overproliferation of accreditors and high-handedness. At the NASU meeting of 1938, simmering complaints against accreditors of professional programs erupted into a great deal of rhetoric and a plan to join other institutional associations in common action. The resulting Joint Committee on Accrediting (JCA) was intended to eliminate some accrediting agencies, simplify procedures, reduce expenses, and reclaim institutional responsibility. Praised by Zook, the venture attracted the cooperation of three other institutional associations.[46]

As a parallel effort, the ACE in 1939 and 1940 called conferences that launched projects to coordinate accrediting agencies. Some accreditation activists grew defensive. The disgruntled chairman of the AAU committee on classification charged the first ACE conference with using steamroller tactics. The principal speakers had complained of pestiferous accrediting bodies. "They implied that presidents no longer had time to manage their institutions and play golf. They further implied that it wasn't our business anyhow to ask too many questions about the intimate affairs of an institution, particularly about the coach's salary and stipends for athletes. . . . A few feeble voices were heard in protest, but they made little impression." As matters turned out, neither the JCA nor the coordinating projects begun by the ACE conferences had much success. But the distractions of World War II considerably lessened the accrediting activities that had irritated presidents and aroused their associations.[47]

The Appraisers Appraised

The direction of academic energies into setting standards, coordinating a system, and arranging accrediting procedures reached well beyond the institutional associations, but they were central to the effort. Their national identities gave them influence that regional accrediting associations and state governments lacked. Their nongovernmental status associated them with American traditions of voluntarism; in fact, the system that emerged was far less coercive than those in centrally administered governmental systems such as the French.

A variety of motives gave heart to the system-makers. They found models in other parts of society. Business was increasingly shifting away from market competition through conscious coordination, as in trade associations and price leadership. Protestant religious bodies moved in the same direction, with national denominational organizations that included specialized bureaucracies and linked themselves in interdenominational federations. The military exemplified order through hierarchy, and the republican polity was a venerated system of levels and branches. In the society so structured, it was easy to argue that higher education must not remain a congeries of autonomous local ventures.

Standardizes claimed that they had not lost sight of the individual, that in fact their control over institutions advanced the freedom of the individual. Recognized degrees, transferable credits, a clearly distinguished ladder—all of these presumably informed students and kept them out of academic cul-de-sacs. To be able to ask if an institution was accredited and by whom allowed the seeker of higher education some protection against the lures of advertisement or mere propinquity.

The benefits of system and standards for institutional association members included the blocking off of competition. Explicit criteria for "higher education" made entry of new units more difficult, while pressuring others to merge or disappear. At the same time, recognized standards and accrediting procedures helped leaders of individual institutions make the case for increased financial support and counseled them on how best to use it.

There were benefits from the standardization movement, no doubt, but it had many flaws. It began with naively numerical criteria. It gave leverage to rigid officials and not just enlightened ones. Its development by a multiplicity of regional, institutional, and professional associations brought public confusion and administrative exhaustion. It reduced institutional variety, embarrassing the idiosyncratic, undervaluing local tradition, and discouraging experimental innovation. As these disadvantages came to light, the institutional associations played an important corrective role.

Even while some participants in associations were dedicated to enforcement of standards, others used the associations as forums to raise objections and poke fun. The counterreform of the 1930s with its shift toward institutional self-appraisal and qualitative considerations began in the North Central Association, but the institutional associations advanced the process. The officiousness of the rapidly increasing professional accrediting bodies affronted institutional presidents. They had thought that universities legitimized professions. Now the process seemed reversed. The AAU began to question all accrediting programs, even its own. The other institutional associations had always denied being accrediting bodies, though occasionally acting as if they were. Now, in reaction to excesses, they were well placed to raise objections and lend support to counterreformers. The ACE, under Zook's leadership, pulled back from quantitative standards and brought accrediting officers and disillusioned institutional administrators together. No one asked for the system to be dismantled. Virtually every academic had some vested interest in it. Zook's bureaucratic meliorism set the tone for alteration.

Notes

1. Charles Maxwell McConn's identification of "The Age of Standards" as the period 1890–1915 seems to me to begin and end too early. See McConn, quoted in William K. Selden, *Accreditation: A Struggle over Standards in Higher Education* (New York, 1960), 28.

2. Selden, *Accreditation*, ch. 1; Harold Orlans, *Private Accreditation and Public Eligibility* (Lexington, Mass., 1975), 1–3.

3. For the AAU and the AAJC foundings, see *The University and the Municipality: Summary of Proceedings of the First Session of the National Association of Municipal Universities* (USBE Bul. 38, Washington, D.C., 1915), 5–6; George F. Zook, *Higher Education, 1918–1920* (USBE Bul. 21, Washington, D. C., 1921), 16–18; Steven Brint and Jerome Karabel, *The Diverted Dream: Community Colleges and the Promise of Educational Opportunity in America, 1900–1985* (New York, 1989), 32–33. For the rise of yet another institutional grouping, see Paul J. Edelson, "Codification and Exclusion: An Analysis of the Early Years of the National University Extension Association, 1915–1923," paper presented at the Kellogg Project Visiting Scholar Research Conference on the History of Adult Education, Syracuse University, Mar. 22, 1990, publication by Syracuse University pending.

4. The immense variety of early patterns for use of Morrill funds is a major theme of Earle D. Ross's *Democracy's College*. See also Eddy, *Colleges for Our Land*, ch. 3.

5. Eddy, *Colleges for Our Land*, 66–67; Rudolph, *American College and University*, 260; "Report of the Committee on Entrance Requirements, Courses of Study, and Degrees," *AAACES Proc.* 10 (1896): 52–54; debate, ibid., 59–62; Williams, "George W. Atherton," 349–354.

6. William Oxley Thompson, *NASU Proc.* 2 (1904); 19, A. B. Storms, "The Distinctive Work of the Land-Grant Colleges: Their Function, Scope, and Organization," *AAACES Proc.* 23 (1909); 51; J. C. Hardy, ibid. 25 (1911): 135; Bettersworth, *People's College* (see ch. 1, n. 18), ch. 2.

7. Henry Suzzallo to "Mr. Perkins," June 8, 1915 ("one great"), HS, box 11; Enoch Albert Bryan, *Historical Sketch of the State College of Washington, 1890–1925* (Spokane, Wash., 1928), 379–388.

8. James K. Patterson, "A Retrospect," *AAACES Proc.* 24 (1910): 31–35.

9. ECR, *AAACES Proc.* 14 (1900): 11 ("mission"); Winthrop Ellsworth Stone, "The Selection and Retention of an Efficient Teaching Force," ibid. 21 (1907): 72 ("stand before").

10. ECR, *AAACES Proc.* 20 (1908): 16; H. S. Pritchett, ibid., 49–51; ibid. 23 (1909): 65–71, 24 (1910): 125–36; A. B. Storms, "Distinctive Work," *AAACES Proc.* 23:57 ("decent"); Enoch Albert Bryan, ibid. 23 (1909): 58 ("national").

11. W. E. Stone, *AAACES Proc.* 23 (1909): 68, 69 ("whole"); ibid. 14 (1900): 73, 15 (1901): 22–25. For another example of emphasis on state particularism, see W. E. Drake, "The Relation of the Agricultural and Mechanical College to the State," ibid. 14 (1900): 183.

12. J. G. Schurman, "Some Problems of Our Universities—State and Endowed," *NASU Proc.* 7 (1909): 36 ("caprice"); G. E. MacLean, "The State University the Servant of the Whole State," ibid. 2 (1904): 34; G. P. Benton, "State Universities and the Educational Challenge of To-morrow," ibid. 16 (1918): 28–41: B. I. Wheeler, "The State Universities as a Factor in American Life," ibid. 173; R. E. Vinson, "Legislative Problems," ibid. 17 (1919): 136; J. K. Patterson, ibid. 6 (1908): 227–228.

13. G. E. MacLean, *NASU Proc.* 6 (1908): 204; similarly, ibid. 5 (1907): 111–112; Edmund J. James, ibid., 113 ("so-called"). For James's related resentment of foundations' advancement of new definitions and standards, see ibid. 6 (1908): 247.

14. "Report of the Committee on Standards of American Universities," *NASU Proc.* 6 (1908): 147–53, 147–48 ("typical"), discussion, pp. 177–220; A. H. Upham, "About Ourselves," ibid. 34:22–23; Fred J. Kelly et al., *Collegiate Accreditation by Agencies within States* (USOE, Bul. 3, Washington, D.C., 1940), 13; Edwin E. Slosson, *Great American Universities* (New York, 1910), 522.

15. *NASU Proc.* 4 (1906): 12–16, 5 (1907): 241; Edward A. Krug, *The Shaping of the American High School* (New York, 1964), 157; Zook and Haggerty, *Principles of Accrediting Higher Institutions* (see ch. 2, n. 8), 38–40; Selden, *Accreditation,* 34–35, 35 ("years"); Howard J. Savage, *Fruit of an Impulse: Forty-Five Years of the Carnegie Foundation, 1905–1950* (New York, 1953), 102–3.

16. *NASU Proc.* 13 (1915): 44–45; Lykes, *Higher Education and the USOE,* 51–52.

17. G. E. MacLean, *NASU Proc.* 7 (1909): 75–76; George E. Fellows to "Dear Sir," Oct. 3, 1906, mimeo., UCPP, box 33; Thomas Kane, "Standardizing the Cost of Departments," *NASU Proc.* 10 (1912): 102; George E. Vincent, "Report of the Committee on Standards of the American Universities and the A. B. Degree," ibid. 13 (1915): 45; Lykes, *Higher Education and the USOE,* 51–52; James H. Baker, "What Influence Should the Carnegie Foundation Have on Entrance Requirements?" *NASU Proc.* 7 (1909): 54–58, 57 ("large"). On the case for diversity as made by Josiah Royce in 1915, see Lagemann, *Private Power for Public Good,* 90–92, 180–83.

18. *AAU Proc.* 9 (1908): 9–11, 74–75, 10 (1909): 66; Selden, *Accreditation,* 69.

19. Samuel P. Capen to Grace Capen, Sept. 19, 1914, SPC, box 12 ("cold-blooded"); Lykes, *Higher Education and the USOE,* 45–52, 48 (quoting Day), 213–15 (for suppressed report and list); *AAU Proc.* 14 (1912): 17; D. J. Cowling, "Report of Committee on Higher Educational Statistics," *AAC Bul.* 2 (1916), no. 3, pp. 97–98; S. P. Capen, "College 'Lists' and Surveys Published by the Bureau of Education," *S&S* 6 (1917): 38–40. For a letter from the AAU to Woodrow Wilson, see *AAU Proc.* 15 (1913): 19. See also David S. Webster, "The Bureau of Education's Suppressed Rating of Colleges, 1911–1912," *HEQ* 24 (1984): 499–511. The USBE had without objection listed women's colleges in a two-level classification between 1888 and 1911. See idem, *Academic Quality Rankings of American Colleges and Universities* (Springfield, Ill., 1986), 31–33.

20. *AAU Proc.* 15 (1913): 55–62, 19 (1917): 20–21, 101–103; Kelly et al., *Collegiate Accreditation,* 13–15, 25; Zook and Haggerty, *Principles of Accrediting Higher Institutions,* 38; Davis, *North Central Association* (see ch. 1, n. 23), 57–64; Louis G. Geiger, *Voluntary Accreditation: A History of the North Central Association, 1945–1970* (Menasha, Wis., 1970), 187; Selden, *Accreditation,* 69–70; *AAU Proc.* 9 (1908): 77 ("approximately"), 78. For the relationship of the AAU list to establishment of Phi Beta Kappa chapters, see Richard Nelson Current, *Phi Beta Kappa in American Life: The First Two Hundred Years* (New York, 1990), 141–145.

21. Kendric C. Babcock, "The Present Standards of Voluntary Associations," *Ed. Rec.* 2 (1921): 93, 94 ("purely"); *AAU Proc.* 25 (1923): 20, 24–27, 26 (1924): 23, 31–35, 40 (1938): 64–65, 42 (1940): 86–97. Expenditures rose from $1,067 in 1923 to $5,518 in 1924, of which $3,794 went toward inspections. For the Fordham case, see Paul A. FitzGerald, *The Governance of Jesuit Colleges in the United States, 1920–1970* (Notre Dame, Ind., 1984), 42–44. For the (successful) efforts of the University of Buffalo to win approval, see Samuel P. Capen to Adam Leroy Jones, May 21, 1924, Nov. 24, 1926, and the printed "Memorandum of Procedure Advised for Institutions Seeking Approval of the Association for Inclusion on Its Accepted List,"

with responses, all in UBPP, box 13. Examples of inspection reports from 1937 are in DBT, box 22. For a general description of the AAU accrediting philosophy and procedures, see Adam Leroy Jones, "The Search for Values—Through Accrediting Agencies: The Association of American Universities," *AAC Bul.* 20 (1934): 111–117.

22. William K. Selden, "AAU: An Enigma," *Graduate Journal* 8:202. See also Webster, *Academic Quality Rankings,* ch. 11. For more on the late 1930s debates, see this volume, this chapter, under "The ACE and the Reshaping of Standardization, 1920–1940."

23. *AAU Proc.* 17 (1915): 22; ibid. 1 (1900): 15 ("separate," "federal"), 17; ibid. 18 (1916): 67–72, 69 ("academic Master's"). For recollections at the time of the committee's dissolution, see ibid. 45 (1944): 84–86.

24. Ibid., 22 (1990): 22 ("research degree"). For the committee's collaboration with professional associations, see ibid., 21–26.

25. Charles W. Eliot, *AAU Proc.* 10 (1909): 62.

26. *AAU Proc.* (Dec. 1902): 50–63, 62 ("cannot"); 5 (1904): 14–21 (discussion of Keppel's paper). See also F. P. Keppel to Benjamin Ide Wheeler, Oct. 28, 1902, UCPP, box 10.

27. *AAU Proc. 9* (1908): 13, 10 (1909): 67–68 (first report), 68 ("institutions"), 11 (Jan. 1910): 90–91 (supplementary report setting definitions for *group, curriculum,* and *division); "Nomenclature," NASU Proc. 7* (1909): 204; ibid. 8 (1910): 39–41. For a later pursuit of the same matter, see David A. Robertson, " Standard Terminology in Education," *Ed. Rec.* 8 (1927), suppl. 4.

28. *AAU Proc.* 20 (1918): 25–26, 21 (1919): 19, 22 (1920): 28.

29. William H. Crawford, "The Place and Function of the Denominational College in Education," *AAC Bul.* 1 (1915): 126–127; ibid., 7, 12.

30. Samuel Capen, "College Efficiency and Standardization; Certain Fundamental Principles," *AAC Bul.* 1 (1915): 143 ("after all"), 146–49; Donald J. Cowling, "Report of Committee on Higher Educational Statistics," ibid. 2 (1916), no. 3, pp. 96–102; Capen, *Resources and Standards of Colleges of Arts and Sciences: Report of a Committee Representing the Associations of Higher Educational Institutions* (USBE Bul. 30, Washington, D.C., 1918), 14 ("to the eye"), 15–17; Kelly, "Audit of Experience," 99.

31. Kelly, "Audit of Experience," 60, 56; Calvin H. French, "The Efficient College," *AAC Bul.* 2 (1916), no. 3, pp. 60–85; Robert L. Kelly, "The Sphere and Possibilities of the Association," ibid., 22–23; Charles Nelson Cole, ibid., 95 ("retard"); similarly, R. Watson Cooper, "The Place and Function of the Proposed Association," ibid. 1 (1915): 45. For comparable worries about too many small hospitals, see Starr, *Social Transformation of American Medicine* (see ch. 2, n. 49), 176.

32. Kelly, *American Colleges and the Social Order* (see ch. 1, n. 30), 85; idem, "Present Standards of Protestant Church Boards of Education," *Ed. Rec.* 2 (1921): 107–113; Thomas Nicholson, "A Proposed Campaign of Christian Education," *AAC Bul.* 2 (1916), no. 2, pp. 2–22; *Forward Movement for Christian Education,* p. [2] ("to assist"), UCPP, box 97; "Denominational Boards in Education," CFAT AR 3 (1908): 172–173. On the assumption that *efficient* had taken on offensive connotations, a later series of papers edited by Kelly for the AAC was entitled *The Effective College* (New York, 1928).

33. Raymond Walters, "Report of the Committee on Classification of Institutions of Higher Education," *AAC Bul.* 20 (1934): 93–94; Edward Everett Rall, "The Report of the National Committee on Standard Reports for Institutions of Higher Education," ibid., 95–97; Kelly, "Sphere and Possibilities," ibid. 2 (1916), no. 3, p. 26 ("significant," "science").

34. Selden, *Accreditation,* 36–38, 98 n. 11; Kelly, "Audit of Experience," 74; *AAC Bul.* 11 (1925): 20.

35. Samuel Capen, *NASU Proc.* 17 (1919): 62; AR, *Ed. Rec.* 1 (1920): 149 ("perhaps"); "Accredited Higher Institutions," ibid., 71–80. For the last list before discontinuation, see ibid. 16 (1935): 363–71.

36. ACE exec. cmte. min., Apr. 4, 1922, Sept. 22, 1923, mimeo., MLB, boxes 5, 13; ACE Committee on Standards min., Jan. 9, 1924, MLB, box 13; AR, *Ed. Rec.* 3 (1922): 186–187; "Preliminary Recommodations [sic] to National, Regional and State Agencies Engaged in Defining and Accrediting Colleges," ibid., 61–63; "Report of the Committee on College Standards," ibid., 210–214; AR, ibid. 4 (1923): 95; George D. Olds, "Conference on Methods of College Standardization," ibid. 2 (1921): 81; D. A. Robertson, "Degrees for Dollars," ibid. 7 (1926): 11–24, esp. 20. The ACE committee soon broadened its purview to include junior colleges and teachers colleges. See "Report of the Committee on Standards," ibid. 5 (1924): 202–208, and *Standards for Accrediting Colleges, Junior Colleges and Teacher Training Institutions* (Washington, D.C., 1924), copy in MLB, box 13. See also Zook and Haggerty, *Principles of Accrediting Higher Institutions,* 29, 41—43.

37. "Report of the Committee on Graduate Instruction," *Ed. Rec.* 15 (1934): 192–226; FitzGerald, *Governance of Jesuit Colleges,* 36–37; Orlans, *Private Accreditation,* 17; Starr, *Social Transformation of American Medicine,* 115–116, 121.

38. "Report of the Committee on College Standards," *Ed. Rec.* 4 (1923): 138; Clark, *Higher Education System* (see ch. 1, n. 7), p. 62, ch. 5; Fritz K. Ringer, *Education and Society in Modern Europe* (Bloomington, Ind., 1979), 247–259.

39. C. R. Mann to D. J. Cowling, Mar. 19, 1925, ACE Ar., 7–14–8; *Financial Reports for Colleges and Universities* (Chicago, 1935); Kelly, "Audit of Experience," 84, 101–103; Lykes, *Higher Education and the USOE,* 97; Cowling to Mann, June 25, 1931, Mann to Cowling, June 29, 1931, both in ACE Ar., 7–14–9.

40. Orlans, *Private Accreditation,* 17 ("presidents"); Zook and Haggerty, *Principles of Accrediting Higher Institutions,* 60–61 ("stifling"); Harry Pratt Judson, "Dangers of the Standardization Movement," *Ed. Rec.* 2 (1921): 114–115.

41. Lotus D. Coffman, "Standardization of State Universities by Outside Agencies," *NASU Proc.* 21 (1923): 66–81; resolution, ibid. 22 (1924): 107 ("seriously"); H. W. Chase to "Gentlemen," Jan. 26, 1924 ("attempt"), copy in UCPP, box 170; Orlans, *Private Accreditation,* 17–18; Henry Suzzallo to "Mr. Henry," Jan. 12, 1925, HS, box 14 ("groups"); similarly, David Kinley to Frank E. Robbins, Dec. 9, 1924, MLB, box 18; "A Study of Recent Standardizing Activities of Certain Associations Affecting University Organizations and Curricula," *NASU Proc.* 24 (1926), part 2 (separately paginated). For a summary of the report presented before another association, see Fred J. Kelly, *The Influence of Standardizing Agencies in Education* (Minneapolis, 1928). See also Selden, *Accreditation,* 70; Zook and Haggerty, *Principles of Accrediting Higher Institutions,* 63–64.

42. Samuel Capen, "Discussion," in Kelly, *Influence of Standardizing Agencies,* 16–23, 17 ("persons"). Other examples of Capen's new position are "Tendencies in Professional Education," *Ed. Rec.* 5 (1924): 15–16; "A Series of Prejudices," *AAC Bul.* 13 (1927): 365–366; "The Principles Which Should Govern Standards and Accrediting Practices," *Ed. Rec.* 12 (1931): 93–103. At the University of Buffalo, Capen's hopes for both an undergraduate tutorial program and a school of library science were undercut by accrediting agencies. See Park, *Samuel P. Capen,* 37, 45n. See also Zook and Haggerty, *Principles of Accrediting Higher Institutions,* 65.

43. Zook and Haggerty, *Principles of Accrediting Higher Institutions,* esp. v–vii; Davis, *North Central Association,* 70–72; Selden, *Accreditation,* 40–41; *Ed. Rec.* 16 (1935): 248; George F. Zook to Raymond B. Fosdick, July 16, 1937, ACE Ar., 9–3–6; Zook, "Who Should Control Our Higher Institution?" *ALGCU Proc.* 52 (1938): 90–99.

44. [Monroe Deutsch] to Charles B. Lipman, Oct. 28, 1936, UCPP, box 416 ("standpoint"); Deutsch to R. G. Sproul, Sept. 26, 1936, UCPP, box 418; Charles B. Lipman, "Professional Associations and Associations of Professional Schools and Some Problems Which They Pose for American Universities," *AAU Proc.* 38 (1936): 131–139, esp. 134–135, and discussion, 140–143; "Memorandum for Guidance of Institutions Seeking Approval of the Association for Inclusion in Its Accepted List," ibid. 40 (1938): 25–28. For more on pharmacists, see L. P. Sieg to John J. Tigert, May 24, 1938, UWPP, 71–34, box 110.

45. Kelly et al., *Collegiate Accreditation,* esp. 212–223; George A. Works, "Voluntary Accrediting Associations," *AAU Proc.* 42 (1940): 86–92; Fernandus Payne, "Discussion," ibid., 96–97.

46. *NASU Proc.* 24 (1926), part 2, p. 1; *NASU Proc.* 36 (1938): 21–48, 79–108. The other JCA participants were the AAU, the ALGCU, and the AUU. See Selden, *Accreditation,* 71–73; Bloland, *Higher Education Associations,* 106–107.

47. Selden, *Accreditation,* 72–73; P&P cmte. min., Oct. 18–19, 1938, ACE Ar., 10–11–8; AR, *Ed. Rec.* 20 (1939): 356–359; Fernandus Payne, "Discussion," *AAU Proc.* 42 (1940): 95 ("implied"); "Report of the Joint Committee on Accrediting," Nov. 14, 1941, AGR, box 56. For a request that accrediting agencies suspend specific requirements that interfered with student acceleration during the war, see min. of joint meeting, P&P cmte. and exec. cmte., Dec. 19, 1941, ACE Ar., 10–20–2.

THE RISE OF UNIVERSITY MANAGEMENT

CHRISTOPHER NEWFIELD

The Bureaucratic Revolution

The end of the Civil War inaugurated a "new economy," the likes of which the country had never seen. This economy emerged from a mixture of new technologies and new forms of administration. The economy developed as it did because firms were able to bureaucratize the administration of their new technologies.

Bureaucracy was something of a magic bullet that solved a variety of problems at once. It increased firms' control over their markets. It coordinated dispersed systems of production and distribution and made these more efficient. It allowed firms to reap great economies of scale. And it increased the firm's power over politics, society, and its own employees.

Business and government intended that the research university should provide both technology and the power to manage it, including above all the management of collectivized work. Capitalism's longstanding tendency was to take relatively autonomous workers and harness them to a common process. Unlike earlier forms of cooperative labor, which tended to reflect the social structures in which they arose, the capitalist form famously organized cooperation around the needs of production for profit. During the infancy of the research university in the United States, Karl Marx was arguing that "co-operation itself, contrasted with the process of production carried on by isolated independent workers, or even by small masters, appears to be a specific form of the capitalist process of production. It is the first change experienced by the actual labor process when subjected to capital." Although cooperative labor had always existed—think of Roman roads, Mayan cities, and plantation cotton—capitalism required a new scale and sophistication in labor management.

The coordination of collective labor became business's central challenge. Although populists, socialists, and many others tried to keep a community or democratic basis for labor cooperation, the main power of coordination was inexorably absorbed by the corporation. This function helped determine the corporation's basic structure as that which "contains many distinct operating units and . . . is managed by a hierarchy of salaried executives." By 1900, the business corporation had established the elaborate bureaucratic systems that allowed this cooperative labor, and the enormous value it created, to be harnessed, extracted, and controlled. There was nothing historically necessary or maximally functional about this trajectory, but it did reflect the general balance of social power and came to dominate the socioeconomic environment. The university contributed both ideas and trained personnel to this bureaucratic system, which needed people that could thrive in spite of, or perhaps because of, its restrictions.

Robert H. Wiebe's description of this new bureaucratic world identified one crucial requirement: continuous adaptation. Bureaucratic ideas, he wrote, were "peculiarly suited to the fluidity and impersonality of an urban-industrial world. They pictured a society of ceaselessly interacting members and concentrated upon adjustments within it. Although they included rules and principles of human behavior, these necessarily had an indeterminate quality because perpetual interaction was itself indeterminate. . . . Thus, the rules, resembling orientations much more than laws,

346

stressed techniques of constant watchfulness and mechanisms of continuous management. . . . Now change was interaction and adjustment, forming elaborate and shifting multilinear patterns." Wiebe overstates the indeterminacy of actual practice, but illuminates the crucial context through which the autonomous, flexible self moved—interaction with a multitude of people, factors, and structures. The graduate would be useless unless he felt at home in the economy, and he would not feel at home unless he were comfortable with managing and being managed in turn. He could not manage and be managed unless he were less an individualist or artisan than an organization man.

The bureaucratic revolution mounted a direct challenge to traditional notions of craft labor. With the development of the factory system and Frederick Taylor's mechanical efficiency studies, individualism came to seem an impediment to valuable labor rather than its precondition. The worker couldn't depend on his or her judgment, desire, or skill to achieve the best possible output, but needed external supervision. Bureaucratic control required not only a supervisory system but supervisors, not only management but managers. Managers would be autonomous enough to run this system without actually standing outside it. Managers were people who possessed knowledge—especially operational knowledge—that would be used to supervise workers who lacked this knowledge. Managers were knowledge workers. But their knowledge functioned within organizational terms.

Where would these managers come from? The institution most involved in developing the kind of person, autonomous and manageable, who could develop and apply knowledge in a bureaucratic environment was of course the research university.

The Discipline of the Knowledge Worker

Managerial efficiency and technological research rose together to the top of university priorities. This was a predictable effect of the university's economic environment.

By the final third of the nineteenth century, Marx had come to see all modern industry as knowledge industry. "Modern industry," he argued, "makes science a productive force distinct from labor and presses it into the service of capital." The evidence for technology's central role was everywhere to see. As the century came to an end, corporations had begun to systematize their research efforts. This involved orchestrating collective scientific labor, of course, and allowed corporations to shift some of their research effort from applied to fundamental inquiries. "Before 1900 there was very little organized research in American industry, but by 1930 industrial research had become a major economic activity."

A "knowledge economy" is an economy in which sustained profit depends on research-based improvement in the production process. In this sense, the United States was a knowledge economy in the nineteenth century. If we narrow the definition so that it specifically denotes an economy in which business firms organize and manage research in the same way they manage production, the United States was a knowledge economy by 1930. Universities were crucial providers of knowledge and knowledge workers alike.

One of David F. Noble's essential insights in his classic book *America by Design* (1977) was that knowledge and the knowledge worker were brought together under one engineering vision of comprehensive corporate management. Parts of this story are familiar, as management practice took shape through Frederick Taylor's scientific management, and through efforts associated with the "human relations" of the 1920s, to reduce invasive supervision and increase job satisfaction. Industry sought not only to engineer its own research but to engineer usable research undertaken by others. Industrial firms looked not only to "trade associations, semiprivate institutes, independent contractors, government bureaus, and private foundations," but to universities. They were especially dependent on universities for expensive basic research. University administrators who desired industry support might feel some need to graft industry's management views onto their own institutions.

If they did, industry was not shy about providing material. Frank Jewett, the head of Bell Labs, defined systematic research as "cooperative effort under control." Dugald Jackson, a GE scientist and chair of the electrical engineering department at MIT, recalled in 1935: "Standardized manufacture demanded 'that the operations of groups of employees and machines . . . be associatively joined, and that individual whims . . . be restrained. . . . The disciplinary relations within the manufacturing organization must be definite and strict.' Dexter S. Kimball, manager of GE'S Pitts-field plant, Dean of Engineering at Cornell University, and a leader in industrial management, had this insight when he noted with some urgency that 'the extension of the principles of standardiza-tion to the human element in production is a most important and growing field of activity.'" Even workers that handled advanced technology needed strict control from managers.

The same discipline applied to college-trained engineers. "If science was to be effectively controlled, scientists had to be effectively controlled; the means to such control was the fostering of a spirit of cooperation among researchers second only to a spirit of loyalty to the corporation. . . . The content of the education had to provide the training necessary for technical work, especially for the early years of employment; it had to instill in the student a sense of corporate responsibility, teamwork, service, and loyalty."

Many industrial managers felt that the university was falling short in preparing individuals for corporate forms of fitting in. Companies like General Electric and Westinghouse had, by 1900, developed supplemental training courses that transformed engineers from soloists to team per-formers. These courses retrained graduates who, fresh out of university, "did not know how to adapt themselves to new conditions, . . . to adjust their personalities to the wishes and desires of their superiors." In corporate school, they learned "to work first for the success of the corporation, and only secondarily to consider themselves, and . . . to subordinate their own ideas and beliefs to the wishes and desires of their superiors,"—that only then could they "really be efficient." In short, engineers learned that "Self-forgetfulness is what is required."

Without assuming that these views also dominated engineering education, we can still detect a strong tendency to see the free agency of the early knowledge worker as damaging the efficient use of that knowledge. University engineering programs knew that corporate employers would see self-direction as a dysfunctional leftover from college days.

It shouldn't be surprising then that some top university administrators wanted to run the uni-versity as a business. In 1900, the *Atlantic Monthly* published this kind of call from a frustrated but safely anonymous administrator: "When the directors of a great commercial corporation or of some transportation company find it necessary to call a new man to the presidency or to the position of general manager, he is at once given almost absolute authority to all executive details. . . . The edu-cational executive or manager, however, has no such freedom of choice as to his associates, has no such right of way." The educational administrator, the author complains, is blocked by the tradition that places the professor "quite beyond the reach of complaint," which presumably includes ready dismissal. The disappointed author correctly noted that nearly every other organization put its mem-bers under the exclusive control of one man, and wondered why universities should be different.

The author struck a perennial note in business-oriented criticisms of higher education: modern-ization means business, and business means centralized authority. The university will fall behind, he concluded, "unless the business of education is regarded in a business light, is cared for by business methods, and is made subject to that simple but all-efficient law of a proper division of labor and of intelligent and efficient organization,—a division of labor which brings men who are students of the classics, of the sciences, of the literatures, of philosophy, of history, under the wise direction and imme-diate control of the man who is necessarily and most desirably a student of humanity; [and who is given] an authority entirely commensurate with his responsibility." For this writer, the research uni-versity's diversity of goals and subjects made top-down command more necessary than ever.

Not Just a Business

Yet most university leaders believed that the university could be businesslike and work with business while refusing to become a business. Individual units such as engineering might form partnerships, but the university as a whole would stand apart. The university had to serve the needs of the larger business community while offering training, services, and environments that business could never provide.

University leaders knew that they were preparing most of their students to enter the era's busi-ness system and often advertised this service. At Chicago, President William Rainey Harper wrote,

"No man who is acquainted with the facts will deny that today special opportunities of the highest rank, in business, are opening to men of college training." While business could use people of every educational level, the "college man" was equipped go beyond "business life" to possess a "business career." University training "is intended to develop in the man systematic habits; to give him control of his intellectual powers; to fit him in such a manner that he may be able to direct those powers successfully in any special direction."

These leaders also understood the premium that business placed on technical training, specialized expertise, and the capacity for change. In this respect, 1900 was hardly different from 2000. Capitalism is fundamentally dynamic, and big future earnings always lie in some "new" economy rather than in the old. University leaders generally accepted technology and change as the basic parameters of specialized knowledge. At the same time, they insisted that the university had a unique niche in the economy and played a unique role.

Presidents with otherwise different theories of education broadly agreed that the university was special. The liberal Eliot insisted that a university's "trustees are not themselves expert in any branch of the university" and should "always maintain a considerate and even deferential attitude towards the experts whom they employ." Eliot rejected the idea that a university could be treated like a market in which services are always for sale at the right price. The personal qualities of "a first-rate university teacher"—"quick sympathy, genuine good-will, patience, and comprehensive learning"—cannot be bought. At the University of Illinois, President Andrew S. Draper did call for a tight financial rein on faculty. "When teachers are not supported by student fees, but are paid from the university treasury without reference to the number of students they teach . . . there is no automatic way of getting rid of teachers who do not teach," But despite his conservatism, Draper admitted that "the university cannot become a business corporation, with a business corporation's ordinary implications. Such a corporation is without what is being called *spiritual aim*, is without moral methods . . . The distinguishing ear-marks of an American university are its moral purpose, its scientific aim, its unselfish public service, its inspirations to all men in all noble things, and its incorruptibility by commercialism."[17] Most presidents agreed that for the university to be useful to society or even to business, it would need to be something other than a business itself. It would have to combine technical training with the training in personal qualities like "quick sympathy, genuine good-will, patience, and comprehensive learning" that underwrote the transmission and creation of knowledge.

As the decades passed, university leaders became if anything more concerned with protecting the university's independence. The full-service university was engrossed in a web of constantly multiplying external entanglements. The stabilization of public funding after 1900 increased legislative involvement in campus politics. World War I brought new political pressures, including demands for political loyalty that cost many faculty their jobs. The interwar years systematized the funding of science by foundations, and World War II introduced the federal government as the new gorilla among external patrons. University administrations needed to combine solicitude and vigilance on a number of fronts at once.

In the early 1960s, President Clark Kerr at California offered a famous warning about the increasingly prosperous university's decreasing autonomy: "Federal support of scientific research during World War II," he wrote, has had a greater impact on higher education than any event since the land-grant movement was enshrined in the Morrill Act of 1862. Kerr detailed the ways in which an indirect form of "federal influence" operated through a nearly irresistible structure of financial opportunities to reduce "the authority of the department chairman, the dean, the president, [and] . . . faculty government." The research university had become a "federal grant university" in which direct state control was avoided in favor of a much more effective system of financial rewards and penalties. "The university, as Allen Wallis, president of the University of Rochester, has remarked, becomes to an extent a 'hotel.' The [federal granting] agency becomes the new alma mater. The research entrepreneur becomes a euphoric schizophrenic. . . . There are . . . especially acute problems when the agency insists on the tie-in sale (if we do this for you, then you must do this for us) or when it requires frequent and detailed progress reports. Then the university really is less than a free agent. It all becomes a kind of 'putting-out' system with the agency taking the place of the merchant-capitalist of old. Sweat shops have developed out of such a system in earlier times and in other industries." This is a harsh assessment of a federal partnership that was, after all, a cornerstone of UC's research prominence. But Kerr had come to feel that federal support had evolved into a shadow government. The early 1960s were arguably the summit of the research university's wealth and power, but it was at this moment that Kerr feared a systemic loss of independence.

Public criticism wasn't the only threat to university sovereignty: positive funding sources threatened it too. The purpose and identity of the research university were shaped through decades of self-defense against even the supportive attentions of business and government.

From Autocracy to Administration

University leaders generally believed in the university's special function and personnel, but they did not find models of conduct in pure craft work or the artistic personality. How would they be able to serve their social and corporate clientele while maintaining their distinctive functions and methods? Leaders were quite certain that the creation of new knowledge and the transmission of advanced skill required a kind of employee freedom not widely admired in business. The development of the technology that allowed Taylorization could not itself be Taylorized. Humanism could draw on both craft labor and artistic traditions for its own vision of the autonomous life that linked creation, thought, and labor. A similar concern for autonomy, however differently expressed, was driven by the university's interest in securing its own unique processes.

The compromise between autonomy and management appeared in the university's rejection of hard Taylorism. In the business world, Taylorism produced opposition in early "human relations" thought. By the 1920s, for example, Mary Parker Follett was arguing that management should replace command with "integration," in which the "desires [of both sides] have found a place," so that "neither side has had to sacrifice anything." Figures such as Elton Mayo and Kurt Lewin would continue the internal resistance to Taylorism into later decades. But years before the anti-Taylorist movement in management theory, many university leaders were denouncing autocratic management as an outdated practice. By the early years of the twentieth century Charles W. Eliot of Harvard had become emphatic on this point: "The president of a university should never exercise an autocratic or one-man power. He should be often an inventing and animating force, and often a leader; but not a ruler or autocrat. His success will be due more to powers of exposition and persuasion combined with persistent industry, than to any force of will or habit of command. Indeed, one-man power is always objectionable in a university, whether lodged in a president, secretary of the trustees, dean, or head of department. In order to make progress of a durable sort, the president will have to possess his soul in patience; and on that account a long tenure will be an advantage to him and to the university he serves." For Eliot, the president-as-ruler didn't fit with the structure of the modern university. About twenty years before liberal management theorists began to criticize autocratic Taylorism, Eliot was defining the leader as a coordinator, facilitator, and supporter.

The university was defining a modernization based on a structural diversity that autocracy couldn't manage. Laurence Veysey notes that universities were experiencing organizational modernity firsthand: "Both intellectually and in terms of its structure, the American university was becoming too diverse easily to define—or to control. The adherence of academic leaders to varying educational philosophies, the emergence of crystallized departments of learning, and the presence of larger number[s] of students all contributed to this result." Eliot was ahead of many of his peers in accepting diversity as systemic rather than deviant.

Autocracy was somewhat more workable in industry, where units could congeal around common functions and measurable outputs. But industry's concern with efficiency also inspired systemic approaches that supplanted and partially replaced the autocrat at the top. In the late nineteenth century, business had discovered that mechanization required more rather than less management; "scientific management" arose to deal with complex coordination problems in operations, ones that the most powerful individual could not solve. Even in industry, autocracy had its limits.

The university was a more complex case, for it was a collection of often unrelated disciplines, projects, and research techniques that lacked the common culture of either the small college or the industrial firm. Unlike the college, the university could presume neither a common purpose nor a set of unifying psychological identifications. Unlike industry, the university could not aspire to tight functional integration. The university was also unable to use the accounting and operational techniques that increased integration in industry. The result made administration vitally important to the university's function. As Veysey put it, "Bureaucratic administration was the structural device which made possible the new epoch of institutional empire-building without recourse to specific shared values . . . Techniques of control shifted from the sermon and the direct threat of punishment toward the more appropriate devices of conference, memorandum, and filing system . . . the multiplicity of cleavages demanded a general submission to regulation, from top to bottom, if all vestiges of order were not to disappear. Bureaucratic codes of conduct serves as a low but tolerable common denominator, linking individuals and factions who did not think in the same terms but who, unlike the students of the 1860's, were usually too polite to require threats." By 1910, bureaucracy had become the research university's standard infrastructure. It was a disjointed bureaucracy, a collection of fragments linked indirectly. In this disarticulation, university administration would find its liberalism. To succeed within it, administrators would need managerial skill rather than collegial familiarity or autocratic strength.

The Meaning of Management

The term "management" has never been widely accepted as applying to universities, but in reality it described key practices of university administration.

Management is a common but complicated word. The English term comes through several steps from the Latin word for "to handle," as in handling horses (which in turn derived from *manus*, "hand"). By extension it generally implied the training and supervising of something of lower capacity. Only after World War II did "management" come to mean the handling of people in *organizations, and the handling of systems and processes along with them.* "Administration" was used far earlier, and remains dominant in universities.

The first fact about management, then, is that it refers to the "right disposition of things" in a *differentiated system* or *"economy."* In this way, it is another word for what the historian and philosopher Michel Foucault called the "art of government." Government, he wrote, initially referred to the governance of a family and all its various members. Government seeks "an end which is 'convenient' for each of the things that are to be governed." Government gradually transferred practices that managed the household to the management of the state. Its goals exist in a "complex composed of people and things," and these goals, and the relations through which they are produced, are invariably plural. Government is bound up in reciprocal ties and multilateral influence, no matter how unequal. The "things with which in this sense government is to be concerned are in fact men, but men in their relations, their links, their imbrication with those other things which are wealth, resources, means of subsistence, the territory with its specific qualities, climate, irrigation, fertility, etc.; men in their relation to that other kind of things, customs, habits, ways of acting and thinking . . . accidents and misfortunes." Management exists to regulate and coordinate a system that consists of disparate elements, dynamic relations, and multiple ends.

Foucault described a second crucial feature of management. The art of government departs from an older notion of authority as sovereignty, embodied in the prince. "The prince stood in a relation of singularity and externality, and thus of transcendence, to his principality." The goal of exercising power is for the prince to maintain a relation of control to what he owns. Under the sovereign, subjects and objects must obey the law that descends from the sovereign power. "The end of sovereignty," Foucault wrote, "is in sum nothing other than submission to sovereignty." "On the contrary," he continues, "with government it is a question not of imposing law on men, but of disposing things: that is to say, of employing tactics rather than laws . . .—to arrange things in such a way that, through a certain number of means, such and such ends may be achieved." The art of government evolved into political science as it confronted the question of "populations," of masses and the inevitable failure of singular, top-down decrees. Government aims at *prosperity* in the broadest sense—at maximizing desirable outputs while maintaining order.

Taking these two features together, we can see that management expresses two major structural aspects of the rising research university. It is decentralized, having diverse elements that must be coordinated yet not assimilated. And it favors (ostensibly neutral) coordination over the commands of a sovereign. Management is theoretically a *post-sovereignty* form of authority. It is also the range of techniques that would allow the fully systematic coordination sought by industrial engineers.

The key word is *theoretically*: sovereignty is rarely abandoned in managerial practice. As Foucault observed, "sovereignty is far from being eliminated by the emergence of a new art of government, even by one which has passed the threshold of political science; on the contrary, the problem of sovereignty is made more acute than ever." Management in practice refers to a hybrid situation in which sovereignty has been complicated rather than eliminated. Power has been decentralized and dispersed in managerial systems, and changes as it moves from level to level and point to point. But much power remains "transcendental" or external to its sites of application. In my usage, the term "management" refers to this *mixed* situation of decentralized structures combined with authority that does circulate horizontally and indirectly but predominantly from the top down.

Faculty as Labor

Speaking abstractly, universities developed a liberal version of available management options. University administration revolved around strong personalities while taking on the major, consistent features of business management. It was hierarchical. It yoked personal relations to explicit, impersonal procedures, procedures which treated individual exceptions as anomalous. Official authority arose from the office rather than from the person. This person, in theory, functioned through his or her specialized expertise. He or she held personal power to the degree to which expertise fit with the larger structure. Finally, the system decentralized power without eliminating the nonconsensual control of superiors over inferiors, that is, without eliminating sovereignty.

The university has had an orthodox chain of command. It had trustees and a president at the top, provosts and deans next, then heads or chairs of departments, rank-and-file faculty, staff, graduate students, and undergraduates. This academic staff was accompanied by a parallel business staff, marked, as Veysey notes, by "its own internal gradations. . . . Generally speaking, power flowed downward throughout this entire organization." Certain faculty wielded what Weber called "charismatic" influence that could override bureaucratic structure and procedure, but only temporarily. Top-down power governed policy making and major decisions. Well before World War I, the term "administration" came to refer to "the president, deans, business staff, and often to a number of senior professors who regularly supported the president's wishes." This group also shared a distinct "state of mind" that had them charging themselves with institutional custody and planning.

Administration was open to selected, individual members of the faculty. The existence within every faculty of a semi-flexible subset of leaders has sometimes been used to suggest that managerial forms do not apply to faculty governance. But disproportionate personal power was fully compatible with managerial procedure. For every junior person who obtained power or resources, there was a senior faculty member or administrator that had exercised an authority to give those things. The senior giver retained sufficient sovereignty to be the source of the gift, which was what distinctive resources generally remained.

As a group, faculty were subordinate to the administrative system. Faculty leadership generally lay with a few trusted "senior" professors rather than with the faculty as a whole or with their legislatures, whose power was generally limited. Even the most influential faculty members, lacking an administrative post, spoke for "the faculty" rather than for the institution as a whole, which was spoken for by the administration. The university's business operations were separated from academic operations, such that the faculty as a whole had negligible input into financial planning and management.

The individual faculty member who lacked important political alliances was powerless and even vulnerable. It wasn't until after World War II that faculty tenure was regularized: for example, the University of California had no formal tenure until 1958. Faculty served in decision-making positions more or less at the pleasure of the administration. The professional standing of faculty did not so much increase their authority as ratify their status as skilled employees. The subordinate position of faculty "was revealed by the fact that whenever an insurgent movement to 'democratize' the structure of an institution took place, it was described as a revolt.'" "The professor had his own quite real dignity," Veysey assures us, "but it was apt to become most apparent when he sat in his book-lined study, not when he met for formal discussions of policy."

Faculty belonged to the professional middle class, and yet they occupied the *position* of labor. Faculty were distinct from and subordinate to management, which retained limited but real authority over their individual affairs. Faculty were sequestered from the business end of the university. When faculty sought authority over the institution as a whole, the move was viewed as it would have been in industry—as insurrection. This system of management was liberal, in the sense that daily faculty labor was not closely supervised, and individuals had the kind of control over the content of their work associated with artisans and professionals. But this individual autonomy did not change the facts of institutional power.

Faculty often contrasted themselves with nonacademic staff, and this contrast allowed them to see themselves as something other than labor in the sense of the clerical, administrative, technical, and facilities workers who kept the university running. Faculty proclaimed their operating principles of collegiality and consent, their research pursued in a "community of scholars," and their teaching as a "high calling." They asserted control over the curriculum and similar matters, and retained many guild privileges by comparison to nonacademic staff. Faculty also retained enormous *supervisory* responsibility. Faculty acted as supervisors to the lowest-status academic workers known as students. Faculty in effect worked on the shop floor, face to face with the students who played the role of "frontline" personnel.

We might therefore think of university faculty as a special kind of "labor aristocracy." Faculty had real control over their individual work and local supervisory authority. But this did not allow faculty *as a group* to wield decision-making power. Faculty occupied a contradictory class location, owning and not owning their academic capital, managing and being managed by turns.

Divided Governance

The underlying reality of the faculty's position as labor was both embodied and concealed by the university's dual management system. The business side generally adapted the corporate look of its particular era, drawing on the practices and the personnel of the business world. The academic side depended on craft skills that remained in the possession of individual faculty. Some academic functions, like lower-division humanities teaching, could be done with untenured labor and be directly controlled by administrators. Other academic functions, like complex and costly scientific research, were utterly beyond the capability of administrators and remained in faculty hands. In spite of constant interaction and negotiation between administrators and faculty, their spheres remained distinct. This meant a reciprocal hands-off ethic, and it also meant, to repeat, the faculty's general exclusion from direct managerial power.

In the absence of this kind of power, how did the faculty protect their positions? The general solution has been a dual system of governance that has sometimes been called "shared governance." Much emphasis was placed on faculty control of academic matters and their right of consultation on policy issues. When it was working normally, a more descriptive term would be *divided governance*. Much of the faculty's sense of freedom and protection depended on the maintenance of this structural division.

Divided governance originally emerged from profound concerns about academic freedom. At the University of California, increasing anger among the faculty at the interventions of President Benjamin Wheeler culminated in the faculty "revolt" of 1919–20, which created UC's Academic Senate. Not far down the road, Mrs. Leland Stanford aroused national attention in 1915 when she got the economist Edward Ross fired for his views on the gold standard. As the century wore on, academic legislatures at various universities, along with the American Association of University Professors, sought to reinforce academic freedom by splitting academics from administration.

As the century advanced, divided governance became the bedrock of academic freedom. In a study based on faculty interviews, Burton R. Clark found that most assumed a clear distinction between business and academic affairs. "The flowering of white-collar bureaucracy [is] largely on the side of 'business' affairs—finance, purchasing, accounting, property management, transportation—and such operations as 'student personnel services.'" On the academic side, "professors look at alternative technologies and decide what is best for their needs. Collectively, they decide on production and distribution, and whether to innovate or continue with the old." Though they had little control over business, faculty members said, they had direct control over academics, which they could prevent from being driven by procedural and financial concerns. But this perception was largely the result of divided governance itself. It was the division that allowed academics to fulfill the wish of most faculty members for the autonomy of their professional sphere. In reality, the larger determinants of academic life were political and financial and, as in other organizations, beyond their reach.

After World War I, some version of divided governance gradually formalized a boundary between educational and business affairs. Business considerations exerted steady pressure on educational policy, but the boundary did correspond to what was in and out of the faculty member's power. She was left with two kinds of freedom: the freedom to manage her individual academic and professional concerns, and the freedom to avoid management contexts where she would be powerless. Faculty were labor within the overall administrative context. They were managers and self-employed professionals in their academic domain. Academic management avoided the Taylorization of its academic functions, but it did this less by democratizing than by dividing authority. Faculty had local and specific craft freedoms in the quasi-private spaces that they sheltered from general management.

Bureaucracy or Democracy

Many faculty have thrived under divided governance. They've had plenty of freedom to do their own work, and they know that they have more personal freedom than they would in nearly any other job. The system has worked particularly well in the sciences, where the university has long served as a kind of communal infrastructure underwriting faculty entrepreneurs. But there are some built-in costs to this kind of freedom, costs that are often overlooked. I'll discuss three of them: a preference for bureaucracy over democracy, a permanent vulnerability to business influence, and a weakening of individual agency.

Most faculty members were inclined toward spending their time in the classroom and lab, where they had freedom and influence, rather than in the larger institution, where they had little of either. They became cynical about mechanisms of participation, like academic senates that spend enormous time ratifying or slightly modifying decisions already made by administrators. Studies have shown that white-collar workers as a whole, when suddenly given authority in contexts where it had long been denied, have difficulty believing in their own authority. Sometimes they have good reason. Their freedom depends on customary protections and guild privileges that are strengthened by a cumbersome bureaucracy. Most faculty members experience university administration less as a system of governance or coordination than as a kind of bomb shelter: the more rigid and dug-in it is, the more secure they are. Whatever their stated politics or personal temperament, most faculty members are invested in a bureaucratic system whose inefficiencies sponsor their academic freedom. Veysey is especially eloquent on this subject:

> The bureaucratic apparatus . . . became a buffer which protected the isolation of the individuals and the small factions on each campus. Thus if the maze of officials and committees grew sufficiently complex, the whole machinery might screen the faculty member from the administration. Surrounded by politely affirmative deans and committees, the university president gradually lost touch with what was going on in "his" classrooms. This could mean that the professor, as long as he avoided sensationalism, became in practice relatively free of intrusion. One speculates that a large measure of academic freedom came about in just such an unintended way.

Freedom from intrusion required a certain refusal of intervention:

> The university throve, as it were, on ignorance. Or, if this way of stating it seems unnecessarily paradoxical, the university throve on the patterned isolation of its component parts, and this isolation required that people continually talk past each other, failing to listen to what others were actually saying. This lack of comprehension, which safeguards one's privacy and one's illusions, doubtless occurs in many groups, but it may be of special importance in explaining the otherwise unfathomable behavior of a society's most intelligent members.

Academic bureaucracy preserves freedom by offering places to hide. This freedom is generally thought to outweigh the ignorance, the errors, even the tacit hostility that circulate in a system predicated on internal exile.

Veysey is describing the situation in 1910, but the next half-century did little but consolidate this management system. Writing at its high point in 1963, President Clark Kerr of UC focused on the power this system had on even its radical members:

> The individual faculty member, and particularly the political liberal of the faculty, is often torn between the "guild" and the "socialist" views of the university. The guild view stands for self-determination, and for resistance against the administration and the trustees; the socialist view, for service to society which the administration and the trustees often represent. The guild view is elitist toward the external environment, conservative toward internal change, conformist in relation to the opinion of colleagues. The socialist view is democratic toward society, radical towards change, and nonconformist. And the political liberal is drawn toward both views. Here is a paradox. Few institutions are so conservative as the universities about their own affairs while their members are so liberal about the affairs of others; and sometimes the most liberal faculty member in one context is the most conservative in another. . . . When change comes it is rarely at the instigation of [the faculty] as a collective body. The group is more likely to accept or reject or comment, than to devise and propose. The group serves a purpose as a balance wheel. . . . The individual faculty member seeking something new has, in turn, often found his greatest encouragement and leverage coming from the outside; the individual scholar is the inventor, the outside agency the force for innovation. . . . Change comes more through spawning the new than reforming the old.

Faculty express their allegiance to bureaucracy through guild conservatism. The freedom of individual faculty becomes dependent on institutional inertia. In contrast, democratic activity threatens freedom by disrupting protective procedure. After 1980 this situation began to change, as individual faculty members, mostly in science and engineering, became increasingly interested in industry partnerships and start-up companies. But this later assault on a formerly protective university bureaucracy did not fly the flag of faculty democracy, but the flag of individual freedom of contract with commercial sponsors. Over time, academic democracy became the implied enemy of academic freedom.

Commercial Vulnerability

The second cost of divided governance appears when we ask this question: if academic freedom depends on withdrawal from general management, what happens when external forces attempt to exert influence?

Most academic fields long ago agreed to remain outsiders on the business side. The active faculty who had administrative power held it through the daily grind in their official positions. The faculty majority lacked detailed information and expertise, and would get involved only by playing one of the roles that bureaucracy is least likely to respect: that of protestor or individual exception. This might not have been such a bad thing if managers and academics had equal status. But managers and academics were not equals. The business environment had the upper hand exactly where faculty had no hand at all.

The university's business side has always appealed to the market power of the consumer. Burton Clark has nicely summarized the problem this poses for universities:

> Sociologists have observed that the social control of expert services may primarily center in professional self-control, governmental-bureaucratic control, or client-consumer control. In American academia, with its pushing back of governmental control and its localization of bureaucrats, the contest comes down primarily to peer-based versus client-based authority, with the latter expressed through organizational management. As they interpret and implement "demand," and sometimes actively shape it, administrators become the active proxies of consumers. In certain institutional locales, their immediate interpretations of service to clientele become controlling: faculty labor trails along, more other- than inner-driven. But in other major settings, the faculty clearly lead, field by field, taking cues from peers and converting administrators to the fiction that "the faculty is the institution." What we find in academic authority in America depends on where we look in the institutional hierarchy.

Although faculty have possessed much "professional self-control," they could be overridden by the administration's built-in power to trump professional concerns with customer needs.

We can make this point in somewhat different terms. Faculty seemed most free to define their work in élite and research contexts where the student customer was subordinate. Where responding to the student customer was primary, it was clear that faculty were not the lead interpreters and definers of customer needs. Research faculty did not control their customers either. They just attended more to one group of customers, external funders, than to the other, their students. Faculty had ceded most institutional governance of self-government to agencies and administrators who were in fact not their democratic proxies. In doing so, the faculty lost most of their control of their markets by World War I. Markets were controlled (defined and interpreted) by agencies and administrators, especially in large public universities, and the faculty were only one among their many constituents.

Corporate Individualism

A third and related cost of divided governance was the restriction of individual agency. By 1900, Veysey writes, "most professors were too contented and the structure of the university had already become too firmly established for basic changes in the distribution of power to be made. The movement for faculty control, unlike the main effort toward academic freedom, became a dated curiosity of the Progressive period. Except for producing some unwieldy academic 'senates' and for encouraging somewhat greater departmental autonomy in the area of appointments, it bore little substantial fruit." In the absence of collective control, individual faculty pursued a prudential care of the self. Hannah Arendt identifies this tendency with Epictetus, who shows that "a man is free if he limits himself to what is in his power, if he does not reach into a realm where he can be hindered. The 'science of living' consists in knowing how to distinguish between the alien world over which man has no power and the self of which he may dispose as he sees fit." There is of course practical wisdom in this: avoid hindrance by ruling in the classroom but not the department, or in the English department but not in the humanities division, or in the humanities but not in the college and so on. This kind of individualism is suited to a republic of scattered estates, where each protects his independence by refusing to interfere with that of others. The fragmented university had a superficial resemblance to exactly that kind of country, with departments ruling themselves but not their neighbors, each on its own freehold.

The psychological impact of this system must also be acknowledged. One of the best studies of white-collar consciousness in bureaucratic systems is that of Charles Heckscher, whose work on downsized corporations in the 1980s and 1990s offers some parallels with faculty reactions in earlier periods. He describes the initial reaction to crisis of middle-class, mid-level employees as "schizophrenia," in which "people alternately and almost in the same breath would express anger at management, hope that the leadership would rescue them, frustration at change, and willingness to suspend judgment." When the intensity of the crisis began to fade, people withdrew "into a cautious individualism. . . . People merely gave up trying to make immediate sense of the situation or to save the company, and focused instead on doing their own jobs well." Often this would be resolved with a "retreat to autonomy." At no point, even when enlisted by upper management, did employees translate their autonomy into an ability to exert leadership in groups.

A similar pattern marked university crises from the start. Faculty members' participation drastically increased in crises, but was rarely sustained. Their participation often lacked the skill, informal knowledge, and determined patience that comes only with daily experience. The faculty tacitly assumed its own belated or secondary status, and except in extreme cases deferred to administrators. Such interventions for the most part confirmed the hierarchical nature of university authority and the rank-and-file faculty member's outsider status within his own institutional politics. Such interventions did not endow faculty members with a sense that their individual perspectives have relevance to the governing of the larger system. Freedom continued to depend on withdrawal from conflict rather than on exerting one's will through it. Freedom did not mean the freedom to revise the social processes in which one's university life was passing. It did not mean opening up Epictetus's boundary between one's freedom and hindrance into democratic participation. Individual agency instead depended on maintaining a détente with bureaucratic inertia.

An autonomy that depends on a routine powerlessness forms what I've elsewhere called "submissive individualism." Public areas of personal action and sovereignty were often abandoned, and this loss of sovereignty had a direct payoff in personal liberty. But this wasn't simply a reasonable liberty, a liberty that knew its own limits. It was a liberty mixed with frustration at its ineffectuality in local as well as large organizational matters. Autonomy was not translating into self-determination over general administrative matters, which were part of a separate and parallel governing system, one that could steer the professional and academic activities that claimed to be beyond its reach.

The university has helped to define professional life in the terms of a somewhat demoralizing compromise. The university agreed that brain work required individual autonomy: Taylorization would not work. At the same time, the university would not support the brain worker's institutional agency. As in industry, the care of the organization would remain in the hands of upper management. Individual conditions were a private matter: freedom was pursued in private (the study, the classroom, the laboratory); collective placement derived not from collective life but from individual performance. The goal of craft work was not a public life based on the principles of freedom, experience, and other aspects of individuality cherished by both liberal humanist and free labor traditions. The goal of craft work was increasingly privatized self-development, motives housed in the structure of individual upward mobility for which the university stood. Upward mobility, in turn, allowed more effective opting out of collective life, defining freedom as a retreat from the collective and tying craft labor to this diminished version. Free labor, that is, became contingent on the shrinking of the individual's agency to his or her sphere of direct influence. Faculty members were Romanized, resembling not so much republican citizens as landowning stoics living under a benign despotism that they could afford to ignore.

Downsizing Individual Agency

The research university "solved" the contradiction in managerial systems between the retaining and the giving up of top-down sovereignty, but did so by splitting its system in two. Faculty members continued to insist on freedom of intellectual inquiry, but preserved it by separating from management rather than by making management their own.

This was convenient to both sides, which has helped the arrangement to endure. But divided governance also helped to reduce the professional middle class's interest in democratic governance. Faculty long ago grew accustomed to the absence of a rewarding democratic experience in their professional life, and to see this absence as protective. Faculty autonomy, in short, became equivalent to a classical, negative form of freedom—freedom from overt coercion—in the very period during which system management, ruling with muted coercion, was making this kind of freedom less effective. Craft labor was central to professional life. At the same time, it was not part of the university's institutional life. The availability of autonomy and craft labor, particularly in the humanities, continued to be associated with a retreat from active management of the commercial forces that support the university. Faculty free labor had come to depend, practically speaking, on the eclipse of democratic processes by a hierarchical bureaucracy abundantly furnished with hiding places.

Faculty members were unable to associate knowledge with democracy. They were equally unable to associate knowledge with their own free agency. The public regarded academic freedom as a workplace perquisite, a reward for having valid knowledge rather than knowledge's cause: good working conditions were a benefit for faculty who produced a unique kind of bankable productivity. The faculty did not, by and large, proclaim autonomous craft labor to be the fountainhead of creativity and progress. They couldn't make the strong case, in the face of regular public doubts, that technological and cultural advantage depended on radical imaginative freedom, wild speculation, unfettered experimentation, the capacity to think about anything, the ability to dream awake. Academic freedom was espoused as the university's special creed, a kind of cultural value that pluralists should respect, but it was not made the source of the university's capacity to fulfill its public missions.

As the university became increasingly well managed, it felt less need for these two traditional virtues of emancipated societies. It sidestepped democratic governance, and it downplayed individual agency. The research university was not a holdout from the "administered world." Its social effect, instead, was to reconcile such a world with the humanist self-image of the professional-managerial class.

Humanist ideals endured nonetheless. The humanities were still associated with the knowledge that taught freedom as well as tradition. It housed knowledges of oneself, and of oneself in formation, and of oneself moving through various social worlds. The humanities were tied to the experience of unfettered interest, and with free labor expressed (partially concealed) as artistic creation. They sustained feelings of enjoyment, by which I mean the *experience* of freedom. The humanities sustained an enjoyment that could exist *within* the collective systems that we call the corporation, culture, and history. The humanities meant historical knowledge and traditional values. They also meant the possibility of free agency and free labor in spite of or because of everything that is known about the constraints of social life.

In this context, would the humanities disciplines "humanize" and transform management? Would they be managed in turn? Would they create some hybrids of freedom in group life that had not been known before?

CHAPTER 6

COLLEGES & NORMAL SCHOOLS

THE ERA OF MULTIPURPOSE COLLEGES IN AMERICAN HIGHER EDUCATION, 1850–1890

ROGER L. GEIGER

The decade of the 1890s in American higher education is properly seen as marking the "Emergence of the American University." Stanford opened in 1891 and the University of Chicago the following year, touching off what Laurence Veysey called "the academic boom of the early nineties." Even Harvard president Charles Eliot, a longtime skeptic, was finally ready to admit the American university had become a reality. But if the future lay with these new educational enterprises, they were still the exceptions as that fateful decade began. In 1890 the majority of students attended denominational colleges, the number of these colleges was still growing, and the majority of men and women students attended single-sex colleges. By 1900 none of this would still be true. The rise of universities and the pressures of standardization displaced the traditional American college from its accustomed central role. The 1890s—more precisely the first half of that decade—thus stand as a major turning point in the evolution of American higher education.

The historiography of American higher education has, not unnaturally, emphasized the rising new elements—research, graduate education, the new disciplinary knowledge base. This study takes the opposite approach. It seeks to explore the "old order" that began to form as early as the 1850s and found itself in a deepening crisis after 1890. More than antiquarian curiosity motivates this inquiry; these developments constitute an unwritten chapter in the history of American higher education.

For the generation following the Civil War, the denominational college was still the characteristic institution of higher education. This institution, however, could no longer be equated with the "oldtime" classical college. The majority of existing colleges (and almost all newly founded ones) implemented some or all of the items on a standard menu of innovations: nonclassical degree courses (bachelor's of science, letters, literature, or philosophy), partial courses for part-time students, varying numbers of electives, and coeducation. In addition, significant numbers of colleges innovated further by entering entirely new markets: the education of teachers; separate schools of science, engineering, or agriculture; and short courses for commercial subjects. Further linkages were forged—and broken—with professional schools of theology, law, or medicine. The modal institution of higher education thus existed in a fluid educational marketplace in which it competed not only with other colleges, but also with other types of schools, including high schools, normal schools, institutes of technology, and commercial colleges. In a time of accelerating educational change, the colleges were forced to make crucial decisions about how to use their generally meager resources to achieve a mix of offerings that would meet the needs of sponsors, traditional constituencies, potential new students, and their own treasuries.

This institution—the multipurpose college—is the missing link in the evolution of American higher education. By the 1850s, many of the country's colleges were expanding the scope of their offerings and assuming such a guise, even as classical colleges of the traditional type continued to be founded. In the succeeding decades, the balance turned decisively in favor of multipurpose colleges (which also describes the new state universities). New and old colleges adapted their degree courses in the face of an expanding academic knowledge base, eclectic student constituencies, and emerging markets for practical, vocational skills. The pace of change varied by institution as well as across regions. However, the inflection point of the early 1890s signaled the onset of a pervasive crisis for these colleges.

In economic terms, the crisis had to do with economies of scale and scope. As these economies began to yield huge payoffs after 1890 for the expanding universities, they essentially ceased to work to the advantage of the smaller multipurpose colleges. The colleges consequently had to redefine their missions, a process fraught with internal conflict and instability. The resolution of the crisis of the 1890s was a long-term development by which the colleges gradually conformed to one of several viable models. Overall, however, they had to assume a new, complementary role as a component rather than the centerpiece of American higher education.

The analysis of this transitional era will start at the endpoint rather than the beginning for two tactical reasons. First, while the denouement definitely lies in the 1890s, its origins are diffuse. Thus, identifying and charting the elements of higher education in this era is an analytical task in itself. Second, abundant data for the later years are available in the annual *Reports of the Commissioner of Education* (RCE). Judiciously interpreted, these data provide a relatively solid depiction of the essential features of the educational system as it was perceived by contemporaries. This foundation, then, permits the structuring of more fragmentary and eclectic information about earlier decades.

"Higher Instruction" in the 1880s

The Bureau of Education was created in 1866, and by 1870 it was able to compile and report statistics for colleges (including women's colleges) and professional schools. It identified 369 colleges, but it noted that "there is very little known" about 80 of them. During that decade, higher education grew considerably, as did the completeness of the data that institutions supplied to the bureau. By 1880, a credible depiction of the entire system was available, even if certain details remained elusive. A decade later this information was being reported in voluminous detail, and the inevitable omissions were largely marginal institutions. The contours of the system can thus be depicted with some confidence for the 1880s (see Table 1).

The many categories of Table 1 are part of its message. Just as the terms employed today, such as *postsecondary* and *research university,* reflect the nature and structure of our current system, the different institutions enumerated by the bureau mirrored realities of that day. Here, though, relations among the parts are more amorphous. Universities, for example, reported separately as colleges, scientific schools, and various professional schools. The different categories of institutions overlapped in some respects, as did the activities they represented.

A relatively fixed point in this array was the undergraduate programs of degree-granting colleges and universities. But land-grant colleges were recorded both separately and as parts of universities, and non-land-grant schools of science were listed apart. Colleges for women generally possessed the right to grant degrees, but contemporaries regarded most of them as inferior, often straddling secondary education in their offerings. Professional schools were more alternatives to colleges than destinations for graduates. Normal schools were clearly below college grade at this date, but some teachers were also trained in high schools and in colleges. Academies, on the other hand, were relegated to secondary education, although they sometimes taught portions of the college curriculum. Given this tangled picture, the Bureau of Education merely tabulated institutions within categories that were self-evident to contemporaries.

The figures in Table 1, imperfect as they are, reveal a significant dynamic. The number of students in all colleges and professional schools grew barely more than the increase in the 15- to 19-year-old population (+30.9 percent). Graduate and professional school enrollments all expanded at a greater rate, accounting for about 11,000 of the 24,000 additional students. The numbers of normal students and those taking business courses (although not part of higher education) also grew relative to the population. Only collegiate enrollments lagged. A closer look reveals a more intriguing finding: when the male/female breakdown is estimated, the number of women in coeducational colleges increased by more than 80 percent, but male undergraduates merely matched population growth. Even preparatory students in these institutions increased by 51 percent. Thus, Americans in the 1880s increased their relative commitment to advanced education in most every category save male undergraduates, traditionally the staple of the American college.

TABLE 1
Institutions and Enrollments in Higher Education, 1879–1880 & 1889–1890

Type	1879–1880		1889–1890	
	Institutions	Students	Institutions	Students
Colleges & Universities (UG)	364	32,142	415	44,414
Resident Graduates, C&U		411		1,717
Schools of Science/Technology (inc. Land Grants)	80	*6,637	63	**7,577
Colleges for Women	227	11,626	179	11,992
SUBTOTAL		50,816		65,700
Schools of Theology	142	5,242	145	7,013
Schools of Law	48	3,134	54	4,518
Medicine		14,006		20,714
Regular	72	9,876	93	13,521
Eclectic	6	833	9	719
Homeopath	12	1,220	14	1,020
Dental	16	730	27	2,643
Pharmacy	14	1,347	30	2,811
TOTAL HI ED ENROLLMENTS		73,198		97,945
Normal Schools, Teaching Programs		25,736		34,814
Commercial Colleges	162	27,146	263	78,920
Population, 15–19		5,011,400		6,557,600
HI ED Enrollments		1.46%		1.49%

*adjusted
**adjusted for double counting

Population Dynamics of the Colleges

No convention governed the nomenclature of the central institutions of American higher education—universities and colleges. While some of the "universities" possessed the same professional faculties that were the hallmark of those institutions in Europe, others taught only at the collegiate level. Most colleges, on the other hand, consisted of more than one part. Except in the Northeast, the great majority maintained preparatory departments, which in 1890 enrolled just 5,000 fewer students (39, 415) than the colleges proper. There was one clear standard for the college course—four years of graded study in Latin, Greek, mathematics, science, and philosophy, leading to an A.B. degree. But a closer look discloses a vagueness about its beginning, duration, and end. Students were admitted according to their proficiency, so that those with strong training entered the sophomore, junior, or even senior classes. One of the liveliest questions of the day concerned the possible shortening of the college course (discussed below). Catholic colleges, on the other hand, considered "college" to consist of an unbroken six- or seven-year course. Nor was it evident why students should persist to graduation, since there was nothing that could be done with a bachelor's degree that could not also be done without one. The term *college* in the latter nineteenth century conjured up definite images, but the actual permutations of this ideal were many and varied.

The "universities and colleges" reported in the RCE were either male or coeducational (women's colleges being a separate category). In 1890, the majority of men enrolled in single-sex institutions, as did their female counterparts. This situation was not destined to persist: gender separation was the rule along the populous eastern seaboard, but throughout the country, nearly two-thirds of the colleges were coeducational. An even larger proportion were associated with a denomination. Just 99 of the 415 colleges in Table 1 lacked formal church ties, and roughly half of those were publicly controlled. In contrast, 74 colleges were associated with some form of Methodism. Roman Catholics operated the next largest number of colleges (51), but this was a particularly volatile group that should be considered a sector in itself (see below). For Protestant colleges, sectarian doctrines were presumed to be banished from the curriculum, and the influence of the church, exerted through president and trustees, varied from traditional association to outright ownership. For all these colleges, however, daily chapel and a religious ambiance were ubiquitous traits of college life. The colleges of 1890 were remarkably young: the majority of institutions in Table 1 were less than thirty years old.

The latter decades of the nineteenth century, far more than the antebellum years, were the era of proliferating colleges. Any effort to enumerate college foundings, however, confronts an imposing obstacle: many of these institutions were discontinuous—in function (operating level), operations, name, and/or location. Precision is thus an impossibility. Table 2 represents a conservative estimate of when and where colleges appeared.

According to Colin Burke, 50 new colleges opened in the 1830s and enrollments grew by 79 percent. The 1840s experienced a lull that produced only 29 new colleges while enrollments virtually stagnated (+19 percent). The 1850s then witnessed the largest antebellum net increase of colleges (73) and substantial enrollment growth as well (67 percent). Table 2 reveals that the dynamics of the 1850s persisted through the next decade, apparently unfazed by the Civil War. The founding of new colleges continued at a lesser but still robust pace for the next two decades, even though enrollment growth probably slowed in the 1870s.

TABLE 2
College Foundings, by Region, 1850s to 1890s

	1850s	1860s 1850–1900	1870s	1880s	1890s 1850	Total Founded	Total 1900	Founded before
New England	1	2	1	2	1	7	22	11
Mid-Atlantic	11	14	7	2	2	41	72	26
South Atlantic	8	6	7	11	6	38	63	21
North Central	28	20	14	6	6	74	96	34
South Central	9	14	12	3	4	42	57	22
West Central	21	24	13	34	20	112	121	8
Western	6	12	7	11	12	48	42	4
TOTALS	84	92	61	69	51	357	473	131
Burke, ACP	88							129
Technical Colleges	1	9	8	9	11		43	5

Sources: 1850s–1870s: RCE, 1880;
1880s: RCE, 1895;
1890s, Total 1900, Technical Colleges: RCE, 1900;
Colin Burke, *American Collegiate Populations*, 15–17.

Viewed in this way, the period from about 1850 to 1890 constitutes a distinct era in American higher education. Its hallmark was the proliferation of colleges at nearly as rapid a rate as student enrollments (Table 3).

Three aspects of this situation are noteworthy. First, although traditional historical treatments of this period emphasize the major new departures in higher education—MIT, Cornell, Johns Hopkins, Eliot's Harvard—the vast majority of new institutions were denominational colleges. Second, the relative stability in average size indicates that the educational technology or modus operandi of the colleges was—again, for the vast majority—largely fixed. Third, the shape traced by the increase in the number of colleges is that of a logistic curve (Figure 1). That is, exponential growth during the 1850s and 1860s gave way to decelerating growth in the following decades, and ceased altogether after 1893—the peak year for traditional colleges. This pattern occurs when the conditions responsible for growth are, in the first phase, self-reinforcing, and in the second phase, self-limiting.

What happened during this era, in the most general terms, was that a variant of the classical college—the multipurpose college—encountered geographical and religious conditions that induced exponential growth during the 1850s and 1860s but became increasingly restrictive thereafter. The potential for growth was entirely exhausted after 1890, when conditions favored the expansion of different kinds of institutions and produced a crisis for the old order of multipurpose colleges.

The growth of colleges after the Civil War, it might be argued, was affected by exogenous events such as the Morrill Act (1862) and the establishment of the historically black colleges (HBCs) for freedmen in the South. Both effects turned out to be small, however. Before 1890, the Morrill land grants and the formation of new western states produced only 15 additional flagship universities (plus Cornell) classified with the colleges. All of these institutions can be considered smaller or larger versions of multipurpose colleges, differing chiefly in lacking denominational ties and, by the end of this period, in possibly receiving public support. Only 3 of them—the Universities of California, Minnesota, and Illinois—counted more than 300 college students in 1890.

Most other public, land-grant colleges were classified during this era with the schools of science. Here a different dynamic prevailed. A linear pattern of steady expansion is evident in Table 2. As for the HBCs, 20 of these colleges were operating by 1890. They nevertheless fit the profile of denominational provision of higher education to underserved populations. Inherently multipurpose, they had only small collegiate enrollments in 1890 (averaging 26). In addition, one might note the founding of "idiosyncratic" institutions in this era—the University of Cincinnati, Johns Hopkins, and Clark. There nevertheless remains a fundamental underlying pattern of logistic growth of, overwhelmingly, denominational colleges.

The distribution of college foundings presented in Table 2 is the product of the interaction of geographical and denominational factors. Geographically, colleges followed settlers into the trans-Mississippi West, but they also increased in density in many settled areas. Two different processes were involved—"extension" and "elaboration" of the collegiate matrix—propelled by the interests of different sets of churches.

The extension of colleges across the trans-Mississippi West resembled in some ways the push across the Appalachians a generation earlier. A difference was that the education of ministers was less urgent a consideration in this era, that task being largely fulfilled by some 140 theological seminaries. These colleges were intended to bring civilization, in the form of advanced Christian education, to the western settlers. The initial wave of colleges, often begun as seminaries or academies,

TABLE 3
Average College Size, 1840–1890

	1840	1850	1860	1870	1880	1890
College Enrollment	8,328	9,931	16,600		32,142	44,133
Colleges	107	136	209		364	415
Average Enrollment	78	73	79		88	106

Sources: 1840–1860: Burke, *American Collegiate Populations*, 54;
1889–1890: Table 1.

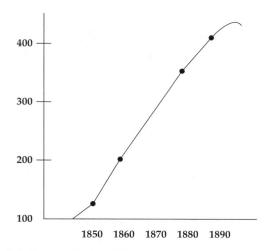

FIGURE 1 Logistic Growth of Colleges, 1850–1890

was often the product of missionary zeal. The early leader of Colorado College, for example, the Congregationalist Edward Payson Tenney, espied a population of Native Americans, Mormons, and Spanish-speaking Roman Catholics, in addition to the boisterous young men of the minefields, all to his mind desperately in need of Protestant culture. A second pattern of founding, usually at the initiative of individuals, occurred largely on what geographer D. W. Meinig has termed "the speculative frontier." In this case, initiatives to found colleges were part of the competitive development of rival settlements—a kind of prospective boosterism. In either case, the founding of colleges in the West was led by the principal denominations. Colorado's first colleges, for example, were Methodist and Congregational, but the Presbyterians too sponsored four institutions, all of which failed. Presbyterians were particularly active in spreading the college gospel in the West, but apparently experienced more failures than successes. Dismay at these results led to the establishment of a central Board of Aid in 1883, which carefully evaluated the prospects for future colleges and achieved better results. All told, 16 enduring Presbyterian colleges were established in the West in the three decades after the Civil War, 11 by direct initiative of church bodies.

East of the Mississippi (roughly speaking), the proliferation of denominational colleges was principally driven by the increasing density and religious fragmentation of the population. The figures in Table 4 can provide only a rough idea of the changes in denominational sponsorship because many colleges were only loosely associated and changes occurred. The principal denominations, in fact, attempted to exert more direct control over their colleges during the latter decades of the century, causing a good number of the older colleges to lapse into nondenominational status. Thus, the figure of 265 Protestant colleges understates the actual situation for 1890. Nevertheless, the contrast indicates the effects of religious fragmentation.

Some 44 of the additional colleges represent independent branches of the main denominations. These churches too felt the need for colleges and added to the overall number. Even when the split was ostensibly regional, the effects could be far-reaching: the 6 colleges of the Cumberland Presbyterians stretched from Pennsylvania to Texas. The growth of a distinctive immigrant population accounted for 14 additional Lutheran colleges. Another 34 colleges were founded after 1860 by smaller denominations, including Friends, United Brethren, and Disciples of Christ. These sects in some ways retraced the experience of Baptists and Methodists in belatedly embracing higher education. Their concern was less the training of a learned ministry than it was to protect their social base. Repeatedly, they expressed concern that young men who attended the colleges of other denominations were lost to the church. The remedy, then, was to establish colleges of their own. Thus, religious fragmentation was the chief impulse behind the elaboration of the collegiate pattern in settled regions.

TABLE 4
Protestant Colleges by Denomination, 1860 & 1890

	1860	1890
Presbyterian	40	35/14*
Methodist Episcopal	35	52/22
Baptist	29	36/8
Congregational	17	22
Protestant Episcopal	15	6
Disciples of Christ	6	20
Lutheran	5	19
United Brethren	2	10
Others	9	21
Total	158	265

*Main church/other branches
Sources: 1860: Burke, *American Collegiate Populations*, 25;
1890: RCE, 788.

A definite pattern of college founding emerged in this era, employed by virtually all denominations. Once a church, through its regional body, decided upon the desirability of establishing a college, it solicited bids from interested communities. The church itself usually contributed some funds, but it expected that the future home of the college would donate land, perhaps buildings, and a certain amount of endowment. The most lucrative offer almost always took precedence over other considerations, such as transportation or population. While this procedure gave the town a certain stake in the new venture, the churches retained fairly close control through the right to name the college trustees. This process of founding colleges had several consequences. It favored small or medium-sized towns, in which pure boosterism could be most readily mobilized, rather than the larger and more heterogeneous cities. The combined resources of church and town gave most of these colleges the vital financial margin for survival, but at the same time, by identifying them with a particular constituency and placing them among a limited population, these arrangements constrained their potential size and scope. Finally, the interests of the churches were clearly paramount in the founding of such colleges.

These two dynamics—geographical extension largely in the West and denominational elaboration elsewhere—underlay the logistic pattern of college expansion in this era. During the 1850s and 1860s, college founding through denominational elaboration was in full force, particularly in the mid-Atlantic and north central states, while geographical extension was accelerating in the Great Plains and the Far West (Table 2). The confluence of both patterns made the 1860s, surprisingly, the most fecund decade for new colleges. The self-reinforcing nature of this growth was undoubtedly due, on the one hand, to the rapid extension of the railroad network and the real estate frontier, which created communities eager to host colleges. On the other hand, the reciprocal effects that denominations had upon one another produced an implicit or protective competition. The momentum behind this dynamic may well have been diminished by the panic of 1873 and its aftermath. In any case, denominational elaboration continued afterward at a much slower pace (although it has never stopped), but most of the foundings of the 1880s and 1890s were due to geographical extension—principally in the Dakotas (7 colleges), Texas (10), Kansas (9), Nebraska (6), Missouri (7), and Florida (5).

Both these processes were self-limiting or, in extreme cases, self-destructive. Where religious fragmentation was high, as in Tennessee, Kentucky, and Missouri, excessive elaboration resulted in the founding of numerous weak and nonviable colleges. Extension also resulted in high mortality rates, as founders often wagered on what turned out to be poor locations. Generally, where population density remained low, colleges faced difficult conditions. In the Midwest, by way of contrast, extension in the 1820s through the 1840s was followed by elaboration as the population grew. For most of the West, however, overextension precluded much subsequent elaboration before the nature of higher education began to change after 1890.

Catholic Colleges

The creation of Catholic colleges contributed to the overall logistic pattern, but differences from their Protestant counterparts made them a kind of parallel system with even less stable population dynamics.

Catholic colleges were founded for essentially the same motives as Protestant ones. Before 1850, Edward Power has noted, they were chiefly founded out of the need to perpetuate the clergy, in this case by preparing students for the seminaries, out of missionary zeal to bring Catholicism to the spreading population, and out of a desire to provide Catholic moral education shielded from hostile doctrines. After 1850, Catholic interests shifted like other denominations toward educating a learned laity—providing higher education appropriate for a Catholic community. Both sets of motives gave Catholics powerful incentives, first for extension of their educational complex and then for full territorial elaboration of colleges. However, whereas each Protestant college was an independent corporation, Catholic colleges were emanations of permanent organizations—extensions of the universal Catholic Church.

The two key entities were the Catholic dioceses, each headed by a bishop and entrusted with authority over education, and the religious orders. Many of the enduring colleges represented some combination of effort by both, since it long proved difficult for a diocese to mobilize the resources needed to sustain a college. Catholics further complicated matters by adopting a variant of the Jesuit seven-year plan of studies. This heavily classical course began with "Rudiments" and proceeded through three years of "Humanities," followed by single years of poetry, rhetoric, and philosophy. This arrangement largely duplicated the preparatory classes and four years of the standard classical A.B. course, but the rigidity of a single course demanded a larger educational enterprise while making such a commitment more formidable to students. Many colleges compromised this pattern out of necessity. Thus, the church was at once ambitious in terms of the elaboration of colleges to serve all Catholics and in curricular requirements, but starved for the resources to sustain such efforts. One might expect large numbers of foundings accompanied by a high rate of failure; indeed, that was what occurred. But the permanence of the church was also a factor. Numerous insolvent Catholic colleges were shuttered, reduced to preparatory schools or seminaries, only to reopen again under more hopeful conditions. Catholic colleges sometimes flickered in and out of existence.

Catholic colleges began to be founded at a rapid rate around the mid-1840s, and this process continued for the next seventy years. From 1850 to 1890, an average of 33 were started each decade, 70 percent of which ultimately closed. This effort of elaboration persisted longer than that of Protestant denominations, and planted Catholic colleges in all but the most sparsely settled western states (Idaho, Nevada, Wyoming). In keeping with the pattern of logistic growth, however, the final efforts were the least productive: Catholic colleges founded from 1890 to 1910 expired at the astonishing rate of 85 percent.

The Nature of Multipurpose Colleges

Multipurpose colleges can be understood only with reference to the classical colleges that preceded and to some extent coexisted with them. The classical denominational college may trace its lineage back to seventeenth-century Harvard, but its early nineteenth-century form nevertheless represented a particular variation of that venerable species. As offered in numerous colleges, the classical course was infinitely varied but essentially the same. The first year was devoted to perfecting the student's skills in Latin, Greek, and mathematics—the subjects required for entry. The ancient languages were employed thereafter in the study of literature (belles lettres) and rhetoric. Natural philosophy (science) was emphasized in the third year, and mental and moral philosophy in the fourth. Interspersed were a variety of classes in history, logic, ethics, and religion. Each year's class studied the entire curriculum together. Students were expected to prepare their lessons on their own and then called upon to recite them in the classroom. The extent to which lectures were employed in the advanced classes depended on the college and the capabilities of its instructors.

The ways in which the classical college might be altered were recognized by contemporaries. Parallel courses might substitute science or modern languages for Latin or, particularly, Greek. Optional courses could be inserted into the fixed curriculum, or a more radical approach was that students might be grouped by proficiency into more and less advanced courses. Students also might be allowed to study only subjects of their own choosing (partial course). During the 1820s, all of these approaches were tried, but met with little success. Instead, the clamor for reform provoked an imposing defense of the classical course—the Yale Report of 1828.

Four essential points are argued in the report. First, the classical college course was not intended for specific intellectual or practical ends, but was the foundation for subsequent professional study and public life. Second, this foundation consisted above all of mental discipline, formed from the "vigorous, and steady, and systematic effort" that the colleges coerced from their students. Third, the study of the classics was superior to all other subjects for acquiring mental discipline and cultural refinement for later life. Fourth, the report thoroughly disparaged all alternate forms of education, establishing in effect the indubitable superiority of the classical course. All four of these points seemed plausible to contemporaries and were repeated almost verbatim for the next sixty years. Only the last, however, was confirmed in an important way by social practice. The reforms of this period foundered due to a variety of circumstances, but they were invariably weighed down as well by the invidious distinction that contemporaries made between the classical course and its alternatives.

Classical colleges nevertheless had distinct drawbacks. In an age when boys of about twelve assumed an economic role and semi-independence from their families, attending college most likely meant the prolongation of dependence and control. Semi-independence harmonized with intermittent forms of schooling, the pattern for most youths, but collegians were expected to undertake thorough preparatory study, followed by a continuous four-year course. And while most young people enjoyed considerable personal freedom, collegians were constrained by myriad rules, enforced in the spirit of petty but inefficient despotism. Considering these traits, a college education probably did produce superior powers of mental application as well as conspicuous verbal skills. Even so, its cachet appealed to a definite but delimited constituency: sons of more affluent families pursuing the genteel route to professional status; aspirants, often mature young men, to the ministry; and a trickle of rural youths defying sociological description who sought better lives through education. For such a clientele, the classical college for long had few rivals.

Although most new colleges of the 1830s largely replicated the classical model, they often began by incorporating reformist ideas. Randolph-Macon College modeled itself after the University of Virginia, for example, and Wesleyan College opened offering a partial course and some electives; but both were brought back to orthodoxy. The few departures from the classical college largely stood alone: Union College—offering nonclassical electives in its A.B. course; Jefferson's University of Virginia—a complete departure from the American college; and West Point—inspiration for a growing number of military academies. In the extension of higher education beyond the Appalachians, however, denominational colleges took the training of a learned ministry as their most urgent mission and clung to the classical course as the surest means to emulate the intellectual standards of the East. Slowly, however, new departures appeared, and by the 1850s the colleges being founded increasingly resembled a new subspecies.

As its primary orientation the multipurpose college embraced the education of a learned laity rather than a learned ministry. At its core there remained the classical college, typically most highly esteemed, but now surrounded by additional courses of the type specifically condemned in the Yale Report. Besides the ubiquitous preparatory departments, these would include nonclassical (or non-Greek) degree courses in science (B.S.) or modern languages (B.Litt. or B.Phil). In addition, these colleges might offer nondegree courses for teachers or for commerce. An inverse scenario frequently occurred when prospering academies upgraded their offerings by obtaining college charters. Academies were already multipurpose in nature, so that a classical course might merely be appended to existing offerings. Finally, and perhaps most characteristic, the multipurpose colleges tended to admit women.

These traits of the multipurpose college are mutually consistent. Usually located in towns that had lured them with an attractive offer, they joined settled communities that had undergone the social and economic effects of the "market revolution" rather than the rudimentary frontier outposts where earlier colleges had begun. They could thus appeal to a proto-middle-class constituency. Their local supporters (and some denominational sponsors) might appreciate the prestige of a classical education, but consistently expressed a desire for more practical and accessible nonclassical courses as well. Teacher and commercial courses might be offered if a demand existed. Such courses would make some financial contribution for these invariably hard-pressed institutions that depended not only on student tuition but on the goodwill of the local community as well.

Coeducation was entirely consistent with these traits, but it was notably antithetical to the spirit of the classical college. Given the prevailing doctrine of separate spheres, women had no need for an education that prepared for professional training or public life. Nor did they require the coercive tactics used to instill mental discipline into recalcitrant boys. College education for women had not yet been contemplated at the time of the Yale Report, but well before midcentury, advanced education in various forms was expanding rapidly in academies, seminaries, collegiate institutes, and ultimately women's colleges. This movement was incorporated rather naturally into multipurpose colleges, in either separate or coeducational departments. Still, higher education for women evoked strong feelings, and thus the incidence of coeducation varied greatly by region and denomination. In the South, colleges or seminaries for women alone were the rule, and in the Northeast, coeducation made only selective inroads after the Civil War. From western New York across the Midwest, however, conditions fostered by the market revolution favored coeducational colleges; and in the Far West, they were the rule. Roman Catholics were most adamantly set against mixed colleges, but the main branches of the Presbyterian, Episcopal, and Lutheran Churches also favored segregation of the sexes. The more populist and evangelical denominations, on the other hand, were far more open to the inclusion of women. These were the denominations, moreover, that were most active in the elaboration of colleges. Although coeducation cannot be considered the litmus test for multipurpose colleges, it is a frequent and telling correlate.

Elaboration of Colleges in Ohio

The market revolution created the conditions that nourished multipurpose colleges. It engendered the prosperity of the towns and countryside that harbored the denominational communities chiefly responsible for this new generation of colleges. Thus, the territories most affected by these forces were the first to sprout such institutions. Nowhere was the transition from a frontier to a market-driven society more rapid and far-reaching than in Ohio. Driven by a boom in canal building in the 1830s and railroad construction during the next two decades, the state in 1860 had the third largest population, the most miles of railroad, and the largest number of colleges.

Oberlin Collegiate Institute, which opened in 1833, was something of a bridge between the classical and the multipurpose colleges. It was founded by evangelical Congregationalists, and its missionary zeal almost immediately pushed it toward a larger role. Its stated purposes were, first, to educate ministers and teachers for the vast lands of the Mississippi Valley; second, to elevate female character through education; and third, to extend a useful and affordable education to all classes of the community. The first goal called for the classical A.B. course, capped by a theological department. The latter was greatly enlarged in 1835 by the defection of a group of abolitionists from Lane Theological Seminary and the arrival of famed evangelist Charles Grandison Finney. So important was theological education that provision was soon made for a short, non-Latin Bible course for impatient preseminarians, who were also permitted to take partial courses in the college. The second goal was met initially by a separate ladies' department, but soon women were admitted to any course. Oberlin graduated the first female A.B.'s in the country in 1841. In order to meet its third goal, Oberlin maintained a large preparatory department and also adopted the manual labor plan, like many colleges of the 1830s. Besides preparing students for the college, the preparatory department offered courses for teaching and commerce. Oberlin was considered radical during its early years, but it also became Ohio's largest antebellum college, attracting many of its students from outside the state. When it was rechartered in 1851 as Oberlin College, the institution was clearly a multipurpose college, although by that juncture it was no longer alone.

After 1840, the college matrix was gradually elaborated in Ohio as each church pursued independently its own denominational interests. Patterns of college founding were diverse or even idiosyncratic, but in total they represent a process that occurred throughout much of the country.

Perhaps most common was the concern of evangelical churches about losing the allegiance of young men educated by rival denominations. Ohio Methodists chafed at Presbyterian control over the two nominally state universities, Ohio and Miami. Their response was to found Ohio Wesleyan College in 1842. Although in the center of the state, Ohio Wesleyan offered little succor to Methodists in the northeastern section who wished to counter the lure of Oberlin. A wealthy layman, John Baldwin, worked with the North Ohio Conference to found an eponymous institute. Raised to collegiate status in 1854, Baldwin College soon surpassed Oberlin in the wide spectrum of its offerings. A third Methodist college, Mount Union (1858), was entirely the work of laymen. Beginning as a seminary in 1846, it also quickly sprouted additional departments. In governance Mount Union resembled earlier colleges in being firmly associated with a church, but not formally affiliated.

Both the United Brethren and the German Reformed Churches were moved to found colleges for the same professed motives as the Methodists. The Brethren had eschewed colleges until they felt pressured into launching Otterbein in 1847. For the German Reformed Church, the long distance to their seminary in Mercersberg, Pennsylvania, was the decisive factor in starting Heidelberg College (1850). The founding of Antioch (1852) might be considered another variation on this theme. Liberal "Christians," who opposed denominational distinctions, sought to found a nonsectarian college of a high rank. They consciously sought the best local offer in New York and Ohio before accepting the bid of the small town of Yellow Springs.

Developments within denominations also generated colleges. Ohio Lutherans were divided between an English branch and a more traditional German branch that controlled the Evangelical Lutheran Seminary in Columbus (f. 1830). After cooperation between the two groups ended in 1840, the English Lutherans protected their interests by organizing Wittenberg College (1844). The German branch countered by founding Capital University (1850).

Presbyterian hegemony over Ohio's first two colleges may have offended other denominations, but it failed to satisfy the church's increasing desire for closer control. The contrasting fates of the two resulting colleges well represent the changing environment. Central College of Ohio (1842) resembled other early colleges in being founded by local Presbyterians acting independently. This institution garnered little support, producing just a single graduate before the Civil War. The two Ohio Synods of the church resolved in the mid-1840s to found a church-sponsored institution, but they apparently felt little urgency. For years they failed to agree on a location, and then the Civil War caused further delay. When the University of Wooster was founded in 1866, however, it had relatively solid underpinnings from both the church and the town.

These colleges in many ways mirrored the denominations they represented. Large denominations, like the Methodists, could support relatively large colleges. Ohio Wesleyan was generally the second largest college in the state (Table 5) and would later harbor university aspirations. Otterbein, which depended almost entirely on the Brethren, remained small and impecunious. Urbana College, founded by the Swedenborgian Church (1850), remained tiny and imperiled throughout the century. Capital University, despite its name, reflected the conservatism of the German Lutherans and remained essentially a classical college into the twentieth century. The more liberal English Lutherans, however, transformed Wittenberg into a multipurpose institution after the Civil War.

Antioch, Otterbein, and Heidelberg were all coeducational from the time of their chartering, and each graduated women from the college course. They reflected support within their respective denominations for the advanced education of women. Muskingum, a United Presbyterian college, adopted coeducation early in contrast to the main church. Methodists generally were conspicuous supporters of women's education. Baldwin, Wilberforce, and Mount Union were coeducational, while Ohio Wesleyan was accompanied by a women's college, with which it merged in 1877. With at least seven antebellum coeducational colleges, Ohio was clearly in the vanguard of this movement. Much the same could be said in curricular matters.

A historian of these colleges has observed that "none of Ohio's antebellum colleges limited itself to the narrow concepts outlined in the Yale Report of 1828." While Capital University might be the exception to this rule, among other traditional institutions, Kenyon taught engineering for a time, and St. Xavier offered commercial subjects in evening classes. Nonclassical degree courses in science or literature were the most common additions to the A.B. in these years, and some colleges offered courses for teaching or commerce.

Colleges that developed from academies (however named) tended to be the most innovative. Baldwin and Mount Union have already been noted, but both were remarkable in this respect. Among its many offerings Baldwin started an extensive commercial course in 1859 that, unlike some others, was never discontinued. In 1858, it started a German department, which met with such success that it was separated five years later as German-Wallace College. The two schools remained closely associated, and later reunited as Baldwin Wallace University. By the 1880s, Baldwin alone counted eight different schools. The founder of Mount Union, Orville Hartshorn, anticipated Ezra Cornell when he stated his intention "to found for the people a cosmic college, where any person may economically obtain a thorough, illustrative, integral instruction in any needed studies." Even as a college, Mount Union operated more like an academy in encouraging students to take elective courses. Hartshorn also seems to have anticipated William Rainey Harper by offering a summer term, largely for teachers.

Fitting into this same mold was Hiram College, chartered in 1867. It was founded by the "Christians" or Disciples, who sought an educational institution for all the usual reasons, but originally opted against starting a college. Instead, they opened the Western Reserve Eclectic Institute in 1850, which fast became a thriving academy offering a wide slate of electives up to and including collegiate course work. This same character was retained after full collegiate courses and degrees were instituted, as Hiram continued to teach large numbers of irregular students.

The most radical departure of the antebellum years was the Farmers' College (f. 1852) located outside Cincinnati. It, too, was preceded by a prosperous academy, but the founders wished to provide a practical collegiate education for business and farming. Ten years before the Morrill Act, they established the functional equivalent of a land-grant college. It offered both a classical course and a scientific course with wide allowance for electives. It also organized an agricultural course with three professors and a model farm. The intent of Farmers' College was to teach the new practical curriculum in association with traditional classical subjects. The college appeared to thrive initially, but it faced continual problems after the war and ceased collegiate operations in 1888.

Looking beyond the Civil War, these same tendencies remained prominent. The matrix of denominational colleges was further elaborated with additions from smaller denominations, but the pace clearly slowed as new possibilities were exhausted. By 1890, nine more Protestant colleges (including Wooster and Hiram) were operating, as well as another Catholic college (Table 5). In addition, several more "eclectic" colleges (to borrow a term from Hiram's predecessor) emerged from academies and normal schools. The traits characteristic of multipurpose colleges became more widespread. By 1890, only four Protestant colleges remained confined to men, and fewer than half of the regular college students were enrolled in the classical course.

A new note in the postbellum era was the distinctive role played by philanthropy as the growing fortunes of the Gilded Age began to affect higher education. Some major gifts produced conventional results, such as denominational colleges for the Universalists (Buchtel College) and the Free Will Baptists (Rio Grande College). However, a few acts of philanthropy produced institutions that clearly would not otherwise have appeared when they did. Four examples stand out, which in time produced institutions that transcended the model of the multipurpose college.

TABLE 5
Ohio Colleges in 1889–1890, by Collegiate Enrollment

College	Year Opened	Denomination	Men	Women	All Departments
Oberlin	1833 #	Congregational	253	356	1,713
Ohio Wesleyan	1844 #	Methodist	266	218	1,117
Scio	1866	Methodist	200	108	402
University of Wooster	1870 #	Presbyterian	173	62	750
Ohio State University	1873 #	state	186	35	425
Mount Union	1846	Methodist	145	30	568
University of Cincinnati	1873 #	municipal	89	31	900
Heidelberg University	1850	Reformed	90	25	347
Wittenberg	1845##	Lutheran	89	26	285
Buchtel	1872##	Universalist	67	42	361
Marietta	1835 #	Congregational	100	*	171
Denison University	1831#	Baptist	96	*	207
Baldwin University	1846 #	Methodist	57	37	344
Western Reserve	1826 #	Congregational	67	5	198
St. Xavier	1840 #	Roman Catholic	71	*	419
Capital University	1850	Lutheran	71	*	154
Muskingum	1837	United Presbyterian	53	18	119
St. Joseph's	1871	Roman Catholic	50	*	225
Ohio University	1809 #	nonsectarian	50	16	171
Franklin	1825	United Presbyterian	54	12	118
Otterbein	1847 #	United Bretheren	35	25	238
Hiram	1867 #	Disciples	40	19	324
Miami University	1824 ##	nonsectarian	44	1	72
Findlay	1886	Church of God	29	12	302
German-Wallace	1864	Methodist	36	5	110
Kenyon	1828 #	Episcopal	38	*	129
Wilmington	1870	Friends	18	17	113
Calvin	1883	Reformed	19	10	143
Twin Valley	1886	Methodist?	12	8	63
Rio Grande	1876	F.W. Baptist	11	7	33
Ashland	1879	United Brethren	9	3	96
Urbana	1851	New Church (Swedenborgian)	6	4	37
Hillsboro	1857	Methodist	4	5	110
Richmond	1835	Congregational?	8	1	110
Wilberforce	1855	A.M.E.	4	3	177
Antioch	1853 #	Christ/Unitarian	— 20	—	146
Farmers'	1852	Methodist	0	0	51
		Total	2,540	1,141	11,197

*men's college
named members of the Association of Ohio Colleges (1878)
subsequent members of the Association of Ohio Colleges
Sources: RCE, 1889–90, 1892–95; and diverse sources.

First, Charles McMicken left a bequest to the city of Cincinnati in 1858 for establishing a men's and a women's college. Implementation was delayed, but grew into a grander conception. The University of Cincinnati (f. 1870) aspired to consolidate all the city's institutions of higher education under its umbrella. Initial progress was slow, with only the School of Design and the Observatory being incorporated by 1890. The next decade saw the addition of professional schools, however, and with them the efflorescence of a unique municipal university. Second, the gift of Leonard Case led to the opening of the Case School of Applied Science in Cleveland in 1881. The school endured numerous difficulties during its first decade, but its substantial endowment assured its eventual success. Third, the Case gift helped to prod Amassa Stone to provide the funds that brought Western Reserve College to Cleveland in 1882. Hitherto a hidebound early college, mimicking Yale and maintaining the classical course "in almost pristine integrity," Western Reserve was propelled toward becoming a true university. Finally, although it may be stretching to regard the land script given to Ohio under the Morrill Act as a gift, its effects were similar to those just described. A new type of institution with an assured income was thereby created, Ohio Agricultural and Mechanical University (f. 1873), which by 1890 would be poised for explosive growth. Each of these four institutions represented new departures for the modern era. As late as 1890, however, they had more features in common than in contrast with the multipurpose colleges.

The Multipurpose Colleges in Ohio

The enrollments noted in Table 5 suggest that Ohio colleges had not yet evolved beyond the multipurpose era in 1890. The great majority of colleges were small and precarious operations. The average collegiate enrollment of the 35 institutions equaled 105, compared to a national average of 106. The situation in Ohio appears representative of the dynamics governing multipurpose colleges.

The multipurpose colleges depended for their vitality or subsistence on some combination of student fees, endowment income, and timely support of benefactors. In practice, each college had to determine for itself how to optimize these potential resources (although there is no evidence they thought systematically about such things). While some students sought the highest standards for the B.A., others might search out the most lenient or inexpensive option. Catering to non-degree students could be an uncertain endeavor. And benefactors might look to reward either traditional high standards or departures from tradition. At any moment, debt, calamities, or inexplicable fluctuations in enrollment might drive a college to the wall. The Ohio colleges during this era appear to have tested myriad possibilities, and thus their experiences provide a laboratory for the complex interactions of academic, market, and external forces.

For an important sector of potential collegians, strong academic standards may have been the paramount consideration. From the earliest foundings, an implicit standard existed that was defined by the practices of the New England colleges. The standard itself was strongly contested, wedded as it was to the classical curriculum most vigorously defended by Yale and Princeton. But for some colleges such an approach fulfilled the expectations of their constituency. This standard in practice called for well-qualified students and faculty, something that all colleges would ostensibly desire, and it was traditionally linked with a controlled residential setting. It also tended to be joined with a commitment to piety and education for the ministry. The oldest denominational colleges largely embraced this formula. Western Reserve, Kenyon, Denison, and Marietta were highly traditional in curricular matters, but so too was Oberlin in its classical course. Such a profile apparently allowed these schools to charge higher tuition and appeal to wealthier families. As of 1880 (before the impact of the new philanthropy), their endowments were the largest among Ohio colleges ($150,000 to $250,000).

If the years surrounding the Civil War were fertile with challenges to the existing order, a conservative reaction became apparent in the mid-1870s. Its vehicle was the Association of Ohio Colleges, which formed in 1867 as a rather informal discussion group among presidents and professors who attended the Ohio State Teachers' Association. Common topics were relations with the high schools and the thorny problem of Greek (discussed below). In the 1870s, the association began to meet on its own, and its interests focused on "elevating the standard of the colleges in the State." They first turned to the matter of regulating the requirements for the bachelor's degree and devised a standard requiring "4 years of solid work with 15 recitations per week." In addition they sought to defend the A.B. as a classical course representing the study of both Latin and Greek. They also stipulated that colleges offering the degree should have a minimum of ten professors. Their disdain for the B.S., on the other hand, was evident. Their reporter remarked: "Nothing probably did so much to cheapen the degrees given by the colleges of Ohio, a few years ago, as the frequent granting of degrees of B.S. for very inadequate and inferior courses." Once degree standards were agreed upon, the association limited its membership to those colleges meeting them (see Table 5).The definition of quality taken by the Ohio Association did not necessarily exclude other kinds of courses, as was common in the East, since most of its approved members were multipurpose colleges with large irregular enrollments. Rather, it chose to man the barricades for the imperiled classical A.B., which throughout the era of the multipurpose college retained its preeminent status.

The general lack of success among colleges that aggressively entered the market for practical subjects is more perplexing. Such programs were the signature of the multipurpose college, but most adopted them selectively and opportunistically. If popular, they boosted enrollments and revenues, but they were often dropped as quickly as they were added. The colleges that placed greatest emphasis on such programs had checkered histories. They tended to thrive from the late 1850s to the 1870s, but faced difficulties by the end of this era. Farmers' College was anemic after the war, eventually converting to a military academy. Scio declined somewhat later and was forced to merge with Mount Union (1911); and that institution, which styled itself a "people's college," barely survived the 1880s.

One explanation is valid but beside the point. The kinds of curricula that reformers had been demanding since the 1820s were scarcely viable prior to 1890. The B.S. may have been an easier route to a college degree, but it did not signify systematic training in science and there was no identifiable demand for such graduates in the American economy. The lack of a knowledge base for agriculture education became painfully apparent after the Morrill Act, and was not appreciably mitigated until well after the Hatch Act (1887) established Agricultural Experiment Stations. The teaching of engineering slowly matured during these years, but even a proponent had to admit that the supply of trained engineers eventually created a demand, not the reverse. Such training, it became apparent, could not adequately be appended to small denominational colleges. Thus, the lack of fit between college, curriculum, and careers may have contradicted the visions of reformers, but it scarcely affected the market-driven programs of multipurpose colleges. These institutions faced a different problem.

As the colleges offered an increasing variety of programs, they tapped into the huge market for intermittent education by irregular students. This was the characteristic pattern for education beyond the common school in mid-nineteenth-century America, and it was met largely by academies and similar institutions. Students mixed periods of education with periods of employment, sometimes into their early twenties. They sought education that would expand their intellect, dignify their social standing, or possibly get them a job. The colleges that developed out of thriving academies were already serving such a clientele, and devised flexible college programs to meet further needs. Other colleges capitalized on their prestige to dabble in these markets. However, results were often disappointing. Students seeking practical instruction attended irregularly and rarely completed degrees. This phenomenon had doomed Francis Wayland's 1850 reforms at Brown; and Cornell opened in 1868 with more than 400 students (332 freshmen), but the attrition rate for the first class approached 90 percent. The industrial classes, whatever their educational aspirations, did not relish spending four consecutive years in cloistered study.

An additional complication was becoming apparent in the last decades of the century. Although the practice of admitting special students was widespread, even in the East, their presence became less compatible with the strengthening collegiate peer culture. Yale president Timothy Dwight was especially blunt: "the special and short course men demoralize the others more than they benefit themselves." If it were true generally, as one conscientious inquiry concluded, that irregular students on the whole were "a drag upon the improvement of the regular students," then their presence in significant numbers would inescapably tarnish the prestige of a college. Such factors may explain why serving irregular students tended to produce substantial enrollments but impecunious institutions.

The colleges of this era are commonly imagined to be tuition dependent, but student fees were seldom adequate to sustain them because they charged so little. In Ohio, tuition ranged from $24 per year at Heidelberg to $75 at Kenyon, with most colleges charging $30 to $45 (1890). If there were 15 students for each teacher (a rough average), a full $40 tuition from each would yield $600, or about half an instructor's salary. Finding the other half of that salary was a continual challenge. Nationally, colleges in the 1890s derived about the same amount of revenues from endowments and other sources as they did from student fees. In Ohio, endowment earnings exceeded income from students. All colleges probably desired robust enrollments, but for financial security they looked above all to productive funds.

In 1900, the majority of colleges reported endowments large enough to support one or more instructors ($25,000). The 171 colleges reporting no endowment were made up largely of public institutions without land grants, Catholic colleges, and most of the small colleges in the South. A similar number (170) reported $100,000 or more, but fewer institutions fell between these two groups. For private colleges to better themselves in the postbellum years—to hire more and better qualified instructors—almost invariably meant accumulating productive funds. Institutional prestige was, as a rule, the critical factor for attracting bequests and benefactions. The distribution of endowments in 1900 indicated a widening distance between have and have-not colleges.

The third and most uncertain element of college financing in this era was deficits. Colleges apparently had only vague notions about their likely income and expenditures. Given good intentions and congenital optimism, colleges overspent virtually every year, ending with a shortfall that had to be somehow met. Trustees at many schools customarily passed the hat; sometimes assets were drawn down; and many colleges actually borrowed funds, deferring the day of reckoning. These perennial deficits, in effect, constituted part of college finance, but they also underlined the colleges' ineluctable dependence on outside support.

Other kinds of support for the colleges changed over time. One frequent recourse was the selling of subscriptions, presentable in lieu of tuition for a set number of years or in perpetuity. This practice was quite widespread in the 1850s and caused subsequent embarrassment to numerous institutions, including Antioch and Ohio Wesleyan. Local enthusiasm for founding a college usually brought an infusion of funds, but this zeal generally proved difficult to duplicate. Direct support from the churches was always problematic. The denominations constituted natural networks for fund-raising, and college agents exploited them. However, actual church organizations were hard-pressed by other needs with higher priorities. The organization late in the century of special boards to coordinate aid to the colleges indicates that such support had to be carefully allotted.

Existing essentially as mendicants created one source of uncertainty for the colleges, but they also found themselves operating in an increasingly competitive marketplace. Although the population and the demand for education were both growing in the late nineteenth century, so too were the alternatives. In offering programs for teachers, colleges competed with the burgeoning normal schools; commercial courses were offered in private business schools as well as high schools; and courses in music and art in all likelihood duplicated the offerings of private teachers. Competitive pressures came from other colleges in the form of rising standards. Hiram College had to extend its degree courses to meet the guidelines of the Association of Ohio Colleges; Mount Union was excluded from the association before 1890 because of its summer term and liberal policy on electives—precisely the features geared to local needs.

As Colin Burke has emphasized, the multipurpose colleges were peculiarly suited for meeting the needs of educationally underserved communities. These were the "island communities" that Robert Wiebe has identified as characterizing the United States of the mid-nineteenth century. The multipurpose colleges were an integral part of small-town America, and they spread across the land at roughly the pace that island communities were formed. They provided the kind of general education that in untold tacit ways permitted enterprising young men to dignify their presence and thus better themselves in commerce, the professions, or public life. For just these reasons, the colleges found the growing cities to be barren ground.

There was not a single urban occupation that required a bachelor's degree, and few where it might be an asset in finding employment. Moreover, the cities were thick with competing institutions. High schools developed from an early date, providing general education as well as an entree into commerce or teaching. A myriad of private schools taught anything for which customers would pay. In Ohio, as elsewhere beyond the Appalachians, the cities tended to be graveyards for nineteenth-century colleges. Cincinnati College was one of Ohio's earliest, but it operated intermittently and closed in 1846. Woodward College failed there too, and the Protestant University of the United States (chartered 1845), whose grandiose vision seems to have been lost in the mists of time, apparently never opened. Farmers' College also foundered on the outskirts of Cincinnati. The single exception was St. Xavier's, which served a well-defined population of Roman Catholics. Cleveland University was launched in 1850 with impressive sponsorship, but was soon defunct. Only private philanthropy gave Western Reserve (after its move) and the University of Cincinnati the staying power to persist into a new and more favorable era.

The other side of this coin is that professional education in law and medicine was located exclusively in Ohio cities. Cincinnati by 1890 had four regular medical schools and four other kinds. Cleveland, Columbus, and Toledo each had two regular medical schools. Law schools were found only in Cincinnati and Cleveland. Large cities, it would seem, were as prolific in sprouting professional schools as the countryside was in breeding colleges. By 1890, however, such compartmentalization was disintegrating along with America's island communities. The multipurpose college, as a result, faced both internal and external challenges.

THE AGE OF THE COLLEGE

W. BRUCE LESLIE

In higher education the period between the Civil War and World War I is conventionally dubbed "the age of the university." The label has obvious justifications. Remarkable developments in universities established the patterns of modern academic life. Graduate school training became the sine qua non for college teaching. The new academic profession's standards were determined by journals and organizations dominated by university faculty. Professional schools within universities became the gatekeepers for the most prestigious professions. Academic research was revolutionized and dominated by a small number of universities. But for most students, donors, and the public, these developments were dimly perceived; it was the colleges and the collegiate aspects of higher education that were visible and attractive. There was a structural reality to this perception; during a period of educational ferment, the American college achieved an important new social and intellectual role.

Parts One and Two presented four case studies. Part Three places them in the context of the educational and social system taking shape in the United States in the early twentieth century. This chapter explains how colleges assumed their unique role as advanced American education was systematized.

The American college traces its intellectual history from colonial, and even medieval, predecessors. However, its modern condition as a freestanding institution operating in a clearly articulated system was a post-Civil War development. In 1870 most colleges were parts of multifunctional institutions; many colleges survived only by offering secondary education.[1] None of the four colleges in this study stood alone for the entire period, and two maintained secondary schools throughout. Frequently noncollegiate students outnumbered collegians (Table 1).

The preparatory branches were not just feeders. They served other educational roles highly valued by denominational sponsors and local citizens. Unfortunately, few left records; Franklin and Marshall Academy is an exception. Formally controlled by the German Reformed church, the college was part of a Reformed educational ladder extending from elementary instruction through advanced theological studies. The academy potentially linked the church's common schools to the college, but initially most students ended their educations at the academy. After 1890 the academy gradually eliminated terminal students and replaced them with college preparatory students recruited from Reformed congregations throughout Pennsylvania. As a result the academy, which furnished about one-third of the college's freshmen in the 1870s and 1880s, produced about 50 percent of the freshmen between 1895 and 1910, hitting a peak in 1909 with forty academy graduates in a freshman class of sixty-eight.[2]

After 1910 the academy's links to the college and the denomination loosened. For years the administration held down tuition to make the academy accessible to the average Pennsylvania German Reformed church member. Continued low tuition depended upon an increased endowment, but members did not respond with sufficient funds. At the same time, Pennsylvania significantly increased its support for public schools, creating free alternatives to the academy. Eventually tuition more than doubled and the fee reduction for Reformed students was eliminated, resulting in a sharp decline in the percentage of Reformed students in the academy (from 73 percent in 1908 to 35 percent in 1920). Increasingly, academy graduates went to other colleges, and Franklin and Marshall recruited from other preparatory schools. The college president tried to eliminate the academy in 1916, but it survived until World War II, annually providing about twenty freshmen to the college.[3]

Princeton briefly maintained a preparatory department, but the college's access to wealth soon provided other sources of students. McCosh's dreams for Princeton required more well-prepared students. The dependence of rivals like Harvard on exclusive private schools disturbed him, but New Jersey's weak secondary schools offered little alternative. He urged the New Jersey legislature to provide Scottish-style extensive free secondary education for the middle class, but his ambitions for Princeton demanded an immediate solution. With a donation from a wealthy alumnus, he created a preparatory department, which functioned from 1873 to 1880 and supplied seventy-five students to the college.

Princeton soon moved into the prep school movement despite McCosh's ambivalence about its aristocratic and Episcopalian traditions. In 1875 John Blair, a devout Presbyterian of Scottish descent, underwrote the revival of what became Blair Academy as a feeder for Princeton. Even more significant was the creation of Lawrenceville School with a bequest from another Presbyterian, John C. Green, Princeton's greatest benefactor in the McCosh years. All of Lawrenceville's trustees were connected to Princeton, and McCosh personally selected the first headmaster, a Scottish Presbyterian immigrant who designed it along the lines of the most prestigious New England prep schools. With its ample endowment and grounds laid out by Frederick Law Olmsted, Lawrenceville was an instant success. By 1890, it was sending about thirty freshmen a year to Princeton. McCosh's successors had no ambivalence about the aristocratic ambiance of prep schools, and Princeton cultivated relationships with them so ardently that it enrolled one of the highest proportions of their graduates of any college in the country by 1900.[4]

Whereas Princeton's short-lived preparatory department was viewed as an unfortunate necessity, Swarthmore's early experience was the opposite. Many early managers and stockholders were primarily interested in secondary education and were suspicious of higher education. Few students in the preparatory classes intended to continue to the collegiate program. From Swarthmore's founding in 1869 until 1886, the secondary (and briefly primary) students outnumbered the collegiate. The preparatory department supplied nineteen of fifty-one freshmen in 1878 and thirteen of fifty-nine in 1888. After a bitter fight, the preparatory classes were phased out in the early 1890s. While the faculty, college students, and some managers wanted a totally collegiate institution, secondary schools were a higher priority for most Hicksites. The collegiate faction won because, unlike the German Reformed church, Hicksite Quakers developed an adequate network of academies to provide a guarded secondary education and prepare candidates for the college.[5]

TABLE 1
Collegiate and Institutional Enrollments, 1869–1910

	Princeton	F&M	Bucknell	Swarthmore
1869–1870	328	72	64	26
		{83}	{151}	{173}
1889–1890	653	136	71	163
		{137}	{214}	{80}
	[118]			[30]
1909–1910	1,266	223	411	359
		{256}	{236}	
	[134]	[18]	[116]	[ca.5]

Source: The figures were compiled from catalogs and other college publications.
Note: Unbracketed numbers indicate undergraduate enrollments. {} = secondary and other subcollegiate enrollments. [ ] = graduate and other postbaccalaureate enrollments. Colleges conventionally included "specials" in undergraduate enrollments, but their work was somewhere between secondary and higher education. Franklin and Marshall figures do not include the theological seminary.

Bucknell University included at various times a theological seminary, a male academy, a female institute, and an institute of music. In 1865, only 99 of the 268 Bucknell students were in the collegiate department; in 1889–90, only 71 of 286. Collegians did not become a majority until the period of rapid growth under President Harris in the 1890s. By 1899–1900, collegians accounted for 315 in a total enrollment of 487. The academy continued to send most of its graduates to the university, preparing about 20 percent of the freshman classes for many years. But the proportion eventually declined while the college grew: in 1914 the academy supplied only seven of the 140 male freshmen. With public high schools providing secondary education to the Lewisburg area and freshmen to Bucknell, the trustees abolished the academy in 1917, although they retained a subfreshman class.[6] Most presidents and faculty resented preparatory work, but colleges were a luxury in the 1870s. The development of freestanding, or at least clearly distinguished colleges by World War I was a victory for their professional ambitions and for the systemization of American education.

The lack of a true educational "system" in the late nineteenth century was evident in the unsystematic nature of the admissions process before 1900. Ante-bellum applicants took oral exams from the faculty; after the Civil War, written exams became standard. Prospective students were examined on campus during commencement week or early September on classical authors, mathematics textbooks, and other materials stipulated by that college. Until the early 1900s, each college set individual admission requirements. By setting very specific measures of achievement, such as four books of the Aeneid or 137 pages of Gage's physics textbook, and requiring different combinations of supplementary subjects, such as geography, history, and English literature, there were almost as many combinations of requirements as there were colleges.[7]

All qualified students were admitted; there was no danger of an oversupply. Underprepared students were sent to the preparatory department or given "special" standing in the college. Financial necessity encouraged flexible standards, especially in hard times; the few surviving records suggest that most candidates were accepted. The faculty admitted some students who had not precisely fulfilled the admission requirements with "conditions," deficiencies to be corrected. Faculty minutes reveal widespread use of this alternative. For instance, the Princeton faculty "conditioned" 83 of 208 freshmen admitted in 1898 and an astonishing 230 to 328 in 1907 during Wilson's campaign to raise standards.[8]

In the nineteenth century, presidents personally administered admissions, corresponding endlessly with parents, headmasters, and candidates about entrance requirements and finances. David Jayne Hill spent his last summer at Bucknell processing admissions letters. President Magill wrote five letters in the summer of 1875 to one student's parents, trying to arrange financial assistance. Even at a larger college like Princeton, every new student reported directly to President McCosh. In the 1890s, the trustee assigned a faculty member to assist McCosh's successor; presidents at the other three colleges were allocated assistants in the 1900s. Presidents continued to oversee admissions into the 1920s and occasionally intervened, as when President Swain asked an alumnus to influence a star athlete to choose Swarthmore over Princeton. "I would be glad if thee would have a talk with Pfeiffer and see if thee cannot turn him this way."[9]

More than secretarial assistance was needed. Admissions was outgrowing the old practices, and the presidents spent much of their time around the turn of the century trying to systematize the process. The colleges' growth could make the work overwhelming. In addition, the colleges were increasingly dealing with institutions unconnected with their local or denominational communities. Admission of students from the colleges' preparatory divisions provided an early shortcut in the admissions process. Other preparatory schools soon developed similar arrangements with colleges, usually those affiliated with the same denomination. At first this certificate system operated informally, as reflected in a letter in 1886 to President Apple at Franklin and Marshall College from the principal of a Reformed church academy describing a group of his students whom he wanted admitted to the freshman class without examination: "They are pretty well prepared except in German. Of course they can get along with [the] class by reason of their knowledge of Pa. German, but for their sake I would suggest that the Faculty condition them in German Grammar. They can study up before the opening of the fall term."[10] The author was a former professor at the college whose ability to get students admitted on his recommendation stemmed from personal ties.

A year later the Franklin and Marshall faculty established a formal certificate system whereby students from approved schools were admitted on the principals' recommendations.[11] Bucknell admitted students informally on principals' recommendations for twenty years before officially offering admission by certificate in 1896 to graduates of all Pennsylvania normal schools and selected academies and high schools.[12]

Swarthmore, the first to establish a list of certified schools, sent faculty members to investigate each institution and by 1884 granted the privilege to nine Friends schools. The faculty slowly expanded the list in the 1890s, examining each request carefully and eventually including non-Friends schools. With the arrival of Joseph Swain from the Midwest where the certificate system was prevalent, Swarthmore considerably expanded its list.[13] A large number of students were admitted by certificate at all of the colleges except Princeton.

Princeton's broader geographic constituency made certificates less feasible. The system depended upon personal contact between the faculties and principals, many of whom had previous connections with the particular college. These relationships sufficed for the three colleges that drew their students primarily from Pennsylvania, but were inadequate for Princeton's national ambitions. In the 1870s, Princeton began giving its admission examinations in midwestern and southern cities. McCosh wrote to one alumnus who volunteered to administer the examinations that, if "there is a fair chance of getting even a few students from Louisville," he should begin to advertise immediately, with Princeton paying the cost. In the 1880s, Bucknell also began holding off-campus examinations within Pennsylvania.[14]

Even when geography was not a problem. Princeton did not cooperate with public high schools. Its social prestige and connections with the elite prep schools eventually enabled Princeton to draw upon them for three-quarters of its students. Despite criticism in the *Educational Review* and by a prominent alumnus-educator, Wilson Ferrand, as late as 1912 the faculty still rejected the certificate system and accepted the New York regents examinations only if reread by Princeton faculty.[15]

Even the certificate system left out many new public high schools that objected to adjusting their curricula to individual colleges. The first instance of intercollegiate cooperation came when nine New England colleges synchronized their entrance requirements for English in 1879. Six years later the formation of the New England Association of Colleges and Preparatory Schools created a permanent organization to coordinate articulation. In the Middle Atlantic states, a group of Pennsylvania colleges met in 1887 on the initiative of Swarthmore's President Magill. They formed the College Association of Pennsylvania and elected President Apple of Franklin and Marshall as the first president. Although formed to deal with the relationship of private colleges to the state government, by 1893 its focus shifted to articulation and its geographic scope broadened as it became the Association of Colleges and Preparatory Schools of the Middle States and Maryland. In 1894, the New England and Middle Atlantic associations agreed upon uniform English entrance examinations for colleges from Maine to Maryland. This led to a National Conference on Uniform Entrance Requirements in English that set national standards in the late 1890s. High schools and academies were told which literary works would be covered in tests for the next few years so they could satisfy all colleges' requirements with a single curriculum.[16]

The work of the Middle States group led to the creation of the College Entrance Examination Board (CEEB).[17] In 1899, Columbia's President Nicholas Murray Butler persuaded the Middle States Association to form committees to consider establishing such an agency. In 1900, they reported favorably, and a year later the CEEB administered its first tests to 973 students. Twelve colleges including Swarthmore were represented on the first board, and a thirteenth, Princeton, participated in its development. Bucknell joined the CEEB in its second year, and Franklin and Marshall, although not a member until after World War I, accepted the results of the board's examinations from the beginning.[18]

At first the CEEB was merely one of several options. In 1913, only one-seventh of Princeton applicants took the board's tests; the remainder took Princeton's own entrance examinations. An even smaller percentage chose the CEEB tests at the other three colleges. However, the precedent set by Columbia, Barnard, and New York University in 1901 of abolishing their own tests and requiring all applicants to take the board's examinations eventually prevailed. In 1915, Princeton, Harvard, and

Yale took the same step. Swarthmore followed suit but retained a certificate system for Friends schools. Both Bucknell and Franklin and Marshall continued holding their own examinations until the 1920s as well as accepting certificates and the CEEB examinations.[19]

Entrance requirements came to be expressed in nationally recognized quantitative measures, an idea suggested by the National Education Association (NEA) in 1899. It proposed that colleges set their requirements in "units," indicating the years spent studying a subject rather than specifying textbooks and areas of coverage.[20] In 1901, Swarthmore followed the NEA recommendation, requiring applicants to take a basic core of high school courses and to choose the others from a list of electives. Bucknell, Franklin and Marshall, and Princeton adopted similar plans over the next twelve years. By 1913, colleges almost universally expressed their requirements in units and permitted a choice of exams rather than examining all subjects. When the CEEB developed comprehensive examinations in 1916, students gained even greater choice. Under this plan, the colleges accepted high school certificates for most units, and students chose four subjects for extensive examination.[21]

Educational reformers hoped to rationalize the whole system. Not only would courses become measurable units, but there would be a uniform, nationally recognized boundary between secondary and higher education. Graduation from a secondary school was not the only path to college admission until well after 1900. Since admission was based on work completed, colleges sometimes accepted students before they graduated from secondary school or on the recommendation of private tutors. Graduates of normal schools, collegiate institutes, and less prestigious colleges entered at various levels. Among the students entering Franklin and Marshall in September 1913 were two graduates of Elizabethtown College admitted to the senior class and three graduates of Millersville Normal School admitted to the junior class; the sophomore class included graduates of Kutztown Normal School, Williamsport-Dickinson Seminary, Schuykill Academy, and Massanutten Academy.[22] On the other hand, early graduates of Swarthmore were admitted to Harvard's junior class. After Swarthmore raised its standards by holding back most students in 1881, Harvard accepted its graduates into the senior class. In the late 1880s, over 10 percent of Swarthmore's graduates went on for a second bachelor's degree, entering the senior class of more prestigious institutions. Princeton admitted graduates of other colleges into its senior class.[23]

Setting admission standards in units of work rather than specific levels of knowledge in effect defined the length of secondary education. The Carnegie Foundation, needing a definition to determine which institutions qualified for its college faculty pension fund, adopted the NEA's approach. It defined colleges as institutions that require "four years of academic or high school preparation or its equivalent in addition to preacademic or grammar schools."[24] The foundation sought to clarify the two levels of education further by urging abolition of collegiate preparatory departments and of the admission of students before high school graduation. Between 1890 and 1915, the line between higher and secondary education became more distinct. Institutions that originated in small-town America—academies, normal schools, and collegiate preparatory departments—had to adjust to a more bureaucratic system demanded by an urbanizing society.

The modern era of selective admissions at prestigious private colleges was a few years off. Princeton hired its first admissions director in 1922 to administer the beginning of selective admissions. Except for a few students turned away due to lack of dormitory space, the four colleges admitted all qualified students before World War I. Those not qualified were usually admitted as "specials" or sent to a preparatory school for further training. The trauma of outright rejection originated when some private colleges decided to limit enrollments in the early 1920s. Princeton and Swarthmore did so primarily for "reasons of space rather than race," though prejudice, especially anti-Semitism, encouraged selective admissions.[25] The confidence to reject qualified students stemmed from the colleges' newly secured role in educating the professions.

The colleges' ambitions intersected with those of powerful members of the professions, transforming professional training and turning liberal arts colleges into influential gatekeepers. In colonial and early republic America, the learned professions were dominated by those with a college degree followed by professional apprenticeship. Evangelicalism and the Jacksonian political spirit of the ante-bellum United States reduced the educational requirements for admission into the professions.

Some professionals, mainly those in elite urban positions, continued to be college educated, but colleges educated only a small proportion of future doctors and lawyers—and not even all ministers. The trend was reversed by a resurgence of professional self-consciousness and a growing public acceptance of the claims of expertise that encouraged stricter licensing procedures. In the mid-1890s, Johns Hopkins Medical School, Harvard Divinity School, and Harvard Law School became the first institutions in their fields to require baccalaureate degrees for admission. Increasingly, the best positions went to those who attended the professional schools that required baccalaureate degrees.[26]

The conflict over training was especially acute in medicine, where training in proprietary schools was rapidly replacing apprenticeship in the 1890s and 1900s. The role of colleges was precarious because they competed directly with medical schools for students. Colleges responded by offering courses that qualified students for advanced standing in the professional schools. In the early 1890s, the College of Physicians and Surgeons agreed to accept Princeton's B.S. degree in place of the first six months of study. Princeton also issued special certificates to graduates who took advanced courses in biology and chemistry, recommending them for advanced standing in medical schools. In the mid-1890s, Bucknell recruited students who wanted one or two years of college before going to medical school. In 1901, Bucknell opened a Department of Medicine purporting to offer most of the nonclinical studies of the first two years of medical college. Swarthmore pledged that its preparatory medical course would lead to admission in the second year of Philadelphia's leading medical colleges. Franklin and Marshall created a bachelor of philosophy degree in 1899 to enable future physicians to study more science and enter the second year of medical school. Even some Franklin and Marshall Academy graduates bypassed the college to go directly into medical colleges.[27]

The pressure from leading medical educators that culminated in Abraham Flexner's famous indictment of American medical schools in 1910 revolutionized medical education. Liberal arts colleges gave up any pretense of professional training. Princeton ceased to list its program in 1905. The Flexner Report led to the abolition of Bucknell's Department of Medicine and Swarthmore's preparatory medical course. In turn, all four colleges increased their offerings in biology and other sciences along the lines Flexner suggested. Flexner went further than even the AMA contemplated and recommended two years of college as a minimum requirement for medical school admission. As none of the eight medical schools in Pennsylvania had previously required any college study, the colleges stood to benefit from the report. Science was to be left to colleges, and professional training to medical schools. Since the medical reforms effectively favored native-born, affluent, Protestant, white males, these four colleges were particularly well positioned to provide the kind of gentlemen that the AMA wanted in medicine. The notice in the *Daily Princetonian* that read, "After 1908 candidates for admission to the Cornell University Medical College must be graduates of approved colleges or scientific schools," reflected a major victory for liberal arts colleges. By World War I, some college science, if not a baccalaureate degree, was required by most medical schools.[28]

The colleges' relationship to the law profession evolved along parallel lines. As in medicine, college control over the profession declined in the face of Jacksonian hostility. Bucknell, Franklin and Marshall, and Princeton made abortive attempts to start law schools before the Civil War. After the Civil War, law schools (many of them proprietary) replaced law office apprenticeship as the most common form of training. Between 1870 and 1910, the proportion of those admitted to the bar who were law school graduates jumped from one-quarter to two-thirds.

In 1893, when Harvard Law School became the first to require a baccalaureate degree for admission, it heralded a greater role for colleges in educating lawyers. As in medicine, educators at leading professional schools led the campaign for higher educational standards. The Association of American Law Schools, founded in 1900, was dominated by prestigious law schools and championed full-time attendance in three-year law programs that required at least a high school diploma for entrance. The four colleges in this study worked as feeders within this system; none of them made a serious attempt to found a law school after the Civil War. Instead, they developed curricula designed either to attract future lawyers for one or two years or to give their graduates advanced placement in existing law schools. In the 1890s, Woodrow Wilson developed a pre-law program based on political science courses after failing to interest President Patton or donors in establishing a law school at Princeton. Bucknell created the most vocational program, which, in addition to political science and economics courses, offered applied courses taught by local lawyers and promised advanced standing in affiliated law schools. A Pennsylvania Supreme Court decree that a college diploma was grounds for waiving the preliminary law exam considerably enhanced these colleges' position.[29]

Reform took place more gradually in legal education than in medical training. A transformation of the magnitude of that following the Flexner Report did not occur until well after World War I. But colleges, especially in the East, benefited from both custom and entrance requirements that made college degrees advantageous for entering the most prestigious law schools and firms. As in medicine, educational reform was intertwined with racial and ethnoreligious predilections. Night schools and other less socially prestigious law schools continued to supply lawyers for the lower end of the profession to serve upwardly mobile new immigrants and African Americans. The four colleges in this study provided students who met the standards for education and "character" desired by the dominant members of the legal profession.

Colleges had much less competition in the third traditional learned profession. Theology had the highest educational standards among the professions. In 1900, most seminaries required a year of college, and almost half required a college degree; in the East the proportions were much higher. Since many seminaries were connected to colleges, their curricula developed naturally in sequence with baccalaureate work. Crozer Theological Seminary, the Theological Seminary of the Reformed Church, and Princeton Theological Seminary were clearly graduate institutions and did not compete with the colleges. Theological seminaries pioneered the professional model that eventually prevailed in the other learned professions and in academia.[30]

A different model developed in engineering, the one area in which most of these colleges offered vocational training. Princeton, Swarthmore, and Bucknell established engineering programs at considerable cost. Civil engineering was the least expensive and most popular. These programs were natural extensions of the science curriculum, but the willingness to spend large sums on them suggests their importance in attracting students and donors.

The approach to business training was quite different. Although a college diploma rapidly gained currency as an appropriate credential for executives in the new corporations, there were relatively few formal business programs before World War I. Economics departments particularly benefited from the growing relationship, but even vocationally minded President Harris of Bucknell did not create a business program. Princeton turned down an offer from Philadelphia's Wanamaker family to underwrite a business program.[31] Liberal education or engineering training combined with the right social credentials sufficiently prepared graduates to enter corporate life.

These colleges, however, were ambivalent about competing for a role in training for another growing profession, public school teaching. State normal schools overlapped the last years of high school and the first years of college. Colleges convinced a few normal school graduates to enter their junior or senior classes. But as long as a college degree was neither required nor expected, they remained a small minority. Early normal school leaders hoped that their graduates would continue to college, but by the 1890s the two institutions were competitors.

Swarthmore's flirtation with becoming a normal school in the mid-1880s was the only venture in explicitly vocational teacher training by these colleges. President Magill wanted to train teachers through the baccalaureate program, but, having saved Swarthmore from becoming a normal school, he refused to consider subcollegiate teacher training. No new teacher training programs were created at Swarthmore until a grant from the Friends General Conference and the college's alumni association underwrote an education department in 1906. James McCosh envisioned Princeton training high school teachers as Scottish universities did, but he made little progress and his successors had little interest in teacher training. A number of graduates from both Bucknell and Franklin and Marshall became teachers, but neither college offered formal training through education departments until the 1910s. The colleges continued to produce teachers, especially for schools in their denomination and for prep schools, but that was a modest market. The job of preparing teachers for the mushrooming public schools remained primarily in the hands of state normal schools.[32] As these colleges secured roles in educating students for more highly paid and prestigious professions, they had little incentive to make special efforts to attract future teachers.

In contrast to normal schools, which overlapped the freshman and sophomore years, graduate study raised new questions about colleges' upper limits. The explosion of knowledge beyond the bounds of theological seminaries and amateur science created the problem of organizing postbaccalaureate studies in the new subject areas. Bucknell, Franklin and Marshall, and Swarthmore responded ambivalently. Each offered the traditional M.A. "in course" after three years of vaguely defined studies, good citizenship, and a small fee. Over the next few decades they experimented with various types of advanced work. In 1872, the *Mercersburg Review* called on the Reformed church to underwrite graduate studies at Franklin and Marshall. Swarthmore had a few "resident graduates" in the 1870s. In the 1880s and 1890s, each college offered a few graduate courses, primarily for their own graduates. In addition to offering on-campus graduate courses, the colleges experimented with credit for courses taken by their graduates at universities or for off-campus work, and with giving degrees by examination.

By 1910, such programs and the M.A. "in course" were disappearing in the face of a consensus that master's degrees required at least a year of study. Franklin and Marshall, perhaps because the theological seminary was across the street, offered only a handful of master's degrees and abolished its graduate program in 1924. Bucknell's graduate student body reached 114 in 1906 before declining to forty-five in 1915 and five in 1920. Swarthmore's small program peaked with six master's degrees in 1908. After awarding a flurry of honorary doctorates to bolster their staffs' credentials in the 1880s and 1890s, none of the three colleges gave serious thought to offering doctoral work. By 1917, graduate work had been standardized, and the three institutions were willing to leave most graduate study to the universities.[33]

Princeton, after decades of ambivalence, developed a medium-sized, prestigious graduate program by World War I. James McCosh arrived at Princeton determined to establish European-style university studies. He urged the establishment of graduate fellowships and badgered the trustees to compete with Harvard. In 1877, he established graduate studies and awarded the first fellowship. Two years later Princeton awarded its first doctorates. But few full-time students matriculated, and only twelve doctorates were awarded, all to Princeton graduates, during McCosh's presidency. He had more luck endowing fellowships to send Princeton graduates to other graduate schools. The trustees refused to underwrite McCosh's desire to compete with the research universities.[34]

In the late 1890s, Princeton brought its degrees into line with policies at the leading universities. The perfunctory M.A. "in course" was abolished, and requirements were standardized for master's degrees and doctorates. Even so, when the College of New Jersey was officially renamed Princeton University in 1896, the graduate program remained modest. In 1905, Bucknell had as many graduate students as Princeton, yet the latter became a founding member of the American Association of Universities in 1900. Apparently Princeton's wealth and social prestige enabled it to join that group and be considered a "university" when its curriculum hardly justified the term. Princeton enrolled only sixty-seven full-time and seventy-six part-time graduate students in 1911. On the eve of World War I, Princeton enrolled eighty-nine full-time graduate students, most supported by fellowships, and forty-eight part-time students.

Unlike most universities, Princeton made no provision for professional preparation; all graduate work was in the disciplines. The two plans for the graduate college over which Wilson and West locked horns both envisioned residential life in Gothic dormitories. They disagreed only about whether to isolate graduate students from undergraduates. Princeton's wealth enabled it to develop top-notch libraries and to provide university-level research facilities for its graduate students and faculty by 1917. Building its graduate college a mile from the main campus guaranteed that the tone of undergraduate life remained very collegiate.[35] As American higher education bifurcated into colleges and universities, Princeton moved into the latter category as a total institution, but for most students and alumni it remained a college.

Speeches and magazine articles by presidents and other college spokesmen at the turn of the century suggested that colleges were on the verge of demotion, if not extinction. Yet these four colleges were all stable or growing. These jeremiads became rhetorical commonplaces, particularly useful for soliciting support from alumni. But there were also honest fears. While the likelihood of fundamental change seems, in hindsight, to have been minimal, collegiate spokesmen may be excused for their concern that the dramatic changes in the role and image of college might not turn out to their benefit.

The clearest perceived threat was movement toward the "university," by which supporters meant not merely adding graduate schools onto existing colleges but adopting a European-style educational system. Admiration for German academic life led some to agree with John Burgess's declaration that he was "unable to divine what is to be ultimately the position of Colleges which cannot become Universities and which will not be Gymnasia."[36] In Germany, students progressed from a restrictive secondary education directly to the social freedom and academic specialization of the university without an intervening collegiate experience. Although the dissimilarity between gymnasia and American high schools made transplanting the German system unlikely, some university reformers adopted it as a model and proposed eliminating or shortening baccalaureate studies. Reducing college work to three years or less was possible, particularly as students going to medical or law school were already doing so de facto by leaving without a degree. Although attacks on the college received considerable publicity, the spirited defenses probably tell more about the insecurity of college leaders than about the reality of the threat.

Most university presidents spoke in favor of preserving the college's role in American education. Daniel Gilman, first president of Johns Hopkins University and founder of the first American graduate school, strongly defended the liberal arts colleges and expected all Johns Hopkins graduate students to have a baccalaureate degree. He maintained that colleges provided intellectual discipline, which had to precede the intellectual freedom of university work. Gilman believed that colleges provided an essential moral as well as intellectual preparation and that, with the growth of universities, colleges "will be recognized as more important than ever, because they lead to higher work."[37] President Jacob Schurman of Cornell wanted to shorten secondary education but retain the four-year college course. His only concern was that colleges might try to do university work and abandon the disciplinary work they did best. The preponderance of discussion in the *Educational Review* and the Association of American Universities shared these positive evaluations of colleges.[38] Even William Rainey Harper, who experimented with a Germanic structure at the University of Chicago, spoke warmly of college life at President Swain's inauguration at Swarthmore.[39] The college was to be a distinctive part of the emerging American system. Vive la différence!

Representatives of all four colleges stressed the need for a broadening and disciplinary experience preceding students' entry into their vocations and, naturally, nominated the college as the appropriate institution to provide it. As President Stahr said of Franklin and Marshall, "It does not claim to be a university. It lays stress on college education as liberal culture fitted to make men, preparatory to their taking up the study of a profession."[40] In 1913, Stahr's successor, President Apple, affirmed that Franklin and Marshall still believed that "the ideal of a college education is mastery of fundamental principles, training toward specific professional education being secondary and incidental."[41]

College and university presidents shared a desire to clarify the line between collegiate and university studies. Former President Edward Magill of Swarthmore wrote to Daniel Gilman that the ideal to be aimed for was "the separate existence of our various grades of Institutions each doing the very best work possible in our own field without aspiring to be more than it really is, or to do more than belongs to its particular grade." Only with a "good solid four-year College course, kept intact between our secondary Schools and universities," would order be restored in the educational system.[42] The withdrawal by 1917 of all except Franklin and Marshall from preparatory work and all but Princeton from substantial graduate work structurally fulfilled the rhetorical commitment.

The distinction between professional and liberal education was more difficult to establish. Although the rhetoric of the time and historians ever since have often counterposed the college and the university, the professional schools outside of universities posed a rarely acknowledged but greater threat. Many potential students bypassed or shortened their college educations in order to attend proprietary medical and law schools. It was probably the increasing numbers of students going into business who were responsible for rising enrollments in four-year college courses. Since graduate business schools were almost nonexistent, there was little incentive to leave without a degree.[43] Once the more prominent medical and law schools began requiring college degrees, the four-year program was safe.

In the 1890s, colleges experimented with balancing liberal and applied studies. In that decade, Swarthmore made its last major effort at teacher training, President Patton at Princeton considered making senior year preprofessional, and John Harris rapidly expanded undergraduate professional curricula at Bucknell.[44] But with the ascendancy of Presidents Swain and Wilson in 1902, Swarthmore and Princeton moved clearly to what Laurence Veysey has labeled "liberal culture." Franklin and Marshall was the most consistent defender of the liberal arts. President Thomas Apple told the College Association of Pennsylvania in 1888 that "the college should preserve its character as ministering first and foremost to high liberal culture, and should keep itself carefully distinguished from the professional school, the technic school, etc."[45] Liberal education, amended to allow some student choice and specialization, was clearly dominant at three of the colleges in the 1900s. Only students in engineering programs and in some of Bucknell's vocational tracks did not share a common liberal arts curriculum in the underclass years. At all four colleges, a majority "majored" in a discipline.

The emerging consensus on the educational role of colleges was reinforced by their considerable success in convincing the public of their unique social and moral atmosphere. The collegiate spirit appealed to the popular mind, an attraction reinforced by collegiate novels and athletics. For most students and parents, the social rewards of college life overshadowed the intellectual pursuits. Presidents repeatedly asserted the social and moral superiority of private colleges in terms that appealed to the values of upper-middle-class parents. College publicity stressed smallness, gentle and personal oversight, healthy activities, and desirable peers. The rapidly growing eastern and midwestern universities, many with enrollments reaching the five thousand range by 1910, could not convincingly make the same claims.

Presidential rhetoric at the four colleges became more confident after 1900.[46] In 1903, Swarthmore President Joseph Swain still portrayed dangers but surmised that colleges would survive if they improved their academic facilities while continuing to provide more contact between students and faculty and closer moral and social oversight than universities. President John Harris of Bucknell more expansively asserted that colleges would soon be deluged with students. Princeton's Dean West proclaimed renewed faith that the four-year college course would endure in 1903, having been convinced a few years earlier that shortening it to three years was unavoidable. President John Stahr told Franklin and Marshall's trustees in 1907 that "the fear which many have entertained as to the future of the denominational colleges and the smaller institutions of learning is really groundless."[47] The educational system that President Magill proposed when he organized the College Association of Pennsylvania had come about; college had become the preferred institution for more privileged youths seeking access to the most prestigious professions. In 1893, Woodrow Wilson defensively pleaded for making a bachelor's degree a prerequisite for professional training in order to return law, medicine, and theology to the status of "learned professions." By contrast, in 1909 the *Reformed Church Messenger* confidently asserted that "in law and medicine as well as in theology the tendency is to insist that students for these professions shall have a college course as a preparation."[48] By World War I, an American educational ladder had been built and colleges occupied a secure rung. Clear distinctions between secondary, collegiate, and graduate or professional studies were gaining acceptance, distinctions that have characterized American education ever since. The ambitions of college authorities intersected with those of the new professional and business classes. The presidents' confident pronouncements suggest that the "age of the university" was also an "age of the college."

The college's intellectual role in transmitting a tradition with classical and medieval origins makes the college appear more venerable than it is. Institutionally, the American college is relatively modern. Although its form derives partially from colonial models, much of it is a twentieth-century development. Historians must be careful not to read history backward and view the college as an ideal type emerging into a predestined future perceived by the wisest educators. Its form was hardly predestined, and its relationship to other types of education was uncertain at the beginning of the century.

The development of the college was one part of the rationalization of a system of education in the United States. The relationship of baccalaureate work to other levels of education changed dramatically between the Civil War and World War I. While the outlines of an educational system were evident in the 1860s, much was not systematized. The relationships of colleges to high schools, normal schools, professional training, and graduate study were neither rationalized nor static. Different configurations of institutions might well have occurred if the colleges' interests had not intersected with those of crucial members of the professions in favor of the freestanding four-year baccalaureate college. Threatened by two emerging giants, the high school and the research university, the college not only survived, but prospered. As the American educational system crystallized, the colleges carved out a major role without parallel in Europe.

Notes

1. According to Frederick Rudolph, *Curriculum: A History of the American Undergraduate Course of Study Since 1936* (San Francisco: Jossey-Bass, 1977), 160, only twenty-six colleges, mostly in the East, operated in 1870 without secondary branches.
2. Of 269 freshmen entering Franklin and Marshall College from 1872 through 1885, 102 were academy graduates, Charles Stahr Hartman, "Franklin and Marshall Academy, 1872–1943" (master's essay, Johns Hopkins University, 1948), 13–117, is a rare and excellent history of a preparatory department.
3. Ibid., 45–72. Also see Franklin and Marshall College, Trustees, Minutes (Franklin and Marshall Archives), 16 June 1877, for an insightful view on the relationship of the academy to the high schools.
4. Princeton University, *Catalogue,* 1873–1874 to 1879–1880; James McLachlan, *American Boarding Schools: A Historical Study* (New York: Charles Scribner's Sons, 1970), 193–207; J. David Hoeveler, *James McCosh and the Scottish Intellectual Tradition: From Glasgow to Princeton* (Princeton: Princeton University Press, 1981), 300–306, 347–348; Patricia Graham, *Community and Class in American Education, 1865–1918* (New York: John Wiley & Sons, 1974), 189–90; Frederick Rudolph, *The American College and University* (New York: Vintage Books, 1962), 285.
5. Statistics compiled from Swarthmore College, *Annual Catalogue,* 1877–1878, 1878–1879, 1887–1988, 1888–1889; Allen C. Thomas and Richard Henry Thomas, *A History of the Society of Friends,* American Church History Series, vol. 12 (New York: Christian Literature Co., 1894), 278; Edward H. Magill, *Sixty-Five Years in the life of a Teacher, 1841–1906* (Boston: Houghton Mifflin, 1907), 149–150.
6. In 1902 Bucknell Academy and the female institute prepared 28 of the 137 new students in the university. Bucknell University, Requirements for Admission, 1902–3 (notebook in Bucknell University Archives). Catalogs show similar ratios in other years. Bucknell University, Board of Trustees, Minutes (Bucknell University Archives), 11 January 1917.
7. The example is from Franklin and Marshall College, *Catalogue,* 1903–1904, p. 17. Much of the information in the following discussion is drawn from the catalogs and faculty minutes of the four colleges.
8. Princeton University, Faculty, Minutes (Princeton University Archives), 19 October 1898; Princeton University, *Annual Report of the President,* 1907. See also Bucknell, Requirements, for liberal use of "conditions."
9. Joseph Swain to James Lippincott, Swain Presidential Papers (Friends Historical Library), 14 January 1904. Magill's correspondence on admissions, which he handled for both the college and the preparatory department, is voluminous; Edward Magill, Presidential Papers (Friends Historical Library). Presidential papers at all four colleges show that great attention was paid to admissions. Bucknell, Trustees, 26 June 1888. Varnum L. Collings, *Princeton,* American College and University Series (New York: Oxford University Press, 1914), 294.
10. Principal Nathan Schaeffer to Theodore Apple, 9 June 1886 (Franklin and Marshall Archives).
11. Franklin and Marshall College, Faculty, Minutes (Franklin and Marshall Archives), 4 May 1887. The assertion that eastern colleges did not use certificates is partially incorrect. Although no state or regional system existed in the East these colleges developed certification systems based primarily on denominational relationships. Two works mistaken on this point are Joseph L. Henderson, *Admission to College by Certificate,* Teachers College Contributions to Education, no. 50 (New York: Teachers College Press, 1912), and Edward A. Krug, *The Shaping of the American High School, 1880–1920* (Madison: University of Wisconsin Press, 1969).
12. Bucknell University, Faculty, Minutes (Bucknell University Archives), e.g., 6 September 1878 and 23 June 1879; J. Orin Oliphant, *The Rise of Bucknell University* (New York: Appleton-Century-Crofts, 1965), 230–231; Bucknell University, *Catalogue,* 1896–1897.
13. Swarthmore College, Faculty, Minutes, 5 and 12 October 1882, 22 January 1894; Swarthmore College, Stockholders, *Minutes of the Annual Meeting of the Stockholders,* 1884, pp. 12–13. A good example of the

system at work in Magill's correspondence is Principal Fannie Pyle (Friends High School, West Chester, Pa.) to Edward Magill, 26 August 1884, Magill Presidential Papers. For an example of a school seeking to be placed on the certificate list, see George Megangee to Charles De Garmo, 2 and 14 March 1896, De Garmo Presidential Papers (Friends Historical Library). Joseph Swain, "Remarks," *Proceedings of the Middle States Association of Colleges and Secondary Schools* 16 (1902): 42.

14. James McCosh to Logan Murray, 26 March 1877, James McCosh Papers (Princeton University Archives). The correspondence continued the next year (11 and 22 May, 2 December). Hoeveler, 305–306; Bucknell, *Catalogue*, 1885–1886, p. 14; Oliphant, 230–231.

15. "Editorial," *Educational Review* 5 18(January 1893): 90–91; Francis L. Patton to Wilson Ferrand, Patton Papers (Princeton University Archives), 11 December 1901; Princeton University, School of Science Faculty, Minutes (Princeton University Archives), 26 February 1902; Princeton, Faculty, 19 February and 13 May 1912.

16. Herbert Malick, "An Historical Study of Admission Practices in Four-Year Undergraduate Colleges of the U.S.; 1870–1915" (Ph.D. diss., Boston College, 1966), 189–190; Krug, 125–129, 363–365. The catalogs list the entrance requirements. For the official action by the Middle States Association, which all four joined, see the *Proceedings* 1 (1894): 61–63.

17. Charles Eliot's Committee of Ten, the Committee on College Entrance Requirements, and the National Conference on Uniform Entrance Requirements in English dealt with the problem in the 1890s. Educational journals such as the *Educational Record* also focused their attention on this issue.

18. Malick, 209–213; College Entrance Examination Board, *Annual Report of the Secretary,* 1901–1913.

19. Malick, 240–241, 288; CEEB, 1902–16.

20. Malick, 196–298, 313. The term "unit" was in use prior to the Carnegie Foundation's adoption of it.

21. See the catalogs of each college. Also, Collins, 328–29; Harry C. McKown, *The Trend of College Entrance Requirements, 1913–1922,* Bureau of Education Bulletin, no. 35, 1924 (Washington D.C.: U.S. Government Printing Office, 1925), 53–54.

22. Krug, 159–163: H.H. Apple, *Report of the President of Franklin and Marshall College,* 1913–1914, p. 6.

23. Swarthmore, Stockholders, 1877; *Phoenix* 6 (1886). "Alumni Notes" lists several such cases; Homer D. Babbidge, Jr., "Swarthmore College in the Nineteenth Century: A Quaker Experience in Education" (Ph.D. diss., Yale University, 1953), 180. For a discussion at Princeton of whether to admit two graduates of other colleges into the senior class, see Francis L. Patton to S. R. Winans, 21 November 1901, and Patton to Robert D. Williams, 30 November 1901, Patton Papers. For Bucknell, see Bucknell, Requirements.

24. Krug, 160, quoting the foundation's *First Annual Report* of 1906, Ellen C. Lagemann, *Private Power for the Public Good* (Middletown, Conn.: Wesleyan University Press, 1983), 94–95.

25. Marcia G. Synnott, *The Half-Opened Door: Discrimination and Admissions at Harvard, Yale, and Princeton, 1900–1970* (Westport, Conn.; Greenwood Press, 1979), 189–193; quote is on 189. Richard J. Walton, *Swarthmore College: An Informal History* (Swarthmore, Pa.: Swarthmore College, 1986), 43. The development of selective admissions has been carefully analyzed in Harold Wechsler, *The Qualified Student: A History of Selective College Admission in America* (New York: John Wiley & Sons, 1977).

26. For a study of the professions before the Civil War, see Daniel H. Calhoun, *Professional Lives in America* (Cambridge: Harvard University Press, 1965), esp. 178–197; Colin Burke, *American Collegiate Populations: A Test of the Traditional View* (New York: New York University Press, 1982), 249–262. For the broader context, see Robert H. Wiebe, *The Search for Order, 1877–1920* (New York: Hill and Wang, 1967), 111–123.

27. Princeton, *Catalogue,* 1892–1893 to 1900–1901; Bucknell, *Catalogue,* 1896–1897, insert; Oliphant, 218–222; Swarthmore, *Catalogue,* 1900–1901; Franklin and Marshall, Trustees, 17 June 1899; Hartman, 45.

28. *Daily Princetonian* 23 (29 April 1908); John Winter Rice, *A History of the Teaching of Biology at Bucknell University* (Lewisburg, Pa., 1952), 3–5; Oliphant, 218–222; John H. Harris, *Thirty Years as President of Bucknell with Baccalaureate and Other Addresses* (Washington, D.C., 1926), 40–42, 81–94; Swarthmore, *Catalogue,* 1900–1901 to 1910–11; Franklin and Marshall, *Catalogue,* 1911–1912 and 1912–1913; Abraham Flexner, *Medical Education in the United States and Canada* (New York: Carnegie Foundation for the Advancement of Teaching, 1910); Lagemann, 61–74; Kenneth M. Ludmerer, *Learning to Heal: The Development of American Medical Education* (New York: Basic Books, 1985), 72–122, 166–190; Paul Starr, *The Social Transformation of American Medicine* (New York: Basic Books, 1982), 116–127; Princeton, *Catalogue,* 1904–1905 and 1905–1906; Gerald Markowitz and David Rosner, "Doctors in Crisis," *American Quarterly* 25 (March 1973): 83–107.

29. Jerold Auerbach, *Unequal Justice: Lawyers and Social Change in Modern America* (New York: Oxford University Press, 1976), 74–129; William R. Johnson, *Schooled Lawyers: A Study in the Clash of Professional Cultures* (New York: New York University Press, 1978), 58–164; Arthur S. Link, ed., *The Papers of Woodrow*

Wilson (Princeton: Princeton University Press, 1966–), 7:63–68, 8:381–83; John M. Mulder, *Woodrow Wilson: The Years of Preparation* (Princeton: Princeton University Press, 1978), 133–134; Harris, 94.

30. Rudolph, *Curriculum,* 179; Natalie A. Naylor, "The Theological Seminary in the Configuration of American Higher Education," *History of Education Quarterly* 17 (Spring 1977): 17–30.

31. Selected correspondence of 1916 and 1917, John Grier Hibben Papers (Princeton University Manuscript Collection); Princeton, *Catalogue,* 1916–1917. The university especially objected to Rodman Wanamaker's desire to have businessmen teach these courses. Kenneth W. Condit, *History of the Engineering School of Princeton University, 1875–1955* (Princeton: Princeton University Press, 1962), 75–96; Princeton University, *Annual Report of the President,* 1916, pp. 9, 31–32. The relationship of colleges and business training has been neglected and needs the same careful scholarship that has recently been devoted to the professionalization of law and medicine.

32. Paul M. Martingly, *The Classless Profession: American Schoolmen in the Nineteenth Century* (New York: New York University Press, 1975), 162–164; Swarthmore, *Catalogue,* 1906–1907 to 1914–1915; Hoeveler, 305–306; Apple, 1912 and 1919.

33. Bucknell, *Catalogue,* 1889–1890 to 1919–1921; Franklin and Marshall, *Catalogue,* 1893–1894 to 1923–1924; Swarthmore, *Catalogue,* 1883–1884 to 1919–1920; Franklin and Marshall College, Alumni Association, *Report,* 1905; "Editorial," *Mercersburg Review* 19 (January 1872): 153–157.

34. McCosh urged the creation of fellowships in his inaugural. Princeton College, *Inauguration of James McCosh* (New York: Carter & Bros., 1868), 82–87; Princeton University, Trustees, Minutes (Princeton University Archives), 22 December 1875; *Princeton College Bulletin* 1 (March 1889): 42–52; Princeton College, *Alumni Directory* (Princeton, 1888), 73–78; Hoeveler, 286–293; Roger L. Geiger, *To Advance Knowledge: The Growth of American Research Universities, 1900–1940* (New York: Oxford University Press, 1986), 1–18.

35. Princeton, *Annual Report,* 1907; Princeton, Trustees, 13 January 1916. In 1906–1907 full-time enrollment was only thirty-eight; in 1915–1916 it was 126. Collins, 255–286. For two statements on Princeton's approach, see Alexander T. Ormond, "University Ideals at Princeton," *Journal of the Proceedings and Addresses of the National Education Association* 36 (1897): 346–357; and Andrew F. West, *The Graduate College of Princeton* (Princeton: Princeton University Press, 1913). The first professional graduate program was a master's degree course in engineering begun in 1921. Condit, 89; Princeton University, *Report of the Librarian* (Princeton, 1921), 1–13. For a sense of a faculty member who was committed to Princeton becoming a research university, see the Edwin G. Conklin Papers (Princeton University Archives).

36. Rudolph, *American College,* 330, quoting Burgess's *American University of 1884.*

37. Daniel C. Gilman, "The Idea of a University," *North American Review* 133 (October 1881): 353–367; quote is from 359.

38. Jacob Schurman, "The Ideal College Education," *Proceedings of the Annual Convention of the College Association of the Middle States and Maryland* 3 (1891): 64–73. A similar worry was expressed in "Editorial," *Educational Review* 1 (1891): 387–388. The debate over the role of the colleges was particularly well recorded in the forty volumes of *Educational Review* (1891–1910). Rudolph, *American College,* 443–449.

39. See, for instance, papers by Stanford's David Starr Jordan and Yale's Arthur Hadley in Association of American Universities, *Journal of Proceedings* 4 (1904): 21–33. Harper's surprising remarks were quoted in *Friends Intelligencer* 59 (22 November 1902): 739.

40. John Stahr, "Remarks," in College Association of the Middle States and Maryland, *Proceedings* 22 (1908): 9.

41. Apple's remarks are quoted in H. M. J. Klein, *History of Franklin and Marshall College, 1787–1948* (Lancaster, Pa., 1952), 160. See also Woodrow Wilson, "Should an Antecedent Liberal Education Be Required of Students in Law, Medicine, and Theology?" *Proceedings of the National Education Association* 32 (1893): 112–117; Andrew F. West, *American liberal Education* (New York: Charles Scribner's Sons, 1907), 65–77; John Stahr, "President's Report: 1907," in Franklin and Marshall, Trustees, 10 June 1907.

42. Edward Magill to Daniel C. Gilman, 12 December 1894 (Gilman Collection, Johns Hopkins University Archives). Also, Richard Schiedt, "College-Need and College Needs," *Reformed Quarterly Review* 41 (January 1894): 117–128.

43. Andrew West, "Remarks," *Proceedings of the Annual Convention of the College Association of the Middle States and Maryland* 17 (1903): 53–60. See also Stahr, "President's Report," for another attack on medical school admissions.

44. Patton's report to the Princeton trustees, 8 June 1896.

45. Thomas G. Apple, "The Idea of a Liberal Education," in College Association of Pennsylvania, *Proceedings* 1 (1887): 13–14.

46. Laurence R. Veysey, *The Emergence of the American University* (Chicago: University of Chicago Press, 1965), 264–83, 441–44, and Rudolph, *American College*, 440–461, find a similar national trend.

47. Stahr's "President's Report"; Joseph Swain, "Remarks," *Friends Intelligencer* 60 (20 June 1903): 393; John Harris, "Remarks," Middle States Association of Colleges and Secondary Schools, *Proceedings* 7 (1903): 79–81; Andrew F. West, "What Should Be the Length of the College Course?" ibid., 53–60; Edward Magill, "The Proper Relation of Colleges to the Educational Institutions of the State," in College Association of Pennsylvania, *Proceedings* 1 (1887): 11.

48. "Editorial," *Reformed Church Messenger,* 4 March 1909, p. 1; Woodrow Wilson, *College and State* (New York: Harper Bros., 1925), 1:223–231.

RETHINKING THE "NONTRADITIONAL" STUDENT FROM A HISTORICAL PERSPECTIVE:

State Normal Schools in the Late Nineteenth and Early Twentieth Centuries

CHRISTINE A. OGREN

Since the mid-twentieth century, a host of political, economic, and societal changes have contributed to the diversification of students in American institutions of higher education. Developments such as the Allied victory in World War II, the decrease in blue-collar jobs, and changing gender attitudes, have encouraged members of minority racial groups, young people with low social-class standing, and women to attend college (Bean & Metzner, 1985). Beginning in the 1960s, governmental and institutional financial-aid and affirmative-action policies explicitly promoted racial, class, and gender diversity for the first time. Not surprisingly, researchers have recently begun to assess the impact of these programs and the implications of an increasingly diverse student body (see Levine & Associates, 1989; Levine & Nidiffer, 1996; London, 1992; Pascarella & Terenzini, 1998; Westbrook & Sedlacek, 1991), using the term "nontraditional" to describe students who are older than typical college students, work because of financial necessity, belong to the first generation in their family to attend college, do not live on campus, attend part-time, or are members of minority racial groups. Bean and Metzner (1985) add, "Nontraditional students are distinguished by the lessened intensity and duration of their interaction with the primary agents of socialization (faculty, peers) at the institutions they attend" (p. 488).

The term "nontraditional" implies that these atypical students are new to higher education and that colleges and universities traditionally have not served people like them. While the intention of research on nontraditional students is to better meet their needs, it may also have the unintended consequence of reinforcing the notion that these students are out of place, indirectly discouraging them from interacting with others on campus. One way to soften the effect of this research would be to emphasize atypical students' rich history in higher education. Indeed, historical research indicates that, even without the encouragement of explicit governmental and institutional policies, students from unsophisticated, lower-social-class backgrounds have a long tradition of attending American colleges and universities (see, for example, Allmendinger, 1975; Nidiffer, 1999). While generations of nontraditional students have attended virtually every type

The author thanks D. J. Chandler, Clif Conrad, Linda Eisenmann, Yvonna Lincoln, Ernie Pascarella, and John Thelin for encouragement and comments on earlier versions of this essay. The National Academy of Education and the NAE Spencer Postdoctoral Fellowship Program supported the research for this article.

Christine A. Ogren is Assistant Professor, Division of Educational Policy and Leadership Studies, University of Iowa.

The Journal of Higher Education, Vol. 74, No. 6 (November/December 2003) Copyright © 2003 by The Ohio State University of higher education institution, they were especially prominent at the precursors of many state colleges and regional universities. S. Y. Gillan, who graduated in 1879 from one of these institutions, Illinois State Normal University, reflected that it "was a school of the people existing for and representing the masses and not the classes."[1]

This article focuses on state normal schools, which resulted from nineteenth-century education reformers' efforts to adapt the German teacher seminary and the French *ecole normale* to train teachers for the growing system of American common schools. Massachusetts established the first state normal schools in 1839, and Connecticut and New York soon followed. By 1870, 39 state normal schools were located in New England, the mid-Atlantic states, the Midwest, and California. During the following decades, southern states established segregated normal schools, and the institutions spread throughout the country and its territories; by 1920, there were more than 180. State normals, which provided elementary-level teacher certification and offered various degrees in pedagogy, were low-status institutions of higher education during a time when the lines between "higher" and "lower" education were blurred (Clifford, 1995, pp. 3–6).

By the end of the nineteenth century, many states began to look to the normals to prepare teachers for burgeoning positions on high-school faculties, which the normals saw as an opportunity to gain prestige. During the 1890s, the schools in Albany, New York, and Ypsilanti, Michigan adopted the name, "normal college." As other normals began to offer four years of college work and grant bachelor's degrees, they usually replaced the title "normal school" with "teachers college." The majority of state normal schools became teachers colleges during the 1920s and 1930s. In the 1940s, the flood of World-War II veterans seeking all-purpose higher education fueled the normals' quest for status, and they began to drop teacher education as their organizing purpose. As a result, the 1940s, 1950s, and 1960s witnessed another flurry of name changes as the former normals added more prestigious programs and became state colleges. By the end of the century, continuing "mission creep" (Selingo, 2000) allowed many to become state universities; institutions that began as normal schools formed the nucleus of state systems from New York to California, and former normals make up the majority of regional universities from Northern Michigan to Southwest Texas.

Although institutions whose roots are nineteenth-century normal schools play a central role in mass higher education at the turn of the twenty-first century, their story is not well known. In their quest for higher status, former normals have tended to bury their history as "an impoverished past thankfully left behind" (Goodlad, 1990, p. 73). Meanwhile, historians of higher education have concentrated on more elite institutions, and historians of teacher education have focused on the normal schools' leaders and official policies. These historiographical approaches virtually ignore normal-school students. (For the few exceptions to this rule, see Burke, 1982; Herbst, 1980; Herbst, 1989; Clifford, 1983; Clifford, 1995; Ogren, 1995; and Schwager, 1987.) Focusing explicitly on the normalites, I conducted extensive historical investigations of more than half of the state institutions that began as normals throughout the United States. I did archival research at seven campuses—in Castleton, Vermont; Geneseo, New York; Florence, Alabama; Pine Bluff, Arkansas; San Marcos, Texas; Oshkosh, Wisconsin; and San Jose, California—and reviewed various sources on close to one hundred other former normal schools. These sources include institutional histories, which I used selectively; like Frederick Rudolph, I "carefully culled episodes and illustrations" (Thelin, 1990, p. xviii) to use as primary material for my own analysis.

This article presents a socio-historical analysis of the students who attended state normal schools and their experiences in the late nineteenth and early twentieth centuries. I profile "normalites" relative to the portrayal of nontraditional students in current literature. Then I discuss the ways in which the state normal schools provided a meaningful higher education experience. While their official mission was preparing teachers, the characteristics of their student bodies forced the normals to expand their unofficial mission to include welcoming unsophisticated students into an engaging intellectual and public life. Indeed, "it was the normal schools . . . that really brought higher education to the people" (Herbst, 1989, p. 142; see also Herbst, 1980). Although the normal schools' specific approaches to serving these students were more appropriate for their time than the present, it is important for current researchers to understand that these institutions did serve atypical students effectively. As student bodies continue to diversify in the twenty-first century, it is helpful to take a look through the lens of history at earlier nontraditional students.

Nontraditional Students

My in-depth examination of state normal schools reveals that their students had much in common with today's nontraditional students. Race (Westbrook & Sedlacek, 1991) and socioeconomic status (Lace, 1986) are prominent issues in literature on nontraditional students. Bean and Metzner (1985) acknowledge that these characteristics, along with gender, "might have differentiated traditional and nontraditional students a century ago (p. 488)." A look at the normalites convincingly confirms this hunch. At a time when women were an unwelcome minority on many coeducational campuses, they were a visible majority at state normal schools. A small number of normals, mainly in the South, restricted their enrollment to women only. But most normal schools were coeducational, with enrollments made up increasingly of women with each passing decade. Before the turn of the twentieth century, the enrollments at coeducational normals nationwide were between 25 and 90 percent female. At coeducational southern normals, only one-quarter to one-half of the students were women. Typical of normals outside the South, the institutions in Cedar Falls, Iowa, and Greeley, Colorado enrolled 70 percent women. After the turn of the century, throughout the country the percentage of students who were women was consistently well over 50, and occasionally higher than 90 percent.[2] The large numbers of female normalites are consistent with the schools' official mission of preparing students for the female-dominated profession of teaching.

In addition to women, state normal schools made higher education available to a significant number of students from minority racial and ethnic groups. Like Arkansas, which established the Branch Normal College at Pine Bluff euphemistically "for the poorer classes," most southern states established segregated normal schools for African-American students. Oklahoma and North Carolina also established segregated normal schools for Native American students.[3] In addition, evidence suggests that several northern, majority-white normals served at least a limited number of minority students. In New York, Albany matriculated twenty-six Native American students in the late nineteenth century and many South-European, Polish, and Jewish immigrants in the early twentieth century, and Oswego graduates of the 1890s remembered "an amiable American Indian girl," "popular young men from the Hawaiin Islands," "a shy, quiet Negro girl," and a "much respected" African American man. African American students, many of whom were from the South, had begun appearing at state normals from Westfield, Worcester, and Framingham, Massachusetts, to Normal, Illinois, soon after the Civil War. The normal schools in Pennsylvania welcomed several students from Puerto Rico and South America beginning in the 1890s, and Cecil E. Evans, who began his presidency at Southwest Texas State Normal School in San Marcos in 1911, once noted, "Very few Mexican students ever get high enough in the grades to reach us," implying that at least a few Mexican students did "reach" the institution.[4]

Regardless of their race or gender, most normalites shared rather low socioeconomic status; they were, for the most part, the daughters and sons of working people, many of whom were struggling financially. Throughout the late nineteenth century, skilled, semiskilled, unskilled, and agricultural workers headed the homes of two-thirds of normalites in Massachusetts. The normal in Worcester reflected the growing industrial city, drawing primarily the children of skilled workers and laborers. During the first decade of the twentieth century, Southwest Texas kept very detailed records of the occupations of its students' parents. Only 6 percent engaged in the professions of medicine and law; physicians, lawyers, teachers, ministers, druggists, engineers, editors, "newspapermen," and architects amounted to only 14 percent. The parents of San-Marcos students were more likely to work in agriculture than any other trade: 47 percent were farmers, and ranchers, fruit growers, stockmen and dairymen were another 10 percent. In fact, farming, which was in economic crisis throughout most of the late nineteenth and early twentieth centuries in the United States, shaped the lives of a majority of normalites. During the late nineteenth century, nearly two-thirds of students at Cedar Falls, Iowa, were from farming families. Likewise, in 1889, the parents of 428 of the 639 students at Emporia Kansas, were farmers. Students at Pine Bluff often had to arrive at school late in the fall and leave early in the spring, in order to help their families with harvests and plantings.[5]

The families of many normal-school students could not afford traditional higher education. For example, George Martin graduated as valedictorian of his Massachusetts high-school class in 1855 and was unable to fulfill his plan to attend Amherst College because of a lack of funds. Martin then worked for seven years and was finally able to enter Bridgewater Normal in 1862. Some normalites were from such impoverished backgrounds that the schools gained a reputation for serving the poor. A Vermont newspaper described the normal in Castleton as catering to the "calico-attired country girl of limited means," and in Westfield, Massachusetts, where the normal school enrolled an especially high number of children of small farmers, "normal" was a disparaging name for a poor person. Similarly, some residents of Oswego, New York, referred to normalites there as "state paupers." Pine-Bluff students made light of their reputation in the following lines from a late-1920s school cheer: "State School, State School, yes we are the state school/Nothing new or formal, no Sir!/Our hair is shaggy and our clothes are baggy/But they'll soon be raggy, Yea!" Throughout the country, many normal-school students could have yelled along.[6]

In addition to being female, minorities, or of low socioeconomic standing, today's nontraditional students often are older than the typical eighteen to twenty-two years (Bean & Metzner, 1985; Bendixen-Noe, 1998; Lace, 1986; Metzner & Bean, 1987; Pascarella & Terenzini, 1998; Zwerling, 1992). Although Bean and Metzner do not acknowledge it, this is another factor that also differentiated traditional and nontraditional students in the late nineteenth and early twentieth centuries. Many normalites—as well as some students at colleges and universities—were mature in age. Throughout the country, most normal-school students were older than the minimum state-stipulated fifteen or sixteen years. Michael Dignam, who graduated in 1882 from Westfield, Massachusetts, remembered, "The pupils were all mature, no one under 20; the ages ranged as high as 26 or 28." A member of the class of 1888 at Oshkosh, Wisconsin lyrically explained: "In age the class varies all the way from the blushing maiden in her teens, filled with anticipation of the future, and the aspiring youth yearning for independence, to the retrospective and reflective minds of maturer years." From Oneonta, New York to Greeley, Colorado, normal schools in the late 1880s and early 1890s reported that on average their entering students were more than 20 years old. In 1886, the first class at Tempe averaged 19.4 years in age; at 26 and 30 years old, respectively, Julia A. McDonald and James M. Patterson were among the oldest students. When the all-female state normal in Greensboro, North Carolina opened in 1892, the average age of entering students was close to 20 years. Throughout the 1890s and 1900s, women students at Oneonta continued to enter at an average age of over 20 years, while their male classmates were closer to 22. In 1903, the first class at San Marcos signed in at 20.1 years, with one student who was 38 years old. The normal school in Plattsburgh, New York, had at least a couple of mature students during the 1910s—there were two mother-daughter pairs on campus.[7]

The literature on nontraditional students further characterizes them as part-time attenders and commuters (Bean & Metzner, 1985; Gilley & Hawkes, 1989; Lace, 1986; Metzner & Bean, 1987; Pascarella & Terenzini, 1998). At West Virginia's normal in West Liberty, some students commuted to campus in an effort to save money. Similarly, many normalites at the Territorial Normal School in Tempe, Arizona, during the decade or so after it opened in 1886, commuted. One male student later explained, "I rode horseback from Mesa to Tempe and returned each day, milked six cows morning and evening, and each morning had to run my horses down before I could go to Tempe. It took nearly 45 minutes to make the distance."[8] Aside from a few scattered examples, however, commuting from home was rare among normalites whose families didn't happen to live within walking distance of campus; after all, transportation was limited. There is no evidence that any students in attendance at a normal school attended part-time. Looking at the normalites serves as a reminder, though, that attending part-time and commuting are not intrinsic personal characteristics in the way that age, race, class, and gender are. Present-day students attend part-time and commute *because* they cannot afford to attend full-time or live on campus and/or their family or life commitments prohibit them from devoting themselves exclusively to the pursuit of higher education. Normalites clearly shared the personal traits that create the special conditions of attendance for today's nontraditional students, but they lived under different historical conditions. Thus, although most were not commuters, many normalites, like today's nontraditional students, arrived with significant work experience and found it necessary to work while attending normal school.

Many state normal-school students had work experience, usually as teachers, prior to matriculation. As early as the 1840s and early 1850s at Bridgewater, "nearly all" of the students had themselves taught school. Of the 2,500 students who enrolled at Oswego between its opening in the mid-1860s and 1880, more than 1,000 had teaching experience, with an average of three years in the classroom. During the late 1880s, more than half of the students at Farmington, Maine arrived with teaching experience. Outside the Northeast, it was also very common for normalites to have work experience as teachers. At Oshkosh in 1879, as well as in 1884, half of the students had taught, and among them the average time spent in front of a class was 2.6 years. Between 1892 and 1908, the collective student body at Oshkosh averaged one year of experience. In their class histories, students conveyed the same idea a bit more creatively: The class of 1895 taught "more than a thousand months," and the brains of members of the class of 1896 bore "unsightly marks . . . caused by patient efforts to impress the American youth in our rural districts with the precept, knowledge is power." Nearly half of the normalites at Emporia, Kansas, in the late 1880s taught before entering the normal, many for five or more years. Tempe's Julia McDonald and James Patterson were former teachers, as were more than 34 percent of the students at Florence, Alabama, around the turn of the century.[9]

Many normalites worked while enrolled, and self-supporting students were not unusual at the state normals. In 1882, President Edwin Hewett of Illinois State Normal University reported, "Many of our students . . . are dependent upon their own exertions for means"; and a decade or so later Principal John Mahelm Berry Sill of the State Normal School in Ypsilanti, Michigan, said, "Our students are working young men and women who earn their little money by the hardest toil." Just after the turn of the twentieth century, one-third of the students at Florence "earned their own money to pay expenses," while Oregon's State Superintendent of Public Instruction expressed concern about the large numbers of "self-supporting" normalites, urging, "Greater precaution must be exercised to prevent the ambitious from overworking than to rouse the sluggards." Gender often determined the term-time jobs normalites were able to find: in New York, female students at Oneonta worked as babysitters or maids, while male students at Oswego shoveled snow, sold various products, or worked as janitors.[10] Throughout the country, it was common for normalites to take leaves of absence to earn the necessary money to continue their education, an earlier approach to being a part-time student. Most often, they taught in rural schools for one or more terms before returning to normal school. For example, a student at Nebraska's Peru State Normal School in 1873 soon found himself short of money. He later remembered:

> My graduation looked far off to me and my limited means made it necessary to quit school for a while and return to the farm. But Dr. Curry, then principal, learning my predicament found me a country school in Otoe county that enabled me to return again after I had finished my school. This I continued to do, alternating between teaching and going to school until I finally graduated in the spring of 1879.[11]

Like today's nontraditional students, normalites found ways to overcome their financial limitations.

Although work experience as well as age must have fostered a certain level of maturity among normal-school students, they were hardly worldly-wise. In fact, socio-historical examination of normalites reveals that many were quite provincial, or lacked sophistication. This significant characteristic is curiously absent from the literature on nontraditional students, but it is unmistakable in accounts of the normal schools. A chronicler of Bridgewater State Normal School observed, "It is hard for us to conceive how provincial these students were. Most of them had never been far from their own towns. . . . ." Sarah A. Dixon, who graduated from Bridgewater in 1885, called herself "a sip of a girl from an isolated shore home." Throughout the country, normalites were predominantly from very small, often very rural, towns and villages. At Arkansas' Branch Normal College for black students, the vast majority of students were from the rural areas surrounding Pine Bluff. Between the 1880s and the 1900s, 23 to 30 percent of all Oshkosh, Wisconsin, students hailed from Oshkosh, which was a booming lumber town. Another 8 percent or fewer of the students came from other lumber towns in the area, and only a few hailed from the bigger cities of Milwaukee, Madison, and, occasionally, Chicago. More than half of the students were from much smaller, rural towns. The 1890s football cheer for the normal in Geneseo, New York, included a line that would also have suited most other normals: "We came to the gridiron fresh from verdant farms." Meanwhile, many of the students at California's state normal in Chico were from very remote mountain settlements in the northern part of the state. When they arrived at the normal, Chico was the largest town they had ever seen.[12]

It is hardly surprising that students from such remote areas tended to be unpolished. For many years after the 1868 establishment of the state normal in Peru, the many students there who had lived "isolated lives" tended to be "ignorant of the social ways incident to more thickly settled portions of the country; hence, they sometimes appeared reserved and awkward." A student at Peru in the late nineteenth century remembered, "Girls with brown faces and plain clothing" and "boys with calloused hands." Early in the twentieth century, the principal at Willimantic, Connecticut, complained, "Many of our students are crude. Their manner of talking, their table manners, their actions often show a decided lack of culture."[13] Sensitive to the implied class prejudice, present-day administrators and researchers would hesitate to make observations such as these. Nontraditional students likely have similar rough edges, however, and a non-pejorative understanding of their provincialism might be an important step toward serving them more effectively. While the normalites' lack of sophistication frustrated Willimantic's principal, it also made them hungry for inspiration. For example, an Oshkosh student declared:

> When one for the first time beholds an imposing structure, whether reared by man's stalwart arm or nature's majestic art, impressions are made upon the delicate parchment of the mind which age can not dim nor time obliterate. Such is the character of my first impressions on beholding the Oshkosh Normal. Its architectural symmetry symbolizes the noble educational system in which it forms an important factor; . . . its spacious assembly room and its commodious recitation rooms silently insinuate to the pupil the possibilities of mental expansion, while each high ceiling proclaims the aphorism, "There is always room at the top."[14]

Attendance at state normal schools was a significant departure in the theretofore unsophisticated lives of many students. As the next section explains, the state normals not only accepted students from nontraditional backgrounds, but they also engaged their sense of awe to create an atmosphere that embraced them.

Embracing Nontraditional Students

This examination of state normal-school students has suggested that the types of students now considered to be nontraditional were prominent in the late nineteenth and early twentieth centuries on state normal-school campuses. A century later, researchers have reported on—and forecasted further—demographic changes in higher education. To meet this challenge, Arthur Levine has called for "better serving the underserved" (Levine & Associates, 1989, p. 172), and much of the literature on nontraditional students is concerned with how to do this (see, for example, Astin, 1993; Gilley & Hawkes, 1989; Lace, 1986; Richardson & Skinner, 1992). It might also be useful for current administrators, as well as researchers, simply to understand that they are not pioneers in their efforts to welcome atypical students to college campuses. State normal schools hardly "underserved" these students, but instead enabled them to take advantage of an engaging intellectual life and to become involved in public life, which encouraged them to move far beyond their humble backgrounds. Normal-school administrators and faculty members' first step, more than a half-century before government programs designed to bring underprivileged students into institutions of higher education, was to ensure that the normals were accessible and affordable for all students.

Admission requirements at state normal schools were fairly loose and somewhat flexible. They did not require matriculants to be high-school graduates until education at that level was attainable by most residents of their states, which generally was not until the early twentieth century. Before they required high-school graduation, normal schools administered admission examinations, but prospective students could present teaching credentials or diplomas instead of sitting for them. Previous years' exams were often published in normal-school catalogues, making them available to students preparing for future admission. In the late 1870s, San Jose, California published questions in arithmetic, grammar, geography, and spelling for admission to the junior class and additional questions for admission to the "middle" and senior classes. Applicants to Oshkosh, Wisconsin, during the 1880s had to score 70 percent or better in reading and spelling, arithmetic, grammar, geography, and U.S. history. In Vermont, Castleton's admission exam in the early 1890s covered spelling, arithmetic, physiology, grammar, geography, Vermont history, U.S. history, and civics.[15] In addition to academic qualifications, other admission requirements were fairly easy to acquire. Applicants had to be 15 or 16 (or 14, at Pine Bluff, Arkansas) years in age, and usually of good "moral character" and health, presumably as prerequisites for being good teachers in the future.[16]

In addition to setting fairly easy standards for admission, many state normal schools assured accessibility by providing detailed directions to campus and individual assistance with settling in. Many normal schools did everything short of printing train schedules in their catalogs. For example, an Oshkosh catalog described the "numerous lines of railroad and river steamers entering the city, as well as its favorable location." Similarly, a bulletin for the normal in Florence, Alabama, explained that the "main line of the Southern Railway from Chattanooga passes through Sheffield, and all passenger trains are met there by electric cars which deliver passengers in Florence in about twenty minutes."[17] After careful instructions helped many students reach campus, the administration—which often consisted solely of the president or principal—literally reached out to individual new students. During the 1870s, 1880s, and 1890s, Oshkosh's Principal George Albee helped each new student get situated and plan a course schedule. The 1907–1908 Geneseo, New York, catalog declared, "Students both old and new are urged to consult the Principal freely regarding their work and their plans for the future." Clark Davis, who attended Ypsilanti State Normal School in Michigan, remembered that upon arrival in Ypsilanti, "I made my first call upon the man whom I had been writing—namely, President Jones. He treated me cordially and courteously, received me at his home, took me to his office, and walked over some of the city streets to show me rooming houses and boarding houses."[18]

While attainable admission requirements and approachable principals eased many students' adjustment to normal school, probably the most important factor in accessibility was affordability. Most state normal schools charged a modest tuition, which they waived for students who signed a pledge to teach in the state after graduation, usually for no more than a few years. The 1879 catalog for Bridgewater, Massachusetts, explained: "Tuition is free to all who comply with the condition of teaching in the schools of Massachusetts." Such contracts were in the states' interest because they increased the teacher supply, but tuition waivers also made a normal-school education affordable for many students. Those who signed pledges to teach had only to buy or rent books, and pay for supplies, transportation, room, board, and perhaps activities fees or music lessons. And at many institutions, financial help from the state was also available for these expenses. The Bridgewater catalog also explained: "The State makes an annual appropriation . . . which is distributed at the close of each term among pupils from Massachusetts who merit and need the aid, in sums varying according to the distance of their residences from Bridgewater."[19] Similarly, during the 1880s the state of Kansas began to reimburse Emporia students three cents per mile for travel beyond one hundred miles; and until 1897, Geneseo students who signed the declaration to teach received reimbursement for travel costs. Ypsilanti's Principal Sill persuaded the state legislature to provide free textbooks, arguing that "the cost of books is often 'the last straw that breaks the camel's back.'" In other states, government officials were directly involved in granting subsidies. Beginning in 1897, each member of the Alabama legislature was able to nominate a student for a two-year normal-school scholarship, which covered tuition and incidental fees; those students appointed by senators also received a grant for boarding costs. Between 1903 and 1909, normalites in Texas could also earn "scholarship appointments," which covered boarding costs, through appointments by their senators, congressmen, or even the governor.[20]

Increasing numbers of campus scholarships and loan funds helped normal students pay expenses that the state did not cover. As early as 1878, Pine Bluff, Arkansas, had an "honorary scholars" program, which provided scholarships for students who passed an exam. For many years beginning in 1882, the Nashville-based Peabody Fund provided for sixteen annual scholarships at Florence, and additional scholarships at other southern normals. Fairly widespread by the early twentieth century, institution-based scholarships were usually funded by and named for former faculty members or graduating classes.[21] If all else failed, the personal efforts of principals and faculty members occasionally enabled individual students to overcome remaining financial obstacles. Long-serving principals, such as Edward Sheldon at Oswego, New York (1861–1897), Percy Bugbee at Oneonta, New York (1898–1933), Cecil Evans at San Marcos, Texas (1911–1942), E. E. Smith at Fayetteville, North Carolina (1883–1933), and many others lent their own money to students in distress. Smith and Pine Bluff's Joseph Corbin (1875–1902), both principals of all-black normal schools, were purposely lax in collecting tuition and fees from students they knew to be struggling; Smith also accepted farm products in lieu of currency.[22] These individual efforts, which filled some of the cracks between state-sponsored tuition waivers and subsidies, as well as campus scholarships and loan funds, helped to make normal schools affordable—so affordable that, during the early 1910s, Geneseo catalogs included the assurance that "no worthy student ever leaves Geneseo because of lack of funds with which to complete the course."[23]

Beyond assuring that students from atypical backgrounds enjoyed easy access, state normal schools offered an atmosphere in which these students thrived. The literature on today's nontraditional students stresses "academic integration" (Metzner & Bean, 1987, p. 30), or "incorporation or support of the students' needs" in "a new, stronger academic community" (Gilley & Hawkes, 1989, p. 34; see also Astin, 1993). Another important issue is scale: the smaller the scale of the institution as a whole or designated programs within it, the higher the comfort level of nontraditional students (Richardson & Skinner, 1992). Most normal schools were small in scale, but size was only one factor in an atmosphere that embraced students from "underserved" backgrounds. Their needs subtly yet ubiquitously shaped these institutions in such a way that serving them was simply intrinsic to the normals' strong academic community. Without special services or programs aimed at nontraditional students, normal schools offered them a comfortable and inclusive intellectual life and numerous opportunities for leadership and involvement in public life. Indeed, state normal schools played a "total adult socializing" (Bean & Metzner, 1985, p. 488) role in the lives of their students, suggesting an alternative to the notion that nontraditional students are "not greatly influenced by the social environment" (Bean & Metzner, 1985, p. 489) in institutions of higher education.

State normal schools created a lively and challenging intellectual life for all students. The bedrock of a strong academic community, the formal curriculum constructively recognized students' limited background and helped them reach further. The normal principals and faculties found that many of their students, especially before the turn of the twentieth century, arrived with little more than an elementary-level education. Because they sought to prepare well-rounded teachers, the normals began from where the students' prior education left off, offering basic and more advanced studies in academic disciplines as well as teaching methods. All students focused on a core of academic studies in mathematics, the sciences, history and civics, and English and language arts. The normals' approach to teaching these subjects allowed students comfortably to gain a certain amount of high-status knowledge.

Western culture wove its way through the required curriculum. Beginning with Greece and Rome, historical studies covered the highlights of Western civilization. In 1894, for example, the catalog for Westfield Normal School in Massachusetts explained that the "General History" course included "Europe from the beginning of the Middle Ages to the present time." Bridgewater imported from London "casts, models, and flat copies" of great art works. The aspect of Western culture that occupied the largest part of the required curiculum was what the normal in Willimantic, Connecticut, called, "The best literary works." There, according to the 1890 catalog, the English literature course covered "Dickens to Burns" during the second term, "Burns to Bacon" during the third term, and "Bacon to Chaucer" during the fourth term. Shakespeare was ever-present on normal-school reading lists; at Westfield, students read *The Merchant of Venice, Julius Caesar, Hamlet* or *Macbeth*, as well as a comedy. In addition to English literature, students at Bridgewater studied American poets and writers such as Longfellow, Whittier, and Hawthorne. Modern and ancient languages were generally optional studies, but institutions as diverse as Castleton, Pine Bluff, and the Territorial Normal School in Tempe, Arizona, required Latin.[24]

Through both required and elective subjects, normal-school students also immersed themselves in another passion of the middle and upper classes in the late nineteenth century: the natural sciences. Between the 1870s and the 1900s, virtually all normal students took short courses in physiology, geography, botany, and natural philosophy (called "nature study" after the turn of the century), as well as at least a few of the following subjects: geology, mineralogy, chemistry, zoology, physics, and astronomy. Together, they performed physical and chemical experiments with rudimentary apparatus, dissected animals, and undertook field expeditions to study local land forms and flora. In keeping with the late-nineteenth-century zeal for scientific collecting, many normal schools amassed sizable collections of mineralogical, geological, physiological, zoological, and even entomological "specimens." For example, beginning in the 1860s, the state normal in Winona, Minnesota, had a growing collection of fossils and minerals from quarries and railway cuts. In 1875, the school purchased a collection of "minerals, fossils, casts, corals, sponges, and shells," which also contained "the partial remains of a Mastodon skeleton." By the 1880s, the normal's museum of natural history also had a bird collection. Science instruction and collections not only enabled students to study fossils, minerals, and animals, but also invited them to share the passion for science.[25]

While the normal schools' formal curriculum established a comfortable academic community, activities outside the classroom strengthened it, intensifying students' intellectual socialization. By the 1870s and increasingly each year thereafter, normal students founded and participated in countless societies, clubs, and publications. These organizations contributed to the vibrant campus intellectual life, which enabled students to grow immensely through intense interaction with one another, their professors, and campus visitors. Academic clubs focused on a variety of topics, primarily in the sciences and foreign languages, and tended to be fairly short-lived. Other student organizations, as well as visiting speakers and performers, exposed students to areas of high culture that were generally outside the formal curriculum, especially classical music and art history.

But it was the literary societies, by far the most long-lived, popular, and far-reaching student organizations, that most facilitated the involvement of these nontraditional students in the life of the mind. Societies met weekly or biweekly, usually on Friday or Saturday afternoon or evening, to execute well-planned programs of orations, debates, moderated discussions, skits, and musical entertainment. In San Jose, the State Normal School's 1900 catalog reported, "The purpose of these societies is to acquaint their members with the customs and practices of deliberative bodies, to give an impetus to literary investigation, and to develop a talent for literary pursuits, public speaking, and extemporaneous discussions." Meetings were occasionally open to the public, and "joint meetings" between two societies were quite common; one at San Jose in 1887 drew over 400 spectators. At the state normal in Greeley, Colorado, the two literary societies were great rivals, and competed each spring in oratory, essays, and debate in the town's Opera House before a large audience. In the South and the East, where social mores were generally traditional, literary societies were usually single-sex. In a unique arrangement, New York's normal schools housed branches of statewide societies. Those for women included Clionian, Arethusa, Alpha Delta, and Agonian; and those for men included Delphic and Philalethean. Gender segregation was less rigid in the Midwest and West. The Lyceum, Literati, and Belles-Lettres societies at Emporia were all coeducational, as were the Roosevelt, Sophoclean, and Emersonian societies at New Mexico Normal University in Las Vegas. Throughout the late nineteenth and early twentieth centuries, the majority of normalites belonged to literary societies. Beginning in the late 1880s, some normals, such as those in Tempe, Arizona, and Cedar Falls, Iowa, had the added incentive of earning credit for society work. A few normals, such as Illinois Normal University, and Oklahoma's Southwestern State Normal School, required membership.[26]

Literary societies enabled students to further pursue some of the topics covered in the curriculum. The main focus, of course, was literature; societies regularly studied a variety of British and American authors. The Browning clubs at Florence and Oshkosh were named for Elizabeth Barrett Browning, a favorite among their members, just as the Shakespeare(n) societies at Cedar Falls, San Jose, and San Marcos were named for the great playwright. Other popular British authors included Charles Dickens, Jane Austin, and Alfred, Lord Tennyson. Studies of the poetry and prose of John Greenleaf Whittier, Henry Wadsworth Longfellow, Washington Irving, Ralph Waldo Emerson, and

Mark Twain, deepened students' familiarity with American literary culture. San Marcos' Every Day Society declared Irving its "patron saint," and imitated him in the 1909 yearbook, presenting a supposed "unpublished tale" in which a lost hunter dreamt of "the girls of the land where the sweet peas grow," who were suspiciously similar to Every-Day members. In many literary societies, students also explored great literature by performing it. At Oneonta, for example, various societies staged Tennyson's *The Princess* in 1892, Shakespeare's *As You Like It* and *The Merchant of Venice* in 1901, and Dickens' *Tom Pinch* in 1905.[27]

Perhaps the most clear illustration of how the normals' academic community allowed students comfortably to broaden their horizons is the societies' vicarious travels throughout the United States and the world. In 1876, members of the Normal School Philologian Society at Westfield enjoyed "an illustrated lecture. . . . An Account of his (Mr. Diller's) Geological Vacation . . . up the Valley in the State of New York." In 1899, "Miss Dopp favored" Oshkosh's Phoenix "society with some of her experiences among the Mormons in Salt Lake City." A decade or so later, a program entitled "Travels in the West" took Florence's Dixie society, figuratively, to Salt Lake City and Yellowstone National Park. Students' vicarious travels also took them to Europe and more foreign locales. In 1880–1881, one literary society at Oshkosh studied Spain and Germany, and in other years both San Marcos' Comenian and Oshkosh's Phoenix studied China. The normal students' world shrank as they acquainted themselves with many distant regions. Together, the literary societies and the formal curriculum created an atmosphere that welcomed normalites into a new intellectual world. Burtt N. Timbie, Bridgewater '96, remembered, "These were years of mind and soul awakening. We came to love learning for learning's sake."[28]

Normalites' socialization was not limited to academic areas; as complete socializing institutions, state normal schools also enabled students to refine the way they carried and presented themselves. The formal curriculum required all students to polish their style of written and oral expression. Rhetoric, composition, and declamation were curricular staples. Through these and other classes, the normals sought to provide "practical training in the correct and effective use of our mother tongue" and "cultivate the individual student's powers of expression in both oral and written language." Students honed their powers of expression through numerous writing assignments, as well as public speaking requirements. Most normal schools required each student to present some sort of schoolwide public declamation at least once, but often on a weekly or monthly basis. For example, "Friday Afternoon Exercises" began at Geneseo in 1877; for the next few decades, classes took turns presenting programs of essays, readings, and recitations. At most normal schools, commencement addresses by all or some of the graduating students, depending on the size of the class, were the culmination of terms of work.[29]

Literary societies also focused on refining their members' styles of expression and composition. Students wrote and delivered orations and essays on different subjects from week to week. Several of the all-male groups, such as The Normal Congress at Bridgewater and The Standard Society at Buffalo, focused on parliamentary procedure. A debate was usually the focal point of the literary society meeting; debating fostered poise, precision, and accuracy in oral communication. In the Midwest, statewide and even interstate normal-school debate and oratorical contests were common and attracted large crowds. After Oshkosh's Elizabeth Shepard won the Wisconsin state contest with her speech on Ulysses S. Grant, her classmates reported, "For Grant when she spoke in electrical tones . . . She made the cold shivers run down our backbones." Buoyed by the normals' vibrant academic community, women commonly orated and debated in public in the Midwest and West, and occasionally in the East. When they did so, they ironically gained cultural polish while violating the gender conventions of high society. Society members also refined their writing skills by producing serial newspapers or magazines; many normal-school student publications began in the societies. Typical titles were: *Normal Thought*, published by the Standard Society at Buffalo; *Normal Ray*, published by the Baconian Literary Society at the State Normal School of Troy, Alabama; and *The Students' Offering*, which was a coordinated effort by all of the literary societies at Cedar Falls.[30]

Not only did the literary societies increase students' comfort with public speaking and writing, but they, along with class organizations and organized athletics, also fostered normalites' self-confidence as leaders and participants in public life. Students took advantage of multiple leadership opportunities. The societies, as well as organizations ranging from academic clubs to YW- and YMCAs all had student officers. By the 1880s, classes elected officers and, beginning in the 1890s, student government associations began to appear. Men served as presidents of coeducational organizations in numbers disproportionately greater than their representation on campus, but women did occasionally serve as president and often occupied other class offices. The constitution of the campuswide self-government association formed at Oshkosh in 1896 stipulated that each class would be represented by one woman and one man. When San Jose's Student Body in 1898 elected Harriet Quilty its first president, *The Normal Pennant* remarked, "Miss Quilty needs no further introduction to our students, her great abilities as a leader are known from Juniors to Seniors." Quilty and other normalites seized the unusual opportunity to serve in a leadership role.[31]

On the athletic fields and basketball courts, normalites gained further experience as public actors in a strong community. Physical activity was a long-standing part of normal life, and by the mid 1890s, athletic competitions were quite prominent. Illinois Normal held its first annual field day in 1895, including running races, shot-put, discus and hammer throws, tennis, and bicycle races. In team sports, men participated in football as well as baseball and basketball, but the relatively small numbers of male students meant a relatively low profile for these intramural and occasional inter-collegiate teams. Basketball was really the territory of female normalites, and it soon became wildly popular. Illinois Normal inaugurated intramural competition among women's teams in 1895, as did Ellensburg, Washington, where a local newspaper reported, "The ladies are getting to be splendid players." In 1902, Ellensburg's women players began interscholastic competition. Beginning at the turn of the century, women and men diversified their athletic endeavors to include sports such as tennis and hockey, but women's basketball continued to draw the most spectators. At Oshkosh, the men reported, "They did make plays and no mistake/Those girls in blue and yellow;/And to spur on the lusty crowd/We cheered them to a fellow." Along with improving their level of fitness, these athletes undoubtedly gained poise as they performed in a public setting.[32]

Finally, the broader social atmosphere of the normals was remarkably vibrant, prompting one observer to write that San Jose exuded "enthusiasm and mutual confidence." At the most formal level, students attended all sorts of anniversary celebrations and building dedications, which brought a sense of history and grandeur to campus. Usually spanning several days, graduation ceremonies generally included a baccalaureate sermon by a local minister, academic speeches by all graduates or student representatives of the senior class, and speeches by the principal or perhaps a visiting dignitary, as well as the ceremonial conferring of degrees. In addition, students created their own tradition of more- and less-formal events. In end-of-the-year "class day" celebrations, they took the stage to read the class history and prophesy and make other speeches. At Castleton in the late 1890s, celebrations included addresses to the juniors that offered advice as well as gentle gibes. From week to week, campus life was alive with other student-initiated events; all sorts of receptions and socials provided normalites with opportunities to grow more comfortable as public actors. At one such reception, sponsored by the YWCA at San Jose, a leader announced at regular intervals new conversation topics including "the last book I read," the weather, and even "women's sphere." This gathering, like countless others on normal campuses, was virtually a seminar on the mores of polite society. With so many opportunities to involve oneself in a robust and inclusive academic community, it is hardly surprising that the "sip of a girl from an isolated shore home" in Massachusetts described attending normal school as, "not unlike birth into another world."[33]

Conclusion

State normal schools in the late nineteenth and early twentieth centuries not only welcomed women, members of minority groups, and students with other nontypical characteristics, but also included them in a rich intellectual and social community and encouraged them to reach beyond their unprivileged backgrounds. While the official mission of the normal schools was simply teacher preparation, the unofficial mission of serving nontraditional students was integral to these institutions. Reflecting on the later transformation of former normal schools into universities, E. Alden Dunham (1969) observed, "One of the ironies of this movement is that a first-class teachers college may become a third-class university as it grows and changes its function" (p. 1). Thus, in the search for status, the former normals gave up their distinctive identity, including the behind-the-scenes yet ground-breaking mission of serving nontraditional students. More than three decades ago, Dunham (1969) saw the "question of model, of institutional purpose" as "the greatest single problem" facing state colleges and regional universities, because they lost "institutional coherence, warmth, and friendliness" as "the atmosphere" changed "from soft to hard" (pp. 155–156). The new "hard" environment marginalized the needs of nontraditional students. Rethinking the notion of "nontraditional" from the historical perspective of state normal schools is an important reminder not only of atypical students' rich history in higher education, but also of what higher education institutions and society stand to lose in turning away from the mission—whether official or unofficial—of serving these students.

Notes

1. Gillan quoted in *Semi-centennial history of the Illinois State Normal University, 1857–1907.* Normal, IL: Illinois State Normal University, 1907, p. 202.
2. David Sands Wright, *Fifty years at the Teachers College: Historical and personal reminiscences.* Cedar Falls: Iowa State Teachers College, 1926, p. 130; William Frederick Hartman, *The history of Colorado State College of Education: The normal school period, 1890–1911.* Unpublished doctoral dissertation, Colorado State College of Education, 1951, p. 153; United States Commissioner/Bureau of Education, *Reports* and *Bulletins.* Washington: U.S. Government Printing Office, 1868–1945.
3. Most black normal schools later became agricultural and mechanical colleges, then universities. North Carolina established a normal school for Native American students in Pembroke, and Oklahoma established one in Tahlequah.
4. William Marshall French & Florence Smith French, *College of the Empire State: A Centennial history of The New York State College for Teachers at Albany.* Albany, 1944, pp. 95, 258; Oswego students quoted in Dorothy Rogers, *Fountainhead of teacher education: A century in the Sheldon Tradition.* New York: Appleton-Century-Crofts, 1961, p. 59; Robert T. Brown, *The rise and fall of the people's colleges: The Westfield Normal School, 1839–1914.* Westfield, MA: Institute for Massachusetts Studies, Westfield State College, 1988, pp. 61–62; Robert McGraw, A Century of Service. In Herb Taylor (Ed.), *The first 100 years: Worcester State College.* Worcester, MA: Worcester State College, Office of Community Services, 1974, Section 4 (no page nos.); Louie G. Ramsdell, First hundred years of the first state normal school in America: The State Teachers College at Framingham, Massachusetts—1839–1939. In *First state normal school in America: The State Teachers College at Framingham, Massachusetts.* Framingham, MA: The Alumnae Association of the State Teachers College at Framingham, Massachusetts, 1959, p. 11; Helen E. Marshall, *Grandest of enterprises: Illinois State Normal University, 1857–1957.* Normal, IL: Illinois State Normal University, 1956, p. 133; Elizabeth Tyler Bugaighis, *Blackboard diplomacy: The role of American normal schools in exporting education to Latin America, 1891–1924.* Paper presented at the annual meeting of the American Educational Research Association, New Orleans, April 2000; Tom W. Nichols, *Rugged summit.* San Marcos, TX, 1970, p. 94.
5. David A. Gould, *Policy and pedagogues: School reform and teacher professionalization in Massachusetts, 1840–1920.* Unpublished doctoral dissertaion, Brandeis University, 1977, p. 87; Brown, *The rise and fall of the people's colleges,* p. 79; Percentages of Southwest Texas parents calculated from data in *Announcement of the Southwest Texas State Normal School for the annual session 1904–1905, 1905–1906, 1906–1907, 1907–1908, 1908–1909, 1909–1910, 1910–1911.* Austin: State Printers, 1903–1910; Irving H. Hart, *The first 75 Years.* Cedar Falls, IA: Iowa State Teachers College, 1951. p. 116; *A history of the State Normal School of Kansas for the first twenty-five years.* Emporia, KS, 1889, p. 45; Elizabeth L. Wheeler. Isaac Fisher: The frustrations of a Negro educator at Branch Normal College, 1902–1911. *The Arkansas Historical Quarterly,* 41 (Spring 1982), 5.
6. Arthur Clarke Boyden, *Albert Gardner Boyden and the Bridgewater State Normal School: A memorial volume.* Bridgewater, MA: Arthur H. Willis, 1919, p. 30; newspaper quoted in Irene Goldgraben, And the glory of the latter house shall be greater than that of the former. In *And the glory of the latter house shall be greater than that of the former: An informal history of Castleton State College.* Castleton, VT, 1968, p. 19; Brown, *The rise and fall of the people's colleges,* p. 89; Rogers, *Oswego: Fountainhead,* p. 58; cheer quoted in *The Arkansasyer.* Pine Bluff, AR: Faculty of Arkansas Agricultural, Mechanical and Normal College, 1 (1928), p. 1. In *Keepers of the spirit: The L. A. Davis, Sr. Historical Collection,* Exhibit, Isaac S. Hathaway-John M. Howard Fine Arts Center, University of Arkansas at Pine Bluff, Pine Bluff, AR, May 1995.
7. Dignam quoted in Work Projects Administration in the State of Massachusetts, *The State Teachers College at Westfield.* Boston: State Department of Education, 1941, p. 53; Class day program, 1888, University of

Wisconsin—Oshkosh Archives, Area Research Center, Polk Library, Oshkosh, WI, p. 18; Carey W. Brush, *In honor and good faith: A history of the State University College at Oneonta, New York*. Oneonta, NY: The Faculty-Student Association of State University Teachers College at Oneonta, 1965, pp. 45, 46, 114; Hartman, *The history of Colorado State College of Education*, p. 154; Ernest J. Hopkins & Alfred Thomas, Jr., *The Arizona State University story*. Phoenix: Southwest Publishing Co., 1960, pp. 85–86; Elisabeth Ann Bowles, *A good beginning: The first four decades of the University of North Carolina at Greensboro*. Chapel Hill: The University of North Carolina Press, 1967, pp. 15–16; ages of San-Marcos students calculated from data in Student Registers, 1903–1910, box 70, series 3, Southwest Texas State University Archives, Special Collections, Alkek Library, San Marcos, TX; Douglas R. Skopp, *Bright with promise: From the normal and training school to SUNY Plattsburg, 1889–1989*. Norfolk, VA: The Donning Company, 1989, pp. 62–63.

8. Frank T. Reuter, *West Liberty State College: The first 125 years*. West Liberty, WV: West Liberty State College, 1963, p. 121; L. B. Johnson (*not* Lyndon Baines) quoted in Hopkins and Thomas, *The Arizona State University story* p. 93.

9. George H. Martin, The Bridgewater Spirit. In *Seventy-fifth anniversary of the state normal school, Bridgewater, Massachusetts, June 19, 1915*. Bridgewater, MA: Arthur H. Willis, 1915, p. 13; Rogers, *Oswego: Fountainhead*, p. 59; Farmington statistics based on information in George C. Purington, *History of the state normal school, Farmington, Maine*. Farmington, ME: Knowlton, McLeary & Co., 1889, pp. 141–174; Oshkosh statistics calculated from *Annual catalogue of the state normal school at Oshkosh, Wis., for the school year 1879–80, 1884–85, 1889–90, 1891–92, 1893–94, 1895–96, 1897–98, 1899–1900, 1901–1902*. Oshkosh, WI, 1880–1902, and *Oshkosh State Normal School Bulletin* (Oshkosh, WI), *1* (June 1904); *3* (June 1906); *5* (June 1908); quotations from Class day programs (Oshkosh), 1895, p. 18; 1896, p. 16; *A history of the State Normal School of Kansas*, p. 43; Hopkins & Thomas, *The Arizona State University story*, 85–86; Florence data calculated using statistics in State Superintendent of Education (Alabama), *Reports, 1899 and 1900*. Montgomery, AL, pp. 31–32; *1901–1902*, p. 117.

10. Hewett quoted in Sandra D. Harmon, The voice, pen and influence of our women are abroad in the land: Women and the Illinois State Normal University, 1857–1899. In Catherine Hobbs (Ed.), *Nineteenth-century women learn to write*. Charlottesville: University of Virginia Press, 1995, p. 95; Egbert R. Isbell, *A history of Eastern Michigan University, 1849–1965*. Ypsilanti, MI: Eastern Michigan University Press, 1971, p. 138; State Superintendent of Education (Alabama), *Report, 1901–1902*, p. 117; Ellis A. Stebbins, *The OCE story*. Monmouth, OR: Oregon College of Education, 1973, p. 46; Brush, *In honor and good faith*, p. 114; Rogers, *Oswego: Fountainhead*, p. 122.

11. J. M. McKenzie, *History of Peru State Normal*. Auburn, NE: *The Nemaha County Republican*, 1911, p. 98.

12. Martin, The Bridgewater spirit, p. 14; Dixon quoted in Boyden, *Albert Gardner Boyden and the Bridgewater State Normal School*, p. 143; State Superintendent of Public Instruction (AR), *Biennial Report, 1905–1906*, p. 70; *Annual Catalogue of the State Normal School at Oshkosh, Wis., for the school year 1879–80, 1884–85, 1889–90, 1894–95, 1899–1900; Oshkosh State Normal School Bulletin 2* (June 1905); *7* (June 1910); Rosalind R. Fisher, "*. . . the stone strength of the past. . .": Centennial history of State University College of Arts and Science at Geneseo, New York*. Geneseo, NY, 1971, p. 146; Maxine Ollie Merlino, *A history of the California State Normal Schools—Their origin, growth, and transformation into teachers colleges*. Unpublished doctoral dissertaion, University of Southern California, 1962, pp. 94–95.

13. McKenzie, *History of the Peru State Normal*, pp. 22–23, 96; Principal's annual report, 1910–1911, quoted in Arthur Charles Forst, Jr., *From normal school to state college: The growth and development of Eastern Connecticut State College from 1889 to 1959*. Unpublished doctoral dissertaion, University of Connecticut, 1980, p. 101.

14. Class day program (Oshkosh), 1888, pp. 17–18.

15. *Catalogue and circular of the California State Normal School, San Jose, 1879*. Sacramento, 1879, pp. 47–51; *State Normal School, Castleton, Vermont*, Flier, 1891, Castleton State College Archives, Vermont Room, Coolidge Library, Castleton, VT; Albert Salisbury, *The normal schools of Wisconsin: A souvenir of the meeting of the National Educational Association held at Milwaukee, Wis., July 6–9, 1897* (1897), p. 17.

16. For admission requirements, see catalogues and bulletins of individual normal schools. See also Fisher, "*. . . the stone strength of the past . . .*," p. 60; Susan Vaughn, The history of State Teachers College, Florence, Alabama. *Bulletin of the State Teachers College, Florence, Alabama, 18* [1930s?], pp. 15, 25; Fredrick Chambers, *Historical study of Arkansas Agricultural, Mechanical and Normal College, 1873–1943*. Unpublished EdD dissertation, Ball State University, 1970, p. 68; Estelle Greathead, *The story of an inspiring past: Historical sketch of San Jose State Teachers College from 1862 to 1928*. San Jose, CA: San Jose State Teachers College, 1928, p. 15; William Herald Herrmann, *The rise of the public normal school system in Wisconsin*. Unpublished doctoral dissertation, University of Wisconsin, 1953, pp. 412–413, 495; John Marvin Smith, The history and growth of Southwest Texas State Teachers College. Unpublished MA thesis, University of Texas-Austin, 1930, p. 53.

17. *Annual catalogue of the State Normal School at Oshkosh, Wis., for the school year 1898–99.* Oshkosh, WI, 1899, p. 111; *Bulletin of the State Normal College, Florence, Alabama, 1* (1912), 9.

18. *The first half century of the Oshkosh Normal School.* Oshkosh, WI: The Faculty of State Normal School, 1921, p. 17; *State Normal School, Geneseo, NY, 1907–1908,* p. 19; Isbell, *A history of Eastern Michigan University,* p. 166.

19. Catalog quoted in *As we were . . . As we are: Bridgewater State College, 1840–1876.* Bridgewater, MA: Alumni Association, Bridgewater State College, 1876, p. 79.

20. *A history of the State Normal School of Kansas,* p. 29; Clayton C. Mau, *Brief history of the State University Teachers College, Geneseo, New York.* Geneseo, NY, 1956, p. 6; Isbell, *A history of Eastern Michigan University,* p. 138; *Catalogue of the California State Normal School, San Jose, 1895.* Sacramento: State Printing Office, 1895, p. 9; *1900* (1900), p. 11; Michael Francis Bannon, *A history of State Teachers College, Troy, Alabama.* Unpublished EdD dissertation, George Peabody College for Teachers, 1954, p. 47; *Announcement of the Southwest Texas State Normal School for the annual session 1908–1909,* p. 44.

21. Chambers, *Historical study of Arkansas Agricultural, Mechanical and Normal College,* p. 80; Vaughn, The history of State Teachers College, Florence, p. 38; on scholarships, see catalogues and bulletins of individual normal schools.

22. Rogers, *Oswego: Fountainhead,* p. 71; Brush, *In honor and good faith,* pp. 32, 102–103; Nichols, *Rugged summit,* pp. 92–93; E. Louise Murphy, *Origin and development of Fayetteville State Teachers College, 1867–1959—A chapter in the history of the education of negroes in North Carolina.* Unpublished doctoral dissertation, New York University, 1960, p. 167; Thomas Rothrock, Joseph Carter Corbin and negro education in the University of Arkansas. *The Arkansas Historical Quarterly, 30* (Winter 1971), 289.

23. *State Normal School, Geneseo, NY, 1911–1912,* p. 28; *1912–1913,* p. 25.

24. Excerpt from Westfield catalog reprinted in Brown, *The rise and fall of the people's colleges,* 134–140; Arthur C. Boyden, *The history of Bridgewater Normal School.* Bridgewater, MA: Bridgewater Normal Alumni Association, 1933, pp. 54, 41–42; Forst, *From normal school to state college: The growth and development of Eastern Connecticut State College,* pp. 68, 70–71; Paul Stoler, Castleton Normal School in the nineteenth century. In Holman D. Jordan (Ed.), *And the glory of the latter house shall be greater than that of the former: An informal history of Castleton State College.* Castleton, VT: Castleton State College, 1968, p. 52; Chambers, Historical study of Arkansas Agricultural, Mechanical and Normal College, 1873–1943, pp. 66–68, 143, 188, 218; Hopkins & Thomas, *The Arizona State University story,* p. 89

25. School catalogs, bulletins and histories (various); C. 0. Ruggles, *Historical sketch and notes: Winona State Normal School, 1860–1910.* Winona, MN: Jones & Kroeger Co., 1910, pp. 143–145.

26. School catalogs, bulletins and histories (various); *Catalogue of the California State Normal School, San Jose, 1900.* Sacramento: State Printing Office, 1900, p. 8; *The Normal Index.* San Jose, CA: Students of State Normal School, *3* (Nov. 1887), 32; Hartman, The history of Colorado State College of Education, p. 159; Mau, *Brief history of the State University Teachers College, Geneseo,* p. 17; W. Wayne Dedman, *Cherishing this heritage: The centennial history of the State University College at Brockport, New York.* New York: Appleton-Century-Crofts, 1969, p. 124; *A history of the State Normal School of Kansas,* pp. 62–73; Deward Homan Reed, *The history of teachers colleges in New Mexico.* Nashville: George Peabody College for Teachers, 1948, p. 136; Hopkins & Thomas, *The Arizona State University Story,* pp. 111–112; Wright, *Fifty Years at the teachers college,* p. 116; Melvin Frank Fiegel, *A history of Southwestern State College, 1903–1953.* Unpublished EdD dissertation, Oklahoma State University, 1968, p. 27.

27. School catalogs, bulletins, and histories (various); Vaughn, The history of State Teachers College, Florence, p. 31; *Oshkosh State Teachers College: The first seventy-five years.* Oshkosh, WI: Oshkosh State Teachers College, 1946, p. 68; Wright, *Fifty years at the teachers college,* p. 74; *The Normal Pennant.* San Jose, CA: Students of State Normal School, *4* (June 1901), 18; *The pedagogue.* San Marcos, TX: Students of Southwest Texas State Normal School, 1905, p. 61; Brush, *In honor and goodfaith,* p. 288.

28. Work Projects Administration, *The State Teachers College at Westfield,* p. 72; *The normal advance.* Oshkosh, WI: Students of State Normal School 6 (Oct. 1899), 33; Dixie Club, Roll and minutes of meetings, Oct. 25, 1912, in Organizations, Files, University Collection, Collier Library Archives, University of North Alabama, Florence, AL (no page nos.); Ladies' Literary Society, Minutes, Oct. 8, 1880 and Feb. 4, 1881, in University of Wisconsin-Oshkosh Archives, Area Research Center, Polk Library, Oshkosh, WI, pp. 127, 136; *The Normal Star* (San Marcos, TX: Students of Southwest Texas State Normal School) 2 (Feb. 23, 1912), 1; *The Normal Advance, 18* (Jan. 1912), 128; Boyden, *Albert Gardner Boyden and the Bridgewater State Normal School,* p. 146.

29. School catalogs, bulletins, and histories (various); Catalogue *and Circular of the California State Normal School, San Jose, 1890* (Sacramento, 1890), p. 31; *Vermont State Normal Schools, 1909–1910* (Catalog, no publication information provided), p. 11; Fisher, ". . . *the stone strength of the past . . . ,*" pp. 86–87.

30. Boyden, *Albert Gardner Boyden and the Bridgewater State Normal School*, pp. 116–117; *New York State Teachers College at Buffalo: A History, 1871–1946*. Buffalo: New York State Teachers College at Buffalo, 1946, pp. 143, 129; *The Normal Advance*, 5 (March 1899), 120–123; Bannon, A history of State Teachers College, Troy, Alabama, 1954, p. 41; Hart, *The first 75 years*, p. 148.
31. School catalogs, bulletins, and histories (various); Class day programs (Oshkosh), 1888; *The first half century of the Oshkosh Normal School*, p. 25; *The Normal Pennant*, 4 (May 1898), 4
32. School catalogs, bulletins, and histories (various); Marshall, *Grandest of enterprises*, pp. 199–200; Samuel R. Mohler, *Thefirst seventy-five years: A history of Central Washington State College*. Ellensburg, WA: Central Washington State College, 1967, p. 97; *The Normal Advance*, 3 (March-April 1897), 78.
33. S. E. Rothery, Some educational institutions: Pilgrimages about San Jose. *The Overland Monthly, 30* (July 1897), 75; School catalogs, bulletins, and histories (various); Commencement Programs, Castleton State Normal School, 1874–1940, Castleton State College Archives, Vermont Room, Coolidge Library, Castleton, VT; *The Normal Index*, 6 (March 25, 1891), 73; Boyden, *Albert Gardner Boyden and the Bridgewater State Normal School*, p. 143.

References

1. Allmendinger, D. F. (1975). *Paupers and scholars: The transformation of student life in nineteenth-century New England*. New York: St. Martin's Press.
2. Astin, A. W. (1993). *What matters in college? Four critical years revisited*. San Francisco: Jossey-Bass.
3. Bean, J. P., & Metzner, B. S. (1985). A conceptual model of nontraditional undergraduate student attrition. *Review of Educational Research, 55*, 485–540.
4. Bendixen-Noe, M. K. (1998). Nontraditional students in higher education: Meeting their needs as learners. *Mid-Western Educational Researcher, 11(2)*, 27–31.
5. Burke, C. B. (1982). *American collegiate populations: A test of the traditional view*. New York: New York University Press.
6. Clifford, G. J. (1983). "'Shaking dangerous questions from the crease": Gender and American higher education. *Feminist Issues*, 3(2), 3–62.
7. Clifford, G. J. (1995). *"Equally in view": The University of California, its women, and the schools*. Berkeley: Center for Studies in Higher Education and Institute of Governmental Studies, University of California, Berkeley.
8. Dunham, E. A. (1969). *Colleges of the forgotten Americans: A profile of state colleges and regional universities*. New York: McGraw Hill.
9. Gilley, J. W., & Hawkes, R. T. (1989). Nontraditional students: A changing student body redefines community. *Educational Record*, 70 (Summer/Fall), 33–35.
11. Goodlad, J. I. (1990). *Teachersfor our nation's schools*. San Francisco: Jossey-Bass.
12. Herbst, J. (1980). Nineteenth-century normal schools in the United States: A fresh look. *History of Education*, 9, 219–227.
13. Herbst, J. (1989). *And sadly teach: Teacher education and professionalization in American culture*. Madison: University of Wisconsin Press.
14. Lace, W. W. (1986). A nontraditional approach. *Currents, 12(5)*, 8–12.
15. Levine, A., & Associates. (1989). *Shaping higher education's future: Demographic realities and opportunities, 1990–2000*. San Francisco: Jossey-Bass.
16. Levine, A., & Nidiffer, J. (1996). *Beating the odds: How the poor get to college*. San Francisco: Jossey-Bass.
17. London, H. B. (1992). Transformations: Cultural challenges faced by first-generation students. *New Directions for Community Colleges, 80(4)*, 5–11.
18. Metzner, B. S., & Bean, J. P. (1987). The estimation of a conceptual model of nontraditional undergraduate student attrition. *Research in Higher Education*, 27, 15–38.
19. Nidiffer, J. (1999). Poor historiography: The "poorest" in American higher education. *History of Education Quarterly*, 39, 321–336.
20. Ogren, Christine A. (1995). Where coeds were coeducated: Normal schools in Wisconsin, 1870–1920. *History of Education Quarterly*, 35, 1–26.
21. Pascarella, E., & Terenzini, P. (1998). Studying college students in the 21st century: Meeting new challenges. *The Review of Higher Education*, 21, 151–165.
22. Richardson, R. C., & Skinner, E. F. (1992). Helping first-generation minority students achieve degrees. *New Directions for Community Colleges, 80(4)*, 29–43.

22. Schwager, S. (1987). Educating women in America. *Signs: Journal of Women in Culture and Society, 12,* 333–372.

23. Selingo, J. (2000). Facing new missions and rivals, state colleges seek a makeover. *Chronicle of Higher Education* (November 17), A40–A42.

24 Thelin, J. R. (1990). Rudolph rediscovered. In Rudolph, F., *The American college and university: A history.* Athens: University of Georgia Press.

25 Westbrook, F. D., & Sedlacek, W. E. (1991). Forty years of using labels to communicate about nontraditional students: Does it help or hurt? *Journal of Counseling & Development, 70* (September-October), 20–28.

26. Zwerling, L. S. (1992). First-generation adult students: In search of safe havens. *New Directions for Community Colleges, 80(4),* 45–54.

PART V

HIGHER EDUCATION
1900–1950

Part V: Higher Education: 1900–1950

American society experienced significant changes at the turn of the twentieth century. Great waves of immigration and the expansion of a middle class hastened the growth of American higher education. The offspring of these groups sought higher learning as a means to enter vocational, managerial, educational, and professional careers. Similar to the European university pattern, American research universities developed, as did affiliated schools of medicine, law, theology, and eventually education. Their subsequent regulation by universities and professional associations that mandated the baccalaureate degree as an entrance requirement played a crucial role in the expansion of the undergraduate programs after World War I. Jurgen Herbst provides an insightful survey of medical, legal, divinity, and professional education as it adapted to and affiliated with these new research universities. Seeking to relinquish its earlier apprenticeship models, professional education embraced *Wissenshaft* inquiry and research ideals and fostered professional accreditation. Importantly, the Carnegie Foundation for the Advancement of Teaching played the major role in the professionalization of medical education as well as other developing professions, as Ellen Condliffe Lagemann presents in her assessment of the *Flexner Report* (published in 1910). As soon as professional schools at older colleges and universities required a bachelor's degree, it became clear that only certain types of persons would be able to study for these occupations. Yet, there were new professions emerging to support the changes in higher education. Jana Nidiffer's chapter explores the changes in student life as deans of women were appointed on various Midwest campuses in 1892; they provided new advising support to women students concerning all aspects of college life. By 1916, they formed a national organization, and later became part of the new profession of student affairs, as described in Jana Nidiffer and Carolyn Terry Bashaw's *Women Administrators in Higher Education*.[1]

The next articles in the Reader fill out the developing system of higher education as universities, colleges, junior colleges, and religious-related colleges sought to meet the new demands of the twentieth century. Individuals who were female, poor, Jewish, or Catholic, and African-American created campus problems for older institutions that preferred to admit historically white Anglo-Saxon Protestant students. Private colleges and universities often blocked their admission. Harold Wechsler's *The Qualified Student* explores the bias that kept "undesirable" groups out of higher education.[2] His overview article for this period in the Reader describes the difficulties that these groups faced in being admitted during the first two decades of the twentieth century. Their difficulties actually advanced institutional differentiation as groups sought to create their own colleges and universities in the face of administrative *subrosa* discrimination. David Levine's chapter from his book, *The American College and the Culture of Aspiration, 1915–1940*[3] further shows how restrictive admissions policies worked at elite colleges, forcing many qualified students to seek higher education elsewhere.

The following articles offer a review of the groups who were barely tolerated on prestigious campuses. James Anderson's portrait of black higher education in the South until 1935 discloses the effects of Reconstruction's "separate, but equal" policies. A compromise of unjust proportions was to be perpetuated. Jennings Wagoner sketches the "American Compromise," as northern educational leaders invoked the ideas of Booker T. Washington and seemed indifferent to southern politicians and administrators' efforts to establish a racially separate and unequal educational system. The establishment of black colleges, black land-grant universities under the second Morrill Land-Grant Act of 1890, and black junior colleges created a *de facto* separate system. With the loss of state revenues, which primarily assisted white institutions of higher learning, as well as the lack of corporate and religious philanthropy by the 1920s, the decline of historically black institutions occurred until the *Brown* decision of 1954. In spite of this prevailing trend, progress was made in the development of colleges and higher education for African Americans. Marybeth Gasman's article provides an insightful historical analysis of the differences between W.E.B. Du Bois's concerns with the progress of black students in higher education and Fisk University President Charles Johnson's success in creating new collegiate opportunities for these students of color as president of Fisk University in the first half of the twentieth century. The two men differed on the use of white philanthropy to achieve their respective goals for African-American colleges and their students.

Describing women's higher education in an expansive chapter from her book, *Gender and Higher Education in the Progressive Era*,[4] Lynn Gordon discusses the successes of women's colleges and coeducation up to 1920. Seeking to overcome Victorian bias against higher education for women, leaders such as Martha Carey Thomas, Alice Freeman Palmer, and Elizabeth Cady Stanton fought for equity in education. Dramatic changes had occurred at certain institutions, especially at the University of Chicago, where women comprised some 40 percent of the enrollments at the turn of the twentieth century.

In a gender counterpose, our next reading refocuses on the institution and the students of privilege during this age. Harvard University had become the citadel of American higher education in all things. President Charles Eliot's 40-year presidency came to a close in 1909; yet his influence, by creating a contrarian undergraduate curriculum and institutional policies, had become the flashpoint for most institutions—how would they follow (or not follow) its precedents. Similarly, Harvard's male students became the supposed pinnacle of collegiate success. However, our understanding of the ideal of "manhood" here is just emerging. Kim Townsend's chapter in his book, *Manhood at Harvard*,[5] offers us a first historical glimpse of the male side of gender studies in higher education.

We end this section of the Reader with many of these groups who also found post-secondary opportunities at public junior colleges. Since the founding of Joliet Junior College in 1901, some 275 institutions were in operation by 1940. Robert Pedersen discusses the beginnings of the public two-year college movement and the societal forces which brought this new institution into being.[6]

Our primary readings also explore the problems encountered by disenfranchised groups. For example, W. E. B. Du Bois describes the predicament of African-Americans and their colleges in 1903. This famous work, "The Talented Tenth," pleaded for America to make education available to this part of the population. From a different perspective, faculty also demanded new rights, as the need to secure academic freedom required a tenure system. Moving beyond one-year contracts, faculty members were free to publicize their research without fear of reprisal. Thus, new historical scholarship on higher education during the first half of the twentieth century has rectified our view of "equity" and "democracy" in American colleges and universities.

As a result of these changes, there were now greater opportunities for individuals to begin higher learning. This postsecondary educational experience gradually came under the purview of professional and regional accrediting associations that attempted to ensure its academic character. Another stage in the Americanization of higher education had occurred. While each of the distinguishing features of American higher education had appeared, their full demonstration would await the most stressful period in American higher education, the boom-to-retrenchment era after the Second World War.

ENDNOTES

[1]Jana Nidiffer and Carolyn Terry Bashaw, *Women Administrators in Higher Education* (Albany, NY: SUNY Press, 2001).

[2]Harold Wechsler, *The Qualified Student* (New York: Wiley-Interscience, 1977).

[3]David Levine, *The American College and the Culture of Aspiration, 1915–1940* (Ithaca, NY: Cornell University Press, 1986).

[4]Lynn Gordon, *Gender and Higher Education in the Progressive Era* (New Haven, Conn: Yale University Press, 1990).

[5]Kim Townsend, "Introduction," *Manhood at Harvard: William James and Others* (New York: Norton and Company, 1996), 15–29.

[6]Robert Pedersen, "Value Conflicts on the Community College Campus: An Examination of Its Historical Origins," in *Managing Community and Junior Colleges: Perspectives for the Next Century*, edited by Allan M. Hoffman and Daniel J. Julius (Knoxville, TN: College and University Personnel Association, 1993), 15–31.

CHAPTER 7

PROFESSIONAL EDUCATION

Rethinking American Professional Education

JURGEN HERBST

It has been the accepted view in American scholarship that the last third of the nineteenth century marked the birth of the modern American university and with it the move of professional education from apprenticeship arrangements and instruction in proprietary schools into the country's institutions of higher education. There, students and instructors pursued their studies in professional schools that were or had become integral parts of the new universities. As Sydney Ann Halpern wrote, American university scholars had come to consider "professional training a central function of higher education and constituted professional schools parallel to letters and science colleges, as major academic divisions. University presidents expected the faculty of these professional schools to engage in scientific research and other scholarly activities."[1]

This view of the incorporation of professional education into the new universities is part and parcel of what Christopher Jencks and David Riesman have called the "academic revolution"[2] and what Richard Hofstadter and Walter Metzger in their book on academic freedom in the United States[3] have defined as the transition period between the age of the college and the age of the university. It has also been described as part of the German influence on American universities between the Civil War and the First World War.[4] American students, so the story goes, had brought back with them an idealized picture of the German university as Wilhelm von Humboldt had conceived it at Berlin in 1810. In that university, teachers and students of all disciplines and faculties were jointly devoted to *Bildung* and *Wissenschaft*, an educational ideal of individual character formation and a common search for knowledge and understanding. In it, research and teaching were parts of the same process of inquiry. So G. Stanley Hall could write glowingly of "the religion of research" that inspired teaching and Richard Ely admired "the spirit of freedom" which pervaded the German university's every laboratory, seminar, and lecture hall.[5] These American scholars set out to model the new American university in the spirit of Humboldt's *Wissenschaft*. Their careers and the careers of their students were to be shaped by a commitment to professionalism that was guided primarily by university inspired scientific principles rather than by the demands of professional practice.

The "academic revolution" and the college-university distinction may well stand as generalized descriptions of the changes wrought in American higher education at the end of the nineteenth century. The incorporation of professional education into the universities and the role played in these events by students returning from Germany were indeed integral parts of these changes. But these

Jurgen Herbst is professor emeritus of educational policy studies and history at the University of Wisconsin, Madison and a Professional Associate of Fort Lewis College, Durango, Colorado.
History of Higher Education Annual 21 (2001): 137–148.

developments were of greater complexity than textbook accounts convey.[6] The history of professional education in the United States was not a simple straight-line transition from apprenticeship to proprietary school to university that played itself out between American collegiate beginnings in the seventeenth and the German influx at the end of the nineteenth century. In fact, the roots of American professional education reach back to the medieval universities and found nourishment in modern Europe's continental universities and professional practice. Furthermore, we must distinguish between the common education in the liberal arts—the German *Bildung*—and the diverse specialized training—the German *Ausbildung*—that, in the nineteenth century at least, were held to be parts of professional education. That distinction also warns us not to speak glibly and in general terms of professional education when practice and traditions differ among the nations and among the professions.

To consider the place of professional schools in American universities let us take a brief look at the history of professional education in the Western world. We should remind ourselves that the medieval universities were assemblies of practicing and aspiring professionals who were incorporated by Pope and Emperor as self-governing faculties for lawyers, physicians, and theologians. These faculties were in effect professional schools. Their masters or professors were in many cases practicing professionals who taught what they practiced. For the preparatory training of their students in the *artes liberales*—the language arts—they relied on teachers in the cathedral schools and in their own non-professional arts faculties.[7] Yet when with the break-up of the Roman Empire and with the Reformation the universities were deprived of their imperial and papal protectors, the masters in the faculties lost their corporate autonomy. They now served their territorial rulers as teachers in the universities that had become training schools for civil servants in the establishments of state and confessional church. From a highly reputed position as master professionals they now had fallen to the lowly status of what Immanuel Kant would call "practitioners of learnedness,"[8] At the same time, the arts faculties suffered from steadily diminishing prestige and sank to the level of secondary schools, the continental *gymnasia illustria* or the English endowed grammar schools.[9]

Toward the end of the eighteenth century, the low repute of the universities on the European continent led to demands that they be abolished and their faculties turned into separate specialty schools.[10] In France such a program was effectively instituted in 1806 as a state monopoly under the Imperial University.[11] In Prussia, however, Wilhelm von Humboldt, well aware of the need for specialized professional training but also disturbed by the fractionalizing and disintegrating effect of specialization, was concerned to preserve "the unity of knowledge" which, to him, constituted the all-embracing concept of university education. He asked his king to join in Berlin the existing scientific academies, institutes, libraries, and collections with the faculties of a university that was neither to exclude any subject nor limit itself to practical exercises. It was to be one organic whole, allowing each part a measure of independence yet working cooperatively for a common purpose.[12] Its organization was to conform to the proposals of Kant, who in his "The Battle of the Faculties," had proposed that the dysfunctional arts faculty be elevated to a non-professional faculty of philosophy. Its mission was to protect the university's freedom of learning, teaching, and research and to serve as a unifying capstone over the specialized and government service oriented professional faculties.[13]

This was the vision that so inspired the American students studying in Germany during the last third of the century. Kant and Humboldt had envisaged the philosophical faculty to stand above the professional faculties as the untainted representative and guardian of *Wissenschaft*. Alas, the American students did not, or did not want to, see that during the half-century after Humboldt, the faculty of philosophy had itself become a specialized professional faculty for the training of Germany's school teachers, scientists, and scholars. It no longer carried any responsibility for the liberal arts education of its students, as that function had been assigned to the country's *Gymnasia*. While the rhetoric of the "unity of science" and *Bildung*—education as character formation and cultivation—continued, in its daily work the university devoted itself to the specialized utilitarian needs of the emerging nation state. Just like its medieval predecessor, the German university of the nineteenth century consisted of an assembly of professional faculties.

Besides, the university was not the only institution for German post-secondary professional education. Specialized schools and institutions, independent of and separate from universities and claiming, and eventually receiving, recognition of university status, provided training in business, engineering, forestry, mining, agriculture, veterinary medicine and other specialties. In their utilitarian emphasis and their separate existence, these institutions resembled the professional faculties and schools of Napoleonic France that had replaced the French universities. Thus, Robert Anderson stated recently that "what happened at the end of the nineteenth century was not so much the triumph of the Humboldtian ideal as a new synthesis in which elements of both [French] Enlightenment and Humboldtian traditions were merged."[14]

The builders of the modern American university also had to take account of American traditions of professional education that went back to the colonial colleges. In his *History of the American College and University*, Frederick Rudolph notes "the university movement did not intrude the spirit of professionalism into the life of American higher education."[15] From the beginning, a college liberal arts education had been held to be the proper education for the ministry, law, and medicine. Specialized training could then be pursued either in a divinity, law, or medical school or in an apprenticeship. Colonial colleges also established professorships in divinity, medicine, and law. The incumbents taught these subjects as liberal arts to undergraduates and as professional studies to graduates who had remained at the college or had returned after an apprenticeship elsewhere. Harvard had appointed its first professor of divinity in 1721; William and Mary, Yale, and the College of New Jersey followed during the next forty years. Medical professorships were established during the 1760s in Philadelphia and New York, and entering students were required to have obtained a bachelor's degree or show competence in Latin, mathematics, and natural philosophy. During the 1770s, both Yale College and the College of William and Mary introduced medical and legal education. Harvard granted its first medical degree in 1788.[16] Colonial colleges saw it as part of their task to provide their society with professionals educated in the liberal arts and trained in their specialties.

The most ambitious project of academically demanding professional education of high quality occurred as an outgrowth of a revolt of conservative churchmen against the liberal theological ministerial education offered at Unitarian Harvard. The revolt led in 1808 to the opening of the Andover Theological Seminary, an institution that, though it was neither college nor university, could claim for itself the rank of a church-sponsored graduate institution. It demanded of its students prior graduation from college and offered a three-year curriculum taught by a professorial faculty of three.[17] Later in the nineteenth century, American colleges introduced scientific and engineering courses into their curricula. Union College, the Rensselaer Polytechnic Institute, and the Massachusetts Institute of Technology are examples of collegiate institutions that provided undergraduate professional education.[18]

These collegiate and academically demanding instances of professional training, however, do not give a representative picture of professional education during the post-revolutionary and Jacksonian period. The majority of America's ministers and preachers, as well as lawyers and physicians, were not college graduates. Whatever professional training they may have received was given in church-sponsored divinity schools, in proprietary medicine and law schools, or under apprenticeship arrangements in parsonages or individual or group legal or medical practices. An end-of-the-nineteenth-century report indicated that in New York State the minimum standard for a license to practice medicine was the equivalent of high school graduation. Other states required no more than a common school education, a high school course, or some evidence of similar academic attainment. As late as 1897, even those professional schools that enrolled college graduates did not always make that a condition of admission. In such theological institutions, only 49 percent of the students held bachelor's degrees. In law schools, college graduates amounted to 24 percent, and in medical schools to only 14 percent.[19] The rationale for not strictly enforcing the bachelor's degree as an entrance requirement was not academic or intellectual, but financial and demographic. Professional schools were in need of income from students, and, given the demand for professionals, college graduates were in short supply. Thus, there were few voices that called for an academically more demanding training.

How, then, did university professional schools gain ascendancy by the end of the century? We find the answer in the growing realization among American professionals that if they wanted to protect their own reputation and credibility among the lay public, they had nowhere else to turn. The reluctance of American state legislatures to impose requirements for admission to the bar or medical practice or to interfere with the appointment of ministers by their congregations had for all practical purposes left professional practice without standards enforceable by professional associations. On the other hand, the chartering of colleges and universities by state legislatures as degree-granting institutions had empowered these to set standards of admission, graduation, and certification for their professional students. A university's reputation for academic excellence assured the public of the competence of its professional graduates. The universities did not hesitate to seize the opportunity and take over private professional schools or create professional schools of their own.[20]

In doing so, American elite universities followed the German example of an institutional separation of a liberal arts education from professional training. As in Germany, the former had been relegated to the *gymnasia* and the latter to the universities in the United States the liberal arts were taught in undergraduate colleges and the professional schools gradually came to be post-graduate institutions. This also meant that university professional schools adopted the German worship of *Wissenschaft* and research and, as Robert Lynn observed of the theological seminary, turned the professional school into a "hybrid creation."[21] Its faculty members had to meet the needs and demands of aspiring professional practitioners and, at the same time, conform to the research and publication requirements set by their tenured colleagues in the university. With regard to their students, they had to ask themselves, as Donald Light phrased it, to what extent their schools's task was "to *train* practitioners and to what extent . . . to *educate* pure disciples of the profession's core knowledge?"[22]

That issue was posed in 1903 by William Rainey Harper, President of the University of Chicago, when he stated that it was in the interest of the university that its School of Theology "partake exclusively of a scientific character" while it also should emphasize "the practical side of this same work," and then wondered "whether both of these things can be accomplished in the same school."[23] Harvard's president Charles W. Eliot had raised it earlier at the occasion of the appointment of James Barr Ames in 1873 to the Harvard law school. Eliot then said:

> In due course . . . there will be produced in this country a body of men learned in the law, who have never been on the bench or at the bar, but who nevertheless hold positions of great weight and influence as teachers of the law, as expounders, systematizers and historians.[24]

Eliot was answered in 1908 by Professor George F. Moore of the Hartford Theological Seminary, who, thinking of the seminary as a "theological university," countered:

> Just as it is not the primary end of the law school, to produce men learned in the history and philosophy of the jurisprudence, but to train men to *practice* law . . . so it is not the primary end of the theological school to send out men learned in the history and philosophy of religion, but to train men for the practice of the ministry.[25]

The contrast could not have been put more starkly.

The issue, however, is by no means only of historical interest. It has remained alive to this day. For the teachers in university professional schools, it has been less a matter of having to choose than of trying to satisfy both claims. "Janus-like," wrote Sydney Halpern in 1987, "they sit facing, on the one side, the university with its commitment to academic standards, and on the other, practicing professions with guild interests and commitments to client-oriented services."[26] Referring specifically to university law schools, Robert Stevens wrote in 1983 that "teaching still took pride of place over scholarship," and the legal literature produced by law school professors "was more likely to be of interest to the practitioner than to the scholar." But as the university's notorious "publish or perish" pressure made itself felt, he concluded, the "inherent conflict" between serving the profession through teaching its newcomers and pursuing scholarship "had developed into a massive case of intellectual schizophrenia."[27]

When in 1960 the dissolution of the University of Chicago's Federated Theological Faculty was announced, it became evident that the conflict affected today's divinity schools as well. The federation had consisted of the university's Divinity School, the Disciples House, the Chicago Theological Seminary (CTS), and the Meadville Seminary. CTS president McGiffert attributed the dissolution to different educational goals held by his Seminary and the Divinity School: "The Divinity School," he said, "felt that the Seminary might become subservient to the immediate needs of the churches; according to the Seminary, the Divinity School, enclosed within the University and lacking a vital connection with the churches, might wither into scholasticism."[28] The strains between church and university were obvious.

Perhaps the most notorious case of professional insecurity is presented by the faculty members of schools of education of major research universities, which stems from their inability to completely satisfy either the demands of practitioners or of their university colleagues. Education professors, wrote Geraldine Clifford and James W. Guthrie, "are like marginal men, aliens in their own worlds. They have seldom succeeded in satisfying the scholarly norms of their campus letters and science colleagues, and they are simultaneously estranged from their practicing professional peers." They are "organizational chameleons, trapped regardless of the coloration they adopt."[29] What makes matters worse, our authors write, is that they are "dominated by the ethos of graduate academic norms," and far more often devote their energies to research than to their professional responsibilities for the training of teachers.[30] Education professors exhibit less the schizophrenia Robert Stevens has ascribed to the faculties of law schools and they are less often caught in the conflict of missions sociologists have found in all fields of professional education than they are beset by a severe case of status insecurity. They feel unappreciated as fellow faculty members in a research university and they regard their tasks as teacher educators of minor prestige and importance.

Medicine appears to be the one area of professional education where, paradoxically, the conflicting demands of teaching neophytes and pursuing research are moderated by the presence of yet a third claim on the professors' time and energy: the care of patients. As professional practitioners, these faculty members generate additional income for themselves and the university, and, by providing hospitals and clinics, the university recognizes patient care as part of their academic duties. As Michael Burrage put it, "Medicine has, in fact, established an unusual relationship with universities in as much as it is the only profession apart from the Church and the academic profession itself that has been able, or allowed, to bring its subject matter and institutions into the university."[31] While university chaplaincies and the teaching done by professors in the Graduate Schools of Arts and Science are integral, not imported, parts of their duties to the university as faculty members and do not yield additional income for either the professor or the university, medical school professors often continue their private practice within the university. No law professor may consult with clients as part of his university work and no university provides courtrooms for his use as legal practitioner. While universities have occasionally provided practice or experimental primary and secondary schools for their education faculties to use as teaching laboratories, most have abandoned them.[32] Few education school faculty members have the opportunity to keep up or improve their practice in public or private school classrooms full- or part-time. To continue a practitioner's professional performance while being a university faculty member is the rare privilege of the medical school professor.[33]

A second issue that historians will have to face is that of professional education's tension between their practitioners' divided loyalties. On the one hand, their commitment to scholarship compels the faculty members of divinity schools to defend the uniform and universal applicability of the results of scientific inquiry; on the other, their allegiance to the doctrines of their confession or denomination sets limits to their freedom to inquire and teach. "Denominationalism," writes Glenn T. Miller, "was the most important single characteristic of nineteenth-century Protestant church life and was a central element in the identity of many American Christians."[34] Can divinity schools claim their teaching to be scientific when they are asked to endorse and abide by the creeds and prayer books of their sponsoring denominations, churches, or sects? Can they belong to the world of scholarship only when they divest themselves of any ties to particular confession? Harvard's President Eliot implied as much when he stated that sectarianism would "impair the public confidence in the impartiality and freedom of the university." Divinity school theologians tried to outflank that issue by maintaining that denominational traditions could be understood as facets of a wider Christian unity embodied in ecumenical organizations. This, wrote Conrad Cherry, "would provide the principal intellectual setting for divinity education."[35] And Glenn T. Miller added that, "if confessionalism divided the schools, scholarship united some of their instructors in a common cause." Still, he observed, "a confession of faith that has become one of many theological causes is not the united voice of the people of God or even of a particular denomination."[36]

For nineteenth century lawyers, the customary introduction into the profession through office apprenticeships and early and continuing socialization on the circuit had inevitably bequeathed a strong local and regional flavor to their professional outlook. As William Johnson has described it so well, the judicial circuit and court days shaped the professional experience of lawyers on the Wisconsin frontier. Their reputation and thus income depended on their success as courtroom advocates. Oratorical ability and familiarity with local conditions, both social and legal, contributed greatly to that success.[37] Given that background, many of the proprietary law school teachers argued that "a standard curriculum based on the development of legal reasoning was less pertinent to the career goals of [their] students than learning the law of their particular jurisdiction." Teachers in the university law schools, however, looked upon the law as a science of a wider than local or regional applicability. They proposed not only to encourage the development of their students' legal reasoning but also to introduce such subjects as jurisprudence, the history and philosophy of law.[38] When that happened, the contrast between university law schools and proprietary law schools, many of them being night schools and specializing in local practice, became even more pronounced.

Historians who study nineteenth century medical education will have to wonder whether a convincing case can be made for scientific medical education as long as physicians were divided among themselves in various camps, the generalists, the Thomsonians, the homeopaths, the osteopaths and the many irregular self-styled doctors?[39] To be sure, when toward the end of the century the germ theory and other developments led to a marked decrease in the threat of infectious diseases, the advances in establishing a scientific knowledge base immeasurably strengthened the scientific authority of university medical schools. As a result, medical schools in the twentieth century have been less endangered than divinity and law schools by sectarian strife or by local and regional differences in their curricular offerings. Still, the presence of chiropractic and herbal medicine, as well as of the varieties of so-called non-western medicine today remind us that the issue persists in medical education as well.

Thirdly and finally, professional schools have found themselves caught in the struggle between those of their faculty members who argue that the push for higher professional school admissions and certification standards is required to meet the public's expectations and those who believe that only low accreditation standards and an open admissions policy that permits access to members of all social, ethnic, and racial groups will restore or maintain the public's confidence. Here, the contrast between the 1910 Flexner Report on medical education and the 1921 Reed Report on legal education are instructive.[40] Abraham Flexner had argued that the subject matter of medical schools rested on scientific investigations and required a uniform application of the highest scientific standards. Medical schools, therefore, should be associated with a university and a teaching hospital. They should not be operated as a business for private profit.[41] Their faculty members should consist of full-time professors committed to research in clinical as well as scientific departments, and their students should have a minimum of two years of college studies in the natural sciences.[42] Alfred Reed, like Flexner commissioned by the Carnegie Foundation for the Advancement of Teaching, did not think that all law schools had to conform to as stringently uniform scientific standards as Flexner had demanded of medical schools. The law, he argued, was a public profession that had to respond to the country's need of "lawyers of differing skills and qualifications serving different purposes and different elements in society.[43] There was room for night schools that were accessible to working people who aspired to work with individual clients and their everyday legal problems, and there was room for university law schools that trained college-educated specialists to deal with government and corporate clients. As it was, America's physicians endorsed Flexner's view of their profession for much the same reasons that America's lawyers, as represented in the American Bar Association, rejected Reed's report. In both cases, professionals sought to protect scientific standards and the prestige they conveyed on them. Critics were later to charge that the Flexner report had severely restricted the supply of physicians and "many of the ills of inadequate medical care in the 1970s can be traced" to its success.[44] Reed's views, too, found their supporters among lawyers who, like Robert Stevens, pointed out that if proprietary law schools had been entirely eliminated, "legal services might have been even more inadequately distributed in this country than they are today."[45] The conflict of view persisted in both professions. During the 1920s and 1930s, it was made all the more virulent when charges of anti-Semitism, xenophobia, and elitist discrimination against racial minorities and the poor entered the debates.[46]

In the similar, though not identical, education of ministers, controversies appeared in the 1920s.[47] The debates between those who wanted to uphold academic standards and those who opted for easy accessibility to and admission into theological schools and the ministry reflected a division between religious modernists and fundamentalists. In general, modernists believed in rational critical inquiry and discourse as the preferred means of theological education. For fundamentalists, the aim of ministerial education was to turn their students into enthusiastic defenders and propagators of the faith of their church. In short, the latter valued faith over intellect. By the time of the Cold War, that dispute was fought between theological liberals and conservatives, with the latter maintaining that the strength and validity of individual faith and religious belief did not depend on higher education. Liberal theologians, on the other hand, looked upon their university divinity schools in much the same way as legal and medical scholars regarded their professional schools as pace-setters of modern science and learning. They, too, were unwilling to reconsider their professional responsibilities in light of what a wider public might need or desire. Lay members of congregations, however, did not ask for ministers who excelled in modern religious scholarship and administrative and social-scientific techniques. While they certainly did not reject these qualities as inappropriate, they would remind the divinity schools that they above all else asked for pastors who were able to strengthen their parishioners' faith and to comfort them in their hour of need. University divinity schools and local congregations not only represent different worlds of educational and theological understanding, they also stand for different social and ideological worlds. For a workable future in professional education in theology as much as in law and medicine, university professional schools may have to rethink their relationship to the diverse social and racial communities in which they live and serve.

For education school faculties, the desire to raise the academic reputation and social respectability of their profession expressed itself differently than it did for lawyers and physicians. If the latter sought to achieve their goal by a policy of exclusion through the applications of raised entrance requirements to professional school and profession, education faculties were stymied in any such effort by the sheer number of teachers needed in the schools.[48] They, therefore, sought to concentrate their efforts on encouraging their students to look upon teaching in elementary or high school as a preliminary step on the ladder of professional success. Their best students, they hoped, would eventually occupy administrative offices as principals or superintendents, and, if they were really successful, professorial chairs in teachers colleges and education schools. They conveyed to their students the message that, as Clifford and Guthrie put it, "the way to get ahead is to get out of the classroom.[49] The result of such an attitude was that as the preparation of classroom teachers came to be seen as a professional task of low repute, the University of Chicago abolished its school of education, and Harvard University severely restricted its teacher training activities in its school of education. As did their brethren in law and medical schools, faculty members in university education schools turned to advanced disciplinary teaching and research, the two chief areas being psychology and administration. It was their way of raising their professional status. This attempt to re-think the history of American professional schools and education has of necessity been limited in its scope. It has taken most of its examples from the traditional academic professions of the ministry, medicine, and the law because their history foreordained them as the preferred candidates for inclusion into American colleges and universities.[50] To what extent other professional fields and their educational institutions share the history and problems outlined here, and to what extent they may differ as I tried to show in the case of education schools, will have to remain a subject of further investigation. What this historical survey points out is that in the United States, colleges and universities have played a dominant role in the development of professional education. This becomes especially clear when one looks at developments in other countries where practitioners and the state have largely determined the course of professional education.[51] This survey also demonstrates that in the United States, university professional school faculties have had to come to terms with three pervasive tensions. From their beginnings, they have been torn by conflicting claims of practitioners and academics. The former wanted the schools to respond to immediate utilitarian needs of society; the latter wanted them to focus their attention on research in order to broaden the professional knowledge base. The second tension has separated practitioners who desired to meet sectarian and local needs while academics preferred to pursue scientific inquiries of universalistic applicability. And thirdly, university professional school faculties found themselves involved in disputes over what should be given priority: maintaining and raising of professional standards or opening access to a socially, racially, and ethnically more diverse membership. Generally, and particularly after their schools attained graduate standing, they opted to defend their scholarly and scientific reputation by favoring high academic standards over open admissions. However conflicted university professional education may appear, it is not likely that it will yield its position as the primary avenue of its graduates to professional success and reputation.

Notes

1. Sydney Ann Halpern, "Professional Schools in the American University," in *The Academic Profession: National Disciplinary, and Institutional Settings*, ed. Burton R. Clark (Berkeley: University of California Press, 1987), 311.

2. Christopher Jencks and David Riesman, *The Academic Revolution* (Garden City: Doubleday & Company, 1968).

3. Richard Hofstadter and Walter P. Metzger, *The Development of Academic Freedom in the United States* (New York: Columbia University Press, 1955).

4. See my remarks in Henry Geitz, Jürgen Heideking and Jurgen Herbst, eds., *German Influences on Education in the United States to 1917* (Cambridge: Cambridge University Press, 1995), 11, and Burton Bledstein's comment in his *The Culture of Professionalism: The Middle Class and the Development of Higher Education in America* (New York: Norton, 1976), 318–19.

5. Richard T. Ely in the *American Economic Association Quarterly*, 3d ser. (April 1910): 68–69, and G. Stanley Hall in his *Life and Confessions of a Psychologist* (New York: Appleton, 1923), 187.

6. Christopher J. Lucas gives a good summary of the German impact on professional graduate studies in his *American Higher Education: A History* (New York: St. Martin's Press, 1994), 170–74. For a critique of the distinction made between the age of the college and the age of the university see James Axtell, "The Death of the Liberal Arts College," *History of Education Quarterly* 11 (winter 1971): 339–52, and my "American Higher Education in the Age of the College," *History of Universities* 7 (1988): 39.

7. See Alan B. Cobban, *The Medieval Universities: Their Development and Organization* (London: Methuen & Co. 1975), and Hastings Rashdall, *The Universities of Europe in the Middle Ages*, eds. F. M. Powicke and A. B. Emden, 3 vols. (Oxford: Clarendon Press, 1951).

8. Immanuel Kant, "Der Streit der Fakultäten," in *Werke in Sechs Bänden*, ed. Wilhelm Weischedel (Frankfurt am Main: Insel Verlag, 1964). VI, 261ff.

9. See my "The First Three American Colleges: Schools of the Reformation," *Perspectives in American History* 8 (1974): 7–52.

10. See Charles E. McClelland, *State, Society, and University in Germany*, 1700–1914 (Cambridge: Cambridge University Press, 1980), 76–77.

11. See Jacques Verger, ed., *Histoire des universites en France* (Toulouse: Bibliotheque historique privat, 1986), 261ff.

12. Application to found the University of Berlin, 24 July 1809, in Withelm von Humboldt, *Gesammelte Schriften*, vol. 10 (Berlin: Akademie der Wissenschaften, 1903–36), 148–54.

13. See Kant, "Der Streit der Fakultäten," and Günther Bien, "Kant's Theorie der Universität and ihr geschichtlicher Ort," *Historische Zeifschrift*, 219 (1974): 551–77.

14. Robert Anderson, "Before and After Humboldt: European Universities Between the Eighteenth and Nineteenth Centuries," *History of Higher Education Annual* 20 (2000): 12.

15. Frederick Rudolph, *The American College and University: A History* (Athens: University of Georgia Press, 1990), 342.

16. See my *From Crisis to Crisis: American College Government, 1636–1819* (Cambridge, Mass.: Harvard University Press, 1982), 160–65.

17. Donald W. Light, "The Development of Professional Schools in America," in *The Transformation of Higher Learning 1860–1930*, ed. Konrad H. Jarausch (Chicago: University of Chicago Press, 1983), 346–49. See also the sections on Andover in Glenn T. Miller, *Piety and Intellect: The Aims and Purposes of Ante-Bellum Theological Education* (Atlanta, Ga.: Scholars Press, 1990), 51–83.

18. See Thomas N. Bonner, "The Beginnings of Engineering Education in the United States: The Curious Role of Eliphalet Nott," *New York History 69* (1988): 35–54.

19. See James Russell Parsons, *Professional Education. Monographs on Education in the United States. # 10*, ed. Nicholas Murray Butler (St, Louis: Universal Exposition, 1904), 7 and 10.

20. For more on this see Michael Burrage, "From Practice to School-based Professional Education: Patterns of Conflict and Accommodation in England, France, and the United States," in *The European and American University since 1800*, eds. Sheldon Rothblatt and Björn Wittrock (Cambridge: Cambridge University Press, 1993), 142–87.

21. Robert W. Lynn, *Why the Seminary: An Introduction to the Report of the Auburn History Subject* (typescript, 1978), 3.

22. Light, "The Development of Professional Schools in America," 346.

23. Quoted in Conrad Cherry, *Hurrying Toward Zion: Universities, Divinity Schools, and American Protestantism* (Bloomington: Indiana University Press, 1995), 7.

24. Quoted in Jerold S. Auerbach, "Enmity and Amity: Law Teachers and Practitioners, 1900–1922," in *Perspectives in American History*, eds. Donald Fleming and Bernard Bailyn, vol. V (1971), 551.

25. Quoted in Light, "The Development of Professional Schools," 350.

26. Halpem, "Professional Schools," 304–05.

27. Robert Stevens, Law School: Legal Education in America from the 1850s to the 1980s (Chapel Hill: University of North Carolina Press, 1983), 264 and 271.

28. Quoted in Cherry, *Hurrying Towards Zion*, 160.

29. Geraldine Joncich Clifford and James W. Guthrie, *Ed School: A Brief for Professional Education* (Chicago: University of Chicago Press, 1988), 3 and 5.

30. Clifford and Guthrie, *Ed School*, 87.

31. Michael Burrage, "From Practice to School-based Professional Education," 156.

32. See Clifford and Guthrie, *Ed School*, 109–16.

33. My thanks to Kenneth M. Ludmerer for bringing this to my attention.

34. Miller, *Piety and Intellect*, 6.

35. Cherry, *Hurrying Towards Zion*, 60.

36. Miller, *Piety and Intellect*, 28 and 33.

37. William R. Johnson, *Schooled Lawyers: A Study in the Clash of Professional Cultures* (New York: New York University Press, 1978), 24–41.

38. Stevens, *Law School*, 41.

39. Light, "The Development of Professional Schools," 361 and Burrage, "From Practice to School-based Professional Education." 174.

40. For a far more incisive comparative analysis of the two reports than I can provide here, see Michael Schudson. "The Flexner Report and the Reed Report: Notes on the History of Professional Education in the United States," *Social Science Quarterly* (September 1974): 347–61.

41. Abraham Flexner, *Medical Education in the United States and Canada* (New York: Carnegie Foundation for the Advancement of Teaching, Bulletin No. 4, 1910), 173.

42. For an excellent overview and analysis of the Flexner Report see chapter 9 in Kenneth M. Ludmerer, *Learning to Heal: The Development of American Medical Education* (New York: Basic Books, 1985).

43. Quoted in Stevens, *Law School*, 116.

44. Quoted in Schudson, "The Flexner Report and the Reed Report," 381.

45. Stevens, *Law School*, 116.

46. See Auerbach, "Enmity and Amity," 579–80.

47. In this paragraph I rely heavily on Cherry, *Hurrying Toward Zion*, 167–82.

48. The *Occupational Outlook Handbook, 1984–85* of the U.S. Bureau of Labor Statistics lists the number of classroom teachers in the United States in 1984 as 2,390,000, of physicians as 480,000, and of lawyers as 465,000. Cited in Clifford and Guthrie, *Ed School*, 18.

49. Clifford and Guthrie, *Ed School*, 14.

50. Note, however, that Abraham Flexner, for reasons I discussed above, did not want to include schools of denominational religion as candidates for university professional faculties. See his *Universities: American, English, German* (Oxford: Oxford University Press, 1930), 29.

51. See Burrage, in "From Practice to School-based Professional Education," 155; "To put it in a nutshell, professional education in England has been dominated by practitioners, in France by the State, and in the United States by the universities."

SURVEYING THE PROFESSIONS

ELLEN CONDLIFFE LAGEMANN

In 1910, the Carnegie Foundation published its most famous report, Abraham Flexner's *Medical Education in the United States and Canada*. Long thought to have originated the reorganization of medical training that occurred in the United States during the early decades of the twentieth century, this report more recently has been shown to have supported and accelerated a trend it did not itself begin. What the Flexner report did initiate, however, was the Carnegie Foundation's professionalizing campaign—its effort to define and institutionalize nationally uniform, science-based, training paradigms that would serve as prerequisites for entrance into the professions.

Obviously, this campaign was an integral part of the Foundation's more general effort to standardize American education, and derived from its concern with developing the university as one of the new institutional hubs of American society, a focal point for a more national and functionally defined social organization. The Foundation's concern was, of course, shared by many "progressive" elements in American society. Most of the leaders of the medical profession, a number of the leaders of the legal profession, and some members of the engineering and teaching professions, among others, also looked to the university to develop, transmit, and certify the special knowledge that would augment and sustain the authority and autonomy they wished to claim. These people became the Foundation's allies in its professionalizing campaign.

With and through the alliances it could build with these other proponents of professionalism, the Foundation was also able to seek recognition for its own related and entirely compatible claims. Its professionalizing campaign supported the assertion that the Carnegie Foundation was not only a pension fund, but also and more importantly, a central agency of educational administration, which would play a role in defining the spheres, the functions, and the relationships among the variety of institutions involved with higher education. By sponsoring surveys that had nothing whatsoever to do with pensioning, it was possible to educate the public to Henry Pritchett's and the trustees' view of the Foundation's most important purpose.

Legally, such surveys were allowed by the power that had been vested in the Foundation when its original 1905 New York State charter was replaced in March of 1906 with a Congressional charter. The charter change had been urged by Pritchett. The first charter had set forth as the Foundation's objectives a variety of activities having to do with pensioning and had also allowed bequests to promote "the cause of science and education." But the Foundation did not have the resources necessary for such bequests. Its actual capacity to do more than pensioning was therefore limited. For this reason, the second charter, which doubtless appealed to Carnegie because of the fuller—Congressional—recognition it gave to his benevolence, was worded in a less specific way. It allowed the Foundation, in addition to pensioning, to "do and perform all things necessary to encourage, uphold, and dignify the profession of the teacher and the cause of higher education" in the United States and Canada.[1]

Technically feasible for this reason, the Carnegie Foundation professionalizing campaign was initially made possible by professional association interest in the possibility of independent evaluations of professional schools. This was made clear in the "Plan for an Examination of the Status of Professional Education" approved by the Foundation's trustees prior to the commissioning of the

Flexner report. Written by Pritchett, this plan stated that "an unsatisfactory situation" was known to exist in the training of American professionals. Low standards, it explained, "permit the unfit and often times the unworthy to enter" even the most elevated callings. But the time for reform was at hand. Carnegie studies, Pritchett had ascertained, would be welcomed by the professional associations, and, because "conditions" were then "fluid," would have a significant "chance to influence in the right direction." As this memorandum concluded, the potential benefit of surveys of professional training to the "cause of education" indicated that it would be "one of the most fruitful projects the foundation could undertake."[2] Circumstances within the professions, particularly within the medical profession, made it possible for the Carnegie Foundation to become the kind of "Great Agency" Pritchett hoped it would be.

The Circumstances in Medicine at the Time of the Flexner Report

By 1908, when the Flexner report was started, many American doctors were eager to raise the requirements for entrance to their field. There had been an increasing supply of doctors: in 1900 there were approximately 25,000 medical students registered in 154 medical schools, compared to approximately 15,000 students in 118 schools ten years earlier.[3] There were also increasing numbers of trained nurses, midwives, and other potentially competitive health practitioners. Higher educational prerequisites for medical practice were of considerable professional interest because they might help curb what was thought to be an excessively competitive market situation worsened by a proliferation of the other, also professionalizing, groups of health practitioners (nurses especially) that might divide the medical field by function, and thereby limit the physician's domain.[4]

Supporting this concern with income, control, and status, was the belief that new patterns of training would result in better medical service. Entrance restrictions to the profession through education were considered in both the profession's and the public's interest. By the turn of the century, physician dissatisfaction with old forms of medical training was increasingly common. The transmission of known techniques and therapies via an apprenticeship, preceded in most cases by no more than elementary school study and supplemented in some cases by attendance at the lectures offered in small, proprietary colleges established, owned, and staffed by local practitioners, had seemed adequate before the rise of scientific medicine. But scientific medicine, which was a demonstrably more effective medicine for the diagnosis and cure of disease, could not be taught in this way.[5]

American doctors had discovered the inadequacy of American medical education through their study in Germany, where approximately 15,000 American medical personnel, about one-half of the nation's leading physicians, received advanced training between 1870 and the First World War. In Germany, they had been exposed to exciting innovations in medical techniques and theories as well as to a research orientation and an emphasis on specialization still unknown in the United States. Many of these doctors found the opportunities that awaited them back in the United States disappointing and constraining.[6] Their experience was not unlike Henry Pritchett's after his return from Germany to Washington University to "teach the Freshman year."

William Henry Welch, the pathologist who became the first head of the Johns Hopkins medical school, on his return to New York from Germany in 1878, found he could not teach medicine within an existing medical college as he wished and was best able to do, and as he thought necessary to transmit the techniques and information he had learned. His immediate solution to the problem was unusually creative. In silent partnership with two other doctors recently back from Germany, William S. Halsted and T. Mitchell Prudden, Welch established what Donald Fleming has described as "a kind of medical faculty of their own, cutting across institutional lines, silently eluding the seniority system . . . of the medical professors, and giving beneath the surface and in the interstices of the formal instruction an almost Germanic tutelage—a shadow medical college of the city of New York uniting the best resources of all the schools."[7] Welch was an unusual man, with a special ability to surmount constraints. He subsequently achieved fame and influence.

Reform had become, by the 1880s and 1890s, a personal and professional necessity for a self-conscious and increasingly powerful cadre of American doctors like Welch. Even the specialization that so often followed from advanced study abroad, which was most immediately evident in the rapid formation of specialized professional societies (sixteen of the eighteen original members of the American Physiological Society founded in 1887 had studied in Germany, and German-trained doctors were disproportionately represented in the ten other special groups formed before 1890), argued for the revamping of medical training along research-based disciplinary lines.[8]

Inspired by admiration for German medicine and by a desire to emulate the educational paradigm on which it was based, interest in reform was furthered by the opening of the Johns Hopkins Medical School in 1893. Joined to both a university and a hospital, and made possible by a large endowment, Hopkins replicated the scientifically-oriented and inquiry-based pedagogy of German medical training. It drew visitors from all over the country. Its remarkable faculty sent out remarkable students to staff what were emerging as the key juncture points of the profession: the most prestigious medical schools, the most important committees of the professional associations, and the leading professional journals. Whether one knew of Hopkins through actual familiarity with the experiment in Baltimore or through acquaintance with Hopkins' graduates, "Welch's rabbits," the favorable consensus of opinion surrounding the new medical school showed even those who had no European training that the didactic classroom lectures of the average proprietary school were old fashioned and second-rate.[9] In consequence, by 1908, a trend toward standardizing the Hopkins model through proprietary school mergers, the establishment of medical school connections with hospitals and universities, and the far more controversial establishment of full-time clinical professorships, all were underway.[10]

Growing professional concern with institutionalizing a new paradigm for medical training had led to the formation in 1904 of an organized lobby—the American Medical Association's (AMA) Council on Medical Education. The Council was composed primarily of doctors associated with the more modern and prestigious medical schools. Its purpose was to coordinate, facilitate, and accelerate the efforts of professional groups interested in reform, for example the National Confederation of State Medical and Licensing Boards and the Association of American Medical Colleges. To achieve this end, the Council had set an "ideal standard" for medical schools; entrance requirements equivalent to university entrance requirements; a medical curriculum including one year of basic science, two years of laboratory science, and two years of clinical science; and a culminating year of internship at the end; and on the basis of this standard it had begun to inspect medical schools and to rate them as acceptable, doubtful, or unacceptable (Class A, B, or C). The Council operated very much like the Carnegie Foundation in determining which institutions would be eligible for its pension fund. Despite these measures, however, the doctors associated with the Council, particularly its president Arthur Dean Bevan of Rush Medical College in Chicago, were dissatisfied with the profession's movement toward reform. The believed that if the "ideal standard" could be raised and the rating a medical school received after inspection could be published, change would be fostered even more effectively and faster.[11]

The Council on Medical Education, although largely self-sustaining, was an arm of the AMA, and presumably for that reason, Bevan was unable to get the Council to adopt the procedures he favored. The AMA, which represented "regular" physicians, had been established in 1847, at a time of great rivalry between medical sects (regular, homeopathic, hydropathic, chronothermal, botanic, and other physicians). It did not establish itself as a closely integrated, national group until the early twentieth century. Only at that time, as a result of an administrative reorganization that linked the national association to state, county, and local medical societies, did the AMA begin to assume its modern form, although even then it did not encompass the entire medical profession. In 1900, it had had approximately 8,400 members and by 1910 it had 70,000 members. Approximately one half of the country's physicians and surgeons belonged.[12]

Many AMA members were associated with medical schools that could not yet meet the Council's "ideal standard." To have raised that standard even further and to have published medical school ratings might well have caused sufficient upset to injure emerging Association and professional unity. Furthermore, since Council ratings were seen as biased in favor of the more modernized schools from which the Council members tended to be drawn, more forceful action would likely have been misinterpreted and discredited. Therefore, as Council president Arthur Bevan explained many years later, it "occurred to some members of the Council that, if we could obtain the publication and approval of our work by the Carnegie Foundation for the Advancement of Teaching, it would assist materially in securing the results we were attempting to bring about."[13]

Council president Arthur Bevan apparently approached Henry Pritchett, and Pritchett then urged his fellow trustees, some of whom were reluctant to venture too boldly beyond Andrew Carnegie's known intentions for the Foundation, to read the new charter as "broad enough to include the study of education at every point where it may affect the higher institutions."[14] The discovery that doctors believed that "if the light can be turned on by an outside agency rather than by those in the profession, it will do great good" led the Foundation to sponsor a report that was designed to make it appear as a prime sponsor of a medical school transformation that was already well underway.[15]

Abraham Flexner and the Flexner Report

In the fall of 1908, Abraham Flexner returned to New York from two years of study in Berlin. He was forty-two-years-old, unemployed and in need of money, ambitious and, as he put it later, eager to make "a layman's contribution to education."[16] Flexner apparently did not want to return to his original calling—he had been a schoolmaster in Lexington, Kentucky—and he did not want to teach in an American college. While in Germany, he had been writing a book, *The American College*, that was severely critical of American higher education and strongly supportive of university ideals. He had made careful note of a newspaper announcement of the Carnegie Foundation's establishment, and throughout his book he referred to Pritchett's early annual reports. Flexner wanted to work at the Carnegie Foundation; and, having secured an introduction to Pritchett from Ira Remson, the president of Johns Hopkins (where Flexner had gone to college) and a Foundation trustee, he met Pritchett just after the Foundation had decided to sponsor professional school studies. Pritchett looked at the proofs of Flexner's new book and hired him to conduct the first study, the medical report that was to be the Carnegie Foundation's Bulletin Number Four.[17]

In the biography Flexner later wrote of Pritchett, he said that when asked to undertake the study he had responded:

> "I am not a physician; aren't you confusing me with my brother Simon at the Rockefeller Institute for Medical Research [who was a prominent pathologist]?"
> "No," rejoined Pritchett. "I know your brother well. What I have in mind is not a medical study, but an educational one. Medical schools are schools and must be judged as such. For that, a very sketchy notion of the main functions of the various departments suffices. That you or any other intelligent layman can readily acquire. Such a study as I have in mind takes that for granted. Henceforth, these institutions must be viewed from the standpoint of education. Are they so equipped and conducted as to be able to train students to be efficient physicians, surgeons, and so on?"[18]

Flexner's fortuitous arrival in Pritchett's office allowed him to secure just the kind of author he needed. Beyond Flexner's full agreement with professional values, the fact that he was not a doctor and that he had been an educator would give the Council what it wanted—"the weight of an independent report of a disinterested body"—and the Foundation what it wanted—the establishment of educators as the arbiters of all training matters, even those that concerned the strongest and best organized of all the professions.[19]

Pritchett took Flexner along to a December, 1908, meeting with members of the Council on Medical Education. According to the minutes of that meeting, it was there agreed "that while the Foundation would be guided very largely by the Council's investigations, to avoid claims of partiality, no more mention should be made in the report of the Council than any other source of information."[20] Then Flexner set off to read about medical education in Germany, to study the Council's medical school reports and ratings, to confer with faculty members at the Johns Hopkins Medical School, and, finally, often accompanied by N. P. Colwell, the secretary of the Council, to visit all of the 155 medical schools in existence in North America at the time.

These visits were brief. Flexner wrote later: "In half an hour or less I could sample the credentials of students filed in the dean's office. . . . a few inquiries made clear whether the faculty was composed of local doctors, not already 'professors' in some other local medical school, or the extent to which efforts had been made to obtain teachers properly trained elsewhere. A single question elicited the income of a medical school. . . . A stroll through the laboratories disclosed the presence or absence of apparatus, museum specimens, library, and students; and a 'whiff' told the inside story regarding the manner in which anatomy was cultivated."[21] Following several visits, Flexner would return to New York, write up his data, mail a copy of his findings to the schools' deans, and then set out again. Within a year, the report was finished. It was a truly brilliant exposé and program for reform.

The report was divided into two sections. The first described the historical and contemporary situation in medicine and presented the case for reform. Its argument may be schematically summarized as follows:

- The American medical school is now well along in the second century of its history. It began, and for many years continued to exist, as a supplement to the apprenticeship system. . . .[22]

- With the foundation early in the nineteenth century at Baltimore of a proprietary school, the so-called medical department of the so-called University of Maryland, a harmful precedent was established. Before that a college of medicine had been a branch growing out of the living university trunk.[23]

- Quite aside from the history, achievements, or present merits of any particular independent medical school, the creation of the (proprietary school) type was the fertile source of unforeseen harm to medical education and to medical practice. Since that day, medical colleges have multiplied without restraint. . . .[24]

- In the wave of commercial exploitation which swept the entire profession . . . the original university departments were practically torn from their moorings. The medical schools of Harvard, Yale, Pennsylvania, became, as they expanded, virtually independent of the institutions with which they were legally united. . . . For years they managed their own affairs along proprietary lines.[25]

- Johns Hopkins Medical School . . . was the first medical school in America of genuine university type, with something approaching adequate endowment, well equipped laboratories conducted by modern teachers, devoting themselves unreservedly to medical investigation and instruction, and with its own hospital, in which the training of physicians and the healing of the sick harmoniously combine to the infinite advantage of both. It has finally cleared up the problem of standards and ideals.[26]

- We may safely conclude that our methods of carrying on medical education have resulted in enormous over-production at a low level, and that, whatever the justification in the past, the present situation . . . can be more effectively met by a reduced output of well-trained men than by further inflation with an inferior product.[27]

- If the sick are to reap the full benefit of recent progress in medicine, a more uniformly arduous and expensive medical education is demanded.[28]

Flexner then moved on to describe what such an education should consist of. It had to be preceded by a minimum of two years of college work in science. It should include during the first two years fundamental laboratory instruction in the basic medical sciences "arranged and organized with a distinct practical purpose in view." It should emphasize during the last two years more advanced hospital-based training in clinical practice, the point being to learn "by doing."[29]

Finally, before presenting in a separate section the results of his medical school visiting, Flexner turned to the all important question of "reconstruction." He described exactly what a reformed national system of medical education should look like. It was to be based on several key principles: for example, the production of enough new physicians to provide one doctor for every 1500 people and the placement of medical schools in cities (usually no more than one per city) so that they could affiliate with the universities that would be best able to develop them. It was to be regional in organization. This is what it projected for the Northeast: "125 new doctors would be needed [50 to cover 1908–1909 population increase, 75 to replace half of those who had died]. To produce this number, two new schools, one of moderate size and one smaller, readily suffice. Fortunately, they can be developed without sacrificing any of our criteria. The medical schools of Harvard and Yale are university departments, situated in the midst of ample clinical material, with considerable financial backing now and every prospect of more. It is unwise to divide the Boston field; it is unnecessary to prolong the life of the clinical departments of Dartmouth, Bowdoin, and Vermont."[30] In the overall reconstruction, 120 medical schools were, in Flexner's words, to be "wiped off the map."[31]

Justified, on the one hand, by the argument with which Flexner began, this plan was further supported, on the other, by his description of the actual colleges. A few colleges had shown themselves to be exemplary: Western Reserve, Yale, Johns Hopkins, and Harvard, among others. A good number (and almost all of those with sectarian associations of any kind) appeared to be scandalously bad. For example, Kansas Medical College in Topeka, Kansas, had only one dissecting room and it was "indescribably filthy; it contained, in addition to necessary tables, a single, badly hacked cadaver, and was simultaneously used as a chicken yard."[32] Most were second-rate. The University and Bellevue Hospital Medical College in New York City had laboratories that "are developed unevenly, as the resources of the school are not equal to uniform promotion of all the medical sciences."[33] The Tennessee Medical College in Knoxville, Tennessee, had a building that "is externally attractive; within, dirty. . . . The dissecting room is ordinary."[34] The Denver and Gross College of Medicine in Denver, Colorado, had a new and "exceedingly attractive dispensary building, "but" its equipment consists of a chemical laboratory of the ordinary medical school type, a dissecting room, containing a few subjects as dry as leather, a physiological laboratory with slight equipment, and the usual pathology and bacteriology laboratories."[35]

The report indicted most medical schools, while offering a clear, specific, and forcefully argued program for change. As everyone involved in planning the report wanted it to do, it documented a discrepancy between the "ideal" and the "real." Indeed, Flexner made this point directly when he said: "Society reaps at this moment but a small fraction of the advantage which current knowledge has the power to confer. That sick man is relatively rare for whom actually all is done that is at this day humanly feasible. . . . We have indeed in America medical practitioners not inferior to the best elsewhere; but there is probably no other country in the world in which there is so great a distance and so fatal a difference between the best, the average, and the worst."[36] The Council on Medical Education had wanted a report like Flexner's to make this discrepancy more widely known. Through a Carnegie Foundation publication it had hoped to persuade those outside the profession that higher and more uniform educational standards, and, in consequence, restricted access to the profession, should be not only a professional, but also a public goal. Flexner had said in the report that "when public interest, professional ideals, and sound educational procedure concur in the recommendation of the same policy, the time is surely ripe for decisive action."[37] And in this instance, as was expected, that certainly proved to be true.

The Outcomes of the Flexner Report

Medical schools had already begun to close and to merge before the Flexner report appeared in 1910. Between 1906, when the Council on Medical Education was founded, and the year of the report's publication, 31 schools went out of existence. But that number increased steadily after 1910. In that year, there were 155 medical schools; by 1920, there were 85; and by 1930, there were 76 (Flexner had recommended 31).[38] More important by far, huge financial investments in medical education had provided the resources necessary for the laboratories, libraries, professors, and hospital affiliations that made the curricular model suggested by Flexner the norm throughout virtually all of the medical schools in the United States.[39]

In some instances, the report helped to win local interest and support for the move toward a new national paradigm. This was true, for example, at Washington University in St. Louis, where a post-report endowment of several millions of dollars realized changes that faculty members had been urging and working toward for some time. The school had been proprietary until 1906, although, as Kenneth Ludmerer has shown, "Flexner's description of proprietary schools as 'essentially private ventures, money-making in spirit and object' did not fit the school."[40] As early as 1872, a Medical Fund Society had been formed with faculty profits to develop the facilities that modern scientific medicine required. It was only after the Flexner report, however, that funds beyond those could be raised. In this instance, as in others, the report quite literally excited public outrage and then interest on the part of the merchant Robert Brookings and other wealthy local businessmen and, as a result, secured for medical reform the levels of financial assistance needed.[41]

In other instances, the capital for medical reform came from philanthropic foundations. The already superior schools were the principal beneficiaries of this aid. For example, between 1911 and 1936, Johns Hopkins received ten million dollars from the Rockefeller's General Education Board (where Abraham Flexner went to work soon after his medical report appeared) and an additional two million from the Carnegie Corporation. One hundred fifty-four million dollars of foundation grants went to medical education between 1910 and the onset of the Depression.[42] Whatever the source, however, the infusion of huge amounts of money clearly made a difference and the result was surely an improvement in the overall quality of American medical education.

Still, not all interests were well served by the changes that came with this new financing. This is particularly evident if one considers the access of black Americans to the medical profession. At the time of the Flexner report there were eight medical schools for blacks; fifteen years after the report's appearance, there were two—Howard Medical School in Washington, D.C., and Meharry Medical College in Nashville, Tennessee. Blacks were of course admitted to some predominantly white institutions, but with medical school-hospital affiliations that too was more difficult, for the hospitals tended to be even more discriminatory than the colleges themselves were. After 1910, it was more difficult for black males to secure medical training than it was even for white females, whose low representation in the profession cannot be attributed to the Flexner report or to the medical reform movement of which it was a part. At the time of the Second World War, there were still fewer than one hundred black students at non-black American medical schools. If only because what had been an increasing number of black physicians (between 1890 and 1910 the number of black doctors had tripled) became after 1910 a decreasing number, one may argue that the Flexner report was in effect, if not intent, discriminatory in some of its outcomes. What is more, though one cannot measure the loss, with longer and more expensive training required for all doctors, financially poor aspirants to the profession were also most likely excluded. In some very important ways, therefore, the Flexner report improved American medicine, while making the profession as well as its services less accessible to many.[43]

Finally, and most important here, the Flexner report provided demonstrable support for an argument for standards in other professions, especially law, which Henry Pritchett had made in 1908 while discussing the Carnegie Foundation's projected professional surveys. In calling attention to what he described as the necessity for doctors to be trained in the sciences fundamental to "regular" medicine, even if they wanted to be homeopaths, osteopaths, Christian Scientists, or faith healers (and in his report, Flexner agreed), he had said:

> The only possible protection and assurance which the public can have is to insist upon this fundamental training as a preliminary to any practice, and it may rightly suspect the motives of any set of would-be practitioners who undertake to evade these reasonable requirements—necessary alike in the interests of the public and of the profession of medicine. With respect to the practice of law, the public interest is dependent likewise on the enforcement of high professional standards. The practitioner of law does not deal so directly with the personal well-being of every citizen as does the physician but no other profession is so closely related to the development of justice and to the progress of sound public policy. There is no way by which the public can tell whether the practitioner of law will develop into a wise advocate or into a sharp attorney. The only criterion it can impose for its own protection is to require such training for entrance to the profession as will fit the ordinary man for good work in it and will at the same time serve as a means to exclude the unfit.[44]

Deeply convinced of these points, Pritchett was calling on the legal profession to invite a study such as the Council on Medical Education had wanted.

Notes

1. Howard J. Savage, *Fruit of an Impulse: Forty-Five Years of the Carnegie Foundation 1905–1950* (New York: Harcourt, Brace, 1953), pp. 56–60 discusses this charter change in greater detail.
2. Pritchett's handwritten draft of the memorandum is in the CFAT Archive, New York City.

3. The figures are from J. Richard Woodworth, "Some Influences on the Reform of Schools of Law and Medicine 1890–1930," *Sociological Quarterly*, 14 (1973): 497.

4. Gerald E. Markowitz and David Karl Rosner, "Doctors in Crisis: A Study of the Use of Medical Education Reform to Establish Modern Professional Elitism in Medicine," *American Quarterly*, 25 (1973): 83–107; Magali Sarfatti Larson, *The Rise of Professionalism: A Sociological Analysis* (Berkeley: University of California Press, 1977), pp. 159–166; and Ellen Condliffe Lagemann, ed., *Nursing History: New Perspectives, New Possibilities* (New York: Teachers College Press, 1983).

5. For a description of early nineteenth-century medical training see Joseph F. Kett, *The Formation of the American Medical Profession: The Role of Institutions 1780–1860* (New Haven: Yale University Press, 1968).

6. Thomas Neville Bonner, *American Doctors and German Universities: A Chapter in International Intellectual Relations, 1870–1914* (Lincoln: University of Nebraska Press, 1963).

7. Donald Fleming, *William H. Welch and the Rise of Modern Medicine* (Boston: Little, Brown, 1954), p. 65. See also Simon Flexner and James Thomas Flexner, *William Henry Welch and the Heroic Age of American Medicine* (New York: Viking Press, 1941).

8. John Field, "Medical Education in the United States: Late Nineteenth and Twentieth Centuries," in *The History of Medical Education*, edited by C. D. O'Malley (Berkeley: University of California Press, 1970), pp. 501–530; Burton J. Bledstein, *The Culture of Professionalism: The Middle Class and the Development of Higher Education in America* (New York: W. W. Norton, 1976), pp. 85–86.

9. Richard H. Shryock, *The Unique Influence of the Johns Hopkins University on American Medicine* (Copenhagen: Ejnar Munksgaard, 1953); and Fleming, *William Henry Welch*, especially chaps. 7–10.

10. The best account of reforms at this time is Rosemary Stevens, *American Medicine and the Public Interest* (New Haven: Yale University Press, 1971), especially chaps. 2 and 3.

11. Ibid., pp. 63–66; James G. Burrow, *AMA: Voice of American Medicine* (Baltimore: Johns Hopkins Press, 1963), esp. chap. 2; James G. Burrows, *Organized Medicine in the Progressive Era* (Baltimore: Johns Hopkins University Press, 1977), chap. 3; and Morris Fishbein, *A History of the American Medical Association, 1847 to 1947* (Philadelphia: W. B. Saunders, 1947), pp. 197–259, 887–922.

12. Kett, *The Formation of the American Medical Profession*, chap. 6; Stevens, *American Medicine*, pp. 26–33, 58–66; and Burrows, *AMA*, chap. 2.

13. A. D. Bevan, "Cooperation in Medical Education and Medical Service," *Journal of the American Medical Association*, 90 (1928): 1173, quoted in Fishbein, *History of the AMA*, p. 897.

14. Savage, *Fruit of an Impulse*, p. 99.

15. Henry S. Pritchett to Alexander C. Humphreys, November 10, 1908, CFAT Archive.

16. Abraham Flexner, *I Remember* (New York: Simon and Schuster, 1940), p. 111.

17. Ibid., chaps. 8 and 9.

18. Abraham Flexner, *Henry S. Pritchett: A Biography* (New York: Columbia University Press, 1943) pp. 108–109.

19. Fishbein, *History of the AMA*, p. 898.

20. Ibid. The CFAT-Council on Medical Education alliance is clearly described in correspondence between Pritchett and Bevan. Writing to Bevan on November 4, 1909, for example, Pritchett stated: "In all this work of the examination of the medical schools we have been hand in glove with you and your committee. In fact, we have only taken up the matter and gone on with the examination very much as you were doing, except that as an independent agency disconnected from actual practice, we may do certain things you perhaps may not. When our report comes out, it is going to be ammunition in your hands" (CFAT Archive).

21. Flexner, *I Remember*, p. 121.

22. Abraham Flexner, *Medical Education in the United States and Canada*, CFAT Bulletin Number 4 (1910), p. 3.

23. Ibid., p. 5.

24. Ibid., p. 6.

25. Ibid., p. 8.

26. Ibid., p. 12.

27. Ibid., p. 16.

28. Ibid., p. 13.

29. Ibid., chaps. 4–7.

30. Ibid., p. 147.

31. Ibid., p. 151.

32. Ibid., p. 227.

33. Ibid., p. 270.

34. Ibid., p. 303.

35. Ibid., p. 197.
36. Ibid., p. 20.
37. Ibid., p. 19.
38. Biennial Survey of Education 1928–1930, 2 vols. (Washington, D.C.: Government Printing Office, 1932), I,547.
39. Any number of recent commentators on the Flexner report have made these points. In addition to Markowitz and Rosner, "Doctors in Crisis," and Stevens, *American Medicine*, chap. 3, see William C. Rappleye, "Major Changes in Medical Education During the Past Fifty Years," *Journal of Medical Education*, 34 (1959): 683–689; Robert P. Hudson, "Abraham Flexner in Perspective: American Medical Education, 1865–1910," *Bulletin of the History of Medicine*, 46 (1972): 545–561; and Carleton B. Chapman, "The Flexner Report," *Daedalus* (1974): 105–117.
40. Kenneth Ludmerer, "Reform of Medical Education at Washington University," *Journal of the History of Medicine*, 35 (1980): 154.
41. Donna Bingham Munger, "Robert Brookings and the Flexner Report: A Case Study of the Reorganization of Medical Education," *Journal of the History of Medicine*, 23 (1968): 356–371.
42. Ernest V. Hollis, *Philanthropic Foundations and Higher Education* (New York: Columbia University Press, 1938); Stevens, *American Medicine*, pp. 68–69.
43. Stevens, *American Medicine*, pp. 71–73; Leonard W. Johnson, Jr., "History of the Education of Negro Physicians," *Journal of Medical Education*, 42 (1967): 439–446; James L. Curtis, *Blacks, Medical Schools, and Society* (Ann Arbor: University of Michigan Press, 1971), especially, pp. 15–17; C. W. Norris, "The Negro College at Mid-Century," *Quarterly Review of Higher Education Among Negroes*, 19 (1951): 7–11; Mary Roth Walsh, *"Doctors Wanted: No Women Need Apply": Sexual Barriers in the Medical Profession, 1835–1975* (New Haven: Yale University Press, 1977), pp. 236–241, and "The Rediscovery of the Need for a Feminist Medical Education," *Harvard Educational Review*, 49 (1979): 451.
44. CFAT *3rd Annual Report* (1908), p. 160.

FROM MATRON TO MAVEN: A NEW ROLE AND NEW PROFESSIONAL IDENTITY FOR DEANS OF WOMEN, 1892 TO 1916

JANA NIDIFFER

Presidents of mid-nineteenth century coeducational colleges hired dormitory matrons as chaperones or disciplinarians. This arrangement was replaced by a new type of woman administrator—dean of women. The deans were highly trained, ambitious women not content with such a limited role. The careers and strategies of four women who were instrumental in transforming the position of dean of women into a profession are examined. This small cadre of women, working in midwestern institutions, developed an expansive vision for their position: Marion Talbot, University of Chicago, 1892 to 1925; Mary Bidwell Breed, Indiana University, 1901 to 1906: Ada Louise Comstock, University of Minnesota, 1906 to 1912: and Lois Kimball Mathews, University of Wisconsin. 1911 to 1918.

The term "dean of women" often conjures up one of two enduring stereotypes: either that of a matronly, curmudgeonly chaperone or an innocuous mother figure (Phillips. 1919, p. 3). Yet neither of those two characterizations, despite their persistence in the popular imagination, is wholly accurate. During the Progressive Era, it became instead a position "in which intelligent, well-qualified, well-educated women could exercise administrative skills and professional leadership and exert a unifying influence on behalf of women" (Treichler, 1985, p. 24). These well-qualified, well-educated deans did help improve the material lot of women students, especially at Midwestern state universities. But most importantly, the deans—at least a small cadre of leaders between the years 1892 and 1916—forged a new professional identity for themselves as the first senior women administrators on coeducational university campuses. Their effort to create a profession for women—its initial success and what is seen as the eventual reversal of fortune—reveals typical difficulties faced by professional women in the early twentieth century.

The position of dean of women also played an interesting historical role by being the first systemic, administrative response in higher education to cope with a new, and essentially unwelcome, population. There was one brief period when the College of William and Mary hired a "Master of the Indian School." to look after the few Native American students, but by 1721, the Indian School had faded away and it was not emulated at other Colonial colleges (Morpurgo, 1976, pp. 67–69). The position of dean of women, on the other hand, was replicated widely.

Early History of Deans of Women

The position of dean of women was born in the antebellum liberal arts colleges of the midwest; it came of age in Midwestern universities in the early twentieth century. Oberlin College opened its doors to women in 1833, an era in which propriety required the close supervision of unmarried young women in proximity to young men. The president and faculty quickly recognized such "problems which demanded the presence and supervision of an older woman" (Holmes, 1939. p. 109). The first woman to serve in this position at Oberlin was Marianne Parker Dascom with the title "Lady Principal of the Female Department" (Kehr, 1938. p.6). The 1835 description of the Female Department in the college catalog indicated both Oberlin's desire to appease trepidation regarding coeducation and the scope of Mrs. Dascom's duties:

> Young ladies of good minds, unblemished morals, and respectable attainments are received into this department and placed under the supervision of a judicious lady, whose duty it is to correct their habits and mould the female character. They attend recitations with young gentlemen in all the departments. Their rooms are entirely separate from those of the other sex, and no calls or visits in the respective apartments are at all permitted (Oberlin, 1835, p. 24).

Antioch College in Yellow Springs, Ohio was also coeducational from its opening in 1854. President Horace Mann acknowledged that "[t]he advantages of joint education are very great. The dangers are terrible." Mann insisted on a boarding house for the young women. He stated. "I should deprecate exceedingly turning them out in the streets for meals" (Holmes, 1939. p. 6–7). The boarding house required a female supervisor.

When members of the Board of Regents of the University of Michigan were contemplating coeducation for their institution in 1858, they solicited opinions from educational experts of the day including Mann and Charles Grandison Finney, president of Oberlin. Finney replied that the results at Oberlin were "satisfactory and admirable" and offered the Board the following advice for ensuring success: "You will need a *wise and pious matron* with such lady assistants as to keep up supervision. . . ." (emphasis added, Holmes, 1939. p. 7). Despite the positive outcome reported by Finney, Michigan remained single-sex for another twelve years until economic pressures by tax-payers forced the university to open its doors to women in 1870.

The experiences of Oberlin and Antioch illustrated two important themes in the earliest history of deans of women. First, the "Lady Principal" was hired as a direct response to prevailing concerns regarding coeducation. Second, her duties were limited to supervision of living arrangements and the moral guardianship of the women students. After the Civil War, coeducation became more prevalent and so did the number of residential colleges employing lady principals, matrons, or preceptresses who supervised the women's housing. Swarthmore College was typical and engaged a "judicious matron" in 1872. By 1880, this practice was more common than not in the liberal arts colleges of the midwest (McGrath, 1936).

The pattern of hiring deans of women at midwestern universities was different, however, and it did not begin until the 1890s. The primary reason why many universities failed to employ a "wise and pious matron" from the outset was because the young state universities had not made provision for on-campus housing for women or men due to lack of resources. The women students were expected to lodge with family members or in local rooming houses. Without a specific dormitory, house, or female college to supervise, university presidents felt little imperative to hire a female administrator. For example, Indiana University experimented briefly with the position when Sarah Parke Morrison, IU's first female graduate in 1869, was hired to be a social advisor to women students in 1873. Morrison resigned her position after only two years, and it remained unfilled for the next quarter of a century (Rothenberger, 1942).

In the late 1880s and early 1890s circumstances changed, leading to the appointment of women administrators. At a few universities, women students, their parents, and sometimes community members as well, agitated for the university to offer some living arrangements for the women students. Without supervised housing, middle-class parents and families who lived long distances from the campuses expressed reluctance to send daughters to college (Gordon, 1990). If boarding houses, residence halls, or sorority houses were created, an administrator was needed.

There were other catalysts, however, beyond the need to monitor a dormitory. As the 1890s progressed, faculty members on several campuses, with or without special residence halls for women, grew increasingly concerned about the extra-curricular activities of students. At the same time, faculty reluctance to handle such matters was intensifying. The growing demand for research productivity placed new pressures on faculty and created an unwillingness on their part to spend vast amounts of time on administrative details or student supervision. Nor would a president interested in research results want a faculty so engaged (Veysey, 1969).

It was interesting that the administrative response to excesses in student behavior, which included class "rushes" and violence in athletics, was a dean of *women*, when it was generally acknowledged that it was male students who exhibited the most troubling behavior. Such reactions suggest that presidents were responding equally to a resurgence of anti-coeducation sentiment at the turn of the century and to the consequent uneasiness felt on many campuses (Rosenberg, 1988).

The battle for coeducation was long and acrimonious. It has been compared by historian Patricia Palmeri (1987) to the abolition debate in terms of the intensity of emotions on both sides of the issue and the numbers of white middle class men and women involved. The high degree of negative feelings toward women on campuses created an environment that ranged from inhospitable to openly hostile. Therefore, administrators at coeducational universities in the 1890s were obligated to worry about the "woman problem." One response was hiring a dean of women. A pioneer in this regard was William Rainey Harper of the University of Chicago. Harper's dream was to make Chicago a Western Yale, and the generosity of John D. Rockefeller gave him the resources to lure prestigious eastern academics to the shores of Lake Michigan (Gordon, 1990).

Harper was determined to fashion a great university quickly by hiring proven administrators and established scholars. Harper was not an enthusiast for coeducation, but the charter of the university demanded it. In keeping with his desire to hire the most talented faculty that he could and the social expectation that college women needed supervision. Harper offered Alice Freeman Palmer, the President of Wellesley College, the position of professor of history and dean of women for the university.

Palmer was reluctant to turn down an opportunity to become a female professor in a coeducational institution, for there were precious few such offers in 1892. She agreed, however, upon two conditions. Because her Harvard professor husband, George Herbert Palmer, was unwilling to leave Cambridge. Alice Palmer said she would only work in Chicago for twelve weeks a year. She also demanded that Marion Talbot, also a professor at Wellesley, be appointed as her deputy. Because of Palmer's schedule, Talbot was, in effect, the dean of women at Chicago (Fitzpatrick, 1989).

From Matron to Maven

With Talbot's appointment in 1892, the position of dean of women began to change. By 1916, the year in which the National Association of Deans of Women (NADW) was founded, a small cadre of women from midwestern institutions had transformed the position into a profession. This article examines the careers of four such women and the strategies they employed. Each woman made a specific contribution to the evolution of the profession. In addition, each woman was, at times, representative of other deans serving in the same era. The four women are: Marion Talbot, University of Chicago, 1892–1925; Mary Bidwell Breed, Indiana University, 1901–1906; Ada Comstock, University of Minnesota's 1906–1912; and Lois Kimball Mathew's University of Wisconsin's 1911–1918. The process they went through to establish a profession is similar to that of myriad other professions that were established in the early twentieth century. Identified are four steps that were especially salient to the deans: laying an intellectual foundation; initiating collective activity; becoming an expert; and creating a professional literature and association.

Laying the Intellectual Foundation

Marion Talbot was a bright and ambitious young woman whose family was part of the Boston intelligentsia—Julia Ward Howe and Louisa May Alcott were in her social milieu. Her father, Israel Tisdale Talbot, was passionate about health reform and the first dean of Boston University's medical school. In 1881, along with her mother. Emily Talbot, Marion founded the Association of Collegiate Alumnae (ACA), the forerunner of the American Association of University Women (Fitzpatrick, 1989). It was the most important organization for college-educated women during the era, dedicated to assisting women graduates in finding employment and intellectual opportunities in adult life.

Talbot's concern for the post-college fate of educated women was transformed at Chicago. She became devoted to making sure that the women students enjoyed the full advantages of the university while on campus. She understood the anti-coeducation sentiment that prevailed, and she, like Breed, Comstock, and Mathews, wanted to change the university and make it a more hospitable environment for women. Talbot articulated a purpose for women's education that she believed would both lay the intellectual foundations for the work of deans and minimize resistance to coeducation. She subscribed to several strains of late nineteenth century thought regarding intelligence and sex role definition, which were challenging conventional assumptions about the place of women in education and society. In terms of her efforts to professionalize deans, two of her beliefs were particularly relevant (Rosenberg, 1982).

First, she believed in a modernist notion about the inherent rationality of all human beings, which implied that women were as capable of intellectual thought as men. As she stated unequivocally in her book, *The Education of Women*, "women have proved their ability to enter every realm of knowledge. They must have the right to do it. . . . Unhampered by traditions of sex, women will naturally and without comment seek the intellectual goal which they think good and fit" (1910, p. 22). Yet, Talbot never completely let go of all the vestiges of Victorian notions of propriety and separate spheres, other than intellectual, so the second component of her belief was that women were unique from men and required an environment that was special or distinct. Her beliefs in the benefits of a separate women's community placed Talbot firmly within the tradition of late nineteenth century feminists who adopted what Estelle Freedman (1979) referred to as "separatism as a strategy." The women "preferred to retain membership in a separate female sphere, one which they did not believe to be inferior to men's sphere and one in which women could be free to create their own forms of personal, social, and political relationships" (Freedman, 1979, p. 514). Creating essentially a separate-but-equal social life for women, as historian Joyce Antler has noted, often reinforced the sexual status-quo by making the separate spheres seem immutable, and, perhaps, this actually limited the choices for women. Yet, the creation of a discrete "social structure . . . was a positive response to the pervasive sexism on campus" (Antler, 1987, pp. 98–99). If any of the four deans engaged the merits of this debate, they left no written record. It was clear from their actions, however, that they followed the separatism strategy common to women prior to World War I and created a distinct women's community on campus.

Talbot was attacked by those opponents of coeducation who argued that women should be in separate classrooms as well. But Talbot firmly stated that mixed classrooms were the only way to insure equivalent educational opportunities and that the needed "special" environment was for the out-of-classroom lives of women. Thus, Talbot acted as an intellectual bridge between the older view that feminine uniqueness implied intellectual limitations—"true womanhood"—and the belief that women were as rational as men, but still distinct—"new womanhood" (Freedman, 1974; Rosenberg, 1982). By asserting that women were academically capable in any field and the need for unique circumstances applied only to the social realm, she secured for women a safe place within the university, maintained propriety, and yet kept all avenues of mental exploration open. Her view laid the foundation for the professional work of deans.

Initiating Collective Activity

Talbot took the next step in professionalization and communicated her beliefs with other deans of women. She published widely in various education journals, especially the *Journal of the ACA*, but most importantly she initiated the first collective activity of deans by organizing the first professional conference. She decided to invite several women from other midwestern colleges and universities for a two-day conference in November of 1903.

Eighteen women, including the young chemistry professor and dean of women at nearby Indiana University—Mary Bidwell Breed—arrived in Chicago in the autumn of 1903 (Minutes of the Conference, 1903, Potter, 1927, p. 212–216). All the deans represented institutions in the midwest (except the dean of the college of Barnard) so it was not surprising that the meeting's official title was the Conference of Deans of Women of the Middle West. Ten of the women were from private institutions while eight represented state universities. Twelve of the women held faculty appointments in addition to their work as deans.

Not surprisingly, the first substantive issue addressed was housing—the most pressing student need that deans faced. But they discussed a few other topics as well including the helpfulness of the League of Women and the YWCA, "Ways of Influencing Young Women," the effectiveness of "at homes"[1] with the dean, and self-government versus direct government (Minutes of the Conference, 1903. p.9). The deans then voted to meet two years hence and passed a series of resolutions summing up the collective opinion of the group. Mary Bidwell Breed was then elected president of the 1905 meeting.

Some time in the two years intervening between the first and second meeting, a decision was made to limit the membership of the group to deans of women in state universities, except for founder Marion Talbot who represented a private institution. No record exists of who made the decision or why,[2] but when the deans met in Chicago in December of 1905, the gathering was convened as the *first* meeting of "The Conference of Deans and Advisors of Women in State Universities." With the exception of Lucy Sprague from the University of California, all participants were from midwestern institutions. The early leadership of the new profession was securely in the hands of women working in the midwestern, public sector (Breed Correspondence, 1901–1906).

One interesting development at the 1905 meeting, however, was that the deans went beyond deliberations of the basic needs of students. The first resolution passed was on ways of making a community of women on campus which they believed was "absolutely necessary" (Potter, 1927, p. 217). Deans of women were probably unique on their campuses in understanding the complexity involved in achieving what would now be termed "full access." Typically, male administrators believed that admission to the institution was all that women needed. Deans, however, recognized that while the immediate concerns of housing, adequate meals, rest, and good health were necessary, the higher needs of women such as intellectual parity, career aspirations, leadership opportunities, and a sense of community must also be addressed. In this vein, the deans also discussed levels of scholarship and the place of domestic science in the curriculum, and were in almost unanimous agreement that the classroom should not be segregated by gender (Minutes of the Conference, 1905).

The biennial conferences not only aided the individual women in the course of their daily jobs by recommending standards of practice, but they were also a mechanism for communication among one another. Most importantly, however, they helped shape an identity for the new profession. A conference illustrated that the number of practitioners was growing, that they had an articulated purpose and a field of expertise, and it placed deans of women within the tradition of all other university administrators of the era who were also forming professional organizations and developing professional identities.

Resistance to their presence and their work was a significant obstacle faced by deans on the state university campuses. Although Breed held a Ph.D. from Bryn Mawr and a record of scholarly accomplishment which included study in a prestigious German university laboratory, her problem of acceptance was illustrative. When she took up residence in Bloomington in the fall of 1901, she met with resentment from both students and faculty. President Swain, who recruited her, believed deans were desirable. He was impressed with both her Eastern "sense of decorum" and her manner which was "strict enough to enforce her code of gentle-womanly behavior" (Clark, 1970, p. 1:320). The fact that he wanted a woman who combined scholarly accomplishment with gentle-womanly grace was again consistent with the prevailing notions of qualifications for the position. But several male faculty members expressed resistance to the idea of a dean of women—not because of her potential effect on students—but because they objected to having a woman with any administrative authority at any level on campus. By the time of Breed's appointment, only three other woman had ever been *employed* by the university; the female contributors to the university had been professor's wives and town women (Rothenberger, 1942; Clark, 1970).

Breed also met resistance from students who believed a dean was an affront to their integrity or feared possible limitations on their newly found freedom (Rosenberg, 1988, p. 118). Gertrude

Martin, who later became a dean herself, recalled her undergraduate days at the University of Michigan when they learned of Marion Talbot at nearby University of Chicago. "We resented that Chicago Dean of Women as an unwarrantable criticism of the conduct of college women in general. We were very certain we needed no disciplining"(Martin, 1911. p.66).

Evidence left by students including letters and diaries suggests that deans on many campuses were successful in reversing resentment and converting it to a respect that sometimes verged on reverence (Haddock, 1952; Antler, 1987; Fitzpatick, 1989; Eisenmann, 1991; Stephens, 1992). Breed's strategy to win over opponents was rather straightforward to a modern reader, but it was new at the time; she expanded her role beyond discipline, involved students in policies and program decisions, and advocated for women in ways that made tangible differences in their lives. For example, she secured membership in the ACA so that Indiana students were eligible for certain scholarships.

Such high regard should not obscure the fact that deans and female students were not always of one mind. There were components of a generation gap and elements of disciplinarian/disciplined relationship. There were also class tensions at times between the largely private-school educated deans and state university students. The deans—Talbot, Breed, Comstock, and Mathews—each came from upper middle class backgrounds, most had powerful fathers, and all had been, before becoming a dean, associated with an elite private institution. One of Comstock's close friends and colleagues, Lucy Sprague of Berkeley, who also came from a privileged background, was more vocal on this issue than other deans. At times, she expressed her uncomfortableness with the rough-hewn nature of the state university women students (Antler, 1987).

Students and deans shared many political objectives, especially in reform-oriented areas, but many women students were pro-suffrage and thought the deans maddeningly silent on this issue. Students agitated for more freedom in male-female socialization, which also caused a split between the two generations of women. Deans thought students were too frivolous; students thought deans were old-fashioned, perhaps sexually unfulfilled, or even "deviant" (Gordon, 1990; Mathews, 1915). But overall, female students had very few adult female role models on coeducational campuses between 1900 and 1920 and even fewer advocates.

Becoming an Expert

The next phase of professionalization called for the development of expertise: deans became experts in women's education in coeducational settings. This phase, roughly from 1905–1912, was marked by a growing professional maturity among the deans. Deans regularly published in educational journals, made connections to other professional women in education (especially the ACA), and became more "scientific," using techniques and language associated with scientific research. In 1911, Dean Gertrude Martin of Cornell conducted and distributed the first statistical research project on the work of deans. This intellectual activity, Lucy Sprague said, saved the profession from the "bog of discipline and decorum" (Antler, 1987, pp. 111–112).

Ada Comstock began her administrative career as dean of women at the University of Minnesota in 1906. She is perhaps best known as the long-term president of Radcliffe College, from 1922 to 1943, who eventually secured full membership (at least in theory) for undergraduate women at Harvard. However, she was also instrumental in helping deans of women develop their field of expertise. When Comstock arrived in 1906, she was immediately able to employ the strategies suggested by her colleagues for coping with the most basic deaning issues such as housing, so she was free to devote energy to other matters. She collected data on students and illustrated a systematic, more "scientific" approach to the job. In journal articles and speeches, she helped articulate the specific expertise needed by deans, building upon the ideas of women's nature previously expressed by Talbot. She then used her expertise as the basis for the campus programs she initiated.

Comstock's initiatives were dedicated to addressing the higher needs of women such as a sense of community, leadership roles, employment, and intellectual opportunities. As far as students were concerned, this was the strategy with the most tangible results. One of Comstock's first acts was to fight the use of the word "coed" in the Minneapolis and campus publications and the ridicule that women faced in the guise of humor. Although she was only partially successful, fighting public mockery became a cause taken up by several of her peers.

Creating a sense of community for the young women was Comstock's highest priority. The Alice Shevlin Hall, which provided women students with a physical place on campus to rest, study, eat, and associate with one another to ease the loneliness and feelings of isolation, was central to her mission (Comstock, 1913, p. 157). In fact, she described Shevlin Hall as her most effective "tool" (Johnson, 1910, p. 194). Comstock recognized that universities were organizations created and run by men "and however kindly the individual members of the faculty may show themselves . . . the close discipleship which the young men may enjoy . . . [is] not so easily attainable to the young women." (Comstock, 1929, p. 413). In several respects, Shevlin Hall was not unlike contemporary women's centers found on many campuses today.

The mechanism Comstock used to develop leadership skills and responsibility in students was the Student Self-Government Association, which was voted in by students in December of 1906 for the purpose of aiding in the care and conduct of Alice Shevlin Hall. Such associations originated in the women's colleges and Comstock herself had participated in self-government while attending Smith College. Comstock believed that student-developed and student-enforced policies achieved more positive outcomes (especially in terms of greater compliance) than those dictated by administrators. In the meantime, the process taught students about leadership, consensus, law and order, and good citizenship (Comstock, 1909, p. 4: Ladd, 1910, pp. 7–8).

A student's need to finance her education, find suitable employment, and develop career aspirations was as important to Comstock as building a dormitory. She wanted to "fit" women for a greater variety of gainful occupations (Johnson, 1910, p. 195). In 1909, it was estimated that the average student needed between $350 and $450 to attend the university (Johnson, 1910). Comstock conducted research and found that fifteen percent of women students were at least partially self-supporting (compared with sixty-four percent of the men). On average, the women earned $191 while their male classmates earned $306 per year on the job. The women worked in very female-oriented occupations including housekeeping, child care, office clerking, tutoring, and other secretarial work. Comstock believed that low salaries obligated women to work longer hours, and she observed that the women often suffered from overwork and exhaustion. She also discovered that despite the hardship, the self-supporting women did as well academically as their non-working counterparts (Comstock, 1910).

Comstock took it upon herself to oversee the employment of women, making sure that it was safe and fairly paid. She once said that "this aspect of the work of my office is of very great interest to me. It brings me in contact with many girls whom I am especially glad to know" (Comstock, 1908, p. 4). She used Shevlin Hall as a clearing house for job listings, but often the choices were limited. To increase employment opportunities, Comstock spent the Christmas vacation of 1911–12 walking up and down the streets of the Twin Cities trying to convince department stores of the sagacity of hiring women. She found that they "were particularly impregnable to the suggestion" (Blanshard, 1974, p. 11).

Creating a Professional Literature and Professional Association

Successfully initiating programs such as those created by Comstock and insuring that women had full intellectual participation in the campus became the *raison d'être* of the young profession of dean of women. Some deans, however, believed that their work on behalf of students and their own sense of self-esteem would be enhanced and legitimized if the overall status of the position were elevated. Lois Mathews at the University of Wisconsin from 1911 to 1918, was of such a mind. She believed that deans of women should also be members of the faculty and have more of the attributes normally associated with a profession—including a professional literature and formal training for aspirants.

Mathews was a protégé of Frederick Jackson Turner and the first women to pass Harvard's Ph.D. examination in history—although her degree was from the Radcliffe graduate school, a bureaucratic anomaly created to award doctorates to women because Harvard would not. She was an assistant professor of history at Vassar and an associate professor at Wellesley College before moving to Wisconsin.

In her long and occasionally heated negotiations with Charles Van Hise, president of the university, she held out for the title of dean (rather than advisor as he suggested) and the rank of associate professor. She argued that an associate professorship carried more weight with students and faculty and contributed to the dignity of her office. She also noted that she might only spend a few years in administration and might choose to resume a full-time academic career, in which case she would need the rank of associate professor to secure her own future. When explaining why she did not relent, she said, "if I were to undertake so great and serious a task as the deanship of women in the University of Wisconsin, it seemed to me it would be my first duty to make it in stature what it is in opportunity; and at the same time to try to make it an example to other universities in that regard" (Van Hise Correspondence).

Mathews' scholarly potential and productivity prior to entering Wisconsin was considerable—she published articles and wrote a very important book in 1909, *The Expansion of New England*, that had its last printing in 1962; her career as an historian was quite disappointing after she was made dean. Although she continued to teach, she did not contribute much after 1912 to the field of history. Unfortunately, Mathews' experience was very typical. All four women in this study were trained as faculty members and all four found their scholarly progress impeded by the exigencies of administrative positions.

Mathews was very dedicated to her new profession and brought to it the same intellectual vigor that she had applied earlier to history. While dean, she had numerous public speaking engagements, published several articles, and spoke frequently at ACA and the biennial deans' conferences. She invited aspiring deans to visit her on the Madison campus to learn about the job. She organized a state-wide conference for all women deans in Wisconsin, including those from small colleges and normal schools. In the summer of 1915, she taught a course in "College Administration for Women," which was the first of its kind taught in a public university and was offered concurrently with the first courses taught on the subject at Teachers College (*The Daily Cardinal*, 1915, 1916).

Her most lasting contribution, however, was her 1915 book, *The Dean of Women*, the first book ever written on the profession that eventually became known as student affairs. A second book on the subject was not written until 1926 (Merrill and Bragdon). Mathews held a particular vision for the profession. She wanted to be "more than a wise and pious matron." She believed deans should be scholars, experts on women's education, and general advocates for women who expanded the social, vocational, and intellectual opportunities available to them. This book represented the collective wisdom of Mathews and her like-minded peers on issues ranging from teaching to supervision in the dormitories to how to organize an office. With all the pieces in place by 1916, the position had the vestiges of a profession.

Reversal of Fortune

The new profession of dean of women opened up the possibility of administrative careers on coeducational campuses. Because of the direct relationship between the number of women students at an institution and the presence of women in the faculty or administration, women's colleges traditionally offered a few opportunities, but prospects at coeducational universities were scarce, especially before 1920 (Clifford, 1989). Coeducational institutions, therefore, held tremendous promise for women who sought professional careers in universities, but who lived in the midwest or other regions of the country where single-sex education was less common. Therefore, deans acted as the "entering wedge" in coeducational institutions (Rossiter, 1982, p. 2). As the first and often the only female administrators who either held a broad range of responsibilities or the sufficient rank needed in the institution to initiate policy proposals, "they had the most consistent effect in bringing more women into the professional community" (Clifford, 1989, p. 13). They also succeeded in making the position of dean *de rigueur*. Although women's needs were hardly an institutional priority, the vast majority of all types of coeducational institutions had a dean after 1920.

One cautionary note on the effect of the position of dean on professional women is in order, however. Like other women in nascent professions, the pioneering deans struggled and strategized to secure professional status, overcome resistance, secure acceptance, and gain recognition. Yet, attaining the position was somewhat of a two-edged sword, perhaps analogous to the experience of academic women who sought appointments within home economics. Like home economics, being a dean provided women with opportunities for professional work, but it also contributed to the ghettoizing of women into administrative roles that became essentially student affairs positions and, consequently, undervalued by the academy. In addition, many of the early deans (those hired in the first years of this century) were women with credentials which should have earned them faculty posts. These highly trained "teaching deans" combined teaching and administration and held faculty rank, but their administrative duties inhibited scholarly advancement. One can only speculate on how many women reluctantly settled for a combined administrative/academic post because they were not offered a purely academic job.

It was this trend toward an exclusively administrative post, away from teaching and in the direction of student affairs, that can be labeled (albeit rather dramatically) as the reversal of fortune. Talbot, Breed, Comstock, and Mathews worked in large universities and simultaneously held faculty positions. However, deans of women were also hired in other types of institutions such as smaller colleges and normal schools. Deans in these environments (and in some universities) began to question the need for dual faculty appointments—they chose instead to emphasize the counseling, guidance, and regulatory nature of their work. A few women with this point of view were studying for a master's degree at Teachers College in the summer of 1916 when they formed the National Association for Deans of Women (NADW)—which eventually became the professional organization for all deans. However, the NADW placed very little emphasis on the importance of faculty rank to the position of dean.

Lois Mathews' vision of deans as scholars lost out to the newer vision of the profession which was shared by the newly created office of dean of men (Catton, 1956). As student affairs practioners, they suffered a lack of prestige within the academy. Therefore, in terms of the administrative influence of deans of women, the era examined, 1892 to 1916, represented a high point. Later decades saw it further reduced in stature when former deans of women, who had once reported directly to the president, subsequently became assistants who reported to male deans of students (Greenleaf, 1968). It is intriguing to speculate on whether the strategy that Mathews proposed—holding dual faculty/administrative appointments—might have helped the profession of dean of women maintain or even increase its prestige on campus. As a result of separating themselves from the faculty, deans were isolated from any important power base within the academy.

Is there a place in a modern coeducational university for a dean of women? It is currently the case that many of the functions historically performed by deans of women such as housing, career advising, discipline, and health care are executed by various student affairs professionals of both genders. But to assume that such functions were the *sine qua non* of the work of the pioneers such as Talbot, Breed, Comstock, and Mathews is to ignore the historical evidence. What drove the pioneering deans to create a new model for the role was a desire to address inequities in coeducational environments, attend to the intellectual development of women students, and move beyond providing basic needs and discipline.

There is still a need to help women combat the effects of sexism, achieve intellectual parity, and find a community on campus. If the work of a dean, in the tradition of the pioneers, is needed, perhaps it is being accomplished today by professionals such as the heads of women's studies programs or the directors of women's centers. So, while a person with the title of dean may not be needed, someone with her agenda most assuredly is.

Notes

1. "At homes" were small gatherings in the dean's office or home. The conversation, accompanied by tea and refreshments, was guided by the dean for the purpose of discussing policies or problems.

2. Several archival and published sources were consulted to establish the fact that no written record of this decision seems to exist, including; the papers and published works of Mary Bidwell Breed (Indiana University) and Marion Talbot (University of Chicago); the archives of the National Association of Deans of Women (currently the National Association of Women in Education) including the minutes of the dean's conferences: other histories of specific deans of women, the position of dean, or the NADW. (See the bibliography for: Catton, B., 1956; Haddock, R., 1952; Holmes, L., 1939; Martin, G. S., 1911: Mathews, L. K., 1915; Merrill, R. A. and H. D. Bragdon, 1926; Phillips, K. S. M., 1919; Potter, M. R., 1927; and Rothenberger, K., 1942).

References

Antler, J. *Lucy Sprague Mitchell: The Making of a Modern Woman*. New Haven: Yale University Press, 1987.

Blanshard, R. Y. "A Louise Comstock: Some of her memories of her life up to 1943, collected for reading to the Saturday Morning Club, March 16, 1974."

Breed, M. B. Correspondence, Dean of Women, 1901–1906. Indiana University Archives, Bloomington, IN.

Cation, B. "Our Association in Review." *Journal of the National Association of Deans of Women* 10 (October 1956): 3–9.

Clark, T. *Indiana University: Midwestern Pioneer*. 2 vols. Bloomington: Indiana University Press, 1970, 1973.

Clifford, G. J., ed. *Lone Voyagers: Academic Women in Coeducational Institutions, 1870–1937*. New York: The Feminist Press, 1989.

Comstock, A. "Report of the Dean of Women." In *The President's Report, 1911–1912. Bulletin of the University of Minnesota*, 6 (January 1913). 157–62.

Comstock, A. "Self Supporting Students." *Minnesota Alumni Weekly* (February 7, 1910): 11.

Comstock, A. "The Fourth R for Women." *Century Magazine* 117 (February, 1929): 411–17.

Eisenmann, L. "'Freedom to be Womanly': The Separate Culture of the Women's College." In *The Search for Equity: Women at Brown University, 1891–1991*, ed. Polly Welts Kaufman, 54–85. Hanover: Brown University Press, 1991.

Fitzpatrick, E. "For the 'Women of the University': Marion Talbot, 1858–1948." In *Lone Voyagers: Academic Women in Coeducational Universities, 1870–1937*, ed. Geraldine Joncich Clifford, 85–124. New York: The Feminist Press, 1989.

Freedman, E. "Separatism as Strategy: Female Institution Building and American Feminism, 1870–1930." *Feminist Studies* 5 (Fall 1979): 512–29.

Gordon, L. D. *Gender and Higher Education in the Progressive Era*. New Haven: Yale University Press, 1990.

Greenleaf, E. "How Others See Us: ACPA Presidential Address." *Journal of College Student Personnel* 9 (July 1868): 225–31.

Haddock, R. "A Study of Five Deans of Women." Ph.D. diss., Syracuse University, 1952.

Holmes, L. *A History of the Position of Dean of Women in a Selected Group of Coeducational Colleges and Universities in the United States*. New York: Teachers College. Columbia University, Bureau of Publications, 1939.

Johnson, E. B., ed. *Forty Years of the University of Minnesota*. Minneapolis: The General Alumni Association, 1910.

Kehr, M. "The Pioneer Days of the Dean of Women." *The Journal of the National Education Association* 27 (January 1938): 6–7.

Ladd, J. "What Student Government Means to the Girls." *Minnesota Alumni Weekly* (May 9, 1910): 7–8.

Martin, G. S. "The Position of Dean of Women." *Journal of the Association of Collegiate Alumnae Series* IV. 2(March 1911): 65–78.

Matthews, L. K. *The Dean of Women*. Boston: Houghton Mifflin, 1915.

McGrath, E. J. "The Evolution of Administrative Offices in Institutions of Higher Education in the United States from 1860 to 1933." Ph. D. diss., University of Chicago, 1936.

Merrill, R. A. and H. D. Bragdon. *The Vocation of Dean*. Washington, D.C.: Press and Publicity Committee of The National Association of Deans of Women, 1926.

Minutes of the Conference of Deans of Women of the Middle West, 1903.

Minutes of the Conference of Deans and Advisors of Women in State Universities. December 19–20, 1905.

Morpurgo, J. E. *Their Majesties' Royall Colledge: William and Mary in the Seventeenth and Eighteenth Centuries.* Williamsburg. VA: The Endowment Association of the College of William and Mary, 1976.

Moniss, M. S. "Cooperation: A.A.U.W. and N.A.D.W." *Journal of the National Association of Deans of Women* 2 (March 1939): 105–08.

Oberlin College. *Second Annual Report,* 1835.

Palmeri, P. A. "From Republican Motherhood to Race Suicide." In *Educating Men and Women Together: Coeducation in a Changing World,* ed. Carol Lasser, 49–64. Urbana: University of Illinois Press, 1987.

Parsons, T. "Professions" In *International Encyclopedia of the Social Sciences,* vol. 12. (New York: Macmillan Publishing, Co., 1968): 536–47.

Phillips, K. S. M. "The Work of a Dean of Women." Master's thesis, Teachers College, Columbia University, n.d. [1919].

Potter, M. R. "Report of Committee on History of the National Association of Deans of Women." *National Association of Deans of Women Yearbook* (1927): 212–27.

Rosenberg, R. "The Limits of Access: The History of Coeducation in America." In *Women and Higher Education in American History,* eds. John Mack Faragher and Florence Howe, 107–29. New York: W. W. Norton & Company, 1988.

Rosenberg, M. W. *Women Scientists in America: Struggles and Strategies to 1940.* Baltimore: Johns Hopkins University Press, 1982.

Rothenberger, K. "An Historical Study of the Position of Dean of Women at Indiana University." Master's thesis, Indiana University, 1942.

Stephens (nee Reed), H. University of Wisconsin, class of 1917, interview with author, 20 July 1992, Madison, WI.

Talbot, M. *More Than Lore: Reminiscences of Marion Talbot.* Chicago: University of Chicago Press, 1936.

The Daily Cardinal, 1 May, 1915. p. 4 and 1 November. 1916, 6.

Treichler, P. A. "Alma Mater's Sorority: Women and The University of Illinois, 1890–1925." In *For Alma Mater: Theory and Practice in Feminist Scholarship.* eds. Paula A. Treichler; Cheris Kramarae, and Beth Stafford. 5–16. Urbana: University of Illinois Press, 1985.

Van Hise, C. Correspondence. To Lois K. Mathews. Dean of Women. 1911–1918, 17 April 1911. University of Wisconsin Archives, Madison, WI.

Veysey, L. R. *The Emergence of the American University.* Chicago: University of Chicago Press, 1965.

CHAPTER 8

DIVERSITY & DISCRIMINATION

AN ACADEMIC GRESHAM'S LAW: GROUP REPULSION AS A THEME IN AMERICAN HIGHER EDUCATION

HAROLD S. WECHSLER

The arrival of a new constituency on a college campus has rarely been an occasion for unmitigated joy. Perhaps such students brought with them much-needed tuition dollars. In that case, their presence was accepted and tolerated. Yet higher-education officials, and often students from traditional constituencies, usually perceived the arrival of new groups not as a time for rejoicing, but as a *problem*: a threat to an institution's stated and unstated missions (official fear) or to its social life (student fear). Most recently, America has witnessed dramas played out between black students and white students and officials, as the former attempted to obtain access to higher education, first in the South and then in the North. *Brown* v. *Board of Education* and its subsequent application to higher education have resulted in only a gradual effort at integration in the South, and then only after almost a decade of outright resistance. In the North, the existence of selective colleges and universities in or near urban ghettos produced persistent demands for the "opening up" of such institutions to a local constituency. In both cases, acquiescence to black demands was feared as inimical to the interests of the college's traditional constituencies and to its missions. The possibility that a new group might "repel" a more traditional constituency has for more than two centuries proved a persistent theme in American higher education and has not been aimed at any one new constituency in particular. Institutional officials (administrators and occasionally trustees; faculty usually played a peripheral role in these issues)[1] often feared the physical exodus of traditional students resulting in a perhaps undesirable change in the institution's status and mission. However, traditional students only infrequently lifted up stakes; more often they simply adopted a policy of segregating themselves from the insurgent group. Depending on whether the traditional group was a positive or a negative reference group, insurgent students would counter-segregate by forming structures either emulating or rejecting majority group arrangements.

In this article, we will discuss four instances of this inverse Gresham's law of academic relations—real or imagined—and analyze official and student responses. In each case, the entrance of a new group brought about less-than-apocalyptic changes. In the case of relatively wealthy students in nineteenth-century New England colleges, the arrival of poorer students led to a decline in activities conducted by the student body as a whole and to a rise of stratified eating and living arrangements. Ultimately, the wealthier students watched as the number of poorer brethren declined. Late in the nineteenth century, the arrival of women on previously all-male campuses led to other forms of social segregation, which apprehensive administrators thought of abetting by segregating academic exercises by sex. Some years later, the arrival of a considerable number of Jewish students on east coast campuses caused concern lest gentile students seek out less "cosmopolitan" surroundings. Most recently, the arrival of significant numbers of black students at previously all-white (or almost so) institutions occasioned fears of "white flight" similar to what was perceived as happening in integrated elementary and secondary schools.

In all of these cases, students adopted modest recourses—various informally segregated arrangements for living, eating, and socializing supplemented or took the place of officially sanctioned arrangements. Usually, college authorities acquiesced in or even abetted these arrangements, believing them preferable to a student exodus.

Rich and Poor

Perhaps American college officials acquired their fear of student exodus from its perceived frequency in the medieval universities. Migrations sometimes led to the founding of rival universities. Even temporary student absences brought about local economic hardship. But in the case of the early Italian universities such migration resulted from disputes not between groups of students, but between local authorities and representatives of these student-run institutions. Early universities were quite heterogeneous, attracting students from much of Europe. By the mid-thirteenth century, the major universities had recognized the existence of "nations" that had fraternal, legal, and educational functions. Each nation contained a diversified membership, but offered cohesion and sanctuary for foreign students in a strange locality by guaranteeing the legitimacy of their members' presence.

In American higher education, which lacked formal groupings such as nations, the questions of incorporation or rejection of an aspirant group onto a campus with a traditional constituency have had to be handled on an ad hoc basis.

During the first two centuries of higher education in America, students from increasingly diverse class backgrounds found such instruction relevant to their interests; for such institutions as reliable information exists, it appears that such heterogeneity could be incorporated within the formal collegiate structure by relaxation of rules calling for continual interaction of the entire student body. Early versions of the laws of Harvard provided that no student could live or eat away from the college without the permission of the president,[2] but seventeenth-century Harvard was not a gentleman's institution. In preparing young men for the clergy and magistracy it often found that the most pious students were also the poorest.[3] Tuition charges were relatively low and meal charges varied according to quantity and quality consumed.[4] "A few resident students had board bills of less than a pound a quarter, a fourth of what their richer friends ate."[5] By the early eighteenth century, the Harvard student body's composition had significantly changed. The increase in enrollment, Samuel Eliot Morison wrote, consisted "of young men [who] came to be made gentlemen, not to study."[6] When the increase forced Harvard to permit some students to live away from the college, a definite bifurcation in the student body ensued. Not only did the pious students domicile and board together, they formed the first student societies—early manifestations of an extracurriculum that wary college officials found themselves forced to tolerate. Thus, the first manifestation of group repulsion consisted of a self-imposed segregation of pious students in response to "the onslaughts and influence of their more licentious classmates' thievery and tormenting."[7]

At other colonial colleges, authorities permitted internal segregation from the outset. William and Mary provided in its 1729 statutes for tuition-paying and scholarship students. For the former, "we leave their parents and guardians at liberty whether they shall lodge and eat within the college or elsewhere in the town, or any country village near the town." Such students simply observed the public hours of study. Poor students aspiring to the ministry would receive scholarship aid according to "their poverty, their ingeniousness, learning, piety, and good behavior, as to their morals." In this case, a college provided for a bifurcated student body in its statutes.[8] Yale and Kings College made provision for domicile outside the college grounds; the latter institution, in fact, had no dormitory during its initial years, and after its completion and enrollment rapidly exceeded the building's capacity.[9] Yale formally "ranked" its matriculants and followed these rankings when it was time to "declame." No formal ranking system existed at Kings College, but President Samuel Johnson did enter each matriculant on the college's rolls in roughly the order of his social status.

The children of New York's elite families readily identified each other and sought each other's company. A "few select ones" gathered regularly for conversation in John Jay's room, and those of high social standing met at a weekly "Social Club."[10] At pre-Revolutionary Princeton as at Harvard and Yale, the poorer students largely aspired to the ministry; their more wealthy classmates, however, were in one way or another also touched by evangelical religion. This, and the lack of housing alternatives to Nassau Hall, may have mitigated some social cleavages existing between rich and poor students.[11]

Thus, in the colonial college, we have evidence of mutual repulsion. The pious students who were initially attracted to each college were joined within a generation or two by students from wealthier backgrounds who attended college more as a means of elite socialization than as a means of curriculum mastery. In most cases, college officials desired attendance of both groups, although they emphatically did not desire the increase in disciplinary problems almost always attendant on the arrival of the children of the more wealthy.

During the years between the Revolution and the Civil War, the trend toward segregation by social class appears to have continued, and as the proportion of students from more modest backgrounds again increased, the fissures became more formal. Perhaps the distinctive feature in this period consisted of official acceptance of many segregated arrangements. In fact, according to one recent study, postcolonial New England colleges systematically courted poor male students. "Provincial colleges devised calendars congenial to seasons to work in nearby fields and schools, and adopted inexpensive living arrangements. Most important, they made tuition cheap, almost a charity."[12] Driven off the land by economic necessity, propelled toward the ministry by the revivals of the Second Great Awakening and attracted by recruiting efforts and special accommodations offered by the provincial colleges, students from modest backgrounds formed significant constituencies at a number of these institutions.[13]

Their absorption by the colleges required further abandonment of the ideal of community often enshrined in the college statutes. Keeping the bill of fare within range of the poorest students meant that students with fuller purses might find the menu unpalatable. Maintenance of spartanlike dormitories often led to demands by wealthier students for the privilege of domicile in more comfortable quarters. Actually, both wealthy and poorer students had motives for living and boarding off campus. The former could often locate more comfortable accommodations and food of better quality. They might move into a boarding house with students of like background, thus cementing the social contacts for which many apparently came.[14] Sometimes such arrangements formed the bases for fraternities, which received their initial impetus in the mid-nineteenth century. College officials tried at first to suppress such illiberal social organizations. "They create class and factions, and put men socially in regard to each other into an artificial and false position"[15] said Mark Hopkins, Williams's president. But the fraternities' rapid proliferation and participation by a sizable number of tuition-paying students argued against actions more drastic than an increasingly perfunctory chapel exhortation against such undemocratic institutions.[16]

The poorer students likewise found other options more attractive than commons. Many boarded in their rooms, while others founded student-run boarding clubs that often provided better and cheaper fare. Not only rich students lived in town; poorer students often found the lodgings offered by a charitable family or in a poor section more satisfactory than rooms in the college halls.

The intensity of this mutual segregation may be discerned from an account in a contemporary novel, in which two financially well-off Harvard students visit a poor classmate who resides in Divinity Hall, the traditional campus abode for poor but earnest students. When a student replied "Oh, down in Divinity," to the question "Where do you room?" the rejoinder was inevitably, "Down in Divinity? What in the name of all that is wonderful, makes you go down there among all those scrubs?" A pious atmosphere and economy provided two answers. A resident found the theological library, located in the Hall, "a delightful place to go into and mouse around when you are tired of study, and have nothing in particular to do."[17] Evening services proved genuinely inspirational. "The music of the choir and organ rolls up through the silent halls, and sounds very beautiful", the resident commented. As for meals, the students "mostly keep themselves entirely. . . . We leave our basket and pail just outside our door over night, and in the morning take in our milk and our fresh loaf; and some of the men down here live on bread and milk for the most part, or make it answer for breakfast and tea."[18] By contrast, one visitor commented that he spent eight dollars a week for boarding out while the Divinity resident replied that he could eat satisfying meals for about a fifth of that sum.[19] Perhaps the greatest fissure between the two groups lay in their respective attitudes toward their studies. The Divinity resident professed a love for mathematics above all else. "I think it a beautiful science: it is all explained and proved so fully and exactly as you go on, and the way is made so smooth and serene, one need never make any mistakes." One visitor, who by his very willingness to visit a student in Divinity demonstrated that his attitudes were far from the most extreme, replied that he enjoyed Greek the best. "But I am afraid I should not do much work of any sort unless I were obliged to," he continued. "We come here for the most part because we do, and without even asking the reason why. . . . I think study is the last thing we come for. Of course, the work is all an imposition, and the instructors are our natural enemies. That is the way most of the fellows feel, I know."[20] The gulf between a student maintaining such an attitude and another who loved his study ("I take the purest and deepest pleasure in it, and I thought everyone else did too; and I still think you must be wrong")[21] was unfathomable, and it is highly unlikely that dialogues such as this constituted normal fare.

In the case of the relations between rich and poor students, officials demonstrated increased tolerance toward student-imposed practices of segregation. Segregation permitted a high level of enrollment, the veneer of adherence to the official goals of inculcating discipline and piety, and the acceptance of tuition from those students more prone to pranks than piety and more often in attendance for social than academic reasons. Perhaps the only time the poor but pious students attained any prestige at the institutions ostensibly founded for them occurred during the religious revivals, which occurred with less frequency as the century progressed. In this example, college authorities accepted the social arrangements devised by the students. When other distinctive groups arrived, their reaction would be less sanguine.

Male and Female

Given the popularity of coeducational living arrangements on the modern campus, and all that such arrangements imply, one reads almost with astonishment a University of Wisconsin alumnus's 1877 statement that "the feeling of hostility [of the men students] was exceedingly intense and bitter. As I now recollect, the entire body of students were without exception opposed to the admission of the young ladies, and the anathemas heaped upon the regents were loud and deep."[22] Perhaps male resistance to coeducation can be traced to a fear that women students might outperform them in the classroom, or to a more generalized desire to retain a specific image of the American woman. The stated objections included women's purported mental incapacity and frail health, and the possibility of increased disciplinary problems. Although time dispelled these fears at the University of Wisconsin, similar concerns at Columbia led to rejection of a coeducation plan. John Burgess, dean of the political science faculty, successfully argued that women students were subject to monthly incapacities, that they would prove too distracting, and that an influx of women would repel Columbia's traditional male constituency, thus reducing the institution to a female seminary.[23] Burgess related that this argument won the day, and Columbia College was thus spared coeducation.[24]

Concern persisted that women students might arrive on campus in such proportions as to pose a threat to the male students and, ultimately, to drive them out. Anxiety increased as the proportion of women among the national undergraduate population rose from 21.0 percent in 1870 to 47.3 percent in 1920.[25] Thus, early in the twentieth century authorities at a number of colleges began to reevaluate their commitment to coeducation and to suggest that some restrictive measures might be in order. A few institutions contemplated a limitation on enrollment of women students; however, the fear of tuition loss and of competitive advantage occurring to nearby colleges led most institutions to opt for less drastic measures. Several major institutions proposed, though few actually adopted, a system of academic segregation whereby course registration might be restricted to members of one sex. President Charles Van Hise of Wisconsin justified such measures as a necessary counteraction to a tendency toward "natural segregation." "With the increase in the number of women in the colleges of liberal arts of coeducational institutions, certain courses have become popular with the women, so that they greatly outnumber the men," he observed. "As soon as this situation obtains there is a tendency for the men not to elect these courses, even if otherwise they are attractive to them."[26] Similarly, he cited instances where the presence of large numbers of male students proved a disincentive for women's registration. Listing language and literature as areas of male reluctance and political economy as unattractive to women in coeducational settings, Van Hise argued that equality of result might best be obtained by segregation.

University of Chicago authorities actually established, albeit briefly, separate junior (freshman and sophomore year) colleges for men and women. As women's enrollment increased so did the debate over the merits of coinstruction. Under President Harper's proposals, social association and equal academic opportunity would continue as would the administration of the junior colleges by a single dean. However, they did provide that, when economically feasible, admission to elective and required junior college courses offered in multiple sections would be restricted to members of one sex.[27] Harper expected that the financial viability proviso would result in continued coinstruction in about one-third of all courses[28] and that other university divisions would retain joint instruction.

Neosegregationists such as Harper or Julius Sachs also defended such arrangements on the grounds that coeducation diminished intellectual standards, or on the basis of current psychological theory. In instructional situations, wrote Harper, "the terms and tone of association are fixed too little by the essential character of the thing to be done and too much by the fact that both men and women are doing it."[29] In his widely quoted chapter, "Adolescent Girls and their Education," G. Stanley Hall remarked that it was comparatively easy to educate boys since they "are less peculiarly responsive in mental tone to the physical and psychic environment, tend more strongly and early to special interests, and react more vigorously against the obnoxious elements of their surroundings." In contrast, woman, "in every fiber of her soul and body is a more generic creature than man, nearer to the race, and demands more and more with advancing age an education that is essentially liberal and humanistic." He concluded that "nature decrees that with advancing civilization the sexes shall not approximate, but differentiate, and we shall probably be obliged to carry sex distinctions, at least of method, into many if not most of the topics of the higher education."[30]

But the fear of higher education's feminization never lurked too deep beneath the surface. "Whenever the elective system permits," wrote Julius Sachs, "the young men are withdrawing from courses which are the favorite choice of the girls, the literary courses; the male students discard them as feminized, they turn by preference to subjects in which esthetic discrimination plays no part."[31]

The coeducationists were fully aware of the psychological and the "diminution of intellectual standards" arguments. "I have never chanced again upon a book that seemed to me so to degrade me in my woman hood as the seventh and seventeenth chapters on women and women's education, of President Stanley Hall's *Adolescence*," wrote President M. Carey Thomas of Bryn Mawr.[32] But the battle would be won or lost on the repulsion argument. Did peculiarly female traits lead women to favor the liberal over the practical to such an extent as to dissuade male students from following a liberal sequence?

Not so, replied University of Chicago Dean of Women Students Marion Talbot. With access to other professions closed off, many college women opted for secondary-school teaching careers. With a next-to-nil chance for a woman to obtain a secondary-school position in chemistry or zoology, Talbot noted, a woman's choice of history or English in college proved to be a shrewd and practical decision—although one that might go against her personal interests. Talbot argued that despite a general belief to the contrary, "considerations of sex are rarely taken into account by women any more than by men on making a choice of studies."[33] President M. Carey Thomas, citing statistics revealing similar registration patterns for electives by male and female students at single-sex colleges, argued that the disproportionate figures reported in western coeducational institutions resulted from external circumstances, not a priori causes. "I am told," she wrote, "that economics in many western colleges is simply applied economics and deals almost exclusively with banking, railroad rates, etc., and is therefore, of course, not elected by women who are at present unable to use it practically, whereas in the eastern colleges for women theoretical economics is perhaps their favorite study."[34] Men and women alike, Thomas said, make rational choices among available subjects, and were unlikely to avoid a subject solely because of a preponderance of registration by members of the opposite sex.

The coeducationists experienced considerable success in avoiding resegregation, but whether statistical, psychological, or economic arguments proved most persuasive is a moot question.

In Wisconsin, the university regents addressed the issue in 1908 and reaffirmed their traditional pro-coeducation policy. The following year the state legislature strengthened the laws concerning university admission by adding a specific provision that "all schools and colleges of the university shall, in their respective departments and class exercises, be open without distinction to students of both sexes."[35]

But if women continued to obtain access to undergraduate education, they found few post-baccalaureate options; in fact, their ability to enter certain professions actually diminished during the early twentieth century. Mary Roth Walsh in her important book on women in the medical profession reported that institutions such as Tufts and Western Reserve, which had heretofore admitted significant numbers of women to the freshmen medical class, ceased to do so. Northwestern decided in 1902 without warning to close the women's division of its medical school. At Johns Hopkins and the University of Michigan, which remained coeducational, the percentage of females in the student body declined respectively from 33 percent in 1896 to 10 percent in 1916 and from 25 percent in 1890 to 3 percent in 1910.[36]

Just as "cheap money drives dear money out of circulation," editorialized the *Boston Transcript* at the time of Tuft's coeducation controversy, "the weaker sex drives out the stronger."[37] Although most authorities cite other factors as prompting a retreat from an elective system, the emergence of distribution requirements at most colleges assured that male students would attend courses in "feminized" disciplines. On the other hand, certain disciplines rapidly evolved into male preserves entered only by women students willing to pay major social and psychological costs. Outside the classroom, many colleges established administrative positions (dean of women students, etc.) that attempted to regulate students' social lives. Officials increasingly tolerated fraternities and sororities on condition that they adopt elaborate sets of rules, many specifically dealing with male-female interactions. Many colleges constructed dormitories and student centers segregated by sex.

Women administrators often supported such policies not simply as a defense—or as making a virtue of necessity—but because they believed that some social segregation would allow women undergraduates to assume leadership roles in activities that, if coeducational, would have inevitably been reserved for men. Thus, although academic practices have been emphasized here, coeducational institutions evolved elaborate social practices as well, permitting in many cases absorption of female students in significant numbers without serious redefinition of institutional missions.

Gentile and Jew

Stephen Duggan's enthusiasm for his Jewish students at the College of the City of New York had few bounds. He admired their motivation, ambitiousness, sincerity, and intelligence; most of all he esteemed their ability to overcome the numerous hardships of life on the Lower East Side and to succeed at an institution with unfamiliar academic and social norms. "No teacher could have had a finer student body to work with," he wrote. "They were studious, keen and forthright. They did not hesitate to analyze any subject to its fundamentals regardless of tradition or age. . . . I do not hesitate to say that I learned a great deal as a result of the keen questioning of these young men. It was fatal to evade; one had always to be on the qui vive. I found these students like students everywhere, very grateful for an evident interest in their personal welfare. . . . Some of their views were quite different from those held by students in a college situated in a less cosmopolitan atmosphere. . . . They formed the most socially minded group of young people that I know."[38]

However, many college and university officials proved far less sanguine concerning the rapid influx of Jewish students into many of America's colleges and universities. "Where Jews become numerous they drive off other people and then leave themselves," wrote Harvard President Abbott Lawrence Lowell in 1922. Denying that moral character or individual qualities created the problem, Lowell attributed its cause to "the fact of segregation by groups which repel their group."[39] He refused to speculate over whether to blame Jewish "clannishness" or Gentile anti-Semitism for the Jewish tendency to "form a distinct body, and cling, or are driven, together, apart from the great mass of undergraduates."[40] Lowell had observed that summer resorts, preparatory schools, and colleges, such as City College, New York University, and Columbia College, had all experienced the same phenomenon.

Lowell's solution, in the words of his biographer, "was a quota, usually called by Jewish writers a numerus clausus." Quotas, Lowell reasoned, had been employed in other social sectors with little or no objection. "Why anyone should regard himself as injured or offended by a limitation of the proportion of Jews in the student body, provided that the limitation were generous, Lowell could not understand."[41]

Others attributed the repulsion between Jew and Gentile to individual, rather than group characteristics. Frederick Paul Keppel, dean of Columbia College from 1910 to 1918, distinguished between desirable and undesirable Jewish students. His Barnard counterpart, Virginia Gildersleeve, wrote that "many of our Jewish students have been charming and cultivated human beings. On the other hand . . . the intense ambition of the Jews for education has brought to college girls from a lower social level than that of most of the non-Jewish students. Such girls have compared unfavorably in many instances with the bulk of the undergraduates."[42]

During the height of nativist sentiment immediately after World War I, many college authorities concluded that a Jewish influx threatened the character of their institutions. They proposed a variety of remedies, all aimed at limiting Jewish enrollment. Williams College, reported Harvard Philosophy Professor William Earnest Hocking, enlisted the aid of Jewish alumni in screening Jewish candidates. Other institutions employed psychological or character tests. Most devices appear to have resulted in a diminution in the number of Jewish students. At Columbia College, the percentage varied from 40 percent just after World War I to less than 20 percent by the mid-1930s. At Barnard the figure hovered around 20 percent while Radcliffe had 12 or 13 percent, Vassar had 6 percent, Bryn Mawr had 8 or 9 percent, and Wellesley had about 10 or 11 percent.[43] Most institutions that restricted Jewish access did not remove the barriers until after a change in national sentiment brought about by the events of World War II.

Other administrators proved more tolerant of the Jewish influx. Some did not believe they posed a threat to institutional missions. Others, shrewdly, cynically, or both, believed that the students could settle any difficulties among themselves and that few direct measures need be taken. When an irate constituent charged the University of Chicago with anti-Semitism because of Jewish exclusion from campus fraternities, President Henry Judson replied that no official discrimination existed and that such exclusionary practices by students were a social, not a religious problem, best left for the students to settle among themselves.

And "settle" they did, with a vengeance. "The University of Chicago," wrote the noted journalist Vincent Sheean, "one of the largest and richest institutions of learning in the world, was partly inhabited by a couple of thousand young nincompoops whose ambition was to get into the right fraternity or club, go to the right parties, and get elected to something or other."[44] Although the administration had segregated many extracurricular activities by sex, Chicago's undergraduate women demonstrated their ability to construct a social system no less rigid or more intellectually oriented than that of their male counterparts. Again Sheean, "The women undergraduates had a number of clubs to which all the 'nice' girls were supposed to belong. Four or five of these clubs were 'good' and the rest 'bad.' Their goodness or badness were absolute, past, present and future, and could not be called into question." Although no sorority houses existed, the women "maintained a rigid solidarity and succeeded in imposing upon the undergraduate society a tone of intricate, overweening snobbery."[45]

Into such a social system, Jews had no access. Sheean related his own encounter with the Chicago students. Just after World War I, he inadvertently pledged a "Jewish fraternity," although not Jewish himself. Lucy, a student with whom Sheean had conducted a flirtatious relationship, warned him to break his pledge. As she explained, "The Jews . . . could not possibly go to the 'nice' parties in the college. They could not be elected to any class office, or to office in any club, or to any fraternity except the two that they themselves had organized; they could not dance with whom they pleased or go out with the girls they wanted to go out with; they could not even walk across the quadrangles with a 'nice' girl if she could possibly escape."[46] Thus, contrary to many administrators' fears, most Gentile students had no intention of abandoning established colleges and universities in face of a Jewish influx. Perhaps it would prove necessary to tolerate their presence in class, but the student culture successfully limited all other interaction.

Jews responded predictably to such restrictions. Jacob Schiff, the financier-turned-philanthropist, anonymously endowed the Barnard Hall student center as a countermove to the self-selecting student culture. Centrally located, its facilities would be open to all. At the same time Schiff and others repeatedly urged that administrators take steps to abolish fraternities and sororities that discriminated against Jews. To such requests most administrators responded that changes in interpersonal relationships could come about only through education; that administrative coercion would probably result in greater anti-Semitism. Even after World War II, many colleges and universities only haltingly pressured local fraternities to abolish discriminatory charter provisions or to disaffiliate from national orders mandating discriminatory policies.

Jewish students responded to social exclusion either by increased emphasis on their academic work (thereby earning the reputation of "grind") or by establishment of predominantly Jewish academic and social organizations. At Harvard College in 1906, a group of Jewish undergraduates organized the first Menorah Society, which had as its purpose "the promotion in American colleges and universities of the study of Jewish history, culture and problems, and the advancement of Jewish ideals."[47] Far more resembling typical nineteenth-century collegiate literary societies than fraternities, Menorah societies florished on a number of colleges before and after World War I.[48]

At a typical meeting a Jewish academic from the campus or from a Menorah speakers' bureau might lecture or lead a discussion, or the society's membership might choose to discuss a book or topic of Jewish interest. The scope included the history and culture of the Jewish people "so conceived that nothing Jewish, of whatever age or clime, shall be alien to it." Its broader purpose was to secure campus recognition of the seriousness or worthiness of its subject matter. "It must demonstrate to the whole student body that the study of Jewish history and culture is a serious and liberal pursuit; it must really afford its members a larger knowledge of the content and meaning of the Jewish tradition."[49] Deliberately eschewing a primarily social purpose (". . . a Menorah Society is not a social organization. Its activities may, indeed, partake of a sociable nature, but only so far as its real objects can thereby be the more fully carried out"), Menorah quickly found itself caught between Jewish student organizations with objectives less lofty than Menorah's academic goals, such as the Student Zionist Organization, and a quickening demand for Jewish fraternities and sororities.

The first Jewish fraternity in America was founded in New York City in 1898. Established under the watchful eye of Columbia University Semitics Professor Richard Gottheil, the Zeta Beta Tau (ZBT) fraternity originally professed ideals more ambitious than friendship and brotherhood. It aimed, wrote an early member, "to inspire the students with a sense of Jewish national pride and patriotism."[50] Although the movement's early Zionist orientation gradually diminished, it attempted to retain the intellectual and service ideals on which it was founded. Richard Gottheil repeatedly expressed concern that the fraternity's uniqueness might be lost. "For the Jew carries with him wherever he goes," Gottheil said, "the great heritage of thought and of impulse which has been handed down from father to son during the last twenty-five centuries." The organization assumed the form of a Greek letter fraternity "in order to fall in with the University habits of the community in which we live." But, he concluded, "we can have no use for those men who are Zeta Beta Tau men simply for the sake of belonging to a Greek Letter Fraternity. We wish to set an example, not to proclaim ourselves a holy people, but to live as such."[51]

Some Jews feared that creation of such groups as ZBT and Menorah might serve to enhance the Jewish stereotype. When some undergraduate Radcliffe women approached their fellow student Ruth Mack, daughter of Harvard alumnus and future Overseer Judge Julian Mack, about Menorah membership, she responded cautiously. She wondered whether the group "would tend to segregate the Jewish girls from the non-Jewish," adding that at Radcliffe "there seems to be so little of this grouping, that I think it a pity to introduce anything which encourages it." Although recognizing the organization's intellectual bent, Ruth Mack feared that banding together "would produce snobbery on both sides." A general student turnout for meetings on Jewish institutions and ideals would be unobjectionable, she explained, but "while we can say that the Menorah is not limited to Jews, we can do little to make the non-Jews come out."[52] The pressures on a woman like Ruth Mack were considerable. On the one hand her strong Jewish identity inclined her to join; on the other she feared alienation from Radcliffe's Gentiles especially because she found the Jewish upperclassmen "less attractive, intellectually, etc., than the parallel class among the non-Jew." Although many at the early twentieth-century college paid lip-service to "democracy"[53] on campus (by which was meant equal opportunity to succeed in the campus student culture), Jews often found themselves arbitrarily disqualified, thus producing dilemmas such as that of Ruth Mack.

By the 1920s, Jewish fraternities had become virtually indistinguishable from their Gentile counterparts and Menorah Societies began to attrophy. "Between 1920 and 1930," wrote Horace Kallen, an original member of Harvard Menorah,

> the tradition of a love of learning which they [Jewish students] brought to college has been dissipated. The adult responsibility which they felt for the problems of their own people and of the community at large, and which was signalyzed [sic] by their membership in such organizations as the Menorah Societies, the Zionist, the Liberal, or the Social Question Clubs, has been destroyed. As their numbers grew, their fields of interest and modes of behavior conformed more and more to the prevailing conditions of undergraduate life. Although excluded by expanding anti-Semitism from participation in that life, they reproduce it, heightened, in an academic ghetto of fraternities, sororities and the like. And they emulate the invidious distinctions they suffer from by projecting them upon the Jews too proud, too poor, or too Jewish to be eligible for "collegiate" secret societies of Jews.[54]

Thus, although on many private college campuses officials limited access by Jewish students, those Jewish undergraduates who obtained admission gradually arrived at an acceptable modus vivendi with their fellow students and with the authorities.

White and Black

During the brief tenure of Harvard President Edward Everett (1846–1848), it became known that a black student would present himself for the college's admissions examination. Although the student had tutored one of Everett's sons, and was the best scholar in his class, rumors spread that Harvard would not permit his matriculation, no matter how well he performed on the exams. The student never entered Harvard (due to "illness" according to contemporary accounts), but Everett took the occasion to announce Harvard's policy. "The admission to Harvard College depends upon examinations," he said, "and if this boy passes the examination, he will be admitted; and if the white students choose to withdraw, all the income of the College will be devoted to his education."[55] The student threat to withdraw from the college to which Everett alluded left him undaunted; however, one of his successors at Harvard, Abbott Lawrence Lowell, took a similar threat quite seriously. In 1914, Lowell closed the freshman dormitories, which supposedly had been built to reduce student social segregation, to black students, claiming, when the practice became public knowledge several years later, that he did not wish to offend the sensibilities of white students. "To maintain that compulsory residence in the Freshman Dormitories—which has proved a great benefit in breaking up the social cliques, that did much injury to the College—should not be established for 99 1/2 percent of the students because the remaining one half of one percent could not properly be included seems to me an untenable position,"[56] wrote Lowell to Roscoe Conkling Bruce, a black alumnus of Harvard seeking dormitory accommodations for his son. After a public controversy arose when Lowell denied dormitory access to the younger Bruce, the Harvard Corporation published an ambiguous rule continuing compulsory dormitory residence (exemptions permitted) and providing that "men of the white and colored races shall not be compelled to live and eat together, nor shall any man be excluded by reason of his color."[57] Whether integrated dormitories would have led to a mass exodus of white students is debatable. In practice, Harvard had few black applicants. But it did wish to attract students from the South, and did not wish to acquire a reputation for forced "race mingling" or for "social equality." As a result, Harvard's dormitories remained segregated de facto until the early 1950s.[58]

By no means was Harvard alone in confronting the housing problem. Various administrations offered different solutions ranging from outright prohibition to integration. The University of Chicago permitted the majority of residents in each dormitory to decide who should join them.[59] Apparently, at Smith, when two Southern students protested the admission of a black student to their dormitory, President William A. Neilson expressed his willingness for the protesting students to move to another dormitory, although it might prove difficult to find accommodations for them. The students replied that they had wanted the black student removed, but Neilson remained adamant. The students thereupon decided they would remain in the same dormitory.[60]

Thus, in a manner reminiscent of officially sanctioned schisms among rich and poor students, a number of colleges created and/or tolerated Jim Crow dormitories, in the process sometimes undercutting claims to formal neutrality in social areas. Colleges could not at the same time argue that education provided the most effective means for overcoming intolerance while in practice facilitating social segregation. Usually hovering between 1/2 and 2 percent, the proportion of black students on northern campuses rarely if ever reached the point where officials feared a massive white exodus. Most probably they wanted to avoid a reputation for liberalism in an area surrounded with many social taboos.

As usual, the dominant student group managed social relations so as not to be inconvenienced by the presence of a distinctive minority. A black freshman enrolling at a predominantly white institution during these years arrived already knowing that he or she would lack much social life. "First of all," wrote one, "being a Negro, I was exempt from all the sororities on the campus. I knew that I would never dance at the Sigma Chi or the Delta Tau houses."[61] A study published in 1942 indicated that, without underestimating the difficulties of economic or academic adjustments, almost all black students were most dissatisfied with their social lives.[62] Some suppressed their aspiration for a full social life and concentrated on their work. "My reaction was to show these people that I was a good student. . . . I cannot help feeling . . . that if I am down scholastically, and a Negro also, I might as well leave this place." But even the students with the strongest defenses could not completely escape the results of social ostracism. "There was the time when I was one among three hundred girls at a social dance, and the instructor and one other girl ventured to drag me over the floor, when all of the other girls had run frantically clutching at each other to dance with everyone else but me, simply because I was a Negro, a brown conspicuous person. That was the time I went home and fell across the bed and cried, cried until I was exhausted. That was the time I hated a white college."[63]

Conditions changed only gradually after World War II. In 1955, the Supreme Court affirmed a lower court ruling that *Brown* v. *Board of Education* applied to segregated institutions of higher education;[64] however, it took another decade for the first black students to gain admittance to several major southern institutions. Only with the successful prosecution of *Adams* v. *Richardson* in the 1970s have a number of southern states been forced to draw up comprehensive programs for the integration of their higher education systems. In the North, the large in-migrations of blacks during the 1950s and 1960s produced major changes in the racial composition of elementary and secondary schools, but did not yield in due course similar changes in colleges and universities.

At first, black students experienced considerable overt hostility in newly integrated campuses. A constant barrage of insults and threats against black students at Louisiana State University (L.S.U.) was supplemented by a series of "pranks" including cross burnings and by several violent occurrences.[65] Although crude manifestations of prejudice decreased over time,[66] black students continued to report incidents, slights, and alienation. At the University of Illinois, an impersonal environment in which white students displayed few initiatives toward blacks (no blacks belonged to any white fraternity) led to disaffection and isolation.[67] As racial tension generally increased in the United States of the late 1960s, black students became less willing to overlook or accept such conditions.

During the 1950s and 1960s, many colleges had undertaken a series of reforms in an attempt to remove any vestige of discrimination against minority students. Some integrated their dormitories; others required fraternity and sorority chapters to drop restrictions against minority group access or to withdraw from national organizations that mandated retention of such restrictions. Sometimes, administrators undertook such reforms vigorously; all too often changes resulted only from outside pressure. There is thus a special irony in the rise of separatist demands by black and other racial minority students, which came just when authorities had concluded that integration could not be left to "education," and that significant minority representation would not necessarily result in a majority exodus. White students, separatist minority students argued, would never fully accept nonwhites as social equals. Instead, they called for a series of exclusively nonwhite extracurricular activities and residential accommodations to supplement their demand for a separate academic program. "The black women [are thinking about] pushing for a Black Women's Living Center," said a junior black woman on a predominantly white campus in the early 1970s.

> We want to get these pockets of black students out of these all-white dormitories and get them into a house of their own. The sororities and fraternities do it; why can't black people live together? Let's face it. Black people are just more comfortable with black people. I don't particularly like being questioned about my hair or style of life by white people. There are certain foods I like to eat which this school ignores or can't cook. Secondly, it would be a unifying device to get every-one together in a living situation. To me it's only natural. Before coming [to this school], I came from an all-black community and it's natural for me to live in one. . . . Of course, those who raise arguments against it don't say or may not realize that . . . unification is a threat.[68]

Black students quickly came to realize the necessity of significant enrollment increases as prerequisite to all such demands. Otherwise, separation would inevitably lead to increased social isolation and would restrict their ability to create an institutionalized social life. A campus with fewer than fifty black students, commented a black undergraduate, "has a vacuum of social activities for blacks."[69] Since most courtship on American campuses is intraracial, a small number of minority students implies an almost nonexistent pool of available dates, even when there are roughly equal numbers of men and women minority students. In addition, small numbers usually mean that attempts at formal social organization will rarely outlast the founders; recruitment often proves difficult even with sizable availability pools.

Unlike other groups, which confronted administrators with an "excess" number admitted by normal entrance processes, black students demanded modifications of admissions policies so as to insure inclusion of an adequate contingent. Many colleges made such commitments. Events at the City University of New York proved most spectacular. After a lengthy sit-in by black and Puerto Rican students at the university's City College, the university adopted an open admissions system in which students would be admitted either by high school grade point average (traditional method) or by high school rank in class (new method).[70]

In more "selective" institutions, that is, in colleges where subjective considerations entered into a competitive admissions process, admissions officers agreed either to take race explicitly into account or at least to make special efforts to recruit minority students who met traditional criteria. Although the absolute number of black students has increased significantly in the last decade, there have been recent signs of "slippage," and on many of the more selective predominantly white campuses the number of minority students remains 3 to 10 percent—lower than the number considered desirable by minority group members.

Conclusion

In many ways, the black separatists of the 1960s wanted precisely what other groups that had been victims of "repulsion" had traditionally attained: the ability to establish a set of social relationships paralleling those of the socially dominant group. However, they put forward their claims at a time when college administrators had finally overcome their fear that group repulsion would lead to an unacceptable change in institutional mission. Whether by compulsion or by volition, authorities in the 1950s and 1960s began to argue that in regulating their internal affairs, they could keep up with changes in "generally socially acceptable boundaries," and, on a number of occasions, go beyond them. Practice often fell short of ideals, and black students who directly or vicariously experienced discrimination proved less hesitant than previous groups to protest. Particularly striking on campuses with sufficient numbers of blacks was a tendency similar to that of other groups herein discussed to emulate certain aspects of the majority extracurriculum. Thus, black fraternities appeared on a number of campuses that, although espousing social consciousness, retained the paraphernalia of fraternities, including distinctive insignias and symbols, and various rites and "customs."

In general we may say that the initial representatives of a new campus group needed the strength to prove themselves academically while surviving socially. Although one might speculate that such pioneers were highly self-selected, we know little about dropout rates for such students. L.S.U. did show rather high attrition among its first classes of black students, but these students were subjected to crass physical abuse as well as the lesser forms of insults often experienced by other groups.[71] We might guess that pioneer students needed rather extraordinary motivation to come to quick terms with an institution whose traditional occupants exhibited attitudes varying from indifference to hostility.

This last points to the potential significance of family in explaining motivation. Lacking numerical peer support, insurgents may have relied quite heavily on their families for needed backing. Marion Talbot's parents strongly encouraged her educational aspirations—so much so that her mother's considerable educational reform activities (she was pivotal in gaining establishment of Girls' Latin School in Boston) partly derived from obstacles faced by Marion.[72] Similarly, majoritarian attitudes may well have been initially acquired off campus, and then subjected to strong peer reinforcement. Sheean at Chicago was surprised to learn that his roommate, who had also intended to pledge the "Jewish" fraternity, had learned, "from his father probably," about anti-Semitism and about "the ridicule, the complicated varieties of discrimination and prejudice, to which any Gentile who belonged to a Jewish fraternity would have to submit throughout four years of college."[73] Although many studies of campus peer groups emphasize discontinuities with the student's previous home life, it may very well be that in some areas peer groups serve to reinforce previously acquired attitudes.

There yet remains to be explored a fundamental set of questions. First, why would members of an insurgent group invade what must have almost appeared to be enemy territory? And, second, why did traditional constituencies not abandon their campuses for "safer" environs, as so many administrators feared they would? Of course, one answer to the latter question is that administrators often retained or obtained the ability to control access by "distinctive" groups. But abandonment rarely occurred even when such measures were not employed.

The fear of group repulsion bears a remarkable resemblance to the contemporary fear of "white flight" often discussed with respect to elementary and secondary education. Should the percentage of minority students in a given school exceed some subjectively sensed percentage, according to the fear, white parents will begin to move into more homogeneous neighborhoods. In due course, the school will become populated almost exclusively by minorities. Current literature contains considerable speculation as to the existence and extent of white flight; a resolution of that debate goes far beyond the scope of this article. But it is very much to the point of this article to say a word about what white elementary and secondary school students are supposedly fleeing from. White parents when interviewed often claim that they withdrew their children not because of the increased presence of minority students per se, but because the quality of education and resources offered appears to deteriorate concomitant with their appearance. In contrast, the quality of most colleges' and universities' educational product remained relatively unchanged despite minority group influxes. If anything, most institutions experienced sizable expansions in endowment, faculty, and facilities. And, by the third decade of the twentieth century, the prestige order among American institutions of higher education had become relatively entrenched; most institutions could "survive" even a sizable onslaught by a significant number of minority students. The more prestigious institutions could provide social and economic mobility to minority students without detracting from the status they accorded members of traditional constituencies. A Harvard or a Swarthmore, for example, could remain attractive to a student from a traditional constituency in a way that an urban high school could not. Apparently the reasoning behind magnet high schools recognizes this, at least implicitly. Such schools aim to provide sufficient educational quality and services to overcome white hesitancy over sending children to schools with a sizable minority constituency.[74] For colleges and universities, majority students usually remained on the rolls despite minority student presence so long as they and/or college officials could devise ways of avoiding undesired social intercourse.

Minorities desired to attend such institutions despite expected exhibitions of prejudice not only because of the expected quality of education and the tangible rewards obtainable for acquiring such education, but also for social reasons. The ability to replicate the majority extracurriculum meant that minority students could learn the same social lessons that extracurriculum taught majority students: how to identify desirable and undesirable acquaintance, how to exercise leadership, how to function in various group settings, cooperatively and competitively, and so forth. Even if in the larger society one found discrimination similar to that existing on the campus, minority students could employ such lessons profitably within their own groups, especially since such college-educated youth usually constituted the recognized future leaders of their groups.

In short, few minority students in the periods discussed in this article found their college careers to be completely clear sailing, but most were convinced that whatever abuse they endured would in the long run be well worth the price.

Notes

1. See Laurence Veysey, *The Emergence of the American University* (Chicago: University of Chicago Press, 1965), pp. 294–302.
2. David F. Allmendinger, Jr., *Paupers and Scholars: The Transformation of Student Life in New England 1760–1860* (New York: St. Martin's Press, 1975), p. 82.
3. Kathryn M. Moore, "Freedom and Constraint in Eighteenth Century Harvard," *Journal of Higher Education* 47 (November/December 1976): 650–651.
4. Margery Somers Foster, *"Out of Smalle Beginnings. . .": An Economic History of Harvard College in the Puritan Period (1636 to 1712)* (Cambridge: Belknap Press of Harvard University Press, 1962), pp. 65–68.
5. Ibid., p. 68.
6. Samuel Eliot Morison, *Three Centuries of Harvard 1636–1936* (Cambridge: Harvard University Press, 1936), p. 60.
7. Moore, "Freedom and Constraint in Eighteenth Century Harvard," p. 653.
8. "Statutes of William and Mary, 1727" in *American Higher Education: A Documentary History*, ed. Richard Hofstadter and Wilson Smith (Chicago and London: University of Chicago Press, 1961), vol. 1, pp. 47–48.
9. David C. Humphrey, *From Kings College to Columbia 1746–1800* (New York: Columbia University Press, 1976), p. 204.
10. Ibid., p. 196.
11. Howard Miller, "Evangelical Religion and Colonial Princeton," in *Schooling and Society*, ed. Lawrence Stone (Baltimore: Johns Hopkins University Press, 1976), pp. 135–139.
12. Allmendinger, *Paupers and Scholars*, pp. 9–11.
13. Ibid. Allmendinger also emphasizes the charitable support offered by the American Education Society and local groups toward meeting educational expenses—see pp. 54–78.
14. Ibid., pp. 85–86.
15. Frederick Rudolph, *The American College and University: A History* (New York: Vintage, 1962), p. 148.
16. Ibid., pp. 149–150.
17. George Henry Tripp, *Student Life at Harvard* (Boston: Lockwood, Brooks and Co., 1876), p. 317.
18. Ibid., p. 318.
19. Ibid., pp. 318–319.
20. Ibid., p. 323.
21. Ibid., p. 324.
22. Statement of James L. High, an 1864 University of Wisconsin alumnus as quoted in Helen R. Olin, *The Women of a State University, An Illustration of the Working of Coeducation in the Middle West* (New York and London: G. P. Putnam's Sons, 1909), pp. 101–102.
23. "And a Hebrew female seminary, in the character of the student body, at that," Burgess commented. John W. Burgess, *Reminiscences of an American Scholar: The Beginning of Columbia University* (New York: Columbia University Press, 1934), p. 242.
24. Ibid., pp. 241–242.
25. Mabel Newcomer *A Century of Higher Education for American Women* (New York: Harper and Brothers, 1959), p. 46.
26. Olin, *The Women of a State University*, pp. 112–113.

27. The University of Chicago, *The President's Report: Administration*, The Decennial Publications, First Series, vol. 1 (Chicago: University of Chicago Press, 1903), p. cxi.
28. Ibid., p. cvi.
29. Ibid., p. cxi.
30. G. Stanley Hall, *Adolescence: Its Psychology and its Relations to Physiology, Anthropology, Sociology, Sex, Crime, Religion, and Education*, vol. 2 (New York: D. Appleton, 1908), pp. 616–617.
31. Julius Sachs, "The Intellectual Reactions of Co-education," *Educational Review* 35 (May 1908): 470.
32. M. Carey Thomas, "Present Tendencies in Women's College and University Education," *Educational Review* 35 (January 1908): 65.
33. Marion Talbot, "Report of the Dean of Women," in The University of Chicago, *The President's Report*, pp. 140, 141.
34. Thomas, "Present Tendencies in Women's College and University Education," p. 73.
35. Olin, *The Women of a State University*, pp. 139–140.
36. Mary Roth Walsh, *Doctors Wanted: No Women Need Apply* (New Haven: Yale University Press, 1977), pp. 200–206.
37. *Women's Journal*, January 1, 1910, as quoted in ibid., p. 201.
38. Stephen Duggan, *A Professor at Large* (New York: Macmillan, 1943), pp. 10–11.
39. Abbott Lawrence Lowell to Rufus S. Tucker, May 20, 1922, A. L. Lowell Papers, 1919–1922. Harvard University Archives, file 1056: "Jews."
40. Abbott Lawrence Lowell to William Ernest Hocking, May 19, 1922, in ibid.
41. Henry Aaron Yeomans, *Abbott Lawrence Lowell 1856–1943* (Cambridge: Harvard University Press, 1948), p. 212.
42. Virginia Gildersleeve to Annie Nathan Meyer, March 31, 1933, Annie Nathan Meyer Papers, American Jewish Archives, "Virginia Gildersleeve" file.
43. Virginia Gildersleeve to Annie Nathan Meyer, May 6, 1929, Barnard College Archives, DO 28–29, box 1, file 1.
44. Vincent Sheean, *Personal History* (Garden City, N. Y.: Doubleday Doran, 1936), p. 9.
45. Ibid., p. 10.
46. Ibid., p. 14.
47. Henry Hurwitz and I. Leo Sharfman, eds., *The Menorah Movement for the Study and Advancement of Jewish Culture and Ideals: History, Purposes, Activities* (Ann Arbor, Mich.: Intercollegiate Menorah Association, 1914).
48. On literary societies see Rudolph, *The American College and University*, pp. 137–146; and James McLachlan, "The Choice of Hercules: American Student Societies in the Early 19th Century," in *The University in Society*, ed. Lawrence Stone (Princeton: Princeton University Press, 1974), pp. 449–494.
49. Hurwitz and Sharfman, *The Menorah Movement for the Study and Advancement of Jewish Culture and Ideals*, pp. 10–11.
50. Zeta Beta Tau, *The First Twenty Years* (New York: Zeta Beta Tau, 1924), p. 15.
51. Ibid., p. 59.
52. Ruth Mack to Julian Mack, November 26, 1914, "Letters and notes used by Harry Barnard in Researching Mack's biography," American Jewish Archives, box 1068, "Letters and notes concerning time period 1900–1929" file.
53. The most famous fictional elaboration of this theme is contained in Owen Johnson, *Stover at Yale* (New York: Collier Books, 1968 [1912]).
54. Horace Kallen, *College Prolongs Infancy* (New York: John Day, 1932), p. 24.
55. Paul Revere Frothingham, *Edward Everett: Orator and Statesman* (Boston and New York: Houghton Mifflin, 1925). My thanks to Richard Yanikoski, who is writing a thesis on Everett, for calling this incident to my attention. It is also recounted in Gordon W. Allport, *The Nature of Prejudice* (Garden City, N. Y.: Doubleday Anchor, 1958), p. 471.
56. Abbott Lawrence Lowell to Roscoe Conkling Bruce, January 6, 1923, as quoted in Nell Painter, "Jim Crow at Harvard," *New England Quarterly* 44 (1971): 629.
57. Painter, "Jim Crow at Harvard," p. 634.
58. Ibid., n. 26. See also Marcia Synnott, "A Social History of Admission Policies at Harvard, Yale and Princeton 1900–1930" (Ph. D. diss., University of Massachusetts, 1974), pp. 368–380, 396–398.
59. William Henderson to E. D. Burton, April 5, 1923, University Presidents' Papers, 1889–1925, The University of Chicago Library, "Racial Issues" file. In 1907 five white students moved out of a dormitory at the University of Chicago when university officials assigned a black student to it. Apparently this was an inadvertent breach of the university's segregationist policy. See S. Breckinridge to H. P. Judson, June

20, 1907, and S. Breckinridge to R. S. Goodspeed, June 20, 1907, University President's Papers, 1889–1925, The University of Chicago Library, "Racial Issues" file.

60. B. S. Hurlbut to E. D. Burton, April 2, 1923, University Presidents' Papers, 1889–1925, The University of Chicago Library, "Racial Issues" file.

61. Edythe Hargrove, "How I Feel as a Negro at a White College," *Journal of Negro Education* 11 (October 1942): 484.

62. William H. Boone, "Problems of Adjustment of Negro Students at a White School," *Journal of Negro Education* 11 (October 1942): 481.

63. Hargrove, "How I Feel as a Negro at a White College," p. 485. The school in question was the University of Michigan.

64. *Frasier v. Board of Trustees of University of North Carolina*, 134 F. Supp. 589 (1955) (M.D. North Carolina); affirmed 350 U.S. 979 (1956).

65. Hansjorg Elshorst, "Two Years after Integration: Race Relations at a Deep South University," *Phylon* 28 (Spring 1967): 41: "A student was threatened with a knife while in his room, another was hit by acid, one was attacked with fists and a girl was hit while in the library."

66. For exceptions see Meyer Weinberg, *Minority Students: A Research Appraisal* (Washington, D.C.: U.S. Department of Health, Education, and Welfare-National Institute of Education, 1977), p. 199.

67. Aaron Bindman, "Participation of Negro Students in an Integrated University" (Ph.D. diss., University of Illinois, 1965), *passim*.

68. Charles V. Willie and Arline Sakuma McCord, *Black Students at White Colleges* (New York: Praeger, 1972), p. 6.

69. Ibid., p. 25.

70. See David E. Lavin, Richard D. Alba, and Richard Silberstein, "Open Admissions and Equal Access: A Study of Ethnic Groups in the City University of New York," *Harvard Educational Review* 49 (February 1979): 53–93; and Harold S. Wechsler, *The Qualified Student: A History of Selective College Admission in America 1870–1970* (New York: Wiley-Interscience, 1977), chap. 11.

71. Elshorst, "Two Years after Integration," p. 51.

72. Richard J. Storr, "Marion Talbot," in *Notable American Women 1607–1958: A Biographical Dictionary*, vol. 3 (Cambridge: Belknap Press of Harvard University Press, 1971), p. 423.

73. Sheean, *Personal History*, p. 16.

74. For a critical study of magnet schools, see James E. Rosenbaum and Stefan Presser, "Voluntary Racial Integration in a Magnet School" *School Review* 86 (February 1978): 156–186.

I wish to thank Ann Breslin, Deborah Gardner, Lynn Gordon, Walter Metzger, and Paul Ritterband for their comments on this paper. I completed this work during my tenure as a Spencer Fellow of the National Academy of Education. I wish to thank the Spencer Foundation and the members of the Academy for their support.

DISCRIMINATION IN COLLEGE ADMISSIONS

DAVID O. LEVINE

In the decade following World War I, a relatively small but critical number of liberal arts colleges enjoyed the luxury of selecting their student bodies for the first time. During this period of unprecedented enrollment expansion, they chose to limit the size of their classes and to seek a national and upper-middle-class student body at the expense of local and more diverse students. New admissions procedures were instituted to select those young people whose backgrounds suggested they should appropriately assume positions of leadership in American society after graduation. Despite the increasing heterogeneity of the American population, the growing importance of education and training in the economic structure of the country, and the emergence of the college student as a cultural ideal, these schools sought deliberately to become bastions of the Protestant upper middle class and to confine their student bodies to young men from socially desirable socioeconomic backgrounds.

Racial and ethnic bias flourished in the American college of the 1920s and 1930s. Restrictive admissions policies could have dictated the selection of students on the basis of their intellectual potential alone, but social class rather than achievement was central to the selection of democratic America's elite college students between the two world wars. Faced with the self-consciously determined opportunity and challenge to prepare a generation of leaders for a technological age, college officials and alumni—predominantly white Anglo-Saxon Protestant (WASP) and often anxious about the loss of status and power of "native" American stock in American society in general—created the model student in their own image. The object of these colleges' affection was the son of the WASP businessman or professional, the alleged twentieth-century spiritual heir to New England ministers' and farmers' sons. The target of these colleges' attention was the son of Eastern European immigrants, and the Russian Jewish student in particular, who was not considered worthy of the economic and social privileges to which his college degree would have entitled him.

Restrictive admissions quotas were developed to solve what was described often as "the Jewish problem."[1] Although Catholic and black applicants also faced discrimination, their numbers were too small to command the attention focused on Jewish students. Surely, anti-Semitism was rampant among the WASP upper middle class and its allies, including many German Jewish Americans. But the establishment of these quotas at the nation's best colleges was more than merely a case of anti-Semitism. Larger questions were at issue: Should America's elite be larger and more heterogeneous than it had been before? Should America's private elite colleges be responsive to democratic ideals in student selection? In the 1920s and 1930s, American higher education witnessed the emergence of the national elite liberal arts college, but it was a selective institution rooted in class and ethnic prejudice, not talent. Let us focus on the development of selective and restrictive admissions procedures at Dartmouth College, perhaps the nation's most popular school in the 1920s.

The Selection Process at the Small Liberal Arts College

Before World War I, institutions of higher learning matriculated essentially all interested young people. A potential student's parents or principal—or, more commonly, his headmaster—simply wrote the president or dean of a college about the student; the boy arrived at the college in September, took the school's entrance examination, and enrolled. The student inquired about only one college; there was no admissions office, no formal application process. As late as the second decade of the twentieth century, all American colleges were still seeking as many students as they could persuade to come, whatever their academic qualifications. The movement toward higher standards in admissions had only just begun at even the so-called best institutions on the eve of the war. In 1911, the founder of Oregon's Reed College studied the number of conditional students—students permitted to enroll with high school records that did not meet the formal entrance requirements—admitted to Harvard, Yale, and other schools and commented, "Oh, spirit of democracy, what scrambles for numbers and fees are performed in thy name." President James R. Angell of Yale later conceded, "The early university seems to have taught any one who appeared and could pay the necessary fee."[2]

By the end of the war, with the improvement in national transportation networks and the growth of the prosperous, mobile, and education-oriented upper middle class, the best American schools could engage realistically in a nationwide search for the most talented and socially desirable young men. Institutions that had formerly operated in similar but separate spheres now recruited students at the same rapidly expanding high schools of the country's metropolitan areas. "In no other civilized country do institutions of higher learning compete for students. Nowhere else are the allurements and advantages of the colleges' training so advertised," observed a 1911 Carnegie Foundation report. "College education in America is a commodity that is sold somewhat after the manner of life insurance and patent medicine."[3] Though their efforts were limited to New England and the Middle Atlantic states, officials of Dartmouth began to show lantern slides of life there at high school assemblies in 1915. Like those of other schools, Dartmouth's trustees and faculty reaffirmed their support for the "natural" enrollment growth of the college by liberalizing admissions requirements to attract students from the West as well as from the public high schools of the nascent eastern and Midwestern suburbs.[4] The competition became fierce to convince young men not only of the value of college attendance generally but also of the special virtues of an individual school.

The rush to the colleges surprised even the most optimistic of educators. At Dartmouth, although the freshman class of 1918–1919 had included fewer than 400 students, 698 young men were accepted to begin college in the fall of 1919—and Dartmouth officials were pleasantly shocked to find themselves rejecting 100 qualified applicants for fear of overcrowding. Within two years, Dartmouth became so popular that its acceptance list was completed in early February, and only half of the applicant pool was admitted. Faced with this unprecedented abundance of qualified potential students, Dartmouth officials realized that an alternative to the "first come, first served" admissions process had to be found. President Ernest M. Hopkins hired Dartmouth's first dean of admissions, E. G. Bill, and worked closely with him to develop one of the nation's first comprehensive selective admissions plans.[5]

Still, few institutions were overwhelmed by the growing interest in higher education in the early 1920s. A 1920 survey of forty of the most renowned colleges and universities showed that only thirteen of them were actually turning away any applicants at all: Dartmouth refused the most (1,600), Princeton was second (1,500), and Pennsylvania was third (750). Harvard rejected only 229 applicants, and Yale accepted all of the young men who fulfilled its entrance requirements. After years of deliberating whether to increase the size of the college or not, the Princeton trustees voted to limit enrollment to the approximately 2,000 students that could fit into the dormitories and eat in the dining halls, but other prestigious institutions were not yet fortunate enough to have this choice. At the University of Chicago, for example, a 1920 faculty committee refused to recommend an enrollment ceiling; it was not until 1923 that Chicago's president could report that an "increase in numbers was a matter of keen interest for many years, but has been decreasingly so for half a decade at least. We have now reached the point when it may properly sink into insignificance and be almost forgotten in comparison with our concern for the quality of our work."[6]

Less prestigious schools had no reason to alter their procedures. Only a few institutions were forced to turn away students because of a lack of facilities. A survey of Methodist colleges at the end of the 1920s pointed out that a student could show up two weeks after the semester began and still be admitted to most institutions. Further, the registrar alone passed judgment on an applicant's qualifications in two of every three of the schools studied; only twenty-five of the thirty-five schools required the filing of a formal application and even fewer requested a personal recommendation, an interview, or an intelligence test score.[7] The lack of admissions standards and formal selection procedures was common at all but a handful of schools between the two world wars.

Yet in the 1920s, several American colleges did choose not to pursue a policy of indefinite expansion and to seek instead the development of a small, carefully selected student body. The opportunity to select and limit students raised the possibility of an intellectual renaissance at many colleges. Frank Aydelotte took over the reins of Swarthmore College in 1921 hoping to attract a small group of highly motivated students and to provide them with a suitable academic environment. Insisting that "quality rather than quantity is the great need of education today," he urged successfully the creation of complementary selective admissions and honors programs. In 1922–1923, 800 students applied for the 170 places in Swarthmore's freshman class; in 1926–1927, just under 1,500 applied for 150 spots. To Aydelotte, the clearest sign of educational progress was that Swarthmore could point with pride "to the multitude that we turn away."[8] Though the number of such schools was insignificant in comparison with the panoply of American institutions of higher education, their influence was great.

As at other institutions, the decision to pursue a policy of selection and limitation was unprecedented at Dartmouth. In October 1919, a faculty committee on admissions proposed that admissions standards be raised to alleviate the problems caused by the sharp increase in qualified applicants, but the committee also favored expanding Dartmouth's facilities and faculty so that any interested young man who could meet the new standards would be able to enroll. The trustees rejected the latter recommendation and discussed the possibility of limiting enrollment. Hopkins convinced the majority that the number of interested and qualified applicants would probably continue to run well above the 500 young men the college could admit. The elder statesman of the board was pleasantly skeptical about the rapid turn of events since the end of the war; Hopkins recalled his reaction some years later:

> When I got done, Mr. Streeter leaned over and said very seriously and without the slightest intention of being humorous, "Mr. President, do I understand rightly that you seriously propose sometime in the future to decline the application of somebody who really wants to enter Dartmouth? . . . Well, now I guess this is all right and I'll probably vote for it, but, by God, I've got to have a little time on it after forty years of watching Dartmouth grab and hogtie every prospect that wandered inadvertently into town with a hazy idea of sometime going to college somewhere."[9]

Mr. Streeter's shock was understandable.

The Dartmouth trustees voted to limit admissions without conditions to those applicants in the top third of their high school class, but a faculty committee soon found it necessary to revise the plan to limit admission to those students in the top quarter of their class. At the time, the trustees did not believe that raising admissions standards would necessarily limit enrollment. But within two years, in 1921, the trustees decided to take further action to limit the size of the college and set attendance ceilings of 2,000 for the entire school and of 550 to 650 for each freshman class.[10] The opportunity to select and limit the size and composition of Dartmouth was welcome; though it ran counter to the value placed on expansion and growth in American economic life, it augured well for the future prestige of the college.

Hopkins' call for an "aristocracy of brains" in September 1922 became the most widely read statement about the advantages of selection and limitation of its time. He asserted that attendance at college was a privilege, not a right, and that college administrators had the responsibility to take great pains to determine just what young people were most deserving of its opportunities. "It would be incompatible with all the conceptions of democracy to assume that the privilege of higher education should be restricted to any class defined by the accident of birth or by the fortuitous circumstance of possession of wealth," Hopkins declared, "but there is such a thing as an aristocracy of brains, to whom increasingly the opportunities of higher education ought to be restricted." Only then would higher education enhance excellence in American society.[11]

Hopkins' goal—and it certainly was an ideal of many other progressive educators—was to provide a valuable intellectual and social experience in a small community for those young people most capable of exercising leadership in society. He believed that economic and social progress was dependent upon the efficient use of the best young men democracy could produce, and he pledged to find those few talented future leaders, "whether these brains be found in the coal pit, on the farm, in the industrial plant, or among the professions."[12] He hoped his new selective admissions plan could bring such a student body together in rural New Hampshire.

Although Columbia University appears to have been the nation's first institution to use a formal application form, Dartmouth was the first to establish a comprehensive selective admissions process. Hopkins' plan was designed to pick a student body that consisted of intellectual-oriented and yet well-rounded students from diverse socioeconomic and geographical backgrounds. He listed nine elements or principles of the process:

1. *Exceptional Scholarship*, which shall be considered sufficient basis for selection.
2. *High Scholarship*, which shall be considered *prima facie* evidence in favor of selection.
3. *Personal Ratings* by school officers and others acquainted with the applicant and distinctive abilities evidenced by *School Activities* submitted by the latter.
4. *Priority of Application.*
5. *The Principle of Occupational Distribution.*
6. *The Principle of Geographical Distribution.*
7. All properly qualified *Sons of Dartmouth Alumni and Dartmouth College Officers* [shall be admitted].
8. *Low Scholarship* shall be presumptive evidence of unfitness for selection.
9. The entire class will be selected on the basis of qualifications and no one allowed to enter simply because he has secured rooming accommodations.[13]

Dartmouth's evaluation process also required a personal application—including a candidate's personal statement—and an interview. Most colleges adopted these innovations but also continued to rely on the traditional method of entrance examinations by fields well after Dartmouth began to use its more flexible applicant review system.[14] Two years in the making, the plan was put into effect in 1922. Over sixty years and many college generations later, it still summarizes the guidelines for selective admissions processes widely followed today.

The rank order of the principles of the plan suggests Hopkins' own priorities. Above all, he wanted to reward those who possessed the intellectual potential to make the best use of the college's facilities and who he hoped would then make the best use of their privileged place in American society. "It is an attempt to winnow out from among the applicants seeking admission to Dartmouth College those men of intelligence and mental power who have the greatest promise of living usefully and helpfully among their fellows in the society of their time," Hopkins told groups around the country.[15] Intellect came first, but even at the outset Hopkins recognized that he, too, had to make concessions to alumni and to other strategic interests within the college community.

The Goal of Diversity

Of greatest significance in the Dartmouth selective admissions plan was Hopkins' frank articulation of the principle of proportionate selection in college admissions. From the outset he self-consciously decided that the composition of an elite student body could be determined neither by intellect nor by socioeconomic background alone. Time and again Hopkins noted that the college's classes could be filled with the graduates of New England preparatory schools, but he wanted to reach out to a variety of occupational and geographical constituencies. No more than twenty-five students could be admitted from any one school, a decision that rankled the preparatory schools. Preference was given to residents of New Hampshire, the South, and the West in an effort to diversify the student body. Hopkins even favored assigning quotas to regional alumni groups. As he informed his friend Felix Frankfurter, Hopkins hoped this plan would enable Dartmouth to accept more students from poorer backgrounds and prevent the student body from becoming "a concentrated extract of American middle-class businessmen."[16]

Hopkins and Bill were justifiably proud of Dartmouth's success at attracting a geographically diverse student body. Of the 552 young men in the first class accepted under the new admissions process, 399 were public high school graduates and represented 323 schools. Over one-fifth of the freshman class received full scholarships. In 1917, two of every five Dartmouth students came from outside New England; by the time of World War II, nearly two of every three did. On the basis of such statistics, Dartmouth was considered one of only ten "national" colleges in a 1931 study.[17]

A close examination of the results of the Dartmouth plan, however, suggests that Hopkins' aspirations for diversity went unrealized. The plan's supporters—which included *The New York Times*—applauded the principles of occupational and geographical distribution, but other pressures compromised Hopkins' democratic-elitist ideals. Critics asserted that the plan was a subterfuge to justify the selection of alumni children and athletes, even if Hopkins' initial proposal assigned them low priority.[18] In addition, Hopkins brought alumni into the admissions process, particularly in areas away from New England, and such men were less committed to a diverse, intellectual-oriented student body than in ensuring the admission of their own children or those others with whom they closely identified.

In time even Hopkins admitted the bias toward upper-middle-class WASPs implicit in the operation of his selective admissions plan. While the number of students from the middle Atlantic and mid-western states climbed throughout the 1920s and 1930s, the evidence indicates that these students were not appreciably different from their New England peers. "We have undertaken to insure the geographical distribution, which has been likewise ours since the men born in New England have begun to emigrate into remote parts of the country and to send their sons back here to college," he explained. "Likewise, in this day of the trend toward the cities, we wish to preserve at least some semblance of the old type country boy constituency from which most of the leaders in urban centers have sprung."[19] Indeed, Hopkins hoped that the composition of Dartmouth's student body and that of the national leadership would continue to remain essentially the same. The hometown could change, but the same socioeconomic background continued to be the only appropriate one. Thus, the plan was not designed ultimately to attract much diversity. By the late 1930s, a decade later, the proportion of farmers' and laborers' children had fallen precipitously to 6 percent and 10 percent, respectively, while the proportion of businessmen's and professionals' children had grown to 43 percent and about 35 percent, respectively.

While Dartmouth was attracting students from across the country, DePauw University, a fine Methodist liberal arts college in rural Indiana, was trying to capture a larger slice of the Midwestern market. Between the two world wars, DePauw recruited the children of the upper middle class, more and more often hailing from suburban areas, and more and more able and willing to pay the rapidly increasing cost of private higher education. In the 1920s, the number of bankers, doctors, teachers, insurance salesmen, and business executives among the fathers jumped by about 50 percent while the size of the student body as a whole increased by less than 19 percent. In 1920, well over four of every five students came from Indiana; by the time of World War II, only two of five did. The number of students from the suburbs of Chicago alone increased to nearly one-quarter of the student body.[20] Despite DePauw's efforts to continue to attract the brightest of Indiana's rural and small-town high school graduates—particularly through the Rector Scholarship program, one of the nation's largest—the college lost its Indiana and socially diverse tone. Each DePauw administration had misgivings about this trend, but chose to adapt its admissions policy to it nonetheless. In 1939, DePauw's president acknowledged that his school had become "cosmopolitan, nondenominational, suburban, rather than rural in its student body," and though for financial reasons he was pleased by the increasing number of well-to-do students there, he was concerned that the college had lost its traditional clientele. Discouraged, he noted that rural students now tended to attend public institutions since the liberal arts college was "a luxury to many."[21] Yet these developments were essential elements in the popularity of DePauw and other schools.

The decisions to limit enrollment, recruit widely, and raise tuition were all fundamental to the effort to develop a high-quality, small, but national liberal arts college. This strategy was tried with varying degrees of success at nearly every liberal arts college, from Dartmouth and its competitors in New England to DePauw in Indiana to Pomona in California. At first, high hopes accompanied the effort to select top-notch student bodies; realistically, however, not every institution could expect to attract an intellectually oriented student body that could pay its own way. In addition, institutional concerns about financial and alumni sources of support appeared to intensify even during the prosperous 1920s. The suburban student market was tapped by schools for a combination of idealistic, financial, and social reasons, but most of all, selective admissions plans were created to project a sense of institutional prestige.

The decision to limit enrollment was thought to give a college a psychological advantage over its competitors. "The most desirable clubs, and the ones that are the hardest to get into, have the longest waiting lines," a DePauw professor observed. "The same is true of colleges." Efforts to appear selective were made even if there was no need for selection; even Harvard and Chicago, for example, having settled on the number of freshmen they would admit, failed to reach the target figure in the late 1920s. Chicago officials frankly conceded within their own community that their decision to limit enrollment had been made "with the hope that we shall thereby arouse students to apply in greater numbers." The enrollment ceiling was set at 750 freshmen, but only 676 students showed up.[22] Institutions were willing to try any policy that would entice upper-middle-class WASPs to apply in sufficient numbers, since they were considered the caretakers of prestige in American society.

The adoption of regional quotas by Dartmouth, Harvard, and other New England colleges was intended to make each school competitive in the hard-fought battle for upper-middle-class suburban WASPs from the Midwest and West. At first educators believed that such students would lead the intellectual renaissance of the American college. Almost immediately, however, educators at Dartmouth and elsewhere found that an emphasis on scholarship in the admissions process did not necessarily produce a student body with the social background considered suitable for the nation's future leaders. Since cultivating this constituency was so important, character soon replaced intellectual potential as the key admissions criterion. Increased attention was then paid to the socioeconomic background of an applicant, and the admissibility of socially undesirable young men, even if talented, was questioned.[23]

Regional quotas, originally intended to increase the diversity of the student body, soon became a tool for discrimination against socially undesirable young men. At Harvard, for example, a faculty committee established by its Board of Overseers in 1923 at first repudiated the idea of a quota on Jewish students and reaffirmed the school's tradition of equality of opportunity. Rather than adopt a selection process that could be seen as a covert means to bar students of undesirable ethnic backgrounds, the committee recommended that all students in the top one-seventh of their high school graduating class be automatically admitted to Harvard College. This strategy would increase the proportion of rural and noneastern students, thereby encouraging regional diversity. But the Harvard plan—and others at similar schools—did not produce the desired social balance. Once it was discovered that Jewish students from urban areas, intellectually competent but socially undesirable, were being admitted in larger numbers than anyone had foreseen, the plan was modified to exclude them. Similarly, national scholarship contests established in the 1920s and 1930s at the major eastern colleges were designed in large part to substitute lower-middle-class WASPs from the Midwest and West for the poor ethnic students in their own backyards.[24] Despite the rhetoric about academic and democratic values, institutional prestige apparently depended on the social homogeneity of a school's student body.

From Selection to Restriction

In the 1920s and 1930s, selective admissions plans became restrictive admissions policies. Many of the nation's best-known colleges gave the appearance of being selective only because they chose to reject deliberately and systematically qualified but socially undesirable candidates in order to placate their alumni and other upper-middle-class WASPs. A critic in *The Nation* opposed regional quotas and proportionate admissions policies because they often led to the acceptance of less qualified but socially acceptable applicants: "An educational institution should not be representative of all people, but only of those with ambition and ability to do its work. . . . To tell a Cohen, whose average on the college board examinations was 90, that he cannot enter because there are too many Jews there already, while a grade of 68 will pass a Murphy, or one of 62 a Morgan, hardly seems in line with the real interests of the college."[25] But such quotas were indeed considered in the colleges' best interest. At such colleges as Harvard, Yale, Princeton, Columbia, and Dartmouth, essentially only the ethnic Americans, particularly the urban Russian Jews, were being turned away. Nearly everyone else, especially if he were in the top one-fifth of his high school class or from outside New England and the middle Atlantic states, was accepted without question to the school of his choice between the two world wars.[26]

That anti-Semitism became critical to a college's ability to call itself an elite school testifies to the rampant nativism in this era. Harvard's Lowell and Dartmouth's Hopkins were not alone in their disdain for most ethnic Americans. The immigrant's disloyalty to the United States was all but assumed: the raids ordered by Attorney General A. Mitchell Palmer were intended to arrest and deport immigrant radicals in 1920, and the decade-long ordeal of the Italian immigrants Nicola Sacco and Bartolomeo Vanzetti, denied a fair trial and later executed for a crime they may not have committed, symbolized Americans' distrust of immigrants. In 1916, Madison Grant's *Passing of the Great Race in America* was hailed as scientific support for widely held racist views on the baneful influence of eastern and southern Europeans on the future of Western civilization and the human race. Even the so-called liberals of the day, those who preached the predominance of environmental over genetic factors in the shaping of individual character, more often than not doubted whether the immigrants were capable of becoming full participants in American democratic life. It is no historical accident that the restrictive immigration laws of 1921 and 1924 were passed and signed into law—one *Los Angeles Times* headline called the latter bill a "Nordic victory"—at the same time that college administrators were looking for ways to limit, if not eliminate, unwanted Jewish and other ethnic students.

Fearful of the rise of the city, with its huge concentrations of ethnic Americans, fearful of the increasing number and visibility of the children of immigrants in American economic, political, and social institutions, many WASPs scrambled for the means to preserve their cultural hegemony. Higher education was not immune to this climate of intolerance. Before World War I, the presence of Jewish students was not a pressing issue, as their number was still relatively small and higher learning had not yet become necessary for social status. In the 1920s, once collegiate training had come to be viewed as a critical avenue of economic and social mobility, it became important to exclude from elite schools those individuals and social groups deemed to be of inappropriate background and character to take advantage of the opportunities and privileges afforded by a college degree. Like the framers of federal immigration legislation, educators first tried a literacy test of sorts—the College Board examinations—to keep Jewish students out. When that strategy failed dramatically, more blatant tactics were adopted.[27]

The presence of even a small number of Jewish students on a college campus sent shudders through the bodies of administrators and alumni. As early as 1910, students demonstrated at Williams College to protest the admission of any Jews; in that same year, E. E. Slosson reported that Princeton officials believed that if Jews were admitted, "they would ruin Princeton as they have Columbia and Pennsylvania." A Menorah Society was formed at Harvard in 1906, and later elsewhere, to bring Jewish students (generally of Russian heritage) together, a sign of the beginning of the social disintegration there.[28] A 1919 survey by the Bureau of Jewish Social Research indicated that with the exception of the colleges and universities located in New York City, Jewish students accounted for no more than 15 percent of the student body at any school: while CCNY was at least 80 percent Jewish, the proportion of Jews at New York University was less than 50 percent, at Columbia about 20 percent, at Western Reserve University and the University of Pennsylvania about 15 percent, at Harvard 10 percent, and at Dartmouth, Princeton, Amherst, and Williams less than 3 percent. While Jews accounted for 1.19 percent of the college students nationwide as late as 1924,[29] the fact that they congregated at the nation's most prestigious schools heightened anxiety about their potential influence in society.

Informal sanctions restricting the number of Jewish students admitted had been accepted practice at several schools before World War I. Without formal admissions procedures, however, the number of such students rose dramatically shortly thereafter. Jews already in attendance were generally accepted by their peers, but with the influx of applications, new questions arose: How would the increasing number of new Jewish students, with their distinctive socioeconomic background and intellectual interests, be assimilated into the predominantly WASP student culture? What if these Jews were successfully integrated into college life and then sought further access to the professions? College officials and their allies not only were uncomfortable in the presence of large numbers of Jewish students, they also felt threatened by those students' aspirations to full participation in American society's economic and social elite.

Limiting the number of Jewish students became an obsession with officials at the elite colleges in the 1920s. Citing the case of City College, the dean of admissions at Yale believed that Yale would become "a different place when and if the proportion of Jews passes an as yet unknown limit." For Yale that acceptable level was about 10 percent of the student body. Sensitive to the fact that his school's "position at the gateway of European immigration [made it] socially uninviting to students who come from homes of refinement," Columbia's dean favored restricting the proportion of Jews there to about 20 percent of the entering class.[30] Some public institutions also confronted the "Jewish problem" in the 1920s: the dean of Massachusetts Agricultural College felt compelled to assure a rural newspaper reporter and local parents that "there is as fine a crowd of good, old New England stock here as you'll find anywhere." A study of collegiate business education in 1931 chronicled what the authors considered to be the indiscriminate acceptance of ethnic students into commerce programs: "A school, like a country, can absorb so much that is different from its accepted pattern or mode," they added. "Beyond that point, only confusion and negation result."[31]

Harvard's Lowell insisted that he had the best interests of Jewish students at heart when he sought to restrict their enrollment in the 1920s. In a letter to *The New York Times* in June 1922, he observed that the amount of anti-Semitic feeling grew in proportion to the increase in the number of Jewish students, and he suggested that if each well-known school limited the number of Jewish students, then anti-Semitic sentiment would be diffused, if not eliminated entirely. The Harvard Student Council Committee on Education in 1926 also emphasized that "no college can admit unassimilables with impunity" when it recommended that Jewish students constitute no more than 10 percent of Harvard's student body. Students who favored a quota system at Harvard supported the concept of proportionate admissions for the nation as a whole, and insisted that Jewish students, conscientious as they were about their studies, destroyed the unity of the college by not mixing well socially. Despite Lowell's and his students' remarks, Heywood Broun and George Britt's 1931 study *Christians Only* found Harvard's restrictions moderate in comparison with those at Yale, Columbia, Cornell, the University of Virginia, and other schools.[32]

At an emotional meeting with Protestant campus leaders in 1922, Harry Starr, president of the Harvard Menorah Society, found out "that it was *numbers* that mattered; bad or good, *too many* Jews were not liked. Rich or poor, brilliant or dull, polished or crude—*too many Jews*, the fear of a New Jerusalem at Harvard" motivated supporters of a quota on Jewish students. WASP students argued that their Jewish peers could not "be prepared in all qualities of mind, character, and personality to assume positions of active, helpful leadership in the world" and did not demonstrate any interest "in the larger life of the college." But the truth was that Jewish students were threatening in large part because of their successful assimilation into undergraduate life, particularly in those programs and activities ushered in by the renewed interest in scholarship. "It is not the failure of Jews to be assimilated into undergraduate society which troubles them," Horace Kallen told *The Nation's* audience. "What troubles them is the completeness with which Jews want to be and have been assimilated."[33]

Kallen's perspective dramatizes the irony of the restrictive admissions policies. The culture of aspiration had proved to be too successful. Too many Jewish and poor students surpassed their WASP peers in intellectual potential and, furthermore, eagerly sought to become integrated into the predominantly WASP world of the college campus. Yet, allegedly for their own good, educators claimed their aspirations had to be restricted, their enrollment limited. Without a vast majority of students from the appropriate upper-middle-class WASP background, these educators and their allies contended, not only would the collegiate community suffer irreparable damage, but the future solidarity and stability of American society would be put in jeopardy. These fears, rampant among his school's competitors for about a decade, soon impelled Hopkins to institute a quota on the number of Jewish applicants accepted at Dartmouth in the winter of 1931–1932.

Anti-Semitism at Dartmouth and Elsewhere

Until the late 1920s there was little anti-Semitism at Dartmouth. In 1920, for example, Hopkins instructed a dean to send admissions information to a Mr. Morris Altman, "who states that he is an Episcopalian—whatever that has to do with it." In a later memo to Dean Bill, he stated emphatically that "the diminution of the Jews never figured in the slightest way in the formation of our plans, nor in our practice" of the selective admissions process. Though he felt that "any college has a right . . . to protect its own individuality . . . if it were true that men of specified race or characteristics were likely to inundate it in such large numbers so as to exclude all others," Hopkins denied privately to Felix Frankfurter and publicly to newspaper reporters that Dartmouth's admissions procedures discriminated against Jewish applicants. Instead, he suggested the school's rural environment did not appeal to urban Jewish students.[34] Even as some schools sharply curtailed the number of Jewish students, the total enrollment of Jews at American colleges and universities climbed dramatically; one 1927 survey of 665 institutions indicated that Jewish students constituted 10.7 percent of the student body.[35] But Dartmouth was still little touched by "the Jewish problem." While Hopkins acknowledged that some undergraduate organizations were anti-Semitic, as late as 1930 a faculty member believed that "discrimination, if it exists, is kept under cover."[36]

"The Jewish problem" emerged suddenly at Dartmouth in 1931. Once other prestigious colleges put severe limits on the number of their Jewish students, the number of Jews applying to and enrolling at Dartmouth increased rapidly. While the classes of 1926 to 1933 averaged about 29 Jews, the class of 1934 (accepted for fall 1930) included 53 Jews and the class of 1935, 75 Jews. Reviewing the composition of the class of 1935 in the *Dartmouth Alumni Magazine* in November 1931, Dean Bill noted that Jewish students comprised over 10 percent of the entering class and that the proportion of entering students indicating no religious preference—considered to be a smoke screen for Jews who wished to hide their background had increased from 8 to 14 percent in a few years. Within the previous decade, the proportion of Jews had increased about five times. "This triumph of the chosen and heathen peoples seems to be a continuing process," Dean Bill concluded in a deliberately provocative remark, "and it will not be long before the above table [on the religious preferences of the freshman class] can be limited to just two or three items." Although the proportion of Jewish students was lower at Dartmouth than at such schools as Harvard and Columbia, even after those two latter schools had established quotas, Hopkins was concerned. "I *know* we have necessity upon us to do something drastic," he conceded to Dean Bill.[37]

On Christmas Eve of 1931, Hopkins proposed that Bill and a Jewish alumnus get together to discuss the imposition of a quota on the number of Jewish students. Echoing Lowell's argument, he considered a quota to be in the best interest of the Jewish students as well as of the college. "Within the last two years," Hopkins informed a sympathetic and influential Jewish alumnus, "[I have realized that] in allowing the percentage of Jews to increase rapidly, and in not being as exacting in regard to qualities of character and personality among Jewish boys as we were among others, we were really not doing justice to those Jewish boys whom we did accept nor to alumni such as yourself." The selective admissions process had put its highest priority on scholarship potential, but, simply put, too many Jewish students had been accepted on that basis. With the same rationale that he had used earlier to cut the proportion of New England students at the college, Hopkins instructed Dean Bill to reduce, "perhaps even drastically," the number of Jewish students admitted to the class of 1936.[38]

To carry out its quota plan, Dartmouth followed established practices to identify and reject Jewish applicants. Its 1932 application form contained three new questions on financial need, religious background, and racial inheritance. In addition, a photograph was required for the first time; it was said that those Jewish students who did not belong at Dartmouth were "of a physical type that is unattractive to the average Dartmouth student."[39] Unlike other schools, such as Columbia and Yale, however, Dartmouth did not use psychological testing to weed out Jewish applicants. The College Board examinations and the Scholastic Aptitude Test were originally tailored to fit the class bias of their designers; as the dean of Columbia told Yale's dean of admissions, "most Jews, especially those of the more objectionable type, have not had the home experiences which enable them to pass these tests as successfully as the average native American boy." But Hopkins was aware that this strategy had proved ineffective in the mid- and late 1920s.[40]

Dean Bill looked carefully—literally—at candidates' applications and photographs and at reports from secondary schools and from alumni who had interviewed applicants. A young man's character now received Dartmouth's close attention: did the applicant possess leadership qualities? did he have good manners? did he engage in "fair play," or was he too competitive? The "good mixer," the upper middle-class WASP, scored high in these criteria, and unwanted Jewish applicants, those considered too "bookish" or ill-mannered to participate fully in the Dartmouth community, could be ferreted out. "Wielding an ax rather than a fine tool," Dean Bill wrote in his *Dartmouth Alumni Magazine* report on the class of 1936, "the Jewish delegation, which was 75 last year, is back to normal." Slightly over 5 percent of the class was Jewish; the actual number of Jewish students accepted, thirty-seven, remained remarkably and assiduously constant each year for at least the rest of the decade.[41]

Not even the Depression could shake the resolve of the Dartmouth administration to continue the quota system. Throughout the winter of 1932–1933, Dean Bill reported to Hopkins that it would be impossible to admit a class of 650 students for the following fall unless the quota were waived. In March, after refusing every Jewish applicant who had had an unfavorable report from an alumni committee and tentatively accepting every other applicant who appeared capable of surviving academically at the college, Dean Bill discovered to his surprise that he had managed to reach the 650 mark only by including no fewer than 90 Jewish boys. He informed Hopkins, "How I am going to throw away 50 or 60 of these boys and still have a class of 650 here in September is more of a problem than I can contemplate." After scribbling in long division on Dean Bill's memo to figure out that such a class would then be over 13 percent Jewish, Hopkins wrote Dean Bill the following day to state in no uncertain terms that he would prefer not to accept a class of 650 if it meant admitting such a high proportion of Jews. He urged Dean Bill to consider accepting a number of "just 'the plain, ordinary bohunks' such as [Dartmouth] used to do" to meet the admissions target figure. The two men also agreed that some offers of financial assistance should be cut sharply in order to discourage the matriculation of even those few Jewish students admitted.[42]

Despite the continued enforcement of a strict quota, and even though the number of Jewish matriculates in each entering class stayed essentially the same, the number of Jewish applicants to Dartmouth continued to rise until at least 1939. Hopkins denied that his school discriminated unfairly against Jewish applicants throughout the decade, and he continued to insist that his policy was appropriate even after World War II. Yet, in an angry reply to a Jewish father who had written him in 1939 to ask if his son had been rejected because of his religion, Hopkins conceded, "It probably is a fact that a boy of Jewish heritage has to have outstanding characteristics in general that are not required of racial stocks a little less aggressive."[43] The facts bear out more than that concession. At the end of the 1930s, when nearly three-quarters of the non-Jewish applicants were accepted by Dartmouth, only about one of ten Jewish applicants was admitted.[44] Dartmouth was still one of America's renowned selective, elite colleges.

As at other institutions, predominantly upper-middle-class WASP alumni influenced the tone and substance of Dartmouth's undergraduate life. They certainly influenced the implementation of the admissions quota policy. Aside from their disdain for socially undesirable Jewish applicants, alumni were concerned that their own children might not be accepted under tighter admissions standards. According to Harvard's former president Charles W. Eliot, Lowell resolved to restrict the number of Jews there in part because of alumni pressure he encountered while on a fund-raising speaking tour in 1922. Yale's board of admissions voted in 1925 that any limitation on enrollment would not exclude any son of a Yale graduate. Dartmouth alumni also exerted this kind of pressure. Hopkins received vigorous support for the quota from alumni class agents at a meeting in March 1932, as he did from the Board of Trustees. He even heard from a friend in the Harvard Corporation who told him he had thought Dartmouth was the only Anglo-Saxon college left in America, and was disappointed and shocked to see so many Jews there when he visited the campus. The number of Dartmouth alumni sons accepted continued to increase throughout the 1930s.[45] Tradition and character counted.

It is important not to underestimate the support that Hopkins' policy received from a group of sympathetic Jewish alumni and students. They agreed that it was best for Jewish students, as well as for the college, that a quota be instituted. In the winter of 1931–1932, Jewish alumni offered to work with Dean Bill to weed out the more undesirable Jewish applicants. The only disagreement came when a Jewish alumnus asked that an exception to the quota be made for all brilliant Jewish students from the public high schools; Dean Bill responded that the alumnus had no idea of how many of those students were already applying, and had to be rejected. An age limitation helped solve the problem. In a March 1933 memorandum, Hopkins reported the satisfaction of Jewish alumni that Dartmouth was admitting only "the better type of Jews rather than . . . the Brooklyn and Flatbush crowd."[46]

The Dartmouth experience confirms the prevalence of what was called the Jewish version of the *Mayflower* social tradition. Most German Jewish leaders in American society held themselves aloof from the Jews of Eastern European extraction who were struggling to become a part of the mainstream of American life. This differentiation between acceptable German Jews and unassimilable Russian and Polish Jews was shared by German Jews and nativists alike. Percy Straus, the only Jewish member of the board of trustees of New York University, agreed publicly to the desirability of a quota on Russian Jewish students there in 1922. During the debate at Harvard, another prominent member of the Straus family told former president Eliot that he viewed the increase in Jewish commuter students as a catastrophe.[47] Well-educated, upper-class Jews generally acquiesced, perhaps with misgivings, in restrictions on less refined applicants of immigrant stock, whether Catholic, Protestant, or Jewish. But the vast majority of these uncouth applicants were Eastern European Jews.

German Jewish alumni were worried about the Russian Jewish students' competitive values and poor manners; the Russian Jews, Hopkins insisted, were "of such aggressive race consciousness on their own part, and so assertive, that they detracted from the community of spirit." Not only were they often too intellectual, but their poverty also embarrassed their wealthier German coreligionists.[48] At schools with a large number of Jewish students, the conflict between German and Russian Jews was reflected, among other ways, in the establishment of separate fraternities. Many German Jewish students were in an awkward position, alienated from the Russian Jews, the "grinds," and yet not always fully accepted by the WASPs. A character in a novel about Harvard was described as a "Manhattan Jew of two generations' money, not clever enough to be taken in by the intellectual Jews, not strong enough to make athletic glory feasible, too fastidious to forgather with the poor Jews to commute from Roxbury and Dorchester, too unconfident of himself to use his wealth to make himself accepted." He sat alone in his room, interrupted only by a Boston aristocrat who wanted to buy his typewriter for less than its value.[49] In the 1930s, their fears roused by the rise of Hitler, German Jewish Americans became even more sensitive to the underlying current of nativism and anti-Semitism in the United States and supported admissions quotas in the hope that they would protect the so-called assimilable Jews and blunt any criticism of their economic and social status. Like non-Jews, German Jews were wary of too much mobility on the part of ambitious Russian Jews and other ethnic Americans.[50]

The WASP-dominated elite college was no longer prepared to heed its own call for the meritocratic selection of its students. Instead, it reinforced the social prejudice and the anti-intellectualism of an anxious American society. In 1922 Hopkins had issued his call for an "aristocracy of brains"; by 1926 he had modified his stand and expressed the hope that Dartmouth's student body would consist of "men who supplement mental capacity with social antennae"; and by 1932, when the quota on Jewish students was instituted, he felt that an applicant's personality was more critical than his potential for scholarship. After all, he conceded, "any college which is going to base its admissions wholly on scholastic standing will find itself with an infinitesimal proportion of anything else than

Jews eventually." The *Yale Daily News* warned that if Yale did not institute "an Ellis Island with immigration laws more prohibitive than those of the United States government," then Yale would become "a brain plant" with too many Jewish students. In *Christians Only: A Study in Prejudice*, Heywood Broun and George Britt blamed anti-Semitism in American colleges on the fact that the Jewish student strove more passionately for a Phi Beta Kappa key than for a football letter.[51] Resentful of Jewish students' academic interests and performance, Hopkins and others resorted to emphasizing the beneficent qualities of collegiate activities that only a few years before they had lambasted as "side shows [which had] swallowed up the circus."

Opposition to this perceived Jewish intellectualism, widespread in the 1920s, became even more bitter in the 1930s, particularly as it was linked to the student radicalism of the Depression era. Open-mindedness toward, if not support for, radical causes exacerbated the tension between Jewish and non-Jewish students. Hopkins, for one, feared that "the unhappiness of soul and the destructive spirit of revolt . . . characteristic of the Jewish race at all times under all conditions" could destroy the spirit of Dartmouth; criticizing the "specious and superficial radicalism" of Jewish students in the 1930s, he insisted that "the jaundiced mulling of that small portion of our undergraduate body which loves to line up against the wailing wall is little indicative of the spirit which education is supposed to produce and is little representative of the traditions of the American college."[52] To Hopkins and others, the American college should train safe leaders; it could do so by preserving social continuity, not by providing a home for social criticism or cultural pluralism.

The private elite liberal arts colleges of the Northeast were not the only institutions that attempted to minimize the number and impact of Jewish students. Historians have pointed out that Jewish students from the urban Northeast migrated to private and public colleges across the country but they were rarely welcomed. Though the University of North Carolina, for example, was long regarded as perhaps the most liberal southern campus, it instituted quotas on the number of out-of-state students and established differential tuition policies on the basis of a student's residence to keep the proportion of Jewish students low enough so that the predominant tone of the campus would not be changed. Administrators and alumni made the same careful distinction between their state's "native" Jews and the "foreigners" from the North as northern alumni and administrators did between German and Russian Jewish applicants.[53] The failure to limit sharply the number of socially undesirable young men, particularly Jews, damaged the reputation of a number of America's finest private urban universities, including Chicago, Columbia, Pennsylvania, and Western Reserve. Chicago representatives stressed that the university wanted "to avoid becoming a city college for day students"; the proportion of Jewish students was limited to the proportion of Jews in the Chicago area, since "the Jews do not want to go to a Semitic school [and] others won't go to one which looks like it tends that way."[54] These schools often sanctioned discriminatory admissions policies and segregated campus activities. Even so, each of these highly respected institutions found that the mere presence of poor, ethnic, and particularly Jewish students drove socially conscious WASPS, their traditional sources of students and support, to "more elite" schools.

Some prestigious colleges continued to use exclusionary admissions quotas as late as the early 1950s. A special Mayor's Committee on Unity in New York City concluded that the situation had worsened during World War II. Women's colleges and less prestigious men's colleges—such as Colgate, which apparently admitted no more than about 5 of its 200 to 300 Jewish applicants—followed the lead of Harvard, Dartmouth, and the others. Hopkins himself still vigorously defended the quota system in a 1945 letter published in a New York City newspaper: the quota still both maintained Dartmouth's tradition of racial tolerance and protected Jews from anti-Semitism. If it did not limit the number of Jewish students, Hopkins argued, Dartmouth would have to exclude them altogether. After all, he concluded little more than two decades after his school had been at the forefront of the intellectual renaissance of the American liberal arts college, "Dartmouth College is a Christian college founded for the Christianization of its students." The *New Republic* called the quota "one of the outstanding blots on American civilization today"; noting the ironic coincidence of Hopkins' public statement and the dropping of the first atomic bomb, it added, "President Hopkins proposes that we handicap ourselves by arbitrarily rejecting certain elements, no matter how high their intellectual capacities, on a basis of religion and (fallaciously assumed) race. We can no longer afford these obsolete myths of racial differentiation." In addition, until after World War II, Jewish scholars were perhaps even more victimized than Jewish students by racial prejudice; in nearly every case, they were prevented from receiving appointments to university faculties even in an age of rising standards and specialization. "Somewhere along the road to democracy," the executive director of the Mayor's Committee wrote in 1946, "American higher education got impeded by a burden of traditions inconsonant with the very ideals ostensibly perpetuated by these traditions—and the schools were left behind."[55] Public pressure mounted to try to force these elite institutions of higher learning to fulfill the promise of American democratic principles, and not merely to meet the interests of their upper-middle-class WASP constituency alone.

Black Students

The treatment of black students provides an even more dramatic example of how WASP educators and their traditional constituencies clung to their racist views. While the number of students at black colleges and universities leaped six times, from 2,132 in 1917 to 13,580 in 1927, the number of black students at predominantly white colleges increased barely at all. Of these schools, Oberlin had the highest proportion of black students during this era—4 percent; but even at this famous school founded by abolitionists, a faculty member admitted, "it [was] impossible . . . to uphold old Oberlin's ideals because of student prejudice." Most white colleges refused to admit black students; the student council at Antioch, a leading progressive school, voted in 1925 that it was "a matter of expediency" not to admit a well-qualified black that year. In 1922, Harvard found itself on the front pages of the nation's newspapers not only because it was slapping a quota on the number of Jewish students admitted, but also because President Lowell refused to permit six black students to live in his school's dormitories. Although the Harvard Overseers and Lowell's own faculty overruled him six months later, Harvard, like most institutions, remained a segregated school until after World War II. The 1,500 blacks who did go to "integrated" colleges in the 1920s and 1930s were essentially pariahs: at some places they were not welcome in the dormitories, in the bathrooms, or at the annual school prom. Black football players were withdrawn from countless games because of "gentlemen's agreements" between schools if an opponent was offended by the prospect of playing against an integrated squad. Blacks were clearly more victimized than even the least desirable white ethnic student.[56]

Prompted by W. E. B. Du Bois's call for the education of the "talented tenth" of America's blacks, middle-class blacks crowded the underfunded black colleges in search of the same professional and status-oriented education that attracted their white peers during the 1920s. E. Franklin Frazier, a 1916 Howard University graduate and a leading sociologist of his day, declared in 1924 that there was "too much inspiration and too little information" in the curricula of black schools. Students at Fisk University went on strike in 1924 to dramatize their desire to establish fraternities and participate in intercollegiate athletics. Not unlike their white upper-middle-class peers, these black students were willing to surrender their identification with less fortunate blacks if the opportunity for a practical education and a middle-class social life became available. Rather than Marcus Garvey, the spokesman for black separatist nationalism, they welcomed "the black rite of Horatio Alger" to their campuses. Most of those few blacks who did go to school had no choice but to attend black colleges, with their vastly inferior facilities and future prospects. By 1940, only 1.3 percent of the total black population had graduated from college, compared with 5.4 percent of white Americans.[57] Between the two world wars, the deck of mobility cards was stacked without question and without regret against young people from lower-class, ethnic, and black backgrounds.

Prejudice and the Pluralistic Vision

In the 1920s and 1930s, American institutions of higher education engaged in egalitarian rhetoric, but their performance was a mockery of American ideals. When an unprecedented opportunity for selection in admissions suggested an intellectual renaissance, character was stressed; when the opportunity presented itself to select a heterogeneous and meritocratic elite, America's best colleges chose openly the sons of native stock, even if they were less qualified. In a courageous speech at Amherst's centennial celebration in 1921, with that exemplar of 1920s political and social conservatism, Amherst graduate Calvin Coolidge, in the audience, President Alexander Meiklejohn spoke out against the perpetuation of what he called an Anglo-Saxon racial aristocracy there and at other prestigious schools and urged Amherst students and alumni to welcome ethnic Americans into the nation's colleges for the sake of the future of society:

> If we are not to have a racial aristocracy, democracy must have a dwelling place within our colleges. . . . We are an Anglo-Saxon college; and so in greater part we must remain. And yet we are American. We may not keep ourselves apart either from persons or from cultures not our own. We dare not shut our gate to our fellow-citizens nor to their influence. . . . And if they do not come, we must go out and bring them in.[58]

The American college should fuse the positive attributes of many cultures, Meiklejohn believed, in order to produce the economic growth and social progress of a distinctive twentieth-century American culture. This meritocratic and pluralistic vision fell mainly on deaf ears.

Critics of the colleges recognized that there was more at stake than the admissions policies of a handful of important schools or the lives of even a few thousand students. If the Jewish student was denied admission to the nation's most renowned colleges, a leading rabbi wrote, he was "defeated in a far more significant battle, namely the right to entrance into the higher spheres of the professions and commerce." Such discrimination was not merely anti-Semitic, then, it was un-American as well. There was something very disquieting, a public high school teacher added, when the colleges' "enthusiasm for democracy is so slight that they demand shelter from its perplexities and from its dangers." The colleges, he asserted, would lose more than they would gain by excluding the "eager, heterogeneous varied amalgam which is America."[59] And so did America's democratic promise. Sadly, between the world wars, by pursuing discriminatory admissions practices, the best American colleges more often than not embodied the worst prejudices and fears of an anxious America.

Notes

1. Harold S. Wechsler, *The Qualified Student* (New York, 1977), and Marcia G. Synnott, *The Half-Opened Door: Discrimination and Admissions at Harvard, Yale, and Princeton* (Westport, Conn., 1979), are the two most complete studies of discrimination in college admissions. See also Harold S. Wechsler, "The Rationale for Restriction: Ethnicity and College Admissions in America, 1910–1980," *American Quarterly* 36 (Winter 1984): 643–667.

2. Burton R. Clark, *The Distinctive College* (Chicago, 1970), p. 100; Crawford, ed., *American College*, p. 184; Fairchild, ed., *Obligation*, p. 22.

3. Quoted in Hofstadter and Hardy, *Development and Scope*, p. 119.

4. James L. McConaughty, "Dartmouth College and the Secondary Schools," *School and Society*, December 18, 1915, p. 891; E. M. Hopkins to Craven Laycock, March 1, 1918, Hopkins Papers, DC; Richardson, *History of Dartmouth*, pp. 674–675, 750.

5. Richardson, *History of Dartmouth*, p. 768; E. G. Bill to Hopkins, April 22, 1927, Hopkins Papers, DC.

6. Widmayer, *Hopkins of Dartmouth*, p. 63; Synnott, *Half-Opened Door*, p. 189; President's Report, 1922–1923, p. xi, UC.

7. Reeves et al., *Liberal Arts College*, p. 361.

8. John Dugdale, "America's Mass Education," *Current History*, April 1930, p. 73; Clark, *Distinctive College*, pp. 186-91; Aydelotte is quoted in Robert L. Kelly, *The Effective College* (New York, 1928), p. 6.

9. Hopkins to Morton C. Tuttle, August 15, 1930, in Hopkins Papers, DC.

10. Laycock to Hopkins, October 1 and December 2, 1919, and Hopkins to Laycock, November 11, 1919, all in Hopkins Papers, DC; Richardson, *History of Dartmouth*, p. 768.

11. E. M. Hopkins, "Aristocracy of Brains," September 21, 1922; Theodore Groves to Hopkins, October 26, 1922, both in Hopkins Papers, DC.

12. Hopkins to Joseph Gollomb, October 5, 1922, Hopkins Papers, DC.

13. E. M. Hopkins, "A Selective Process," 1922, in Hopkins Papers, DC.

14. E. M. Hopkins, "Talk on the Selection of Students," 1925; Bill to Hopkins, February 1927, both in Hopkins Papers, DC.

15. E. M. Hopkins, *This Our Purpose* (Hanover, N. H., 1950), pp. 178–179.

16. Hopkins to Felix Frankfurter, February 26, 1923, Hopkins Papers, DC.

17. E. G. Bill, "The Class of 1926," p. 6, in Hopkins Papers, DC; Hopkins, *This Our Purpose*, p. 272. A national institution was defined as one that enrolled students from at least three-quarters of the states and enrolled less than 30 percent of its students from its home state. The ten were Antioch College, Asbury College of Kentucky, Sweetbriar College, Washington & Lee College, Wellesley College, Georgetown College, Smith College, Yale University, Dartmouth College, and Notre Dame University. See *Dartmouth Alumni Magazine* 24 (October 1931): 29.

18. *The Dartmouth*, December 6, 1921, p. 1; Richardson, *History of Dartmouth*, p. 782.

19. Hopkins to Editor of *Louisville* (Ky.) *Post*, December 29, 1921, Hopkins Papers, DC. The geographical distribution of each entering class in the 1930s was presented in a table in each year's November issue of the *Dartmouth Alumni Magazine*.

20. *DePauw Daily*, May 5, 1922, p. 1; *Bulletin of DePauw University*, 4th ser., 16, no. 7 (September 1929): 51; Annual Report of the Officers, 1939–1940, pp. 51,86, DPU; *Bulletin of DePauw University*, 3d ser., 7, no. 9 (1920): 3.

21. President's Report to the Trustees, June 10, 1938, pp. 910, and November 3, 1939, pp. 2–A, DPU. See also George B. Manhart, *DePauw through the Years* (Greencastle, Ind., 1962), p. 329.

22. W. W. Carson, "The College and the Coming Years," *DePauw Magazine* 8, no. 3 (March 1927): 32; Wechsler, *Qualified Student*, p. 226; David H. Stevens to Harold P. Swift, January 25, 1928, Presidential Papers, 1925–1945, UC.

23. Heywood Broun and George Britt, *Christians Only* (New York, 1931), p. 108; *New York Times*, June 2, 1922, p. 1.

24. Jewish students constituted 42 percent of those accepted under Harvard's "top seventh" plan when it was first adopted; see Synnott, *Half-Opened Door*, pp. xvii, 92, 107, 110, 202. See also Stephen Steinberg, *The Academic Melting Pot* (New York, 1974), pp. 29–30; Lipset and Riesman, *Education and Politics*, pp. 147–148.

25. William T. Ham, "Harvard Student Opinion on the Jewish Question," *Nation* 115 (September 6, 1922): 225–227.

26. In 1922 E. M. Hopkins told one alumnus: "I do not know whether it would be well to tell this to men who are selecting their college, but it is a fact that it is not so hard to get into Dartmouth College under the selective process as it is popularly supposed. Practically any chap who has a record of good character and good scholarship and has diverse interests, though he may not be an exceptionally good scholar, can gain admission" (Hopkins to S. S. Larmon, December 8, 1922, Hopkins Papers, DC).

27. Gavit, *College*, pp. 204–206; Synnott, *Half-Opened Door*, pp. 14, 26–57; Carey McWilliams, *A Mask for Privilege* (Boston, 1948), pp. 28–38, 68.

28. Slosson is cited in Synnott, *Half-Opened Door*, pp. 150–151, 174; Morison, *Three Centuries of Harvard*, p. 417.

29. Synnott, *Half-Opened Door*, pp. 15–16; Reynolds, *Social and Economic Status*, pp. 31–34.

30. Synnott, *Half-Opened Door*, pp. 154–155. At Yale, the classes of 1911–1914 included 5.5 percent Jews; the classes of 1923–26 had 10.2 percent Jews; the class of 1927, 13.3 percent Jews; and each class thereafter, about 10 to 12 percent Jews. See also Wechsler, *Qualified Student*, p. 135.

31. The April 15, 1921, clipping can be found in the Historical Collection files, UM; Bossard and Dewhurst, *University Education for Business*, p. 558. See also Broun and Britt, *Christians Only*, p. 113, and *The Campus* (CCNY), October 28, 1930.

32. Events at Harvard are discussed in Steinberg, *Academic Melting Pot*, pp. 21–31; Lipset and Riesman, *Education and Politics*, pp. 144–146; Broun and Britt, *Christians Only*, pp. 89–90.

33. Starr is quoted in Synnott, *Half-Opened Door*, p. 75; Kallen is in Steinberg, *Academic Melting Pot*, p. 28.

34. Hopkins to Laycock, January 1, 1920; Hopkins to Bill, July 15, 1922; Hopkins to Frankfurter, July 15, 1922; Hopkins to *New York World*, April 30, 1926 (telegram), all in Hopkins Papers, DC.

35. Wechsler, *Revolt on the Campus*, p. 354.

36. Hopkins to Rabbi Harry Levi, November 21, 1922, Hopkins Papers, DC; Broun and Britt, *Christians Only*, pp. 120–121.

37. *Dartmouth Alumni Magazine*, November 1930, p. 22; November 1931, p. 99; and November 1932, p. 20; Hopkins to Bill, October 14, 1931, Hopkins Papers, DC.

38. Hopkins to Bill, December 24, 1931; Hopkins to Judge William N. Cohen, February 1, 1932, both in Hopkins Papers, DC. In a later memorandum to Bill, dated March 7, 1932, Hopkins wrote: "I shrink from and abhor the whole necessity [but] in the last analysis there is no more reason why we should withhold from doing this than from letting the College become exclusively a rich man's college or exclusively a Massachusetts institution" (ibid.).

39. Bill to Hopkins, October 12, 1932, and January 3,1933, Hopkins Papers, DC.

40. The dean of Columbia is quoted in Synnott, *Half-Opened Door*, p. 18, and see pp. 18–19 and 109–110; Reports of the President and Other Officers, 1926–1927, pp. 61–62, CWRU; Sinclair, *Goose-Step*, pp. 357–359; Wechsler, *Qualified Student*, p. 159; and Steinberg, *Academic Melting Pot*, pp. 17–21, for more discussion of the testing issue. Even the Commission of the College Board agreed that the initial Scholastic Aptitude Test in 1926 was biased; see Claude M. Fuess, *The College Board: Its First Fifty Years* (New York, 1950), p. 107.

41. The number of Jewish freshmen remained at 37 or 38 for the rest of the decade; see the November issues of the *Dartmouth Alumni Magazine* each year in the 1930s. See also Herbert A. Wolff to Hopkins, April 14, 1932; Hopkins to Wolff, May 5,1932, Hopkins Papers, DC; *Dartmouth Alumni Magazine*, November 1932, p. 20.

42. Bill to Hopkins, March 24, 1933; Hopkins to Bill, March 25, 1933, Hopkins Papers, DC. The following is an example of a favorable alumni committee report on a Jewish candidate, as reported by Bill to Hopkins, January 19, 1933: "I would very much like to see him come to Dartmouth, and if the well pigmented Phibetes are to be reduced materially and a somewhat more gentlemanly lot from the same ethnic roots introduced, I know of no more suitable than Don Frank, Toledo, Ohio." Hopkins expressed his willingness—owing to widespread support—to do whatever was necessary to keep the proportion of Jewish students down: "I have not yet heard one single reservation expressed in regard to the reduced proportions of Jews in the last class, and I have heard over-whelming satisfaction expressed even among some of the Jewish alumni and boys themselves. I think I would rather take the hazards of what appears to be a group of less scholastic promise, distributed among Anglo-Saxons, Hibernians, Scandinavians, and those from other outlying districts, than to let the Jewish proportion again rise above the admirable proportion that you established in this year's class" (Hopkins to Bill, February 20, 1933, DC).

43. Hopkins to Myer Segal, May 18, 1939, Hopkins Papers, DC.

44. Robert C. Strong to Hopkins, April 4, 1939, Hopkins Papers, DC.

45. Synnott, *Half-Opened Door*, pp. 58, 152; Hopkins to Bill, April 25, April 28, and June 24, 1932, Hopkins Papers, DC. See also the data on the increasing number of alumni children in the November issues of the *Dartmouth Alumni Magazine*.

46. Judge William N. Cohen to Hopkins, January 29, 1932; Bill to Hopkins, April 12, 1932; Hopkins to Bill, March 25, 1933, all in Hopkins Papers, DC.

47. Broun and Britt, *Christians Only*, pp. 50–53, 63–64, 111, 299; Synnott, *Half-Opened Door*, pp. 78–79.

48. Hopkins to Arthur Cohen, March 16, 1932, Hopkins Papers, DC; see also Synnott, *Half-Opened Door*, pp. 142–143.

49. Weller, *Not to Eat*, pp. 250–251, 6, 39, 47, 319.

50. Hopkins expressed this point of view as early as his lengthy March 25, 1933, memorandum to Bill: "The impulses and motivations which have led to Hitlerism and the Jewish pogroms in Germany will presumably not be allowed to get out of hand in other parts of the world but the will is sufficiently near the surface, even in a lot of our communities in America, so that it is about as essential for the Jews themselves as for us that we should not intensify the demand already existent in some quarters that we adopt the Princeton system of no Jews at all" (Hopkins Papers, DC).

51. Hopkins, *This Our Purpose*. p. 179; Hopkins to Bill, April 28,1932, Hopkins Papers, DC; Broun and Britt, *Christians Only*, p. 57; *Yale Daily News* is cited in Synnott, *Half Opened* Door, p. 159.

52. Hopkins to Allan H. MacDonald, May 5, 1936; Hopkins to Bill, August 19, 1932, both in Hopkins Papers, DC.

53. The view that noneastern schools were unusually receptive to Jewish students is intimated in Steinberg, *Academic Melting Pot*, p. 21. My research, however, indicates otherwise. See Robert M. House Papers for a copy of the out-of-state application form; *Tar Heel Topics*, April 1938, p. 2; Kemp Battle to Frank P. Graham, November 17, 1936, Graham Papers, UNC. See also McWilliams, *Mask for Privilege*, p. 133.

54. For the University of Chicago, see "Report on Student Promotion" (1930), box 79, and C. F. Huth to Emery T. Filbey, October 20, 1927, box 76, both in Presidential Papers, 1925–1945, UC; Wechsler, *Qualified Student*, pp. 221–230, 375–377. For a contemporary view of Columbia, see Keppel, *Columbia*, pp. 111, 179–181. For the University of Pennsylvania, see Slosson, *Great American Universities*, pp. 346, 361–363; Samuel Lipshurz, "Four Years of College," *American Mercury*, October 1929, pp. 131–135; Cheyney, *University of Pennsylvania*, p. 475; Broun and Britt, *Christians Only*, pp. 72–76; Baltzell, *Protestant Establishment*, p. 211; Baltzell, *Puritan Boston and Quaker Philadelphia* (New York, 1979), pp. 258–268. For Western Reserve University, see Report of the President and Other Officers, 1922–1923, p. 12, and Survey Commission of the Cleveland Foundation, 1925, pp. 42–43, both in CWRU. See also Steinberg, *Academic Melting Pot*, pp. 9–10, 17; Rudy, *College of the City of New York*, pp. 292–294. Finally, Baltzell has

shown that the proportion of men listed in the 1940 Social Register who had graduated from Harvard, Yale, Princeton, and Stanford after 1920 was about twice as high as among earlier college graduates (*Protestant Establishment*, pp. 209–210).

55. Hopkins' defense of the quota is discussed in "Anti-Semitism at Dartmouth," *New Republic*, August 20, 1945, pp. 208–209; "Sense or Nonsense," Time, August 20, 1945, p. 92; McWilliams, *Mask for Privilege*, pp. 130–140; Dan W. Dodson, "College Quotas and American Democracy," *American Scholar* 15 (Summer 1946): 267–276 (Dodson was executive director of the Mayor's Committee); Lewis S. Feuer, "The Stages in the Social History of Jewish Professors in American Colleges and Universities," *American Jewish History* 71 (June 1982): 432–465. The imposition of an admissions quota at Sarah Lawrence College was the topic of a controversial article in *Commentary*, May 1983, by Louise Blecher Rose, titled "The Secret Life of Sarah Lawrence," and of many letters from readers published in the August 1983 issue.

56. The finest monograph on black colleges and black students in the 1920s is Raymond Wolters, *The New Negro on Campus* (Princeton, 1975), esp. pp. 17,314–329. The Oberlin anecdote can be found in ibid., p. 322. The Antioch story is in Kirkpatrick, *American College*, pp. 183–184. Lipset and Riesman, *Education and Politics*, pp. 142–143, 177–178, cover these years at Harvard. See also Wechsler, *Revolt on the Campus*, pp. 362–373, for a contemporary view.

57. Seventeen of the 69 land-grant schools that received federal funds were black colleges. Of these 17, none had more collegiate-grade than secondary-grade students until the 1930s. In 1930, only three met accreditation standards of library size; by 1940, 15 of the 17 did. In the early 1930s, while blacks constituted nearly one-quarter of the total population of the 17 southern states, black colleges received less than 6 percent of the funds appropriated to those states for the support of the land-grant colleges. See Eddy, *Colleges for Our Land*, pp. 257–266, for more on black land-grant schools. See also Wolters, *New Negro*, pp. 18–30, 82–83, 339–348; Eagan, *Class*, pp. 34–36. Frazier is quoted in Wolters, *New Negro*, pp. 82–83.

58. Alexander Meiklejohn, "What Does the College Hope to Be in the Next Hundred Years?" *Amherst Graduates' Quarterly* 10 (August 1921): 337–338, 344.

59. Louis I. Newman, *A Jewish University in America?* (New York, 1924), esp. pp. 11–13, 15–22; Ralph P. Boas, "Who Should Go to College?" *Atlantic Monthly*, October 1922, pp. 441–448. See also Broun and Britt, *Christians Only*, p. 86; McWilliams, *Mask for Privilege*, pp. 114–115.

TRAINING THE APOSTLES OF LIBERAL CULTURE: BLACK HIGHER EDUCATION, 1900–1935

JAMES D. ANDERSON

From the Reconstruction era through the Great Depression, black higher education in the South existed essentially through a system of private liberal arts colleges. During this period, the federal government gave scant aid to black land-grant schools, and the southern states followed with a few funds for black normal schools and colleges. Between 1870 and 1890, nine federal black land-grant colleges were established in the South, and this number increased to sixteen by 1915. In that same year, there were also seven state-controlled black colleges in the South. These black federal land-grant and state schools, however, were colleges or normal schools in name only. According to the 1917 survey of black higher education conducted by Thomas Jesse Jones, only one of the sixteen black federal land-grant schools in the former slave states taught students at the collegiate level. The Florida Agricultural and Mechanical College enrolled 12 black college students. The seven black state colleges or normal schools had no black students enrolled in collegiate grades. Of the 7,513 students enrolled in the combined twenty-three black land-grant and state schools, 4,061 were classified as elementary level students, 3,400 were considered secondary level students and, as mentioned above, only 12 were actually enrolled in the collegiate curriculum. In 1915, there were 2,474 black students enrolled in collegiate grades in the southern states and the District of Columbia, and only 12 of them attended land-grant and state schools. Hence, as late as World War I, virtually all of the black college students in the southern states were enrolled in privately owned colleges. This structure of black higher education, albeit significantly improved, persisted into the late 1920s. Arthur J. Klein's 1928 survey of black higher education demonstrated that the private black colleges were nearly all the sole promoters of higher education for Afro-American students. For the academic year 1926–1927, these were 13,860 black college students in America, and approximately 75 percent of them were enrolled in private colleges. By the mid-1930s, this situation had changed and black college students in public institutions accounted for 43 percent of the total black college enrollment in the sixteen former slave states and District of Columbia. Until this time, however, private philanthropy largely determined the shape and even the survival of southern black higher education.[1]

In the South the history of black higher education from 1865 to 1935 involves largely a study of the interrelationship between philanthropy and black communities—or at least black leaders—in the development of colleges and professional schools for black youth. Three separate and distinct philanthropic groups formed the power structure in black higher education during this period. At the beginning of the Reconstruction era, northern white benevolent societies and denominational bodies (missionary philanthropy) and black religious organizations (Negro philanthropy) established the beginnings of a system of higher education for black southerners. The third group of philanthropists was large corporate philanthropic foundations and wealthy individuals (industrial philanthropy). They had been involved in the development of black common schools and industrial normal schools since the Reconstruction era, but in 1914 they turned their attention to plans for the systematic development of a few select institutions of black higher education. From the late nineteenth century through the first third of the twentieth century these various groups of philanthropists debated the role of higher education in the overall scheme of black education and the relationship of classical liberal training to larger issues of black political and economic life. At the core of different educational ideologies and reform movements lay the central goal of preparing black leaders or "social guides," as they were sometimes called, for participation in the political economy of the New South. Each philanthropic group, therefore, took as its point of departure a particular view of the relationship of higher education to the "Negro's place" in the New South and shaped its educational policy and practices around that vision. The different philanthropic groups, particularly the missionary and industrial philanthropists, were in sharp disagreement over the ends and means of black education in general. Most visible were their divergent conceptions of the value and purpose of black higher education.

The northern mission societies, which were most prominent in the early crusade to establish institutions of higher education for the ex-slaves, were also largely responsible for sustaining the leading black colleges. The American Missionary Association (AMA) colleges for the freed people included Fisk University, Straight University (now Dillard), Talladega College, and Tougaloo College. The Freedmen's Aid Society of the Methodist Episcopal church founded Bennett College, Clark University, Claflin College, Meharry Medical College, Morgan College, Philander Smith College, Rust College, and Wiley College. The American Baptist Home Mission Society (ABHMS) administered Benedict College, Bishop College, Morehouse College, Shaw University, Spelman Seminary, and Virginia Union University. The Presbyterian Board of Missions for Freedmen maintained Biddle University (now Johnson C. Smith), Knoxville College, and Stillman Seminary. The major nondenominational colleges operated by independent boards of northern missionaries were Atlanta University, Howard University, and Leland University.[2]

The leading Negro philanthropic organization was the African Methodist Episcopal church, which paved the way for black religious denominations to establish and maintain colleges for black students. The leading AME colleges were Allen University, Morris Brown College, and Wilberforce College. Other AME schools were Paul Quinn College, Edward Waters College, Kittrell College, and Shorter College. The college work fostered by the African Methodist Episcopal Zion church was confined to one institution, Livingstone College. The Colored Methodist Episcopal church owned and operated four colleges: Lane, Paine, Texas, and Miles Memorial. The bulk of educational work on the college level promoted by black Baptist denominations was carried on in schools under the control of the American Baptist Home Mission Society. Still, several state conventions of black Baptists undertook to provide higher education for black youth in pressing areas not provided for by the ABHMS. Black colleges founded by the black Baptists included Arkansas Baptist College, Selma University, and Virginia College and Seminary. Most of the colleges financed by black religious organizations were small and inadequately equipped, but so were those administered by white religious organizations. According to Arthur Klein's 1928 survey of black colleges, black church organizations had been able to provide an average annual income for their colleges in excess of that for institutions operated by the northern white denominational boards. Black religious organizations owned so few of the total number of black colleges, however, that less than 15 percent of the total number of black college students were enrolled in institutions sponsored by those organizations. The black colleges supported and controlled by white missionary philanthropists enrolled a sizable majority of black college and professional students.[3]

The missionary philanthropists rallied their colleagues to support classical liberal education for black Americans as a means to achieve racial equality in civil and political life. They assumed that the newly emancipated blacks would move into mainstream national culture, largely free to do and become what they chose, limited only by their own intrinsic worth and effort. It was supposed axiomatically, in other words, that the former slaves would be active participants in the republic on an equal footing with all other citizens. Education, then, according to the more liberal and dominant segments of missionary philanthropists, was intended to prepare a college-bred black leadership to uplift the black masses from the legacy of slavery and the restraints of the postbellum caste system. The AMA's "civilizing mission" demanded permanent institutions of higher education that could educate exceptional black youth to become leaders of their people. Thus, the missionary philanthropists valued the higher education of black leaders over all other forms of educational work. To these philanthropists, black leadership training meant, above all, higher classical liberal education. This view reflected, on one hand, their paternalistic tendencies to make unilateral decisions regarding the educational needs of blacks. On the other hand, such enthusiastic support for black higher education expressed—making due allowance for exceptions—the missionaries' principled liberalism, which was innocent of any inclination to doubt the intellectual potential of black Americans. As the Freedmen's Aid Society put it, "This society (in connection with similar organizations) has demonstrated to the South that the freedmen possess good intellectual abilities and are capable of becoming good scholars. Recognizing the brotherhood of mankind and knowing that intellect does not depend upon the color of the skin nor the curl of the hair, we never doubted the Negro's ability to acquire knowledge, and distinguish himself by scholarly attainments." It was the mission societies' primary duty, argued one philanthropist, "to educate . . . a number of blacks and send them forth to regenerate their own people."[4]

To be sure, missionary philanthropists were not proposing social changes that were revolutionary by national standards, but they were radical within the southern social order. Equality was carefully defined as political and legal equality. They consented to inequality in the economic structure, generally shied away from questions of racial integration, and were probably convinced that blacks' cultural and religious values were inferior to those of middle-class whites. Their liberalism on civil and political questions was matched by their conservatism on cultural, religious, and economic matters. Missionary philanthropists held that slavery had generated pathological religious and cultural practices in the black community. Slavery, not race, kept blacks from acquiring the important moral and social values of thrift, industry, frugality, and sobriety, all of which were necessary to live a sustained Christian life. In turn, these missing morals and values prevented the development of a stable family life among Afro-Americans. Therefore, missionaries argued, it was essential for education to introduce the ex-slaves to the values and rules of modern society. Without education, they concluded, blacks would rapidly degenerate and become a national menace to American civilization. In vital respects, such views are easily identified with the more conservative retrogressionist ideologies of the late nineteenth century. Generally, retrogressionist arguments, as George Fredrickson and Herbert Gutman have shown, supported the advocacy of various forms of external control over blacks, including disfranchisement and increasingly rigorous legal segregation.[5]

For the equalitarian missionaries, black economic and social conditions merely reflected the debasing effects of slavery and had nothing to do with racial characteristics. They saw no reason not to extend equal civil and political rights to black Americans. Moreover, because blacks were mentally capable and entitled to equal rights under the law, education was viewed as a means to liberate the former slaves from the effects of enslavement. In the words of the Freedmen's Aid Society, "Let us atone for our sins, as much as possible, by furnishing schools and the means of improvement for the children, upon whose parents we have inflicted such fearful evils. Let us lend a helping hand in their escape from the degradation into which we have forced them by our complicity with oppressors. Justice, stern justice, demands this at our hands. Let us pay the debt we owe this race before we complain of weariness in the trifling sums we have given for schools and churches." Consequently, the missionary philanthropists conducted a continual criticism of the political disfranchisement, civil inequality, mob violence, and poor educational opportunities that characterized black life in the American South. From this perspective, they supported the training of a black college-bred leadership to protect the masses from "wicked and designing men."[6]

The mission societies started their educational crusade by concentrating upon schools for elementary level training, but by the early 1870s their emphasis had shifted to the establishment and maintenance of higher educational institutions. In 1870, the AMA, for example, had 157 common schools. By 1874, that number had declined to 13. In the meantime, however, the number of AMA colleges, high schools, and normal schools increased from 5 in 1867 to 29 in 1872 with the primary objective of training black youth as teachers. The AMA and other missionary philanthropists believed that common school and eventually secondary education were a state and local responsibility to be shared by private societies only until it could be assumed by state governments. Their colleges, however, were to be permanent. From the outset, the missionaries named their key institutions "colleges" and "universities," although most of their students were scarcely literate and virtually all of them were enrolled at the subcollegiate level. These labels, as Horace Mann Bond stated, "tell us that the founders took emancipation seriously, believing that the Civil War had settled, indeed, the issue of human inequality in the nation; they also tell us that the founders were applying, to the newly freed population, the ancient faith in the efficacy of higher education to elevate a people." The missionary colleges did not, as was often charged, offer their black students collegiate studies before they were ready. For instance, classes opened at the AMA's Talladega College in November 1867. All 140 students were in the elementary grades. Officials did not begin planning college work until 1878, and no such courses were outlined in the catalog until 1890. The first bachelor's degree was not granted until 1895. Generally, the missionaries developed their institutions of higher education at a reasonable and responsible pace.[7]

Consistent with their view of the need for a well-trained black leadership, the missionaries made liberal culture rather than industrial training the chief aim of their curriculum. The courses in the black colleges controlled by missionaries were similar to those in a majority of contemporary liberal arts schools. Freshmen studied Latin, Greek, and mathematics. Sophomores were taught Greek, Latin, French, mathematics, and natural science. Juniors studied the same courses with additional work in German, natural philosophy, history, English, and astronomy. Mental and moral science and political science were added for the seniors. Regular studies were supplemented at stated times with required essays, debates, declamations, and original addresses. Missionary colleges offered at least a smattering of industrial courses—mainly agriculture, building trades, and domestic science—but normally these courses were offered in the secondary or grammar grades. Some college students took manual training courses because these courses were usually connected with student work programs that allowed them to work their way through school. Industrial training, however, had no major role in the missionaries' philosophy and program of training a leadership class to guide the ex-slaves in their social, economic, and political development. In 1896, Henry L. Morehouse became the first to use the words "talented tenth" to describe this philosophy and program of black education. W. E. B. Du Bois would soon make the concept central to his writings on higher education. As Morehouse put it, "In all ages the mighty impulses that have propelled a people onward in their progressive career, have proceeded from a few gifted souls." The "talented tenth" should be "trained to analyze and to generalize" by an education that would produce "thoroughly disciplined minds." From the missionaries' vantage point, this could be accomplished only through a solid grounding in the classical liberal curriculum.[8]

Between 1865 and 1900, there were tensions between the denominational missionary societies and the black leadership, but generally not over the question of curriculum. Black leaders also believed that the "Negro problem" could be solved most quickly through the training of southern black youth—mostly males—in the best traditions of New England culture and by sending such college-bred persons among the masses as scholars, ministers, doctors, lawyers, businessmen, and politicians. Colleges such as Fisk, Atlanta, and Howard were viewed as social settlements that imparted the culture of New England to black boys and girls along with the culture of the Greeks and Romans. During the first third of the twentieth century, blacks would begin to modify this philosophy of education to include the scientific study of black life and culture as Du Bois so successfully inaugurated at Atlanta University in 1900 and as Carter G. Woodson initiated with the founding of the *Journal of Negro History* in 1916. But until this time, black leaders and missionary philanthropists generally agreed that the transplanted New England college in southern soil was the proper way to educate the sons and daughters of ex-slaves. This shared conception of the appropriate education of black leaders was reflected in the curriculum of colleges owned and operated by black religious organizations. Languages and mathematics received greater emphasis than the other courses in these colleges. The required subjects usually included Latin, Greek, English, mathematics, elementary sciences, history, and mental and moral philosophy. The electives included Latin, French, German, chemistry, physics, and biology. Thus, it was agreed that prospective black leaders could not be properly educated for teaching and leadership positions through industrial education. When the time came that white students who planned to become teachers, doctors, lawyers, ministers, and professors "should learn to hoe and plow and lay bricks rather than go to literary and classical schools," wrote President James G. Merrill of Fisk in 1901, "it will be the right policy to shut off all our literary and classical schools for negroes in the South." Consequently, despite sharp tensions between missionaries and black leaders over questions of black participation in the administration and faculty of missionary colleges, the two groups shared a common conception of the appropriate training of black leaders, and this common ground kept relations fairly harmonious. Both groups believed in the "talented tenth" theory.[9]

How did the "talented tenth" theory work out in practice? Between 1865 and 1900, the positive accomplishments of black higher education were impressive. Of all the evaluations that could be cited, the most profound and most eloquent was penned by Du Bois, who praised the early missionary philanthropists as "men radical in their belief in Negro possibility." By 1900, Du Bois continued, the black colleges supported by northern missionary and black religious organizations had "trained in Greek and Latin and mathematics, 2,000 men; and these men trained fully 50,000 others in morals and manners, and they in turn taught the alphabet to nine millions of men." The black colleges were far from perfect, concluded Du Bois, but "above the sneers of critics" stood "one crushing rejoinder: in a single generation they put thirty thousand black teachers in the South" and "wiped out the illiteracy of the majority of the black people of the land."[10]

Yet in 1900, the mission societies and black religious organizations knew that their existing institutions had many defects, that they had nowhere near the amount of capital needed to correct those defects, and that the production of black college and professional students and graduates was minuscule compared to the number needed merely to fill the educational, medical, legal, and ministerial positions in a segregated black community. As illustrated in Table 1, in 1900 there were 3,880 black students in colleges and professional schools and fewer than 400 graduates of college and professional programs. These new graduates were added to the existing pool of about 3,000 other graduates in a total black population of nearly 10 million. A decade later less than one-third of 1 percent of college-age blacks were attending college compared with more than 5 percent among whites. The ratio of black physicians to the total black population was 1 to 3,194 compared to 1 to 553 among whites; for lawyers the black ratio was 1 to 12,315 compared with 1 to 718 among whites; for college professors, 1 to 40,611 among blacks and 1 to 5,301 among whites; and in the teaching profession there was 1 black teacher for every 334 black persons compared with a ratio of 1 to 145 for whites. The small number and percentage of blacks enrolled in colleges and professional schools demonstrated clearly that nowhere near 10 percent of the college-age black population benefitted from higher education. However aggressively missionary and black religious leaders defended the wisdom of providing classical liberal education for the "talented tenth," they admitted to themselves that they had fallen far short of their goal, and they saw no light at the end of the tunnel.[11]

Meanwhile, beginning in the 1880s, industrial philanthropy, which had paralleled the growth of missionary and black religious philanthropy, placed its emphasis almost exclusively on industrial training. Industrial philanthropy began in the postbellum South with the educational reforms of the northern-based Peabody Educational Fund, which was founded in 1867 and was boosted by the establishment of the John F. Slater Fund in 1882. From the outset, the leaders of the industrial philanthropic foundations favored racial inequality in the American South and attached themselves early on to the Hampton Idea. Encouraged by Hampton's success, the trustees of the Slater Fund decided to concentrate their grants on industrial education. After 1890, J. L. M. Curry, former slaveholder and congressman in the antebellum South, assumed the position of field agent for both the Peabody and Slater funds and advanced further the Hampton-Tuskegee program of industrial education. With so much emphasis on Negro industrial training by such wealthy and prominent organizations and individuals, the black colleges came in for a good deal of direct and indirect criticism. Much was said of black sharecroppers who sought to learn Latin and knew nothing of farming, of pianos in cabins, and of college-bred Afro-Americans unable to obtain jobs.[12]

TABLE 1

**Black College and Professional Students and
Graduates in Southern States and the District of Columbia, by Sex, 1900**

State or District of Columbia	Colleges students		Professional students		College and professional students	College graduates		Professional graduates		College and professional graduates
	Male	Female	Male	Female	Total	Male	Female	Male	Female	Total
Alabama	23	10	206	35	274	3	1	6	7	17
Arkansas	49	21	66	0	136	3	1	0	0	4
Delaware	12	8	0	0	20	1	0	0	0	1
District of Columbia	357	125	326	32	840	3	0	47	11	61
Florida	1	0	16	0	17	0	0	0	0	0
Georgia	223	67	183	67	540	6	3	23	1	33
Kentucky	18	18	23	0	59	0	0	3	0	3
Louisiana	23	12	41	12	88	6	3	11	7	27
Maryland	10	1	19	0	30	0	0	5	0	5
Mississippi	46	6	0	0	52	13	2	0	0	25
Missouri	12	1	0	0	13	0	0	0	0	0
North Carolina	348	81	178	13	620	39	4	33	5	81
South Carolina	45	31	65	0	141	6	6	0	0	12
Tennessee	220	77	281	0	578	13	2	59	0	74
Texas	97	91	41	0	229	3	0	1	0	4
Virginia	47	6	108	0	161	9	0	18	0	27
West Virginia	0	0	0	0	0	0	0	0	0	0
Total	1,561	606	1,553	159	3,880	105	22	206	31	364

Source: U.S. Commissioner of Education, *Report, 1899–1900* (Washington, D.C.: U.S. Government Printing Office, 1901), 2: 2506–2507.

The industrial philanthropic foundations established in the early twentieth century followed the same pattern at least until the post–World War I period. The General Education Board, Anna T. Jeanes Foundation, Phelps-Stokes Fund, Carnegie Foundation, Laura Spelman Rockefeller Memorial Fund, and Julius Rosenwald Fund, all established between 1902 and 1917, cooperated in behalf of the Hampton-Tuskegee program of black industrial training. Moveover, industrial philanthropists viewed the missionary program of black higher education as the futile and even dangerous work of misguided romantics. In 1899, Tuskegee trustee William H. Baldwin, Jr., expressed the industrial philanthropists' general disappointment with the missionary colleges. Summarizing the missionary educational work from the Reconstruction era to the end of the nineteenth century, Baldwin commented:

The days of reconstruction were dark for all. Their sting has not yet gone. Then appeared from the North a new army—an army of white teachers, armed with the spelling-book and the Bible; and from their attack there were many casualties on both sides, the southern whites as well as the blacks. For, although the spelling-book and the Bible were necessary for the proper education of the negro race, yet, with a false point of view, the northern white teacher educated the negro to hope that through the books he might, like the white men, learn to live from the fruits of a literary education. How false that theory was, thirty long years of experience has proved. That was not their opportunity. Their opportunity was to be taught the dignity of manual labor and how to perform it. We began at the wrong end. Instead of educating the negro in the lines which were open to him, he was educated out of his natural environment and the opportunities which lay immediately about him.

Convinced that what Afro-Americans needed most to learn was the discipline of manual labor and the boundaries of their "natural environment," Baldwin, like other industrial philanthropists, generally opposed the development of black higher education. "Except in the rarest of instances," Baldwin proclaimed, "I am bitterly opposed to the so-called higher education of Negroes." To be sure, he recognized that racial segregation of necessity required the existence of limited black higher education and professional opportunities to train needed professionals such as doctors, nurses, and social workers. Explicit in Baldwin's statements was the philosophy that higher education ought to direct black boys and girls to places in life that were congruent with the South's racial caste system, as opposed to providing them with the knowledge and experiences that created a wide, if not unlimited, range of social and economic possibilities. Further, the needs of the South's racially segregated society were to determine the scope and purpose of black higher education, not the interests and aspirations of individual students or the collective interests of black communities. As the first chairman of the General Education Board and an influential voice among northern industrial philanthropists, Baldwin helped channel the funds of these philanthropic foundations into black industrial schools and white colleges. Yet, he was not alone in this effort. Industrial philanthropists in general were opposed to black higher education, except in the rarest of instance, and did not change their position until after World War I.[13]

Thus, a convergence of circumstances—the lack of federal and state support for the development of black higher education, the opposition of industrial philanthropy, and the impoverishment of missionary and black religious philanthropy—combined to retard the development of black higher education during the first two decades of the twentieth century. Most important, the key promoters of black higher education, missionary and black religious societies, could not accumulate the large amounts of capital required to place black colleges on solid financial grounds. Though they plodded on persistently, preserving a modest system of black collegiate education, their nineteenth-century momentum declined sharply after 1900. By the turn of the century, the mission societies were virtually bankrupt, and their campaign to develop black higher education was rapidly diminishing in scope and activity. In looking at the future of their black colleges, the missionary philanthropists had many reasons to be downhearted. By any standard, the material and financial status of black higher education was bad. Black colleges were understaffed, meagerly equipped, and poorly financed. The combined efforts of the missionary and black organizations could not raise sufficient funds to meet annual operating expenses, increase teachers' salaries, expand the physical plant, improve libraries, or purchase new scientific and technical equipment. Indeed, almost all of the missionary black colleges lacked sufficient endowments to ensure their survival. Of the one hundred black colleges and normal schools in 1914–1915, two-thirds had no endowment funds; and the remaining third had a combined total of only $8.4 million. Most of this sum belonged to Hampton and Tuskegee Institutes, which had attracted large gifts from industrial philanthropists in support of industrial education. In 1926, the total endowment of ninety-nine black colleges and normal schools had risen to $20.3 million, and more than $14 million of this belonged to Hampton and Tuskegee Institutes; the ninety-seven remaining institutions had a combined total of $6.1 million. As late as 1912, seventy-five black colleges had either a negligible endowment or none at all.[14]

The relative impoverishment of black "colleges" and "universities" made it difficult for them to increase their college-level enrollments, which were already extremely small. In the academic year 1899–1900, only fifty-eight of the ninety-nine black colleges had any collegiate students. The proportion of collegiate and professional students in these ninety-nine institutions was small in relation to their precollegiate enrollment, which amounted to 27,869. These precollegiate students constituted more than nine-tenths of the total number of students enrolled in black colleges. This pattern had not changed significantly by World War I. In 1915, only thirty-three black private institutions were "teaching any subjects of college grade." The lack of good academic elementary and secondary schools for southern black students forced the black colleges to provide training for pupils at lower levels to help meet the educational needs of local black communities. Of the 12,726 students attending these institutions in 1915, 79 percent were in the elementary and secondary grades. Many institutions were endeavoring to maintain college classes for less than 5 percent of their enrollment. Thus, lacking an adequate supply of high schoolers to enter the freshman course, the black colleges enrolled elementary and secondary students mainly as a means to feed their college departments. These enrollment patterns in black colleges differed significantly from the national pattern. In 1900, approximately one-quarter of all students enrolled in American colleges were in precollegiate programs. As late as the 1930s, the black precollegiate enrollment represented about 40 percent of the total enrollment in black institutions of higher learning.[15]

Another important development, which threatened the survival of the missionary colleges and black higher education in general, was the establishment of national and regional accrediting agencies. In the late nineteenth century, regional accrediting agencies such as the Middle States Association of Colleges and Secondary Schools, the Southern Association of Colleges and Secondary Schools, and the New England Association of Colleges and Secondary Schools were formed to give more fixed meanings to the terms "high school," "college," and "university." In the early twentieth century, these regional accrediting agencies were joined by national standardizing organizations such as the College Entrance Examination Board and the Carnegie Foundation for the Advancement of Teaching. Before 1913, accrediting agencies worked mainly to establish closer relations among institutions of higher learning, to standardize college admission requirements, and to improve the academic quality of college and university education. Beginning in 1913, however, the North Central Association of Colleges and Secondary Schools issued the first list of regionally accredited colleges and universities, which signaled the movement to define institutions of higher learning by specific, factual, mechanical, and uniform standards. This movement, financed by foundations like Carnegie, increased the pressures on black colleges to become full-fledged institutions of higher learning.[16]

In one sense, standardization or accrediting was a voluntary action. No institution was surveyed for the purpose of accreditation except upon application. Nevertheless, it was virtually impossible for a college or university to exist as an important institution without the approval of these rating bodies. The nonattainment or removal of accreditation, whether by a regional or national accrediting agency, was a serious detriment to the welfare of an institution. The mere publication of accredited schools had an adverse effect upon institutions that did not appear on the lists. Whether students were graduates of accredited or nonaccredited institutions figured significantly in job opportunities, acceptance to graduate and professional schools, and the acquisition of required state certificates to practice professions from teaching to medicine.[17]

Although no formal accrediting agency took black colleges seriously until 1928, when the Southern Association of Colleges and Secondary Schools decided to rate black institutions separately, there were several evaluations of black higher education from 1900 to 1928. In 1900 and 1910, W. E. B. Du Bois made the first attempts to evaluate and classify the black colleges. In 1900, Du Bois listed thirty-four institutions as "colleges" with a total collegiate enrollment of 726 students. He concluded, however, that these 726 students could have been accommodated by the ten institutions which he rated as first-grade colleges. In 1910, Du Bois made a second and more careful evaluation of black higher education in which he attempted to classify thirty-two black colleges. Institutions like Howard, Fisk, Atlanta, Morehouse, and Virginia Union were classified as "First-Grade Colored Colleges." Lincoln, Talladega, and Wilberforce were examples of the "Second-Grade Colored Colleges," and schools such as Lane, Bishop, and Miles Memorial were included under the label "other colored colleges." Du Bois's evaluation was, on balance, a friendly one designed to strengthen the black college system by concentrating college-level work in about thirty-two of the better black institutions. But in 1917, Thomas Jesse Jones, director of research for the Phelps-Stokes Fund, published a critical attack upon black higher education that questioned the legitimacy of nearly all black institutions of higher learning. From 1914 to 1916, Jones conducted a survey of black higher education for the Federal Bureau of Education that resulted in a two-volume book. In the volume on black colleges, he identified only two institutions as capable of offering college-level work. These were Howard University and Fisk University. In Jones's words, "hardly a colored a college meets the standards set by the Carnegie Foundation and the North Central Association." These rating agencies required, among other things, that accredited colleges maintain at least six departments or professorships with one professor giving full time to each department. The college's annual income had to be sufficient to maintain professors with advanced degrees and to supply adequate library and laboratory facilities. The rating agencies also held that the operation of a preparatory department at the high school level was undesirable, and in no case could it be under the same faculty and discipline as the college. Finally, the North Central Association of Colleges and Secondary Schools recommended that accredited colleges possess an endowment of at least $200,000. At that time, Hampton and Tuskegee were the only black institutions with substantial endowments, and these industrial normal schools did not offer collegiate courses. For Jones, his findings strongly suggested that only two or three black institutions were equipped to become accredited colleges. Hence he recommended that the remaining "colleges" convert to secondary, elementary, and normal schools. Undoubtedly his views were harsh and unwarranted, reflecting significantly his bias toward the Hampton-Tuskegee model of industrial education. Still, Jones's survey, backed by the Federal Bureau of Education and northern industrial philanthropic foundations, underscored a major crisis in black higher education. Black colleges, however segregated, could not exist apart from the power and control of white standardizing agencies. It had become apparent to missionary philanthropists and black educators that their institutions were compelled to seek admission to the society of standardized colleges and on terms defined by all-white regional and national rating agencies. Thus, for black institutions of higher learning, rating by accrediting agencies was a primary goal in the post-World War I era.[18]

The crucial threats to the survival of black higher education could not be met effectively by missionary philanthropists or black organizations, and the black colleges were forced to seek help from industrial philanthropists. As early as 1901, Thomas J. Morgan, then corresponding secretary for the American Baptist Home Mission Society, requested fellow Baptist John D. Rockefeller to "assume the expense of fully equipping" eight of the society's leading colleges. Writing to Wallace Buttrick, Rockefeller's adviser in philanthropic affairs, Morgan suggested several ways to support black colleges: "(a) by endowing each school separately; (b) by placing in the hands of the ABHMS a lump endowment sum; (c) the creation of a fund placed in the hands of trustees especially selected for the purpose; or (d) the donation of Mr. Rockefeller annually of such a sum of money as may be essential to carry on the work." Between 1901 and 1908, the ABHMS's leading members, Morgan, Malcolm MacVicar, Henry L. Morehouse, George Sale, and George Rice Hovey, wrote to Wallace Buttrick pleading for grants to keep their black colleges financially solvent. In January 1908, George Sale made a specific request for funds to improve the ABHMS's Virginia Union University. He listed four important needs: a dormitory that would cost at least $40,000; two residences adjoining the campus for the accommodation of teachers that would cost $3,000 each; increases in the salaries of continuing instructors; and most urgently, to raise the quality of its instructional program by adding faculty positions in pedagogy, history, and social science. For these purposes, Sale asked the General Education Board to make appropriations as follows: $20,000 toward the cost of the dormitory; $3,000 toward the purchase of the two residences for teachers; and $3,000 for faculty salaries. All requests were denied. The missionaries' correspondence with Wallace Buttrick and the General Education Board reveals the growing impoverishment of their societies relative to the financial resources necessary to keep their colleges abreast of modern standards. In 1901, Morgan wrote: "Reflecting upon the future of our educational work it seems to me we have reached an actual crisis that demands very careful consideration. Suppose, for instance, that the Society is obliged to carry on the work as heretofore. What shall we do? It is exceedingly difficult to secure money to keep the schools up to their present degree of efficiency and it is uncertain whether the present interest in the schools can be kept up among the churches and individuals." In Morgan's view, black colleges simply could "not expect too much of the Society in the immediate future with reference to enlargement, improvement, and increased costs." Likewise, George Rice Hovey, president of the ABHMS's Virginia Union University, said to Buttrick: "We, I fear, can never accomplish the work that we ought to do if we rely solely on the missionary society." Hovey's assessment characterized the general state of northern missionary societies for, by the turn of the century, they had become too weak financially to keep their colleges abreast of modern standards. Unfortunately, the missionaries became bankrupt at a time when black colleges depended almost exclusively upon private aid.[19]

Significantly, although some of the missionaries threw themselves upon the mercy of the General Education Board—knowing full well the board's practice of contributing funds only to industrial schools—they were unwilling to compromise their primary mission of sustaining classical liberal colleges for the training of the black "talented tenth." George Sale, though careful not to attack industrial education, informed Buttrick that "the wisest policy for Virginia Union University is to place emphasis on its college and college preparatory work." Thomas J. Morgan recalled that from the beginning the ABHMS's schools had incorporated a smattering of industrial courses. Although he was favorable to the engrafting upon missionary colleges courses in industrial training, Morgan believed it would be a great misfortune to convert them to the trade school mission. In his letters to Buttrick, he constantly reaffirmed the ABHMS's commitment to its traditional philosophy of black education. As he wrote in January 1901,

> The one all-important function of these institutions, the work to which they must give their strength for many years to come is that of raising up a competent leadership; men and women who can think; who are independent and self-reliant; who can persuade and lead their people; they should be men and women who are themselves models and examples of what their people can and ought to become, especially should they be persons capable of teaching and preaching. No modification of their curriculum or their spirit and purpose should be allowed to interfere in any manner with this as the supreme purpose of their existence.

A day later, lest Buttrick forget, Morgan repeated the same philosophy: "I feel very keenly the sense of responsibility for using what little influence I may have in developing our schools to a high grade, so that they may offer to the ambitious and competent young Negroes the best possible opportunities for self-culture, development, training and preparation for life's duties." What worried the industrial philanthropists was the probability that such ambitious and competent young college-bred Negroes would impart their knowledge and culture to secondary and normal school students who would in turn transmit classical liberal education to the common schools, leaving no central role in the basic structure of black education for the Hampton-Tuskegee model of industrial training.[20]

On the surface, it appeared that the two camps might reach a compromise because one group emphasized college training and the other precollegiate education. Booker T. Washington, for example, publicly supported higher education for black elites. Washington stated: "In saying what I do in regard to industrial education, I do not wish to be understood as meaning that the education of the negro should be confined to that kind alone, because we need men and women well educated in other directions; but for the masses, industrial education is the supreme need." No compromise was practical, however, because both the supporters of classical liberal and industrial education looked to the same group to spread their ideas to the masses of black citizens. They both believed that the education of black teachers was most critical to the long-term training and development of the larger black community. If the teachers were to be, as Morgan said, "models and examples of what their people can and ought to be," there was little chance that the two camps could reach a compromise regarding the proper training of black teachers. Their conceptions of what black people could and ought to be in the American South were simply too divergent and conflicting to reach any sound agreement on the training of teachers of black southerners. In the pre–World War I period, therefore, industrial philanthropists could not bring themselves to support the expansion of black higher education because they viewed it as an infringement upon terrain they aspired to occupy and control. In 1914, Buttrick expressed a fundamental difference between the missionaries' and industrialists' view of the appropriate structure of black higher education. "I have long believed that there should be developed in the South two or three strong institutions of higher learning for the Negroes and, further, that something should be done to develop two, or possibly three, of the medical schools for Negroes," wrote Buttrick to John D. Rockefeller, Jr. "The difficulty in any attempt to promote institutions of higher learning," continued Buttrick, "is the fact that most of the Christian denominations have each founded several such schools." Indeed, altogether they had founded more than one hundred such schools. Buttrick wanted to reduce the number of black colleges and professional schools to six and thereby leave the larger field of teacher training to industrial normal and county training schools. The denominations wanted not only to maintain their more than one hundred "colleges" and professional schools but to improve and expand them. The missionaries' plans were diametrically opposed to the industrial philanthropists' conception of the proper scope and function of black higher education.[21]

Although the industrial philanthropists refused to support the missionaries' plans for the development of black higher education, they had no intentions of abandoning black collegiate and professional education. Because industrial philanthropists appropriated virtually no money for black higher education before 1920, they were often perceived as committed exclusively to the idea of Negro industrial education. This was a misperception. In 1907, Buttrick stated well his colleagues' attitude toward black higher education: "I am convinced that all members of the [General Education] Board believe that there should be a sufficient number of thoroughgoing colleges for colored people in the southern states." Further, he was inclined to agree with his fellow trustees "that the matter of collegiate education for the colored people should be taken up as a whole by this Board." In fact, as Buttrick informed George Sale, superintendent of Negro education for the ABHMS, the board had already designated one of its "School Inspectors" to make "a careful study of the whole question" of black higher education. This report, completed in May 1907 by W. T. B. Williams of Hampton Institute, set forth basic reasons to develop a small number of strong black colleges in the South. First, these institutions would produce college-bred leaders to acculturate black Americans into the values and mores of southern society. Second, it was very important that black leaders be trained in the South by institutions "in touch with the conditions to be faced by the young people in later life rather than in the North by institutions . . . out of touch with southern life." Third, and most important, the development of a few strong institutions was viewed as a strategic means to reduce the number of existing black colleges. Williams argued:

> If more strong men and good college courses, and better equipment both in the way of dormitories and apparatus could be added in a few places, and some scholarships or student aid in the college department, could be provided, as is common in the great northern universities, the mass of Negro college students would congregate in these few institutions and their numbers would steadily increase. This would render impossible many of the weaker college courses and would make for strength in organization and economy in the management of college training, for it would minimize duplication.

Williams expressed an interesting and noteworthy effect of standardization which was not so marked and known. If a few outstanding black colleges were established, industrial philanthropists could use these institutions to pressure the remaining ones into discontinuing their collegiate courses because of their inability to keep pace with the rising standards of college-level work. Buttrick regarded Williams's report as "so valuable that in my judgement all the members of the Board ought to read it just as it stands."[22]

Despite an apparent similarity in principle, there was a fundamental difference between Williams's and Du Bois's proposals to reduce the number of black colleges. Du Bois believed that a smaller number of financially solvent black colleges, about thirty-three, was preferable to the larger number (one hundred) of weaker schools in constant danger of folding. Further, starting from the position that the black college enrollment was much too small, he believed that a smaller number of sound institutions could both improve their academic quality and expand their physical capacity to increase the overall number and proportion of black college students. Williams's report, consistent with the philanthropists' interests, recommended the concentration of black higher education in a few institutions, about four or six, as a means to reduce dramatically the opportunities for black students to pursue higher education. This proposal reflected the philanthropists' belief that far too many black students aspired to attend college, a belief that would not change significantly until southern states began requiring all teachers to have bachelor's degrees. In short, Du Bois recommended concentration and efficiency in black higher education to increase opportunities, whereas the Williams report to the General Education Board recommended concentration and efficiency to reduce the scope of black higher education. Though their means were similar, they envisioned very different ends.

Williams's report impressed the board's trustees and spurred them to develop a formal rationale for the support of black higher education. Wallace Buttrick and Abraham Flexner were primarily responsible for formulating the board's policy. In 1910, Flexner became nationally known for writing Carnegie Foundation Bulletin No. 4, a detailed study titled "Medical Education in the United States and Canada." This survey and the policies derived from it foreshadowed the board's approach to black higher education. Flexner inspected 155 medical schools and reported their "appalling deficiencies," which led him to conclude that all but 31 of them should discontinue. After this report appeared, the Council of Medical Education of the American Medical Association intensified its efforts to eliminate "inferior" medical colleges. Much of the financial support for the medical reform movement was provided by the General Education Board. In 1911, the board appropriated $1.5 million to Johns Hopkins Medical School for the purpose of setting standards in American medical education. Flexner was placed in charge of the board's medical reform program. His main goal was to develop a model of medical education that would force weaker institutions to shut down because of their inability to approximate the new standards. Clearly, this policy followed closely the suggestions contained in the Williams report, though there was no direct relation between the two.[23]

In 1914, Flexner became a trustee of the General Education Board and assistant secretary to Wallace Buttrick. In this capacity, he began to apply his medical model to the field of black higher education. Fortunately, Flexner did not have to conduct a study of black higher education comparable to his investigation of American medical education. Both he and Buttrick were acutely aware of the survey of black higher education being conducted by Thomas Jesse Jones for the Federal Bureau of Education. They were in close contact with Jones and realized, early on, that they could rely upon his forthcoming survey as a "Flexner report" of black higher education. Buttrick informed John D. Rockefeller, Jr., in February 1914, that he was in "frequent conference" with Jones, and he assured Rockefeller that Jones's survey would "throw light" on the whole question of black education. Though Jones's survey was not published until 1917, by December 1914, Flexner was already convinced that it would sound the death knell for many black colleges as his medical report had done for the vast majority of American medical schools. Writing to Oswald Garrison Villard about the value of the Jones survey, Flexner proclaimed:

> Dr. Jones is a disinterested and competent outsider whose report will separate the wheat from the chaff. After its appearance the public will have a source of information the accuracy and impartiality of which cannot be discredited. The situation here is not different in principle from that which once existed in reference to medical schools. There was an association of American medical colleges that could enforce no standards just because it meant that the members, in order to do this, would have to legislate against one another. After, however, the Carnegie Foundation Bulletin appeared, an entirely new situation was created. Since then things have been run by the better schools and the others are rapidly disappearing.

Jones, however, was not a disinterested outsider. As a former member of Hampton's faculty, he had helped develop the Hampton-Tuskegee approach to black education and as the director of the Phelps-Stokes Fund played a critical role in adapting the Hampton-Tuskegee philosophy to Britain's African colonies. His two-volume survey of black education, published in 1917, espoused the Hampton-Tuskegee philosophy. Anticipating the impact of the Jones survey, the General Education Board held its first interracial conference on Negro education in November 1915. The invited participants represented both the major black industrial and liberal arts institutions. Presidents Fayette A. McKenzie of Fisk University and John Hope of Morehouse College represented two of the most outstanding black private colleges. Others included Principal R. R. Moton of Tuskegee Institute, Principal H. B. Frissell of Hampton Institute, Abraham Flexner of the General Education Board, Thomas Jesse Jones of the Phelps-Stokes Fund, W. T. B. Williams, field agent for the John F. Slater Fund, and James H. Dillard, president of the Anna T. Jeanes Foundation. This conference brought together the forces that represented the industrial philanthropists' overall approach to the development of black education. On one hand, Frissell, Moton, Williams, Jones, Flexner, and Dillard exemplified the movement to spread industrial education throughout the Afro-American South as the all-pervasive educational curriculum. On the other, McKenzie and Hope symbolized the industrial philanthropists' developing commitment to influence the direction of black higher education.[24]

The discussions at this conference illuminated fundamental flaws in the Hampton-Tuskegee movement that ultimately forced industrial philanthropists to reshape their approach to the promotion of industrial education for the masses of black children. The discussions also pointed to the pressing need for industrial philanthropists to become involved in the development of black colleges and professional schools if they were to be successful in redirecting the scope and function of black higher education. The original Hampton-Tuskegee Idea had run its course by 1915 and was rapidly falling behind modern educational standards. It was based largely on a program of unskilled and semiskilled agricultural and industrial training, the discouraging of college and even high-quality secondary work, and a heavy emphasis on moral development and ideological training. This program had broken down under its own weight. The extreme emphasis on routinized labor, or "learning by doing," produced graduates who found it increasingly difficult to meet state and local academic requirements for teacher certification. In certain respects, southern state and local school authorities wanted Hampton-Tuskegee graduates as teachers because they were advertised as young black men and women who "knew their place" and who were uncontaminated by the pompous ideals of classical liberal education. Yet the South, as the nation, was emphasizing and implementing certain required standards of education for teachers and even demanding college degrees to teach in public high schools and normal schools.

Such changes presented serious challenges to the traditional Hampton-Tuskegee program. Defending this tradition, Hampton principal H. B. Frissell said: "To us at Hampton the doing of the thing is the important thing, and what we might call the academic side is comparatively secondary. We have got to learn to do by doing . . . the academic training is really secondary to the actual doing of the thing." The fundamental flaw in this approach was pointed out to Frissell and the other members of the conference by two of Hampton's prominent graduates, Robert R. Moton and W. T. B. Williams. Moton said: "I am a Hampton man. I went to the summer school [for teachers] two or three summers, and took gymnastics, nothing else, only on the physical side pure and simple." Williams maintained that such a poor academic program caused Hampton graduates to fall down on the job: "Even when they go to teach the elementary subjects they cannot bring any fresh information to the children." The ultimate defeat and embarrassment, as Moton recalled, was that Hampton could not find one of its own graduates sufficiently qualified to fill a teaching position at the Whittier Elementary Lab School located on Hampton's campus. In Moton's words: "We had to go to Howard University to get a man to help Miss Walter. With all our 1,200 graduates, we should have had a man we could have put in that place. We had no one with sufficient academic training for the Whittier school. That is what Miss Walter thought, and she is very loyal to us, so you see that is at our own Hampton school; after twenty-five years or so we ought to have been able to pick out some Hampton man for that work." Moton, who was in the process of leaving the Hampton staff to become principal of Tuskegee Institute, admitted that Tuskegee had similar problems. Its graduates were being kept out of the teaching profession because of poor academic training. Bruce R. Payne, president of the George Peabody College for Teachers, asked the next logical question, "What is the use of the Hampton training if we are not allowed to use it?" Hampton and Tuskegee were thus compelled to meet more modern and higher academic standards or continue producing students with insufficient academic training to pass certification standards required of entry-level teachers.[25]

The conference then shifted to the question of black higher education. H. B. Frissell asked the central question: "What is sound policy in respect to the number, scope, support, and development of higher academic institutions for Negroes?" Only John Hope questioned the relevance of engrafting vocational education on the college curriculum and stated firmly that he stood for the "modern sort of education" for black and white children. Flexner, speaking for the industrial philanthropists, insisted that black collegiate work was "very pretentious, and not calculated to get anywhere." Having tested some black college students in Latin, physics, and literature, he concluded ironically that "if it had been Greek they could not have been more puzzled." Flexner then asked for Hope's reaction to the General Education Board's thoughts about means to reduce the number of existing black colleges: "Dr. Hope, what would be the effect of selecting four or five Negro colleges and building them up, making them good, honest, sincere, effective colleges so far as they went, and letting the others alone, not try to suppress them or consolidate them, but just let them 'sweat,' would that tend in the long run, to stigmatize the inferior institutions that they would give up, the way the poor medical schools are giving up?" Hope admitted that such a policy might pressure weaker colleges to discontinue, but he did not sanction this approach.[26]

Shortly after this conference, the General Education Board formed a Committee on Negro Education to review its overall policy for the development of black education, paying particular attention to the questions of supporting schools for the training of black teachers and the shaping of black higher education. The committee's report was submitted to the board on 27 January 1916. "A crying need in Negro education," the committee reported, "is the development of state supported schools for the training of Negro teachers." The committee realized, however, "that many decades will elapse before Negro education is adequately provided for through taxation." Therefore, the committee recommended that the board use its resources to strengthen private institutions that promised to render "important educational service." "It should perhaps be explained," the committee stated, "that in making this recommendation the Committee has in mind, first, industrial schools, such as those at Fort Valley, Manassas, Calhoun, and St. Helena—schools which, on a much smaller scale, are doing for their own vicinities the valuable work which Hampton and Tuskegee have done for the country at large." Second, the committee had in mind academic institutions. It observed:

> The Negro is determined to have some opportunity for higher education, and certain Negroes have made good use of such opportunities as are open to the race. Of course, there are far too many Negro colleges and universities; and of this large number, not one is well equipped and manned on a sensible, modest scale. Wise cooperation with one or two institutions would be the most effective way of bringing order out of chaos, of distinguishing the real from the imitation.

Finally, the committee recommended support for black medical education. "The Negro physician has, in our judgment, a place in the South." It was recommended that the board support one or two black medical schools. Thus, in time, with these recommendations, the committee formulated principles calling first for support of industrial normal schools, second, for assisting one or two black colleges, and, third, for aiding one or two black medical schools. The board moved immediately to provide financial support for the smaller industrial schools, but a few years passed before any major campaigns were launched to assist black colleges and professional schools.[27]

Meanwhile, a confluence of changing political and social developments in black America heightened the industrial philanthropists' interest in the scope and purpose of black higher education. Most important were the emergence of more militant post-World War I black leaders and the subsequent realization that the Hampton-Tuskegee coalition was rapidly losing political ground to the college-bred "New Negro." During the war, blacks became increasingly intolerant of economic and social injustices, especially in the South, where white terrorist groups increased their brutal attacks upon black civilians while black soldiers fought on the battle front to "make the world safe for democracy." There developed in the South, and to a significant degree in other sections of the nation, a grave interracial crisis. Inflammatory rumors filled the air, suspicion and fear were rife, lynchings multiplied, race riots broke out in several northern and southern cities, and the embers of discontent smoldered in many more. The widespread racial repression in the South, coupled with labor shortages in the North, escalated the migration of blacks to northern urban areas. The white South, fearing the loss of a major proportion of its agricultural laborers, opposed the migration and used both legal and extralegal means to keep blacks from boarding the trains bound northward. Efforts to deprive blacks of even so basic a freedom as the right to migrate only served to exacerbate racial tensions. Robert R. Moton, then the leading black spokesperson for the Hampton-Tuskegee coalition, was awakened to the pervasive undercurrent of social unrest among black civilians when he toured the South in 1918. Indeed, Moton was so alarmed that he felt compelled to alert President Woodrow Wilson to the ever-present danger. In June 1918, Moton wrote a confidential letter to the president:

> There is more genuine restlessness and dissatisfaction on the part of the colored people than I have before known. I have just returned from trips in Alabama, Georgia, North Carolina, and South Carolina. It seems to me something ought to be done pretty definitely to change the attitudes of these millions of black people; and this attitude, anything but satisfactory, not to use a stronger word, is due very largely to recent lynchings and burnings of colored people. The recent lynching in Georgia of six people in connection with a murder, and among them a woman, who it is reported was a prospective mother, has intensified tremendously this attitude of the colored people.

In Moton's view, blacks en masse were on the brink of becoming "indifferent or antagonistic" or "quietly hostile."[28]

After the signing of the Armistice in 1918, race relations in America deteriorated further. The South and the nation were shaken by the "Red Summer" of 1919, when a series of major riots threatened to precipitate widespread race warfare. Significantly, the Hampton-Tuskegee moderates, who traditionally served as mediators in such crises, had little influence among the post-World War I black leaders. By 1920, there was no powerful segment of the black leadership that favored the Hampton-Tuskegee accommodationist approach to race relations and political conflict. In March 1920, the NAACP's *Crisis* published a revealing article by Harry H. Jones, which argued that, except for R. R. Moton, few black leaders accepted the Hampton-Tuskegee philosophy of racial accommodation. The liberal and radical wings of the black intelligentsia were the dominant political voices in the black community, and the philanthropists understood the impact of this influence on their own political program. Philanthropist George Peabody, having read the Jones article, informed Hampton's principal, James Gregg, of its implications: "It is clear to me, with the Negro people having found themselves in a general way, during the war excitement, there is some danger of sharp definitely conscious line of division. We must, I think, give great weight in the present temper of susceptibility to the advertising influence of the *Crisis* and other publications, including James Weldon Johnson and The New York *Age*." The problem, then, from the standpoint of the philanthropists, was how to secure an articulate black conservative wing with sufficient status within the race to counter the influence of such men as Du Bois, Trotter, and Johnson.[29]

Peabody wanted a conservative black leader to "write the most effective reply, which I have in mind, to the article in the March issue of the *Crisis*." But he did not believe that Moton or Fred Moore, the New York *Age's* editor, who sympathized with Moton's accommodationist philosophy, had sufficient status to challenge Johnson and Du Bois. In fact, Peabody could only think of Isaac Fisher as a potentially effective ideologue of the industrial philanthropic view of black educational and social affairs. Interestingly, Fisher, a Tuskegee graduate who took his ideology from Booker T. Washington, was appointed to the Fisk University administration shortly after McKenzie became president. When McKenzie suspended the student-operated *Fisk Herald* in 1917, he established the conservative *Fisk University News* and made Fisher its editor. Following the bitter race riots of 1919, in a period of rising black militancy, Fisher called for the return of the "conservative Negro." He castigated the liberal and radical segments of the existing black leadership, claiming that they had "muzzled" the voice of the conservative Negro and taken away his "mandate to speak for his race." Fisher defined the conservative Negro leader as one who urges his people to lay a foundation in economic efficiency, submits willingly to the laws and customs of the South, and works for better race relations through the guidance of the "best white South." Toward this end, he instituted at Fisk in 1917 a seminar on race relations and later became a member of the southern white-dominated Commission on Inter-racial Co-operation. Yet such conservatives as Fisher and Moton could not really challenge the intellectual leadership the liberals and radicals had achieved in the black community by 1919. Du Bois probably expressed the dominant black view of the conservative wing when he informed the Commission on Inter-racial Co-operation that "Isaac Fisher represents nothing but his own blubbering self. Major Moton is a fine fellow, but weak in the presence of white folks." To Du Bois and many other black leaders who demanded full American rights for blacks, Moton and Fisher were "the sort of Colored men that we call 'White Folks' Niggers.'" Whether they were such accommodationists was less important than their lack of influence among the postwar black leaders and especially among the masses. The black leaders of the postwar period reflected the self-determinist and militant character of the larger Afro-American society. Marcus Garvey and his Universal Negro Improvement Association epitomized some of the core values and fundamental political thoughts of the masses of Afro-Americans. Garvey arrived in the United States from Jamaica in 1916 and by 1922 had several hundred thousand followers. He led the largest mass movement among Afro-American before the civil rights movement of the 1960s. The political thrust toward self-determination and militant demands for equality and racial justice were also manifested in the emergence of a more liberal black press and the literary tenor of the "Harlem Renaissance." Historian V. P. Franklin argues convincingly that the postwar self-determinist political and literary activities reflected values deeply embedded in black culture and tradition.[30]

These developments reaffirmed the industrial philanthropists' growing convictions of the necessity to take hold of black higher education and to influence more directly the training of black leaders. Hence, during the early 1920s they launched two national endowment campaigns that incorporated several of their major goals to shape postsecondary black education and develop the "right type" of black teachers and leaders. One campaign was to raise a million-dollar endowment for Fisk University. This campaign embodied the industrial philanthropists' plan to develop one or two black private colleges to the point that they would set new standards for black higher education and thus stigmatize the "inferior" or less fortunate ones, possibly pressuring them to discontinue or convert to secondary schools. The other endowment campaign aimed to raise at least $5 million to be split equally between Hampton and Tuskegee. This campaign reflected the industrial philanthropists' continuing commitment to the Hampton-Tuskegee Idea. They recognized, however, that Hampton and Tuskegee must meet higher educational standards if the graduates were to continue to obtain teaching jobs and other positions of leadership. Together these campaigns, conducted by the same group of industrial philanthropists, were also intended to develop sympathetic harmony between the liberal arts colleges and the industrial schools.

Not surprisingly, the industrial philanthropists selected Fisk University as the college to be developed into a model institution of black higher education. Fisk was at the financial crossroads that precipitated the transformation of the power structure in black private higher education from missionary to industrial philanthropy. President George A. Gates, who headed Fisk from 1909 to 1913, faced a drying up of the old missionary sources of revenue and, in turn, made a strong plea for southern white friendship and financial support. Booker T. Washington had been appointed to the Board of Trustees in 1909 with the hope that he would bring some of his sources of revenue to Fisk. Fisk was also selected because the industrial philanthropists regarded it as the "capstone" of black private higher education. Wallace Buttrick said: "Perhaps the most promising of the academic institutions for the higher education of the Negro is Fisk University." Outside of Howard University, Fisk had nearly 20 percent of the private black college students enumerated in Thomas Jesse Jones's 1917 survey of black higher education. Fisk enrolled 188 of the 737 college students in private black colleges (this figure excludes the 1,050 college students enrolled in Howard University); Virginia Union University, with 51, had the next largest enrollment. Thus, when the General Education Board held its 1915 conference to discuss the reorganization of black higher education, Fisk University's newly appointed white president, Fayette Avery McKenzie, was invited as a key representative of black higher education. Convinced that McKenzie was sympathetic to the board's policy, the industrial philanthropists selected him and his institution to spearhead their campaign to reshape black higher education.[31]

McKenzie, a professor of sociology at the Ohio State University before coming to Fisk in 1915, came to Nashville as a representative of industrial philanthropy. He dedicated his presidency to modernizing the curriculum (that is, emphasizing physical and social sciences) and raising a sizable endowment for the university. Industrial philanthropists regarded him as a leader who would break with the missionary or egalitarian past and lead Fisk down a path of conciliation and cooperation with conservative northern and southern whites. More than any of his predecessors, McKenzie sought to make Fisk acceptable to the white South and northern industrial philanthropists. He urged Fisk students and graduates to eschew political and social questions and concentrate on interracial cooperation and economic development. In his inaugural address, McKenzie paid homage to Fisk's liberal arts tradition but emphasized the concept of education for "service." In this context he promised that the university would help restore the South to economic prosperity: "It was the function of Fisk to increase the material wealth of the nation. . . . Fisk University claims the right to say that it will be one of the chief factors in achieving larger prosperity for the South. Every dollar spent here in the creation of power may mean a thousand dollars of increase in wealth of the South within a single generation." In line with these goals and priorities, McKenzie favored autocratic rule over his students and faculty, sought personal associations mainly with the teachers and administrators of the white schools in Nashville, and cultivated the goodwill of the city's white business community. These actions pleased the industrial philanthropists, and they regarded McKenzie's reign as a new and wise departure from the missionary tradition.[32]

From the outset, industrial philanthropists reinforced McKenzie's behavior by contributing their economic and political support to his regime. Julius Rosenwald, who visited Fisk at McKenzie's installation, was initially ambivalent about the possibility of transforming the college into an accommodationist institution. In revealing his "mixed feelings" about Fisk students to Abraham Flexner, Rosenwald stated, "There seemed to be an air of superiority among them and a desire to take on the spirit of the white university rather than the spirit which has always impressed me at Tuskegee." Rosenwald and other industrial philanthropists believed that Tuskegee was training black leaders to maintain a separate and subordinate Negro society. They were primarily interested in supporting black institutions committed to this mission. Thus, Flexner assured Rosenwald that McKenzie, with the help of industrial philanthropy, was working to transform Fisk into an institution more acceptable to southern white society. Toward this end, the General Education Board began appropriating in 1916 about $12,000 annually to help Fisk pay its yearly operating expenses. In 1917, the board contributed $50,000 to Fisk for endowment and building purposes and persuaded the Carnegie Foundation to give the same amount. Still, Fisk had no substantial endowment, was deeply in debt, and suffered from a deteriorating physical plant and a poorly paid faculty. According to Hollingsworth Wood, vice-chairman of the Fisk Board of Trustees, "$1,600 has been the maximum salary of a professor at Fisk University. This has meant lack of food in some cases." Fisk authorities knew that the college could not survive without a sizable endowment, and the industrial philanthropists were the only source of sufficient money. These circumstances, however, required compromise. As McKenzie put it, "Intimation has been made to me from several sources that if we continue to behave ourselves, if we are efficient in teaching and administration and continue to hold the right relationship to our environment, we can expect large and highly valuable financial aid in carrying out a great program at Fisk."[33]

The philanthropists' financial assistance to Fisk University was accompanied by a new coalition of Negro accommodationists, southern whites, and northern industrialists who took control of the university's administration from the old alliance of black educators and northern white missionaries. McKenzie and the philanthropists restructured the Fisk Board of Trustees to reflect the new power structure. In October 1915, Thomas Jesse Jones informed Flexner of the changes: "The Board of Trustees is being strengthened. Governor Brumbaugh and two influential colored men have been added in the last few weeks. With Mr. Cravath and Dr. Washington as trustees and the constant attention which I can give to the institution, we have at least a guarantee of fairly sound educational policy." By 1919, Jones was executive secretary of the Fisk Board of Trustees and one of five members on the Executive Committee. In 1920, the philanthropists, acting through the General Education Board, agreed to spearhead a campaign to obtain for Fisk a $1 million endowment, and their strength on the university's Board of Trustees increased. William H. Baldwin, son of the General Education Board's first chairman, was appointed by the board to chair the endowment committee. He was immediately appointed to the Fisk Board of Trustees and became, in 1924, the chairman of the trustees' Executive Committee. Other conservatives were added as the philanthropists moved in a quiet and forceful manner to reorganize the school's administration. In May 1920, Hollingsworth Wood notified the president of the General Education Board that "Dr. Moton of Tuskegee is now on the Board; Miss Ella Sachs, daughter of Samuel Sachs, and a close friend of the Rosenwalds, is an eager new member; and Mrs. Beverly B. Mumford of Richmond, Virginia adds an excellent influence from the southern viewpoint." The traditional missionary equalitarians were gradually pushed off the Fisk Board of Trustees. They were replaced mainly by northern industrialists, southern whites, and a few Negro accommodationists who were virtually handpicked by industrial philanthropists. The philanthropists were raising an endowment for a new Fisk that was largely controlled by their agents and supporters.[34]

These philanthropists no doubt hoped that their economic and firm political hold on Fisk would squelch the school's equalitarian tradition and open the way for the development of a more conservative black leadership class. In 1923, the General Education Board generated a memorandum on the Fisk endowment campaign which emphasized the urgent need to train "the right type of colored leaders" who would help make the Negro "a capable workman and a good citizen." The industrial philanthropists, as the memorandum stated, aimed primarily at "helping the Negro to the sane and responsible leadership that the South wants him to have." To the white South, "sane" Negro leaders were those who encouraged blacks to "stay in their place." The philanthropists recognized that they were facing a new situation between the races. "How the Negro is going to get on in this country and what his relations are to be with the whites, are no longer problems of a single section; they are national," the memorandum stated. To the philanthropists, this new situation, in the context of growing racial friction, increased the necessity of training "the right kind" of black leaders. The report maintained:

> Due to various experiences during and since the World War, there is a growing disposition among the Negroes to suspect all white men and their motives and therefore to break all contacts with them and go it alone. Because such a movement by ten percent of the population is obviously futile, is no reason to overlook the fact that ten percent is a large enough proportion to cause considerable harm if permitted to go off at a tangent from the general interest. This very real menace to the public welfare makes the strengthening of school facilities for Negroes a matter of national significance.

Both McKenzie and the industrial philanthropists shared the belief that the new type of black college should help curb and even extinguish the self-determinist and equalitarian character of the emergent black leadership.[35]

Toward this end, McKenzie, as Raymond Wolters has shown, set out to convince the industrial philanthropists that "Fisk students were not radical egalitarians but young men and women who had learned to make peace with the reality of the caste system." Thus, McKenzie disbanded the student government association, forbade student dissent, and suspended the *Fisk Herald*, the oldest student publication among black colleges. He would not allow a campus chapter of the NAACP and instructed the librarian to excise radical articles in the NAACP literature. Student discipline was rigorously enforced, special "Jim Crow" entertainments were arranged for the white benefactors of the university, and Paul D. Cravath, president of the Fisk Board of Trustees, endorsed complete racial separation as "the only solution to the Negro problem." McKenzie would not allow certain forms of social intercourse such as dancing and holding hands, and he justified his code of discipline on the grounds that black students were particularly sensuous beings who needed to be subjected to firm control. In short, McKenzie attempted to repress student initiative, undermine their equalitarian spirit, and control their thinking on race relations so as to produce a class of black intellectuals that would uncomplainingly accept the southern racial hierarchy. Historian Lester C. Lamon concluded that "McKenzie's autocratic policies took away means of self-expression, created second-class citizens, and relied upon fear instead of reason to bring societal control." Although discipline and repression of student initiative and self-expression were strict before McKenzie became president, they became harsher and more racist during his administration.[36]

By June 1924, the industrial philanthropists had successfully completed their campaign for Fisk's million-dollar endowment. The following pledges were then in hand: $500,000 from the General Education Board; $250,000 from the Carnegie Foundation; and $250,000 secured elsewhere, including sizable pledges from such philanthropists as Julius Rosenwald and George Peabody. This endowment fund was not, however, collectible until Fisk's accumulated deficits were met. The outstanding indebtedness at the time was $70,000. To solve that problem, a special campaign to raise $50,000 led by Nashville's white citizens was successfully completed by June 1924. This campaign was organized by Nashville's Commercial Club, which included Tennessee's governor, Nashville's mayor, and many of the city's leading businessmen. From 1915 to 1924, Fisk had become so conservative that the Commercial Club was inspired to call Fisk the "key" to interracial cooperation and understanding in the South. "He came into our midst unknown," the Commercial Club said of McKenzie, "and by his wise administration and official methods won our hearty cooperation." With such backing, plans were perfected for raising the money to eliminate the school's deficits and thereby secure the endowment for Fisk's financial rehabilitation.[37]

At this juncture, however, McKenzie's conservative administration was attacked by black students, intellectuals, and community organizations. Led by W. E. B. Du Bois, the Fisk alumni attacked McKenzie's Draconian code of student discipline and expressed outrage at the humiliation and insults perpetrated on the student body. Du Bois openly challenged the school's administration in 1924, when he was invited to give the commencement address. He especially criticized the administration's campaign to suppress Fisk's equalitarian tradition so as to obtain economic support from industrial philanthropy. The students, long dissatisfied with McKenzie's regime, were reinforced by alumni support and escalated their protest against the school's repressive policies. In February 1925, the *New York Times* reported that Fisk's alumni were organizing in "all sections of the United States to agitate for the removal of Dr. Fayette McKenzie, the white president of the University." The following month the students went on strike against McKenzie's administration, and they were backed in their protest by the alumni, the black press, and the local black community. On the day following the student rebellion, more than twenty-five hundred black citizens of Nashville convened and formally declared that McKenzie's "usefulness as president of Fisk is at an end." This protest forced McKenzie to resign in April 1925. Fisk University trustee Thomas Jesse Jones attributed McKenzie's problems to black self-determination, the very force that he and other industrial philanthropists were trying to counter. As he wrote to fellow trustee, Paul Cravath,

> The present unfortunate and unfair criticism of Dr. McKenzie's policies is partly the result of misunderstandings, but largely the result of an effort on the part of a few designing Negroes to obtain control of Fisk University for a policy of Negro self-determination, so extreme in extent as to undermine all cooperation between whites and Negroes. Such an extreme attitude has appeared within the last few years in many parts of the world. While it is natural and in its more reasonable forms desirable, self-determination, as advocated by those who oppose Dr. McKenzie, is dangerous not only to the well-being of Fisk University, but to sound race-relationships throughout America.[38]

Du Bois praised the students' victory over McKenzie and hailed them as a new breed of black intellectuals sorely needed to challenge the power of industrial philanthropy: "God speed the breed! Suppose we do lose Fisk; suppose we lose every cent that the entrenched millionaires have set aside to buy our freedom and stifle our complaints. They have the power, they have the wealth, but glory to God we still own our own souls and led by young men like these at Fisk, let us neither flinch nor falter, but fight, and fight and fight again." But many black intellectuals, especially those responsible for black colleges, could not easily afford to attack the policies of industrial philanthropy. After the Fisk rebellion, the General Education Board withheld the endowment pledges on the grounds that they were not collectible until Fisk eliminated all its deficits. The Nashville Commercial Club, which was expected to raise the capital to cover the deficits, withdrew from the campaign following McKenzie's resignation. Convinced that McKenzie's successor, Thomas Elsa Jones, did "not conceive himself to be a leader or an emancipator of the Negro group," the philanthropists eventually granted Fisk the endowment. Fisk, however, was still dependent on industrial philanthropy throughout the period and into the present.[39]

Although northern philanthropists sought to move Fisk and other black colleges closer to the philosophy and practice of racial accommodation throughout the first third of the twentieth century, they seemed comfortable only with Hampton, Tuskegee, and similar industrial normal schools. This attitude was revealed through their parallel involvement in the Hampton-Tuskegee endowment campaign. To be sure, they recognized that educational standards at these institutions had to change to keep abreast of minimum requirements for teacher certification, but they saw no need to modify the basic social philosophy of black accommodation to white authority. The campaign for $5 million was organized during the summer of 1924 by Clarence H. Kelsey, chairman of the Title Guarantee and Trust Company and vice-chairman of the Hampton Board of Trustees. Anson Phelps-Stokes was appointed from the Tuskegee Board of Trustees as chairman of the Special Gifts Committee. The John Price Jones Corporation was engaged to prepare the publicity for the campaign and to help with the organizational work. As a result of these efforts, the following subscriptions had been secured by the end of the first year: George Eastman, $4.3 million; General Education Board, $1 million; John D. Rockefeller, Jr., $1 million; Arthur Curtis James, $300,000; Edward H. Harkness, $250,000; Julius Rosenwald, $100,000. Amounts equal to or greater than $25,000 were pledged by the Phelps-Stokes Fund (the largest contribution it ever made to any single object), Slater Fund, George Foster Peabody, William M. Scott, William G. Wilcox, and the Madame C. J. Walker Manufacturing Company. George Eastman, largely as a result of this campaign, became deeply impressed with the importance of the Hampton-Tuskegee Idea to the nation and on 8 December 1924 announced that in the distribution of the major portion of his estate, Hampton and Tuskegee would each obtain securities valued at $2 million. This pledge was conditional on his requirement that the Hampton-Tuskegee endowment campaign reach its $5 million goal by 31 December 1925. Eastman also contributed another $300,000 toward the goal of $5 million. Anson Phelps-Stokes believed that Eastman's gift resulted from a visit to his home by Julius Rosenwald, Clarence Kelsey, and Robert Moton in November 1924.[40]

The "Special Memorandum" to promote the Hampton-Tuskegee campaign was prepared for Kelsey by the Jones Corporation, and it detailed the reasons for the endowment campaign and the continuing importance of the Hampton-Tuskegee Idea. Part Two of the memorandum, "Our Most Grave and Perplexing Domestic Problem," was introduced with the following quotations:

> "The Color line is the problem of the present century."
> "The relation of Whites and Negroes in the United States is our most grave and perplexing domestic problem."
> "The Negro problem is one of the greatest questions that has ever presented itself to the American people."

These quotations were attributed to J. W. Gregory, the Chicago Commission on Race Relations, and William Howard Taft, respectively. This problem, according to the memorandum, had been exacerbated because the "rise of world-wide race consciousness and ideal of self-determination has had special effect on the American Negro." Consequently, "a wide variety of leadership has sprung up to give them expression." This development was viewed largely as a crisis of leadership:

> Some of this leadership, as is natural under the circumstances, is demogogical or otherwise self seeking. Some of it is patently visionary. But there are thousands of earnest, intelligent Negroes today who are fired with a belief in the possibilities within their race and with the ambition to help realize those possibilities sanely and constructively. This whole movement, in all its various forms, has taken deep root. It is not confined to the big city groups but permeates every part of the country. A remarkable Negro periodical and daily press has grown up within the past few years devoted, almost wholly, to advancing, directly or indirectly, these ideas.

The memorandum pointed out that it was "impossible, even if it were desirable, to stop this movement." The important thing was to assure its development in "a sound and constructive form."[41]

The industrial philanthropists believed that the right black leaders could direct the masses along "constructive" lines. "As the Negro progresses," the report stated, "the ideals of at least the sound thinking majority will be most influenced by those of advanced education and experience." Herein were the reasons to raise Hampton and Tuskegee to a level of "advanced education" and to influence the attitudes of emergent black leaders, whether they were trained in advanced industrial schools or academic colleges. From the philanthropists' standpoint, the solution to the race problem was self-evident. First, "The Negro problem has been happily and permanently solved by the application of the Hampton-Tuskegee method in many individual communities." Second, "The Hampton-Tuskegee Idea, therefore, of solving the race problem in America is to *multiply these local solutions and the national problem solves itself.*" Third, "The proposed method for doing this is to *multiply the number of Hampton and Tuskegee men and women adequately trained for present day leadership.*" Although Armstrong had died in 1893, Booker T. Washington in 1915, and H. B. Frissell in 1917, the industrial philanthropists remained steadfastly committed to the Hampton-Tuskegee methods as the fundamental solution to the race problem. Anson Phelps-Stokes said in a letter to John D. Rockefeller, Jr.: "Personally, I am increasingly convinced that Hampton and Tuskegee provide the most important contribution yet found towards the solution of the race problem in this country, and towards the development of the Negro people so as to make them fitted for the highest citizenship." Throughout the endowment campaign, the industrial philanthropists reminded themselves and the larger society that the Hampton methods produced Booker T. Washington, "the outstanding Negro leader of the past," and that every president of the United States, from Grant to Calvin Coolidge, had supported the Hampton-Tuskegee Idea. President Garfield was a trustee of Tuskegee, and William Howard Taft became a trustee of Hampton while president of the United States and was, in 1925, president of Hampton's Board of Trustees. For the industrial philanthropists, the Hampton-Tuskegee Idea had become a matter of tried and true methods, of tradition, and had congealed into a permanent policy.[42]

The basic social philosophy underlying the Hampton-Tuskegee program for the training of black leaders remained unchanged. It was still a program of interracial harmony predicated on a social foundation of political disfranchisement, civil inequality, racial segregation, and the training of black youth for certain racially prescribed economic positions. The central question was whether this social and educational philosophy could remain intact as Hampton and Tuskegee were transformed from normal schools to secondary schools with certain forms of collegiate work. Nearly one-half, or $2 million, of the Hampton endowment was earmarked for "teacher training of collegiate grade now required by southern States." Attached to the endowment campaign's "Special Memorandum" were regulations governing certificates for teachers in North Carolina and Alabama. In 1925, North Carolina required for a high school teacher's certificate, graduation from a "standard A Grade college in academic or scientific courses, embracing 120 semester hours," 18 of which had to be in professional educational subjects. Alabama required three years of standard college work approved by the State Board of Education, including nine hours of professional study. Such requirements forced Hampton and Tuskegee into the world of collegiate education. They started by offering the Bachelor of Science in agriculture and teaching, trying hard to hold closely to their traditional emphasis, but were soon compelled to expand the collegiate departments to cover a range of liberal arts fields.[43]

This very yielding to the new educational standards changed the social composition of the institution's student population, and the question of whether the Armstrong-Washington philosophy could prevail at the collegiate level was answered in part by the Hampton student strike of 1927. Traditionally, the Hampton-Tuskegee Idea rested on a denigration of academic subjects, which was easier to maintain when the institutions were composed of half-grown elementary students, regimented to strict military discipline, and overworked in simple agricultural and industrial tasks. But the new collegiate programs attracted different students. Although the total number of students enrolled at Hampton remained at about a thousand throughout the 1920s, the number of students in the college division grew steadily, from 21 in 1920 to 417 in 1927. By 1929, no new high school students were admitted. The new college-level students repeatedly insisted that academic standards be raised. In 1924, Hampton's Student Council charged that the director of the trade school had so little formal education and used such poor English that he was not qualified to teach. Similar accusations were lodged in 1925 against several teachers in the school of agriculture. There were additional complaints that white teachers were less concerned with academic subjects than with teaching manners and morals. Indeed, five of Hampton's white teachers participated in a Ku Klux Klan parade in support of a law requiring racial segregation on Hampton's campus, and other white instructors established a segregated club and openly opposed the employment of qualified black teachers. In response to Hampton's low academic standards and repressive racial policies, the students went on strike in October 1927. They demanded an end to racism and paternalism and insisted that "our educational system be so revised that we shall no longer be subjected to instructions from teachers whose apparent education is below that of the average student." The students' demands, breaking with tradition, called essentially for an abandonment of the Hampton-Tuskegee Idea. Such matters were not easily settled on a campus that had devoted more than half a century to a philosophy of racial subordination and industrial training. Student unrest and contention between the faculty and administration persisted into the spring of 1929. Confronted with this disorder, James E. Gregg, successor to H. B. Frissell, was forced to resign his office. The Hampton Board of Trustees quickly concurred. Thus, both the principal of Hampton and the president of Fisk University, men who presided over the institutions' first significant endowments, were forced to resign their office because the students rejected the very policies and social philosophy that underlay the endowment campaigns.[44]

The Hampton students put the final nail in the coffin of the old Hampton-Tuskegee Idea. As Robert A. Coles, one of the leaders of the student revolt, said, Hampton's new students possessed "a Du Bois ambition" that would not mix with "a Booker Washington education." Such attitudes reflected an increasing demand for collegiate education among black youth of the 1920s. Despite the industrial philanthropists' efforts to reduce the number of black colleges (through their scheme of making one or two vastly superior to the others) and their attempt to transform industrial training into a collegiate program, black youth and their parents pushed for and achieved more and better higher educational opportunities. The enrollment of college students in public colleges in the sixteen former slave states and the District of Columbia grew from 12 in 1915 to 12,631 in 1935, and, as illustrated in Table 2, the enrollment in private colleges in 1935 was 16,638. In 1915, there were only 2,474 students enrolled in the black private colleges. These accomplishments and the beliefs and behavior that brought them about specifically rejected the Hampton-Tuskegee Idea and its philosophy of manual training and racial subordination. The industrial philanthropists, as evidenced by their contributions of time, money, and effort during the Hampton-Tuskegee endowment campaign, did not voluntarily abandon the Hampton-Tuskegee Idea. Rather, the philosophy was decisively rejected by the black students and leaders of the 1920s, and the key institutions were compelled by changing educational requirements and student demands to become standard institutions of higher learning. Thus was ushered in a new and different era in black higher education, and all concerned parties, blacks, missionaries, industrial philanthropists, and southern whites, had to adjust to this new departure. The battles for control and influence over the training of black leaders did not cease, but they were fought on a different terrain.[45]

TABLE 2
Black College and Professional Students in Private and Public
Colleges in Southern States and the District of Columbia, by Sex, 1935

State or District of Columbia	Private college students		Public college students		Public and private college students
	Male	Female	Male	Female	Total
Alabama	793	676	325	554	2,348
Arkansas	138	203	173	172	686
Delaware	0	0	33	50	83
District of Columbia	1,069	894	148	587	2,698
Florida	132	141	267	241	782
Georgia	907	1,078	136	198	2,319
Kentucky	0	0	288	510	798
Louisiana	575	569	273	270	1,687
Maryland	163	298	66	188	715
Mississippi	184	297	127	79	687
Missouri	0	0	215	340	559
North Carolina	652	830	782	1,722	3,986
South Carolina	542	770	254	247	1,813
Tennessee	881	945	460	793	3,079
Texas	740	1,097	453	700	2,990
Virginia	960	1,103	495	523	3,081
West Virginia	0	0	464	494	958
Total	7,736	8,902	4,963	7,668	29,269

Source: Blose and Caliver, *Statistics of the Education of Negroes*, pp. 37–40.

The progress of black higher education during the 1930s was mixed. The northern missionaries and black educators who presided over the black colleges entered the 1920s extremely worried about the financial and material conditions of black colleges. Then, during the 1930s, northern industrial philanthropists presented black college educators with good opportunities for improving the material conditions of black higher education. To be sure, financial solvency was critical, but it was only a means to the more important and long-standing mission of black higher education. For the northern missionaries and black educators, the great mission of black colleges was that of training a competent leadership, men and women who could think, who were independent and self-reliant, and who could persuade and lead the black masses. This mission was contradicted by the wonderful material improvements in endowments, physical plants, and faculty salaries because the industrial philanthropists who provided these gifts pressed continuously for the spontaneous loyalty of the college-bred Negro. As black colleges became increasingly dependent on donations from northern industrial philanthropists, the missionaries and black educators found it extremely difficult, if not impossible, to accept philanthropic gifts and assert simultaneously that many of the political and economic aims of the philanthropists were at variance with the fundamental interests of the black masses. From 1915 to 1960, the General Education Board alone expended for black higher education (exclusive of grants for medical education) over $41 million. The board disbursed over $5 million to Atlanta University; $5 million to Fisk University; $3.8 million to Tuskegee Institute; $3.5 million to Spelman College; $2.15 million to Dillard University; $1.9 million to Morehouse College; and $1.1 million to Clark College. The board symbolized the central place that northern philanthropists had come to occupy in the development of black higher education in the South. Given the industrial philanthropists' demand for a conservative black leadership that would cooperate with instead of challenge the Jim Crow system, a certain amount of compromise, indifference, apathy, and even fear developed among black college educators and students.[46]

Observers of the black colleges during the 1930s were dismayed at the apparent shift in consciousness among black college educators and students which paralleled the colleges' increasing dependence on the purse strings of northern industrial philanthropy. As early as 1930, W. E. B. Du Bois, in a commencement address at Howard University, chastised the black college male students for their nihilistic behavior:

> Our college man today is, on the average, a man untouched by real culture. He deliberately surrenders to selfish and even silly ideals, swarming into semiprofessional athletics and Greek letter societies, and affecting to despise scholarship and the hard grind of study and research. The greatest meetings of the Negro college year like those of the white college year have become vulgar exhibitions of liquor, extravagance, and fur coats. We have in our colleges a growing mass of stupidity and indifference.

Du Bois and other prominent black intellectuals worried that black college students and educators had forsaken their obligation to become socially responsible leaders of their people. Historian and educator Carter G. Woodson argued in 1933 that the "mis-education" of black students had resulted in the creation of a highly educated bourgeois that was estranged from ordinary black people, "the very people upon whom they must eventually count for carrying out a program of progress." In 1934, writer and poet Langston Hughes denounced the "cowards from the colleges," the "meek professors and well-paid presidents," who submitted willingly to racism and the general subordination of black people. The following year, George Streator, business manager of the *Crisis*, proclaimed that black college faculty were much too conservative, "years behind the New Deal." "Further," said Streator, "Negro college students are not radical; they are reactionary." Such critics showed little sympathy for the black college educators' inability openly to protest against the system of racial caste and still expect to be well received in philanthropic circles.[47]

Some educators in black colleges, however, were also disturbed by the growing apathy and social irresponsibility of black college students. In 1937, Lafayette Harris, president of Philander Smith College in Little Rock, Arkansas, castigated black students for their general apathy and particular estrangement from common black folk: "Probably nothing gives one more concern than the frequently apparent fatalistic and nonchalant attitude of many a Negro college student and educated Negro.

With him, very little seems to matter except meals, sleep, and folly. Community problems are never even recognized as existing. They know nothing of their less fortunate fellowmen and care less." The following year Randolph Edmonds, a professor at Dillard University, blamed black college educators for the attitudes of black students toward the masses. "The Negro youth is being educated to regard the race with contempt, not only by white teachers in mixed schools, but by Negro instructors in Negro colleges." The central contention of much of this criticism was that the college-bred Negroes, or "talented tenth," were not being educated to think and act in behalf of the interests of black people. Rather, they were internalizing a social ideology nearly indistinguishable from that of the philanthropists who helped finance black higher education. As one black student assessed the social consciousness of black educated leaders in 1938, "The American race problem has brought us many anomalies. But it may be some time before it equals the Negro leader, supported by workingmen's dollars, leading a working population, and yet enunciating a philosophy which would do credit to the original economic royalist or the most eloquent spokesman for America's 'sixty sinister families.'" In vital respects, the fate of black higher education during the 1930s was closely related to the attitudes and interests of the nation's wealthiest families. Only black college educators could appreciate fully the difficulty of depending on this wealth while being urged to articulate a philosophy that challenged the philanthropists' conceptions of proper race and social relations.[48]

Undoubtedly, the verbal attacks upon black college educators and students during the 1930s were engendered in part by the growing liberalism of the era. The social critics may have been excessively harsh and even off the mark in their judgments of the social consciousness of black college educators and students. Black college educators had to steer between two equally critical courses. On one hand, they were dependent on the benevolence of industrial philanthropists for the very survival of the private black colleges that formed the backbone of black higher education. On the other hand, it was their mission to represent the struggles and aspirations of black people and to articulate the very source of the masses' discomfort and oppression. One course propelled them into conflict with the other because the industrial philanthropists supported black subordination. Black college educators had no noble path out of this contradiction and sought to contain it by placating northern industrial philanthropists while training black intellectuals who would help lead black people toward greater freedom and justice. Indeed, it was a painful and difficult course to steer that frequently brought down upon black college educators the wrath of both sides. This was a moment in the history of black higher education when presidents and faculty could do little more than succeed in keeping their institutions together while maintaining themselves and their students with as great a sense of dignity as was possible. When their students helped launch the civil rights movement of the 1960s, the hard work of these educators seemed far more heroic in the hour of harvest than it did during the years of cultivation.

Notes

1. Logan, "Evolution of Private Colleges for Negroes," p. 216; Jones, *Negro Education*, 2: 310; Klein, *Survey of Negro Colleges and Universities*; Holmes, *Evolution of the Negro College*, p. 201.
2. Holmes, *Evolution of the Negro College*, pp. 163–177.
3. Ibid., p. 216; Klein, *Survey of Negro Colleges and Universities*, pp. 5–33.
4. Richardson, *Christian Reconstruction*, p. 173; missionary philanthropists quoted from Holmes, *Evolution of the Negro College*, p. 69; Wright, "Development of Education for Blacks in Georgia," p. 31.
5. Butchart, "Educating for Freedom," p. 353; Fredrickson, *The Black Image in the White Mind*, p. 244; Gutman, *The Black Family in Slavery and Freedom*, p. 532.
6. Freedmen's Aid Society quoted from Holmes, *Evolution of the Negro College*, p. 69; Bond, "Century of Negro Higher Education," p. 187; Butchart, "Educating for Freedom," pp. 453–490; Wright, "Development of Education for Blacks in Georgia," p. 29; Logan, "Evolution of Private Colleges for Negroes," p. 216.
7. Richardson, *Christian Reconstruction*, pp. 113, 123, 128; Bond, "Century of Negro Higher Education," pp. 187–188.
8. Richardson, *Christian Reconstruction*, p. 125; McPherson, *Abolitionist Legacy*, pp. 213, 222; Morehouse quoted in ibid., p. 222.

9. Richardson, *Christian Reconstruction*, p. 125; Merrill quoted in McPherson, *Abolitionist Legacy*, p. 220.

10. Du Bois quoted in McPherson, *Abolitionist Legacy*, p. 223.

11. Ibid.

12. Ibid., p. 213.

13. Baldwin, "Present Problem of Negro Education," pp. 52–60; Anderson, "Education for Servitude," pp. 208–216.

14. Weinberg, *A Chance to Learn*, p. 280.

15. Ibid., pp. 267, 280; Badger, "Negro Colleges and Universities"; Jones, *Negro Education*, 1:59.

16. Selden, *Accreditation*, pp. 32–37; Green, "Higher Standards for the Negro College"; Cozart, *History of the Association of Colleges and Secondary Schools*.

17. Selden, *Accreditation*, pp. 35–37.

18. Du Bois, *College-Bred Negro*, Du Bois and Dill, eds., *College-Bred Negro American*, Jones, *Negro Education*, 1: 58, 64; Green, "Higher Standards for the Negro College"; Cozart, *History of the Association of Colleges and Secondary Schools*. Hampton and Tuskegee, the two black educational institutions most favored by industrial philanthropists, were excluded from consideration because they were normal schools and it was their mission to provide precollegiate education for the training of common school teachers.

19. Morgan to Buttrick, 25, 29, 31 Jan. 1901, Sale to Buttrick, 23 Dec. 1909, 8 Jan. 1908, Box 716, Sale to Buttrick, 1 Jan. 1908, MacVicar to Buttrick, 7 June, 12 Aug. 1902, Buttrick to MacVicar, 18 Aug. 1902, Hovey to Buttrick, 30 Mar. 1908, Box 170, GEB Papers; Jones, *Negro Education*, 1: 7–8.

20. Sale to Buttrick, 8 Jan. 1908, Box 170, Morgan to Buttrick, 31 Jan., 1 Feb. 1901, Box 717, GEB Papers.

21. Harlan and Smock, eds., *Booker T. Washington Papers*, 3: 620; Buttrick to Rockefeller, 5 Feb. 1914, Box 203, GEB Papers.

22. Buttrick to Sale, 29 May 1907, Box 59, Report of Williams to Buttrick, 22 May 1907, Buttrick to the General Education Board, 22 May 1907, Box 716, GEB Papers.

23. Fosdick, *Adventure in Giving*, pp. 151–155; Hine, "Pursuit of Professional Equality," pp. 176–177.

24. Buttrick to Rockefeller, 5 Feb. 1914, Flexner to Villard, 1 Dec. 1914, Box 203, "General Education Board's Conference on Negro Education," 19 Nov. 1915, GEB Papers; Du Bois, "Thomas Jesse Jones," p. 253; Berman, "Educational Colonialism in Africa," pp. 183–194; King, *Pan-Africanism and Education*, pp. 43–57.

25. "General Education Board's Conference on Negro Education," 29 Nov. 1915, pp. 133–134.

26. Ibid., pp. 130–138, 149–152, 162–164.

27. Report of Committee on Negro Education, 24 Jan. 1916, Box 722, GEB Papers.

28. Logan, *The Negro in the United States*, pp. 74–83; Moton to Wilson, 15 June 1918, Box 303, GEB Papers.

29. Jones, "Crisis in Negro Leadership"; Peabody to Gregg, 5 Apr. 1920, Box 58, Peabody Papers.

30. Peabody to Gregg, 5 Apr. 1920, Box 58, Peabody Papers; *Fisk University News*, Sept. 1919, pp. 2–4; Du Bois to Eleazer, 12 Mar. 1926, Commission on Inter-racial Co-operation Collection; Franklin, *Black Self-Determination*.

31. Jones, *Negro Education*, 1: 310, 314–315; "General Education Board's Conference on Negro Education," 29 Nov. 1915, GEB Papers; Lamon, "Black Community in Nashville," p. 231.

32. McKenzie, *Ideals of Fisk*, p. 7; Aptheker, ed., *W. E. B. Du Bois*, pp. 52–57; Du Bois, "Fisk"; Wolters, *New Negro on Campus*, pp. 35–39.

33. Rosenwald to Flexner, 15 Jan. 1917, Flexner to Rosenwald, 17 Jan. 1917, Box 138, Flexner to Swift, 2 Apr. 1917, Appleget to Thorkelson, 12 June 1928, "Appropriations Made by the General Education Board to Fisk University"; for endowment contributions, see Baldwin to General Education Board, 6 Oct. 1924, Wood to General Education Board, 6 May 1920, Box 128, GEB Papers; *Fisk University News*, Dec. 1924, p. 20.

34. *Fisk University News*, Apr. 1923, p. 7; ibid., Oct. 1920, p. 21; Jones to Flexner, 4 Oct. 1915, Wood to Buttrick, 6 May 1920, Thorkelson to Wood, 5 Nov. 1926, Box 138, GEB Papers. For the philanthropists' role in actively recruiting trustees, see Flexner to Rosenwald, 8, 17 Jan. 1917, Rosenwald to Flexner, 13 Jan. 1917, Flexner to Swift, 2 Apr. 1917, Flexner to Judson, 27 Mar. 1917, Judson to Flexner, 30 Mar., 13 Apr. 1917, Box 138, GEB Papers.

35. Flexner, Memorandum on the Fisk Endowment Campaign, 25 May 1923, Box 23, GEB Papers.

36. The most thorough accounts of McKenzie's repressive educational practices are Wolters, *New Negro on Campus*, pp. 26–69; Lamon, "Fisk University Student Strike"; Richardson, *History of Fisk University*, chaps. 6 and 7.

37. "Fisk University," a 1926 memorandum, Box 138, GEB Papers; "Fisk Endowment Drive in Nashville," *Fisk University News*, May 1924, pp. 31–32; "First Million-Dollar Endowment for College Education of the Negro in the History of America," ibid., Oct. 1924, pp. 1–13; Commercial Club of Nashville to General Education Board, 24 Jan. 1920, Box 138, GEB Papers; Jones, *Negro Education*, 1: 314–315, 320–321.

38. Wolters, *New Negro on Campus*, pp. 34–40; *New York Times*, 8 Feb. 1925, sec. 2, p. 1; Jones to Cravath, 20 Sept. 1924, Box 3, Folder 20, McKenzie Papers.

39. Du Bois quoted in Wolters, *New Negro on Campus*, pp. 62–63; "Fisk University," a 1926 memorandum, Box 138, GEB Papers. For General Education Board contributions, see Fosdick, *Adventure in Giving*, pp. 329–332; "Fisk University," Report by Jones to the General Education Board, 27, 28 Sept. 1928, Box 138, GEB Papers.

40. Stokes to Rockefeller, 8 Jan. 1925, Box 17, Folder 8, "Special Memorandum Prepared for Clarence H. Kelsey, Esq.," 24 Oct. 1924, Box 17, Folder 5, Stokes to Rosenwald, 9 Dec. 1924, Box 17, Folder 6, Rosenwald Papers.

41. "Special Memorandum," 24 Oct. 1924, pp. 8, 23, 31–33, Box 17, Folder 5, Rosenwald Papers.

42. Ibid., pp. 10, 20; Stokes to Rockefeller, 8 Jan. 1925, Box 17, Folder 8, Rosenwald Papers.

43. "Special Memorandum," 24 Oct. 1924, p. 32, Appendix C, Box 17, Folder 5, Rosenwald Papers.

44. Wolters, *New Negro on Campus*, pp. 233, 248, 258, 273; Du Bois, "The Hampton Strike," *Nation* 125 (2 Nov. 1927): 471–472.

45. Wolters, *New Negro on Campus*, p. 267.

46. Fosdick, *Adventure in Giving*, pp. 328–329.

47. Franklin, "Whatever Happened to the College-Bred Negro?" (Du Bois, Woodson, and Hughes are quoted in Franklin's article); Hughes, "Cowards from the Colleges"; Streator, "Negro College Radicals."

48. Harris, "Problems before the College Negro"; Edmonds, "Education in Self-Contempt"; Allen, "Selling Out the Workers."

THE AMERICAN COMPROMISE: CHARLES W. ELIOT, BLACK EDUCATION, AND THE NEW SOUTH

JENNINGS L. WAGONER, JR.

It is generally accepted that by the beginning of the twentieth century, most Northerners, including many who in earlier decades had been zealously involved in Southern affairs, had turned their attention away from the plight of the Southern black. Reconstruction officially ended in 1877 and, as one Northern journal then announced, "Henceforth, the nation as a nation, will have nothing more to do with him [the black]."[1] Although lynching reached its peak in Southern states in the 1890s and Jim Crow legislation steadily relegated blacks to a position of political, economic, and social inequality,[2] many Northerners were apparently anxious to believe that the "wisest and best" men of the South could solve the Southern race problem and that indeed, a "New South" free from the legacy of racial injustice was in fact becoming a reality.[3]

The extent to which some Northern liberals abandoned the freedmen and the cause of civil rights around the turn of the century is an issue that invites further study. David W. Southern, in *The Malignant Heritage: Yankee Progressives and the Negro Question*, strongly indicts such national political leaders as Theodore Roosevelt, William H. Taft, and Woodrow Wilson for their racial attitudes and policies during this period. Southern condemns as well a number of leading liberal intellectuals and journalists for their blindness to racial injustice during the so-called "Progressive Era."[4] Other studies[5] have added credence to the argument that progressivism was for whites only and that many Northerners who were former allies of the freedmen had, with but few exceptions, become increasingly disillusioned with the slow pace of black progress by the opening years of the new century and in consequence reconstructed their notions of equality to exclude blacks and other "colored" peoples.

James Anderson and Donald Spivey, among others, have even more pointedly argued that those Northerners who did remain involved in Southern affairs, especially in the arena of black education, did so in order to help create an educational program "deliberately calculated to fit the freedmen to a new form of servitude in the caste economy of the post-war South."[6] Northern industrialists who had economic interests in the South are especially singled out by these historians for censure. Anderson's economic analysis, for example, leads him to contend that the "main end of the Southern industrialists, Northern philanthropists, and educational reformers was to force blacks into a workable scheme of social organization that would permit the structuring of a caste economy least removed from slavery. The problem of the school was to help fit blacks into that scheme."[7]

If Anderson's analysis resounds too strongly with conspiratorial tones, one must nonetheless confront the fact that, during this period of retreat from reconstruction, widespread support was given to the philosophy of accommodation and compromise espoused by Booker T. Washington. While it has become fashionable to portray Washington as a Judas for the stand exemplified in his Atlanta address of 1895, such a simplistic view ignores the fact that many of America's most liberal spokesmen, for a wide range of reasons, good and bad, played a vital role in legitimizing and, to a large degree, orchestrating the position to which Washington gave voice. There is more than coincidence in the fact that Washington was awarded an honorary M.A. degree from Harvard University in 1896, only months after making his famous "Atlanta Compromise" speech. Harvard's gesture was symbolic of the fact that many Northerners as well as Southerners were indeed ready to lay aside the "bloody shirt" and to move toward the new century with the myopic assurance that all had been done that could or should be done for the black man. From here on, ran the conventional wisdom, the rise from slavery would largely depend upon the black man's own initiative and ability.

In the context of the paradox presented by the rising tide of progressive reform on the one hand and the capitulation of many American liberals to the concept of a racially separate and unequal society on the other, an examination of the views of selected liberal reformers can be instructive. In this study, the racial attitudes and reform prescriptions of Charles W. Eliot, president of Harvard University for forty years (1869–1909), are presented as a case study in order to portray the evolving position of a widely respected educational reformer and New England liberal. Eliot, who was sometimes characterized as the nation's "first private citizen" and "our greatest moral force as an individual,"[8] was noted for his leadership in liberal causes. He was outspoken in support of "progressive" reforms in such areas as municipal government, civil service, capital-labor relations, conservation, sex hygiene, and international peace as well as in education. His direct and authoritative manner of speaking could quickly rankle those who held contrary views, but his was a voice that demanded an audience and not infrequently provoked a response. Eliot's tendency to offer judgments on issues across the spectrum of human events caused him to become, in Ralph Barton Perry's phrase, "adviser-at-large to the American people on things-in-general."[9] Although certainly Eliot cannot be said to have represented the views of all Northern whites any more than Booker T. Washington can be pictured as a spokesman for all Southern blacks, still his posture is revealing as one strand of Northern liberal thinking on the race issue. When considered in this context, the parallels between the views of Eliot and Washington, as well as the paradoxes inherent in Eliot's own "liberal" attitudes, take on special significance. It becomes apparent that as Eliot and other Northern liberals added their endorsement to the "Atlanta Compromise," the solution to the "Negro problem" became more than a matter of regional accommodation. The compromise, if we must call it that, took on national proportions. It become an "American compromise."

Eliot and Washington: Paradoxes and Parallels

Clearly, there was little in the backgrounds of the son of a slave and the son of a mayor of Boston to cause them to reach somewhat similar conclusions regarding the place of the black man in American society.[10] When Washington was born in a crude slave hunt on a Virginia plantation in 1856, Eliot had already completed his B.A. at Harvard and was serving as tutor of mathematics at his alma mater. After Emancipation, young Washington struggled to obtain snatches of schooling while also working in a salt furnace and coal mine. During the same period, Eliot achieved the rank of assistant professor at Harvard and then, from 1863–1865, observed the closing years of the Civil War from newspaper accounts and letters while traveling in Europe. In 1865, Eliot returned to the states to become professor of analytical chemistry at the newly formed Massachusetts Institute of Technology. It was from this post in 1869 that Eliot was called, at the age of thirty-five, to become president of Harvard University, a position he held until 1909. Eliot was thus beginning his third year as president of Harvard when sixteen-year-old Booker T. Washington proved himself worthy of entry into Hampton Institute by sweeping the floors to the satisfaction of the matron. And it was at Hampton that Washington mastered those principles of fidelity, honesty, persistence, and a devotion to the ideals of individualism and self-help that were so highly praised by the Puritans and their descendants, men like Charles W. Eliot.

As an educational reformer, Eliot was so involved with the internal restructuring of Harvard during the first two decades of his tenure as president that he gave only passing notice to larger social currents. Strengthening the professional schools, expanding the elective system, upgrading the quality of the faculty and the student body, reforming the curriculum—these and other immediate tasks absorbed his energies and tended to divert his attention from external matters. As far as the South was concerned, Eliot's main interest during the early phase of his administration was with wooing Southern students back to Harvard. In an address before the New York Harvard Club in 1872, Eliot observed with noticeable pleasure that Harvard could number in its ranks thirty-three students from the former slave states, not counting Missouri. Noting that Yale had twenty students from the same states, Eliot held forth the olive branch by proclaiming that "we are beginning to welcome back again the South." Encouraged as he was by these signs, however, Eliot was nonetheless sensitive to the wounds of war and reconstruction and expressed his concerns that among the casualties of the war was Harvard's loss of students from the leading Southern families. "We still miss," he lamented, "the old South Carolina, Virginia, and Louisiana names, and we may be sure that the wisdom of our legislators will not have perfectly solved the difficult problem of Southern reconstruction until the Pinckneys and Barnwells, the Middletons, Eustises and Lees go to colleges again with the Adamses and Lincolns, the Kents, Winthrops and Hoars."[11]

In part, at least, Eliot's strong desire to enroll more students from the "better" Southern families at Harvard eventually motivated him to concern himself with Southern conditions. There is little question but that Eliot's own Brahmin heritage predisposed him to view the plight of the South from the perspective of the former patrician class. At the same time, however, he was struck by the sluggish pace of progress in the South when compared with the tempo of growth and industrialization in the North. He despairingly observed in 1900 that the Southern situation was "depressing" and that "the backward condition of our Southern States is one of the saddest facts in all the world."[12] Eliot's specific desire to attract Southerners to Harvard and his more general but no less genuine wish to see the South enter the mainstream of national progress prompted him by the turn of the century to investigate more closely the problems and the prospects of the region in an effort to promote both ends.

Lessons from the South

Not a few Southerners saw themselves as capable of educating the president of Harvard as to the unique dimensions of the Southern race problem. Southerners of both races and all classes made their views known to Eliot on questions regarding the social and political ramifications of suffrage for blacks, on the advisability of a dual school system, on the efficacy of industrial education or any education at all for blacks, on the moral habits and inclinations of Southern blacks as compared with whites, and even on the appropriateness of Booker T. Washington dining with President Theodore Roosevelt.

Not all correspondents were as forthright as one writer from Louisiana, who identified himself as "of the 'poor white trash' of the South—that is to say I'm only a skilled workingman—owning neither a great plantation nor a newspaper" and whose only "Harvard' was a log schoolhouse, and not since the age of 13 at that." Apologizing for thus not being able to "produce a finished essay on the subject," the writer nonetheless proceeded to advise Eliot that the workingmen of the South had "*no interest* whatsoever in the education of the negro" and challenged that newspapermen and politicians who said otherwise were as far from representing the correct "Southern Sentiment" on the race question as was Roosevelt from approaching greatness! Should any "Tuskegeeized" or Harvard-educated black threaten to take his job, the writer advised Eliot, his response would be to "shoot him just as soon as dark gave the better opportunity! And never be in a moment's dread of indictment by a grand jury of my neighbors!" Convinced that social equality and miscegenation were the only outcomes of political and educational equality, the writer closed his letter by asserting: "The negro must move! So long as he is here so long will there be dissension. Let him go into Old Mexico and Central America and have done with this country for all time. Then will you and I be friends and not until then."[13]

A correspondent from Savannah, rejecting the idea that blacks possessed the ability to advance at all, informed Eliot that "those portions of Africa where the negro has full sway are as much of a wilderness as they were thousands of years ago." This Southerner took strong exception to the view that the black had made substantial progress in the forty years since slavery. "A forced, hothouse 'advance' is not true progress," he reasoned. "As well might driftwood be considered as swimming while transported downstream by the current. *No other race in history has been carried along on the back of another race as has the negro.*"[14]

Most of the letters that Eliot received from those anxious to inform him of the racial situation in the South were more moderate in tone, and in some cases the correspondence between the Harvard president and selected Southern advisers spanned a period of several years.[15] Moreover, Eliot's connections with Northern philanthropists such as Robert C. Ogden, William H. Baldwin, and John D. Rockefeller, Jr., exposed him to the perspectives and efforts of men who were themselves involved with Southern educators and upper-class paternalists in a campaign of Southern uplift.[16] Thus, when in 1904 Eliot ventured to speak on "The Problems of the Negro"[17] before a gathering of the Armstrong Association of Hampton Institute in New York and two years later when at Tuskegee he spoke to the topic "What Uplifts a Race and What Holds It Down,"[18] he was by no means uninformed as to Southern attitudes and options. Yet whatever the insights and sympathies some Southerners and their Northern allies may have aroused in Eliot, his clear and uncompromising assertions in private correspondence and his conciliatory yet forceful public addresses suggest that Eliot characteristically, if not always consistently, endeavored to reason from liberal principles. Responding, for example, to a Southern minister who interpreted Roosevelt's inviting Booker T. Washington to dinner as a deliberate insult to the South, Eliot firmly expressed his own position:

> As a rule, I select my companions and guests, not by the color of their skins, but by their social and personal quality. It would never occur to me not to invite to my house an educated Chinaman or Japanese because their skin is yellow or brownish, or to avoid asking a negro to my table if he were an intelligent, refined and interesting person. It is the intelligence, refinement and good judgment of Mr. Booker Washington which makes him an agreeable guest at any table; and to many of us Northern people, the fact that nearly half his blood is African is a matter of indifference.[19]

It may well be, as Hugh Hawkins contends, that Eliot's stance in this instance was at best only "superficially tolerant" and reveals formidable standards to which others had to conform.[20] Yet it is clear that Eliot outwardly rejected race as a criterion for social intercourse. However elitist as judged by contemporary standards Eliot may appear, he was in his own day among a liberal minority who were prone to interpret racial differences as legacies of culture as well as genetics. While Eliot understood that genetically inherited traits were not immutable (short of undesirable "amalgamation"), he contended that the possibilities of cultural assimilation were vast and believed that somehow the process of assimilation could gradually qualify and "render less visible" some racial differences. At the same time, he maintained that "the diversities of race need no more be extinguished under free institutions than the diversities between human individuals." "Freedom," he proclaimed, "should encourage diversity, not extinguish it."[21] It is hardly surprising then that Eliot, who stood fast against nativism and the clamor to restrict immigration, should be singled out by one historian as an example of the "minority with faith" during the years when restrictionism was on the rise.[22]

For all of Eliot's commitment to libertarian principles and dependence upon his inner-directed moral sense, however, he proved on more than one occasion not in the least hostile to the pragmatic temper. If he was a staunch individualist, he was also sensitive to the demands of a rising corporate state and could in time speak with conviction about the necessity of individualism yielding to collectivism and the needs of the larger society.[23] And, while he can be viewed as an exponent of fair play and equality of opportunity, and as an outspoken foe of racial discrimination, he must also be seen as one who, in assessing popular sentiment, could convince himself that there could perhaps be in some contexts racial distinctions without unjust racial discrimination.[24]

What then were the solutions offered by this liberal Northern reformer to the Southern race problem? What encouragement, what direction did he give those who searched for a way up from slavery and second-class citizenship into the promise of American life? And what assurances did he give those in the South and elsewhere who were prone to reject the idea that blacks and whites could ever live as coequal citizens, socially as well as politically? It is in searching out the answers to these questions that the dimensions of the American Compromise become clear.

Shaping the American Compromise

Sharing the platform with Andrew Carnegie, Hollis B. Frissell (the white principle of Hampton Institute), and Booker T. Washington, Eliot took the occasion of an address before the Armstrong Association meeting in New York City in 1904, to give public hearing to his views on the Southern race question. Eliot, then seventy years of age, was careful to note that there were fundamental points on which Northern and Southern sentiment was identical, foremost among these being the desire to preserve racial purity. "The Northern whites hold this opinion quite as firmly as the Southern whites," Eliot stated, "and," he continued, "inasmuch as the negroes hold the same view, this supposed danger of mutual racial impairment ought not to have much influence on practical measures." Sexual vice on the part of white men accounted for the limited degree of racial mixture which already existed, Eliot claimed, and nobody "worthy of consideration" would advocate racial intermarriage as a policy.[25]

It was against the backdrop of this assurance that racial mixture was anathema to the whole of American society—blacks as well as whites, Northerners as well as Southerners—that Eliot then proceeded to speak in more specific terms about differences in the treatment accorded blacks above and below the Mason-Dixon line. Noting that in the South separate provisions were made for blacks in schools, in public conveyances, and in public facilities, Eliot discounted the difference from practice in the North as being "socially insignificant." Indeed, Eliot observed, "with regard to coming into personal contact with negroes, the adverse feeling of the Northern whites is stronger than that of the Southern whites, who are accustomed to such contacts. . . ."[26] Eliot noted further that while the North had not moved toward a dual school system, "in Northern towns where negro children are proportionally numerous there is just the same tendency and desire to separate them from the whites as there is in the South," a separation, he added, which if not effected by laws may well result "by white parents procuring the transfer of their children to schools where negroes are few."[27] As Eliot thus evaluated the differences in practice between the North and South, he concluded that the underlying racial attitudes of the two regions appeared much the same. No greater feeling of brotherhood, no deeper commitment to liberalism, no fervent devotion to ideals of liberty, equality, or justice were needed or warranted in explaining differences in practice. The fundamental explanation, Eliot contended, rested with the difference in the proportions between the races. Eliot described the situation accordingly:

> Put the prosperous Northern whites into the Southern states, in immediate contact with millions of negroes, and they would promptly establish separate schools for the colored population, whatever the necessary cost. Transfer the Southern whites to the North, where the negroes form but an insignificant fraction of the population, and in a generation or two they would not care whether there were a few negro children in the public schools or not, and would therefore avoid the expense of providing separate schools for the few colored children.[28]

In setting forth these propositions, Eliot was speaking not in terms of what "ought" to be, or even necessarily what he wished were the case, but rather in terms of observed social realities in the North and his understanding, based on his secondhand knowledge of the South, of conditions and attitudes in that region. However much he might personally feel that race should not be the determining consideration in regard either to dinner guests or schoolmates, he judged popular sentiment to be of a different mind. And in so judging, he gave Northern liberal endorsement to the Southern system of dual schooling.

On another matter of popular sentiment, however—at least Southern sentiment—Eliot saw less national unanimity. A real difference existed, Eliot felt, between Northern and Southern views as to the supposed connection between political equality and social equality. The "Southern view" was perhaps most directly stated by Frederick Bromberg, a Mobile attorney and frequent correspondent with Eliot on the Southern problem. According to Bromberg, Southern objection to black suffrage had nothing to do with "the ignorance of the emancipated race." Rather, Bromberg asserted:

> . . . no amount of intelligence or culture upon the part of any one with negro blood in him can overcome the objection to him as a coequal citizen. . . . [We] do not object to negro suffrage because of the Negro's incapacity, but because he is a negro—because suffrage and the right to hold

office are usually associated with each other, and holding office means possession of power, and possession of power means social equality, and social equality tends to miscegenation, and miscegenation is what we will not tolerate, and therefore oppose the beginnings. . . .[29]

In correspondence as well as in public forums, Eliot labored to undermine what he perceived as the illogic of this Southern syllogism. Using European as well as Northern experience, Eliot argued repeatedly that possession of the ballot had never had anything to do with the social status of the individual voter. Eliot favored, as he felt most Northerners did, educational qualifications for suffrage, but he refused to accept the idea that blacks, as blacks, should be denied the ballot or right to hold office. Political rights, he maintained, were separable from social intercourse. "In Northern cities," he reasoned,". . . the social divisions are numerous and deep; and the mere practice of political equality gives no means whatever of passing from one social set to another supposed to be higher. The social sets are determined by like education, parity of income, and similarity of occupation, and not at all by the equality of every citizen before the law."[30] It was indeed this very logic that informed Eliot's administration of Harvard University. He frequently and fondly proclaimed that Harvard recognized among its officers and students neither class, race, caste, sect, nor political party. While in one instance denying that there was a tendency in the North "to break down the social barriers between the white race and the negro race," Eliot at the same time firmly asserted that, as far as Harvard was concerned, any person who could pass the admission examinations would be received as a student and, upon completion of his studies, would "receive the degree without the least regard to his racial quality or religious or political opinions."[31] But as far as social relations were concerned, individual preferences (indeed prejudices) superceded institutional policies. "Membership in the societies and clubs of Harvard," he wrote in 1907, "is determined entirely by social selection—this social selection being made on the basis of similar tastes, habits and ambitions." Japanese students had been admitted to some of the desirable clubs at Harvard, Eliot noted, but he could recall no instance of blacks being invited to join a social club and thought the possibility of such "extremely unlikely."[32]

Thus, on the matter of social equality, Eliot's attitude closely paralleled the public pronouncements of Booker T. Washington. In social matters, at Harvard or elsewhere in the nation, individuals or groups were free to include or exclude according to their own preferences or prejudices. But in matters political, whether it be university admission or universal suffrage, meritocratic standards only should be invoked. There need not be, Eliot insisted, any connection between political equality and social equality.[33]

Education: Separate but Equal

Access to political equality (and the way toward gaining the tastes, habits, and ambitions that might make one socially acceptable), however, depended in part upon educational opportunity. Having acknowledged the apparent necessity of separate education in the Southern states, Eliot would not yield ground to those who argued for grossly unequal education for blacks. As Eliot interpreted Southern attitudes on the type and amount of schooling black children should receive, three different opinions seemed to emerge. "Some Southern whites, educated and uneducated," Eliot said, "think that any education is an injury to the negro race, and that the negro should continue to multiply in the Southern States with access only to the lowest forms of labor." Another segment of the population, he continued, "holds that negro children should be educated, but only for manual occupations. . . . This section approves of manual training and trade schools, but takes no interest in the higher education of the negro." There was, however, a third, and to Eliot, proper attitude held by still other white Southerners, one which recognized "the obvious fact that a separate negro community must be provided with negro professional men of good quality, else neither the physical nor the moral welfare of the negro population will be thoroughly provided for."[34] Thus, to Eliot, beyond the ideal of political equality and the requirements for public safety, there existed a compelling justification for adequate provisions for higher education of blacks. "The provision of a higher education for negroes," Eliot proclaimed, "is the logical consequence of the proposition that the black and white races should both be kept pure. . . ."[35] Separate education was thus a basic requirement for the maintenance of a segregated society.

Sympathetically recognizing the "peculiar burden upon the Southern States caused by the separation between the black and the white races in the institutions of education," Eliot closed his address before the Armstrong Association by calling for federal aid to Southern education.[36] The national government, he said, should make it possible for black schools in the South to be kept open eight months of the year instead of four. Separate colleges for agriculture and the mechanical arts should be provided throughout the South and separate professional schools for blacks should be established within existing Southern universities, all made possible by national support. "It was in the supreme interest of the whole nation that the Southern States were impoverished forty years ago by a four years' blockade and the destruction of their whole industrial system," Eliot reasoned. "It is fair that the nations should help rebuild Southern prosperity in the very best way, namely, through education."[37]

Concern with fairness—even with public security and racial purity—might have little impact on a man like Mississippi's James K. Vardaman who could ask "Why squander money on his education when the only effect is to spoil a good field hand and make an insolent cook?"[38] But Eliot's appeals, like Washington's, were primarily addressed to moderates and liberals who recognized that the problems of the blacks were also the problems of the whites, Northern as well as Southern. Yet Eliot believed, as did Washington, that provision of educational opportunities was only part of the struggle up from slavery. In the final analysis, both men maintained that the place of the black man in American society depended primarily upon the use he made of available opportunities, however limited. That their own and later generations would often twist this formulation into a cruel mechanism for "blaming the victim" was a consequence these "self-made" men could hardly appreciate.

Education and the Doctrine of Self-Help

When Eliot was invited to make an address at Tuskegee in 1906, he chose as his theme, "What Uplifts a Race and What Holds It Down." Eliot identified four essentials which must be sought after by any race which hoped, as he put it, to lift itself "out of barbarism into civilization." First among the elements necessary was a commitment to steady, productive labor. Eliot stated:

> Every race that has risen from barbarism to civilization has done so by developing all grades of productive labor, beginning with agricultural labor, and rising through the fundamental mechanic arts, and mining, and quarrying, to manufacturing, elaborate transportation, trade, commerce, the fine arts, and professional labor. Respect for labor of all sorts, for the simplest as well as the most complex forms, will be manifested by every rising race. This respect is founded not only on the conviction that productive labor yields comfort, security, and progressive satisfactions, but also on the firm belief that regular labor in freedom develops the higher intellectual and moral qualities of the human being.[39]

Second to the uplift provided by honest labor, Eliot told the Tuskegee students, was devotion to Christian family life. "Respect for family life," he said, "fidelity in the marriage relation, and appreciation of the sacredness of childhood are sure signs that a race is rising."[40]

Education held third place in the scale of values Eliot sought to impress upon Tuskegee students. Observing that Americans in general seemed to place more faith in education as an agency for uplifting a race than any other avenue, Eliot contended that "habitual productive labor and family life must precede education; and the education of children cannot prevent the decline of any people whose habit of labor or family life has been impaired." Third in importance though it might be, education, especially education that would contribute to industrial efficiency, was heralded by Eliot as vital. In a line which must have warmed the heart of Washington, Eliot declared: "This effort to make education contribute immediately to industrial efficiency is thoroughly wholesome in all grades of education; and particularly it is wholesome for a race which has but lately emerged from the profound barbarism of slavery; for it unites in one uplifting process all three of the civilizing agencies I have already mentioned—productive labor, home-making, and mental and moral training."[41]

Before he proceeded into a discussion of the fourth agency of the civilizing process—respect for law—Eliot acknowledged that current educational conditions in the South were inadequate, not only for black children but for whites as well. Poorly trained teachers, short school terms, early leaving age, and limited curricula offerings all were hindrances to educational opportunity. Sounding again the theme of federal aid, Eliot declared that at least one institution like Tuskegee or Hampton should exist in every Southern state.[42]

Even though Eliot publicly praised Tuskegee and was doubtless convinced that Washington's uplift philosophy, which he endorsed, was in most respects appropriate, he observed inadequacies in the program he saw in operation. Eliot's uneasiness with the Tuskegee program was no doubt heightened by information provided him by Roscoe C. Bruce, a Harvard graduate, then a teacher at Tuskegee, who had earlier complained to Washington that industrial activities too frequently encroached upon the academic and that "the education of the pupil is largely sacrificed to the demands of productive labor." The charges Bruce, an insider, leveled against Tuskegee—that standards of scholarship were woefully inadequate, that a student's capacity for productive labor and "goodness of heart" counted more toward promotion than intellectual attainment, that the teaching staff was inferior, that students "who plan to teach school have not one minute more for academic studies than the pupils who plan to make horseshoes or to paint houses"[43]—were not lost on Eliot. Several months after his visit to Tuskegee, Eliot was moved to inform Washington of areas in which the institute needed to improve. After questioning the ability of Tuskegee to offer adequate training in nursing and the ministry and making some recommendations regarding the use of capital outlay funds, Eliot then hit the problem of academic training. He noted his impression that the manual labor dimension of the Tuskegee program threatened to overshadow the mental labor side. "Is it not important," Eliot asked, "that the graduates of Tuskegee should have acquired not only a trade or an art, but the power to read and cipher intelligently and a taste for reading?"[44]

In responding to Eliot's concerns, Washington endeavored to justify the work being done at Tuskegee with rural ministers and defended the institute's nursing program by noting that prior to Tuskegee's efforts, "there was no trained nurse within a radius of a hundred miles." "The question is," Washington stated, "whether we should turn out people who can partially relieve suffering, or wait until we, or some other institution, are in a position to turn out those who are much better equipped than our nurses are now." Promising nonetheless to lay all of Eliot's suggestions before the board of trustees, Washington spoke to Eliot's concern for the academic side of Tuskegee by briefly noting, "We have already reorganized our course of training so that we are spending more time in strictly academic work than was true when you were here."[45]

If in these particulars the Harvard president and Tuskegee principal differed in their emphases, on most other matters of what has been termed "accommodationist philosophy," the two found grounds for common agreement. The month before Eliot made his "Uplift" speech at Tuskegee, he had solicited Washington's advice as to the treatment of certain topics. Washington seconded Eliot's call for the creation of Tuskegees in every Southern state and felt that Eliot's "placing emphasis upon the fact that there is a difference between social intermingling and political intermingling" would prove helpful. But Washington expressed reservations regarding Eliot's suggestion that he speak in specific terms as to just and unjust examples of racial separation. "There is a class of white people in the South and in the North," Washington advised, "who are always ready to insist on unreasonable and unjust separations to the extent that I very much fear that anything you might say in this direction would be twisted into an endorsement of unjust and unreasonable separation." Washington in particular cautioned Eliot against repeating the statement made before the Armstrong Association to the effect that Northern whites might feel segregation in public schools justified in areas were the Negro population is large. "I am wondering," Washington said, "whether or not the result might not be that the colored people would receive inferior opportunities for education rather than equal opportunities?" While Washington doubted that it would "be desirable or practicable on the part of either race to attempt to bring about coeducation in the South," he did not wish to see present Southern circumstances used to excuse segregation in other regions of the country. Concluding this appeal to Eliot with a slightly different twist to the theme made famous in his Atlanta Compromise speech, Washington stated: "In all things that are purely social, the colored people do not object to separation . . . but the difficulty is in the South in many cases civil privileges are confounded with social intercourse."[46]

Apparently satisfied with the merits of Washington's observations, Eliot contented himself in his Tuskegee address with only general references to proper and improper modes of racial accommodation. "The Republic desires and believes," Eliot stated, "that all competent men within its limits should enjoy political equality, the tests of competence being the same for all races." But he felt compelled to add: "Of course the Republic does not include under political equality social equality; for social equality rests on natural or instinctive likes and dislikes, affinities and repulsions, which no political institutions have ever been able to control."[47]

Eliot as Ambassador of Accommodation and Compromise

In 1909, on the eve of Eliot's retirement from the presidency of Harvard and one year after he become a member of the General Education Board, he was prevailed upon to undertake a Southern tour. Seeing the trip as a way to further cement the growing bridge between Harvard and the South, Eliot also looked upon a period of Southern travel as an opportunity to study first-hand conditions in that region as well as an occasion to spread further the doctrines of the American Compromise. With extended stops in various cities in Tennessee, Texas, Louisiana, Alabama, Georgia, and South and North Carolina, Eliot praised Southern progress, assured Southerners that their white counterparts in the North were at one with them on the matter of social separation between the races, delivered messages of "uplift" at black churches and colleges, and counseled whites to be just in their dealings with blacks. In Montgomery, Eliot was quoted as saying that "the policy of the South regarding the negro is a wise one. The white people and the negroes should be kept apart in every respect." Taking direct aim at the critics of accommodationism, Eliot reportedly added: "The work being done by Booker T. Washington, I believe to be good for his race, and that done by Professor Du Bois, harmful."[48]

In comforting Southerners with assurances that Northerners not only understood their problem but shared it, Eliot made yet another pronouncement that sparked quite a controversy in Northern, and even a few Southern newspapers. "In the North we have our race problem," Eliot declared in Memphis and elsewhere on his trip. "I do not believe," he was quoted as saying, "in the admixture of even white races. For instance, the Irish, Jews, Italians, and other European nationalities should not intermarry with Americans of English descent."[49] Newspaper accounts as to Eliot's precise wording varied, and while some publications, such as *Harper's Weekley*,[50] chose to suspend judgment until confirmation of Eliot's remarks could be obtained, other papers were less patient. The *Boston Pilot* charged that Eliot was an ancestor worshipper and editorialized that he had for too many years been "talking altogether too much on every subject."[51] Other papers wrote that Eliot deserved watching, one New York paper, *Town Topics*, venturing the opinion that perhaps Eliot had "reached the period of senility."[52] Even the *Charleston News and Courier* expressed puzzlement, arguing that surely Eliot recognized that the "American" was the product of intermarriage among stocks differing "in minor degree." The *News and Courier* resolved the riddle by asserting: "Of course, the intermarriage of the races when the term connotes peoples of different color, as Chinese, Malays, and Negroes, ought to be prohibited and that is probably all that Dr. Eliot has said."[53] A week later the same paper editorialized enthusiastically for Eliot, saying: "He has learned a great many things in the last twenty-five years, and has displayed remarkable familiarity with the peculiar problems with which our people have had to deal all these weary years."[54]

If Eliot's overzealous concern for racial purity caused a temporary controversy in the Northern press, it was an episode that rather quickly faded away. What remained from Eliot's Southern tour was a testimony to the very ideals of goodwill, patience, responsibility—and accommodation—that formed the platform of the American Compromise. Eliot had laid out, as had Washington earlier in Atlanta, a program of self-help and "uplift" that gave vague promise of allowing the black to earn a "respectable" place for himself in a socially segregated American society. To blacks whose ambitions and frustrations led them to demand or expect "too much" immediately, and to those whites who doubted that progress on the part of the black man was ever possible,

Eliot could paternalistically pass on the wisdom of one of America's leading educational reformers and liberal statesmen:

> Why, you believe that your race problem is a new one, but it has been experienced before, only it is intensified here [in the South]. The negro cannot be expected to be ready for all phases of civilization only a few decades removed from the time when he first began to enjoy civilization as a free man. After 500 or 1000 years we may expect more substantial growth.[55]

Conclusion

If the tonic of self-help, educational endeavor, dependence upon white paternalism, and faith in the gradual process of cultural assimilation seemed at best an inappropriate placebo if not a near-fatal opiate, such a prescription must nonetheless be judged in the context of prevailing American liberal thought, not merely in the narrower context of black capitulation to Southern racism. Charles Eliot was but one in a long line of Northern liberals at the turn of the century who approached the race issue with counsel of compromise and accommodation. The strategies of accommodation tacitly agreed upon by Northern philanthropists and Southern reformers and endorsed by liberals such as Eliot were intended to dampen the appeal of racist demagogues and soften the demands of impatient freedmen, all for the sake of Southern progress and racial harmony. However, advocacy of accommodationist policies served in time to weaken the position of liberals as guardians of the interests of blacks and other minorities in the North as well as in the South. Eliot, for example, although a consistent champion of political equality and an opponent of racial bigotry, discounted the significance of social discrimination and came to accept as a matter of necessity the existence of a racially segregated society. While he advocated educational opportunity, he nonetheless gave his blessing to the system of dual schooling in areas where the black population was sizeable. And although he sincerely believed in the efficacy of the Puritan ethic, he preached the values of patience as well as hard work and calmly asserting that significant advance on the part of black Americans as a whole would result only after generations of effort.

Even though such strategies of accommodation and deferred commitments were condemned by those who assumed a more militant stand, the difference between "liberal-conservatives" such as Booker T. Washington and Charles W. Eliot and their more radical critics may well have been, as Eugene Genovese has argued, more a difference in emphasis, tactics, and public stance than one of fundamental ideology.[56] The goal of Washington no less than Du Bois was the attainment by blacks of full rights of citizenship. As August Meier has noted, "The central theme in Washington's philosophy was that through thrift, industry, and Christian character Negroes would eventually attain their constitutional rights."[57] Thus, the accommodationist tactics of Washington were immediate means toward an ultimate end of racial equality and justice. In adopting tactics that won the approval of liberal and moderate whites, North and South, Washington was seeking allies in the struggle, recognizing that without white support, no amount of effort on the part of blacks would bring positive results. Similarly, it was W. E. B. Du Bois in his celebrated critique of Washington who asserted that "While it is a great truth to say that the negro must strive and strive mightily to help himself, it is equally true that unless his striving be not simply seconded, but rather aroused and encouraged by the initiative of the richer and wiser environing group, he cannot hope for great success."[58] Certainly the encouragement and endorsements given by Charles Eliot, a respected member of the "richer and wiser environing group," were not the only directives he could have set forth, but his axioms were unquestionably representative of the major doctrines of what had become an American Compromise.

Notes

The author wishes to thank Professors Hugh Hawkins, Robert Bremner, Louis Harlan, and Ronald Goodenow for their helpful comments on earlier drafts.

1. *Nation*, April 5, 1877, as cited in Paul H. Buck, *The Road to Reunion*, 1865–1900 (New York: Vintage Books, 1959), p. 294.

2. C. Vann Woodward, *The Strange Career of Jim Crow*, rev. ed., (New York: Oxford University Press, 1966). Cf. Woodward's *Origins of the New South, 1877–1913* (Baton Rouge, La.: Louisiana State University Press, 1951), p. 351, where he notes that nationally lynchings averaged 187.5 per annum between 1889 and 1899 and dropped to 92.5 during the next decade. However, the percentage of lynchings in the South increased from about 82 percent in the 1890s to about 92 percent in the 1900–1909 decade and almost 90 percent of the victims were blacks.

3. The metamorphosis from "creed" to "myth" of a "New South" based on a reconciliation of sectional differences, racial peace, and a new economic and social order based on industry and scientific, diversified agriculture is insightfully examined in Paul M. Gaston, *The New South Creed: A Study in Southern Mythmaking* (New York: Alfred A. Knopf, 1970). On the dynamics of sectional reconciliation also see Buck, *The Road to Reunion* and Stanley P. Hirshon, *Farewell to the Bloody Shirt: Northern Republicans and the Southern Negro 1877–1893* (Bloomington, Ind.: Indiana University Press, 1962).

4. David W. Southern, *The Malignant Heritage: Yankee Progressives and the Negro Question, 1901–1914* (Chicago: Loyola University Press, 1968). Southern points to the Clergyman Lyman Abbott and former abolitionists Carl Schurz and Charles F. Adams, Jr., as liberals who changed their views on racial equality. Ray Stannard Baker, Herbert Baxter Adams, John R. Commons, Josiah Royce, Walter Lippmann, Herbert Croly, and Walter Weyl all in varying degrees began to consider blacks a separate caste which blighted the "promise of American life." See Chapter III, especially.

5. Charles B. Dew in "Critical Essay on Recent Works" in Woodward, *Origins*, pp. 517–628, provides an excellent survey of studies on this topic. See especially pp. 577–584. See also Arthur S. Link and Rembert W. Patrick, eds., *Writing Southern History: Essays in Historiography in Honor of Fletcher M. Green* (Baton Rouge, La.: Louisiana State University Press, 1965).

6. James Douglas Anderson, "Education for Servitude: The Social Purposes of Schooling in the Black South, 1870–1930," (Ph.D. diss., University of Illinois, 1973), p. 3; Donald Spivey, *Schooling for the New Slavery: Black Industrial Education, 1868–1915* (Westport, Conn.: Greenwood Press, 1978).

7. Anderson, "Education for Servitude," p. 4.

8. Eugen Kuehnemann, *Charles W. Eliot: President of Harvard University* (Boston: Houghton Mifflin Co., 1909), pp. 1–4, as cited in Hugh Hawkins, *Between Harvard and America: The Educational Leadership of Charles W. Eliot* (New York: Oxford University Press, 1972), p 290.

9. Ralph Barton Perry as quoted in Hawkins, *Between Harvard and America*, p. 298.

10. Booker T. Washington, *Up From Slavery: An Autobiography* (New York: A. L. Burt, Co., 1901) is Washington's most polished account of his life. A more objective analysis is provided in Louis Harlan, *Booker T. Washington: The Making of a Black Leader* (New York: Oxford University Press, 1972). On Washington's thought (as opposed to his biography) the standard work is still August Meier, *Negro Thought in America 1880–1915* (Ann Arbor, Mich.: University of Michigan Press, 1963). On Eliot, in addition to Hawkins cited above, see Henry James, *Charles W. Eliot: President of Harvard University, 1869–1909*, 2 vols. (New York: Houghton Mifflin, 1930).

11. Charles W. Eliot, Speech at New York Harvard Club, February 21, 1872, Charles W. Eliot Papers, Harvard University Archives, Box 334 (hereafter cited as Eliot Papers.)

12. Eliot to William G. Brown, July 26, 1900 (Eliot Papers, Letterbook 92).

13. Forrest Pope to Eliot, March 2, 1904 (Eliot Papers, Box 234).

14. Charles Kohler to Eliot, March 2, 1904 (Eliot Papers, Box 234). Emphasis on original.

15. See, for example, the series of letters from Frederick G. Bromberg to Eliot (Eliot Papers, Box 123) and William B. Watkins to Eliot (Eliot Papers, Box 234).

16. On the "Ogden Movement" and the work and racial views of the men who formed the interlocking directorate of the Southern Education Board and the General Education Board, see Charles W. Dabney, *Universal Education in the South*, 2 vols. (Chapel Hill, N. C.: University of North Carolina Press, 1936); Louis R. Harlan, *Separate and Unequal: Public School Campaigns and Racism in the Southern Seaboard States 1901–1915* (Chapel Hill, N.C.: University of North Carolina Press, 1958); and Woodward, *Origins of the New South*, especially Chapter 15, "Philanthropy and the Forgotten Man." While Eliot was not formally a part of the Southern Education Movement, he was on its fringes and after 1908 became more directly involved in Southern educational developments as a member of the General Education Board.

17. Charles W. Eliot, "The Problems of the Negro," in *The Work and Influence of Hampton*, Proceedings of a meeting held in New York City, February 12, 1904, under the direction of the Armstrong Association (Eliot Papers, Box 337).

18. Charles W. Eliot, "What Uplifts a Race and What Holds It Down," Address at Tuskegee Institute, April 1906, TS (Eliot Papers, Box 338).

19. Eliot to Rev. S. A. Steel, October 25, 1901 (Eliot Papers, Letterbook 92).

20. Hawkins, *Between Harvard and America*, p. 182.
21. Charles W. Eliot, "The Contemporary American Conception of Equality Among Men as a Social and Political Ideal," Phi Beta Kappa Oration, University of Missouri, June 2, 1909 (Eliot Papers, Box 340).
22. Barbara Miller Solomon, *Ancestors and Immigrants: A Changing New England Tradition* (Cambridge: Harvard University Press, 1956), pp. 99–102, 186–188. Cf. Hawkins, *Between Harvard and America*, pp. 182, 353. See also Eliot to Edward Lauterbach (President of National Liberal Immigration League), January 10, 1911 (Eliot Papers, Box 341).
23. See, for example, Charles W. Eliot, "Individualism vs. Collectivism," Address, New England Society in City of New York, 1905 (Eliot Papers, Box 337) and "Address at the Second Annual Conference on No-License Workers of Massachusetts," October 29, 1908, TS (Eliot Papers, Box 339).
24. Cf. Hawkins, *Between Harvard and America*, p. 191.
25. Eliot, "The Problems of the Negro," p. 9.
26. Ibid., p. 10.
27. Ibid., p. 9.
28. Ibid.
29. Frederick G. Bromberg to Eliot, October 29, 1901 (Eliot Papers, Box 123). Bromberg was a Harvard graduate of the class of 1858, a Unionist during the war, and a member of Congress during Reconstruction. While Eliot could not agree with Bromberg's position on suffrage restrictions, he nonetheless recommended him to Theodore Roosevelt as a suitable candidate for the office of district attorney for the southern district of Alabama. See Eliot to President Roosevelt, December 17, 1901 (Eliot Papers, Letterbook 92).
30. Eliot, "The Problems of the Negro," p. 10. See also Eliot to Frederick G. Bromberg, December 6, 1901 (Eliot Papers, Letterbook 92).
31. Eliot to Bruce L. Keenan, August 9, 1907 (Eliot Papers, Letterbook 96).
32. Ibid. The number of blacks at Harvard during the Eliot years was small. Eliot's secretary, Jerome Greene, when asked in 1904 about the number of "full blooded Negroes at Harvard," confessed that accurate statistics were not available but that estimates placed the number at about fifteen, or one-third of one percent of the student body. He guessed that there had probably been forty or fifty black students at Harvard during the preceding ten years. See Jerome D. Greene to J. N. Hazelhurst, October 24, 1904 (Eliot Papers, box 284). See also W. E. B. Du Bois's description of his years at Harvard in *The Autobiography of W. E. B. Du Bois* (New York: International Publishers, 1968), pp. 132–153.
33. Eliot, "The Problems of the Negro," p. 11.
34. Ibid., p. 13.
35. Ibid.
36. Ibid. Eliot framed a resolution to this effect for NEA consideration in 1905. See "Resolutions Suggested to Dr. Wm. H. Maxwell at his Request for the NEA Convention of 1905," TS, June 12, 1905 (Eliot Papers, Letterbook 95).
37. Ibid., p. 15.
38. As quoted in Roger M. Williams, "The Atlanta Compromise," *American History Illustrated 3* (April 1968), p. 18. For an examination of Vardaman's several variations on this theme, see William F. Holmes, *The White Chief: James Kimble Vardaman* (Baton Rouge, La.: Louisiana University Press, 1970), especially pp. 78, 122 and passim.
39. Eliot, "What Uplifts a Race and What Holds It Down," pp. 1–2.
40. Ibid., p. 3.
41. Ibid., p. 3–4.
42. Ibid., p. 5–6.
43. Roscoe C. Bruce to Booker T. Washington, April 12, 1906, copy, (Eliot Papers, Box 234).
44. Eliot to Washington, September 7, 1906 (Eliot Papers, Letterbook 95).
45. Washington to Eliot, October 20, 1906 (Eliot Papers, Box 255). Bruce had earlier confirmed that "to my surprise and delight Principal Washington has already granted in modified form some of the things I have so long been asking for." Roscoe C. Bruce to Eliot, April 23, 1906 (Eliot Papers, Box 204).
46. Washington to Eliot, March 7, 1906. See also Jesse Max Barber to Washington, April 23, 1906 in Louis R. Harlan and Raymond W. Smock, eds., *The Booker T. Washington Papers*, vol. 8, (Urbana, Ill.: University of Illinois Press, 1979), p. 585 in which Barber states: "I am glad to have had the opportunity of reading this letter which you wrote to President Eliot. Evidently, Mr. Eliot was going to make a speech that would have done us a great deal of harm, and I am glad you influenced him not to deliver the address that he had in mind. In doing so, you have rendered the race a valuable service."
47. Eliot, "What Uplifts a Race and What Holds It Down," p. 8.

48. As quoted in *The Advertiser*, Montgomery, Alabama, March 9, 1909 (clipping, Eliot Papers, unnumbered box). Du Bois's attack on Washington in *The Souls of Black Folk* (Chicago: A. C. McClurg & Co., 1904) and his leadership in the founding of the Niagara Movement had clearly marked him as Washington's chief rival. See Du Bois, *Autobiography*, pp. 236–253.

49. Ibid.

50. *Harper's Weekley*, April 3, 1909 (clipping, Eliot Papers, unnumbered box).

51. "Is He an Ancestory [sic] Worshipper?," *The Pilot*, Boston, March 6, 1909 (clipping, Eliot Papers, unnumbered box).

52. *Town Topics*, New York, March 11, 1909 (clipping, Eliot Papers, unnumbered box).

53. *News and Courier*, Charleston, S. C., March 10, 1909 (clipping, Eliot Papers, unnumbered box).

54. As quoted in ibid., March 17, 1909.

55. Ibid. In responding to a pointed letter from William Monroe Trotter, editor of *The Guardian*, Eliot similarly stated: "As to the most expedient treatment of colored people who are removed by four or five generations from Africa or slavery, I am in favor of leaving that problem to the people of a hundred years hence." Eliot to W. Monroe Trotter, May 5, 1909 (Eliot Papers, Letterbook 98).

56. See Eugene D. Genovese, *In Red and Black: Marxian Explorations in Southern and Afro-American History* (New York: Random House, 1968), pp. 143–144. Cf., however, Herbert Aptheker, "Comment," *Studies on the Left*, 6 (November/December 1966): 27–35.

57. Meier, *Negro Thought in America*, p. 103.

58. Du Bois, *The Souls of Black Folk*, as quoted in Genovese, *Marxian Explorations*, p. 143.

W.E.B. Du Bois and Charles S. Johnson: Differing Views on the Role of Philanthropy in Higher Education

Marybeth Gasman

Introduction

Philanthropy is typically defined as a charitable act, a gift, or an organization that dispenses such gifts. Rarely do we think negatively about gifts. However, as the literature in this area tells us, there is much mistrust of philanthropy and those behind it. Some critics have pointed toward the ulterior motives underlying the gifts of philanthropists.[1] Is it really a gift or does it serve the philanthropist more than the recipient? Others have drawn attention to the unethical business practices of the corporations behind the philanthropies.[2] How can "tainted" money promote good? Still others have questioned the amount of control that many philanthropists gain once their benefactors become dependent on them.[3] Are philanthropists giving money just to extend the reach of their power? Despite these criticisms, philanthropy, in the words of Robert Bremner, "has been one of the principal methods of social advance."[4]

The history of black colleges is interwoven with that of philanthropy. Since the post-Civil War era, northern industrialists have been actively providing financial support to black colleges. Initially, they supported primarily industrial education, which provided blacks with manual training and skills. This lack of wholehearted support for the liberal arts aroused the ire of W.E.B. Du Bois and led to his well known, and often misunderstood, debate with Booker T. Washington. Du Bois advocated a liberal arts education for at least a "Talented Tenth" of the black population—in order to create an intellectual elite that could advance the civil rights of all black people.[5] Washington urged the majority of blacks to "cast down your bucket where you are" and work within the system of segregation in the South.[6] He believed that blacks should be committed to economic improvement and eventually civil rights would follow. Economic improvement would come through a steadfast commitment to hard work and the ownership of property.[7] Du Bois was not opposed to industrial education; he "believed that we should seek to educate a mass of [Negroes] in the three R's and the technique . . . and duty of good work." But, he also thought that the "race must have thinkers and leaders" who possess a liberal arts education.[8] In Du Bois's opinion, what was most unsettling about Washington was his willingness to be a pawn to the northern philanthropists and southern whites.[9] Louis Harlan notes that Washington". . . frequently played upon the desire of southern whites to have a docile, subordinate black population and the desire of northern capitalists to have a skilled, tractable, and hard-working black laboring class."[10] This fundamental difference between Du Bois and Washington caused a rift between the two black leaders.[11]

In the second decade of the twentieth century, the industrial philanthropists shifted their emphasis toward higher education for African Americans and decided to concentrate their efforts on a few elite institutions such as Fisk and Dillard.[12] Despite this change in philosophy, Du Bois

513

continued to be hesitant about philanthropic support of black higher education. He had witnessed the impact of philanthropy on curriculum at his alma mater, Fisk, in 1908[13] and was not convinced that the "enlightened philanthropists" would change their ways.[14] As late as 1946, he wrote, "Education is not and should not be a private philanthropy: it is a public service and whenever it becomes a gift of the rich it is in danger."[15] According to Du Bois, philanthropy stood in the way of the African American's "truthful" education.[16] However, not all African-American intellectuals agreed with him. One who did not was Charles S. Johnson, and Du Bois would later criticize Johnson just as he had Washington thirty years earlier. An analysis of the disagreement between these two men exposes a new and more complex layer of issues concerning higher education for African Americans and philanthropy.

Unlike Du Bois, sociologist and educator Charles S. Johnson worked closely with white philanthropists beginning in the early 1920s and continued to do so until his death in 1956. He saw the foundations as a means for making advances for African Americans—a way of cultivating scholars and leaders. This essay will examine the views of both Du Bois and Johnson with regard to philanthropy. It will not attempt to provide a comprehensive treatment of either figure but will instead compare and contrast their views and experiences with respect to philanthropy. It will illustrate why Du Bois thought that philanthropy was, and would remain, an obstacle to higher education even though it was being used to support many of the goals he had advocated. The paper will also examine Johnson's belief in philanthropy as a pragmatic route with which to create opportunities for African Americans. Through an exploration of Johnson's background, it will uncover the experiences that led to this belief. Finally, it will point to some of the difficulties and limitations of both men's perspectives.

To assess the views of both scholars, this research draws upon their papers, available at Fisk University (Charles S. Johnson Papers, Special Collections) and the University of Massachusetts (W.E.B. Du Bois Special Collections). The author reviewed speeches, letters, unpublished autobiographies, and reports. This essay incorporates material from the large number of publications authored by both Du Bois and Johnson. Information was gathered from interviews conducted by both the author and historian Patrick J. Gilpin.[17] Further, the research draws upon secondary sources written about both Du Bois and Johnson.

Understanding Du Bois—Radical Intellectual

Born in 1868 in Great Barrington, Massachusetts, W.E.B. Du Bois grew up in a mostly white community in the Northeast. He had his first encounter with "southern" segregation only after enrolling at Fisk University in Nashville, Tennessee, in 1885. Although Jim Crow laws had not yet appeared on the books in Nashville, Du Bois experienced the discriminatory "social norms" and separation of the races upon arrival in the community.[18] It was at this point that he began to understand his purpose and developed his sense of activism. In his words, "So I came to this region where the world was split into white and black halves, and where the darker half was held back by race prejudice and legal bonds, as well as by deep ignorance and dire poverty. But facing this was not a lost group, but at Fisk a microcosm of a world and a civilization in potentiality. Into this world I leapt with enthusiasm. A new loyalty and allegiance replaced my Americanism: henceforward I was a Negro."[19] Du Bois graduated from Fisk and moved on to earn multiple degrees from Harvard—culminating in a Ph.D. in history in 1895. While at Harvard, Du Bois received a research grant for study in Europe from the Slater Fund.[20] This was his first "hands-on" interaction with industrial philanthropists. The Slater Fund had claimed in national newspapers that it was looking for "colored" men worth educating.[21] To obtain the grant, Du Bois had worked diligently, writing letter after letter to former United States President Rutherford B. Hayes, the head of the Fund. Despite the fund's national call and Du Bois's excellent credentials, Hayes replied, upon receiving Du Bois's application, that scholarships were no longer available. After two years of writing to Hayes, Du Bois finally persuaded the fund to give him a scholarship. As if to deny that Du Bois had beaten them, the fund made him pay back half of the scholarship upon completion of his studies in Europe.

After graduating from Harvard, Du Bois worked as an instructor at Wilberforce College in Ohio. Eventually, he moved to Atlanta University. There, Du Bois's outrage over racism grew—fed by the increasing discrimination and the horrible practice of lynching taking place throughout the South. At this point, "legalized" Jim Crow had become commonplace and the gains of Reconstruction were all but reversed.[22] No longer able to remain a "detached scientist," Du Bois began to wield his intellect and voice. With the publication of the landmark book, *The Souls of Black Folk*, he identified for the American people the century's most pressing problem—that of "the color line."[23]

Du Bois's experience at Atlanta University fueled his frustration with white philanthropy. He appealed to railroad baron Jacob Schiff and steel magnate Andrew Carnegie for financial backing for a scholarly journal and social science center at Atlanta University. Both journal and center would aim at the black intelligentsia and would focus on race issues in the United States. Both philanthropists refused, and Du Bois attributed this to their connections with Booker T. Washington's Tuskegee "machine."[24] In many cases, Washington had final authority over which black colleges and scholars received philanthropic funds. At this point, Du Bois felt that Atlanta University was suffering the loss of potential philanthropic contributions due to his presence. He noted, "Young President Ware had received almost categorical promise that under certain circumstances increased contributions from the General Education Board and other sources might be expected, which would make the University secure. . . . I was sure that I was at least one of these 'circumstances,' and so my work in Atlanta . . . faded."[25]

As a result of his frustration and desire for change, Du Bois began the Niagara Movement in 1905 and helped found the National Association for the Advancement of Colored People (NAACP) in 1909.[26] Initially, the NAACP's board of directors hoped that Du Bois would use his prominent stature to raise funds for the organization. He refused that role. In a frank admission, he stated, "I knew that raising money was not a job for which I was fitted. It called for a friendliness of approach and knowledge of human nature, and an adaptability which I did not have."[27] Instead of being a fund-raiser, Du Bois became the director of publications and research. In this position, he acted as a social critic and provided opportunities for many of the Harlem Renaissance artists, writers, and poets.

While at the NAACP, Du Bois, once again, clashed with white philanthropists. Of note were his dealings with NAACP board member Oswald Garrison Villard, the owner of the *New York Evening Post* and grandson of noted abolitionist William Lloyd Garrison. Du Bois felt that Villard expected blacks to be humble and thankful—to be respectful of his wealth and willingness to share it.[28] Du Bois, of course, would neither acquiesce to racist social norms nor bow down to riches—his personality would not allow it. Not long after Du Bois started to edit the *Crisis*, Villard clamped down on its content. In an effort to draw attention to the horrors of mob violence against blacks, Du Bois frequently published a list of lynchings in *The Crisis*, sometimes accompanied by graphic photographs. Villard suggested that he also include a list of black crimes. Du Bois refused, noting the ridiculous nature of this request.[29] When there was a clear situation in which to stand up and say, "enough is enough," Du Bois showed courage and resolve.[30]

In 1911, a frustrated Du Bois took aim at white philanthropy and its role in the education of blacks. With the publication of his literary piece *The Quest of the Silver Fleece*, he caricatured the members of the General Education Board as arrogant, conniving, and unconcerned about the "higher" education of African Americans. For example, John D. Rockefeller appeared as John Taylor, a northern businessman whose bank accounts increased daily and whose promise to southern whites was "We'll see that . . . you Southerners get what you want—control of Negro education."[31] Through the farcical style of the novel, Du Bois showed his contempt for the northern industrial philanthropists and their manipulation of African-American education during the early part of the twentieth century.[32]

In 1917, the publication of a particularly critical report on black education by the Phelps Stokes Fund, with the support of the General Education Board, infuriated Du Bois. Written by Thomas Jesse Jones *Negro Education: A Study of the Private and Higher Schools for Colored People in the United States* called for the elimination and consolidation of the majority of black institutions of higher education.[33] White sociologists and philanthropists lauded the report's findings. In 1918, Du Bois fired back at Jones and the philanthropists in a *Crisis* article entitled "Negro Education." "Here, then, is the weakness and sinister danger of Mr. Jones' report. It calls for a union of philanthropic effort with no attempt to make sure of the proper and just lines along which this united effort should work. It calls for cooperation with the white South without insisting on the Negro being represented by voice and vote in such 'cooperation,' and it calls for a recasting of the educational program for Negroes without insisting on leaving the door of opportunity open for the development of a thoroughly trained class of leaders at the bottom, in the very beginnings of education, as well as the top."[34] According to Eric Anderson and Alfred Moss, Jr., Du Bois' critique "permanently marked Jones' reputation."[35] Du Bois's scathing but insightful portrait of the northern philanthropists' actions did not earn him their favor.

W.E.B. Du Bois's willingness to speak out on issues and his unpopularity with white northerners contributed to his rocky relationship with many in the NAACP, in particular its executive secretary Walter White. Frustrated by the constant battles with that organization, Du Bois left in 1934. A quiet offer from friend and Atlanta University President John Hope was the sanctuary Du Bois needed. This institution proved to be an inspirational setting for Du Bois. It was here that he began *Phylon*, published *Black Reconstruction in America*, completed important sociological studies, and wrote several autobiographical pieces.

However, it was also at Atlanta University that Du Bois had one of his most frustrating experiences with philanthropy.[36] This experience would be a thorn in his side for many years and would eventually lead him to give up any hope that philanthropy could make significant change in society.[37] From the age of twenty-nine, Du Bois had longed to publish an Encyclopedia of the Negro. He first mentioned his idea publicly at the Academy of Political and Social Science meeting in Philadelphia in 1897 but was unable to find any support for it. In 1906, he wrote to Andrew Carnegie to request funds for the encyclopedia—again, to no avail. Determined to realize his goal, he continued to contact foundations, including Rockefeller's General Education Board. Although his efforts were commended by the GEB, sponsorship could not be found. When the Phelps-Stokes Fund finally held a conference on the issue in 1931, Charles S. Johnson and Walter White were included but Du Bois was not. Thus, "the most important group scholarship enterprise of the twentieth century was convened without Du Bois being invited" or even credited for his idea.[38] Thomas Jesse Jones, the Phelps-Stokes's education director, saw Du Bois as "the definition of radicalism, a brilliant troublemaker bloated with racial pride and devoid of political common sense."[39] On the day of the conference, the blacks present noted Du Bois's absence and, under pressure, the Fund promised to include him in future meetings. At the second meeting, Du Bois expressed his anger over the Phelps-Stokes Fund's suggestion that the editor of the encyclopedia be white: he did not think it was possible for white editors to express the black point of view. The Fund countered with the rather twisted idea that in true social science the one who knows everything about a topic (as Du Bois did about the Negro) cannot be objective.[40] In his typically conciliatory manner, Charles S. Johnson suggested joint editors—one black and one white. Eventually, Du Bois and sociologist Robert E. Park were chosen for the project.

In 1934, the Phelps Stokes Fund presented the encyclopedia project to the GEB in an attempt to secure funding. They were confident that the GEB would support the project and that their approval would lead to the Carnegie Corporation's backing as well. However, the GEB turned them down. According to David Levering Lewis, "Du Bois' involvement . . . would preclude favorable foundation action for an indefinite period."[41] Although the idea was revived when he moved to Ghana, Du Bois' Encyclopedia of the Negro was never published. To "dodge the credibility of Du Bois' proposal for the encyclopedia," the philanthropists commissioned what they thought would be an equally interesting project—a psychological study of race that would become Gunnar Myrdal's *American Dilemma*.[42] The failure of this lifelong pursuit cemented Du Bois's mistrust of philanthropy.

Under John Hope's presidency, Du Bois had flourished at Atlanta University. However, when Rufus Clement became president, Du Bois began to have difficulty and was soon dismissed from his position. Despite receiving offers, in 1944, from the sociology departments of both Howard and Fisk Universities, Du Bois was persuaded to return to the NAACP.[43] But only four years later, he would have another disagreement with the leadership, this time over his public support of 1948 Progressive Party presidential candidate Henry Wallace. He left the NAACP and spent the remainder of his life writing, speaking, and traveling internationally. Despite his lack of affiliation with a university or the NAACP, Du Bois maintained his influence among blacks in the United States and abroad.[44] His work was interrupted briefly, in 1951, when the United States Department of Justice indicted him on charges of failing to register as a foreign agent. Du Bois was eventually acquitted of this Cold War smear. In 1961, Du Bois left the United States to live in Ghana where he died in 1963 at age 95.[45] Du Bois had spent a lifetime criticizing racial injustice in the United States. Initially, he made attempts to work against racial discrimination and ignorance with the support of the power elites—attempting to garner funds from major philanthropists. With repeated failures on this front, however, Du Bois may have become convinced that the American capitalist system was in and of itself the engine of racism. Hence, it is no surprise he spent his last years in exile.

Understanding Johnson: Liberal Educator and Race Relations Pioneer

Twenty-five years after W.E.B. Du Bois's birth and just a few years prior to *Plessy v. Ferguson's* "separate but equal" ruling, Charles S. Johnson was born in Bristol, Virginia. In contrast to Du Bois, Johnson experienced southern segregation and discrimination from an early age. As the Jim Crow laws went into effect, many of the places that Johnson's family frequented suddenly became unavailable to blacks. In particular, Johnson recalled an incident in an ice cream parlor that "was the beginning of a new self-consciousness that burned."[46] After newspapers carried a short statement about new legislation pertaining to "Negros," Johnson and his mother were suddenly refused a seat at the counter where they had sat each Sunday. According to Johnson, incidents like this from his youth spurred his commitment to alleviating racial problems.[47]

After graduating from high school in 1913, Johnson enrolled in Virginia Union College and earned a bachelor's degree in sociology in 1916. He then moved north to the University of Chicago to study with Robert E. Park who became Johnson's mentor and the two remained close friends until Park's death in 1944. Johnson interrupted his studies at the University of Chicago to enlist in the military during World War I.[48] Upon returning to Chicago in 1919, he found himself in the midst of a race riot caused by the stoning of a young man who accidentally swam into the "White side" of a Chicago beach. According to Martin Bulmer, this incident led Johnson to a deeper interest in "interpreting 'colored people to whites and white people to Negroes.'"[49] Further, that riot sparked his involvement with the Chicago Race Relations Commission as associate executive secretary. The Commission published *The Negro in Chicago: A Study of Race Relations and a Race Riot*; Johnson received national acclaim for his involvement with the study and the commission. It was at this time that Johnson became acquainted with Sears and Roebuck tycoon Julius Rosenwald. Both Rosenwald and Edwin Embree, the president of the Rosenwald's philanthropic foundation, admired Johnson.

Embree and Johnson had a close professional relationship throughout their careers. It was well-known among the black and white liberal communities that Embree relied on Johnson to make recommendations as to what the Rosenwald Fund should support.[50] Embree provided most of the financial backing for Johnson's ideas, including the internationally known social science department that he would later establish at Fisk.[51] Not only did Embree steadfastly endorse Johnson, but Johnson acted as a conduit to the black community for Embree. Embree was greatly concerned with race relations ("the Negro problem") and saw Johnson as the type of black leader who offered a solution. This is evident in Embree's book *Thirteen Against the Odds* (1946), in which he highlights the influence and accomplishments of prominent African Americans and greatly lauds Johnson.[52] In 1934, Johnson and Embree collaborated with Will W. Alexander to produce a study entitled *The Collapse of the Cotton Tenancy*, which challenged the federal government to intervene in the southern situation: "buy up huge acreages of farm lands now in the hands of insurance companies, land banks, and others, and distribute this land in small plots of minimum size required to support farm families."[53] Johnson's work with Embree, which began in the 1920s, would lead to a lifetime of working with the nation's leading philanthropists.

In 1921, Johnson moved to New York to work as the director of research and investigations at the National Urban League. Much like Du Bois, Johnson was offering a forum to Harlem Renaissance luminaries through his editorial position at *Opportunity*, the Urban League's literary magazine.[54] While in New York, Johnson began to "rub elbows" with the city's white philanthropists.

According to Harlem Renaissance artist Aaron Douglas, [Johnson's] "subtle sort of scheming mind had arrived at the feeling that literature was a soft spot of the arts and in the armor of the nation, and he set out to exploit it."[55] This strategy would become a hallmark of Johnson's approach to creating opportunities for African Americans. Sociologist and Johnson contemporary Blyden Jackson portrayed the Renaissance as a stage on which Johnson thought "America [would be] utterly emancipated from the color caste." Jackson points to a dinner hosted by Johnson at the Civic Club in New York on March 21, 1924, as his most significant contribution to the Harlem Renaissance: "It was a dinner at the 'white' Civic Club, one of the very few places in downtown Manhattan where an interracial group, be it ever so elite, in the 1920s could have broken bread together undisturbed."[56] Johnson invited over 300 people—white and black—who identified themselves with the Renaissance. The guests included: Alain Locke, James Weldon Johnson, W.E.B. Du Bois, William Baldwin III, Jessie Fauset, Albert Barnes, and many influential white publishers. Before the event, many black writers and poets had to entrust their manuscripts to unscrupulous agents, but with the success of the evening came interest from prominent American publishers.

Near the close of the Harlem Renaissance in 1928, Charles S. Johnson returned to the South to take a position as director of the social science department at Fisk University. The Julius Rosenwald Fund and the Laura Spelman Rockefeller Memorial handpicked him for that position. These foundations granted Fisk money to support the social science department and made clear their interest in Johnson.[57] While at Fisk, he propelled the department to national prominence and created an internationally known race relations institute. He was a prolific writer and published *Shadow of the Plantation* (1934), *The Negro College Graduate* (1938), and *Patterns of Negro Segregation* (1943) among others. Throughout his work, Johnson focused on the study of racial oppression through the eyes of those who were experiencing it rather than those who were responsible for causing it. He spent years developing ethnographic case studies through the use of "human documents" and identifying "vectors of social change."[58] Johnson thought that by gauging people's attitudes and ideas, it was possible to reveal the information that would lead to political emancipation. He believed in cooperation along racial lines and looked for allies within the white community. For Johnson, cooperation met working within the power structure—specifically national government and philanthropy—and using his connections within these institutions to bolster his public stature on issues of race relations. He favored a steady "chipping away" at segregation and inequality rather than large-scale protest or "radical" attacks. In Johnson's words, "No strategy is sound that does not envisage the total picture in such a way that a person can be helped in deciding, in some smaller individuals cases, what is soundest and most important to stress and what on the whole, is of minor consequence."[59]

This less confrontational approach has made Johnson the subject of much criticism by both black scholars, such as E. Franklin Frazier, and white liberals, such as August Meier.[60] In addition to his work on race relations within the academic setting, Johnson served as a trustee for the Julius Rosenwald Fund from 1934 to 1948, working specifically as the codirector of the race relations program. From 1944 to 1950, he served as the director of the race relations division of the American Missionary Association. In addition, Johnson served on various international committees, including the United Nations Educational, Scientific, and Cultural Organization (UNESCO), and was an advisor to the Supreme Commander for the Allied Powers in Japan after World War II.

In 1946, after a heated national debate led by Fisk alumni, Johnson became the first black president of the institution. At the request of a vocal group of alumni, W.E.B. Du Bois publicly opposed his appointment and, in a September 7, 1946: *Nation* article, suggested that Johnson might be a pawn of philanthropy: ". . . here can be no doubt as to the present situation; the Northern white trustees [philanthropists] hesitate to put a Negro into the presidency; they would prefer a complacent, even second class, white man. The white Southern trustees would consent to a Negro president provided he was a Negro amenable to their guidance and not "radical" that is, not an advocate of the FEPC, the abolition of the poll tax, or any New Deal policies. It is rumored that they are in partial agreement on a man of this sort."[61] It was clear to Fisk alumni and all involved that Du Bois was talking about Johnson.[62] However, Du Bois was mistaken in his assessment of Johnson and the situation at Fisk. As part of an informal network of advisors to the Roosevelt administration, Johnson did much to support the very New Deal policies that Du Bois mentioned.[63] Further, Johnson was not the favorite candidate of the white northern philanthropists on the Fisk board. They saw him as much more valuable in the field of sociology. In the end, it was the actions of several black board members, who recognized Johnson's skill in dealing with philanthropy, which led to his selection. The university needed to meet an endowment challenge set forth by the Rockefeller Foundation, and the board knew that Johnson was better situated to accomplish this task than the other contender, Charles H. Wesley (Du Bois's candidate of choice). According to John Hope Franklin, a Fisk board member during Johnson's presidency, "Charles Wesley's world was a black world. Johnson's world was a white world. Wesley would not have been able to attract funds as Johnson did."[64]

In less than a decade under Johnson's leadership, Fisk built five major buildings, acquired a world-class fine art collection compliments of artist Georgia O'Keefe, and was awarded chapters of *Phi Beta Kappa*, the *American Association of University Women*, and the *Association of Schools of Music*.[65] Under Johnson, Fisk's budget was doubled and over a million dollars was added to its endowment. Always looking to the future, Johnson was cognizant that Rockefeller and Rosenwald monies for black education were dwindling. Thus, he eagerly cultivated new relationships with Clarence Faust of the Ford Foundation and New York socialite John Hay Whitney, securing money from both men to begin the Basic College program—an early college entrance program for Du Bois's "Talented Tenth" at Fisk. That program nurtured scholars and leaders such as Johnnetta B. Cole, David Levering Lewis, and Hazel O'Leary. The Basic College was the culmination of both Johnson's efforts to promote racial equality and his relationships with white philanthropy.[66] However, his work was cut short in 1956 when, on the way to a Fisk board meeting in New York, he died of a heart attack.

Uncovering their Goals

Despite their different backgrounds and perspectives, W.E.B. Du Bois and Charles S. Johnson shared several goals in their pursuit of quality black higher education. Du Bois believed in the need for black colleges and their ability to acclimate students to the larger society: [The student] "may adjust himself, he may through the help of his own social group in the neighborhood of this school successfully achieve an education. . . ." Further, in discussing the needs of black students, Du Bois stressed "individual attention, close acquaintanceship with their fellows and that skilled guidance that only can be gotten in the small college."[67] Johnson not only agreed with these goals but also worked toward their accomplishment in many of his programs.

Du Bois differed from Johnson over the funding of black colleges. In 1946, he proclaimed that to provide the most benefit to black students, a college president must "be not a financier and collector of funds but an educational administrator capable of laying down an education program and selecting the people who will carry it out."[68] He believed that any use of philanthropy in this regard interfered with the search for "truth" in the educational process. According to Du Bois, if "colleges are going to depend on the gifts of the rich for support they cannot teach the truth. . . . [The] impoverishment of the truth seekers can only be avoided by eventually making the state bear the burden of education and this is socialism."[69] Du Bois believed that support and leadership by the state would provide for the growth of strong and secure black colleges. "The state must in the future support and control higher education because of its large and increasing cost."[70] Black colleges could rely on neither unstable church support nor "undesirable" philanthropic support.[71] Stability and consistency, according to Du Bois, would lead to a college experience that nurtured the black student.

While Johnson would not have opposed the use of government funds for black colleges, he clearly believed that there was a role for philanthropy. In some ways, Johnson's career shows the drawbacks of philanthropic support for education. The control given to him by the foundations lent an authoritarian tendency to his leadership style.[72] He determined how much funding was allocated, and in many cases, what types of projects were funded. Johnson did much to support black higher education; however, he tended to squelch ideas that were different from his own. According to Butler Jones, Johnson controlled "the race relations research territory available to blacks [and] exercised suzerainty over fellowships and grants."[73] Likewise, Patrick J. Gilpin notes that Johnson, "had the last word on foundation and other philanthropic grants. Academic, social, and economic leaders relied heavily, sometimes exclusively, upon his judgment, recommendation, or disapproval. Often, it was only with his blessing that the South could get needed funds from outside the area."[74] Johnson's connections created a "power base" that stretched far and wide. He had the funding, respect, and support of white liberals in both the North and South.

But, unlike Booker T. Washington, Johnson worked to create a liberal arts program that was identical to the one favored by Du Bois. Throughout his career, Johnson held a great interest in the welfare of black college students. Not only did his research relate to this area, but his philanthropic service and affiliations coincided with the advancement of African Americans. Johnson helped direct Rosenwald money toward scholarships for black students and later went on to create the Basic College with foundation monies. This program is perhaps the best example of Johnson's overall philosophy pertaining to students and student learning. Unsure of the possibility of integrated black education in the South, Johnson created the Basic College early entrant program, to give promising black students the opportunity to learn in a nurturing, stimulating environment. Students were taught in cohesive learning groups and benefited from the presence of artistic, literary, and political figures whom Johnson invited to the Fisk campus. They studied, ate, and lived together in small cohorts that provided support within the academic setting. According to Peggy Alsup, one of the Basic College students, "Charles Johnson believed in the whole concept of identifying young Black bright kids who thrive in an environment where they have good teachers and encouragement. He was trying to demonstrate too that it did not matter what your color was as long as you have the potential."[75] Johnson was providing students with exactly the college environment prescribed by Du Bois. However, he was doing it in a way that was ideologically opposed to Du Bois's perspective. In fact, according to Basic College graduate David Levering Lewis, "The two sociologists could not have been temperamentally and ideologically more dissimilar."[76]

Philanthropy: Obstacle or Avenue?

If Johnson was able to achieve success, one might expect Du Bois to soften his views on the use of philanthropy and perhaps be more cordial toward Johnson himself. However, the opposite was true. Long after the foundations ceased to meddle in the curriculum and even after they began to embrace a more pro-civil rights agenda, Du Bois continued to oppose them. His hard line perspective on white philanthropy was based on two essential elements. One was personal experience, and in particular, a seemingly purposeful repression of his research agenda. The other was an ideology that was highly complex and distinctly to the left of most of his peers.[77]

Among the most vexing of Du Bois's negative experiences with philanthropy were those that involved Booker T. Washington. In Washington, Du Bois saw a man who had been corrupted by philanthropy and whose work undermined the pursuit of black progress. And to Du Bois, Johnson looked a lot like Washington. Certain connections between the two men were quite compelling. As demonstrated, Johnson was the "golden child" of the Rosenwald Fund. During the early years of that Fund, Washington had played a similar role—assisting Julius Rosenwald with his school-building projects by deciding which counties would receive one.[78] Another connection between Washington and Johnson was their close relationship with Robert E. Park. Park had served as a ghostwriter and advisor to Washington and said of this experience, "I think I probably learned more about human nature and society, in the South under Booker Washington, than I learned elsewhere in all my previous studies."[79] Of course, Johnson studied under Park at the University of Chicago and considered him one of the greatest influences on his career, thought process, and life. Lastly, there was Johnson's involvement with the Urban League. This organization was founded in part by Ruth S. Baldwin, the widow of William H. Baldwin, Jr.—a close friend of Washington, a Tuskegee trustee, and a major industrial philanthropist. Washington gave his support to Baldwin's widow when she started the Urban League. He felt that the League was much more in line with his ideas than the NAACP. Because of these similarities between Johnson and Washington, it is likely that Du Bois viewed the Fisk sociologist as being in the mold of the "Wizard of Tuskegee." This view persisted in spite of Johnson's accomplishments in the area of liberal education.[80]

But Du Bois's views were more than just a matter of personal bias. As shown, his work was unfairly rejected on numerous occasions because of meddling by the foundations. His negative experiences and leftist views reinforced one another over the course of his life. In Du Bois's words, "philanthropy [was a force] which organized vast schemes of relief to stop at least the flow of blood in the vaster wounds which industry was making."[81] Thus, in his mind, philanthropy was merely interested in Band-Aid solutions rather than attacking the root causes of social ills.[82] According to historian Sterling Stuckey, "Du Bois was struck by the essential vulgarity of the Andrew Carnegies and was opposed to any alliance of black workers with a system responsible for the enslavement of their fathers."[83]

The philanthropists had shown time and time again that they were not willing to support the kind of scholarship that Du Bois thought was crucial to the future of the United States. The fact that only Johnson's more mainstream type of research was funded was to Du Bois evidence that the philanthropies were not fully ready to cooperate in the advancement of blacks. Du Bois thought that Johnson "split the difference endlessly and that what passed for wisdom was cliché with the apparatus of scholarship behind it."[84] He was, in Du Bois' words, "if not reactionary, certainly very cautious."[85]

Johnson shared Du Bois's sense of outrage over the injustices black students faced, but his experiences led him to take a much different approach. From Johnson's perspective, the philanthropists seemed more enlightened—they valued his opinions and trusted him. The Rosenwald Fund and the Laura Spelman Rockefeller Memorial made Du Bois's vision of a center for social science research possible at Fisk, under the direction of Johnson. The Fisk sociologist was convinced that through cooperation across racial lines, blacks would benefit and succeed.[86] In fact, students on the Fisk campus left the insulated environment fostered by Johnson with the notion that "the only thing wrong with [this] country was that it was a little slow at embracing [blacks]. And it soon would. [Students] were persuaded that [they] could compete, and to use race as an excuse was really quite demeaning."[87] This attitude toward racial issues was also prevalent in Johnson's writings and speeches. While addressing the Southern Sociological Society, in Atlanta, Georgia, in 1944, Johnson said, "There is fairly widespread agreement that race relations in the South have deteriorated in character since the beginning of the war. [However, it is my] thesis [that] the emotional disturbances of the present period, involving racial issues, are symptoms of accelerated social changes, and that these changes are wholesome, even if their temporary racial effects are bad."[88] Thus, Johnson's essentially optimistic view of the American system explains his faith in the ability of American institutions to ameliorate the racial climate. In a *New York Times* article written after the *Brown* decision, Johnson affirmed his whole-hearted support of the American way of life: "Basically, this is a struggle today not between North and South, or whites and Negroes, or between the national and international points of view. It is a struggle between those who believe in democracy and those who do not."[89] For Johnson a solution to the racial problems he had experienced throughout his life was possible through democracy and through the free enterprise system that included industrial philanthropy.

For Du Bois, the final rejection of his *Encyclopedia of the Negro* was an equally strong denial that United States's style democracy and capitalism offered a solution to race problems. Du Bois would offer other proposals for racial uplift including a black self-tax to support education. He proposed such a plan in a speech given in 1946 entitled, "The Future and Function of the Negro College." In the spirit of black self-determination, he called on the black college alumni and local constituency to "tax themselves. . . . I say 'tax' and I mean tax: a payment as regular and recognized as just as compulsory as any tax. I believe it would be possible but only possible if this kind of contribution was lifted out of the class of ordinary miscellaneous giving to which we are so used and stressed throughout the college course as an absolute necessity for the maintenance of independent methods of education."[90]

Only a few months after his "self taxation" speech, Du Bois conceded that fund-raising and associations with philanthropy might just be needed in the educational process. Upon hearing of Johnson's selection for the presidency of Fisk, Du Bois reluctantly wrote to a trustee who was also aligned against Johnson's candidacy: "He has the ear of the foundations and he will probably get the money that Fisk sorely needs. He will probably rebuild the university physically and may be able to get a faculty about him of the sort of teachers that Fisk needs. At any rate, the only thing that we can do now, it seems to me, is to keep still and give him a chance."[91] Despite his shaky admission that philanthropy may be necessary to the education of blacks, Du Bois himself would not work in this way. Although he had brief interactions with philanthropists in his early years, he was true to his words and convictions. In a 1958 statement to historian Merle Curti, Du Bois wrote, "During my whole career, I have tried not to be put in a position where collecting money from philanthropists would be any considerable part of my work. For that reason I have always declined to [be a] candidate for the presidency of any college or organization where I had to raise funds. Philanthropy is being guided by Big Business to ward off Socialism and Communism, to control labor unions, and to curb all sorts of 'radical' thought."[92] In light of this continuing commitment to a leftist perspective, it is not surprising that Du Bois left the United States to spend his last years in Ghana.[93]

Conclusion

According to historian David Levering Lewis, W.E.B. Du Bois had "influence, not power." Du Bois himself was aware of his situation, noting in 1932 that one who agitates must be willing to pay the price.[94] He was an agitator—one who was skilled at bringing attention to issues. He did not need philanthropy to accomplish this task.[95] He was stubborn and fought vehemently for his ideas. Because this put him in conflict with the powerbrokers of his time, he often acted from the position of "respected outsider."[96]

Charles S. Johnson, on the other hand, has been described as "one of the race's foremost diplomats, whose hands were on the purse strings of numerous foundations."[97] Johnson was a builder who needed monetary support to realize his goals. He worked hard to gain the trust of white philanthropists and eventually was able to make independent decisions in his roles as director of the social science department and president of Fisk University. He studied the ways of philanthropists and acted upon this knowledge. He took the lead by bringing ideas to the philanthropists and seeking their funding. According to Richard Robbins, "The foundations had the money, and they allocated it. They had confidence in Johnson. He needed their resources to get the work done; he went to them. . . . Nowhere is there any record of Johnson being compelled to submit his work to censorship imposed by the foundations. In the milieu of his time, in an era of extreme racism, he managed to obtain the grants, get the studies done, and conceivably, advance the understanding of racial oppression and what strategies could be deployed against it."[98] This is a much different relationship than that of earlier black college presidents who were sometimes manipulated by white philanthropists. The level of independence that Johnson had achieved allowed him to accomplish many of the goals set forth by Du Bois—an African-American social science center, a race relations institute, and the education of the "Talented Tenth." Johnson, however, was not able to be an agitator. Unlike Du Bois, he would sometimes back down from direct confrontation if it meant losing funds for a key program or a position of power.[99] His personality was quieter, and he was a firm believer in working across racial lines.

Although Johnson was accused of compromising in some situations, he did so with a strategy in mind.[100] Johnson was cognizant of the political situation in the United States. He was willing to seek funding from the sources Du Bois favored (i.e., alumni and government), but as a realist, he knew these groups had their limitations. The major drawback to Johnson's approach was his inability to make his innovative programs flourish after his death. While this criticism has been applied to other African-American leaders, the fact that Johnson was working within an educational context makes it particularly severe. Responding to ad hoc concerns, political leaders often expect that their influence will fade after the agenda has been accomplished. Educational leaders like Johnson, however, put programs in place to deal with ongoing concerns—student learning, research, etc. This usually allows for the continuation of those programs after their term in office. In Johnson's case, however, the programs disappeared, and he was virtually forgotten for a long period of time. As a result of his tight hold on power, he entrusted no one with his strategies for working with philanthropists. Only after the processing of his presidential and personal papers many years later, were we made aware of these strategies.

What makes it worthwhile to revisit Johnson is the example he provides in his interactions with the philanthropists. Johnson brought a global awareness to his work in education and race relations. His understanding of changes in the social and economic conditions at mid century, coupled with his shrewd knowledge of the ways of the philanthropists, allowed him to direct funds toward programs that advanced the situation of African Americans in the South. Because he had done extensive writing and research on the southern economic structure, Johnson was well aware of the possibilities for the social changes that were emerging. The collapse of cotton tenancy meant that segregation was no longer a linchpin in the southern economic system. Therefore, northern industrial philanthropy did not have to be as cautious about programs that challenged segregated norms. As a result of Johnson's participation on international committees, including UNESCO, he was also cognizant of the impact of global events at home. In fact, he understood that the defeat of fascism in Europe and the developing Cold War made segregation an embarrassment to the capitalist system. Johnson was aware of these changes and used them to his advantage.[101] He inserted himself in situations—such as United Nations' committees, foundation boards, and governmental advisory committees—that gave him access to prominent personalities. He came to virtually every foundation meeting with a proposal tucked into his briefcase, allowing him more control of the agenda and use of funds.[102] During face-to-face interactions with philanthropists, Johnson was a master of the spoken word. Thus, he was able, through the use of white monetary support, to help students find the "truth" that Du Bois sought on the college campus. He was a strong advocate of research and under his auspices many academic careers were spawned.

In Du Bois's eyes, however, the fact that industrial philanthropy wanted to give African Americans access to education as part of its Cold War agenda was no great victory for blacks.[103] It is important to note that his later criticisms of philanthropy no longer focus on the curtailment of academic freedom and acquiescence in southern segregation, but on the problem of capitalism in general and its complicity in racism. Although supportive of and involved in civil rights efforts,[104] Du Bois realized that a victory against segregation might come at the expense of the global emancipation of people of color—that the end of legal segregation might be a propaganda tool for international capitalism.[105] And this led him to support socialist governments abroad.

At first glance, the fact that Du Bois is reluctant to recognize Johnson's accomplishments in educating the "Talented Tenth" seems like a change in his position on black education. However, when examined in the context of his overall worldview this position is quite consistent.[106] Of many of his fellow black intellectuals, Du Bois wrote in *Dusk of Dawn*, "[They] were deeply American with the old theory of individualism, with a desire to be rich or at least well-to-do, with suspicion of organized labor and labor programs; with a horror of racial segregation."[107] Of their approach, he held, "The bulk of my colleagues saw no essential change in the world. It was the same world with the problems to be attacked with the same methods as before the war. All we needed to do was continue to attack lynching, to bring more cases before the courts, and to insist upon our full citizenship rights."[108] Du Bois believed that as mid century approached, the problems of the world were quite different and that the old liberal solutions would no longer work. Whereas the debate between Du Bois and Washington focused mainly on the narrowing of curricula through the influence of philanthropy, the Du Bois/Johnson disagreement came to encompass questions of the use of capital in the larger society and its impact on issues of race and power. The fact that the latter debate took place, in large part, during the Cold War era made it different in nature and scope from the former. According to Du Bois, few in the race relations circles, including white philanthropists, "moved from [the] undisturbed belief in the capitalist system toward the left, toward a conception of a new democratic control of industry."[109] Du Bois believed that this restructuring of power was critical to worldwide racial emancipation.

When these beliefs got him into trouble during the McCarthy Era, who came to his defense but Johnson. Of this, Du Bois said, "[Of the] 50 presidents of Negro colleges, every one of which I had known and visited—of these only one, Charles S. Johnson of Fisk University, publicly professed belief in my integrity before the trial. . . ."[110] Given Johnson's views and experience with Du Bois, it is likely that he did this not as a gesture of friendship, but as a part of his commitment to the ideal of free speech. In spite of this support, Du Bois continued to shun Johnson. Thus, each man was true to his own beliefs—Johnson, to his belief that the freedoms promised by the American system would bring advancement to blacks and Du Bois, to his belief that they would not.

Notes

Marybeth Gasman is an assistant professor at The University of Pennsylvania. Her interests include philanthropy and historically black colleges, fundraising rhetoric, African-American leadership, and black philanthropy. An earlier version of this paper was presented at the History of Education Society Annual Meeting, San Antonio, Texas, 2000. For their thoughtful comments on earlier drafts, the author would like to thank Derrick P. Aldridge, V. P. Franklin, Philo A. Hutcheson, Edward Epstein, Anthony E. Hargrove, and the *History of Education Quarterly's* anonymous readers. Funding for this research was provided by the Indiana University Center on Philanthropy.

1. James D. Anderson, *The Education of Blacks in the South, 1860–1935* (Chapel Hill: University of North Carolina Press, 1988); Edward Berman, *The Influence of the Carnegie, Ford, and Rockefeller Foundations on American Foreign Policy: The Ideology of Philanthropy* (Albany: State University of New York Press, 1983); Stephen J. Peeps, "Northern Philanthropy and the Emergence of Black Higher Education—Do-gooders, Compromisers, or Co-conspirators?" *Journal of Negro Education* 50:3 (Summer 1981): 251–269; John Stanfield, *Philanthropy and Jim Crow in American Social Science* (Westport, CT: Greenwood Press, 1985); Teresa J. Odendahl, *Charity Begins at Home: Generosity and Self-Interest Among the Philanthropic Elite* (New York: Basic Books, 1990).

2. Washington Gladden, "Tainted Money," *Outlook* 52 (1895): 886–87; William H. Rudy, *The Foundations. Their Use and Abuse* (Washington, D.C.: Public Affairs Press, 1970).

3. Anderson, *Education of Blacks in the South*; Berman, *Influence of the Carnegie, Ford and Rockefeller Foundations*; Stanfield, *Philanthropy and Jim Crow*; E. Franklin Frazier, *Black Bourgeoisie* (Glencoe, IL: Free Press, 1957); Vincent P. Franklin and James D. Anderson, eds. *New Perspectives on Black Educational History* (Boston: G.K. Hall & Co., 1978); Harold J. Laski, *The Dangers of Obedience and Other Essays* (New York: Harper and Brothers, 1930).

4. Robert Bremner, *American Philanthropy* (Chicago: University of Chicago Press, 1988), 2. Eric Anderson and Alfred A. Moss, *Dangerous Donations: Northern Philanthropy and Southern Black Education, 1902–1930* (Columbia: University of Missouri Press, 1999).

5. W.E.B. Du Bois, "The Talented Tenth, "*The Negro Problem: A Series of Articles by Representative American Negroes of Today* (New York: J. Pott & Company, 1903), 33–75.

6. Washington was not opposed to a liberal arts education and in fact, he sent his children to liberal arts colleges. However, for the majority of the freedmen, he advocated industrial education.

7. Booker T. Washington, *Up From Slavery* (New York: A.L. Burt, 1901); Booker T. Washington, "Atlanta Compromise," Cotton States and International Exposition, September 1895, Atlanta, Georgia; Louis R. Harlan, *Booker T. Washington, I, The Making of a Black Leader, 1856–1901* (New York: Oxford University Press, 1972); Louis R. Harlan, *Booker T. Washington, II, The Wizard of Tuskegee, 1901–1915* (New York: Oxford University Press, 1983).

8. W.E.B. Du Bois, "The Hampton Idea," *The Education of Black People, Ten Critiques, 1906–1960* ed. Herbert Aptheker (New York: Monthly Review Press, 1973): 5–15, 5.

9. Of course, Washington was not wholly a pawn. He, in many cases, manipulated white philanthropists and used their money to support progressive causes such as voting rights. See Harlan, *Booker T. Washington: The Wizard*, 144.

10. Harlan, *Booker T. Washington: The Wizard*.

11. Sterling Stuckey, *Slave Culture. Nationalist Theory and the Foundations of Black America* (New York: Oxford University Press, 1987). As Du Bois's influence grew stronger, Washington grew paranoid and spied on him. In some cases, Washington's meddling curtailed Du Bois' potential successes. For example, in 1903, after the "Boston Riot," Washington became angry with Du Bois and his colleagues for disturbing his public speech. From this point on, Du Bois was on Washington's black list. See Harlan, *Booker T. Washington: The Wizard*, 47–49 for more information. Of course, Du Bois was also constantly trying to stay one step ahead of Washington. In many cases, Du Bois blamed him for difficulties with publishers and funders.

12. Anderson, *The Education of Blacks*. For more information, please see Derrick P. Aldridge, "Conceptualizing a Du Boisian Philosophy of Education: Toward a Model for African American Education," *Educational Theory* 49:3 (Summer 1999): 359–379.

13. W.E.B. Du Bois, "Galileo Galilei," (1908) *The Education of Black People, Ten Critiques, 1906–1960*, ed. Herbert Aptheker. (New York: Monthly Review Press, 1973): 17–30.

14. In 1906, Du Bois discovered that money from the Slater Fund supported an "applied science" Department at Fisk. He was outraged that Fisk, a traditionally liberal arts institution, would succumb to such

a request from a northern philanthropist. For more information see, Joe M. Richardson, *The History of Fisk University* (Alabama: The University of Alabama, 1980). In actuality, the Slater Fund grant was only used for the secondary and normal school students who attended Fisk. The college students did not participate in the department of applied sciences.

15. W.E.B. Du Bois, "The Future and Function of the Private Negro College," *The Education of Black People*, 142.

16. W.E.B. Du Bois, *A Soliloquy on Viewing My Life from the Last Decade of Its First Century. The Autobiography of W.E.B. Du Bois* (New York: International Publishers, 1968).

17. Interviews conducted by Patrick J. Gilpin are located in the Fisk University Special Collections (in vault) and were conducted in the 1970s.

18. C. Vann Woodward, *The Strange Career of firm Crow* (New York: Oxford University Press, 1966).

19. Du Bois, *A Soliloquy*, 108.

20. The Slater Fund was created with monies from John Fox Slater's textile manufacturing business in Norwich, Connecticut. The Fund supported industrial education at black colleges during the nineteenth century.

21. Du Bois, *A Soliloquy*, 151

22. Woodward, *The Strange Career of firm Crow*.

23. Du Bois, *The Souls of Black Folk*.

24. Du Bois, *A Soliloquy*.

25. W.E.B. Du Bois, *Dusk of Dawn. An Essay Toward an Autobiography of a Race Concept* (New York: Harcourt, Brace, and Company, 1940): 94.

26. The Niagara Movement was a short-lived attempt to secure full civil rights and political participation for African Americans. The NAACP is an interracial organization, which called for integration and an end to lynching. It also supported much of the artistic talent present during the Harlem Renaissance.

27. Du Bois, *A Soliloquy*, 257–258.

28. Ibid. Despite their squabbles, Du Bois gave Villard credit for changing his believe in the capitalist system to a more leftist perspective which supported a more democratic control of industry. (See also Du Bois, *Dusk of Dawn*, 290).

29. Du Bois, *A Soliloquy*. Du Bois may have also resented Villard for pushing for cooperation between he and Booker T. Washington. Despite leaning toward Du Bois's side philosophically, Villard thought that Washington and Du Bois could work together—this would accomplish more. According to Louis Harlan, "Oswald Garrison Villard "dreamed of joining the forces of Washington, whose work at Tuskegee he admired and supported, and W.E.B. Du Bois, the champion of human rights . . . he was virtually alone in his belief that the two leaders could be reconciled." Harlan, *Booker T. Washington: The Wizard*, 360.

30. Manning Marable, *W.E.B. DuBois. Black Radical Democrat* (Massachusetts: G.K. Hall & Co., 1986).

31. W.E.B. Du Bois, *The Quest for the Silver Fleece* (Miami, Florida: Mnemosyne Lewis, 1969), 161; Lewis, *W.E.B Du Bois. Biography of a Race*, 447.

32. Anderson, *Education of Blacks in the South*.

33. Thomas Jesse Jones, ed. *Negro Education: A Study of the Private and Higher Schools for Colored People in the United States* [1917] (New York: Arno Press and the New York Times, 1969).

34. W.E.B. Du Bois, "Negro Education," reprinted in David Levering Lewis, *W.E.B. Du Bois. A Reader* (New York: Henry Holt Publishers, 1995): 261–269:269.

35. Anderson and Moss, *Dangerous Donations*, 204.

36. This controversy began while Du Bois was at the *Crisis* but came to a head during his tenure at Atlanta University.

37. Lewis, interview with author, 3 August 2001.

38. Ibid. According to David Levering Lewis, Thomas Jesse Jones, the education director for Phelps-Stokes, said that the foundation's idea was sparked by Monroe Work's *Negro Year Book*. Work's book was published by Tuskegee the same year. For a detailed explanation of the situation, see Lewis, *W.E.B. Du Bois. The Fight for Equality*, 426–433.

39. Thomas Jesse Jones quoted in David Levering Lewis, *W.E.B. Du Bois. The Fight for Equality*, 427.

40. David Levering Lewis, interview with author, 3 August 2001.

41. Lewis, *W.E.B. Du Bois. The Fight for Equality*, 434.

42. David Levering Lewis, interview with author, 3 August 2001.

43. It was Charles S. Johnson who persuaded then president of Fisk University, Thomas Elsa Jones, to make an offer to W.E.B. Du Bois. Charles S. Johnson to W.E.B. Du Bois, 26 May 1944, located in Charles S. Johnson Papers [hereafter Johnson Papers], Special Collections, Fisk University, Nashville, Tennessee.

44. Gerald Horne, *Black and Red. W.E.B. Du Bois and the Afro-American Response to the Cold War, 1944–1963* (Albany: SUNY Press, 1986).

45. Du Bois, *A Soliloquy*, 391.

46. Charles S. Johnson, "A Spiritual Autobiography," n.d. [1947], 4, Johnson Papers.

47. Ibid.

48. Although often referred to as "Dr. Johnson," Johnson did not have a Ph.D. He was awarded a Ph. B (Bachelor of Philosophy) from the University of Chicago in 1919. (See University of Chicago Registrar).

49. Martin Bulmer, "Charles S. Johnson, Robert E. Park, and the Research Methods of the Chicago Commission on Race Relations, 1919–22: An Early Experiment in Applied Social Research," *Ethical and Racial Studies* 4:3 (1981): 2899.

50. Patrick J. Gilpin, "Charles S. Johnson. An Intellectual Biograpy," (Ph.D. diss., Vanderbilt University, 1973).

51. Patrick J. Gilpin and Marybeth Gasman, "Charles S. Johnson: Sociologist, Race Relations Diplomat, and Educator during the Age of Jim Crow," (Albany: State University of New York Press, forthcoming).

52. Edwin R. Embree, *Thirteen Against the Odds* (New York: The Viking Press, 1946).

53. Charles S. Johnson, Edwin R. Embree, and W. W. Alexander, *The Collapse of Cotton Tenancy: Summary of Field Studies & Statistical Surveys, 1933–35* (Chapel Hill: University of North Carolina Press, 1935): 65.

54. Perhaps it is indicative of their contrasting personalities that Johnson's journal was entitled *Opportunity* while Du Bois' was entitled *Crisis*.

55. David Levering Lewis, *When Harlem was in Vogue* (New York: Oxford University Press, 1981): 125.

56. Blyden Jackson, "A Postlude to a Renaissance," *Southern Review* 25, 4 (1990): 746–765, 753.

57. Gilpin and Gasman, *Charles S. Johnson*.

58. Charles S. Johnson, *Shadow of a Plantation* (Chicago: The University of Chicago, 1934); idem., *Patterns of Negro Segregation* (New York: Harper & Row, 1943); and idem., *The Negro College Graduate* (New York: Negro Universities Press, 1969). Richard Robbins, *Sidelines Activist: Charles S. Johnson and the Struggle for Civil Rights* (Jackson: University of Mississippi Press, 1996), 179.

59. Charles S. Johnson, "Famous Sociologist Asks, Answers Some Key Questions for Negroes," *The Chicago Defender* (September 26, 1942): 32.

60. For more information see, August Meier, *A White Scholar in the Black Community* (Amherst: University of Massachusetts Press, 1993); Anthony Platt, *E. Franklin Frazier Reconsidered* (New Brunswick, New Jersey: Rutgers University Press, 1991).

61. W. E. B. Du Bois to Ernest Alexander 11 July 1946; Carter Wesley to Ernest Alexander, 15 July 1946; James Stamps to Ernest Alexander, 18 July 1946; James Stamps to Ernest Alexander, 26 June 1946; Confidential memo to the president of the alumni association and alumni representatives on the Fisk board of trustees, 12 July 1946; Ernest Alexander to W.E.B. Du Bois, 20 July 1946; Sadie St. Clair Daniels to Ernest Alexander, 23 July 1946; W.E.B. Du Bois to Ms. Freda Kirchway, editor of *Nation* Magazine, 26 July 1946, all located on Reel 58 in the W.E.B. Du Bois Papers [hereafter Du Bois Papers], University of Massachusetts, Amherst. W.E.B. Du Bois, "A Crisis at Fisk," *Nation* (September 7, 1946): 269–270, 270.

62. W.E.B. Du Bois to Ernest Alexander 11 July 1946; Carter Wesley to Ernest Alexander, 15 July 1946; James Stamps to Ernest Alexander, 18 July 1946; James Stamps to Ernest Alexander, 26 June 1946; Confidential memo to the president of the alumni association and alumni representatives on the Fisk board of trustees, 12 July 1946; Ernest Alexander to W.E.B. Du Bois, 20 July 1946; Sadie St. Clair Daniels to Ernest Alexander, 23 July 1946; W.E.B. Du Bois to Ms. Freda Kirchway, editor of *Nation* Magazine, 26 July 1946, all located on Reel 58 in the Du Bois Papers. W.E.B. Du Bois, "A Crisis at Fisk," *Nation* (September 7, 1946): 269–270, 270.

63. Robbins, *Sidelines Activist*; Katrina Sanders, "Building Racial Tolerance Through Education: The Fisk University Race Relations Institute, 1944–1969," (Ph. D. diss., University of Illinois, 1997).

64. John Hope Franklin, interview with author, 5 June 1999.

65. For more information on these programs, see Charles S. Johnson Papers, 1955–56 clipping file, located in the Fisk Archives. Specifically, Charles S. Johnson to Marie Johnson, July 25, 1956, box 144, folder 8, Johnson Papers. In this letter, Johnson notes the growth of the university. See also, Gilpin, "Charles S. Johnson. An Intellectual Biography."

66. Marybeth Gasman and Edward Epstein, "Modern Art in the Old South: The Role of the Arts in Fisk University's Campus Curriculum," *Educational Researcher* 4:2 (March 2002): 13–20.

67. Du Bois, "The Future and Function of the Private Black College, (1946)" *The Education of Black People*, 144, 146. For more information on Du Bois' views on higher education, please see Aldridge. "Conceptualizing a Du Boisian Philosophy;" Frederick Dunn, "The Educational Philosophies of Washington,

Du Bois, and Houston: Laying the Foundations for Afrocentrism and Multiculturalism," *Journal of Negro Education 62*, 1 (Winter 1993): 24–34; James B. Stewart, "The Legacy of W.E.B. Du Bois for Contemporary Black Studies," *Journal of Negro Education* 53, 3 (Summer 1984): 296–312.

68. Du Bois, "The Future and Function of the Private Black College (1946)," *The Education of Black People*, 144. This speech was given at the commencement of Knoxville College, in Tennessee on June 10, 1946. Charles S. Johnson became president of Fisk University in July the same year—much to Du Bois' dismay. Du Bois' opposition to Johnson's selection is evident in the continual theme in the speech of presidents not being a financier or someone who solicits monetary gifts.

69. Du Bois, "The Future and Function of the Private Black College, 157.

70. Ibid., 140.

71. One of the reasons Du Bois, at one point, called for the elimination or consolidation of the weaker black college is their lack of stable financial support. State funding would, in Du Bois's mind, lead to security for black colleges.

72. Marybeth Gasman, "A Renaissance in Nashville: Charles S. Johnson's Use of Philanthropy to Build Fisk University in the Post-War Period," (Ph.D. diss., Indiana University, 2000). Gilpin and Gasman, "Charles S. Johnson."

73. Butler Jones, "The Tradition of Sociology Teaching," in John Bracey, August Meier, and Elliot Rudwick, eds. *The Black Sociologists: The First Half Century* (Belmont, CA: Wadsworth Publishing Company, 1971): 137.

74. Gilpin, "Charles S. Johnson," 631.

75. Peggy Alsup, interview by author, 31 March 1999.

76. Lewis, *W.E.B. Du Bois. The Fight for Equality*, 157.

77. Ibid.; Adolph Reed, *W.E.B. Du Bois and American Political Thought* (New York: Oxford University Press, 1997); Hugh Murray, "Review Essay. Du Bois and the Cold War." *The Journal of Ethnic Studies* 15:3 (Fall 1986): 115–124; Dan S. Green and Earl Smith, "W.E.B. Du Bois and the Concepts of Race and Class," *Phylon* XLIV 4 (December 1983): 262–272.

78. Harlan. *Booker T. Washington. The Wizard*.

79. Ibid., 291.

80. Ironically, Charles S. Johnson wrote an article entitled "The Social Philosophy of of Booker T. Washington," in the April 1928 issue of *Opportunity*. His ability to see the best of Washington's ideas may have contributed to Du Bois' mistrust of Johnson.

81. W.E.B. Du Bois, *Darkwater: Voices from Within the Veil* (New York: AMS Press, 1920, reprinted 1969): 136.

82. Lewis, interview with author, 3 August 2001.

83. Stuckey, *Slave Culture*, 272.

84. Lewis, interview with author, 3 August 2001.

85. W.E.B. Du Bois to George Padmore, 17 March 1950 in Herbert Aptheker ed. *W.E.B. Du Bois, The Correspondence of W.E.B. Du Bois, Volume III, Selections, 1944–1963* (Amherst: University of Massachusetts Press, 1978), 281.

86. Gasman, "A Renaissance in Nashville."

87. Lewis, interview with author, 3 August 2001. Lewis was a student at Fisk University during Johnson's presidency. Other students have corroborated his statements including: Richard Thornell, interview with author, 23 August, 2001, Peggy Alsup interview with author, 31 March 1999, Prince Rivers, interview with author, 25 March 1999, Vivian Norton, interview with author, 11 May 1999, Earl Daily, interview with author, 22 April 1999, Jane Forde, interview with author, 27 April 1999, Richard Thornell, interview with author, August 24, 2001.

88. Charles S. Johnson, "The Present Status of Race Relations in the South," *Social Forces*. 23, 1, October 1944: 27–32, 27. For similar rhetoric, see idem., "The Negro in Post-War Reconstruction: his Hopes, Fears and Possibilities," *Journal of Negro Education* 11:4 (October 1942): 343–348; idem., "Social Changes and Their Effects on Race Relations in the South," *Social Forces* 23:5 (March 1945): 343–348; and idem., "The Decade in Race Relations," *Journal of Negro Education*, 13:3 (Summer 1944): 441–446.

89. Charles S. Johnson. "A Southern Negro's View of the South," *New York Times Magazine* (September 23, 1956): 15, 64–67, 65.

90. Du Bois, *Education of Black People*, 145–146.

91. W.E.B. Du Bois to Ernest Alexander, 9 November 1946, Reel 58, W.E.B. Du Bois Papers.

92. W.E.B. Du Bois to Professor Merle Curti, 4 June 1958, Herbert Aptheker, ed. *The correspondence of W.E.B. Du Bois. Volume III Selections, 1944–1963* (Amherst: University of Massachusetts Press, 1976), 430.

93. Lewis, *W.E.B. Du Bois. The Fight for Equality*.

94. Ibid., 431.

95. Cornel West, "W.E.B. Du Bois: An Interpretation," Africana: An Encyclopedia of the African and African American Experience," eds. Kwa Authony Appiah and Henry Louis Gates (New York: Basic Civitas Books, 1999).

96. Lewis, interview with author, 3 August 2001.

97. Richard Bardolph, *The Negro Vanguard*. (New York: Vintage Books, 1959): 327.

98. Robbins, *Sidelines Activist*, 9.

99. Gilpin and Gasman, "Charles S. Johnson." In 1945, Johnson was selected to be the first black president of the Southern Sociological Society. The following year he presided over the society's annual meeting in Atlanta, Georgia. The conference announcement included information about housing at the Biltmore Hotel. However, when Juliette V. Philter, a black member of the society, sent in her hotel reservation she was told, by Johnson, that accommodations were not available for black participants. Alternative housing was made available for black participants at Atlanta University. Rather than risk his position in the society, Johnson acquiesed in southern norms. Charles S. Johnson to Juliette V. Phifer, May 7, 1946, Charles S. Johnson Papers.

100. Gilpin, "Charles S. Johnson," 635.

101. Marybeth Gasman, "Passport to the Front of the Bus: The Impact of Fisk University's International Program on Segregation in Nashville Tennessee," 49th Parallel: An Interdisciplinary Journal of North *American Studies*, 7 (Winter 2001): online journal at: artsweb.bham.ac.uk/49th parallel/backissues/issue7/Frontpg7.htm

102. Prince Rivers, interview with author, 25 March 1999.

103. Lewis, interview with author, 3 August 2001.

104. Horne, *Black and Red*.

105. Lewis, interview with author, 3 August 2001; Lewis, *W.E.B. Du Bois, The Fight for Equality*.

106. Reed, *W.E.B. Du Bois and American Political Thought*.

107. Du Bois, *Dusk of Dawn*, 290.

108. Ibid.

109. Ibid.

110. Du Bois, *A Soliloquy*, 391.

FROM SEMINARY TO UNIVERSITY: AN OVERVIEW OF WOMEN'S HIGHER EDUCATION, 1870–1920

LYNN D. GORDON

Victorian Culture and Women's Education to 1870

The conventions of middle-class Victorian culture prescribed separation of the sexes. The public, political, and economic world belonged to men, whereas women's sphere was limited to household and children. This ideology of separatism described middle-class life in nineteenth-century urban northeastern America: men worked for wages outside the home, while women toiled within it. But even outside the cities and in other regions of the country, Victorians accepted scientific and theological theories of profound, inherent male-female differences.

Victorian sex roles, and in particular the cult of domesticity, glorified the responsibilities of home and sentimentalized motherhood. Separate spheres allowed women no political voice, limited economic options, and few legal rights, even concerning their sacred duty of mothering. Clearly, men held the reins of power. Yet domesticity gave homebound women moral and spiritual authority within the family, and thus a role in urban, bourgeois society.

Historians have also noted that separatism promoted the development of a women's culture. In their domestic lives and intimate same-sex friendships, Victorian women embraced religious, moral, communal, and emotional principles opposed to the competitive materialism and individualism of nineteenth-century American life. Moreover, although confining women within the home, the cult of domesticity laid the ideological groundwork for their leaving it. The very qualities attributable to good wives and mothers—purity, piety, moral superiority, and gentleness—made women necessary actors in the public arena. The notion of "social housekeeping" and the idea that suffrage itself extended domestic duties to the world outside the household did not fully develop until the turn of the century, but began in the northeast during the antebellum era, with women's participation in missionary work, teaching, temperance, moral reform, and abolition.

In practice, then, the lives of Victorian men and women resembled overlapping circles more than separate realms. The incessant public discussion and debate over sex roles throughout the nineteenth and into the early twentieth century reveal that separatism was difficult to maintain, its definition and implications troubling men and women alike. As women moved beyond the home, albeit proclaiming their actions as logical extensions of domesticity, male and female critics complained that such behavior destroyed family life and ruined the health of women and children, thereby undermining the social order. These fears surfaced time and again as Victorian women challenged sex role boundaries, defining and redefining the meaning of masculinity and femininity and the interplay between public and private life. Conservatives, who insisted on a narrow, household-bound definition of women's roles, as well as liberals, who argued that femininity was not incompatible with certain public activities, believed that the sexes had inherently distinct natures.[1]

Even before the Victorian era, education was an important arena for the expansion of women's sphere under the rubric of improving family life. Since the mid-eighteenth century, reformers and radicals, including Mary Wollstonecraft, had asserted that lack of education made women frivolous and socially irresponsible, unfit to be companions to their husbands, good mothers to their children, or self-supporting in the absence of a male provider. The ideology of the American Revolution suggested the importance of family education for the creation of good "republicans," and Americans came to agree that educated mothers raised better citizens. Between 1780 and 1830, this association of women's education with family needs opened the doors of primary schools to girls. And in the nineteenth century, evangelical Christianity sanctioned education for women as a means of enhancing and enforcing their spiritual authority within the home.

In the antebellum North, economic issues also advanced the cause of women's secondary education. The exodus of labor from households into shops and factories meant that older children had to earn a living outside the home before they married. Northern women who remained single, through choice or necessity, turned to teaching as a "respectable" way of supporting themselves. The growth of primary education in the North and West during the antebellum era led districts, desperate for teachers, to hire women at half the salary paid to male teachers. Moreover, teaching as a female occupation represented one of the first cases of domesticity extended. Proponents argued that women made better teachers because they could draw upon innate maternal instincts in dealing with students.[2]

Thus, many women who attended seminaries, academies, or normal institutes did so in preparation for running their own classrooms. The need to train women to earn a living caused northern schools to emphasize professional courses as much or more than preparation for domesticity. Prominent women's educators such as Emma Willard, Mary Lyon, and Catharine Beecher claimed that women's secondary education enriched home life and enhanced Christian practice but also channeled their efforts into the development of a teaching profession.[3]

The quality of seminary education varied greatly, but some of the best schools, including Willard's Troy Female Seminary and Lyon's Mount Holyoke, offered a rigorous curriculum, featuring reading, writing, study of the Scriptures, grammar, mathematics, composition, arithmetic, history, geography, French, Latin, and natural history. The devoutly religious founders of many women's academies and seminaries demanded high standards of conduct and disciplined students sternly. Students observed the Sabbath, attended prayer meetings, and followed a schedule of bells indicating classes, study times, recreation periods, and sleep. Antebellum academies trained women to think and reflect, gave them access to books, companionship, and the example of their teachers, while preparing them to earn a living. Studies of individual institutions show that graduates worked at a variety of jobs and participated in community activities throughout their lives.[4]

Southerners also believed that women's education would uphold, not subvert, their slaveholding patriarchal culture. In the South, the high cost of a seminary education (around $150 a year for two to five years, with extra charges for music, dancing, drawing, and needlework) limited attendance to women who would not have to support themselves. Graduates of southern seminaries returned home to marry, raise children, and assume the duties of running a plantation or urban middle-class household. The diversity of denominational allegiances, the male-dominated hierarchy within evangelical Protestant churches, and the isolation of white women on farms and plantations kept antebellum southern white women from developing the bonds of womanhood, and thus the intimacy necessary for the creation of a separate women's culture. As Catherine Clinton put it: "Antebellum southern women were confronted by the irony of their education." Exposed to new forms and varieties of knowledge, they were nevertheless confined to the same domestic duties as their uneducated mothers and grandmothers.[5]

For some southern women, however, education may well have bred high expectations and ultimately dissatisfaction. The courtship of Bessie Lacy and Thomas Dewey in the 1850s offers one such example. At Edgeworth Female Seminary in Greensboro, North Carolina, Lacy became part of a world with larger concerns and possibilities than her parents' household. Her friendships with other women led her to hope that marriage would be a similar meeting of intellect and sensibility. In his analysis of Bessie Lacy's letters to her parents, friends, and Dewey, Steven M. Stowe demonstrates her gradual though reluctant acceptance of the nineteenth-century realities and constrictions of male-female relationships.[6]

By proving women's intellectual mettle, maintaining the rhetorical connections between domesticity and schooling, and training some young women to support themselves, nineteenth-century seminaries and academies expanded woman's sphere, paving the way for higher education. Indeed, the boundary between nineteenth-century secondary schools and colleges remained indistinct, particularly for women's education. Willard's and Lyon's schools compared favorably to the men's colleges of their day; several southern institutions even called themselves colleges.

Institutional distinctions were nonetheless clear to Americans of that era; and in the 1830s and 1840s, women's desire to attend college inaugurated a century-long debate over female higher education. Once again, neither side refuted gender distinctiveness. Conservatives claimed that higher education would destroy women's desire to remain within the home, while liberals asserted that colleges would produce better wives and mothers. Yet women students and their families had their own agendas. They made the decision for higher education independently, often in opposition to the rhetoric around them, and many did not define their purposes in terms of domesticity.[7]

Why Go to College? The Pioneers

Nineteenth-century advocates of women's higher education linked their cause to enhanced domesticity and "cultured motherhood." Protests came from doctors, clergy, and writers already uneasy about the expansion of women's public roles. Opponents claimed that by going to college, women would sever the tenuous connections between education and domesticity and enter the domain of men. In these years before the founding of well-established women's colleges, conservatives mixed arguments against female college attendance with objections to coeducation.

By the mid-nineteenth century, most Americans accepted coeducation in primary or secondary schools. As Victoria Bissell Brown has pointed out, Victorians were so sanguine about inherent sex-based characteristics that they did not believe prepuberty association of boys and girls endangered the formation of gender identity. Higher education, however, was another matter. As the final stage before the assumption of adult roles, collegiate coeducation put issues of separatism to the forefront. Most contemporary adult social institutions and organizations either excluded one sex or separated the two; coeducational colleges and universities were a major exception. How would students and faculty cope with such a situation, requiring them to treat men and women in the same manner, and simultaneously observe sex-role norms? And, most important, what effect would such associations have on the long-term relations between the sexes? Many feared that women educated with men would seek more than access to liberal culture and teacher training and want the privileges and duties of men. Would not collegiate coeducation, by its very nature, move women outside the home, their proper sphere?[8]

In the antebellum era, a few private colleges, notably Oberlin (established in 1833) and Antioch (1853) pioneered collegiate coeducation. Early in their histories, these institutions, both founded by Christian social reformers, struggled with the definition and implications of coeducation. Oberlin women studied the Ladies' Course (although they were permitted after 1841 to elect the men's course if they so wished). They were not allowed to deliver graduation orations, or any other public speeches, and were expected to perform domestic work, while male students did the heavier chores. Oberlin's first president, evangelist Charles Finney, and future administrators and faculty felt that coeducation provided a healthy social atmosphere, as well as practice for future ministers in dealing with women who would one day be their congregants or spouses. Social and extracurricular organizations and activities were sex-segregated; relationships between men and women took place in an atmosphere of evangelical piety and propriety. Similar conditions prevailed at Antioch, where President Horace Mann separated men and women completely except in the classroom. Women students and women faculty at both colleges resisted separatism. Oberlin students and future women's rights activists Lucy Stone and Antoinette Brown opposed their college's policies, while at Antioch women students broke the rules of social propriety so dear to Mann's heart by attempting to combine their literary society with the men's.[9]

In contrast, Lori Ginzberg's reinterpretation of Oberlin's early history depicts a more benign separatism, emphasizing the college's positive view of womanhood. Ginzberg maintains that the founders of Oberlin wanted men to live up to women's higher social and moral standards; separatism indicated respect for women's special qualities. She points out that male as well as female students performed the college's domestic work; that both sexes founded separate moral reform societies; and that the presence of women, according to contemporaries, inspired piety and correct behavior. Although Antioch and Oberlin administrators and faculty strictly limited women's roles on the campuses, the religious, reform-oriented atmosphere at these schools favored the presence of women and the development of their intellect. Women's rebellion against restrictions demonstrates self-confidence about their place at Oberlin and Antioch.[10]

Women's higher education continued to be controversial, despite the success of Oberlin and Antioch, Congress's passage of the Morrill Act (1862), providing for the establishment of state universities, and the founding of authentic women's colleges in the 1860s and 1870s. Harvard's Dr. Edward Clarke fanned the flames of opposition with his popular books, *Sex in Education, or a Fair Chance for the Girls* (1873) and *Building a Brain* (1874). Adding the authority of science to older arguments that religion and morality prescribed "woman's proper sphere," Clarke maintained that biology was destiny. Too much study, he said, drew blood away from the ovaries to the brain, particularly if the female student overtaxed herself during the "catamenial function" (menstruation). College women thus endangered their health and perhaps rendered themselves incapable of bearing healthy children. Although he particularly opposed coeducation, Clarke also condemned women's colleges like Vassar for educating women in the same manner as men.[11]

Given the controversy and the possibility of long-term deleterious effects, why did women want to go to college during the latter half of the nineteenth century? After all, domestic enhancement and even a teaching career were possible through a normal school, high school, seminary, or academy education. Why risk social opprobrium or one's health to go to college?

Some families apparently did not believe the "experts." The mother of young Martha Carey Thomas, future president of Bryn Mawr College, reassured her daughter that neither she nor her friends knew any women like those Clarke described in his book. For other families, rhetoric about domesticity took second place to ensuring their daughters' future; college was a good investment. Many families preferred state universities as a less costly educational choice; seminaries and normal schools were usually private and not universally available. Most states did not have significant licensing laws for teachers until the early twentieth century, but university credentials quickly became a useful asset for landing a more prestigious or better-paying urban teaching position. Families sometimes relocated near a state university, so that their children could live at home and attend classes.[12]

White southern women had little access to higher education until the 1880s and 1890s, almost a generation later than their northern counterparts. Yet arguments promoting their education had begun earlier, after the Civil War left many white women without husbands or financial resources. For these women, and subsequent generations caught in the throes of the modernizing and urbanizing southern economy, teaching became the road to self-support, as it already was in the North. And like northerners, southern proponents of women's higher education emphasized its applicability to Christian home life.[13]

If most aspiring college women equated the impetus for higher education with the need to earn a living, others had a wider, more idealistic vision. Although most advocates of women's higher education did not support women's rights, the Declaration of Sentiments, written in 1848 by the first women's rights convention in Seneca Falls, New York, listed lack of access to colleges on its roster of gender inequalities. In succeeding years, women's rights periodicals promoted higher education as the key to full social and economic participation. After deciding to devote her life to the women's rights movement, Kentuckian Laura Clay spent a year at the University of Michigan in preparation for her work in the cause.

Women's rights advocates sometimes played a leading role in women's admission to specific campuses and in refuting Dr. Clarke's theories. The *Woman's Journal*, the leading women's rights publication, printed highly critical reviews of Clarke's book by distinguished doctors and nonmedical authorities. Three volumes of essays, edited by suffragists Julia Ward Howe, Eliza B. Duffey, and Anna C. Brackett, proclaimed Clarke's ignorance about women's health and education. College women were certainly conscious of the women's rights movement, if only because critics of women's higher education usually linked the two causes. And whatever their political views upon entering college, some alumnae went on to become prominent in suffrage organizations and other women's rights causes.[14]

Higher education also offered intellectual and aesthetic fulfillment. Women's clubs, amateur scientific societies, home study, lyceums, and lectures provided forums for discussion and companionship outside the academy, but many women found that only in universities and colleges could they stretch their minds and test their capabilities. Writing about her experiences at Cornell, Florence Kelley said, "My freshman year was one continued joy. Anhungered and athirst for learning . . . here was indeed delight. Little did we care that there was no music, no theater, almost no library; . . . Our current gossip was Froude's life of Carlyle . . . I embarked upon a schedule of twenty-five hours a week of ancient and modern languages and mathematics . . . I listened and recited, studied, memorized, and acquired."[15]

In the nineteenth century, the "family claim" often kept unmarried women of the middle classes at home to look after parents and siblings, but some families supported their daughters' efforts to get the best education possible and move into the professions. In her analysis of Wellesley College's all-female faculty, Patricia Palmieri has described the nurturing and enabling New England family culture of the late nineteenth century. The women in Palmieri's study learned to value books and education early in life, and parental encouragement continued after graduation. In 1890, Wolcott Calkins successfully negotiated with Harvard's president, Charles William Eliot, for the admission of his talented daughter, Wellesley professor Mary Whiton Calkins, to the university's graduate psychology program.[16]

Nor was this phenomenon confined to potential Wellesley professors from New England families. A survey of Vassar alumnae from the classes of 1865 through 1890 (most of whom were from the New York–New Jersey–Pennsylvania area) revealed that these women had attended college because their parents wanted them to. Fathers were mentioned five times more frequently than mothers as sources of inspiration for college attendance.[17]

Less frequently, families outside the northeast also adopted progressive ways of raising daughters. William Campbell Preston Breckinridge, Kentucky lawyer, congressman, and Confederate colonel, was initially dubious about the decision by his daughter, Sophonisba, to attend Wellesley in 1884. He worried about the consequences, for her and for the family, of life outside their close-knit network of friends and relatives. "You have been tenderly reared & always treated with rather peculiar and affectionate esteem," he wrote to her. "Dutiful, loving, and unselfish; you were appreciated and perhaps a little spoilt in our not very large circle. At Wellesley you are but one of five hundred—a new, unknown one at that." On another occasion, he wrote: "One of the best results of education at home is common friends—that all the members of a family have in a certain sense mutual friendships & common associations . . . I doubt if what you gain compensates for this."

Breckinridge, however, was an empathetic father who had assumed responsibility for his daughter's care in infancy and nursed her through childhood illnesses. Above all, he wrote, "[I] persisted in my purpose to give your brain a fair chance to show its power." He urged Sophonisba to make the most of her opportunities at college, to explore Boston, accept the proffered class presidency, and remain for the full four-year course of study. Finally, the colonel reminded his daughter that "you ought to look squarely in the face that if I die, you will have to make your own living: & if I live you may have to do so anyhow . . . God preserve you . . . from the aimless . . . life of the young girls you would associate with here."[18]

For the first generation of college-educated women, the choice between single-sex and coeducational institutions determined the nature of their campus experiences. Most students, male or female, attended the tuition-free or inexpensive state universities. Yet as American higher education expanded and research universities developed, faculty involvement with scholarship left students without caretakers. Violence, indifference toward academic pursuits, an obsession with class competitions, and increased distance from faculty marked male student life in the 1860s, 1870s, and 1880s. Struggling for intellectual acceptance and social survival, the female pioneers of coeducation formed literary societies and other clubs but existed only on the social margins of college life.

Women at Men's Colleges, 1860–1890

Colleges and universities did not enthusiastically open their doors to women in the late nineteenth century, overwhelmed by egalitarian considerations. A few private men's colleges admitted women for local, idiosyncratic reasons or when pressured by women's rights advocates to do so. Women gained access to state universities, however, when parents, teachers' associations, or women's organizations, using the rhetoric of domesticity, petitioned legislatures and boards of regents to provide vocational preparation for the daughters of taxpayers.

At the secular state universities, founded outside the aegis of reformers, women encountered limitations similar to those at Oberlin and Antioch, but fewer mitigating circumstances. Hostility, ridicule, and neglect characterized the experiences of pioneer women students at Michigan, Wisconsin, and Cornell.

In 1855, the State Teacher's Association of Michigan proposed admitting women to the state university. Throughout the 1850s and 1860s the regents, legislature, and people of the state debated the issue. In 1858, responding to the application of three young women for admission, the regents appointed a committee to study the advisability of coeducation. Supporters of women's admission claimed that the university's charter required it to accept all "persons" residing in the state who met certain academic qualifications, and that "the basis of our national and state system is equal rights." The regents agreed that future mothers and teachers needed a good education and indignantly denied reports of a "women's rights" influence among female applicants:

> Woman is the parent and nurse of the human race. . . . Our statesmen and scholars, our moral and intellectual teachers, and our spiritual guides . . . receive from her their earliest and most lasting impressions. . . . We give no heed to those who attempt to connect or identify the application of the young ladies . . . with the political or social movements known as "women's rights," "Free Love," etc. etc. This application has no such connections in our minds, and we would not have the question prejudiced or the request of these young ladies spurned because some persons who advocate the Free Love Movement or attend Women's Rights conventions may also advocate coeducation of the sexes.[19]

The regents' committee wrote for advice to college administrators across the country. Not surprisingly, officials at the all-male eastern colleges replied negatively to the question of admitting women, but Oberlin's Finney and Antioch's Mann also issued grave warnings (influenced, no doubt, by women's resistance to regulation on their own campuses), indicating that they, at least, considered unsuccessful the attempts to elevate college life through women's superior morality. Mann stated that the administration of a coeducational college required "constant vigilance." Michigan authorities should be prepared, he said, to provide separate dormitories and eating places and to supervise women students. Finney doubted the success of coeducation in any atmosphere less evangelical than Oberlin's.

These reports reinforced the opposition of Michigan's faculty and administrators, and the regents declined approval of coeducation, concluding that it would, as a local newspaper reported, "unwoman the woman and unman the man." Advocates of coeducation did not give up, however. Stalled during the Civil War, the movement to admit women to the University of Michigan regained momentum shortly thereafter. The resignation of President E. O. Haven and pressure from taxpayers, women's organizations, and James and Lucinda Stone, teachers at the university preparatory college in Kalamazoo, opened the doors of the university to women in 1870. Although the state of Michigan would have preferred to educate women separately, it could not afford to do so.[20]

Consideration of coeducation at the University of Wisconsin began in the 1850s, also inspired by the state's teachers. The regents established a normal department in 1863, when the Civil War took away so many male students that they feared for the university's survival. In 1867, after the war, President Paul A. Chadbourne (1866–1870), who opposed coeducation, established a female college. During the early 1870s, however, after Chadbourne's departure, the university gradually abolished separate instruction; the 1874 commencement was the last at which men and women graduated separately. Although an 1877 report by a Board of Visitors stressed the adverse effects of coeducation on women students' health, a faculty committee disputed the report. Objections to coeducation appeared from time to time in the university's publications, but women students remained.[21]

At newly founded, private Cornell University, not the state's taxpayers and teachers, but reformers and women's rights advocates, especially Elizabeth Cady Stanton and Susan B. Anthony, pushed for coeducation in the belief that it would form the basis for healthier relationships between the sexes and for marriages based on mutual intellectual interests and respect. They pressured founder Ezra Cornell, first president Andrew Dickson White, and trustee Henry Williams Sage to admit women. Mary Ann Cornell and White's first wife, Mary, and his second, Helen Magill (who held the first Ph.D. ever awarded to an American woman), also urged the higher education of women (although Susan Linn Sage, Henry's wife, did not).[22]

Cornell's motto, "I would found an institution where any person can find instruction in any study," encouraged the application of women students, but White was not eager to confront the difficulties of coeducation. He asked women to stop seeking admission until the university weathered an initial storm over its nonsectarian character. When women students continued to come to Ithaca, demanding admission, he relented and began construction of a dormitory and social hall for them.[23]

In Rochester, New York, women's organizations struggled for thirty years to coeducate the University of Rochester, a private men's liberal arts college. In 1898, the trustees bowed to community pressure, agreed to admit women if they brought with them a "dowry" of $100,000 to pay for additional faculty and classroom space, and imposed a two-year deadline for raising the funds. By the spring of 1900, the women of Rochester had raised $40,000. The trustees agreed to reduce their demand to $50,000, but in September the women still lacked $8,000. At that point, Susan B. Anthony, a Rochester resident, took a direct role in the struggle. Although long an interested observer and behind-the-scenes participant in the campaign for women's admission to the University, she had not openly associated herself with the cause, for fear of damaging it with the taint of women's rights. During the waning hot days of the summer, Anthony dashed around the city in her carriage, collecting pledges. Ultimately she put up her only personal financial resource, a life insurance policy worth $2,000, purchased for her by the suffrage associations, in time to meet the deadline. The first women students entered the University of Rochester a few weeks later, in time for the fall semester of 1900.[24]

The interest of older women in seeing the next generation go to college is a highly significant feature in the history of women's access to coeducational institutions. Collegiate coeducation usually did not come about naturally or because of American democratic traditions. For nineteenth-century Americans, there was nothing "natural" about young men and women of marriageable age associating as equals. Despite the arguments that college-educated women would thereby make better teachers, and ultimately better wives and mothers, conservatives believed that collegiate coeducation had the potential to alter gender roles. Access to higher education in the North, Midwest, and West became a reality when women themselves—mothers, civic leaders, potential students, or women's rights advocates—pressured state and university officials to open the doors of colleges and universities. And with one exception (the University of Arkansas in the 1880s), southern state universities, too, coeducated because women campaigned for admission.[25]

Pioneer women students rejoiced at their newfound opportunities. Women like Martha Carey Thomas, Alice Freeman Palmer, and Elizabeth Cady Stanton (who wanted to send her daughter Harriot to Cornell but had to settle for Vassar) believed that coeducational schools represented social freedom and intellectual excitement, as opposed to the new women's colleges, which they regarded as little better than seminaries.

But even when access was no longer an issue, the appropriate relationship between men and women students was as troublesome at the new universities as it had been at Oberlin and Antioch a generation earlier. During the first thirty years of widespread collegiate coeducation (1860–1890), women students were ignored, ridiculed, and isolated from campus life. This hostility sometimes extended to the classroom, where male instructors, themselves educated at single-sex schools, had neither experience nor interest in teaching female students.[26]

In her novel, *An American Girl and Her Four Years in a Boys' College* (1878), Olive San Louis Anderson (Michigan '75) discussed the situation of women students at her alma mater. The book dealt with problematic issues and significant themes for the first generation of college women: the purpose of women's higher education, relationships between women students and their families, the uneasiness of male and female students with each other, and women's experiences with male faculty.

Anderson's heroine, Wilhelmine Elliott, struggled to define herself—to create a new image of womanhood—in a world with strictly defined gender roles. With her masculine nickname, "Will," her robust health, tomboy activities, distaste for organized religion, and high scholastic standing, Elliott was the very prototype of the "New Woman"—that masculinized female much feared by late nineteenth-century Victorians. She was also, however, startlingly beautiful, warm, and loving, with both male and female friends.[27]

Women liked and admired Will even when they did not understand her; men's feelings were more complex. Some had difficulty treating "Miss Elliott" as just another student, whereas others felt that if she were a student, she could not also be a lady. After her entrance examinations, a classics professor "conditioned" her acceptance until she did further work in Greek. He recommended a tutor, a young man working his way through college, but remarked: "If Jerry Dalton can be closeted for an hour a day with that face and eyes and never think of anything but 'The Retreat of the Ten Thousand,' he is a very remarkable young man." The professor's prediction proved accurate. Carried away by Will's beauty, the tutor tried to make love to her, and she walked out in disgust. In another incident, on her way to class, Will got caught in a "rush" (fight) between freshmen and sophomore men and received a bloody nose. The men ignored her plight, but the other women students helped her get home. As she put it, "There is not one of those boys but, if you find him out of college, would have run to a lady's assistance and begged a thousand pardons for having had any hand in such an accident; but, would you believe it, not one of those two hundred and fifty boys offered any help or sympathy, simply because they feel that we are trespassing upon their domains."[28]

Will's college experiences contrasted sharply with those of her friend Mary Palmer ("Mame"), who went to Vassar College. In their letters, Will adopted the stereotypic attitude toward women's colleges popular among women's rights advocates of her day when she referred to them as "boarding schools," and argued that the students should live with families in the town where it could be taken for granted that they would "conduct themselves properly without surveillance, and have the college provide for nothing but their intellectual wants." She praised coeducation for providing women with both social and intellectual freedom and claimed that the presence of "boys" taught "girls" about competition, achievement, and enthusiasm. Ironically, however, the early women's colleges, although they did institute social restrictions, taught women far more about "competition, achievement, and enthusiasm" than Will learned in her male-dominated environment.

Women's Colleges: Moving Beyond the Seminary, 1860–1890

The percentage of students nationwide attending women's colleges peaked in 1879–1880 (28.3 percent), then declined to 19.1 percent in 1899–1900 and to 8.1 percent in 1919–1920 (with an additional .09 percent in women's Catholic colleges). Women's colleges had the greatest impact in the East and the South, where the strength of prestigious men's schools, and local or regional preferences for single-sex education, barred women from many private and state institutions until well into the twentieth century. Although they borrowed from the traditions of both men's colleges and female seminaries, women's colleges created unique institutional forms and practices.[29]

Founders and supporters of the eastern women's colleges, later known as the Seven Sisters, argued that their schools met the demand for women's higher education without sacrificing femininity. At single-sex colleges, women, they promised, could develop their minds without becoming like men. From the beginning, women's college administrators identified institutional intellectual goals with men's colleges, though their social aims remained conservative.

Late nineteenth-century American colleges and universities debated the merits of the traditional classical curriculum, with its prescribed courses and emphasis on Latin and Greek. Few institutions went to the extreme that Harvard did under Charles William Eliot (1869–1909) in abolishing all requirements for the bachelors degree. Most steered a middle course, expanding the percentage of electives in a students program and gradually modifying the curriculum to emphasize laboratory sciences, social sciences, modern languages, and fine arts. Although they made it a point of honor to offer Latin and Greek courses, the eastern women's colleges also taught an impressive array of natural and social sciences and pioneered in the development of fine arts. Determined to prove the inaccuracy of Edward Clarke's theories, the colleges included hygiene and physical education in their curricula.[30]

To fulfill their promises that college women would remain womanly, founders and administrators looked to successful, well-established female seminaries like Mount Holyoke, instead of to men's colleges, when building their campuses and regulating students lives outside the classroom. In her study of campus architecture at the Seven Sisters colleges, Helen Lefkowitz Horowitz noted that Vassar and Wellesley initially expected students to live in one main building, under the close surveillance of resident teachers, and to follow the rigid daily schedule made famous by Mary Lyon at Mount Holyoke in the mid-nineteenth century. Women's college founders continued the seminary's association of women's education with religion, requiring chapel attendance, prayer meetings, Bible study and placing heavy pressure on students to "convert."[31]

Discipline, religiosity, and the lowering of academic standards for a preparatory department caused women's rights advocates and some prospective students, like the fictional Will Elliott, to prefer coeducation in the late nineteenth century. And the students and faculty at women's colleges cast aspersions on female seminaries, resentful about their legacy of regulations and religious dogmatism. Yet the new institutions also adopted positive seminary traditions. Long before Progressive Era college students became interested in social reform, female seminaries had promoted an ethic of social service, passing it on to their institutional successors. Women's colleges thus combined insistence on collegiate level instruction with a commitment to social amelioration.

We can see these themes most clearly in the higher education of Jane Addams, who would have preferred to attend Smith College but, at her father's insistence, entered Rockford Seminary in 1877. Finding Rockford's religious atmosphere oppressive, Addams resisted pressures from faculty and from the school's founder and long-time principal, Anna Peck Sill, to convert and become a missionary. She did not, however, reject the push toward social service permeating Rockford, the "Mount Holyoke of the West." In a speech delivered during her junior year, Jane Addams revealed her philosophy of higher education. She sympathized with the intellectual aims of the women's colleges but emphasized her desire to combine these with an ethic of secular social service. Speaking of the modern woman's educational agenda, she stated:

> She wishes not to be a man, nor like a man, but she claims the same right to independent thought and action. On the other hand, we still retain the old ideal of womanhood—the Saxon lady whose mission it was to give bread unto her household. So we have planned to be "Breadgivers" throughout our lives, believing that in labor alone is happiness, and that the only true and honorable life is one filled with good works and honest toil.

Although women could, of course, be breadgivers in their traditional domestic capacities, Addams and other college women of her generation sought to be breadgivers for all of American society. In later life Addams continued to support research, scholarship, and higher education and to urge that college women (and men) use their knowledge for the greater social good.[32]

Early in their history, the eastern women's colleges functioned as closely knit communities serving students and faculty's needs, often in defiance of administrators and trustees. These institutions provided professional homes for talented women academics who could not have found jobs in men's or coeducational colleges. And, as that faculty's sole constituency, women's college students did not have to compete with men for attention and recognition; their work and aspirations were taken seriously. Extracurricular activities, with or without administrative sanction, provided leadership opportunities. Moreover, students and faculty engaged in constant questioning about women's issues and the future of educated women, including the publication of serious and thoughtful articles on such subjects in their campus newspapers. Although such discussions undoubtedly took place among coeducated women, they did so privately, without the advantage of public campus forums for debate and sharing viewpoints.

At the women's colleges, the community was more socially homogeneous, and thus more cohesive than at coeducational institutions, particularly the state universities. Female seminaries had educated women from a wide variety of backgrounds; some, like Mount Holyoke, made it a point to offer an education to the daughters of farmers and the "middling classes." In contrast, Seven Sisters students came from upper-middle-class households, with fathers who were professionals, merchants, or businessmen. With financial aid very limited, few women from less comfortable homes could afford the tuition, living expenses, and foregone income to attend a private college.[33]

The history of the founding and earliest years of Wellesley College shows the determination of first-generation women faculty and students to make these institutions their own. Bostonians Henry Fowle Durant and his wife, Pauline, evangelical social reformers whose children died quite young, wanted to create a family and community for themselves and their "Wellesley daughters." The Durants believed higher education would strengthen women's minds and bodies, prevent sentimentality and idleness, and prepare them to make the world a better, more Christian place. They hired only women faculty to exemplify the qualities they wanted students to emulate. Determined that his students would have all the advantages of young men attending Harvard, Henry Durant purchased the latest scientific and library resources for Wellesley. Forced to open a preparatory department when only thirty of the three hundred initial students met standards for college-level work, the Durants closed it within ten years.

Notwithstanding Wellesley's ambitious programs, rigorous academic standards, and highly intellectual women faculty, the Durants, partly from personal inclination and partly to demonstrate the propriety of women's higher education to a dubious public, cast college life in the seminary mold. Henry Durant, a Mount Holyoke trustee, admired the seminary's religious discipline and well-ordered daily life. He was particularly eager to convert Wellesley women to his own brand of evangelical Christianity. Although he changed the institution's name from "Wellesley Female Seminary" to "Wellesley College" before opening its doors, the first students found themselves in a closely and carefully regulated environment.

Wellesley students and faculty defied the Durants and first president, Ada L. Howard, creating instead a true college community with few vestiges of the seminary. They resisted attempts to convert them, broke college rules, and staged a rebellion in 1876 (the year after Wellesley opened) following Durant's dismissal of three popular teachers for refusing to interrupt their classes to provide an exhibition before the Board of Visitors. This incident led to the loss of Durant's authority over the college, and he gradually withdrew from its affairs. Ada Howard retired after Henry Durant's death in 1881 and was succeeded by Alice Freeman, a young University of Michigan graduate with a secular, intellectually ambitious plan for Wellesley's development.[34]

Similarly, at Mount Holyoke Seminary, the transition to collegiate status pitted a modernizing elite of teachers and students against trustees and administrators who wished to maintain the seminary's reputation for offering a Christian education, oriented toward enlarging, but maintaining, woman's sphere. In the 1880s, Mount Holyoke students complained about required prayer meetings, domestic work, the self-reporting system for transgressions against the rules, lack of free time, and the difficulty of developing friendships in an environment where every hour of every day had its assigned purpose.

Teachers like Lydia Shattuck, a seminary alumna from the class of 1851, began to change Mount Holyoke's curriculum. Shattuck, whose personal acquaintance with founder Mary Lyon gave her much prestige, taught science, introduced laboratory experiments and discussed the theory of evolution in her classes. When queried about the compatibility of her work with the seminary's religious ethos, she replied, "Perhaps your question means to ask whether we have thrown the Bible overboard. I reply; we never did use it as a textbook for science, and we do not now."

The establishment of Vassar (in 1865), Wellesley, and Smith Colleges (both in 1875) challenged Mount Holyoke's primacy, not only within New England, but as the nationally acknowledged leader in women's higher education. In 1884, changes in the composition of the Board of Trustees and the selection of a new principal, Elizabeth Blanchard, swung the pendulum toward change. Although insisting that Holyoke had a unique mission, namely, the education of Christian women for social and religious benevolence, officials agreed to institute a college department. Many faculty responded by seeking college and graduate degrees themselves; by 1893 the transition to college was complete.[35]

The First Graduates: After College, What?

Both contemporary observers and modern scholars have viewed this first generation of women college students, educated between 1860 and 1890, as a serious and dedicated band of pioneers, eager to prove themselves intellectually, and with little time or inclination for frivolity. Before the ink had dried on their degrees, social commentators began scrutinizing the marriage and career patterns of these graduates. Unfortunately, most colleges did not keep alumnae records. Thus, we have no comprehensive survey of this group's choices; nor can we say a great deal about differences between women's college graduates and coeducated alumnae.

Most researchers who went beyond analysis of a single institution's alumnae took their data on college women's lives from members of the Association of Collegiate Alumnae (the ACA, founded in 1881). Since this organization admitted only the graduates of fifteen select colleges, the statistics did not represent a typical group. Whatever the average college graduate of the 1860s, 1870s, and 1880s did with her life, several trends became clear. First, although some women returned home to marry, raise children, or care for aging parents, higher education did not necessarily lead to quiet but enriched domesticity. Second, college graduates married later and less frequently than their counterparts in the general population, and had fewer children. And finally, higher education became, for some women, the prelude to prominence in the public sphere and to professional achievements.

Working alumnae made their influence felt mostly as teachers at all levels of the educational system, raising academic standards at schools across the country and inspiring their female students to go on to college themselves. Alumnae also staffed the women's colleges as deans, administrators, and occasionally professors at coeducational institutions. Less frequently, college women went into medicine, law, the ministry, and business. By the turn of the century, 12 percent of Vassar alumnae held graduate degrees from Yale, Cornell, Chicago, Columbia, Harvard, and Bryn Mawr. The class of 1891, with thirty-six members, had five Ph.D.'s. Finally, the unpaid labor of college women, as members of school boards, college trustees, organizers and directors of societies and charity groups, constituted a major social contribution.[36]

For some ambitious graduates, however, the world outside the campus gates remained the province of men. In their early postgraduate years, women such as Jane Addams, Sophonisba Breckinridge, Julia Lathrop, and Florence Kelley, wanting to carry out their college ideals, unsuccessfully sought socially significant work. Depressed and floundering, they ultimately found a home in the social justice movements of the Progressive Era and established the modern profession of social work. Combining masculine expertise and training with the attitudes and values of women's culture, these college graduates drew national attention to the need for social reform, formulated and campaigned for legislation to ameliorate the problems they identified, and served as officials to enforce it.[37]

Women who did not go to college also made their mark on the world, but increasingly college women led others in achievement. Of the entries in *Woman's Who's Who In America* (1914), 63.4 percent had some advanced education, 43.8 percent had bachelor's degrees, and 22.7 percent had done postgraduate work. The correlation between higher education and achievement becomes even more impressive when we recall how few women actually attended college in the late nineteenth and early twentieth centuries.[38]

The pioneers often chose nontraditional personal lives as well. Although a precise accounting is impossible, it seems likely that half of them did not marry. In 1895, using a sample of 1,805 alumnae from the ACA register, one researcher reported that 28.2 percent of the women were married, compared to a rate of 80 percent for women over twenty years of age in the general population. When she restricted her sample to women over forty, the numbers changed, but the trend remained the same: 54.5 percent of the college graduates were married, compared to 90 percent of women in the general population. Undoubtedly, most of the career women in the group had remained single, for various reasons. Some prominent professional women, such as Dr. Alice Hamilton, felt that a mother could not adequately attend to both her children and her job. And Martha Carey Thomas, struggling with her attraction to an interesting man, prayed to overcome her feelings so that she could get on with her career. Still others may not have wished to assume the burdens of marriage in a patriarchal society in an era when divorce was difficult or impossible; or they did not find men who wanted intelligent, professionally active wives.[39]

Unmarried women college graduates did not necessarily lead lonely lives; many found emotional fulfillment and familial attachments in relationships with each other. Carroll Smith-Rosenberg has written compellingly about these intimate friendships, flourishing within the homosocial women's culture of Victorian America. As college women of the pioneer generation moved into social activism, professional careers, and suffrage work, they carried these friendships with them, maintaining lifelong partnerships and family ties with other women.[40]

Victorian reticence makes it difficult to know whether these friendships, many clearly erotic and sensual, were sexual as well. In the 1920s, Katharine Bement Davis (B.A. Vassar, Ph.D. Chicago), head of the Bureau of Social Hygiene, surveyed twenty-two hundred "normal" middle-class women, most of them college graduates. She found intense same-sex friendships to be common among all her subjects, though most prevalent among the alumnae of women's colleges. Respondents differentiated between emotionally close relationships and those with a strong erotic component (expressed or not) but moved easily between the two, making rigid categorization of nineteenth- and early twentieth-century college women as homo- or heterosexual ahistorical.[41]

The first generation of college women realized some, though not all, of the conservatives' fears, as they demonstrated the potential of higher education to alter gender roles. Yet despite their boldness, ambition, and successes, the pioneers did not completely abandon woman's sphere. Many regarded their careers as successful precisely because they brought the values of women's culture—empathy, nurturance, compassion, and concern for the community—into the public arena. Women's personal and professional networks shaped their lives and were of critical importance to their achievements. Because higher education had meant so much in their lives, they served as mentors to the young women who succeeded them on the college campuses of the Progressive Era. For some, however, this was a disappointing and disillusioning project. Alumnae, women faculty, and administrators frequently complained about a lack of purpose and direction among the young women they advised.[42]

Historians have also taken the second generation to task for not carrying forward the aims of its predecessors, noting the flowering of student activities and the rise in the marriage rate for college women after the turn of the century. They concluded that these women came from a higher social class than the pioneers and attended college to have fun, participate in student life, and meet eligible men.[43]

Evidence below and in subsequent chapters, however, demonstrates a great deal of continuity from the first generation to the second, as well as highly significant changes. Although sharing the intellectual and political goals of their predecessors, the second generation gradually shifted its vocational orientation from service and social reform to individual achievement. And, more strongly than their mentors, Progressive Era college women felt the competing pulls of marriage and motherhood.

Continuity and Change: College Women and Student Life during the Progressive Era

By the turn of the century, American women had greatly modified the practices if not the ideology of Victorian gender culture. Living in a less isolated and self-contained female sphere than had their mothers, they entered and influenced the male worlds of higher education, the professions, and politics. The ideas and behavior of Progressive Era settlement workers, academics, and physicians had several sources and emphases, including a growing reliance on science, efficiency, and technology. Still, the values of women's culture, particularly concerns with democracy, community, compassion, and social gospel Christianity pervaded the rhetoric and informed the activities of many reformers and professionals. Suffragists argued that women's enfranchisement would further extend female cultural and moral influence to all segments of American life.[44]

American college campuses during this period reflected the social and cultural values of the progressive middle classes. Disturbed by the violence and elitism among male collegians of the mid-nineteenth century, and unable to rely on an increasingly research-oriented faculty to curb student excesses, presidents hired personnel administrators, such as deans of men or women, vocational counselors, and other support staff. Changes in the tone of campus life, however, came more from the students themselves than from administrative initiatives. Men de-emphasized brawling, hazing, and fighting to become involved in student self-government, honor systems and honor societies, civic and political clubs, and the regulated, organized competition of debate and intramural athletics. Such activities allowed individual recognition and achievement but also focused on service to the university community. White Protestant male college students used the extracurriculum as preparation for professional, business, and civic leadership in the larger society.[45]

The growing numbers of women college students found that the social and political climate of the Progressive Era provided a rationale for their own participation in student activities, while the presence of the first generation as faculty, administrators, and visiting alumnae smoothed their path. Women faculty and deans of women invited prominent reformers, civic activists, and feminists to visit the campus as speakers and to meet with students, and eagerly promoted female students' participation in campus activities. In their view, student life helped women transfer energies from the family to the more public world of the college community, where they learned leadership, organizational skills, and developed friendships. Without the extracurriculum, women students, especially at state universities, took courses and went home at night, or perhaps attended an occasional dance, untouched by the special experience of higher education and unprepared to assume postgraduate social and civic leadership. The importance women faculty and students attached to college activities demonstrated their expectations that alumnae would take on public as well as private responsibilities.

The curriculum, the example of their women teachers, and the social reform climate on and off campus encouraged female college students to bring womanly influence to bear in the public sphere. Like men of that era, they used collegiate culture as a blueprint for their future, a way of trying out their social responsibilities as educated women. Activities organized around women's rights did not attract many students, but reform and feminism shaped the second generation's aspirations and achievements. In the North, students participated in the social reform programs of campus Young Women's Christian Associations (YWCAs), the Settlement League, Consumers' League, suffrage clubs, and the Intercollegiate Socialist Society. Southern students also expressed interest in progressive social justice reforms, although more often in church or education-related activities than through suffrage or settlement work.

Women faculty and students argued for the adoption of courses on settlement work, socialism, sociology, and particularly sanitary science, or home economics, which was not always a nuts and bolts subject. Women scientists and social scientists of the Progressive Era, whose research focused on women, children, families, and communities, often became home economics professors, sometimes because they could not get positions in conventional science departments. Women studying home economics usually planned to teach the subject or work in federal and state institutions, as dietitians, food chemists, and county agricultural agents. In the attempt to place women's concerns into the curriculum, sanitary science of the Progressive Era resembles today's women's studies programs.[46]

The demand for home economics courses reflected another common concern of women faculty and students. By the turn of the century, college women found it desirable and necessary to seek jobs outside of elementary and secondary education. Through speakers, articles in campus publications, vocational conferences, job counseling, campus employment bureaus, and alumnae networks, the two generations of college women worked together to create and exploit women's career opportunities. Themes of service or nurturance continued to characterize most jobs considered appropriate for women. Increasingly, however, women took pre-business courses, planned graduate study, or attended professional schools. And the professionalization of such occupations as social work, medicine, and education required a bachelor's degree and postgraduate training.[47]

Women students of the second generation did not spend all their free time soberly pursuing social reform and careers. Yet even their purely recreational activities challenged the boundaries of Victorian gender roles, combining features of both men's and women's spheres in their campus lives. Women students formed and ran self-government associations, voted in campus elections, held mock political campaigns in presidential election years, debated, played basketball or soccer with teams from other schools, and put on plays in which women played men's parts. At women's colleges, students created class traditions: sophomores gently harassed freshmen, and juniors served as "sisters" to freshmen, just as seniors did to sophomores. Designed to initiate newcomers into the community and increase campus privileges as students became upperclasswomen, class activities had been largely the province of men until women's colleges adopted such practices at the turn of the century.

In her analysis of student life at Bryn Mawr College, folklorist Virginia Wolf Briscoe described a year-long cycle of class traditions, practiced since the early twentieth century, incorporating freshmen into the community and bidding farewell to seniors. In Briscoe's view, class customs are significant, rather than frivolous, helping women find places and status in a public, nondomestic world.

In an elaborate ceremony at the beginning of the school year, freshmen receive lanterns, symbols of wisdom and of the intellectual prestige of women's higher education. Immediately afterward, the fun of Parade Night teaches them to combine work and play at college. During Hell Week, freshmen carry out the silly requests of upperclasswomen. Finally, on Flower Day, freshmen receive flowers and cards, symbolizing their acceptance into the community and completing the cycle. Lanterns at the beginning of the school year signify the entry of Bryn Mawr women into the formerly all-male world of intellect and study. The flowers in the spring show that studying like men need not bar women college students from the more traditional aspects of female lives. After Flower Day, attention turns to the seniors, honored on May Day with gifts, dancing, and awards ceremonies, while they distribute their college possessions to underclasswomen. In this sequence of traditions, seniors are "noticed, given precedence, admired, and finally symbolically excluded from the community." In the final ritual of the year, seniors roll hoops away from the center of campus, toward the world they will soon face.[48]

When Patty Went To College by Jean Webster detailed the lighter side of college life. Written by a Vassar alumna of the class of 1901, the novel had the ring of authenticity, and students called it "realistic" and "clever." The book depicted women students, like their male counterparts, developing a group identity and defying official attempts to control them and subdue their youthful good spirits. Patty Wyatt's college career consisted of escapades to outsmart teachers who wanted her to study, of evading rules, playing tricks on friends and underclasswomen, and treating outsiders to baffling but dazzling displays of Vassar wit. In one such episode, Patty met her visitor in the college parlor, where he sat in the middle of the annual doll show. Each Christmas, the Vassar Christian Association asked students to dress dolls as presents for children in the slums. Before sending the dolls off, the association held a show to benefit the College Settlement Association. Mr. Todhunter asked Patty about the dolls:

> "I say, Miss Wyatt, do—er—the young ladies spend much time playing with dolls?"
>
> "No," said Patty candidly: "I don't think you could say they spend *too* much. I never heard of but one girl actually neglecting her work for it. You mustn't think that we have as many dolls as this here every night," she went on. "It is rather an unusual occurrence. Once a year the girls hold what they call a doll show to see who has dressed her doll the best."
>
> "Ah, I see," said Mr. Todhunter. "A little friendly rivalry."
>
> "Purely friendly," said Patty.
>
> As they started for the dining room, Mr. Todhunter adjusted his monocle and took a parting look at the doll show.
>
> "I'm afraid you think us rather childish, Mr. Todhunter," said Patty.
>
> "Not at all, Miss Wyatt," he assured her hastily. "I think it's quite charming, you know, and so—er—unexpected. I had always been told that they played somewhat peculiar games at these women's colleges, but I never suspected they did anything so feminine as to play with dolls."

Mr. Todhunter appeared ridiculous not only because he did not recognize that Patty was mocking him but also because he thought of women students as feminine children who dressed dolls in preparation for lives of postgraduate domesticity. Any Vassar insider reading the book would find that presumption especially amusing, given the socially activist nature of their own Christian Association and of the national College Settlement Association.

As the book progressed, Patty outgrew her student pranks and learned a code of communal honor and service. She shammed to avoid a test but confessed to the professor after she realized her high mark on the makeup examination would raise the grade curve, thus hurting her classmates' standing. She successfully pleaded with the faculty to give Olivia Copeland, a talented but failing freshman, another chance. When she overcut chapel, a visiting bishop persuaded her to report herself to the Students' Association, and she did so, although it cost her the right to chair the Senior Prom Committee.[49]

Women students' activities, organizations, and sometimes their courses thus mirrored the complexities of their lives and their hopes for the future, as they sought to perpetuate the new type of womanhood created by the pioneers. They combined beliefs in female distinctiveness, moral superiority, and the social service imperative with attitudes and activities said to be the province of men—namely, an intellectually rigorous education and political activism. And, with the example of the pioneers before them, Progressive Era college women expressed great interest in postgraduate professional and political activities.

But despite shared projects, social goals, and a common culture, the two generations of women on the college campuses of the Progressive Era discovered important differences between themselves and gradually drew apart. This generation gap began off-campus, in northern and western middle-class homes, with changes in child-rearing practices. Benefiting from a half century of health reform, education, and public discussion of women's rights, girls born after 1880 enjoyed more personal and social freedom and shared more activities with boys, including attendance at coeducational high schools. As they experienced greater closeness with and greater likeness to boys and men, educated women of the second generation found heterosexual intimacy and sexual expressiveness more desirable than had their predecessors.[50]

Less progressive values also led to the new popularity of marriage among educated women. Whatever the social benefits of woman's expanding sphere, many feared a resulting effeminization of American life and institutions because of the entry of women's culture into the public domain. Thus, during the very period when women's progress and influence reached its height, a cultural backlash appeared. Through "muscular Christianity," the Boy Scouts, wild West dime novels, competitive athletics, quotas for female admissions to colleges and graduate schools, and other measures, Americans reasserted the masculinity of their society. Unmarried career women living as female couples or in women's communities seemed particularly threatening, and a negative appraisal of women's homosocial relationships and networks accompanied reactions against women's culture. Modern marriage became the only socially and psychologically correct choice for the college woman.[51]

Finally, Nancy Cott has pointed to the growing individualism among feminists who attended college in the early twentieth century. For these women, the nineteenth-century woman's movement with its emphasis on the shared identity and culture of all females, was a less important frame of reference than the equal rights of individuals, regardless of gender, to fulfillment in both their personal and professional lives.[52]

These changes became most evident on college campuses during the 1910s, as women students and faculty sharply disagreed about appropriate clothing, social regulations, and above all, male-female relationships, while continuing to cooperate in political and vocational enterprises. Contemporary charges of frivolity and lack of purpose made against women students of the Progressive Era stemmed from their elders' perception that these young women were entirely too concerned with what men thought of them. For their part, women students began to view their unmarried teachers as unfulfilled or even sexually deviant old maids.

Even earlier than the 1910s, however, the short stories of Progressive Era women college students revealed their hopes and fears. Like the pioneers, they looked forward to lives of purposeful social, civic, and professional activity, bringing women's culture into the public sphere; at the same time, this generation longed for heterosexual romance and marriage. In stories coming from coeducational institutions, the men usually appeared as attractive, superior creatures who knew best what would make women happy, and whose wishes prevailed. In stories written by students at women's colleges, the men were often foolish or unworthy. Regardless of the depiction of male characters, however, the stories rarely had happy endings; usually the female protagonist lost man or job.

In the South, students experienced this transition somewhat differently. White southern college women of the Progressive Era constituted a first generation, struggling to establish some independence from the family claim. Although they acknowledged the need for women's higher education, southern parents tried to minimize its effects. With exceptions like Colonel Breckinridge, most southern families clung to their daughters and to conservative notions of southern womanhood. Short stories by southern college women stressed themes of separation; often a fictional family member became ill or died when the daughter went to college.

Southern women's separate networks, organizations, and cultural influence began only after the Civil War and were less powerful and effective than in the North. Independent spinsterhood and women's communities never became the significant alternatives to traditional families that they were elsewhere in Progressive Era America. By the 1890s, a small group of unmarried northern women faculty with impressive professional credentials held positions at southern women's colleges, but their students, while fond of them, did not regard them as role models. In her research on Greenville, North Carolina, and the East Carolina Teachers Training School during the Progressive Era, Sally Brett found an "estrangement of female professor and female community member." Women professors were, by definition, not southern ladies; as such, their students could not identify with them. Although southern college women expressed interest in graduate study and careers, for the most part they functioned as wives and mothers, looking to married alumnae for guidance on performing the special social obligations of educated womanhood.[53]

Although region played an important part in setting campus trends and agendas, the choice of a single-sex versus coeducational college was, as it had been for the first generation, the most significant predictor of a woman's campus experiences. At Progressive Era coeducational institutions women, excluded from men's student life, created a world of their own and wrestled with the meaning and consequences of separatism as a cultural and political strategy for women's advancement in the modern world.

Separatism and the Road to Equality: Coeducational Campuses of the Progressive Era

With the cooperation of male students, Progressive Era college and university presidents tried to curb violence and rechannel student life. They sought the development of a true university community, appealing to new national middle-class ideals of service, democracy, and self-government. Competition between institutions, usually in athletics or debate, replaced destructive interclass wars on campus. Fraternities took on new importance as organizations in which members of all four classes mingled freely, but they did not dominate college life. Instead, the community ideal became the focus of student activities. Service clubs, YMCAs, and political groups provided alternatives to fraternity life.

Building a progressive campus community seemed to resolve the social problems of coeducation. Beginning in the 1890s, coeducational institutions hired women as deans, physicians, hygiene and physical education instructors, and sometimes faculty. Just as older women had helped the pioneers gain access to higher education, so these new administrators and teachers, mainly first-generation college graduates, improved the second generation's campus experiences. They created important alliances with club women, reformers, suffragists, and alumnae. Their own status as college graduates, often with advanced degrees as well, was the most crucial element in their success, winning them at least the grudging respect of male colleagues. These women helped the second generation on coeducational campuses build a separate structure of social and extracurricular activities, rivaling the men's in number and variety.

The social and extracurricular separatism of Progressive Era college women may be viewed in a number of ways. As Harold Wechsler has wryly observed, "The arrival of a new constituency on a college campus has rarely been an occasion for unmitigated joy." When rich and poor male students coexisted at antebellum colleges, males and females at coeducational universities of the late nineteenth century, Jews and Gentiles in the 1910s and 1920s, and, more recently, whites and blacks, social separation has alleviated fears on both sides of conflict or amalgamation. Women students were not welcome in men's campus organizations; rather than accept exclusion from university life, they formed their own groups. At all times, however, men students dominated coeducational institutions, holding exclusive control over publications, student government, competition with other schools, debate, and campus politics. The growing importance of men's athletics, particularly football, further diminished the status of women on campus.[54]

Although separatism did not constitute equality on campus, anymore than it did elsewhere, it gave coeducated women a power base, drew them together to form a community, connected them with older women on and off campus, helped them to develop leadership skills, and provided forums for discussion of career opportunities. Moreover, separatism calmed fears about the possible negative effects of overly close associations between men and women. Both sexes felt more comfortable with some degree of separation, thereby ratifying Victorian notions about the unique capacities and possibilities of men and women.

Women faculty and administrators promoted and encouraged separation in campus life, not finding it inconsistent with intellectual equality. Lois Kimball Mathews, dean of women and associate professor of history at the University of Wisconsin, had previously taught at Vassar, and wanted coeducational universities to provide women with the same self-assurance promoted at single-sex institutions. Mathews explained her support of women's separate self-government as contributing to female independence and supporting the values of women's culture: "The young men's standard of judging their fellow students among the young women is commonly that of social availability, and that only. Young women judge one another by a quite different measure."[55]

At its best, separatism attempted to put women's values at the center of university life. Even when separatism was solely a response to exclusion, it often developed into a positive force, as women pushed their fellow students and the university to acknowledge that separate should mean complementary, but equal. In the process, many came to a new understanding about their own lives and prospects. During the 1910s, as the off-campus movement for women's rights gathered momentum, culminating in the federal suffrage amendment in 1920, women college students on some campuses openly challenged men's right to shape and dominate campus activity.

In spite of their high ideals and substantial achievements, women's campus communities had serious flaws, especially their exclusion of students from the "wrong" backgrounds. The daughters of farmers and the less well-to-do made up a significant minority of women students at state universities. These women had to work their way through school or live at home while attending college. They had neither the time nor the right clothes to participate in campus activities and were rarely elected to sororities or special honor societies. Jewish, Catholic, and black students, also socially disadvantaged, sometimes had to form their own organizations, or have no stake in campus life.

Faculty behavior further isolated minority women, exacerbating the treatment meted out by their fellow students. When Laura Zametkin (the future Laura Z. Hobson, author of *Gentleman's Agreement*) entered Cornell University in the fall of 1919, she enrolled in a "baby Greek" course. After several months of hearing the instructor address her as "Miss Zamooski," "Miss Zimenky," or "Miss Djimorskey," she decided to speak up. "Professor Jones . . . if we're supposed to pronounce names like Clytemnestra correctly, and Iphigenia, and Agamemnon, and Aeschylus, don't you think you could say Zametkin? It's really quite easy." Zametkin's assertiveness saved her from further embarrassment in Greek class, but she could not prevent what she later described as "the great wound of my youth.' Eligible for Phi Beta Kappa, she was denied the key because of the faculty's fear that too many "greasy little grinds from New York" had altered the honor society's "character" in unacceptable ways.[56]

Black women suffered the most from the intolerance of older students and faculty. And the small numbers of black students on northern and western coeducational campuses made it difficult for them to develop alternatives to the white social structure. When Gregoria Fraser entered Syracuse University in 1901 as a music student, the dean told her that dishwashing and scrubbing floors would make her hands unfit for piano practice. After she assured the dean that she had never done such work, the chair of the music department "informed me that ambition was a dangerous thing; some had to be hewers of wood and drawers of water." Fraser found the students equally unwelcoming; only a German man, a Jewish woman, and a Catholic woman, also marginal to campus life, spoke to her.[57]

Then too, the very success of social separatism and its promotion by college women themselves, inspired male administrators and faculty to use it as a precedent for academic separation. The growing numbers of women attending college and their considerable academic achievements alarmed the male educational establishment. After years of coeducation, many universities and colleges considered banning or limiting women's access; others established a separate women's college or segregated classes. As part of the general backlash against women's culture at the turn of the century, concern over possible effeminization of the university and its men, and masculinization of women students created a furor in the popular press as well, rivaling the outcry over Clarke's work in the 1870s and 1880s.[58]

Female faculty had favored social and extracurricular separatism, believing that women brought special gifts to the university and had, in turn, special needs to be fulfilled, but they vehemently opposed classroom segregation. In this respect they resembled women doctors and suffragists; the former felt that gender-specific qualities made them different and better physicians than men but nonetheless wanted coeducated medical schools; the latter argued for equality in political power so that women might bring their unique perspective to the electorate. Women faculty, alumnae, students, club members, suffragists, and reformers believed that classroom separation would erase gains of the past fifty years, during which women had struggled to prove their intellectual and physical fitness for higher education.[59]

Women's successes on the coeducational campuses of the Progressive Era proved their undoing. The numbers of female students rose steadily throughout this period, until, by 1920, they constituted 47.3 percent of American undergraduates; over 90 percent attended coeducational schools. Women's culture influenced student life, and women's campus communities flourished. Inspired by the fear that women were overrunning the campuses of America, dominating the liberal arts courses, and effeminizing higher education, male educators tried to curb this dangerous phenomenon.

Between 1902 and 1915, Wesleyan College banned women students; the University of Rochester, Tufts University, and Western Reserve University set up women's coordinate colleges; and Stanford and Michigan adopted quotas for women's admission. Chicago established separate classes for freshmen and sophomore men and women, while Wisconsin reluctantly decided that it was too costly to do so. On campuses with no formal barriers, educators and male students made it clear that they would not tolerate equality, even the equality of separate, complementary spheres. At some institutions, these restrictions on women lasted until the 1950s or 1960s.[60]

Growing differences between the first and second generations of college women represented a third problem for the cohesion and success of campus women's communities. Older women worried about what they viewed as a lack of educational and professional commitment in the second generation, while students moved away from their women teachers, and toward more intense relationships with men.

The chronicle of the University of California illustrates the growth of a female community and the resulting empowerment of women students, which eventually led to their demands for equality. At Chicago in the 1890s, women of both generations quickly built such a strong campus life that male faculty and administrators moved decisively in 1902 to weaken its influence with classroom segregation. At both institutions, the two generations of college women defined common educational, political, and reform purposes, but the younger women began to assert new personal priorities.

The pioneers had found coeducational universities liberating, but female students discovered, early on, that single-sex colleges had many advantages. These advantages, derived from institutional assumptions about the importance of women's intellectual development and faculty commitment to women students, made single-sex schools, especially the eastern women's colleges, the leading national model for women's higher education during the Progressive Era. Women deans, faculty, and students at coeducational institutions consciously patterned their efforts to improve curriculum and extracurriculum on what women were doing at Vassar, Smith, Wellesley, Radcliffe, and Mt. Holyoke, and even at newly founded Barnard and Bryn Mawr (both opened in 1889).

"Little Edens of Liberty": Women's Colleges of the Progressive Era

The Progressive Era brought recognition, expansion, and important changes to the eastern women's colleges. Freed from the need of members of the first generation to prove themselves, and aided by extraordinary women faculty and alumnae with graduate degrees from distinguished European and American institutions, second-generation students created a fascinating and intricate campus life. While popular literature continued to tout women's colleges as havens for the preservation of femininity, Progressive Era college life at the Seven Sisters schools offered women all the opportunities available to college men elsewhere. Self-government associations, athletics, and campus organizations flourished. The curriculum expanded to include courses in sociology, socialism, economics, and other topics with social relevance. Using faculty and alumnae as resources, students explored career and service options other than teaching. In 1912, graduates of women's schools in the East founded the Intercollegiate Bureau of Occupations in New York City. Social reform and political activity, including woman suffrage, became important features of campus life.[61]

Eastern women's colleges also served as the prototypes for a new form of women's higher education. Because reaction against coeducation during the Progressive Era made life at some universities difficult for women, some proposed "coordination," that is, the creation of women's colleges within universities. By linking a women's undergraduate college to a men's college or university, coordinate institutions represented a compromise between single-sex education and coeducation. Proponents of coordination argued that women students thereby received the advantages of both systems, but in fact the specifics of coordination varied widely. Barnard and Sophie Newcomb functioned largely as independent women's colleges with their own faculty, endowment, and campus. The women of Barnard and Newcomb fought to enhance their schools' standards and prestige. They used their endowment as leverage to gain access to the resources of Columbia and Tulane, while successfully protecting themselves against administrative interference from the universities.

In other cases, however, coordination simply excluded women, without offering them any advantages. Some coordinate colleges were founded and promoted by Progressive Era male educators eager to rid their universities of women's effeminizing presence. In 1900, the University of Rochester's new president, Rush Rhees, was dismayed to find himself president of a coeducational university, following Susan B. Anthony's successful campaign for women's admission. As English professor John R. Slater, Rhees' biographer, put it, Rhees determined to do his duty. "That he endured it," said Slater, "showed his patience and power of detachment,. . . for the women's mere presence in the crowded rooms and corridors conduced in the minds of some hostile critics to a high school atmosphere and hindered both study and college spirit." Male students at Rochester were equally unwelcoming, banging their feet loudly when a woman entered the classroom or slamming doors in her face. They sneered openly and formed crowds in front of campus buildings, forcing women to elbow their way through to get to their classes.

Rhees initiated a movement to replace coeducation with coordination and in 1912 threatened to accept the presidency of Amherst College unless the Rochester trustees agreed to his plan. In 1913, the Women's College of the University of Rochester opened its doors, with separate classes and social activities for female students. The situation quickly deteriorated as fewer resources were allocated to women students each year. When the men's college, graduate schools, and medical center moved to the new River Campus in the 1930s, women students had difficulty arranging access to advanced classes and libraries. The university did not reunite its undergraduate colleges until 1955.[62]

During the Progressive Era, the eastern women's colleges continued to be socioeconomically and ethnically homogeneous communities, admitting a few minority women but resisting significant diversification of the student body. College officials rarely discriminated openly; instead, they argued that applicants of a certain type would feel more "comfortable" elsewhere. In 1900, James Monroe Taylor, Vassar's president, explained to Harriet Giles, principal of Spelman Seminary, that he did not personally oppose admitting "colored girls" to the college but that white southern Vassar students would object, making normal campus life strained or impossible. Taylor told Giles that if a black woman applied to Vassar he would raise the matter with the trustees, but his lack of enthusiasm made such applications unlikely. Similarly, when Frances W. Williams sought admission to Mount Holyoke College in 1915, administrators told her mother that the academically talented young black woman would be happier at a different institution. Mrs. Williams, a Berea College graduate, replied: "Frances's happiness is none of your business; that's my business. I want to know if you will admit her." Holyoke did accept Frances Williams, who graduated Phi Beta Kappa four years later.[63]

In contrast, Wellesley continued to welcome a small number of black students, as it had during Alice Freeman's presidency, and supported their rights as members of the college community. Virginia Foster Durr, a white student from Birmingham, Alabama, who attended Wellesley from 1921 to 1923, enjoyed getting to know other southern students from Harvard and Wellesley and joined the Southern Club to attend its dances. On the first night of her sophomore year, Durr saw a "Negro girl" sitting at her assigned table in the dining room. She promptly walked out and told the head of her house that she could not possibly eat with a Negro. The head crisply informed Durr that she could either abide by the rules of Wellesley College or withdraw from the institution. After much soul-searching, Durr decided that "if nobody told Daddy, it might be all right." She ate with her black table mate and discovered that they shared certain southern tastes and distastes. Many years later, Durr, by then a committed civil rights activist, wrote: "That was the first time I became aware that my attitude was considered foolish by some people, and that Wellesley College wasn't going to stand for it. That experience had a tremendous effect on me." Wellesley became noted for accepting not only black but also Asian students and for insisting that they be well treated.[64]

Wellesley's record on the admission and treatment of Jewish women was less exemplary, possibly because their presence on campus challenged the opportunity to exercise the college's Christian missionary spirit. Like men's colleges and coeducational universities, the eastern women's colleges faced a "Jewish problem" from the 1910s until after World War II. The Ivy League and Seven Sisters colleges in particular felt that having too many Jewish students lowered the social prestige of their institutions. As with blacks, administrators did not like to speak openly about discrimination and restrictions. At Barnard College, whose New York City location and Jewish trustees prompted many applications from Jewish women, Dean Virginia Crocheron Gildersleeve (1911–1947) denied that the college employed admissions quotas. However, Barnard's more subtle policies of "geographic diversity" and psychological testing effectively limited Jewish enrollments.[65]

Jewish women who did enroll at Seven Sisters colleges generally received courteous but aloof treatment. Ruth Sapinsky Hurwitz '10 praised Wellesley's commitment to intellectual, aesthetic, and altruistic values. While some girls, she said, came to college for fun and to pass the time before marriage, the majority were "training for some kind of service." Hurwitz immersed herself in the study of English literature, paying particular attention to the Victorians. Her interest in writing, developed through creative writing courses, blossomed into the publication of a prize-winning story in the *New England Magazine*. Under the influence of Professors Vida Dutton Scudder and Emily Greene Batch, she volunteered for settlement work, relinquishing cultural and recreational excursions to Boston to do so, since she could not afford travel to the city oftener than once a week. She was "fascinated by the little Syrian and Italian girls I taught, and by the first-hand contact with problems of child welfare, housing and health." Not limiting herself to intellect and altruism, Hurwitz also attended dances at Temple Emanu-El in Boston, worked on the *Wellesley Magazine*, played basketball, participated in the class operetta and Tree Day dancing, and sang in the Glee Club.

A midwesterner from a progressive family, Sapinsky did not find Wellesley's Christian character offensive. She enjoyed the required Old and New Testament courses and found chapel services beautiful. She defended Wellesley when her Harvard friends told her about quotas at other colleges and the growing resistance to Jewish presence in the universities and the professions. Still, she acknowledged that Wellesley's Jewish women were not elected to important offices in student organizations or admitted to the secret societies; nor were they often invited to visit the homes of non-Jewish students. Stung by her growing awareness of Ivy League anti-Semitism, Sapinsky began to meet with Harvard students for discussions of Jewish life and issues and eventually married one of the participants, Henry Hurwitz, founder of the Menorah Society.[66]

Generational differences between the pioneers and women of the Progressive Era first appeared at the eastern women's colleges in the 1890s, as students sought increased opportunities to entertain young men on campus. During that decade, the colleges began allowing students to dance with their male prom guests, instead of merely "promenading" with them up and down the college corridors. Students' growing interest in heterosexual relationships eventually created distinctions and distance between them and the women faculty, especially in the 1910s, when weekending at men's colleges became popular, thus modifying the close residential nature of Seven Sisters schools.

Founded mostly between 1880 and 1900, and modeled on the successful and prominent eastern women's schools, colleges for white southern women nevertheless had a distinctive atmosphere and followed a different timetable of educational development. In the South, the later founding of women's colleges and the shortage of good secondary education meant that academic standards remained an issue into the twentieth century.

Graduates of southern women's colleges before the 1920s often found it necessary to get a second bachelor's degree, from a northern college, before undertaking master's or doctoral work. In spite of her B.A. from Statesville Female College in North Carolina in 1889, Elizabeth Avery Colton could not be admitted to the freshman class at Mount Holyoke Seminary without a year of preparatory study. She subsequently chaired the English department at Meredith College in Raleigh, North Carolina, and founded the Southern Association of College Women (SACW) in 1903, which worked to raise academic standards in southern women's colleges. She surveyed southern colleges, normal schools, and seminaries for white women, publishing her evaluations in a series of bulletins between 1911 and 1916. The SACW did not achieve its major goal of obtaining state legislation to set minimum standards for chartering colleges, but did draw regional and national attention to the issues and influence curricular development. In 1921, the SACW merged with the northern Association of Collegiate Alumnae to form a new national organization, the American Association of University Women (AAUW).[67]

Formal denominational ties and required religious observances characterized southern women's colleges long after the Seven Sisters schools dropped such practices to identify themselves as secular institutions. Similarly, as Seven Sisters students and faculty successfully battled for relaxation of seminary-type rules, southern colleges maintained and even increased such regulations. In her study of campus life of the 1920s and 1930s at Hollins, Queens, Salem, Sweet Briar, and Wesleyan Colleges, Amy Thompson McCandless found numerous social restrictions governing on- and off-campus behavior. In the 1920s, southern colleges warned students to avoid "extravagance and freakishness" in dress and not to wear jewelry. Drinking, smoking, and dancing were taboo, and chaperonage required. Queens College closed its campus to all visitors on Sundays, chaining the entrance and posting a sign proclaiming "Sabbath Day. No Admittance."[68]

Like Seven Sisters students, southern college women had homogeneous socioeconomic backgrounds. In her study of Wesleyan Female College and Randolph-Macon Women's College between 1893 and 1907, Gail Apperson Kilman called students "daughters of the New South." Wesleyan and Randolph-Macon students came from families in which fathers were involved in commerce or manufacturing (30.5 percent at Wesleyan, 24.8 percent at Randolph-Macon) or the learned professions (24.3 percent at Wesleyan and 30.3 percent at Randolph-Macon), or were white-collar workers (9.3 percent at Wesleyan and 10.2 percent at Randolph-Macon). Only 18.5 percent of the Wesleyan students and 13.3 percent of the Randolph-Macon students came from farming families; they were most likely the children of planters. There were fewer non-Protestant women in the South than in the North. Thus, southern women's colleges never had many applications from Jewish and Catholic students, although they seem to have admitted those who did apply. The charters of these institutions explicitly limited them to "white women"; no racial integration occurred at southern women's colleges before the 1960s.[69]

Internally cohesive as these white women's colleges were, external ties hindered the growth of campus life. Parents wanted their daughters to become self-supporting but also expected them to retain close family loyalties. Throughout the Progressive Era southern educators strongly encouraged students to focus their attention on studies and campus life instead of on home duties and social obligations. These efforts were, for the most part, successful; between 1900 and 1910, southern women's colleges formed student governments, campus publications, debate teams, dramatics groups, and active alumnae associations.

During the Progressive Era, students in the South constituted a first, not a second, generation, and as such had fewer opportunities to call on the support and advice of older college women. By the first decade of the twentieth century, the faculties of the best colleges included some northern-educated pioneer college graduates, although students did not develop a strong identification with these women. Given southern conservatism, it is hardly surprising that women's colleges of that region did not have the close ties to urban progressivism or the interest in women's politics that we find at the eastern schools. Yet, self-conscious about their status as educated women, southern college students explored avenues to make their mark on society, particularly through civic and religious activism. By the end of the Progressive Era, students had begun to demonstrate more interest in careers and in progressive social reform.

Chapters examine the evolution of campus life at Vassar, Sophie Newcomb, and Agnes Scott Colleges. Common themes united these institutions, most notably the determination to make women's higher education the intellectual equivalent of the best available to men. All three began with preparatory departments and evolved into liberal arts colleges—Vassar in the 1890s, Newcomb and Agnes Scott by the 1910s. Founders and administrators proclaimed the most traditional purposes for educating women, namely the enhancement of domesticity, but students, faculty, and alumnae at all three schools shaped institutional purposes for their own ends, creating a rich campus life combining aspects of men's and women's spheres.

Differences among the colleges reflect varied regional and local societies. Social-justice progressivism, suffragism, interest in careers, and the closeness of students and faculty marked Vassar College during the Progressive Era. Working together, the two generations of college women utilized "men's" privileges but modified them to fit the imperatives of women's culture. Women students enjoyed the fun of competition, whether in hockey, debate, or class elections, but, with faculty assistance, tried to control its effects on friendships and community cohesion. They sought information on new professional careers opening up to women, such as law and business, but also looked for ways to implement social reform ideals. Conflicts over the role and conduct of hetero-social relationships did not prevent the two generations of college women from cooperating in political and reform projects.

Compared to their sisters at Vassar, students of Agnes Scott and Sophie Newcomb had fewer ties to faculty, less enthusiasm for careers, and little interest in suffrage. Yet the two southern schools also differed from each other. As an urban, nonsectarian, and nonresidential college associated with southern women progressives, Newcomb contrasted with Agnes Scott's Presbyterian character, more isolated residential life, and student interest in religiously based social service.

At the turn of the century, single-sex colleges allowed women the luxury of exploring curricular and extracurricular options without encountering, on their own campuses, the objections and resistance of men. However, even the dignity of a separate institution did not command equality for women outside its gates. When Vassar women, for example, challenged Princeton students to a debate, the invitation drew anger and outrage from the men, who did not consider the two colleges equal. Like coeducated women, women's college students found separatism an essential prerequisite, but not a guarantee, of gender equality in American society.

Notes

1. Cott, *The Bonds of Womanhood*, provides an excellent description of the emerging cult of domesticity and the development of woman's sphere. The other critical book on this subject, stressing intellectual and theological history, is Sklar, *Catharine Beecher*. The essays of Caroll Smith-Rosenberg, collected in her *Disorderly Conduct*, are indispensable for understanding the origins, development, and decline of Victorian women's culture. See especially "The Female World of Love and Ritual: Relations Between Women in Nineteenth Century America," 53–76. Examples of Victorian women using domesticity to subvert the social order may be found in Glenda Gates Riley, "The Subtle Subversion", Smith-Rosenberg, "Beauty, the Beast, and the Militant Woman," in *Disorderly Conduct*, 109–128; Anne Firor Scott, "The Ever-Widening Circle." On the values of women's culture in the public sphere, see Rousmaniere, "Cultural Hybird in the Slums," and Lynn D. Gordon, "Women and the Anti-Child Labor Movement in Illinois, 1890–1920." For discussion and conceptualization of the liberal-conservative debate over women's nature and social roles, see Rosalind Rosenberg, *Beyond Separate Spheres*, especially the introduction and chap. 1.
2. The classic statement of the relationship between women's education, the American Revolution and republicanism is Kerber, *Women of the Republic*. See also Kerber, "Daughters of Columbia: Educating Women for the Republic, 1787–1805," in *The Hofstadter Aegis*; Glenda Gates Riley, "Origins of the Argument for Improved Female Education," *History of Education Quarterly* 4 (Winter 1969): 470; and Hoffman, ed., *Woman's True Profession*.
3. For general descriptions of nineteenth-century academy and seminary education, including detailed accounts of curricula and institutions, see Woody, *A History of Women's Education in the U.S.*, especially vol. 1; Solomon, chap. 2. More specific and thematic studies include Sklar, *Catharine Beecher*; Sklar, "The Founding of Mount Holyoke College"; Scott, "The Ever-Widening Circle"; Scott, "What, Then, Is the American, This New Woman?" Green, *Mary Lyon and Mount Holyoke*; and Kerns, "Farmers' Daughters." For a critical assessment of the literature on women's secondary education, see Schwager, "Educating Women in America."
4. Scott, "The Ever-Widening Circle"; Sklar, *Catharine Beecher*; Rota, "Between True Women and New Women"; Kerns, "Farmers' Daughters;" Allmendinger, "Mount Holyoke Students Encounter the Need For Life-Planning."
5. Clinton, "Equally Their Due;" Fox-Genovese, *Within The Plantation Household*; Friedman, *The Enclosed Garden*; Blandin, *History of Higher Education of Women in the South Prior to 1870*.
6. Stowe, "The *Thing*, Not Its Vision"; Stowe, "The Not-So-Cloistered Academy."
7. M. Carey Thomas, "Present Tendencies in Women's College and University Education," Association of Collegiate Alumnae *Publications* (February 1908).
8. Brown, "Golden Girls"; Schwager, "Arguing For the Higher Education of Women"; Wallach, "The Dilemmas of Coeducation."
9. Hogeland, "Coeducation of the Sexes at Oberlin College"; Schwager, "Arguing for the Higher Education of Women"; Rury and Harper, "The Trouble With Coeducation."
10. Lori Ginzberg, "The Joint Education of the Sexes; Oberlin's Original Vision," in *Coeducation in A Changing World*, ed. Carol Lasser (Urbana: University of Illinois Press, 1987): 67–80.
11. Clarke, *Sex in Education*, and Clarke, *Building a Brain*.
12. Thomas, "Present Tendencies," 49.
13. Scott, *The Southern Lady*, especially chapter on post-Civil War South; Mayo, *Southern Women in the Recent Educational Movement in the South*. See especially, the introduction by Dan T. Carter and Amy Friedlander to the new edition of Mayo's work (Baton Rouge: Louisiana State University Press, 1978): xi–xxiii.
14. Butcher, "Education For Equality: Women's Rights Periodicals and Women's Higher Education"; Duffey, *No Sex in Education*; Brackett, ed., *The Education of American Girls* Howe, ed., *Sex and Education*. For a fascinating discussion of Clarke's work and its impact, see Morantz-Sanchez, 54–55, 206. On Laura Clay, see Fuller, *Laura Clay and the Women's Rights Movement*.
15. Florence Kelley, "When Co-education Was Young," *The Survey* 57 (1 February 1927): 557–561, 600–602.
16. Palmieri, "In Adamless Eden": Scarborough and Furumoto, *Untold Lives*.
17. Rogers, *Vassar Women*.
18. Letters from William Campbell Preston Breckinridge to Sophonisba Breckinridge, 20 September 1884–30 March 1885, in Breckinridge Papers, Library of Congress, Washington, D. C. Quoted in Horowitz, "With More Love Than I Can Write." I am grateful to Natalie Zemon Davis for the reference to this source.
19. D. McIntyre, Luke H. Parsons, and B. L. Baxter, "Report on the Admission of Females," 29 September 1858, *Regents' Proceedings*, 795.
20. McGuigan, *A Dangerous Experiment*, 19–22.

21. Curti and Carstensen, *The University of Wisconsin 1848–1925*, 1: 369–81; Olin, *The Women of a State University*; Hague, "What If the Power Does Lie Within Me?"

22. Conable, *Women at Cornell*.

23. Haines, "Coeducation and the Development of Leadership Skills in Women."

24. May, "History of the University of Rochester," unpublished MS; Harper, *The Life and Work of Susan B. Anthony*, vol. 4.

25. Ihle, "The Development of Co-Education in Major Southern Universities."

26. For a lively account of women's admission and campus experiences at one land grant university, see Treichler, "Alma Mater's Sorority."

27. Anderson, *An American Girl and Her Four Years in A Boys' College*.

28. Ibid., 52.

29. Newcomer, *Century of Higher Education*, 49.

30. Rudolph, *Curriculum*; Boas, *Women's Education Begins*, 256–258.

31. Horowitz, *Alma Mater*, 9–55.

32. Davis, *American Heroine*, 29; Lagemann, "The Challenge of Jane Addams."

33. Solomon, *In the Company of Educated Women*, 62–77; Rogers, *Vassar Women*; Sarah H. Gordon, "Smith College Students"; Rota, "From True Women to New Women."

34. Palmieri, "In Adamless Eden," chap. 1 and 2.

35. Rota, "From True Women to New Women"; Shea, "Mount Holyoke College, 1875–1910"; Glazer and Slater, *Unequal Colleagues*, chap. 2.

36. Abbott, "A Generation of College Women" and "The College Woman and Matrimony"; Shinn, "The Marriage Rate of College Women" and "Etc.," Thwing, "What Becomes of College Women"; Olin, *The Women of A State University*. For a modern assessment of the first generation's choices, see Cookingham, "Bluestockings, Spinsters, and Pedagogues."

37. Rousmaniere, "Cultural Hybrid in the Slums"; Gordon, "Women and the Anti-Child Labor Movement."

38. Campbell, *The Liberated Woman of 1914*.

39. Shinn, "The Marriage Rate of College Women" and "Etc.", Sicherman, *Alice Hamilton*; Dobkin, *The Making of a Feminist*; Herman, "Loving Courtship or the Marriage Market?" Davis, "Why They Failed to Marry."

40. Smith-Rosenberg, "Female World of Love and Ritual"; Palmieri, "In Adamless Eden."

41. Davis, *Factors in the Sex Life of 2200 Women*.

42. Criticism of the second generation of college women can be found in Mathews, *The Dean of Women*; Talbot, *The Education of Women*; and Talbot, *More Than Lore*.

43. Horowitz, *Alma Mater* and *Campus Life*.

44. Brown, "Golden Girls," chap. 1; Morantz-Sanchez, *Sympathy and Science*.

45. Rudolph, *The American College and University*.

46. Rossiter, *Women Scientists in America*. My own view of the home economics movement is more positive than Rossiter's. See also Vincenti, "A History of the Philosophy of Home Economics"; Marion Talbot, "The Vocational and Cultural Value of Domestic Science," *Journal of Home Economics* 5:3 (1913): 232–236; Talbot, *The Education of Women*.

47. Institutional efforts to broaden women's career opportunities are described in subsequent chapters of this book. See also the Association of Collegiate Alumnae's *Publications*, 1898–1911. For a discussion of the professionalization of social work, see Roy Lubove, *The Professional Altruist: The Emergence of Social Work As A Career* (Cambridge: Harvard University Press, 1965).

48. Briscoe, "Bryn Mawr College Traditions."

49. Jean Webster, *When Patty Went to College* (New York: Grosset and Dunlap, 1903), 53–57.

50. Victoria Bissell Brown, "Golden Girls," chap. 1.

51. Nancy Sahli, "Smashing"; Filene, *Him/Her/Self*; Simmons, "Companionate Marriage and the Lesbian Threat"; Smith-Rosenberg, "The New Woman as Androgyne: Social Disorder and Gender Crisis, 1870–1936," in *Disorderly Conduct*, 245–296.

52. Cott, *The Grounding of Modern Feminism*.

53. Brett, "A Different Kind of Being."

54. Wechsler, "An Academic Gresham's Law."

55. Mathews, *Dean of Women*, 160. For a theoretical discussion of women's separatism in the nineteenth and early twentieth centuries, see Freedman, "Separatism as Strategy."

56. Hobson, *Laura Z*, 16, 64–66.

57. Memoir dated 21 December 1962, box 36, file 2, no. 26, in Gregoria Fraser Goins Papers, Moorland-Springarn Research Center, Howard University, Washington, D.C.

58. Woody, *A History of Women's Education in the United States*, 2: 280–294.
59. Morantz-Sanchez, *Sympathy and Science*, 64–89, discusses the debate over medical coeducation and women physicians' concept of their professional mission.
60. For a useful description of one institution's response to the coeducational crisis, see Knight, "The Quails." My thanks to Rosalind Rosenberg for drawing my attention to this source.
61. Emily James Smith, "Some Further Considerations."
62. Slater, *Rhees of Rochester*; May, "History of the University of Rochester."
63. James Monroe Taylor to Harriet Elizabeth Giles, 1900, "Racial Matters" file, Spelman College Archives; transcript of interview with Susie Williams Jones, 11 April 1977, p. 20, by Merze Tate, Black Women's Oral History Project, Columbia University.
64. Durr, "A Southern Belle Comes North." My thanks to Leah Fygetakis for sending me this article.
65. Wechsler, *The Qualified Student*; Gordon, "Annie Nathan Meyer and Barnard College."
66. Hurwitz, "Coming of Age at Wellesley."
67. Dutton, "History of the Southern Association of College Women"; Lemmon, "Elizabeth Avery Colton"; *Proceedings of the Southern Association of College Women*, 1912, 1913.
68. McCandless, "Preserving the Pedestal."
69. Kilman, "Southern Collegiate Women."

MANHOOD AT HARVARD:
WILLIAM JAMES AND OTHERS

KIM TOWNSEND

Introduction

WEDNESDAY, JUNE 24, 1908, was an unusually hot and humid day, but nothing dampened the spirits of those who had gathered for Harvard's Two Hundred and Sixty-sixth Commencement.[1] Certainly not the weather. One minor adjustment seemed advisable. The conferring of degrees in Massachusetts Hall began at 10:30 instead of 10:00, thus shortening the time between it and the forming of the procession that would march through the Yard and across Cambridge Street to Memorial Hall for the afternoon ceremonies. During those ceremonies, the weather was only a source of amusement: noting "the savage heat," one honorary degree recipient, the governor of Kentucky, Augustus E. Willson (class of 1869), recommended his own state as a "summer resort"; Edward Kent (class of 1883), the chief justice of the Supreme Court of Arizona—a territory that would become the forty-eighth state four years later—was introduced as not caring whether it was hot or not. If Kent did care, being the last speaker, he cared just as much about the lateness of the hour. Comparing himself to the dying sinner who had asked his doctor to pray with him, he said he would be "brief and fervent."

Justice Kent's urgent message was that it was harder for the Harvard man in the West than for the one in the East to represent Harvard's ideals, and that it was incumbent upon Harvard to support the Western man in his efforts. "The farther away we get from Harvard, the more is expected of the Harvard man in spreading the faith," he said. The Harvard men of Arizona needed help; their alma mater had to send out men bearing libations "from the fountainhead of our inspiration." He beseeched the president—Charles William Eliot—to come himself. Dean Briggs' visit the year before had done wonders, but now "Mahomet must come to the mountain." It would hasten the day "when Harvard will be the Harvard of our whole country, our national university." Kent was more than half serious about faith and inspiration and Mahomet. The Harvard he had in mind had the potential of saving the country's soul.

According to the governor of Massachusetts, Curtis Guild (class of 1881), the day when Harvard would enlighten the entire nation had already arrived. Being the second speaker (after President Eliot), Governor Guild was not brief at all, but his concluding words were every bit as fervent as Justice Kent's: "Whatever patriotism of American manhood comes to the fore, Harvard memory, Harvard ideals, instinctively rise, because Harvard is not merely Massachusetts, Harvard is not merely New England, Harvard is the ideal of America." Harvard men were always imbued with America's ideals, he claimed; after they graduated, they were continually embodying those ideals in their service to their country. Wherever one turned—Guild turned to Kansas and Florida, and even beyond, to the Philippines, for his examples—one came upon the inspiring words of Harvard men. "How far does the influence of Harvard extend?" he asked. "How far does it not extend? Imagine any crisis or any determining event in any young man's life that you will," he replied, and "see how naturally the Harvard idea comes to the fore." He called that idea the "patriotism of American manhood."

Previous generations of Americans had been more concerned with generic man's relationship to his God. Although they made clear gender distinctions in their attempts to understand and strengthen that relationship, and also the family relationships that they created with God's blessings, they did not linger over the question of what constituted their earthly existences *as men*. Or if they did—as had been the case for so long as anyone could remember—they took manhood to be simply a quality possessed by courageous and honorable individuals. In the nineteenth century, according to the *Century Dictionary* (an American equivalent to the *Oxford English Dictionary*), the word "manly" denoted "the highest conception of what is noble in man and worthy of his manhood." According to one of Harvard's most eminent graduates, Ralph Waldo Emerson, even a woman could, at least by implication, possess such manhood. A modern reader of "Self-Reliance" might assume that when Emerson said, "Society everywhere is in conspiracy against the manhood of every one of its members," he was speaking only of men, but we are obsessed by gender. Emerson was not. His vision was broad and embracing. "We want men and women who shall renovate life and our social state," he said in the same essay. There was no more powerful educational presence in the young Emerson's life than in that of his aunt, Mary Moody Emerson; his wife Lidian's advocacy of women's rights (and of abolition) predated and influenced his own; his friendship with Margaret Fuller was one of intellectual equals. He knew, finally, that "superior women are rare anywhere, as are superior men . . . and every country, in its roll of honor, has as many women as men."[2]

But the Civil War brought about a marked narrowing of the common definition of manhood. The exemplary man who had once been closest to God, or who had been most valiant in his pursuit of intellectual or moral betterment, was supplanted by a figure who had distinguished himself on the battlefield—still an honorable man, but now a stronger, a tougher, a less thoughtful man. After the Civil War, men were more concerned about character traits, attitudes, and appearances than about deeds. They felt pressure to be masculine. The word itself took on new meaning, and the word "masculinity" made its way into the language. By the end of the century, "masculine"—once used simply to differentiate traits distinguishing men from women ("masculine clothing" or "masculine occupations," for example)—had become useful to men looking for ways to describe and explain the authority they sought to establish. By 1890, the noun "masculinity" was in the *Century Dictionary*.[3] During this period, men approached all the issues that men face—physical, educational, domestic, and social issues—with a new sense of having to present themselves as manly, and a clear sense of how womanly they would be considered if they did not measure up.

James Russell Lowell reflected the change at ceremonies commemorating the end of the war. "Yea, Manhood hath a wider span/And larger privilege of life than man," he wrote in his "Ode Recited at the Harvard Commemoration, July 21, 1865." What separated the manly from mere men was their willingness to fight and, if necessary, to die for the "Truth." Lowell acknowledged that Harvard men might take other routes to "Truth":

> Life may be given in many ways,
> And loyalty to Truth be sealed
> As bravely in the closet as the field,
> So bountiful is Fate,

but the closeted or the scholarly life was clearly inferior. "Many loved Truth, and lavished life's best oil/Amid the dust of books to find her," Lowell said. A few lines later, though, the phrase "ashes of the burnt-out mind" makes clear how unproductive, and finally unheroic, Lowell considered the man who spent or used up "life's best oil" in his study. And it followed—in lines that look forward to talk of racial superiority at the end of the century—that warriors made infinitely better breeders:

> That is best blood that hath most iron in't
> To edge resolve with, pouring without stint
> For what makes manhood dear.

Of the Harvard men being honored on that July day in 1865, Lowell said, "These hold great futures in their lusty reins/And certify to earth a new imperial race."

When Governor Guild spoke about the "patriotism of American manhood" forty-three years later, he evoked memories of the Civil War and of the Union forged in 1865. He also indicated just how far America's influence had extended in the intervening years. In his consideration of its citizenry as "a new imperial race," he had much more to draw on than James Russell Lowell did. By 1908, America was—to the satisfaction of most of its citizens—fulfilling the "manifest destiny" that had been first defined for it when Texas was annexed in 1845. Having expanded beyond its continental boundaries to possess Hawaii, the Philippines, Puerto Rico, Guam, and the Panama Canal Zone in the years just before and after the turn of the century, the country seemed well on its way to becoming the redeemer and civilizer of the world.

Guild gave evidence of Harvard men spreading the word throughout America's growing domain. He cited a sergeant reading *A Man without a Country*, by Edward Everett Hale (class of 1839)—"And for your country, boy, and for that flag, never dream a dream but of serving her as she bids you, though the service carry you, through a thousand hells"—to boost the morale of the "ragged soldiers" under his command in the Philippines; he told of the time during the Spanish-American War when he heard a Northern band play "Dixie," a Southern band play "Yankee Doodle," and then both bands spontaneously strike up with "My Country Tis of Thee," the words of which had been written by "S. F. Smith of Harvard." But of course everyone in Guild's audience had in mind a much more impressive example of Harvard's preeminence as a producer of men who could reshape the world in America's image. They were thinking of the man who had just completed his second term as president of the United States—"just now voluntarily retired from that great office which in his hands had become the greatest seat of power in the world," as the next speaker put it. Though he was not present on this occasion, at the very mention of his name—"Roosevelt of the Class of 1880"—"a hearty greeting" went up in the form of a "Harvard cheer."

But as Guild made clear, proof of the "patriotism of American manhood" was not limited to scenes of civil strife or international conquest. In his speech he called for "a little more earnest everyday patriotism among the educated classes." An educated man could prove his devotion to his country by demanding respect for the law, by working for civil service reform, and by curbing his own desire for mere wealth. He could prove his patriotic manhood by doing battle with dishonor, corruption, and greed. America being a democracy, he said not *noblesse* but *sagesse oblige*.

In these contexts, Harvard's example was also pervasive and compelling. Harvard was not a martial institution. It was, however, an increasingly powerful institution, possessed of tremendous wealth and privilege, and in its day-to-day operation it demonstrated how wealth and privilege could be used efficiently. Harvard was coming into its own as a great educational institution at the same time that America was beginning to emerge as the richest and most powerful nation on earth. It was becoming—arguably—"our national university," not just because it tapped that wealth, but because it devised ways to control and direct it. And it set itself the task of teaching its students how to develop their considerable financial, physical, and intellectual resources as well, to put them to responsible use. It created an educational and social environment in which—ideally, at least—young men learned to become professional and business leaders, an environment in which—again ideally—they learned to be responsive to the forces and energies of the age while at the same time contriving ways to improve or reform them. In doing so, they would join the men who served their country in uniform as exemplars of patriotic American manhood.

Their new theater of operations changed radically in the decades following the Civil War. Between 1870 and 1900, the country's population almost doubled (from just over 38 million to almost 76 million); in another ten years it was 92 million. Immigrants accounted for almost a third of the increase, even as between a fourth and a third of them eventually returned to their native lands. Accounting for about a third of the industrial work force as well, immigrants joined the hundreds of thousands who left their farms and rural homesteads; together they converted the country into an urban industrial empire.

The story of this decidedly material (rather than religious) conversion is a familiar one. The country's seemingly unlimited natural resources—coal and oil, copper and iron, gold and silver, lumber and animal life—were discovered and exploited so fast that by the end of the century there was no longer any wilderness to tame. Or so the story went—most famously—in the lecture called

"The Significance of the Frontier in American History," which Frederick Jackson Turner delivered at the Columbian Exposition in 1893. So the story went from the perspective of those who were "destined" to seize this unprecedented historical moment. From the perspective of those whose lands were seized—the *native* Americans—the story reads differently. After the Civil War, settlers moving west overcame Indian resistance and, in 1887, received government approval in the form of the Dawes Act, which endorsed the breakup of communally owned reservation land and established rights of way for telegraph and railroad companies. Indian resistance effectively ended at Wounded Knee in 1890; by 1900, Indian holdings were about half of what they had been in 1887.[4]

In a matter of a few decades, the country had the ability to communicate with itself—by telegraph (Western Union having established itself as America's first monopoly by 1866), by rail (the first transcontinental track was completed in 1869), by telephone (Bell's invention in 1876), by automobile (Selden's in 1877, Ford's in 1892), and thanks to the typewriter (1868), the mimeograph (1876), and the Linotype machine (1885). Countless other inventions and innovations—the Bessemer steel plant (1864), the oil pipe line (the first going from Pithole, Pennsylvania, to a railroad connection five miles away in 1866), the refrigerated railroad car (1868), the silo (1870), barbed wire (1876), a store lighted by electric lamps (Wanamaker's in 1878) and streets by arc lights (Cleveland in 1879), the hydroelectric plant (1879), and the steel-framed skyscraper (1884), to name a few—made it possible for men to transform the country's natural resources into goods and services, and then to transport and to sell them.[5]

Out of the competition and struggle for riches, "trusts"—companies and business alliances controlling the oil, steel, lumber, meat-packing, railroad, and other industries—came into being. It was the Gilded Age. Politicians' pockets received new linings, especially during the administration of Ulysses S. Grant (1869–77). Legendary fortunes were made, and the men who made them—Diamond Jim Brady, Jim Fisk, Mark Hopkins, Collis Huntington, Cornelius Vanderbilt—built monuments to themselves and lived lives that might have shamed even the "barons" to whom they are routinely compared. The first, largest, and most exemplary trust was that of John D. Rockefeller, whose Standard Oil Company of Ohio, incorporated in 1870, controlled about 90 percent of the industry within a decade. "The growth of a large business," he said, "is merely a survival of the fittest, the working out of a law of nature and a law of God."[6] It was his homely expression of Social Darwinism, the philosophy—developed by Herbert Spencer in England, and disseminated most effectively in America by John Fiske (an occasional lecturer at Harvard between 1869 and 1871) and William Graham Sumner (a permanent and highly influential fixture on the Yale faculty beginning in 1872)—that argued that social evolution was a slow and cruel but ultimately beneficent process, and that any tinkering with it, any effort to improve social conditions, could only make the process more painful. No matter that by 1890 some 1 percent of families owned 51 percent of the country's wealth, and that the lower 44 percent owned just over 1 percent of it, with an estimated 23 to 30 percent of the work force being unemployed part of every year during this era. No matter that 5,000 businesses failed in 1873, 10,000 in 1878, and 15,000 in 1893, or that between 1881 and 1905 almost 37,000 strikes were recorded, some of them (at the Coeur d'Alene mines, in Idaho, at Homestead, Pennsylvania, at Pullman, Illinois) involving pitched battles and loss of life. Nor could much be said about race riots and lynchings against Chinese in Los Angeles (in 1871) or Seattle (in 1886), against Negroes in Vicksburg (1874, 75 killed) and Italians in New Orleans (1891, 11 killed). Evolution was taking its course; there were some peoples who were apparently not destined to survive.[7]

Rockefeller also defended his business practices by explaining that someone had to "bring some order out of what was rapidly becoming a state of chaos," and in fact—whatever the incalculable costs—American economic and social life became more orderly by the end of the century. Symptomatically, in 1882, Frederick W. Taylor, a gang boss for the Midvale Steel Corporation, introduced a system of "scientific management" that would be applied to industrial operations nationwide; the next year standard time was established, with the railroads dividing the country into four time zones; the captains of industry were replaced by financiers (J. P. Morgan leading the attack) who merged and controlled their trusts; and the number of professional associations and societies ballooned around the turn of the century.

At the commencement of 1908, there was ample evidence that Harvard had grown and prospered in the decades since the Civil War—that it had progressed right along with the nation. It had benefited from the country's successes in obvious ways. Although the number of graduating seniors (only 445, as against 530 the year before) might have been cause for concern, the only reference to enrollments was to their increase over the years, and more than enough gifts received were mentioned to allay any fears for Harvard's future. More to the point, there were specific indications that Harvard had been consciously addressing the question of how men could become successful in whatever business or professional field they entered, and that it had itself evolved into a model of administrative efficiency. Of the several "parts" delivered after the prayer that opened the ceremonies in Memorial Hall—"Commencement Day," "Literature and Life," "Harvard Hymnody"—one was titled "The Responsibilities of the Business Man of the Future." President Eliot talked almost exclusively about how Harvard was being managed, about the practical relevance of a Harvard man's education, and about what manly qualities a Harvard man would have to possess if he expected to succeed.

In the address that he gave when he took office in the fall of 1869, President Eliot had said specifically, "The principle of divided and subordinate responsibilities, which rules in government bureaus, in manufactories, and all great companies, which makes a modern army a possibility, must be applied in the University."[8] In 1908, almost forty years later, at what would be his last commencement as president of Harvard, he said that "the best issue" of the preceding year was that "we have accomplished something considerable . . . toward the better organization of Harvard University." First, what had been three undergraduate departments—Harvard College, the Lawrence Scientific School, and the Bussey Institution (devoted to agriculture and horticulture)—had been rolled into one. Harvard College now granted the bachelor's degree in arts and sciences. Secondly, the Bussey Institution had itself become a graduate school, and another, an entirely new one—"a novel experiment in our country"—had come into existence: the Graduate School of Business Administration. (The signals were clear: the nation was no longer a predominantly rural republic; students of business administration and agriculture were passing in the night, the former to become more and more prominent, the latter fated to be absorbed—in the early 1930s—by the Biological Institute at Harvard.) And finally, with one exception (the Dental School), the undergraduate department had become "the gate to all the professional schools of the University." The Department of Dentistry was not yet a graduate school. When that happened, Eliot said, "then will Harvard have accomplished first and alone in our country the true organization of a University—a single undergraduate department and all the professional schools on top of that department and all of them requiring a degree in arts, letters, or science for admission." The requirements of the University as Eliot had defined them in 1869 were all but met.

In his remarks, Eliot devoted an equal amount of time to making the point that there was a direct correlation between "success in college scholarship and success in after-life." He told of a study by Professor of Government Abbott Lawrence Lowell (who the following June would stand—as the next president of Harvard—right where Eliot stood), a study showing that one out of five of the first four scholars in the last twenty-seven classes appeared in Who's Who, whereas only one out of 13.3 of the "average" graduates had achieved that honor. Eliot said that he himself could not "arrive at statistical demonstrations." He agreed with Lowell wholeheartedly, but his support was not that of a social scientist. He spoke, instead, as the man who had presided over the moral and physical education of young Harvard men since just after the Civil War.

In language that had become commonplace thanks to "Roosevelt of the Class of 1880," Eliot appealed to the Harvard man's manhood: "It is in college that men begin to prepare for the strenuous competitions of the world, and win the mental power, the nervous power to succeed in them." He acknowledged that many families considered social or athletic distinction truer indications of future success. Indeed, during the preceding decades, many undergraduates—most, some argued—paid much more attention to Harvard's clubs and Harvard's athletic teams than to Harvard's professors. But "social distinction or athletic distinction" were not "the main object of college life." Eliot maintained, "The real road to success is through scholarship, and the acquisition of the power to work hard, and to endure fatigue and have a steady nerve under intellectual and moral stress."

Clearly, a young man's coming of age as a man in post-Civil War America would not be easy. The toll on his nerves would be especially heavy. George Beard explained why in 1881, in his book *American Nervousness: Its Causes and Consequences*. The cause was "modern civilization," which, he said, was characterized by "steam-power, the periodical press, the telegraph, the sciences, and the mental activity of women." From these ills that modern man was heir to, secondary and tertiary causes fanned out, including climate—inexplicably, Beard instanced New England's dry air—institutions of every sort, and personal habits, including "indulgence of appetites and passions."[9] President Eliot's words describing what the ambitious student faced echo Beard's diagnosis: the strenuousness, the drive to succeed, might result in no more than fatigue; the otherwise steady nervous system might collapse under the stress. But nevertheless, the Harvard undergraduate would strive to represent patriotic American manhood—manhood that was distinctly American, the manhood of men who typified America.

Lowell's contemporaries and students would speak another language, but the older men—most of the men—at the 1908 commencement referred often and variously to an ideal manhood that had been developed and represented— even taught—at Harvard since Eliot had become president in 1869. The new ideal of manliness had been realized during the Civil War. Lowell testified to that fact in his commemoration ode. When T. W. Higginson—famous for having commanded a Negro regiment during the war—gathered and published ninety-five memorials to Harvard men who had lost their lives in the conflict, he suggested in his preface that patriotic manhood was to be expected of men who had been "highly educated": "If there is one inference to be fairly drawn from these memoirs, as a whole, it is this: that there is no class of men in this republic from whom the response of patriotism comes more promptly and surely than from its most highly educated class."[10] Harvard education had to have been working in order to produce such martyrs.

In the decades after the war, Harvard would continue to foster manliness. It could not provide a war, but it could provide the next-best thing—combat on playing rather than battle fields. And provide it did, as it developed first a physical education program and then an intercollegiate athletic program that rivaled and (after great effort) often surpassed that of Yale. The men who possessed the qualities of a good athlete—competitiveness, perseverance, strength, endurance—would be rewarded by ending up at the top of their classes. And they would go on to succeed in life—life, at any rate, as most of the speakers imagined it, the active life of business and the professions.

At one point in the commencement proceedings, Governor Willson of Kentucky listed the raw materials out of which Harvard would fashion this man. He described the American man, who, he claimed, was the same the country over, in his own state as well as in Massachusetts, in Texas or South Carolina:

> He is the real thing, all wool and a yard wide. He is in earnest; he has courage; he is sometimes a little hardheaded, and it takes a little more than moral suasion to veer him around in the course if he gets set wrong; but he is a man all the time, wherever he is, and a real man who intends to do things.

He was itemizing the same "stuff" that Frederick Jackson Turner had said characterized the frontier man—"coarseness and strength combined with acuteness and acquisitiveness; that practical, inventive turn of mind, quick to find expedients; that masterful grasp of material things . . . that dominant individualism."[11] The Harvard man who was being honored on this hot and humid June afternoon hour was "a real man," an earnest and courageous, acute and practical, individual, but he was neither coarse nor hardheaded, and moral suasion had been enough to enable him to stay the course. In a word, he had had the benefit of a Harvard education.

In his preface to his *Memorial Biographies*, Higginson had defined the "most highly educated class" as an aristocracy "with only an admixture, such as aristocracies now show, of what are called self-made men." The self-made man of which he spoke had become an inspiring household word with the publication of Horatio Alger's (Harvard, class of 1852) *Raggedy Dick* in 1867. As he evolved into the fittest man in the industrial jungle, it was apparent that he needed to be educated in honor, fair play, and social responsibility. Or rather, for the aristocracy to remain in place, it would have to make sure that America's self-made man—or wooly, or frontier, man—shared its values.

Very little was said about his origins. Governor Guild alluded to a recent speech in which President Eliot had advised "citizens of a certain race and creed" to join the Massachusetts Volunteer Militia. In his evasiveness, he seemed to suggest—it seemed to go *almost* without saying all afternoon—that the man about whom everybody was speaking was an "Anglo-Saxon." In fact,

Harvard did not turn its back on the thousands of recent immigrants; men of surprisingly diverse backgrounds had recently attended Harvard. A man commenting on the *Harvard Quinquennial Catalogue* in the fall of 1908 said, "During the past 25 or 30 years the numbers of foreign names have increased, and the nationalities represented would reach at least a score." He listed "Scandinavians, Poles, Russians, Italians, Hungarians, Armenians, Greeks, Icelanders, Bulgarians, Chinese, and Japanese."[12] But wherever the student came from, whoever he was, he would feel the pressure to fit himself into the mold of the Harvard gentleman, a figure who was more than likely to be relatively wealthy and to have a name that one would not think of as "foreign." Whatever his beginnings or social situation, he obviously had the potential of embodying manhood as Harvard conceived of it.

The same could not be said of a woman. Radcliffe had celebrated its twenty-fifth commencement the day before, but on this occasion her only appearance was in her traditional supporting role as described by Governor Willson: "the character of the American man" was "fortified and ennobled by the influence of the American woman," he said. By 1908, in the country at large, the number of women entering colleges, and then the professions, rather than into the holy state of matrimony, and the amount of political and social activity involving women in the sixty years since Lucretia Mott and Elizabeth Cady Stanton convened the first woman's rights convention in Seneca Falls, New York, made it increasingly difficult to assume that her place was in the home. But though Harvard kept up with—or instructed—the culture on every other front, it purposely and determinedly did not do so when faced with questions about women's worth and their appointed destinies. Put simply, Harvard could not do that while insisting on the value of manhood as much as it did.

Before the war it had been possible to imagine women possessing manly qualities and to admire them for it. After the war, the thought of strong women—autonomous, independent-minded, educated women, for example—forced a man to try to become that much more manly. Or to reverse the logic, if a man felt he was about as manly as he could be—or his efforts about as intense as his constitution could bear—he could relax them so long as he could be sure that women remained relatively womanly. As we will see in the pages that follow, that was the logic that dictated Harvard's response to the evolution of Radcliffe College from its beginnings in 1879.

Governor Willson's hopes for Harvard, Governor Guild's assumptions about the institution, President Eliot's boasts, their way of speaking (or not speaking) about the "admixture" of students, and their exclusion of women—the commencement exercises as a whole—are all typical of a period of about forty years in which Harvard developed its ideal of manhood. The ideal both reflected ideas about manhood that prevailed after the Civil War and—as these men preferred to claim—expressed those ideas in their original and most inspiring form. It is still at work in the culture.

Manhood at Harvard: William James and Others is about that ideal and about the men who created or questioned it. My subtitle recalls the title of an autobiographical work by James' brother Henry: *A Small Boy and Others*. Like Henry James, William was one among many others—not a family as in Henry's volume, but a group of extraordinarily distinguished colleagues and, in time, students. In retrospect he may be somewhat diminished by that very fact, but he is still the one who is—like his brother Henry—the most interesting figure in his group. And inasmuch as Harvard strove to become the most influential educational institution in the country during the years that James taught there, all the while that higher education itself was becoming the means by which young men made their way in society, there is ample justification for imagining William James at the center of a much larger circle.

In *The Confident Years, 1885–1915*, Van Wyck Brooks (Harvard, class of 1907), a foremost student of American culture, called James "a type of the epoch," along with Theodore Roosevelt, on the basis of their common commitment to a "philosophy of 'toil and risk.'"[13] It is a characterization that is all the more interesting for my purposes because Roosevelt was a student of James' and a man with whom James debated educational, national, and international issues. They talked the same language, so to speak. James was an extraordinary man in his own right; he was also—for all the important differences—very much a man among men like Roosevelt. He was a man who put his stamp on his community and on his society; he was also a part of that society.

John Jay Chapman, a student and friend of James'—and, in his day, another prominent social critic—called it "a secret society." "Every generation is a secret society," he said, "and has incommunicable enthusiasms, tastes and interests which are a mystery both to its predecessors and to posterity."[14] There is nothing unusual about a generation's being something of a closed society, or about a man's withholding secrets, but Chapman's figure is especially apt for this group of privileged men, who bonded in clubs and societies in elite educational institutions during this particular era. It also echoes one of James' own modest—and startling—accounts of himself, one in which he appears *less* rather than more distinguishable in the shrouded atmosphere in which the men of his generation lived. He was, he said, like a dark planet, "believed to be greater than all the shining ones, because of the many correspondences with the illustrious, all treating him with deference," but in fact saying nothing all the while—"having the wit to suppress his answers." He shone, he confessed, because he so successfully reflected others' light.[15] Positioning him there at the cultural center, among his colleagues and his students, we may also see the world as it was illuminated by them. "There is a Zeitgeist," Chapman went on to say, "about all hero-worship." To a degree, the spirit of an age determines who will turn out to be its heroes. James' greatness lay not only in the way he brought out the spirit of his age but also in the way his own dark spirit reflected it.

In a lecture called "Great Men and Their Environment," delivered before the Harvard Natural History Society in 1880, James expressed his own views on the relationship between distinguished individuals and the era in which they lived.[16] He framed his discussion in the context of a debate with Herbert Spencer and his disciples, the Social Darwinists who so misread their Darwin as to argue that change was due primarily to environmental influences, to mere circumstance to physical geography, to ancestry, to anything but what James considered vital—namely, "the accumulated influences of individuals." James acknowledged that the environment acted upon a great man just the way it did on what Darwin called "the accidental variations" with which an animal was born, but his primary interest was in "the vital importance of individual initiative." By the same token, whereas many of his opponents thought only of groups, or tribes, or races, and the differences among them, James said he was interested in "the small difference between the genius and his tribe." In a short follow-up essay— titled unambiguously "The Importance of Individuals"—he summed up his argument with a proposition that he claimed he learned from an uneducated carpenter: "There is very little difference between one man and another," the carpenter had said, "but what little there is, *is very important*."[17]

Even as he spoke, James himself was beginning to play a key role in altering the structure and tone of Harvard University. In the opening minutes of his lecture, he had asked what it was that made "communities change from generation to generation," and he had used the fact that "the Harvard College of today [was] so different from that of thirty years ago" as one of his examples. Though the question as to what made the difference was left open, the obvious answer in 1880 was Harvard's president, Charles William Eliot. But it would not be long before William James would be a correct answer too. From a Spencerian perspective, he was only one member of the faculty that Eliot had brought to Harvard in the last quarter of the nineteenth century. But from the perspective that James encourages us to take in "Great Men and Their Environment," he was distinctive, the "greatest" among that group of men.

James stood out from his colleagues, and from students of the stature of Du Bois and Santayana, on the basis of his monumental *The Principles of Psychology* (1890), *The Will to Believe* (1897), *The Varieties of Religious Experience* (1902), or *Pragmatism* (1907), but equally important was something in his tone, something about his presence. It was discernible in the man himself, and it was what was remarkable about his thinking. "Let me repeat once more," James said in "The Types of Philosophic Thinking" (1908),

> That a man's vision is the great fact about him. Who cares for Carlyle's reasons, or Schopenhauer's, or Spencer's? A philosophy is the expression of a man's intimate character, and all definitions of the universe are but the deliberately adopted reactions of human characters upon it.[18]

What made James great was the "vision" that was both his response to life and the philosophical reflection of his "intimate character."

The year before he died, James took the time to read a draft of a Ph.D. thesis in which he noted, "utterances of mine written at different dates, for different audiences belonging to different universes of discourse," were strung together to form a "philosophy," and then pronounced incoherent. He reacted "with admiration and abhorrence." The thesis deserved a degree summa cum laude, he thought—certainly he would have seen to it that Harvard gave it highest honors—but by the same token, it represented everything he disliked about what he had memorably called "The Ph.D. Octopus." Had the author been a man, he would have left it at that. "Being a woman," however, he said chivalrously, "there may be yet a gleam of hope!" He urged "Miss S——" to devote her talents "to the study of reality in its concreteness," to be constructive and substitute an alternative to his "humanism," to supersede him. But first she had to appreciate his "vision." "The whole Ph.D. industry of building up an author's meaning out of separate texts leads nowhere," he wrote, "unless you have first grasped his centre of vision, by an act of imagination."[19]

This book attempts to approach what I think lies at the center of his vision, and at the center of his contemporaries' vision as well. As I try to show in my first chapter, James' own personal perspective was very much a man's perspective, a masculine or manly one. In two subsequent chapters, I bring out how much it befit the times—how Harvard responded to the pressures of the era and, in turn, how perfectly James represented Harvard's response. In a fourth, I consider how the "highly educated" men of this era responded to women, to African-Americans, to anyone who did not mirror their conceptions of themselves as men. In a fifth, I focus on the simplest and most enduring construction of manhood that emerged during this period: the Westerner, as he was imagined by Owen Wister, Harvard' 82, and as he was represented by Theodore Roosevelt, Harvard' 80.

"The truth is," Van Wyck Brooks reported in his last year at Harvard, "we deliberately acquire our ungraceful ways in an effort to be manly," and he exclaimed, "How morbid we are on the subject of manliness!"[20] His was a nice choice of words. Most of the men in this book limited, even damaged, their lives trying to be "manly." In the process they were often literally ungraceful. Imagining their bodies as so many forces to be controlled, they reined them in, fought and subdued them. And they often thought of themselves as graceless in the sense of being without Grace, their lives as lonely struggles unto death. One could add that they were also lacking in graciousness, because these manly men tended to be wary of and to exclude anyone who undermined their assumptions about what it was to be a man.

Many years later, Brooks refused to make an exception of James. "He was unable to create values because he had never transcended his environment," Brooks said in 1932.[21] But when he was an undergraduate he would have thought it sacrilegious to speak about James like that. He was "a great man"—"Our greatest teacher," he called him upon his retirement, "one of the great serene figures of Time, above all little disagreements, large, sane, clear, simple, universal."[22] The discrepancy, reflective of the difference between James the dark planet and James the illuminating star, only reconfirms the fact of his central and fascinating presence.

It also throws us back upon ourselves. "The preferences of sentient creatures are what *create* the importance of topics," James wrote at the end of his article "The Importance of Individuals."[23] What are we to make of him? What are we to make of the manhood that he and his colleagues and students represent? What are our preferences?

The subject of manhood was indisputably important to James and his contemporaries. What James made of himself (and they of him) was always influenced by their understanding of what was required of them as men. That much is clear. But it is hard to gauge the effect of their case on others, especially in the past. In the pages that follow, we will hear many claims like Brooks', and like those of the men who spoke at the Harvard commencement of 1908, about the representativeness of individual Harvard men's views and of Harvard's influence, but these are, after all, the claims of Harvard men.

Nevertheless, by the end of the nineteenth century, Harvard was preeminent among educational institutions. Speaking of President Eliot, Yale's historian was prepared to say that "by 1900 it was generally conceded that he had made Harvard into America's strongest and most celebrated university."[24] When one considers Eliot's, and Harvard's, determination to know and to teach the ways of a newly industrialized and secularized world, and to allow the young men in their charge to find out for themselves—in their free election of courses—what was most important to them individually, then Harvard turns out to be preeminent by these more specific criteria too. To extend the obvious comparison with Yale: Yale's first lay president took office in 1899, Harvard's in 1829; Harvard abolished required chapel in 1886, Yale in 1926; Harvard dropped Greek as an entrance requirement in 1884, Yale in 1903; Yale never did allow so free an elective system as Harvard; Harvard was far wealthier, its funds having grown to thirteen million by 1900, Yale's to only five.

For many people such preeminence would be synonymous with more rapid decline (not to mention the fact that to untold millions such distinctions matter not at all). Or, to make the comparison with Yale once again, it could signal deplorable compromises with the world as it is—at one extreme, inattention to students' religious faith; at the other, only halfhearted efforts to generate school or team spirit. More generally, it could mean the loss of a prized sense of community and of tradition. Be that as it may, Harvard's rise to prominence both helped cause and accompanied the emergence of a particular kind of manly individual a century ago, and insofar as we are at present concerned about who and what is a man—and thus, ineluctably, who and what is a woman—we have much to learn from the men in this book. They were an extraordinarily distinguished group of writers and thinkers; they were also the first to raise these questions in their modern form.

Notes

1. This assumes that Harvard held a commencement every year, after its first in 1642. The proceedings of the 1908 commencement are reported in *Harvard Graduates' Magazine*, XVII (September 1908), 55–78 (hereafter cited as *HGM*).
2. Robert D. Richardson Jr., *Emerson: The Mind on Fire* (Berkeley: University of California Press, 1995), p. 534.
3. Gail Bederman, *Manliness & Civilization: A Cultural History of Gender and Race in the United States* (Chicago: University of Chicago Press, 1995), pp. 18–19; Michael Kimmel, *Manhood in America: A Cultural History* (New York: Free Press, 1996), pp. 119–20.
4. Nell Irvin Painter, *Standing at Armageddon: The United States, 1877–1919* (New York: W. W. Norton, 1987), pp. 162–63.
5. Howard Mumford Jones, *The Age of Energy: Varieties of American Experience, 1865–1915* (New York: Viking Press, 1971), pp. 157–58; Irving S. and Nell M. Kull, *A Short Chronology of American History, 1492–1950* (New Brunswick: Rutgers University Press, 1952).
6. Alan Trachtenberg, *The Incorporation of America: Culture and Society in the Gilded Age* (New York: Hill and Wang, 1982), pp. 84–85.
7. Kull and Kull; Painter, p. xx; Thomas J. Schlereth, *Victorian America: Transformations in Everyday Life, 1876–1915* (New York: Harper Collins, 1991), pp. 33–34.
8. *Educational Reform: Essays and Addresses* (New York: Century, 1898), p. 34.
9. (New York: G. P. Putnam's Sons, 1881), pp. vi–vii.
10. *Harvard Memorial Biographies*, 2vols. (Cambridge: Sever and Francis, 1866), I, iv–v.
11. *The Frontier in American History* (New York: Henry Holt, 1920), p. 37.
12. *HGM*, XVII (September 1908), 34.
13. (New York: E. P. Dutton, 1952), pp. 19–20.
14. *The Selected Writings of John Jay Chapman*, ed. Jacques Barzun (New York: Minerva Press, 1957), p. 217.
15. Charles H. Compton, *William James: Philosopher and Man* (New York: Scarecrow Press, 1957), p. 111.
16. *Writings, vol. 1, 1878–1899* (New York: Library of America, 1992), 618–46 (hereafter cited as *Writings*). All references to James' writings are to this volume and to *Writings*, vol. 2, *1902–1910* (New York: Library of America, 1987), unless otherwise noted.
17. Ibid., I, 648.
18. Ibid., II, 639.
19. *The Letters of William James*, ed. Henry James, 2 vols. (Boston: Atlantic Monthly Press, 1920), II, 355 (hereafter cited as *Letters*).
20. James Hoopes, *Van Wyck Brooks: In Search of American Culture* (Amherst: University of Massachusetts Press, 1977), p. 39; *Harvard Advocate*, LXXXIII (April 12, 1907), 35–37.
21. *Sketches in Criticism* (New York: E. P. Dutton, 1932), p. 40.
22. *Harvard Advocate*, LXXXIII (April 26, 1907), 50.
23. *Writings*, I, 651.
24. George Wilson Pierson, *Yale College: An Educational History, 1871–1921*, 2 vols. (New Haven: Yale University Press, 1952), I, 48.

Value Conflict on the Community College Campus: An Examination of Its Historical Origins

Robert T. Pedersen

Over the last few years, Dr. S., the dean of humanities at a large suburban community college, has grown tired of a continuing controversy within the college's English department. Younger members of the department, all with doctoral degrees from well-known universities, believe strongly that scholarship is closely tied to teaching effectiveness and their professional identities. Older faculty, most with only their master's degree, see their colleagues' interest in scholarship as a diversion from the real task at hand: instruction in basic composition and remedial English. This division becomes especially heated at budget time, when the younger faculty demand more money for travel and computer time, while the older faculty call for more dollars to be spent on teaching materials and additional tutor support in the department's learning lab.

As the dean finally confesses to a colleague, it seems as if the institution is confused as to its real purpose. If it is truly part of higher education, community college faculty must keep abreast of changes in their disciplines, if only so that their students, when they transfer, do not discover that their instruction was outmoded. At the same time, greater faculty involvement in their disciplines often comes at the cost of teaching and student contact. And, in all honesty, such involvement can be costly—conventions, support for research, and even the occasional sabbatical. The dean is fully aware that while the community college may claim to be part of higher education, it must operate with the funding of a public high school.

Conflict over ends and means is commonplace on community college campuses, and its source is not difficult to locate. The community college, as any number of observers have pointed out, is mired in an identity crisis, confused both as to its purpose and its place within the American schooling system.[1] As Garms has observed, "There is consensus neither on what the community colleges are, nor on what they should be doing."[2] When an institution's purposes are many and varied, poorly integrated, and incompletely understood, conflict arises among those it charges with carrying out these purposes. Under such conditions, an action taken by one member of the organization to further the institution's mission and purpose will almost certainly be challenged by another as directly threatening some fundamental institutional value.

It is possible that some community college practitioners—faculty, campus administrators, and trustees—would question the proposition that theirs is an institution of confused or uncertain purposes and values. In defending the community college's integrity of purpose, they would most likely point to the highly focused mission statements found in virtually every community college catalog. Such statements, they would argue, not only define an institutional vision but also, in the process, lay the foundation for an integrated system of values that guide practitioners in the realization of that vision.

However, if these practitioners engaged in a moment of honest and critical self-appraisal, they would acknowledge that there is a yawning gap between community college mission statements and the values that currently inform institutional practice. They would find a community college culture that is essentially derivative, an eclectic and often perplexing mixture of values, traditions, and practices borrowed from the public schools, the university, and even the settlement houses—all without apparent rhyme or reason. More often than not, community colleges are financed and governed much like a high school, describe themselves in the language of higher education, and yet champion the kind of community renewal once sought by Jane Addams through Hull House.

The derivative nature of the community college is most readily apparent in the often ambiguous circumstances of community college faculty. With respect to their basic working conditions, the values that guide them as professionals, and their graduate-level preparation, community college instructors far more closely resemble university faculty than high school teachers. The 12- or 15-hour workload of the average community college instructor approximates the three-course assignment of a public university's junior faculty far more than the 30 hours expected of public high school teachers. Likewise, claims of academic freedom, as voiced recently by faculty at New York's Nassau County Community College, reflect a university tradition of faculty autonomy unknown to high school instructors.

In other respects, however, community college instructors are indistinguishable from public high school teachers. The limited involvement of community college faculty in institutional governance, their preference for unionization, and the relative ease with which they earn tenure reflect the traditions and conventions of the public high school rather than the research university.

The marriage of university and secondary school values and practices on the campus of the community college has not been altogether happy. The opening of this chapter offered one example of the value conflict commonplace on many community college campuses; experienced faculty, department chairs, and deans can no doubt supply others. Such conflict is neither historical accident nor the outgrowth of purely local conditions. Rather, it arises inevitably in any institution, such as the community college, that not only derives its core values from other institutions but then fails to integrate and marry these values into an internally consistent system of values and practices. If the community college is ever to overcome its "identity crisis" and move beyond the type of conflict faced by Dr. S., its practitioners must first understand the historical forces that brought about the present confusion surrounding institutional values and practices. Armed with this knowledge, they must then fashion a consistent and socially responsive body of institutional practices for their colleges that is no longer founded on the shadows of the past, but that embraces those "new ideals" first described by University of California at Berkeley professor and lecturer, K. Patricia Cross.

The Historical Origins of the Community College Value Conflict

For the community college practitioner who wishes to explore the historical basis of the campus value conflict, what insight and guidance can be expected from the literature? Surprisingly little. Those who have written on the history of the community college have focused almost exclusively on broad issues of ideology and, in the process, have restricted their inquiries to the writings of a small cadre of national community college leaders, such as Koos, Eells, and Medsker.

Particularly within the last two decades, this preoccupation with questions of ideology has polarized the historical literature of the community college into two fundamentally opposed camps. To one side are those scholars collectively described as the "critics," among whom are generally counted Clark, Zwerling, and Karabel.[3] For these scholars, the egalitarian rhetoric of community college leaders only masks their institutions' true social mission: the diversion of socially and economically disadvantaged students away from the baccalaureate and into vocational programs, leading to careers of inferior status and limited opportunity.[4] In its most extreme form, this perspective holds that the community college and its leadership are willing partners in a complex and socially regressive conspiracy on the part of unnamed national elites to regulate access to positions of power and prestige to the advantage of these elites, and to the disadvantage of those students community colleges claim to serve.

On the debate's other side are the community college proponents, such as Medsker, Gleazer, and Parnell. As a group, the proponents cast the community college's social purpose in a far more positive light. They extol its success as a democratizer of access and as the principal means by which higher education has been brought within the reach of virtually all Americans. This basic theme took form in the earliest writings of Koos, for whom the two-year college was the nation's best hope for "the economic and social democratization of educational opportunity,"[5] and would change little over the next seven decades. The recent claim by Gillett-Karam, Roueche, and Roueche that the community college was "established to redress the grievances brought about by the practices of elitist or meritocratic educational systems" would have most likely received the assent of not only Koos, but also Metzker and Brick.[6]

For both critic and proponent, the community college is merely a foil—a silent adjunct—in a larger ideological struggle that is played out in the writings of university leaders and other national figures. Given its cosmopolitan perspective, this debate fails to offer the practitioner a framework for understanding the community college's derivative nature and the conflict that such a nature prompts. It neither explains how seemingly inconsistent values and practices came to coexist on community college campuses nor points the practitioner in the direction of a fully integrated value system.

Among the historians of the public two-year college, only Frye has recognized the irrelevancy of this debate to a practitioner's understanding of the historical development of the colleges themselves.[7] Perceptively, Frye has argued that the community college did not develop in isolation, shaped solely by the ideology of a small cadre of national leaders. Rather, the community college has been influenced by those institutions upon which it initially depended for either its day-to-day existence or its legitimacy—the high school and the university—and, to even a greater degree, by the social and economic interests of its sponsoring community.

The practitioner who follows Frye's lead will find that the community college has no more gained its distinctive, if frequently confused, character from the conspiratorial designs of distant university leaders than from some native American desire to democratize higher education. Rather, he or she will discover that many of the seemingly conflicting traits of the community college culture took shape in response to specific social and economic conditions presented between 1900 and 1940, the period during which the first great wave of junior colleges were founded. It will become apparent, for example, that the close association of the junior college with the public high school was born during this period, and developed not by design, but rather out of necessity. It was an association dictated by the economic constraints confronting civic leaders of this period, and not by the theoretical vision of a new schooling system proposed by the likes of Harper, Lange, and Koos. Further, it will also become apparent that the influence of the university was felt through the university's control of a process then known as "standardization," and now known generally as accreditation. Moreover, the university's impetus for bringing certain aspects of junior college practice into conformity with university norms stemmed largely from external pressure on the university to strengthen its own academic standards, and not from any great desire on its part to "colonize" the junior college.

Why Were Junior Colleges Established in the First Place?

Between 1900 and 1940, approximately 275 public junior colleges were established in the United States and its possessions. Hailed at the time as a "revolutionary phenomenon," these colleges were still far from a universal or national movement. With surprisingly few exceptions, these colleges were established in small and medium-sized cities of the Middle and Far West. Public junior colleges east of the Alleghenies, as found in Newark, New Jersey, and Springfield, Massachusetts, were the exceptions, and most did not survive the period. To understand the junior college, and especially those forces that gave it life, shaped its early development, and whose influences are still felt today, one has to look instead to such cities as Holtan, Kansas; Hibbing, Minnesota; and Bakersfield, California.

While university encouragement was certainly important to the success of the first junior colleges (it is difficult to imagine that communities would have opened junior colleges in the face of outright university opposition), this support does not sufficiently explain their highly regionalized popularity or their concentration in cities of between 10,000 and 25,000 residents. It simply strains credibility to believe that civic leaders in Iola, Kansas, and Pipestone, Minnesota—cities well removed from the influence of Stanford, Chicago, and Berkeley—took on the cost of a junior college primarily to allow some distant university to be rid of troublesome freshmen and sophomores, when small city leaders in both Illinois and Missouri—states whose university leaders actively supported the junior college—did not.

Fortunately the practitioner who wishes to search out a more adequate explanation for the founding of junior colleges in such cities as Iola and Pipestone is not without resources. School records, local newspaper accounts, community histories, and other similar sources, while not nearly as accessible as the pronouncements of university presidents or the publications of Koos and Eells, are available to those who search them out. Indeed, from these records it is possible to construct a history of the origins and early development of the two-year college that is not only complete and reasonable, but that also contains more than a few surprises for those who have traced the origins of the history of the community college as it begins with Harper.

Most conventional histories of the two-year college, for example, appear to assume that early twentieth-century communities learned of the junior college from its university advocates and then chose to sponsor one without seriously exploring any alternatives. Reflecting such thinking, many historians have credited Harper with exerting such influence in the communities surrounding Chicago, while Brint and Karabel have similarly argued that the early junior colleges of California were the product of "lobbying" by the University of California's Alexis Lange. Community records, however, cast doubt on these assumptions. It is unclear how civic leaders came to learn of the junior college, although local newspapers in California, at least, favorably reported on the spread of this new institution quite independently of any efforts by university leaders. It is clear, however, that for many communities, a junior college was often their *last* choice, either following in the wake of failed efforts to secure more traditional forms of higher education or as an ad hoc solution to the threat to community status posed by the unexpected closure of a private college.[8]

Some historians of the junior college have also assumed that the immediate impetus for the establishment of most junior colleges was the advocacy of a school superintendent and his or her board.[9] Where a record of the events surrounding a junior college's founding have been preserved, such was rarely the case. Far more often, the driving force behind a new junior college was a city's civic and commercial leadership.[10] While the motivations of these leaders were complex and varied, the strongest was a desire to establish a community's commercial and cultural leadership within a large, primarily agricultural region. In these cities, the establishment of a junior college was not an isolated event, but an integral part of a general strategy to achieve regional leadership by replicating the full range of those institutions generally associated with civic life: a comprehensive high school, a library, a hospital, a courthouse, and a college.

In their aspirations, the civic leaders of such small cities as Tyler, Texas, and Burlington, Iowa, differed little from their large city counterparts, who were attempting to assert a broad claim to metropolitan status through institutional acquisition. At roughly the same time that Rochester, Minnesota, established its junior college, the civic leaders of Atlanta purchased Emory University from its trustees, moved the institution to their city, and built a complete campus. During this period, the civic leaders of small and large cities alike shared an enthusiasm for the future, a willingness to take risks, and a measure of opportunism—a spirit often summarized in the popular press of this period by the term "boosterism." It was just this quality that is reflected in the call of one small city editor for the citizens of his town to "boost" the establishment of a proposed junior college:

> We don't get good things by passively waiting and hoping they will come in their own good time.

What the civic leaders of Rochester and other small American cities lacked were resources. Whereas, Atlanta could rely on a $1 million gift from Coca Cola's Asa Candler to underwrite its acquisition of Emory, the civic leaders of small city America had to make do with the often meager resources at hand.

Both the single-mindedness of small city leaders in pursuing a college for their community and the social and economic factors that eventually led to the opening of many high school-based junior colleges are exemplified by the 1926 founding of Temple Junior College in Texas. Unable to tap the kind of wealth that had allowed Atlanta to acquire a university, and after several failed attempts to secure a more prestigious form of higher education, Temple's civic leaders finally turned to the public high school as the only remaining means through which they could realize the dream of bringing a college to their community.

As in most other communities during the 1920s, civic and business leaders provided the impetus for a series of attempts to secure a college for the growing city of Temple, Texas. To achieve this end, the leaders were willing to explore every available option, and they committed substantial time and energy to the process through their chamber of commerce. Population growth of more than 50 percent in the decade before 1925 certainly provided a positive stimulus to their civic boosterism. As Temple's population approached 15,000, a college must have seemed a natural and appropriate addition to the city's growing collection of institutions. However, at first, Temple's civic leadership, through the chamber, showed no interest in a junior college, choosing instead to secure the more conventional form of American higher education: a denominational, four-year college. It was with this hope that, in 1924, chamber representatives offered the Missouri Synod of the Lutheran Church some 20 acres of land and a pledge of $20,000 in a bid for a college the Missouri Lutherans were planning to open in Texas. The Missouri Synod rejected Temple's offer, choosing instead to locate their new college in the far larger and more prosperous city of Dallas.

Rebuffed, but undaunted, the chamber next looked to the University of Texas, whose president had demonstrated his interest in extending the university's presence beyond its main campus at Austin when he opened a two-year branch campus at El Paso in 1925. That same year, a subcommittee of the Temple chamber negotiated an agreement with the University of Texas in which the university agreed to place a branch in Temple, on the condition that the Temple chamber would fully underwrite all costs associated with the venture.

Unfortunately for the chamber, shortly after its deal was struck with university officials at Austin, the Texas attorney general ruled the university's El Paso branch, and any other similar arrangement, unconstitutional. It was only at this point, with all of its most prestigious options closed off, that Temple's chamber of commerce proposed the organization of a public junior college as part of the city's public high school. Initially, it appears that the Temple school board did not receive this proposal with much enthusiasm, being concerned with the potential cost of a junior college to local taxpayers. It was, in fact, only after the chamber agreed to match the school board's commitment to the university, and accept full financial responsibility for the venture, that the board authorized the organization of a junior college under its general jurisdiction. The chamber, in keeping with its pledge, immediately secured $5,000 from local businesses and parents for a library and laboratory equipment, then secured an additional $20,000 to ensure the college's solvency during its first two years of operation. With these financial assurances, the Temple city school board proceeded to select a college president, and the city's junior college admitted its first class in late 1926.

In the public debate leading to the opening of Temple's junior college, one finds no hint of egalitarian idealism. Temple's leaders were aware that a college—like a library hospital, or courthouse—was needed to bolster their growing city's claims to regional leadership. Only after more prestigious alternatives were lost did they turn to an unenthusiastic school board and settle for what was their best available option.

The circumstances surrounding the opening of Temple Junior College were far from unique. Small town civic leaders of the early twentieth century recognized the limits of both their power and resources, being especially conscious of the resistance of many community elements to any increase in public expenditures. Where these leaders could not realize their goal through more conventional means, and where the state had not specifically forbidden junior colleges, they followed the same course as their counterparts in Temple, and placed their junior colleges under the formal governance of the public schools.[11] In their decision to rely on the public schools as an incubator for the junior college, these civic leaders not only took advantage of the faculty and facility resources of public high schools, they also, more importantly, avoided the far more costly and politically difficult option of creating a free-standing public college—something that had been done by the wealthier and more populous cities of New York, Toledo, and Cincinnati in the nineteenth century.

But expediency brings cost, and in this instance the costs have been bourne by the two-year college. Housed in a public high school, drawing its faculty from the high school's staff, and governed by a common board during its early and most formative stage, the community college could not avoid the imprint of the values and culture of the public high school. Yet, this influence was neither destined or intentional. It was a secondary consequence of decisions dictated by the political and fiscal constraints under which the colleges' founders operated.

The motivations of civic leaders in such cities as Temple, Texas, and Everett, Washington, were not ideological. They were not driven by a desire to extend the common school, or to democratize access, or to advance meritocratic notions of higher education. Their objective was civic development, and they saw this goal being realized primarily through an aggressive program of institution building. In the absence of other, more prestigious options and compelled to conserve resources, these leaders saw the grafting of the junior college to the public high school as both an expedient and reasonable strategy for adding an important institution to their community at a price the community would accept. That a long-term consequence of this decision would be an institution of confused purpose and uncertain mission was of no great concern.

The University Influence on Two-Year College Values and Practices

Just as the early influence of the public schools upon the two-year college was more historical accident than expression of its founders' progressive ideology, could the university's influence also have been coincidental? If these early junior college founders were motivated largely by civic concerns and were not blindly implementing the vision of a reformed and progressive American schooling system advocated by various university leaders, how then did university values and norms find their way into the two-year college? Could it be that the extent to which the practices and values of the community college imitate those of the university reflects nothing more than an attempt by two-year colleges to usurp some small measure of collegiate prestige? Or, could university standards and norms have been imposed upon these parochial institutions by cosmopolitan interests bent on a form of educational colonization?

A clue to the source and nature of the university's influence over the community college is to be found in the erratic nature of that influence during the first years of the public junior college. Where governance, finance, and certain other aspects of the junior college and its operations went largely untouched by university practice, other facets of institutional life were profoundly influenced by the university. The evidence suggests, however, that this erratic pattern was neither irrational nor arbitrary but reflected the manner by which universities exercised oversight of the junior college in the years before 1950. Before the modern system of institutional accreditation was established, the vast majority of junior colleges were regulated by state universities through a process known as standardization. It was the nature of this process, concerned with a relatively small number of easily measured standards of "quality," that limited the scope of university influence upon the junior college and left major aspects of junior college life largely untouched by the university and its values.

Standardization did not begin with the establishment of the first junior college, but actually took form in the late nineteenth century as several of the nation's larger public high schools began to regularly offer collegiate-grade courses to their graduates. Since those who completed these "upward extension" courses typically applied for transfer credit once they entered a college or university, Michigan, Illinois, and the larger state universities felt the need to establish a mechanism by which they could judge the quality of such courses—if for no other reason than to preserve the integrity of their own degrees. By the 1920s, the process of standardization became widespread, with three-quarters of the state legislatures that had adopted junior college legislation specifically charging their state universities with oversight of public junior colleges. Importantly, this development occurred largely as a response to cultural forces well beyond the influence and control of either the universities or the junior colleges, and it was these external developments that led to the transformation of an essentially collegial and informal process into a rigid, directive, and intrusive one.

While the fact is virtually ignored by junior college historians, larger public high schools before 1900 frequently offered college-level courses to those graduates who, for whatever reason, were unable to enroll immediately in a college or university. Such schools as Indiana's East Chicago High School and Illinois' Joliet Township High School offered a varied series of transferable courses in mathematics, science, and foreign languages as early as 1890. By 1915, according to a report of California's Superintendent of Public Instruction, more students in that state were actually enrolled in high school postgraduate courses than in recognized junior college programs.

Both universities and colleges appear to have been more than willing to award credit for "upward extension" courses, although they took steps to ensure the integrity of their own degrees by formally evaluating the academic quality of these courses. Robert Smolich, in his history of Joliet Junior College, offers some insight into the relatively informal system of course evaluation that developed during the late nineteenth century. Typically, a university team of two faculty members would visit a high school campus, meet with the faculty who taught the upward extension courses, and observe their classes. A report would be made to the university by the team, followed by a letter to the school superintendent summarizing the team's findings and recommendations. If the report was favorable, students from the high school might be admitted in certain subjects with advanced standing—often equal to a full year of college work.

In 1898, for example, Professor Joseph Drake of the University of Michigan visited Joliet High School to review its postgraduate program. Apparently after some delay, Drake wrote to Joliet's superintendent, J. Stanley Brown, with an assessment of Joliet's upward extension program that centered almost exclusively on its Latin offerings. Apart from suggesting that the Joliet course might consider giving more attention to the "reading of Latin as Latin," Drake spoke glowingly of the program and indicated a willingness by the university, apparently in response to a request from Brown, to extend college credit to Joliet graduates whose high school preparation in Latin would exceed the university's minimum requirement for admission.

Joliet was not alone in receiving this recognition from Michigan. As Drake noted in his letter to Brown, "a majority of our better [high schools] are doing a little more than is required for entrance and the result is good. The University is glad to give some advanced credit for work done in this way."[12] Nor was Michigan alone in granting advanced standing. As Brown noted in a speech commemorating the opening of Joliet's new high school, the University of Illinois was also willing to admit the high school's "recommended graduates" with sufficient advanced credit to enable them "to complete a four years' course [work] in three years."[13]

However, by the 1920s this collegial approach to standardization was supplanted by a far more focused, directive, and intrusive process. Where Michigan's Drake had concerned himself with only matters of pedagogy and course content, by the 1920s university accreditors extended their inquiries to include issues of governance, student access, and faculty qualifications and working conditions. While the rapid multiplication of junior colleges in the years after 1915 undoubtedly contributed to the emergence of a rigid and even bureaucratic process, an even more significant factor was the increasing concern among the public at large with standards and their measurement—a concern that touched the universities themselves and to which a more rigorous form of standardization was but one response.

A fairly extensive body of literature describes university accreditation of the junior college as it developed after 1900. Typical of this literature is the "Circular of Information to Accredited Junior Colleges," first issued by the University of Missouri in 1919, and issued again in revised form in 1926.[14] Jesse H. Coursault, then Dean of Education for the University of Missouri, used these circulars to describe the standards junior colleges would be required to meet in order to qualify for his university's accreditation. The circulars included detailed standards in such areas as laboratory equipment and the maintenance of student records, and spelled out the range of subjects appropriate to a junior college curriculum and the specific textbooks that could be assigned by junior college faculty.

That university accreditation standards were not mere guidelines, but were actually enforced through systematic site visits by university accreditors is evidenced by the unpublished 1929 rating of Burlington (Iowa) Junior College by the University of Illinois' Committee on Admissions from Higher Institutions (CAHI). CAHI's evaluation of Burlington not only provides some indication of the areas of institutional life the University of Illinois sought to influence, but also the extent to which the Iowa junior college actually conformed to university expectations. What we find is that many features traditionally associated with the two-year college, most notably open admissions and a comprehensive curriculum, were not found at Burlington, because of Illinois' accreditation requirements.

CAHI's report makes apparent that Burlington was in no respect an open admissions institution. The Deegan and Tillery belief that there was an "awareness" among the early junior colleges that they were to provide access to higher education for academically unprepared students is without basis.[15] To maintain its accreditation, Burlington could admit only those who would be eligible for regular admission to the university. In the case of Illinois, this meant students were expected to present a minimum of 14 units of high school work, a requirement that all but 5 of the 97 students at Burlington met. Those who failed to meet this minimum were expected by CAHI to either be privately tutored or to complete the appropriate high school work before entering a junior college course study.

As Whitney documented in 1929, CAHI's admission standards were not unusually strict, with a similar standard having been mandated by the vast majority of the state universities and other state agencies legally charged with accrediting junior college. In most instances, these universities, like Illinois, required a minimum of 14 or 15 high school units for admission to a junior college, although one required 16 units, and another, just 12. Moreover, nine universities also required that a "major part" of a student's high school curriculum "shall be closely related to the junior college curriculum,"[16] effectively eliminating the admission of high school vocational program graduates. It should be little wonder, given the restrictive admissions policies of the early public junior college, that Koos found both the tested mental abilities and parental occupations of public junior college students to be comparable to freshmen and sophomores at prestigious senior colleges and universities.[17]

While, for reasons that go beyond the scope of this paper, two-year colleges eventually threw off the restrictive admissions standards of the universities, the university's influence on faculty standards would be felt well after standardization had been replaced by regional accreditation. It appears to have been the universities that established both the master's degree and preparation in an academic field as the minimum prerequisites for employment as a two-year college instructor. Illinois, like other accrediting universities, specifically required junior colleges to restrict their teaching assignments to "suitably prepared" faculty, and over the course of the early part of this century these universities pressured junior colleges to tighten this requirement. While Illinois had initially allowed junior college instructors to teach with only a baccalaureate and one year of graduate study, by 1928 all "new teachers of academic subjects" were expected to hold a master's in the discipline in which the instructor was to teach.

Universities also ensured that the working conditions of junior faculty at least approximated those of the university's own junior faculty. To this end, they stipulated maximum teaching loads (Illinois' maximum was 20 hours) and frequently required that junior college faculty be supervised separately from high school faculty, typically under a dean.

While Harper, Lange, and Jordan's impact upon the evolving junior college would end with their deaths, the effect of university accreditation upon the junior college persists. Where the junior college might well have become an integral department of the high school, university accreditation standards ensured that junior college faculty would be set apart from high school teachers by their traditional academic credentials, their lighter teaching loads, and their collegial governance, making possible the partial replication of the collegiate culture within the context of a small city high school.

But this still fails to explain the university's interest in junior college standardization. The simplest, and also most cynical, explanation is that the kind of accreditation process practiced by the University of Illinois reflected an imperialist tendency on the university's part, a desire of university administrators and faculty to re-create, in the university's own image, academic colonies throughout small town America. But nothing in the available record corroborates this harsh judgment.

Moreover, this cynical analysis of university interests and motives fail to explain the dramatic change in the scope and thoroughness of standardization between Michigan's visit to Joliet in 1898 and Illinois' visit to Burlington in 1929. The actual condition of collegiate-grade programs in public junior college had changed little over these years. The programs were still small (most junior colleges of the 1920s enrolled fewer than 150 students), most were concentrated in first-year coursework, and the curriculum was still narrowly academic. What then, led such universities as Missouri and Illinois to adopt comprehensive standardization programs?

The one thing that had clearly changed for these universities during this period did not, in fact, directly involve the junior colleges. As Higgins has noted, the early part of this century was an "age of standards" in which individuals and organizations were increasingly measured and judged according to fixed, quantitative standards.[18] As individuals were measured using Alpha and Beta tests, so, too, were institutions. And universities and senior colleges did not escape this scrutiny.

Evidence of the growing national concern with university quality, and of the universities' collective fear of the concern, can be seen in the controversy that surrounded the attempt, in 1911, by the federal Bureau of Education to classify colleges and universities. Under Commissioner Claxton's guidance, the Bureau of Education evaluated the quality and reputation of most senior colleges and universities operating in the United States between 1910 and 1911. Based on this evaluation, the bureau divided these colleges and universities into four classes. Those of the first class were judged to provide a program study that would enable a graduate to complete a master's degree in one year. Colleges and universities of the second class offered a program that, in the bureau's judgment, would require its graduates to complete some additional work beyond a year's graduate study in order to earn the master's. The curricular standards of third-class institutions (notably the Universities of Florida and Arkansas) were "so low, or so uncertain, or so loosely administered" that their graduates would require at least two years to earn the master's, while the degrees of fourth-class institutions (which included Texas A&M and the Citadel) were judged to be equivalent to no more than a two-year program at a "standard" college.

The bureau's attempt at institutional classification would never be formally issued, although its contents were widely reported in the press, much to the consternation and outrage of those colleges and universities not included among the first-class schools. The protests of university presidents injured by the bureau's report were so vigorous and forceful that the Taft administration decided to withhold issuance of the actual report until the matter could be reviewed by the new Wilson administration, which also chose to suspend its publication. While America's universities and colleges were able to forestall a federal attempt to impose a unified system of institutional classification based on quality, the attempt itself demonstrates a growing public awareness of, and even desire for, greater accountability among institutions. While unhappy with the form this change in public sentiment first took at the instigation of Commissioner Claxton, universities and colleges were not insensitive to the public interest, and the introduction of more rigorous and measurable standardization practices in their accreditation of junior colleges in subsequent years was but one indication of their responsiveness to changing public sentiment and their more self-interested desire to preclude any further attempts at classification by the Bureau of Education.

Conclusion

From a close examination of Temple Junior College's founding and the accreditation experience of Burlington, today's community college practitioner should come to see that much of the value conflict now found on community college campuses was not destined by the historical forces that gave rise to the two-year college. Not only can the origins of this conflict be traced to the often contradictory influences of the high school and university upon the two-year college during the first part of this century, but much of this influence was coincidental and unexpected. As we have seen, the early and close ties of the junior college to the public school were not the product of conscious design, but were born of simple necessity and very practical considerations of cost and opportunity. In much the same way, the subsequent imposition of certain university norms upon the junior colleges was not arbitrary or imperialistic extension of university control over "democracy's college" but simply one facet of a broader and fundamentally self-interested response by the universities to increasing public demands *upon them* for greater academic rigor and accountability.

The community college practitioner, in recognizing that many of the values and practices uncritically accepted on his or her campus were derived from other institutions that serve very different social purposes, is then freed of this legacy. He or she may then fashion an internally consistent and socially responsive set of values and practices for the modern community college. This practitioner is under no compulsion to replicate values of either the high school or the university, but only to ensure that these values and practices further the community college's realization of the fundamental ideals of access and equity.

It is not the intent of this work to suggest the outline of such a new value system. A lasting and constructive resolution of such issues as whether, for example, discipline-based research and scholarship by faculty should be valued, or whether instruction in basic academic skills falls within the proper scope of the community college curriculum, will only be achieved when community college practitioners—faculty, staff, and trustees—work with their community to bring campus values and practices in line with institutional mission. There is a clear risk to such an undertaking, particularly for those community college faculty and administrators who derive prestige from the imitation of university practices. But the cost of value conflict, particularly as it currently exists on two-year campuses, is far too great in an era of scarce resources for public institutions and public employees to allow such concerns to preclude the renewal of an institution whose services are critically important to communities in need.

Notes

1. Jennings L. Wagoner, "The Search for Mission and Integrity: A Retrospective View" in *Maintaining Institutional Integrity*, D. E. Puyear and George Vaughan (San Francisco: Jossey-Bass, 1985), 14; John Frye, *7th Vision of the Public Junior College, 1900–1940*, (New York: Greenwood Press, 1992), 3.
2. Walter L. Garms, *Financing Community Colleges*, (New York: Teachers College Press, 1977), 31.
3. George B. Vaughan, (ed), "Questioning the Community College Role" in *New Directions for Community Colleges*, 8 (4) (1980), 1–14; Kevin James Dougherty, "The Policies of Community College Expansion: The Cases of Illinois and Washington States" (Ph.D. diss., Harvard University, 1983), 6–9.
4. Steven Brint and Jerome Karabel, *The Diverted Dream: Community Colleges and the Promise of Educational Opportunity in America, 1900–1985* (New York: Oxford University Press, 1989), 225.
5. Leonard Koos, *The Junior College*, (Minneapolis: University of Minnesota, 1924), 143.
6. Rosemary Gillett-Karam, Suanne D. Roueche, and John E. Roueche, *Under-representation and the Question of Diversity—Women and Minorities in the Community College* (Washington, D.C.: Community College Press, 1991), 6; Leland Medsker, *7th Junior College: Progress and Prospect* (New York: McGraw Hill, 1960), 33.
7. Frey, in *Vision of the Public Junior College*, 136.
8. No tabulation has been made of the junior colleges established following the closure of a private college, but the number may have been substantial, particularly during the early part of this century. It is known that at least three junior colleges were founded under such circumstances: Holton (1917) and Fort Scott (1921), both in Kansas, and Nebraska's Grand Island (1931). In two of these cases, the junior college was also closed within two years in the absence of widespread public support.
9. Dougherty, "The Policies of Community College Expansion."
10. Frye gives two examples of the central role played by a community's commercial and business interests in establishing a junior college. See Frye, *The Vision of the Public Junior College*, 83.
11. In some states, the opposition of a state government to such local initiative forced civic leaders to place their junior colleges under ostensibly "private" governance. Such was the case in Washington state, where the earliest junior colleges operated for several years as "private" junior colleges until the state finally adopted permissive legislation in 1941.
12. R. Smolich, *An Analysis of Influences Affecting the Origin and Early Development of Three Mid-Western Public Junior Colleges: Joliet, Goshen, and Crane.* (University of Texas at Austin: 1968), 71–72.
13. *loc cit.*, 72–73.
14. Jesse H. Coursault, "Circular of Information to Accredited Junior Colleges," University of Missouri *Bulletin* 19 (4) Education Series 12 (February 1918); Jesse H. Coursault, "Circular of Information to Accredited Junior Colleges" (revised), University of Missouri *Bulletin*, 27 (37) Education Series 21 (October 1926).
15. Deegan, William L. and Dale Tillery and Associates, *Renewing the American Community College.* (San Francisco: Jossey-Bass, 1985), 6–7.
16. Whitney, Frederick L., *The Junior College in America* (Greeley: Colorado State Teachers College, 1928), 65–66.
17. Koos, *The Junior College*, 103–104.
18. Arthur S. Higgins, "The Rating of Selected Fields of Doctoral Study in the Graduate Schools of Education: An Opinion Survey" (Ed.D. diss., Columbia University Teachers College, 1968).

PART VI

HIGHER EDUCATION AFTER WORLD WAR II

Part VI: Higher Education After World War II

Given the difficulties of archival access (many institutions retain 50-year restrictions on their holdings, and copious institutional documentation after 1945), fewer historians of education have assessed the dramatic changes that occurred at colleges and universities during this time. Nevertheless, the third edition of this Reader reflects greater historical research on these problems and issues. In large part because of the tremendous influence of national public policy on post-secondary education, many of our primary and secondary readings focus on the rise of federalism. Three developments characterize the readings for this half century: federal policies and funding, the dramatic increases in the college-age population, and student revolts. Each contributed to this boom period in American higher education between 1955 and 1970.

Our primary readings include this important expansion of federal support for higher education. For example, the G.I. Bill of Rights facilitated access to higher education for World War II, Korean War, and Vietnam War veterans. President Truman's commission on higher education encouraged the education and training of all citizens and the growth of community colleges. The Higher Education Act of 1965 enabled many institutions to build classroom buildings, libraries, residence halls, and research laboratories as well as offer students graduate scholarships. Each of these readings (found on the companion website) signifies the growing federalism of higher education. Other federal laws, especially the earlier National Defense Education Act of 1958, enabled emerging universities to accommodate increased student demands for undergraduate, professional, and graduate education as well as to make tremendous strides in research. Federal monies also were sought to satisfy the need for vocational training through the now over 1,600 community colleges. These federal enactments enabled universities and colleges to meet the extraordinary demands of society.

Our first reading provides a contextual framework for the period by looking at institutional, faculty, and student developments. Martin Trow's critical overview of this period in his "American Higher Education: Past, Present, and Future" (1988) places these dramatic developments in a broad perspective. Calling this period one of "mass higher education" (over 40 percent of the college-age cohort enrolled in higher education), he reviews the shifts in clientele, markets, governance, and finance. The results of these extensive changes fully democratized American higher education and solidified its distinctive features. Furthermore, the research productivity of the sciences and the humanities in American colleges and universities earned universal acclaim for the quality of higher education in the United States. Richard Freeland's in-depth exploration of Massachusett's universities from 1945 to 1970 from his book, *Academia's Golden Age*,[1] reflects how federal policies from the Truman to the Johnson administrations affected universities and their research. Yet, greater governmental intervention can also compromise academic freedom. During the McCarthy decade of the 1950s, institutions and faculty faced dramatic threats to their activities. Philo Hutcheson offers an in-depth portrayal of the American Association of University Professors' hobbled efforts to stem the congressional pillaging of academic freedom, and the revitalization of the association in the face of its dramatic failures during this period.[2] His assessment discloses the strengths and weaknesses of the movement that created the contemporary professoriate. Perhaps, the most dramatic state development in higher education during this period was the creation of the California idea for a three-tiered university system through state master planning. John Douglass presents a narrative account of this great public policy enactment in his chapter from *The California Idea and American Higher Education*, involving its primary architect Arthur Coons and University of California President Clark Kerr.[3]

As in the previous era, institutional diversity continued to meet growing changes in student populations. The increasing intervention of the courts and the assistance of federal funding can be dramatically seen in the developments in Historically Black Colleges and Universities (HBCU), American Indian, Chicano, and Puerto Rican colleges. Walter Allen and Joseph Jewell's article provides an expansive history of HBCUs from 1865 to the present challenges. Similarly, Joy Williamson in her portrayal of private black colleges reviews how the state of Mississippi sought to blunt post-secondary African-American civil rights activism and maintain segregationist policies during the 1960s, resulting in the demise of a college, the firing of a college president, and the weakening of a third college. On the other hand, Jon Reyhner and Jeanne Eder offer a helpful narrative of the major Native American institutions of higher learning beginning with the 1887 normal school in North Carolina that became Pembroke State University (which still enrolls approximately 25 percent Native American students), as well as other four-year and two tribal institutions, and a discussion of the 17-member Native American Higher Education Consortium. Finally, Fred Beuttler's study of the developing University of Illinois' Circle Campus in Chicago enables us to see the administrative struggles to create a public urban research university for the commuter student.

In large part, the federal attention during this period and even its withdrawal in favor of state policies reflects the major emphasis on the student. It was the "Age of the Student," and our last readings appropriately explore this central focus. David Lavin and others describe how student and faculty demands for change during the 1960s brought about governance, administrative, professorial, and pedagogical developments unparalleled in the history of higher education. In addition to these internal strides for democratization, societal pressures influenced colleges and universities to open their doors even wider to women students and faculty members. In her 2004 presidential address to the History of Education Society, Linda Eisenmann gave a broad picture of women's advocacy and activism in higher education from the post-World War II era up to 1965. These women's stories, as presented in this address, show the gains they have made as campuses changed dramatically. As viewed from the turn of the twentieth century where women made demonstrable gains among college constituencies, the restoration of their participation in the period is clear.

Other groups also brought greater diversity to higher education. Lin-Chi Wang contributes a valuable overview of the Asian American's historic and contemporary participation in higher education, from her entry in the extensive two-volume encyclopedia, *Higher Education in the United States* (2002). Victoria Maria MacDonald and Teresa Garcia further offer an insightful first overview of the Latino experience in higher education through five eras, beginning in the nineteenth century with early experiences at the University of Texas and Santa Clara University in California to the dramatic developments for students during the past 50 years. Finally, Philip Altbach brings us up to date with his commentary on student life in the past two decades where "me-ism" and vocationalism refocused student attitudes and activities on more practical concerns.

A deep concern for equity and abhorrence of racism created campus environments where student demands for political correctness turned attention to the underlying needs for greater civility and justice—for example, student demands for divestment. In sum, few aspects of higher education have remained unchanged during this period. Marvin Larzerson's sobering concluding commentary on this era points to the problematic results of extensive growth, which was due to the student demographic upsurge, the complications of public higher education expansion, and the attractions of professionalism and vocationalism in academe. His realistic portrayal leaves the reader with a more nuanced understanding of the so-called "Golden Age" of

American higher education. Nevertheless, these now 4,200 colleges and universities have become institutional vehicles for creating an expansive middle class for all people, places of incredible scientific discovery, and the research engines for enabling the United States to claim the twentieth century as the "American Century."

ENDNOTES

[1] Richard M. Freeland, *Academia's Golden Age: Universities in Massachusetts, 1945–1970* (New York: Oxford University Press, 1992).

[2] Philo A. Hutcheson, "The AAUP from 1946–1950: McCarthyism and Reconstruction Effects," in *A Professional Professoriate: Unionization, Bureaucratization, and the AAUP* (Nashville: Vanderbilt University Press, 2000).

[3] John A. Douglass, "Negotiating the Master Plan and the Fate of Higher Education in California," in *The California Idea and American Higher Education: 1850–1960 Master Plan* (Stanford: Stanford University Press, 2000).

CHAPTER 9
CONTEXTUAL, INSTITUTIONAL, AND FACULTY ISSUES

AMERICAN HIGHER EDUCATION: PAST, PRESENT, AND FUTURE

MARTIN A. TROW

American higher education differs from all others in offering access to some part of the system to almost everyone who wants to go to college or university, without their having to show evidence of academic talent or qualification. Private attitudes and public policy—so consensual across the political spectrum that they occasion hardly any comment—affirm that the more people who can be persuaded to enroll in a college or university, the better. The budgets of most American colleges and universities are directly keyed to their enrollments: the private institutions through tuition payments, the public institutions through a combination of tuition and funding formulas that link state support to enrollment levels. And this linkage is incentive indeed for almost every institution to seek to encourage applications and enrollments.

Enrollment levels are central to the financial health and social functions of American higher education. I begin this article by reviewing current enrollment trends and forecasts. I then explore the social and historical forces that gave rise to and sustain this unique system and conclude by examining the system's prospects for responding to change, given its peculiar and deeply rooted characteristics.

Enrollment Trends and Forecasts

American higher education is the largest and the most diverse system of postsecondary education in the world. In 1947, just after World War II, 2.3 million students were enrolled in some 1800 American colleges and universities, about half in public and half in private institutions (Andersen, 1968, p. 8009). Although both sectors have grown over the past forty years, the enormous growth of enrollments during the 1960s and 1970s was absorbed largely by public institutions, both four-year and two-year colleges. Thus, by 1986, enrollments in America's roughly 3300 colleges and universities were running at 12.4 million and holding fairly steady, with 77 percent enrolled in public institutions (see Table 1). No central law or authority governs or coordinates American higher education: the roughly 1800 private institutions are governed by lay boards; the 1500 public institutions (including some 900 public community colleges) are accountable to state or local authorities, but usually have a lay board of trustees as a buffer, preserving a high, if variable, measure of institutional autonomy.

Forecasts of future growth in higher education are almost uniformly wrong, not only in the United States but also abroad. The efforts of the British to predict the growth of their system after the *Robbins Report* in 1963 were consistently wrong, within a few years and by large amounts (Williams, 1983, p. 13). Clark Kerr has noted that the Carnegie Commission's early estimates of aggregate enrollments in the United States, of the numbers of new institutions, of faculty salaries, and of the proportion of the gross national product spent on higher education were all too high (Kerr, 1980, pp. 6–8). And more recently, nearly everyone concerned with American higher education was predicting a marked decline in enrollments starting in 1979, a decline that was inevitable, given the decreased size of the college-age cohorts starting in that year. Indeed, the number of high school graduates did reach a peak of some 3 million in 1979 and did, in fact, decline to about 2.6 million in 1984, a drop of about 13 percent. The demographic projections point to a further decline in the number of high school graduates, down to a four-year trough of about 2.3 million from 1991 to 1994 (McConnell & Kaufman, 1984, p. 29). But the fall in college and university enrollments that was anticipated has simply not occurred; on the contrary, aggregate enrollments grew between 1979 and 1984 by about 6 percent, and "colleges and universities had close to 1.5 million more students, and 56 billion more revenues than predicted by the gloom and doomers" (Frances, 1984, p. 3).

Although the nation faces a further fall of about 10 percent in the numbers of high school graduates by 1991, it is unlikely that enrollments in higher education will suffer an equivalent fall. In fact, the Center for Education Statistics projects that college and university enrollments will remain fairly stable through 1991 ("Mostly stable," 1987). Among the reasons for not anticipating any large decline over the next decade are these:

- *First, there has been a steady growth since the early 1970s in enrollments of older students.* During the decade 1972–1982, the greatest percentage increase in enrollments was among people 25-years-old and older; those 35-years and older increased by 77 percent, and the enrollments of 25 to 34-year-old students increased by 70 percent, as compared with a growth of 35 percent in total enrollments during that period ("Statistics," 1984).

- *Second, increasing numbers of students are enrolled part-time.* During the decade 1972–1982, part-time enrollments increased by two-thirds, while full-time enrollments were growing by less than a fifth.

- *Third, the past decade has seen very large increases in the enrollments of women and minorities.* The number of women in colleges and universities grew by 61 percent in that decade, and minority enrollments grew by 85 percent, as compared with 15 percent for men, and 30 percent for all white students.

The growing enrollments of older students, of working and part-time students, and of women and minorities are all trends that are not dominated by the changing size of the college-age population.

TABLE 1
Higher Education Enrollment, 1947–1985

Year	Total Enrollment in thousands	Percent of Enrollments	
		Public Institutions	Private Institutions
1947	2,338	49 (1,152)	51 (1,186)
1950	2,297	50	50
1955	2,679	56	44
1960	3,789	59	41
1965	5,921	67	33
1970	8,581	75	25
1975	11,185	79	21
1980	12,097	78	22
1985	12,247	77 (9,479)	23 (2,768)
1986	12,398	77 (9,600)	23 (2,797)
	(numbers in parentheses in thousands)		

Sources compiled from: A Fact Book on Higher Education (p. 8009) by C. J. Andersen, 1968. Washington, D.C. American Council on Education. *1984–1985 Fact Book* (pp. 56, 59) by C. A. Ottinger, 1964. New York: American Council on Education and MacMillan Publishing Company.
"Fact-file Fall 1985 Enrollment." 1986, *The Chronicle of Higher Education*, p. 42.
"Mostly Stable: College and University Enrollments: 1985–1991," 1987, *The Chronicle of Higher Education*, p. A2.

For example, relatively small proportions of Mexican American (Chicano) students in California currently go on to higher education. But the number of Chicanos in California's population, and especially among its youth, is very large. In 1981–1982, they were about a quarter of all public school students, and, by the year 2000, will begin to outnumber whites in the under-20 age group (Project PACE, 1984, p. 11). Even small changes in the propensity of Chicanos to graduate from high school and go to college would have a major impact on enrollment levels in California colleges and universities. We would predict a long-term growth in the numbers of Chicanos going on to college, simply on the basis of trends among other ethnic groups throughout American history. Moreover, long-term changes in the occupational structure, such as the growth of the knowledge and information industries, increase the numbers of jobs for college-educated people. And many of our colleges and universities are more than eager to welcome back older people who want to upgrade their skills and equip themselves for jobs in the new industries.

Enrollment levels may yet fall over the next few years. Population movements, changes in the economy, and change in the size of age cohorts will, however, affect various states and regions and their institutions differently. Not only will there be an obvious disparity in the effects for, say, Ohio and Texas, there will also be equally great differences in the effects for each region's public community colleges, minor and elite private four-year colleges, and research universities. Some private colleges will certainly close over the next decade, and perhaps some public institutions will consolidate, though recent figures show an increase in the number of private four-year colleges in recent years that one would not have predicted (Tsukada, 1986, p. 101, Figure 5.3). But the birth and death of colleges in large numbers throughout our history has been and continues to be a natural outcome of the market's great influence over our diverse and decentralized system of higher education. And although there may be closures, they will be mostly of weaker institutions and may well leave the system as a whole even stronger (Glenny, 1983).

But if it is not prediction in the sense of forecasting, the value of this exercise lies elsewhere. The effort to think about what higher education will look like in 20 or 40 years forces us to think more clearly abut the historical forces that have shaped American higher education's unique qualities and character. Eric Ashby has said that we cannot know "what the environments of tomorrow's world will be like," but "we already know what its heredity will be like" (Ashby, 1967). And, as Clark Kerr has observed, heredity in higher education is a particularly strong force. The universities of today can draw a direct line back to Bologna, Paris, Oxford, and Cambridge. Even religious institutions—those vehicles for the eternal verities—have changed more, and political and economic institutions incomparably more, than universities.

The Social and Historical Background[1]

Certain features leap out when one compares American higher education with the systems in other advanced industrial societies. American colleges and universities are indeed exceptional, made so by characteristics built deeply into our history and institutions that shape their capacity to respond to unanticipatable events.

First, the market and market-related forces have a deep, pervasive influence. Second, and related to the first, the structural diversity among institutions is enormous, in their size, functions and curricula, sources of support, configurations of authority, and academic standards, a diversity their student bodies mirror in their age distributions, purposes and motivations, class, ethnic and racial origins, and much else.

Third, the internal differentiation in our comprehensive universities and many of our larger state colleges in academic standards and educational missions gives them great flexibility to respond to the markets for undergraduates, faculty, graduate students, and research support. This internal differentiation among academic departments and professional schools complements the structural differentiation between public and private, large and small, selective and open-access colleges and universities.

Fourth, a cluster of shared characteristics marks our curricula, teaching styles, and patterns of assessment: the unique role of general education as a component of nearly all American first degree courses; the considerable extent of student choice in the selection of courses; and the modular course earning *unit-credits,* an academic currency that makes a system of 3300 separate institutions.

Fifth, our mode of college and university governance is unparalleled. Lay boards and strong presidents, certainly strong by comparison with their counterparts elsewhere, command large administrative staffs located inside the institutions rather than in some central ministry or governmental agency.

The great, unique feature of American higher education is surely its diversity. It is this diversity—both resulting from and making possible the system's phenomenal growth—that has enabled our colleges and universities to appeal to so many, serve so many different functions, and insinuate themselves into so many parts of the national life. And it is through the preservation of diversity that our system will be best prepared to respond to changing demands and opportunities in the years ahead. To see why this is so, review briefly the historical roots of this diversity and the benefits we derive from it today.

America had established nine colleges by the time of the Revolution, when two—Oxford and Cambridge—were enough for the much larger and wealthier mother country. The United States entered the Civil War with about 250 colleges, of which over 180 still survive. Even more striking is the record of failure: Between the Revolution and the Civil War, perhaps as many as 700 colleges were started and failed. By 1880, England was doing very well with four universities for a population of 23 million, whereas the state of Ohio, with a population of 3 million, already boasted 37 institutions of higher learning (Rudolph, 1962, pp. 47–48). By 1910, we had nearly a thousand colleges and universities with a third of a million students—at a time when the 16 universities of France enrolled altogether about 40,000 students, a number nearly equaled by the American faculty members at the time.

The extraordinary phenomena of high fertility and high mortality rates among institutions of higher learning are still with us. For example, between 1969 and 1975, some 800 new colleges (many of them community colleges) were created, and roughly 300 others were closed or consolidated, leaving a net gain of nearly 500. This is a phenomenon unique to the United States—one that resembles the pattern of success and failure of small businesses in modern capitalist economies. It is in sharp contrast with the slow, deliberately planned creation of institutions of higher and further education in most advanced industrial societies or their even slower and rarer termination. And this points to the very strong link between higher education in the United States and the mechanisms of the market. This link has been a major factor in the emergence and persistence of large numbers of diverse institutions.

Two important features of markets, as compared with other forms of social action, are (a) that their outcomes are not the result of planning or central purposive decision, and (b) that when producers are relatively numerous, their behaviors are marked by their competition for buyers, which strengthens the buyers' influence over the product's character and quality, indeed, over the producers' very character.

In higher education, we can see this when the buyers are students, and the producers, the colleges and universities, compete for their enrollment. We can see it also when the sellers are graduates competing for job openings. The two together translate opportunities in the job market into the size of academic departments and programs. The key is the considerable autonomy of American colleges and universities, which enables them to move resources between departments in response to changes in student enrollment and demand. Similarly, when research groups compete for scarce funds, funding agencies gain power over the character, direction, and quality of the research they buy. In the United States, apart from the quite unusual period of rapid growth between 1955 and 1975, the supply of places has on the whole outstripped demand; and buyers or potential buyers at both ends, students and the employers of graduates, have had a powerful influence on the behavior of the producers. This influence of buyer over seller is likely to be relatively constant in the decades ahead.

The Influence of Market Forces

We can see the emergence of strong market forces in the early history of American higher education, we can see them today in the very structure and workings of our institutions, and we can compare their strength here with the systems of other societies.

A multiplicity of forces and motives lay behind the establishment of colleges and universities throughout our history: religious motives; fears of relapse into barbarism at the frontier; the need for various kinds of professionals; state pride and local boosterism; philanthropy; idealism; educational reform; speculation in land, among others, and in all combinations. But the number and diversity of institutions, competing with one another for students, resources, teachers, bringing market considerations and market mechanisms right into the heart of this ancient cultural institution—all also required the absence of any restraining central force or authority. The states could not be that restraining force; under the pressures of competition and emulation they have tended throughout our history to create institutions and programs in the numbers and to the standards of their neighbors. Crucially important has been the absence of a federal ministry of education with the power to charter new institutions, or of a single preeminent university that could influence them in other ways.

The closest we have come as a nation to establishing such a central force was the attempt, first by George Washington, and then by the next five Presidents, to found a University of the United States at the seat of government in Washington, D.C. In fact, Washington made provision for such a university in his will and mentioned it in his first and last messages to Congress. His strongest plea came in his last message to Congress, where he argued that a national university would promote national unity, a matter of deep concern at a time when the primary loyalties of many Americans were to their sovereign states, not the infant nation.

Washington saw also the possibility of creating one first-class university by concentrating money and other resources in it. As he noted in his last message to Congress: "Our Country, much to its honor, contains many Seminaries of learning highly respectable and useful; but the funds upon which they rest, are too narrow, to command the ablest Professors, in the different departments of liberal knowledge, for the Institution contemplated, though they would be excellent auxiliaries" (Hofstadter & Smith, 1961, p. 158). Here, indeed, Washington was right in his diagnosis. The many institutions that sprang up between the Revolution and the Civil War all competed for very scarce resources and all thus suffered to some degree from malnutrition. Malnutrition at the margin is still characteristic of a system of institutions influenced so heavily by market forces.

Defeat of the national university meant that American higher education would develop, to this day, without a single capstone institution. As it was, until after the Civil War, whatever the United States called its institutions of higher learning, it simply did not have a single genuine university— an institution of first-class standing that could bring its students as far or as deep into the various branches of learning as could the institutions of the old world.

A national university would have profoundly affected American higher education. As the preeminent university, it would have had an enormous influence, direct and indirect, on every other college in the country, and through them on the secondary schools as well. Its standards and educational philosophies would have been models for every institution that hoped to send some of its graduates to the university in Washington. It would, in fact, have established national academic standards for the bachelor's degree, for the undergraduate curriculum, for the qualifications for college teachers, even for entrance to college, and thus for the secondary schools. Eventually, it would have surely constrained the growth of graduate education and research universities in the United States.

Similarly, a national university of high standard would surely have inhibited the emergence of the hundreds of small, weak, half-starved state and denominational colleges that sprang up over the next 170 years. They simply could not have offered work to the standard that the University of the United States would have set. The situation would have been familiar to Europeans, for whom the maintenance of high and, so far as possible, common academic standards has been a valued principle, almost unchallenged until recently. In the United States, after the defeat of the University of the United States, no one has challenged the principle of high academic standards across the whole system because no one has proposed it—there have been no common standards, high or otherwise. Indeed, if Europe's slogan for higher education has been "nothing, if not the best." America's has been "something is better than nothing." And in that spirit, we have created a multitude of institutions of every sort, offering academic work of every description and at every level of seriousness and standard. And, by so doing, we have offered Europeans nearly two centuries of innocent amusement at our expense.

Ironically, however, without any central model or governmental agency able to create one or more national systems, all of our 3300 institutions, public and private, modest and preeminent, religious and secular, are in some way part of a common system bound by membership in a series of markets for students, support, prestige, faculty.

Another event in the early history of the Republic that had powerful effects on the shape and character of American higher education was the 1819 Supreme Court decision in the Dartmouth College case. In 1816, the New Hampshire legislature had passed a bill giving the state government broad powers to "reform" Dartmouth. The rationale for proposed changes in its charter was the plausible argument that, as the college had been established (though as a private corporation) to benefit the people of New Hampshire, this could best be accomplished by giving the public, through the legislature, a voice in its operation. Chief Justice Marshall, ruling in favor of the college trustees, declared that state legislatures were forbidden, by the Constitution, to pass any law "impairing the obligation of contracts," and that the charter originally granted the college was a contract (Hofstadter & Smith, 1961, p. 218). This landmark decision affirmed the principle of the sanctity of contracts between governments and private institutions. In so doing, it gave expression to the Federalist belief that the government should not interfere with private property, even for the purpose of benefiting the public welfare. John Marshall, the then-Chief Justice, had written earlier: "I consider the interference of the legislature in the management of our private affairs, whether those affairs are committed to a company or remain under individual direction as equally dangerous and unwise." He and his colleagues on the Court decided, in the Dartmouth College case, that a private college or university charter was a contract that a state could not retroactively abridge. That decision of 1819 had massive repercussions both for the growth of capitalist enterprises and for the future development of higher education in the United States.

The Dartmouth College decision sustained the older, more modest role of the state in educational affairs against those who looked to the government to take a greater role in the working of society and its institutions. Marshall's decision had the practical effect of safeguarding the founding and proliferation of privately controlled colleges. Thereafter, promoters of private colleges knew that once they had obtained a state charter they were secure in the future control of the institution. By this decision, state university development was slowed or weakened, though, paradoxically, it may be that by making it more difficult to create them, state universities were ultimately strengthened.

The failure of the University of the United States and the success of Dartmouth College in its appeal to the Supreme Court were victories for local initiative and private entrepreneurship. The first set limits on the federal government's role in shaping the character of the whole of American higher education; the second set even sharper limits on the state's power over private colleges. Together, these two events constituted a kind of license for unrestrained individual and group initiative in the creation of colleges of all sizes, shapes and creeds. As a result, colleges' and universities' behavior came to resemble living organisms' behavior in an ecological system—competitive for resources, highly sensitive to the demands of environment, and inclined, over time, through the ruthless processes of natural selection, to be adaptive to those aspects of their environment that permitted their survival. Their environment also has included other colleges, and later universities. So we see in this frog pond a set of mechanisms that we usually associate with the behavior of small entrepreneurs in a market: the anxious concern for market demands and the readiness to adapt to its apparent preferences; the effort to secure a special place in that market through the marginal differentiation of the product; and a readiness to enter into symbiotic or parasitic relationships with other producers for a portion of that market.

We are employing a language that Europeans tend to find strange and often a bit distasteful when used in connection with institutions of higher learning. But distasteful or not, an American must insist on this as a central and distinguishing characteristic of American higher education—that it has developed as a network of institutions that, in many respects, resembles in its behavior the myriad of small capitalistic enterprises that were springing up everywhere, at the same time and in the same places, and often in response to the same forces.

We are, and have been from the beginning, an acquisitive society, confronted by a continent whose ownership had not been settled by sword and custom since medieval times. In America, as Louis Hartz has noted, the market preceded society, a central and powerful fact whose ramifications can be seen in all of our institutions and throughout our national life (Hartz, 1955). We are, to put it crudely, unembarrassed by the market. By contrast, Europeans and their governments, now, as in the past, dislike market mechanisms and processes in education and do everything they can to reduce their influence. And this difference arises out of our profoundly differing feelings about culture and about cultural competence. Markets threaten the "cultural integrity" of cultural institutions by increasing the power of consumers as over against producers—that is, as over against the people who are presumably most competent to supply some given kind of cultural entity, whether it be a performance of music or higher studies in philosophy or physics. In colleges and universities, the consumers, ordinarily students or their parents, are by definition incompetent, or at least less competent than the teachers and academic administrators who together provide instruction. Europeans try very hard to reduce the influence of the incompetent mass on high cultural matters and to preserve a realm of elite determination of cultural form and content.

We in the United States, surely the most populist society in the world, accept a larger role for the influence of consumer preference on cultural forms—even in the provision of what and how subjects are taught in colleges and universities. Europeans try to reduce the influence of consumer preference in a number of ways. Most importantly, they try to insulate their financing of institutions of higher education from student fees. By contrast, in the United States, enrollment-driven budgets in all but a few institutions, both public and private, ensure that most institutions are extremely sensitive to student preferences.

Another example of the comparative hospitality of American institutions to market forces in higher education can be seen in the ways Congress has decided to provide major public funding for colleges and universities. After sharp debate in the early 1970s, this country chose to fund colleges and universities chiefly by providing grants and loans to students, rather than through direct support to the institutions themselves; the decision was to subsidize higher education through the consumers, not the producers. The result was to strengthen the relative power of consumers over producers substantially, without increasing the power of central government over the producers.

The Character and Structure of our Institutions

We can look at broad patterns of organization and finance of higher education (for example, multiple versus single sources of support) and see the differences between market systems and those dominated by other principles of organization and political decision-making. But we can also see the influence of market mechanisms in the private life of higher education, in the very processes of teaching and learning. Our peculiar system of earned and transferable "credits," a kind of academic currency that we all take for granted in American institutions, is one example. The unit-credit system is not found in other countries, where degrees are earned by passing examinations or writing dissertations. But our credits, units that can be accumulated, banked, transferred, and, within limits, automatically accepted as legal academic tender toward an earned degree throughout the country, make possible the extraordinary mobility of our students between fields of study, and between institutions. Moreover, credits that can be accumulated and transferred also allow students to drop out, or "stop out," and return to college in ways that are increasingly familiar to us.

An inventory of the unique qualities of American higher education must include a reference to the multiplicity of subjects taught, a product of the extraordinary hospitality of our institutions to almost any subject that might have a claim to be useful or to be rooted in a body of skill and knowledge that can be studied and taught. But this range of studies, often the subject of somewhat derisive comment by Europeans, would not be possible if we had a central agency maintaining "high standards" and scrutinizing new subjects for their appropriateness as judged by traditional criteria. The openness of our institutions to new subjects is linked to the absence of a central administrative body that certifies institutions and subjects, as well as to our consequent reliance on market forces to sustain our many weak and impoverished institutions.

Or we could point to the intimate links between our colleges and universities and local industry, governments and other institutions and private organizations of all kinds, relationships that are envied and emulated elsewhere but rarely matched in scope (Eurich, 1985).

This inventory leaves us with the question of how these unique characteristics are all related, both in their origins and in their current functioning. Let us look, for example, at a cluster of phenomena embedded in American higher education: the lay board, the strong presidency, a weak professoriate, the internal administration, the absence of a central ministry of higher education. The origins of the external nonacademic board of trustees lie in the precedent set at Harvard. The founders of Harvard had intended to "carry on the English tradition of resident-faculty control" (Rudolph, 1962, p. 166). But Harvard had to be founded and not just developed. There simply was not a body of scholars to be brought together to teach and to govern themselves. A *president* could be found to take responsibility for the operation of the institution, and he might find some young men to help him with instruction as tutors. But Harvard had been established for more than 85 years before it had its first professor; Yale for more than 50. "For over a century and a half, American collegiate education relied chiefly on the college president and his young tutors." And for a very long time indeed, well into the nineteenth century, "The only secure and sustained professional office in American collegiate education was that of the college president himself. He alone had, in the community and before the governing boards, the full stature of a man of learning. To this situation can be traced the singular role and importance of the American college or university president" (Hofstadter & Metzger, 1955, p. 124).

The lay boards that arose to govern America's first college and the great majority of those that followed were created by groups of individuals, not by the state. These boards *had* to govern; there was no one else. They could appoint a president, and, as busy men themselves, they had to delegate to him the day-to-day running of the institution. He held his office, however, and everywhere in the U.S. still does, wholly at the pleasure of this external board; the president has no security of tenure as president (though he may hold tenure as a professor in the institution). But for a very long time there was no body of learned men making academic life a career and, thus, no challenge to the president's authority, so long as he had the support of his board of trustees.

The near absolute authority of the college president in running an institution was lost over time, especially with the rise of the great research universities and the emergence of a genuine academic profession. In this century, especially in the stronger institutions, a great deal of authority over academic affairs has been delegated to the faculty. But the American college and university president is still more powerful than his counterpart in European institutions, who faces the power held jealously by the professoriate, or by the academic staff more broadly, and by government ministries, trade unions, or student organizations (Trow, 1985a).

The relatively great power and authority of the American college and university president also insured that, when some institutions became very large and needed a big bureaucratic staff to administer them, that staff would be an extension of the president's office, rather than responsible to a faculty body or to state authorities. By keeping the administrative staff within the university, the strong presidency has helped preserve the autonomy of the public university in the face of state authority.

I have mentioned how weak, indeed for a long time nonexistent, the academic profession in America was. When professors did begin to appear, they did not command the enormous prestige and status accorded to the European professor. They were neither part of a prestigious civil service, nor were they recruited from the highest social strata. Indeed, in a society that prized action and worldly success, they were rather looked down on as men who had stepped aside from the real challenges of life. America, for the most part, has given its honors and respect chiefly to men of action rather than reflection; the very choice of an academic career for a long time suggested that a person was incapable of managing such important matters as the affairs of a university (Hofstadter, 1963, pp. 24–51; Rudolph, 1962, pp. 160–161). This tended to strengthen the hand of the president, who *may* have been a scholar, but almost certainly was also a man of affairs.

The relatively low status and weakness of the professoriate also meant that, as the academic profession grew, it was not dominated by a handful of prestigious professors. The academic ranks were established during the growth of the research universities after the Civil War, but with almost the whole teaching faculty holding the title of professor of some rank, and with remarkable independence for even young assistant professors. That is partly due to the egalitarian elements in American cultural life, which are still very strong, but partly also to the historic weakness of the senior professor—his lack of real power, social prestige, even scholarly distinction. Academic ambition directed itself not so much to rank—that could be assumed—but to national reputation and to the distinction of the institution or department in which one gained an appointment.

Indeed, many of the most important qualities of American higher education have arisen not from design but from the weakness of its component institutions. For example, as I have suggested, the relatively egalitarian character of American academic life and the independence and authority of its junior members are products not of plan or policy, but of the slow formation of the academic profession and the professoriate and its relative poverty, low status, lack of tenure or civil service rank. But that has meant that we have avoided the bitter struggles between the professors and the other ranks of the academic profession that have marked European systems since World War II. In America, the rank of professor was no great honor and held no great reward; it was, in fact, the rank that every young instructor or assistant professor (and not just the few most talented ones) could expect to achieve in the fullness of time. That ease of access has helped to keep its status relatively low both within the university and outside it—where the title "Professor" still has slightly pejorative or comic overtones.

The connections among a weak academic profession, strong presidents, lay boards, and the power of the market in American higher education lie in the more general lack of other forces that constrain the self-interested actions of individuals and institutions. Most commonly, those constraining forces in other countries are the state authorities allied with the academic professions and its organizations or guilds. In the United States, central state power was initially weak, and in relation to higher education remained weak, in part as a result of the failure of the University of the United States and the Dartmouth College decision which guaranteed an essential role to the private sector. In addition, the weakness of the professoriate greatly reduced its constraint on the market. On the other hand, strong presidents and their administrative staffs could act in pursuit of the self-interest of individual institutions, and lay boards could ensure that those institutions would continue to be responsive to the larger society, and to its markets for students and graduates, rather than to the state or professional guilds. And that certainly has been and will be a source of strength as these institutions face an uncertain future and a changing environment.

Trends in Higher Education Finance

I have been looking backward but now look at the present and near past for trends and developments that might point in the direction of larger changes in the future.

In 1985–1986 expenditures of all kinds on American colleges and universities were estimated to be over $102 billion, an increase in current dollars of 32 percent, and in constant dollars of 17 percent, over 1981–1982. This represents roughly 2.5 percent of the Gross National Product ("Higher education is," 1986, p. 3). One important and distinctive characteristic of American higher education is the diversity of its sources of support. The diversity of funding sources has large consequences for the autonomy of American colleges and universities and for their traditions of service to other institutions, both public and private, as well as for their finances. Taken in the aggregate, American colleges and universities get support from federal, state and local governments; from private sources such as churches, business firms, foundations, and individuals; from students, in the form of tuition and fees, living expenses in halls of residence, food services, health services, and the like; and from their own endowments, as well as from the sale of their services to others.

Government at all levels together provide nearly half of all current revenues for American higher education, and that excludes federal aid given directly to students, which shows up, for the most part, as tuition and fees from the students. The federal government provides only about 13 percent of the support for higher education overall, and that includes its support for research and development in the universities, but excludes the aid it provides directly to students. State and local governments (mostly state) provide a third of all support for higher education. Students themselves provide another third, including federal aid they have received. The institutions themselves contribute about 15 percent from their own endowments and other sources. If we count federal aid to students as federal support to higher education, it increases the federal proportion to about 23 percent of total support and reduces the student contribution to about the same proportion. Another 6 percent is provided by individuals, foundations, and private business firms, in the form of gifts, grants, and contracts.

These proportions, of course, differ between public and private colleges and universities, though it must be stressed that all American colleges and universities are supported by a mixture of public and private funds. For example, whereas in 1981–1982 public four-year colleges and universities got over 44 percent of their operating budgets from their state governments, the private institutions got less than 2 percent from state sources. (But note, private colleges received a slightly larger proportion of their support funds from the federal government than did the public institutions.) The other big difference lies in the importance of students' fees and payments directly to the institution for services: These account for less than a quarter of the revenues to public institutions, but about a half of the support for private institutions (Plisko, 1985, p. 114, Table 2.14). These proportions differ sharply among even finer categories of colleges and universities; for example, as between public research universities and public four-year colleges.

In 1985–1986 student aid from all sources was running at over $21 billion a year, 23 percent higher than in 1980–1981. In real terms, however, student support from all sources had fallen by 3 percent since 1980–1981, and aid from federally supported programs by 10 percent, when adjusted for inflation ("*Trends in*," 1986, p. 2). The federal government in fiscal 1985 provided directly and indirectly about $23.7 billion to higher education, of which $10.2 billion was in a complex combination of student grants and loans (derived from "Higher education funds," 1986, p. 12). Student aid has widespread support in the Congress as well as in society at large. And although the Reagan administration regularly proposed cuts in that aid, many of its proposals were defeated. In 1985, Congress "blocked virtually all the cuts in aid to college students that the Reagan Administration proposed . . ." and was "drafting legislation to keep grants, loans and work opportunities essentially intact for five years" (Friendly, 1985, p. 15). Although pressures on the federal budget arising out of the large deficits may be reflected in further pressures on federal student aid programs, there is little likelihood of cuts so deep as to endanger the programs. Federal support for students is here to stay.

Increases in student aid at the state and the institution levels (which now comprise 22 percent of the total student aid reported from all sources) have helped to offset the drop in federal aid. At the federal level, the distribution of student aid has greatly shifted from grants to loans: in 1975–1976, 75 percent of federal student aid was awarded in the form of grants, but by 1984–1985 the share of grant aid had dropped to 29 percent, whereas the share of loans had tripled, from 21 percent in 1975 to 66 percent (see Table 2).

Many states did cut their support for public colleges and universities during the severe recession of 1980–1982, but thereafter the levels of state support tended to rise about as fast as economic recovery and rising revenues permitted. State tax funds for the operation of higher education (this does not include capital costs) was nearly $31 billion for 1984–1985, up 19 percent over 1983–1984. "Over the last decade, [1974–1984, state] appropriations [for higher education] increased 140 percent nationwide. Adjusted for inflation, the increase was 19 percent" (Evangelauf, 1985, p. 1 ff.).

With regard to federal support for research, also perceived by many as endangered by the Reagan administration, between 1982 and 1985, federal obligations to universities and colleges for research and development increased by 16 percent in real terms, reaching $6 billion in 1985. Moreover, in that year nearly two-thirds of all federal academic R & D support was committed to basic research projects, compared to about one-half in 1975 (National Science Foundation, 1985, p. 2; see also, "Higher education funds," 1986, p. 12).

TABLE 2
Shift of Federal Student Aid from Grants to Loans

	1975–1976	*1984–1985*
Grants	75%	29%
Loans	21%	66%
Work-Study	4%	5%

Source: "1986 Major Trends Shaping the Outlook for Higher Education" by C. Frances, 1985, *AAHE Bulletin*, p. 5.

Other Supports and Benefits of the System[2]

We need not place very great weight on recent trends in enrollments and support. We know, especially from the sad example of British higher education, how rapidly these figures can change when they are built on shallow foundations. In Britain, where the university system has few friends in industry, in the professions, in the trade unions, or the political parties, its few friends in the civil service and elsewhere are unable to protect it against economic and political pressures from government.

But American higher education has many friends and, more important, many supporters in the society, not just in government. The absence of any strong central governing and standardizing authority that can control (and limit) the growth of American higher education and the concomitant responsiveness of our colleges and universities to market forces have allowed and indeed required them to find ways to serve other institutions and groups in their constant search for support. We have not been able to afford the luxury of high academic standards across all our degree-granting institutions. The result is the diversity of standards and functions in our colleges and universities that we find so familiar and that Europeans find so strange. So long as the governing assumption of a system of higher education is that only a minority of students can work at the required standard, that system is constrained both in its size and in the functions it can perform for its students and for the larger society. Such a system may perform the functions of elite selection, preparation, and certification, as most European universities have done and still do. But it cannot penetrate as deeply or broadly into the life of society as American higher education has.

Some of the effects of mass higher education on American society are not, I believe, well recognized. Economists often say that it is best to measure and assess carefully what can be measured, and leave to others—historians, sociologists, educators, politicians—the discussion of higher education's larger effects on society. We cannot measure these very precisely; they are long delayed in their appearance, are "outcomes" rather than intended effects, and have sources only partly within the system and partly within the society at large. (For an economist whose views are similar to those I express below, see Bowen, 1977, pp. 359–387.)

Let me suggest some of those effects here:

- *Higher education has substantial effects on the attitudes of those exposed to it.* A large amount of research supports this assertion—and also that changes in attitudes occurring during the college years persist throughout life (Hyman, Wright, & Reed, 1975; Feldman & Newcomb, 1969). For example, higher education achieves some of what it intends by broadening the perspectives of students, giving them an appreciation of other cultures and groups, making them more tolerant of cultural differences, and weakening the prejudices characteristic of uneducated people. And those changed attitudes in a population, in turn, make possible real changes in social structures, if and when they are accompanied by changes in law and institutional behavior.

In the United States, the years after World War II saw a steady decline in hostility toward black people and growing readiness on the part of whites to give blacks equal treatment and fair access to education, housing, and jobs. These changes can be seen in studies of attitudes both in the general population as well as among college students during the college years and after (Hyman & Wright, 1979; Stember, 1961; Stouffer, 1955; Clark, Heist, McConnell, Trow, & Yonge, 1972). I believe that the considerable progress the United States has made in race relations since World War II has been made possible by the growth of mass higher education and the marked decline in racial prejudice that accompanied it. If that is true, then it represents a very great contribution to the life of the society, one that is almost never acknowledged by economists as a benefit of American higher education.

Higher education has also played a visible role in this revolution by helping to expand and educate black, Hispanic, and Asian middle classes. In 1985, the University of California at Berkeley for the first time admitted a freshman class made up of a majority (52 percent) of those minority group members. In the next century, those students will be assuming leadership positions in every institution in our society.

- *People who have been to college or university, on the whole, view public issues in a longer time perspective than do less well-educated people.* Such perspectives are important to assessing the significance and recognizing the origins of a problem or issue, yet we do not measure them or give them value, certainly not as outcomes of higher education. Nations and industries cannot plan or develop programs without the help of people who take the long view, who can imagine the outcome of projects that may lie years in the future. And that perspective is very much a benefit of mass higher education.

In an increasingly complex society, it is not enough that a small number of elites have these longer time horizons; the successful development and implementation of plans require such people throughout the society, especially at the middle levels of the civil service in central, regional, and local governments, and in public and private enterprises. Long-range plans require continual adjustments and modifications at the levels where they are implemented; people at those levels must be able to understand the purposes of long-range programs and be able to implement and modify them within planning guidelines.

- *The capacity of citizens to learn how to learn is another skill that is gained or enhanced by exposure to higher education.* So much of what we learn in college or university is obsolescent in 10 years, obsolete in 25, that it is impossible to exaggerate the importance of the ability to continue to learn after finishing formal schooling. Wherever facilities are provided for adult education, they are now quickly filled by people with a degree or some postsecondary education, who already have, as adults, developed a desire to learn (Organization for Economic Co-operation and Development, 1977, p. 27). Modern societies need citizens with that quality of mind, which is also a product, if often a by-product, of higher education. I believe that mass higher education in the United States, especially in its generous provision of education for adults, engenders and distributes more widely the habit of "life-long learning" than is true in most other countries.

The qualities of mind (they are more than attitudes) that I have mentioned—tolerance of cultural and class differences, a longer time perspective that helps sustain initiative among middle-and lower-level administrators, the ability to learn how to learn—are all created or enhanced by exposure to postsecondary education. As I have suggested, they are usually by-products of that education, but immensely important by-products for the life and progress of any society.

- *In American political life, higher education has a familiar role as home of the cultural critic of the established political order and the nursery of radical and even revolutionary student movements. But less dramatically and visibly, the expansion and democratization of higher education may also work to legitimate the political and social order by rewarding talent and effort rather than serving merely as a cultural apparatus of the ruling classes by ensuring the passage of power and privilege across generations.*

In a time of rising expectations among all social strata around much of the world, nations must provide real opportunities for social mobility to able people from poor and modest origins. They must do so for social and political reasons, as well as for economic growth. In many countries, the armed forces have provided an avenue of mobility, and they have often gained the support of the poor even when other institutions have lost it. But, for many reasons, higher education is a better instrument for strengthening the legitimacy of a political democracy, and, where it performs that vital function, as it has in the United States, it goes unrecorded on the accounting sheets of the cost benefits analyst.

A further large benefit of American higher education, yet to be achieved, is the help and guidance extended by colleges and universities to secondary education in other ways than through teacher training and educational research. The many reports and books on public secondary education that have appeared since 1983 (e.g., National Commission on Excellence in Education, 1983; Boyer, 1983; Goodlad, 1983) have led to the creation of a large number of programs by colleges and universities that establish new links between higher and secondary education. Some of those programs are designed to strengthen the academic and college preparatory work of the high schools, not just provide remediation for ill-prepared students after they reach college (Trow, 1985b). It may be that the task is too large and that the structural characteristics of American high schools will defeat all efforts to overcome their "bias against excellence" (Clark, 1985, p. 391). But it will not be for want of trying. Already hundreds of programs that aim to correct or ameliorate deficiencies in the schools have been developed by colleges and universities. Results can already be seen in individual schools, but the larger effects will be long delayed and obscured by many other inputs and forces. My point here is to illustrate the continuing propensity of American higher education to respond to national needs of almost every kind and to try to provide some service, some program, to meet those needs.

Conclusion

I have chosen to look to the past and the present to assess characteristics of our unique system of colleges and universities that may shape the future. It is futile to make specific predictions—they all fail in a few years, even in societies that manage their systems more closely than we do. But my review of the central characteristics of American higher education leads me to believe that it is well equipped to survive major changes in the society and to respond creatively to almost any developments, short of a catastrophe. The strength of our system lies precisely in its diversity, which allows it to respond to different needs and demands on different segments of the system. Over the past forty years, enrollments have grown from about 2.3 million to 12.4 million and, along with this enormous growth, there has been further diversification and democratization of access. By the end of World War II, and perhaps much earlier, we had a system that had the capacity to grow by a factor of five without any fundamental change in its structure or functions, a system able to provide access to a broad spectrum of American society, while still providing education of the highest standard for a small fraction of our youth and research at an equally high standard in the broadest range of scholarly and scientific disciplines.

What besides this massive growth has changed significantly in American higher education over the past forty years? First, the federal government has become a major source of support, both for university-based research and through student aid. Yet it still supplies less than a quarter of all support for American higher education. Moreover, the government's influence on the system has been further muted, precisely because that support has gone to individual scientists and students rather than directly to the institutions. Of course, the federal government has become a major actor in shaping the agenda of American science. And yet science still retains a large measure of autonomy to pursue problems and issues that arise internally, rather than at the initiative of the government.

As the fifty states have increased their support for the public sector of higher education, they have demanded greater accountability from the colleges and universities for the use of these funds. Not long ago, these demands by public authorities were seen as the forerunners of a dangerous shift of authority and initiative away from the state colleges and universities to the state houses and governors' office (Trow, 1975). Relations between public universities and state authorities vary too much for any easy generalization, yet my sense is that public authorities and university leaders in many states have been coming to a more reasoned and mutually acceptable relationship than was seen as possible or likely even ten years ago (Newman, 1987).

Higher education has expanded its relationships with industry in many ways. On the one hand, business firms provide very large and growing amounts of education and training at all levels of skill and sophistication, including degree-granting programs (Eurich, 1985). On the other hand, universities have provided the ideas and professional staffs for new science-based industries and are at the center of their physical clusterings from Boston to Silicon Valley. They also provide an organizational model and style of work for many other institutions, from consulting firms and industrial labs to legislative committees (Muir, 1982). Moreover, community colleges enroll increasing numbers of students who already hold a bachelor's degree but want further training in another specialty—new patterns of continuing education and professional development.

Certainly, the democratization of the student body has meant more mature, part-time, and working students; these kinds of students in fact have confounded the predictions of enrollment decline after 1979. There seems no limit to this development: American higher education, or at least a large segment of it, seems ready and eager to provide some useful educational service to all nontraditional students. And we have no reason to believe that this will be less true in the future, as more and more of our labor force comes to work in industries whose very survival is predicated on rapid change, new skills, and new ways of thinking.

All of this suggests that American higher education will be an even more important institution in this society in the decades to come: as a supplier of more advanced skills, as well as a source of greater social equality, continuing social commentary and criticism, and the transmission of an ever-broadening cultural heritage. Higher education is, today, I believe, the key institution in American society, the source of many of its most important ideas, values, skills, and energies. That will be true, and increasingly true, as far ahead as anyone can see.

Acknowledgment: Revised from State and Welfare, USA/USSR: Contemporary Policy and Practice, *edited by Gail W. Lapidus and Guy E. Swanson, Berkeley: Institute of International Studies, University of California (forthcoming 1988). My thanks to Janet Ruyle for her help with this paper.*

Notes

1. This section draws, in part, on my essay "Aspects of Diversity in American Higher Education," 1979.
2. This section draws on my paper, "The State of Higher Education in the United States," 1986.

References

Andersen, C. J. (Comp.). (1968). *A Fact Book on Higher Education* (Issue No. 1). Washington, DC: American Council on Education.

Ashby, E. (1967, November). Ivory Towers in Tomorrow's World. *The Journal of Higher Education*, pp. 417–427.

Bowen, H. R. (1977). *Investment in Learning: The Individual and Social Value of American Higher Education*. San Francisco, CA: Jossey-Bass.

Boyer, E. (1983). *High school: A Report on Secondary Education in America*. New York: Harper & Row.

Clark, B. R. (1985, February). The high school and the university: What went wrong in America, Part I. *Phi Delta Kappan, 66*, 391–397.

Clark, B. R., Heist, P., McConnell, T. R., Trow, M. A., & Yonge, G. E. (1972). *Students and Colleges: Interaction and Change*. Berkeley, CA: Center for Research and Development in Higher Education, University of California.

Eurich, N. P. (1985). *Corporate Classrooms: The Learning Business*. Princeton, NJ: Carnegie Foundation for the Advancement of Teaching.

Evangelauf, J. (1985, October 30). States' spending on colleges rises 19 pct. in 2 years, nears $31-billion for '85–'86. *The Chronicle of Higher Education*, p. 1 ff.

Fact-file fall 1985 enrollment. (1986, October 15). *The Chronicle of Higher Education*, p. 42.

Feldman, K. A., & Newcomb, T. M. (1969). *The Impact of College on Students (Vol. 2)*. San Francisco, CA: Jossey-Bass.

Francis, C. (1984, December). 1985: The economic outlook for higher education. *AAHE Bulletin*, p. 3.

Francis, C. (1985, December). 1986: Major trends shaping the outlook for higher education. *AAHE Bulletin*, p. 5.

Friendly, J. (1985, September 24). Budget ax fails to make dent in aid programs for students. *The New York Times*, p. 15.

Glenny, L. A. (1983, July). *Higher education for students: Forecasts of a golden age*. Paper delivered at a seminar sponsored by the Higher Education Steering Committee, University of California, Berkeley, CA.

Goodlad, J. I. (1983). *A Place Called School. Prospects for the Future*. New York: McGraw-Hill.

Hartz, L. (1955). *The Liberal Tradition in America: An Interpretation of American Political Thoughts Since the Revolution*. New York: Harcourt Brace.

Higher education funds in President Reagan's fiscal 1987 budget. (1986, February 12). *The Chronicle of Higher Education*, p. 12.

Higher education is a U.S. industry. (1986, July 28). *Higher Education and National Affairs*, p. 3.

Hofstadter, R. (1963). *Anti-intellectualism in American Life*. New York: Alfred A. Knopf.

Hofstadter, R., & Metzger, W. P. (1955). *The Development of Academic Freedom in the United States*. New York: Columbia University Press.

Hofstadter, R. & Smith, W. (Eds.). (1961). *American Higher Education: A Documentary History* (Vol. 1). Chicago, IL: University of Chicago Press.

Hyman, H. H., & Wright, C. R. (1979). *Education's Lasting Influence on Values*. Chicago, IL and London: University of Chicago Press.

Hyman, H. H., Wright, C. R., & Reed, J. S. (1975). *The Enduring Effects of Education*. Chicago, IL and London: University of Chicago Press.

Kerr, C. (1980). The Carnegie policy series 1967–1979: Consensus, approaches, reconsiderations, results. In *The Carnegie Council on Policy Studies in Higher Education*. San Francisco, CA: Jossey-Bass.

McConnell, W. R., & Kaufman, N. (1984, January). *High School Graduates: Projections for the Fifty States (1982–2000)*. Boulder, CO: Western Interstate Commission for Higher Education.

Mostly stable: College and university enrollments: 1985–1991. (1987, November 25), *The Chronicle of Higher Education*, p. A29.

Muir, W. K. (1982). *Legislature: California's School for Politics*. Chicago, IL: University of Chicago Press.

National Commission on Excellence in Education. (1983). *A Nation at Risk: The Imperative for Educational Reform*. Washington, DC: U.S. Department of Education.

National Science Foundation. (1985, May 9). Federal academic R&D funds continue strong growth through 1983. *Science Resources Studies Highlights*. Washington, DC: Author.

Newman, F. (1987). *Choosing Quality: Reducing Conflict Between the State and the University*. Denver, CO: Education Commission of the States.

Organization for Economic Co-operation and Development. (1977). *Learning Opportunities for Adults, General Report*. (Vol. 1). Paris: Author.

Ottinger, C. A. (Comp.). (1984). *1984–1985 Fact Book:* New York: American Council on Education and Macmillan Publishing Company.

Project PACE, (1984). *Conditions of Education in California, 1984* (No. 84–1). Berkeley, CA: University of California.

Plisko, V. W., & Stern, J. D. (Eds.). (1985). *The Condition of Education, 1985 edition*. Washington, DC: National Center for Education Statistics.

Rudolph, F. (1962). *The American College and University*. New York: Alfred A. Knopf.

Statistics you can use: Growth in nontraditional students, 1972–1982. (1984, June 18). *Higher Education & National Affairs*, p. 3.

Stember, C. H. (1961). *Education and Attitude Change*. New York: Institute of Human Relations Press.

Stouffer, S. A. (1955). *Communism, Conformity and Civil Liberties*. Garden City, NY: Doubleday.

Trends in Student Aid: 1980 to 1986. (1986). Washington, DC: The College Board.

Trow, M. (1975, Winter). The public and private lives of higher education. *Daedalus*, 2, 113–127.

Trow, M. (1979). Aspects of diversity in American higher education. In H. Gans (Ed.). *On the Making of Americans: Essays in Honor of David Riesman* (pp. 271–290). Philadelphia, PA: University of Pennsylvania Press.

Trow, M. (1985a). Comparative reflections on leadership in higher education. *European Journal of Education*, 20, 143–159.

Trow, M. (1985b). Underprepared students and public research universities. In J. H. Bunzel (Ed.). *Challenge to American Schools* (pp. 191–215). New York and Oxford: Oxford University Press.

Trow, M. (1986). The state of higher education in the United States. In W. K. Cummings, E. R. Beauchamp, S. Ichikawa, V. N. Kobayashi, & M. Ushiogi (Eds.). *Educational Policies in Crisis: Japanese and American Perspectives* (pp. 171–194). New York: Praeger Publishers.

Tsukada, M. (1986). A factual overview of education in Japan and the United States. In W. K. Cummings, E. R. Beauchamp, S. Ichikawa, V. N. Kobayashi, & M. Ushiogi (Eds.). *Educational Policies in Crisis: Japanese and American Perspectives* (pp. 96–116). New York: Praeger Publishers.

Williams, G. (1983, November 18). Making sense of statistics. *The Times Higher Education Supplement*, p. 13.

THE WORLD TRANSFORMED: A GOLDEN AGE FOR AMERICAN UNIVERSITIES, 1945–1970

RICHARD M. FREELAND

In the years following World War II, academic leaders in Massachusetts participated in a national debate about the social role of higher education in the era that lay ahead. They also experienced the beginnings of a period of expansion for universities that would continue, more or less uninterrupted, for twenty-five years. Change in this postwar golden age involved an ongoing interaction between ideas and opportunities: the first concerning the public purposes of higher education; the second promising glory for institutions and advancement for academic interest groups. For most of the period, the dominant view—inside and outside of higher education—was that expansion was improving the academy as well as the country, but the turmoil of the late 1960s raised fundamental doubts about the character of postwar change.

Academic Ideas and Developmental Opportunities in the Postwar Years

Impact of World War II

Although World War II entailed difficulties for universities, their extensive involvement in the military effort stirred a new awareness of the social importance of academic work. This habit of thought extended into the postwar period, as educators, exhilarated by wartime patriotism, looked for new ways to contribute to social problem solving. As they did so, they exhibited a further effect of their recent experience: a tendency to focus on national concerns—as distinct from regional or local ones—far more intensively than they had done before 1940.

The country's agenda was long. The human costs of the war, and the even more-frightening possibility of atomic conflict, made the importance of maintaining peace evident. Europe had precipitated two wars in a generation and now lay in ruins. The United States, suddenly the preeminent power of the globe, would have to pioneer in shaping a stable world order. In some, the nation's new international prominence aroused a sense of urgency about discrimination and inequality at home. More broadly, world leadership implied a need to maintain military and economic power and the technological vitality on which they depended. Many educators believed they had important roles to play in all these contexts—through training leaders, forming attitudes, and advancing knowledge. As one college president put it: "Events . . . have shaken the complacency of many university communities and compelled educators to . . . make [their] maximum contribution to a decent, well-ordered, free and peaceful society."[1]

Belief in the importance of addressing social issues was paralleled among academics by conviction that their wartime activities would have a positive effect on attitudes toward higher education. Indeed, even as they struggled with war-related problems, many educators saw the crisis as a chance to prove the value of intellectual work to a skeptical society. Mindful of the financial pressures of the long pause, they anticipated stronger public support in the postwar period—and new opportunities to pursue developmental plans delayed by adverse circumstances.

The comment of M.S C.'s Baker was typical: "Out of the bitter struggle of war will come future demands for . . . greater opportunities for all people . . . The promise for state supported growth of colleges and universities . . . is great." The heightened expectations included hopes that the federal government, whose assistance had been vital during the Depression, would continue channeling resources toward academia. Carmichael of Tufts expressed this idea frequently. "It is possible," he wrote, that "patterns of connection between the government and the colleges now evolving as war expedients will allow the endowed educational institutions of the country to serve the nation's welfare in peacetime as well."

As the references to their particular types of universities in the comments of Baker and Carmichael implied, the prospect of new government aid raised important questions about what kinds of support might go to various campuses. The war created a new context for competition among universities even as it revealed new opportunities for public service.[2]

Two war-related federal programs were particularly important for higher education: during the conflict itself, the organization of scientists to develop military technology; in the latter years of the war and the early postwar period, the inclusion of educational entitlements among the benefits for veterans in the G.I. Bill. Both programs offered opportunities for individuals and campuses to contribute to the military effort. Both dramatized the significance of higher education for governmental officials, political and business leaders, and even the general public. Both revealed an awareness among educators of the advantages that could derive from participation in national programs.

The story of academic science during World War II began with the conviction among leading scientists and engineers, as the crisis developed in Europe, that their expertise was essential to the government's preparations for American involvement. One of these men, Vannevar Bush, president of the Carnegie Institution in Washington, persuaded President Roosevelt to charge a small group to plan for the mobilization of the nation's scientific capabilities. Roosevelt gave the job to Bush, who created the National Defense Research Committee. The N.D.R.C. quickly became the key link between the military hierarchy and academic science. As the nation's participation in the war intensified, the committee evolved into a new federal agency, the Office of Scientific Research and Development (O.S.R.D.). This organization was based on an important innovation in the relationship between the federal government and the scientific community. Rather than creating freestanding, government-managed research-and-development facilities, as had been done during World War I, Bush's group subcontracted specific projects to campus-based scientists, who continued to work in university laboratories. Using this system, Bush and his colleagues produced a series of technical achievements, the most spectacular of which was the atomic bomb, widely assigned a crucial role in the Allied military effort.[3]

So impressive was the record of O.S.R.D. that, as the war ended, Roosevelt asked Bush for an analysis of science's potential to contribute to national development in peacetime. Bush's 1945 report was a passionate statement of the role of scientific research in industry, defense, and medicine and of the importance of federal funds in guaranteeing the strength of science. The following year, President Truman appointed a cabinet-level committee, the President's Scientific Research Board, chaired by his close advisor John R. Steelman and including Bush himself, to consider the federal interest in scientific work. The board's report, published in 1947, affirmed Bush's views and recommended that "by 1957 we should be devoting at least one percent of our national income to research and development." The report also proposed a National Science Foundation to administer federal grants for basic research and urged the government to adopt O.S.R.D.'s practice of channeling support directly to university-based investigators.

In arguing that the nation had an interest in basic research, Bush was voicing ideas about science that academics like Compton and Conant had been advancing for years. In particular, the idea that the federal government should finance scientific work had been a prewar cause of Compton's, and he had used his platform as chair of the Science Advisory Board in the 1930s to promote ideas similar to those of the Scientific Research Board. In fact, Bush had been Compton's vice president before going to the Carnegie Institution, and the two shared an awareness of M.I.T.'s difficulties in obtaining financial support for research. Not surprisingly, therefore, both Bush and Compton were quick to see the possibilities of the war for demonstrating the importance of science and establishing a precedent for federal funding. As early as 1941, Compton wrote that "the military emergency is serving to bring educational staffs into closer contact with industry and . . . government" in a way that "presage[s] a new prosperity for science and engineering after the war."

Bush drew heavily on his former associates in the Cambridge scientific community, especially at M.I.T., to staff his wartime agency. Compton himself was one of the first men to join the Central Committee of the O.S.R.D. The group also included Frank Jewett, president of the National Academy of Sciences and of Bell Labs, member of the M.I.T. Corporation, and a close friend of Compton's who had actively supported the effort to strengthen science at M.I.T. during the 1930s. The fourth member of the Central Committee was Conant, and the fifth was Richard Tolman, an M.I.T. alumnus on the faculty of Cal Tech. The men brought in to staff the O.S.R.D. at the second and third levels further tightened the connection between Washington and Cambridge.[4]

The experience of the O.S.R.D.'s leaders in working for increased support for science during the prewar years and their perception of the potential significance of the war in advancing their cause inevitably affected their thinking about the operations of the wartime agency, including the all-important decision to award federal funds directly to campus-based scientists. In this context, the report of President Truman's Scientific Research Board should be seen not only as a general indication of the war's impact on science but also as a specific and aggressively pursued victory for Bush, Compton, and their colleagues. As the postwar era dawned, they had reason to hope that the federal government would become the adequate source for financing scientific work—and the development of academic institutions devoted to science—that for so long had eluded them.

The veterans' education program, like the O.S.R.D., was created by government officials to serve purposes related to the war, but like the scientific agency, it became a vehicle through which segments of the academic community advanced their own agenda—in this case, the expansion of educational opportunities. The fundamental purpose of the G.I. Bill was to help integrate returning soldiers into civilian life. Those planning for demobilization worried that problems would arise if large numbers of veterans sought jobs in an economy no longer stimulated by the war. Realizing that a program to encourage former soldiers to enter college would be helpful, they asked for assistance from the American Council on Education, headed by Dr. George Zook.

The A.C.E. recognized that any program of educational entitlements for servicemen would affect colleges even as it served the nonacademic purposes of the government. Most important, a veterans' program would boost enrollments decimated by the war. The idea raised, however, a number of long-term issues that proved divisive within the A.C.E. For example, the program had the potential to bring higher education within reach of many who could not previously afford college. For some, this was a welcome chance to open the academic gates. Included in this group was Zook himself, a New Deal liberal and former president of the University of Akron, who for years had advocated the use of public funds to expand access to higher education. Others, including Conant, believed that higher education should remain elite and favored a limited program for veterans.

The prospect of federal support for tuition also uncovered tensions between private and public institutions. The latter worried that reimbursing students for full costs would favor the former. In the end, the A.C.E. suggested compromises on all these issues, while presenting a united front on the question that concerned educators most: that the program preserve the independence of all academic institutions from federal control.

Although questions about the impact of the proposed veterans' program on academia were important to educators, who saw the entitlements as a precedent, such considerations were marginal for governmental planners as well as legislators. In testimony before Congress, the primary force behind the G.I. Bill was the American Legion, which wanted the broadest possible program for its constituents. It won benefits more generous than the compromise put forward by Zook's organization: support for one year of college for nearly all veterans with a year's service or less and a further year for each additional year served.

Throughout the deliberations, academics cast themselves as willing participants rather than lobbyists for an education bill. This stance, as well as the relative ease with which factions within the A. C. E reconciled their differences, reflected the fact that few regarded educational entitlements as a central element of the demobilization effort. Estimates of potential college attendance under the veteran's legislation ranged from one hundred fifty thousand to several hundred thousand per year, with total participation over the life of the program not likely to exceed seven hundred thousand. An activity on this scale, while helpful to universities and interesting as an experiment, was not likely to produce major change in higher education.[5]

The veterans surprised everyone and grasped the chance to attend college in totally unexpected numbers. For most of 1946, M.I.T. received four thousand applications per month—an extreme example of a common pattern. Between 1945 and 1949, about 2,200,000 former servicemen enrolled in college through the G.I. Bill, more than three times the maximum figure projected during the war. Sixty thousand former soldiers applied to Harvard alone. Educators responded with the spirit of patriotism—and gratitude—characteristic of the early postwar years. Conant told his Overseers: "The society of free men on this continent has another chance to realize its aspirations; the world has another chance to organize for peace. The youth of our country made this possible."

Although caught by surprise, educational leaders took every possible step to accommodate the demand. Enrollments at many institutions rose far beyond normal capacity. Special administrative and counseling mechanisms were created. Curricula were streamlined to help veterans complete their work rapidly. Year-round schedules were adopted, and graduation requirements were relaxed. Credit was awarded for work done in military service. Refresher courses and noncredit programs for poorly prepared veterans were implemented. It was an inspiring and generous time, providing a challenge that elicited from academics a maximum desire to adapt themselves and their institutions to the unusual needs of a special group.[6]

For educators like Zook, the enthusiasm of the veterans and the response of academics constituted a political bonanza. The popularity of higher education had been strengthened by the war; now it soared. A federally assisted effort to enlarge the educational system suddenly seemed possible. President Truman was, after all, seeking ways to extend the New Deal into new areas of domestic life. Eager to seize the moment, Zook persuaded the president to appoint a commission on the national interest in higher education—the first review of this subject ever ordered by a chief executive. Zook himself won appointment as chair, and most of the members shared his prospective.

The President's Commission on Higher Education was dominated by individuals from teaching and service-oriented public institutions and experimental private colleges with disciplinary backgrounds in education and in occupational and technical fields. The influence of the progressive education movement of the prewar years, with its emphasis on socially responsive schools, was clearly in evidence. Representatives of the academic establishment—people, like Conant, who were skeptical about Zook's democratizing agenda and who had resisted the idea of turning the veterans' program into a pilot project for it—were scarcely visible at the table. There were few commissioners with backgrounds in the arts and sciences or the elite professions, and none were from the nation's most distinguished universities, private or public, or the most prestigious colleges. The commission's report, issued in several volumes in late 1947 and early 1948, expressed the hopes of its constituency for a vastly expanded, socially engaged system of higher education, supported by an infusion of federal dollars. Specific recommendations included scholarships and direct aid to public institutions.[7]

The reports of the two presidential commissions of the early postwar years contained recommendations for national policy on issues that had preoccupied the academic community in the years before World War II. The President's Scientific Research Board was concerned with supporting research in science and technology as well as with graduate and professional education in scientifically oriented fields, matters of concern to men like Compton and Conant. The Zook commission focused on questions of interest to those—like Ell of Northeastern or Murlin of B.U.—who had fought to make higher education less oriented toward social elites, less dominated by tradition, and more concerned with the practical affairs of life. In proposing new federal programs to address these issues, the two commissions advocated sweeping changes, with highly unpredictable consequences, in the nation's institutions of higher education.

Both reports were bound to be controversial. They were issued, moreover, at a time when academics, inspired by the war and hopeful about new developmental opportunities, were already considering academia's postwar role. Many colleges and universities formed planning committees. States and educational associations established special commissions. The aggregate result was an intense and wide-ranging public debate. As the president of the Carnegie Foundation exclaimed in 1950: "At no time in the history of this country has there been so much ferment and stir about the ends and means of education." Competing opinions appeared in the pages of newspapers and popular journals. The recommendations of the presidential commissions provided a focus for much of this discussion.[8]

Among the many reactions to these two reports, none contained a more thoughtful or comprehensive alternative perspective than the work of the Commission on Financing Higher Education, jointly sponsored by the Rockefeller Foundation and the Association of American Universities. Officers of the foundation shared the view of many educators that the financial problems produced by the Depression—especially among endowed institutions—remained unaddressed. After a series of preliminary conferences with institutional leaders revealed not only continuing economic worries but also widespread discomfort with the recommendations of the two presidential commissions, the foundation decided to sponsor a broad examination of higher education, with particular reference to financial problems.

In contrast to the two governmental commissions, the Rockefeller group was dominated by representatives of leading private universities. It chair was Paul Buck, dean of Arts and Sciences at Harvard, and its membership included senior officers of Johns Hopkins, Cal Tech, Stanford, and Brown. In essence, the Rockefeller group was a vehicle through which academia's traditional elite responded to the reforming propositions of the two public bodies on the central issues facing higher education: who should go to college and for what? And how should graduate education and research be developed? In offering different answers to these questions, the three reports summarized much of the postwar debate. Moreover, they each addressed the most fundamental questions of all: what system of higher education would best serve the nation? And how should that system be organized and financed?[9]

Who Should Go to College and for What?

The most controversial recommendation of the Zook commission was that facilities for higher education should be enlarged so that, by 1960, 49 percent of the country's eighteen- to twenty-one-year-olds would receive at least two years of college, and 32 percent would attend for a full four years. Increased public expenditures, including the new program of federal scholarships, would subsidize the expansion. While arguing that these proposals were consistent with recent trends and responded to needs made clear by the veteran's program, the commission recognized that its ideas would appear revolutionary to many Americans. Less than 16 percent of the college-age population was receiving advanced education in 1940.

The commission justified its recommendations on two grounds. First, it pointed out that current enrollments were artificially depressed by nonacademic barriers, including finances, regional variations in opportunity, and discrimination against religious and racial groups, especially Negroes and Jews. These inequities, the commission argued, denied the nation the full talents of many citizens, were inconsistent with American ideals, and were intolerable at a time when democratic and totalitarian values battled for popular allegiance. The commission also criticized universities for focusing excessively on "verbal skills and intellectual interests" and for ignoring "many other aptitudes—such as social sensitivity and versatility, artistic ability, motor skills and dexterity, and mechanical aptitude and ingenuity." The commission's estimates of the numbers that could benefit from higher education assumed that programs would be developed for the wider range of talents that, in its view, should be cultivated. It recognized that "if these proportions of American youth are to be admitted to institutions of higher education, we shall have to provide a much greater variety of institutions than we now have to meet the needs."[10]

The Rockefeller report agreed that admission policies should be free of bias, and it joined the Zook commission in urging admission policies based on merit. It also acknowledged the "startling fact" that less than 50 percent of the most gifted young Americans attended any form of college, and it advocated an expansion of financial aid programs. Unlike the Zook commission, however, the Rockefeller group did not emphasize educational inequality as a major problem for academic institutions. It stressed that "colleges and universities are among the least discriminatory institutions in American society" and argued that the main difficulties lay in individual motivation, secondary schooling, and family finances. The Rockefeller group had little inclination to expand the interests and talents with which colleges were concerned. "The primary purpose of higher education," it observed, "is the development of . . . intellectual promise and . . . [the capacity to] deal with abstract ideas . . . and to reason . . . upon the basis of broad conceptual schemes." The Rockefeller report estimated that 25 percent of the population—half the figure suggested by the Zook commission—could profit from college and argued against educating a significantly enlarged proportion of young people. It opposed any federal scholarships beyond the veterans' program.[11]

At the heart of the differences between the two reports were divergent views about the implications of "democratic" values for higher education. For the Rockefeller group, there was no conflict between democracy and elitism. Admission procedures must be fair and accessible, but they could also be highly selective. The Zook commission was less ready to accept a system that limited its advantages to the few. In its view, democracy implied not only fairness of treatment but also equality of status for a wide range of abilities and fields.

The comments of academic leaders in Massachusetts typified the spectrum of campus-level responses to the Zook-Rockefeller debate. Conant, true to his prewar ideals, insisted with the Rockefeller group that the national interest required recognizing differences in individual ability. He wanted to make Harvard more, not less, exclusive in terms of academic standards, and he doubted the wisdom of conferring social status on an expanding set of "semiprofessional" occupations by requiring four or more years of postsecondary education not demanded by the fields themselves. In contrast, Marsh of B.U. and Ell of Northeastern, siding with Zook, argued that democratic admission policies implied opening their doors as widely as possible. Both thought their universities should embrace the changing requirements of employment markets by continuously developing new occupational programs.[12]

Liberal Education, General Education, and the Quest for Democratic Community

During the twenty years preceding World War II, one of the liveliest topics of academic discussion involved the educational consequences of the increased emphasis on science and the corresponding decline of the traditional curriculum. This change, some argued, had weakened attention to the development of character by making undergraduate work too intellectual and also had shattered the ability of college to transmit a common culture. Sectarian institutions, especially Catholic ones that had chosen to retain requirements in philosophy, theology, and ancient languages, had avoided curricular disintegration, but most American institutions could not rely on religious imperatives to achieve coherence or maintain values.

In the prewar years, these concerns gave rise to two broad movements to reform the curriculum. The first stressed exposure to the arts and sciences through required courses. Although it took many forms, this pattern was associated particularly with Columbia in the 1920s and the University of Chicago in the 1930s. The second movement emphasized the nonintellectual elements of undergraduate education: emotional capacity, physical health, and social skills. Initially conceived—for example, in the General College at the University of Minnesota—as an alternative to the liberal arts for students in two-year colleges, this movement influenced four-year institutions as well. It was especially evident in the development of guidance programs, residential facilities, and extracurricular activities. Both of the movements were referred to as "general education" at one time or another, though they were rooted in markedly different conceptions of the boundaries of academic work.[13]

Concern about the social contributions of higher education at the end of World War II introduced new intensity into the debate about general and liberal education. The Zook commission asserted that "liberal education has been splintered by overspecialization" and argued that "the failure to provide any core of unity in . . . higher education is a cause for grave concern." It concluded that "the crucial task of higher education today . . . is to provide a unified general education" that will transmit a "common cultural heritage towards a common citizenship." Zook and his associates recommended a series of goals for all college programs—including several concerned with family life, physical health, emotional adjustment, and ethical behavior—that aimed at both intellectual breadth and personal and social development.

The Rockefeller report also stressed the importance of shared goals for undergraduate learning, but it set much narrower limits on college curricula. Liberal education, the Rockefeller group argued, should seek "a quality of mind" by "liberat[ing] the spirit of man from superstition and ignorance while cultivating . . . enduring values and the capacity of discriminating judgment." The two committees agreed on the goals of undergraduate education but differed on the means. The Zook commission argued that socially constructive behavior should be taught directly by "redefining liberal education in terms of life's problems as men face them," while the Rockefeller report asserted that desirable personal qualities could best be nurtured indirectly, through studying the academic disciplines of the arts and sciences.[14]

Among many institution-based efforts to address the issues of common learning in the postwar years, the most conspicuous was the report of the Harvard Committee on General Education in a Free Society—frequently called the "Redbook" because of its crimson cover. The committee included humanists and social scientists and was charged by Conant and Buck to produce "a concept of general education that would have validity" not only at Harvard but also at colleges and schools throughout the country. Published in 1945, the Redbook argued that general education should "look first of all to [the student's] life as a responsible human being and citizen." Education must be concerned not only with imparting knowledge and skills but also with producing the "good man" and the "good citizen" by developing values, wisdom, a sense of cultural tradition, and the capacity for an emotional and gregarious life. The committee translated its formulations into concrete terms by proposing that Harvard create three required, interdisciplinary courses for undergraduates—one from each of the disciplinary divisions—to provide a shared body of knowledge and also design a series of upper-class electives infused with the spirit of general education. Conant hailed the document as "the dawn of a welcome day" in which colleges and universities could organize themselves to "both shape the future and secure the foundations of our free society."[15]

The Harvard Redbook found a wide readership and had a major impact on discussions of undergraduate curriculum reform. Its inspired defense of general education expressed the social idealism of the period. It applied the imprimatur of the nation's leading university to a cause hitherto considered marginal by most academics. In suggesting, moreover, that the ambitions and goals of general education could be achieved by restructuring traditional materials in a limited portion of the curriculum, the Harvard committee offered a middle course between broadening undergraduate studies to include nonacademic concerns—as the Zook commission would suggest—and standing pat with the traditional liberal arts—as the Rockefeller group would prefer.

Despite the eloquence and apparent practicality of the Redbook, events quickly demonstrated that the academic community would not agree on a single conception of general education. As many approaches to this issue were offered as there were faculties to debate it, and agreement proved elusive even with institutions. Sometimes, as in the famous programs at Harvard and Amherst College, general education courses were specifically designed as broad introductions to areas of knowledge. In other instances, general education more closely resembled a distribution requirement, and students simply chose from more or less standard disciplinary courses. Even at Harvard, the Faculty of Arts and Sciences was unable to overcome disciplinary boundaries and rejected the notion of a single basic course in the three areas of knowledge, voting instead to offer several options in each category. Tufts's Carmichael represented an extreme position. Intensely conscious, as a psychologist, of differences among students, he was fundamentally opposed to common requirements and preferred his institution's prewar emphasis on individually tailored programs.[16]

Beyond basic requirements, the general education movement provoked a wide variety of programmatic innovations in the late 1940s and early 1950s. Several institutions, including Harvard and Boston University, strengthened international coursework, as had been recommended by the Zook commission, to support the nation's new position of world leadership. A more controversial topic was religious studies. The Zook commission had not made reference to religious belief, and the Redbook explicitly rejected religion as a basis for infusing values or unity into undergraduate education. The advice naturally went unheeded in schools like B.C. and B.U. with strong religious traditions or church sponsorship, but even M.I.T. made new efforts to support the religious lives of students from different faiths. The strengthening of campus life offered another important context for general education. Marsh proposed a new student-faculty assembly to help train students in the workings of democracy. M.S.C. created programs in health and guidance to aid the maturation of the whole student.[17]

In the end, postwar debates on general education more clearly reflected diversity of perspective and cultural tradition than the new unity that Conant had welcomed so hopefully. Indeed, despite the tendency among academic leaders to explain their initiatives in terms of newly perceived national needs, the programs actually instituted, as well as the concerns that lay behind them, were remarkably continuous with patterns of development during the 1930s. With few exceptions, the atmosphere of the late 1940s impelled institutions and their leaders to redouble efforts along lines charted before World War II, and the Cold War infused them with a new sense of democratic urgency.

Research and Graduate Education for a Technological Age

The recommendation of the President's Scientific Research Board that the national government support research and graduate education presented the Rockefeller group with a dilemma. The panel's members agreed that universities could foster progress in defense, health, agriculture, and industry, and as officers of leading universities, they appreciated the benefits for higher education of federal funding. They were particularly enthusiastic about grants for basic research through a National Science Foundation, as distinct from the applied and development-oriented projects typically sponsored by the armed services.

The Rockefeller group believed, however, that the Scientific Research Board, composed largely of nonacademics, had failed to consider troubling questions. Some concerns involved matters of balance within and among academic institutions. What would be the impact on instruction of a sudden outpouring of money for research? Would support for natural science weaken general education, social science, and the humanities? On the other hand, if federal support were extended into the social sciences, would it not lead educators into controversial policy issues for which academic research could not produce definitive answers? There was also concern that the proposals would benefit some institutions more than others. What, for example, would the Scientific Research Board's program do for liberal arts colleges that did little research in natural science? Alternatively, was there not a danger that political pressures would force the government to distribute funds too widely, thus dooming the entire effort to mediocrity? Administrative issues lurked as well. By what criteria would government officials make awards? Would bureaucrats enforce an unwelcome uniformity or place unacceptable controls on the work they supported?[18]

As the Rockefeller group deliberated in the late 1940s, the burgeoning Cold War resulted in a continuing flow of federal funds for defense-related work, though in amounts much reduced from wartime levels. The Office of Naval Research played a particularly important role in this phenomenon. The need to write contracts gave academic leaders and government officials opportunities to resolve some of the administrative issues associated with the Scientific Research Board's recommendations. Design work on the National Science Foundation also proceeded during these years, and the enabling legislation, adopted in 1950, contained important protections for academic institutions, including peer review of requests for funding.

These developments relieved some of the anxieties of the Rockefeller group, but questions about the implications of federal aid remained. In its report, the panel took a middle position, endorsing the programs already in existence, including the National Science Foundation, but opposing any expansion. "Higher education . . . needs time," the group asserted, "to digest what it has already undertaken and to evaluate the full impact of what it is already doing under federal government assistance." It urged academic institutions to seek alternative sources of funding for postwar development.

As the ambivalent conclusions of the Rockefeller group implied, the lines of postwar debate were less starkly drawn on questions related to academic research than on enrollment policies and general education. This was not surprising, since most universities regarded teaching as their primary responsibility. The Zook commission and the Rockefeller group actually agreed on most issues in this area. In an atmosphere dominated by uncertainty about the impact of new federal action, individual institutions worked out policies according to the logic of their positions and their goals.[19]

The differing perspectives on government investment in science among academic leaders whose universities focused on research were illustrated by the views of Compton and Conant. Not surprisingly, given his history of advocacy, Compton embraced the opportunity to undertake federally assisted work. While he was eager to strengthen basic research, he stressed the country's need for help in defense and announced that M.I.T. would continue to manage large-scale military projects similar to those undertaken during the war. Conant was more wary. A fiscal conservative, he worried that acceptance of contract work would expose Harvard to financial risk. Governments were political bodies and policies could shift suddenly. Moreover, while Conant's wartime experience had increased his appreciation of applied work, he thought fundamental knowledge was the country's most pressing need. For these reasons, Conant barred Harvard from involvement in the large technical projects that Compton was ready to accept.

The two leaders also disagreed about classified work. Compton regarded secret research as undesirable in a university setting but unavoidable under conditions of the postwar years. Harvard adopted a general rule against research contracts under which results could not be published freely.

The contrasting attitudes of Conant and Compton expressed divergent institutional interests as well as alternative philosophies. Harvard was not oriented toward applied research, having reduced such activities during the Lowell years, and its scientists had little interest in projects that did not involve basic questions and the possibility of publication. M.I.T. retained a central focus on engineering, despite Compton's new emphasis on science. Harvard was, moreover, much richer than M.I.T., and its leaders could hope, in a way their Institute counterparts could not do, to accomplish their developmental goals through funding sources other than the national government. Finally, since science and technology had always been the Institute's central interests, leaders at M.I.T. were not worried about programmatic imbalances that might result from increased funding for those fields. Thus, the two leading universities in Massachusetts became prominent exponents of opposing positions on federal support: Conant's Harvard sought to limit reliance on government funds and to strengthen itself through other means; Compton's M.I.T. welcomed federal contracts as both duty and opportunity.[20]

Research was always linked to graduate and professional education. Interest in advanced training had been moderated during the decades prior to World War II by the same forces that had produced the general education movement, but the postwar atmosphere put graduate studies high on the academic agenda. Bush pointed out in his 1945 report, for example, that the development of science required not only support for current work but also the training of future scholars. Conant suggested limiting federal financial aid to graduate students in a handful of scientific and medical fields. There was even talk at M.I.T. of abandoning undergraduate education to concentrate on graduate training. The issue was broader than science, however, since the war had demonstrated the importance of specialists in a variety of academic, technical, and managerial fields. Both the Zook commission and the Rockefeller group wanted to increase the supply of professionals.[21]

Two major questions were raised about graduate education in the early postwar years. One was advanced by the Zook commission, which criticized universities for past tendencies to stress specialized academic studies rather than fields of national need. Pointing out that most holders of Ph.D.s spent their lives doing something other than scholarly research, the commission advocated programs for teaching and nonacademic careers. A second concern involved the potential for graduate education to reduce attention to undergraduate teaching. This issue was repeatedly introduced in faculty discussions at M.I.T. in response to Compton's proposals to strengthen graduate education and research. Compton's response provided a model for advocates of advanced work at all institutions: graduate and undergraduate education, like teaching and research, were mutually reinforcing, not conflicting, priorities. A heightened effort in graduate work, he claimed, would inevitably enrich the educational environment for undergraduates.[22]

University and Society: Academic Values, Institutional Diversity, and Interinstitutional Competition

Debates of the late 1940s on questions ranging from enrollment policy to curriculum change to research often turned on underlying disagreements about the social functions of universities. At the same time, the thoughts of academics on social issues were affected by the possibility that the federal government might channel large sums toward their institutions precisely because they could assist in solving national problems. The contrasting perspectives of the two presidential committees—the Zook commission and the President's Scientific Research Board—and the Rockefeller group illustrated the complex interplay within the institutional complex of academic ideas and interinstitutional competition for support.

The presidential commissions began with a common charge: to identify ways in which colleges and universities could meet national needs. The members of the President's Scientific Research Board, all government officials, were asked to consider how scholarly expertise could foster technological progress. The task given Zook and his colleagues was broader: to examine the "objectives, methods, and facilities [of higher education] . . . in light of the social role it has to play." The commission responded with a statement of fundamental assumptions:

> The social role of education in a democratic society, is at once to ensure equal liberty and equal opportunity . . . and to enable the citizens to understand, appraise and redirect forces, men and events as these tend to strengthen or to weaken their liberties. In performing this role education will . . . [be most successful] if its programs and policies grow out of and are relevant to the characteristics and needs of contemporary society. Effective democratic education will deal directly with current problems.

Did the society need more trained people in occupational fields? Higher education should add the necessary programs. Did the country face social problems ranging from racial prejudice to poverty to troubled families? Academic institutions should alter their curricula to address such questions. Did technical problems need to be solved? Academia should put its shoulder to the wheel. The country needed scholars with "a passionate concern for human betterment, for the improvement of social conditions and of relations among men" who could "apply at the point of social action what the social scientists had discovered regarding the laws of human behavior."[23]

In viewing universities as social agencies that should assume whatever functions they could usefully undertake, the Zook commission was drawing on educational ideas with deep roots. Academic institutions typically grew out of the religious, economic, or social purposes of particular communities, and continuing ties to external groups perpetuated their concern with nonacademic issues. Other patterns reinforced the social involvement of universities. One was the rise of public service during the second half of the nineteenth century. A second was the spread, during the same period, of career-oriented programs. The clearest expression of the social theme was the development of state universities and land grant colleges with their central commitment to promoting economic progress.

Other strands of academic tradition, however, pulled educators in a different direction. American universities inherited from their European antecedents an impulse toward self-regulation and separation from the outside world rooted in the medieval church. In modern times, the desire for autonomy was strengthened by Germanic ideas about academic freedom. From these perspectives, universities were best understood not as creatures of society but as independent entities dedicated to transcendent goals like "truth" and "knowledge." So conceived, they should not constantly adapt to social needs. Indeed, the evolution of universities in the United States fostered an association between academic autonomy and scholarly achievement, since the most prestigious institutions were those with a high degree of independence from external, nonacademic control.

Contending perceptions of the proper relationship between universities and external communities had turned the nation's academic history into an ongoing saga of battles between "insiders" and "outsiders." The rise of professionalism in the late nineteenth century was only one example of a phenomenon that began with disputes between Puritan governors and Harvard scholars in seventeenth-century Cambridge. The academic debates of the late 1940s made it clear that the postwar period would be an important new chapter in this ancient story.

Many educators were appalled by the views of the Zook commission. The members of the Rockefeller group, for example, stressed limits on the social involvements of academic institutions. Their report began not with an analysis of contemporary concerns but with an explication of academic traditions. It identified four functions of universities and colleges: liberal education, professional education, graduate education and research, and public service. Of these, public service, direct efforts to address social problems, was accorded least emphasis. Higher education's primary response to societal needs, in the view of the Rockefeller group, should be to "contribute the trained experts, the scholars, and the leaders" who could work on these issues. The Rockefeller report affirmed many characteristics of higher education that the Zook commission attacked: its relative exclusivity, its emphasis on the development of individuals, and its focus on specialized knowledge. The report resisted the notion that major change was needed. "What higher education has been doing," the group argued, "must still be done."[24]

It would be a mistake, however, to draw the lines between the Zook commission and the Rockefeller group too sharply. Zook and his associates respected academic freedom, pure scholarship, and liberal learning. The Rockefeller report praised public service and urged colleges to help individuals become citizens. Both acknowledged that historical conditions had produced many kinds of academic institutions in the United States. Indeed, both reports saw this diversity as the special genius of American higher education, a clear difference from the centralized national systems of Europe. Both linked diversity with democracy and stressed that federal policy must protect this aspect of academia. The Zook commission advocated federal support to promote diversity, but the Rockefeller group felt that government involvement would threaten diversity by concentrating influence in Washington.[25]

The philosophical disagreements between the Zook commission and the Rockefeller group could not be separated from the financial interests of their respective constituencies. The institutions represented on Zook's panel were likely to benefit from extensive federal involvement in higher education. For example, the funding of scholarships for large numbers of Americans not previously equipped, financially or academically, to attend college was bound to strengthen enrollments at the nonelite, practically oriented institutions that dominated this commission. On the other hand, the Rockefeller group's conservative estimates of the numbers of Americans who could profit from college were a logically essential element of their effort to demonstrate the viability of a system heavily dependent on private support.

The Zook commission's recommendation that institutional aid be granted only to public institutions would produce a windfall for a sector of the academic community with which it was strongly aligned. This possibility was bound to frighten the establishment figures on the Rockefeller group, since it would shift the balance of academic power against private schools. Even proposals that would allow everyone to benefit, such as the call for research aid by the President's Scientific Research Board, were worrisome to the authors of the Rockefeller report, since the long-term pressures of politics on any governmental program would diffuse funds widely among regions and campuses, inevitably weakening the positions of well-established universities. At the same time, such institutions were likely to prosper if nongovernmental sources of funding continued to be dominant, as the Rockefeller panel urged, since they possessed the strongest ties to philanthropists, foundations, alumni/ae groups, and private industry.

The impact of the Zook commission's recommendations and the Rockefeller report, as well as of the numerous other studies and statements produced during the postwar years, is hard to measure. These documents clearly affected academic debates at the campus level, but government response was thin. The National Science Foundation was one specific outcome, and some federal funding for research and technology-based development continued to flow. No legislation, however, was proposed or enacted based on the recommendations of the Zook commission. At a minimum, these debates on the functions and values of higher education documented the concerns of a generation of educators on the eve of the greatest period of academic development in the nation's history. In terms of the institutional complex, they provided benchmark statements of academic ideas against which observers of a later time could assess postwar change.[26]

The Three Revolutions: Enrollments, Finances, and Faculty

During the 1950s and 1960s, the traditional scramble for resources as well as the balance of academic power underwent striking transformations. Both students and dollars, which had been in short supply between 1930 and 1945, became much easier to acquire as young people applied to college in greatly increased numbers and financial support from a variety of sources became available at levels unimaginable before World War II. As institutions grew in response to the new conditions, demand for faculty—the third key resource for universities—intensified. This phenomenon greatly improved the historically weak organizational position of the professoriate. Other factors, especially the rise of government-funded research, further empowered professional scholars. Thus, as educational leaders considered the debates of the late 1940s in relation to their own institutions, they confronted changes in the context of interinstitutional competition for resources and shifts in the relative power of subgroups within campus communities.

The Revolution in Patterns of College Attendance

The question of who should go to college, so intensely discussed in the postwar years, was only partially susceptible to the determinations of educational leaders. They could urge governments to encourage or limit attendance. They could make admission policies receptive or restrictive. But the disposition of potential students to apply or not to apply, the capacities of families to support their children's educations, and the reactions of politicians to public pressures to expand educational opportunities were important and uncontrollable factors in the equation. The response of the veterans to the G.I. Bill demonstrated how widely actual conditions could diverge from prior expectations. The educators of the postwar years knew all this, and, even as they argued about who *should* go to college, they wondered who *would* do so.

Uncertainty about enrollments after the servicemen completed their studies dominated the late 1940s and early 1950s. Some, like Conant and Baker, argued that the veterans' program had introduced higher education to a new group of Americans who could not have afforded college before the war and that demand from younger siblings and friends of the former soldiers would generate continuing growth. Others, like Ell, remembered the falling birthrates of the 1930s and regarded the postwar expansion as a temporary aberration. In 1947, the United States Office of Education issued a report leaning toward Ell's side of the argument: national enrollments would peak at about 3.3 million in the late 1940s, the U.S.O.E. projected, and then would decline toward about 3 million, at which level they would remain for a decade.[27]

Difficulties in predicting enrollment trends were compounded by uncertainty about federal policies. The Zook commission's recommendations for federal scholarships and institutional aid resulted in several years of fruitless debate and anticipation. During these same years, the nation's continuing need for military manpower posed new threats to enrollments. Discussions of peacetime conscription, like wartime planning for veterans' benefits, did not focus on education, but academic leaders had to consider the impact of legislation in this area on their institutions.

The crucial question was whether students would be allowed to defer military service to complete their studies. Some, like Conant and the A.A.U., opposed deferments as fundamentally unfair; this position was strongest, however, among academics whose institutions were not worried about enrollments. Most educational leaders favored deferments, and the A.C.E. lobbied vigorously to obtain them. Their success led Conant to comment derisively on a draft policy "designed to keep the colleges full of students." The new selective-service law was a victory of sorts for academia, but the outbreak of the Korean war in 1950, followed by federal legislation extending the G.I. Bill to veterans of the new conflict, created additional uncertainties about enrollments.[28]

While various federal proposals were alternately promising prosperity or disaster, academics were learning firsthand about educational demand in the wake of the veterans' program. Enrollments of ex-servicemen rose to 1.1 million in the fall of 1947, then dropped to less than 400,000 by 1951. Despite this reduction, total enrollments increased in 1948 and 1949, lending support to the view that postwar trends would not follow the patterns anticipated in the late 1930s. When enrollments did fall in 1950 and again in 1951, many observers thought the long-anticipated decline associated with the end of the veterans' subsidy was arriving. But in 1952, the numbers turned upward, confounding the expectations of planners yet again. Additional confusion arose from the differential impact on institutions of postwar shifts in student demand. The bulk of the post-veterans' growth occurred in the public sector, while many private universities experienced a decline in applications.[29]

The atmosphere of uncertainty about long-term demand for higher education began to change in the early 1950s. Ralph Van Meter, Baker's successor as president of M.S.C., renamed the University of Massachusetts in 1947, was among the first to identify the new situation. "It appears certain," he wrote in the fall of 1951, "that pressure for admission will increase sharply in the last part of the decade." Tying together the increased birthrates that began in the early 1940s and the higher rates of attendance of the late 1940s, Van Meter argued that applications would overwhelm academic facilities by the 1960s. After 1952, national enrollment statistics lent support to Van Meter's contention that a basic change had occurred in the percentage of young Americans wishing to attend college. The upturn in enrollments of that year initiated a new pattern of steady expansion at a time when the impact of high birthrates during the 1940s was still years away. Between 1952 and 1960, the number of young Americans enrolling in college increased from 2.1 million to 3.6 million, while the proportion attending rose from 14 percent to 22 percent.

By the mid-1950s, there was a consensus among academics that higher education faced fundamentally new conditions. In 1955, the American Association of Collegiate Registrars and Admissions Officers issued a report called "The Impending Tidal Wave of Students." A year later, President Eisenhower's Committee on Education Beyond the High School gave even more visible attention to the issue. The expansion was going to be rapid and sustained. Both the Association of Registrars and the president's committee estimated that by 1970 colleges and universities would be enrolling triple their current numbers. The new projections radically altered the focus of academic planning. Leaders stopped worrying about maintaining their institutions in uncertain times and concentrated on ensuring adequate places—and appropriately trained faculty—to accommodate the expanded applicant population that would appear after 1960.[30]

Several analyses were offered to explain the increased interest in college. To a substantial degree, the pattern continued a trend dating from the nineteenth century, but World War II seemed to have changed the country in basic ways. The Zook commission, though much criticized, appeared to have anticipated accurately a new impatience with restrictions on social mobility and with privileges based on class and race. Men from all social groups had died in battle, and Nazi Germany had made clear where racial prejudice could lead. The accomplishments of expatriate Jews were dramatizing the blindness of bigotry, not least within higher education.

Institutions, also affected by the democratic emotions of the war, actively encouraged applicants from all segments of society. The veterans' program not only stirred an appetite for higher education among new groups, but also engendered an appreciation among academics of admission policies based on merit rather than family history. Moreover, the increasingly technical and bureaucratic character of industry, combined with the interest of employers in applicants with formal training and credentials, was convincing young Americans that college was an economic necessity. At the same time, an unprecedented prosperity, which began almost immediately after the war, brought college within reach of many more Americans than had been the case in the 1930s.[31]

The long-anticipated "tidal wave" of applications for college admission arrived as predicted in 1960, and the nation's system of higher education expanded to accommodate it. During the following decade, college and university enrollments grew from 3.6 million to 7.9 million, and the proportion of the nation's youth attending college—32 percent in 1970—came to approximate the figure that the Zook commission, to the distress of many academics, had advocated. The number of colleges and universities jumped by a third during the 1960s, while average institutional size tripled. The expansion occurred in every region and among all types of institutions, though the shift in enrollments from private to public institutions that began right after the war continued. In 1950, about 50 percent of the college population was attending a publicly supported campus; by 1960 the figure had grown to 59 percent; and by 1970, to 73 percent.[32]

Not everyone was enthusiastic about the growth in numbers of those seeking higher education, as would be expected from the debates on enrollment policy of the early postwar years. John Gardner, president of the Carnegie Corporation, expressed the doubts of many as the momentum of expansion was building in the 1950s:

> We send great numbers of our youth on to college without any clear notion of what they will get out of it, but simply in pursuance of a vague notion that "college is an opportunity that should not be denied them." This makes no sense at all.[33]

Such reservations, however, counted for little in the rush of postwar development. During the 1950s and 1960s, with only passing attention given to the issues raised by Gardner and others, educators and political leaders, responding to overwhelming public pressures, concentrated on building the world's first system of mass higher education. The task of evaluating this phenomenon would be the work of another time.

The Revolution in Financial Support

Postwar change in the financial circumstances of higher education was even more dramatic and less expected than the new patterns of college attendance. In the late 1940s, as educators considered the enlarged social role they hoped to play, the most worrisome obstacles were economic. Inflation was making it difficult to maintain the activities established before 1940. Faculty salaries, which had made little progress during the Depression and war, were losing ground in comparison to those of doctors, dentists, and lawyers. Higher costs compounded long-neglected problems of maintenance and rendered new construction especially difficult. The authors of the Rockefeller report summarized the situation in 1952: "The educational administrators of our day are so preoccupied with the effort to protect the educational achievements of the past . . . that they can give little attention to educational advancement." One question haunted all discussions of new academic possibilities in the early postwar years: who would pay the bill?[34]

The economic position of higher education was illustrated by the nation's wealthiest institutions: endowed, private universities. These schools historically had depended on private philanthropy, but this income source was becoming less reliable. Endowment income, which provided 30 percent of the revenues of private universities in 1930, contributed only 16 percent in 1950. Several factors explained the change, including reduced returns on investment since 1929, lower rates of giving resulting from the progressive income tax as well as the Depression and war, and postwar enrollment expansion that outstripped investment growth.

Institutional leaders hoped to offset some of the loss through annual fund drives, especially campaigns oriented toward alumni/ae, a technique that few universities had exploited systematically before the war. There was little reason to believe, however, that annual giving, which historically had contributed less than 10 percent of current income, could make up for a continued erosion of endowments. A 1947 report sponsored by the Rockefeller Foundation noted that academics felt "bewilderment and doubt about the appropriate solution" to the loss of support from investments.

The severity of the situation varied among institutions. At Harvard, with the largest endowment in the country, the importance of fund income declined only moderately between 1930 and 1950. Still, Conant told the Corporation that additional funds would be needed to make any new ventures possible. At Tufts, with its modest financial base, the change was more severe, and Carmichael identified the weakness of endowments as his institution's most urgent problem. Compton observed that M.I.T. needed new capital comparable in significance to the gift from George Eastman in 1912 that had financed the Cambridge campus. All these presidents were convinced, moreover, that no conceivable program of private giving would be adequate to sustain research programs at needed levels, especially in the physical sciences. In this area, a federal program of the type proposed by Bush and the President's Scientific Research Board seemed essential. Even Conant moved toward this position, albeit reluctantly.[35]

As endowments declined in significance, payments from students became more important. Private university income from tuition and fees increased as a proportion of total income from 56 percent in 1940 to 65 percent in 1950. Some of this change was merely the mirror image of reduced contributions from investments. The major explanation, however, was the expansion of enrollments, coupled with increases in tuition. The enlarged role of tuition and fees was problematic for several reasons. Since it resulted partly from higher prices, it represented a trend that could restrict access to college and also limit the student market. If inflation in the general economy continued, moreover, it was doubtful that prices could be pushed higher, even though costs would climb. Finally, the association of higher revenues from students and enrollment growth linked budgets to a source that most educators considered highly uncertain. These concerns were particularly pertinent at institutions where traditions of philanthropic support were strong and where revenues from expanded enrollments held the key to institutional development.[36]

While both philanthropy and student payments seemed unreliable in the late 1940s, government support appeared likely to increase in scale and importance. Publicly supported institutions were less vulnerable to economic pressures between 1930 and 1945 than their private counterparts. Indeed, during years when most private universities were neglecting facilities and postponing new construction, state universities experienced a building boom. The value of the physical plant at public institutions doubled during the 1930s and doubled again in the 1940s, a result of New Deal public works programs and postwar financial surpluses of state governments. Moreover, state appropriations for academic institutions grew slightly during the 1930s and rapidly during the 1940s. In the early postwar years, state universities experienced growth in total appropriations and in support per student, while private universities faced declining per-student income. There were differences from state to state, but even in Massachusetts, with its tradition of low support for public higher education, the late 1940s were years of enlarged government funding.

The strength of state appropriations at a time of financial uncertainty for their own campuses aroused fears among leaders of independent institutions that the balance of power between the two sectors was shifting permanently. Compton noted that the financial situation "threatens the continued leadership and even the continued relative effectiveness of privately supported institutions," and he emphasized the need to position M.I.T. securely in an educational world dominated by state schools. Public educators were, indeed, optimistic about the future in the early postwar years, though they had worries of their own. They were particularly concerned that, over time, political pressures would push up enrollments more rapidly than appropriations, a pattern illustrated by the experience of Massachusetts State in the 1930s. They also shared their private counterparts' apprehensions about inflation, increased dependence on student payments, and even endowments, which were important at a number of public campuses.[37]

The first and most important indication that the postwar economic position of higher education was going to be radically different from what most educators of the late 1940s anticipated came from innovations in federal policy. As so often had been the case, the change stemmed not from increased appreciation of the inherent value of academic work but from the perception that colleges and universities could serve a nonacademic purpose.

In the early 1950s, the decisive developments were the Cold War and the Korean conflict, which generated support for applied, defense-related research-and-development projects. For several years in the 1950s, federal funding for university-based research, both basic and applied, grew incrementally to a total of $169 million in 1955. Then, in 1957, the Soviet launching of *Sputnik I* created the shocked impression that America was falling behind Russia in science. Government support for academic work jumped quickly to $356 million in 1959. For the next decade, federal aid grew steadily, reaching close to $2 billion by 1968. In the mid-1960s, the federal government accounted for more than 70 percent of all separately budgeted, university-based research support.

Throughout the period, defense-related work was a mainstay of government spending. Within this context, however, aid for basic work grew more prominent, effectively realizing Bush's vision of universities as the nations' primary resource for scientific progress. During the mid-1960s, federal support also broadened into new areas. As domestic policy issues moved to the top of the political agenda, research allocations from the domestic departments of government—especially Health, Education and Welfare—became more important. The government also created two new funds, paralleling the N.S.F., to support the arts and humanities. The direct impact of all this spending on academia was, however, highly concentrated. During the 1960s, ten institutions—Harvard and M.I.T. among them—received approximately 30 percent of all research support, and twenty institutions received between 45 and 50 percent. There was little movement in and out of this select group.[38]

Research was not the only area where federal policies had a major effect on academia. In the immediate postwar years, in fact, educators were as concerned with student aid and direct institutional support as with research, though the Zook commission's proposals in these areas were not enacted. Discussions of federal action to expand the nation's academic system were kept alive, however, by the prospect of the tidal wave of students projected for the 1960s, and in 1957, President Eisenhower's Committee on Education Beyond the High School recommended a comprehensive program, including support for facilities construction, student aid, and institutional grants.

The *Sputnik I* crisis finally created a political environment in which an enlarged federal role was viable. The first significant legislation was the National Defense Education Act of 1958, establishing scholarships and fellowships, together with aid for new programs in specified fields. Additional training programs were created in the National Institutes of Health, the Atomic Energy Commission, and the National Science Foundation. After 1960, as higher education became a concern of social policy as well as national security, federal programs came rapidly. Bills were enacted to support campus building, expand educational opportunities in the health professions, strengthen the study of other countries and foreign languages, and increase aid to students from low-income backgrounds. Support for educational programs through the three endowments was expanded. A new G.I. Bill for veterans plus amendments to the Social Security Act provided additional sources of financial aid.[39]

By the late 1960s, Congress had created an array of programs that channeled money toward academia, although no overall national policy with respect to higher education had been formulated. There were, however, some general trends. The most important was that nonresearch support was directed largely to student aid, some granted directly to individuals and some administered by institutions. By 1968, student aid programs equaled sponsored research in total dollar support, and these two areas accounted for two-thirds of the federal budget for higher education. The largest part of the remaining third paid for facilities and equipment, while only 10 percent supported educational programs. During the 1960s, moreover, student aid was increasingly concerned with ensuring access to college, and financial need became a dominant consideration in determining eligibility for federal support.

Overshadowing particular programs and legislative patterns was the aggregate effect of federal funding during the 1950s and 1960s. Prior to World War II, revenue from federal sources was a negligible part of the current income of the country's private institutions of higher education—less than 1 percent in 1940; by 1970, the national government was providing nearly 23 percent of the operating funds of these schools. The change for public campuses was less pronounced but still substantial: from 10 percent of current funds in 1940 to 17 percent in 1970.[40]

Federal support was not the whole story of the postwar revolution in the economics of higher education. As public systems expanded to absorb increased enrollments, state allocations also grew markedly, rising from $492 million in 1950 to $5.8 billion in 1970, a gain of over 1,000 percent. At the same time, a strong economy and sustained public support enabled institutions to mount fundraising campaigns for amounts that could not have been imagined before 1940. Much of the money came from traditional sources—alumni/ae, private individuals, and foundations, but new tax incentives prompted corporations to greatly expand their donations to academia. Between 1950 and 1970, voluntary annual giving from all these sources increased by 675 percent, from $240 million to $1.86 billion. In addition, with demand for college places intense and family income growing, colleges and universities increased tuition charges rapidly, vastly expanding revenue from this historic source.

Annual receipts from students rose by over 1,000 percent in twenty years, from $395 million in 1950 to $4.4 billion in 1970.[41]

Educators had difficulty grasping the significance and scale of the new financial environment, but the basic story was evident in the summary numbers. Aggregate spending by all institutions of higher education rose from $2.2 billion in 1950 to $21 billion by 1970. This golden age of financial support, when funding could be found for almost any worthwhile educational proposal, stood in stark contrast to the gloomy expectations of educators in the early postwar years and to the difficult realities of the long pause. A single comparison highlighted the change. Between 1930 and 1950 institutional expenditures per student had risen somewhat more slowly than per capita G.N.P. During the next two decades, the relationship was reversed with a vengeance as academia's outlays increased at more than double the rate of national productivity.[42]

The Triumph of the Professoriate

The perception of the mid-1950s that academia was approaching a period of expansion generated widespread concern about faculty shortages. Estimates of new Ph.D.s that would be needed varied with enrollment projections, but no one disputed the basic problem. An influential report in 1955 by the Ford-sponsored Committee of Fifteen summarized the situation as follows:

> . . . between now and 1970 about 135,000 doctorates will be awarded . . . Even if all these new Ph.D.s were to become teachers, we would, by 1970, need approximately 350,000 more college teachers than we shall probably train in our doctoral programs . . . To expect that by 1970 the proportion of college teachers holding the Ph.D. degree will have declined from the present 40 percent to 20 percent is not statistical hysteria but grassroots arithmetic.

President Eisenhower's Committee on Education Beyond the High School incorporated a similarly alarming appraisal in its 1957 report.

As higher education grew in the late 1950s, the Ph.D. shortage seemed to materialize. Biennial surveys by the National Education Association reported that the proportion of doctorates joining faculties of four-year colleges and universities was well below the 40 percent baseline identified by the Committee of Fifteen. These reports encouraged a conventional wisdom that the mismatch between supply and demand was producing a deterioration of faculty quality. This perception, in turn, moved educators to focus on raising salaries to attract talent. The president's 1957 committee noted that the economic circumstances of faculty had eroded in recent decades and urged a doubling of salaries over a five- to ten-year period. Fearful of competition for professors and aided by an improved financial environment, institutional leaders made salary enhancement a priority.

Nathan Pusey, Conant's successor at Harvard, exemplified the attitudes of the time. Pusey was conscious that Harvard traditionally had set national standards for faculty pay, and he recognized a threat from rapidly growing and well-financed universities in other regions. Improving salaries became the central goal of his presidency. Nationally, faculties achieved their prewar purchasing power by 1958. For the next ten years, real income grew steadily as pay rose at rates well above inflation. Working conditions got better in other ways as well: fringe benefits were expanded, support staff and facilities were improved, and teaching loads were reduced.[43]

The actual expansion of college faculties between 1955 and 1970 approximated the predictions of the Committee of Fifteen, increasing from two hundred thousand in 1952–1953 to five hundred thousand by 1970. The Ph.D. shortage, however, turned out to have been a false alarm—at least in terms of formal credentials and aggregate numbers. Existing graduate programs expanded, and additional institutions moved into doctoral-level education. Between 1948 and 1969, annual production of Ph.D.s increased from about four thousand to over twenty-six thousand. As a result, the proportion of terminally trained faculty at four-year colleges and universities actually increased somewhat across the period. A number of factors explained the new attractiveness of professorial careers, including improved material rewards, the high status of academia during the 1950s and 1960s, and the social idealism of college graduates. The true situation became clear only in retrospect, however, and the perceived shortage of teachers dominated discussions of graduate education into the late 1960s. Such perceptions were encouraged by the limited availability of highly talented scholars and the increased number of campuses trying to attract them. Competition in the top layer of academia bid up compensation levels for the entire professorate.[44]

The position of college faculties was further strengthened, both economically and politically, by the growth of support for scholarly work from noninstitutional sources, especially the federal government. The new dollars were, of course, part of the general prosperity that supported better pay and conditions. Equally significant was the fact that faculty were able to obtain funds as direct grants to themselves. As Carl Kaysen put it, this development "had the effect of supporting the community of professionals—the professor and his peers—as against the power of the educational institution and its administrators." Indeed, a faculty member able to win outside funding not only achieved a measure of independence but also became a source of institutional income. With academic jobs plentiful, scholars gained a major advantage in negotiating terms of employment—and in asserting other interests.[45]

The position of faculties was enhanced also by the increased emphasis on research that flowed from federal policies. In the 1950s and 1960s, American scholars, especially scientists, achieved the international eminence Conant and Compton had envisioned twenty years earlier. The graduate school replaced the college as the most important component of many universities, and research productivity became a vital measure of institutional standing. In this context, well-known scholars became increasingly valuable contributors to campus reputations, and judgments about research carried greater weight in decisions on hiring and promotion. Moreover, the trend toward ever more sophisticated and specialized research, already a source of professional power in the late nineteenth century, continued to erode the capacity of administrators to evaluate specific research achievements. In combination, these facts shifted power in matters of academic personnel toward the faculty.

The circumstances of the postwar decades spawned an era of professional ascendancy that involved much more than improved working conditions. The discipline-oriented professional associations that were formed in the late nineteenth and early twentieth centuries flourished as never before. Their memberships increased along with their influence. Part of their new strength resulted directly from academia's growth. As large numbers of Ph.D.s joined new or expanding institutions, often in remote locations, the disciplinary societies provided them with crucial links to others in their fields. The new emphasis on research reinforced this phenomenon.

As faculty members became more specialized, they were more likely to find colleagues with common interests in professional groups than on their own campuses. Institutions also came to rely on scholarly associations in new ways. For example, universities planning Ph.D. programs turned to them for guidance and sometimes for formal accreditation, just as administrators used them to assess faculty scholarship. As learned societies achieved greater authority, activity within them—service on committees and election to key offices—became important measures of scholarly standing.

The associations also influenced national policy. This was especially true outside the hard sciences, which were well established in Washington by the end of World War II. Social science organizations lobbied for research support for their fields and for protecting funded projects from political control. The American Council of Learned Societies was influential in promoting the National Endowment for the Humanities.[46]

The expanded role of the professional societies on matters of interest to specific disciplines proceeded in tandem with a more assertive stance by the American Association of University Professors on matters of general policy. The A.A.U.P. was especially concerned with issues of compensation and scholarly autonomy. Its decision in the 1950s to publish information on salaries at individual campuses promoted interinstitutional competition in faculty pay.

Even more important were the A.A.U.P.'s guidelines on the standing and treatment of faculties. The most fundamental of these was the 1940 Statement of Principles on Academic Freedom and Tenure. This document not only asserted the central importance of academic freedom but also argued that tenure was its indispensable adjunct and that clearly stated norms and procedures were vital in matters of academic personnel. In subsequent years, these guidelines were supplemented by others, including the 1958 Statement on Procedural Standards in Faculty Dismissal Proceedings, the 1961 Statement on Recruitment and Resignation of Faculty Members, and the 1964 Statement on Standards for Notice of Nonreappointment. In combination, these A.A.U.P. policies provided the basis for investigations by the association of complaints by aggrieved faculty members against their institutions, actions that occasionally led to formal censure. The guidelines also emboldened faculties on individual campuses to advocate change in local policies.[47]

The new power of faculties, both substantive and political, transformed the manner in which academic decisions were made at the campus level. Bolstered by A.A.U.P. guidelines, faculties at universities in Massachusetts worked to replace the administrative discretion common in the prewar decades by formal statements of faculty rights, including rules, procedures, and criteria. At Boston University, the first published statement of academic personnel policy was issued in 1946. Revisions of this document during the 1950s and 1960s steadily expanded faculty prerogatives and protections. At less-developed institutions, the process progressed more slowly. The Northeastern faculty did not establish an A.A.U.P. chapter until Ell retired in 1959. The first formal statement of personnel policy came shortly thereafter, as did a conventional tenure system. By 1970, however, with some local variation, especially at Harvard, codified rules governing personnel decisions were the norm at universities in Massachusetts.[48]

As in the late nineteenth century, the expanded role of professional societies developed simultaneously with enhanced power for academic departments. Here, again, the most dramatic shifts involved academic personnel decisions, where departments and faculties gained much greater power than they had possessed before World War II.

The evolution of M.I.T. illustrated the change. The Institute traditionally had maintained a high degree of central administrative control over academic matters. In the postwar decades, however, as federal money flowed and Compton's vision of a campus focused on research and graduate education became a reality, administrators learned that advanced, specialized work in basic fields could not be supervised with organizational tools appropriate for undergraduate programs in engineering. They were forced to grant more autonomy to subunits as well as individuals, not only in judging faculty qualifications but also in setting research priorities and building graduate programs.

The same process was replicated at campus after campus around the country. By the end of the period, academic personnel decisions at low-status institutions like Northeastern were being made, as they were at elite campuses like Harvard, on the basis of recommendations from departments and faculty committees with which administrators differed at their peril.[49]

Perhaps the most impressive indication of the faculty's altered position was the broadening of its formal involvement in institutional policy-making. A crucial early step was typically the formation of an elected senate (or its equivalent) to represent faculty interests to campus administrators. The B.U. faculty, with memories of reduced salaries and longer hours during the Depression and war still fresh, organized a Senate in the late 1940s. Their colleagues at the University of Massachusetts did so in 1957, and Northeastern came along in the 1960s. While senates often focused initially on issues of compensation and personnel policy, in time they expanded their concerns to include priorities in program development, resource allocation, and even administrative organization.

An additional arena for the assertion of faculty power was the selection of administrative leaders, from department chairs to presidents. In the 1930s, presidents were typically appointed by trustees with no formal—and little informal—consultation with the faculty. Deans and chairs were chosen by presidents. With some notable exceptions, especially the selection of presidents and deans at Harvard, formal mechanisms for involving faculty in choosing administrators became normal in the postwar years. The A.A.U.P.'s Statement on Government of Colleges and Universities in 1966, issued jointly with the A.C.E. and the Association of Governing Boards of Colleges and Universities, expressed the expanded expectations of the professoriate and acceptance of the new rules by administrative leaders.[50]

Notes

1. On new social orientation of academics, see D. Henry, 1975, Chapt. 3 and pp. 69, 86; Oscar Handlin and Mary F. Handlin, 1970, pp. 74–75; J. Brubacher and W. Rudy, 1976, p. 295; A. Powell, 1980, pp. 231–232. For Massachusetts examples, see NUAR (1943), 17; (1944), 6; (1949), 3–6; BUAR (1941), 22; Boston College Building Fund Committee, 1946, p. 20. Quote from BUAR (1951), 15.

2. For perception of changed public attitudes, see O. and M. Handlin, 1970, pp. 74–75. For Baker quote, see MSCAR (1942), 4–5. For Carmichael, see TUAR (1942); R. Miller, 1966, p. 707. See also MITAR (1941), 6–7; (1944), 30. For view that federal research support would probably decline after the war to prewar levels, see MIT, Committee on Educational Survey, 1949, p. 55. Not all institutional leaders thought public subsidies were a good idea; see, for example, Ell's perspective in NUAR (1947), 8–9.

3. On NDRC and OSRD, see J. Conant, 1970, Chapt. 19; V. Bush, 1970, pp. 31ff.; N. Pusey, 1978, pp. 61ff.; R. Geiger, 1986, pp. 264–265; MITAR (1940), 13.

4. For Bush report, see Vannevar Bush, 1945; V. Bush, 1970, p. 64; see also A. Rivlin, 1961, p. 37; N. Pusey, 1978, pp. 67–70. For Scientific Research Board, see President's Scientific Research Board, 1947, recommendations are on 6–7. For Compton, see MITAR (1941), 16. For MIT/HU in OSRD, see V. Bush, 1970, pp. 32, 48–53; J. Conant, 1970, p. 242; John E. Burchard, 1948, p. ix; MITAR (1940), 13.

5. For general discussion of G.I. Bill, see Keith W. Olson, 1974; Davis R. B. Ross, 1969; D. Henry, 1975, Chapt. 4. For Congressional Hearings, see U.S. Congress, House, 1943; U.S. Congress, Senate, Committee on Education and Labor, 1943. For wartime estimates of participation, see Henry, 1975, pp. 59–60.

6. For MIT, see J. Burchard, 1948, p. 315. For overall participation, see D. Henry, 1975, pp. 62–63. For HU, see R. Smith, 1986, p. 60. For Conant, see HUAR (1946), 5. For national patterns in accommodating vets, see Henry, 1975, pp. 61–68. For Massachusetts examples, see HUAR (1952), 14–15; NUAR (1944), 12; (1946), 8–10; Burchard, 1948, p. 316. MITAR (1946); K. Olson, 1974, p. 36; TUAR (1944), 4; (1946), 1–2; BUAR (1946), 7–8.

7. For background of commissions, see Diane Ravitch, 1983, p. 15. For report, see U.S. President, Commission on Higher Education, 1947–1948, 6 vols.; report is excerpted in Gail Kennedy (ed.), 1952. For biographical information on commission members, see *Who's Who*, 1946–1947. For pre-WWII sentiment on expanding educational opportunity, see J. Brubacher and W. Rudy, 1976, pp. 234, 241–250, 258. For influence of progressive education, see F. Rudolph, 1962, Chapt. 22; Ravitch, 1983, Chapt. 2.

8. For campus-level planning activities in Massachusetts, see as follows: for HU, see references to Committee on General Education in a Free Society (below, n. 15); for BU, see discussion of Committee on the University in the Postwar World, BUAR (1942), 30; for MIT, see Committee on Educational Survey, 1949; for NU, see discussion of General Committee on Postwar Planning, NUAR (1943); for MSC, see discussion of Faculty Defense Council and Subcommittee on Postwar Planning, MSCAR (1941), 3, 15; for Jesuits, see discussion of Committee on Postwar Jesuit Education in JEA, Executive Committee, Minutes, Nov. 5, 1943; April 8, 1944; Oct. 7, 1944; and Oct. 17, 1944; also JEA, Executive Director, 1943 and 1944. For national patterns, see D. Henry, 1975, pp. 46–54; 70–71. For Carnegie quote, see Henry, pp. 1975, p. 70.

9. For Rockefeller, see Commission on Financing Higher Education, 1952. For comparison of Zook and Rockefeller, see D. Henry, 1975, pp. 80ff. For background on Rockefeller, see Exploratory Committee on Financing Higher Education and Research, Rockefeller Foundation, Aug. 17, 1948.

10. For discussion of enrollments, see U.S. President, Commission on Higher Education, vol. 1, 1947, Chapt. 2. Quote is from ibid., 41; also G. Kennedy, 1952, p. 13, and O. and M. Handlin, 1970, p. 76.

11. Commissions on Financing Higher Education, 1952, pp. 12–15, 45–54, 158.

12. For Conant on admissions, see James B. Conant, 1948, pp. 195–98; also "Education for A Classless Society: The Jeffersonian Tradition," May 1940, reprinted in G. Kennedy, 1952. For Conant on curriculum, see Conant, 1948, pp 153–163, 195–203. For Marsh on Zook, admissions, see BUAR (1948), 6–12; (1950), 15. On BU curriculum, see Committee on the University in the Postwar World, reprinted in BUAR (1944), 13ff. For Ell on Zook, admissions, see NUAR (1949), 7–8, (1950), 6. For Ell on curriculum, see NUAR (1946); quote is on 7; also (1948), 6.

13. For general education in twenties and thirties, see Frederick Rudolph, 1977, pp. 252ff.; F. Rudolph, 1962, pp. 455ff.; C. Jencks and D. Riesman, 1968, pp. 493–504; Daniel Bell, 1968; J. Brubacher and W. Rudy, 1976, pp. 259–260, 265, 271–278. For Massachusetts examples of these movements, see following references: for Tufts, TUR, Dean of Liberal Arts (1939); TUAR (1941), 1–8; R. Miller, 1966, pp. 618–621. For MSC, MSCAR (1938), 14–15; (1939), 6.

14. For general education after WWII, see F. Rudolph, 1977, pp. 256ff.; C. Jencks and D. Riesman, 1968, p. 494. For Zook, see U.S. President, Commission on Higher Education, vol. 1, 1947, pp. 23–31. For Rockefeller, see Commission on Financing Higher Education, 1952, pp. 15–19.

15. For discussion of Redbook, see F Rudolph, 1977, p. 257–259; Phyllis Keller, 1982, Chapt. 1; N. Pusey, 1978, pp. 160ff.; S. Lipset and D. Riesman, 1975, pp. 347, 376, 385–386; R. Smith, 1986, pp. 160ff. For Conant on Redbook, see J. Conant, 1970, Chapt. 27; HUAR (1942), 12ff.; (1944), 11–12; (1945), 10–14; (1952), 25; see also A. Powell, 1980, p. 207; quote is from Harvard Committee, 1945, pp. vi, x.

16. For impact of Redbook, see F Rudolph, 1977, p. 257. For Harvard, see S. Lipset and D. Riesman, 1975, pp. 347–48. For Tufts, see TUAR (1952), 16. For other Massachusetts examples, see following references: for BU, BUAR (1946), 12; (1950), 10; W. Ault, 1973, pp. 143ff., 172. For MIT, Committee on Educational Survey, 1949, pp. 81ff. For NU, NUAR (1946), 6.

17. For international emphasis, see U.S. President, Commission on Higher Education, vol. 1, 1947, pp. 14–20; N. Pusey, 1978, pp. 38ff.; HUAR (1946), 20–21; BUAR (1943), 8–10; (1944), 9ff.; (1947), 22. For religion, see D. Henry, 1975, p. 102; Harvard Committee, 1945, pp. 76ff.; BUAR (1951), 15ff.; MITAR (1953), 29; (1954), 29ff.; Wilfred M. Mallon, "Proceedings on the Institute . . . ," Aug. 3–13, 1948, pp. 4ff. On student life, see BUAR (1950), 15ff.; MSCAR (1945), 10–11; UMAR (1951), 4–6. For MIT, see MITAR (1947), 17ff.

18. Commission on Financing Higher Education, 1952, Chapt. 4; Exploratory Committee on Financing Higher Education and Research, 1948, pp. 53–54.

19. For Rockefeller on research, see Commission on Financing Higher Education, 1952, pp. 21–24, 176; quote is on 163; for Zook on research, see U.S. President, Commission on Higher Education, vol. 1, 1947, pp. 92ff. For Office of Naval Research, see J. Killian, 1985, p. 61.

20. For MIT, see MITAR (1944), 25ff.; Committee on Educational Survey, 1949, Chapt. 4 and p. 60; John E. Burchard (ed.), 1950. For HU, see HUAR (1946), 244–245; (1952), 15–16; J. Conant, 1970, pp. 244–245; J. Conant, 1948, p. 171; McGeorge Bundy, Summer 1970, p. 536.

21. For pre-WWII status of graduate education, see Everett Walters in Lewis Mayhew, 1967, pp. 131ff.; Bernard Berelson, 1960. For Conant, see HUAR (1946), 9–10; also J. Conant, 1948, pp. 197–198. For MIT, see Committee on Educational Survey, 1949, Chapt. 2. For Zook, see U.S. President, Commission on Higher Education, vol. 1, 1947, pp. 75–90; G. Kennedy, 1952, p. 21. For Rockefeller, see Commission on Financing Higher Education, 1952, Chapt. 1. See also N. Pusey, 1978, p. 62–65; Dael Wolfle, 1954.

22. For Zook, see U.S. President, Commission on Higher Education, vol. 1, 1947, Chapt. 4. For a characteristic Compton statement on relation of undergraduate and graduate education, see MITAR (1931).

23. For Science Board, see President's Scientific Research Board, vol. 1, 1947, Appendix 1. For Zook charge, see U.S. President, Commission on Higher Education, vol. 1, 1947, "letter of appointment." For Zook quote, see ibid., pp. 5–6, 91.

24. For controversy stirred by Zook, see G. Kennedy, 1952, esp. essays by Farrell and Hutchins; see also D. Henry, 1975, pp. 73ff. For Rockefeller, see Commission on Financing Higher Education, 1952, pp. 26–27 ("trained experts"), 25–26 ("still be done"), 27–30.

25. For Zook on diversity, see, for example, U.S. President, Commission on Higher Education, vol. 1, 1947, pp. 44–46 and vol. 3, 1947, pp. 1–2; see also D. Henry, 1975, p. 74. For Rockefeller on diversity, see Commission on Financing Higher Education, 1952, pp. 31–32, 157–164.

26. For impact of Zook, see D. Ravitch, 1983, p. 18.

27. For Conant, see HUAR (1946). For Baker, see MSCAR (1944), 26; (1946); 12. For Ell, see NUAR (1950), 18. For USOE projections, see NUAR (1947), 6; MITAR (1947), 8. For other perspectives on enrollments, see U.S. President, Commission on Higher Education, vol. 1, 1947, pp. 1–2; O. and M. Handlin, 1970, p. 74; Commission on Financing Higher Education, 1952, pp. 77ff.

28. For debates on draft, see D. Henry, 1975, pp. 85–88; J. Conant, 1970, Chapts. 26 and 38; Commission on Financing Higher Education, 1952, pp. 81ff.; TUAR (1951), 5; UMAR (1950), 2, 14–15. For Conant, see HUAR (1952), 20.

29. U.S. Office of Education, 1956. See also J. Millett, 1952, pp. 68–70, 271.

30. For Van Meter, see UMAR (1951), 3, 15; (1952), 2–3. For national figures, see U.S. Office of Education, 1956, p. 2; U.S. Bureau of the Census, 1975, Series H700–715, p. 383; U.S. Bureau of Census, 1985, Table A-6, p. 52. For consensus on new conditions see D. Henry, 1975, pp. 99–100; N. Pusey, 1978, pp. 56–62.

31. For increased attendance rates, see O. and M. Handlin, 1970, pp. 72–73; Commission on Financing Higher Education, 1952, p. 133; J. Brubacher and W. Rudy, 1976, pp. 257–58; D. Henry, 1975, pp. 99–103.

32. For statistics on growth, see U.S. Bureau of Census, 1975, Table H700–715, p. 383; U.S. Bureau of Census, 1985, Table A-6, p. 52; John A. Dunn, "Some Trends in Higher Education in the 1960's and 1970's" in "Tufts: The Total University," 1973, Appendix C, 11–16.

33. Gardner cited in D. Henry, 1975, p. 112.

34. For financial problems of higher education, see J. Millett, 1952, pp. 132, 136; U.S. President, Commission on Higher Education, vol. 5, 1948, pp. 13, 26; Commission on Financing Higher Education, 1952, esp. Chapt. 3. For Rockefeller quote, see Commission on Financing Higher Education, 1952, p. 114.

35. For general discussion of endowments and annual giving, see J. Millett, 1952, Chapts. 16 and 18; Commission on Financing Higher Education, 1952, pp. 139–42, 165–84; U.S. President, Commission on Higher Education, vol. 5, 1948, pp. 30–31, 48. For Rockefeller quote, see Exploratory Committee on Financing Higher Education and Research, Aug. 1, 1948, pp. 7, 20. For HU, see HUAR (1945), 14–16; (1947), 9; (1952),

7, 15; HUTR (1930); (1948). For TU, see TUAR (1952); TUTR (1930); (1948). For MIT, see MITAR (1947), 19–20; see also (1948), 7–12.

36. On trends in student payments, see J. Millett, 1952, Chapt. 15; see also N. Pusey, 1978, p. 102. BU and BC exemplified the national trend among Massachusetts institutions.

37. On publics vs. privates, see Commission on Financing Higher Education, 1952, pp. 64, 86; J. Millett, 1952, pp. 256–257; R. Geiger, 1986, p. 61. On growth of public funding after war, see N. Pusey, 1978, pp. 105ff.; Malcolm Moos and Francis Rourke, 1959, p. 11, Fig. # 1; R. Geiger, Dec. 1986, draft Chapt. 2, pp. 62–63. For MSC in 1940s, see MSCAR (1952), 2. For MIT, see MITAR (1947), 7–14; (1948); quote from 1948, p. 11; see also Committee on Educational Survey, 1949, pp. 16, 18.

38. Excellent general treatments of postwar trends in federal funding for academic research can be found in the following: A. Rivlin, 1961; Chester E. Finn, 1978; Bruce L. R. Smith and Joseph J. Karlesky, 1977. See also D. Henry, 1975, pp. 123ff.; Commission on Financing Higher Education, 1952, Chapts. 4 and 5; N. Pusey, 1978, pp. 72ff.; A. Touraine, 1974, pp. 133–135; J. Ben-David, 1977, p. 117; MITAR (1952), 29; (1956), 5.

39. On nonresearch support, see A. Rivlin, 1961, Chapt. 4; C. Finn, 1978; for table summarizing allocation of federal funds among categories of aid in 1968 and 1977, see Finn, 1978, p. 12; see also D. Henry, 1975, pp. 12ff.; J. Brubacher and W. Rudy, 1976, p. 249; MITAR (1956), 2–4; N. Pusey, 1978, p. 107.

40. For general patterns, see C. Finn, 1978, esp. Chapt. 1; Frank Newman et al., 1973, Chapt. 5. For aggregate federal support as percent of current funds, see Finn, 1978, p. 14.

41. Statistics on state spending, voluntary giving and student payments from: U.S. Bureau of the Census, 1975, Series H 716–727; U.S. Dept. of Education, Office of Educational Research and Improvement, 1988, Tables 226 and 227.

42. For aggregate expenditures, see U.S. Bureau of the Census, 1975, Series H 728–738. For expenditures in relation to GNP, see C. Jencks and D. Riesman, 1968, p. 111n.

43. For Ph.D. shortage, see Allan M. Cartter, 1976, Chapt. 2; quote is on 13. See also D. Henry, 1975, pp. 105ff.; C. Jencks and D. Riesman, 1968, p. 13; W. Metzger, 1987, pp. 150ff. For Pusey, see below, Chapt. 3, n. 40.

44. For faculty in 1952, see D. Henry, 1975, p. 105. For 1970, see H. and S. Bloland, 1974, p. 11. For myth of Ph.D. shortage, see A. Cartter, 1976, Chapt. 2; see also C. Jencks and D. Riesman, 1968, pp. 113–114; for studies that repeat myth of shortage, see L. Mayhew, 1967, p. 5; J. Brubacher and W. Rudy, 1976, p. 214. For annual production of Ph.D.s, see Cartter, 1976, pp. 83, 129. See also Seymour Harris, 1972, pp. 317, 379; National Science Board; 1969.

45. For impact of external funding, see R. Nisbett, 1971, Chapts. 5 and 6; A. Touraine, 1974, pp. 137–139; C. Kaysen, 1969, p. 26.

46. For professional associations, see H. and S. Bloland, 1974, Chapt. 2. For rise of professionalism generally, see C. Jencks and D. Riesman, 1968; O. and M. Handlin, 1970, pp. 74–75; A. Touraine, 1974, Chapt. 4; Logan Wilson, 1979.

47. For AAUP, see Louis Joughlin (ed.), 1967.

48. For BU, see BUAR (1947), 13ff.; also Faculty Manual for following years: 1950, 1957, 1962, 1967, 1970. For NU, see Faculty Handbooks for following years: 1957, 1961, 1962, 1966, 1967, 1971.

49. For MTT, see below, Chapt. 3, "Organizational Dimensions of Academic Change." For a general discussion of faculty vs. administration on control of academic appointments, see Peter Blau, 1973, Chapt. 7.

50. For BU, see Faculty Manual for 1950, VI–1. For UMass see below, Chapt. 6, n. 51. For NU, see below, Chapt. 5, n. 55. For general role of senates, see J. Brubacher and W. Rudy, 1976, pp. 375ff. For AAUP, see L. Wilson, 1979, p. 104; L. Joughlin, 1967, pp. 90ff.

THE AAUP FROM 1946 TO 1958: MCCARTHYISM AND RECONSTRUCTION EFFORTS

PHILO A. HUTCHENSON

McCarthyism and Reconstruction Efforts

The federal government acted immediately upon the end of World War II to address the country's educational needs. The first of these efforts was the massive G.I. Bill of Rights program, enacted into law in 1944. As a result of the G.I. Bill, approximately one-third of U.S. World War II veterans entered colleges and universities.[1] The second reflected the sentiments of the egalitarian nature of the G.I. Bill; the President's Commission on Higher Education stated in its 1947 report, "It is obvious, then, that free and universal access to education, in terms of the interest, ability, and need of the student, must be a major goal in American education." The commission noted later in its report that according to results of the Army General Classification Test, "the most inclusive testing program ever conducted, that even with the present inflexibility of college curricula, a minimum of 49 percent of the college-age population of this country has the ability to complete at least the first two years of college work, and at least 32 percent has the ability to complete additional years of higher education."[2] The third effort, however, focused on a very different aspect of higher education, its research capabilities. In 1945, Vannevar Bush, who was then director of the Office of Scientific Research and Development, submitted to President Roosevelt his report, *Science, the Endless Frontier,* in which Bush urged the nation to invest heavily in basic research. That report is generally regarded as the basis for the establishment of the National Science Foundation, an institution at the vanguard of massive federal financial support of research.[3] Both universal access and high-quality basic research were important national goals following World War II. Both of these goals also had consequences for higher education and the professoriate.

The federal government, through both unprecedented levels of funding and the issuance of policy reports, created a context of institutional growth and an emphasis on research. In view of higher education's commitment to enrollment growth and the long-standing tradition of scholarship, it would not suffice to ascribe the reasons for bureaucratization and professionalization to the federal government. Nevertheless, its substantial commitment to the uses of higher education provided a powerful set of contributing factors.

Enrollment in higher education increased from 2,078,095 in the fall of 1946 to 2,446,693 in the fall of 1955.[4] The enrollment of first-time students in the fall of 1946 was relatively large compared to following years, the result of the G.I. Bill. There were 696,419 first-time students in 1946, compared to 592,846 in 1947, and in ensuing years the number stayed below the 1947 level until 1954, when there were 624,910 first-time students.[5]

The growth in the number of professors appears to have surpassed the growth in the number of students. In 1945–1946 there were 125,811 college instructors, and in November 1955 there were 197,791 college instructors.[6] During the late 1940s the supply of potential professors did not meet the demand. It was a time "when standards were relatively low for entering college teaching, a high proportion of young people entered college teaching with only master's degree credentials or were content to remain ABDs."[7] Nevertheless colleges and universities typically appointed new professors in accordance with the institutions' levels of prestige. The major study of the academic labor market in the mid-1950s reported that the type and prestige of the employing institution, the level (master's degree or higher) and prestige of the professor's education, and the professor's discipline, age, and rank all proved to be powerful factors in the academic labor market.[8] Institutions at the top of the academic hierarchy continued to attract new professors with doctorates. Graduate-level research, the demonstration of expertise, continued to be of primary importance to highly influential and prestigious institutions. To a substantial degree in the first decade after World War II, there continued to be a dual labor market for professors, one focused on securing instructors for burgeoning enrollments and one for institutions emphasizing research expertise. Yet labor market issues were of minimal importance in those years; instead, the serious and sustained attacks on professors during the era of McCarthyism attracted the most attention.

The AAUP from 1946 to 1955: Oligarchy and McCarthyism

In the decade following the end of World War II, the AAUP confronted two obstacles that restrained its activities. One was internal, the presence of a singularly powerful and relatively unresponsive general secretary and a compliant elected leadership. The other was external, the continuous and often virulent attacks upon professors and the professoriate typically led by Senator Joseph P. McCarthy, allied legislators, and business people. The eventual responses of the AAUP elected leadership and the membership to the association's silence established an organizational framework that would eventually facilitate direct representation of professors' working interests.

Three internal factors apparently combined to create the organizational silence in alleged academic freedom violations. First, General Secretary Himstead was not a competent administrator; he did not delegate the detailed and lengthy tasks of correspondence and investigation in alleged academic freedom violations.[9] Furthermore, "he was timorous when it came to any opposition to Senator [Joseph] McCarthy and the actions of universities in that period of Communist hysteria," and he told the council several times that if the AAUP opposed McCarthy and anti-Communism, the association "would just disintegrate."[10] Second, the association had not operated completely during World War II. Only the council met from 1942 to 1946, and after the war the organization and the members and leaders had to turn from the national focus on the war back to association programs.[11] Third, most of the charter members, those professors who had shared the vision of a national professional association, were, by reason of age or death, no longer participating in the AAUP.[12]

Himstead handled most of the association's correspondence and affairs by 1946. Loya Metzger argues that Himstead dominated the association and was vague regarding the work of the staff.[13] It appears that Himstead did not respond to much of the association correspondence and affairs because of the burden of those activities as well as his picayune attention to details and his desire to maintain control of the association.[14] An early example of the burden and attention to detail appears in an October 1947 letter to *Bulletin* readers. Himstead wrote that the staff was back to two professional members despite a net increase of 8,000 members in the past two years.[15] Equally troublesome was the upcoming and unexpected move of the Central Office, and Himstead implored readers to be patient with slow responses to inquiries.[16] As he continued, his sense of his central importance to the organization and his attention to details appeared:

> In the nature of the case we must be the judge of what constitutes "first things." In determining the parts of our work that are to be given priority, the paramount consideration is the welfare of the profession. Another very important consideration is the quality of our work. We must never sacrifice quality for quantity.[17]

Despite his concerns about organizational demands, Himstead's reports on association activities indicated a healthy organization. In the Winter 1950 issue of the *Bulletin*, he reviewed the AAUP's growth in membership and financial resources since 1936. The association had experienced consistent growth in its membership, from 12,713 members in 1936 to 39,092 as of January 1950. From 1938 to 1949, the AAUP had enjoyed surpluses each year, and its reserve fund showed steady growth since 1937.[18] Yet Himstead concluded his report by reminding AAUP members that the staff was the same size as it had been in 1937.[19] There was only one addition to the AAUP staff from 1947 to 1955: Warren Middleton was appointed staff associate in February 1952.[20] With the addition of Middleton, there was one staff member for every 13,746 AAUP active members.[21]

In the middle and late 1940s, Himstead was the AAUP's primary force not only in such areas as academic freedom but also in studies of the economic status of the profession and faculty participation in college and university government. In fact, he identified himself, perhaps unwittingly, as such. In the investigation of the alleged academic freedom violations at the University of Texas, Himstead used the first-person singular pronoun, an extremely unusual occurrence in AAUP reports.[22] In 1947, the council gave Himstead five hundred dollars to assemble data on faculty salaries. He met with representatives of the AAC, American Council on Education (ACE), and the United States Office of Education and reported that he had regular discussions with the chair and the executive secretary of the President's Commission on Higher Education, again using the first-person singular pronoun.[23] In January 1948, Himstead handled a Committee T survey of faculty participation in governance at forty institutions, sending out duplicates of the 1939–1940 survey to those institutions' chapters.[24]

Following the censure of the University of Texas, the AAUP began a period of inaction, especially in the area of investigations of alleged violations of academic freedom. The only noticeable association work in the area was the result of extensive negotiations between the AAUP and the AAC, which began in 1943, to develop the Statement of Principles on Academic Retirement. The negotiations ended in 1950, and both the AAC and the AAUP endorsed the statement in 1951.[25] The association did not publish any investigations of alleged violations of academic freedom and tenure from the summer of 1949 until the spring of 1956.[26] The exceptional nature of national and local attention to professors in this period accentuated the consequences of AAUP inactivity.

From the late 1940s to the mid-1950s, the profession was under attack, often the subject of vituperative charges against its members' loyalty to the nation and the society. Senator Joseph P. McCarthy is the foremost example of the attacks on the professoriate, but requirements such as loyalty oaths for faculties or trustees' condemnations of irreligious professors went far beyond McCarthy's work in the U.S. Senate.[27] The attacks came from a variety of sources—state as well as federal investigating committees (from both the legislative and executive branches), local business people, newspaper editors and columnists, and even a "professional" anti-Communist network.[28] The attacks on professors also ranged from coast to coast at public and private colleges and universities.[29] Professors felt vulnerable and scared during this time. Even in professors' most valued professional activity—the review of peers for appointment, promotion, and dismissal—the fear took hold. Trustees, administrators, and even professors often refused to support attacked professors, and many professors alerted administrators and faculties to the alleged undesirability of their attacked peers.[30] Very often these attacks on professors constituted violations of the principles of academic freedom. The attacks persisted until the mid-1950s, when U.S. Senate witnesses began to challenge successfully McCarthy's undocumented claims of Communist conspiracies, thereby generally discrediting the attacks.

Even in the case of the 1950 attempt of the Board of Regents of the University of California to require a loyalty oath of faculty members, a case which generated national publicity and support for California faculty members from professors all over the nation, the AAUP did not report its investigation until 1956.[31] The University of California AAUP chapter members emphasized the need for an investigation, even going so far as to fly to Washington, D.C., to discuss the situation with AAUP staff members. Although two AAUP members investigated the situation in the spring of 1951 and sent their final report to the Central Office in December 1951, the report (even in partial format) remained hidden from public review until the spring of 1956.[32]

As Lazarsfeld and Thielens show, the academic profession itself was thoroughly afraid of attacks on professors.[33] Himstead reinforced that fear by claiming that any AAUP response to the anti-Communist attacks would "paralyze the Association."[34] He was a major factor in the paralysis of the predominant program of the association, the work of Committee A. It is important to remember, however, that there was also a national elected leadership that acquiesced to a considerable degree as Himstead slowed the organization, thus constituting the other major factor.

From 1946 to 1955, there was the beginning of a transition in the AAUP institutional experience of association presidents. The last president who was a charter member, Frederick Deibler at Northwestern University, served from 1940 to 1942.[35] AAUP presidents after Deibler had joined the association increasingly, if irregularly, in later years of the organization—ranging in this period from 1923 to 1930. Only one president, Edward Kirkland (history, Bowdoin College), who served from 1946 to 1948, had been chair of Committee A, and only one other had been a member of Committee A, William Britton (law, University of Illinois, AAUP president from 1954 to 1956).[36] These presidents began their experience with the AAUP after the organizational membership standards had changed and organizational activity had broadened beyond the initial work of Committees A, P (on Pensions), and T. They also had limited direct experience with the association's predominant program, the protection of academic freedom and tenure, suggesting a gap between AAUP goals and leadership experience.

More problematic, however, was the composition and activity of Committee A. Its leadership and membership were static from 1946 to 1955. There were only two chairs of the committee from 1946 to 1954. The first, George Pope Shannon, served as chair in 1946 and 1947.[37] William Laprade, former AAUP president, was chair of the committee from 1948 until 1954.[38] Committee members tended to come from elite colleges and universities where academic freedom problems were less likely to occur, and there was little change of membership from 1946 to 1954.[39] The Committee A annual reports, while indicating the receipt of complaints from professors and often noting the informal negotiations resulting in resolved cases, were general in their approach; they did not name specific institutions. Despite repeated insistence upon adherence to academic freedom and tenure principles and practices with such phrases as "teachers and scholars cannot afford to be silent when danger threatens," the committee's formal investigative practices were at a standstill.[40] Although Loya Metzger, and to a lesser degree Ellen Schrecker, focus blame for AAUP inactivity on Himstead, Committee A inactivity indicates that elected leaders must share the blame.[41] At the least, Committee A leaders and members paralyzed by Himstead's arguments allowed hundreds of professors' cases to remain in the files. The "timid" professors of the nation whom Schrecker questions were well represented on Committee A of the AAUP. Laprade suggested in his final report as chair of Committee A that only the Central Office staff was in the proper, central place for the conduct of Committee A affairs. Nevertheless, he chose to support Himstead *despite* Central Office inactivity, in his final report and in his nine-year presence as chair of Committee A.[42]

Nor was the AAUP Council active from 1946 to 1955, with only one *Bulletin* report of activity, its 1946 censure of the governing board at the University of Texas. Annual meeting reports typically noted that the council had met, but there were no statements concerning council activity, and other reports indicate that local leaders pushed the council into action.[43] In general, as was the case with Committee A, council members came from elite colleges and universities.[44] The sense of the profession, even under attack from external forces, from the AAUP perspective derived from professors at institutions that were less likely to experience such attacks.

AAUP Activity and Salaries and Governance

AAUP interest in salaries and governance continued at about the same level from 1946 to 1955 as had existed prior to World War II. The 1946 *Bulletin* carried two articles on the deteriorating state of professors' salaries. Himstead introduced the two articles and wrote that the association "has never been as specific or as vigorous as the significance of the subject warrants."[45] Later that year, the members at the annual meeting passed resolutions urging national and chapter studies of salaries and research by Committee Z ("A Symposium on the Economic Status of the Profession") on salary problems and the study of faculties' role in college and university government.[46] In 1948, the Harvard University chapter issued another Committee Z report, this one the result of a survey of 119 colleges and universities, indicating that since 1939 the nation's cost of living had risen faster than professors' salaries or tuition charges.[47]

In the Summer 1948 issue of the *Bulletin*, Himstead announced that the newly revitalized national Committee Z was preparing a study of forty-six colleges and universities. Among the committee's first recommendations were the establishment of annual salary surveys and the addition of a staff member to the national office to assist the study of faculty salaries.[48] The Summer 1948 issue also included an article on professors' salaries that identified a critical problem. A study of 21 percent of U.S. colleges and universities found that there was no agreement about an appropriate salary scale.[49] Without that consensus, faculties and the AAUP would obviously have difficulty convincing administrations and governing boards as to appropriate levels of salaries, even within the context of professional standards. Committee Z offered an extensive report in the Winter 1953–1954 *Bulletin* and stated:

> The most striking conclusion evidenced by the comparison of all the salary data now collected by the Committee is that instructional salaries have not, since 1939–40, kept pace with living costs, with improvements in the incomes of other professions, or with the per capita growth of the national income.[50]

Yet, as the committee indicated, its data were from institutions with "good practices with respect to instructional salaries and related matters."[51] Those practices were apparently unlikely to have parallels at many other institutions.

In 1948, Committee T issued a report on its study of forty colleges and universities that the association had surveyed in 1939–1940; twenty of them had shown the lowest rates of faculty participation in government and twenty the highest rates of participation. Thirty of the institutions responded, and the Committee T report concluded that there was no trend in faculty participation in college and university government nor any evidence of more participation among faculties. The report suggested that professors should have more participation in college and university government.[52]

Committee T announced in 1953 its continued research into faculty participation in college and university government, finding that there was some increase in administrations' consultations with faculties.[53] A spring 1955 report compared current faculty participation in college and university government with such participation in 1939 and concluded:

> The implication which the data force upon us is that the general picture, so far as faculty participation in the selection of institutional policies is concerned, is somewhat better; in some spots it is a little worse, but in other spots it is very much better. A slow but pervasive shift toward more consultation of the faculty by the administration is evidently in process.[54]

Only one group that had worsened was specifically identified, six small liberal arts colleges. The committee noted, however, some improved groups. They were the "'less democratic'" state universities of 1939, teachers colleges that "were conspicuously autocratic" in 1939, women's colleges, and, to a lesser degree, five private research universities. One group of institutions, engineering colleges, changed very little in faculty participation.[55]

Committee T suggested in its 1955 report that the association pursue the possibility of a joint statement with the Association of American Colleges, one similar to the 1966 Statement on Academic Freedom. And it asked that the committee serve in continuous form, rather than in its previous "periodic efforts."[56] Issues of professional influence at colleges and universities seemed slightly improved in the mid-1950s despite McCarthyism, and Committee T members wanted a procedural statement about professional participation in university governance.

Members' interests in salaries and governance went beyond the national work of Committees T and Z, as local activity increased in the AAUP. In the Southeast and Ohio, there was some membership activity, including annual meetings. In the Southeast, concerns about economic status "always occupied a prominent place in the meetings."[57] Ohio members were particularly concerned about academic freedom and also considered in detail faculty participation in government.[58]

Whatever the interests of AAUP leaders and members, they could do very little about those interests in operational terms as long as the Central Office under Himstead remained inactive and the council and Committee A were acquiescent. Members at the local and regional levels appeared to have generated much of the protest against national AAUP inactivity. The details of the actions indicate substantial interest in the association's capacity and failure to act as a custodian of the interests of higher education.

The Collapse of the Oligarchy

By 1953, the University of Minnesota chapter was sufficiently disturbed by the inactivity of the national AAUP that it sent a delegate, Werner Levi (political science), to the annual meeting to attend to the chapter's complaints.[59] At that meeting, the concern of members and leaders about Himstead reached a peak "when exceedingly bitter and well-documented complaints were loudly voiced."[60] In opposition, the "national office 'steam-rolled its wishes and almost succeeded in a machine-like domination of the Chicago meetings.'" Levi reported back to his Minnesota colleagues that a fellow group of "rebels" had "forced a vote instructing the national headquarters to take action on the grievances" of the members, grievances that focused on Committee A inactivity.[61] The council responded by reactivating Committee O on Organization and Policy and instructed the chairman and members to examine Central Office operations and communications with members and chapters.[62]

The *Bulletin* report of the 1953 Annual Meeting included an unusual "Addendum" written by Himstead in which he offered rebuttals to the objections raised at the annual meeting. As concerned the lack of communication between the Central Office and chapters and state conferences, he indicated that he had repeatedly requested reports of their meetings for publication in the *Bulletin* but had received none. Although he had received thirty-seven invitations to attend chapter or state conference meetings in 1952–1953, he had refused them all because of office demands. These two rebuttals appear to be accurate, given the previous publication of "Association News" and the small size of the association staff. On the issue of alleged violations of academic freedom, however, Himstead was at once evasive and excessively blunt. He wrote that at times the Central Office did not respond to inquiries about academic freedom cases because the situations were under investigation and thus were confidential; he offered no explanation for those cases not under investigation. He then proceeded to offer two provocative, albeit accurate, statements. He indicated that chapter involvement in academic freedom cases made the investigative process more difficult and was also in violation of the AAUP Constitution.[63] At a time when he had a choice between inclusive and exclusive behavior toward local activities, he chose the latter. He concluded his "Addendum" with a review of the demands on the AAUP staff, suggesting that in the past year the Central Office received one hundred thousand communications (telephone calls, letters, telegrams) of which twenty thousand could be handled only by professional staff members.[64] He argued again that the staff was too small and the financial resources were too limited for the demands on the association.[65]

Himstead avoided Committee O meetings, canceling three appointments with it scheduled for the fall of 1953, until members met with him in February 1954. The committee reported to the council that the Central Office should be reorganized with "specifically designated" associate secretaries for academic freedom and for chapters and membership. The council responded with an approval in principle, a secret-ballot expression of confidence in Himstead, and the appointment of a two-member subcommittee for further investigation. The subcommittee's report "seemed to exonerate Himstead's management," suggesting that the professional staff be increased by two members and that the association increase dues, and it "termed the need for these moves urgent." Although Himstead liked the report, he submitted his resignation as general secretary to the council before the 1954 Annual Meeting, requesting to be retained as *Bulletin* editor. His letter noted that he had lost the members' confidence; Loya Metzger suggests that he was trying to generate sympathy.[66]

While the national leaders were providing a weak defense of Himstead, members at the local level were planning a change. Werner Levi organized a regional meeting of AAUP members, contacting many officers at "first-rank institutions" who were concerned about the association's current operations. Thirty-nine members from twenty-one institutions attended the meeting, and they agreed on the importance of greater regional activity and decided to begin drafting a formal protest.[67] The first section of the protest statement addressed national AAUP operations in the area of academic freedom, especially its "failure to act," to communicate with chapters on its actions, and to reinstate censured institutions without "excessive delay." The second section criticized the lack of usable information in the *Bulletin,* while the third spoke to the Central Office's inefficiency and concentration of power. The statement's recommendations included establishing a national academic freedom defense fund and appointing a full-time academic freedom investigator in the Central Office. The AAUP members drafting the protest agreed to circulate it among chapters in the region, make any changes necessary, and then send a final version to the Central Office.[68]

In February 1954 the University of Minnesota chapter hosted the second regional meeting. By that time, members at Minnesota had evidence of national inactivity in the area of academic freedom as the result of their contacts with colleagues at the University of Nevada, where a difficult case had developed. This information, in combination with the standing dissatisfaction with the national organization, generated discussion that suggested local activity supplementing national activity. The AAUP members at the meeting reviewed several topics, including development of local public relations programs to inform professors and the public about academic freedom issues, forming a regional academic freedom defense panel, and "plans for acting whenever a need might be unmet by the national organization." In addition, they examined the annual meeting and the procedures "blocking full discussion of criticisms of the national office." They instructed Professor Levi to ask if the motions of the 1953 Annual Meeting had any results in order to focus attention on the members' grievances.[69]

The members at the 1954 Annual Meeting were even angrier than those at the 1953 meeting. Levi reported:

> "There was strong tension between sections of the audience and Secretaries Himstead and Shannon, which at times deteriorated into almost personal insults. At one point Mr. Himstead was shouted down and on another occasion several members of the Council felt obliged to speak against Mr. Himstead."[70]

Nor did Himstead enjoy the same organizational control that he had somewhat effected at the 1953 Annual Meeting. He objected to the appointment of two new staff members (although he himself had noted the inadequate size of the AAUP staff), stating that he could not train them quickly in the "delicate work" of the association. The council overrode his objection and authorized the appointments. When Himstead opposed the rescheduling of discussion on his report, members reminded him that he had been instructed in 1953 to schedule more time for the general secretary's report.[71] George Pope Shannon, associate secretary of the AAUP, attempted to defend Himstead, but the members at the annual meeting would not countenance supporters either. Shannon read letters from members as an attempt to illustrate the diverse demands on the Central Office and was accused of trying to filibuster.[72]

The council voted at the 1954 Annual Meeting to accept Himstead's resignation, effective 1 February 1955.[73] He fought the council action, including arranging his appointment to the search committee and suggesting in an interview with the committee's choice, Ralph F. Fuchs, that AAUP finances were too uncertain for a strong future. In August 1954, Himstead suffered a heart attack, and subsequent illness forced him to miss the 1955 Annual Meeting; at that meeting, the council announced his retirement from the general secretaryship.[74]

Yet Himstead continued to fight his removal and refused to announce the appointment of Ralph F. Fuchs as general secretary "despite direct instruction from the president of the Association to do so."[75] On 8 June 1955, Himstead collapsed at his desk, stricken by a cerebral hemorrhage. The news release that he had written for Fuchs' appointment lay on his desk. Himstead died the next day, and following his death Fuchs assumed the general secretaryship.[76] In the same period, Himstead and McCarthyism ended as obstacles to AAUP activity.

Revitalizing the Association, 1955 to 1958

Ralph F. Fuchs had considerable local and national AAUP experience; the association appointed as general secretary an experienced member with disciplinary distinction in law at a time when the organization needed strong and inclusive executive leadership.[77] When Fuchs began his new position, he saw several important association tasks, two of which were to address the backlog of academic freedom cases and to meet the demand for other types of association activity. In regard to the latter, he wanted to develop "an expanded and more diversified program of activities, involving widespread membership participation and enhanced Association influence in a broad range of professional matters."[78] The council supported Fuchs, approving in March 1955 the appointment of two more staff members and directing Committee A to prepare short reports on the academic freedom cases at University of California and University of Washington, two cases from the late 1940s and early 1950s.[79] The two current AAUP staff members also supported Fuchs' goals, and in the summer of 1955 they completed several important tasks to give the association "a smooth transition."[80]

Within months of Fuchs's appointment he was effecting a rapid increase in association activity. Most important, Fuchs accelerated the removal of the backlog of Committee A cases by appointing a special committee to report on alleged violations since 1948 that involved anti-Communism.[81] The membership of the committee was announced in the Autumn 1955 *Bulletin* with the accompanying statements that the committee had been authorized by the council's written vote and would report to Committee A, the council, and the annual meeting. Fuchs also coordinated activities with the AAUP Council and AAUP President Britton in California.[82]

The presentation and approval of the report, "Academic Freedom and Tenure in the Quest for National Security," at the 1956 Annual Meeting allowed the AAUP to clear most of its backlog of academic freedom cases and thus move ahead with its business. As the Special Committee explained, the association accomplished a great deal by addressing the troubling issue of academic freedom and national security:

> The Association has not, however, expressed itself publicly on these particular situations. The insistence that it do so is widespread among its members; and this committee believes that, at the present hour in national and world affairs, we may gain much by announcing the Association's position in reference to these situations, and by stating anew, in the present context, the principles upon which the Association relies.[83]

The committee's report discussed the context of the actions of administrations and boards of trustees during the McCarthy era, noting the "growing realization of the Communist strategy of infiltration." The report accepted "unhesitatingly the application to colleges and universities of needed safeguards against the misuse of specially classified information important for military security" in the case of persons with access to that information.[84] The committee also included "conspiracy against the government," established by evidence and reviewed under due process, as a specific justification for the removal of a professor. The 1940 Statement on Principles refers only to incompetence in teaching or scholarship and to moral turpitude as causes for dismissal, and it was published in the pages preceding the Special Committee's report; the Special Committee placed additional limitations on academic freedom. The committee also narrowed professors' personal freedom in its interpretation of the use of the Fifth Amendment, arguing that professors had the duty to reveal information about their teaching to their institutions.[85] The Special Committee even offered criticism, albeit light, of faculties and faculty committees, indicating for example that the faculty at Kansas State Teachers College at Emporia "may not have realized that academic freedom is the right of every teacher."[86] The committee exercised considerable caution in its report in response to the still powerful anti-Communism sentiments; the report also reflected, however, AAUP commitment to the interests of higher education and professors as opposed to only the interests of professors.

The AAUP report appeared to be immediately successful, as the report and censures received widespread public notice, perhaps the most the AAUP has ever received. Many national and local newspapers carried editorials on the AAUP action, and college and university educators responded as well.[87] The AAUP had resumed in full its predominant program, with some exceptional internal procedures, and had suggested institutional and professorial practices, and the nation had taken notice.

The Special Committee report also allowed the organization to develop programs in other areas of interest to faculty members since it demonstrated that the AAUP could effectively respond to issues of academic freedom and tenure. As part of that development, the association needed to examine its capacities and its members' interests.

The Committee O on Organization and Policy report at the 1956 Annual Meeting assessed the state of the association. It noted that the staff had three full-time members (the most in years because of previous illnesses) and that by June 1956 there would be five full-time staff members. Other staff members were already working with representatives from the Commission on Academic Freedom and Tenure of the Association of American Colleges to develop procedural standards in dismissals. The national leadership had "either reconstituted entirely or created" six committees, including Committee A.[88]

The council further formalized association structure and operations when in October 1956 it approved a new committee structure that included descriptions of each committee.[89] The three most extensive descriptions were of Committees A, T, and Z; Committees T and Z were the only two of the thirteen described that had subcommittees. In addition, Committee A had district panels with members to assist Committee A work in their geographic regions.[90] This attention to issues of governance and economic status, as well as to local interest in the work of Committee A, indicated that the AAUP was ready to return to its perceived role and perhaps to expand upon it.

The expansion of association activity following the Special Committee's report on academic freedom indicates the extent to which the organization was committed to revitalizing its efforts and to addressing a broader range of professional issues. Both the elected and staff leaders were moving the association toward changes in policies and practices, yet it was an activism of professionals. In the Spring 1956 *Bulletin*, the association reprinted the 1938 statement on the nature of the AAUP by then—general secretary H. W. Tyler; in which he argued that the association was not a union.[91] George Pope Shannon, the *Bulletin* editor, added a note to the reprint indicating that the letter was published "because of its relevance to continuing or recurrent problems of the Association."[92] AAUP national leaders remained careful in their activism. The first major step in the association's commitment to expansion was the development of a thorough national graded survey of professors' salaries.

The Economic Interests of AAUP Members

Members, chapters, and state and regional conferences urged the national AAUP to focus on the economic status of the profession during this reconstruction period. For example, the Committee O analyses revealed a strong occupational interest among some members:

> Another group of responses can be understood only as conscious or unconscious pressure for a shift toward a pattern of organization and performance more largely protective of the immediate interests, economic and other, of the members of the academic profession. The Committee is aware of the fact that circumstances have, over the years, forced our Association, as they have similar professional groups, to assume a greater degree of responsibility for the security of the individual member. It may well be, as some members insist, that the social context in which higher education now functions is such as to require of us both a more aggressive and protective policy in the area in which we have traditionally operated and an extension of such policy into other areas once thought not to be within the limits of our concern.[93]

The committee recommended careful examination of potentially appropriate changes in "traditional policies and practices" in order to achieve traditional association goals given the current circumstances.[94]

National attention to the economic status of the profession also occurred at the 1957 Annual Meeting when members changed the AAUP Constitution, adding the word "welfare" to the phrase "to advance the standards and ideals of the profession" following the initial amendment to add "economic welfare."[95] Members at the 1957 Annual Meeting also approved a resolution on economic status:

> The Meeting further resolves that the Association be requested to establish as immediate objectives the discovery of tactical ways and means of securing proper salary levels throughout the country and the implementation of these ways and means at national and local levels, and that the Council report to the Forty-Fourth Annual Meeting on the progress achieved in this program.[96]

Members wanted the AAUP to achieve as quickly as possible the new constitutional goal of advancing the welfare of the profession.

There was also increased interest in association examination of faculty salaries at the local level. In April 1957, delegates from the chapter at American University wrote a letter to the Central Office suggesting that the AAUP should work to make adherence to national salary minima a criterion for accreditation.[97] Later that year the chair of the District of Columbia Conference sent a proposal to the presidents of state and regional conferences and chapters as well as council members suggesting "we must initiate a *National Campaign to make Economic Welfare a Major Objective of the AAUP.*"[98] The Illinois Conference passed a resolution in support of the proposal in October 1957.[99]

The District of Columbia proposal examined the welfare of the profession beyond economic status. The first recommendation of the proposal emphasized faculty participation in college and university government because problems of economic status or academic freedom and tenure were "symptoms [rather] than the real disease." The proposal suggested using full-time staff members (instead of professors volunteering their time and energy) to implement the recommendations, including the use of a professional public relations person. Despite the assertive nature of the statement, the District of Columbia proposal stated that even "hard-minded and unabashed assertion of our national importance" should model the assertion of such importance by members of the medical and legal professions.[100] Although the District of Columbia and Illinois Conferences wanted AAUP activism, those leaders saw themselves in the same context as that of the national leaders: members of a profession analogous to the professions of medicine and law.

The enthusiasm and concerns in the AAUP paralleled national sentiment increasingly favorable toward higher education. In 1957, shortly after the attacks on the professoriate subsided, the Union of Soviet Socialist Republics launched *Sputnik.* One of the immediate responses in the United States was to identify the importance of education in achieving superiority in the technological and scientific race for space. President Eisenhower suggested expanding the work of the National Science Foundation and implementing the National Defense Education Act; the United States Congress agreed, and by 1958 the federal government began to spend even greater sums of money on scientific and technological research and on financial assistance for students.[101] President Eisenhower's Commission on Education Beyond the High School affirmed the national importance of professors in its *Second Report,* The commission recommended "the goal of doubling the average level [of professors' salaries] within five to ten years, and with particular attention to increasing the spread between the bottom and the top of each institution's salary structure."[102]

In 1958, Committee Z began a remarkable program to address members' concerns about their low salaries and benefits. Fritz Machlup of the committee and members of a subcommittee of Committee Z proposed that the AAUP grade the academic salary scales of United States colleges and universities.[103] Machlup noted that chapters and conferences had increasingly demanded "greater activity on the part of the Council, the national committees, and the Washington office in promoting the material welfare of the members of the profession."[104] He stated that the purposes could be construed as "to safeguard the standards of the profession and the quality of higher education; or, in the most mundane terms, to raise faculty salaries as quickly as possible." Machlup and Committee Z had considered numerous proposals for means to raise salaries, including "the employment of 'skilled organizers' and of 'high-caliber public-relations experts.'" Machlup and the committee felt, however, that most of the proposals were "impractical or inappropriate" and that some "would create ill-will and antagonism toward the profession." With the skilled use of econometrics and data from about four hundred colleges and universities, Machlup developed a scale, with grades A through F. Each grade was for a minimum salary for each rank, professor to full-time instructor. The proposal suggested that the scales first be used to grade 1957–1958 salary reports, and its spring 1958 publication allowed ample time for association discussion and implementation.[105]

The salary scales were moderate ones, as the lowest grades were less than the salaries of teachers at urban public secondary schools.[106] Nevertheless, Committee Z was clearly intent upon improving salaries since the top grade did *not* include any salaries at any colleges or universities. The committee established a goal for top salaries that was above current practice "to accelerate the adjustment of salary scales to the realities of the market for highly qualified academic personnel."[107]

Despite the activity to improve faculty salaries, association leaders maintained their insistence that the AAUP met professional ideals. Helen C. White (English, University of Wisconsin), 1956–1958 AAUP president, reminded members at the 1958 Annual Meeting of the nature of academic freedom:

> We must be ready to explain again and again that academic freedom is not a matter of personal indulgence, not a self-interested union privilege, but the basic premise of the job which we have to do—that we are asking academic freedom not to exploit impulse or escape scrutiny for efficiency, but to do the work we have to for society.[108]

Association activity to promote better salaries did not mean that the AAUP would lose its professional face and become a union.

AAUP Ideals of Academic Freedom, AAUP Standards of Membership

Whatever the programmatic efforts in the area of faculty salaries, Committee A and academic freedom remained the primary professional program of the AAUP. Yet even in that arena, the association evidenced forms of activism. And, while the organization had a pro forma membership process that modeled professional standards, it was readying to change that process.

At the 1958 Annual Meeting, the association awarded its first Alexander Meiklejohn Award to the president and the trustees of the University of New Hampshire "for their 'significant contribution to academic freedom during the year.'"[109] The monies, and apparently even the conception of this award, came from outside the AAUP. In 1957, alumni and former professors of the Experimental College of the University of Wisconsin offered a three-thousand-dollar fund to the AAUP for an annual award in Meiklejohn's name, which the council accepted.[110] The AAUP had a new method for the advancement of academic freedom in the Meiklejohn Award.

Association efforts in 1958 to advance and protect academic freedom and tenure extended beyond censure and award. The members at the 1958 Annual Meeting, upon recommendation of the council, endorsed the Statement on Procedural Standards in Faculty Dismissal Proceedings as developed by representatives of the AAUP and the AAC.[111] The statement was detailed in its attempt to ensure due process, indicating that

> . . . formal proceedings should be commenced by a communication addressed to the faculty members by the president of the institution, informing the faculty member of the statement formulated [by the president and a faculty committee, concerning particular grounds for dismissal], and informing him that, if he so requests, a hearing to determine whether he should be removed from his faculty position on the grounds stated will be conducted by a faculty committee at a specified time and place.[112]

The statement furthered faculty participation, peer review, in a college's or university's consideration of dismissing a professor, through a carefully articulated series of steps. This statement went beyond principles of academic freedom and tenure and addressed the issue of faculty participation in college or university operations, identifying specific practices. Such participation not only furthered the professional goals of the association, securing influence if not control of working conditions, it also furthered bureaucratic procedures.

Local and national leaders also wanted to simplify the membership application process, and in 1958 the council voted to discontinue "publishing in the *AAUP Bulletin* the names of nominees for membership." Council members instructed Committee F on Membership and Committee O on Organization and Policy "to formulate a constitutional amendment establishing a system of membership by application to supersede the present system of membership by nomination."[113] Bertram H. Davis, staff associate, was in charge of membership at that time, and he identified the length and cost of the lists of nominees in the *Bulletin* as two of the three primary factors in the council decision. The third was:

> In part because the chapters objected; it took too long to get people in. They wanted to have somebody who had sent in his dues, . . ., [to] become active in the chapter right away. The waiting period was an inconvenience, and there wasn't much need for it. It seemed fine when the Association was starting—you had to be a full professor, it was far more of an elite organization. But it had outworn its usefulness, and I don't think anyone seriously regretted that we scrapped that.[114]

The public face of the association as an elite group requiring nomination for membership changed to a professors' association requiring a simple application for membership.

Getting members in quickly also meant that the association was also able to increase membership quickly, which was important because membership declined during this time. As of 1 January 1955, the AAUP had 42,144 active members (those allowed to vote at annual meetings and in elections), 39,748 of whom were at colleges and universities.[115] One percent was composed of professors at public and private two-year colleges, 30 percent was at public four-year colleges, 15 percent at private universities, and 10 percent at private colleges. Under one-half of the membership was at institutions from which the AAUP traditionally drew its leaders; 6 percent at selective private colleges, 7 percent at selective private universities, and 28 percent at public research and state flagship universities.[116] By 1 January 1959, the association had 38,347 active members of whom 36,631 were at colleges and universities.[117] In contrast, the number of college instructors nationally increased from 197,791 in November 1955 to 226,536 in 1957–1958.[118]

In a critical policy area, academic freedom, and a central organizational characteristic, membership, the association was evidencing some ambiguity in regard to professional ideals and standards. Bureaucratic procedures were having an impact on AAUP activities in terms of academic freedom, and the association was evidencing less concern about standards of membership.

Summary

The period from the spring of 1955 to the spring of 1958 was a very busy one for the AAUP following the organizational lull from the mid-1940s to 1955. Committee A and members at the annual meeting broke the tremendous backlog of academic freedom and tenure cases. Committee O and members at the annual meetings examined the Constitution and structure of the association and approved changes considered necessary "to advance the standards, ideals, and welfare of the profession." Committee Z began the implementation of grading salary scales at colleges and universities. The staff size increased to five members, one for every 7,669 active members.[119]

Committee structure among and within association committees changed in this period. The AAUP expanded the number of standing committees as preparation for addressing membership concerns and problems of higher education and the professoriate. By the end of 1958, there were thirteen standing committees, including committees on association investments, professorial ethics, and college and university accreditation, compared with apparently only four (A, O, T, Z) in 1955.[120] The AAUP leaders revived the committee structure, its basic organization for decision making and policy creation, from 1955 to 1958.

The completion of reconstruction of the association, however, needed the assurance of continuous executive staff leadership. In April 1957, General Secretary Fuchs announced that he had decided to return to teaching law at Indiana University.[121] Fuchs had done the association a tremendous service, leading the revitalization of AAUP. He identified the importance of attracting new members and leaders to the association (two of whom, Clark Byse and Ralph S. Brown, Jr., would become presidents) and providing broader and greater opportunities for involvement in the organization.[122] He also saw the need to act upon many issues facing professors and had begun the organizational process of addressing those issues. The council selected Robert Carr, one of the AAUP vice-presidents, to succeed Fuchs as general secretary.[123] The transition from Ralph Fuchs to Robert Carr was apparently a smooth one, perhaps in part because they worked together in the Central Office during June 1957.[124]

Yet Carr stayed in the position less than a year. He announced his resignation in the June 1958 *Bulletin*, stating that his decision was "a step taken in accordance with the agreement by which I assumed the office." Although there was no mention of such an agreement in any of the *Bulletin* announcements about Carr's appointment, the brevity of his stay apparently had no impact on the association's operations. The council appointed William P. Fidler, who had joined the AAUP staff in 1956, as general secretary—with his "acceptance of the post . . . not restricted as to time."[125] The AAUP was now strong enough to continue through some rapid changes at the senior administrative level.

Association activity ranged from quietude to considerable efforts at reconstruction in the period from 1946 to 1958. Himstead and national elected leaders had allowed the AAUP to remain inactive on issues of academic freedom, the organization's predominant program. The strong reaction of chapter and conference leaders to oligarchy and McCarthyism as they rapidly addressed the organizational inactivity proved that the AAUP could act. The national leaders' implementation of new programs and organizational structure proved their commitment to an active organization and to effecting the suggestions of chapter and conference leaders. In fact, the reinvigorated association could move toward more active and expansive application of membership and leadership solutions to the problems of higher education and the professoriate. The association had just effected one of those solutions, the Committee Z salary grading scale, and the coming years would prove to be ones of further expansion and activism.

Although the AAUP had begun to change its membership criteria, both within the AAUP and nationally college professors tended to be members of the academic profession as defined by Logan Wilson. Professors continued to teach mostly at four-year institutions in the mid-1950s.[126] Those teaching at two-year colleges tended to have backgrounds different from those at four-year institutions; more than 64 percent of the teaching staffs at seventy-six institutions surveyed in 1957 had taught at elementary or secondary schools.[127] Yet professors recognized some of the problems they faced. In 1957, Logan Wilson described professors as apparently "restive" about their working conditions, salaries, promotion policies, and the problem of arbitrary college and university administrations.[128] The AAUP had begun to address those issues, and the late 1950s and early 1960s would bring further expansion.

Notes

1. Bradford Morse, "The Veteran and His Education," *Higher Education* (1960): 16–19 as cited by Frederick Rudolph, *The American College and University: A History* (New York: Vintage Books, 1965), 486n. 6. See also *Keith W. Olson, The G.I. Bill, The Veterans, and The Colleges* (Lexington: University Press of Kentucky, 1974).
2. *Higher Education for American Democracy: A Report of the President's Commission on Higher Education*, 2 vols. (Washington, D.C.: United States Government Printing Office, 1947), I: 36 and II: 7.
3. Vannevar Bush, *Science, the Endless Frontier* (Washington, D.C.: United States Government Printing Office, 1945), 31–40. See John T. Wilson, *Academic Science, Higher Education, and the Federal Government, 1950–1983* (Chicago: University of Chicago Press, 1983), 2–3 on Bush and the development of the National Science Foundation. See also Dael Wolfle, *The Home of Science: The Role of the University* (New York: McGraw-Hill, 1972), 107.
4. *Digest of Educational Statistics: 1969 Edition* (Washington, D.C.: United States Government Printing Office, September 1969), table 85, 65.
5. *Digest of Educational Statistics: 1973 Edition* (Washington, D.C.: United States Government Printing Office, 1974), table 91, 76.
6. Federal data collection efforts concerning the number and type of professors (full-time, part-time, senior or junior staff, etc.) are erratic. Not only is information only available for occasional years but also the methods of reporting data vary. Readers should treat any longitudinal comparisons of faculty members in this work with care. *Statistics of Higher Education 1945–46*, table IV, 6 for 1945–1946 data; *Digest of Educational Statistics, 1971 Edition* (Washington, D.C.: United States Government Printing Office, 1971), table 104, 78 for November 1955 data.
7. Allan M. Cartter, *The Ph.D. and the Academic Labor Market* (New York: McGraw-Hill, 1976), 155.
8. Theodore Caplow and Reece McGee, *The Academic Marketplace* (Garden City, N.Y.: Basic Books, 1958), 93–166.
9. Loya Metzger, "Professors in Trouble," 75.
10. H. Bentley Glass, interview in Stony Brook, New York, on 4 March 1986. Glass was chair of the Special Committee that reviewed several alleged violations of academic freedom that the association had *not* addressed during the McCarthy era. See also Loya Metzger, "Professors in Trouble," 77; and Ellen Schrecker, *No Ivory Tower: McCarthyism and the Universities* (New York: Oxford University Press, 1986), 327–328.
11. "Thirty-third Annual Meeting," 5.
12. Frederick S. Deibler, AAUP president from 1940 to 1942, was the last president who was a charter member. "Report of the Nominating Committee," *Bulletin of the A.A.U.P.* 25 (October 1939): 437.
13. Loya Metzger, "Professors in Trouble," 72.
14. Ibid., 74–76. Loya Metzger emphasizes Himstead's concerns about details and power. As will be shown in the case of General Secretary William P. Fidler, the burden of running the association was excessive. Himstead complained in the *Bulletin* about the burden of his office, and the membership and chapters grew considerably during this period, increasing the workload. On Himstead's complaints, see [Ralph E. Himstead], "A Letter to the Membership," *A.A.U.P. Bulletin* 32 (Spring 1946): 163–165; and [Ralph E. Himstead], "A Letter to the Membership," *A.A.U.P. Bulletin* 33 (Autumn 1947): 579–585. The latter documents organizational growth, 584.

15. [Himstead], "A Letter to the Membership" (Autumn 1947), 583–584 on resignation of staff member Robert Ludlum and number of members, 581–583 on Shannon appointment.

16. Ibid., 584–585 on move and 585 on request for patience.

17. Ibid., 585.

18. [Ralph E. Himstead], "The State of the Association, 1936–1950," *A.A.U.P. Bulletin* 36 (Winter 1950): 758 on membership growth, 762 on reserve fund.

19. Ibid., 762–763.

20. [Ralph E. Himstead], "The Association's New Officers," *A.A.U.P. Bulletin* 38 (Spring 1952): 8–9.

21. "Record of Membership for 1951," *A.A.U.P. Bulletin* 38 (Spring 1952): 159 indicates a total of 41,238 Active Members as of 1 January 1952, a month before Middleton's appointment.

22. [Himstead], "Academic Freedom and Tenure at the University of Texas," 629, 632, and 633. This report is also interesting because Himstead quotes the University of Texas regents as accusing the AAUP of being "a 'CIO-like Union' that is attempting to control education in Texas." See 632. External observers continued to apply the union label.

23. Ralph E. Himstead, "Economic Status, Professional Standards and the General Welfare," *A.A.U.P. Bulletin* 33 (Winter 1947): 771–772.

24. Paul W. Ward, "Report of Committee T on the Place and Function of Faculties in College and University Government," *A.A.U.P. Bulletin* 34 (Spring 1948): 61.

25. "Academic Retirement, Statement of Principles," *A.A.U.P. Bulletin* 37 (Spring 1951): 90.

26. "Academic Freedom and Tenure, Evansville College," *A.A.U.P. Bulletin* 35 (Spring 1949): 74–111. The next reports on an investigation occurred in 1956; "Academic Freedom and Tenure: Saint Louis University" and "Academic Freedom and Tenure: North Dakota State Agricultural College," *AAUP Bulletin* 42 (Spring 1956): 108–129 and 130–160, respectively. See the index for the *A.A.U.P. Bulletin* for the intervening years. See also "Disposition of Committee A Cases: January 1, 1950–September 15, 1956," *AAUP Bulletin* 42 (Winter 1956): 706–708.

27. Paul Lazarsfeld and Wagner Thielens, Jr., *The Academic Mind: Social Scientists in a Time of Crisis* (Glencoe, Ill.: Free Press, 1958), table 2–6, 50. Forty-six percent of the reported attacks on professors were based on issues other than political ones. Lazarsfeld and Thielens also address the virulent anti-Communism, 35–39, 47, 49–58.

28. Schrecker, *No Ivory Tower*, 77, 95, 113,116, 279–280.

29. The AAUP's belated examination of these attacks provides a comprehensive description (and attempted evaluation) of the widespread nature of the problem. "Academic Freedom and Tenure in the Quest for National Security," *AAUP Bulletin* 42 (Spring 1956): 49–107 and particularly 96–100 on the widespread nature of the controversies. In general the reported attacks were more likely to occur at institutions other than the elite colleges and universities, although those institutions also faced serious problems. See Philo A. Hutcheson, "McCarthyism and the Professoriate: A Historiographic Nightmare?" *Higher Education: The Handbook of Theory and Research*, ed. John C. Smart, vol. 12, (New York: Agathon Press, 1997), 435–460.

30. Lazarsfeld and Thielens, *The Academic Mind*, chapter 3, "A Measure of Apprehension," 72–91; Theodore Caplow and Reece J. McGee, *The Academic Marketplace*, 137; Jencks and Riesman, *The Academic Revolution*, 202–204; Schrecker, *No Ivory Tower*, 171–181.

31. On faculties' and professors' support, George R. Stewart, *The Year of the Oath* (Garden City, N.Y.: Doubleday, 1950), 38–41, On the eventual AAUP report (a brief one), see "Academic Freedom and Tenure in the Quest for National Security" (Spring 1956), 64–66.

32. David P. Gardner, *The California Oath Controversy* (Berkeley: University of California Press, 1967), 208–209. Gardner reports that the AAUP delay in action did not help the faculties when they needed assistance. On AAUP quiescence, see Max Radin, "The Loyalty Oath at the University of California," *A.A.U.P. Bulletin* 36 (Summer 1950): 237–248 (including addenda for updates by the author and *Bulletin* editor, the latter based on information from media reports); Ralph E. Himstead, "Two Chapter Letters," *A.A.U.P. Bulletin* 36 (Autumn 1950): 585–587 (includes request for Committee A investigation); "The University of California Loyalty Oath Situation," *A.A.U.P. Bulletin* 37 (Spring 1951): 92–101 (report on the District Court of Appeal decision that the loyalty oath was invalid); [Ralph E. Himstead], "Editor's Note," *A.A.U.P. Bulletin* 37 (Autumn 1951): 441 (publication of Himstead telegram to university president on reinstatement of professors who did not sign the oath and president's response that the regents had not yet made a decision). On the eventual AAUP censure of the Board of Regents, see "The Forty-second Annual Meeting," *AAUP Bulletin* 42 (Summer 1956): 341.

33. Lazarsfeld and Thielens, *The Academic Mind*, 72–91. Himstead and the AAUP as an organization were not the only ones excruciatingly slow to respond to the attacks, and with strong reason.

34. H. Bentley Glass, interview in Stony Brook, New York, on 4 March, 1986.

35. "Twenty-sixth Annual Meeting," *Bulletin of the A.A.U.P.* 26 (February 1940): 7; and "List of Members," *Bulletin of the A.A.U.P.* 2 (March 1916): 36.

36. First years of AAUP membership and Committee A experience are from "Report of the 1945 Nominating Committee," *A.A.U.P. Bulletin* 31 (Autumn 1945): 510 for Edward Kirkland; "Report of the 1947 Nominating Committee," *A.A.U.P. Bulletin* 33 (Autumn 1947): 574 for the 1948–1950 president, Ralph Lutz; "Report of the 1949 Nominating Committee," *A.A.U.P. Bulletin* 35 (Autumn 1949): 561 for the 1950–1952 president, Richard Shryock; "Report of the 1951 Nominating Committee," *A.A.U.P. Bulletin* 37 (Autumn 1951): 590 for the 1952–1954 president, Fred Millett; "Report of the 1953 Nominating Committee and Proposed Constitutional Amendment," *A.A.U.P. Bulletin* 39 (Autumn 1953): 516 for William Britton.

37. George Pope Shannon, "Academic Freedom and Tenure, Report of Committee A for 1946," *A.A.U.P. Bulletin* 33 (Spring 1947): 70; George Pope Shannon, "Academic Freedom and Tenure, Report of Committee A for 1947," *A.A.U.P. Bulletin* 34 (Spring 1948): 132.

38. William T. Laprade, "Academic Freedom and Tenure, Report of Committee A for 1948," *A.A.U.P. Bulletin* 35 (Spring 1949): 65 and 49 on his statement that he was chair in 1941. William T. Laprade, "Academic Freedom and Tenure, Report of Committee A for 1949," *A.A.U.P. Bulletin* 36 (Spring 1950): 44. William T. Laprade, "Academic Freedom and Tenure, Report of Committee A for 1950," *A.A.U.P. Bulletin* 37 (Spring 1951): 82. William T. Laprade, "Academic Freedom and Tenure, Report of Committee A for 1951," *A.A.U.P. Bulletin* 38 (Spring 1952): 114. William T. Laprade, "Academic Freedom and Tenure, Report of Committee A for 1952," *A.A.U.P. Bulletin* 39 (Spring 1953): 120. William T. Laprade, "Academic Freedom and Tenure, Report of Committee A for 1953," *A.A.U.P. Bulletin* 40 (Spring 1954): 79. William T. Laprade, "Academic Freedom and Tenure, Report of Committee A for 1954," *A.A.U.P. Bulletin* 41 (Spring 1955): 31.

39. As selected, representative samples: Shannon, "Academic Freedom and Tenure, Report of Committee A for 1946," 70; Laprade, "Academic Freedom and Tenure, Report of Committee A for 1950," 82. Laprade, "Academic Freedom and Tenure, Report of Committee A for 1954," 31–33.

40. See, for example, Laprade, "Academic Freedom and Tenure, Report of Committee A for 1954," 27.

41. Loya Metzger, "Professors in Trouble," 73; Ellen Schrecker, *No Ivory Tower*, 336, where she identifies Himstead as suffering from a "strange pathology" that caused his inaction.

42. Laprade, "Academic Freedom and Tenure, Report of Committee A for 1954," 29–31, in defense of Himstead.

43. On the 1946 censure, see [Edward C. Kirkland], "Academic Freedom and Tenure, The University of Texas," 384–385. On the lack of reports on council activity, see "Index for 1946," *A.A.U.P. Bulletin* 32 (Winter 1946): 782; "Index for 1947," *A.A.U.P. Bulletin* 33 (Winter 1947): 229–233; "Index for 1948," *A.A.U.P. Bulletin* 35 (Spring 1949): 180; "Index for 1949," *A.A.U.P. Bulletin* 36 (Spring 1950): 194; "Index for 1950," *A.A.U.P. Bulletin* 36 (Winter 1950): 230; "Index for 1951," *A.A.U.P. Bulletin* 37 (Winter 1951–1952): 838; "Index for 1952," *A.A.U.P. Bulletin* 38 (Winter 1952–1953): 675; "Index for 1953," *A.A.U.P. Bulletin* 39 (Winter 1953–1954): 720; "Index for 1954," *A.A.U.P. Bulletin* 40 (Winter 1954–1955): 689. The report of the March 1955 council meeting began a continuing series of *Bulletin* reports on council activity. The spring 1955 meeting focused on reviving Committee A investigations and strengthening the organization—assigning the new president the authority to appoint new committees, for example. [George Pope Shannon], "Record of Council Meetings of American Association of University Professors," *A.A.U.P. Bulletin* 41 (Spring 1955): 104–109. The next section details local leaders' push to action.

44. "Report of the 1945 Nominating Committee," 510–514; and "Officers and Council," *A.A.U.P. Bulletin* 32 (Summer 1946): 232; "Report of the 1946 Nominating Committee," *A.A.U.P. Bulletin* 32 (Autumn 1946): 576–580; and "Thirty-third Annual Meeting," 8; "Report of the 1947 Nominating Committee," 574–578; and "Thirty-Fourth Annual Meeting," *A.A.U.P. Bulletin* 34 (Spring 1948): 11; "Report of the 1948 Nominating Committee," *A.A.U.P. Bulletin* 34 (Autumn 1948): 613–617; and "Thirty-fifth Annual Meeting," *A.A.U.P. Bulletin* 35 (Spring 1949): 11; "Report of the 1949 Nominating Committee," 561–565; and "Thirty-sixth Annual Meeting," *A.A.U.P. Bulletin* 36 (Spring 1950): 17; "Report of the 1950 Nominating Committee," *A.A.U.P. Bulletin* 36 (Autumn 1950): 592–596; and "Thirty-seventh Annual Meeting," *A.A.U.P. Bulletin* 37 (Spring 1951): 70–71; "Report of the 1951 Nominating Committee," 590–595; and "The Thirty-eighth Annual Meeting," *A.A.U.P. Bulletin* 38 (Spring 1952): 104; "Report of the 1952 Nominating Committee," *A.A.U.P. Bulletin* 38 (Autumn 1952): 473–478; and "Thirty-ninth Annual Meeting," *A.A.U.P. Bulletin* 39 (Spring 1953): 101; "Report of the 1953 Nominating Committee and Proposed Constitutional Amendment," 516–521; and "The Fortieth Annual Meeting," *A.A.U.P. Bulletin* 40 (Spring 1954): 123; "Report of the 1954 Nominating Committee, "*A.A.U.P. Bulletin* 40 (Autumn 1954): 484–488; and "The Forty-first Annual Meeting," *A.A.U.P. Bulletin* 41 (Spring 1955): 103.

45. Ralph E. Himstead et al., "A Symposium on the Economic Status of the Profession," *A.A.U.P. Bulletin* 32 (Autumn 1946): 428–442 on report, 428 on Himstead's comments.

46. "Thirty-third Annual Meeting," 8–9.

47. Seymour E. Harris, "Professorial Salaries and Tuition, 1947–48: Background and Proposals," *A.A.U.P. Bulletin* 34 (Spring 1948): 98 on survey, 108 on rises of cost of living, salaries, and tuition.

48. Ralph E. Himstead, "The Association and the Economic Status of the Profession," *A.A.U.P. Bulletin* 34 (Summer 1948): 420 and 424.

49. Henry G. Badger, "Constitution of College Teachers' Salary Schedules," *A.A.U.P. Bulletin* 34 (Summer 1948): 407.

50. "Instructional Salaries in 41 Selected Colleges and Universities for the Academic Year 1953–54," *A.A.U.P. Bulletin* 39 (Winter 1953–54): 633.

51. Ibid., 632.

52. Paul W. Ward, "Report of Committee T on the Place and Function of Faculties in College and University Government," *A.A.U.P. Bulletin* 34 (Spring 1948): 61 on previous rates of faculty participation; 61–62 on lack of trend; 58–59 on report's suggestion.

53. "The Role of Faculties of Colleges and Universities in the Determination of Institutional Policies," *A.A.U.P. Bulletin* 38 (Winter 1952–53): 637–644 for Himstead's announcement of a survey of faculty participation and a copy of the survey and see [Paul W. Ward and Ralph E. Himstead], "The Place and Function of Faculties in College and University Government, Report of Progress," *A.A.U.P. Bulletin* 39 (Summer 1953): 300–318. See 311 on administrations' consultations with faculties.

54. Paul W. Ward, "The Place and Function of Faculties in College and University Government, Report of Committee T," *A.A.U.P. Bulletin* 41 (Spring 1955): 77.

55. Ibid., 74–75 on small colleges, 72–75 on other institutions.

56. Ibid., 78 on joint statement, 80–81 on continuous service.

57. James Holladay, "The Role and Activities of Region VII of the Association," *A.A.U.P Bulletin* 41 (Spring 1955): 84–87.

58. Warren Taylor, "The Ohio Conference of Chapters of the American Association of University Professors," *A.A.U.P. Bulletin* 41 (Winter 1955): 677–679.

59. Ibid., II: 354–355.

60. Loya Metzger, "Professors in Trouble," p. 78.

61. R. Beck, "Chapter Minutes, 26 May 1953," AAUP Files, as quoted by Wiberg, "A History of the University of Minnesota Chapter of the American Association of University Professors, 1916–1960," 2 vols., Ph.D. dissertation, University of Minnesota, II: 355.

62. Loya Metzger, "Professors in Trouble," p. 78.

63. [Ralph E. Himstead], "The Thirty-ninth Annual Meeting," *A.A.U.P. Bulletin* 39 (Spring 1953): 102–103 on lack of communication and chapter invitations; 103 on academic freedom violations; 103–104 on chapter involvement.

64. Ibid., 104–105. Loya Metzger writes that Himstead's numbers are "pure fabrications" and that mail was never counted. Metzger, "Professors in Trouble," 73 and 73n. 1, on mail not counted. Simple division, however, indicates that Himstead's numbers would mean 398 communications for each day of the year, using 251 working days. Given the intensity of the McCarthy attacks, their widespread publicity, and the level of chapter activity (as documented in this work), it is reasonable to guess that Himstead took a busy day's communications and exaggerated, but not extraordinarily so. In further support of this assessment of the level of communications, see [George Pope Shannon], "Central Office Notes," *A.A.U.P. Bulletin* 41 (Summer 1955): 366, in which he states that in three months the AAUP staff members wrote 2,500 letters. Assuming 66 working days in three months, the staff members wrote 38 letters per day. Himstead's claim of 20,000 communications best handled by professional staff members would mean 80 per day (using again 251 working days) and would include telephone calls as well as letters.

65. [Himstead], "The Thirty-ninth Annual Meeting," 105.

66. Loya Metzger, "Professors in Trouble," 78–79 on avoiding Committee O, 79–80 on Committee report and Council response, 80 on subcommittee's report, 80–81 on resignation.

67. Wiberg, "A History of the University of Minnesota Chapter," II: 354 on regional meeting; II: 356–357 on attendance and suggestions.

68. Ibid., II: 356 on first section; II: 356 on second and third sections; II: 357–358 on recommendations and delivery to the Central Office.

69. Ibid., II: 358 on second meeting; II: 358 and 359 on discussion; II: 358, 358–359 on annual meeting and instructions to Levi.

70. Werner Levi, "Report on the Annual Meeting of the AAUP, 1954," AAUP Files, as quoted by Wiberg, "A History of the University of Minnesota Chapter," II: 361n. 33.

71. Ibid, II:361.

72. Ibid.
73. Loya Metzger, "Professors in Trouble," 81. See Wiberg, "A History of the University of Minnesota Chapter," II: 359 on effective date of resignation.
74. Loya Metzger, "Professors in Trouble," 81–82 on fighting Council action, 82 on retirement.
75. Ibid, 82–83.
76. Ibid., 83. See also Ralph F. Fuchs, "A Letter From the General Secretary," *A.A.U.P. Bulletin* 41 (Autumn 1955): 423–424.
77. Ralph F. Fuchs, "Report, 1955–57, by the Retiring General Secretary," *AAUP Bulletin* 43 (September 1957): 415; [William E. Britton], "The General Secretaryship," *A.A.U.P. Bulletin* 41 (Spring 1955): 6. He had been the president of the Washington University chapter (elected to the position two years after joining the AAUP in 1931) and vice-president of the Indiana University chapter in 1949–1950. He had national leadership experience as a member of the council from 1945 to 1947, first vice-president from 1950 to 1951, and chair of the Resolutions Committee for the 1951 and 1952 Annual Meetings. Fuchs had also been a member of the staff of the U.S. solicitor general and active in the Indiana Civil Liberties Union as well as the Association of American Law Schools (serving as chair of that organization's Committee on Academic Freedom and Tenure in 1953). He published widely in the field of administrative law and was reported to be "one of the twelve people who shaped the most important piece of administrative law legislation in our country's history, the Administrative Procedure Act." See [George Pope Shannon], "The General Secretaryship of the American Association of University Professors," *A.A.U.P. Bulletin* 41 (Summer 1955): 212; and "Special Commemorative Meeting of the Indiana University School of Law Faculty in Honor of the Memory of Professor Ralph Follen Fuchs: Transcript of Proceedings" (Bloomington, Ind.: 4 March 1985), 11 and 17.
78. Fuchs, "Report, 1955–57, by the Retiring General Secretary," 416.
79. [Shannon], "Record of Council Meetings of American Association of University Professors," 104–105. The council made these decisions at the awkward time when Himstead was fighting to stay in the office but Fuchs was to assume the general secretaryship. Thus, although Himstead was at the time general secretary, the decisions appear to respond to Fuchs's anticipated arrival. Elected leadership activity continued beyond committing funds for staff members and urging quick investigations into alleged academic freedom violations. As requested by the council, President William E. Britton began to scrutinize committee membership, and he appointed three new committees, on annual meeting programs, AAUP publications, and eligibility for membership. See [George Pope Shannon], "Central Office Notes," *A.A.U.P. Bulletin* 41 (Summer 1955): 367.
80. [Shannon], "Central Office Notes," 366.
81. Fuchs, "A Letter from the General Secretary," 423 and [Shannon], "Central Office Notes," 366. Although the AAUP president was responsible for appointments, Fuchs assembled the Special Committee according to its chair, H. Bentley Glass. H. Bentley Glass, interview in Stonybrook, New York, on 4 March 1986.
82. [Ralph F. Fuchs], "Central Office Notes," *A.A.U.P. Bulletin* 41 (Autumn 1955): 592–593 on committee membership and requested reports; 592 on contacts.
83. "Academic Freedom and Tenure in the Quest for National Security," 52.
84. Ibid, 50 on Communist infiltration and 56 on needed safeguards.
85. "Academic Freedom and Tenure in the Quest for National Security," 58 on conspiracy; "Academic Freedom and Tenure: Statements of Principles," *AAUP Bulletin*, 42 (Spring 1956): 41–44, and 43–44 on incompetence and moral turpitude; "Academic Freedom and Tenure in the Quest for National Security," 60 on personal freedom. One scholar's examination of the AAUP during World War I suggested that even in those early years the association was willing to sacrifice values of scholarship to the service of the nation; see Carol S. Gruber, *Mars and Minerva: World War I and the Uses of Higher Learning in America* (Baton Rouge: Louisiana State University Press, 1975), 115–117. Another author offered a stronger statement on AAUP activity in defense of academic freedom and tenure principles, stating that the association "sacrificed individuals and substantive principles in order to gain compliance for procedural safeguards from university officials for the profession as a whole." That author also called the Special Committee's report "a massive and pathetic equivocation." See Sheila Slaughter, "The Danger Zone: Academic Freedom and Civil Liberties," *Annals of the American Academy of Political and Social Science* 448 (March 1980): 47–48. Slaughter softened her stance in a more recent article, suggesting that "the degree of academic freedom varies with historical circumstance." See Sheila Slaughter, "Academic Freedom in the Modern University," in *Higher Education in American Society,* ed. Philip G. Altbach and Robert O. Berdahl, rev. ed. (Buffalo: Prometheus Books, 1987), 84.
86. "Academic Freedom and Tenure in the Quest for National Security," 71.

87. [Ralph F. Fuchs], "Outside Reaction to Last Spring's Special Committee Report and Censure Actions," *AAUP Bulletin* 42 (Autumn 1956): 566–570. See also R. H. Eckleberry, "Editorial Comments: A Double Standard," *Journal of Higher Education* 47 (April 1956): 223–225.

88. "Organization and Policy—Report of Committee O," *AAUP Bulletin* 42 (Spring 1956): 166–167.

89. "Committees of the Association," *AAUP Bulletin* 43 (Spring 1957): 93–99.

90. Ibid., 93–95 on A, T, and Z; 98–99 on district panels.

91. H. W. Tyler, "What the Association Is and Is Not," *AAUP Bulletin* 42 (Spring 1956): 163–165.

92. Ibid., 163.

93. "Organization and Policy—Report of Committee O," 170.

94. Ibid.

95. "General Recommendations and Projections," *AAUP Bulletin* 51 (May 1965): 191n. 1, on addition of "economic welfare." See "Proposed Revision of the Constitution," *AAUP Bulletin* 43 (Spring 1957): 85 on the version to be amended as approved by the council. The original phrase dates back to the 1914 call to organize the association; see the brief history of the association's early years in the first chapter.

96. "The Forty-third Annual Meeting," *AAUP Bulletin* 43 (June 1957): 364.

97. American University chapter delegates to council, 26 April 1957, in "Council Meeting—November 15–16, 1957 Washington, D. C.," file in AAUP Archives, Washington, D.C.

98. "Recommendations of the District of Columbia Regional Conference to the Council" (1 September 1957), 2, in "Council Meeting—November 15–16," file in AAUP Archives, Washington, D.C.

99. "Resolution Adopted at the Annual Meeting of the Illinois Conference of the American Association of University Professors, October 26–7, 1957" in "Council Meeting—November 15–16, 1957," file in AAUP Archives, Washington, D.C.

100. "Recommendations of the District of Columbia Regional Conference to the Council," 1 on symptoms, 1 and 4 on staffing recommendations, 3 on professions.

101. John Wilson, *Academic Science, Higher Education, and the Federal Government*, 45. The National Defense Education Act was also an indication of concern about loyalty in education having subsided rather than ended as it included a required loyalty oath that was not rescinded until 1961. See Wilson, 46–47.

102. President's Commission on Education Beyond the High School, *Second Report to the President* (Washington, D.C.: United States Government Printing Office, July 1957), 4.

103. Fritz Machlup, "Grading of Academic Salary Scales," *AAUP Bulletin* 44 (March 1958): 219. "Report of the Subcommittee on Standards of the Committee on the Economic Status of the Profession," *AAUP Bulletin* 44 (March 1958): 217–218.

104. Machlup, "Grading of Academic Salary Scales," 219–220.

105. Ibid., 219 on purposes of survey, 220 on proposals, 225–226 on construction of scale, 226 on timing of report.

106. Ibid., 225, 231.

107. Ibid., 226 on top grade; See "Report of the Subcommittee on Standards of the Committee on the Economic Status of the Profession," 217 on acceleration.

108. Helen C. White, "The Association in 1958," *AAUP Bulletin* 44 (June 1958): 395–396. White also notes the recent strong change in public attitudes about higher education, 394.

109. "Forty-fourth Annual Meeting," 503.

110. "Record of Council Meeting," *AAUP Bulletin* 43 (September 1957), 538. See also H. Bentley Glass, interview in Stonybrook, New York, on 4 March 1986.

111. "Statement on Procedural Standards in Faculty Dismissal Proceedings," *AAUP Bulletin* 44 (March 1958): 271–274; "Record of Council Meeting," 281 on council approval; "Forty-fourth Annual Meeting [Completed Report]," *AAUP Bulletin* 44 (September 1958): 652–653.

112. "Statement on Procedural Standards in Faculty Dismissal Proceedings," 272.

113. "Record of Council Meeting," *AAUP Bulletin* 44 (September 1958): 658.

114. Bertram H. Davis, interview in Tallahassee, Florida, on 7 March 1986.

115. "Distribution of Membership and Record of Chapter Officers: Record of Membership for 1954," *AAUP Bulletin* 41 (Spring 1955): 170.

116. Ibid., 135–169. The remaining active members at colleges and universities were at professional and technical institutions or foreign colleges and universities.

117. "Membership: Record for 1958," *AAUP Bulletin* 45 (March 1959): 135.

118. *Digest of Educational Statistics: 1971 Edition*, table 104, 78.

119. Staff size was temporarily down to four members at the end of 1958 because General Secretary Carr had resigned, but a new staff member was to be appointed shortly. See "Record of Council Meeting," *AAUP Bulletin* 45 (March 1959): 90 on Fidler's proposal for another member. Staff size of four noted in

"Officers and the Council," *AAUP Bulletin* 45 (March 1959): 229 [unnumbered] and active members in "Membership: Record for 1958," 135.

120. "Committees of the Association," *AAUP Bulletin* 44 (December 1958): 792–796 and "Index for 1955," *A.A.U.P. Bulletin* 41 (Winter 1955): 822–823 on committee reports in 1955. There are no published lists of more committees in 1955, although more may have been operating at the time.

121. Ralph F. Fuchs, "Council Election, and Appointment of New General Secretary," *AAUP Bulletin* 43 (June 1957): 247.

122. Clark Byse, interview in Cambridge, Massachusetts, on 2 March 1986. Ralph S. Brown, Jr., interview in New Haven, Connecticut, on 3 March 1986.

123. Fuchs, "Council Election and Appointment of New General Secretary," 248. Carr was the author of books on civil rights and civil liberties, and since 1937 he had been a professor of law and political science at Dartmouth College. His AAUP activities included council membership and service on Committee A and the Special Committee on Academic Freedom and Tenure in the Quest for National Security. See [Ralph F. Fuchs], "The New General Secretary," *AAUP Bulletin* 43 (September 1957): 411.

124. Fuchs, "Council Election and Appointment of New General Secretary," 248.

125. Robert K. Carr, "The Association's New Officers, Council Members, and General Secretary," *AAUP Bulletin* 44 (June 1958): 390–391 on Carr's announcement, 391 on Fidler's appointment.

126. *Statistics of Higher Education: 1955–56, Faculty, Students, and Degrees* (Washington, D.C.: United States Government Printing Office, 1957), table V, 14.

127. Leland Medsker, *The Junior College: Progress and Prospect* (New York: McGraw-Hill, 1960), 172.

128. Logan Wilson, "A President's Perspective," *Faculty-Administration Relationships*, ed. Frank C. Abbott (Washington, D.C.: American Council on Education, 1958), 3.

Negotiating the Master Plan and the Fate of Higher Education in California

John Aubrey Douglass

If they don't come up with something, we will do it ourselves . . . we have to move ahead on this Master Plan.

—Governor Edmund "Pat" Brown, 1959

As California struggled to find a common vision for its higher education system in the late 1950s, other states were engaged in a similar debate. Commenting on the lack of state coordination within rapidly growing state systems of higher education, James Conant, the former president at Harvard, described his "sense of horror at the disarray [he] found in a number of large and important states." After touring the nation to assess the future of America's education system, he urged states to "plan more carefully for the development of education beyond the high school."[1]

The post-World War II era was a significant period of reorganization in American higher education. Of the approximately seventeen states during the late 1950s and early 1960s that modified their public and private systems to promote coordination and control costs, most looked toward reducing the autonomy of their public higher education institutions. As Lyman Glenny observed in 1959, state governments found it imperative to develop formal coordinating mechanisms: "Legislatures, in response to the competition for funds, have increasingly turned to superboards or commissions of lay persons with a professional staff for information and recommendations on public higher education. They expect such a board to make the higher educational system more productive, efficient, and economical."[2]

Conscious of the national trend toward centralization of state systems of higher education, and the predilections of powerful political leaders such as state senator George Miller, Clark Kerr and others in California's education community recognized that the Master Plan negotiations might be their last chance to influence reform. Failure to create a politically palatable plan would almost certainly guarantee significant if not radical reform of the tripartite system. For University of California officials, there was a fear that lawmakers might elevate the programs and role of the state colleges; more worrisome, legislators and Governor Brown might attempt a constitutional amendment that would erode the university's autonomy and provide greater regulatory control by both the legislature and state agencies.

State college officials such as San Diego's Malcolm Love imagined another scenario: Kerr might successfully revive the idea of university control of the state colleges, winning the support of the new Democratic leadership in Sacramento. Pressure was building to come to some resolution. An editorial in the *Los Angeles Times* noted, "The patchy development of the State Colleges may reflect regional necessities, but it has become clear that the state must have a master plan for higher education, not only for the state colleges, but for the branching University of California."[3]

Kerr later claimed that the path to the Master Plan was not the end result of a clearly constructed strategic plan either by university officials or other members of the higher education community in

California. "We were not on the Acropolis looking back on events," Kerr reflected in 1990, "but down in the Agora, the marketplace, making deals under the discipline of time and deadlines." [4] Yet the ultimate approval of the plan by the two boards and lawmakers was the result of Kerr's efforts and the outcome of a clear, if at times risky, strategy. At the opening of the negotiation process, it was understood that the stakes were extremely high for the University of California and the state colleges, and for the people of California.

The Love Plan

A week after the California Legislature passed Dorothy Donahoe's resolution calling for a Master Plan, Kerr and Simpson agreed that the plan should be completed by a nine-member Joint Advisory Committee (JAC) to the Liaison Committee. The JAC had been established in the early 1950s to assist the Liaison Committee on key issues. It now consisted of three state college presidents, three university chancellors, and three representatives from the junior colleges. Staff for the JAC included Thomas C. Holy from the university and Arthur Brown from the Department of Education.[5] Both served as staff to the Liaison Committee as well. Kerr and Simpson asked the JAC to immediately negotiate one of the most contested questions facing California public higher education: what was the appropriate function of each segment of the public system? Kerr and Simpson agreed that two other key issues, governance and enrollment expansion, would follow the resolution of segmental functions. However, placing the burden of negotiating the Master Plan on the JAC would prove problematic for the university.

In preparing for the first JAC meeting, Dean McHenry suggested a scheme for Kerr and university officials. Kerr had known McHenry since their days in graduate school at Berkeley, where they had been roommates. McHenry was born in Lompoc, California, and had received his B.A. from UCLA in 1932. Four years later, he had earned his Ph.D. at Berkeley. McHenry then accepted a faculty position at UCLA in the Department of Political Science. After serving in the Navy during World War II, he returned to UCLA and, between 1947 and 1950, served as the dean of the social sciences. McHenry had a scholarly passion about California politics and the workings of state and local government—a passion he then converted into an attempt at a political career. He was an active member of the California Democratic Council and ran unsuccessfully for the State Assembly in the early 1950s. When Kerr became president in 1958, he asked his politically astute and good friend to become an "academic assistant." McHenry accepted, while still retaining his faculty position at UCLA.[6]

McHenry became Kerr's primary strategist and confidant in the difficult days that lay ahead. He told Kerr that the university needed to assess those "areas most vital . . . to the university system, the loss of which would be disastrous, and the sharing of which would lead to the depletion of quality and/or the slow starvation of the portion of functions left with UC." At all costs, argued McHenry, the university must prevent the state colleges from being called universities and should never relinquish doctoral degrees. He was also adamant, as Sproul had been, that the university obstruct any attempt to enlarge the research functions of the state colleges. A change in name or new degrees, noted McHenry, should require legislative action to amend the *Education Code* or, possibly, the state constitution. He advised Kerr that, among legislators, "we must build up such strength that they will fear to propose lest they fail." To do so, the university must "tell them frankly what our vital interests are." In short, he claimed, if a joint agreement fails, "we will fight them in the first house, second house, the governor's office, etc. If they get a bill through we hold it up in referendum."[7] McHenry hoped that, with the help of junior college representatives, the university might "score regular six-to-three victories," in JAC meetings.

The state college presidents had other ideas. They had already circulated their three-point plan for higher education in Sacramento. Now they brought it to the negotiation table with some interesting twists. At the next meeting of the JAC in late March, Malcolm Love offered a radical "redefinition" of state college and university functions. Under the "Love Plan," the state colleges would become universities offering undergraduate liberal arts and occupational and professional curricula, with "specialization continued at the graduate level and culminating in an advanced degree." This would include the Ph.D., a research function with state support for buildings, and a reduction in the teaching loads of faculty. At the same time, the University of California would reduce its admission of undergraduates and focus on the training of advanced research scholars. Terminal master's degrees would cease to be given, and the university would admit students from the top tenth of the high school graduating class—down from approximately the top 15 percent it had accepted since the Progressive Era.[8]

Kerr asked McHenry to attend all the JAC meetings and report their activities to him. He was traumatized by the acquiescence of the university's representatives. Chancellors Glenn Seaborg (Berkeley), Verne Knudsen (UCLA), and Stan Freeborn (Davis) had been appointed to uphold the university's interests. Despite Kerr's instructions, the Love Plan entranced them. The three chancellors—each highly respected scientists, with Seaborg a Nobel Prize winner and one of the discoverers of plutonium—listened intently as Love and his politically savvy colleagues, San Francisco State President Dumke and San Jose State President Wahlquist, explained the advantages of the plan. As McHenry silently watched, deferring to his superiors, the three chancellors immediately noted their general agreement, indeed, enthusiasm, for the proposal. They were attracted to the graduate and research emphasis that appeared to them the true calling of the University of California—an image that had captured the imaginations of Benjamin Ide Wheeler and David Starr Jordan fifty years before.

McHenry reported back to Kerr with alarm. "Having failed to do their homework, these boys have practically given on a silver platter what we have kept from them by force of logic and by power of the legislature," complained McHenry to Kerr. "Deliver us from naive scientists!"[9]

The Love Plan would fulfill the major objectives of the state college presidents. McHenry analyzed President Love's opening move, noting to Kerr: "tactically, it appears that we were outmaneuvered. . . . [T]he state colleges are to take over nearly everything." What remained was a university "pricing itself out of the undergraduate market and living in the stratosphere with Ravel and the Deity . . . shooting [the University of California] into space. Sad thing is that there is little in the way of refueling up there and some solid BTU's and dollars are required to keep such an expensive mechanism operating."[10] Vernon Cheadle, a professor of botany at Davis and chair of that campus' Education Policy Committee, noted that "the University has been beaten to the punch, consciously or unconsciously, and has been thrown into a defensive position."[11] An academic senate committee called Love's proposal "unacceptable." It would create "a second University system in California" and mark the beginning of the end of the university's dominant position in the state's hierarchy of public higher education.[12]

Several days after the Love Plan was unveiled, Chancellor Knudsen innocently sent Kerr an outline of segmental functions that reflected Love's proposal, noting its advantages and conceding doctorate programs to the state colleges as inevitable. Why "give away our heritage," exclaimed an upset McHenry. He urged Kerr to immediately replace Seaborg, Knudsen, and Freeborn on the JAC or to insist that their views represent those of the university president and the regents. Otherwise, McHenry warned, Kerr's presidency would be a black mark in the history of the University of California. "During the Kerr era, the Empire becomes Commonwealth," eulogized McHenry. "Another 'babes in the woods' act like that and Kerr may preside over the liquidation of the new Commonwealth. Or its twilight?"[13]

President Kerr responded by sending a letter addressed to university vice president Harry Wellman and routed to Freeborn, Knudsen, and Seaborg. Kerr noted that he was "disturbed" by the discussion at the JAC. He felt that the "University must have a unified position at this time of great crisis in its external relations. . . . The Love proposals on the functions of the University would make it such an elitist institution that it might no longer endure." Under no circumstances, noted Kerr, should the university accept such a broad definition of the state college mission. Less than a month later, Kerr replaced Knudsen and a retiring Freeborn with the new chancellor at Davis, Emil Mrak, and the new chancellor at Riverside, Herman Spieth. By the end of July, Seaborg had also been replaced on the JAC by the new chancellor at Santa Barbara, Samuel B. Gould. All three replacements were viewed by Kerr and McHenry as more politically adept for the challenges ahead.

Kerr then forcefully told Superintendent Simpson that the Love Plan was unacceptable. At a meeting of the state college presidents, an angry Malcolm Love retorted that Kerr had "prematurely rejected the statement. . . without full study and consideration by everyone concerned." Love noted his worry that Kerr and the university were attempting to forge a consensus among lawmakers in Sacramento toward absorption of the state colleges under the regents. This would presumably end all hope of new graduate programs and make the state colleges second-class citizens within the university system. Glenn Dumke also reported that Governor Brown now seemed to be in favor of this change or a similar reform, joining Senator Miller.[14]

In the wake of the Love Plan, Kerr considered abandoning the Master Plan negotiations. Valuable time had been lost, and the bold and populist demands of Malcolm Love and his compatriots posed a serious challenge to the university. Kerr asked key faculty for their advice. William S. Briscoe, a professor of education at UCLA, advocated the swift absorption by the regents of the state colleges. "I feel we are facing a crisis," he exclaimed.[15] Tom Holy agreed. He had been the university's staff member on the JAC since its creation in 1953 and now warned that the system of voluntary coordination was collapsing. In his opinion, it probably could not be resurrected.[16] It was perhaps time for the university to launch a hostile takeover of the state colleges. "Statements of public officials, legislators and others," he explained, "leave the impression that chaos reigns and that millions of dollars of the taxpayers' money is being wasted in the struggle between the University and the state colleges." This, combined with "the fact that president Kerr is in his 'honeymoon period'" with lawmakers and the public, Holy argued, "offered an opportune time for the University taking control of the colleges."[17]

McHenry thought differently. Reflecting the consternation of former university president Robert Sproul in the 1930s and 1940s, McHenry warned that such a bold move would raise substantial political opposition and result in legislation abhorrent to the university. Even if the university was successful in its conquest, the regents would then face the difficult task of managing two competing groups of institutions. The resolve to protect the university's teaching and research mission might fade over time. There would be pressure for the state colleges to reach some form of parity with the campuses of the university. This pressure might eventually come from within the board as new governors chose new regents with allegiances to the state colleges. He urged Kerr not to abandon the negotiations.

Kerr's legal counsel also advised against absorption of the state colleges: It was bound to raise questions regarding the proper level of autonomy for the university and possibly a movement to end the university's status as a constitutionally protected public trust. Kerr decided to keep with the negotiations but to abandon the JAC as a forum to complete the planning study.[18] Chancellors within the university system appeared consumed by the interests of their own campuses. At the same time, the formidable state college presidents on the committee had a clear agenda that promised little if any compromise. A new forum for negotiating the plan was needed, with new players. At the same time and as a contingency plan, Kerr would keep open the option of a constitutional amendment to place the state colleges under the regents.

Organizing the Plan

In late May of 1959, a little over a month after Love's gambit, Kerr gained Superintendent Roy Simpson's agreement to create a "Master Plan Survey Team." The team would include representatives from the university, the state colleges, the junior colleges, and the addition of private institutions who had been lobbying in Sacramento for a role in the negotiations. Most importantly, it would include as chair an arbitrator without ties to either the university or the state colleges.[19] Though Simpson remained a reluctant supporter of the Master Plan, he was cognizant of the need to complete the plan to maintain, indeed rebuild, his reputation with lawmakers. The Board of Regents and the California State Board of Education then approved the concept of the survey team.

The state college presidents were angry over the abandonment of the JAC and Simpson's capitulation to a new forum for negotiations. University officials, they believed, had created a new negotiating environment by adding a university ally: representatives from the private institutions. However, the key to the negotiations, the state college presidents realized, lay perhaps in the selection of the chair of survey team. Here they found some comfort with the naming of Arthur G. Coons.

Kerr and Simpson considered several people before agreeing on Coons as the survey team chair. A. Alan Post was one candidate, because of his ties with the legislature as the chief budget analyst and his excellent reputation. Another candidate was Wilson E. Lyon, president of Pomona College. Finally, in early June they agreed on Coons, the longtime president of Occidental College and a political scientist who had published in the area of political economy. "It was clear I would be under the necessity of trying to get the 'warring' factions into sufficient agreement fast enough to fulfill the Legislature's demands," reflected Coons in 1968. He agreed to chair the survey team, even though two Occidental trustees strongly opposed his decision. It would take him away from his duties at the small liberal arts college. Friends and trustees at the college told him that any attempt to resolve the fighting within the higher education community on the one side and the reckless abandon of legislators on the other would certainly "ruin his health." Coons had already experienced a heart attack in early 1957.[20]

A native of Los Angeles, Coons began his academic career as a teacher at Fullerton Junior College before becoming a faculty member at the Claremont Graduate School. In 1950, he was named president of Occidental. Glenn Dumke had spent most of his academic and administrative career at Occidental and had served under Coons as a dean before becoming the president of San Francisco State in 1957 at the age of forty. Dumke reported to his fellow state college presidents that Coons could be counted on to provide a fair hearing for their interests.

The other eight members of the survey team were also chosen by Kerr and Simpson and included Glenn Dumke for the state colleges and Dean McHenry for the university. Henry T. Tyler was selected to represent the junior colleges. Tyler was the executive secretary for the California Junior College Association. The Association of Independent Colleges and Universities appointed Robert J. Wert, vice provost at Stanford University. Also appointed to act as staff on the team were Thomas C. Holy for the university, Arthur Browne for the State Department of Education, and retired superintendent of the Los Angeles Public Schools Howard A. Campion.[21]

Coons and the survey team were to consider six major issues. None assumed any major shift in California's commitment to expanding access to higher education; rather they focused on ways to make modifications in the tripartite system that had emerged largely in the Progressive Era. The first concerned enrollment: What was their projection of student enrollment demand from 1960 to 1975, and how might they be distributed among the three public segments?[22] The second issue related to segmental functions—a source of heated debate. "In light of new and changing circumstances," explained the survey team's mandate, "what modifications should be made in the existing agreements on the differentiation of functions among the junior colleges, state colleges and the University of California?" After addressing these two issues, the team needed to provide a priority list and schedule for establishing new campuses, an estimate of the cost of capital and annual operations to the state, and an assessment of the ability of the California government to pay for the expansion plan. The sixth and final challenge of the survey team was to recommend the appropriate model for the governance and coordination of the system.[23]

To assist the work of the survey team, six "technical committees" were established, each focusing on the six planning issues stated in the charge for the survey team.[24] (See Figure 10.) These committees were chaired by faculty and administrators from the public tripartite system and were largely fact-finding groups with representatives from all the public and private segments.[25]

Arthur Coons initially favored a single governing board for all public higher education in California. In his view, it needed to have "inclusive and extensive authority and power" over the tripartite system.[26] In no small part, this position reflected his experience as president of Occidental College. "Coons was one of the old line college presidents," later reflected Glenn Dumke, "who operated very autocratically and with insistence that there be central control. . . . [H]e ran a very tight ship."[27]

Coons saw in California public higher education a level of disarray that needed to be forcefully addressed. This was a viewpoint he brought openly to the first meeting of the survey team on June 16, 1959. Coons' predilection was reinforced by a comparative study of other state higher education governance systems conducted by Tom Holy and Arthur Browne two months earlier.[28] Holy and Browne reported that three general organizational structures could be found in state

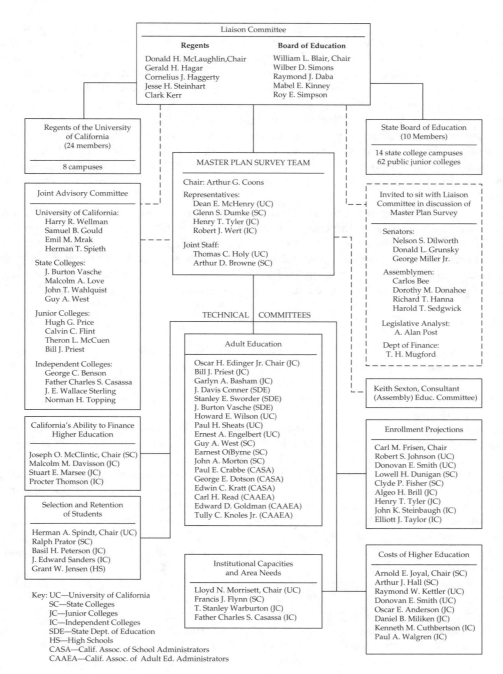

Figure 10 Organization of Master Plan Study, 1959

SOURCE: Graphic presented in the *California Master Plan for Higher Education,* 1960

systems of public higher education in the United States. The first model offered no central governance mechanism and reflected a laissez-faire approach: Each institution, or campus, had its own board that would then report directly to the legislature. Approximately ten states, they noted, functioned in this manner.[29]

The second model, that of a single board with authority over all public higher education, could be found in twenty states. In most of these states, a single board governed all public colleges and universities. In New Mexico, New York, North Carolina, Oklahoma, Texas, and Wisconsin, a super-board was imposed over existing boards for the teachers colleges and the other public colleges and universities in the state. Local boards were subservient to the superboard, whose responsibilities included approving all academic programs, establishing all new campuses, and preparing a single budget for all state-supported higher education.[30] Seven other states were in the process of shifting to a single board model (sometimes called a "coordinating agency") with various levels of authority, including Arkansas, Colorado, Illinois, Louisiana, Michigan, Tennessee, and Utah.[31]

The third model, with two separate boards for the state land grant university and state colleges, could be found in approximately eighteen states, including California. Within this model, only three states had a voluntary coordinating mechanism, California, Ohio, and Indiana. In Ohio and Indiana, voluntary boards were formed in the face of a legislative threat to establish a single board.[32]

In Coons' opinion, there was little if any chance to resurrect a workable voluntary mechanism, like the Liaison Committee, in California. In the face of a rising tide of enrollment demand and the often bitter feuds between the university and the state colleges, a single board seemed the most effective and responsible course. He knew that finding an agreement among the survey team was going to be extremely difficult. He hoped to first settle the issue of the function of the various public segments of the public tripartite system before focusing on governance.

✳✳✳

The first meeting of the survey team, held on the Berkeley campus, opened with Glenn Dumke, the main spokesman for the state colleges, on the attack. Dumke emerged as the most politically adroit state college president. The other state college presidents hoped that Dumke's personal relationship with Coons might prove a valuable, perhaps decisive, influence on the outcome of the pending negotiations.

At the survey team meeting, Dumke insisted that they take a fresh look at the functions of each of the public segments. He reiterated the complaint of the state college presidents at the outright rejection by Kerr and other university officials of the Love Plan. He then set out a new proposal to extend the doctorate in the field of education to the state colleges. Dumke explained that the "degree would not be a research degree, but a teaching degree." There was a clear and documented need for additional doctoral-level teachers, he insisted. The state colleges were in the best position to provide training in this area, Dumke argued. The state colleges needed the degree for another reason: to "enhance morale and professional advancement" of their faculty. If the colleges were denied this function, he concluded, the effect would be the creation of a permanent "caste system," relegating the colleges to "a second-rate status."[33]

McHenry's response was strong and adversarial. He told Dumke that if he and the other state college presidents continued to "make passes at the Crown Jewels," they could expect "to encounter the firmest resistance" from the university. It was "essential for the well being of the State, and of the institutions themselves," he and Holy stated, to maintain this structure of academic programs that "has been officially and almost universally accepted."[34] They both cited the Restudy Report, which stated that, unless there were "new and compelling factors," doctoral programs at state colleges should not be considered until 1965. According to McHenry, there were no compelling factors. He further insisted that in the "fields in which doctorates are advocated, education, social sciences etc., additional space for students exists in the university and private institutions." The problem in these fields, he claimed, was to recruit students, not to create new programs.

McHenry and Holy told Dumke and Browne that the state college presidents had it all wrong. They should concentrate on improving the quality of their master's degree programs "and achieving eminence within their regular sphere of activity." Sanctioning the doctorate within the state colleges, they concluded, would destroy the concept of differentiation of functions and erode any hope of maintaining a rational public system of higher education.[35] For McHenry, Holy, and other university officials, holding the line on state college functions was the most important goal in the negotiations. The survey team's first meeting, thought Coons, was a disaster.

At the survey team's next meeting in July, Dumke insisted that the state college proposal did not refute the premise of different functions among the three segments of California's higher education system or the basic findings of the previous Strayer and Restudy Reports. Though he did not agree completely with the "flatly vocational concept of education" for the state colleges professed by the Restudy Report, even under this rubric Dumke claimed there was room for innovation. In the field of education and possibly other areas of graduate training, noted Dumke, "clearly it is possible to have each set of institutions doing something different." There already existed this type of differentiation within master's level programs between the University of California and the state colleges in areas such as engineering. The same argument, Dumke explained, could be made to support a research function for state college faculty.[36] The gulf between McHenry and Dumke and their respective institutions was deep and wide.

In the opening months of their negotiations, the survey team found no common ground. A worried Coons abandoned his strategy to tackle the difficult issue of segmental functions first before moving onto other key issues such as governance, admissions standards, enrollment projections, and new campuses. The wrangling at the negotiation table reinforced Coons' view that a single board was the only solution to the vexing problem of creating an ordered system of higher education in California. After numerous meetings, Coons proposed that the survey team move on to the issue of governance and return to the contentious issue of functions at a later date. He was not optimistic about reaching any agreement. "My reaction to the deliberations of the past month," he wrote in his personal diary, "is that I am wasting my time and the State's money. It is evident at this moment to me that no segment of the state supported higher education is willing to retreat. . . . If there is no yielding on major and fundamental issues on each side all along the line, this survey will be doomed."[37]

Debating a Single Board

Meeting on the Berkeley campus in late July and with five months until the legislative deadline for the plan, Arthur Coons offered his proposal for a single governing board. Under this plan, the junior colleges, with their strong link to local districts, would remain under the State Board of Education. Coons explained his view that the lack of "differentiation of functions is forcing California toward a single system." Writing on a blackboard, Coons outlined his plan for a new board to be composed of some forty members, including sixteen former regents, ten lay members from the State Board of Education, five or six new lay members to balance the representation between the university and the state colleges, and eight ex officio members, ranging from the speaker of the assembly to the governor.[38] In form and content, Coons's proposal looked much like the plan forwarded in the 1932 Suzzallo Report.

The monstrous size of the proposed board brought a wince from the rest of the survey team. McHenry and Dumke immediately expressed great reluctance to embrace any proposal for a single board, no matter what its composition. Thomas Holy noted that moving to one board would in fact make it even more difficult to maintain the differentiation of functions between the university and the state colleges—as outlined in his earlier report to Kerr. This differentiation, remarked Holy, was what "made California's system great." McHenry added that the new board would abrogate the existing powers of the university and the regents. This, he insisted, would be rejected by President Kerr.[39]

Dumke protested for different reasons. He explained that even with a balance in representatives on the proposed single board, the political influence of the university would be dominant. Coons' proposed superboard would "so firmly fix their second-class status that it would be unacceptable." Dumke then articulated another objection that would prove a powerful argument against the single board idea. Because of the huge size of the two public segments—the two largest four-year institutions in the nation—Dumke noted the need to retain some form of separate governing boards. How could a single board, he asked, properly manage such a huge conglomeration of campuses? Inevitably, he concluded, the state colleges would suffer a similar level of neglect they now experienced under the State Board of Education.[40]

Although for different reasons, Dumke and McHenry were for the first time standing on common ground. Dumke once again proposed the creation of a new board for the state colleges that could be accompanied by a new "coordinating council" with the power to review the separate budgets of the segments and to approve new degree programs and campuses. Hence, California could create something like a superboard without the direct powers associated with such entities. It might prepare and defend a single statewide budget for higher education, review academic programs to help reduce duplication of programs, and help plan new campuses.[41] Such a system, he noted, could be found in Wisconsin and Utah. Dumke's proposal was, in fact, similar to one that McHenry offered to Kerr two months earlier. For both sides, this governance model provided an attractive balance of autonomy and a central coordinating body. It might also distract the interest of influential lawmakers, including state senator George Miller, in forcing a marriage between the University of California and the state colleges.[42]

In the course of the debate over governance, there was some concern over the management of the junior colleges, although, clearly, this was a secondary concern for the survey team. A proposal was offered to create a separate board for the junior colleges, but it was rejected. It implied an infringement on local authority that, in the survey team's opinion, would be wildly unpopular among local communities and their representatives in the California Legislature. A separate board might also require or imply a large increase in the state government's financial responsibility.[43]

For some three months, the survey team debated Dumke's proposal for a new board for the state colleges and a coordinating council with largely advisory powers. Before the survey team, Lyman Glenny, in the midst of his study on state coordination of higher education, warned that the council would likely prove a weak coordinating mechanism, particularly if it had only advisory powers and was largely a reconstituted Liaison Committee. Glenny also assumed that the council would be unattractive to legislators such as Miller. The most significant problem, observed Coons, "was how a legal agency could be established over a constitutionally independent group," such as the regents. A legal structure could exist only if the regents accepted the arrangement, "thus limiting their autonomy in certain respects."[44]

Five months into the deliberations, the survey team finally came to its first major agreement. In October, under a joint proposal offered by Dumke, McHenry, Tyler, and Wert, the survey team agreed to the concept of a separate board for the state colleges and a new coordinating council. The council would need to be established as an amendment to the California Constitution. It would have broad budgetary powers and the final authority to establish new programs and new campuses. The council would review and possibly revise the proposed budgets of the university and the state colleges and would present and then defend the budgets as a package to the legislature. Along with the authority to review new program proposals, this would provide a method for reducing duplication and inefficiencies in the two segments that, it was hoped, legislators would find attractive. Unlike the failed Coordinating Council established in 1933 in California, the council would include primarily members of California's higher education community, and hence it would not be a lay board. The proposal also required the hiring of a research staff and an "executive officer" on the level parallel to that of Superintendent Simpson and President Kerr.[45] (See Figure 11.)

Coons backed away from his insistence on a single board and embraced the idea of the coordinating council. It remained unclear how this proposed "solution" would play in Sacramento. In the legislature, Assemblywoman Donahoe and Senator Miller had already asked Legislative Counsel Ralph N. Kleps to outline the legal wording necessary to create a single board for the University of California and the state colleges, with possible authority over the junior colleges.[46] There was also a diversity of opinion over governance and coordination within the higher education community. State college faculty relished the idea of gaining their own board, relatively free of what was viewed as stifling regulatory controls of state agencies. Among university faculty, however, there remained a strong "contingent convinced that only a single board could control the thirst of the state colleges for parity with the university.[47]

Students and New Campuses

The agreement on governance was a major achievement. For the first time, Arthur Coons sensed that the completion of the plan was a possibility. With the issue of governance and coordination apparently settled, he hoped that other major agreements would quickly follow. The survey team proceeded to

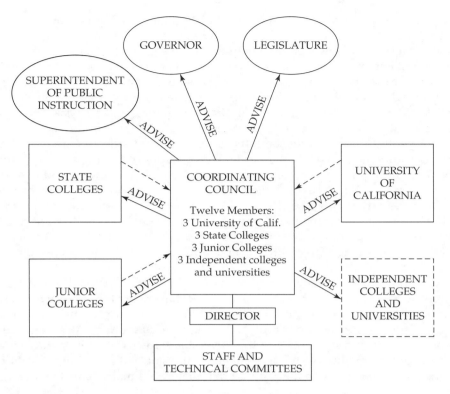

Figure 11 1960 Master Plan Proposed Coordinating Council
SOURCE: Graphic presented in the *California Master Plan for Higher Education,* 1960

consider the criteria for determining future enrollment demand in California. The flow of students into the respective segments had huge budgetary implications for the state and for the aspirations of the public segments. Since the Progressive Era, the appropriation of state funds for operating costs was directly proportional to student enrollment. Enrollment-driven budgets were the lifeblood of the university, the state colleges, and the junior colleges. Capital costs were also related to projected student enrollment growth.

In yet another surprise move by state college representatives, Arthur Browne presented the survey team with his analysis of how the state might save vast sums of money. California should channel a greater number of the projected freshmen entering the public system into the junior and state colleges, explained Browne, where he claimed that costs per student were much lower. The state, he projected, could save some $45 million by such a shift—a projection later reiterated in the *San Francisco Chronicle* and other newspapers in support of Browne's plan. To accomplish this, Browne proposed raising the admissions requirements of the university. "Why not save money by curbing university expansion?" he asked.[48]

Accompanying Browne's presentation was a large chart displaying the cost of educating a student at each of the public segments. To the great frustration of McHenry and Holy, it showed a huge cost differential between the university and the other two public segments. Browne also implied that California was sinking large sums of public funds into the university while the junior and state colleges did the lion's share of work. Both segments, he noted, had surpassed the university in total enrollments. While the university enrolled only 16 percent of the students in 1958, Browne explained, it received 54 percent of the total state appropriations for higher education. The university also got 62 percent of the capital outlay funds, while the state colleges received only 38 percent. The junior colleges, he explained, received no funds for capital construction from the state. The burden of physical expansion fell solely on local governments.

Browne also presented projections of costs for new campuses. He assumed that each new and planned university campus would cost the state approximately $100 million—an estimate given by Regent Pauley in a speech. However, he remarked, the seven state college campuses proposed by Simpson at the first joint meeting of the two boards would cost a total of only $150 million. Browne was appealing to the members of the legislature. For cost reasons alone, he was implying, state funds needed to be shifted to both the junior and state colleges and away from the university.

McHenry and Holy disagreed sharply with Browne's figures and analysis. For one, they stated, Browne's assessment of costs used head-count numbers, equating the costs associated with part-time students to those with full-time status. Both the junior and state colleges enrolled substantial numbers of part-time students. "I asked whether he would support curbing state college expansion," noted McHenry in his report to Kerr, "if our cost studies showed that we spend less per student on Lower Division then they did. Dumke intervened to try to save him, but Holy read the Lower Division cost figures from Restudy [Report], and we had him nailed."[49] At a subsequent meeting of the survey team, McHenry stated that the university had "modest goals . . . [W]e want to educate about the same proportion of the college age group that we did in 1940 and 1950." This meant maintaining an admissions policy that offered enrollment to approximately the top 15 percent of high school graduating classes.[50]

Browne had argued that the university should reduce its admission pool, while the state colleges should enlarge theirs. In subsequent discussion at the next meeting of the survey team, Dumke noted his concern that the state colleges should, along with the university, reduce their own admission pools. He now distanced himself from Browne's projections and offered this as a formal proposal. The raising of university and state college admissions standards would both reduce costs to the state and increase the overall quality of students attending the state colleges. It would shift prospective students to the junior colleges with the promise that they could matriculate to either the university or the state colleges.[51]

McHenry and university officials agreed with Dumke's proposal. Despite the auspicious opening discussion on eligibility, another general agreement was in the making. Two questions remained regarding future enrollment: What should be the revised admission pool for the university and the state colleges, and how might the state support the subsequent expansion of the junior colleges to accommodate more students? The answer would have a tremendous impact on the flow of students through California's higher education system and on the personal lives of thousands of Californians.

The benefits of diverting more lower-division students to the junior colleges appeared substantial to the survey team. It would certainly make the final Master Plan recommendations more politically attractive. "The probability is that capital outlay for the junior colleges will be much lower than for the other segments," explained McHenry. "[E]ven if instructional costs should prove equal, this fact plus the saving to parents and students through living at home would argue for considerable cost savings to the state and its residents. . . . Further, junior colleges are better able to screen and do remedial work and counseling than are the other segments."[52] In light of the strong sense of competition between the state colleges and the university, Dumke, McHenry, and Coons agreed that the shift of students needed to be equitable and, at the same time, not overburden the junior colleges. To make the plan work, the survey team concluded that state government would need to compensate local districts by providing additional funds for junior college operations and capital costs.

The survey team looked to their technical committee on "Selection and Retention of Students," chaired by Herman A. Spindt, for recommendations on how to accomplish this equitable shift. Dumke proposed that Spindt consider establishing a mandated ratio for both the university and the state colleges of approximately one lower- to two upper-division students within both the university and the state colleges. By establishing this mandate for each campus, it would ensure that state colleges and the university would focus on upper-division courses and students. Spindt's committee, however, returned several weeks later with an unexpected answer. There "should be no attempt to control the size of the lower division in the university and the state colleges on the basis of the 'floor' type of admissions procedure," stated Spindt. The desired enrollment shift could be achieved, he insisted, on a voluntary basis, by having "all public four-year colleges participate

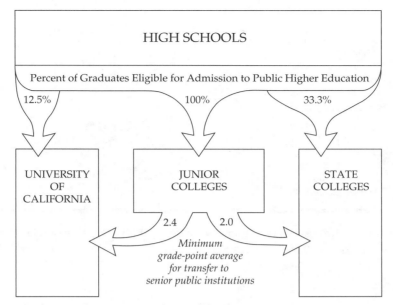

Figure 12 1960 Master Plan Agreement on Student Admissions
SOURCE: Graphic presented in the *California Master Plan for Higher Education, 1960*

whole-heartedly in a 'persuasive guidance' program aimed at increasing the proportion of freshmen and sophomores attending the junior colleges." The survey team rejected this innocuous recommendation. There needed to be a clearly stated policy on admissions and a set percentage of lower- to upper-division students, they concluded. It offered the best method to ensure a shift in students.[53]

In November, less than two months before the Master Plan was due before the legislature, an agreement was reached on admissions. The survey team first determined the current ratio of lower- to upper-division students within state colleges and the university. Taken together, California's public institutions enrolled approximately 180,000 full-time students. Of these students, 88,000 (72,000 undergraduates and 16,000 graduate students) attended the state colleges and the university. In both segments, lower-division students represented approximately 51 percent of the undergraduate population. The survey team agreed that "the percentage of undergraduates in the lower division of each segment [be] reduced to approximately ten percentage points below that [projected] in 1960." This eventually boiled down to a stated policy that would drive new admissions standards and shift students to the junior colleges. The university and the state colleges would have 40 percent lower-division students (freshman and sophomores) and 60 percent upper-division (juniors and seniors).

Based on this shift in ratios for the year 1960, Carl Frisen of the Department of Finance determined that the university should no longer be able to draw from the top 15 percent of California high school graduates but from the top 12.5 percent. Similarly, the state colleges would need to shift from approximately the top 40 percent to the top 33.3 percent.[54] Here was the basis for California's contemporary policy on admission to the state's four-year public institutions—a choice heavily conditioned by the need to reduce costs to taxpayers.

These new admissions standards then allowed Frisen to analyze the impact on future student enrollment between 1960 and 1975. Frisen projected that California could expect to enroll 436,000 additional full-time equivalent students in all higher education institutions, both public and private, by 1975. Of that total, Frisen expected that nearly 94 percent would enter California's public tripartite system, a total of 409,000 additional students. This would represent a 228 percent increase over enrollment in 1958. The change in admissions standards, he estimated, would divert some

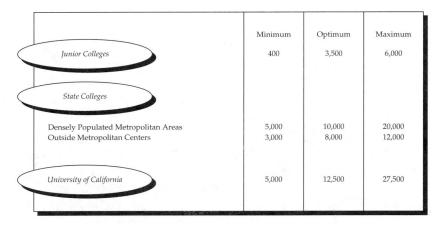

	Minimum	Optimum	Maximum
Junior Colleges	400	3,500	6,000
State Colleges			
Densely Populated Metropolitan Areas	5,000	10,000	20,000
Outside Metropolitan Centers	3,000	8,000	12,000
University of California	5,000	12,500	27,500

Figure 13 Master Plan Full-Time Student Enrollment Ranges for Public College and University Campuses
SOURCE: *California Master Plan for Higher Education,* 1960

50,000 students to locally funded junior colleges where operating costs were lower. In addition, it would reduce the need for state government to fund the construction of new university and state college campuses.[55] Yet how much it would save was subject to unresolved planning assumptions. The need for new campuses was not driven exclusively by projected enrollment demand. It also was contingent on an assessment of the most cost-effective enrollment sizes for existing and planned campuses.

✳✳✳

Kerr, McHenry, and other university officials were upset when one of the survey team's technical committees recommended that the maximum enrollment for new state colleges should be 12,000 students, while the goal for all university campuses should be 27,500. Such a low ceiling for the state colleges and a high ceiling for the university implied a potential flood of new state college campuses.[56] McHenry complained that "the political strength of the state colleges will be further accentuated, and the relative influence of the University will decline."[57] McHenry found support from John E. Carr, the new director of finance in the Brown administration. Carr stated that the suggested campus enrollment limits needed to be revised; they would unnecessarily increase state costs. At the request of Coons, the technical committee proceeded to modify their recommendations, creating two categories of state colleges: those in metropolitan areas with a maximum of 20,000 students and those in less densely populated areas at the previous maximum of 12,000 students. Here was another key element of the emerging Master Plan study.

In recommending the location for new campuses of the university and the state colleges, the survey team essentially reiterated the recommendations of the 1957 Additional Centers Report. It was politically expedient to adopt the findings of this study, completed only two years earlier. The survey team recommended that state funds be provided for three new University of California campuses: in San Diego, the Los Angeles-Orange County area (what would become Irvine), and the south central coast area (what would become Riverside). The list of state college campuses was also familiar. A total of four colleges were proposed, two that already had legislative approval: Northridge, another in the north San Francisco Bay Area (Sonoma), and new campuses at San Bernardino and Dominguez Hills. Each of these campuses, it was explained, should be established before 1965. Beyond 1965, the new coordinating council could conduct "careful studies . . . of the need for additional University facilities in the San Joaquin Valley and the Los Angeles area." They also anticipated the possibility of five other university or state college campuses being built by 1975.[58]

The survey team agreed to a list of twenty-two new junior colleges to be established by 1975. To support the expansion of the junior college system, including the anticipated shift of 50,000 students, they recommended that state government increase its share of the operational budget of the junior colleges from 30 to 42 percent. For the first time, this included a proposed program of state bonds for college construction—capital costs that previously had been borne exclusively by local government.[59]

Reducing Future Costs

Arthur Coons and the survey team members knew that the political appeal of their proposed Master Plan would rest largely on its method of controlling costs. "One of the early issues debated," explained a report by the survey team, "was the extent to which educational policies were to be based on, or determined by, economic factors." There was a great need to make the public system more efficient; but it was not the intention of the team, they argued, simply to make significant adjustments in admissions policies to match a presumed level of state funding in future years. "Good educational planning," they stated, "requires consideration of many factors other than the price tag." Yet the issue of providing a more "efficient" system of higher education, one that promised substantial savings for state government and ultimately for California taxpayers, was clearly a major factor in the survey team's deliberation. Besides shifting students to the junior colleges, the survey team also proposed that all public higher education move to a "full-year calendar."[60] This, it was presumed, would maximize the use of existing campus facilities and lessen the need for new and costly campuses of the university and the state colleges. Improved coordination would, in theory, reduce the unnecessary duplication of programs and would regulate financing to the public segments.

The survey team also recommended a substantial expansion of the state-sponsored undergraduate scholarship program that could be applied at any public or private institution.[61] The scholarship program had been established in 1955 by lawmakers despite the university's opposition, but now university officials saw its advantages. This state scholarship program, it was thought, would encourage some students to attend private colleges and would broaden the political appeal of the Master Plan.

Joseph O. McClintic, chairman of the technical committee that worked on estimating future costs, reported that the shifting of students to the junior colleges and other proposed modifications would provide immediate savings for the state. By 1966, McClintic estimated that the Master Plan would cut the yearly operating and capital costs by $41.5 million. The total amount of savings, however, would decrease in future years. There would be increasing state costs associated with expanding the junior colleges. By 1970, McClintic estimated that the Master Plan would result in substantial yet less spectacular savings: approximately $18 million.[62] (See Figures 14 and 15.)

With the assistance of the Department of Finance, McClintic's committee also offered a projection of future state revenues. Would California state government have the funds to pay for the projected price tag of the Master Plan? Even with the proposed methods for saving costs, the available state revenues would be inadequate by as early as 1962. California state government would need to either reallocate existing revenue to higher education or raise taxes. The survey team concluded that the state should raise revenue. California was a relatively wealthy state, they argued, yet state tax collections represented only a moderate percentage of the state's total income. The percentage of personal income allocated to higher education was comparatively low, only thirty-fifth in the nation. As the survey team later reported to the legislature, "Even though this state possesses the taxable wealth, a critical question concerns its willingness to use larger proportions of this wealth for its educational welfare."[63]

The Impasse

By November 1959, with the January deadline for submittal to lawmakers approaching, Arthur Coons and the survey team had made progress on governance and coordination, admissions standards,

Fiscal Year 1965–66	Lower Division (%)	Upper Division (%)	Grad Division (%)	Total (%)
A. Operating Costs				
Junior Colleges	+8.7	—	—	+8.7
State Colleges	−3.7	−1.6	—	−5.3
University of California	−8.7	−7.3	−6.3	−21.8
B. Capital Costs				
State Colleges	−6.0	—	+0.4	−5.6
University of California	−6.1	−6.4	−5.0	−17.5
Total Savings to the State	−15.3	−15.3	−10.9	−41.5
Fiscal Year 1970–71				
A. Operating Costs				
Junior Colleges	+24.5	—	—	+24.5
State Colleges	−11.6	+1.2	+1.0	−9.4
University of California	−12.4	−13.2	−5.8	−31.4
B. Capital Costs				
State Colleges	−7.3	+3.0	+0.6	−3.7
University of California	−4.5	+3.1	+3.5	+2.1
Total Savings to the State	−11.3	−5.9	−0.7	−17.9

Figure 14 Estimate of Annual Savings and Costs for Higher Education Under the Master Plan, 1965–1966 and 1970–1971

SOURCE: *California Master Plan for Higher Education,* 1960

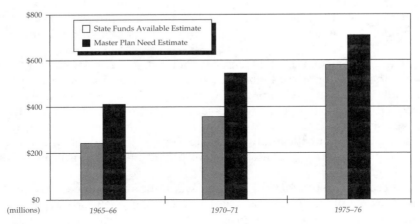

Figure 15 1960 Master Plan Estimate of State General Funds and Capital Outlay Needed for Expanding Enrollment

SOURCE: *California Master Plan for Higher Education,* 1960

new campuses, and methods for reducing future costs. Yet there remained one unresolved issue: the functions of the state colleges and particularly a resolution to their demand for the doctorate and state funding for research. As Coons readily acknowledged, what had been agreed to thus far by the survey team was tenuous. The months of arduous discussions and agreements could quickly unravel.

When the survey team met with lawmakers to discuss the plan, Coons, appraised them of the unfinished business. Kerr and other members of the Liaison Committee attended as well.

A. Alan Post told Coons, "[F]rankly I don't see how you can do it at this point." A frustrated Coons responded, "You are no more worried than I am." The "warring factions" made it difficult to resolve certain aspects of the negotiations. Coons noted that, indeed, the "team has blocked off just about as much time for chatter as they can." The difficulty, he concluded, was gaining agreement on "whose ox is being gored." With Assemblywoman Donahoe, Senators Miller, Grunsky, and Dilworth, and Donald Leiffer from the governor's office looking on, Kerr insisted that the study would be completed in one form or another. It would be a "plan to end all plans" he remarked, seemingly sending a message to both legislators and state college officials. Kerr's resolve was clear.[64]

Despite the best of Coons's efforts and Kerr's promise, the survey team remained entrenched in a bitter battle over the future of the state colleges. The university, stated Dean McHenry, would not support the desires of the state colleges. Dumke told the survey team that in light of the position of university officials, the state college presidents were now opposed to the proposed changes in admission standards. Dumke and his constituents were raising the stakes, hoping to force Kerr and the university to a compromise.

In the next Liaison Committee meeting in mid-November, Coons begged for an agreement before December 7, the scheduled date for the submittal of the plan. In a fit of frustration and fatigue, Coons told legislators that the Master Plan negotiations were in deep trouble. "We are like Montana," Coons analogized. "Montana is snowed in and so are we. But, whereas Montana happens to be way below zero, we happen to be working at temperatures on occasions that have gone well above a hundred."[65]

At the next meeting of the survey team a week later, the intractable positions were once again highlighted. In earlier meetings, Glenn Dumke and Arthur Browne insisted that the new board for the state colleges should have the freedom to review the appropriate functions of the colleges. McHenry and Kerr had clearly stated that this would be vehemently opposed by the university. In preparing for the meeting, McHenry told Kerr they had perhaps four out of eight votes on the survey team. "The junior college boys will be decisive. I think we have hope for Campion but I think Tyler will side with the state colleges." Dumke now presented a revision: an independent commission made up of nine members from the education and business communities could decide the issue at a later date and after the approval of the other aspects of the Master Plan. The plan, explained Dumke, then could be completed on schedule, and possibly California's public tripartite system could be preserved. It was a brilliant countermove, made before several legislators. Frustrated with the stalemate, junior college representatives stated their support.[66]

McHenry and Holy, however, rejected the idea of a commission. It was clearly a tactic to keep the aspirations of the state colleges alive and to shift the decision to a more favorable forum. McHenry and Holy, based on their earlier consultation with Clark Kerr, used the meeting to insist that there be no delay on decision-making. University officials wanted to fix the functions of the colleges in the state constitution—to create a plan to end all plans.[67]

Superintendent Simpson had deliberately played a low-key role in the negotiations, deferring to Dumke and Browne. He had been asked, however, by McHenry and Kerr several weeks earlier to officially state why the state colleges should enter the world of doctoral training. Simpson replied that the great need for additional doctoral-trained professionals and teachers was amply documented. Several state colleges were more appropriate for providing the doctorate, explained the superintendent, than, for example, was the university campus in Santa Barbara with its small number of faculty.[68]

Armed with Simpson's remarks and a recent State Department of Education study on the need for doctoral programs in the state, Dumke argued before the survey committee: "Those who say there are no new and compelling factors to justify the doctorate in the state colleges are giving opinions based on inconclusive evidence." Specifically, noted Dumke, an earlier university study on the need for doctoral programs and graduates was seriously flawed. For instance, it underestimated the demand for faculty with Ph.D.s in the state colleges by assuming that these institutions would attract the same proportion of out-of-state faculty as in the past. The university study also assumed that only 40 percent of the future faculty hires in the state colleges would have a doctorate. "Not only are there shortages of doctorates to satisfy teaching needs, but also in industry, science, and research throughout the nation," insisted Dumke. "If what has happened in other states is any criterion, sooner or later the doctorate will be given to the state colleges. The University cannot maintain its monopoly point of view forever."[69]

Over the course of the two-day meetings, McHenry and Holy stood their ground, although the tone of their arguments seemed more desperate. They were confronted by a solution, the establishment of an independent commission that might gain political support within the legislature and the governor's office. "The state college's house is not fully in order," McHenry countered. "Before allowing a change in function, the state colleges should be helped to get their freedom" in the form of their own board. Sensing that Coons and the junior and private college members of the survey team were sympathetic to Dumke and Browne's position, McHenry even suggested that "the doctorate in certain state colleges might be favored if these colleges were to become a part of the University system." Perhaps three or four colleges could be transferred, they noted.[70]

Concerned with the impasse in the negotiations, Kerr had already approached four state college presidents, including Dumke, Love, Wahlquist, and Joyal, to see if they would be interested in having their campus become part of the university. In the end, however, Kerr found no takers.[71] Kerr's surreptitious offer simply reinforced the opinion of most state college representatives that, if all failed, the university would attempt to absorb all or a part of the state college system, despite the inherent risks. The veracity of Kerr, McHenry, and the regents was something to fear. Indeed, a bid to absorb the state colleges was a possible course of action for Kerr. The university's contingency plan remained an unstated threat but a threat just the same.

***

With the November meetings concluded, Coons found the December 7 deadline quickly approaching. There was no plan, and there were no further meetings of the survey team scheduled. McHenry sadly wrote to Kerr, "[I]t now appears that the state colleges are unwilling to accept real differentiation of functions that will keep them out of doctorates and the higher professions." Something had to be done, insisted McHenry. Reaching no agreement would bode poorly for the university, possibly lead either to radical reform by legislators or to the continued proliferation of the state college programs and campuses. McHenry now conceded to Kerr that perhaps the only option was a university-derived constitutional proposition to absorb the state colleges.[72]

The deadlock was not a surprise to most lawmakers. Six months earlier and at the beginning of the survey team negotiations, Governor Pat Brown insisted that the education community had better provide a solid plan for higher education. Failure to do so or the presentation of a plan consisting of "mutual log-rolling by which each approves the projects of the other in order to have license for its own," proclaimed Brown, could compel the state "to consider other structural possibilities."[73] With only days left to resolve basic issues of function and in turn governance, Governor Brown, Assemblywoman Donahoe, and Senator Miller renewed this threat. Brown insisted that he and the legislature would make their own Master Plan. Assemblywoman Donahoe complained that she was tired of the fight: "I keep hearing 'mine, mine, mine.' But what we need to hear is 'our state.'"[74] Senator George Miller thought the survey team's efforts doomed. "We can no longer afford this competition," he told reporters on December 2, "and in light of it, as in public utilities, we must establish a monopoly."[75]

Arthur Coons, however, still sought a last-minute agreement. On December 2, he called a special meeting of the survey team at the Bowman House on the Stanford campus. It was a last ditch effort. For two days, the survey team deliberated. To Coons's joy, a compromise was reached. Under great pressure, Dean McHenry and Tom Holy agreed that the proposed "Coordinating Council" could decide the issue of doctoral degrees in the state colleges. The survey team also agreed to the submittal of a proposed constitutional amendment with three major components: Beyond the issue of the doctorate, it would set segmental functions for the tripartite public system, establish a new and autonomous state college board, and create the Coordinating Council.[76] The proposed constitutional amendment would protect the university's historical mission as the primary graduate training and research institution. The primary function of the state colleges would be undergraduate education, teacher training, and graduate education through the master's degree, with the issue of doctoral training to be decided by the Coordinating Council. While "large-scale" research was not a primary function of the colleges, the survey team agreed, "nothing in the Constitution shall be construed to restrict or preclude the allocation of support and facilities adequate for professional research." No major changes were proposed in the functions of the junior colleges.[77]

Per their discussion on the Stanford campus, the state colleges would be governed by a new Board of Trustees. Like the regents, the new state college trustees would be "a public trust, to be administered by a body corporate . . . with full powers of organization and government, subject only to such legislative control as may be necessary." The Trustees would have six ex officio members: the governor, lieutenant governor, speaker of the assembly, superintendent of public instruction, president of the University of California, and chief executive of the state college system. Similar to the regents, sixteen members would be appointed by the governor for twelve-year terms. The survey team also added the recommendation that the present members of the State Board of Education serve as the first members of the trustees "to assume an orderly transition." New trustees would be appointed as the terms of the board members expired.[78]

Finally, the Coordinating Council would decide on issues of segmental functions, enrollment expansion, and "budget coordination," including the submission to the legislature of a budget for all three public segments. New campuses and the establishment of "any new graduate degrees," the survey team agreed, would require the affirmative recommendation of the council and, when it required additional state funding, the legislature. As noted, the council would include twelve members, each representing a member of the higher education community: three representatives each for the university, state colleges, junior colleges, and the Association of Independent California Colleges. For the university, this included the president and two regents. For the state colleges, representatives on the council included the new chief executive and two members of the new Board of Trustees. Superintendent Simpson would sit along with two members of the State Board of Education as representatives of the junior colleges.[79]

Reflecting the extreme caution of all members of the survey team not to abrogate the authority of the regents or the proposed state college trustees, the power of the council had many serious limitations. In matters related to funding, expansion, and curriculum of the university and state colleges, only their respective representatives could vote. The independent college representatives had no voting authority on any of these matters. In addition, because of the status of both the regents and the proposed state college trustees as "public trusts," the council as constituted seemed to have no more authority than the voluntary Liaison Committee.[80]

***

Arthur Coons left the two-day meeting at Stanford thinking he had achieved an agreement on all the key points of the survey team's charge. The seemingly impossible was accomplished. He had remained in good health, despite his friends' warnings that the ordeal might very well kill him. Several days later, however, McHenry returned with shocking news. President Kerr did not accept a key aspect of the agreement, specifically, the proposal to have the Coordinating Council decide on the issue of the doctorate in the state colleges. He wanted the proposed constitutional amendment to state that only the university could grant the doctorate. Otherwise, Kerr insisted that the university would not support the proposal for a state college Board of Trustees, and he was considering abandoning the work of the survey team altogether to pursue a constitutional initiative for a single board. Coons was livid. Kerr was holding the compromise hostage. At an emergency meeting with the survey team, he chastised university officials. Their demand for a renegotiation, he warned, would not stop him from presenting the previously agreed-upon plan, or some version of it, to the two higher education boards and lawmakers at a Liaison Committee meeting scheduled in four days.[81]

In University Hall across from the Berkeley campus, Coons opened the long-awaited Liaison Committee meeting. It had been scheduled to last for two days, but Coons requested that it be extended to a third. He hoped that the extra time might help him broker a new compromise. "This is what is commonly called in the novel the 'moment of truth,' when your team is called upon to bring to you certain final recommendations," he stated to a large audience that included regents and board of education members, lawmakers such as Donahoe and Miller, members of Governor Brown's staff, and the press. He and other survey team members spent the day explaining their enrollment projections, the plan to shift 50,000 lower-division students to the junior colleges, and the priority list of new campuses—all of the agreed-upon elements.

On the second day, a presentation was made on utilization and space standards used to assess the need for capital construction. The team also reviewed the projected need for faculty. Coons concluded the day's meeting by stating that the survey team had met the previous evening. He announced bitterly that there was as yet no unanimity on the most important agenda items: segmental functions and, in turn, governance. Notwithstanding, he would present his personal recommendations the next day.[82]

A Last-Minute Compromise

Desperate to find a solution and worried by Coons's increasing hostility to the university, that evening Kerr asked for a meeting in his office on the Berkeley campus. This important summit included Coons, McHenry, Dumke, Board of the Regents Chair Donald McLaughlin, State Board of Education Chair William Blair, and State Superintendent Simpson. Only an hour earlier, Coons had given a press conference despairing that an agreement was elusive. In Kerr's office, a frank discussion ensued. Without an agreement on the issues of the doctorate and state college research, reiterated Kerr, the university would refuse to back the creation of the state college trustees or the Coordinating Council. The Master Plan would be dead. Dumke and Blair knew the likely result: a university or legislatively induced superboard. In either case, the state colleges would lose their bid for an autonomous board. For Dumke and the other state college presidents, gaining a board similar to the university's remained the most important goal. It held the promise of greater independence from legislative caprice and the regulatory world of state agencies. It might gain the political power and influence to expand the scope of state college programs. Dumke did not want to lose the board, and Blair agreed.[83]

Kerr presented a series of "solutions" that offered a method for university faculty to regulate doctoral training in the state colleges. One option was to have state college faculty appointed as adjunct professors at the university. They could then direct doctoral degrees at state college campuses but only as university employees. Dumke complained that the state colleges needed recognition as institutions of advanced learning, not as satellites of the University of California. Based on a program sponsored by Wayne State University in Michigan, Kerr also proposed the creation of "joint doctoral" programs. State college faculty could approach university faculty to codevelop a doctoral program. Faculty at both campuses would participate; but the university would always have the ability to simply disband the doctoral program.[84] Details of the joint doctorate needed work, and it was assumed that initially most programs would be in the field of education.[85] If Dumke, Blair, and Simpson could agree to the joint doctorate in principle, Kerr and McLaughlin promised to support the rest of the Master Plan. They would fight for the creation of the Board of Trustees as a public trust within the state constitution. Dumke and Blair acquiesced, but only if there was a more liberal interpretation by the university of the research role of state college faculty. They agreed to the following language for inclusion in the Master Plan: "Research which stimulates professional and scholarly growth of individual faculty members is appropriate for the state colleges and should be authorized." The deal was struck.[86]

***

The next day, the Liaison Committee and an audience of more than thirty legislators and government officials heard Arthur Coons describe the compromise. The joint doctorate, he explained, would allow the state colleges to meet an apparent need in California's economy while also retaining the university's historic control of doctoral programs. Coons then stated an important contingency: If either the new state college board or the joint doctorate program failed to gain the endorsement of the two boards or the legislature, the whole deal should be called off. The strategy was to have the Master Plan passed as a package and to discourage its dismemberment in the legislative process.[87]

Coons, Kerr, Dumke, and the other major players in the formulation of the Master Plan were relieved to have finally created a meaningful "compact." It was, they thought, a plan that was politically attractive. While it shifted the university and the state colleges toward a more selective admissions policy at the freshman level, the expansion of the junior colleges promised a dramatic increase in access to higher education.

The proposed Master Plan also reaffirmed California's commitment to a tuition-free public tripartite system. With a largely homogeneous population, the primary barrier to higher education, thought the authors of the plan, was economic class. There was little concern about the role of race and inequities in local schools. Low costs for students and their families and a wide geographic distribution of public institutions, they believed, would provide the primary basis for equitable access to all students who could benefit from a higher education—elements of California's higher education system outlined over fifty years ago by Alexis Lange and other Progressives.

The Master Plan was simply a proposal. There remained the approval by both the regents and the State Board of Education, the legislative process, and a constitutional measure. No state had ever placed in either statute or in its constitution such a comprehensive outline of duties of its state-supported colleges and universities, let alone created two distinct and highly autonomous public trusts to govern them. The proposed Master Plan clearly moved against the tide of centralization and increasing legislative authority found throughout the nation.

Notes

1. Conant, *Shaping Policy,* 15, 48.
2. Glenny, *Autonomy of Public Colleges,* 18.
3. Budgetary considerations, noted the editorial, were paramount. There was no room to increase the $232 million budgeted by the Brown administration for higher education. "A Master Plan for Colleges," *Los Angeles Times,* April 24, 1959.
4. Kerr, "The California Master Plan of 1960 for Higher Education: An Ex Ante View," speech delivered at a meeting of the Organization of Economic Cooperation and Development, May 21, 1990, Berkeley, 20–21.
5. They included university Vice President Wellmen, Chancellors Seaborg, Allan, and Freeborn, and state college Presidents Love, Dumke, and Wahlquist. The other three members were junior college Presidents Calvin Flint from Foothill College, Bill Priest at American River Junior College, and Theron L. McCuen from Kern County Junior College. After the April 2 meeting, the new group would be called the "Joint Advisory Committee" and, for the purposes of the up-coming Master Plan study, would include an equal representation from the private colleges and universities. "Constitution of the Technical Advisory Committee to the Joint Staff for the Liaison Committee," January 15, 1959, CSA.
6. Dean E. McHenry, interview with author, March 29, 1989, McHenry Library.
7. Dean McHenry to Clark Kerr, March 17, 1959, UCA, McHenry File.
8. Malcolm Love, "Functions of the Three Segments of Public Higher Education in California," March 26, 1959; Robert S. Johnson to Clark Kerr, "Analysis of President Love's Proposal for Redefinition," March 31, 1959, UCA, LCF.
9. Dean McHenry to Clark Kerr, March 31, 1959.
10. Dean McHenry to Clark Kerr, "How Much was Lost at the JAC Meeting Last Week," March 31, 1959, UCA, McHenry File.
11. Vernon I. Cheadle (chair EPC–Davis) to C. W. Jones (chair EP–northern division of the Academic Senate), April 10, 1959, UCA, LCF.
12. Dean McHenry to Harry Wellman, May 19, 1959, UCA, LCF.
13. *Ibid.*
14. Council of State College Presidents, Minutes, May 6–7, 1959.
15. William S. Briscoe to Chancellor Vern O. Knudsen, May 22, 1959, UCA, LCF.
16. T. C. Holy to Clark Kerr, Harry Wellman, Jim Corley, and Stan McCaffrey, April 27, 1959, UCA, LCF; T. C. Holy, "Some Factors Indicated the Need for Overhaul," April 22, 1959, UCA, LCF.
17. *Ibid.;* see also "It'll Be Tougher to Get Into College," *San Francisco Chronicle,* April 13, 1959; "Coordinating Higher Education," *San Diego Union,* April 15, 1959.

18. Clark Kerr to Harry Wellman (copies to S. B. Freeborn, V.O. Knudsen, and G. T. Seaborg), April 9, 1959; Clark Kerr to Herman Spaeth, June 5, 1959; Joint Advisory Committee, Minutes, July 29, 1959, UCA, JACF.

19. T. C. Holy to Clark Kerr, May 14, 1959. Holy and Browne provided the general proposal for a Master Plan survey team, although they had different ideas on how it should be structured. Browne suggested a fifteen-member commission directed possibly by John W. Gardner, head of the Carnegie Foundation for the Study of Higher Education. Holy argued that there was no time to form such a large group of outsiders, which would be "too unwieldy."

20. Coons, *Crises*, 33–34; Dean McHenry to Clark Kerr, May 27, 1959, UCA, McHenry File. As it turned out, "I had my second [heart attack] in January 1960," explained Coons.

21. *Master Plan*, 21–22; T. C. Holy to Clark Kerr, May 14, 1959; Liaison Committee, Minutes, June 3, 1959; Bill J. Priest of the California Junior College Association and a representative on the JAC, requested the addition of another junior college representative in his June 11, 1959, letter to Roy Simpson (UCA, LCF). Wert was added after R. J. Wig, president of the Association of Independent California Colleges and Universities, requested representation in a letter to Roy Simpson and Clark Kerr, June 25, 1959, UCA, LCF.

22. Browne and Holy, "Plan Recommended to the Liaison Committee for the Master Plan Study Authorized by ACR 88," May 26, 1959, CSA, LCF.

23. *Ibid.*

24. Coons, *Crises*, 42. In addition, while three state senators, four assembly members, A. Alan Post, and T. H. Mugford from the Department of Finance were all invited to attend subsequent Liaison Committee meetings, it was thought wise to have only one legislative representative attend the survey team meetings. Keith Sexton, Donahoe's young assistant, was assigned to keep "selected persons of the two legislative houses informed, and to [maintain] contact with the governor's staff, channeling back to the team reactions to ideas as proposed." Sexton was part of the first group of "legislative interns" hired to staff several legislative committees, which included Jack Smart (future vice chancellor for the California State University system), Stan Anderson, and Jan Stevens. Sexton, interview, May 3, 1989.

25. All Technical Committee reports, stated Coons, "will be forwarded to the Liaison Committee, the two executive officers [Kerr and Simpson], and the JAC two weeks before discussion in the Liaison Committee."

26. Coons, *Crises*, 43.

27. Dumke, interview by Judson A Grenier, July, 1981, Oral History Pilot Project on the Origins of the CSU System, CSA.

28. Holy and Browne, "Materials Presented to the Joint Meeting of the State Board of Education and the Regents of the University of California," March 14, 1959, CSA, LCF.

29. *Ibid.*

30. *Ibid.*

31. Working with the help of T. R. McConnell at Berkeley, Glenny was completing the first detailed survey of the varied governing systems for higher education employed in the states. "Without exception," observed Glenny, "since 1950 [most] state surveys of higher education conducted by recognized experts have recommended coordinating some or all of the major activities of the colleges and universities." Lyman Glenny, as quoted by Holy and Browne from his pending book, *State Coordination and Control of Higher Education*.

32. Stanley B. Freeborn to Clark Kerr, August 13, 1959, UCA, JACF. The Ohio plan was created in 1935 and included an "inter-university council," consisting of one member of the Board of Trustees and the president and business manager of each of the state's six public higher education institutions. In 1940, the council said of the functions of doctoral-level work: "Specialized technological and professional training should be the sole property of the main land grant campus at Columbus." The other state universities were to be limited, much like California's state colleges, to "liberal arts (including fine arts), education, business and commerce through undergraduate curricula leading to the Bachelor's degree and in graduate work for the Master's degree."

33. Master Plan survey team, Minutes, June 16, 1959, California Postsecondary Education Commission Library.

34. *Ibid.*; Dean McHenry to Clark Kerr, June 24, 1959, UCA, McHenry File. "Past experience reveals the ineffectiveness," argued a university senate committee, "once authorization to grant a given degree has been given to the state colleges, of even direct prohibitions against its extension to unauthorized fields, under the most detailed conditions, restrictions, and procedures."

35. Master Plan survey team, Minutes, June 16, 1959.

36. Glenn Dumke to the Joint Advisory Committee, July 9, 1959, UCA, JACF.

37. Arthur G. Coons Papers, Binder 1, Occidental College Library.

38. Master Plan survey team, Minutes, July 27–28, 1959.

39. *Ibid.;* Dean McHenry to Clark Kerr, July 28, 1959, UCA, McHenry File.

40. Master Plan survey team, Minutes, July 27–28, 1959.

41. Stanley B. Freeborn to Clark Kerr, August 13, 1959, UCA, JACF.

42. Dean McHenry to Clark Kerr, July 28, 1959, UCA, McHenry File.

43. Presley C. Dawson to Arthur G. Coons, "Junior Colleges and the Master Plan for Higher Education in California," December 10, 1959; Master Plan survey team, Minutes, Regents Room, UCLA, September 29–30, 1959.

44. Master Plan survey team, Minutes, President's Conference Room, San Francisco State College, July 6–8, 1959.

45. Master Plan survey team, Minutes, October 12, 1959; Master Plan survey team, Minutes, November 23–24, 1959; Dean McHenry to Clark Kerr, October 23, 1959, UCA, LCF; Glenn Dumke to the Master Plan survey team, "Coordination of Higher Education in California," October 10, 1959, UCA, LCF.

46. Dean McHenry to Clark Kerr, July 28, 1959, UCA, McHenry File.

47. Dean McHenry to Clark Kerr, October 23, 1959, UCA, LCF.

48. It was estimated in a Joint Staff study, made prior to the survey team's establishment, that some 50,000 students could be channeled into the junior colleges by a change in the admission policies of the university and the state colleges. As reported in the *San Francisco Chronicle,* cost savings over a ten-year period or more could come to approximately $45 million because of their lower operating costs. Dean McHenry to Harry Wellman, March 22, 1959, UCA, JACF.

49. Master Plan survey team, Minutes, July 27–28, 1959; Dean McHenry to Clark Kerr, July 28, 1959, UCA, McHenry File.

50. Dean McHenry to Clark Kerr, July 28, 1959, UCA, McHenry File.

51. Master Plan survey team, Minutes, July 29–30, 1959.

52. *Ibid.*

53. "Major Recommendations of the Technical Committee on Selection and Retention of Students, with Comments by the Master Plan Team," as presented to the Liaison Committee, October 14, 1959.

54. Master Plan survey team, Minutes, Occidental College, November 2–4, 1959; Master Plan survey team, Minutes, University Club, Los Angeles, November 16–18, 1959; Master Plan survey team, Minutes, Occidental College, November 23–24, 1959.

55. Master Plan survey team, Minutes, Occidental College, November 23–24, 1959; *Master Plan,* 51–63. As later stated in the final Master Plan report, "under this plan, lower division enrollments in the state colleges in 1975 are 67,400 as compared with 91,750 under the status quo projections. For the University of California, comparable figures are 28,800 and 45,900." Junior college enrollment could jump from 246,350 to 288,950 under the proposed change in admissions.

56. Dean McHenry to Lloyd N. Morrisett, November 10, 1959, UCA, McHenry File.

57. *Ibid.*

58. *Master Plan,* 111–14.

59. *Ibid.*

60. *Ibid.,* 97.

61. *Ibid.,* 189.

62. *Ibid.,* 192–93.

63. *Ibid.,* 188–91.

64. Liaison Committee, Minutes, State Education Building, October 14, 1959, Sacramento.

65. Liaison Committee, Minutes, Los Angeles State College, Dining Room, November 18, 1959.

66. Joint Advisory Committee, October 13, 1959; "Functions of a Commission to Investigate the Potentialities for Increasing the Number of College and Universities Programs at the Doctoral Level," October 9, 1959, CSUA; Master Plan survey team, Minutes, November 23–24, 1959.

67. Dean McHenry to Clark Kerr, November 13, 1959, UCA, McHenry File.

68. Lloyd D. Bernard, Lowell H. Dunigan, and Charles E. Young, "Faculty Demand and Supply: Preliminary Report of the Technical Committee on Institutional Capacities and Area Needs," November 4, 1959, CSA, LCF; Roy Simpson to Arthur G. Coons, "Doctoral Programs," October 29, 1959, UCA, LCF; Master Plan survey team, Minutes, October 12–14, 1959.

69. Master Plan survey team, Minutes, November 23–24, 1959.

70. *Ibid.*

71. Clark Kerr, interview with author, February 11, 1994; Coons, *Crises,* 33–34.

72. Dean McHenry to Clark Kerr, November 29, 1959, UCA, LCF.

73. Op-Ed, *San Francisco Chronicle,* April 15, 1959.

74. "Brown Asks Action on College Issue," *Berkeley Daily Gazette,* November 30, 1959.

75. "Master Plan on College Policy Due," *Berkeley Daily Gazette,* December 2, 1959; "Higher Education Program Still Faces Many Hurdles," *Berkeley Daily Gazette,* December 1, 1959.

76. Master Plan survey team, Minutes, December 2–3, 1959.

77. *Ibid.*

78. *Ibid.*

79. *Ibid.*

80. Master Plan survey team, Minutes, December 2–3, 1959.

81. Coons, *Crises,* 56.

82. Liaison Committee, Minutes, December 7–8, 1959.

83. Kerr, interview, February 11, 1994.

84. Master Plan survey team, Minutes, December 8, 1959; Coons, *Crises,* 57–60.

85. After the meeting, Kerr called key senate members. Later that evening, he then called Coons and stated that sufficient support was available to allow a tentative commitment on the joint doctorate.

86. However, there was no direct statement supporting state funding for this college function placed in the Master Plan. Further, the plan would state: "The superiority and supremacy of the University of California as the state-sponsored research agency should be recognized." Liaison Committee, Minutes, December 9, 1959.

87. *Ibid.*

CHAPTER 10

DIVERSITY

A BACKWARD GLANCE FORWARD: PAST, PRESENT, AND FUTURE PERSPECTIVES ON HISTORICALLY BLACK COLLEGES AND UNIVERSITIES

WALTER R. ALLEN AND JOSEPH O. JEWELL

The American dream lies at the very heart of the American cultural ethos. At the center of the American dream is the emphatic conviction that, in this society, education opens the door to success. The belief that even the poorest American can achieve greatness with talent and hard work is one of this society's cherished cultural ideals (Hochschild, 1995). In most instances, talent is equated with educational attainment. African Americans have embraced these beliefs to the extreme. Dating back to when Black slaves were forbidden to learn to read and write under threat of physical harm or death, we have invested education with mythic qualities, seeing it as our hope and salvation for the future. No matter how much education African Americans achieved, they still suffered discrimination based on skin color. Nevertheless, Black people have continued to crave and to embrace education as the ultimate solution. Despite the paradox of societal stereotypes of Blacks as lazy, ignorant and mentally inferior—even as America developed history's most elaborate institutional barriers to deny African Americans equal access to learning and knowledge—Black people continued to pursue education. Historically Black Colleges and Universities (HBCUs) grew out of and were shaped by this striving of African Americans for education. These institutions have embodied the hopes and frustrations of a people seeking the Promised Land.

Education has long been seen as an essential foundation of democracy. The extent to which individuals are afforded the opportunity to obtain knowledge speaks volumes about openness and power relations within any society. Yet for African Americans, the centuries-old struggle for access

WALTER R. ALLEN is Professor of Sociology at the University of California, Los Angeles. He is codirector of CHOICES, a longitudinal study of college attendance among African Americans and Latina/os in California. His research and teaching focus on family patterns, socialization and personality development, race and ethnic relations, and social inequality and higher education. Dr. Allen's more than 80 publications include *The Color Line and the Quality of Life in America* (1987), *Enacting Diverse Learning Environments: Improving the Climate for Racial/Ethnic Diversity in Higher Education Institutions* (1999), *College in Black and White* (1991), and *Black American Families, 1965–84* (1986). He has also been a consultant to industry, government, and the courts on issues related to race, education, and equity. JOSEPH O. JEWELL is an Assistant Professor of Sociology at Texas A&M University in College Station. His substantive areas of interest are the sociology of education, race and ethnicity and comparative/historical sociology. His work explores the intersections between race and class with a focus on the role of noneconomic capital in the process of class formation. He is currently at work on a manuscript that deals with the experience of nonWhite minorities with middle-class formation in the United States in the late nineteenth and early twentieth centuries. Address queries to Allen at Department of Sociology, 264 Haines Hall, Box 951551, Los Angeles, CA 90095–1551; telephone: (310) 206–7107; fax: (310) 825–776; e-mail: wallen@ucla.edu.

and parity in higher education has been emblematic of their larger fight for equality and group recognition in America. As direct outgrowths of this struggle, Historically Black Colleges and Universities (HBCUs) embody the African American quest for education. In the face of numerous obstacles, HBCUs have functioned as multifaceted institutions, providing not only education, but also social, political, and religious leadership for the African American community. While rooted in a long, rich tradition of achieving against the odds, they are now presented with new challenges as well as opportunities for growth and change. HBCUs are called upon to continue effectively serving a community that is itself in the grip of profound change. This article looks at the past, present, and future of HBCUs, examining the contributions, key issues, challenges, and trends in their development.

THE FREEDMEN'S EDUCATION MOVEMENT, 1865–1877

From their very beginnings, HBCUs were faced with outright opposition to their existence. In the years following the American Civil War, African Americans, no longer constrained by the bonds of slavery, seized every opportunity to formalize and expand upon the clandestine educational practices that had functioned in slavery. Indelibly marked by their slave experience where they had been forcibly kept in a state of ignorance, Blacks invested education with great importance. Formal education was a chief means for African Americans to distance themselves unequivocally from slavery and their subordinate status in society. Education also enabled African Americans to achieve social mobility while "defending and extending" (Anderson, 1988, p. 3) their newly gained rights as citizens. Thomas Webber (1978), James Anderson (1988), and V. P. Franklin (1992) characterize the efforts of African Americans to gain and secure educational access through institution building and legislation as a social movement. By working to establish a system of universal public education, which included poor Whites as well as Blacks, in a region where education had largely been the privilege of the White upper class, African Americans were in essence attempting to transform the Southern social order.

African Americans were not alone in their struggle to secure educational access. In addition to the fierce drive for Black institutional development, the post-Civil War years also witnessed the en masse arrival of Northern missionary societies. Organizations affiliated with various religious denominations and composed of men and women who had been sympathetic to the Abolitionist cause now saw the "social uplift" of freedmen as the second phase of their work. However, these missionaries perceived Blacks as hapless victims of a corrupt and immoral system that inculcated values antithetical to "civilization" and viewed as their God-given task to both "civilize and educate" the freedmen, in so doing ensuring the survival of American society. To this end, they ventured into urban and rural Black communities throughout the South as teachers, where they established and operated educational institutions of varying levels.

The continued drive for group advancement and community empowerment by African Americans in this period necessitated the development of institutions that would produce a highly educated, politically astute generation of leaders, capable of representing Black interests within the White power structure while remaining independent from it.

> Ex-slave communities . . . believed that the masses could not achieve political and economic independence or self-determination without first becoming organized, and organization was impossible without well-trained intellectuals—teachers, ministers, politicians, managers, administrators, and businessmen. (Anderson, 1988, p. 20)

Blacks and their White allies faced opposition from Southern conservatives-representatives of the old regime who saw higher education for African Americans as a threat to White supremacy (Allen, Hunt, & Gilbert, 1997; Morris, 1984). Their resurgent power after the demise of Radical Reconstruction, coupled with a lack of funds and insufficient numbers of qualified teachers, made Black independent support of institutions of higher learning next to impossible. To this end, Blacks accepted the assistance of White missionary groups, embracing the normal schools and colleges they had established and benefiting from the high level of training offered. However, the persistent conflict between Black desires for empowerment and White desires for assimilation and social control shaped these institutions in the years that followed.

WHITE PATERNALISM AND BLACK EDUCATION, 1865–1920

As the turn of the century approached, African Americans had made definite inroads into securing access to higher education. Twenty-five years after the Civil War, there were approximately 100 colleges and universities for African Americans, located primarily in the South. While a minority of these institutions (most notably those founded by the AME church) were operated and controlled by Blacks themselves, the vast majority were governed by White philanthropic agencies and missionary societies (e.g., the American Missionary Association, the American Baptist Home Mission Society, and the Freedmen's Aid Society of the Methodist Episcopal Church). As such, African Americans found their collective voice in the education of their leaders limited by the paternalism of their White allies.

Despite their differing origins, all HBCUs addressed in some form or fashion three primary goals: (a) the education of Black youth, (b) the training of teachers, and (c) the continuation of the "missionary tradition" by educated Blacks (Ogden et al., 1905). Having built, staffed, and controlled institutions like Howard University, Fisk University, Atlanta University, Hampton Institute, Straight College (later Dillard), Bennett College, Clark College, Morehouse College, Spelman College, and Shaw University, the cultural biases of White missionaries largely dictated the curricular means by which these goals would be achieved. Most missionary institutions employed the traditional liberal arts curriculum found in elite White colleges which, as James Anderson writes, many Blacks accepted as necessary for leadership training (Anderson, 1988). In practice, however, this curriculum often reflected the biases of the culturally dominant majority. Scholars like Carter G. Woodson (1933) have noted that even the best of the missionary colleges employed curricula that focused on the contributions of Europe and the West, while viewing the non-White world (particularly Africa) as benighted and in sore need of Christianizing and civilizing. While some schools broke from the liberal arts tradition and focused on industrial education, a similar undercurrent of Black cultural inferiority existed. Hampton Normal and Agricultural Institute, perhaps the best-known of the industrial institutions and the model for those which followed, concentrated on a program of "manual training" mandated by the school's White missionary founder who believed Blacks to be "morally inferior" and incapable of efffectively utilizing liberal arts training. This curriculum taught basic academic competence, stressed manual laboring skills, and encouraged political accommodation through strict adherence to the South's racial codes (Bullock, 1967; Spivey, 1978).

Beyond the immediate missionary presence at HBCUs, White philanthropy as a major source of funding for HBCUs also affected the educational destiny of African Americans. Nowhere is this influence seen more clearly than in the emergence of the Booker T. Washington/W.E.B. Du Bois controversy. Booker T. Washington, a graduate of Hampton Institute, established his own school on the Hampton model in Tuskegee, Alabama, and became famous, not only for his advocacy of self-help and industrial education for Blacks, but also for his conservatism on race issues. Largely through his efforts, the Hampton/Tuskegee model of education was accepted and avidly encouraged by White Northern philanthropists and Southern politicians as an effective compromise between maintaining White supremacy and satisfying Black educational aspirations in the South. An 1890 modification of the 1862 Land Grant Colleges Act, combined with the immense popularity of the Hampton/Tuskegee model, spawned the growth of state-supported technical and industrial colleges for Blacks in the region (e.g., Alabama A&M, Tennessee A&I, North Carolina A&T universities) (Anderson, 1988; McPherson, 1975).

The overwhelming support for the Hampton/Tuskegee model and Washington's national prominence as a leader and spokesman for African Americans generated controversy within the African American community. W.E.B. Du Bois, a liberal arts graduate of Fisk University and Harvard University, opposed both the industrial model and Washington's influence, arguing instead for the education of African Americans "according to ability" and for continued political agitation against segregationist customs and laws in the South. This debate effectively split the African American intellectual community and HBCUs themselves into two separate camps. As a result of Washington's influence, many liberal arts institutions with staunchly integrationist traditions were required to adopt aspects of the Hampton/Tuskegee philosophy to maintain financial support from Northern philanthropists and Southern state governments (Bullock, 1967; Du Bois, 1969). While the Washington/Du

Bois controversy is significant as an effort by African Americans to retain a voice in deciding their educational (and by extension, social, political, and economic) destiny, its outcome was, in fact, largely decided by those with the power and resources. The decisions to fund industrial rather than liberal arts colleges for Blacks and to adopt industrial courses at traditionally liberal arts schools were largely out of the hands of African Americans. These decisions were made by White-controlled state governments, White individual and corporate philanthropists, and White-dominated agencies such as the General Education Board, the Phelps-Stokes Fund, and the Julius Rosenwald Fund (Bullock, 1967).

The problem of White philanthropy and missionary control remained an issue for Black colleges well into the 1920s. As Raymond Wolters (1975) notes, the advent of the "New Negro" movement in the 1920s saw the alumni and students of schools like Howard, Fisk, Hampton, and Tuskegee become more vocal, insisting on greater Black representation among the faculties and administrations of these schools and lobbying for changes in curriculum and rules governing student life. To make their voices heard, African Americans typically resorted to protests, both on campus and in the surrounding community. In more than a few cases, these protests succeeded in achieving the intended goal. This tradition would resurface in the late 1960s and 1970s, as Black student activists turned their attention toward self-definition and self-determination, renouncing the vestiges of the cultural paternalism that had been intrinsic in the founding of many HBCUs (Wolters, 1975).

In many ways, HBCUs were far more than educational institutions. Du Bois referred to them as "social settlements" where the "best traditions of New England" were made known to the sons and daughters of former slaves through close contact with White missionaries (1989, p. 100). Many missionary teachers sought to divest Blacks of their "peculiar" cultural past and to teach them the ways of middle-class White Americans. However, their modernist/evangelical fervor produced a system of draconian rules that rigidly defined "appropriate" behavior, dress, speech, and extracurricular activity for the future "leaders" of the Black race. These rules were roughly similar to those enforced at predominantly White institutions in the early years but, at HBCUs, were predicated to an extent upon Blacks' supposed moral laxity. As such, these rules lasted well into the twentieth century, long after they had been relaxed or modified at traditionally White institutions (TWIs) (Flemming, 1983; Jewell, 1998; Little, 1981).

HBCUs also played an important role in structuring the social stratification system within African American communities, primarily by acting as gateways for social mobility. The professional classes in African American communities were trained almost exclusively in HBCUs in the era prior to the 1954 *Brown* ruling. Even today they account for a disproportionate number of the advanced and professional degrees awarded to African Americans (Allen & Jewell, 1995; Nettles & Perna, 1997). While these institutions produced the highly educated and skilled class of leaders that the Freedmen's Education Movement had envisioned, they were also (in keeping with the desires of their missionary founders) a group thoroughly assimilated into middle-class Anglo-Protestant culture. These institutions gave a distinct and definite cultural meaning to class and status among African Americans. Adelaide Cromwell theorized that the process of stratification within minority communities—i.e., status estimations of the majority group (e.g., wealth, education, occupation) and the minority group (e.g., skin color, antebellum status)—is "synthesized" into a mutually agreed-upon class structure. This synthesis was facilitated within HBCUs, where Blacks were routinely exposed to the cultural knowledge, behavior, and tastes of the Anglo-Protestant elite.

The regular social contact with middle- and upper-class Whites afforded by HBCUs served as an important resource for Blacks seeking social mobility in an America socially and culturally dominated by Whites (Jewell, 1999). Having successfully assimilated this knowledge, college-educated African Americans felt that it was their responsibility to hand the "principles of Western culture" to "the masses below" (Miller, 1905, p. 15). As Kevin Gaines (1996) notes, late nineteenth- and early twentieth-century notions of racial uplift that were partially instilled and nurtured at HBCUs contained visible elements of cultural paternalism and class privilege. Though gallantly committed to the struggle for civil rights and racial equality, some of these men and women were often as paternalistic towards the Black masses as their White missionary teachers had been towards African Americans as a whole. The result often placed Black elites summarily at odds with the community they were pledged to uplift, a split that lasted well into the civil rights era and beyond.

SEGREGATION AND BLACK HIGHER EDUCATION, 1896–1954

While HBCUs met with a great deal of success, their effectiveness was also limited by the realities of segregation. Despite the language of "separate but equal" in the U.S. Supreme Court's decision in *Plessy v. Ferguson* (1896), Black public education was dramatically underfunded on the state and local levels. In fact, the public educational system for African Americans was described as "inadequate" by federal investigators some fifty years after the end of the Civil War, leaving HBCUs (which continued to be operated mainly under the auspices of the Northern missionary societies) primarily responsible for what educational opportunities existed for Blacks in the South, particularly at the secondary and post-secondary levels. Although missionary societies and philanthropic agencies had intended to help lay the groundwork for a system of public and higher education for Blacks, they often found themselves solely responsible instead for providing the only quality education available for Blacks. Across much of the South, Whites remained overtly hostile to the inclusion of African Americans in the statewide system of public education (Anderson, 1988). To compensate for the lack of state funding, African American communities—with vital assistance from these missions and foundations—were called on to establish and maintain quality schools, provide teachers, and fund building construction.

HBCUs were also compelled to function as multilevel institutions, including students at the secondary, college preparatory, and college levels, thereby serving the varied educational needs of the African American community. These burdens had a decidedly negative impact upon the development of HBCUs as full-fledged collegiate institutions. White power structures in the South carefully monitored the curricula of state-funded colleges, keeping them colleges in name only (Morris, Allen, Maurrasse, & Gilbert, 1995). In most state colleges for Blacks, precollegiate courses were offered along with limited vocational and industrial education. Because of their large secondary departments, the vast majority of these institutions were not recognized as college-grade institutions by federal and state agencies and, for many years, were denied accreditation.

In time, as the secondary departments were phased out, Black educational institutions took their place in the college community, although on a limited basis. With White administrators in charge of hiring and firing Black teachers at many state-run industrial schools, qualified liberal arts graduates were often passed over for those with inadequate education so long as they demonstrated the proper political outlook. Funding was often inadequate, and curricular offerings were severely restricted. Graduate education at Black institutions was significantly less available than quality elementary, secondary, and college-level education. In the 1930s, lawsuits filed in Southern states challenged the "separate but equal" concept in higher education in attempts to break the "glass ceiling" imposed on Black education for the past 70 to 75 years. While Blacks gained severely limited access to professional schools funded by the states, little change resulted until 1954 when the Supreme Court reversed its decision in *Plessy* with *Brown v. Board of Education of Topeka, Kansas.* After another decade marked by Southern resistance to integration, African Americans began to gain access to previously segregated colleges and universities (Jewell, 1999).

INTEGRATION OR DESEGREGATION? 1955–1978

While many believed that *Brown* signaled an end to the Black struggle for educational opportunity, in many respects this Supreme Court decision was, in fact, just the beginning. Across the South, school districts resisted the Supreme Court's mandate for integrated education with legal maneuvers and outright defiance. Nationally, White parents fled to the suburbs and/or enrolled their children in private schools, intending to thwart the court's ruling. As a result, to the present day, the nation's schools remain largely segregated by race (Orfield et al., 1996).

After some delay and further resistance, previously segregated universities grudgingly opened their doors to African Americans in the decade following *Brown.* Predictably this process moved faster in institutions of higher education outside the South. The national enrollment of African Americans in college grew significantly, increasing from 83,000 in 1950 to 666,000 in 1975 (U.S. Bureau of the Census, 1979). More dramatic, however, was the shift in patterns of where African Americans attended college. In 1950, the overwhelming majority of Blacks in college attended HBCUs; but by 1975, fully three-quarters of all Blacks in college attended predominantly White institutions. During the 20 years following *Brown*, African Americans participated in a second "Great Migration." This time, however, the move was not from the South to the North, but instead consisted of an enrollment migration from HBCUs to traditionally White colleges and universities (Allen, Epps, & Haniff, 1991). It should be noted that this "educational migration" reflected, in sizable part, significant gains in the overall numbers of African Americans enrolling in college.

Over this period, HBCUs made important contributions as catalysts and agents for social change. Students and faculty from these institutions played instrumental roles as leaders and foot soldiers in the civil rights and Black power movements. Leaders of the student sit-ins of Greensboro, participants in mass civil disobedience at Birmingham, and contributors to the voter registration drive across Mississippi were often students at HBCUs (Morris, 1984; Payne, 1994; Robnett, 1997; Ture & Hamilton, 1992). Alumni from HBCUs were liberally represented among the leadership of civil rights organizations and among the attorneys pursuing legal challenges for equal opportunity in education. Graduates from HBCUs were also disproportionately represented among Blacks who were "pioneers" in fields, occupations, and positions that had traditionally been closed to Blacks (Nettles & Perna, 1997).

Assisted by favorable social attitudes, a strong economy, and sustained government and university commitment, African Americans made great strides in college enrollment and degree attainment during this period. For example, in 1976–1977, 58,636 African Americans earned bachelors' degrees. By 1994, this number had grown to 83,576 (a 43 percent increase). Unfortunately, African American gains in earned doctoral degrees were much more modest. While total earned doctoral degrees increased nationally by 30 percent from 1977 (33,232) to 1994 (43,185), the increase in earned doctorates was only 73 percent for African Americans (from 1,253 in 1977 to 3,344 in 1994). Over this same period, the number of doctoral degrees awarded by HBCUs increased by 218 percent (from 66 in 1977 to 210 in 1994) (Blackwell, 1981; Nettles & Perna, 1997).

The number of African Americans enrolled in college grew from 1.033 million in the fall of 1976 to 1.5 million in the fall of 1994. In 1976, African Americans constituted 9.4 percent of all enrolled college students in the nation; by 1994, nearly 20 years later, they were only 10.1 percent of the total (Nettles & Perna, 1997). The contributions of HBCUs to African American college enrollment and earned degrees have always been disproportionate. In 1995, 230,279 (17.3 percent) of the total 1,334,000 African Americans enrolled in college attended HBCUs. Similarly, the 23,434 baccalaureate degrees awarded to African Americans in 1993–1994 by HBCUs represented 28 percent of all B.A.'s awarded to African Americans nationally. These enrollment and degree statistics loom especially large when we remember that only 2 percent of the nation's institutions of higher learning are HBCUs.

However, storm clouds loomed just beyond this period of phenomenal success in the form of a less sympathetic political climate, a declining economy, and court challenges to race-based admissions programs. The subsequent reversal in fortunes is best symbolized by the *Bakke* case. In 1978, Bakke challenged the race-based admissions procedures of the University of California-Davis, claiming that his rights had been violated by an admissions process that selected less academically qualified Black and other applicants over him. The Supreme Court ruled in Bakke's favor, striking down the University of California-Davis Medical School admissions program as "racially discriminatory." The court ruled that, while race could not be the sole or determining factor in admissions, it was permissible for race to be one of several factors employed in the admissions process. *Bakke* continues to be the U.S. Supreme Court standard for national legal precedence on the permissible role of race in college admissions decisions.

A quarter century after *Brown* saw the paradox of great educational advances by African Americans amid persistent racial inequities. The dream of integrated education had given way to the bitter reality of, at best, partly desegregated education. De jure segregation in the nation's schools had evolved into de facto segregation—with the same result for the vast majority of African Americans (Orfield et al., 1996). Separate and unequal education in racially segregated schools with few resources and low achievement levels continued to be characteristic for significant segments of the African American population. Further, within racially desegregated schools and universities, African American students were overrepresented among low achievers and in weaker academic tracks or programs.

The Deracialization Of Black Higher Education, 1978–Present

In 1978, William Julius Wilson published his enormously influential book *The Declining Significance of Race*. Wilson argued that race relations have evolved to the point in the United States where socioeconomic class is more significant than race as a basis for discrimination. He concluded that life opportunities for African Americans are now shaped more by economic status than by racial identity. Wilson's thesis coincided with several other trends, events, and shifts in society, which combined to fuel the argument that race no longer mattered in America. More significantly, the thesis suggested that race-based policies were no longer needed to address (redress) the status inequalities of African Americans. In short, society declared the battle for racial equality a victory and announced that America was now officially color blind or "de-racialized" (Thernstrom & Thernstrom, 1997).

Several key trends motivated and sustained the deracialization hypothesis, despite persistent evidence to the contrary in the form of continuing inequities in education, employment, wealth, and well-being. The 1970s and 1980s were characterized by an upsurge in political conservatism. For most of these two decades, Republicans dominated the national political scene (Cohen, 1999). The political climate was cool toward and restrictive of any activist role for government in addressing racial inequality. The growing mood in the country was that government had done enough in the decade of the 1960s to address racial discrimination and Black inequality (Dawson, 1994).

In the courts, a string of key decisions (often issued by conservative Nixon, Reagan, and Bush judicial appointees) questioned, weakened and in some instances overturned precedents that had favored equal opportunity and affirmative action programs. The emerging consensus in these rulings was that the courts and judges had become too activist and were overreaching their appropriate roles by becoming agents for social change, as, for instance, ordering busing to achieve school desegregation. The courts' shift toward less interventionist stances coincided with systematic, well-funded campaigns by entities such as the Center for Individual Rights to reshape the national landscape. Legislation embodying hard-won civil rights and equal opportunity guarantees was held legally suspect or even unnecessary. So on both the political and legal fronts, a coordinated effort was mounted to force acceptance of a new vision of America as a color blind or deracialized society.

It is no coincidence that these trends occurred during a period of massive economic and demographic upheaval. Liberalization in immigration laws was followed by exponential increases in the number of immigrants to the United States from Mexico, Central and Latin America, and Asia. This increased demographic diversity had reverberations for racial and economic relationships in U.S. society (Omi & Winant, 1994). Racially, the country was forced away from the simplistic—and never truly accurate—dichotomous racial paradigm of White or Black to a much more complicated, elusive rainbow continuum formed by skin color, ethnicity, nationality, social class, etc. More specific to this paper, in this period higher education saw dramatic increases in Asian and Latino students. Indeed, some campuses in California, Florida, New York City, and Texas experienced demographic shifts that threatened the majority status of Whites. Gradually, the previous rhetorical emphasis in higher education on equal opportunity (read: the inclusion of African Americans) gave way to a broader rhetoric of diversity (read: all groups of color, women, gays/lesbians, and the physically challenged). In the process, African Americans were redefined from a group uniquely deserving "educational compensation" because of past racial injustice to just one of many groups vying for college admission under the goal of "increased diversity."

On the economic front, the country experienced a severe downturn. America and the rest of the world were battered by a series of consecutive recessions. This economic decline and instability bred insecurity and fueled racial scapegoating (Cohen, 1999). Many Whites felt economically insecure and threatened by African American socioeconomic gains. They felt that any economic progress made by African Americans (and the largely colored immigrants) came only at their expense. The media drumbeat of court cases charging "reverse discrimination" in hiring and promotions that violated White constitutional rights by favoring "unqualified" Blacks and minorities over Whites only exacerbated these feelings. Thus, increasing numbers of Whites resented and resisted the continued pressure from African Americans for expanded economic opportunities by asserting White privilege and White supremacy. This backlash grew even as the country continued to craft a new vision of itself as color blind.

Consistent with this notion of the "new America" as color blind were the changes noted in White responses to surveys of racial attitudes. Some surveys reported dramatically positive changes in the views Whites expressed about and toward Blacks and other people of color with the result that some researchers were skeptical of surveys that reported continued racial hostility and negative attitudes by Whites toward Blacks. Bobo and Smith (1997) documented that, in fact, negative White attitudes toward Blacks persisted, albeit in more subtler forms. Bobo and Smith argued that the old Jim Crow racism had become *laissez faire* racism. A series of voter propositions that followed seemed to support their conclusion. In California, Proposition 209 outlawed affirmative action for students of color while Proposition 187 denied public education to illegal immigrants. In Washington, voters outlawed affirmative action, and similar drives nationally received widespread support. The result clearly communicated the continuing racial animus of a majority of Whites toward—if not African Americans themselves— programs whose purpose was to advance racial equity between Blacks and Whites.

Forming a backdrop to these developments was a growing chorus in the scholarship of writers such as Charles Murray, Shelby Steele, Thomas Sowell, Dinesh D'Souza, Glen Loury, William J. Wilson, and Stephan and Abigail Thernstrom. This body of writings argued aspects of the new racial orthodoxy, which proclaimed that America was now color blind, that African Americans had achieved equality, and that the need for government equal opportunity programs was past.

Interestingly, the racial lines in employment, housing, and education remained rigidly drawn and, for the most part, unbroken over this period. African Americans were as nearly segregated residentially in 1980 as they had been in 1950 (Farley & Allen, 1989). As a consequence, the patterns of school attendance, largely dictated by geographic neighborhood, continued to be distinctly drawn along racial lines (Orfield et al., 1996). Under the new, less supportive regime, a series of court-ordered busing plans and government-administered monitoring functions (e.g., Civil Rights Commission, Equal Educational Opportunities Program) were deemphasized and/or discontinued. *Bakke* was followed by *Podberesky* (1992), *Hopwood* (1996), and several other court decisions that signaled clearly the expressed position that affirmative action programs were without legal basis or support. Put more simply, the time when government felt the need to, could be expected to, or would legally intervene on behalf of Black compensatory claims had ended.

Evidence of substantial Black progress in education and employment was also regarded as proof that America was color blind (Hochschild, 1995). The growth in the ranks of African American professionals and the Black middle class was often cited to support the view that racial discrimination was now a thing of the distant past. African Americans were subdivided into the "truly disadvantaged" (i.e., Blacks with legitimate claims for government intervention to achieve racial equity) versus affluent, middle-class Blacks who were making illegitimate claims (Wilson, 1987). Indeed, an emerging court standard or test of racial discrimination required that *individual* African Americans be able to provide evidence of specific acts of discrimination directed against them personally to receive redress for racial discrimination—as opposed to previous court standards that accepted the notions of *historical* discrimination against African Americans as a class or group of people (Thernstrom & Thernstrom, 1997).

FACING THE FUTURE: NEW CHALLENGES AND OPPORTUNITIES FOR HBCUs

The 1970s and 1980s witnessed new challenges (alongside persistent old ones) for many HBCUs with regard to student enrollment, academics, and resource availability. These challenges have only intensified in the last decade of the 20th century. The civil rights gains of the 1960s and 1970s opened doors for middle-class African Americans. Historically Black institutions, perhaps for the first time since their beginnings, were required to compete with traditionally White institutions for students. Thompson (1973) notes that Black colleges had in the past practiced a "modified form of open enrollment," recruiting the vast majority of their students from the lower socioeconomic classes (rural and urban) who were often unprepared for college-level instruction. Webster, Stockard, and Henson (1981) note that the 1970s saw a sharp decline in the already small percentage of high-achieving and affluent students enrolling at HBCUs, a trend that continued into the 1980s. This enrollment trend, coupled with the steady decline of American public schools which, according to census data, educate roughly 80 percent of African American school-age children, has led to a corresponding change in the academic environments of many HBCUs. By continuing to assume responsibility for repairing deficiencies in the education received by most Black students, many colleges now commit greater resources to remedial instruction than they have in the past. This added burden continues to put a strain on HBCUs, often taking time and energy away from college-level instruction and hampering their recognition as high-quality academic institutions (Jencks & Reisman, 1968).

Yet for a select set of historically Black colleges and universities, the late 1980s and 1990s revealed a totally different story. The experiences of institutions such as Spelman College, Morehouse College, Xavier University, Hampton University, Howard University, and Florida A&M University differed dramatically from the challenges described above. Not only were these schools able to maintain strong academic programs and to build strong endowments, but they also competed successfully with predominantly White institutions for the "brightest of the bright"—the offspring of the growing Black middle class. In many instances, these jewels in the crown of HBCUs surpassed their White competitors on commonly accepted indicators of academic excellence and institutional success. For instance, Spelman College, Morehouse College, and Fisk University were all named among the best liberal arts colleges in the nation in the 1999 *U.S. News and World Report* educational rankings. Similarly, Xavier University has been acknowledged as the nation's leading institution for the production of Black undergraduates who enter medical school. For consecutive years, Florida A&M University held the record for the largest number of National Merit Achievement Scholars enrolled.

Interestingly, such shining successes brought, along with the celebration, concerns in some quarters over whether the high-academic status historically Black colleges and universities had in fact lost their way. Questions were raised about whether these schools had turned away from their traditional constituency to attract the children of African American elites through increased emphasis on high standardized test scores, exclusive honors programs, and high national rankings. Ironically, many of these African American elite parents were once themselves beneficiaries of opportunities for advanced education provided by HBCUs dedicated to developing the raw academic talent of first-generation college students. In any case, HBCUs continued to make striking, disproportionate contributions to the higher education of African Americans. Although the 100 or so HBCUs represent roughly 2 percent of the nation's 3,000-plus institutions of higher learning, in any given year HBCUs enroll over 25 percent of all African Americans attending undergraduate programs and graduate just under 30 percent of all African Americans who receive bachelor's degrees (Carter & Wilson, 1997).

HBCUs have a long and distinguished history of challenging the racial and gender status quo in American higher education. In addition to offering educational opportunities to African Americans, they were among the first institutions to open their doors to students regardless of race, creed, color, gender, or national origin, despite the existence of segregationist customs that severely limited the practice of this ideal. Native American, African, Asian, Latin American, and Caribbean students have all benefited from the educational and social commitment of HBCUs, as have White women and Jews who enrolled in professional schools at these institutions when gender-, religion- and race-based quotas kept many of them out of traditionally White institutions (TWIs) in significant numbers. As Gabrielle Simon Edgcomb (1993) documents, this "open door policy" with regards to race has not been limited to students. During the second World War, refugee scholars from Europe joined the faculties of Atlanta, Fisk, Howard, Xavier, Lincoln, and other schools after arriving in the United States. In the ensuing years, HBCUs have continued to employ international scholars, mainly from Africa and Asia, as faculty (Edgcomb, 1993; Logan, 1969).

African American communities are uniquely positioned to assist this nation's quest for a redefined multicultural, diverse reality. African Americans led the struggle for inclusion and provided a model for the various "Others," who were excluded because of differences defined by gender, ethnicity, religion, race, class, region, and sexual orientation (Morris, 1984). HBCUs are therefore called upon to provide leadership and to make important contributions in the quest for a truly inclusive society. The more complicated landscape of "difference" in contemporary society challenges HBCUs to do a better job of valuing and incorporating women, gays, lesbians, Asians, Latinos, Muslims, Jews, Whites, and the less affluent. While HBCUs have been at the forefront in managing and accommodating difference, these campuses are no panacea. Certain categories of people have been and continue to be discriminated against at HBCUs because of their gender, national origins, social class, sexual orientation, religion, race, or ethnicity. To simply argue that HBCUs are in many respects less discriminatory than predominantly White institutions misses the point. In fact, this argument is hard to sustain when the focus is on certain types of discrimination, e.g., gender, sexual orientation, social class status, or national origin. There is a need to recognize the invidious nature of structured inequality in our society—that all systems of domination and degradation are intertwined and that there is violence done to human beings and relationships when they are allowed to function against *any* group (Carbado, 1999; Cohen, 1999; Collins, 1998). Inevitably, these patterns of hierarchy and discrimination take root and are reflected in HBCUs, since the larger society leaves its footprints, to a greater or lesser degree, on these institutions. The challenge confronting HBCUs is how to best define and realize a new vision wherein all types of difference are appreciated and celebrated rather than feared or persecuted.

The worsening racial climate nationally, and at TWIs for Blacks and other minorities, presents HBCUs with a monumental opportunity to continue to expand upon their established traditions of inclusion by recruiting Latinos, Asians, Native Americans, and even lower-income Whites as students. HBCUs can draw upon the lessons from the past, where White missionary teachers and their families interacted with Blacks inside and outside of the classroom. There are lessons to be learned as well from the increasingly multiracial and multiethnic reality of contemporary American society. HBCUs can experiment with and perfect the implementation of a truly multicultural campus environment while offering educational opportunities to the youth of other groups who, like African Americans, are facing severely limited access to higher education (Hurtado, Milem, Clayton-Pedersen, & Allen, 1999). In so doing, HBCUs might reaffirm their commitment to community empowerment and racial equality by taking a leading step in promoting concrete political and economic coalitions between communities of color as well as with lower-income Euro-Americans.

It is especially ironic, given their long history as institutions that taught racial tolerance and the work of their distinguished alumni in promoting equality and cross-cultural understanding, that HBCUs should play so small a role in the current debates on multiculturalism in American higher education. Having been among the first such institutions in America, they should by rights occupy a leading position in such discussion, offering the insight that only they have gained from their distinctive traditions of opening doors to students and faculty regardless of race, class, religion, or gender. Those who control debates over multiculturalism in higher education fail to understand the rich multicultural contributions of HBCUs toward resolving the problems. Though direct descendants of the Black/White paradigm in American race relations, HBCUs have continued to expand their vision beyond these stereotypic constraints.

BACK TO THE FUTURE: HBCUS, THE NEW MILLENNIUM, AND THE CONTINUING STRUGGLE FOR BLACK HIGHER EDUCATION

Sankofa, an oft-seen African cultural symbol, shows the body of a bird facing forward while the head looks backward. The message is explicit: the past shapes the future. As we reflect on the future of HBCUs at this dawning of a new millennium, it is appropriate to look backward to better see what is ahead. One inescapable lesson is that African Americans have found the road to higher education stony, fraught with obstacles and resistance. In many respects, the Black struggle for higher education is an apt metaphor for the larger Black struggles for citizenship, self-determination, and personhood in this society. Education generally, and higher education in particular, has been and continues to be fiercely contested ground for African Americans. Black educational gains have been hard won. Because our victories tend to be partial and/or precarious, African Americans often find themselves revisiting the same battlefields. Currently, national political movements against affirmative action in higher education (e.g., California's Proposition 209) and for "high stakes" standardized tests (e.g., to determine high school graduation or college admission) pose very real threats to African American access and success in higher education. Along with several court decisions that withdrew legal support for compensatory programs (e.g., *Hopwood*) and a societal-wide retreat from a commitment to equity, these trends place the future of African American higher education at risk.

Hearing that African American progress in higher education is at risk, some will find such a pronouncement alarmist. They will argue that U.S. cultural ethos and practices have changed so fundamentally that African Americans are ensured continued access to higher education. We, however, are less sanguine on this point. Looking backward, we see eerie resemblances between the systematic efforts to turn back the clock of Black progress at the end of the twentieth century and similar efforts during the post-Reconstruction period at the end of the nineteenth century. Concretely, the 1998 implementation of the University of California Board of Regents' decision to end affirmative action in admissions (subsequently ratified in a statewide referendum, Proposition 209) resulted in a 40–50 percent reduction in the enrollment of African American and Chicana/o/Latina/o students at UCLA and UC-Berkeley. At the same time, several HBCUs have "converted," that is, they now have—or will soon have, given current trends—a majority of White students. Examples are Bluefield State University in West Virginia and Lincoln University in Missouri. Further, extreme fiscal crisis threatens the continued viability, if not existence, of several public and private HBCUs. In short, at the very moment when higher education options for Black students at predominantly White institutions are shrinking, we are also seeing constriction in the options available at HBCUs. Today, as in the past, HBCUs are called upon to complete the herculean task of contributing disproportionately to the higher education of African Americans.

Although greatly outnumbered and comparatively impoverished in economic and physical resources, HBCUs continue to rise to the challenge. The over 100 HBCUs represent roughly 3 percent of all institutions of higher learning in the nation; yet during the 1990s, these institutions enrolled around one-quarter of all Black students in U.S. higher education. These institutions also granted over 25 percent of baccalaureate degrees, 15 percent of master's and professional degrees, and 10 percent of Ph.D.'s to African Americans (Carter & Wilson, 1997; Nettles & Perna, 1997).

The accomplishments of HBCUs are truly impressive by any standard. HBCUs have helped to liberate and empower Black aspirations for the American dream. HBCUs were conceived at the intersection between ideal aspirations and racial restriction. Despite White racism and White paternalism, these institutions managed to form "free spaces," racially segregated arenas where African Americans were able to forge and pursue visions of equality and self-determination, removed from the gaze and direct control of White power structures (Morris, 1984; Robnett, 1997). However, as Robnett (1997) reminds us, rarely are free spaces completely free; thus, they tend to have both positive and negative aspects. HBCUs were never left entirely alone; the reach of White domination, whether benevolent or hostile, constricted, distorted, or destroyed the interior of HBCUs to control expressions of independence and self-determination. These efforts to direct and/or suppress the higher education and development of African Americans were motivated by what W.E.B. Du Bois refers to as "The Great Fear"—the fear felt by oppressive forces of the moment "when a human being becomes suddenly conscious of the tremendous powers lying latent within him." Du Bois continues: "When this happens in the case of a class or nation or a race, the world fears or rejoices according to the way in which it has been trained to contemplate a change in the conditions of the class or race in question" (qtd. in Aptheker, 1973, pp. 8–9). For Du Bois, education represented a vital tool for empowerment, education that had been systematically denied Blacks to maintain a system of White supremacy. The goal of this oppressive system was to educate African Americans to "put their rights in the background; emphasize their duties—say little of ambition or aspiration[;] . . . if their young men will dream dreams, let them be dreams of corn bread and molasses" (Du Bois, qtd. in Aptheker, 1973, p. 9). By Du Bois's account, the salvation of African Americans lay in HBCUs: "I regard the college as the true founding stone of all education, and not as some would have it, the kindergarten" (qtd. in Aptheker, 1973, p. 3).

To prosper in this new millennium as academic institutions of the first order and not, as some uniformed observers view them, as relics of America's less enlightened racial past, HBCUs must continue to evolve and change to reflect America's new reality. They must maintain and solidify the worldview and traditions that have anchored them and kept them viable for more than a century. At the same time, these institutions will need to adapt to the new reality best exemplified by the increasing number of racially, culturally, and economically diverse student bodies that they will be called upon to educate.

Certainly HBCUs will be affected by the general transformations sweeping U.S. higher education and will respond to a variety of questions as they reassess their missions and decide how best to serve their constituencies. Among these questions are: How to do more with less? What will be the role of faculty governance? How viable is distance education? What are the information and technology needs of the future? What are effective strategies for upgrading institutional budget, records, and facilities infrastructure? How should capital campaigns be managed? What are essential elements for the twenty-first century curriculum? What changes will be required to recruit and serve multiracial/multicultural student bodies? What are pressing faculty needs? The list goes on.

Beyond these relatively common, utilitarian questions is another set of questions about the "heart and soul" of HBCUs, questions about their *raison d'être*, special place, and distinctive roles. These conversations are best left to my colleagues who live and work daily in these institutions. However, I would suggest that W.E.B. Du Bois's articulated vision of the nature, theory, content, and purposes of the education of Black people is an appropriate starting point for such inquiries. To be truly education, according to Du Bois, it must be partisan and—given the realities of the social order—fundamentally subversive. In this sense, he was concerned in the first place with the education of his people in the United States and with education as part of the process of the liberation of his people. He insistently called on Black people to exercise great energy and initiative in controlling their own lives, engaging in continued experimentation and innovation (Aptheker, 1973).

References

Allen, W. R., Epps, E. G., & Haniff, N. (Eds.). (1991). *College in Black and White: African American students in predominantly White and historically Black public universities*. Albany: State University of New York Press.

Allen, W. R., Hunt, D., & Gilbert, D. I. M. (1997). Race-conscious academic policy in higher education: The University of Maryland Banneker Scholars Program. *Educational Policy 11*(4), 443–478.

Allen, W. R., & Jewell, J. O. (1995). The mis-education of Black America: African American education since *An American Dilemma*. *Daedalus 124*(1), 77–100.

Anderson, J. D. (1988). *Education of Blacks in the South, 1865–1930*. Chapel Hill: University of North Carolina.

Aptheker, H. (Ed.). (1973). *The education of Black people: Ten critiques, 1906–1960, by W.E.B. Du Bois*. New York: Monthly Review Press.

Blackwell, J. E. (1981). *Mainstreaming outsiders: The production of Black professionals*. Bayside, NY: General Hall.

Bullock, H. A. (1967). *A history of Negro education in the South: From 1619 to the present*. New York: Praeger.

Carbado, D. W. (Ed.). (1999). *Black men on race, gender and sexuality*. New York: New York University.

Carter, D. J., & Wilson, R. (1997). *Minorities in higher education*. Washington, DC: American Council on Education.

Cohen, C. (1999). *The boundaries of Blackness: AIDS and the breakdown of Black politics*. Chicago: University of Chicago Press.

Collins, P. H. (1998). *Fighting words: Black women and the search for justice*. Minneapolis: University of Minnesota Press.

Dawson, M. C. (1994). *Behind the mule: Race and class in African-American politics*. Princeton, NJ: Princeton University Press.

Du Bois, W.E.B. (1969). The Niagara movement. In W.E.B. Du Bois, *An ABC of color* (pp. 30–33). New York: Workman Press. (Original work published 1963)

Du Bois, W.E.B. (1989). *The souls of Black folk*. New York: Penguin. (Original work published 1903)

Edgcomb, G. S. (1993). *From swastika to Jim Crow: Refugee scholars at Black colleges*. Malabar, FL: Krieger.

Farley, R., & Allen, W. R. (1989). *The color line and the quality of life in America*. New York: Oxford University Press.

Flemming, C. G. (1983). The effect of education on Black Tennesseans after the Civil War. *Phylon 44*, 209–216.

Franklin, V. P. (1992). *Black self-determination: A cultural history of African-American resistance*. 2d Ed. Brooklyn, NY: Lawrence Hill Books.

Gaines, K. K. (1996). *Uplifting the race: Black leadership, politics and culture in the twentieth century*. Chapel Hill: University of North Carolina.

Hochschild, J. (1995). *Facing up to the American dream: Race, class and the soul of the nation*. Princeton, NJ: Princeton University Press.

Hopwood v. Texas. (1996). 78 F.3d 932, 932–937.

Hurtado, S., Milem, J., Clayton-Pedersen, A, & Allen, W. R. (1999). *Enacting diverse learning environments: Improving the climate for racial/ethnic diversity in higher education.* ASHE-ERIC Higher Education Report, Vol. 26, No. 8. Washington, DC: George Washington University, Graduate School of Education and Human Development.

Jencks, C, & Reisman, D. (1968). *The academic revolution.* Garden City, NY: Doubleday.

Jewell, J. O. (1998). *Black ivy: The American Missionary Association and the making of Atlanta's Black upper class, 1867–1915.* Unpublished Ph.D. dissertation. University of California at Los Angeles.

Jewell, J. O. (1999, August). *From Black sheep to dusky shepherds: The American Missionary Associations First Congregational Church and Atlanta's Black upper class.* Unpublished paper delivered at the American Sociological Association annual meeting in Chicago.

Little, M. H. (1981). The extracurricular activities of Black college students, 1868–1940. *Journal of Negro History* 65, 135–148.

Logan, R. W. (1969). *Howard University: The first hundred years, 1867–1967.* New York: New York University.

McPherson, J. M. (1975). *The abolitionist legacy: From Reconstruction to the NAACP.* Princeton, NJ: Princeton University Press.

Miller, K. (1905). Howard University. In R. C. Ogden et al., *From servitude to service.* Boston: American Unitarian Association.

Morris, A. (1984). *The origins of the civil rights movement.* New York: Free Press.

Morris, A., Allen, W. R., Maurrasse, D., & Gilbert, D. (1995). White supremacy and higher education: The Alabama higher education desegregation case. *National Black Law Journal* 14(1), 59–91.

Nettles, M. T., & Perna, L. W. (1997). *The African American education data book* (Vols. 1, 3). Washington, DC: Frederick Patterson Research Institute of The College Fund/UNCF.

Ogden, R. C., et al. (1905). *From servitude to service.* Boston: American Unitarian Association.

Omi, M., & Winant, H. (1994). *Racial formation in the United States: From the 1960s to the 1990s.* 2d Ed. New York: Routledge.

Orfield, G., Eaton, S. E., & the Harvard Project on School Segregation. (1996). *Dismantling desegregation: The quiet reversal of Brown v. Board of Education.* New York: New Press.

Payne, C. (1994). *I've got the light of freedom.* Berkeley: University of California Press.

Podberesky v. Kirwin. (1992).956 F.2d 52–4th Cir. (Case No. JFM-90-1685 [D.MD.]).

Robnett, B. (1997). *How long? How long?: African American women in the struggle for civil rights.* New York: Oxford University Press.

Spivey, D. (1978). *Schooling for the new slavery: Black industrial education, 1868–1915.* Westport, CT: Greenwood Press.

Thernstrom, S., & Thernstrom, A. (1997). *America in Black and White: One nation indivisible.* New York: Simon and Schuster.

Ture, K., & Hamilton, C. (1992). *Black power: The politics of liberation.* New York: Vintage.

U.S. Bureau of the Census. (1979). *The social and economic status of the Black population in the U.S.: An historical view, 1790–1978.* Washington, DC: U.S. Department of Commerce, Bureau of the Census.

Webber, T. L. (1978). *Deep like the rivers: Education in the slave quarter community, 1831–1865.* New York: Norton.

Wilson, W.J. (1978). *The declining significance of race.* Chicago: University of Chicago Press.

Wilson, W.J. (1987). *The truly disadvantaged.* Chicago: University of Chicago Press.

Wolters, R. (1975). *The new Negro on campus: Black college rebellions of the 1920s.* Princeton, NJ: Princeton University.

Woodson, C. G. (1933). *The mis-education of the Negro.* Washington, DC: Associated Publishers.

"Quacks, Quirks, Agitators, and Communists": Private Black Colleges and the Limits of Institutional Autonomy

Joy Ann Williamson

Private black colleges and their students played a vital role in the Civil Rights Movement of the middle twentieth century. The colleges' corporate structure shielded the colleges and their students from direct state intervention, and students took advantage of the liberal campus climate. Private philanthropic support and control enabled a more active form of participation in the movement, but insecure economic situations, internal dissention, and other convenient liabilities left the colleges vulnerable. State agencies found creative ways to interfere in campus affairs and capitalize on institutional weaknesses. This piece examines the battle for institutional autonomy as it played out in the state of Mississippi. It offers a picture of the lengths to which racists would go to crush the Civil Rights Movement, an evaluation of the public role of private institutions, and a window into the role of higher educational institutions in society.

The end of the Civil War forced the nation to grapple with integrating freedmen and freedwomen into the social order. Benevolent societies and denominational bodies created what are now labeled private, historically black colleges and universities (HBCUs) throughout the South to train African American leaders to uplift the race. These private institutions depended on private donations, tuition, and philanthropic gifts to sustain them and remained outside the state's purview. The campuses were tiny islands that promoted racial equality but rarely challenged the existing Southern social order. Racist state officials paid little attention to the internal affairs of private HBCUs until the middle twentieth century when students joined the campaign for black liberation. Private HBCUs enjoyed political and economic autonomy not shared by their state-supported counterparts, and students took advantage of the liberal campus climate. The corporate structure of private HBCUs buffered them from the most intense forms of state interference and allowed them and their students to play an active role in the Civil Rights Movement. But, their private status did not shield them completely from state pressures, particularly when college aims collided with state interests. Private HBCUs battled with state legislatures, racist citizen's organizations, and other groups hostile toward the colleges' role in the black freedom struggle. The public role of the private colleges made them enemies of the state.

This piece examines the battle between the state of Mississippi and private HBCUs and its consequences for institutional autonomy during the civil rights era. Mississippi, more than any other state, aggressively attacked all sources of activism. Its agency of choice, the Mississippi Sovereignty Commission, vowed to preserve and defend racial segregation at any cost. It targeted three private HBCUs in particular: Campbell College, Tougaloo College, and Rust College. Other private HBCUs existed in the state, but the Commission considered these three institutions the greatest threat to

History of Higher Education Annual 23 (2004): 49–81.
© 2004. ISBN: 0-7658-0839-0

Mississippi laws and customs. The Commission never succeeded in destabilizing any of the colleges by itself, but it created conditions under which private HBCUs weighed the benefits and costs of remaining involved in civil rights. Its success hinged on its ability to act as a parasite that capitalized on institutional vulnerabilities. The weakest institutions suffered dire consequences, and none of the colleges were immune to the Commission's agenda. The colleges fought back, and in some ways were successful, but the tug-o-war for ultimate control of campus affairs exacted a toll. The experience of the three colleges demonstrates the value of civil society in an oppressive state and the price private HBCUs paid for assuming an active role in the Civil Rights Movement.

The Mississippi Context

Mississippi, like other Southern states, created public HBCUs to insure social stability, to create a separate black professional class, and to keep African Americans from attending historically white institutions.[1] Public college curricula taught respect for the racial order and the proper limits of black aspirations. The all-white Board of Trustees of Institutions of Higher Learning, the state legislature, and campus administrators carefully controlled the institutions to thwart radical notions of black equality. Religious philanthropists created a separate set of private HBCUs. Rather than fit African Americans to the racial status quo, these institutions educated African Americans for full political and civic equality. Religious philanthropists argued that a classical curriculum, paired with religious training, equipped future leaders in the black community with the skills and knowledge necessary for full citizenship. The campuses maintained an uneasy agreement with the surrounding white community: they instilled racial pride, a sense of entitlement, and leadership skills but accepted the segregated Southern reality.[2]

The growth of the Civil Rights Movement dissolved the compromise between the private colleges and hostile whites. The state aggressively attacked individuals and institutions sympathetic to the movement. The high rate of HBCU student participation, particularly by those at private campuses, marked HBCUs as prime targets. The use of campus facilities for integrated events and civil disobedience planning sessions infuriated segregationists. The state completely controlled the public HBCUs and felt confident about its control of some private HBCUs. The state, however, encountered resistance at Campbell College, Tougaloo College, and Rust College. In 1960, the three colleges, combined, educated 1,300 students total. An even smaller number participated in active protest. The number of students meant less than the colleges' private status, role in the movement, and key geographic locations in the state. Mississippi racists increasingly monitored events at private campuses as civil rights activism escalated.

The state of Mississippi organized its anti-desegregation efforts after the Supreme Court's 1954 *Brown* v. *Board of Education* decision, which declared racial segregation unconstitutional. The state legislature passed a parade of bills that ranged from repealing the state's compulsory education laws to an interposition resolution. It also created the Mississippi Sovereignty Commission, a tax-supported implementation agency and "a permanent authority for the maintenance of racial segregation."[3] Incorporated on 29 March 1956, the Commission sought to "do and perform any and all acts and things deemed necessary and proper to protect the sovereignty of the state of Mississippi, and her sister states, from encroachment thereon by the Federal Government or any branch, department, or agency thereof."[4] The Commission hired informants, conducted investigations on suspected integrationists, and distributed segregationist propaganda to defend Mississippi's racial hierarchy. It also allocated funds to the White Citizens' Council, a private citizen's organization whose agenda paralleled that of the Sovereignty Commission.[5] The Commission and the Council became part of an extensive network of racist public officials who closed ranks to protect the racial hierarchy.

Meanwhile, students at HBCUs across the South joined the Civil Rights Movement and inaugurated a period of sustained mass activism beginning in 1960. Their brand of activism broke with the past and shifted civil rights agitation from the courts to the streets. Four students from North Carolina A&T, a public HBCU, staged a sit-in at the local Woolworth's to protest segregation and discrimination in eating establishments (1 February 1960). Other HBCU students in North Carolina followed their example, and HBCU students in other states soon conducted their own sit-ins. Shaw University, a private HBCU in North Carolina, hosted a conference to organize the sit-in movement in April. The Student Non-violent Coordinating Committee (SNCC) grew out of the conference and enabled students across the South to coordinate their activities. SNCC turned its attention to voter registration as proprietors desegregated their facilities. HBCU students and interested others traveled to the deep South and provided voter education classes, transportation to registration and voting locations, and psychological sustenance to disenfranchised African Americans.[6] Activists used local churches, homes, and HBCU campuses to organize their assault on racial domination.

Conditions in Mississippi stalled full-blown direct action in the state. White political and economic terror reigned, and conservative civil rights leaders worried that direct action would lead to violent retaliation and counseled activists to be patient.[7] Militant activists ignored the advice. Medgar Evers, Jackson resident and Mississippi Field Secretary for the National Association for the Advancement of Colored People (NAACP) since 1954, organized an Easter boycott of downtown Jackson stores to protest poor treatment and discrimination in 1960. Local students from Tougaloo College, Campbell College, Jackson State College (a public college), and black high schools canvassed door-to-door to solicit support, but only for a short while and with limited success.[8] The same April, NAACP members on the Gulf Coast organized a wade-in in Biloxi to protest regulations that prevented African Americans from patronizing beaches along the Gulf of Mexico. A white mob chased and assaulted the swimmers as police watched.[9] Intense white scrutiny and reprisals forced Mississippi activists to regroup. Almost an entire year passed before black Mississippians initiated another direct action attack on Mississippi's racial caste system.

In 1961, Jackson became the center of increasing civil rights activity after nine Tougaloo College students staged a sit-in at the whites-only public library in March. The sit-in inaugurated a period of sustained and massive civil disobedience across the state and Jackson in particular. Local NAACP branches and other interested individuals organized and executed a variety of attacks on segregation and discrimination in the city in the next few years. Between 1961 and 1964, activists in Jackson launched another longer lasting and more effective boycott of white stores, conducted sit-ins, pickets, mass marches, and letter writing campaigns, and initiated a school desegregation suit. Police arrested over six hundred people in 1961 and 1962 alone.[10] The assault on Jackson, the urban center and capital of the state, angered white Mississippians. The Citizens' Council, local police, and the Sovereignty Commission jailed, harassed, and killed activists to stem the tide of protest. They also targeted the organizations and institutions in which activists pooled their resources and devised plans of action. Campbell College and Tougaloo College, both of which were located in Jackson, fell under heavy scrutiny.

Mississippi's dismal record on civil rights brought increasing media attention and more civil rights workers in 1964. During the summer months, SNCC spearheaded the Mississippi Summer Project. SNCC hoped to force the state to change its racist policies or coerce federal intervention, highlight the rabid resistance to racial equality, and develop local leadership to sustain the movement.[11] The Project brought hundreds of mostly white volunteers to Mississippi to teach in Freedom Schools and to work in voter registration alongside local activists. After completing a week of training in Oxford, Ohio, in classroom pedagogy, Mississippi history, and nonviolent self-defense, volunteers made the long drive to Mississippi. Their journey often took them through Holly Springs. Some workers remained in Holly Springs and joined other SNCC workers and local activists in a major campaign against segregated facilities and voting rights violations. As one of the only sizable towns in northern Mississippi, Holly Springs and its independent institutions, including Rust College, became invaluable for movement purposes. They also became targets for state intervention.

The Institutional Consequences of Involvement in the Civil Rights Movement

The Sovereignty Commission and the Board of Trustees of Institutions of Higher Learning policed public HBCU campuses and expected full compliance from their presidents. As an arm of the legislature, on which public HBCUs were economically dependent, college presidents followed the Commission's advice and fired any faculty labeled as an agitator. Tenure did not exist at state-supported HBCUs, nor did the state pretend to value institutional integrity. The Commission also forced the presidents to be agents in its fight against student participation in the movement. Students at Mississippi Vocational College staged a thirty-six-hour walk-out to demand a student government in 1957, the first boycott in an HBCU in Mississippi. The president stalled the issue for four years before allowing the students to form an association. He guaranteed the student government's compliance with college regulations against activism by requiring the presence of two faculty members and the Dean of Students at all meetings.[12] Also in 1957, the Board of Trustees fired the president of Alcorn A&M College after he sided with students boycotting classes to protest pro-segregation editorials written by an Alcorn professor. The Board demanded his immediate resignation, expelled the entire student body, and appointed a new president more amenable to its attitudes on proper student behavior.[13] In 1961, Jackson State College's president dissolved its Student Government Association after accusing it of instigating civil rights activities and "embarrassing" the school when Jackson State students rallied in support of the Tougaloo students arrested at the whites-only library.[14] He also provided the Sovereignty Commission with the names and home address of activist students.[15] Students at public institutions were not dormant, but the nature of state control and the severe consequences leveled by the administration negatively influenced participation in the movement.

Conditions at Mississippi's private HBCUs were different. The high rate of private HBCU student participation in the movement, paired with the fact that college presidents refused to expel or punish activist students for their involvement, infuriated Mississippi racists. Segregationists and their allies railed against what Lieutenant Governor Carroll Gartin called havens for "quacks, quirks, political agitators and possibly some communists."[16] The Sovereignty Commission enlisted the assistance of campus informants and sponsored court injunctions to prevent campus constituents from participating in direct action. The Citizens' Council initiated its own investigations and accused various campus officials of conspiring with communists to overthrow the United States government. Local police regularly visited the campuses and recorded license plate numbers in an effort to gather information and to harass campus constituents and off-campus activists. In extreme cases, the legislature itself entertained creative sanctions against the colleges. The state's organized and interconnected network marshaled its forces to intimidate the colleges into compliance with state laws and social codes.

Private status buffered the institutions from direct state intervention since the legislature did not finance the colleges or appoint their boards of trustees. But, institutional vulnerabilities provided the entrée through which the state forced the private colleges to reevaluate their role in the Civil Rights Movement. Campbell, Tougaloo, and Rust were not wealthy institutions. Defending the campuses and their constituents from constant state harassment diverted funds away from college development projects. The state also exploited dissention on each campus. Individual campus constituents maintained different ideas on the path and pace of social reform. Conservatives accused activists of hijacking education for civil rights aims and transforming the colleges into centers for political activity. As white Tougaloo professor John Held stated, "I am in favor of the Negro having every right that he can obtain—but I do not believe it to be the purpose of Tougaloo College to sponsor agitation."[17] Campbell, Tougaloo, and Rust fought back, and private status prevented unilateral Commission success. But, the colleges differed in their ability to negotiate the internal and external pressures threatening to undermine their autonomy.

Of the three institutions, Campbell College was the most vulnerable to state intervention and suffered the most dire consequences. A variety of factors set Campbell College apart. First, it was supported by black religious philanthropy, namely the African Methodist Episcopal (AME) church. It was one of only two black-controlled higher educational institutions in the entire state of Mississippi.[18] The entire Campbell College constituency, from its Board of Trustees, faculty, administrators, staff, and students, was African American. Racial separation was not an anomaly in Mississippi, but black control of a higher educational institution was. Second, AME doctrine supported full racial equality and likened forced segregation with second-class citizenship. White religious philanthropists, including those who created Tougaloo College and Rust College, did not share the same overtly political theological principles though campus constituents often professed radical interpretations of Christian theology. Not all AME members translated church doctrine into direct confrontation with the Southern racial hierarchy, but some did, particularly when the Civil Rights Movement gained momentum.

Beyond its black philanthropic roots, the particular nature of funding also set Campbell apart and made it more vulnerable to Commission aims. The college was uniquely quite poor. The Eighth Episcopal District of the AME church, consisting of Louisiana and Mississippi, supported the institution. The AME church had a nationwide network, but different districts took on the financial responsibilities of particular schools. Campbell, a combined high school and junior college, received little national AME attention as the denomination concentrated its funds and energies on its four-year institutions. Campbell had only a small pool of money on which to rely for support. Lastly, the level of internal dissention on campus regarding the role of Campbell College in the Civil Rights Movement was extreme. Each campus had its own conservatives calling for a return to pure academic education, but disagreements within the Campbell Board of Trustees and between the trustees and the campus administration threatened to disintegrate the institution. The Sovereignty Commission exacerbated the college's problems and pushed Campbell toward ruin.

Tougaloo, on the other hand, was in a stronger position to resist Sovereignty Commission efforts. The nature of philanthropic support buffered it. The American Missionary Association (AMA), a group of white religious philanthropists, supported Tougaloo. More importantly, AMA colleges received funding from a nationwide network, not individual districts. AMA headquarters were located in New York, another factor that marked them as different from Campbell and provided an important sense of autonomy since philanthropic agencies with headquarters and donors outside the South were more immune to state pressure. Tougaloo's financial scaffold provided it with more security, but it was far from wealthy. Tougaloo received less money from the AMA than some of the association's other colleges, but it still received more financial assistance than other private colleges in Mississippi. The AMA cared enough about Tougaloo to work toward costly accreditation requirements before any other philanthropic group did the same for its colleges. In 1948, Tougaloo became the only accredited HBCU in Mississippi, a distinction it kept until the 1960s.[19]

Tougaloo and Campbell were located a mere six miles from each other near the seat of government in Jackson, and students often coordinated civil rights activities and visited each other's campus. What marked Tougaloo as different was the level of campus participation in the Civil Rights Movement. Tougaloo students, faculty, and staff spearheaded some of the most public and most disruptive assaults on Mississippi's racial hierarchy. Tougaloo also had more extensive campus facilities than Campbell College, which made Tougaloo more attractive for off-campus activists seeking a meeting place in Jackson. On-campus events and off-campus demonstrations garnered the college and the movement increasing publicity in national and local media outlets. These factors combined made Tougaloo the Sovereignty Commission's biggest college target. Commission director Erle Johnston Jr., associated his own career advancement with his ability to quash the activism emanating from Tougaloo.[20] Tougaloo was stronger than Campbell, but it was also a bigger threat to Mississippi laws and customs—a fact illustrated by the common racist nickname for the institution, Cancer College. Accordingly, the Sovereignty Commission more aggressively harassed the institution and focused its energies on finding an entrée to exploit. A fortuitous fundraising campaign and a unique charter controversy provided the Commission with the fodder it needed to undermine Tougaloo's role in the movement and make civil rights activism a campus liability.

Rust College was the least influenced by external pressure and was able to protect itself from punitive measures for a variety of reasons. Like Tougaloo, it was funded by white religious philanthropy (Methodist Episcopal Church), maintained a Board of Trustees headquarters outside Mississippi, and was supported by a nationwide financial network. The fact that Rust did not have any peculiar vulnerabilities, like Tougaloo, or extreme financial trouble, like Campbell, frustrated the Sovereignty Commission's agenda. Also, the Commission reserved much of its energy for events in Jackson and at Tougaloo in particular. Sit-ins, demonstrations, and boycotts in the capital embarrassed the state and drew much of the Commission's attention. The Commission monitored the Rust campus, particularly when activist students became more aggressive, but Rust's isolated geographic location made it a secondary target. Even the Mississippi media ignored much of the movement in northern Mississippi as Rust students and their civil rights projects received little noteworthy press.[21] Lastly, the Sovereignty Commission learned from its mistakes in Jackson. Local and national newspapers repeatedly carried pictures of Jackson activists (including some from Tougaloo and Campbell) being attacked by hostile whites and chased by police dogs. The Commission resented the bad publicity, particularly since one of its missions was to soften Mississippi's image and convince the American populace that Mississippi blacks were content with the existing social structure. Commission representatives put their hard lessons to use in Holly Springs and at Rust, but the campus withstood the pressure.

Campbell College[22]

> We think it wise to keep this record of [Negro AME ministers] in case they crop up in future meetings or incidents.[23]

AME ideology on racial equality influenced the campus ethos, but Campbell College and its constituents did not directly confront the existing racial order until the growth of the Civil Rights Movement in the mid-twentieth century. The Sovereignty Commission matched Campbell's increasingly public role in social reform with increasing scrutiny. Investigators monitored church events and, in December 1957, reported that a Bishop admonished members attending a regional conference: "I warn you here and now, in the presence of God and this audience, that if any one of you permit any person, white or black, to advocate segregation in any form, your appointment will be immediately revoked. Further, you will be brought to trial for violation of the honor and traditions of this great denomination."[24] AME publications in the early 1960s articulated an overtly political agenda for AME schools: "The basic concern of the A.M.E. Church in education is training Christian leaders for the struggle of the Negro to secure by his own efforts full rights, privileges and benefits of citizenship and respect for the worth and dignity of human personality without regard to race, creed or nationality—for realization of Christian and democratic ideals of liberty and justice."[25] This aggressive stance put the AME church and its schools in direct conflict with Mississippi's racial hierarchy.

Campbell College, with an enrollment of three hundred in the early 1960s, hosted a few of the civil rights events centered on the economic boycott of white Jackson stores. Chaplain and Dean of Religion, Charles Jones, became heavily involved and invited the NAACP to use the campus for organizing sessions and press conferences by Medgar Evers.[26] The enrollment of almost one hundred black high school students expelled from Burglund High School in McComb, Mississippi, in October 1961, drew the campus deeper into the movement and, in turn, increased Campbell College's visibility in the state. The previous summer, several Burgland students participated in a voter registration drive and sit-ins, and some had been arrested. Fifteen year-old Brenda Travis was sentenced to one year at the Oakley Training School, a school for juvenile delinquents. At a Burgland assembly the following fall, students quizzed the principal about Travis's return. He hedged his answer, and the students initiated an impromptu march through downtown McComb. Police arrested them as they prayed on the steps of City Hall.[27] The principal refused to allow the one hundred sixteen arrested students to re-enroll unless they signed a pledge promising to refrain from participating in any further demonstrations. Many students refused, and Campbell College president Robert Stevens extended offers of enrollment.[28]

The Sovereignty Commission watched in horror as Campbell College constituents joined demonstrations against the state and used the college facilities to plan direct action tactics. President Stevens did not join any demonstrations or participate in the planning of civil disobedience, but he allowed these activities to occur on campus and refused to curtail the involvement of both students and staff. The state of Mississippi considered his offer to enroll expelled Burgland High School students a slap in the face. The Commission, however, reserved some of its harshest criticism for Charles Jones and treated him as a primary cause for concern. Jones made headlines with an attempt (by himself) to integrate the Jackson Trailways Bus Terminal the same day the Interstate Commerce Commission ordered segregated signage to be removed and with his participation in an interracial pray-in at the Jackson Federal Post Office to protest police brutality.[29] Jackson police arrested him and a court convicted him of breach of the peace after both demonstrations. His active involvement in the movement and the support of President Stevens earned both men the dubious distinction of being added to the Sovereignty Commission's "trouble-makers list."[30] As Campbell's role in the movement increased so, too, did Commission efforts to destabilize the institution. In 1960, the Commission sent a list of Campbell's Board of Trustees to local Jackson police to solicit ideas for how to deal with them, and at least one Trustee joined the Commission payroll.[31] But, Campbell's private status insulated it from direct state intervention.

Campbell College officials gave the Commission the opening it could exploit. Conservative AME and Board of Trustees members held gradualist attitudes toward the pace of societal reform and admonished students and staff that a college should focus on academics and not political education. Fearing the campus had spun out of control, four members of the Board of Trustees requested an injunction preventing President Robert Stevens, Dean Charles Jones, and other Campbell College administrators from performing their campus duties in February 1962.[32] The state did not act as a plaintiff, but the ends sought by the plaintiffs certainly buoyed the Commission's cause. The plaintiffs linked their disgust for campus-based civil rights agitation with accusations that Campbell College officials abused its charter, the laws of the state of Mississippi, and financial donations. The Sovereignty Commission kept a record of the court proceedings and watched the situation carefully.[33]

The plaintiffs in the injunction focused part of their argument on Charles Jones. They charged that Jones's election as Dean of Religion was "for the express purpose of preaching to, and disseminating among the students of the college, the radical and unorthodox views held by him, and in order to create dissention among students of the college and to agitate and incite them into a violation of the laws of the State of Mississippi." Jones's aggressive attacks on white supremacy colored the campus atmosphere. He and other activists transformed Campbell from a respected private institution into a hotbed for political activism. The plaintiffs argued: "he invited and encouraged the so-called 'freedom riders' to congregate on the campus of the College, and he undertook to persuade the students of the college to join in the movement, and to violate the laws of the State of Mississippi; and he himself did, in fact, join in said movement and for his willful violation of the laws of the State of Mississippi, he was arrested by the Police of the City of Jackson, and was tried and convicted, and is now out on bond."[34] His actions, according to the plaintiffs, jeopardized the institution.

Campbell's admission of the ousted Burgland High School students aggravated the situation. Plaintiffs complained that the enrollment of the students flouted the laws of Mississippi and unnecessarily politicized the campus. Campbell had been involved in the movement prior to their arrival, but few people outside of Jackson had paid any attention to the college. Their enrollment brought the campus unwanted and negative attention in the white press, a fact that made the plaintiffs very wary. Plaintiffs also attacked the students' right to attend. Their suit argued that the students took the spots of deserving and qualified children of AME church members. President Stevens admitted the high school students "without any regard whatsoever to their educational and scholastic qualifications or good character, and without requiring them to pay the usual enrollment and tuition fees."[35] Complainants considered these actions a violation of the charter agreement and evidence of bad judgment.

The injunction also illuminated a split in the Board of Trustees. The plaintiffs accused Chairman Frederick Jordan and Dean Jones of mismanaging large sums of money. They complained that the men diverted donations, church assessments, and rent from College-owned property in Mound Bayou for personal gain. Jordan, the suit declared, practiced duplicitous behavior on a regular basis. The plaintiffs offered the example of the purchase and sale of property located near the campus. According to the suit, R. A. Scott, one of the plaintiffs and former president of the College, owned land adjoining the campus. Jordan persuaded individual AME church members that Campbell College should purchase the land for educational purposes and raised the necessary funds. The College bought the land, but Jordan immediately sold it to the state for $2,500. The plaintiffs accused Jordan of keeping the funds for himself rather than depositing the money in the College's accounts. Their final insult came when Jordan, Jones, and President Stevens conspired to solicit funds under the guise of the McComb high school student episode. The accused not only wrongly enrolled the students, they did so "as a publicity 'gimmick' to raise money for their personal gain."[36]

Three weeks after the plaintiffs filed their plea the Chancery Court ordered that the Board of Trustees be reconstituted and demanded that the Council of Bishops remove Jordan as presiding Bishop of the

Eighth Episcopal District. But, the Court allowed Charles Jones to continue as Chaplain and Dean of Religion until the trustees election, and it did not object to President Stevens's reinstatement by the new Board if it so desired.[37] Four months later, AME members reelected fifty percent of the former Board of Trustees and reinstated President Stevens and Dean Jones.[38] The AME effectively reasserted its authority over Campbell and demonstrated the broader AME church's support for the administration. It is unknown if the Court or the Sovereignty Commission expected the trustees to reinstate President Stevens and Dean Jones. It is possible that Commission officials miscalculated the broad base of support for the administrators, and by extension, the Civil Rights Movement. Campbell College regained an important sense of autonomy in its tug-o-war with the Sovereignty Commission.

Campbell College looked very much the same before and after the litigation. The staff remained largely intact, and the Burgland high school students left the college at the end of the academic year. The Campbell College student body remained active in the movement after 1962, and the campus continued to host civil rights events. The difference was that the Eighth Episcopal District of the AME church and Campbell College grew poorer in the process. The court injunction cost the church money, particularly since it pitted campus officials against each other. Campbell College never maintained a large endowment and had been under-funded for years. Neither the Court nor the plaintiffs offered incontrovertible evidence that Trustee Jordan, President Stevens, or Dean Jones mismanaged money, but the validity of the claim was irrelevant as far as the Court was concerned. The financial claims provided a perfect opportunity to exploit institutional weakness. The state stepped in, and this time it sealed the college's fate.

In 1964, the state of Mississippi seized the Campbell College property by right of eminent domain. The campus had deteriorated and gone into debt, and the legislature wrestled control from the Board of Trustees. Legislators never called it an act of retribution, but Campbell's place in the Jackson movement clearly influenced the decision. Campbell College administrators planned to move the campus to Mound Bayou, 174 miles northwest of Jackson, but needed time to do so. They applied to the Board of Trustees of Institutions of Higher Learning, which chartered the creation of any new private or public college, for two separate extensions before vacating the premises. The new presiding Bishop even used the removal of President Stevens as a bargaining chip: more time to build a college in Mound Bayou for Stevens's forced retirement. The Board refused to be swayed, particularly since "the takeover of the property automatically will remove Dr. Stevens."[39] The state clearly never supported a rebuilding campaign and did all in its power to prevent it from succeeding. The state purchased the Campbell College property and deeded it to Jackson State College for its expansion program under the leadership of Jacob Reddix, Jackson State president and friend of the Sovereignty Commission.[40] A new campus was never constructed due to lack of funds.

The demise of Campbell College provides an extreme example of private HBCU vulnerability to state attempts to quash the Civil Rights Movement. Campbell's role in the movement made it a target for the state, and its financial situation provided an opportunity the state refused to ignore. The nature of its philanthropic support made the campus susceptible to external pressure. Colleges supported by black philanthropy were notoriously under-funded. Tuition, church assessments, and donations rarely yielded enough for basic operating costs. Their racial make-up made funding agencies wary, and Northern foundations preferred institutions with, if not a white president, a predominantly white board of trustees.[41] The intense internal dissention also facilitated the Commission's efforts. Campbell trustees unwittingly primed the institution for the state's successful intervention. Mississippi racists not only halted the college's role in the movement, they killed Campbell College.

Tougaloo College

Tougaloo College is finally surrendering to intimidation.[42]

Though enrollment was only five hundred in 1960, Tougaloo College had a national reputation and attracted students from across the country. It maintained high academic standards, had a well-respected faculty, and was headed by a strong and independent Board of Trustees located in New York. The state paid little attention to the campus until the 1940s and 1950s when a few campus constituents initiated individual attacks against the racial hierarchy. In 1946, William Albert Bender, Tougaloo's African American chaplain, attempted to vote in the Democratic primary but was denied. He later filed a complaint with the state attorney general. Hostile whites burned a cross on the Tougaloo campus in retaliation.[43] In 1958, Tougaloo professor Ernst Borinski, a German Jew, invited Tougaloo students to join his German classes at Millsaps College, a private white institution in Jackson. Borinski taught courses at Millsaps during the summer months, and a Tougaloo student enrolled in his class two weeks after it began. The White Citizens' Council blasted Millsaps in the press, and campus officials moved the class to Tougaloo since Millsaps maintained strict policies on racial segregation.[44] The state monitored these men and other campus constituents who actively challenged the social order but did not consider them much of a threat until the Civil Rights Movement gained momentum and transformed isolated acts of resistance into full-blown civil disobedience. The state and its allies easily contained individual activism but worried about an organized assault on Mississippi laws and customs.

By the early 1960s, the Sovereignty Commission identified Tougaloo as one of its primary targets. The degree of activism on campus was unmatched at colleges across the state. Tougaloo students in the campus NAACP chapter inaugurated the sustained Civil Rights Movement in Mississippi with the sit-in at the Jackson Municipal Library in March 1961, and continued to play a vital role in a variety of other very public attacks on Mississippi's racial hierarchy. Off-campus activists from across the nation identified Tougaloo as a hospitable environment and frequently used campus facilities to plan direct action activities. Key Tougaloo faculty and administrators joined with students to support the Civil Rights Movement in Jackson. Chaplain Ed King and Professor John Salter, two of the most active white staff members on campus, received national media attention for their involvement in certain civil rights projects.[45] President Adam D. Beittel, a white man, supported civil rights efforts, defended the students' right to protest, and was photographed with students, Ed King, and John Salter at a sit-in at the local Woolworth's.[46] By 1964, four white students enrolled at Tougaloo making it the only voluntarily desegregated institution in the entire state. It seemed, at least to the State of Mississippi, the entire Tougaloo campus was involved in the Civil Rights Movement.

The Sovereignty Commission escalated its attacks on the campus as years passed and employed some of the same tactics it used to destabilize Campbell College. In June 1963, the Sovereignty Commission sponsored a court order naming President Beittel, Chaplain King, Professor Salter, student Bette Anne Poole (an African American) along with other individuals, the NAACP, Congress of Racial Equality, Tougaloo trustees, and "their agents, members, employees, attorneys, successors, and all other persons in active concert with them" in a writ of temporary injunction preventing them from demonstrating in any way, shape, or form.[47] The point of the injunction, ending civil rights activism, paralleled the mission of the injunction at Campbell, but it was different in important respects. First, the impetus for the Tougaloo injunction came from an external source, not campus officials. The Campbell injunction revealed a serious ideological split and created an opportunity the Sovereignty Commission happily manipulated. The Commission attempted to create a similar exploitative situation at Tougaloo but failed. Second, the injunction against Tougaloo requested a halt to demonstrations not the termination of employment for individual staff members. The Campbell injunction pitted campus officials against each other and split the campus while the Tougaloo injunction, by the sheer number and variety of campus constituents named in the court order, unified the campus by pitting it against the state. The plaintiffs in neither injunction succeeded in ending campus activism, but they did weaken the institutions by draining scant resources away from other campus projects. At Campbell, the plaintiffs unintentionally weakened the institution beyond financial recovery. The Commission attempted to create dire financial consequences at Tougaloo, but Tougaloo's national financial network was less rocked by the immediate fiscal requirements of defending itself against a court injunction.

Tougaloo withstood the first phase of the tug-o-war, but the state was not easily dissuaded from its task. The Sovereignty Commission tried another tactic and attempted to capitalize on the fact that some Tougaloo constituents resented the college's involvement in the Civil Rights Movement. Dr. John Held, chairman of Tougaloo's Department of Philosophy and Religion, volunteered to become an informant in early April 1964. Held accused Beittel and others of appropriating the college for civil right aims and transforming Tougaloo into a center for political activity. He also had designs on the presidency. While on an invited visit to the Commission's office, Held informed Director Johnston about "the dissension among faculty and students" regarding the policies of President Beittel and Chaplain King, threatened to resign if Beittel was not removed, and offered to identify documents linking Beittel to a communist organization. Johnston, grateful for the assistance, requested a list of students and faculty opposed to and in support of Beittel and King as well as the names of trustees who might be open to Commission concerns. Held and Johnston "worked out a code system for communication and relaying information which would not involve Dr. Held with those at Tougaloo who would be opposed to his contact with the Sovereignty Commission."[48] Days later, "Mr. Zero" [Held?] submitted a list of trustees considered "most vital and influential" (all of whom were white) and those "probably more easily influenced by pressure" (all of whom were African American). The communication also included a list of notable students and a Tougaloo College catalog in which Mr. Zero categorized the faculty.[49]

Meanwhile, Tougaloo's Board of Trustees attempted to broaden the campus financial base. The campus's annual expenses jumped when Tougaloo experienced a rapid increase in student attendance that forced the college to institute a major new facilities campaign in the late 1950s.[50] President Beittel worked hard to solicit funds from individual donors and philanthropic agencies and was in large part successful, but increasing college costs made the task a daunting one. Also, certain financial sources turned away from Tougaloo. The Mississippi branch of the Christian Churches (Disciples of Christ) withdrew its financial support after Tougaloo activists targeted its segregated churches for pray-ins in 1963.[51] Trustees looked to the Ford Foundation's Fund for the Advancement of Education for financial assistance. The Fund supported partnerships between HBCUs and predominantly white northern colleges. Tougaloo and Brown University already shared a friendly relationship, and both institutions entertained a more formal association. In fall 1963, Tougaloo and Brown began the application process for Ford funds.

Tougaloo trustees hinged their financial hopes on the Ford grant and attempted to clear a path for a speedy decision. Tougaloo's public role in the movement became a point of concern. Brown University President Barbaby Keeney warned the Tougaloo trustees that the Ford Foundation was wary of donating the money for the partnership because of the siege situation created by constant state harassment. Brown University shared the same set of concerns. Keeney then targeted Tougaloo's President Beittel, a vocal supporter of the Civil Rights Movement, and urged that the Tougaloo trustees fire him. Keeney believed that Beittel's refusal to curb campus activism was irresponsible and that Beittel's actions unnecessarily politicized the campus and brought it unwanted scrutiny. He warned the trustees that Beittel's firing was imperative to secure Ford funding: "They will not do much, if anything, until they have this assurance."[52] Certain Tougaloo trustees agreed with Keeney's assessment and set about undermining Beittel's presidency. A self-selected group of trustees, the same trustees Mr. Zero identified as most vital and influential, arranged a special meeting with Beittel at Board headquarters in New York in January 1964. They explained to Beittel that the partnership program funded by the Ford Foundation needed consistent leadership for at least ten years, an impossibility for him because he was sixty-five. They then requested his resignation.[53] Their next task was to convince the other trustees, a racially mixed group, that their actions were appropriate and necessary. A few of the trustees expressed anger at the sub-committees' unilateral decision, but they presented a united front in public.[54] Rather than announce the decision immediately, the trustees decided to wait for the official Board meeting in April.

Beittel fought the decision. The Board hired him in 1960, and was fully aware of his liberal leanings since Beittel had been equally involved in civil rights issues while president at Talladega College, a private HBCU in Alabama and Tougaloo's sister-institution under the American Missionary Association.[55] One of his conditions for employment at Tougaloo had been that the Board assure him of job security until age seventy, provided he remained healthy, with the option to continue on a yearly basis after age sixty-five.[56] Beittel found the Board's violation of his contract highly suspicious and accused the trustees of using him as a bargaining tool: "It was indicated that Brown University would not continue our promising cooperative relationship unless I am replaced, and that without Brown University the Ford Foundation will provide no support, and without Ford support other Foundations will not respond, and without foundation support the future of Tougaloo College is very uncertain."[57] The Board resented the implication that an external source prompted their actions, discounted Beittel's claims in a variety of forums, and refused to alter their decision to fire President Beittel.[58]

Meanwhile, the legislature itself employed measures to punish Tougaloo for its role in the Civil Rights Movement. Legislators used materials gathered by the Sovereignty Commission to devise two bills meant to cripple the institution and never pretended otherwise. On 17 February 1964, Lieutenant Governor Carroll Gartin called for an investigation of the College's role in demonstrations and civil rights activities.[59] Other state leaders joined his cause, and three days later, three senators introduced a bill to revoke Tougaloo's ninety-four-year-old charter in the name of "public interest."[60] The argument was twofold. First, Tougaloo's original charter restricted the campus to five hundred thousand dollars worth of assets, a figure Tougaloo passed years earlier with no repercussions. Second, and more to the heart of the matter, Gartin and others accused the College of neglecting its charter all together: "The big question to be decided is whether the school has substituted civil disobedience instruction for the curriculum it was authorized to have under its charter."[61] The legislature also contemplated a bill that allowed discretionary powers to the Commission on College Accreditation.[62] Passage of the bill revoked Tougaloo's reciprocal accreditation from the Southern Association of Colleges and Schools, and the state. The loss of state accreditation prevented education students from receiving state teacher's licenses. The state hoped the loss of accreditation would tarnish Tougaloo's reputation, limit attendance, and force those teachers who received their degrees from Cancer College to leave Mississippi.

Tougaloo mounted an aggressive publicity campaign to call attention to the situation and embarrass Governor Paul Johnson into either vetoing or limiting the influence of each legislative bill. President Beittel, at the same time he was fighting for his own job, aggressively protected Tougaloo from the state's onslaught. He enlisted the assistance of the American Association of University Professors, the United Church of Christ, Tougaloo's sister institutions, the Southern Association of Colleges and Schools, and other institutions and organizations with a vested interest in protecting higher educational autonomy. Tougaloo's allies wrote the legislature and the governor expressing their horror at such a public and offensive disrespect for institutional integrity.[63] Tougaloo's efforts were successful. The bill to revoke Tougaloo's charter died in the Judiciary Committee. The bill separating accreditation passed but held no teeth. The legislature was increasingly disturbed by the bad press created by the situation and did not use the Act against Tougaloo.

The Sovereignty Commission took matters into its own hands in April 1964, months prior to the resolution of the legislative bills. Harassing Tougaloo became a top priority for Director Erle Johnston Jr. With the list of powerful and influential trustees provided by Mr. Zero, Johnston requested a private meeting with a group of Tougaloo trustees to plead his case:

> At the meeting it was our purpose to show that the image of Tougaloo as represented by the President, Dr. A. D. Beittel and [Reverend Ed King], had inspired such resentment on the part of state officials and legislators that a show-down clash appeared imminent. We suggested that if Tougaloo had a good man as president and a good man as [chaplain], the institution could be restored to its former status as a respected private college. We also suggested that if such a move could be made by the trustees, the college would have ample time to prove good faith and a change of attitude and possibly avoid punitive action from the Legislature,[64]

Johnston and Shelby Rogers, a Jackson attorney and Commission confidant, flew to the Board of Trustees headquarters in New York. They met with a subcommittee of trustees—the same trustees who, unbeknown to the Commission, had already requested and spearheaded Beittel's forced resignation in January.[65]

The Board of Trustees announced Beittel's retirement at their annual meeting only days after the subcommittee's appointment with the Sovereignty Commission. The timing could not have been worse. The subgroup of powerful trustees delayed the announcement of Beittel's resignation until the April Board meeting to avoid having his resignation associated with Brown University or the Ford Foundation. Meanwhile, the Sovereignty Commission visit became public knowledge and turned into a public relations fiasco. Trustees adamantly denied that Beittel's active support for civil rights contributed to the decision to request his resignation, but the local press and angry campus constituents coupled Beittel's termination with Sovereignty Commission aims. The Commission itself promoted this interpretation: "Our pipeline of information from Tougaloo says the trustees gave as their reason for dismissal of Dr. Beittel that he was 'inefficient.' This will certainly work to our advantage. Had Dr. Beittel been asked to resign because of racial agitation or collaboration with communist front organizations, he could have made a martyr out of himself."[66] The self-congratulation was misplaced. The Commission's visit with the Tougaloo trustees did not prompt the Board's decision, which had been made months earlier, but Tougaloo's involvement in the Civil Rights Movement did. The legislative bills, court injunctions, and constant harassment became costly. The trustees spent time and money needed to improve the college on defending it instead. Tougaloo's role in the Civil Rights Movement became a liability. Trustees made a decision they believed would protect the college and insure its financial future.

The Campbell College situation looked like a cakewalk compared to the battle between the state and Tougaloo. Many of the factors that saved Tougaloo from Campbell's fate became like a double-edged sword. Tougaloo's prestige and private status made it the most important black college in the entire state but also made it the Commission's number one target. Tougaloo's ability to garner national support and media attention prevented the legislature from closing the campus, but the state merely turned to other tactics to rein in the campus. Internal dissention did not reach a level in which the campus disintegrated from the inside out, but it did provide fodder for Commission aims in the guise of informants and conservative trustees. Tougaloo's relative financial security, made possible by a national network and a unique funding opportunity, prevented an immediate fiscal catastrophe. At the same time, the funding opportunity and desire for increased donations made Tougaloo vulnerable and the college's role in the movement a liability. The Commission did not precipitate Beittel's retirement or have an immediate effect on daily campus life and activism, but the immense amount of energy, time, and money spent on destabilizing Tougaloo was not in vain. The Commission and its allies made it costly for Tougaloo to remain in the movement and forced the trustees to take a particular course of action, one they may not have considered without constant harassment by the state of Mississippi.

Rust College[67]

> Holly Springs, in my thinking, is one of the most explosive spots in Mississippi for racial trouble due to the fact that Rust College is located there.[68]

Rust College's geographical location in northern Mississippi made campus facilities particularly important for the movement in that part of the state. In 1962, the campus played a tangential role in James Meredith's enrollment at the University of Mississippi, marking the end of legal segregation in higher education institutions in the state. The Mississippi press reported that Meredith and his legal team drove from Oxford, Mississippi, to Memphis, Tennessee, during his repeated attempts to enroll at the University of Mississippi, but Meredith sometimes spent the night at Rust College instead.[69] Holly Springs was closer to Oxford, and the Rust College campus offered a friendly and secret space to recuperate from the white racist reaction to his enrollment. Two years later, SNCC's Summer Project made the campus invaluable. Student volunteers often traveled through Holly Springs and spent time at Rust before heading to their respective assignments throughout the state. The campus also became a clearinghouse for Freedom School materials. Books poured in from Northern states and found their way to Rust where students and staff sorted them for distribution.[70]

Rust students also used the campus to launch their own attack on Mississippi's racial caste system. Leslie Burl McLemore, a student at Rust from 1960 to 1964, chose the institution because of its private status, "I wanted to go to a place where I knew I wouldn't have any difficulty with my political activity." He used the shield of the campus to help organize and become the first president of the campus chapter of the NAACP in 1962. He and other students participated in SNCC, the Mississippi Freedom Democratic Party, and various direct action initiatives in Marshall County and other surrounding counties. The Student Government Association, of which McLemore became president, fed the civil rights cause.[71] Students also created a Speaker's Bureau that dispatched its members to local black churches to discuss voting rights issues. Frank Smith, a SNCC organizer sent to Holly Springs to help with voter registration, joined their effort and was impressed by what students had accomplished. According to Smith: "the image of students knocking on doors, the fact of their speaking at churches on Sundays, and the threat of demonstration have served to build respect for them and has challenged the local ministers to no end. They see this and are beginning to work to try to build their images and redeem themselves."[72]

Activist students also spearheaded boycotts against local merchants. In May 1961, Leon Roundtree, a theater owner, received a letter signed by the Rust College student body declaring their intent to boycott the theater if he continued to practice segregation and discrimination against black patrons. Worried about the loss of revenue and the possibility that the boycott would spread to students at Mississippi Industrial College, a private HBCU located across the street from Rust and run by the Colored Methodist Church, Roundtree arranged a meeting with the Student Government Association. He offered to build a colored theater of equal quality, but students rejected his compromise. They demanded, "Permit us to sit where we please, by whom we please, and use the same facilities that everyone else uses."[73] Roundtree refused, and Rust students inaugurated the boycott. The theater keenly felt the economic ramifications, and the boycott spread to other white merchants. In December 1962, Rust College students boycotted local drugstores. Rather than encouraging patrons to avoid the stores, the boycott called for sit-ins. Students visited each drugstore and made polite inquiries about the possibility of desegregating lunch counters. None of the druggists agreed to desegregate, and one threatened to remove tables and chairs if students attempted to use them. The students held meetings on Rust's campus to discuss the issue and invited each druggist to attend. None accepted the invitation.[74]

As students devised a plan of action so, too, did the Sovereignty Commission. Informed of the events by the druggists, the Commission swung into action. The Commission counseled the Holly Springs police to return the students to campus rather than transport them to jail. The Commission learned valuable lessons from the Jackson police who found pictures of themselves in local and national media brutalizing students with billy clubs and attack dogs. Television cameras hoping to catch Holly Springs police officers abusing students and carrying them to jail would instead find little newsworthy behavior. The Commission advised the police to warn Rust College President Earnest Smith about continued activism and remind him "that good relationships between Holly Springs and the negro colleges had always been maintained in the past."[75] This type of reaction, the Commission believed, would be a "tremendous set-back" and "psychological defeat for Rust College as well as Rust College students."[76] The students, however, were not deterred.

Several Rust College faculty and staff supported the activist students. Most faculty refused to use grades and attendance as a way to deter activism. Leslie Burl McLemore remembered, "No one penalized me because I was not in class, but they made it very clear that they expected me to do my work."[77] Some key faculty members actively supported the movement by loaning vehicles to activist students transporting registrants to the County Courthouse and joining the Regional Council of Negro Leadership, a Mississippi organization that sponsored voter registration drives and economic boycotts and was considered radical by the white establishment.[78] President Smith never participated in any civil rights demonstrations, but he refused to punish campus constituents for their involvement in the movement. When students treated the National Guard convoy escorting James Meredith from Memphis to the University of Mississippi like a celebratory parade, Smith was pressured to rein in the students, particularly after such a public display of disrespect for Mississippi laws and customs. He refused. He also assisted activist students by calling special faculty meetings to solicit money for bail and demonstrated by example through his membership in the NAACP.[79] Smith's actions angered racist whites, including the mayor of Holly Springs, who asked why President Smith refused to punish activist students the way that President Ed Rankin of Mississippi Industrial College did: "President Rankin made it crystal clear to all students attending M.I. that the institution was a place of learning in which those who would take advantage of it could better qualify themselves for any vocation in life; whereas, Rust College appears to defend those who violated the law."[80] Presidential and faculty support for the movement and student participation in it marked the college as a threat to the state.

Rust College and Holly Springs received less attention than institutions and events in Jackson, but the Sovereignty Commission kept close watch on campus affairs, particularly since "It was the general consensus of everyone that evidently not just one racial agitator was busy agitating out at Rust College, but there were quite a few agitators out there."[81] The Commission began identifying allies as early as the late 1950s, and considered two African American Board of Trustees members potential informants since both publicly opposed the NAACP.[82] Rust's Board of Trustees also included a white Holly Springs bank president, Glen Fant, who maintained close contact with the Commission. In 1961, Fant offered information to the Commission, persuaded fellow trustees to take particular actions, and promised his resignation before he would become a party to "spawning an integration crew at Rust College."[83] Rust students continued to agitate, and Fant resigned his trusteeship when his term expired in 1963.[84] The Commission made little headway in destabilizing the college in part because it focused most of its time and energy on events in Jackson. But, SNCC's 1964 Freedom Summer Project and Rust's geographic importance to it brought the campus under increasing scrutiny.

The Sovereignty Commission, buoyed by its "success" at ousting the leadership at Tougaloo College, set its sites on Rust College and President Earnest Smith in the summer of 1964: "We have put into action a plan for Rust College similar to the plan we used at Tougaloo College. . . . It is hoped that the case against President Smith will be ready to present to trustees at Rust College within a short time with the recommendation that the president be removed and a new administration return the college to the educational purposes for which it was established."[85] A Commission employee and a member of the Board of Trustees traveled to Holly Springs to reason with Smith and discern what was happening on the campus, but Smith refused to meet with them and ordered them off the campus.[86] Undeterred, the Commission interviewed campus informants who accused Smith of employing a large number of "suspected homosexuals" as faculty, impregnating a young girl, refusing to discipline a white male and black female "caught in the act," and employing a "bunch of white beatniks" to teach summer courses.[87] The Commission gathered the evidence and returned to the Board of Trustees hoping to get Smith fired. Other public officials joined the cause and attempted to undermine Smith's authority. Mayor Sam Coopwood wrote to the Mississippi branch of the Methodist Church and encouraged it to investigate the college and President Smith.[88] Senator George Yarbrough, from Marshall County, pressured the Board of Trustees in New York to take action against Smith.[89] The Commission and its allies attempted to marshal their forces to compel the trustees to take action.

The attempts to oust President Smith failed. He remained president until 1966 when he retired of his own volition. A series of miscalculations frustrated the Commission's efforts. The Commission's assessment of the Board of Trustees was somewhat accurate. Several trustees wanted to insulate Rust from the Civil Rights Movement, and the Board's lukewarm support of civil rights activism frustrated President Smith and contributed to his voluntary departure.[90] But, the Commission miscalculated the level of the Board's antipathy toward the movement. Many of the white Board members from the Mississippi branch of the church were angry about the campus's place in the movement, but the Mississippi Methodist Church donated only a small amount of funds to the college. Rust received most of its financial sustenance from the national church so financial threats from the Mississippi branch carried little weight. The Commission also overestimated the level of dissention between the Board and President Smith. Board members may have tempered their support for the campus-based movement, but they found the Commission's morals charges against Smith distasteful and obvious. The Commission's crass attempts offended the Board, which refused to take any action.

The Commission also misjudged its power over private HBCUs. It did not, by itself, precipitate the president's firing at Tougaloo College or the demise of Campbell College. Tougaloo's charter and fund-raising crisis and Campbell College's financial situation provided the Commission with a rare opportunity. Rust College's financial situation was not as dire as that at Campbell College, though it was far from wealthy. Nor was Rust in the middle of a charter crisis or a funding campaign like that at Tougaloo College. The Commission considered Rust a threat to the state, but it could not capitalize on fortuitous vulnerabilities. Rust was able to withstand state pressure in part because it received less concerted attention from the Commission, but also because it did not provide the Commission with an entrée to exploit.

Implications

The examination of Campbell College, Tougaloo College, and Rust College during the civil rights era offers implications beyond discrete battles with the Sovereignty Commission. Their experiences offer civil rights scholars evidence of the importance of independent, self-sustaining institutions and the depths of Southern racism. The advent of the Civil Rights Movement severed the uneasy compromise between private HBCUs and the Southern power structure. The state easily dealt with individual campus constituents who confronted the Southern system. Quelling group dissent proved another matter. Government agencies aggressively attacked the institutions and their constituents, an attack made easier by the insecure economic situation of the colleges, internal dissention, and other convenient vulnerabilities. Their private status forced segregationists to invent creative strategies to curtail activism. The state was not the only destabilizing force, but it created conditions under which the colleges struggled to function and were forced to take drastic and costly measures to protect themselves if possible. The experiences of Campbell, Tougaloo, and Rust demonstrate the volatile nature of the era and the lengths to which racists would go to crush the Civil Rights Movement.

Also, the experiences of these three small and isolated institutions illuminate broader themes in the history of higher education. First, the battle between the colleges and the state contributes to the debate over the role of a college in society: should it remain aloof and practice neutrality or should it be pressed into service toward specific social and ideological goals.[91] The state of Mississippi admonished private HBCUs to stay out of the Civil Rights Movement. Activists drafted Campbell College, Tougaloo College, and Rust College to play a role in societal reform despite the state's threats. The institutions became what Aldon Morris describes as movement centers: organizations or institutions that enable a subjugated group to engage in sustained protest by providing communication networks, organized groups, experienced leaders, and an opportunity to pool social capital.[92] Activists used their respective campuses as a protective shield to coordinate an attack on racial domination and eschewed the notion that participation in social reform should wait until after graduation. Student-status protected activists, but the HBCUs themselves became targets. The Sovereignty Commission, legislature, government officials, Board of Trustees of Institutions of Higher Learning, local police, the state legal system, and Citizens' Council marshaled their forces to punish the private colleges and force them to take a more conservative position on the role of a college in society. Private status prevented direct intervention, but the state and its allies were able to make the public role of private colleges a liability.

Second, the experiences of these private HBCUs force a reevaluation of the dichotomy drawn between public and private institutions. The category has proven useful in examinations of higher education, but the experiences of these institutions put a different spin on the question: What is (should be) the relationship between the state and higher education institutions? The Supreme Court addressed the potential danger of the situation in its 1819 *Dartmouth College* decision. The Court found that a privately funded college should not be subjected to legislative whims, public opinion, or the rise and fall of political parties. Education was a public matter, but the faculty and philanthropic interests had the right to act as a private entity.[93] The decision had nothing to do with private black colleges; none existed at the time. But, missionary philanthropists set up private HBCUs with the same assumption: financial and political autonomy from the state and the right to develop curricula, campus policies, and other matters without the fear of state intervention in college affairs. The state violated the autonomy of private colleges after they became involved in the Civil Rights Movement. The campuses were free to encourage group esteem and practice desegregation as long as their campus reality did not directly confront the Southern racial order itself. Private institutions, as Rust's President Smith put it, "were not as free as everyone thought we were."[94]

Third, an examination of private HBCUs in the Civil Rights Movement offers an alternative interpretation of the role of private and public institutions in a democracy. The history of higher education tells us that public institutions democratized higher education. State-supported institutions expanded the educational opportunities for youth previously excluded in a system of private colleges. Under certain conditions, however, private institutions became vital to democratic aims while public institutions could not perform the same role. In the 1960s, when Southern state interests collided with constitutionally protected freedoms, private institutions provided a forum for dissent. Private HBCUs—*because they were private*—were invaluable. Their freedom from state control allowed the colleges latitude not available to public institutions. They paid heavily for their choice and intense external pressures left its mark, but private HBCUs played a pivotal role in the protection of egalitarian aims.

Notes

1. See David Sansing, *Making Haste Slowly: The Troubled History of Higher Education in Mississippi* (Jackson: University Press of Mississippi, 1990), 61–64, 79–80.

2. James D. Anderson, *The Education of Blacks in the South, 1860–1935* (Chapel Hill: University of North Carolina Press, 1988), chapter 7.

3. *Journal of the House of Representatives of the State of Mississippi, 1956,* regular session, 107–108, cited in Yasuhiro Katagiri, *The Mississippi State Sovereignty Commission: Civil Rights and States' Rights* (Jackson: University Press of Mississippi, 2001), 5.

4. *General Laws of the State of Mississippi, 1956,* chapter 365, section 5, 521.

5. "Citizen Council Grant" [1964], Sovereignty Commission Record (hereafter cited as SCR) 99-30-0-46-1-1-1 to 2-1-1, Mississippi Department of Archives and History (hereafter cited MDAH; all Sovereignty Commission Files are located at the MDAH).

6. Clayborne Carson, *In Struggle: SNCC and the Black Awakening of the 1960s* (Cambridge, Mass.: Harvard University Press, 1981).

7. John Dittmer, *Local People: The Struggle for Civil Rights in Mississippi* (Urbana: University of Illinois Press, 1994), 85–86.

8. Ibid., 86–87.

9. J. Michael Butler, "The Mississippi Sovereignty Commission and Beach Integration, 1959–1963: A Cotton-Patch Gestapo?" *Journal of Southern History* 68, no. 1 (February 2002): 107–48.

10. Charles Payne, *I've Got the Light of Freedom: The Organizing Tradition and the Mississippi Freedom Struggle* (Berkeley: University of California Press, 1995), 286.

11. Carson, *In Struggle,* chapter 9.

12. "Negro Students Stage Boycott," *Greenwood Commonwealth,* 22 February 1957; "Negro Student Boycott Settled," *Greenwood Commonwealth,* 23 March 1957; and J. H. White, *Up from a Cotton Patch: J. H. White and the Development of Mississippi Valley State College* (Itta Bena, 1979), 111.

13. Jerry Proctor, "King Tries to Stop Student Walk-Outs," *State Times,* 8 March 1957; and Board of Trustees of Institutions of Higher Learning, Minutes of Special Meeting, 9 March 1957, MDAH.

14. "Report Classes Boycotted at Jackson State," *Jackson Daily News,* 7 October 1961, SCR 10-105-0-4-1-1-1; John A. Peoples Jr., *To Survive and Thrive; The Quest for a True University* (Jackson: Town Square Books, 1995), 58.

15. Jacob Reddix to Albert Jones, 1 April 1961, SCR 10-105-0-2-1-1-1.

16. "Tougaloo Bill Appears Dead," *Clarion-Ledger,* 14 April 1964, Subject Files Tougaloo College, 1960–1969, MDAH. The statement was made about Tougaloo, specifically, but it fits securely with the government's attitude toward the other private HBCUs in the state.

17. John Held to [Wesley] Hotchkiss, 2 June 1964, American Missionary Association Archives, Addendum (1869–1991, n.d.), Series A, Subseries Tougaloo Correspondence, Box 110, folder 19, Amistad Research Center, Tulane University, New Orleans, Louisiana (hereafter cited ARC).

18. The other was Mississippi Industrial College, supported by the Colored Methodist Church.

19. Clarice Campbell and Oscar Allan Rogers, Jr., *Mississippi: The View from Tougaloo* (Jackson; University Press of Mississippi, 1979).

20. Erle Johnston to John Salter, 17 August 1981, Tougaloo Office File Register, Brown University-Tougaloo College Cooperative Program, Brown University Archives, Providence, Rhode Island (hereafter cited BUA).

21. See Leslie Burl McLemore, interview by Joy Ann Williamson, 20 August 2003, Jackson, Mississippi.

22. All of Campbell College's records were either lost or destroyed. The following information is gathered from other available sources.

23. "Note," [December] 1957, Sovereignty Commission investigator notes on 88th Session of the West Tennessee and Mississippi Annual Conference of the African Methodist Episcopal Zion Church, SCR 2-5-1-53-54-1-1-1. Charles Jones attended this conference.

24. Hal DeCell to Governor J. P. Coleman, 16 December 1957, 1, SCR 2-5-2-16-1-1-1.

25. Sherman L. Greene Jr., "The Urgency for Unification of the A.M.E. Church System of Education," *A.M.E. Church Review* 78, no. 210 (October-December 1961), 28.

26. Zack J. Van Landingham, "Memo to File 1–23," 2 June 1960, SCR 1-23-0-70-1-1-1.

27. Hopkins and Downing, "Investigation of Student 'Walk-out' from Burglund Negro High School, McComb, Mississippi; Parade and Demonstrations; Their Arrest, and Hearing in City and Youth Court," 19 October 1961, SCR 1-98-0-25-1-1-1; Payne, *I've Got the Light of Freedom,* 125; and Jacqueline Byrd Martin, interview by Joy Ann Williamson, 27 August 2003, McComb, Mississippi.

28. Dittmer, *Local People,* 110–11, and Martin, interview.

29. John Salter, Jr., *Jackson, Mississippi: An American Chronicle of Struggle and Schism* (Malabar, Fla.: Robert E. Krieger Publishing, 1979), 146–147; and John Her[unreadable], "City Declares Segregation Not Enforced in Terminals," *Clarion-Ledger,* 10 April 1962, SCR 2-72-2-36-1-1-1.

30. Tom Scarbrough to File, 8 May 1961, 2, SCR 2-65-0-42-2-1-1.

31. Zack Van Landingham to Meady Pierce, 13 April 1960, SCR 2-72-1-56-1-1-1; and Requisition, Sovereignty Commission payment to Percy Greene and T. S. J. Pendleton, 22 January 1962, SCR 97-98-1-317-1-1-1. Percy Greene was the editor of the *Jackson Advocate,* a black newspaper, and was a well-known informant. T. S. J. Pendleton was a black school principal, minister, and Campbell College Board of Trustees member.

32. *R. A. Scott, et al. v. J. P. Campbell College, et al.,* February 1962, Chancery Court of the First Judicial District of Hinds County, Mississippi, SCR 3-78-0-1-1-1-1 through 19-1-1.

33. A. L. Hopkins to Members of the Sovereignty Commission, 1 May 1962, SCR 7-4-0-77-1-1-1.

34. *Scott v. Campbell College,* 3 (both quotes).

35. Ibid., 3–4.

36. Ibid., 4.

37. *R. A. Scott, et al. v. J. P. Campbell College, et. al., Agreed Decree,* 29 March 1962, SCR 3-78-0-2-1-1-1 through 3-1-1.

38. "Suit Settled at Campbell," *Jackson Daily News,* 28 March 1962, and "Stevens Restored as President of Campbell," *Jackson Daily News,* 2 July 1962, SCR 10-35-1-136-1-1-1.

39. Erle Johnston to File, 13 July 1964, 1, SCR 3-78-0-4-1-1-1.

40. Ibid.

41. Daniel Thompson, *Private Black Colleges at the Crossroads* (Westport, Conn.: Greenwood Press, 1973).

42. Reverend Bernard Law, Reverend Duncan M. Gray Jr., and Rabbi Perry E. Nussbaum to Board of Trustees, 4 May 1964, 2, American Missionary Association Archives, Addendum (1869–1991, n.d.), Series A, Subseries Tougaloo Correspondence, Box 110, folder 18, ARC.

43. United States Senate, 79th Congress, 2d Session, *Hearings Before the Special Committee to Investigate Senatorial Campaign Expenditures, 1946* (Washington, D.C.: Government Printing Office, 1947), 19, 88–90, cited in Dittmer, *Local People,* 3.

44. "Integrated Class at Millsaps College Sent to Tougaloo," *State Times,* 4 July 1958; Gabrielle Simon Edgcomb, "Ernst Borinski: 'Positive Marginality' 'I Decided to Engage in Stigma Management,'" in *From Swastika to Jim Crow: Refugee Scholars at Black Colleges* (Malabar, Fla.: Krieger Publishing, 1993), 124.

45. Ed King joined the Mississippi Freedom Democratic Party, an alternative to the state's Democratic Party that barred black participation, and ran as its vice presidential candidate in a mock election in 1963. John Salter became the North Jackson NAACP Youth Council's adviser and gained national media attention after his picture at the Woolworth's sit-in appeared in the national media in 1963.

46. See Salter, *Jackson, Mississippi,* and Ed King, interview by Joy Ann Williamson, 28 August 2003, Jackson, Mississippi.

47. *Writ of Temporary Injunction,* Chancery Court of the First Judicial District of Hinds County, Mississippi, 6 June 1963, Ed King Papers, Box 8, folder 374, Tougaloo College Archives, Tougaloo, Mississippi (hereafter cited TCA).

48. Erle Johnston to File, 13 April 1964, 1, SCR 3-74-2-17-1-1-1 through 2-1-1.

49. Mr. Zero to Sovereignty Commission, 5 May 1964, 1, SCR 3-74-2-19-1-1-1 through 2-1-1.

50. In 1954, Tougaloo merged with Southern Christian Institute, and the Tougaloo campus absorbed the Institute's student body.

51. "Church Group Cancels Support of Tougaloo," *Jackson Daily News,* 20 September 1963, Box A.D. Beittel Unprocessed, Folder Board of Trustees, Fall 1963, TCA.

52. Barnaby Keeney to Lawrence Durgin, 9 March 1964, 1, Barnaby Keeney Office File Register, Tougaloo College, 1964–65, Miscellaneous Correspondence, BUA.

53. Wesley Hotchkiss to Robert Wilder, 10 April 1964, Barnaby Keeney Office File Register, Tougaloo College, 1964–65, Miscellaneous Correspondence, BUA.

54. Ed King, interview.

55. For a discussion of Beittel's liberalis at Talladega, see Henry N. Drewry and Humphrey Doermann, *Stand and Prosper: Private Black Colleges and Their Students* (Princeton: Princeton University Press, 2001), 148–52.

56. Robert O. Wilder to A. D. Beittel, 20 April 1960, American Missionary Association Archives, Addendum (1869–1991. n.d.). Series A, Subseries Touglaoo Correspondence, Box 110, folder 17, ARC.

57. A. D. Beittel to Barnaby Keeney, 5 April 1964, American Missionary Association Archives, Addendum (1869–1991, n.d.), Series A, Subseries Touglaoo Correspondence, Box 110, folder 18, ARC.

58. Wesley Hotchkiss to Mr. and Mrs. George Owens, 20 April 1964, American Missionary Association Archives, Addendum (1869-1991, n.d.), Series A, Subseries Tougaloo Correspondence, Box 110, folder 18, ARC.

59. "Tougaloo Bill Appears Dead," *Clarion-Ledger,* 14 April 1964.

60. Senate Bill No. 1672, Regular Sess., 1964, Box Tougaloo College History, Folder Accreditation Revocation (State), TCA.

61. "Action on Tougaloo is Due for Delay," *Clarion-Ledger,* 6 March 1964.

62. Senate Bill No. 1794, Regular Sess., 1964, Box Tougaloo College History. Folder Accreditation Revocation (State), TCA.

63. A. D. Beittel to William Fidler (AAUP), 6 June 1964, A. D. Beittel to Hollis Price (President, LeMoyne College), 27 May 1964, and A. D. Beittel to Gordon Sweet (Southern Association of Colleges and Schools), 6 June 1964, Box Tougaloo College History, Folder Accreditation Revocation (State), TCA.

64. Johnston to File, 24 April 1964, 1, SCR 3-74-2-16-1-1-1 through 2-1-1. Ed King's name and title were blacked out in the record, but it is certain that he is the individual to whom the report refers.

65. Wesley Hotchkiss to Robert Wilder, 10 April 1964, Barnaby Keeney Office File Register, Tougaloo College, 1964–65, Miscellaneous Correspondence, BUA.

66. Erle Johnston to Paul Johnson and Carroll Gartin, 5 May 1964, 1, SCR 3-74-2-23-1-1-1.

67. Rust College experienced several different fires that destroyed the college's records. The following information is gathered from other available sources.

68. Tom Scarbrough (Sovereignty Commission investigator), "Marshall County," 19 April 1963, 2, SCR 2-20-1-67-1-1-1 through 2-1-1.

69. McLemore, interview.

70. "No Room for Communists," *South Reporter,* 30 July 1964; and "Book Boom," *Bearcat,* 15 July 1964, Folder *Bearcat* 1964, Rust College Archives, Holly Springs, Mississippi.

71. McLemore, interview, quote p. 8.

72. Frank Smith, "A Second Beginning of the End," 11 May 1963, [n.p.] Voter Education Project Papers, James Lawson Files, cited in Payne, *I've Got the Light of Freedom,* 197.

73. Tom Scarbrough, "Marshall County-Mrs. Clarice Campbell, White Female Teacher at Rust College-Also Rust College-All Negro School," 29 May 1961, 5, SCR 2-20-1-50-1-1-1 through 7-1-1.

74. Tom Scarbrough, "Marshall County," 14 December 1962, SCR 2-20-1-63-2-1-1 through 3-1-1.

75. Ibid., 2–3.

76. Ibid., 3.

77. McLemore, interview.

78. Dittmer, *Local People,* 29–33, and Payne, *I've Got the Light of Freedom,* 31–33.

79. Earnest Smith, telephone interview by Joy Ann Williamson, 13 February 2004.

80. Tom Scarbrough, "Marshall County (Rust College)," 30 June 1964, 5, SCR 2-20-1-78-1-1-1 through 5-1-1.

81. Tom Scarbrough, "Marshall County-Mrs. Clarice Campbell, white female teacher at Rust College-also Rust College-all Negro School," 29 May 1961, 7, SCR 2-20-1-50-1-1-1 through 7-1-1.

82. M. L. Malone to Zack Van Landingham, 9 February 1959, SCR 2-94-0-2-1-1-1; Zack Van Landingham to Director of the State Sovereignty Commission, 6 March 1959, SCR 2-4-10-6-1-1-1; Tom Scarbrough, "Lowndes County," 1 September 1961, SCR 2-94-0-56-1-1-1 through 2-1-1.

83. Tom Scarbrough, "Marshall County-Mrs. Clarice Campbell, white female teacher at Rust College-also Rust College-all Negro School," 29 May 1961, 4, SCR 2-20-1-50-1-1-1 through 7-1-1.

84. Rust College General Catalogue, 1963-1964, Rust College Archives, Holly Springs, Mississippi.

85. Erle Johnston, Jr., to Herman Glazier, 9 June 1964, SCR 2-20-1-77-1-1-1.

86. Smith, interview.

87. Tom Scarbrough, "Marshall County (Rust College)," 30 June 1964, 2 (first quote), 3 (second and third quotes), SCR 2-20-1-78-1-1-1 through 5-1-1.

88. Sam Coopwood to Bishop Marvin Franklin, 29 June 1964, SCR 2-20-1-80-1-1-1.

89. Tom Scarbrough. "Marshall County-Mrs. Clarice Campbell, white female teacher at Rust College-also Rust College-all Negro School," 29 May 1961, SCR 2-20-1-50-1-1-1 through 7-1-1.

90. Smith, interview.

91. Derek Bok discusses this debate in *Beyond the Ivory Tower; Social Responsibilities of the Modern University* (Cambridge, Mass.: Harvard University Press, 1982), though he does not address the dilemma faced by black colleges in the Civil Rights Movement.

92. Aldon Morris, *Origins of the Civil Rights Movement: Black Communities Organizing for Change* (New York: Free Press, 1984), 282.

93. This discussion of the Dartmouth case is taken from Frederick Rudolph, *The American College and University: A History* (Athens: University of Georgia Press, 1990), 207–10.

94. Smith, interview.

Higher Education of American Indians

JON REYHNER AND JEANNE EDER

Many Indians have been upset about the elementary and vocational emphasis of BIA education. However, leaving close-knit Indian communities for large, impersonal non-Indian colleges and universities to obtain advanced education can be too traumatic, expensive, and harsh a sacrifice for many Indians. Various solutions to the problem have been proposed, including Indian-only colleges and universities, Native American Studies programs as a "home" for Indians at large universities (Reyhner 1997), and tribal colleges that target their courses and programs to local needs (Tribal Colleges 1989; Boyer 1997).

As indicated in chapter 1, Harvard, the College of William and Mary, and Dartmouth were established with Indian education missions, but the ambitious rhetoric of their founders was not matched by deeds. In the late nineteenth century, several new institutions were set up for Indians. Although the surviving schools now educate a majority of non-Indian students, they still retain a substantial Indian student body. In addition, Harvard, Dartmouth, and other colleges and universities responded to the increased interest in Indian education in the 1970s by establishing Native American studies programs. This chapter looks at the various efforts in the nineteenth and twentieth centuries to provide higher education for American Indian students.

Ottawa University

The historian William Unrau (1983) has documented that education was used in the nineteenth century to defraud Indians. In 1860, C. C. Hutchinson worked with a member of the American Baptist Home Mission Society to charter Roger Williams University in Ottawa, Kansas (renamed Ottawa University in 1865), with the help of prominent Baptists. In 1861, Hutchinson was appointed an Indian agent and used his position to get a treaty through that included setting aside almost one-third of the reservation for establishing a university for Indians. He was dismissed the same year but wrangled another appointment as agent for the Ottawa until he was suspended for not keeping adequate financial records. Fifty thousand dollars were spent building the university, which had only one Indian student. An act was passed to sell the university in 1872 and give the proceeds to the Ottawa Indians, but most of the money from the sale went to lawyers. It was not until 1960 that, through the Indian Claims Commission, the Ottawa, now in Oklahoma, received $406,166 in compensation for the fraud that had been perpetrated against them.

Cherokee Indian Normal School of Robeson County

A more successful effort at Indian education occurred in North Carolina. One of the earliest institutions of higher education established exclusively for Indian students was the Croatan Normal School. The Lumbee Indians were recognized in 1885 by the North Carolina General Assembly and authorized to have their own schools because they did not want to be educated in segregated schools with blacks. The Croatan Normal School opened its doors with fifteen students in fall 1887.

The school's early curriculum was described by the historians David Eliades and Linda Oxendine (1986) as nonstandard and nontraditional and below an eighth-grade level. Students originally

694

had to be fifteen years old to enter. In 1911 the school was renamed the Indian Normal School of Robeson County because of the negative connotations given by North Carolinians to the word "Croatan." In 1913 it was again renamed, this time Cherokee Indian Normal School of Robeson County, a name it retained until 1941, when it became Pembroke State College for Indians. In 1949 the name was shortened to Pembroke State College, From 1941 to 1953, when it was opened to non-Indians by court-ordered desegregation in schools, Pembroke was the only four-year state-supported college for Indians in the United States.

In 1926 a regular two-year normal course was added to the curriculum, and elementary courses were phased out so that by 1928 the school offered only high school and teacher training studies. The school was opened to all Indians in 1945. It was accredited regionally as a four-year liberal arts college in 1951. As Pembroke State graduated more Indian students, pressure was put on the state universities to open their graduate and professional schools to Indians.

The school remained small until the 1960s. It experienced tremendous growth after the courts forced desegregation, and white students soon outnumbered Indian students. In 1969 the school was renamed Pembroke State University, and in 1971 it became part of the University of North Carolina System. In reaction to the de-Indianization of the university and the Indian militancy of the early 1970s, a Native American Studies department was added in 1972, and that department was authorized to offer a major in 1984–one of only two such majors offered east of the Mississippi River at the time. In 1981 the school's enrollment was 24 percent Indian. This percentage has remained relatively steady, and in 1992, 24 percent of the 3,041 students were again categorized as American Indians.

Bacone's Indian University

Three years after the founding of the Croatan Normal School, Almon C. Bacone, an instructor at the Cherokee National Male Seminary, helped to found the Indian University in Tahlequah with support from the American Baptist Home Mission Society. The school started with three students in 1880 in the Cherokee Baptist Mission and was chartered by a close vote a year later by the Muscogee-Creek Nation with the stipulation that the school be open to all Indians. John D. Rockefeller, the oil magnate and a friend of Bacone's wife, became the school's major benefactor.

The first annual catalog in 1881 for the Baptist Normal and Theological School declared that "[i]ts primary object is to prepare native teachers and preachers for a more effective Christian work among the Indian tribes" (quoted in Williams and Meredith 1980, 15). The school awarded its first bachelor's degree in 1883, and construction on Rockefeller Hall began in 1884 in Muscogee, Oklahoma, with the old site in Tahlequah becoming the Cherokee Academy. Between 1883 and 1888, there were five graduates, all Cherokee. The 1889–90 Tenth Annual Catalog listed fifteen students in a normal class and ten in a theological class. It reported that sixty students had been prepared for teaching and thirty-three for the ministry. The catalog stated, "Daily Bible instruction is imparted to all. All are required to be present at the weekly prayer meetings, the Sunday School, and the regular Sabbath services" (35). Rule 7 for students was as follows: "The young men and women will not be allowed to walk or ride in company, or have any place of meeting, only as they are brought together in their regular school duties, and religious and society meetings. Their correspondence will be subject to the approval of the teachers" (36). Students could not go to town without permission, and there were to be no amusements on Sunday. The Board of Trustees included the chiefs of the Creek Nation and the Delaware. Seniors took German, juniors Spanish, sophomores French, and freshmen Latin for a year. Graduates received a master's of science degree. The 1889–90 catalog reported twenty-two students, nine of them white, including all three seniors.

Alcoholism was considered the major illness among students, and they were closely supervised; for example, their correspondence was censored, and coeds were required to have teacher escorts outside of the school. Most of the faculty in the early days spoke one of the Indian languages of Oklahoma. Bacone graduates entered a variety of professions, including medicine, law, journalism, and business. There were only ten students in the college department in the 1904–5 school year, and from 1911 to 1916 there were no college-level students. Vocational training in farming was emphasized to prepare students to work their allotments.

In 1910, after Bacone's death, the college was renamed Bacone College. The student body represented fifteen tribes in 1919, twenty-four tribes in 1922, and forty tribes in 1933. In 1925, only Indians were accepted because of overcrowding. In 1928, there were ten Indians on the faculty, and the curriculum emphasized Native music and art. Bacone became known for its school of traditional Indian art. Commissioner of Indian Affairs John Collier recognized its contributions to Indian education when he laid the cornerstone in 1937 for a new boys' dorm.

From 1943 to 1948, the Reverend Early Louis Riley, a Creek Indian and an alumnus, served as president. During World War II, school enrollment declined, and by the end of 1943, 160 students had joined the armed forces. During the summers of 1943 and 1944, Bacone hosted Summer Linguistic Institutes, with more than one hundred students and fifteen faculty members in attendance.

After World War II, the school focused on providing programs that other Indian schools did not offer, and more non-Indian students were enrolled. In the late 1950s, the school received regional accreditation. Dean Chavers, a Lumbee with a Ph.D. from Stanford and experience in establishing the Native American Studies program at the University of California, Berkeley, was president from 1978 to 1981. In 1992, 43 percent of Bacone's 623 students were American Indians. Its fall 2001 enrollment of 436 students was 45 percent Indian, representing twenty-three tribes.

Tribal Colleges

Despite the long histories of Indian higher education at Pembroke State University and Bacone College, these schools served only a tiny fraction of Indians. Both schools remained small, with only a few hundred students or less until after World War II. As the Bureau of Indian Affairs improved its educational system, it began to think about postsecondary education. In 1932, Secretary of the Interior Ray L. Wilbur reported that Indian students could get educational loans from federal and tribal funds, get room and board at nearby Indian schools in return for part-time work, and receive federal funding for tuition and scholarships (Fischbacher 1967). However, Indian students enrolling in mainstream colleges had a 90 percent attrition rate (Stein 1992). Some colleges would not even accept Indian students. K. Tsianina Lomawaima describes how her father worked his way through high school and graduated in 1939 with an Honor Society scholarship. He was admitted to a small midwestern college. On arrival, however, "a dean informed him they had no place for Indians and told him to pack his bags and go" (Lomawaima 1994, 170). The failure of off-reservation colleges and universities to recruit and retain Indian students led to the exploration of alternative routes to higher education for American Indians. Tribal colleges were a direct outgrowth of OEO adult education programs and attempts by Indians to control their own schools.

As knowledge of what worked in cross-cultural education increased and began to be applied in schools, it became apparent that mainstream colleges were not designed to develop the skills provided by community-based schools. Thus, immediately after the founding of Rough Rock, Robert Roessel and others turned their attention to the higher education needs of Native students. Specialized colleges and universities for Indian students were not a new idea. However, the system of tribal colleges that developed, starting with the founding of Navajo Community College in 1968, was unprecedented.

Navajo Community College

In 1957, the Navajo tribe established a scholarship fund financed by oil royalties. However, more than 50 percent of the students dropped out in their freshman year. This high failure rate led Navajo leaders to explore the possibility of setting up their own college. In the early 1960s, Navajo educator Dillon Platero, traditional elder and chairman of the tribal council's Education Committee Allen Yazzie, and tribal council man Guy Gorman worked to establish a Navajo institution of higher education as a solution to the problem of high dropout rates. In 1965, they helped to convince the OEO, a Johnson-era War on Poverty agency, to finance a feasibility study. The study concluded that a tribally controlled community college should be established. Across Indian country, OEO programs after 1965 provided leadership, career-ladder opportunities, and funded graduate education for young Indians.

With the example of Rough Rock Demonstration School in mind, formal and informal meetings were held, with the result that a non-Indian with grant writing skills, Robert Roessel, former director for the Center for Indian Education at Arizona State University and director of Rough Rock Demonstration School, was brought into the planning process. A proposal was submitted to the OEO at the start of 1968 that was strongly supported by OEO officials in Washington, D.C. The OEO funding bypassed the BIA, which tended to be obstructionist. A public meeting was held in May 1968 in Window Rock at which Navajo tribal chairman Raymond Nakai strongly supported the founding of a community college.

On July 17, 1968, the Navajo tribal council passed a resolution founding Navajo Community College (NCC). An interim Board of Regents was appointed. In recognition of the work he did to gain initial funding for the college, Roessel stepped down from directing Rough Rock Demonstration School and was appointed the first president of NCC. Classes began in January 1969 in the BIA high school facility at Many Farms, Arizona. NCC started as an open admission institution, and 309 students (196 full-time equivalent [FTE] students) enrolled at NCC that first spring. Approximately 60 percent passed their courses the first semester, a much better percentage than Indians had attending mainstream institutions. By 1978, the enrollment had reached 1,241 students (1,034 FTE), 110 of whom were non-Indian. Roessel's Navajo wife, Ruth, became director of the Navajo Studies Department.

Yazzie Begay donated family lands at Tsaile, Arizona, and ground was broken in 1971 for a permanent campus, which opened in 1973. Ironically for a community college, this location was some distance from any Navajo population center, making it necessary for most students to live in dorms or to commute thirty miles or more one way to the main campus. Branch campuses were soon established in population centers, including Shiprock, Tuba City, and Chinle.

A staunch advocate of local control, Roessel soon stepped aside as president and became the college's chancellor, and in July 1969 Dr. Ned Hatathli became the first Navajo president. Both Roessel and Hatathli envisioned Navajo Studies as the centerpiece of the college and intended to replace non-Indian staff as qualified Indians became available. However, Roessel "was distressed" when non-Indian faculty members at NCC were denied a voice in school decision making (Szasz 1977, 177). Hatathli, disregarding the source of funding for the college, declared, "This is an Indian owned and an Indian operated institution, and we certainly don't want any people other than Indian to dictate to us what is good for us" (quoted in Szasz 1977, 177–78). While in 1970 the faculty was only 40 percent Indian, Hatathli considered the non-Indian faculty as just "working themselves out of a job" (quoted in Szasz 1977, 178). Faculty served without tenure on one-year contracts. Because of geographic isolation, cultural differences, and sometimes outright anti-white hostility, there was a high turnover of non-Indian faculty. Navajo faculty members tended to have less formal education than the non-Indian faculty but brought an intimate knowledge of Navajo language and culture to their teaching.

Although Szasz (1977) emphasized Roessel's role in starting NCC based on interviews and published sources, former tribal college president and Montana State University professor Wayne J. Stein (1992) put more emphasis on the role of Navajo leaders. However, assigning credit is a fruitless debate, since both local community support and the tribal leadership of Guy Gorman, Allen Yazzie, Dillon Platero, and others were needed as well as the expertise of Roessel and the support of government officials both in the BIA and the OEO. Navajo Community College was the result of collaboration between local desires and outside expertise; however, the tension created by that interplay continues today in the debate about what role tribal colleges should play.

On the one hand, extremists would reject much of mainstream thinking on what should comprise a college curriculum. On the other hand, there is a potential in the words of American Indian Movement leader Ward Churchill (1992, 36) that tribal colleges will do "the training of the colonized to colonize themselves." This conflict over what Indian tribal colleges would be was played out early on the NCC campus. Tribal traditionalists saw the tribal college playing a leading role in preserving tribal culture; modernists saw tribal colleges preparing students to get jobs or to leave the reservation to enter mainstream four-year colleges. On December 15, 1971, the U.S. Congress passed the Navajo Community College Act (P.L. 92–189) to provide federal support for the college.

Hatathli died unexpectedly in 1972 while still president of NCC. According to an account in the biography of one of his relatives:

> He died at a young age in the bedroom of his home of a shotgun blast. He had been drinking, friends say, and was despondent. He had just been passed over for a job as head of the BIA area office, a high-ranking job in the BIA bureaucracy. It is not clear whether his death was suicide or an accident. (Benedek 1995, 242)

After Hatathli's death, the new president, Thomas Atcitty, moved NCC, with the support of the new tribal chairman, Peter MacDonald, toward a more mainstream non-Indian community college against the wishes of the Board of Regents. MacDonald grew up herding sheep, and he first attended the BIA day school at Teec Nos Pos in northeastern Arizona pretty much on his own initiative. However, later he ran away twice from the boarding school at Shiprock, New Mexico, because of the "teasing, taunting, [and] the regimentation" there, and he became a "sixth grade dropout" (MacDonald and Schwarz 1993, 45, 87). After serving as a code talker in the Marine Corps, he was allowed to enroll in Bacone, at that time a Baptist Indian junior college, on the G.I. Bill in spite of his lack of a high school education.

After getting a General Equivalency Diploma at Bacone, MacDonald majored in sociology and studied both Christianity and Indian history. On graduation from Bacone, he majored in engineering at the University of Oklahoma. He worked nights at the state mental hospital and was encouraged by the BIA to enter a trade school when his G.I. Bill funding ran out. MacDonald chose instead to work two years to save enough money so that he could return to the University of Oklahoma in 1955. He completed an electrical engineering degree in 1957.

After being wooed by several companies, MacDonald accepted a job at Hughes Aircraft. His autobiography describes a successful career at Hughes, where he learned about Polaris missiles and other cutting edge technology. He also was impressed by the lifestyle of the corporate leaders at Hughes, who had offices on "Mahogany Row" (1993, 107). Despite opportunities for advancement at Hughes, the new Navajo tribal chairman, Raymond Nakai, convinced MacDonald to take a sabbatical leave to head OEO programs on the Navajo Reservation. He used that position as a springboard to the tribal chairmanship in 1971. As tribal chairman, MacDonald worked to separate the tribal government from BIA control and to get a better deal for the tribe on their oil, gas, and coal contracts. He wrote in his autobiography:

> Looking back, I realize that the BIA program was poorly planned and unrelated to the needs of the Navajo children. The hostile attitude toward my people was emotionally devastating, of course. We were taught that we were superstitious savages, and we were forced to go to church without being given an understanding of the Christian religion. We were made to feel that our parents, our grandparents, and everyone who had come before us was inferior. . . . We were constantly told that we were truly inferior to them and that we would always be inferior. (1993, 49)

MacDonald refused to accept an inferior position, and he learned to appreciate the good things in life. He also wanted the Navajo elite to have the same luxuries as the non-Indian world. He and his wife sponsored the Navajo Academy for the best high school students, and his final political downfall came when during his fourth term he made his office literally into a Mahogany Row and was imprisoned in 1990 for accepting bribes and inciting a riot after efforts were made by the tribal council to dismiss him from office. President Bill Clinton pardoned MacDonald, releasing him from jail, just before he left office in 2001.

MacDonald wanted Navajo Community College to have greater prestige, and admission standards were instituted. Atcitty, while gaining national recognition serving as a leader of the tribal college movement, was absent frequently from Tsaile and lost touch with his home base. He helped to found the American Indian Higher Education Consortium and later became its president. Robert Roessel (1979) bitterly resented that under Atcitty Navajo Studies ceased to be a separate entity and were to be integrated into the various traditional college departments. A coalition of faculty, students, and staff petitioned successfully for Atcitty's resignation in January 1977. In 1976, 77 percent of the 304 college employees were Indian, and about 65 percent of the faculty were non-Indian. After two short-term presidents, the Navajo educator Dean C. Jackson became NCC's sixth president, serving from 1979 to 1989. Jackson, who had chaired a committee developing a Navajo (Diné) philosophy of education while at Window Rock Public Schools, brought curricular balance and administrative stability back to the institution and promoted a Diné philosophy of learning:

> The educational philosophy of Diné College is Sa'ah Naagháí Bik'eh Hózhóón, the Diné traditional living system, which places human life in harmony with the natural world and the universe. The philosophy provides principles both for protection from the imperfections in life and for the development of well being. (*Diné College NCA* 2002, 25)

Jackson needed such a philosophy. As president, he was forced to deal with a federal funding cut, from $6 million to $3 million per year, for operating expenses.

Sometimes, in reaction to the many years of coercive assimilation in BIA schools that devalued all that was Indian, tribally controlled schools went to the other extreme and devalued everything that was "white." Deborah House, who took Navajo Studies classes and taught at NCC in the 1990s, wrote:

> [N]on-Navajo students (Anglo, Hispanic, and others) were encouraged to disparage their own upbringing and cultural experiences. Furthermore, their language, literature, religion, family life, and ethnic identities are routinely, and at times painfully, denigrated and devalued by Navajo and non-Navajo instructors, administrators, and other students. (2002, 38)

House found that although there was a great deal of talk about the importance of revitalizing Navajo language and culture at NCC, very little was actually being done. The ideal Navajo lifestyle that was promoted in some NCC classes—"sheepherding and growing a small garden, living in a hogan, and driving a team of horses"—was not really viable, especially considering the great increase in Navajo population over the last century (House 2002, 87). According to the 2002 North Central Accreditation (NCA) Self Study, "[I]n recent years the DEP [Diné Educational Philosophy] office has provided little or no support for faculty in integrating the philosophy into instruction" (*Diné College NCA* 2002, 27).

In 1997, NCC was renamed Diné College. "Diné" means "the people" in the Navajo language and is their name for themselves. In addition to the main Tsaile campus, there were seven satellite campuses in 2002. Finding the money to keep these campuses in repair was a major problem, as was balancing the financial needs of the main campus with the demands of local constituencies for local services. In part as a result of the conflicting demands and severe financial constraints, the 1990s were characterized by administrative instability, according to the the Diné College 2002 NCA Self Study report. In 1996, a four-year teacher education program was started, with the cooperation of Arizona State University. However, independent accreditation for this program was denied because of the college's lack of resources. FTE enrollment averaged 1,387 students per semester between 1997 and 2002, an enrollment substantially higher than that at any other tribal college.

Other Tribal Colleges

Deganawidah-Quetzalcoatl (D-Q) University near Davis, California, established originally as a joint Hispanic-Indian school in 1971, was among the pioneer tribal colleges. Jack D. Forbes, a Powhatan-Delware, helped to found the California Indian Education Association in 1967, and that group worked to set up an Indian college. After a nonviolent takeover of an abandoned army installation, the founders were able to get the facility turned over to the college. But funding was precarious in the early years. Most of the students were urban Indians, and Lakota was the only Indian language taught at the college. The activist founders hired the AIM leader Dennis Banks as an instructor in 1975 and as assistant to the president in 1976 (employment was a condition set by then California Governor Jerry Brown to keep Banks from being extradited to South Dakota to face charges stemming from the second Wounded Knee incident). In 1978, to obtain funding through the Tribal College Act, the Hispanic board members resigned.

Oglala Lakota College (OLC) on the Pine Ridge Reservation in South Dakota was started in 1969 by volunteers in association with the University of Colorado. In the 1978 mission statement, the trustees stressed "the importance of maintaining the Lakota culture and fostering tribal self determination" while also preparing students" to understand the ways of the larger society" (quoted in Stein 1988, 99). To serve better the dispersed communities on the reservation, the college had nine centers rather than one central campus. The vision of the four-year teacher preparation program at OLC is "[t]o graduate highly qualified, professional, motivated, committed teachers who possess and who will teach *Wolakota* in a multicultural, changing world" (2001, 79). (*Wolakota* refers to the whole person in balance and in harmony spiritually, physically, mentally, and socially.)

OLC is currently working on an assessment format that identifies seven ability-based outcomes. The college's goal is for students to be able to demonstrate and use these qualities as a source of empowerment for lifelong learning. They are the ability to (1) develop and maintain an individual wellness program and nurture the mind, body, heart, and spirit; (2) model self-identity, founded on cultural practices, customs, values, and beliefs; (3) demonstrate basic understanding and usage of the Lakota language; (4) demonstrate community involvement or service; (5) reflect and document real-life examples of character (courage, honesty, generosity, etc.); (6) demonstrate and document effective communication skills; and (7) demonstrate and document professional abilities of critical thinking and problem solving. Assessment results are being gathered throughout the collegewide network using a Medicine Wheel view of abilities that emphasize *wolakolkiciyapi* (living in peaceful balance).

Sinte Gleska College on the Rosebud Sioux Reservation in South Dakota was chartered in 1971 and began with six centers. From the beginning, Sinte Gleska had a large non-Indian enrollment, sometimes representing over 50 percent of the student body. One of the founders, Gerald Mohatt, went on to help to form the American Indian Higher Education Consortium in 1972. In 1973, Lionel Bordeaux became its president. The tribal chairman tried to dismiss him several times, but he was still president in 2003. A four-year program in human services and education was started in 1977.

American Indian Higher Education Consortium

The American Indian Higher Education Consortium (AIHEC) was founded in 1972 at a meeting of representatives from all existing Indian postsecondary institutions. Gerald One Feather of Oglala Sioux Community College was chosen as its first president. The organizers' first priority was to start an American Indian accreditation agency, but finding a stable funding source quickly became the overriding priority and external accreditation helped the struggling colleges to establish credibility with Congress. In addition, the North Central and North Western Association of Schools regional accreditation associations proved very supportive of the infant tribal colleges and helped boards of trustees and college administrators to distance themselves from tribal politics and to gain legitimacy in the eyes of the outside world.

In her 1994 Ed.D. dissertation, "The Tribally Controlled Community Colleges Act of 1978: An Expansion of Federal Indian Trust Responsibility," former Little Big Horn College president Janine Pease-Windy Boy (Crow) gave a blow-by-blow analysis of AIHEC's work to find a stable source of funding for tribal colleges. Tribal college presidents Lionel Bordeaux of Sinte Gleska College, James Shanley of Standing Rock College, Thomas Atcitty of Navajo Community College, and Phyllis Howard of Fort Berthold College led the fight for a tribal college act. Between 1973 and 1975, AIHEC's executive director, David M. Gipp, and Bordeaux visited every congressional representative whose district had a tribal college lobbying for support (Stein 1990). Key support came from South Dakota Senator James Abourezk, who had grown up on the Rosebud Reservation.

According to Pease-Windy Boy, the BIA and the U.S. Office of Education consistently opposed the tribal college bill, and there was Indian opposition as well. Patricia Locke, a Hunkpapa Lakota and White Earth Chippewa, of the Western Interstate Commission on Higher Education and president of the National Indian Education Association in 1977, initially fought a tribal college amendment to the 1975 Indian Self Determination and Educational Assistance Act because it "undermined tribal sovereignty and self-determination" (Pease-Windy Boy 1994). Her efforts contributed to a name change from Indian-controlled to tribally controlled community colleges and the requirements that they be chartered by a tribal government, have all-Indian boards of trustees, and majority Indian student enrollment.

AIHEC leaders unselfishly supported new, struggling tribal colleges even though it meant spreading inadequate federal funding even thinner. Between 1968 and 1978, the seventeen colleges listed in Table 6 were established that have survived into the twenty-first century. In 1978, stable if not bountiful funding for these colleges was achieved, despite BIA opposition, with the passage of the Tribally Controlled Community College Assistance Act (P.L. 95–471). It was sponsored by Senator Abourezk and signed by President Jimmy Carter. In that Act, Navajo Community College received special funding status. In 1994, federal legislation awarded tribal colleges land grant status. In 1999, AIHEC listed twenty-eight tribally chartered colleges, most of them fully accredited, and three federally chartered Indian colleges in twelve states; four offered bachelor's degrees and two offered master's degrees. Accreditation requirements have helped tribal colleges to remain independent of tribal politics.

American Indian and Native American Studies

Responding to calls by university administrators and American Indian representatives, the South Dakota State Legislature authorized the founding of the Institute of American Indian Studies at the University of South Dakota in 1955. The Institute collected oral histories and, among other books, published *An Indian Philosophy on Education* (1974), edited by John Bryde. That book was described as "the first publication of its kind[,] . . . a collection of essays by American Indian professionals describing how American Indian children should be educated" (Bruguier and White 2001, 7).

As Indians moved to cities because of the BIA's relocation program promising jobs, many found that promise hollow. Some of the disappointed immigrants became community activists who along with college students began to protest the treatment of Indians in various ways. One of the most highly publicized protests was the takeover of Alcatraz Island in San Francisco Bay by activists and students from the University of California, Berkeley, the University of California, Los Angeles, and San Francisco State College. It was these institutions that first established Native American Studies (NAS) programs and associated courses (De La Torre 2001).

During the 1970s, NAS programs were established in colleges and universities across the United States and Canada. Within these programs, courses were developed in Native American literature, American Indian legal-political studies, Native American arts, Native American religion and philosophy, Native American education, American Indian languages, American Indian tribal and

TABLE 1
Original Tribal Colleges Still Open (Some Now with New Names) in 2003

	Date Chartered	1979 Enrollment
Navajo Community College, Tsaile, Ariz.	1968	1,118
Oglala Sioux Community College, Kyle, S. Dak.	1970	282
Sinte Gleska College, Rosebud, S. Dak.	1971	173
Standing Rock Community College, Ft. Yates, N. Dak.	1972	111
Turtle Mountain Community College, Belcourt, N. Dak.	1972	107
Fort Berthold Community College, New Town, N. Dak.	1973	60
Lummi Community College, Lummi Island, Wash.	1973	85 (1980)
Nebraska Indian Community College, Winnebago, Neb.	1973	115 (1997)
Sisseton Wahpeton Community College, Sisseton, S. Dak.	1973	96
Little Hoop Community College, Ft. Totten, N. Dak.	1974	51
Cheyenne River Community College, Eagle Butte, S. Dak.	1975	138
Dull Knife Memorial College, Lame Deer, Mont.	1975	231
Blackfeet Community College, Browning, Mont.	1976	304
Little Big Horn College, Crow Agency, Mont.	1977	102
Salish Kootenai College, Pablo, Mont.	1977	507
D-Q University, Davis, Calif, (originally founded 1971)	1977	163 (1978)
Fort Peck Community College, Poplar, Mont.	1978	135

SOURCE: Adapted from Oppelt 1984, 42–43.

community development, and related areas (Forbes and Johnson n.d. [1971?]). Jack D. Forbes, who was involved in establishing the NAS programs at the University of California, Davis, wrote in 1969 that the "thrust of Indian Studies is not primarily to study the Indian community but to develop practical programs for and by the Indian community" (Forbes and Johnson n.d. [1971?], 29).

Higher Education Goals

The central question for tribal colleges in particular and Indian education in general is whether the education supplied will be for the purpose of assimilation into the non-Indian world or for a purpose that is more in line with Indian cultures. W. Larry Belgarde, founding president of Turtle Mountain Community College, examined the struggle between tribal members operating the colleges and the demands of the federal funding agencies that provided the resources necessary for the colleges' existence. Using Turtle Mountain Community College and Little Big Horn College as case studies, Belgarde documented that "[t]he colleges have installed formal administrative structures that resemble those of the external society but have moved towards using Indian social norms for day to day interaction" (vi). The colleges need to conform to outside norms both to continue receiving funding and to confer on their students an education that is recognized by outside employers. However, the higher education structure allows considerable autonomy, and strong tribal studies departments have grown up in many colleges, and Diné College has a tribal press that focuses on the publication of oral history and other materials on Navajo culture.

Tribal colleges serve students who would not otherwise have a chance to go to college and retrieve students who have gone off to mainstream colleges and failed. They were in the vanguard of improving the quality of life on their reservations. A two-year study of tribal colleges by the Carnegie Foundation concluded. "The idea of Indian-controlled colleges offers great hope to the Native American community and the nation as a whole" (*Tribal Colleges* 1989, 87). Longtime president of Sinte Gleska College, Lionel Bordeaux (1991, 12), declared that "these founders [of the tribal colleges] foresaw the need to preserve the Indian culture so cultural preservation is really the foundation of the tribal colleges."

In the 1990s, there was a move by some tribal colleges to become four-year institutions. Sinte Gleska College became Sinte Gleska University in 1992. Sinte Gleska and Oglala Lakota College in South Dakota developed four-year teacher preparation programs, and Sinte Gleska also developed a master's degree program in education (Bordeaux 1991). Both Diné College in Arizona and Haskell Indian Nations University in Kansas began developing teacher education programs in the mid-1990s.

Unlike many white college graduates, many American Indian college graduates have had unsuccessful K-12 school careers. A Montana case study showed that their high school teachers did not encourage them to go to college, most had low grade point averages, and they heard little or nothing positive about Natives in their classrooms. Yet with family support, they went on to receive associate of arts, bachelor's, and master's degrees. Tribal colleges and organizations such as the American Indian Science and Engineering Society visited high schools and demonstrated to students that American Indians could be successful in technological society and at the same time retain their tribal cultures (Davis 1992). Table 2 shows the rapid increase in the number of degrees earned by American Indians and Alaska Natives between 1981 and 1998.

TABLE 2
Degrees earned per year by American Indians and Alaska Natives: 1981–1998

	1981	1985	1990	1995	1997	1998
Associate's degrees	2,584	2,953	3,530	5,492	5,927	6,220
Bachelor's degrees	3,593	4,246	4,392	6,606	7,409	7,894
Master's degrees	1,034	1,256	1,101	1,621	1,924	2,049
Ph.D.'s	130	119	99	130	173	187

SOURCE: US. Census Bureau, *Statistical Abstract of the United States* 2001, 175.

ENVISIONING AN URBAN UNIVERSITY: PRESIDENT DAVID HENRY AND THE CHICAGO CIRCLE CAMPUS OF THE UNIVERSITY OF ILLINOIS, 1955–1975

FRED W. BEUTTLER

In the decades after World War II, numerous states expanded universities to handle the wave of students. The Chicago Circle campus of the University of Illinois opened in 1965, but its particular mission was unclear. U of I president David Henry was a leading national spokesman for the new urban universities, but his vision of an "urban mission" for Circle clashed with the political realities of campus expansion and especially with faculty aspirations for comprehensive research. This early controversy over mission has shaped the further history of the university, helping it over a period of retrenchment and laying the foundations for UIC's development as a significant model of American higher education, the comprehensive urban research university.

"Just as universities make great cities, so a great city makes a great university," proclaimed Mayor Richard J. Daley, in October 1963, during the groundbreaking ceremony for the new Chicago Circle Campus of the University of Illinois. Daley had worked for over twenty-five years to bring a major public university to Chicago, a dream that finally saw its fulfillment when Circle Campus opened in February 1965. But what was to be the relation of the new university to the city? While there was some talk nationally in the mid-1960s of an "urban land grant" on the model of the Morrill Act of 1862, there was no clear consensus as to what this type of institution should look like, or even whether it was a good model.[1]

In 1955, the same year Richard J. Daley became mayor of Chicago, the University of Illinois Board of Trustees selected David Dodds Henry, a former president of Wayne University and then chief academic administrator of New York University, as president of the University of Illinois. The Board gave Henry an explicit mandate to establish a permanent campus for the university in the Chicago metropolitan area. While the issue of the site for the campus was hotly contested, with the trustees preferring a suburban site and Mayor Daley insisting upon a downtown location,[2] the main area of concern was over its so-called "urban mission." In an unpublished memoir, Henry commented that there was "too little understanding of the urban mission," and that many faculty "had no notion of the meaning of the charge to the Circle campus."[3] Conflict over the priority given to research also dogged relations between the Urbana campus and Chicago, with persistent and lingering impressions by Chicago faculty that Urbana, and Henry in particular, had little desire to see the Chicago Campus fulfill a significant research and service role for the urban community.

What was this "charge" to the new Circle Campus? Henry referred to Circle's "urban mission," but what was it, and how was it to be accomplished? Was its urban mission to be defined by the students it served, or by its research on the urban environment? Should its courses and research have

History of Higher Education Annual 23 (2004): 107–141.
©2004. ISBN: 0-7658-0839-0

a specific focus upon the city and its problems, seeing the city as a laboratory? Or should the campus concentrate on service, confining itself to a more limited role, which would not unduly compete with the state's flagship university in Urbana? These questions created significant controversy in 1960s and still are areas of current confusion.

These questions recur in the history of higher education, but perhaps more sharply in the case of Illinois. In the three decades after the end of World War II, higher education was transformed by both the G. I. Bill and the massive increase in enrollment of the baby-boom generation. In many states, such as California, New York, Pennsylvania, and Wisconsin, educational coordination became paramount in order to manage the wave of students.[4] The increasing dominance of urban regions also forced a reorientation in higher educational thinking, as universities began to be located, by plan or demand, in highly concentrated urban areas. The University of Illinois' expansion into Chicago was by no means unique, but because of the specifics of Illinois and Chicago, it is more than just an illustrative case study. Illinois was comparatively late in setting up structures of higher education governance, and its regional politics even further limited the time available to manage the growth of higher education. Because of this, the common questions of the meaning and purpose of higher education became especially acute at Circle Campus.

David Henry's vision of an urban university dramatically shaped the historical development of the University of Illinois at Chicago.[5] He was not a minor character, but one of the major academic statesmen of his generation. To understand his vision may help illuminate the larger history of the rise of urban higher education. Henry's conception of a distinctive urban mission of the university underwent a process of development from his early years as president through the construction, staffing, and programming of the Circle Campus, but they generally centered around two concepts: access and service. As his later reflections suggest, he was not able to persuade the University of Illinois, Chicago Circle (UICC) faculty, which continued to push for the Chicago Campus to become a comprehensive research university.

Many new urban universities were created or dramatically expanded in the 1950s and 1960s, and there are many parallels in their histories. A number were quite ambitious, sharing with the Circle Campus faculty the desire to build first rank research universities. Most of the new urban universities, however, developed into at best only second tier institutions. Circle Campus in the 1960s and 1970s was typical of this pattern. But the university that developed after that was not, for in less than twenty-five years it achieved the coveted status of a Carnegie Research I institution. Now, almost forty years after its birth, it boasts of over $200 million in funded research, with a budget of over a billion dollars. Only part of this was due to the merger of the Circle Campus with the University of Illinois Medical Center, which created the University of Illinois (UIC) at Chicago in 1982. Rather than attempt to write a brief history of the rise of UIC here, a task that properly requires a book length study, this article will focus on the distinctive mission of Circle Campus through a close examination of the vision of the university president who ruled over its creation. David Henry was the most important president of the University of Illinois from 1920 to 1980, and it was Henry who oversaw Illinois' growth into a major graduate research university, with a student body of over fifty thousand on three campuses. Henry's vision for an urban campus was significant historically, for the idea evolved in the midst of difficult circumstances.

The growth of Circle Campus into a research university was due in large part to the early controversy over its distinctive mission. Most universities accept their mission willingly, without undergoing an enormous amount of controversy. Circle was different. In its founding years, two visions competed with each other, and in that struggle the intellectual groundwork was laid for its later development into a research university. In this sense, a close examination of David Henry's vision, and how this changed during the historical development of Circle Campus, holds a key to understanding the particular place and mission of urban universities in late-twentieth-century America. Looking at UICC's history from 1955 to 1975, UICC struggled over whether it was to be primarily an urban university emphasizing access and service, David Henry's vision, or whether its destiny was to be a comprehensive research university. It seems that what it was working towards institutionally in this period was a reconciliation of these two visions, to develop a new model in American higher education, the comprehensive urban research university.

The Preparation of an Administrator: David Henry's Early Career

David Dodds Henry was one of the major academic administrators of the middle-twentieth century. While not as widely known as his contemporaries, Robert Maynard Hutchins of the University of Chicago or Clark Kerr of the University of California, he was a leader in a wide variety of fields. Over the course of his career, he was chief academic officer and president of Wayne University, provost of New York University, and the longest serving president of the University of Illinois, from 1955 to 1971. In addition, he was a nationally recognized educational leader, one of the few who served as president or chairman of six national organizations: the Association of Urban Universities, the American Council of Education, the National Association of State Universities and Land-Grant Colleges, the National Commission on Accrediting, the Association of American Universities, and the Carnegie Foundation for the Advancement of Teaching. In addition, he served on several national study groups, including the Carnegie Commission on Educational Television, the President's Committee on Education Beyond the High School, the Carnegie Commission on Higher Education, and the national Board on Graduate Education. He was even chairman for a term of the United Negro College Fund.

Personally, Henry was a rather humorless individual, stubborn and obstinate at times, but he was a hard-working administrator who avoided controversy and seldom tolerated dissent. He was relatively unimaginative, with few original ideas, for he was a reformer and a manager. He knew he was not "brilliant," but he made up for it as "work was my recreation as well as my stress."[6] In examining David Henry, the task is, as one historian put it, to face "the dramatic problem of portraying a bore without allowing the bore to bore us."[7] This is not necessarily a slight at Henry, who realized this about himself. In his first memoirs, he admitted,

> I have not regarded myself as having the personal qualities that are of special interest to other people. Certainly, I am not "charismatic" in any way. I have been submerged in my work so completely that I have often felt that I have no personality or personal interest to others apart from career. While the career has had many dramatic moments, including some crises for me and for my work, they have been isolated incidents in a rather colorless progression of duties and responsibilities, albeit heavy and important ones.[8]

He admitted one exception, however. He approached his vision of education out of a sense of "missionary zeal" for, as he put it. "I started my academic life in the outreach department at Penn State, and it was that early experience, with the Wayne emphasis, that led to my deep and abiding commitment to extending educational opportunity. Indeed, this became the central motiff [sic] in my whole career, a crusade, a cause."[9]

Henry was born in October 1905 in Western Pennsylvania, about 25 miles from Pittsburgh. His paternal grandfather, surnamed Heinrich, was a coal miner who had emigrated from Germany in the 1880s. He settled in the west Pennsylvania coal country, where he worked in the mines until retiring around 1915. Henry's father was a machinist for the railroads, until he brought the family to Chicago around 1913 to attend the Moody Bible Institute. His father was unschooled, at least not beyond eighth grade, but felt called to religious service. He was a rather strict fundamentalist and ambitious for the ministry. In Chicago, the Henrys lived in a number of one-room apartments, around Chicago and Wells streets, "within walking distance" of Chicago's Navy Pier.[10] An only child, young David would occasionally accompany his father on street missions. After Moody Bible Institute, his father was called to a succession of small Baptist churches in Colorado and Pennsylvania. As David Henry remembers, his father "had a violent temper, easily aroused," and relations between them were quite strained. His parents later divorced.[11]

As a child Henry was a loner, not active in sports and with few friends, although he did join the "Lone Scouts of America," an organization that brought the values of the Boy Scouts to rural children. His chief childhood activity, in addition to household chores, was reading. The family returned to the Pittsburgh area in time for David to attend Schenley High School, several blocks from the University of Pittsburgh and Carnegie Tech. Henry thrived at Schenley, a new school which emphasized college preparation, and excelled in social and academic activities, becoming president of the Classical Club, president of the senior class, valedictorian at commencement, and the recipient of the Civic

Honor Award. He moved away from the strict fundamentalism of his father, becoming president of the "Hi-Y" club at the YMCA and assistant superintendent of the Y's Sunday School.

From Schenley, he attended The Pennsylvania State University, excelling in liberal arts and finishing fifth or sixth in his graduating class of 500. To support himself, he got a typing job copying letters in the president's office. His extracurricular activities were in preparation for his later work, involving varsity debate, editor of the yearbook, editor of a new literary magazine, and finally president of the senior class. The *New York Times* took notice of him, calling the young Henry "the busiest college student in America." Upon graduation in 1926, he was awarded a fellowship for graduate study, so he continued at Penn State, earning his M.A. in English in 1927 and his Ph.D. in 1931, writing a biography of the poet William Vaughn Moody for his dissertation.

In 1927, he was hired full time in the Department of Engineering Extension, where he was to prepare liberal arts courses and organize classes throughout the state. This experience oriented him to the needs of commuting and adult students. From the extension department, he moved into an instructorship in English, later joining the faculty of Battle Creek College, where he finished his dissertation. Battle Creek had been founded by Dr. John Harvey Kellogg to train professionals for his Battle Creek Sanitarium. Henry was rapidly given administrative assignments, becoming Dean of Men after his first year, and later the director of the School of Liberal Arts. Henry later considered this a key "turning point" in his life, as he discovered his talent for administration.[12]

With the Depression, Battle Creek College experienced serious financial difficulties, which soon led to its closure. Battle Creek's president had foreseen the looming disaster, so he ran as a Democrat for State Superintendent of Public Instruction for Michigan, and won. Henry accompanied him to Lansing, where he became Assistant Superintendent for Higher Education in 1933. Henry threw himself into the work, helping to win Michigan's first substantial appropriation for the public schools, organizing the Michigan Council on Higher Education, and even administering the New Deal WPA program in adult education.

When the Republicans took back the superintendent's office in 1935, Henry accepted a position as assistant to the executive vice president at Wayne, which was then under the control of the Detroit Public School system. He was to remain at Wayne for seventeen years, as it grew from Junior College, to City College, to Colleges of the City of Detroit, and to Wayne University. It was Henry who laid the groundwork for its later development into Wayne State University.[13]

In 1939, upon the retirement of the executive vice president, Henry was appointed to the position, which made him *de facto* head of the university. Detroit's Board of Education was the board of trustees for the university, which caused some serious difficulty over authority as the superintendent of schools was also president of the university. This structural flaw was soon corrected, however, as the board separated the office of superintendent from the university president in 1945, naming Henry to that role. One of Henry's major goals in this period was to push the board to yield jurisdiction to the state if Michigan would take financial responsibility, a move that was not fully completed when Henry left Wayne, but well on its way at that time. Wayne was one of the first to move from municipal university to state university, a move initially opposed by most of the other municipal universities in the country, but which they eventually followed.[14]

Henry and the university were embroiled in some controversy, which seemed to foreshadow his future at Illinois. Wayne's location made it vulnerable during the Detroit race riots of 1943, and a change of location was seriously contemplated. Henry seemed to prefer a suburban site for the university, but inability to secure significant funding forced an incremental expansion of the campus. In addition to race, there was the threat of domestic subversion, and like other states around the country in the late 1940s and early 1950s, Michigan created its own investigative commission to expose communists. In the spring of 1949, David Henry vetoed a lecture by Herbert Phillips, a communist philosopher recently dismissed from the University of Washington. Defending his action, Henry, who two years earlier had claimed that "the University has no right to differentiate among American citizens on the basis of political belief," this time insisted that "it is now clear that the Communist is to be regarded not as an ordinary citizen . . . but as an enemy of our national welfare . . . I cannot believe that the university is under any obligation in the name of education, to give him an audience."[15]

By 1952, Henry felt that he had accomplished all he was going to accomplish at Wayne. He had administered the university for thirteen years, from age 34 to 47. He felt himself somewhat worn out physically, after a seven-day a week, day and night schedule, and he was admittedly rather thin-skinned, taking any criticism towards the university personally. A state referendum on educational funding had just been turned down. In addition, a teachers union with a chapter at the university had just formed, which was increasingly taking an adversarial stance towards the administration. It was time to leave.

David Henry left Wayne after a fond farewell ceremony, which included a gift of a personal car. He accepted a position as chief academic officer at New York University (NYU), under Henry Heald, who had recently been head of the Illinois Institute of Technology, and who later would run the Ford Foundation. The shift from a public to a private institution was not great, David Henry later recalled, as the missions of NYU and Wayne had much in common: "Both were urban, emphasizing service to commuting students. Both had comprehensive professional programs. Both had severe financial problems." Henry settled into his new position, but after only a couple of years allowed his name to be circulated for possible presidencies. He was approached by the University of Illinois' trustees, who offered Henry the position.

Henry had some misgivings about accepting Illinois' presidency. After the war, Illinois had as its president George Stoddard, a dynamic leader who sought to awaken what he called the "sleeping giant" in Urbana. An internationalist active in UNESCO, he sought to move Illinois up into prominence, but soon fell afoul of a rather politicized trustee board.[16] At midnight on a Friday night in July 1953, a rump board summarily fired Stoddard and his provost, Coleman Griffith, ostensibly over Stoddard's handling of a scandal in the medical school, but in reality over long-standing political differences. In his place, the trustees appointed an internal caretaker as interim, and began searching for a new president. The public and faculty were outraged over the midnight firing, and few candidates would consider taking over a university with such a board, so the search dragged on. Interestingly, Stoddard ended up at NYU, where he and Henry consulted frequently about the situation at Illinois.[17] After a change in the presidency of Illinois' trustee board, Henry decided to accept the position.

Bringing Public Higher Education to Chicago

After the passage of the G.I. Bill, the University of Illinois had agreed to admit all qualified Illinois veterans, but quickly found that it simply could not meet the demand at the Urbana campus. In 1946, it created two temporary campuses for the incoming students. These branches offered only the first two years of instruction, although they were not junior colleges, for admission requirements and courses were the same as at Urbana. One branch was in western Illinois, at Galesburg, where the University occupied part of the wartime Mayo Hospital complex. About three thousand students enrolled, many of them disabled veterans recuperating at the hospital. The university administration closed it after three years, when the Urbana campus could absorb the transfer students. The second campus was the "Chicago Undergraduate Division," housed in warehouse space on Chicago's Navy Pier. When the Navy Pier campus opened in October 1946, there was no public university in the entire Chicago area, only two small teachers colleges, although there were of course a number of private universities. Student demand was heavy for this U of I branch campus, with around four thousand students attending each semester, and this demand continued after the initial wave of veterans. Within a few years, student and community pressure forced the trustees to keep the campus open, as a first step towards a permanent degree granting institution.[18]

One of the key individuals behind this community pressure was Richard J. Daley. As a first-term legislator in 1936, he had introduced a resolution calling for a public university in Chicago. In 1945, he introduced four bills into the state senate, to direct the University of Illinois to establish a branch in Chicago, "to provide liberal and practical education customarily offered at the college or university level."[19] These bills were referred to the senate education committee, then under the control of senators favorable to Urbana's interests, who subsequently tabled it, where it died on adjournment. In 1951, Daley's allies in the state house were able to introduce another bill, with similar language. It was amended by Urbana Republicans to limit the branch campus to only offer a "full undergraduate education," and in this form passed that same year.

This was the mandate from the state, and it is significant that it took political pressure from a powerful Chicago politician to secure passage in the state legislature, which forced a very reluctant university to build a branch in Chicago. The political context here is important. The president of the U of I at that time was George Stoddard, who generally opposed expanding the Navy Pier branch, believing that it was premature and would dilute the state's resources for the flagship campus in Urbana. This opinion was widely shared among the Urbana faculty. Stoddard's firing in the summer of 1953 had delayed planning for the Chicago campus, making the situation increasingly urgent by the time David Henry assumed the presidency.

One of the main reasons for the sense of urgency was the rising tide of enrollments that demographers and university planners predicted in the mid-1960s. In addition, the larger percentage of college-age students attending college raised the potential tide to enormous proportions, possibly doubling or even tripling college populations within ten years. One practical difficulty, however, was that Illinois at that time was operating under two handicaps—first, there was no central coordinating body for state higher educational planning, so each university had to make its case individually before the legislature; and second, the state was operating under biennial budgets, which meant that if appropriations for expansion were not sufficient in a given biennium cycle, it would delay planning by two full years. In addition, the state was strongly segmented politically, with the nation's second largest city heavily Democratic, its growing suburbs almost exclusively Republican, and the rural downstate countries mixed between the Republican northern and central counties, and the far south, which was southern Democratic. These political alliances would shape the expansion of higher education into urban Chicago.

Upon taking office as president of the University of Illinois in 1955, David Henry knew the university trustees' "highest priority among new developments" was progress "toward the realization of plans for a permanent undergraduate degree granting division" in Chicago, From the very beginning of his administration then, David Henry concentrated on fulfilling this mandate for a permanent campus. University plans, however, raised serious debate within Chicago and downstate, as private universities in Chicago questioned the need for a new institution, and downstate legislators were "uneasy about the open-endedness" of the Chicago campus. Because of this, Henry devised a strategy "to advocate limiting the immediate commitment to a permanent home for the current program, as longer-range polices and issues were debated."[20] In the fall of 1955, Henry began delivering public addresses before varied audiences, pushing for a new campus and implying longer-range goals for the campus, but without listing any controversial specifics. At the student convocation on the Navy Pier campus on 20 October 1955, Henry outlined some of his concerns, seeing the development of a permanent urban campus as essential. "The urban student body of America is a very large and important one. The commuting students represent half the college population. The growth of the urban universities has made a major impact upon the equalization of educational opportunity and will continue to do so."[21]

In January of 1956, speaking before U of I alumni in Chicago, Henry called for a permanent Chicago "undergraduate center." Continuing the strategy of putting need before program specifics, Henry stressed issues of demand, equity and expense, arguing for a "regional distribution of educational service." "The University undergraduate center in Chicago located where its students live, meets the logic of demand, the equity of need, the expedience of minimum expense in serving the greatest number." Henry stressed the urgency of the task ahead: "We must make immediate progress in providing permanent facilities for the present program, even while the question of expansion of that program is under review."[22]

The following fall was the tenth anniversary of the Navy Pier campus, supposedly only a temporary institution. Convocation on 18 October 1956, was a celebration of the accomplishments of the campus and its faculty, as Henry praised the fact that over 37,000 students had attended the Chicago Undergraduate Division since its inception. Henry projected a permanent campus in 1963, seven years in the future, to the restrained applause of students, parents, and faculty. He announced that the University trustees had recommended a suburban site for the permanent campus site, in forest preserve land called "Miller Meadows," about twelve miles from Chicago's Loop. "The University has made its recommendation in the best interests of the students who will use the campus, with a view to economy, accessibility, and the future growth of the community," but Henry did not elaborate, for as he put it, the "question is a highly technical one."[23] Henry placed the Chicago branch within the context of the larger University's needs. The U of I was growing by approximately one thousand students per year, necessitating new staff, faculty wage increases, new support for expanding academic programs in nuclear physics, computers, agriculture and medical research, student housing at Urbana (which had the lowest percentage of student housing in the Big Ten), and limitations on program facilities. While a priority, Henry made it clear that the Chicago campus was only one of many, in an age of overall university expansion.

Henry's discussion of the potential site for the new Chicago branch campus was significant, however, as he was generally supporting the proposed suburban location. Traditionally, the flagship Urbana campus had drawn students primarily from northern and central rural counties and from Chicago's suburbs, both wealthier and heavily Republican, while the students and faculty at the Navy Pier branch were in large part urban, ethnic, and Democratic. Most were first generation college students. This not-so-subtle political divide would shape the future of a new urban campus, both in its location and in its mission. While obviously aware of this division, Henry's main concern was in first rallying support for a new campus, one in which he had to raise financing for campus construction, while avoiding alienating potential supporters by making the new campus's mission too ambitious. As this was a common problem among many states as they expanded into urban higher education in the 1960s, it is useful to examine closely Henry's thinking as it evolved.

Henry's "Urban University" Ideal, 1958–1960

By the late 1950s, David Dodds Henry had emerged as one of the key national spokesman for the new "urban university." In a series of addresses at various urban universities around the country, such as at Wichita, Wayne University, Akron, as well as before the Association of Urban Universities (AUU), David Henry developed his understanding of the mission of an urban university. In late 1958, he collected his speeches together for an extended introduction to a proposed publication by the AUU on urban higher education, although it was never published. These texts provide an essential source for understanding Henry's thinking before the development of the program at U of I's Chicago campus. Here, he stressed two main themes: access and service.

In Henry's view, as higher education developed in the twentieth century, there was a move away from pastoral settings due to the "economic impossibility of taking all students to rural areas." Strangely, though, he avoided addressing the Jeffersonian tradition, which had made educators suspicious of cities and urban life. Still, urban universities were to "emphasize functional education" and "vocational service," to "relate itself to the life of the community." Henry sought to articulate a distinct philosophy for the urban university, but he had a better idea of what it was not, rather than what its positive role could be:

> The urban university in the generic sense is still not widely recognized as a distinct type among the colleges and universities, nor are its mission and its character understood by the general public. It is much more than a poor man's college, proud as one may be of that designation; much more than an educational service station for the part-time student, vital as is that function; much more than a second-choice institution for those who would prefer to go somewhere else but cannot.

What he saw as primary was its service responsibility to its community. The urban university had "a special obligation to respond to the immediate educational needs of the community in which it is set"; consistent with appropriate university standards. Within those bounds, "it plans its offerings with direct reference to these needs; and that within the limits of its resources it is hospitable to all local requests for those intellectual services which a university may legitimately render."[24]

He placed special emphasis upon increasing access and opportunity to what a later generation would call the "non-traditional student." In an address at Wayne in 1954, reaffirmed years later in

Illinois, Henry called for programs for "the adult searching for avocational and recreational satisfactions or self-improvement." He also expanded the concept of university research for the urban university, "to include application of research to any and all efforts that make for improvement in living, or add to our prosperity." Seeing little utility in the dividing line between basic and applied research, something that was increasingly becoming an important rhetorical device to defend the designation of "university" to an urban campus, Henry considered "any effort arbitrarily to exclude the university from applied research" as "an unnecessary, harmful limitation on free inquiry and comprehensive graduate training."[25] Yet in practice, and as any university researcher knows, this has the effect of collapsing basic research into applied training.

Community service then became central to Henry's conception of the urban university: "Thus, the urban university has come to be defined not only as one located in an urban center, serving the young people of the urban community, but as one which in many ways seeks to relate itself to its community. In thus interacting with its community, the urban university has deepened the dimension of direct community service from higher education." This was a common refrain:

> In the concept of a free and prosperous America, the university must be wholly in the service of the community—a service complete by the definition of those served and complete in the scope and variety of offerings." That community orientation would make the urban university as "an influence for community harmony," at the "core of community integration," a potential "neutral ground where partisans on all other issues may join in a common effort for furthering the public interest. The university has political immunity and commands social understanding and respect.

It was to focus on social research, staff consultation, hospitality to community organizations, and problem-solving. The urban university then could be "an instrument for the harmonization of the various elements in the general social structure."[26]

What Henry envisioned by 1960 was what he called the "community-centered urban university," which would emphasize two things: applied research, often of a contract nature with industry and government; and an openness to adult and continuing education students, which would include large numbers of part-time evening students in an "urban evening college."[27]

The Founding Years of the University of Illinois, Chicago Circle

This was Henry's vision for an ideal urban campus, but this vision was to undergo serious modifications over the next few years, as it clashed with the specifics of Chicago and Illinois politics. Henry's initial strategy for university expansion in Chicago was to concentrate on the physical construction of the campus, before the school's academic program was fully developed, as site selection, acquisition, campus planning, development, and construction were more dependent upon outside funding and the State's biennial budgeting structure than the academic program. Concerns involving the physical plant drove campus planning, as did the selection by Henry of Norman Parker to head the new campus. Parker, an engineer and head of Urbana's mechanical engineering department, had prepared some of the initial campus program planning documents in the late 1950s, but this was focused primarily on departmental space needs and location, rather than on academic programs.

In order to get the funding necessary for the construction of the Chicago Campus, it was essential to pass a large bond issue. The first bond issue had failed in 1958 and only narrowly passed in 1960. Even though the majority of funding went for universities throughout the state, only Cook County and the two downstate counties near St. Louis voted for the bond issue; downstate voters were generally opposed. Without the elective power of Mayor Daley's Democratic organization, the bond issue clearly would have failed. The city-downstate split in Illinois' political culture was to limit the expansion of the Circle Campus, and provided a restrictive context for its further development. In addition to downstate opposition to university expansion in Chicago, there was also hostility on the part of the region's private colleges. In order to get support in Springfield for the bond issue, David Henry and U of I needed to make a number of quiet commitments to the Chicago area private colleges, especially DePaul, Loyola, Roosevelt, and the Illinois Institute of Technology, that would limit the Chicago campus' growth. "We were narrowly prescribed as to what we could do," Norman Parker recalled later. "We were told to stay out of graduate work, we couldn't have a night program and we couldn't even offer evening courses without at least a year's notice." This "gentleman's agreement" also limited Circle Campus' expansion into dormitories and professional programs, such as law and business administration. Evening courses were not offered at Circle until over a decade later, and it was almost twenty years before a full night program was begun in limited disciplines. These two issues: downstate political opposition and the "gentlemen's agreement" with Chicago's private colleges, served to narrow Henry's original vision of UICC's "urban mission."[28]

The demand for a new campus was clear by the mid-1960s, as the Chicago Circle Campus soon became the fastest growing campus in the nation. Classes began at the new Circle Campus in February 1965, and the student body rapidly grew from around 5,000 at Navy Pier in fall 1964, to almost 8,500 in winter 1965–66, to 17,500 by winter 1970–71, Henry's last year as president. This was an increase of over 340 percent in six short years.

After the opening of Circle Campus, David Henry continued to sell his vision of an "urban university," but with a more limited scope due to the restrictions on a night school and professional programs. He was optimistic in speaking with the university's Citizen's Committee on 13 May 1966, in Chicago: "The Urban University in an urban America will be at the center of American thrust in days ahead," with its emphasis upon "issues of urban living," urban government, arts, and culture. His optimism, however, was tempered by a note of uncertainty: "Non-urban scholars will also have their contributions but the potential of the urban-located and community oriented campus remains to be fully defined."[29]

That December the campus was awarded a prize by the "Chicago Builder's Congress," where Henry took the opportunity to emphasize the direct and indirect economic impact of the university on the city. "Only recently have economists begun to treat education as economic capital, not just human capital and assess the measuring devices." He boasted of the $10 million annual payroll, plus the almost $100 million in building costs. About the only thing Henry did not boast about was the amount of concrete used in its construction, although that was probably why the builder's association awarded the prize. While clearly a sales pitch, this was how Henry sold the Circle Campus to its urban environment. Of greatest importance was its "indirect economic benefits," for with the commuter campus, students lived, worked, and spent money in Chicago, with graduates often remaining in the city to work. Henry pointed to the campus's potential to attract business and industry, along with the availability of faculty expertise. "Someday," Henry hoped, "we may be able to put all of this into a formula."[30]

Intellectual Infrastructure: Towards a Comprehensive University?

While Henry and Parker were concentrating on building the physical infrastructure, other administrators were creating the intellectual infrastructure of the new campus. University Provost Lyle Lanier, a psychologist and a member of the "Southern Agrarians,"[31] seemed to have wanted to create a research university in Chicago with an emphasis upon urban affairs, but still focused upon basic research.[32] In that aim, he was assisted by another psychologist, Glenn Terrell, who was dean of liberal arts at Chicago Circle, later becoming "dean of faculties," the school's chief academic officer. In 1967, he left to assume the presidency of Washington State University. While at Circle, Terrell concentrated on building up a strong, research-minded faculty, by hiring aggressive department heads, major scholars, and promising younger faculty. The watchword was to create a "UCLA in Chicago," a comprehensive research school which would rival Urbana. What this meant was a rapid expansion, not just to undergraduate education, but especially into graduate study, including the Ph.D., as quickly as possible.

However, Henry's vision of the Circle Campus was as an "urban university," defined by access and service, expanding educational opportunity for undergraduates and providing service to the city. Many of the new department heads, however, saw this as a limiting role that would relegate the new university to second class status, rather than as a potential equal to Urbana, Northwestern, and even, someday, the University of Chicago. Growing rapidly, with little direction from Circle chancellor Norman Parker, ambitious department heads were pretty much left to their own initiative to create new graduate programs. Most aggressive were the departments of philosophy, history, chemistry, and mathematics, which developed doctoral programs within two years of the move to the Circle Campus. Other departments under less aggressive leadership only slowly tried to catch up. An internal division quickly developed in the Circle Campus, between those faculty who emphasized teaching and who often had been retained from the Navy Pier campus, and the new research oriented faculty.[33] The latter soon came to feel that Henry was consciously restricting the growth at Circle Campus by trying to limit its role to that of an urban service school for undergraduates.

Internal dissension over the direction of the Circle Campus reached a crisis point in 1966, a little over a year after the campus had opened. In April, David Henry and Provost Lyle Lanier met with about forty-five of the key department heads and deans at the Circle Campus, trying to explain university organization and governance. Speaking from handwritten notes, Henry explained that the "objective for Chicago Circle administration has been maximum operational autonomy within university-wide structure." He was careful to explain the focus of the central administration, emphasizing that the "central administration is NOT an Urbana administration," and that department heads should make that clear to their faculty. Henry asked for "understanding and patience." A further concern was that "internal administrative unity" was "essential for progress," for external elements in the state were "quick to take advantage . . . to create uncertainty and lack of confidence." Competition for graduate work, new buildings, and new programs in the state and at the Board of Higher Education level was fierce, and "taking internal gripes and criticisms" to students, press, and legislature, "plays into the hand of those who would hold back the U of I." In his notes he had crossed out, but still thought, "some damage already done."[34]

The research-oriented faculty were not persuaded, for they doubted David Henry's and the larger University of Illinois' commitment to graduate study in Chicago. "There is evidence that the administration of the University, while now making public acknowledgment of the necessity for graduate study at Chicago Circle, is as a matter of fact impeding its development by means of its internal policies." In a publicly released memo, the research-oriented faculty listed numerous arguments, such as the need for graduate training in numerous fields as an entry for employment, and the lack of graduate training in anything but private universities in Chicago. One major argument was over faculty recruitment, for outstanding faculty "cannot be induced to join the university unless they have available the possibility of teaching at the graduate level and the means for pursuing their scholarly interests and research." They were skeptical of Henry's vision of a high-quality university devoted only to undergraduate instruction, pointing out as well that federal money was available for infrastructure construction, but only contingent on graduate instruction. This was especially true in the natural sciences and engineering.[35]

The faculty charged that the operating budget for Circle Campus was adequate to only maintain the campus, not rapidly to develop graduate programs. Especially damning, in their view, was the lack of serious funding for the library and inadequacies of laboratory space and equipment.

> If the delays in construction materialize, Chicago Circle will be without a minimum graduate library, without research laboratories, and without major graduate programs in essential areas, until the fall of 1971. This five-year delay would not only damage our graduate programs extensively, but would also hurt the quality of our undergraduate instruction. It is inconceivable that Chicago Circle could assemble and retain a high quality faculty for the instruction of our undergraduates if library, laboratories and graduate programs are not at hand. The damage inflicted on this institution would extend far beyond the five-year period under discussion. It is not unreasonable to state that, with this delay, the Chicago area would be deprived of a first-rate full university for another generation.[36]

By 1966, it was the perception of many faculty at Circle that Henry and his administration were "insensitive" to the needs of the Chicago campus. Within two years of its opening, the Circle Campus had seen some of its major faculty, with national reputations in their fields, resigning for other, more promising universities. Dean Glenn Terrell left in 1967, which further eroded the research emphasis on the Chicago campus. Faculty agitation for advanced graduate instruction was not completed, however, when a more serious challenge developed, although this time not between the Urbana campus and Chicago Circle, but rather at the state level.

Excursus: The Wayne State Centennial, 1968

In the midst of the increasing controversy in Chicago and in down-state Illinois, David Dodds Henry accepted Wayne State's invitation to keynote their centennial celebration on June 18, 1968. Henry spoke on the program theme, "The Urban University and Urban Society," and his address provides an important snapshot of his thinking in the midst of the Circle Campus controversy. Henry had been a national spokesman for urban university education for over fifteen years by that point, but his experience at Circle had chastened him. His own faculty was undermining his vision of access and service. Returning to Wayne gave him an opportunity to reflect on these experiences, but more significantly, they gave him a platform to respond to his most persistent critics, the research faculty at UICC. This speech should be interpreted as a rhetorical defense of his own work in Chicago, raising up Wayne as a successful model of an urban university, against the research faculty's vision of Circle Campus.[37]

David Henry was, of course, deeply honored to be chosen as centennial speaker, as he had spent almost half his professional life at Wayne University. He pointed to the rapid growth of the institution, with praise to the builders of the institution: "Let those under 30 remember that they were not the first idealists; that they were not the first missionaries of social service; that they were not the first to dream of improvements in our social structure." Educational opportunity was one of the chief purposes of the university, and Henry singled out for special praise Wayne's "urban commitment:" "Wayne was ahead of its time in its urban commitment," a position "not academically fashionable" in the 1930s and 1940s. Wayne's leaders "conceived of this institution as being uniquely related to this metropolitan community in the supply of graduates, in the applications of research and in extramural research to the community at large. We were told in those day that these objectives constituted a parochial approach to higher education, that the University's high academic goals would be blunted, that the search for relevance to the City would make the University educationally irrelevant," or, in perhaps a better phrase, though crossed off in his draft, "an educational service station rather than an educational powerhouse." Henry was pleased to call the critics wrong, for Wayne was able to attract capable faculty "into the laboratory which every great city constitutes," and its reputation has increased as the "problems of the cities are now seen as primary problems of the Nation."[38]

In that contentious summer, midway between the riots after Martin Luther King's assassination in April and the Democratic Convention in Chicago in August, Henry pointed to the nationwide expectation of "university contributions to the solution of urban problems." He noticed some limitations on that mission, first in "the epidemic of student convulsions on our campuses" especially when race was involved: "If public confidence in the university system can be weakened, all institutions will be irreparably damaged." Like many defenders of the university that summer, Henry reemphasized "reason, intellectual analysis, and rational debate" as the framework for university policy and governance. He defended institutional neutrality, seeing a second serious threat to the urban university in "the insistence of those who would alter its corporate character from one of neutrality in community conflict to one of social activism." Henry feared the loss of relative autonomy if universities as institutions were perceived as agencies of social transformation.[39]

The third great threat to urban higher education, he believed, was "the policy drift that transmutes institutional service into retailing of training at a low level of educational achievement. In my view, the concept of the 'urban grant' university as a parallel to the land-grant university of the nineteenth century is a false analogy." In a new note, he stressed the need to concentrate resources and focus on maintaining quality: "In servicing society, the highest utility [of universities] is in their distinctive functions, and if they become unduly enmeshed as agencies of social welfare, these functions will be eroded. We must be on our guard, therefore, against the inadvertent kind of mayhem which attenuates core purposes in a vast disarray of welfare services."[40]

Finally, with an interesting comparison, he drew explicit parallels between Wayne State and Chicago Circle, for each derived "its strength from its character as a people's university," with broad concern for public welfare, "unrestricted by elitism of any kind." He emphasized again the service function of the urban university: "Education for relevance must remain a constant in the changing public university." Both Chicago and Wayne, as "people's universities," emphasized the key functions of the university: "discovery of new knowledge, its useful application, the preparation of specialists and the broad education of all who seek it." There were many in Illinois, however, who would seek to use Henry's rhetorical vision of Circle to restrict its development, an irony that would be lost on Circle's research faculty and Henry, but one that was to be extremely significant for UICC's future.[41]

State Battles: The Attempted Dismembering of the University of Illinois

David Henry struck a new note at Wayne State with his emphasis upon the concentration of resources and the maintenance of quality, for there were serious threats to limit the University of Illinois' growth. Illinois in the mid-to-late 1960s was in the midst of serious turmoil over the governance of higher education. Before World War II, the University of Illinois was the only comprehensive public university in the state; the other institutions of higher education were basically normal schools or community colleges. U of I's Board of Trustees were state constitutional officers, elected on staggered six-year terms, like senators. After WWII, the normal schools throughout the state began expanding, leading to increased calls for state appropriations. Southern Illinois University, under a dynamic president and supported by a powerful state legislator, grew exponentially, gaining southern Illinois as its territory and seeking to supplant the University of Illinois' extension service in that part of the state.[42] University expansion was basically seen by legislators and the public as yet another interest, with legislators competing against each other to see who could bring state education money home to their districts. By the late 1950s, the situation called for coordination, if not state control, so a study commission was formed which recommended the creation of a central state Board of Higher Education (IBHE). The IBHE was created in 1961, after the funding had been secured and planning was underway for Circle Campus. The IBHE was given a mandate to coordinate the further growth of higher education in the state and to create a series of master plans to manage its expansion.

The most important executive director of the IBHE in the 1960s was Lyman Glenny, who had been involved in the creation of the California system. Glenny definitely did not want to see Illinois develop a centralized system like that in California. Instead, he proposed what came to be known as the "systems of systems" approach, where university expansion would be governed under five different boards of trustees, with the IBHE to act as a coordinating and budgetary agency. Each "system" would govern a different "type" of university, such as the "multi-campus comprehensive land-grant" institution, the U of I; an "emerging multi-campus comprehensive university," such as the Southern Illinois University (SIU); the "liberal arts colleges"; and the regional normal schools. The fifth governing board would control the expanding community colleges.[43] Glenny and the IBHE informally adopted the "system of systems" approach in 1965, over the protests of David Henry and the University of Illinois, who saw the "systems of systems" as limiting U of I's ability to expand. The IBHE was also to manage the relations between the public universities and the private colleges and universities within the state, and the privates had representation on the IBHE. The rapid expansion of the student population in the late 1960s pushed the IBHE to propose, in addition to Circle Campus and SIU's branch in Edwardsville, near St. Louis, the creation of at first four, then two "senior colleges," which would provide the last two years of undergraduate education along with selected master's degree programs.[44]

In this context, David Henry had hoped for an increased role for the University of Illinois, to manage and in large part control the expansion of other universities in the state. But now, instead of having direct access to the legislature as he did before the creation of the IBHE, Henry had to go through this coordinating institution. The IBHE philosophy was based on regional balance and managed competition between schools, and thus was structurally, and with Glenny, personally, opposed to an increased role for Urbana. As the Circle Campus was being built, Henry sought to continue a two-year branch at Navy Pier, but this proposal was rejected, to the amusement of many at the IBHE. As the IBHE planned for two "senior colleges" in 1966–67, Henry sought to gain control over a proposed campus in the state capital in Springfield. At one private meeting, Henry pleaded with the chair of the IBHE's committee on governance, Jim Worthy: "Goddamn it Jim, we can have the new school open and running this fall, not sometime a couple of years from now. We've got curricula. We've got faculty. We've got the resources. All we have to do is rent a few store fronts and we'll have a new university." Yet this was exactly what the IBHE did not want; instead, they wanted innovative and tailored curricula, and that was felt could only be done outside Urbana's control.[45] Henry lost on his bid to increase the dominance of Urbana, and he watched as its relative share of the state budget diminished, as resources went to build up other institutions around the state.

The victory of Republican Richard Ogilvie in the 1968 governor's race dramatically changed the context of Henry's plans for the University of Illinois in general, and specifically the Circle Campus. Henry's limited vision of UICC's urban mission back-fired when the new governor appointed the former vice-chancellor at UICC, James Holderman, as executive director of the Illinois Board of Higher Education. The highly ambitious son of a prominent downstate Republican politician, Holderman had received his doctorate in political science, moving rapidly from the Urbana faculty to various administrative posts at Circle Campus, and finally vice chancellor in charge of administration. Barely thirty years old, Holderman had attempted to force out UICC's chancellor Norman Parker, but failing that, he jumped at the chance to head the IBHE. Assuming the executive director's position in July 1969, Holderman immediately sought to reorganize governance within the state university system, hoping eventually to dismember the University of Illinois by establishing Circle Campus as a freestanding institution.

Circle Campus had long had difficulties with autonomy from Urbana. All major hiring decisions, plus numerous minor administrative matters, had to be cleared with the Urbana administration. Earlier, in 1964, UICC head Norman Parker had complained of his limited, subsidiary role, but the only thing that had really changed since then was his title. One extremely telling example of Parker's limited authority was during the worst snowstorm in Chicago's history, in January 1967. Chancellor Parker had to get permission from President Henry before he could close the campus during the peak of the emergency, and that only after great difficulty and long delay.[46] In addition, there were severe restrictions placed on faculty involvement with City of Chicago departments, which seriously weakened the flexibility of faculty to develop working relationships. Most faculty and staff at UICC and at the IBHE realized that Circle needed increased autonomy.

Holderman used this desire for autonomy to build up pressure for a freestanding campus. Frequently declaring "the days of educational empire building in Illinois are over," Holderman attacked the expansion of graduate education. "During the 1960s," Holderman argued, "an extremely high demand for PhDs was created by the space program, plentiful foundation and defense funds for basic research . . . and ambitious industrial research programs. Unfortunately, much of the demand has now evaporated, but our massive national capacity for producing graduate degrees remains."[47] Holderman seized on the idea of "urban mission" as a means to break Circle Campus off from the University. He specifically targeted graduate programs, arguing that they unnecessarily duplicated private-university programs and competed with Urbana. He defined Circle Campus's "urban mission" like David Henry had earlier, as one of opportunity and service rather than graduate research. Under Holderman's administration of the IBHE, graduate programs at Circle Campus began to be turned down, and he moved to restrict ones that were already approved.

David Henry found himself increasingly on the defensive by 1970, as his earlier vision of "urban mission" was now being used to pressure for the dismemberment of the University of Illinois. Henry argued in stormy public hearings for the necessity of maintaining the link between Circle Campus and Urbana, for only then could it become a research institution. The establishment of the "senior colleges" was also a threat, for these further diluted increasingly limited state educational dollars. As the concept of "urban mission" became increasingly restrictive under Holderman and the IBHE, Henry sought to argue that the UICC was to become a research university, like Urbana, rather than like the more limited senior colleges: "Any change of campus governance at this critical point in [Circle Campus's] development would set the timetable for the development of the institution back many years, and would permanently deprive Chicago of a comprehensive state-supported educational institution if accompanied by the apparent change in mission contemplated for the Chicago Circle Campus under all three of the governance proposals." All three plans would all have made Circle a stand-alone institution and limited it to an urban mission of service and access.[48]

According to Henry, the university's long-range educational mission for the Circle Campus was "that the nation's second-largest metropolitan area should have a public university of the first rank—offering graduate, research, and public-service programs commensurate in scope and diversity with the varied needs of the area's people and with the magnitude of the problems of its physical environment."[49] It was not to be "a mere replica" of Urbana, for it would have "greater emphasis . . . upon professional education and applied research related to the problems of urban society," but it must remain "an integral part" of the University, "dedicated to the basic educational values of the land-grant movement, and determined to find creative expression for them in the complex and turbulent urban environment of the 1970s." Chicago needed a campus with "a level of quality in its unique spectrum of educational functions that would be essentially equivalent in general" to the main campus in Urbana. In addition to the need for a "broad spectrum of educational opportunity" that Circle Campus provided, Henry argued that "Only a public university *of the kind* conceived for the University of Illinois at Chicago Circle . . . would enable an urban society to make the kinds of investment in its human resources that are necessary to its viability and to its capability for self-improvement." To further emphasize the integral link between campuses, Henry pointed to the wide variety of advanced intercampus programs, for example, with the Medical Center campus in bioengineering, public health, and psychopharmacology, along with several joint plans with Urbana, such as in social work and survey research. The most significant reason, however, was the availability of federal and private funds for advanced graduate and research programs. If the Chicago campus was separated, "it is a virtual certainty that several hundred million dollars would be lost to the State and to the Chicago metropolitan region during the critical remainder of this century," for without the link to the University of Illinois, it "would be unable to attract the kinds and level of resources that will be available only to a major public university of top rank." Henry strongly defended the multi-campus system, for it is "the University's general thesis that all three of its campuses share common goals, even though each has a distinctive mission within the University system," for they "comprise a unified educational whole greater than the mere aggregation of its parts."

There are numerous ironies here as Henry sought to prevent the dismemberment of the University of Illinois. While in the earlier period, he had sought to limit Circle Campus to an urban service school, a "people's university" on the model of Wayne State, now, when powerful forces sought to create a fully autonomous campus that would emphasize urban service, Henry switched to defending Circle's research mission, in some ways conceding the point of the research faculty. Henry's vision of an urban university was modified in the face of the reality of competing political pressures.

Interestingly, the Chicago Circle faculty now strongly backed Henry and his rhetorical support for research at the UICC. As a colleague of Holderman's at the IBHE put it, "We felt very strongly Circle ought to be severed from Urbana so it could fulfill its unique urban mission. To our astonishment, we ran into extraordinarily loud and angry resistance from the faculty at Circle."[50] Indeed, one of Henry's most vocal opponents in 1966, chemistry department head Bill Sager, now was one of the chief defenders of the linkage between Urbana and Circle Campus. Holderman's strategy had backfired, for the strong research minded faculty at Circle, which had earlier clashed with Henry over his vision of a restrictive "urban mission," now publicly supported Henry and the ties of Circle to the Urbana Campus.

Retreat, Retrenchment, and Retirement

David Henry, with strong vocal support from the UICC faculty, was able to prevent the dismemberment of the University of Illinois, but another blow to his plans came soon afterwards. Governor Ogilvie, in his third budget that took effect on July 1, 1971, returned the proposed budgets for the public universities, saying that they were "outlandish." "We must take a hard look at our commitment to higher education in Illinois," Ogilvie declared in his budget message on 3 March 1971. "It is essential that we begin asking whether this system which has doubled its expenditures in the past four years has produced corresponding results. In the face of widespread student dissatisfaction and public impatience with the quality of higher education, it is essential that we ask why the system has failed to satisfy the very people it exists to serve."[51] Ogilvie's budget kept higher education equal to fiscal 1970, but redistributed the share, increasing support to private institutions and community colleges. The University of Illinois budget was reduced by $7 million, as was SIU's, but "state aid to private institutions (mostly medical) increased by $10 million, state support for community colleges rose by $7 million, as did student aid." As one later interpreter put it, "Although these developments were detrimental to the University of Illinois's ability to maintain its stature as a research university, they were far more damaging to the developing state universities with immature programs and less tradition," such as Chicago Circle.[52]

By this point, David Henry was sixty-five and ready to retire. He had served as president of the University of Illinois for seventeen years, longer than any other president to that point, and he realized that it was time to step down. In his last commencement address as President of the University, delivered in both Urbana and Chicago, in June 1971, one can sense the mood of foreboding and crisis: "American higher education is in a state of flux matched by few periods in its centuries-old history. The turbulent reassessment of traditional values and procedures so characteristic of the current generation of youth continues to affect the University as a whole and society in general." Henry saw that one of the key failures of universities was their inability to gain the understanding of the public that it was a special purpose community—with a specific purpose different from the larger society. Because of this, there was a broad loss of confidence in higher education, leading to a looming "financial crisis of major proportions," leaving universities "the prospect of receiving what is left over, after other public service needs are fulfilled."[53] Overall, the mood was of decline.

This dark outlook for the future of higher education continued, as Henry passed into his role as educational statesman. He served on Clark Kerr's Carnegie Commission on Higher Education, and later wrote a gloomy history of higher education, *Challenges Past, Challenges Future: An Analysis of Higher Education Since 1930*.[54] His thesis was that the 1970s were a far more serious crisis for higher education than the height of the Great Depression of the 1930s. He spent much of the decade organizing his papers and drafting a long, defensive memoir. A decade later, in the early 1990s, he drafted yet another memoir, privately published and dedicated to his grandchildren, entitled *Recollections in Tranquility*.[55] This second memoir emphasized the Wayne years, and had very little on Illinois. If it is true, as Garrison Keillor suggests, that, "no innocent man buys a gun, and no happy man writes his memoirs,"[56] it is significant that David Henry wrote two memoirs before he died.

Towards a New Model: The Urban Research University

The professional depression Henry felt in the mid-1970s was reflected at Chicago Circle as it approached its tenth anniversary. Enrollment had climbed over 300 percent since 1965, from 5,400 to over 18,000, where it roughly stabilized. Still, it lacked a sense of a distinctive identity. The chancellor at Circle, Norman Parker, stepped down when David Henry did, and Parker was replaced by physicist Warren Cheston. Cheston sought to move Circle towards open admissions, looking towards the model of the City College of New York, which had adopted that policy in 1969. Unwittingly, Cheston used the same rhetoric of "urban mission" that had proved so divisive before, and which predictably led to a faculty revolt almost immediately. Faculty opposition, budget pressures, plus personal scandal, plagued Cheston's tenure, and he soon announced his resignation.

In early June 1975, the *Chicago Sun-Times* published an extensive five-part report on the campus, entitled "UICC's 'Urban Mission?'" The first article was entitled: "Circle: university in name only?" under a heading "A 10-year identity crisis." The reporters found the university "still mired in confusion over what it means to be an urban university." While some of the problem was due to the "strife-worn, lame-duck chancellor" at Circle, more significant was its lack of central purpose or plan. Rather than a unified institution, it was "more a collection of medieval-like fiefdoms—the departments or colleges—led by feudal lords perpetually at war with each other and with the crown prince—the administration."[57]

The reporters reiterated the central problem with the university: "For 10 years, Circle has been unable to determine clearly what it should be about—its 'mission.' . . . Should it become a comprehensive, traditional university like UCLA, Michigan or Urbana? Or ought it be a unique, urban-oriented institution tailored to the particular needs of city students and metropolitan issues?" The reporters did not mention it, but perhaps Circle Campus was becoming an urban university after all, as it reflected the malaise of the city of which it was a part.[58]

David Henry continued his fight against the Circle faculty in his memoirs, where he strongly criticized the seeming failure of the UICC faculty to embrace an "urban mission." They had "too little understanding of the urban mission. Many of the faculty came from non-urban institutions and had no notion of the meaning of the charge to the Circle Campus. Worse, some had little enthusiasm for it." They modeled their efforts on traditional research universities, rather than embracing the "urban mission." But if the new faculty failed to understand this "urban mission," it was because Henry did not understand the significance of the attachment of the Chicago Circle Campus to the University of Illinois. Central to the mandate of the University of Illinois was graduate research, but Henry was critical of the speed by which aggressive faculty pushed for graduate research in Chicago. He insisted that his administration was "committed to the development of graduate work in due course, but felt that the first obligation was to fulfill the pledge made to the people of Illinois . . . completion of the undergraduate program, physically and educationally, would have priority."[59]

Yet given the nationwide dynamic of higher education in the mid 1960s, it was probably not possible to build a strong university without a serious commitment to advanced graduate training. The rapid expansion of the 1960s was followed by severe cutbacks in the 1970s throughout the nation. Loss of public confidence was part of it, but external factors also limited funds available for higher education. Practically speaking, the University of Illinois had only about six years to create a university in Chicago of any type, and whatever was created, that was all that it had for the next two decades at least. Henry's vision of an "urban university" was based upon service and access, a limited role, and if this had been fully implemented, Circle Campus would have remained a limited institution. His vision clashed with many of the new faculty, who sought to create a "Harvard on Halsted"[60] or a new UCLA, which would have challenged Urbana. But given the competitive and democratic environment in Illinois, this was not realistic either, for the private schools successfully limited the Circle Campus at its founding with a "gentlemen's agreement," and the other colleges and universities in the state, both public and private, were able to distribute funding and resources throughout Illinois, balancing institutions rather than concentrating on a few peaks of excellence. Henry's idea of an urban university was a limited one—research, but limited to applied, rather than the basic research of a comprehensive research university. Yet the research faculty's position was also limited in its vision—in not seeing the significance of its location, and the possibilities of both the strategic situation and the University's position in a restricted and competitive environment. The research-minded faculty were right in pushing for rapid growth in graduate programs, for that was the way to develop a strong, nationally known faculty, and also to win the federal funding that was contingent upon graduate instruction, but they were not able to see the larger context of higher education in Illinois. Only when graduate research at Circle Campus was threatened by the IBHE's attempt to explicitly mandate a restrictive "urban mission," were David Henry and the research-oriented faculty able to make common cause. But by then it was too late for any major expansion, and thus Circle Campus was barely able to maintain its position.

Each of these visions for the University of Illinois at Chicago Circle was unrealistic, as it did not take into account the needs of Chicago and the dynamic of the advancement of knowledge. What was needed was to see the campus as a new model for a university, as a comprehensive urban research university. This would not be merely an analogy of the nineteenth-century land-grant model, but rather one which emphasized basic fundamental research in urban, regional, and national issues. Perhaps one smaller-scale example is the University of Chicago's first department of sociology in the early twentieth century, which, by focusing on local and regional issues, built one of the strongest research traditions in sociology, helping to make it an internationally known university. What was not seen in the 1960s, either by David Henry, the Circle research faculty, or even the IBHE, was that the University of Illinois at Chicago Circle was in the process of developing a new model of higher education, of the comprehensive urban research university.

Epilogue: Becoming a Research University

The story of the Circle's "urban mission" does not end in the 1970s, of course. Circle Campus struggled throughout the decade, limping along with limited finances and an undergraduate student body recruited through open admissions. As a commuter campus, it was known by many in the Chicago area as a school of last resort: "If you couldn't get in anyplace else, you could always go to Circle." In most disciplines, however, the strong, research-oriented faculty that had been hired during the period of expansion between 1965 and 1970 did not disappear, but continued to be productive scholars. Among fellow academics, Circle was known as a campus where its faculty were better than its students, a mediocre undergraduate campus with good graduate programs.

By the late 1970s, Circle's administration and faculty began to incrementally improve the campus, with a slow but steady increase in admission standards, the development of an evening program, and an expansion of graduate degrees. While these improved Circle, what really transformed the campus was the vision of a new University of Illinois President, Stanley O. Ikenberry, who took over U of I in 1979. Ikenberry had come from Penn State, and saw the university's potential. It was Ikenberry who transformed the Circle Campus into a research university.

Circle Campus had been built in the 1960s on Chicago's near west side, a little over a mile east of the University of Illinois' Medical Center campus. The Medical Center had had a long and distinguished tradition, with some of its academic units dating back to the mid-nineteenth century. After World War II, the Medical Center had expanded, adding colleges of nursing and allied health professions to its professional colleges of dentistry, medicine, and pharmacy, and developing strong graduate programs in the life sciences. Under David Henry's administration, there was virtually no contact between the Medical Center and the new Circle Campus. Each reported directly to Henry as president in Urbana, and virtually the only time Circle and Medical Center faculty and administrators came together was at Urbana.

When, in the late 1970s, Henry's successor as president, John Corbally, suggested publicly that perhaps the Medical Center should merge with Circle, Henry warned him against it. Corbally let it drop, and soon retired from the university. His suggestion was a shrewd one, however, for it allowed his successor significant flexibility. Ikenberry, as a new president, could safely explore the possibilities. If the merger idea failed, he could always blame his predecessor; if it succeeded, it would be his accomplishment. There was significant opposition from some at Circle Campus, and the College of Medicine was almost unanimously hostile to the idea. Ikenberry debated whether merging the campuses was the right decision.

Ikenberry realized that it was essential to consult with David Henry. Henry was still at Urbana as an elder statesman, where he served as an emeritus professor while writing his memoirs. Henry considered a possible merger as a disaster, saying that it was against Circle's urban mission, which was to be an undergraduate division of the university, without any graduate or research programs. Henry also believed that it would ultimately be a threat and rival to the flagship campus. After meeting with Henry, Ikenberry knew what he needed to do. "For me, that confirmed that I was doing exactly the right thing," Ikenberry later recalled.[61]

On his first day as president, Stanley Ikenberry walked through the neighborhood from the Medical Center to Circle Campus, symbolically linking the two and signaling that the merger would be his major policy goal. After three years and in the face of significant opposition, he succeeded in consolidating the two campuses, creating the University of Illinois at Chicago in 1982. That made the new campus the largest, most comprehensive research university in the Chicago area.

Ikenberry rejected the remedial "urban mission" idea for the new campus. "My view of the urban mission was that it ought to be our urban mission to become the very strongest university that we could possibly become in the inner city of Chicago."[62] Working with the faculty, Ikenberry continued the gradual rise in admissions standards, and he even created an Honors College at the Chicago campus. In 1987, the Carnegie Foundation published its new rankings, and it acknowledged the fact that UIC had become a Research I university, based on its funded research and production of doctoral degrees. In the mid-1990s, UIC developed its "Great Cities Commitment," as a major interdisciplinary research effort directed at urban issues, not only in Chicago, but also for urban areas worldwide. Through special funding, the Great Cities program implements hundreds of teaching, research, and service programs, ranging from urban transportation studies to neighborhood planning to public health initiatives. With a goal of "civic engagement," the Great Cities initiative has developed numerous partnerships with community and government agencies.

Within thirty years of its opening, UIC emerged as one of four major research universities in Illinois. The conflict over visions of its relation to the city had been resolved. While there was a strong institutional memory of David Henry's vision of an "urban mission," the campus had embraced the ideal of academic excellence, graduate education, and basic research. In becoming the University of Illinois at Chicago, the campus reconciled the two visions, possibly developing a new model in American higher education, the comprehensive urban research university. Only time will tell if this is indeed a distinct model for the future of higher education.

Notes

1. The origins of an "urban grant" idea has been traced to Paul Ysvilaker of the Ford Foundation, who first proposed a system of urban-grant universities at the annual meeting of the Association of Urban Universities in 1958. Maurice R. Berube, *The Urban University in America* (Westport, Conn.: Greenwood Press, 1978), 125. See J. Martin Klotsche, *The Urban University: And the Future of Our Cities* (New York: Harper and Row, 1966). Klotsche was chancellor of University of Wisconsin at Milwaukee. See also Clark Kerr's speech before the New York City College's Phi Beta Kappa chapter, "The US today needs 67 Urban Grant Universities to stand beside its 67 Land Grant Universities," *New York Times*, 22 October 1967. It was printed by City College in a pamphlet, entitled "The Urban-Grant University: A Model for the Future" (New York: City College, 1968).
2. See George Rosen, *Decision-Making Chicago Style: The Genesis of a University of Illinois Campus* (Urbana: University of Illinois Press, 1980), and Adam Cohen and Elizabeth Taylor, *American Pharaoh: Mayor Richard J. Daley: His Battle For Chicago and the Nation* (Boston: Little, Brown, 2000).
3. David Henry, *Career Highlights and Some Sidelights*, Memoir, June 1983, p. 256. University Archives, President's Papers, David D. Henry Papers, 2/12/20, Box 25 (hereafter cited as DDH Papers). David Henry's papers are located in the University Archives, Urbana, Illinois. Henry had all his speeches as Illinois' president bound in orange bindings, with a concluding memoir, written between 1976 and 1984, bound separately. He later wrote a second memoir that was also privately published.
4. For a general history, see Roger L. Geiger, *Research and Relevant Knowledge: American Research Universities since World War II* (New Brunswick, N.J.: Transaction Publishers, 2004 [1993]).
5. The University of Illinois at Chicago (UIC) was officially formed in 1982, with the merger of Circle Campus with the University of Illinois Medical Center.
6. David Henry, *Recollections in Tranquility*, memoir, privately published in Florida (1993), p. 30. A copy is in the DDH Papers, Box 29. Other copies exist at Wayne State and The Pennsylvania State University.
7. Daniel Boorstin, "Universities in the Republic of Letters: A Review of Laurence Veysey's, 'The Emergence of the American University,'" *Perspectives in American History* 1 (1967): 371.
8. David Henry, *Career Highlights*, iii.
9. Ibid., 93.
10. An interesting irony, as Navy Pier would be the site of the temporary Chicago undergraduate campus of the University of Illinois, from 1946 to 1965.
11. Henry, *Recollections*, 12.
12. Ibid., 42.
13. Leslie L. Hanawalt, *A Place of Light: The History of Wayne State University. A Centennial Publication* (Detroit: Wayne State University Press, 1968).
14. See Henry, *Recollections*, 60.
15. Quoted in Ellen Schrecker, *No Ivory Tower: McCarthyism and the Universities* (New York: Oxford University Press, 1986), 91–92.
16. Winton Solberg, "Academic McCarythism and Keynesian Economics: The Bowen Controversy at the University of Illinois," *History of Political Economy* 29, no. 1 (1997): 55–81.
17. George D. Stoddard, *The Pursuit of Education: An Autobiography* (New York: Vantage Press, 1981).
18. There was suspicion in Chicago that the Urbana administration did not particularly favor a permanent branch in Chicago. The previous president, George Stoddard, had publicly dismissed calls for a full undergraduate campus, and the legislature had to force the trustees to do it, passing a bill to that effect in 1951. It took fourteen years for that campus to be opened.
19. Illinois State Senate, 64th General Assembly, Senate Bill No. 388 (1945).
20. David Henry, "A Call for Action," 1955, DDH Papers.
21. David Henry, "Convocation at Navy Pier," 20 October 1955, p. 3, DDH Papers.

22. David Henry, "Statement on 'Chicago Undergraduate Center,'" at alumni meeting, LaSalle Hotel, Chicago, 19 January 1956, DDH Papers, "A Call to Action," pp. 4, 6.

23. David Henry, "Navy Pier Convocation Speech," 18 October 1956, p. 5, DDH Papers.

24. David Henry. "Collection of Speeches for AUU," 1958, p. 9, DDH Papers.

25. Ibid., 14.

26. Ibid., 20–21.

27. Ibid., 18.

28. *Chicago Sun-Times,* 1 June 1975, p. 46.

29. Remarks before Citizen's Committee, 13 May 1966, Chicago Circle File, DDH papers, 2/12/20, Box 27.

30. David Henry, "Award of 'Chicago Builder's Congress,'" 1 December 1966, pp. 5, 9, Chicago Circle File, DDH Papers, 2/12/20, Box 27.

31. See Lyle Lanier, "A Critique of the Philosophy of Progress." in Twelve Southerners *I'll Take My Stand: The South and the Agrarian Tradition,* (New York: Harper, 1930).

32. There is some significant controversy over Lanier's role in Circle's development. As University Provost, Lanier had control of university academic affairs and Circle's expanding academic program, but he also worked very closely with Henry. What appears to be the case is that Lanier sought to increase the quality of Circle by encouraging the hiring of research faculty, while at the same time limiting their ambitions to expand into doctoral level programs that would unduly compete with the flagship campus in Urbana. This was an unsustainable position, although most of the Circle research faculty's anger was directed at Henry, rather than Lanier.

33. See Milton Rakove, "Research vs. Teaching: Our Circle Campus Opportunity," *Chicago Sun-Times,* 16 May 1965, sec. 2, p. 3.

34. David Henry, DDH Papers, 2/12/20, Box 3, and Adm. Org-Chicago Circle.

35. "Memo by Research Oriented Faculty," April 1966, Office of the UIC Historian Files, UIC.

36. Ibid.

37. David Henry, "The Urban University and Urban Society," address at the Wayne State University Centennial, 28 June 1968, p. 11, DDH Papers, 2/12/20, Box 12, manuscript 308.

38. Ibid.

39. Ibid.

40. Ibid.

41. Ibid.

42. Speaker of the Illinois House Paul Powell held the University of Illinois budget hostage until they acquiesced to Powell's desire to create a separate board of trustees for Southern Illinois University. See Robert E. Hartley, *Paul Powell of Illinois: A Lifelong Democrat* (Carbondale: Southern Illinois University Press, 1999), 50.

43. See Illinois Board of Higher Education, *A Master Plan for Higher Education in Illinois* (Springfield, Ill.: 1964).

44. Carol Everly Floyd, "Centralization and Decentralization of State Decision Making for Public Universities: Illinois, 1960–1990," *History of Higher Education Annual* 12 (1992): 101–18.

45. James Worthy memoir, privately published, chapter 11, p. 14, Office of the UIC Historian files, UIC.

46. Ibid., 28.

47. Taylor Pensoneau, *Governor Richard Ogilvie: In the Interest of the State* (Carbondale: Southern Illinois University Press, 1997), 173–75.

48. "University's Official Response to Board of Higher Education Study on Governance," *Faculty Letter From the Office of the President, University of Illinois,* no. 206, 6 November 1970, p. 8.

49. *Provisional Development Plan,* p. 34, quoted in Ibid., at 10.

50. *Chicago Sun-Times,* 2 June 1975, p. 26.

51. Pensoneau, *Governor Richard Ogilvie,* 183–84.

52. Roger Geiger, *Research and Relevant Knowledge,* 265.

53. David Henry, "A Crucial Confrontation in a Turbulent Time," Commencement address, 19, 20 June 1971, p. 10. in *Interpreting the Public University and the Land-Grant College Tradition, 1955–1971,* ed. David D. Henry (December 1976), 796, DDH Papers.

54. David D. Henry, *Challenges Past, Challenges Future: An Analysis of Higher Education Since 1930,* The Carnegie Council Series (San Francisco: Jossey-Bass Publishers, 1975).

55. David Henry, *Recollections in Tranquility* (1993).

56. Garrison Keillor, *Lake Wobegon Days* (New York: Viking, 1990).

57. *Chicago Sun-Times*, 1 June 1975, p. 5.

58. See, for example, Janet Abu-Lughod, *New York, Chicago, Los Angeles: America's Global Cities*, (Minneapolis: University of Minnesota Press, 1999), especially her chapter on Chicago from the 1970s to the 1990s, entitled, "Postapocalypse Chicago."

59. David Henry, *Career Highlights*, 257.

60. The main street through the Circle Campus was called Halsted.

61. Stanley O. Ikenberry, interview by Fred Beuttler, Office of the UIC Historian, 9 November 2000, p. 13.

62. Ibid., 16.

CHAPTER 11
STUDENTS

PERSPECTIVES ON OPEN-ACCESS HIGHER EDUCATION

DAVID E. LAVIN AND DAVID HYLLEGARD

As we approach the end of the century, uncertainty clouds the direction and form of opportunity policies for higher education in the United States. These policies have their roots in a national preoccupation with equality of opportunity that began to take shape at midcentury. Education was one of the most volatile topics of debate during the struggle to broaden opportunity for the members of disadvantaged minority groups. The Supreme Court desegregation decision of 1954 was a fundamental step toward reducing inequalities in schooling. By the early 1960s, the focus on higher education had become sharper, as the federal government intervened in the South to begin the racial integration of universities. Throughout the 1960s and during the early 1970s, a variety of public and private efforts were undertaken to lower the barriers to college. Although the specific influence of individual policies cannot be precisely gauged, federal and state grant and loan programs, proliferation of postsecondary institutions, and special admissions programs targeted to minorities all stimulated the increase of enrollment—especially minority enrollment—in higher education. Indeed, the racial gap in the college enrollment of high school graduates practically disappeared: the rate of college enrollment by black graduates, which was 77 percent of the white rate in 1960, reached 98 percent of that rate by 1975 (U.S. Bureau of the Census 1987a, table 233), though, to be sure, this trend was less impressive than it appears because the high school graduation rate of blacks remained below that of whites.

In the latter half of the 1970s, these gains began to erode, and by 1985 the rate of college enrollment for black high school graduates had fallen back to 76 percent of the white rate—just where it had been in 1960 (U.S. Bureau of the Census 1987a, table 233). Although the relative weights of different factors influencing the resurgent gap in college participation are uncertain, one source undoubtedly was the decline in federal support for higher education under the Reagan administration. Part of the decline in black enrollment can be attributed to cuts in student financial aid and to shifts in the types of aid available—away from grants and toward loans. Presumably these changes in financial aid disproportionately affected minorities, who were far more likely than whites to come from low-income families (College Board 1985).[1]

Coincident with federal reductions in support for higher education was a change in the climate of debate about educational policy. Through the 1960s and early 1970s, a liberal perspective, based on a belief that educational attainment has a major influence on an individual's life chances, had been ascendant. This belief was the foundation of various policy efforts to narrow inequality of educational opportunity. After the mid-1970s, a conservative reaction to liberal programs gathered momentum. A spate of reform proposals blamed higher education for an alleged decline in academic standards and for encouraging a pluralism that led to "cultural dilution" of college curricula.[2] Moreover, higher education was sometimes perceived as responsible, at least in part, for diminishing educational quality at lower levels of schooling. In one of the most important reports, the National Commission on Excellence in Education (1983) claimed that the economic position of the United States was at risk because its educational institutions were "being engulfed by a rising tide of mediocrity that threatens our very future as a Nation." Asserting that educational decline was a source of U.S. global economic decline, the report's authors warned that the nation had, in effect, "been committing an act of unthinking, unilateral educational disarmament." Among its many recommendations for reform, the commission called for more stringent requirements for both high school graduation and admission to four-year colleges and universities. In response to the perception of a decline in standards, some states—Florida, for example—instituted standardized testing procedures in an effort to ensure that college students were meeting minimum criteria of academic competence.[3] The conservative trend may have disproportionately discouraged college enrollment and depressed educational attainment among minority students, who were more likely than whites to have serious weaknesses in their high school academic preparation.

Neither the climate of debate nor the changes in policy were informed by any systematic evidence about the results of higher education opportunity programs begun in the 1960s and early 1970s. Indeed, when the conservative reaction was gaining ascendancy, the results of these programs were not in. Indeed, one detailed review of the major reform proposals concluded that they were based on weak arguments and poor data (Stedman and Smith 1983); the authors asserted as well that the reformist agenda exhibited a shift away from concern for equal educational opportunity. Though data cannot definitively resolve the policy disputes between liberals and conservatives, they can help to clarify some of the issues in the debate about "equity versus excellence." Given the changing policies and shifts in value priorities over the past three decades, this seems an appropriate time to take stock of college access policies.

One way to assess equity issues in higher education is to examine an institution that made an unusual effort to create educational opportunity. We shall do this for the seventeen-campus, two hundred thousand—student system of the City University of New York (CUNY), the nation's third-largest higher education system and its largest urban university. In 1970, CUNY initiated its open-admissions policy, arguably the nation's most ambitious attempt to expand college access for minorities.

Although the program was limited to a single university system, its outcomes have more general implications for higher education policy. The university is located in a city that contains large concentrations of lower-class blacks and Hispanics, two of the most disadvantaged minority groups in the nation, and typically the main foci of opportunity programs in higher education. Moreover, the CUNY open-admissions policy was designed to create more educational opportunity than other open-access models, and thus it may be regarded empirically as a limiting case from among a range of possible opportunity programs: its results provide an indication of the outcomes possible under the most favorable conditions.

The City University of New York and Its Open-Admissions Program

The open-admissions policy at CUNY evolved from a complex historical context. The university has its origins in the founding in 1847 of the City College of New York (CCNY), the best-known school in today's multi-campus system of nine four-year (senior) colleges and eight two-year community colleges. Founded through a public referendum, CCNY had a populist mission from the outset. In the words of its first head, Horace Webster, at the inaugural ceremonies, "The experiment is to be tried, whether the highest education can be given to the masses; whether the children of the whole people can be educated; and whether an institution of learning, of the highest grade, can be successfully controlled by the popular will, not by the privileged few, but by the privileged many" (Rudy 1949, 29).

These words were more rhetoric than reality in the college's early years, for the student body consisted mainly of the sons of prosperous merchants and professionals. But by the end of the nineteenth century and the beginning of the twentieth, the college began to play a significant role in the lives of impoverished immigrants, especially Jewish families arriving from eastern Europe. In the 1930s, CCNY students were regarded as among the most able in the nation, and the college came to be known as the "proletarian Harvard." Its graduates' achievements in diverse walks of life contributed to a faith in the college as a path out of poverty.

Partly as a result of growing demand, new institutions were added to the municipal college system. Hunter College had been founded in 1870 as a teacher-training school for women, and in the 1920s and 1930s, three more four-year schools were established in Brooklyn, Queens, and the Bronx.[4] In spite of these expansions, the colleges could not accommodate all who wanted to attend, especially after World War II. Even the addition of three community colleges in the 1950s failed to provide enough seats.

Although the increasing demand for college was not based on a precise understanding of the stunning economic changes in the United States and especially in New York since the turn of the century, rising educational aspirations were no doubt partly attuned to economic aspirations. Broadly speaking, the transition from an agricultural to an industrial system that began in the 1800s was essentially completed by the first half of this century, and a new transition was gaining momentum: a shift from a goods-producing economy to a service-rendering one, typically referred to as the emergence of postindustrial society.

Trends in the American occupational profile clearly reflect these developments. The decline in agricultural employment has been spectacular: in 1900 more than a third of all workers were in farming; by mid-century only about 10 percent were so employed; and by the 1980s fewer than four in one hundred were.[5] Decline is also apparent within the lower levels of the blue-collar work force: in 1900 about one in eight workers was an unskilled laborer; by mid-century the figure was one in fifteen. Since mid-century the proportion of semiskilled workers has also fallen, probably as a consequence of the vulnerability of this tier of the labor force to automated production (Featherman and Hauser 1978, Chapter 2). Shrinkage in the agricultural and blue-collar sectors of the labor force has been offset by explosive growth in the share of jobs in the white-collar sector: between 1900 and the 1980s, clerical and sales jobs more than tripled (from 7.5 percent to 25 percent), while the share of the top tier of the white-collar category—professional, technical, and managerial workers—expanded from about 10 percent to almost 30 percent of the work force.[6]

As Bell (1973) and others (Featherman and Hauser 1978) have suggested, perhaps the fundamental characteristic of this transformed economy is its implied demand for a college-educated work force. Although scholars may disagree about the mechanisms that link education and the economy and about whether economic changes have brought about an overall upgrade in the skill levels of occupations, educational requirements have risen coincident with change in the occupational structure.[7] Rumberger (1981), for example, estimates that based on changes in the skill levels of jobs between 1940 and 1970, the percentage requiring four or more years of college increased from 8 to 22 percent, while those requiring less than a high school degree declined from 29 percent to 15 percent.

The national trend from goods production to service has been even more evident in New York. After World War II, the city's manufacturing sector began a sharp decline. Accounting for thirty percent of jobs in 1950, manufacturing provided only 20 percent in 1970 and little more than 10 percent by the mid-1980s (Mollenkopf 1988).[8] By contrast, the service sector—including education, the arts and culture, business and financial services, government, health, and social welfare—experienced enormous growth. In 1950, these services accounted for a third of all jobs in the city; by 1970, they provided almost half the jobs. In the 1980s, nearly 60 percent of the city's workers were employed in such positions. The pace of change in New York makes it a leading example of a postindustrial city.[9]

These changes in the New York labor market were associated with rising educational requirements for entry-level jobs. Partly because the demand for seats in the city's municipal colleges outstripped available places during the 1950s, entrance requirements rose throughout that decade. Indeed, between 1952 and 1961, the number of new admissions to baccalaureate programs actually declined from 8,859, or 17 percent of high school graduates in the city, to 8,563, or 13 percent (Holy 1962, 91). Because admission to the municipal colleges was becoming more difficult as demand was increasing, questions were being raised about the appropriateness of such a policy in a publicly supported university (Holy 1962, 68–69, 73, 127–28).

In the 1960s, requirements stiffened even further: a high school average in the mid- to upper 80s was generally required for admission to CUNY's four-year colleges, and some years an average in the 90s was needed at certain schools. Gaining a seat at many of these institutions was virtually as difficult as in selective private colleges. Even for admission to a community college, students needed at least a 75 average.

The combination of a changing labor market and the growing selectivity of New York's public colleges coincided with a major demographic transition that began in New York during the 1950s. In that decade, nearly seven hundred thousand blacks and Hispanics came to New York City, in effect replacing a similar number of whites who left during that time in the postwar exodus to the suburbs.[10] The newcomers typically had little education and few job skills. Unlike earlier periods when much work was available for immigrants with few skills, the changing labor market provided fewer employment opportunities for the new arrivals. As a result, they were often unemployed or under-employed, and when they found work it was typically in positions at the bottom rungs of the occupational ladder. Welfare rolls swelled accordingly.

Adding to the difficulties of blacks and Hispanics was their severe disadvantage in the public education system of the city. They typically attended segregated schools where grades generally were quite low; they were much more likely than whites to attend vocational high schools or to be placed in nonacademic tracks within general high schools. Consequently, they were far less likely than white students to receive college preparatory diplomas. These factors limited the number who could qualify for traditional college programs. By the time minority students finished high school, they were poorly positioned in the increasingly rigorous competition for places in the City University. Limited access to college at a time when educational requirements of the labor market were rising foretold a gloomy outlook for life chances in New York's minority communities.

A look at the historical experience of various groups in the university suggests that by the 1960s, CUNY was serving different groups in very unequal ways. Around the turn of the century, the student body had been composed largely of the sons and daughters of Jewish immigrants of eastern European origin. They remained the numerically dominant group through the first half of the century. After the Second World War, enrollments became ethnically more diverse in some respects: students of Irish and Italian ancestry in particular began to attend the university in increasing numbers, and by the late 1960s members of these ethnic groups accounted for a third of entering classes.[11] But what the university had done for these earlier groups arriving from Europe it had failed to do for the new arrivals from the American South and from the Caribbean. Because of the disadvantages to which they were subject in the city's public education system, the latter were largely excluded from CUNY's senior colleges and underrepresented at the two-year level.

Framed by the national preoccupation of the 1960s with issues of equal opportunity in American society, the question of minority access to CUNY grew in importance in that decade. One of the driving forces was the increasing militancy of the civil rights movement. Across the country, civil disobedience, strident demonstrations, and riots had riveted national attention on various issues of racial inequality. A developing sense of urgency about equal opportunity was expressed in the enactment of such "great society" programs as Head Start and the "war on poverty." These programs reflected a belief by the liberal establishment that social policy could and should be used to advance equity.

New York City echoed the tenor of the times, both in the racial tensions that arose with minority efforts to gain greater control over the public schools in their communities, and in efforts to establish a civilian review board to investigate complaints of police brutality toward minority individuals.[12] It was in this broad context that the question of minority representation at CUNY took center stage.

Movement toward a policy of open admissions developed on two fronts.[13] One was institutional. In 1963, Albert H. Bowker left his post as dean of the Stanford University graduate school to become chancellor of the CUNY system.[14] Paradoxically, one of the main reasons that the university's trustees had hired Bowker was to spur the development of a centralized program of doctoral studies in all of the major academic areas, which he accomplished. But soon after his arrival, he was struck by CUNY's unresponsiveness to the burgeoning college-age population and to the demographic changes in the city. He perceived that political support for the university might erode if it maintained its highly selective admissions policies. He believed that the long-term interests of CUNY required a major expansion of access—one that involved substantial revision of admissions standards.

The transition from the exclusive admissions practices of the early 1960's to the open-admissions policy of 1970 began modestly. In an initial effort in 1964 to increase minority enrollment, Bowker obtained funds from the state to set up in the community colleges an experimental program known as College Discovery. Two years later he gained state support for a special minority admissions program in the four-year colleges. Known by the acronym SEEK (Search for Education, Elevation and Knowledge), it began in fall 1966 and immediately became the major avenue of minority entry to CUNY's senior colleges.

The establishment of these programs added momentum to the drive for broader access to the university. By 1968, Bowker had persuaded the CUNY trustees to approve a 100 percent admissions plan, beginning in 1975. To meet the broad demand for college and to provide further opportunity for minority students, a stratified admissions scheme was proposed in the university's 1968 master plan:

1. The top 25 percent of high school graduates would be offered admission to a senior college baccalaureate program;

2. The top two-thirds of graduates would qualify for community colleges (the top 50 percent of this group would be eligible for transfer programs, while the rest would qualify for career programs);

3. About 6 percent would be admitted to senior colleges through the SEEK program—and thus outside of the regular admissions procedure—and about 4 percent would be admitted to community colleges via the College Discovery program;

4. All others could enroll in educational skills centers, which would provide job-oriented technical training. These centers also would provide "college adapter" courses designed to identify students with potential for community college–career programs (Board of Higher Education 1968).

Though highly stratified, this plan represented a significant step forward in broadening access to the university. In light of what was coming, however, it seemed quite modest. Indeed, Bowker's foreword to the master plan was prophetic: "Change, however well anticipated, has a way of making the most forward looking plans obsolete. This plan is not likely to be an exception" (Board of Higher Education 1968, vii).

CUNY proposals in this period were sometimes couched in rhetoric about proportions of minority students in the university and whether their representation was in line with their proportions among high school graduates in the city. Such rhetoric helped to crystallize a growing concern among whites, particularly those who formed the traditional Jewish constituency of CUNY: during a period when admission was highly selective, were places being allocated to students who did not meet traditional criteria—at the expense of other qualified students? References to "proportion" in trustee meetings irritated a particularly sensitive nerve in the Jewish community: the noxious concept of the quota, which had once been used against them by private colleges (Steinberg 1974; Wechsler 1977).

At the same time that whites were worried that merit in the admissions process was being eroded by a competing principle of quotas—and hence, that some seats of deserving students would be taken by other less academically able ones—minorities were increasingly dissatisfied, feeling that not enough was being done to advance educational opportunity. Their perception of the university was epitomized by City College, sitting high on a hill in the middle of Harlem, historically the most important and most famous of New York City's black communities. Black and Hispanic students had been criticizing the college on a variety of counts for not doing enough to expand minority enrollment. Even with the SEEK program, blacks and Hispanics in 1968 constituted only about 10 percent of the CCNY student body although they comprised close to a quarter of the New York City high school graduating class (City University of New York 1968–70). In February 1969 a minority student organization called upon the administration to alleviate "conditions that deny the very existence of the Black and Puerto Rican community" (*Observation Post* 1969). The students issued five demands and insisted that the CCNY president, Buell Gallagher, "utilize whatever means necessary" to meet them. In the confrontation to come, these demands formed the agenda for negotiations (*Observation Post* 1969):

1. A separate school of black and Puerto Rican studies;

2. A separate orientation program for black and Puerto Rican freshmen;

3. A voice for students in setting guidelines for the SEEK program, including the hiring and firing of personnel;

4. Assurance that the racial composition of all entering classes would reflect the black and Puerto Rican population of the New York City high schools;

5. The requirement of black and Puerto Rican history and the Spanish language for all education majors.

President Gallagher met with the students, but no specific agreements were reached. The group then occupied a part of the administration building for several hours in an effort to demonstrate that it could shut down the college if it so chose (Penzer 1969).

A developing budget crisis at the university intruded upon events at CCNY. The university faced a substantial reduction in the budget for the following year, and Bowker stated that without more funding, there would be no freshman class in the fall. This served to galvanize various student and community groups into action, the most significant manifestation of which was a rally of thirteen thousand CUNY students at the state capitol in Albany in March. Although some progress was made on the budgetary crisis, minority students, apparently fearing that a dollar shortfall would result in "virtually no Black or Puerto Rican students in the University," called for a strike in support of the five demands that had been made earlier (*Campus* 1969). Shortly thereafter, some two hundred minority students, joined later by some whites, occupied campus buildings and announced that the "University of Harlem" would remain closed until the college administration met the five demands (Ackerman 1969).

The propriety of closing the college became an issue in the upcoming mayoral primary, in which John V. Lindsay sought renomination. His base of support included blacks, Puerto Ricans to a lesser extent, and a substantial number of high-status Jews and Protestants, along with a sprinkling of affluent Catholics. Lindsay supported the closing of the college and conciliatory efforts. His main rival, Mario Procaccino, a CCNY alumnus, attracted working-class and lower-middle-class Irish, Italians, and Jews who resided largely in the boroughs outside Manhattan. He and other politicians saw the shutting down of the college as "appeasement." The controversy reflected a larger issue in the city: whether Lindsay had done too much to help minorities, at the expense of whites from the working and lower-middle classes (Glazer and Moynihan 1970, xxvi–xxix).

Shortly thereafter, Procaccino and Mario Biaggi, a Bronx congressman representing a white working-class constituency, along with the militant Jewish Defense League, obtained show-cause orders against the college for shutting down and a court order that set a date for reopening. Congressman Adam Clayton Powell of Harlem urged the insurgents to defy the injunction. By early May the students did vacate the buildings, but matters then became chaotic, with daily incidents of violence that culminated in the burning of the auditorium in the college's main student center (*New York Times* 1969). Such incidents brought an end to the negotiations which had been taking place and Gallagher resigned.

Subsequently, negotiations resumed between the dissidents and the college administration, which now was headed by an acting president designated by the CUNY trustees. The fruit of these sessions was a proposal for what was in effect an ethnically based dual admissions plan, whereby 50 percent of the CCNY freshman class in fall 1970 would be drawn from poverty areas or designated ghetto high schools, while the other half would be selected under the traditional competitive admissions criteria, high school grades and Scholastic Aptitude Test scores (Board of Higher Education 1969a).

The proposal was sent to the college faculty senate for approval, but scathing public reaction pre-empted faculty discussion. All of the mayoral candidates attacked the proposal. Procaccino threatened to initiate legal action to prevent its implementation, claiming that it was "unfair and discriminatory" and would exclude "intelligent, qualified, and ambitious students" from CUNY (Fox 1969a; McNamara 1969). Mayor Lindsay, initially noncommittal, later asserted that "if this is a quota system, I am against it" (Fox 1969a; Greenspan 1969; McNamara 1969).

Eventually, the faculty senate voted to reject the dual admissions plan and recommended instead the admission over the next two semesters of a few hundred additional students from poverty areas, who were not to take the place of any students who qualified for admission under the competitive criteria (Fox 1969b, 1969c). But the senate, in sending this proposal to the university's Board of Higher Education, also stated that "a large disadvantaged segment of the City population, for social, economic and education reasons, has been unable to receive these benefits [of higher education]. The most equitable way to attain this stated goal is by a system of 'open enrollment' financially supported by the City, State, and Federal Governments" (Faculty Senate 1969).

In June, the spotlight shifted to Bowker and the CUNY trustees. Public hearings underscored the conflicts inherent in any plan that used ethnicity as a principle for admissions. The perceived conflict between merit and quotas seemed irreconcilable. Ultimately, a way out of the quandary was found in a proposal put forth by the powerful New York City Central Labor Council, a coalition of major unions. Representatives of this group argued that many members of white ethnic groups— particulary Catholics of Irish and Italian ancestry—would be shut out of any plan that gave special preference to minorities and imposed stringent admissions criteria for everyone else. The Labor Council proposed that the only proper plan was one that would guarantee admissions to all (Board of Higher Education 1960b). Only this idea seemed to put to rest the fear that increased representation of some groups would come at the expense of others. Both within and outside the university, a consensus seemed to form around the approach of letting everyone in.

By early July, Bowker and his staff had decided that an open-admissions program was the solution to the impasse over the expansion of access to the university and that the plan of 100 percent admissions by 1975 should be moved up to fall 1970. The proposal to guarantee to every graduate of a New York City high school a place in the university beginning in the fall of 1970 was approved by the trustees, not only for City College but across all the colleges of the university (Board of Higher Education 1969c). In effect, Bowker's early drive for expanded access, which he promoted not only as a matter of equity but also as one of institutional self-interest, coalesced with the concerns voiced in the student uprising. Together, both institutional and student interests formed a mechanism for a huge expansion of the university.

The funding for this expansion was by no means assured at the time the open-admissions resolution was passed, but Bowker was ultimately able to obtain the support of Mayor Lindsay and— grudgingly—Governor Nelson Rockefeller (Gordon 1975).

The CUNY board's open-admissions decision left a major question unanswered: what should be the mechanism for allocating students to the various CUNY colleges? The process of hammering out an actual admissions model engendered further controversy. A special commission had been appointed and charged with the task of developing a set of admissions criteria. The members of the commission represented important constituencies of the university, including groups that were traditional beneficiaries of CUNY education as well as advocates for minority group aspirations. These groups had different conceptions of a proper admissions plan. A key issue was not merely access to the university but access to *senior colleges*. Minority members of the admissions commission perceived the four-year schools as far more valuable in the struggle to overcome disadvantaged status (University Commission on Admissions, 1969, 62):

> Less than fifty percent of Black and Puerto Rican students who enter high school graduate; the majority of the survivors fall in the bottom halves of their classes, with large numbers graduating with averages below seventy (70). What, one must ask, will be their earning capacities and ability to provide for their families twenty years hence, in competition with their white contemporaries who will have gone to the senior colleges and graduate schools? What will be their relative earning capacities even if they finish two-year career programs in community colleges and go on to become X-ray technicians and low-level managers in factories? In short, we see unending societal clash unless this vicious educational cycle is smashed. We propose to do this by giving *all* high school graduates a fair and equal chance to achieve a B.A. degree.

On the other side, traditional constituents of the university continued to be concerned that the effort to broaden access would undermine admissions criteria based on academic merit. Some feared that increased opportunity for minority students might come at the expense of seats for previously qualified students (Board of Higher Education 1969d). There was, in short, a perceived conflict between equity and excellence in the admissions process.

Ultimately, the university formulated an admissions model that addressed both concerns. The plan created two admissions pools, one for the senior colleges and the other for the two-year schools. Students who graduated from high school with at least an 80 average (in academic, college preparatory courses) *or* who ranked in the top 50 percent of their high school graduating class were guaranteed a place in a senior college if that was their preference (Board of Higher Education 1969e).[15] The two criteria combined a traditional admissions standard with one intended to provide greater access. The high school-average criterion meant that students who would have qualified for a senior college before open admissions would continue to do so; the primary aim of the class-rank criterion was to increase minority representation in the senior colleges by creating a pathway for students from ghetto high schools where averages tended to be low. Students who fell short of the senior college criteria were placed in the community college pool.[16]

In September 1970 a freshman class of almost 35,000 students took their seats at CUNY—a 75 percent increase over the previous year's entering class. The open-admissions era began under a glare of media publicity, both national and local. That the national spotlight focused on CUNY may seem curious, for open-access higher education is hardly a new idea in American higher education. Indeed, its roots go back to the middle of the nineteenth century, when the land-grant colleges were established under the first Morrill Act of 1862. These colleges, most located in the Midwest, offered admission to all high school graduates; in the 1930s, the general college of the University of Minnesota was open to any student with a high school diploma (Wechsler 1977, 241–42). After World War II, California had established its so-called differential access version of open admissions, wherein any high school graduate could attend one of the levels of the state's public higher education system. Part of the reason for the attention given to CUNY was that the events leading to open admissions embodied so clearly the political and racial conflict that characterized American society in the 1960s. Also striking was the sheer abruptness of change: no major educational institution had ever moved so quickly from a highly selective admission standard to a policy of guaranteed access for all high school graduates.

CUNY's program incorporated other unique features. One was the admissions model itself. At least on paper, the plan was less stratified than the three-tiered California model, in which the university level accepts only the top 12.5 percent of high school graduates, the state colleges admit the top third, and the two-year community colleges accept all others. The CUNY system formally distinguished only two- and four-year colleges, thus constituting a two-tiered system. Its open-admissions model was designed to generate a less rigid sorting of students between senior and community colleges than the California system allowed. In effect, the CUNY effort was more senior college–oriented and was especially intended to increase minority enrollment in these institutions.

A second feature of the university's effort to increase educational opportunity concerned mobility between its two- and four-year colleges. To further enhance their chances of earning a baccalaureate degree, all graduates of the community colleges were guaranteed admission to a senior college with full credit. According to the plan, the community colleges would not be dead-end institutions whose primary function was to provide terminal vocational education.

A third unique aspect of open admissions was CUNY's concept of educational opportunity, which embraced not only access but also outcome. In its decision to commit the university to a policy of open admissions, its board of trustees stated that opportunity would be merely an illusion if access were followed by a high rate of student failure. Accordingly, the university developed extensive programs of remediation, counseling, and related services that were designed to enhance students' academic chances. In addition, the board decided that students should not be dismissed for academic reasons during the grace period of the freshman year. In effect, the responsibility for academic success lay not only with the students but also with the institution.

Overarching the open-admissions program was a financial-aid policy that had been in place since CCNY's founding in the nineteenth century: free tuition. CUNY's colleges were tuition free for all matriculated students, including those who were attending part-time.

Open Admissions and Academic Standards

CUNY's program was in the forefront of the egalitarian efforts of the time, arguably the most ambitious effort to create educational opportunity ever attempted in American higher education. Its far-reaching nature produced great concern in many quarters. One source of anxiety was the university's rapid transformation from one of the nation's more selective institutions into its most accessible. Some questioned whether the open-admissions policy could reverse the effects of prior economic and educational disadvantage, which were especially severe among New York City's minority youth. Given their handicaps, there was concern that academic standards would be swept away in a deluge of incompetent students. Ultimately, the degradation of CUNY diplomas might, it was feared, undercut graduates' chances of landing good jobs and acceptance for postgraduate study. Vice President Spiro Agnew, for example, denounced the CUNY plan as a giveaway of "100,000 devalued diplomas" (1971, 81). Others saw in open admissions a threat that ultimately would erode even the standards of the professions:

> Though I know many brilliant people I would not care to have as my doctor or my children's teacher, it is undoubtedly true that a unidimensional measure of academic excellence can be used to set a special, higher floor for many occupations and professions. The ardently egalitarian . . . are fundamentally unconvincing: one can dismiss them with the curse that they should cross the river on a bridge designed by an engineer from an engineering school where students were admitted by lottery; and that their injuries should then be treated by a doctor from a medical school where students were admitted by lottery; and that their heirs' malpractice suit should then be tried by a lawyer from a law school where students were admitted by lottery. (Mayer 1973, 47)

Others anticipated that the program would cruelly thwart the aspirations of students whose appetites for educational attainment would be whetted only to be frustrated as they flunked out in droves. From a deluge of entrants would emerge a trickle of graduates. In the way this public debate was framed, CUNY had launched a no-win policy: if many of the new students graduated, standards had gone down the drain. If they flunked out, open admissions had failed because it could not eradicate the effects of severe disadvantages that students brought with them to college.

Overview of the Issues

In assessing what actually happened under the open-admissions policy, we shall examine a number of questions that pertain to outcomes of the program. The open-admissions blueprint was designed to broaden access to the university for minority students—mostly blacks and Hispanics—who had been largely shut out beforehand.[17] How well did the program succeed in attracting students who could not have gotten into CUNY otherwise? Other higher education systems have attempted to enhance educational opportunity by expanding their community college tier. CUNY's effort focused more on providing access to baccalaureate programs, especially for minority students. To what extent were entering students actually placed in senior rather than community colleges? Whatever their initial level of placement, how much success did students experience in their college careers, and how well did minority students do compared with whites? We shall address this question by examining graduation rates for both associate's and bachelor's degrees. More broadly, we shall examine educational attainments over the long term, more than a decade after college entry. This investigation will give a sense of how far students ultimately were able to go in higher education; what proportion went away empty-handed, starting college but never earning a degree; what proportion earned an undergraduate degree; and what proportion were able to use the opportunity provided by open admissions to complete postgraduate programs, not only at CUNY but the broader system of higher education.

The open-admissions policy was an intervention that aimed to boost the life chances of educationally and economically disadvantaged students who would otherwise have had no opportunity for college. To what extent did the program actually foster success in the labor market? That is, how did the educational attainments translate into socioeconomic attainments? Did the program do as much for black and Hispanic students as it did for whites? What factors other than educational credentials influenced job-market experiences? For example, it is well known that women typically earn less than men. Does that inequity mean that women received less benefit from the open-admissions program, even when their educational attainments were comparable to men's? Another consideration is the effect of employment sector: do individuals in the public and private spheres differ in how well they do in their careers and how rapidly they move ahead? By examining such variables as gender and employment sector, we can evaluate the importance of educational attainments relative to other influences. Such an examination can provide a sense of both the potentialities and the limits of educational policy in a larger social context. In addressing these questions and issues, we shall look at different types of job rewards. Although status and earnings are fundamental aspects of work, they are not the only important features. Other significant considerations include whether a job is challenging and interesting, whether it requires judgment and responsibility, and whether it includes authority over the work of others.

The ramifications of the open-admissions policy extend beyond the results for its immediate beneficiaries, the students who were admitted to CUNY under the provisions of the program, beginning in 1970. The large majority of the students who took advantage of open admissions represented the first generation in their families to attend college. By extending a collegiate opportunity to them, the program aimed, implicitly at least, to set in motion an educational momentum that would carry over to their children. The gains to individual students might thus be transmitted across the generations, so that a self-sustaining class of college-educated men and women would begin to develop in heretofore educationally disadvantaged communities. To what extent might this have happened among the offspring of the students who came to CUNY in the early 1970s? To address this question we shall examine the familial and educational environments of children of former CUNY students. What proportion were living in households in which both parents were present, and what proportion were with a single parent? It is arguable that the household configuration producing the most favorable life chances for children is a two-parent family in which the spouses have high levels of educational attainment (a B.A. or more), while single parents without college credentials provide less favorable chances for their offspring. What were the various family and educational configurations in which the children of our respondents were living, and were minority children distributed differently across these configurations than were white children? In addressing such questions, we will assess the extent to which open admissions may have helped to consolidate intergenerational gains among whites, blacks, and Hispanics.

Beyond the leverage that college provides in obtaining more–highly rewarded jobs, it is also thought to produce nonmaterial benefits. For example, evidence suggests that college enhances such critical thinking skills as the ability to identify and question the assumptions made in arguments. It also appears that college encourages commitment to civic participation, increases interest in cultural activities, helps to produce a positive sense of self-esteem, and contributes to feelings of satisfaction with life. If such nonmaterial outcomes are desirable and if education enhances the likelihood of attaining them, then access to those outcomes constitutes an equity issue much like those that concern job status and income. In effect, we shall examine whether the open-admissions policy, by contributing to greater educational attainments, increased students' chances of realizing some of the nonmaterial benefits of college.

The Stages of Open Admissions

The questions and issues that we have described to this point will be assessed with data collected on students who entered CUNY in the initial few years of the original open-admissions policy (1970–72). As we observed earlier, that policy appears, at least on paper, to have produced a noteworthy degree of educational opportunity, embodied in its focus on access to baccalaureate study, in its provision of various supportive features designed to enhance students' chances for academic success, and in the provision of free tuition. These features of open admissions were in effect during the period from 1970 through the 1975–76 academic year—an interval during which one might say that the form of the policy remained pure. Our analyses of this initial stage of the program are designed to assess what it could do when, in effect, it provided more favorable conditions to facilitate students' academic progress.

By the mid-1970s a grave fiscal crisis had overtaken New York. As the city entered an era of scarcity, CUNY received a severe buffeting. The university was thrown into crisis as it struggled over ways to deal with sharp and sudden budget reductions and an even bleaker future. The open-admissions program was undercut as important changes in academic and fiscal policies were instituted. Beginning in fall 1976, CUNY's century-old tradition of free tuition was swept away, criteria for admission to its four-year colleges became more stringent, and in other important ways the academic climate at the university became more difficult. Did these changes influence students' educational chances? Was their academic progress affected—was there a change, for example, in the rate at which they earned credits? As indexed by the grades they earned, did the quality of their academic performance change? Ultimately, were graduation rates diminished? Were the academic chances of disadvantaged minority students affected more than others'? To explore such questions, we shall compare the academic careers of freshmen who entered CUNY in 1970 (before the fiscal crisis) with the class that entered in 1980 (after the crisis). Looking at academic careers in two decades separated by major policy changes in the university will provide a context for assessing the long-range significance of the open-admissions experiment. In effect, we will look at what happened to student academic outcomes as CUNY shifted from its liberal open-admissions policy to a more conservative approach to access and academic requirements.

Sociological Perspectives on Open Admissions

The questions that we have been discussing resonate with a long-standing controversy among social scientists about the effect of education on socioeconomic life chances. The debate revolves around the interpretation of a central conclusion that emerges from research: educational attainment is the single most important influence on occupational success, overshadowing by far the direct effects of family background.[18] According to one perspective, sometimes referred to as the "functional" view, this preeminence of education indicates that high status in American society can no longer be directly inherited but must be gained in accordance with universalistic achievement criteria, the most important of which are educational attainments.[19] Those who earn the more valuable credentials—bachelor's and postgraduate degrees—do so by displaying competence in an educational system that selects and sorts on the basis of academic performance. According to this perspective, the processes of educational sorting and selection are based mostly—though not exclusively—on merit, and therefore individuals can go as far in education as their talents will take them. From this vantage point, then, individuals from low-status origins can find in the educational system an opportunity for social and economic mobility. Education serves to loosen the linkages between social origins and social destinations.[20] According to this line of thinking, such policies as open admissions, which enhance educational opportunity, would be expected to facilitate access to good jobs.

Not all scholars share such optimism about education's egalitarian function. Although they accept the findings about the important influence of educational attainment on labor-market rewards, many are unconvinced that family background has waned as a determinant of socioeconomic success. As Karabel and Halsey (1977b, 19) have stated, social inheritance has taken on a new but no less important form:

> If . . . the inheritance of status in modern societies takes place through the transmission of "cultural capital," then the distinction between ascription and achievement becomes a misleading one. . . . The privileged no longer reproduce their positions solely through property but also through the acquisition of superior education for their children. Rather than describing this process as heightened universalism it would seem more accurate to view it as a new mechanism performing the old function of social reproduction. Social inheritance, whether through the transmission of property or through the transmission of cultural capital, is still social inheritance.

In this *critical perspective* on education then, schools are less agents for social mobility than institutions that serve to reproduce inequality from generation to generation. Although the various critics differ about how schools contribute to the reproduction of inequality, they share a skepticism that the selection and sorting functions of schools are fundamentally meritocratic. They see in the curriculum and assessment procedures of schools a playing field on which students from advantaged social backgrounds are better positioned for the academic competition than are those from lower social classes and minority ethnic status.[21] Because children from higher-status families typically have better-educated, more affluent parents, they tend to bring with them to school more of the characteristics that schools reward. Because schools prefer some forms of language usage to others, for example, students from higher-status families may be advantaged because their linguistic socialization enables them to read, write, and speak in ways that more closely match school expectations than do the language styles of lower-status children.[22] More broadly, the cultural capital held in higher status families—predispositions including tastes in music, literature, cinema, and theater; periodicals and newspapers read; uses of leisure; types of vacations taken, styles of dress, styles of social interaction, and so on—gives their children more familiarity with the content of the school curriculum and probably facilitates interaction with teachers.[23]

Part of the academic edge provided by parents who have high levels of cultural capital is that, because of their greater educational attainments, they typically are better able to help their children with schoolwork. Moreover, as Lareau (1989) has shown, high-status parents more frequently interact with teachers on behalf of their children. All in all, the advantages that accrue to higher-status children are reflected in their greater likelihood of placement in high-ability classroom groups. Ability grouping in turn tends to enhance further their academic performance. Students in low-ability groups tend to learn less, most likely as a consequence of lower teacher expectations and less demanding curriculum content. Of course, all of this works to the advantage of higher-status children, thus ratifying their status as strong students.

These disparities in elementary school performance have a continuing influence on academic careers; students who were in the upper-ability groups, for example, might be expected to outperform lower-group children on standardized achievement tests, which often play an important role in high school curriculum placement. Low test scores may lead to placement in lower, nonacademic tracks. Because of track differences in curriculum content and, possibly, more negative teacher attitudes toward lower-track students, these youngsters do not do as well in high school and are less likely to enter college than those in academic tracks.[24] If they continue their schooling, they are more likely to enter community colleges. These two-year schools are far less valuable than four-year ones; students who begin college in the former are significantly less likely ever to earn a bachelor's degree, even if they aspire to one, and if they receive a two-year associate's degree, its leverage in the labor market is typically very modest relative to that of the B.A.[25]

In the end, then, proponents of the critical perspective believe that the educational system serves to transmit inequality from generation to generation while at the same time preserving an illusion of equality. Standardized tests and the seemingly hard currency of grades give the schools a patina of objectivity and fairness that make their function of social reproduction less visible. Ultimately, a stratified system of education—in which ability grouping at the primary school level is linked with curriculum tracking in high school, which is connected in turn to four-year and two-year tiers in higher education—provides niches into which students are sorted, with significant consequences for their respective life chances.

The two views of education that we have summarized here may not be as diametrically opposed as they appear. As one writer has pointed out (Bielby 1981), there are no studies that show schooling to be independent of social origins, nor are there any showing that schooling is completely determined by the circumstances into which one is born. Differences between perspectives are mainly ones of emphasis. Nonetheless, each perspective generates contrasting expectations about the results of a policy such as open admissions. Compared with the functional view, the critical perspective leads to much less optimistic expectations that the policy could make a deep dent in class or ethnically based inequalities. But taken together, these perspectives provide a broad theoretical context that can be useful in interpreting the outcomes of the open-admissions program.

Assessing the Outcomes of Open Admissions

Three data sets have been used to analyze the questions and issues that we have been describing. The first, an anonymous annual census conducted by the university, allows us to distinguish blacks and Hispanics from non-Hispanic whites in order to examine important changes that took place in the ethnic composition of CUNY's four-year and two-year colleges after the open-admissions policy was initiated.

We have assembled a large longitudinal data set. Its origins go back to the fall of 1970, when CUNY's seventeen senior and community colleges initiated the open-admissions policy. As part of the study, large samples of the first three freshman classes to enter after the program began—the 1970, 1971, and 1972 entrants—were surveyed by questionnaire, generally either at registration or in required freshman courses. The numbers of students in the sample surveys for each year and the size of their corresponding populations were as follows: 1970, 13,525, or 43 percent of the 31,596 entrants; 1971, 8,527, or 24 percent of 35,639; 1972, 12,725, or 36 percent of 35,545.[26] The survey data include information on socioeconomic background, including race and ethnic group membership, gender, age, family income on entry to CUNY, parental educational attainments, educational aspirations, reasons for attending college, and self ratings of academic ability.

Subsequently, these survey data were integrated with students' official academic records, including: (1) high school background information, such as high school average and the number of college preparatory courses taken; (2) information on placement in CUNY, including the level of college (senior or community) at which students began their studies and, for two-year entrants, their initial curricular placement (liberal arts vs. career or vocational programs); and (3) academic performance information covering the period from fall 1970 through spring 1975, including grade point averages, credits earned, whether students took remedial courses and how many they took, whether they dropped out or "stopped out" (temporarily suspended their college education), whether they transferred from a community to a senior college, and what CUNY degrees they earned.

These samples provide good representations of the populations and have been the basis for a number of studies analyzing various outcomes of the open-admissions policy over its first five years, including academic performance processes and graduation rates (Lavin et al. 1979, 1981; Alba and Lavin 1981).[27] This five-year interval was adequate to delineate many of the important results of the program and to analyze ethnic differences in academic success. Nonetheless, at the end of that time, the record seemed incomplete for some key bottom-line educational results, like graduation. By spring 1975, large proportions of students had neither graduated nor dropped out—they were persisting in college. Others, who appeared in our records as dropouts, may have temporarily interrupted their studies because of the need to work full-time, or for other reasons; still others may have transferred out of CUNY and ultimately graduated from other colleges (the initial studies were able to report only what happened within the university). Obviously, an unfolding of the full graduation and dropout picture required more time.

To complete that picture, we conducted a follow-up survey in 1984 for a subsample of approximately 5,000 respondents who were members of the samples from the original 1970–72 cohorts. The new survey expanded the time frame of the data set, adding information on educational attainments as of 1984. It included all degrees earned (ranging from high school diploma through advanced postgraduate and professional degrees), not only from CUNY but also from the wider higher education system. The survey also provided information on labor-market experiences, including employment status as an undergraduate, year of first full-time job and job title, number of years employed since 1970, employment status in 1978 and 1984, job title in 1978 and 1984, salary for the 1978 and 1984 jobs, and the type of organization for which the respondent worked in these years. Information was also collected on marital status (including, among those who were married, employment status and salary of spouse), number of dependent children living with the respondent, attitudes about work, self-image, and satisfaction with various aspects of life.

The new survey data were merged with the original 1970, 1971, and 1972 freshmen cohort files, which were then combined to form a single file. It contains information on the lives of respondents from the time they were in high school and in their teens, to a time twelve or more years after they had begun college, when typically they were in their early to mid-thirties. This file allows us to explore what happened to them and what their experiences during and subsequent to formal education tell us about the success of the open-admissions policy.

Because this data set contains about 5,000 respondents from the combined original or "mother" sample of about 34,700 cases, we wanted to assess how well the characteristics of the former matched those of the latter. To do so, we compared the two, using a large number of variables common to both. The details of this procedure are presented in the. . . . In some respects, the subsample differs from the mother sample. Most notably, CUNY graduation rates as of 1975 are higher among the members of the follow-up sample, implying that subsequent educational attainments in this subsample would exceed those in the mother sample. To adjust for nonresponse bias, we developed a weighting procedure. . . . It adjusted the values for variables in the subsample so that they closely matched those in the mother sample. Although we obviously do not have measures in the latter sample for every variable measured in the former, the adjustments produced by our weighting model add to our confidence in the validity of the conclusions that we have drawn from our subsample.

As we said earlier, the open-admissions policy was undercut by the severe fiscal crisis that hit New York City in the mid-seventies. To assess the impact of changes in the program on educational opportunity at CUNY and on students' college careers, we have used a third data source: a longitudinal file that tracked the academic progress of students who entered CUNY in 1980, after the policy changes. The academic success of these entrants will be compared with that compiled by the students who entered in 1970 under the original open-admissions policy. This 1970 data set was, of course, put together for the initial studies of open admissions. Our comparison of academic outcomes in the 1970 and 1980 cohorts will help to deepen our understanding of the long-term success of open admissions.

Notes

1. Possibly in reaction to the aid cuts, minority high school graduates, as Hauser (1988) has suggested, may have increased their rates of enlistment in military service as a means of acquiring entitlements for higher education, thus contributing to the decline in minority enrollments.

2. An analysis of the major proposals appears in Dougherty and Hammack (1990a, Chapter 10). See also a discussion by Hammack (1985). A leading example of the conservative attack on higher education is Bloom (1987), probably the best-selling book about education ever written by an academician. Critics claimed that higher education had abandoned the traditional curriculum and called for a renewed commitment to the idea that "the core of the American college curriculum—its heart and soul—should be the civilization of the West" (Bennett 1984, 30). This camp demanded a focus on works by classical philosophers, European writers, American literature and historical documents, which "virtually define the development of the Western mind" (Bennett 1984, 10). For a good analysis of the pleas for a renewed commitment to the teaching of the "canon," see Aronowitz and Giroux (1988).

3. Minimum competency assessment at different educational levels is reviewed in Dougherty and Hammack (1990a, Chapter 10).

4. In 1917 a branch of CCNY was established in Brooklyn. An independent Brooklyn College was founded in 1930. A branch of Hunter College was established in the Bronx in 1929; it became Herbert H. Lehman College in 1968. Queens College opened its doors in 1937.

5. These figures were compiled from U.S. Bureau of the Census (1975, series D, 182–232, p. 139) and U.S. Bureau of the Census (1983a; no. 693, p. 417).

6. Undoubtedly the proportion of managers and officials has grown even more than these figures indicate, because proprietors, who also are included in this category, have been a shrinking part of the work force.

7. Broadly speaking, "functionalists" may be contrasted with a variety of critical theorists regarding the relation between education and the economy. The former, exemplified by Bell (1973), Featherman and Hauser (1978), Treiman (1970), and Parsons (1959), hold that the transition from industrial to postindustrial society leads to growth in more complex jobs that require a more highly educated population. Others, like Randall Collins (1979), disagree that educational requirements have increased because work has become more complicated. Some, most notably Braverman (1974), have argued that technology

has played a key role in deskilling of jobs. Whatever the effects of economic change on the quality of work, the proportion of high-status jobs has risen, and so have educational requirements. For a broad review of the literature on this debate, see Spenner (1985).

8. This trend reflects a decline not only in manufacturing's relative share of the labor market but also in the absolute number of jobs in the sector.

9. The city's place at the forefront of the national trend is based upon a comparison of New York data (Mollenkopf 1988, table 9.1, p. 226; table 9.2, p. 228) with national data (Singelmann 1978, table A.1, pp. 145–46). National figures are calculated from the sum of percentages employed in production, social, and personal services. New York figures are calculated from the sum of the percentages employed in financial and related services and in government. From a reading of Singelmann, the New York categories appear to match the national ones.

10. In that decade about 90 percent of the Hispanic immigrants were from Puerto Rico. The estimates of the numbers of blacks and Puerto Ricans are made from figures provided by Glazer and Moynihan (1970, pp. 25–29, 91–94, and table 3).

11. Irish and Italian Catholics had earlier been less likely to attend the municipal colleges in part because the church discouraged attendance at secular institutions. Moreover, numerous Catholic colleges in the New York metropolitan area attracted a large share of Catholic youth. A more detailed discussion of this topic may be found in Lavin et al. (1981, Chapter 1). The rise in the enrollment of these groups in CUNY is consistent with their generally increased educational attainment, especially among the generations that completed their education after World War II. A more extensive consideration of this point is given in Alba (1990, chapter 1). See also Steinberg (1974).

12. Disputes over school decentralization and a civilian review board are discussed in Berube and Gittell (1969) and Glazer and Moynihan (1970).

13. A more detailed description of events leading to the open admissions initiative may be seen in chapter 1, Lavin et al. (1981).

14. Until 1961, the municipal colleges were semiautonomous entities that were related to one another through their ties to a New York City Board of Higher Education. In 1961, they were established as a more closely linked set of institutions that were designated the City University of New York. The chancellorship was established at the same time to formulate and coordinate university-wide academic and fiscal policies.

15. High school average and class rank were calculated for all applicants, regardless of the type of high school they attended. Among graduates of vocational high schools or among those from nonacademic tracks in comprehensive schools, for example, average and rank were based just on the academic courses taken. In effect, CUNY's program made the type of high school or curriculum track irrelevant to the admissions process.

16. In spite of what its name seems to imply, the open-admissions policy did not guarantee that every applicant could attend the college he or she preferred. Within the two pools, admission to a particular college was competitive. If there were more students who picked a certain college than there were places available at that school, the available seats went to those with the higher averages. Those who were not admitted to the college of their first choice in this competition would then be placed with the candidates for the college of their second choice, and the competitive process would begin again if the demand for places exceeded the supply.

17. At the time the open-admissions program started, few Asian students—less than 1 percent—were enrolled in CUNY. Indeed, because there were so few of them, they were not included as a separate category in the annual ethnic censuses conducted by the university. Because of their small numbers, it was not possible to include them in the statistical analyses of this study.

18. According to results reported in Blau and Duncan (1967), about 14 percent of the variance in a son's occupational status is explained by the occupational status of his father, whereas the son's educational attainment explains about 30 percent. (The measure of occupational status is son's first job.)

19. Of course, educational attainment is not the only basis for increased universalism in occupational attainment. Antinepotism rules and legislation against ethnic and gender discrimination in employment have helped to create broader employment opportunity.

20. A considerable literature reflects this point of view. Some of the best examples are Bell's exposition of the development of postindustrial society (1973), the classic analysis of status attainment and social mobility by Blau and Duncan (1967), and Clark's work on the "expert" society (1962). One of the most important theoretical statements is that presented by Talcott Parsons (1959). A good summary of this position, often referred to as the "functional perspective" is to be found in Hurn (1993, see especially chapter 2). Parsons explicitly notes that family background factors play a role in educational attainment, but he is very clear in asserting that in the main, universalistic standards of achievement are the primary

bases for evaluating students' school performance. For a discussion of the mobility function versus the social reproduction effects of schools in the context of research on status attainment, see Bielby (1981).

21. Critiques of the functionalist position are expressed in the work of a number of scholars. One of the best known is the neo-Marxist study of Bowles and Gintis (1976), who see schools as a major institution for reproducing the hierarchical social and economic relations of capitalism. Another position is represented by the work of Collins (1979), who argues that, for the most part, educational credentials are unnecessary for effective job performance. Rather, credentials represent a cultural "currency" that provides their holders with eligibility for the better-rewarded jobs. In the race for credentials, individuals from high-status groups are better able to compete, thus maintaining their advantage vis-à-vis other aspiring groups (i.e., minorities, lower social class groups).

22. This perspective on language as been developed most notably in the work of Basil Bernstein (1977). See also his article (1973) in Karabel and Halsey (1977a). Whereas Bernstein focuses on social class differences in linguistic usage, the work of Labov (1972) addresses race differences through analysis of black dialectical usage.

23. The concept of cultural capital has been developed most notably in the work of Pierre Bourdieu. See, for example, his article (1977) in Karabel and Halsey (1977a), as well as Bourdieu and Passeron (1970). A good overview of Bourdieu's work is provided by Swartz (1990).

24. There is an extensive literature on tracking which in its broad outlines indicates that track placement is partly determined by socioeconomic status, that track influences how much is learned, and that tracking adds to, rather then diminishes, preexisting academic inequalities. Nonetheless, the consequences of tracking appear to be more complex than has been portrayed by some reproduction theorists. Some important analyses of tracking may be found in Oakes (1985), Gamoran (1992), Gamoran and Mare (1989), Gamoran and Berends (1987).

25. Over the past three decades, a large literature has accumulated in response to controversy about the functions of community colleges and the socioeconomic value of the associate's degree. Some of the more important examples are Clark (1960), Karabel (1972), Brint and Karabel (1889), Dougherty (1987, 1994), and Cohen (1990). Other citations regarding the issue of community colleges will be made, as appropriate, in succeeding chapters.

26. The number of entrants does not include students who were admitted under special admissions programs instituted in the 1960s. These programs involved minority students almost exclusively. Because special program students received services, including stipends, at levels not generally received by students entering under the open-admissions program, including them in our analyses would have further complicated an already complex study.

27. Detailed comparisons of the samples with the populations have been presented in Lavin et al. (1981). The samples contain a slightly higher proportion of able students than the populations. This bias is small with respect to high school grades, transfer, and college grades, larger but still modest with respect to graduation rates. Across all samples, the graduation rate is less than 5 percentage points higher than the rate in the population. Overall, we concluded that the samples provided good representations of the populations, and there seemed little reason to suspect that findings based on the samples were invalid.

A Time of Quiet Activism: Research, Practice, and Policy in American Women's Higher Education, 1945–1965

Linda Eisenmann

This exploration of American women's post–World War II higher education begins with three stories. These narratives reflect issues women faced when, as educators, they tried to plan curricula and programs for female students, and when, as professionals, they tried to manage their own careers in an era that frequently sent mixed messages about women's roles and opportunities. They also reveal a quiet type of activism practiced by postwar women educators, an approach which often pales in comparison to the firmer efforts of postsuffrage and World War II activists, or to the lively and boisterous work of late-1960s feminists. However, I will argue that this more muted style, when combined with the era's predilection for individualized solutions to women's concerns, marks a particular postwar approach to advocacy that may be different from other eras but that suited the contextually complicated postwar period.

The initial story belongs to Agnes Meyer. Meyer was an unusual woman and rather a free spirit in mid-twentieth century America.[1] In 1907, as Agnes Ernst, she graduated from Barnard College with a love for both art and travel and soon took a job as one of the very few female reporters with the *New York Sun*. Ernst traveled to Paris, where she became involved in the culture of artists and writers including Thomas Mann, Auguste Rodin, Constantin Brancusi, and Gertrude Stein. She advised Charles Freer on his unparalleled collection of Asian art, which later became the base for his huge donation to the Smithsonian Institution. At age twenty-three, Ernst married the thirty-four-year-old millionaire financier Eugene Meyer, who in 1933 purchased *The Washington Post*. Returning to the United States, the Meyers had five children over the next eleven years; the fourth child was Katharine, who as Katharine Graham in 1963 succeeded her husband Philip as publisher of *The Washington Post*.

Meyer was an unorthodox mother, particularly during an era when family and motherhood carried enormous public expectation as women's most important roles. She distanced herself from her family, both emotionally and physically, living alone for long periods of time, and frequently traveling without either husband or children. Meyer wrote for *The Washington Post*, lectured widely on public affairs, exerted notable influence in Democratic party politics, and dispensed considerable philanthropy. As her interest in education grew after World War II, Meyer encouraged creation of the Urban Service Corps, tangled publicly with Catholic churchmen over the issue of federal aid to public schools, and held seats (although nearly fifteen years apart) on both Harry Truman's Commission on Higher Education and John Kennedy's President's Commission on the Status of Women. *Newsweek* magazine called Meyer "a one-woman reform movement."[2]

Yet this woman who proved so comfortable acting alone in the world frequently emphasized in interviews her primary devotion to family, insisting that "a woman could have her own work but always had to take care of her husband first." Commenting on her mother's surprising and perhaps confusing assertion some years later, daughter Katharine Graham hardly hid her bitterness in countering that "motherhood was not exactly Mother's first priority."[3]

Turning from Meyer, a woman dealing with expectations of the family claim, the second story presents educator Kate Hevner Mueller. Mueller had joined Indiana University as dean of women in 1937.[4] She was well-known in the professional circle of deans, particularly for editing the journal of the National Association of Deans of Women and writing an influential book on collegiate women.[5] However, Mueller became caught in a professional reorientation of deans' work that surfaced after World War II as a new focus grew on student development. Over time, the new approach led to the elimination of both "deans of women" and "deans of men" in favor of a more efficiently and expertly organized "dean of students" position that emphasized what became known as "the student personnel point of view." Not only were the new deans of students usually men, but the jobs were often given to men who had served in the military during World War II or who had led the universities' stateside military programs during the war.[6]

At Indiana, where 5,000 veterans arrived on campus shortly after the war, President Herman B. Wells was already planning to reorganize student affairs into a new Division of Student Personnel. Wells named as the new dean of students Colonel Raymond B. Shoemaker, the man who had managed Indiana's wartime student programs. Wells demoted the previous deans of men and women, and Kate Mueller, who had long functioned as an autonomous dean of women, became an "assistant dean and senior counselor to women." In actuality, most of her duties, as well as her title, disappeared.[7] Compounding the personal effects of the change, Mueller was not consulted about the staff revisions and was informed of her new job by a junior male colleague.

In fairness, concerns had been raised earlier about Mueller's lack of administrative skill, and she later admitted that she brought little particular expertise to the dean's position. Even so, her demotion matched a pattern of older women deans being replaced by ex-military men across the country. In response, both the American Association of University Women (AAUW) and the National Association of Deans of Women (NADW) launched a protest—albeit unsuccessfully—in 1944.

The third story involves Mary Church Terrell who, in 1946, agreed to serve as a test case in suing the AAUW over its racially restrictive membership policies.[8] As the nation's largest organization for college women graduates, with a membership over 100,000, the association did not specifically prohibit African-American members. However, it limited membership to liberal arts graduates from approved institutions that could meet a series of curricular and financial requirements established by the association. Although not intentionally discriminatory, the AAUW set its standards in a way that most historically black colleges, still struggling in the 1940s to upgrade their curricula, programming, and facilities, were unable to earn association approval. Black graduates of qualifying white institutions could join as national AAUW members, but often found that many local branches would not accept African-American members. In an organization that conducted policy at the national level but fostered sociability and networking via its branches, black colleagues limited to the national association missed a very important aspect of AAUW membership.

Throughout most of the twentieth century, AAUW's national office had followed a hands-off approach toward membership decisions, allowing considerable differences to develop among branches, and between national headquarters and the locals. In 1945, only seven local branches across the nation were racially integrated.[9]

A group of members in the District of Columbia (DC) branch decided to push the issue of integration. That branch provided primary financial support for an AAUW clubhouse in the Washington area that was used not only by the DC branch but also by national members when visiting Washington headquarters. Traditionally, the dining room would serve African-American members, but many awkward moments had occurred around what was perceived as forced racial mixing. A group within the DC branch decided to advance black women for local membership, aiming to open not only their branch but also the clubhouse.

Mary Church Terrell, among the black community's most respected activists, had left a privileged life for work in race uplift. In 1896, she cofounded the National Association of Colored Women and, over many decades, had applied social and economic analysis to her club work on behalf of African Americans.[10] Since the AAUW issue coincided with her own strengthened commitment to desegregate public facilities throughout Washington, DC, Terrell agreed to try to reinstate her lapsed

AAUW membership. Her application sharply divided the branch, which ultimately voted against admitting a black member.

Although the national board had generally kept its distance from local membership decisions, they chose in this case—after lengthy consideration—to notify the branch that it would be expelled if it refused to admit a member solely on the basis of race. As long as Terrell met the educational qualifications, the board ruled, she was entitled to membership in both the national and the local organizations.

That ruling did not resolve the dispute, however. The DC branch sued the national AAUW in United States District Court, charging that the board had no authority to expel branches for ignoring its policy interpretation on membership. To the great surprise of association leaders, the DC court ruled in favor of the branch, and, five years prior to the 1954 *Brown v. Board of Education* decision, a subsequent federal appeal produced the same result.[11] The courts ruled not on the issue of race, but rather found that the AAUW's by-laws held only that members *could* be admitted if they met requirements, not that they *must* be. Further, since the national organization had followed a pattern of not interfering with local membership decisions, the rulings effectively meant that branches could continue operating as they wished, rejecting any members they perceived as unsuitable.

Each of these narratives reflects an issue that affected American women's participation in higher education during the first twenty years after World War II. Agnes Meyer's story reveals the challenges women faced in dealing with expectations about their appropriate role and contribution in postwar society. A set of expectations—so strong that they became virtual ideologies in this period—held that women should heed their patriotic duty by defending the nation from Cold War threats, both at home and abroad.[12] This expectation meant that, from an economic point of view, those women with special skills needed in the work force should contribute their labor, while others should provide safety and stability by serving their families. From cultural and psychological perspectives, women were encouraged to give family life and motherhood their main attention and to seek personal fulfillment through familial achievement and equilibrium. Agnes Meyer preferred an unconventional approach to career and family, yet felt it necessary to proclaim support for a model that did not satisfy her.

Kate Mueller's story of being eased out of her dean's role demonstrates challenges women faced as professionals in higher education. As the twentieth century progressed, women had become an increasingly larger proportion of students in college and, to a lesser extent, in graduate school. During World War II, women's presence as faculty and as one-half of the student body kept many schools afloat.[13] Yet, just as many "Rosie the Riveter" workers were pushed out of the work force when male veterans returned to the job market, so, too, were some female educators eased from jobs when new approaches and new job candidates emerged after the war. Mueller personifies the frustration and surprise that women educators confronted in trying to sustain their contributions in the postwar era.

Finally, Mary Church Terrell's story of integrating the AAUW shows the internal dilemmas facing postwar women's educational organizations as external developments pressured for change. AAUW, as well as the National Association of Deans of Women, had long avoided confronting their own racism, preferring instead to foster a parallel collegiality where segregated networking hardly provided equal benefits.

These three examples suggest that women's postwar experience was neither as quiet nor as simple as our stereotypic image of the 1950s would hold. Our popular view of this early postwar era—from war's end in 1945 to the period just before the women's liberation movement in the mid-1960s—is often captured by televised images of family sanguinity like "Father Knows Best" or "Leave it to Beaver," with bemused, but authoritative, white-collar husbands surrounded by supportive mothers dedicated to raising slightly mischievous but always good-hearted suburban children. Movies, magazines, and newspapers generally affirmed this view, emphasizing family values in a time when nuclear and global insecurities were real threats.[14] In higher education, the popular impression of postwar college campuses was as quiet, stable places where dutiful veterans prodded college boys and girls to understand the value of their privileged educational opportunity and where many women persisted just long enough to find a suitable husband.[15] Like the mixed 1950s messages captured in the 2003 movie "Mona Lisa Smile," women's curriculum was often more geared to helping women accommodate to their family roles than preparing them for further education or careers.[16]

Yet, some women—like Agnes Meyer—chafed against expectations. Some professionals—like Kate Mueller—resisted replacement by male veterans. And some activists—like Mary Church Terrell—challenged discriminatory practice. Just as the postwar era saw rhythm and blues and rock and roll develop alongside the Top 40; just as the civil rights movement grew alongside Eisenhower calm; and just as Beat poetry grew next to more traditional literature, cultural challenges were budding throughout the early postwar period. And, just as these newer developments struggled for a place within the dominant popular scene, so did women activists seek a role within a culture permeated by domesticity.

In women's history, scholars frequently focus on the more immediately appealing World War II era, when women's roles shifted widely to accommodate necessary contributions to the war effort and women actively responded. In industry, in higher education, and in the labor movement, wartime women took on new roles created by the smaller number of male leaders and the nation's shifting demands for wartime support. Similarly, women's historians are drawn to the late-1960s and 1970s era, when new feminists challenged cultural, economic, sexual, and psychological expectations for women, including the role that education could play in preparing women for modern lives.[17] This activism, too, seems lively, creative, and appealing.

Fewer scholars, however, have yet examined the threads of advocacy or activism on behalf of women in the twenty years between the war and the new rise of feminism.[18] The Eisenhower era rarely evokes images of female advocacy. Although advocacy for and interest in women existed, the era seemed to require a quieter, less activist approach. Higher education, although recognized generally by many scholars as playing a role in women's personal and professional advancement, has been regarded in the postwar period as a confused and not very rich site for understanding women's professional ambitions, their preparation for a variety of possible roles, or the foundation for later developments.[19]

The larger work on which this discussion is based suggests that activism on behalf of women did occur in the postwar era, but with a quieter voice and a less radical face than found in prior or subsequent periods.[20] Generally, women's early postwar efforts leaned more toward "reform" than "revolution." Postwar advocates for women—sometimes based on their own experiences—often employed a stance of individualism, recommending a personal calculus that could allow each woman to satisfy the variety of societal expectations facing her. With such a wide array of messages reaching postwar women, each individual—at least those with the economic means to do so—needed to choose her own best combination of education, family, and career. Aware of the complicated context, advocates of the 1950s emphasized individual choice rather than the sort of collective action that would characterize women's efforts two decades later.

By focusing on individual decision-making, the postwar approach made its activism seem more muted, less organized, and less effective than what would develop later, after a new language and political framework developed around women's issues. In the early postwar, however, this individualistic and quiet approach marked a quite reasonable response to the mixed demands facing women, one that continued to embrace the patriotic expectations for Cold War citizens who supported their country as needed. In other words, postwar advocacy must be understood and analyzed within its own context.

With so little scholarly attention yet paid to women's postwar higher education, paths to its analysis remain open. One line of inquiry, as suggested in the opening narratives, would be to use individual stories to illuminate the experience of women in college, as graduate students, or as administrators and scholars who persevered during an era of muted support. My work employs an organizational perspective, finding in women's professional associations and educational organizations threads that guide an examination of women's issues through the postwar era. This organizational lens examines short-lived commissions and projects that provide benchmarks of thinking about women's issues, explores professional organizations that produced research and generated advocacy for women, and studies educational movements that arose in response to particular situations, sometimes fading as those issues changed.

Two of the shorter-term projects explore research and policy related to women. First is the Commission on the Education of Women, supported by the American Council on Education from 1953 to

1962. Throughout a difficult ten-year existence—continually marked by an uphill fight to secure funding—that commission was one of few postwar groups to foster and encourage research on women's education. Just as it closed, a second group took up consideration of women's issues from a different perspective; John F. Kennedy's President's Commission on the Status of Women from 1961 to 1963 explored women's conditions and offered recommendations for enhancing their wider contributions. Both commissions, especially through their publications, offer benchmarks that summarize thinking about women's postwar options. The ACE Commission highlights the era's *research* efforts, and the President's Commission reflects *policy* related to women.

A longer view of *practice* regarding women appears through two organizations with similar goals but different means: the large-scale AAUW, open to women graduates of approved colleges, whether pursuing professional work or not, and the NADW, comprising collegiate professionals, but one-tenth the size of the AAUW. Although the former held more money, members, and lobbying power than the latter, both groups aimed to disseminate information about women's education, foster professional opportunities, and sustain networks of education professionals. An examination of these four organizations illustrates the nature of postwar women's advocacy, including ways in which it was encouraged, sustained, and often frustrated.

The ACE's Commission on the Education of Women, created in 1953 during the Korean War, grew out of concern for how women could contribute to the Cold War effort. The commission envisioned a wide variety of roles for women, including "as effective individuals, as members of families, as gainfully employed workers, as participants in civic life and as creators and perpetuators of values."[21] The commission recognized all five roles as necessary but was less clear about how modern women should fill all of them. Examining the relationship among these roles, as well as how higher education could foster women's efforts, constituted a main task of the ACE Commission.

One tool at the group's disposal was the era's growing attention to research, particularly work on women's education and psychology. Over its ten-year life, the commission's main contributions resided in clarifying the research base on women, fostering support for its expansion, and disseminating knowledge to practitioners and scholars. The fact that it hoped to do more—including conducting and supporting research, as well as generating new lines of inquiry—remained an ongoing frustration. Starting with a one million-dollar research agenda in 1953, the commission closed in 1962, having raised only one-tenth that amount. In the end, the ACE Commission had limited success with all of its goals, but nonetheless created several benchmark studies about women's education and psychology.[22]

Taken together, these studies suggest the absence in the 1950s of a widespread analysis of how discrimination affected women as a group, including the combined operation of economic and cultural forces. For many researchers, differences in individual motivation seemed the most convincing explanation for why some women pursued education and careers while others chose the less intellectually demanding (although more immediately satisfying) role of motherhood. The commission examined evidence about within-sex differences which suggested that not all women made their choices for the same reasons. The key for educators was deciding how to help which women with which decisions.[23]

New research explored by the commission suggested that the cumulative effect of women's individual and specific decisions affected their ultimate investment in education and their subsequent job choice. John Anderson and Lester Sontag, for example, had shown that girls often made inconsistent decisions as they considered paths toward career and motherhood. Sontag found that by age ten, girls' "feminine motive" dominated, leading them away from college and career. Other work showed that girls' grades and intelligence test scores declined when they perceived that being smart lessened their popularity and femininity. Some suggested that society's valuing of masculine traits, such as self-expression and individualism rather than female virtues of supporting others and "bearing the culture," led women to more popularly accepted choices.[24]

Psychoanalytic explanations also complicated women's decision-making. Many researchers, influenced by the era's strong Freudianism, recognized the particular psychological pressures women faced, holding that only by satisfying their "feminine core" could women reconcile the dilemma they often felt around the choice between college or marriage.[25] This view helped collegiate educators understand why the adult "identity crisis" typically hit men in their sophomore year of college while choosing a major, but confronted women in their senior year when marriage or further study posed the big choice.[26]

Ultimately, the commission took a safe middle road in the era's debate over how to apply such research to creating a collegiate curriculum for women. On one side were educators who, recognizing that most women would first satisfy their roles as wives and mothers, advocated curricula that supported home and community. On the other side were planners who advocated training that would prepare women for a variety of service-oriented roles, depending on their individual choice. In the end, the commission tried to support all these ideas, stressing that a generous dose of the liberal arts would offer women the broadest educational preparation.[27]

At the end of its tenure, the commission turned to a new idea in women's education that seemed well-suited to the preference for individual choice: the notion that women lived their lives in phases, moving in and out of education, work, and family roles. This "lifespan" approach sought to give women the strongest possible base while in college but tried to assign no blame if they left before completing. If such women, after meeting family responsibilities, sought a later return to formal schooling, continuing education could ease their return and prepare them for a second phase of adult life.[28]

Although the development of continuing education and its lifespan approach served many women well and acknowledged the complexity of their choices, it nevertheless represented an adaptive approach to higher education that best served a middle-class clientele. Lifespan thinking constituted a sensible response to 1950s expectations, but as the 1960s generated new ideas about civil rights and feminism, such an approach began to seem outmoded and insufficient.

John F. Kennedy's President's Commission on the Status of Women provided an opportunity for policy-oriented educators to apply to higher education new ideas spurred by the civil rights and feminist movements. However, its deliberations, as well as its final report to the public in 1965, instead reveal missed opportunities for wider conceptions of how education might advance social change.[29] Although hints appear in the report of newer, more collective approaches to meeting women's needs, the commission's education committee (which greatly influenced the thinking of the entire commission) ultimately relied on extant ideas about the power of individual choice in guiding women's lives.

As the first national effort to assess the status and potential of American women, the President's Commission assumed a wider purview than had the ACE Commission on the Education of Women. Organized within the Department of Labor and led by Assistant Secretary Esther Peterson in her role as director of the Women's Bureau, the President's Commission pursued a quite specific governmental focus on protective labor legislation, social security taxes, and government contracting—all with a side agenda of forestalling the controversial Equal Rights Amendment (ERA) that was beginning to attract popular interest and scattered support.[30] Education was actually an afterthought to the commission's work, added to its list of committees only after the first meeting.

Much of the President's Commission's agenda resembled that of the ACE a decade earlier. How could women balance home and career? How should they meet their duties as citizens? What role might education play? Yet, unlike the ACE Commission throughout the 1950s, the President's Commission appeared during a moment in postwar history when several new ideas were rising in the national spotlight, and each of these issues affected its efforts. One was the potential of the ERA that, if passed, would forcefully proclaim gender equality in legal, employment, and social realms. A second was the increasingly vigorous national challenge around civil rights. Third was a new awareness—one that would blossom in the Great Society era-of education as a possible lever for social change, an idea fostered by the work of scholars like Michael Harrington, Daniel Patrick Moynihan, and James Coleman.[31]

Ultimately, the President's Commission sidestepped strong recommendations on each of these issues. The ERA proved too controversial, and Kennedy did not favor it as a way to enhance women's opportunities. Instead, the commission recommended a less-radical approach that would use the Fourteenth Amendment to foster test case litigation on behalf of women's needs.[32]

Concern over civil rights was visible in the commission's deliberations; it organized a special "consultation," outside its regular committee structure, of key African-American leaders to advise on issues of poverty, race, and class. Among other areas, this group explored how the concentration of black women in lower-paid, insecure jobs limited their long-term advancement, as well as how African-American women's use of college for vocational purposes stymied both their own achievement and the growth of black institutions. But the decision to have a special group rather than the regular committee structure deal with civil rights ultimately diminished the power of the commission's arguments about race and class. Brief mentions were scattered throughout the commission's recommendations, but the final report showed little impact from race and class concerns.

Only on the issue of education did the President's Commission take a somewhat stronger stand. Although it backed away from the implications of truly claiming education as a lever for change, the commission did embrace newer thinking about education's power by identifying it as a key factor in the lives of girls and women.

Initially, the group had considered the forceful idea of using education to ameliorate America's social and economic deficiencies. Members of the education committee had offered a draft report with the powerful opening statement that education has "a deeper effect on [a woman's] life and status than anything else within the range of immediate social action."[33] Such a view could have guided the commission's work, pushing for an overhaul of education not just for women, but for all Americans disadvantaged by differences in opportunity. However, by the final report, this potent language had been reduced to a bland statement about the "great importance" of improving "the quality of early education available to all the nation's youth."[34]

Education became a safe way to address more challenging issues. Rather than lead with its discussions about the ERA or economic approaches to poverty, the commission opened with a general discussion of education, hailing it as the ideal way to prepare women for the set of choices facing them. Advocating education as the best preparation for individual choice proved easier than advocating other policies that might more directly impact social, economic, and class differences.

Finally, although education had barely been discussed within deliberations by the full commission, the final report claimed that, "as our work progressed, we became convinced that greater public understanding of the value of continuing education for all mature Americans is perhaps the highest priority item on the American agenda."[35] This unlikely conclusion revealed the influence of the commission's subcommittee on education, which was filled with proponents of the lifespan approach to higher education.[36] Although that committee—designed to consider education in its broadest reach—briefly mentioned younger girls, high school students, and the "culturally deprived," its main attention focused on middle-class college women who had experienced interrupted educations. The commission's presentation made it seem as if decisions about educational preparation were entirely matters of individual choice, with little acknowledgement of ways that cultural, economic, and social issues affected personal decision-making—an approach quite typical of the era.

Turning our lens from research and policy to educational practice draws on the history of two women's organizations, the American Association of University Women and the National Association of Deans of Women. Because of their lengthy histories, and in contrast to the two national commissions, these two groups allow examination of women's issues across a longer period of time. AAUW had origins in the 1881 Association of Collegiate Alumnae, morphing into its modern form in 1921; NADW appeared in 1916 through the efforts of practitioner deans seeking mutual support.[37] Yet, even with such long histories, two issues centered in postwar developments confounded both groups in the 1950s and early 1960s: racial integration and women's own professional progress.

As the opening story of Mary Church Terrell reveals, the AAUW proved no more successful than the President's Commission in addressing postwar issues of race and discrimination. When the federal appeals court ruled against the national organization's interpretation of its membership rules, the AAUW realized that its only recourse for fostering integration was a national effort to change its bylaws. Association President Althea Hottel—who five years later would become the first director of the ACE Commission on the Education of Women—led the association through a successful change of bylaws, personally visiting branches and reassuring members that the organization would continue to serve them, even with more open membership requirements.[38]

Like AAUW, the deans' group also faced charges of internal racial discrimination. NADW's African-American members boycotted one annual meeting held at a whites-only hotel. The next year, the white NADW president personally escorted black members through the lobby of the conference hotel; eventually (although not immediately), the organization passed a resolution against holding its meetings at segregated facilities.[39]

Yet, these somewhat dramatic developments did not resolve racial issues for the two organizations. In fact, parallel groups to the AAUW and the NADW were created by African-American professionals who felt unwelcome and unserved by the larger organizations. Lucy Diggs Slowe, the influential African-American dean at Howard University, helped create and sustain both the National Association of College Women as a black counterpart to AAUW, and the Association of Deans of Women and Advisers to Girls in Negro Schools as a complement to NADW. These smaller groups faded when AAUW and NADW eased their requirements and discriminatory practices and black members felt more comfortable in the larger associations. However, African-American members continued to bear primary responsibility for integrating the larger groups and for keeping organizational attention attuned to issues of racial equity.[40]

Race and civil rights represented one area where external developments prompted change within women's educational organizations. The professional challenge that Kate Hevner Mueller experienced in her demotion at Indiana University represented another. Since the beginnings of the dean of women's position around 1900, these female professionals had advocated for women's place on coeducational campuses. Often viewed as mere disciplinarians, the deans also represented a rare collegiate model of an educated female professional on campuses where women scholars were hardly numerous.[41] In fact, the growth of the dean's role, for both men and women, was spurred by women's efforts to professionalize their work with students.[42]

After World War II, however, women's place on campuses, both as students and professionals, was diminished as policies and practices increasingly focused on men returning to campus. Facilities and programming for women—rarely an easy sell in coeducational settings—became less significant as collegiate women became increasingly incidental.

The demotion that Mueller and other deans experienced across the country symbolized the diminishing role of women's concerns in the postwar era. Women constituted significant numbers on these campuses (usually at least one-third of the student body), but they rarely attracted educators' attention in matters of policy and planning. Mueller's experience also marked a generational change as older women deans who had pioneered the role were eased aside in favor of a newer conception of student development that downplayed a gendered basis for campus services.

Although Mueller and others waged protests against their treatment and what it portended for women's issues, they lacked a collective understanding of how to challenge developments beyond their individual cases. In fact, the associations' journals carried notably self-critical articles in which women deans blamed themselves for insufficient preparation, for inability to respond to changes in the field, and for personal timidity in challenging campus decisions. A vague sense of being discriminated against did not translate into an analysis of structural explanations. A particularly pointed assessment came from one dean who charged, "It is time women quit pleading lack of recognition and concentrated on earning it."[43]

Just a few years after this dean lambasted her colleagues, Betty Friedan's *Feminine Mystique* would capture an approach that offered women educators a different language and framework for understanding their experience. As the 1960s progressed, this older generation of women campus professionals would experience complicated reactions to the new feminist movement, often feeling left out and left behind by the turn to collective action and the loud expressions of dissatisfaction with women's campus roles. Comparing themselves to the new feminists, they often failed to recognize their own contributions and frequently judged their efforts harshly; one dean, for instance, lamented how she and her colleagues had "unaccountably suffer[ed] from timidity, self-effacing meekness, and virtuous silence.[44]

In hindsight, the educators of the 1950s and early 1960s may seem gratuitously meek and self-effacing. In comparison to later efforts, their activism can appear unnecessarily limited and too adaptive. Yet, the nature of the advocacy practiced by these postwar educators suited itself to the opportunities and the thinking of an era filled with ambivalence about how women should balance home with career, community work with national service, and personal fulfillment with societal expectation. Faced with the task of guiding female collegians through these varied expectations—and with understanding the impact on their own careers—women's advocates turned to personal, individualized solutions. Yet, their unquestionable commitment to women, enacted through a more quiet activism, remains potent, significant, underexamined, and undervalued.

Linda Eisenmann is Dean of the College of Arts and Sciences at John Carroll University in Cleveland, Ohio. Prior to that she was Associate Professor and Director of the doctoral program in Higher Education Administration at the University of Massachusetts Boston. This work is adapted from her forthcoming book, *Reclaiming the Incidental Student: Higher Education for American Women, 1945–1965*. This article was presented as the presidential address to the History of Education Society's annual meeting, Kansas City, MO, November 4–7, 2004.

Notes

1. Information about Meyer's life is drawn from Barbara Sicherman and Carol Hurd Green, eds., *Notable American Women: The Modern Period: A Biographical Dictionary* (Cambridge: Belknap Press of Harvard University Press, 1980), 471–173, and Katharine Graham, *Personal History* (New York: Alfred A. Knopf, 1997).

2. Graham, *Personal History*, 173.

3. Ibid., 252, 27.

4. Mueller's story is told in Kathryn Tuttle, "What Became of the Dean of Women? Changing Roles for Women Administrators in American Higher Education, 1940–1980" (Ph.D. diss., University of Kansas, 1996), chapter 4.

5. Kate Hevner Mueller, *Educating Women for a Changing World* (Minneapolis: University of Minnesota Press, 1954).

6. See Tuttle, "What Became of the Dean of Women?"; and Robert Schwartz, "Reconceptualizing the Leadership Roles of Women in Higher Education: A Brief Note on the Importance of the Dean of Women," *Journal of Higher Education*, 68:5 (September-October 1997): 502–22.

7. Tuttle, "What Became of the Dean of Women?" especially 167–195.

8. The lawsuit, as well as AAUW's experience with racial issues, is discussed in Susan Levine, *Degrees of Equality: The American Association of University Women and the Challenge of Twentieth-Century Feminism* (Philadelphia: Temple University Press, 1995), especially chapter 6.

9. Ibid., 33.

10. Beverly Jones, "Mary Eliza Church Terrell," in Darlene Clark Hine, ed., *Black Women in America: An Historical Encyclopedia* (Brooklyn: Carlson Publishing, 1993), 1157–1159.

11. *Washington Branch of American Association of University Women v. American Association of University Women et al*, 79 F. Supp. 88, July 16, 1948; *American Association of University Women et al v. Washington Branch of American Association of University Women*, 85 U.S. App. D.C. 163, 175 F.2d 368, 1949.

12. A discussion of four prominent postwar ideologies - patriotic, economic, cultural, and psychological— appears in Linda Eisenmann, "Educating the Female Citizen in a Postwar World: Competing Ideologies for American Women, 1945–1965," *Educational Review* 54:2 (June 2002): 133–141.

13. During the war, women held nearly 30 percent of all higher education teaching posts, having gained a few points with men's wartime absence. In 1944, women constituted 50 percent of all undergraduates, although their proportions declined with the advent of G.I. Bill of Rights recipients. See National Education Association, "Teacher Supply and Demand in Degree-Granting Institutions, 1954–55," *Research Bulletin of the National Education Association*, 33:4 (1995): 127–162; National Center for Educational Statistics, 120 *Years of American Education: A Statistical Portrait* (Washington, DC: Office of Educational Research and Improvement, 1993), 76.

14. For general discussions of the era, see Eugenia Kaledin, *Mothers and More: American Women in the 1950s* (Boston: Twayne Publishers, 1984); Elaine Tyler May, *Homeward Bound: American Families in the Cold War Era* (New York: Basic Books, 1988); William Chafe, *The Paradox of Change: American Women in the Twentieth Century* (New York: Oxford Press, 1991); Sara Evans, *Born for Liberty: A History of Women in America*, 2d ed. (New York: Free Press, 1997).

15. A good discussion of college campuses during the height of the G.I. Bill era, which pays particular attention to women's roles, is Daniel Clark, "The Two Joes Meet-Joe College, Joe Veteran': The G.I. Bill, College Education, and Postwar American Culture," *History of Education Quarterly*, 38:2 (Summer 1998): 165–189.

16. A good discussion of how cultural demands translated into curricular confusion for women is Paula Fass, *Outside In: Minorities and the Transformation of American Education* (New York: Oxford University Press, 1989), especially chapter 5, "The Female Paradox: Higher Education for Women, 1945–1965," 156–188.

17. See Chafe, *The Paradox of Change; Evans, Born for Liberty*; Kaledin, *Mothers and More*; May, *Homeward Bound*; and Alice Kessler-Harris, *Out to Work: A History of Wage-Earning Women in the United States* (New York: Oxford University Press, 1982).

18. A noteworthy exception is the anthology by Joanne Meyerowitz, ed., *Not June Cleaver: Women and Gender in Postwar America, 1945–1960* (Philadelphia: Temple University Press, 1994). Its various articles discuss women's activism in politics, race relations, organizations, culture, and sexuality. Little mention is made of education, however. For a small but growing historiographic investigation of the era, see also Nancy Gabin, *Feminism in the Labor Movement: Women and the United Auto Workers, 1935–1975* (Ithaca, NY: Cornell University Press, 1990); Susan Ware, "American Women in the 1950s: Nonpartisan Politics and Women's Politicization," in Louise Tilly and Patricia Gurin, eds., *Women, Politics, and Change* (New York: Russell Sage Foundation, 1990), 281–299; Melody Miller, Phyllis Moen, and Donna Dempster-McClain, "Motherhood, Multiple Roles, and Maternal Well-Being: Women of the 1950s," *Gender and Society*, 5:4 (December 1991): 565–582; Susan Lynn, *Progressive Women in Conservative Times: Racial Justice, Peace, and Feminism, 1945–the 1960s* (New Brunswick, NJ: Rutgers University Press, 1992); Wini Breines, *Young, White, and Miserable: Growing Up Female in the Fifties* (Boston: Beacon Press, 1992); Abby Scher, "Cold War on the Home Front: Middle Class Women's Politics in the 1950s" (Ph.D. diss., New School for Social Research, 1995); and Susan Hartmann, *The Other Feminists: Activists in the Liberal Establishment* (New Haven: Yale University Press, 1998).

19. Fass, "The Female Paradox."

20. See *Reclaiming the Incidental Student: Higher Education for American Women, 1945–1965* (Baltimore: Johns Hopkins University Press, forthcoming).

21. Lucile Allen, 26 May 1952 memorandum, American Council on Education, Commission on the Education of Women, collection B-22, box 1, folder 2, Schlesinger Library, Radcliffe Institute for Advanced Study, Harvard University.

22. Significant Commission publications include: Althea Hottel, *How Fare American Women?* (Washington D.C.: American Council on Education, 1955); *The Education of Women: Signs for the Future*, ed. Opal David (Washington D.C.: American Council of Education, 1958); *The Span of a Woman's Life and Learning* (Washington D.C.: The Commission on the Education of Women of the American Council on Education, 1960); and *Education and a Woman's Life*, ed. Lawrence Dennis (Washington D.C.: American Council on Education, 1962).

23. Work on motivation is best covered in *How Fare American Women?* and *Signs for the Future*. The Commission relied heavily on work by psychologist Elizabeth Douvan of the University of Michigan.

24. Hottel's discussion of this research is presented in *How Fare American Women?*

25. See especially David Tiedeman, "Career Development of Women: Some Propositions," in *Signs for the Future*, 64–74.

26. Nevitt Sanford, "Motivation of High Achievers," in *Signs for the Future*, 34–39.

27. Fass, *Outside In*, lays out the parameters of the curriculum debate. My work differentiates among three approaches to curricular decisions: cultural conformism, economic utilitarianism, and equity-based planning. Exemplars of advocates of each approach include, as a cultural conformist, Lynn White Jr., *Educating Our Daughters: A Challenge to the Colleges* (New York: Harper & Brothers, 1950); as an economic utilitarian, Dael Wolfle, *America's Resources of Specialized Talent: A Current Appraisal and a Look Ahead* (New York: Harper and Bros., 1954); and, as an equity-based planner, Mirra Komarovsky, *Women in the Modern World: Their Education and Their Dilemmas* (Boston: Little, Brown, 1953).

28. The Commission's pamphlet, *Span of a Woman's Life and Learning*, as well as the book, *Education and a Woman's Life*, best outline their thinking about "lifespan" education. Continuing education for women became a significant movement after 1960, with its attempts to reclaim the educational careers of women who had dropped out before completing college. See, for example, Helen S. Astin, ed., *Some Action of Her Own: The Adult Woman and Higher Education* (Lexington, MA: Lexington Books, 1976); and Linda Eisenmann, "Advocacy, Research, and Service: The Pioneering Origins of the University of Michigan's Center for the Education of Women," University of Michigan, Center for the Education of Women Research Paper Series, Winter 2001.

29. See *American Women: The Report of the President's Commission on the Status of Women and Other Publications of the Commission*, eds. Margaret Mead and Frances Kaplan (New York: Charles Scribner's Sons, 1965).

30. A good discussion of the President's Commission is Cynthia E. Harrison, *On Account of Sex: The Politics of Women's Issues, 1945–1968* (Berkeley: University of California Press, 1988).

31. Michael Harrington, *The Other America: Poverty in the United States* (New York: Macmillan, 1962); U.S. Department of Labor, Office of Policy Planning and Research [Daniel Patrick Moynihan], *The Negro Family: The Case for National Action* (Washington, DC: Government Printing Office, 1965); James S. Coleman, et al, *Equality of Educational Opportunity* (Washington, DC: Government Printing Office, 1966).

32. Harrison, *On Account of Sex*, covers this strategic shift in depth.

33. Committee on Education, "Summary of Report of Committee on Education" (27 March 1963), box 6, folder 41, Schlesinger Library, Radcliffe Institute, Harvard Library, Cambridge, Mass.

34. Mead and Kaplan, *American Women*, 25.

35. Ibid., 23.

36. The Education Committee of the President's Commission was chaired by Mary Ingraham Bunting, president of Radcliffe College, who had chaired the ACE Commission on the Education of Women just prior to assuming her college presidency. As Bunting left the ACE Commission, it was focusing closely on the idea of lifespan education. Several of the people whom Bunting and Esther Peterson chose as members of the Education Committee (especially Esther Raushenbush of Sarah Lawrence College and Virginia Senders, formerly of the University of Minnesota) were well-known advocates, and even programmatic founders, of women's continuing education.

37. The origins and history of AAUW are discussed in Levine, *Degrees of Equality*; for NADW, see Lynn Gangone, "Navigating Turbulence: A Case Study of a Voluntary Higher Education Association" (Ph.D. diss., Teachers College, Columbia University, 1999).

38. Hottel's efforts as national AAUW president, as well as the wider story of race in the organization, are found in Levine, *Degrees of Equality*, especially chapter 6.

39. Ruth Brett, Edna Calhoun, Lucille Piggot, Hilda Davis and Patricia Bell-Scott, "A Symposium: Our Living History: Reminiscences of Black Participation in NAWDAC," *Journal of the National Association of Women Deans, Administrators, and Counselors* 33(2): 3 (Winter 1979), 49–51.

40. The story of the NACW is in Mary Carter, "The Educational Activities of the National Association of College Women, 1923–1960" (masters thesis, Howard University, 1962), and Linda Perkins, "The National Association of College Women: Vanguard of Black Women's Leadership and Education, 1923–1954," *Journal of Education* 172:3 (1990): 65–75. For "the Colored Deans of Women," as members often called it, see Hilda Davis and Patricia Bell-Scott, "The Association of Deans of Women and Advisers to Girls in Negro Schools, 1929–1954: A Brief Oral History," *Sage* 6:1 (Summer 1989): 40–44; Darlene Clark Hine, ed., *Black Women in America: An Historical Encyclopedia* (Brooklyn, New York: Carlson Publishing, 1993), 1157–1159; and Brett, Calhoun, Piggot, Davis and Bell-Scott, "A Symposium."

41. For discussion of the early deans' work, see Jana Nidiffer, *Pioneering Deans of Women: More than Wise and Pious Matrons* (New York: Teachers College, Columbia University, 2000).

42. Schwartz, "Reconceptualizing the Leadership Roles of Women."

43. Eunice Roberts, "Keynote Speech," *Journal of the National Association of Women Deans and Counselors* 22:4 (Summer 1959): 152–153.

44. Helen Schleman, "The Committee's Report of the AAUP as Viewed by the Dean of Women," *Journal of the National Association of Women Deans and Counselors* 27:4 (Summer 1965): 147–148. See also Sarah Blanding, "The Dean's Contribution to the Life of Our Times," *Journal of the National Association of Deans of Women* 9:4 (Summer 1946): 148; and Eunice Hilton, "'The Feminine Mystique': A Special Message to Counselors of Women," *Journal of the National Association of Women Deans and Counselors* 27:2 (Winter 1964): 61–62.

© 2005 History of Education Society

ASIAN AMERICANS IN HIGHER EDUCATION

L. LING-CHI WANG

Asian Americans in Higher Education

Asian Americans are the most visible racial minority among two types of institutions of higher education in the United States today: the most selective national research universities and elite liberal arts colleges, on the one hand, and the state universities and community colleges located in major metropolitan areas, on the other hand. The former students are mostly the motivated children of well-educated business and professional families. They attract both positive and negative media attention, and their presence at these elite universities contributes to the popular stereotype of Asian Americans as "the model minority" and to frequent allegations of and even resentment of their so-called overrepresentation. The latter students, the forgotten majority of Asian Americans in higher education, are mostly children of working-class Asian Americans. The vast majority are children of poor immigrants and refugees, trying to learn English and acquire basic job skills and struggling to adjust to U.S. life and make ends meet.

This unusual bifurcation is a reflection of the diversity and complexity within the Asian American population. Asian Americans include the children of earlier working-class immigrants from China, Japan, Korea, India, and the Philippines, from the period before World War II. And they include more recent immigrants and refugees of all socioeconomic classes, from virtually all countries in East, Southeast, and South Asia and many countries in Latin America and the Caribbean, from the Cold War period. The bifurcation in the Asian American population is also the result of historical immigration policies, settlement patterns, race relations, admission policies, and opportunities in the changing labor market, both real and as perceived by Asian American parents and children alike. The convenient label "Asian Americans" obscures the diversity of ethnicity, national origin, language, culture, gender, and, above all, class within the Asian American population. It diverts public attention from resources for and service to the people who need help the most, whether they attend the first or the second type of universities and colleges.

History and Diversity

Like Native Americans, African Americans, and Chicano/Latino Americans, the earlier Asian American immigrants were excluded from and discriminated against by institutions of higher education. In fact, the children of Asian immigrants were systematically excluded from public education. From 1859 to 1885, Chinese Americans waged protracted legal, political, and diplomatic battles to win access to public education, including the case of *Tape v. Hurley* (1884/1885) in California.

Even after they won the right of access, Asian Americans found that in the second half of the nineteenth century and the early part of the twentieth century, they were still admitted only into segregated schools. They still had to resort to litigation, such as *Aoki v. Deane* (1907) in California and *Rice v. Gong Lum* (1925) in Mississippi, to tricky diplomatic maneuvers between the United States and Japan, and to political interventions by President Theodore Roosevelt. The school segregation law in California was not repealed until 1947, even though integration had occurred long before that.

Similar exclusionary practices occurred in higher education. In spite of more enlightened policies in admissions based on merit, Asian Americans faced similar practices of exclusion. Interestingly enough, the national research universities and elite liberal arts colleges had a history of offering Oriental studies courses and admitting foreign Asian students, recruited by U.S. missionaries and business interests, from China, Japan, Korea, and the Philippines. Motivated by trade and mission, Oriental studies (the name later changed to the more enlightened "Asian studies" or "East Asian studies") in these institutions concentrated mostly on the study of Chinese language, religion, philosophy, and classical literature and on the training of missionaries, businessmen, and diplomats. (The study of the history, society, politics, and economies of Asia did not receive full legitimacy and financial support until the Cold War, when social sciences were brought into something called International and Area Studies). To assist U.S. business and missionary penetration into Asian countries and to bring both authenticity and authority into their studies of Asia, these same institutions also recruited outstanding students from China, Japan, Korea, and the Philippines each year to receive education and training. The Ivy League universities established the models for both Oriental studies and admissions for foreign Asian students. Yale University led the way with the admission of Yung Wing in 1850. This model was replicated in the second half of the nineteenth century by other Ivy League universities and by the emerging elite liberal arts colleges (e.g., Amherst, Wellesley, Swarthmore, and Oberlin Colleges), the leading land-grant universities (e.g., the University of Michigan; the University of Illinois; the University of California, Berkeley; and the University of Washington), and other private universities (e.g., Duke University in the South, the University of Chicago in the Midwest, and Stanford University in the West). Invariably, after graduation these students returned to their home countries, where they played influential roles in educational, business, and governmental affairs. The possibility of admitting home-grown Asian Americans from the Chinatowns, Japan-towns, and Manilatowns and establishing ethnic studies or Asian American studies courses did not occur to the leaders of higher education until the late 1960s.

In fact, one of the most peculiar outcomes of racism was the way higher education treated the emergence and arrival of Asian American students. Because successive waves of Asian immigrants were recruited mostly as contract laborers in the second half of the nineteenth century and the first thirty-five years of the twentieth century, and because, as such, they lived relatively harder lives, died younger, and married and procreated less often than European immigrants, U.S.-born generations of Asian Americans emerged relatively slower and in proportionally smaller numbers than did those of European immigrants. Chinese laborers arrived in significant numbers beginning in 1852. When they were no longer needed, they were excluded, denied citizenship by the Chinese Exclusion Act of 1882, and confined to urban ghettos. Japanese immigrants started coming shortly after the Chinese exclusion, and in 1924, they too were excluded and ostracized. Filipino immigrants came after Japanese exclusion, and in 1934, like the earlier groups, they too were excluded.

Nevertheless, by the 1920s and 1930s, a significant number of highly motivated U.S.-born Chinese and Japanese began to emerge from the ghettoized Chinatowns and Japantowns in major cities and to graduate from West Coast high schools and even colleges with outstanding academic credentials. By all social indicators and behavioral patterns, they were well educated and thoroughly Americanized, and they had career ambitions in law, engineering, medicine, and the sciences. Yet they were unable to find jobs commensurate with their education and training because of strict racial discrimination in the job market.

This emerging group soon caught the attention of sociologist Robert Park of the University of Chicago and social psychologist Edward Strong of Stanford University. Park, through his and Strong's colleagues and collaborators, recruited a small but steady stream of these college-educated Asian Americans to be the subjects of their research on the social process of assimilation and, at the same time, their graduate students, research assistants, and ethnographic informers in their studies of the Asian ghettos. Strong used the same group to pioneer and develop what eventually came to be known as the Strong Vocational Aptitude Test, a test designed to gather "scientific data" on its subjects' vocational aptitudes; reinforced by "professional counseling," these tests would help steer these highly ambitious Asian Americans away from occupations that the test's developers deemed unrealistic and inaccessible to them.

With perfectly good intentions, the two research projects in fact aided and abetted the institutional racism of their time and provided neither help nor consolation to these motivated and professionally oriented young Asian Americans as they tried to use higher education to overcome racial barriers. Strong's subjects found themselves debating whether their future lay in their parents' homelands, where their skills and knowledge would be appreciated and put to good use, or in the United States, where they would have to settle for second-class citizenship and accept jobs on their parents' farms and in their laundries, grocery stores, and restaurants in the ghettos. As brilliant as many of them were, Park's students were unable to break out of the rigid intellectual ghetto imposed by their mentor to find both rewarding teaching positions and intellectual liberation with their doctoral degrees. It was not until after World War II that the U.S.-born generation finally found the first crack in the job market in the postwar military-industrial complex and in selected technical sectors of the civil service: midlevel jobs in engineering and accounting for men and clerical jobs for women.

The phenomenal Nisei adjustment to and assimilation into middle-class professions after their release from military services and U.S. concentration camps rekindled the intellectual curiosity of such postwar social and educational psychologists as William Caudel and George DeVos in the 1950s. They established a link between Asian culture and the development of certain personality traits that these researchers deemed crucial to the Nisei ability to overcome adversity and achieve occupational success. Their studies planted the seed for the creation of the "model minority" idea during the height of the African American civil rights movement in the late 1960s. But it was a concurrent trend, the postwar intellectual migration of Chinese to the United States, that enabled the construction and persistence of the idea, which is both a blessing and a curse for Asian Americans.

The Model Minority

After World War II, Asian immigrants in the United States were also allowed to be naturalized, but the exclusion of Asian immigrants persisted until 1965, when the law setting quotas on immigrants of various national origins was finally replaced by a new law based on principles of racial equality, family reunion, and skills needed in the U.S. economy.

The ongoing exclusion, however, did not prevent the universities from continuing their tradition of recruiting and training the best foreign students and intellectuals from U.S. allies in Asia throughout the forty-five years of the Cold War. In fact, each year, thousands of the best and brightest Asian foreign students were carefully screened and admitted into U.S. colleges and universities, especially Chinese graduate students from Taiwan and Hong Kong and from countries in Southeast Asia, where affluent ethnic Chinese experienced anti-Chinese policies under post-colonial nationalism. Many of these foreign students successfully completed their Ph.D.'s with distinction. Unfortunately, the existing exclusionary immigration laws forced them to choose between returning to their essentially inhospitable countries of birth or, as many did, staying in the United States, either by working toward a second Ph.D. degree or by becoming illegal aliens.

The 1965 immigration law finally enabled them to change their status to that of permanent resident and eventually citizen. These are the scientists and engineers who were part of the backbone of U.S. superiority in science and technology—from computer science to space exploration, from physics to biotechnology—in the second half of the twentieth century. A very large number of them became leading scientists and engineers, winning Nobel Prizes and national honors. It was this group of intellectual immigrants that was cited repeatedly as evidence of educational and scientific success by the media and social scientists alike. It was this group of intellectual immigrants that contributed to the construction of the notion that Asian Americans were a model minority during the height of the civil rights movement in the late 1960s and early 1970s.

According to the proponents of the model minority theory, the fact that members of a discriminated-against racial minority were able to pull themselves up by their bootstraps proved conclusively that the United States was a land of unlimited opportunity, as long as racial minorities were willing to work hard to overcome hardship, including racial discrimination. This artificially constructed notion was offered as a counternarrative to the African American civil rights and welfare rights discourses. Needless to say, there is no basis for linking the success of the cream of the intellectual immigrants from Asian countries directly to the motivated and educated U.S.-born Asians. In fact, a labor market segmented by race and gender before the advent of the civil rights movement sent the U.S.-born

Asian Americans back to the farms and ghettos to till land, do laundry, wait on tables, and peddle "Oriental gifts."

The post–World War II foreign students and, later, the huge influx of both immigrants and refugees since the 1970s have swelled the Asian American population since the 1960s. Included among this demographic deluge were highly educated and wealthy immigrants. Their children and the children of the tens of thousands of successful postwar foreign students have largely been the ones entering the national research universities and liberal arts colleges since the artificial barriers to minorities and women were finally removed. Hardly noticeable, but no less important, are the children of the working-class immigrants and refugees. These are the students who have been swamping the state universities and community colleges in major metropolitan areas where their parents settled.

Thus, it has been largely class that bifurcated the enrollment patterns of Asian American students. And the media have artificially constructed the model minority myth, which has neither historical nor material foundation. In this sense, the counternarrative is both ideological and political: It reinforces the myth of the United States as a land of unlimited opportunity, and it drives a wedge between Asian Americans and other racial minorities.

Major Issues and Concerns

Just how well are Asian Americans doing in higher education? According to the *Almanac 2000–2001* issue of the *Chronicle of Higher Education,* there were 859,200 Asian Americans enrolled in higher education in 1997: 743,700 were undergraduate students, 82,600 were graduate students, and 32,900 were enrolled in professional schools. Among the undergraduates, 518,500 attended four-year colleges and universities (349,300 in public and 169,200 in private) and 340,700 attended two-year colleges (331,100 in public and 9,600 in private). These figures appear to be relatively small when we consider that in 1997, there were 14.5 million students enrolled in all types of institutions of higher education; Asian American students were a mere 6 percent of that total. However, this percentage is significant considering the fact that according to the 1990 census, Asian Americans constituted only 2.9 percent of the U.S. population. Asian American participation in higher education becomes even more significant if we examine the types of institutions and the geographic distribution of the institutions in which they are found.

In general, Asian American college students tend to enroll heavily in the nation's most selective institutions of higher education, on the one hand, and in state universities and two-year community colleges located in major metropolitan areas with high concentrations of Asian American populations, on the other hand. The bifurcated pattern, in fact, reflects the complex socioeconomic status of Asian Americans.

Asian Americans are well represented in the top national universities and in the elite national liberal arts colleges across the United States. For example, among the top private universities, the Massachusetts Institute of Technology has 28 percent Asian American students; the California Institute of Technology, 24 percent; Stanford, 23 percent; Carnegie-Mellon, 23 percent; the University of Chicago, 22 percent; Johns Hopkins, 20 percent; the University of Pennsylvania, 19 percent; Harvard, 17 percent; Yale, 16 percent; Rice, 16 percent; Columbia, 14 percent; Emory, 14 percent; Northwestern, 14 percent; Princeton, 13 percent; and Duke, 13 percent. Among the public research universities, the nine-campus University of California system has more than 30 percent; University of Washington, 23 percent; SUNY, Stony Brook, 21 percent; University of Michigan, Ann Arbor, 11 percent; SUNY, Binghamton, 17 percent; University of Texas, Austin, 14 percent; University of Illinois, 13 percent; University of Virginia, 10 percent; and University of Minnesota, 8 percent. And among the small private liberal arts colleges, Wellesley has 24 percent; Barnard, 24 percent; Pomona, 18 percent; Bryn Mawr, 17 percent; Swarthmore, 13 percent; Amherst, 11 percent; Carleton, 9 percent; Williams, 9 percent; Wesleyan, 8 percent; and Mount Holyoke, 8 percent.

At the same time, the children of Asian American working-class parents are also very well represented at four-year state universities and two-year community colleges in the nation's top metropolitan areas, such as Boston, Chicago, Honolulu, Houston, Long Beach, Los Angeles,

Minneapolis–St. Paul, New York, San Diego, San Francisco, San Jose, and Seattle. For example, the campuses of the California State University in the Los Angeles–Long Beach area include Fullerton, 24 percent of whose students are Asian American; Long Beach, 24 percent; Los Angeles, 22 percent; and Northridge, 15 percent; the campuses in the San Francisco Bay area include San Jose State, 37 percent, and San Francisco State, 33 percent. At the community college level, San Francisco is the best example: It has 75,000 students, of whom 42 percent are Asian Americans.

By far the most favored subject for research on Asian Americans has been their educational success, using such popular categories as years of schooling, test scores, degrees acquired, and professional accomplishments. From the 1930s to the 1970s, the literature has highlighted Asian Americans' educational achievements and has invariably tried to put forward cultural explanations for their success. These studies were reinforced by studies on the successful adjustment and assimilation of Indochinese refugees in the 1980s and 1990s. However, since the advent of Asian American studies in the 1970s, most Asian Americanists tend to challenge the validity of the success thesis, which by the 1960s had become known as the model minority thesis. Their challenge tends to focus mostly on methodology, accusing the earlier scholars of ignoring the diversity of the Asian American population, including their diverse national and linguistic origins, class backgrounds, regional concentration, and so on.

Since the 1980s, controversies over Asian American admissions into the top colleges and universities and over whether affirmative action policy has helped or hurt Asian Americans have attracted some scholarly attention on both sides of the debate.

Like so many phenomena involving Asian Americans, the perceptions of Asian Americans in higher education, both within the Asian American communities and in the mainstream United States, rarely correspond with realities. These perceptions, in fact, often contradict each other. Defining the campus issues and problems facing Asian American faculty, staff, and students in national research universities, elite liberal arts colleges, or community colleges becomes a chronic contest between Asian Americans and campus administration, between Asian Americans and professional organizations in education, and, not infrequently, even among Asian Americans, usually along national origin, gender, and class lines.

Here are a few obvious examples of such contentious issues: Are Asian American applicants to the national research universities being subjected to discriminatory admission policies and procedures? If there are underrepresented minorities in higher education, is there such a thing as an over-represented minority, such as Asian Americans? If so, how and by whom is the notion of over-representation defined? Even more important, what are the policy implications of such a notion of over-representation? Is Asian American studies a legitimate intellectual enterprise like European studies, American studies, Judaic studies, Asian studies, and African American studies? Are Asian Americans being hurt or aided by the policy of affirmative action aimed at correcting past injustices and ensuring equality of opportunity? Why are Asian Americans so disproportionately underrepresented in the faculty and administration in research universities and in national professional organizations, especially among those academic disciplines, such as math, science, and engineering, in which their numbers of Ph.D.'s are disproportionately high? Are Asian American students so successful and well adjusted in campus life that they have none of the legitimate personal problems or concerns routinely found among white students and other minority students? Finally, are the Asian American scientists and engineers who are working in research laboratories in universities and corporations being subjected to racial profiling and discrimination, as was illustrated by the case of Dr. Wen Ho Lee of the Los Alamos National Laboratory?

For each of these questions, there are at least two or three contradictory answers. They are just a few of the more obvious examples of conflicting perceptions that are heard frequently on campuses with a significant Asian American presence. As usual, there is some truth in these perceptions, even in the pernicious model minority myth.

The challenge for Asian Americans in higher education is what to do about these conflicting perceptions. The high visibility of Asian Americans at the most select research universities, liberal arts colleges, and scientific research facilities in both public and private sectors across the nation is undeniable. Just as significant is the "over-representation" of Asian American students at state universities and community colleges in major metropolitan areas throughout the United States. Equally undeniable is the conspicuous absence of Asian American faculty across the disciplines, in administration, and throughout student affairs and services. In essence—and quite ironically—Asian Americans have the dubious distinction of being the most visible yet most marginalized population in all types of institutions of higher education.

Sources and Further Reading

1. Asian Pacific Americans in Higher Education (APAHE). 1996. *Affirmative Action and Discrimination: Proceedings of the Ninth Annual Conference of APAHE.* Sacramento: Asian Pacific Americans in Higher Education.
2. Chan, Sucheng, and Ling-Chi Wang. 1991. "Racism and the Model Minority: Asian-Americans in Higher Education." In *The Racial Crisis in American Higher Education,* ed. P. G. Altbach and K. Lomotey, 43–68. Albany: State University of New York Press.
3. Chronicle of Higher Education. *Almanac 2000–2001* issue of *Chronicle of Higher Education,* September 1.
4. Hsia, Jayjia. 1988. *Asian Americans in Higher Education and at Work.* Hillsdale, NJ: Lawrence Erlbaum Associates.
5. Hune, Shirley, and Kenyon Chan. 1997. "Special Focus: Asian Pacific American Demographic and EducationTrends." In *Minorities in Higher Education, Fifteenth Annual Status Report, 1996–1997,* ed. Deborah J. Carter and Reginald Wilson, 39–67 and 103–107. Washington, DC: American Council on Education.
6. Nakanish, Don, and Tina Nishida, eds. 1995. *The Asian American Educational Experience: A Source Book for Teachers and Students.* New York: Routledge.
7. Takagi, Dana Y. 1992. *The Retreat from Race: Asian-American Admissions and Racial Politics.* New Brunswick, NJ: Rutgers University Press.
8. Woo, Deborah. 2000. *Glass Ceilings and Asian Americans: The New Face of Workplace Barriers.* Walnut Creek, CA: AltaMira Press.

HISTORICAL PERSPECTIVES ON LATINO ACCESS TO HIGHER EDUCATION, 1848–1990

VICTORIA-MARÍA MACDONALD AND TERESA GARCÍA

In *A Darker Shade of Crimson* Rubén Navarrette, Jr. (1993) recalls his first days at Harvard College in 1985:

> Of an entering class of just over 1,600 freshmen, I was one of only 35 Mexican-Americans . . . Was this the browning of the academy that affirmative action critics on Sunday morning talk shows foretold so ominously? Furthermore, aside from the low numbers, it was impossible not to notice the "quality" of those who had made it through Harvard's half-opened door. We had been carefully chosen it seemed. We were valedictorians, star athletes, class presidents, and National Merit Scholars. We were, in short, the *crema* of the Mexican crop.

Contemporary post-affirmative action discussions concern the loss of policies that brought large numbers of underrepresented groups into higher education during the last half of the twentieth century (Lindsay & Justiz, 2001; Ibarra, 2001). However, as an educational research community we have barely constructed an adequate history of the relatively recent entrance of some of these groups, particularly Latinos, Asians, and Native Americans into postsecondary education. The 2000 U.S. census suggests that growth of the Latino population will continue unabated throughout the twenty-first century. Resultantly, researchers have scrambled to fill in the holes of our sparse knowledge of the Latino population—one that is hardly new but dates back to sixteenth-century colonial America (MacDonald, 2001). This essay provides a social and historical backdrop designed to frame and explain the long and uneven historical trajectory of Latino access and participation in higher education from the nineteenth century through the 1980s. Of critical importance for understanding collegiate participation are the deeply rooted barriers of segregation and discrimination that have generally accompanied the Latino elementary and secondary experience. Numerous scholars including Nieto (2000), Donato (1997), Moreno (1999), San Miguel, Jr. (2001), and others have examined facets of these historical barriers to schooling. A comprehensive examination of those works is outside the scope of this chapter. However, one key to understanding higher education is to realize that the pipeline to college for Latinos has generally been blocked at the lowest levels of schooling, often prior to high school. As a result, it was not until the last quarter of the twentieth century that Latinos entered higher education in significant numbers. Their political fight for access during the 1960s forced the academy and federal government to confront the issues and potential of a large and underserved population.

Historians of higher education have virtually ignored the presence of Latino students and faculty. In the only journal specifically devoted to this topic, *The History of Higher Education Annual*, not one article on Latinos has appeared in almost twenty years of publication. Commonly used texts in higher education foundations and history courses provide only passing reference to Latinos (Lucas, 1994; Goodchild & Wechsler, 1997). Donato and Lazerson (2000, p. 11) pointed out these inadequacies in the literature: "We still know little about how peoples of color were limited in their use of higher education and the ways they advanced through it, issues that are central to current debates over affirmative action and the outcomes of schooling." Scholars of Chicano or Puerto Rican studies have pioneered the majority of research on the historical relationship between Latinos and higher education. Aurora Levins Morales argues that "the role of a socially committed historian is to use history, not so much to document the past as to restore to the dehistoricized a sense of identity and possibility" (1998, p. 1). This essay brings to light the history of Latinos in American higher educational history through an examination of five major eras.

The first period, "Southwestern Class Exceptionalism, 1848–1920s," illustrates how Latino collegiate participation waxed and waned in the Southwest from the mid-nineteenth through the early twentieth century. Historians have documented the social and economic decline of Mexicans after the 1848 Treaty of Guadalupe Hidalgo. Promised the preservation of Spanish land grants, citizenship, and language rights, Mexicans encountered instead a series of discriminatory measures which resulted in significant socioeconomic decline (Pitt, 1966; Alonzo, 1998; Menchaca, 2001). Opportunities for higher education, linked closely to social class status during this era, subsequently also declined.

The second focus, "Imperial Conquests: The Case of Puerto Rico, 1898–1920," examines imperialistic policies imposed upon the newly acquired Puerto Rican lands in 1898. The University of Puerto Rico's creation during this era provided an important avenue of upward mobility for later generations of Puerto Ricans. During Puerto Rico's era of colonial tutelage, 1898–1948 (Carrión, 1983), however, appointed American educators narrowly defined the form of higher education Puerto Ricans should receive. On both the island and mainland, Puerto Ricans were slanted towards narrow industrial education and normal school curricula.

In the third stage, "Slipping in the College Gates: 1920s–1950s," several factors, including the role of philanthropical organizations and the GI Bill are examined to explain the first generation of working-class Latino college students who entered higher education. This generation, entering against the odds, became role models for the student activists of the 1960s and 1970s.

In the fourth era, "El Movimiento in Higher Education, 1960–1980," the critical role of Latino youth in demanding higher educational access, curriculum, and faculty/staff recruitment is explored. This era was clearly the watershed of the entrance of Latinos into higher education.

The fifth and last period, "The Federal Government Steps In—the 1980s and 1990s," explores how the activism and demands of the previous generation is co-opted into federal policy. The important lobbying efforts of the Hispanic Association of Universities and Colleges, for example, resulted in the federal designation of Hispanic Serving Institutions (HSIs).

The complex history of Latina and Latino access to higher education corresponds to the complexity of contemporary issues related to Latina and Latino access and success in higher education. Diversity of national origin and generation in the United States, gender, socioeconomic status, and other factors impact a broad array of issues in higher education. This brief overview thus offers a foundation for understanding Latina and Latino access to higher education from a historical perspective that may inform efforts to examine and address contemporary issues.

Trajectories of Minority Higher Education

Minority groups have pursued pathways to higher education specific to their linguistic, political, racial, and socioeconomic position in American history. For example, federal policies concerning forced relocation, assimilation, and reservation schooling of Native Americans shaped the late twentieth-century passage of the 1975 Indian Self-Determination and Education Assistance Act and subsequent Tribally Controlled Community College Assistance Act in 1978 (Olivas, 1982/1997; Adams, 1995). In contrast, federal higher educational policies for African Americans emerged earlier in U.S. history. After the Civil War, the U.S. government and religious missionary organizations sent money and personnel to rebuild the South. Furthermore, African Americans themselves demanded and pooled resources for educational opportunities (Anderson, 1988).

From that era came the genesis of our Historically Black Colleges and Universities (HBCUs). The U.S. government founded Howard University in 1867. Dozens of private Black colleges such as Tuskegee, Morehouse, and Spelman arose during this era. Because Blacks were denied access to White colleges and universities in the American South, HBCUs received federal funds from the Second Morrill Land Grant Act of 1890, which provided monies for segregated Black state universities (Brown & Davis, 2001). In the twentieth century, the War on Poverty, Title III of the 1965 Higher Education

Act stipulated aid for "Strengthening Developing Institutions." HBCUs were well positioned to take advantage of these additional federal resources.

The Latino experience is distinct from both that of Native Americans and African Americans. Neither the federal government nor missionary organizations created historically Hispanic colleges. The rise of what Black intellectual W. E. B. DuBois called the "Talented Tenth," a college-educated elite from which to draw leaders, was thus absent among most Latino communities until after World War II. The post-1980 era witnessed the fastest growth among minorities in general. Lee (2002) pointed out that Asian, Black, Hispanic, and Native Americans were only 18 percent of all enrolled undergraduates in 1980 and increased to 27 percent by 1995. This chapter explores historical factors shaping the relative newcomer status of one of these groups, Hispanic Americans, within the context of rising minority participation in higher education during the latter part of the twentieth century.

Identity issues and census classification pose considerable challenges to historians of the Latino experience. The word "Latino/a" is utilized here to collectively denote the diversity of peoples including Mexican Americans, Puerto Ricans, Cubans, and Latin Americans who are linked to U.S. history through immigration, acquisition of lands, or political upheavals. The counting and labeling of Latinos, however, generally did not occur until the late twentieth century, posing difficulties for historians (Oboler, 1995; Rodríguez, 2000). Securing reliable data on the numbers of Latinos in postsecondary institutions prior to 1980 is problematic. Federal and state governments generally did not create a census classification for Hispanics until the 1970s (NCES, 1980).

As a result, many pre-1970 case studies that exist are based upon estimated counts of Hispanic surnames. The difficulties with this methodology include an undercounting of Latinos who possess Anglo surnames and an inclusion of South American or Iberian Spanish foreign students as U.S. Latinos. Despite these limitations, primary and secondary sources supplement statistical data to create a historical portrait of Latino higher education participation.

Southwestern Class Exceptionalism, 1848–1920s

As a result of the Treaty of Guadalupe Hidalgo (1848), the United States acquired the vast territories that include modern-day Arizona, Colorado, California, New Mexico, and Texas. The terms of this Mexican-American War treaty provided several rights to Mexicans who elected to remain in the United States. These rights included citizenship, preservation of former land grants, and Spanish language rights. The Gold Rush of the 1840s and early 1850s, with accompanying land grabs and a rapid influx of Anglo settlers to the West resulted in the erosion of these rights for the *Californios* (early Mexican settlers in the Northern New Mexico region known as California) and *Hispanos* (settlers in New Mexico and Colorado who claimed pure Spanish ancestry). Higher education participation during this era thus arose in a context in which the rights and status of many Southwestern Hispanics were eroding (León & McNeill, 1992; Menchaca, 2001; Weinberg, 1977). Historians have pointed out that the more resilient economic and political strength of Hispanos in New Mexico and Colorado protected bilingual traditions and equitable educational access well into the twentieth century (Donato, 1999; Getz, 1997). In contrast, conditions for Mexican Americans in Texas and California were more difficult, negatively impacting higher education access.

The possession of a college degree or even collegiate participation in mid-nineteenth-century America was rare for anyone regardless of race, gender, or ethnicity. Geiger (2000) concluded that college graduates represented only one percent of the male workforce before the Civil War. The small number of Latinos in nineteenth-century colleges were thus drawn from among the most privileged classes in the new territories as well as families from northern Mexico who sent their sons to receive a bilingual education (McKevitt, 1990/91). State universities in the Southwest provided one pathway for students seeking higher education during this era. The University of California opened its doors in 1869 with forty students. The university quickly found itself in a situation familiar to many nineteenth-century institutions—few students were adequately prepared for collegiate-level work. As a result, the university opened a preparatory department called the Fifth Class. Standards for admission were lower and during its brief existence from 1870 to 1872 the Fifth Class enrolled almost two dozen Mexican-born and *Californio* students. Furthermore, two Latino students passed

the entrance examination and proceeded to the freshman class (León & McNeil, 1992). The abolition of the preparatory department in order to "raise standards" two years later resulted in the
"virtual disappearance of Spanish surnamed students from the University of California" (León &
McNeil, p. 194). Although some Latino students attended the Berkeley campus at the University of
California during the next one hundred years, it was not until after 1970 that the Latino student
was more than a rarity.

In Texas, the flagship campus opened in the fall of 1883. Kanellos (1997) pointed out that a Manuel
García was the first Mexican American to graduate from the University of Texas in 1894. Little is know
about other Latinos in the Texas university system during this early era. When researchers began count-
ing Hispanic-surnamed students in the Texas university system in 1928, only 57 undergraduates
(1.1 percent) at UT-Austin possessed Hispanic surnames out of a total of 5,390 enrollees. Only one
Hispanic-surnamed graduate student enrolled that year out of 465 (0.2 percent) (Carter, 1970). (See
Table 2.1.) Latino participation in late-nineteenth-century higher educational institutions in Arizona,
Colorado, and New Mexico has received very little attention, but the sociohistoric context suggests par-
ticipation may have been higher than Texas or California. Kanellos (1997, p. 45) noted that Mariano
Samniego was appointed a member of the first board of regents for the University of Arizona in 1886;
his
presence may have encouraged Latino access among the student population during an era in which
Latinos still maintained political power.

The role of Catholic higher educational institutions in providing access during this first era appears
to yield promising answers to where Latinos found easier pathways to college. The emerging Anglo
public schools of California and Texas quickly enacted English-only laws, forbidding the Spanish
language. Furthermore, the Catholic religion and culture was denounced in the Pan-Protestant
curriculum of primary and grammar public schools. In contrast, Catholic schools and colleges were
more accepting of Hispanic bilingual and Catholic traditions (San Miguel, Jr., & Valencia, 1998).

For example, McKevitt (1990/91) documented the popularity of Santa Clara College (now university) in California as a choice for Hispanic college attendance. Between 1851 and 1876, almost
four hundred Hispanic-surnamed students had attended. By 1867, one-quarter of the student population was Spanish-speaking. McKevitt (1990/91, p. 322) argues that the Jesuits in charge "actively
recruited Spanish-speaking students" through the publication of a Spanish language catalogue. Similarly, in nearby Notre Dame College for women, the student population was largely Hispanic and
even report cards and bills were printed in Spanish. By the late 1850s, Notre Dame offered parallel
courses in English and Spanish. Additional scattered references in local histories mention the presence of Latinos at institutions such as St. Mary's Catholic College in San Francisco in the late 1800s
and the College of San Miguel in Santa Fe, New Mexico (Kanellos, 1997, p. 44).

Further research into the early state universities of the southwest territories and Catholic institutions will provide a fuller portrait of early Latino participation. The little that is known about these
early students suggest that their socioeconomic positions allowed them entry to college. As the status of many Latinos declined in the late decades of the nineteenth century, collegiate participation
among Latinos may have also dropped (Pitt, 1996). Unlike the African American experience, specific
racial codes did not formally prohibit Hispanics from White universities and colleges, yet their numbers remained miniscule except perhaps in Catholic colleges. The political status of Latino youth, as
demonstrated in the next section, also shaped their educational offerings. Anglo American's limited
expectations for the youth of newly acquired Puerto Rico impacted participation of Puertorriqueños
on the mainland during colonialism.

Imperial Conquests: The Case of Puerto Rico, 1898–1950

Over one hundred years ago, U.S. acquisition of Puerto Rico in the Spanish-American War of 1898
resulted in the introduction of American schools and the English language in Puerto Rico. A massive
Americanization campaign in the Puerto Rican schools extended to the university level. In 1903, the
University of Puerto Rico was created and emphasized normal (teacher training) and industrial departments. The university's emphasis upon teacher training for American assimilation, and agricultural

and mechanical arts rather than classical studies, resembled that of many post-Civil War institutions on the mainland for African Americans and Native Americans (Anderson, 1988; Adams, 1995).

One form of Americanization involved sending youth to mainland colleges to become inculcated with American values. The colonial government sponsored approximately forty-five "poor young men of robust constitution and good conduct" per year between 1901 and at least 1907 to attend colleges in the United States. The colonial legislation (Section 73) narrowly specified the institutions available; "The colleges or institutions designated to which the said students shall attend are Hampton Institute, Hampton, Va., and Tuskegee Institute, Tuskegee, Ala., and such other similar educational institutions as the commissioner of education may from time to time specify" (U.S. Commissioner of Education Report, 1907, p. 331).

Tuskegee and Hampton, African American industrial education colleges, were also the recipients of advanced students from Native American reservations (Lindsey, 1995). A loophole in the legislation enabled the commissioner to permit some Puerto Rican scholarship students to attend institutions with broader academic missions than Tuskegee and Hampton. For the school year 1903–04, the Commissioner of Education in Puerto Rico reported eighteen students in their third academic year at institutions as varied as Haverford, Rutgers, Cornell, Wesleyan, MIT, University of Michigan, University of Maryland Medical School, and Lehigh University (U.S. Commissioner of Education Report, 1905, p. 333). By 1905, almost five hundred Puerto Ricans were attending American institutions as a means of building pride in the United States and educating officials to staff the colonial government (Rodríguez-Fraticelli, 1986).

The University of Puerto Rico in Río Piedras was opened in 1903 and was typically free for students pledging to teach in Puerto Rico. However, financial and logistical difficulties often blocked access to higher education. The case of Ana Peñaranda Marcial illustrates the perseverance required of Puerto Rican students desiring a postsecondary education. Peñaranda Marcial began her baccalaureate degree at the University of Puerto Rico in 1921. Like many of her teaching colleagues, she could only take classes on Saturdays. The university created centers in rural areas where Peñaranda Marcial and other teachers could have more access. It was not until 1943, however, that she finally completed her degree (Sánchez-Korrol, 1994).

Serious socioeconomic conditions resulting from colonization spurred migration from the island to the mainland during the 1940s and 1950s. (Sánchez-Korrol, 1994). Puerto Ricans arrived in New York and Chicago and worked in low skill jobs (Padilla, 1985). Even teachers with B.A. degrees and teacher certification from Puerto Rico were unable to utilize their full economic potential on the mainland. Few Puerto Rican educators could pass the speech test required by New York City's Board of Examiners (Sánchez-Korrol, 1994). Furthermore, Puerto Rican children arriving to the mainland were often placed in classes for slow learners and one or two grades below their level because of lack of fluency in English. As a result, few went on to secondary school and completed the requirements necessary for college. Puerto Rican associations in New York lobbied on behalf of bilingual education during the 1930s through 1950s but received little government support (Sánchez-Korrol, 1994). Except for some unusual cases, access to higher education was deferred for a later generation of Puerto Rican youth who had migrated to the mainland.

Slipping in the College Gates, 1920s–1950s

> I assumed that there were other Mexicans like me on campus, and occasionally I would notice a Spanish surname, perhaps in some school publication. However, with the exception of some professors, the only other Hispanic I ever met at Berkeley in four years [1949–1953] was an Argentine student whom I dated for a short while. (Francis Esquivel, in Twyoniak & García, 2000, p. 163)

Frances Esquivel Tywoniak's recollection of growing up in California's Central Valley and entering the University of California at Berkeley in 1949 with an academic scholarship captures a little-known but significant era in Latino higher education. Historians have often referred to adult Mexican Americans of the 1930s through the 1950s as the Mexican American Generation. (García, 1989; Sánchez, 1993). García defines this group as "the first extensive bilingual, bicultural cohort of Mexican

TABLE 2.1   Enrollment of Spanish-Surname Students and Total Number of Students at the University of Texas at Austin for Selected Years

Year	Total No. of Undergrads	Spanish-Surname Undergrads	Spanish-Surname Undergrads	Total No. of Graduate Students	Spanish-Surname Graduate Students	% Spanish-Surname Graduate Students	Total No. of Students	Spanish-Surname Total Students	% Spanish-Surname Total Students
1928–1929	5,390	57	1.1	465	1	0.2	5,855	58	1.0
1938–1939	10,103	152	1.5	818	3	0.3	10,921	155	1.4
1948–1949	16,356	395	2.4	2,177	37	1.7	18,533	432	2.3
1958–1959	15,533	518	3.3	2,229	49	2.2	17,762	567	3.2
1966–1967	22,559	634	2.8	4,786	126	2.6	27,345	771	2.8

Source: Carter, Thomas P. 1970. Mexican Americans in School: A History of Educational Neglect. p. 30.

Americans in the United States" after 1848, when Mexico was conquered (Twyoniak & García, 2000). The Mexican American Generation's relationship to higher education remains shadowed.

The history of Midwestern Latino higher education within this era is also limited. Valdés (2000), a leader in this field, noted that in St. Paul, Minnesota's Mexican colonia of 3,000 inhabitants "not a single person" entered college until 1941. The young woman who broke the mold attended Duluth State Teacher's College (now University of Minnesota–Duluth). In Chicago, home to the second largest Puerto Rican population after New York, by the 1960 census only one percent of Puerto Rican men and women had attended four years of college. The median number of school years completed was only 7.9 (male) and 7.2 for women (Padilla, 1987). How many other Latino men and women attended the newly opened state and two-year institutions that accompanied the rapid expansion of public higher education in the mid-twentieth century is still undocumented. While knowledge about specific institutions such as that available for the University of Texas at Austin since 1928 provides some information, it is only a partial portrait because Latino youth of this era were most likely entering the college gates at smaller, less prestigious and more teaching-oriented schools.

What is apparent, however, is that during these decades an increasing number of Mexicans in the Southwest and Midwest, and Puerto Ricans in Chicago and New York, began entering the college gates after two decades of minimal participation. Philanthropy, increasing numbers of middle-class Latinos, and the GI Bill were major contributors to this shift. These twentieth-century pioneers, often the only Latinos in their classes, provided leadership and talent for the formation of the Chicano/Puerto Rican civil rights movement of the 1960s and 1970s.

The college-going pioneers in the years between 1930s and 1950s were clearly exceptional. Unlike the late nineteenth-century participation of Latinos from older, elite Hispano families, students from middle- and working-class families were finally entering higher education. The barriers to high school graduation (or even entrance) for Mexican Americans in particular, were formidable. In some areas of the Southwest, Mexican children were segregated into either separate schools or classrooms based upon their accents, skin color, or surname (Donato, 1997). Lack of enforcement of school attendance laws, language difficulties, immigration, classroom harassment, and racism resulted in few Mexican American children even reaching eighth grade (Valdés, 2000). The pipeline to higher education was thus choked off early in most Latino children's lives. Despite these obstacles, which impeded most Mexican Americans from collegiate participation prior to the 1960s, at least four factors contributed to the few who broke through the barriers.

First, community and charitable organizations became involved. During the Great Depression of the 1930s, the Protestant Young Men's Christian Association (YMCA) in Los Angeles committed $30,000 to work with Mexican American youth. The YMCA hired role model and social worker Tom García to head this project. García created boys' clubs, organized the first Mexican Youth Conference, and provided training and leadership to adolescent boys (Muñoz, 1989). Significantly, YMCA officials provided contacts with leaders in higher education. Scholarships, admissions information, and important networks were opened to Latino male youth. As an offshoot of the YMCA club, Mexican American students at UCLA created the first Latino student organization called the Mexican-American Movement (MAM). Under the direction of student Felix Gutierrez, the first Latino college student newspaper, *The Mexican Voice*, was in operation at UCLA from 1938 until 1944. After 1944, the title was changed to *The Forward*, and the tone of the paper changed as it focused on war-time activities of members of MAM (Navarro, pp. 49–50).

A second factor opening access to higher education from non-elite Latino families involved what Muñoz (1989, pp. 24–25) described as the "active support of individual teachers, clergy, or social workers that were sympathetic and in a position to identify youth with exceptional intelligence." For example, Frances Esquivel secured a UC Berkeley alumni scholarship through the efforts of her high school history teacher, Miss Helen Grant, a UC Berkeley alumna (Twyoniak & García, 2000). Similarly, the writer and scholar Ernesto Galarza entered Occidental College in 1923 and then became the first Mexican American to enter Stanford through the active assistance of interested teachers (Muñoz, 1989).

Third, the passage of the Servicemen's Readjustment Act of 1944 (the GI Bill), also assisted in expanding higher education access in the mid-twentieth century. Muñoz (1989, pp. 48–49) argued that "among the thousands of returning Mexican American veterans who took advantage of this opportunity to pursue a higher education were Américo Paredes, Octavio Romano V; and Ralph Guzmán. They were destined to become . . . significant contributors to Mexican American intellectual life." Both Muñoz (1989) and Navarro (1995) concluded that post-World War II Chicano students were "studious," and "self-oriented" rather than active contributors to larger goals of social activism.

Other researchers portray a less passive role for Latino World War II veterans. Donato (1999) demonstrated how Hispano veterans in Colorado demanded local access to higher education and were responsible for creating the San Luis Institute, a public two-year college. One San Luis veteran recalled, "I remember that almost all of us who discharged from the military went to college." According to Donato, "the sense of camaraderie among San Luis students who went on to Adams State" eased their access and retention at a four-year institution. The creation of the American G.I. Forum in Texas in 1948, an activist group designed to protect the civil rights of returning Mexican American GIs further suggests that veterans were not uniformly interested in individual success (Allsup, 1982).

Fourth, we must look to Latino communities themselves for efforts resulting in increased college participation during the 1920s through the 1950s. The League of United Latin American Citizens (LULAC) was founded in 1929 and worked to improve conditions for Mexican Americans. This largely middle class Texas organization provided college scholarships and challenged educational segregation (San Miguel, Jr., 1987). In New Mexico, the continued political strength of Hispanos was evident in the 1909 founding of the Spanish-American Normal School at El Rito. The legislature charged the institution to educate "Spanish-speaking natives of New Mexico for the vocation of teachers in the public schools of the counties and districts where the Spanish language is prevalent" (New Mexico Department of Education, 1917–18, p. 30). The school enrolled over one hundred students by 1918. In the 1930s, the bilingual state teacher training college was still open and eventually absorbed into the New Mexico higher education system (Getz, 1997).

The 1920s through the 1950s also witnessed the entrance of Latino faculty into higher education. Anecdotal evidence suggests that prior to the 1940s, Hispanic-surnamed faculty at White colleges and universities were generally from Spain and clustered in the Romance Language and Literature Departments (Twyoniak & García, 2000). Key role models and intellectuals who trained the leaders of the Chicano generation include George I. Sánchez, first at the University of New Mexico in the 1930s and then from 1940 until his death at the University of Texas at Austin. Historian Carlos Castañeda was also a significant figure at UT–Austin. He devoted his life's work to documenting and correcting Latino history as a professor in the Department of History (García, 1989). The pioneers on the faculty of White colleges most likely shared the limelight with peers at normal schools, two-year colleges, and Catholic institutions at mid-century. After these "firsts" and "greats" in Latino history, in stepped Latinos no longer content with the status quo, bringing their activism and energy with them.

El Movimiento in Higher Education, 1960–1980

It is a fact that the Chicano has not often enough written his own history, his own anthropology, his own sociology, his own literature. He must do this if he is to survive as a cultural entity in this melting pot society which seeks to dilute varied cultures into a gray upon gray pseudo-culture of technology and materialism. The Chicano student is doing most of the work in the establishment of study programs, centers, curriculum development, and entrance programs to get more Chicanos into college. This is good and must continue, but students must be careful not to be co-opted in their fervor for establishing relevance on the campus. Much of what is being offered by college systems and administrators is too little too late. [Manifesto of El Plan de Santa Barbara, 1969. In Muñoz (1989, p. 200)]

The pioneers of the pre-1960 era demonstrated that Latino youth could succeed in college if they attained access. Furthermore, the first generation of Latino faculty appearing on campuses served as role models. Civil rights activism, anti–Vietnam War protests, and all forms of antiauthoritarianism converged in the 1960s and 1970s on U.S. campuses. This era brought unprecedented numbers of Latinos into academe and clearly represents a watershed in higher educational history. No longer isolated individuals and small groups on campus, the new Puerto Rican and Chicano college students across the nation organized to demand their rights.

The parallel Chicano and Puerto Rican activism emerged with a concrete agenda to change the role of Latino students on campus as other than privileged exceptions. These radicalized youth demanded a broad range of services aiding access and retention for Chicano and Puerto Rican students. Often connected to organizations that pushed for reform in K-12 schools and community improvements, the Latino student youth movement nonetheless had its own leadership and momentum. The histories of the Chicano (Mexican American) and Boricuan (Puerto Rican) movements in the 1960s will be examined separately, since regional and sociohistoric contexts varied these experiences.

The early 1960s were a period of identity development for many Mexican Americans as they looked to inspiration from their indigenous roots rather than pathways of assimilation. As the Black civil rights movement for access to White colleges and universities gained visibility in the national media, Latino students examined their own status and numbers in the academy (Navarro, 1995). Available data suggest that on the eve of the turbulent 1960s, Latino students were still on the margins of academe. Valdés (2000, p. 159) noted that in 1960 Michigan, 40 percent of all seventeen- to twenty-four-year-olds in the state were attending some form of postsecondary institution, compared to only 7 percent of its Mexican population. In Houston, Texas, only 3 percent of Mexican American adults older than twenty-five had completed four years of college in that same year (de León, 2001). Researcher Herschel T. Manuel found in 1958 that only 5.7 percent of freshmen in 146 southwestern colleges had Hispanic-surnames (Carter, 1970, p. 31). By the mid-1960s however, numbers had increased to 12.8 percent (see Table 2.2). Finding strength in numbers, they organized *el movimiento*. One of the issues which engaged students was the small number of Latino faculty.

At the beginning of the movimiento's heyday (1968–1973), Muñoz (1989, p. 142) pointed out that "fewer than one hundred scholars of Mexican descent held doctorates in the United States. Of these, most held doctorates in education (Ed.D.s), which located them in a distinctly different research network with a very different emphasis from those scholars holding a Doctor of Philosophy." The low number of faculty who might be interested in teaching or researching Latino issues was a principal issue addressed in the youth movement's conferences and lists of demands.

Several simultaneous external events also sparked the creation of a militant Chicano movimiento that spread through the Southwest. The national attention given to Cesar Chávez and the farmworkers' movement, the politicization of Latinos through Viva Kennedy clubs, and a growing desire to take advantage of federal War on Poverty programs contributed to the formation of student groups. The fall of 1967 witnessed the birth of several Mexican American student organizations. The Mexican American Youth Organization (MAYO) began at St. Mary's College in San Antonio, Texas, and then at UT–Austin. In Los Angeles, the United Mexican American Students (UMAS) formed several chapters in area institutions including UCLA and Loyola. At the large East Los Angeles Community College, the Mexican American Student Association (MASA) was formed (Muñoz, 1989, p. 58). Frustrated with the lack of attention to Latino demands for more faculty and relevant courses, the students engaged in a series of conferences and protests to change the academy.

The Chicano movement received inspiration and training from African American organizations, particularly the Black Panther Party and the Student Non-Violent Coordinating Committee (SNCC) (Navarro, 1995, p. 86). Campus dynamics between Chicano and Black protest organizations were often tension-fitted, however. Both Muñoz (1989) and Olivas (1982) note that Chicanos often felt slighted by an overemphasis on the recruitment of Black students. As a result "bitter and intense conflicts between Mexican Americans and Blacks on several campuses, [made] viable coalition politics difficult, if not altogether impossible" (Muñoz, 1989, p. 85).

The first Latino protest activity on a college campus occurred at San José State College (CA) in 1968. Approximately two hundred graduating seniors and members of the audience walked out of commencement exercises to protest the underrepresentation of Chicano students and lack of bilingual and cultural training for professionals (teachers, social workers, and policmen) who worked in

TABLE 2.2   Spanish-Surname Student Population at a Selection of Colleges and Universities, 1966–1967

Class	Total	Percent*
Freshman	1,006	12.87
Sophomore	652	8.34
Junior	810	10.36
Senior	759	9.71
Graduate school	631	8.07

*Percentages are based on the authors' calculations with estimated total enrollment of 7,816.
Source: Adapted from Carter, Thomas p. 1970. *Mexican Americans in School: A History of Educational Neglect*, p. 31. The enrollment of Spanish-surname students is the combined enrollment of University of Arizona, University of California at Riverside, University of Colorado, California State College at Los Angeles, Northern Arizona University, The University of Texas, and New Mexico Highlands University.

Latino communities. The San José State walkout was the beginning of a series of conferences and strikes that changed the image of Mexican Americans as "passive" to that of a visible and militant group. Dolores Delgado Bernal's study of the East Los Angeles blowouts also illustrates the significant leadership roles of Chicanas in the movement (1998).

Among the many conferences and strikes which students engaged in, the conference in 1969 at University of California at Santa Barbara holds the most significance for Latino higher educational history. Emerging from the conference was El Plan de Santa Barbara; the plan represented the clearest and most detailed articulation of the demands of Latino college youth. Although El Plan Spiritual de Aztlán, created at the National Chicano Youth Liberation Conference in Denver in March of 1969 was a pivotal "magna carta" of the general Chicano movement, El Plan de Santa Barbara specifically concerned higher education.

The Chicano Coordinating Council on Higher Education, a coalition of students, faculty, and staff from California institutions of higher education organized the Santa Barbara conference to develop a unified platform for higher education reform in the area of Chicano studies programs, access, and retention. The conference resulted in the call for individual student groups to forego their current names and become the Movimiento Estudiantil Chicano de Aztlán (MEChA). Many groups joined MEChA, others retained their individuality. The manifesto "El Plan de Santa Barbara" focused on three key areas. First, it emphasized the obligation of college and university Chicanos to maintain ties with the barrio community. Second, it stressed the importance of changing institutions of higher education to open their accessibility to Chicanos. The hiring of Chicano faculty, administrators, and staff was viewed as a key step in achieving this objective. Lastly, the Santa Barbara plan called for the alteration of traditional European White interpretations of history, literature, and culture to incorporate Third World viewpoints and particularly Chicano perspectives (Navarro, 1995; Muñoz, 1989; Valdés, 2000). El Plan de Santa Barbara served as a model that was circulated throughout the nation as Chicanos and Puerto Rican students not only entered academe in the 1960s and 1970s in significant numbers but also worked to change academe itself.

While Chicano students on the West Coast and in the Southwest forged a largely Chicano identity on campuses, Puerto Rican students in the urban Northeast and Midwest also joined with community-based groups or created their own organizations. The population of Puertorriqueños swelled in the mid-twentieth century. In New York, the Puerto Rican population rose tenfold from 70,000 in 1940 to 720,000 in 1961. The work of ASPIRA ("aspire" in Spanish) for bilingual and bicultural educational programs in New York City set the groundwork for future militancy. Founded by educator and leader Antonia Pantoja in 1961, ASPIRA focused on raising educational levels and preparing Puerto Rican youth for leadership. At the time of its founding, few Puerto Ricans were graduating from high school, and among those who did graduate, few received academic diplomas (Pantoja, 1998). For example, in 1963 only 331 of 21,000 Puerto Rican high school graduates in New York earned academic diplomas. (Sánchez-Korrol, 1994, p. 230). The numbers of Puerto Rican students in the city colleges were correspondingly low. Traub (1994, p. 44) found that in 1964, City College, although located in Harlem, did not enroll more than 2 percent of its students from the Black community and "a much smaller number of Puerto Ricans."

The Puerto Rican youth movement did not arise in a vacuum but built upon decades of Puerto Rican American associations that had raised awareness of deficiencies in the community and local governments' response to Puerto Rican poverty, discrimination, and lack of bilingual assistance (Sanchez-Korrol, 1994). Similar to Mexican American youths who had shifted their identities to embrace both the spiritual homeland and signify a new activist stance, Puerto Ricans chose "Boricua" as a symbolic term. The name "Boricua" appears in the titles of numerous 1960s student organizations, the founding of Boricua College in New York City in 1973 and Universidad de Boricua (a university without walls founded by Antonia Pantoja). Boricua, explained Santiago (1995, p. xviii), stands for the word "Borinquén" or "Land of the Brave Lord," which the Arawak Indians called the island prior to Columbus's arrival. In contemporary times, Boricua is a term of endearment used among the Puerto Rican community. In the 1960s and 1970s, Boricua served as a rallying cry for activist youth.

The radicalization of Puerto Rican youth is attributed to the small increase of college students as a result of early 1960s programs such as City University of New York (CUNY)'s SEEK (Search for Education, Elevation, and Knowledge), College Discovery, and SUNY Educational Opportunity Programs (EOP) (Serrano, 1998). These pioneer students created several organizations, including the Puerto Rican Student Movement (PRSM) for ASPIRA members in the CUNY system. In addition, Puerto Ricans for Education Progress (PREP) was a network of private college students who worked to get more students into prestigious private schools such as Princeton and Yale (Serrano, 1998). Although these early organizations were not long-lasting, they provided early leadership for the more radical movement that followed.

The pivotal turning point in the Puerto Rican student movement was the successful fight for open admissions at City College, generally considered the flagship campus of the CUNY system. In 1969, conditions were ripe for a showdown between minority students and administrators. Black and Puerto Rican students organized a strike and campus shutdown. The controversial Open Admissions policy at CUNY resulted in a flood of Puerto Rican and Black students. By 1975, Puerto Rican undergraduates had increased to 18,570 or 8.3 percent of the population. In 1969, Puerto Rican students had only numbered 5,425 or 4 percent. (Rodríguez-Fraticelli, 1986). Similarly, at Brooklyn College, students from the Black League of Afro-American Collegians (BLAC) and the Puerto Rican Alliance (PRA) occupied the president's office and issued a series of demands. Throughout the greater New York area, public and private colleges experienced demonstrations and strikes during the tumultuous years of 1969 and 1970 as underrepresented students fought their way into college (Serrano, 1998).

In addition to increasing college enrollment for Puerto Rican, then Dominican, and other Latino groups in the greater New York area during the 1970s and beyond, the movement created Puerto Rican research centers critical to the rewriting and reinvigoration of a Puerto Rican history and culture. In 1971, after two years of battles, CCNY finally approved the creation of a Department of Puerto Rican Studies. Dr. Frank Bonilla of Stanford was brought to assist in the design of the program. Furthermore, CCNY agreed to open an office of Puerto Rican Development to increase Latino admissions and bolster retention rates. At Hunter College, the Puerto Rican Student Union (PRSU) facilitated the creation of the Centros for Estudios Puertorriqueños in 1972, an archival and scholarly research center with a continuing presence in the research community.

Students at the Chicago Circle campus of the University of Illinois (now UIC) successfully fought for the inclusion of a Latino curriculum and assisted in the creation of Rafael Cintrón-Ortiz Latino Cultural Center. Similarly, the Center for Chicano-Boricua Studies at Wayne University in Detroit was founded in 1971 and continues its presence as a Midwestern research center (Valdés, 2000, p. 200). The peak of the Puerto Rican student movement was reached between 1969 and 1973. After 1973, many student organizations declined in numbers and militancy. The end of the open admissions experiment at CUNY in 1975 impacted Puerto Rican youth. The combination of new tuition charges—the first ever in the institution's history—and the general economic recession of the 1970s led to a decline in the steady Puerto Rican enrollment growth of the early 1970s (Traub, 1994).

Throughout the country, the student youth movement began to wane as government programs, private foundations, and institutions implemented many of their demands. Affirmative action

TABLE 2.3   Percentage of College Students Enrolled in Different Types of Institutions, by Racial or Ethnic Group, Fall 1978

Racial or Ethnic Group	Public Institutions			Private Institutions		
	Universities, %	Other Four-Year Institutions, %	Two-Year Colleges, %	Universities, %	Other Four-Year Institutions, %	Two-Year Colleges, %
Whites	19.7	24.8	33.2	6.5	14.6	1.3
Blacks	9.7	30.6	39.3	4.3	13.5	2.7
Hispanics	8.6	25.0	53.3	4.1	7.9	1.1
Native Americans	12.5	22.4	53.0	2.9	7.1	2.1
All students	18.4	25.2	34.5	6.4	14.1	1.4

Source: Brint, Steven, and Jerome Karabel. 1989. The Diverted Dream: Community College and the Promise of Educational Opportunity, 1900–1985, p. 128.

initiatives among many institutions of higher education in the 1970s brought Latinos into colleges, many of whom are now faculty members (Keller, Deneen, & Magallán, 1991). In the long continuum of Latino higher educational history, the 1960s and 1970s was a permanent watershed, although Latinos remained clustered overwhelmingly in public two-year institutions (see Table 2.3). Although Mexican Americans and Puerto Ricans had not been previously barred from White colleges and universities on account of racial policies, their participation prior to the mid-1960s was negligible. The Latino student movement introduced the possibility not only of access to White institutions, but the creation of uniquely Hispanic colleges. The U.S. government's growing acknowledgment in the 1970s that "minority" was not only African American had a significant impact on subsequent state and federal court rulings and policies. President Richard Nixon's O.M.B. Statistical Directive 15 of 1973 finally created a separate federally identified group. As the controversial Richard Rodriguez wrote in *Brown, The Last Discovery of America* (2002), the result of this federal directive was that "several million Americans were baptized Hispanic". The intervention of the federal government in shaping policies towards Hispanic higher education had began.

The Federal Government Steps In, 1980s and 1990s

> While the increase in Hispanics pursuing a postsecondary education is significant, it is insufficient to assure parity in the workforce. From *1973 to 1994, the overall number of high school graduates enrolled in a four-year institution doubled, from 16 to 31 percent*. College-bound Hispanics in four-year institutions, however, only increased from 13 to 20 percent. Plainly, postsecondary Hispanic student enrollment and graduation rates are not keeping pace with the Hispanic American presence in the general population nor with the available pool of Latino high school graduates. (President's Advisory Commission on Educational Excellence for Hispanic Americans, 1996)

The most recent discernible stage in Latino higher educational history recognizes the controversial and critical role of the federal government as a stakeholder in identifying and actively participating in Latino issues. The surging Latino population of the 1980s and 1990s with accompanying predictions of becoming the "largest" minority—and yet the least educated—caught the attention of the federal government. The creation of the term "Hispanic" in 1973 as OMB Statistical Directive 15 was received with skepticism from many scholars and activists. The "homogenization" of diverse peoples with individual social and historical ties to the United States raised debate and concerns (Oboler, 1995). From the longer historical perspective, however, the counting and documentation of Hispanics signaled unprecedented recognition and attention. In particular, Hispanics joined Blacks, Asians, and Native Americans as ethnically identifiable groups. This status permitted not only visibility but also a larger share of public funds. The combination of federal recognition of Hispanics as a separate minority group, and advocacy from the Hispanic Association of Colleges and Universities, the National Council of La Raza, the Puerto Rican Legal and Defense Fund, and others brought postsecondary needs and concerns from the preliminary inroads of the student movement to permanent recognition and status.

The year 1980 represented another turning point in Latino history. Latinos were the fastest growing minority group in the United States according to the U.S. census, and the 1980s were heralded as the "Decade of the Hispanics." Sheer numbers alone, however, could not alter the almost stagnant postsecondary enrollment. The 1980 census revealed that while 20 percent of Californians were Hispanic, only 2.7 percent possessed college degrees. Nationally Latinos received only 2.3 percent of all baccalaureate degrees in 1980–81 yet earned 3 percent of all doctorates (U.S. Congress, 1985, p. 3). Detailed examination of these statistics revealed that the majority were clustered in community colleges. With the exception of Native Americans, Latino college students since 1980 have not fared well compared to African Americans and Asian Americas (see Figure 2.1). Furthermore, Puerto Rican students enrolled in universities on the island of Puerto Rico were counted along with Latinos in the United States, creating a misleadingly high figure of collegiate participation (U.S. Congress, 1985, p. 4). Most disturbing in the early 1980s was the decline in gains made in the 1970s. The percentage of Hispanic high school graduates attending college for example, decreased from 35.4 percent in 1975 to 29.9 percent in 1980 (Olivas, 1986, p. 2). As a result of the severe disconnect between Latino educational achievement, the

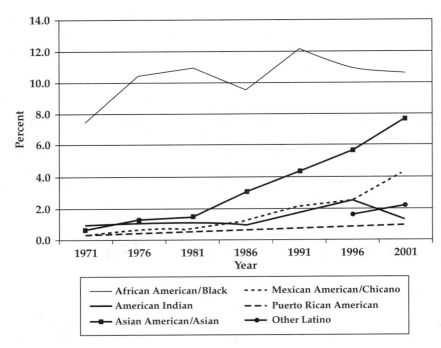

Figure 2.1 Minority representation of students in four-year colleges, 1971–2001.
Data courtesy of Linda J. Sax, Director, Cooperative Institutional Research Program and Associate Professor-in-Residence, University of California, Los Angeles.

size of its population, and its relative underachievement compared to other ethnic groups, a series of steps were taken in the 1980s to regain advances begun in the 1970s.

Michael Olivas, through his supervision of the influential National Center for Education Statistics report, *Condition of Education for Hispanic Americans* (NCES, 1980), spurred reform in Hispanic education. Chairman of the Subcommittee on Postsecondary Education Paul Simon initiated the Hispanic Access to Higher Education Project after reviewing Olivas's work (U.S. Congress, 1985, p. 1). A series of hearings on the topic of Hispanics and higher education subsequently took place on several campuses during 1982 and 1983. Simon introduced H.R. 5240, The Higher Education Act Amendments of 1984, which recommended several reforms to aid Hispanic access and retention. These included the modification of Title III to provide direct aid to institutions with high concentrations of Hispanic students; specific monies for Hispanic students in the TRIO Programs;[1] a special emphasis on Teacher Preparation (Title V) programs to train teachers for Hispanic populations; and increased monies for the Graduate and Professional Opportunities Program (G*POP) to channel more Latinos towards graduate and professional schools. Although H.R. 5420 was not approved, subsequent legislation adopted the bill's key points. Furthermore, publication of the Staff Report on Hispanics' Access to Higher Education (1985) provided data to support future reforms.

The creation of the Hispanic Association of Colleges and Universities (HACU) in 1986 brought together Hispanic leaders in business and two- and four-year colleges and universities with large numbers of Latinos into one powerful advocacy organization. The mission of HACU, to improve the access and quality of college education for Hispanics, has been carried out through offices in San Antonio, Texas, and Washington, D.C. (Laden, 2001). HACU's most successful victory was the establishment of Hispanic Serving Institutions (HSIs) as a federally recognized category. Hispanic

---

[1]The name "TRIO" refers to a set of three federal outreach programs funded under Title IV of the Higher Education Act of 1965. The programs expanded beyond the original three—Upward Bound, Talent Search, and Student Support Services—but the name TRIO persists.

Serving Institutions, unlike HBCUs or Tribal Colleges, do not necessarily have a specific historic mission towards Latino education. Instead, the Department of Education defines HSIs as postsecondary institutions with at least 25 percent Hispanic full-time equivalent enrollment and also 50 percent or more low-income students. Laden (2001) credits HACU with successfully having HSIs recognized in the reauthorization of Title III of the Higher Education Act of 1992, thus securing eligibility for federal funds. Furthermore, in the reauthorization of the Higher Education Act of 1998, HSIs were included with Tribal Colleges and HBCUs under Title V, allowing them a larger slice of the federal pie.

The specific developments accompanying federal categorization received increased visibility in numerous private and publicly sponsored commissions created to examine the Latino educational condition at all levels. For example, President William Jefferson Clinton signed Executive Order 129000, "Educational Excellence for Hispanic Americans" in 1995. The order created a special task-force "to advance the development of human potential, to strengthen the nation's capacity to provide high-quality education, and to increase opportunities for Hispanic Americans to participate in and benefit from federal education programs (President's Advisory Commission on Excellence, 1996, p. 8.). The National Council of La Raza (Fisher, 1998) also sponsored a major study on education that differentiated achievement levels between the numerous Latino groups. The 1990s also witnessed emergence of a new field of studies called Latino Critical Theory and more attention to gender issues within the Hispanic experience (García, 1997; de la Torre & Pesquera, 1993; Valdés, 1997; and Stefancic, 1997).

Conclusions: 2000 and Beyond

The reality to many Latinos is that affirmative action did not cure all of their problems. For instance the income and education gap between Latinos and Euro Americans has increased dramatically in the last two decades. At the same time, however, the Mexican American middle class has expanded significantly since 1965. Undoubtedly, affirmative action along with the Voting Rights Act of 1965 played a role in this expansion . . . As a result, today more Mexican Americans attend universities than at any time in our history, something that would not have happened without the environment created by affirmative action. Affirmative action gave us the justification for our being at the university, and the right that administrators listen to our demands. (Acuña, 1998, pp. 1–2)

The long trajectory of Latino higher educational history does not suggest a never-upward linear path of progress. Latinos in the middle and late nineteenth century enrolled in state and private, particularly Catholic, colleges. The declining social and economic status of Latinos after the turn-of-the-nineteenth century appears to have negatively influenced postsecondary enrollment. Nevertheless, the creation of the University of Puerto Rico in 1903 established an historical legacy of higher education on the island that has not extended to mainland Puerto Ricans (Rodríguez-Fraticelli, 1986). By the mid-twentieth century, only middle-class or exceptional working-class Mexican Americans and Puerto Ricans had entered higher education. The GI Bill and private organizations, including the YMCA and LULAC, provided support for some of these post-World War II students.

The 1960s and 1970s were the watershed years for Latinos in higher education. The successful mobilization of student groups who targeted goals to enhance Latino college access and retention resulted in a permanent presence in academe. Universities, foundations, and state and federal governments created policies, centers, and curricula designed to meet student demands. Unfortunately, successes of this era lost momentum in the economic recessions of the 1970s and into the 1980s.

The 1990s witnessed a political backlash against Latinos and affirmative action. For example, California voters approved the California Civil Rights Initiative of 1996, commonly referred to as Proposition 209, which ended affirmative action programs in the state. Proposition 209 occurred in a climate in which affirmative action was likewise being challenged in the courts. Conflicting decisions in cases such as *Hopwood v. State of Texas* (Fifth Circuit, 1996) and *Smith v. University of Washington* (Ninth Circuit, 2000), respectively repudiating and permitting the use of race in admissions, called into question the future of affirmative action programs as well as the future of *Bakke v. Regents of University of California* (1978), the U.S. Supreme Court decision permitting the use of race in college admissions.

Researchers point to future agendas impacting Latino higher education. One development concerns lawsuits filed to stop the use of Advanced Placement (AP) courses for admissions to college. The American Civil Liberties Union contends that many students in California and Texas simply do not have these offerings at their schools and should not be punished for unequal school resources (Chapa, 2002).

A further issue concerns undocumented Latino college students. Many students were raised in the United States, but their parents did not have them naturalized; as a result, they are being rejected from college admissions and financial aid packages. The complicated legal status of these students was brought to the attention of legislators, who introduced the Development, Relief, and Education for Alien Minors Act (DREAM Act) in the summer of 2002. The bill would grant legal residency to undocumented students with no criminal records who have been U.S. residents for at least five years and graduated from an American high school or received a GED (Torrejón, 2002).

Lastly, although promising gains have been made in higher education enrollment among Latinos, recent studies note that students continue to drop out at high rates for financial reasons. Furthermore, Latinos remain clustered in two-year colleges (40 percent) compared to 25 percent of White college students (Fry, 2002). Overall, researchers predict that Latinos will be underrepresented by 500,000 students by the middle of the twenty-first century, a devastating loss of human potential.

The perilous political climate of the late 1990s for affirmative action and other programs such as bilingual education suggests that Latino higher education may again cycle backward instead of forward. As this narrative has highlighted, numerical dominance of Latinos as the largest minority group in the United States does not *readily* translate into equity. History teaches us that an equitable higher education for Latinos in the future requires vigilance and activism today.

References

1. Acuña, R. F. (1998). *Sometimes There is No Other Side: Chicanos and the Myth of Equality.* Notre Dame, IN: University of Notre Dame Press.
2. Adams, D. W. (1995). *Education for extinction: American Indians and the boarding school experience 1875–1928.* Lawrence, KS: University Press of Kansas.
3. Allsup, C. (1982). *The American G.I. Forum: Origins and evolution.* Austin: Center for Mexican American Studies, The University of Texas at Austin: Distributed by the University of Texas Press. Monograph/Center for Mexican American Studies, The University of Texas at Austin, No. 6.
4. Alonzo, A. C. (1998). *Tejano legacy: Rancheros and settlers in south Texas, 1734–1900.* Albuquerque: University of New Mexico Press.
5. Anderson, J. (1988). *The education of southern Blacks, 1860–1930.* Chapel Hill: University of North Carolina Press.
6. Brown, M. C., & Davis, J. E. (2001). The historically Black college as social contract, social capital, and social equalizer. *Peabody Journal of Education, 76,* 31–49.
7. Carrión, A. M. (1983). *Puerto Rico: A political and cultural history.* New York: W. W. Norton.
8. Chapa, Jorge. (2002). Affirmative Action, X Percent Plans, and Latino Access to Higher Education in the Twenty-first Century. In M. Suárez-Orozco and M. M. Páez. (Eds.), *Latinos Remaking America,* pp. 375–388. Cambridge, MA: David Rockefeller Center for Latino American Studies, Harvard University and Berkeley: University of California Press.
9. Carter, T. P. (1970). *Mexican Americans in school: A history of educational neglect.* New York: College Entrance Examination Board.
10. de la Torre, A., & Pesquera, B. M. (1993). *Building with our hands: New directions in Chicana studies.* Berkeley: University of California Press.
11. de León, A. (2001). *Ethnicity in the sunbelt: Mexican Americans in Houston.* College Station, TX: Texas A&M University Press.
12. Delgado Bernal, D. (1998). Grassroots leadership reconceptualized: Chicana oral histories and the 1968 East Los Angeles school blowouts. *Frontiers: A Journal of Women Studies, 19* (2), 113–142.
13. Donato, R. (1997). *The Other Struggle for Civil Rights.* Albany, NY: State University Press of New York.
14. Donato, R. (1999). Hispano education and the implications of autonomy: Four school systems in Southern Colorado, 1920–1963. *Harvard Educational Review, 69* (2), 117–149.

15. Donato, R., & Lazerson, M. (2000). New directions in American educational history: Problems and prospects, *Educational Researcher, 29* (8), 4–15.
16. Fisher, M. (1998). National Council of La Raza, "Latino Education Status and Prospects: State of Hispanic America 1998."
17. Fry, R. (2002). *Latinos in higher education: Many enroll, too few graduate*. Pew Hispanic Center Research Report. *www.pewhispanic.org*
18. García, M. T. (1989). *Mexican Americans: Leadership, ideology & identity, 1930–1960*. New Haven: Yale University Press.
19. Geiger, R. L. (2000). New themes in the history of nineteenth-century colleges. In Geiger, R. L. (Ed.), *The American college in the nineteenth century* (pp. 1–36). Nashville: Vanderbilt University Press.
20. Getz, L. M. (1997). *Schools of their own: The education of Hispanos in New Mexico, 1850–1940*. Albuquerque: University of New Mexico Press.
21. Goodchild, L. F., & Wechsler, H. (Eds.) (1997). *ASHE reader in the history of higher education*. (2nd ed.).
22. Ibarra, R. A. (2001). *Beyond Affirmative Action: Reframing the Context of Higher Education*. Madison: University of Wisconsin Press.
23. Kanellos, N. (1997). *Hispanic firsts: 500 years of extraordinary achievement*. Detroit, MI: Visible Ink Press.
24. Keller, G. D., Deneen, J. R., & Magallán, R. J. (1991). *Assessment and Access: Hispanics in Higher Education*. Albany, NY: State University of New York Press.
25. Laden, B. V. (2001). Hispanic-serving institutions: Myths and realities. *Peabody Journal of Education, 76* (1), 73–92.
26. Lee, S. M. (2002). Do Asian American faculty face a glass ceiling in higher education? *American Educational Research Journal, 39*, 695–724.
27. León, D. J., & McNeil, D. (1992). A precursor to affirmative action: Californios and Mexicans in the University of California, 1870–72. *Perspectives in Mexican American Studies 3*, 179–206.
28. Lindsay, B., & Justiz, M. J., (Eds.). (2001). *Quest for equity in higher education: Toward new paradigms in an evolving affirmative action era*. Albany: State University Press.
29. Lindsey, Donal F. (1995), *Indians at Hampton Institute, 1877–1923*. Urbana, IL: University of Illinois Press.
30. Lucas, C. J. (1994). *American higher education: A history*. New York: St. Martin's Press.
31. MacDonald, V.-M., (2001). Hispanic, Latino, Chicano, or "Other"?: Deconstructing the relationship between historians and Hispanic-American educational history, *History of Education Quarterly, 41* (Fall 2001), 365–413.
32. McKevitt, G. Hispanic Californians and Catholic higher education: The diary of Jesús María Estudillo, 1857–1864, *California History 69* (Winter 1990–1991), 320–331, 401–403.
33. Menchaca, M. (2001). *Recovering history, constructing race: The Indian, Black, and White roots of Mexican Americans*. Austin: University of Texas Press.
34. Morales, Aurora Levins. (1998). The Historian as Curandera. JSRI Working Paper No. 40. East Lansing, MI: Julian Samora Research Institute.
35. Moreno, J. F., (Ed.). (1999). *The Elusive Quest for Equality: 150 Years of Chicano/Chicana Education*. Cambridge: Harvard University Press.
36. Muñoz, C. (1989). *Youth, identity, power: The Chicano movement*. London: Verso Books.
37. National Center for Education Statistics [NCES]. (1980). *The condition of education for Hispanic Americans*. Washington, DC: Government Printing Office.
38. Navarrette, R. (1993). *A Darker Shade of Crimson: Odyssey of a Harvard Chicano*. New York: Bantam Books.
39. Navarro, A. (1995). *Mexican American youth organization: Avant-garde of the Chicano movement in Texas*. Austin: University of Texas.
40. New Mexico Department of Education. (1917–1918). *Annual Report of the State Superintendent of Instruction*. Albuquerque, NM: Printing Co.
41. Nieto, S. (Ed.). (2000). *Puerto Rican Students in U.S. Schools*. Mahwah, NJ: Lawrence Erlbaum.
42. Oboler, S. (1995). *Ethnic labels, Latino lives: Identity and the politics of (re)presentation in the United States*. Minneapolis: University of Minnesota Press.
43. Olivas, M. (1982/1997). Indian, Chicano and Puerto Rican Colleges: Status and Issues. In L. F. Goodchild & Wechsler, H., (Eds.), *The History of Higher Education* (2nd ed.) 1997.
44. Olivas, M. (1986). Research on Latino College Students: A Theoretical Framework and Inquiry. In M. Olivas, (Ed.), *Latino College Students* (pp. 1–25). New York: Teachers College Press.
45. Padilla, F. M. (1985). *Latino ethnic consciousness: The case of Mexican Americans and Puerto Ricans in Chicago*. Notre Dame, IN: University of Notre Dame Press.
46. Padilla, F. M. (1987). *Puerto Rican Chicago*. Notre Dame: University of Notre Dame Press.

47. Pantoja, A. (1998). Memorias de una vida de obra (Memories of a life of work): An interview with Antonia Pantoja, *Harvard Educational Review, 68* (2), 244–258.

48. Pitt, L. (1966). *The decline of the Californios: A social history of the Spanish-speaking Californians, 1846–1890.* Berkeley, Los Angeles, and London: University of California Press.

49. President's Advisory Commission on Educational Excellence for Hispanic Americans. (1996). *Our Nation on the Fault Line: Hispanic American Education.* Washington, DC: GPO.

50. Rodríguez, Clara E. (2000). *Changing Race: Latinos, the Census, and the History of Ethnicity in the United States.* New York: New York University Press.

51. Rodriguez, R. (2002). *Brown: The last discovery of America.* New York: Viking Press.

52. Rodriguez, R. (October 6, 1994). Black/Latino relations: an unnecessary conflict. *Black Issues in Higher Education, 11*, 40–42.

53. Rodríguez-Fraticelli, C. (1986). *Education and imperialism: The Puerto Rican experience in higher education, 1898–1986.* Centro de Estudios Puertor riqueños Working Paper Series. Higher Education Task Force. Hunter College, New York.

54. San Miguel, Jr., G. (1987). "Let All of Them Take Heed:" *Mexican Americans and the Campaign for Educational Equality in Texas, 1910–1981.* Austin: University of Texas Press.

55. San Miguel, Jr., G. (2001). *Brown, Not White: School Integration and the Chicano Movement in Houston.* College Station, TX: Texas A & M University Press.

56. San Miguel, Jr., G., & Valencia, R. (1998). From the treaty of Guadalupe to Hopwood: The educational plight and struggle of Mexican Americans in the Southwest. *Harvard Educational Review, 68*, 353–412.

57. Sánchez, G. J. (1993). *Becoming Mexican American: Ethnicity, culture and identity in Chicano Los Angeles, 1900–1945.* New York: Oxford Press.

58. Sánchez-Korrol, V. (1994). *From colonia to community: The history of Puerto Ricans in New York City.* Berkeley: University of California Press.

59. Santiago, R. (Ed.). (1995). *Boricuas: Influential Puerto Rican writings—An anthology.* New York: Ballantine Books.

60. Serrano, B. (1998). Rifle, Cañón, y Escopeta! A Chronicle of the Puerto Rican Student Union. In Torres, A & Velásquez, J. (Eds.), *The Puerto Rican Movement: Voices from the Diaspora* (pp. 124–143). Philadelphia: Temple University Press.

61. Stefancic, J. (1997). Latino and Latina Critical Theory: An Annotated Bibliography. *California Law Review, 85*, 1509–1581.

62. Torrejón, V. (2002, July 18). Residency urged for some kids of entrants. *Arizona Daily Star*, p. B8.

63. Traub, J. (1994). *City on a hill: Testing the American dream at City College.* New York: Addison-Wesley Publishing.

64. Tywoniak, F. E., & Garcia, M. T. (2000). *Migrant daughter: Coming of age as a Mexican American woman.* Berkeley: University of California Press.

65. U.S. Commissioner of Education. *Annual reports of the secretary of education, department of Porto Rico.* (1901–1910). Washington, DC: Government Printing Office.

66. U.S. Congress. Committee on Education and Labor. (1985). Staff Report on Hispanics' Access to Higher Education. 99th Congress, 1st Session. Serial No. 99-K. Washington, DC.

67. Valdes, Francisco. (1997). Under Construction: LatCrit Consciousness, Community and Theory. *California Law Review. 85*, 1087–1142.

68. Valdés, D. (2000). *Barrios Norteños: St. Paul and Midwestern Mexican Communities in the twentieth century.* Austin: University of Texas Press.

69. Weinberg, M. (1977). *A Chance to learn: The history of race and education in the United States.* Cambridge, UK: Cambridge University Press.

AMERICAN STUDENT POLITICS: ACTIVISM IN THE MIDST OF APATHY

PHILIP G. ALTBACH

The 1960s, of course, saw the flowering of American student political activism.[1] The American university was in turmoil, and students, for the first time since the 1930s, were playing on a national political stage. A sitting president, Lyndon Johnson, decided not to run for reelection in part because of student demonstrations against his Vietnam policies. Students were also at the forefront of a major change in American values and attitudes—particularly in areas such as relations between the sexes, reproductive rights, music, and social norms. For a short period in the late 1960s, public opinion polls indicated that the most important concern of the American population was campus unrest. It is certainly true that the two decades following the sixties have, in contrast to the decade of turbulence, been characterized by quiet. In reality, the situation is much more complex. There has been some activism, and the revolution in attitudes and values started in the sixties has not completely disappeared.[2] The one major upsurge of student activism, the anti-apartheid "divestment" movement of 1984–86, involved thousands of students nationwide and indicated a new trend in student activism. The quarter century since the sixties has seen a few blips of activism, but seems apathetic only in contrast to the benchmark decade. It may, in fact, be just about at the norm for activism on campus.

Several things are clear about the past quarter century. The first is that activism is not entirely dead. There have been modest upsurges from time to time. There was a flurry of concern about such issues as Nicaragua and campus racism, and there was significantly more involvement with the anti-apartheid movement. It is significant that these are precisely the sorts of issues that have energized American students in the past—issues that have a clear moral content and that may relate to foreign policy. It is also clear that although American student attitudes have become somewhat more conservative politically, the campus remains fairly liberal in orientation on issues of political ideology and particularly on "lifestyle" questions.

Some have detected the embers of activism on campuses, and that the right combination of circumstances might reignite a major student movement.[3] These analysts point to a range of localized student political efforts, and the existence of several national liberal and left-oriented groups. Others look at student volunteerism and the willingness of significant numbers of students to spend time on social service activities as an important force on campus and perhaps a harbinger of political activism.[4] However, the circumstances of both American politics and American higher education in the 1990s are so different that such a resurgence seems very unlikely.

At the same time, American students have certainly turned "inward" in many respects. They have become more concerned with careers in a difficult economy, and the increase in interest in religions—first "alternative" faiths such as Hinduism and Zen Buddhism and, more recently, fundamentalist Christianity and conservative Judaism—shows a concern for spiritual issues.

In sum, the period since 1970 exhibits a variety of somewhat contradictory trends among American students. There is neither sustained activism nor total apathy; neither complete "careerism" nor widespread altruism. The fact is that the past two decades have been characterized by brief sparks of activism in a general context of quiet and even political apathy. There are undercurrents of concern for social issues, with a significant minority of students participating in social service volunteerism. But there are no national or regional activist organizations with significant campus support or the ability to project a political voice for students nationally.

The Legacy of the Sixties: Causes of Decline

The contemporary campus scene is frequently seen in the mirror of the sixties—despite the fact that this era was quite atypical. The legacy of that decade may have some lessons for the recent period. The student movement of the sixties declined for a number of complex reasons. It is not possible to provide a quantifiable explanation for the decline or even to assess accurately the relative weights of the causes. Nonetheless, it is important to catalog some of the key factors.

1. The key motivating force for student activism, the war in Vietnam, gradually wound down during the early 1970s. The war was the factor that mobilized the largest number of students and generated the most dissent. The Vietnam War was a unique phenomenon in American history—it was, at least by the late sixties, widely unpopular not only on campus but among the American middle classes.[5] Students were being drafted into the army, and there was an undercurrent of guilt and resentment among large numbers of students. The end of the war brought an immediate end to mass student activism.

2. The economic situation dramatically changed. The prosperity of the sixties helped to generate a feeling among students and the middle classes generally that individual economic success was assured in the context of a steadily expanding economy. In this respect, among others, the sixties were a rather unique decade. The economic "costs" of activism were seen to be minor in terms of risks to careers—through temporarily suspending studies, and the like. Economic realities changed dramatically in the following decades. The 1970s were characterized by rapid inflation, several "oil shocks" with resulting economic dislocation, fairly high levels of unemployment, and a generally gloomy feeling about the economy. Basic structural changes in the American economy also became evident. American world economic hegemony ended with the rise of Japan and other Pacific Rim nations as major industrial and technological forces. Productivity declined as global competition increased and trade deficits grew. Students began to worry about the job market and how to fit into an increasingly uncertain economy. Not only were traditional middle class jobs declining, but the employment market was in the process of significant change. Students increasingly chose "safe" fields for majors, such as business administration, computer science, pre-law, and pre-medicine—fields in which job prospects were perceived to be favorable. Enrollment patterns on campus shifted dramatically, with majors in the traditional liberal arts declining.

3. The fields that became increasingly popular—in the sciences and professions—were not fields that tend to contribute to activism. Many activists traditionally came from the social sciences, and these fields rapidly lost popularity during the 1970s.

4. The tactics and to some extent the ideology of the student movement of the sixties, particularly in its later more militant and sometimes violent phases, did not lead to success. On the contrary, the majority of American students were alienated by both violent tactics and the hyperrevolutionary rhetoric of the Weathermen and other factions.[6] It must be remembered that the activist leaders of the sixties felt that they were unsuccessful in their major goals—ending the Vietnam War and stimulating revolutionary social change in America. Many were bitter, and some turned to ever more radical approaches, including bombing buildings, violent bank robberies, and supermilitancy on campus. The movement itself sowed some of the seeds of its own destruction. In some ways, the ideological and tactical self-destruction at the end of the sixties made it more difficult for activist movements in the following decades.

5. Media attention was an important part of the student movement of the sixties, and when the mass media turned to other topics, the activist movement lost an important focus.[7]

6. The changing American political climate had a key influence on the decline of the student movement. American politics moved sharply to the right and have remained there throughout the past two decades. The election of Richard Nixon as president in 1968 was the beginning of this trend, and the "Reagan Revolution" of the 1980s solidified it. There is no question that the political center in America has moved significantly to the right. Traditionally, student activist movements have benefited from a relatively liberal social milieu.

7. The student population itself significantly changed. Expansion slowed, and the proportion of students from working class and minority backgrounds increased. Many more students studied part-time, and the percentage of students working while studying ballooned. These demographic facts tend to diminish the potential for activism, since activists have traditionally been middle class in social class origins and are full-time students with the time to devote to extracurricular activities.

The decline and, by 1972, virtual collapse of perhaps the largest student activist movement in American history left a tremendous vacuum on the campus. Ever since then, the trend has been to compare activist campaigns to the sixties, a comparison that is unfair, because the more recent period has not been characterized by the social unrest and crisis of the sixties. Recent activist movements have had to grow in the shadow of both the accomplishments and the failures of the sixties.

A Complex Configuration of Attitudes

There is no question that student attitudes have become more conservative on many issues since the sixties. In 1987, only 2.3 percent of American freshmen identified themselves as being on the far left with another 22.2 percent liberal. On the other hand, only 1.3 percent claimed a far right affiliation, and 18.3 percent were conservative.[8] In 1995, these proportion remained fairly stable—with 2.7 percent claiming far left views, 21.1 percent liberal, 20.3 percent conservative, and 1.6 percent far-right. This is down, particularly in the far left category, from the 1960s. The large majority are "middle of the road." A configuration of attitudes concerning political and lifestyle issues indicates that students express a variety of liberal to middle-of-the-road attitudes. General trends in political and lifestyle attitudes remained fairly steady from the mid-1980s to the mid-1990s. For example, 23.8 percent favored the abolition of the death penalty in 1988. In 1995, 20.9 percent agreed. In 1988, there was majority support for nuclear disarmament, consumer protection, busing to achieve racial balance in the schools, and other items on the liberal agenda. A majority of students believed that couples should live together before marriage (52.1 percent), and 58.7 percent believe that abortion should be legal. Yet, only 19.3 percent support the legalization of marijuana and 23.8 back the abolition of the death penalty.[9] By 1995, 33.8 percent supported the legalization of marijuana, while support for the abolition of the death penalty dropped to 20.9 percent. Ninety percent of American students claim religious affiliation, and 80.6 percent in 1995 reported that they attended a religious service at least once in the previous year.

Religion is an interesting indication of change in student interest and perspectives. During the sixties, campus religious organizations continued to exist and some were involved in the activist movement. In the past two decades, there has been a resurgence of interest in religion, reflecting, it seems, a concern for personal values and orientations as opposed to societal issues.

Except during the 1960s, American student attitudes have not been notably different from those of the mainstream of the American population—particularly the middle class from which a large proportion of the students come. Student attitudes tend to be modestly more liberal on ideological issues and significantly more liberal on "lifestyle" questions. In 1984, for example, Ronald Reagan had 7 percent less support among students than he had among adults. All in all, however, there is general consistency.

Students in the 1980s and 1990s indicated that they did not participate to any great extent in political activities. Only 14.8 percent in 1995 indicated that they discussed politics frequently, and 7.6 percent worked in an off-campus political campaign. On the other hand, 70.3 percent performed volunteer work during the previous year.[10]

Arthur Levine and Keith R. Wilson have written persuasively about the "me-generation" that they felt dominated campus culture during the 1970s and, for the most part, up to the present time.[11]

The "me-generation" is characterized by student attitudes that place much greater stress on individual values and needs than did the socially conscious students of the 1960s. "Me-generation" students have chosen academic fields that promise the best and most lucrative opportunities for jobs and careers, and when asked, they have named the achievement of wealth as an important goal. They have been interested in a variety of self-fulfillment movements, from EST to Hare Krishna, and there has been a modest return to traditional religious faiths. During this period, Americans, in general, expressed a lack of confidence in social institutions of all kinds: for example, confidence in the United States Supreme Court dropped from 50 percent in 1966 to 31 percent in 1977. Confidence in institutions of higher education dropped from 73 percent to 55 percent in the same period; people tended to rely more on individual orientations and concerns.

"Me-ism" has had a significant impact on campus life. Self-help groups have, for example, expanded significantly. Students have been more willing to bring lawsuits against academic institutions and have been much more concerned with the quality of campus life. There has been more competition—for admission to the best colleges, for entry into the major fields that will yield high-paying careers, and for grades in courses and the like. Social and sexual mores also seem to be affected, although here causes—and effects—are less clear, in part due to the concern about AIDS.

"Me-ism" and Activism

The configuration of attitudes that emerged in the 1970s is reflected in a new style of campus activism. Without question, there is less activism and political concern in general. Further, the nature of the organizations changed during the 1970s, as did the tactics of student political groups. The rebirth of the student government organizations, which were a mainstay of campus life and one of the foci of political concerns during the 1950s, is an indication of the change.[12] Student governments have been concerned not only with the quality of campus life and with student service enterprises, but also with the representation of students in a wider forum within the university—and in some cases in a broader one.[13] These groups seem to remain a minority phenomenon, however, since only 22.7 percent of students in 1995 indicated that they voted in student government elections.

Directly related to student governments were student lobbies, which emerged in many states and at the national level in the 1970s and 1980s, but seem to have waned by the 1990s. The National Student Lobby has been sporadically active in Washington, trying to press for their interests in Congress and elsewhere. It was estimated that such lobbies were established on 22 percent of the nation's campuses in thirty-nine states by the early 1970s. The lobbies were mainly concerned with ensuring that student interests are respected; they have tried to maintain guaranteed student loan programs, opposed tuition increases at state universities, argued against restrictions on student rights, and so on. One of the most successful student lobbies was the Student Association of the State University (SASU) at the State University of New York (SUNY), but even this active group had run its course by the end of the 1980s, and has been less active, even in a period when SUNY experienced serious cuts. SASU represented most of SUNY's thirty-four campuses at the state capitol in Albany and employed a full-time staff to work with SUNY officials and the state government. On many occasions SASU has cooperated with SUNY on legislative initiatives, but occasionally it opposed SUNY officials on tuition increases. It occasionally sponsored large-scale demonstrations in Albany to press for student issues. The organization also provided reduced rate travel, block concert tickets, and student shopping discounts.

Another notable trend among student organizations during the 1970s, which has seen a decline in the 1980s, was the re-establishment of the Public Interest Research Groups (PIRG). The idea for the PIRG was proposed by Ralph Nader in 1970, and by 1978 PIRGs had been formed at 11 percent of American colleges and universities in twenty-eight states.[14] The PIRGs, which do research on environmental and other social issues, and also engage in lobbying for legislation and in public education, proved to be popular. They were able to combine student concerns for social issues that affected their own lives, such as the environment, with a tradition of social activism. The PIRGs were not generally involved in activist demonstrations, but rather worked with government officials, provided educational materials, and tried to raise public consciousness about their concerns. By the mid-1980s, however, the PIRGs experienced a dramatic decline and were much less evident on most campuses.

Although students continue to be committed to environmental concerns, they are not active in this or in the other areas stressed by the PIRGs.

Although the "me-generation" was primarily focused on activism and the level of campus political concern was at a low ebb during the 1970s, "me-ism" did have some political and social ramifications.[15] The kinds of student organizations that seemed to be most effective during the 1970s reflected student interest in issues that directly affected their lives and futures. The ideologically based social action groups that were much in evidence during the 1960s virtually disappeared from the campuses. It is significant that the areas of activism that have been most successful in the 1970s and early 1980s were those that combined individual interests and social concerns.

The Eighties and the Nineties—Modest Concern in the Midst of Apathy

The 1980s and to some extent the early 1990s show something of a paradox in student political activism in the United States. On the one hand, the configuration of attitudes evident in the post-sixties period has continued without significant change, with the marked decline in radical attitudes but with the continuing social concerns noted earlier. There continues to be a strong focus on careers and worry about ensuring a safe position in the middle class. Yet, in the nineties, there has also been a modest resurgence of interest in the social sciences, education, and other fields that had lost favor in the previous two decades. There has also been a sporadic resurgence of student activism.[16] It has been activism more reminiscent of the earlier nonviolent period of the early 1960s than the hypermilitant late sixties student movement. Students have also reacted with some activism to campus racial tensions that were marked at the end of the 1980s.[17] As in earlier periods, most activism and social concern has emanated from the liberal left, although there has also been some conservative political involvement as well.[18]

A detailed analysis of the broader political and economic context of the past two decades is beyond the scope of this discussion. However, it is important to mention several key elements. The fairly severe economic problems of the 1970s abated considerably, although the middle class did not fully regain its sense of prosperity. The impact of the several "oil shocks" wore off, and rampant inflation ended. Unemployment, while quite high early in the 1980s, also declined, although the pattern of employment changed, with many jobs clustered in low wage fields. Students remained concerned about finding good jobs, and choices of majors reflected an uncertain job market.

The "Reagan Revolution" downplayed the welfare state. Wall Street boomed and declined, a record number of large corporations merged, the savings and loan industry collapsed, and the scramble for wealth dominated the national scene more completely than it had at any time since the 1920s. By the end of Reagan's first term, the campuses seemed to be little more than yuppie breeding grounds, politically quiescent places where by far the leading undergraduate major was business administration. A *Newsweek on Campus* cover story summarized this mood in a cartoon showing collegians dropping the rebellious 1960s' slogan "Don't trust anyone over 30," and replacing it with a more yuppie/80s' sentiment, "Never trust anyone under $30,000."[19]

The rejuvenation of conservatism wrought by the Reagan revolution from 1980–1988 inhibited progressive activism on the two key issues that traditionally had mobilized the student Left: peace and civil rights. President Reagan effectively promoted a new Cold War nationalism against the Soviet's "Evil Empire," obtaining Congressional funding for a significant military buildup. His invasion of Grenada in 1983 and the United States' military victory there yielded much flag waving, which even affected the campuses, where rallies in support of the invasion outnumbered protests. Though there was some student involvement in the nuclear freeze movement and in demonstrations against the Contra war in Nicaragua, the conservative national mood prevented these causes from generating mass student support during Reagan's first term. Moreover, the Reagan administration's assault on affirmative action left civil rights groups reeling and promoted a campus backlash against minorities, which helped to stifle student activism on civil rights issues and stimulated a rash of campus-based racial incidents by decade's end.

The Reagan landslide in 1984 seemed initially to seal the fate of the student left as an impotent minority in a conservative era. Ironically, however, the landslide had the opposite effect, stimulating rather than suffocating campus protest. Because the election had made it clear that neither Reagan nor the nation's rightward drift could be halted at the polls, student activists now concluded that protest was the only way to challenge Reaganism. And this challenge would occur on the one issue upon which the Reagan administration (and American university administrators) seemed most vulnerable: South Africa.

Anti-Apartheid and Divestment: An Eighties' Activist Movement

During the 1984–1985 academic year, the apartheid regime in South Africa faced the greatest black insurgency in a quarter century. Black protest against white minority rule and the new "reform" constitution was met with repression that was brutal even by South African standards, culminating in March 1985 with a police massacre of unarmed demonstrators near Sharpeville. In response to these events and stimulated by extensive television and press coverage of them, a solidarity movement took root in the United States, centered in black churches and civil rights organizations. This movement demanded that the Reagan administration enact sanctions against South Africa. But the administration, clinging to its "constructive engagement" policy, vigorously opposed sanctions. The solidarity movement escalated its protests through a dramatic civil disobedience campaign, orchestrating sit-ins at which demonstrators, including prominent political leaders, were arrested at the South African embassy. The anti-apartheid protests in both the United States and South Africa captured the imagination of American undergraduates in spring 1985, sparking the largest student protests since the 1960s.[20]

Both on campus and off, the anti-apartheid movement grew substantially in the wake of a national day of protest held on April 4, 1985, commemorating the seventeenth anniversary of Martin Luther King Jr.'s assassination. Some 4,000 demonstrators marched outside the South African embassy in Washington, D.C., and 58 were arrested. On this same day, several hundred Columbia University students brought the anti-apartheid movement to their campus. Chanting and sitting outside the main entrance to Hamilton Hall, they vowed to stay until Columbia divested all of its holdings in companies doing business with South Africa.[21]

The Columbia protest lasted three weeks, and it inspired similar divestment protests on some sixty campuses. Several of these protests were far larger than the Columbia sit-in. At the University of California at Berkeley, well over 10,000 students joined a one-day strike in protest against the arrest of 158 divestment protesters. More than 1,000 Cornell University students were arrested in a series of divestment sit-ins.

Though engaging in protests that evoked memories of the 1960s, the divestment movement sought to avoid the polarization of that earlier decade. The spring 1985 protests were nonviolent and directed more toward raising the divestment issue than disrupting or attacking the university. This tone was set from the beginning at Columbia, where the protesters sat outside rather than inside Hamilton Hall and posted notices that though they were blocking the main entrance, the basement entrances would remain open. "We don't hate President Sovern," explained one Columbia protest leader. "We think we have a better argument than he does." *Newsweek* noted that "compared to the purple-hazed 60s" the divestment protesters "are exceedingly polite." Students at the University of Colorado at Boulder, for example, carefully negotiated with school officials before staging a demonstration that one administrator called "the most civilized on the face of the earth."[22]

The divestment protesters also seemed more studious and "high tech" than their predecessors. Students at Columbia and other campus sit-ins rotated on the front lines of the protest so that they could attend their classes. The activists also made good use of the personal computer revolution, quickly setting up a computer network linking over one hundred campuses to share the latest news about their protests.

The unambiguous moral issue of apartheid was at the heart of student protests. The activists focused most of their attention on pressuring the university and the nation to use their economic leverage against Pretoria's racist regime. But beyond South Africa itself, the divestment protesters were seeking to send America the message that the political conscience of the campus had not disappeared and that their generation was ready and willing to raise its voice against the administration's right-wing policies. Soon after the divestment protests began, the *New York Times* reported that across the United States student activists were unanimous in agreeing that among their strongest recruiting points were the Reagan administration policies and even the personality of the President himself. "A lot of what's going on is in reaction to Reagan," explained a Berkeley divestment activist. "People are frustrated and aggravated with what's going on in El Salvador and Nicaragua. People with a lot of pent-up energy finally see a chance to do things constructively."[23]

This was a revolt against not only the president's foreign policy, but against the self-centered materialism of the Reagan era. The student protesters were saying that morality must take precedence over profitability, that regardless of the financial costs the university had a civic obligation to sever its economic ties to South Africa. Moreover, student activists were trying to make a similar point about themselves, seeking to show that contrary to media stereotypes, many collegians were not avaricious yuppies. Berkeley divestment leader Ross Hammond explained that at his university the movement was "in part a reaction against the media for portraying Berkeley as a dead campus. That idea annoys people no end, people who really care. This is still a progressive campus." Similar sentiments were expressed by student protesters across the nation, including Yale divestment organizer Tom Keenan who proudly credited the demonstrations with "disproving the idea that we're one homogeneous student body heading for business suits."[24]

Though the surge of activism in spring semester 1985 was confined primarily to divestment, there were also protests on behalf of peace and affirmative action. At the University of Colorado, over 450 protesters were arrested during a demonstration against CIA recruiters. Anti-CIA protests also occurred at Yale, Wesleyan, and the University of Wisconsin at Madison—where students sought to make a citizen's arrest against a CIA recruitment officer. Minority students incorporated into their divestment protests a call for greater minority representation on campus. And at Brown University affirmative action took center stage, as minority students led a brief strike and building occupation in April, demanding increased minority admission, financial aid, and a more Third World-oriented curriculum.[25]

Underestimating the political strength and appeal of the divestment movement, most campus administrators initially turned down its demand for total severance of all university investments in companies doing business in South Africa.[26] The Columbia administration led the way in setting this hard line. Soon after the sit-in began, Columbia spokesman Fred Knubel announced, "Columbia has no plan to meet the students' demands." In justifying this refusal to negotiate, Columbia president Michael Sovern insisted, "no university can allow some of its members to force a position on it." Campus officials at many institutions stressed that total divestment would violate their fiduciary responsibilities, and some claimed that divesting would lessen America's economic leverage and its ability to press for reform in South Africa. The depth of this administration opposition meant that the movement would not win divestment overnight: a lesson driven home by the Columbia sit-in, which ended with no promises by the administration that it would move toward total divestment.[27]

Campus administrators also reinforced their antidivestment position by clamping down on the demonstrators. They initiated disciplinary proceedings against leaders of sit-ins and in several cases denied diplomas to students who had broken campus regulations. College officials began holding national meetings to discuss ways to control protesters. This led to the enactment of tighter campus disciplinary procedures at Cornell and other activist-oriented universities and colleges. At Berkeley and Columbia, campus police were authorized to videotape demonstrations to facilitate the prosecution of students involved in unlawful protests. Divestment protesters denounced these policies, claiming that they could have a chilling effect upon free speech.[28]

What these administrators had not counted on in taking this hard line was the groundswell of public support that would quickly strengthen the divestment movement. Divestment leaders such as Jon Klavens of Columbia understood, as college officials had not, that America's revulsion against apartheid—exacerbated daily by the televised atrocities from South Africa—gave their movement an edge over campus administrators, who appeared Scrooge-like in refusing to part with their South African investments. "We have as much of a moral high ground as the abolitionists, maybe more," Klavens said. Despite early setbacks in the face of administration intransigence, divestment protesters remained confident that ultimately, in the words of Stanford organizer Steven Phillips, "we will be effective because apartheid offends everyone's sense of justice."[29] Such confidence was well placed.

The campus divestment movement had never stood alone in demanding a change in university investment policies. During the first week of the Columbia sit-in, Rev. Jesse Jackson came up to Morningside Heights and warmed the rain-drenched divestment protesters with a speech praising them for "setting a moral example for America."[30] Similar praise came from Bishop Desmond Tutu. Joining these civil rights leaders were labor leaders, faculty, and hundreds of public officials across the nation who advocated divestment of state and municipal funds from banks with South African connections. The call for federal sanctions against South Africa was also beginning to gather support in Congress. This increasingly favorable public mood gave the divestment movement powerful allies in the community. When, for instance, UCLA and Berkeley students sat-in, demanding divestment, several California state legislators, including House Speaker Willie Brown, endorsed the protest and warned the university that its budget would get bottled up in Sacramento unless it divested. The combination of campus and community pressure led more than twenty-five campuses nation-wide to partially or totally divest between April and October 1985.

The pressure for divestment increased dramatically during the 1985–1986 academic year. Building on the organizational base constructed the previous spring, a national divestment mobilization in October 1985 orchestrated demonstrations on over one hundred campuses—nearly doubling the size and geographical scope of the movement.[31] If the 1983–1984 academic year had been the year of the yuppie on campus, 1985–1986 was the year of the shanty, as divestment protesters across the nation constructed shabby huts, and placed them on their campuses to symbolize the poverty and oppression of South African blacks.[32]

With the movement gaining momentum, university administrators, regents, and trustees began to back down from their original refusal to divest. The first big symbolic victory of the academic year came in October 1985 when the Columbia administration committed itself to total divestment. Columbia also provided other administrators with a face-saving argument for reversing their earlier anti-divestment position. The Columbia administration claimed that it had opted to divest not because of student protest, but because the recent state of emergency imposed in South Africa had created a new political environment and rendered unrealistic the hope that United States companies could, through their presence and egalitarian employment policies, reform that social system and end apartheid. But Columbia was only the beginning; by the end of the 1985–1986 academic year, 120 colleges and universities had divested their South African holdings either partially or completely.[33]

The biggest divestment occurred in July 1986, when the University of California opted to pull its $3.1 billion investment out of companies doing business in South Africa. This victory was perhaps the most striking demonstration of the degree to which the divestment movement had influenced public opinion and thereby caused a shift in the position of politicians. Where the previous spring California's governor, George Deukmejian had vigorously opposed divestment, this conservative Republican now—up for reelection and recognizing the widespread and rising public support of the student movement's goal—endorsed divestment and used his considerable political influence with the Board of Regents to bring about a surprising reversal of its earlier vote against divestment.

The End of the Divestment Movement

Unlike the student movement of the 1960s, which self-destructed because of its sense of failure (its leaders wrongly thought the movement was failing to stop the Vietnam War), the divestment movement's demise was a product of its own success. The movement not only won divestment on campuses across the nation, it helped transform public opinion sufficiently so that even President Reagan had been forced to modify his position by supporting very limited sanctions against South Africa. Having won so many major divestment battles, the movement now had to face the problem of determining a new goal and a more extended political agenda. But having, in effect, lost its raison d'être, the movement was unable to solve this problem or shift its focus; instead it faded in the 1986–1987 academic year almost as quickly as it had emerged.

The movement's collapse was linked to the fading of another important motivation for the student activism—the need to halt Reagan and the nation's rightward drift. The Reagan revolution no longer aroused fear among students because it had dissipated in the wake of both the 1986 elections, which restored Democratic dominance in Congress, and the Iran-Contra scandal, which paralyzed the Reagan White House. With its two major opponents—university investments in South Africa and President Reagan, now weakened, the student movement of the 1980s came to an end.

The demise of the divestment movement left some activists wondering whether their much-lauded pragmatism and moderation had turned out to be a weakness rather than a strength. By focusing so intently on the limited demand of divestiture, the movement had inadvertently given the universities a way of opting out of the controversy: allowing administrators to render apartheid a nonissue on campus simply by purging their investment portfolios of South Africa-linked stocks. Thus, after winning many divestment battles in 1985–1986, campus protests ended, though the apartheid regime continued its repression. The divestment movement's collapse, moreover, coincided with the press blackout instituted by the Botha regime, which kept news of South Africa's anti-apartheid struggle out of the reach of the American media. Movement activists watched helplessly as public interest in South Africa, which they had labored so hard to build, declined both on campus and off. The movement had mobilized campus opinion against apartheid, Reaganism, and yuppieism, but it could find no way of sustaining mass anti-apartheid protest in the United States once the issue of university complicity with South African racism had been resolved.

Unlike the divestment effort, which tried to build a national movement through coordinated demonstrations and meetings, the antiracism movement remained local and there was no national coordination. By the end of the 1987–1988 academic year, there was little evidence of a significant campus protest movement. In addition to these two major activist thrusts in the mid-1980s, there has been concern about American policy in Central America, and significant campus opposition to supporting the Contras in Nicaragua. As in the past, civil rights issues and foreign policy were key elements of a modest rebirth of campus political concern. At the end of the 1987–1988 academic year, there were no major national activist organizations seeking to coordinate political developments on campus.

Conservative Trends: The Media Exaggerates

Not all students, however, welcomed these divestment victories and the appearance of shanties and mass protest on campus. Since the early Reagan years, small but well-organized and well-funded groups of right-wing student activists had appeared on campus. The most vocal and well known of these groups was at Dartmouth. It published an ultraconservative magazine, the *Dartmouth Review*, which received financial support from conservative alumni. The *Review* was well connected to the right-wing Republican establishment; it drew attention and praise from William F. Buckley's *National Review*, and it served as an Ivy League recruiting ground for the Reagan White House—several editors went on to become administration officials. Dinesh D'Souza, who was one of the main organizers of the Dartmouth activities and was an editor of the *Dartmouth Review*, went on to write an influential book attacking affirmative action, multiculturalism, and other liberal initiatives on campus.[35] The *Dartmouth Review* was known not only for its conservative ideology, but also for its sarcastic and nasty editorials, which included gay bashing and minority baiting. A 1982 article opposing affirmative action, charged that Dartmouth had lowered its academic standards in order to recruit blacks; it was headlined "DIS SHO AIN'T NO JIVE."[36]

With the emergence of an active divestment movement on the Dartmouth campus, the *Dartmouth Review* crowd had an opportunity to move beyond rhetorical attacks on the left. Enraged by the appearance of shanties on campus, a dozen right-wing students (ten of whom were *Review* staffers) went out late at night armed with sledge hammers and destroyed shanties in January 1986. The *Review's* next issue praised the assault and crowed that it would have been even better had the shanties been destroyed much earlier.

This incident provoked a wave of indignation at Dartmouth, particularly since the destruction of the shanties had been timed to coincide with the Martin Luther King, Jr., holiday. In protest against the destruction of the shanties, students occupied the administration building for thirty hours, until the administration agreed to hold a day-long teach-in on racism. At the teach-in, nearly two-thirds of the student body turned out and heard black students complain of the discriminatory environment they confronted at Dartmouth.[37]

The controversy at Dartmouth attracted national attention to the issue of collegiate fascism. "The shanty project," observed one reporter, "designed to focus attention on racism far away, forced many to face allegations of bigotry in their own backyard."[38] Similar attacks on shanties occurred at the University of Utah, Johns Hopkins University, California State College at Long Beach, and at UC Berkeley. But such attacks were rare and aroused far more opposition than support among a national student body sympathetic to the anti-apartheid movement.

It is fair to say that there is little campus support for the right-wing politics expressed by the *Dartmouth Review* and similar newspapers and journals on other campuses. Conservative initiatives have been supported by right-wing foundations, which have provided funds to "conservative alternative" campus newspapers nationwide. These funds have permitted newspapers to continue to publish. By the 1990s, little remained of the modest conservative upswing—mainly the externally-funded newspapers. Conservative campus activism received considerable attention in the media, especially in conservative newspapers and magazines, in part because there has been very little other activism to report.

Racism and Antiracism

Many campuses experienced racial incidents aimed against African-Americans and, to a lesser extent, other minority groups, in the mid-1980s and early 1990s. The causes for this surprising wave of campus racism are not entirely clear. The attitudes expressed by President Ronald Reagan and members of his administration opposing affirmative action and other programs to assist minorities, and the general lack of sensitivity to minority issues during this period, played a role. So, too, did growing resentment by many whites against affirmative action, set-asides, and other programs aimed at helping minorities, which were perceived by some as causing problems for whites. A racial climate punctuated by the Clarence Thomas court hearings, the beating of Rodney King and ensuing riots, and other incidents contributed to tensions on campus.[39]

While it would be an exaggeration to say that campus race relations dramatically deteriorated by the mid-1980s, there were a variety of racial problems at American colleges and universities, some of which remain unsolved. The most dramatic—and disturbing—issue was the emergence of acts of racism against minority students. It is difficult to estimate the number of incidents nationwide. The National Institute Against Prejudice and Violence cited 174 incidents of ethnoviolence on college campuses in the 1986–1988 academic years.[40] The same organization noted that one in five students of color indicated that they had been victims of some sort of harassment on the campus of the college they attended.[41] These incidents generally consisted of anonymous racist graffiti or slogans, defacing of posters or other petty incidents.[42] Such acts were deeply offensive to African-American students, and generally resulted in soul searching and sometimes in anti-racist activism on campus. Many colleges and universities adopted anti-hate speech codes intended to eliminate racist expression. Some faculty and students opposed these codes as violations of free speech and academic freedom, and in a few cases the matter was taken to the courts, where judicial rulings in some cases overruled the codes while in others supported them.

Campus racial and ethnic tensions proved to be a highly complex and contentious set of issues and concerns. The entire academic community agreed that expressions of racial and ethnic prejudice were reprehensible. There was less agreement about the trend toward dormitories and other facilities which were based on race or ethnicity, and many were dismayed by the noticeable self-segregation of groups on campus. Racial preferences in admissions and in the award of scholarships became controversial issues on campus in this period as well, and this further enhanced campus racial tensions.

The activist organizations that emerged to oppose campus racism were, in all cases, limited to single colleges and universities. No national movement emerged, and in general activism diminished once the specific racist incident was dealt with. Ad hoc student groups were organized to deal with the crisis, generally under the leadership of minority students, but these organizations did not last. In some universities—Stanford, Columbia, Cornell, and Arizona State University among them—the incidents were not handled sensitively by administrators, and protest escalated, resulting in a few cases in arrests.[43] In most cases, crises were soon defused, and the situation returned to normal. Anti-racist groups succeeded in raising campus consciousness about prejudice and bigotry on campus, and focused discussion on racial issues. They may have had a positive impact on campus relations. But they did not engender a continuing student movement.

Campus race relations were, however, affected by these incidents. National media attention exacerbated the situation by focusing attention on campus racial problems. Many African-American students felt unwelcome on some predominantly white campuses. This feeling, combined with an already existing trend toward racial separation on campus, pulled African-Americans out of the campus mainstream into separate social groups, and sometimes into separate dormitories. By the 1990s, campus subcultures became based to some extent on race and ethnicity, and in some cases, political activism devolved on these groups to a considerable degree.

The Curriculum and "Interest Politics"

The undergraduate curriculum has undergone a number of significant changes during the past two decades. Students influenced these changes to some degree. Perhaps the most significant change was the re-establishment of the general education "core" curriculum on many campuses. This restoration was mainly an initiative of the faculty, and there was little student involvement, pro or con. Indeed, the general education movement was in considerable part a reaction to the student-induced abolition of specific curricular requirements in the sixties. As students chose to major in preprofessional fields, engineering, and other vocationally oriented subjects, and the humanities and social sciences experienced low enrollments. The recent curricular "restoration" of the general education movement was stimulated in part by faculty wishing to restore the traditional base of the university, and in part as an effort to increase enrollment in some fields.[44]

The new model general education curriculum that was put into place differed, on most campuses, from the model that dominated American higher education in the 1950s. It included, in addition to the traditional arts and sciences, a multicultural component, and often options for such new fields as women's studies or minority studies. The inclusion of these new fields in the curriculum, as well as the establishment and nurturing of minority studies programs on many campuses, was stimulated in considerable part by students and supported by influential student groups. In many cases, student activism to establish or institutionalize minority studies or women's studies programs and departments was of central importance. Traditional faculty members often opposed these new initiatives, with students providing the balance of influence.[45]

Without student support, women's studies and minority studies programs, would not have achieved their current level of success. In some cases, students were the initiating force for these programs, while in many others they provided central support for their establishment or maintenance. Women's and minority studies courses and programs are now entrenched in most universities, and are established as important fields of scholarship.[46] Feminist student groups are also widespread and have been active in both campus affairs and self-help for women students. Black student organizations are also widespread, and have had an impact on Black Studies academic programs. Newer phenomena are gay and Asian-American student groups. These have also been active in supporting academic programs to reflect their concerns, and by the 1990s, academic programs in these areas were being established on some campuses.

None of these efforts have led to the creation of significant national organizations or regional or national student activist movement. The struggles have been focused on specific campuses. Many of the campus-based movements have attracted faculty support, and have been successful in establishing academic programs. Local organizations have, however, maintained their existence and have provided a focus for social and intellectual activity.

The establishment and maintenance of these new fields has been one of the most significant influences of students on American higher education, perhaps in the past century. It is, in this respect, worth noting that the various demands for university reform and the participation by students in academic governance made during the 1960s had little lasting impact. A small number of colleges and universities gave students significant voice in governance, but virtually all of these withdrew the reforms once student interest and faculty support waned in the 1980s. Students did gain participation in token numbers on academic committees in many institutions, but this did not significantly alter established patterns of governance.[47] While the history of the establishment and institutionalization of women's and minority studies program is a complex one, students played a central role.

Other Campus Political Developments

Students did not organize protest movements concerning the several American foreign policy involvements of the past decade. The case of the Persian Gulf War is especially interesting. The crisis built up over a number of months in 1990 and 1991. There was only minor campus concern, and few protests, although there was time for campus organizing and the crisis received considerable attention from the mass media. The large majority of students supported American policy in the Gulf.[48] There were more campus manifestations of support for the Gulf war (such as putting up American flags) than against it. No national protest movement emerged, and there seems to have been little coordination of campus activism. The Gulf crisis was relatively short-lived, involved few American causalities, and took place when students were not being compelled to enter military service. Yet, public opinion in the early period of the U.S. build-up in the Gulf was somewhat divided, and there was vocal Congressional opposition to the use of military force. The lack of a strong student response is perhaps indicative of the significant changes in the American student population since the 1960s, as well as the general campus quiet during the past decade.

The "collapse of the Soviet Union and the end of the Cold War had a modest impact on campus. One of the pillars of American foreign policy, opposition to the Soviet Union, was removed, as were many of the bipolar assumptions about America's role in the world. The collapse of communism was a blow to radical ideology, and the traditional stances of the left came into question. The small radical organizations on campus were affected. Other foreign policy initiatives during this period that might have aroused significant opposition were met with general campus apathy. The U.S. invasion of the Caribbean island of Grenada during the Reagan administration to topple a "pro Castro" regime was widely opposed on campus, but attracted little activism. The ongoing crisis in the former Yugoslavia produced no student response or initiatives, nor was there any reaction when the United States decided to commit troops to the NATO peace-keeping mission in 1996. In short, foreign policy, traditionally the mother lode of student activism in the United States has not stimulated significant interest since the anti-Apartheid protests of the mid-1980s.

Students have, in small numbers and without a major national movement, been exercised about several issues. Environmental issues have always had considerable resonance on campus. When asked in surveys, students have supported environmental issues—in 1995, 83.5 percent of freshmen said that the federal government was not doing enough to control environmental pollution.[49] At the end of the 1980s, Earth Day had widespread campus support and was marked by meetings and demonstrations in many colleges and universities.[50] Greenpeace and other pro-environmental groups claim many campus chapters, and a dozen other organizations focus at least to some extent on campus environmental concerns.[51] Students support recycling efforts on campus. The environmental movement has not stimulated a national student movement, although several national organizations that work on campuses exist. The focus of most of the activism has been at the local campus level.

As noted earlier, participation in volunteerism has increased among students. While numbers are not available, it is likely that more students are involved in social service volunteer activity than in any other kind of activism, and perhaps more than all other kinds combined. Campus volunteerism is especially impressive because social service activity must compete with increasingly common part-time employment. Deborah J. Hirsch calls this volunteerism the activism of the 1990s and argues that it may pave the way for more militant activism.[52] So far this has not occurred, and if past trends are any indication, social service work focused on local organizations and relating to quite specific issues will not turn into campus-based national activist student movement.

Conclusion

The past quarter century has seen several campus trends, but overall it has been a period of general quiet. The one significant national political movement that emerged, the anti-apartheid struggle, was of short duration and little lasting significance. A deteriorating racial situation on campus in the 1980s was accompanied by some anti-racist involvement. There are few activist national student political organizations, and none that can claim significant campus support. Activism has been overwhelming focused on specific campuses and has not coalesced into a regional or national movement. The significant changes in the American economy and in the world situation have not favored campus activism. The composition of the student population has itself changed, and again these shifts do not favor political involvement. Fewer students are full-time, there is more diversity in terms of social class and ethnic background, and larger proportions of the student population are studying part time or working to earn money to pay for their education.

The configuration of attitudes remains basically unaltered, although with a modest shift toward the center and away from leftist positions. On lifestyle questions as well as some social issues, students remain liberal in their views. There have been some interesting changes in curricular choices; the dramatic shift toward vocationalism in the late 1970s and early 1980s has been at least in part countered by a partial return to the liberal arts fields. There is some increase in interest in careers in teaching. Focus on the social science, traditional breeding ground of activists, is modestly up.

Compared to the volatile sixties, the past two and one half decades have, of course, been notably apathetic with regard to student political involvement. But in the broader historical context of American student activism, the recent period is by no means unusual. The decade of the 1970s might well have been below the norm for American activism, but that of the 1980s is probably somewhat above average. The basic patterns seem to hold. The issues that appear to motivate students are those with a high moral content—issues such as repression in South Africa, racism on American campuses, or U.S. intervention in Central America. The campuses that have exhibited most activism in the recent past are the same universities that were prominent in earlier periods—the more cosmopolitan and prestigious universities on both coasts, a sprinkling of major public universities in between, and some traditionally progressive liberal arts colleges. Students from the social sciences seem to be more interested in political participation than those in professional programs or the sciences. Thus, the basic configuration of American student political involvement seems to have been maintained over time.

Given the imposing historical reputation of the student movement of the 1960s, it is understandable that most commentators on student politics of the past two decades have used the heyday of the New Left as a benchmark for comparative analysis. But this is the faulty comparison. American society was in the process of change. American student activists during most of the 1970s and 1980s attended college when the nation as a whole was shifting rightward as it had in the 1950s.

The lobbying, electoral work, and nonviolent demonstrations that collegians organized on behalf of federal student aid; peace; affirmative action; women's, gay and disabled rights over the past two decades transcends anything students were able to organize in previous conservative eras. Indeed, student divestment protesters in the mid-1980s achieved what no previous generation of campus activists had ever managed to do: they created a mass student movement during the term of a conservative president (in contrast to both previous mass student movements, in the 1930s and 1960s, which had been born during reformist eras when liberals occupied the White House). There has been a persistence of liberal values and modest activism despite the resurgent conservatism in the nation.

The early 1990s saw a downward trend in activism. No doubt influenced by the dramatic political changes on the world scene and the decline of the left in general, student activism has been at a very low ebb in terms of national organizations and movements. There has nonetheless been an increase in voluntary social service activity, indicating that students retain a sense of moral concern and involvement. And there have been some local student activist initiatives around environmental issues and incidents of racism on campus.

While it is impossible to predict the future of student activism, the immediate future does not look to be one of significant campus political involvement. Demographic, economic, and societal factors affecting the student population do not favor activism. Current foreign policy issues are not the sort that lend themselves to campus activism. It is hard to see a campus-based national movement flourishing under current circumstances. But circumstances change, and no one predicted the emergence of the student movement of the 1960s.

Notes

1. This chapter first appeared as an article in the *Journal of Higher Education*, 61 (January-February 1990): 32–49. In that version, it was coauthored with Robert Cohen. It has been extensively revised and updated for this volume.
2. For a discussion of the sixties, see Todd Gitlin, *The Sixties: Years of Hope Days of Rage* (New York: Bantam, 1987). See also Paul Berman, *A Tale of Two Utopias: The Political Journey of the Generation of 1968* (New York: Norton, 1996).
3. For two analyses which argue that activism is not dead, see Paul Rogat Loeb, *Generation at the Crossroads: Apathy and Action on the American Campus* (New Brunswick, N.J.: Rutgers University Press, 1994), and Tony Vellela, *New Voices: Student Activism in the '80s and '90s* (Boston: South End Press, 1988).
4. Arthur Levine and Deborah J. Hirsch, "Undergraduates in Transition: A New Wave of Activism on American College Campuses," *Higher Education* 22 (September 1991), 119–128.
5. See Tom Wells, *The War Within: America's Battle Over Vietnam* (New York: Henry Holt, 1994).
6. H. Jacobs, *Weatherman* (San Francisco: Ramparts Press, 1970) See also Cyril Levitt, *Children of Privilege: Student Revolt in the Sixties* (Toronto: University of Toronto Press, 1984).
7. Todd Gitlin, *The Whole World Is Watching: The Mass Media in the Making and Unmaking of the New Left* (Berkeley: University of California Press, 1980).
8. "Fact File: Attitudes and Characteristics of This Year's Freshmen," *Chronicle of Higher Education*, January 20, 1988, A36, and *Chronicle of Higher Education*, September 2, 1996, 19.
9. Ibid.
10. All of the data cited here is from the UCLA-American Council on Education annual survey of college freshmen as reported in the *Chronicle of Higher Education* and in Linda J. Sax, et al., *The American Freshman: National Norms for Fall 1995* (Los Angeles: Higher Education Research Institute, University of California at Los Angeles, 1995). Attitudes for other categories of students may vary, although other research indicates general consistency.
11. Arthur Levine and Keith Wilson, "Student Politics in America: Transformation Not Decline," *Higher Education* 8 (November 1979): 636–638.
12. Philip G. Altbach, "The National Student Association in the Fifties: Flawed Conscience of the Silent Generation," *Youth and Society* 5 (December 1973): 184–211.
13. Helen Lefkowitz Horowitz, *Campus Life: Undergraduate Cultures from the End of the Eighteenth Century to the Present* (Chicago: University of Chicago Press, 1988).
14. Levine and Wilson, "Student Politics in America."
15. Arthur Levine, *When Dreams and Heroes Died: A Portrait of Today's College Student* (San Francisco: Jossey Bass, 1980).
16. For more positive analyses, see Loeb, *Generation at the Crossroads* and Vellela, *New Voices*.
17. For a general discussion of the campus racial climate, see Philip G. Altbach and Kofi Lomotey, eds., *The Racial Crisis in American Higher Education* (Albany: SUNY Press, 1991).
18. One of the most visible examples of conservative activism was at Dartmouth College, where a right-wing student newspaper was quite active in the 1980s. See Dinesh D'Souza, *Illiberal Education: The Politics of Race and Sex on Campus* (New York: Free Press, 1991).
19. "The Conservative Student," *Newsweek on Campus*, March 1985.
20. J. Nesses, "Student Struggle: Agenda for Change," *Guardian Supplement* (Spring 1986), 3.
21. Eric L. Hirsch, "Sacrifice for the Cause: Group Processes, Recruitment, and Commitment in a Student Social Movement," *American Sociological Review* 55 (April 1990): 243–254.
22. "A New Wage of Campus Protest on Apartheid," *Newsweek*, April 22, 1985, 71.
23. *New York Times*, April 25, 1985.
24. "'The Times They Are a Changin,'" *Time*, April 29, 1985, 44.
25. *Chronicle of Higher Education*, April 24, 1984, 17.
26. Ibid.
27. "The Divestment Controversy," *Daily Californian Special* (Berkeley, Calif.) (1985), 1–4.
28. *Chronicle of Higher Education*, September 18, 1985, 25.

29. "A New Breed of Activism," *Newsweek*, May 13, 1985, 62.
30. "'The Times They Are a Changin.'"
31. *Chronicle of Higher Education*, October 6, 1985, 32.
32. J. Weiner, "Divestment Report Card: Students, Stocks and Shanties," *Nation*, October 11, 1986, 337.
33. Ibid.
34. D'Souza, *Illiberal Education*.
35. "Shanties on the Green," *Newsweek*, February 3, 1986, 63–64.
36. Ibid.
37. Ibid.
38. Philip G. Altbach, "The Racial Dilemma in American Higher Education," in Altbach and Lomotey, eds., *The Racial Crisis in American Higher Education*, 3–18.
39. Mfanya D. Tryman, "Racism and Violence on College Campuses," *The Western Journal of Black Studies* 16 (No. 4, 1992), 222.
40. Ibid.
41. Denise K. Magner, "Racial Tensions Continue to Erupt on Campuses Despite Efforts to Promote Cultural Diversity," *Chronicle of Higher Education*, June 6, 1990, 1, 29–30. See also Jon C. Dalton, ed., *Racism on Campus: Confronting Racial Bias Through Peer Interventions* (San Francisco: Jossey-Bass, 1991).
42. Altbach and Lomotey, *op. cit.*, pp. 199–248.
43. See Allan Bloom, *The Closing of the American Mind* (New York: Simon and Schuster, 1987). This was one of several influential books arguing that American higher education had lost its direction, and advocating the restoration of a traditional core curriculum. See also Nicholas H. Farnham and Adam Yarmolinski, eds., *Rethinking Liberal Education* (New York: Oxford University Press, 1996).
44. For different perspectives, see Patricia Aufderheide, ed., *Beyond PC: Towards a Politics of Understanding* (St. Paul, Minn.: Graywolf Press, 1992) and William Casement, *The Great Canon Controversy: The Battle of the Books in Higher Education* (New Brunswick, N.J.: Transaction, 1996).
45. Jayne E. Stake, et al., "The Women's Studies Experience: Impetus for Feminist Activism," *Psychology of Women Quarterly* 18 (1994): 17–24. See also Frances A. Maher and Mary K. T. Tetreault, *The Feminist Classroom* (New York: Basic Books).
46. Ibid., pp. 1991994) and G. R. Bowles and R. Duelli Klein, *Theories of Women's Studies* (London: Routledge and Kegan Paul, 1983).
47. Alexander Astin, et al., *The Power of Protest: A National Study of Students and Faculty Disruptions with Implications for the Future* (San Francisco: Jossey Bass, 1975).
48. Elizabeth A. Williams and Gary D. Malaney, "Assessing the Political Ideology and Activism of College Students: Reactions to the Persian Gulf War," *NASPA Journal* 33 (Winter 1996): 145–160.
49. "Attitudes and Characteristics of Freshmen," *Chronicle of Higher Education*, September 2, 1996, 19. See also Darren E. Sherkat and T. Jean Blockerm, "Environmental Activism in the Protest Generation: Differentiating 1960s Activists," *Youth and Society* 25 (September 1993): 140–161.
50. Julian Keniry, "Environmental Movement Booming on Campuses," *Change*, September-October 1993: 42–49.
51. Ibid, 48.
52. Deborah J. Hirsch, "Politics Through Action: Student Service and Activism in the '90s," *Change*, September-October, 1993): 32–36.

CHAPTER 12

SUMMING UP

THE DISAPPOINTMENTS OF SUCCESS:
HIGHER EDUCATION AFTER WORLD WAR II

MARVIN LAZERSON

ABSTRACT: From a historical perspective, Marvin Lazerson gives an account of the unprecedented growth of higher education in the years following World War II, its transformation from a public good to a private benefit that confers economic rewards, and the current problems that it faces during an era of retrenchment. He demonstrates how higher education's postwar success was built on three already established patterns and beliefs: vocationalism, public higher education, and multiple sectors of postsecondary schooling. He then discusses how the world of higher education changed after 1970, when critics began to voice concerns over unchecked expansion, and how its current problems emerged during the 1980s and 1990s, as the costs of attending college began to outpace the economic returns.

In the half-century after World War II, higher education in the United States triumphed. Few industries grew as fast, gained as much prestige, or affected the lives of so many people. Higher education received remarkable sums of money from federal and state governments; alumni and foundations also gave generously. Families reached into their savings, postponed purchases, and went into debt so that their children could go to college. Higher education came to simultaneously embody both a public good—beneficial to the nation's economy, protective of its national defense, opening up new avenues of knowledge, and able to realize equality of educational opportunity—and a private benefit, so that everyone who possessed it substantially improved their access to higher income, status, and security.

Most remarkably, higher education built upon prewar trends to do what almost no one would have predicted: it achieved a virtual monopoly on middle-class status. It became the licensing agency for Americans who wanted to enter the professions. Every occupation seeking to increase its prestige and income made going to college and beyond the requirement for entry. For countless Americans, college was the route upward; they expected their governments at every level to help facilitate that mobility, through grants and loans to students, as well as establishing branch campuses of state universities and local community colleges. Even when economic returns to higher education plateaued during the 1970s and 1980s and the costs of going to college escalated, families and students—especially older students—dug down into their savings and took out loans in order to attend. Higher education had been converted from a land of opportunity to a necessity for many in order to prevent the loss of status.

Marvin Lazerson is Carruth Family Professor at the Graduate School of Education, University of Pennsylvania. He is a widely published educational historian and commentator on current issues in higher education.

NOTE: I would like to thank Jesse Minier and Barbara Jaffe for providing much of the data, posing many of the most intriguing questions, challenging the interpretations, and aiding in the writing. The work reported herein is supported under the Educational Research and Development Center Program, agreement number R309A60001, CFDA 84.309A, as administered by the Office of Educational Research and Improvement (OERI), U.S. Department of Education. The findings and opinions expressed in this report do not reflect the position or policies of OERI or the U.S. Department of Education.

Higher education has become a victim of its own successes, however. Able to assume a continuing clientele, to capitalize on the aspirations for upward mobility that so marked American society in the postwar era, and to attract a seemingly unending stream of government funds, higher education charged what the traffic would bear. By the 1980s, those costs would so substantially outpace inflation and the growth rate of median family income that higher education looked like yet another greedy industry.

By the 1990s, higher education had come to look like other monopolies and powerful industries of postwar America. Like the U.S. auto industry in the 1970s, it dominated the market, produced the best products, and paid off for those who invested and worked in it. But also like the auto industry, higher education failed to recognize its hubris and the environmental changes occurring around it. Even the complaints about higher education mirrored those hurled at corporate monopolies: overpriced and poor-quality products, poor service and inattention to customers, inefficient and bureaucratic, unwilling to adapt to new markets, technologically backward, administratively bloated, too concerned with frills rather than the core product. Shocked and confused by criticism and reluctant to change, higher education at the end of the century faced a new world. It was unclear whether it would be routed by the imports and alternatives or made better for the competition.

The Markers of Success

By almost any measure, the half-century since 1945 was good for higher education, even with the strains of the 1970s and 1980s. Two kinds of data tell the story: institutional and enrollment growth, and fiscal growth. Between 1950 and 1990, the number of colleges and universities almost doubled, from 1851 to 3535. The number of students increased from 2.66 million in 1949–50 to 8.00 million in 1969–70, and to 13.54 million in 1989–90. In those same years, the percentage of 18- and 19-year-olds in school (overwhelmingly, in postsecondary schools) doubled from 29.7 percent of the age group to 57.2 percent; the proportion of 20- to 24-year-olds in school tripled, from 9.2 percent to 28.6 percent. The most rapid growth occurred during the 1960s, but, after a sluggish decade in the 1970s, the trend was again upward (National Center for Education Statistics [NCES] 1994).

Where students went and who they were also changed. The proportion of students in public colleges—at around 50 percent in 1950—continued to increase, reaching 59 percent in 1960 and a whopping 73 percent in 1970 (Freeland 1992, 88). Women, who composed 30 percent of the student population in 1949–50, were the majority by 1979–80 and rose to 54 percent in 1989–90 (NCES 1994, tabs. 168 and 169). Among African Americans, the proportion of 18- to 24-year-olds in college increased from under 10 percent in 1964 to 20 percent in 1972, and Hispanic Americans showed similar growth in enrollment (Gumport et al. 1997). By 1990, 25 percent of African American youths and 16 percent of Hispanic American youths were enrolled in college (Gumport et al. 1997). The number of non-traditional-age and part-time students also rose after 1970. By 1990, the proportion of students 22 years of age and older were the "new majority" in college, and more than 40 percent of all college students were going part-time (Gumport et al. 1997).

Spending on higher education soared, from $2.66 billion in 1949–50 to $7.14 billion a decade later, to $25.27 billion in 1969–70, to $62.46 billion in 1979–80, and $151.76 billion in 1989–90 (NCES 1994, tab. 32). Higher-education expenditures as a percentage of the gross national product (GNP) rose from 1.7 percent in 1961 to 2.1 percent in 1970; after stabilizing during the 1970s, they rose again to 3.0 percent in 1990 (NCES 1994, tab. 31). Between 1950 and 1970, higher education increased its spending per student by more than double the rate of the GNP. In contrast, between 1930 and 1950, the rate of increase per student rose more slowly than the rate of per capita growth in the GNP. In recent years, the rise in spending on a per-student basis has been enormous, going from $3947 (in 1990–91 constant dollars) in 1949–50 to $7460 in 1969–70, declining over the next decade but rising sharply to $8225 in the 1980s (NCES 1994, tab. 328).

The numbers tell a compelling story: more students, more money, more status. Higher education became one of the most successful industries of postwar America—perhaps the single most successful.

It was hard to imagine a world without colleges, without large numbers of people attending them, without higher education's contributions to the resolution of the nation's most complex and important economic, technological, social, and health problems. Its colleges and universities illustrated what made the United States great.

Neither the ride nor the progress was smooth, however. Just as American industry would find itself troubled—by foreign imports and global competition, managerial miscalculations, worker demands for higher wages, and shorter workweeks—so, too, did higher education find itself troubled. The immediate postwar period witnessed the McCarthyism of anti-Communists who were convinced that "Reds" and their fellow travelers had invaded the campuses. The Soviet Union's launch of *Sputnik* in 1957 raised doubts about whether American standards of academic achievement were stringent enough for the Cold War era. Demonstrations, strikes, and violence during the 1960s and early 1970s divided higher education from within and diminished enthusiasm for it among politicians and the public at large as they questioned whether higher education had become yet another mistaken entitlement of the welfare state. A slowdown in income returns to college education during the 1970s combined with the rising costs of going to college.

The industry seemed unable or unwilling to rein in its expenditures, opening higher education to more strident criticism than ever before—this time matched by legislative efforts to reduce federal and state expenditures. During the 1980s, state appropriations, the largest governmental source of funds for higher education, increased only slightly per student but appeared flat when measured in constant dollars. Overall government funding as a percentage of funding for higher education declined during the 1980s. Critics challenged whether colleges and universities were teaching students anything and whether "higher education" was a misnomer as remedial programs proliferated. The media found itself with yet another institution that seemed corrupt, was politically incorrect, and misused funds, leading higher education to become more defensive than at any time in its history.

Nonetheless, before the end of the 1980s, the times of trouble were blips in the trajectory. By turns, they were threatening, annoying, confusing, raising questions, and sometimes lessening the flow of dollars, but they were almost always transitory. Each rocky moment was followed by renewed enthusiasm, more applications for admission, expansiveness, and money. McCarthyism shook some campuses, frightened many faculty, and ruined careers, but it hardly made a dent in the industry's growth or prestige. *Sputnik* produced considerable criticism and a great deal of hand-wringing, but from it came the National Defense Education Act of 1958, which gave unprecedented fiscal support for the sciences, foreign languages, area studies, and campus growth. In the 1960s and 1970s, campus rebellions shocked the nation, leading to angry diatribes directed at overly entitled youths, but the public's shifting attitudes toward the Vietnam war ultimately gave greater legitimacy to the demonstrations. Few, if any, students turned away from attending college because some of their peers had protested. The most obvious direct impact of student demonstrations was to give everyone more freedom. Campus restrictions on student life practically disappeared as "in loco parentis" became a dirty word. The number of required courses declined; the size of the overall curriculum increased. Students and faculty had more choices of what to take and what to teach. Income and status returns to college attendance remained high: even though the rate of growth slowed and may have even trailed off after 1970, attending college, compared to not going beyond secondary school, was still a wise decision, particularly in the 1980s, when the job market for high school graduates collapsed.

Finally, at the start of the 1980s, when it seemed that the declining number of 17- to 21-year-olds in the population would substantially diminish the market for students, higher education discovered the non-traditional student, who, in turn, found that it was never too late to go to college. While it became more and more difficult for families to pay for a college education during the 1980s—as higher education raised tuition faster than the rise in inflation and the average income of workers—the numbers scrambling to get into college kept going up, as community colleges in particular burst their seams enrolling high school graduates and dropouts, adults seeking job preparation, and others simply wanting a place to learn more about the world and themselves.

For all of the ups and downs, during almost a half-century after World War II, higher education was truly a success story. Build a college and students would come. Expand facilities and resources would arrive. By and large, it was truly a golden age.

Dimensions of the Past

Higher education's postwar success built upon three already established patterns and beliefs, each of which sowed the seeds of conflict: vocationalism, public higher education, and multiple sectors of postsecondary schooling.

Vocationalism—the direct application of schooling to jobs and economic opportunities—had been apparent since the late nineteenth century. Seeking students and public approbation, many nineteenth-century colleges adapted their liberal arts traditions to become multipurpose schools, diversifying their curricula and becoming sensitive to local and regional economic needs and job opportunities (Geiger 1995). For women especially, vocationalism was always central; overwhelmingly, women college students prepared for teaching. At the University of California, Berkeley, early in the twentieth century, 90 percent of the women students expected to become teachers (Gordon 1990).

Between 1880 and the 1930s, vocationalism took full form, with the development of professional schools, the creation of an educational ladder between high school and college, and, increasingly, a reliance by employers on college credentials as a criterion for hiring. Each of these factors was important. The appearance of schools of business, engineering, education, social work, nursing, and dentistry and the growth of law and medical schools defined higher education in terms of its direct application to specific occupations. The creation of an education ladder that went from elementary and secondary schools through college and then to graduate school sharpened the distinction between college and other educational institutions and reduced the undergraduate college's nineteenth-century competitors—academies, high schools, one- and two-year normal schools, private proprietary schools, and apprenticeships—to institutions preparatory to college or to a lesser status. By the 1930s, the high school no longer paralleled the college but had become its subordinate; without a high school degree, there was no entry to college, and more and more professions were requiring graduate training beyond college.

The shift in the criteria for employment, partially due to the growth of white-collar jobs within corporate and public agencies, generated much of the consumer-driven growth in postsecondary enrollments in the first decades of the twentieth century. What David Levine has called "the culture of aspiration," a variation of the Horatio Alger story of rags to riches—or at least, to middle-class respectability—was connected to higher education (Levine 1986). The movement was hardly massive before World War II; too many obstacles still lay in the way of nearly universal higher education, especially the continuing low proportions of youths graduating from high school, but the terms of the postwar expansion had been laid. Going to college meant greater income returns and status than not going.

A second critical ingredient of postwar expansion had also been put in place earlier: the growth of the public sector in higher education. Although we tend to associate public higher education with the post–World War II period, large proportions of young people had always attended publicly supported colleges and universities. Indeed, the perception of a separate private versus public sector was an invention of the nineteenth century. The Morrill Acts of 1862 and 1890 furthered the notion that higher education was a public responsibility. While there was a private gain to the individual from going to college, the primary gain was to the public good. College enrollments strengthened the nation, state, and locality.

This view of higher education as a public good also laid the basis for its politicization. Before postwar expansion, the number of students going to college and the amount of public funds invested in higher education had been small enough to mute political antagonisms. As higher education became a mass system in the postwar decades, however, the politicization inherent in its public character intensified.

The third critical ingredient that fed postwar expansionism comprised the organizational characteristics of decentralization and segmentation. Because higher education was always a decentralized industry, made up of relatively autonomous institutions competing within a deregulated market, it expanded in whatever ways it thought necessary. Often, this meant changing admission requirements to attract more students (or, in a few cases, to become more selective), providing fiscal incentives to students to attend, revising the curriculum to make it more attractive, expanding student life activities, and seeking funding from alumni and philanthropists. Higher education thus established its entrepreneurial orientation in its relationship to students and vendors before the mid-twentieth century.

Segmentation was also important. Higher education accepted the equation that access to college could be widespread if the system was segmented. A complex web of different kinds of postsecondary institutions was already formed by the late 1930s, from junior and community colleges through the small number of selective liberal arts colleges and research universities. Providing for gradients of status within a system of increasing access to higher educational opportunity, the web of sectors joined with the ideas of equality of opportunity, meritocracy, the preservation of institutional status, and market sector competition to lay the basis for extraordinary growth.

The Enthusiasms of Success

In a simple fashion, the remarkable expansion of higher education in the first two and a half decades after World War II can be easily stated: large numbers of Americans subsidized higher education because they were convinced that it was a public good that substantially furthered national defense, economic growth, and equality of educational opportunity. Students and their families read the postwar labor market correctly: going to college meant better jobs, more income, higher status, and greater security.

It is hard at the end of the twentieth century to imagine the extraordinary enthusiasm for the postwar growth. Even elite private universities, initially worried that high levels of public investment would diminish their place and would open the doors to unqualified students, soon found themselves caught up in the opportunities of expansion. The Cold War, the ideology of equality of opportunity, state and local pride, the high stature of research, and federal investments all fueled an expansion that was inconceivable a few decades earlier. In particular, by providing direct grants to institutions to be redistributed primarily in student aid, the federal government helped keep the opportunity costs to attending college low, while allowing colleges to increase their charges, a situation in which everyone seemed to win.

Students and their families responded. College going provided opportunities for young people to do better than their parents. In absolute terms, between 1950 and 1970, income returns to college graduation increased in a steady fashion. Each annual cohort of college graduates was likely to earn more money than the previous cohorts as employers heavily recruited college graduates. Relative to high school graduates and high school dropouts, returns to college graduates during those 20 years grew or remained stable annually, again peaking around 1970. College graduates seemed to have little trouble finding jobs (Gumport et al. 1997; Hecker 1992).

In those 25 years after the war, there was, it seemed, little restraint on the possibilities for higher education. Although student rebellions in the 1960s provoked substantial criticism, the decade ended with the largest growth that higher education had ever seen. Substantial state and federal funding existed; the commitment to civil rights and educational opportunity opened doors for minorities; women were a growing proportion of the college population. Income returns to college graduates were high and had been growing in a seemingly unending progression. There was little reason to think that during the 1970s the surfacing doubts would become more than that, little reason to believe that higher education was about to be seriously challenged.

The Era of Disappointments

The world of higher education changed after 1970. The preceding rise had been meteoric and substantial. Higher education had become self-confident, assured that it was a public and a private good that strengthened the nation and provided high rates of return to individuals. The criticisms emerging after 1970 were a surprise; the disenchantment, unsettling; the anger, a shock.

As early as 1971, commentators like Earl Cheit, in *The New Depression in Higher Education*, worried that higher education had lost its capacity to manage itself and suggested that a number of colleges and universities were in serious fiscal trouble. Others criticized the continuing lack of access for minorities despite substantial gains, the neglect of the teaching of undergraduates, the uniformity across institutions, the remoteness of higher education from society, and its excessively close association with government and social concerns. That there were contradictions between the various criticisms was more or less irrelevant. The critics' voices coalesced in the public's mind around the notion that there was something terribly wrong with higher education (Freeland 1992, 97–115).

Initially, the sourest notes were sounded around the behavior of students. The protests of the 1960s and early 1970s, the in-your-face dress and language of that period, and the violence raised questions about whether the entitled were worth the expenditure. President Nixon's urban and domestic affairs adviser, Daniel Patrick Moynihan, may have spoken for countless other Americans when he proclaimed to one of his former graduate students that "even the mathematics students were protesting," and, in the wake of the demonstrations and violence at Columbia University, he was apoplectic because parents were bailing their children out of jail and protesting against undue violence on the part of the police. Why did these parents, he fumed, not let their children take responsibility for their illegal and uncivil actions?

But there was also a deeper malaise affecting higher education after 1970, one that would have an even more substantial impact: the intersection of the costs of college and the income returns to attending. Higher education presumed that its importance allowed it to increase its expenditures substantially faster than the GNP and the rate of inflation. That thinking quickly became an albatross. As the U.S. economy faced soaring inflation, high unemployment, oil crises, wage and price controls, loss of markets to Japanese and German goods, and corporate downsizing in the 1970s and 1980s, the seemingly unconstrained costs of higher education came to look obscene.

Concern about costs coincided with uncertainties about the income returns to higher education. After 1970, depending upon the source, income returns to college graduates either flattened, declined, or increased only modestly over the next two decades (Zemsky 1997; Levy and Murnane 1992).[1] A consensus quickly emerged that going to college was no longer paying off in the ways that it had over the previous decades. Why this was so is the source of intense controversy, with interpretations pointing to an oversupply of college graduates, the deskilling of many managerial and technical jobs, corporate downsizing, the poor quality of elementary and secondary schools, declines in the quality of academic and technical skills possessed by college graduates, lowered college admission standards, the larger proportion of women college graduates entering the labor market, and a mismatch between the skills that college graduates possessed and those required in the advanced labor market.

If enthusiasm waned in the 1970s and 1980s, it also became even more imperative to play the game. Relative to high school graduates, the differential wage increases associated with college graduation declined during the 1970s. In 1971, male college graduates aged 25 to 34 earned 22 percent more, on average, than male high school graduates of the same age. In 1979, the earnings differential had shrunk to 13 percent. For women aged 25 to 34, the changes were similar, with the earnings premium associated with college education declining from 41 percent in 1971 to 23 percent in 1979 (Levy and Murnane 1992, 1354–57). It was thus reasonable to have doubts about going to college in the 1970s.

During the 1980s, the world became even more complicated. The educational premium for male college graduates aged 24 to 35 over high school graduates of the same age jumped from 13 percent in 1979 to 38 percent in 1987, For women in the same categories, the premium rose from 23 percent to 45 percent but with a substantial difference, Whereas the median real earnings of male high school graduates working full-time declined by 12 percent in the 1980s—as did the likelihood of even working full-time—it did not decline for women high school graduates working full–time (Levy and Murnane 1992, 1356–57). In the case of both women and men, the gap between high school and college earnings was even higher, since the likelihood that high school graduates would hold full-time jobs year-round declined considerably during the 1980s. With women entering new professions and with the income inequality gap between men and women closing, the experiences of college going for the two sexes had shifted. For men, graduating from college after 1970 was considerably less positive than during the golden era between 1945 and 1970; for women, college graduation had become, at least in terms of earnings, much more positive. For both, however, the gap between going to college and not going was huge. It paid to go to college, but it cost more and more to attend.

The psychology of college attendance was also changing. The postwar generation of college students went with great expectations, promises that were fulfilled. From the 1970s on, however, an increasing number of students went to college in order not to suffer the fate of high school graduates. It was a subtle shift in social psychology, from optimism to defensiveness. One went not to get ahead but to avoid falling behind (Zemsky 1997).

The evidence suggests that students and their families agreed that college was, if not a good thing, necessary to getting ahead. The percentage of recent high school graduates enrolled in college, which had climbed from 45 percent in 1960 to a high of 55 percent in 1968, slid down during the 1970s but then began to rise again in the 1980s. While there was a brief drop in full-time undergraduate enrollments in the early 1970s—partly a result of the elimination of the draft deferment for college students—and again around 1977 and between 1983 and 1985, the trajectory was up, sharply so between 1973 and 1975, then more gradually between 1977 and 1983 and again after 1985. The number of part-time undergraduates showed a slightly different profile, but the overall trend between 1971 and 1991 was decidedly up. Among African Americans, participation rates increased in the 1960s, declined in the early 1970s, increased briefly, then flattened or declined until the mid-1980s, and turned upward again. Among African Americans, sharp differences by gender appeared, with the enrollments of women increasing between 1976 and 1985, while the rates for men declined. Between 1986 and 1990, when participation rates went up for both sexes, they did so by almost 16 percent among African American women and by about 9 percent for African American men. Between 1976 and 1990, participation rates for Hispanics and Asian Americans also increased, with the enrollment of women in each group increasing mare rapidly than that of men (Hauptman and McLaughlin 1992, 168–78).

Much of this growth came as a surprise. As David Breneman (1994) has pointed out, the 1980s began on a dreary note, punctuated by demographic fears: an anticipated 25 percent decline in the number of 18-year-olds over the next 15 years. Even if larger proportions of high school graduates enrolled in college, the likelihood of actual enrollments dropping by 5 percent to 15 percent was substantial. Combined with high inflation and unemployment, little if any productivity gains, and anticipated drops in real income, the situation did look bleak.

The catastrophic projections at the beginning of the 1980s did not come true, but three things did happen during the decade that would effectively shake higher education's foundations. First, higher education expanded because older, nontraditional students enrolled, many of them attending part-time. Although their participation had been growing since the 1960s, between 1970 and 1975, the number of students aged 22 or older increased by more than 50 percent, while the number of traditional-age students remained relatively constant. Between 1978 and 1989, the number of college students aged 25 and older grew by 44 percent, while the number of 18- to 24-year-olds in college increased by only 7 percent. The number of women college students in that same period grew by 26 percent, accounting for the largest growth among older students.[2] After 1975, students aged 22 or older became the majority of the college-going population; in the late 1980s, those 30 and older were the fastest-growing percentage of matriculants (Gumport et al. 1997). Older students were also much more likely to enroll part-time, accounting for almost all the growth in part-time attendance in the 1980s. In their determination to enroll in college, older students affirmed what was higher education's greatest triumph: college was the necessary license for middle-class status.

Second, the expansion of enrollment in the 1980s was not matched by a parallel expansion in degree attainment. As Robert Zemsky points out, between 1950 and 1982, the portion of those who started college but left before finishing it dropped from over half to less than 30 percent. Over the next decade, over 40 percent who started college quit before they earned their bachelor's degree. Americans became convinced that it was necessary to go to college—this was an especially striking phenomenon among those over age 30—but they were not receiving the degree they so desperately sought (Zemsky 1997; Gumport et al. 1997).

Third, higher education became caught in a price-income squeeze that was more serious than at any time in the previous half-century. The direct costs of going to college—tuition, fees, room and board—increased dramatically during the 1980s, especially at private universities (the increases hit the public universities in the late 1980s and early 1990s), substantially outpacing inflation and the family incomes of most Americans. At the same time, median income in constant dollars either stayed the same, declined, or increased only slightly for male college graduates aged 25 to 34.

Taken together, these developments revealed both higher education's continuing success and its vulnerability. The proportion of high school graduates aged 18 to 24 going on to college had grown once again, from a low of 30 percent in 1973 to 34 percent in 1986. New populations were attending in record-breaking numbers, signifying how powerful higher education's license to middle-class respectability and status had become. For the selective colleges and universities, which promised entry to the upper class, the fight to get in had all the characteristics of a gold rush. Income returns to college vis-à-vis high school grew dramatically. As David Breneman (1994) has written, "Largely because the bottom fell out of the job market for high school graduates (especially for males), the economic returns to a college education reversed itself, with the wage premium for college graduates increasing between 1979 and 1986 to larger than those found in any earlier period" (31–32).

Yet the promise of success was all too shaky. A greater proportion of those who believed it was necessary to go to college were finding it harder and harder to attain a degree. Those who hoped that higher education would translate into high incomes were finding that just paying for college was harder and harder and, when they got out, worried about finding or holding a job and paying their debts. A person had to go to college, because if he or she did not, the result was to face even bigger financial trouble. At a time when choice was being trumpeted as the new American ideal, higher education's monopoly over access to the middle class—its greatest triumph—was becoming an incitement to condemn it. The public stood ready to unleash a critical onslaught beyond anything higher education had ever witnessed. The disappointments were overshadowing the industry's successes.

Notes

1. The measurement of earnings returns to education is one of the most technically complex areas in the economics of higher education. Zemsky (1997) and Gumport et al. (1997) argue that returns to higher education for men have been declining in constant dollars since the mid-1970s. Levy and Murnane (1992), in contrast, argue that between 1979 and 1987, there was "an eight percent increase in the median earnings of 25–34 year old male college graduates" and a "21 percent increase in the median earnings of 25–34 year old female college graduates," in both cases based on working full-time for the entire year (1355–57), Every analyst agrees that the most significant development of the 1980s was the decimation of the labor market for high school graduates. For a summary of studies on returns to college, see Pascarella and Terenzini 1991.

2. The importance of women in these trends is significant and not well appreciated. Women grew from 40 percent of the student population to a majority during the 1970s and up to 54 percent by 1990. The income returns for women college graduates also rose faster than those for men, so that by the end of the 1980s, while women with comparable education and jobs still earned less than men, the wage inequality gap was closing. Women were thus beginning to get more out of going to college than did men. Most of the scholarly and popular discussion about costs and returns, unfortunately, is based on male income data. The price-income squeeze may be most severe—and generating the most anger—among men, with women having a somewhat different perception of what has been happening.

References

1. Breneman, David W. 1994. *Liberal Arts Colleges: Thriving or Endangered?* Washington, DC: Brookings Institution.
2. Cheit, E. F. 1971. *The New Depression in Higher Education.* New York: McGraw-Hill.
3. Freeland, Richard M. 1992. *Academic's Golden Age: Universities in Massachusetts, 1945–1970.* New York: Oxford University Press.

4. Geiger, Roger L. 1995. The Era of Multipurpose Colleges in American Higher Education, 1850–1890. *History of Higher Education Annual* 15:51–92.

5. Gordon, Lynn. 1990. *Gender and Higher Education in the Progressive Era*. New Haven, CT: Yale University Press.

6. Gumport, Patricia, Maria Iannozzi, Susan Shaman, and Robert Zemsky, 1997. The United States Country Report: Trends in Higher Education from Massification to Post-Massification. In *RIHE International Seminar Reports*. No. 10. Hiroshima: Hiroshima University, Research Institute for Higher Education.

7. Hauptman, Arthur M. and Maureen A. McLaughlin. 1992, Is the Goal of College Access Being Met? In *American Higher Education: Purposes, Problems and Public Perceptions*, ed. Aspen Institute. Queensland, MD: Aspen Institute.

8. Hecker, Daniel E. 1992. Reconciling Conflicting Data on Jobs for College Graduates, *Monthly Labor Review* (July): 3–12.

9. Levine, David. 1986. *The American College and the Culture of Aspiration, 1915–1940*. Ithaca, NY: Cornell University Press.

10. Levy, Frank and Richard J. Murnane. 1992. U.S. Earnings Levels and Earnings Inequality: A Review of Recent Trends and Proposed Explanations. *Journal of Economic Literature* 30(Sept.): 1333–81.

11. National Center for Education Statistics (NCES). 1994. *Digest of Education Statistics, 1994*. Washington, DC: Department of Education.

12. Pascarella, Ernest and Patrick Terenzini. 1991. *How College Affects Students: Findings and Insights from. Twenty Years of Research*. San Francisco: Jossey-Bass.

13. Zemsky, Robert. 1997. Keynote Address: Seminar on Post-Massification. In *RIHE International Seminar Reports*, No. 10. Hiroshima: Hiroshima University, Research Institute for Higher Education.